Human Sexuality

SEVENTH EDITION

Human Sexuality

DIVERSITY IN CONTEMPORARY AMERICA

William L. Yarber
Indiana University

Barbara W. Sayad
California State University, Monterey Bay

Bryan Strong
Late of University of California, Santa Cruz

Published by McGraw-Hill, an imprint of The McGraw-Hill Companies, Inc., 1221 Avenue of the Americas, New York, NY 10020. Copyright © 2010, 2008, 2005, 2002, 1999, 1997, 1996. All rights reserved. No part of this publication may be reproduced or distributed in any form or by any means, or stored in a database or retrieval system, without the prior written consent of The McGraw-Hill Companies, Inc., including, but not limited to, in any network or other electronic storage or transmission, or broadcast for distance learning.

This book is printed on acid-free paper.

2 3 4 5 6 7 8 9 0 DOW / DOW 0

ISBN: 978-0-07-337088-0
MHID: 0-07-337088-6

Vice President Editorial: *Michael Ryan*
Publisher: *Mike Sugarman*
Executive Marketing Manager: *James Headley*
Marketing Manager: *Yasuko Okada*
Director of Development: *Dawn Groundwater*
Developmental Editor: *Cheri Dellelo*
Editorial Coordinator: *AJ Laferrera*
Production Editor: *Catherine Morris*
Manuscript Editor: *Margaret Moore*

Art Manager: *Robin Mouat*
Design Manager: *Ashley Bedell*
Text Designers: *Linda Beaupré and Elise Lansdon*
Cover Designer: *Irene Morris*
Manager, Photo Research: *Brian J. Pecko*
Senior Production Supervisor: *Tandra Jorgensen*
Composition: *10.5/12 Garamond by Aptara®, Inc.*
Printing: *45# New Era Matte, R. R. Donnelley & Sons*

Cover: Clockwise from top left: © Image Source/Corbis; © Ed Freeman/Getty Images; © Kei Uesugi/Getty Images; © Getty Images/OJO Images

Credits: The credits section for this book begins on page C-1 and is considered an extension of the copyright page.

Library of Congress Cataloging-in-Publication Data

Yarber, William L. (William Lee), 1943-
Human sexuality : diversity in contemporary America / William Yarber, Barbara Sayad, Bryan Strong.—7th ed.
    p. cm.
  Prev. ed. cataloged under the title: Human Sexuality.
  Includes bibliographical references and index.
  ISBN-13: 978-0-07-337088-0 (alk. paper)
  ISBN-10: 0-07-337088-6 (alk. paper)
  1. Sex. 2. Sex customs. 3. Hygiene, Sexual. I. Sayad, Barbara J. II. Strong, Bryan. III. Title. IV. Title:
Human Sexuality.

HQ21.Y29 2010
306.7—dc22   2009034028

The Internet addresses listed in the text were accurate at the time of publication. The inclusion of a Web site does not indicate an endorsement by the authors or McGraw-Hill, and McGraw-Hill does not guarantee the accuracy of the information presented at these sites.

Brief Contents

Contents

Perspectives on Human Sexuality   1

Studying Human Sexuality 28

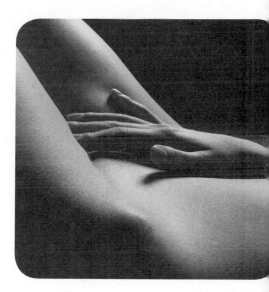

Gender and Gender Roles 125

Love and Communication in Intimate Relationships 220

Sexual Expression   259

Variations in Sexual Behavior   296

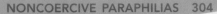

11

Contraception, Birth Control, and Abortion 323

Conception, Pregnancy, and Childbirth   361

The Sexual Body in Health and Illness 397

Sexual Function Difficulties, Dissatisfaction, Enhancement, and Therapy 440

Sexually Transmitted Infections   489

16

HIV and AIDS 526

Sexual Coercion: Harassment, Aggression, and Abuse 564

18

Sexually Explicit Materials, Prostitution, and Sex Laws   605

About the Authors

William L. Yarber

WILLIAM L. YARBER is a senior research fellow at the Kinsey Institute for Research in Sex, Gender, and Reproduction and the senior director of the Rural Center for AIDS/STD Prevention at Indiana University, Bloomington. He is also professor of applied health science and professor of gender studies at IU. Bill has authored or co-authored over 135 scientific reports in professional journals on sexual risk behavior and AIDS/STI prevention. At the request of the U.S. federal government, he wrote the country's first secondary school AIDS prevention curriculum. He chaired the National Guidelines Task Force, which developed the Sexuality Information and Education Council of the United States (SIECUS) publication *Guidelines for Comprehensive Sexuality Education: Kindergarten–12th Grade*. Bill, who received his doctorate from Indiana University, is past president of the Society for the Scientific Study of Sexuality (SSSS) and past chair of the SIECUS board of directors. He has received over $4 million in federal and state grants to support his research and AIDS/STI prevention efforts. His awards include the Professional Standard of Excellence Award from the American Association of Sex Educators, Counselors, and Therapists, the SSSS Award for Distinguished Scientific Achievement, the Research Council Award from the American School Health Association, the President's Award for Distinguished Teaching, and the Graduate Student Outstanding Faculty Mentor Award at Indiana University. Bill has been a consultant to the World Health Organization Global Program on AIDS. He regularly teaches undergraduate and graduate courses in human sexuality. He was previously a faculty member at Purdue University and the University of Minnesota, as well as a public high school health science and biology teacher. This edition of the book is the fourth he has co-authored. Bill is married and is the father of two adult daughters.

Barbara W. Sayad

BARBARA W. SAYAD is a full-time faculty member at California State University, Monterey Bay, where she teaches human sexuality, women's health, behavior change, marriage and family, and wellness with a focus on service learning. Barbara holds a Ph.D. in Health and Human Behavior, an M.P.H. in Community Health Education, and a B.S. in Foods and Nutrition. Additionally, she has co-authored six editions of *Human Sexuality: Diversity in Contemporary America* (McGraw-Hill). She has also co-authored *The Marriage and Family Experience* (Wadsworth) and has contributed to a number of other health-related texts, curricular guides, and publications. In addition to her 25 years of teaching and mentoring in the university setting, Barbara has facilitated a number of training programs, presented at professional organizations, and worked as a training and curriculum consultant in nonprofit and proprietary organizations. Barbara is married and with her husband has three children.

BRYAN STRONG and Christine DeVault were married to each other when they wrote the first and second editions of *Human Sexuality*. Sadly, at the young age of 53, Bryan died of melanoma. Bryan received his doctorate from Stanford University and taught at the University of California, Santa Cruz. His fields of expertise included human sexuality, marriage and the family, and American social history. Christine DeVault is a Certified Family Life Educator, educational writer, consultant, and photographer. She received her degree in sociology from the University of California, Berkeley. Christine is the mother of three children and grandmother of two.

To my research colleagues, Cindy, Rick, Robin, and Stephanie—with appreciation, admiration, and love, I dedicate this book.

—W. L. Y.

To my parents, Robert and Elsie; my husband, Bob; and children, Sarah, Elizabeth, and Sam—I dedicate this book with love and gratitude.

—B. W. S.

Behind every McGraw-Hill education product is research.

Thousands of instructors participate in our course surveys every year providing McGraw-Hill with longitudinal information on the trends and challenges in your courses. That research, along with reviews, focus groups, and ethnographic studies of both instructor and student workflow, provides the intensive feedback that our authors and editors use to assure that our revisions continue to provide everything you need to reach your course goals and outcomes.

Some KEY FINDINGS from our Human Sexuality Course Survey

78% of human sexuality instructors state that teaching their students to think critically and evaluate research quality is a top goal of their course.

60% of human sexuality instructors state that teaching their students through the use of video clips is a top goal of their course.

think about it

"Do You Know What You Are Doing?" Common Condom-Use Mistakes Among College Students

For those wanting to prevent STIs and pregnancy, condom use is necessary for *all* sexual episodes. But consistent use is only part of the answer—the condom must be used correctly if it is to be effective.

Very little research has been conducted on correct condom use, but the first comprehensive study of college male students produced some startling and alarming results. Researchers at The Kinsey Institute for Research in Sex, Gender, and Reproduction and the Rural Center for HIV/STD Prevention at Indiana University determined the prevalence of male condom–use errors and problems among samples of undergraduate, single, self-identified heterosexual men (N = 158) who applied the condom to themselves and single, self-identified heterosexual women (N = 102) who applied a condom to their male partner at a large, public midwestern university. Participants were asked to indicate if the error or problem occurred at least once during the past 3 months during sex, defined as when the male put his penis in a partner's mouth, vagina, or rectum. The percentage of the errors and problems that occurred at least once in the past 3 months were remarkably similar whether or not the male applied the condom to himself or whether his female partner applied the condom to him. The table indicates some of the most important errors and problems.

Error/Problem	Male Appliers	Female Appliers
Put condom on after starting sex	42.8%*	51.1%*
Did not hold tip and leave space	40.4%	45.7%
Put condom on the wrong side up (had to flip it over)	30.4%	29.6%
Used condom without lubricant	19.2%	25.8%
Took condom off before sex was over	15.3%	14.8%
Did not change to new condoms when switching between vaginal, oral, and anal sex (for those switching)	81.2%	75.0%
Condom broke	29.0%	19.3%
Condom slipped off during sex	13.1%	19.3%
Lost erection before condom was put on	21.6%	14.3%
Lost erection after condom was on and sex had begun	19.6%	20.2%

*Percentage reporting that the error or problem occurred at least once in the past 3 months.

A subsequent focus group study of undergraduates who reported male condom use for other-sex behavior in the previous month found that they had concerns about male condoms, including mistrust of each gender in supplying and properly using condoms, inadequate lubrication during condom use, condoms partially or fully slipping off during sex, "losing" part or all of the condom in the vagina, delayed applications, and irritation and reduced sensation (Yarber et al., 2007).

The researchers concluded that the condom-use errors and problems reported in these studies indicate a possible high risk of exposure of the participants to HIV/STIs and unintended pregnancy. They also stated that the effectiveness of condom use against HIV/STIs and unintended pregnancy is contingent upon correct condom use.

Think Critically

- Did the types and frequency of condom-use errors and problems found in these studies surprise you? Explain.
- Why do you think these errors and problems occurred?
- Is it really that difficult to use condoms correctly—why or why not?
- What can be done to promote correct condom use?

SOURCES: Crosby, R. A., Sanders, S. A., Yarber, W. L., Graham, C. A., & Dodge, B. (2002). Condom use errors and problems among college men. *Sexually Transmitted Diseases, 29,* 552-557; Sanders, S. A., Graham, C. A., Yarber, W. L., & Crosby, R. A. (2003). Condom use errors and problems among young women who put condoms on their male partners. *Journal of the American Medical Women's Association, 58,* 95-98; Yarber, W. L., Graham, C. A., Sanders, S. A., Crosby, R. A., Butler, S. M., & Hartzell, R. M. (2007). "Do you know what you are doing?" College students' experiences with male condoms. *American Journal of Health Education, 39,* 322-331.

> Students learn to think critically about high-interest topics in sexuality such as "Surrendering to Sexual Pleasure," "The First Kiss: A Deal Breaker?" "Is Intercourse Enough? The Big 'O' and Sexual Behaviors," and "Are Gay and Lesbian Couples Any Different from Heterosexual Ones?"

> Students learn about major course topics with short video clips designed to prompt critical thinking.

62% of human sexuality instructors state that teaching their students a healthy lifestyle is a top goal of their course.

The Sexual Body in Health and Illness

13
chapter

MAIN TOPICS

Living in Our Bodies: The Quest for Physical Perfection

Alcohol, Drugs, and Sexuality

Sexuality and Disability

Sexuality and Cancer

Additional Sexual Health Issues

> *Human Sexuality* features four significantly revised chapters that have the most direct impact on students and their well-being— Chapter 11: Contraception, Birth Control, and Abortion, Chapter 13: The Sexual Body in Health and Illness, Chapter 15: Sexually Transmitted Infections, and Chapter 16: HIV and AIDS—and offers the most current data.

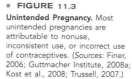 **FIGURE** 11.3

Unintended Pregnancy. Most unintended pregnancies are attributable to nonuse, inconsistent use, or incorrect use of contraceptives. (*Sources:* Finer, 2006; Guttmacher Institute, 2008a; Kost et al., 2008; Trussell, 2007.)

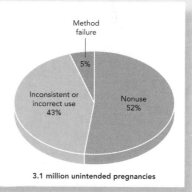

Method failure

5%

Inconsistent or incorrect use
43%

Nonuse
52%

3.1 million unintended pregnancies

If you would like to participate in any of the McGraw-Hill research initiatives, please contact us at **research@mcgraw-hill.com**.

Preface to the Instructor

HUMAN SEXUALITY: DIVERSITY IN CONTEMPORARY *America* continues to be a pioneering text in many ways. It is the first text to achieve a full integration of cutting-edge research with a contemporary "sex-positive" approach that encourages students to become proactive in and about their own sexual well-being. By stressing critical thinking about human sexuality, this text prompts students to examine their own values and the ways they express their sexuality. It also strives to represent the contemporary, diverse world that students encounter outside the classroom.

Both within the text itself and throughout the exemplary art and photo program, the focus is on inclusion. Written by leading sexuality researchers who are also experienced teachers of courses in human sexuality, this book has been lauded by students and instructors alike for providing the most integrated and nonjudgmental view of sexual variation available. This modern theme, along with the thorough and empirical coverage of sexuality and culture, an engaging writing style, and a biopsychosocial orientation, defines the book's approach. The new seventh edition builds on these strengths and adds updated information, a revised design, and a highly crafted resource program to make the book more useful than ever.

Sex-Positive Approach: Health and Well-Being

We strongly believe that studying human sexuality is one way of increasing the healthy lifestyle of students. With that in mind, we have significantly revised four chapters that have the most direct impact on students and their well-being: Chapter 11: Contraception, Birth Control, and Abortion, Chapter 13: The Sexual Body in Health and Illness, Chapter 15: Sexually Transmitted Infections, and Chapter 16: HIV and AIDS.

Sex-Positive Approach: Thinking Critically about Sexuality through Print

Think about It features prompt students to think critically about high-interest topics in sexuality such as "Surrendering to Sexual Pleasure," "The Kiss: A Deal Breaker?" "Is Intercourse Enough? The Big 'O' and Sexual Behaviors," and "Are Gay and Lesbian Couples Any Different from Heterosexual Ones?"

Sex-Positive Approach: Thinking Critically about Sexuality through Videos

SexSource Online offers short video clips with further perspective about major course topics. Each video is accompanied by pre- and post-viewing questions that prompt critical thinking. You will find the video icon in the margins of your book directing you to the site.

● New in This Edition

In writing this seventh edition of *Human Sexuality: Diversity in Contemporary America,* we continue to be struck by the ever-changing nuances and complexity in the nature of human sexuality. Like a partnership that changes and evolves with time, we have in this edition remained loyal to the foundation of our book and deepened our exploration and presentation of topics. What we provide the reader is what we feel are the most relevant and current data, patterns, and variations available in the field. We hope that in reading this text, you agree.

Continuous developments in the field of human sexuality demand a text that reflects the dynamic changes of our society and the current state of sexuality research. So, once again, we have gone line-by-line through the text to ensure that concepts and facts are current and representative of the most recent findings in the field. Because of the effectiveness reported by students and instructors, we have chosen to continue using the same instructional approach in this seventh edition. We have made several major changes and chapter content updates that we believe will enhance learning. These include:

- Significant revisions on the following chapters: Chapter 11: Contraception, Birth Control, and Abortion; Chapter 13: The Sexual Body in Health and Illness; Chapter 15: Sexually Transmitted Infections; and Chapter 16: HIV and AIDS. See other chapter by chapter content changes to the dynamic field of human sexuality on page xxvi under Chapter Content Changes.

- Streamlined text and reduced the overall number of pages by 12 to retain the book's accessibility to students

- Added provocative and engaging "Critical Thinking Questions" to each Think About It box

- Replaced a variety of Think About It boxes with ones that are more reflective of college students' interest and behaviors, such as "Why College Students Have Sex," "Hooking Up Among College Students," and "The First Kiss: A Deal-Breaker?"

- Updated and moved menopause content from "The Sexual Body in Health and Illness" (Chapter 13) to "Sexuality in Adulthood" (Chapter 7)

- Increased focus on inclusive, nonjudgmental language and nomenclature

- Expanded global perspective in content coverage and in illustrations program

- Increased focus on issues and policies concerning gay, lesbian, bisexual, transgender, and intersex individuals

- Revised graphic design to improve the functionality and visual appeal of tables, figures, and features

- Updated material related to STIs, HIV/AIDS, emergency contraception, assisted reproductive technologies, menopausal hormone therapy, managing HPV, sexual function difficulties, and laws related to sexuality
- Increased focus on social networking and Web-based resources

● Chapter Content Changes

Chapter 1: Perspectives on Human Sexuality

- New material on online social networking
- New research on sexuality in television and film
- New research on parents' response to sexual content in the media
- Expanded discussion of sexuality and evolution

Chapter 2: Studying Human Sexuality

- Updated discussion of the campus newspaper sex advice column
- New material on the distortion of sex-related research by the media
- New example of a sex questionnaire
- Expanded presentation of the findings from the National Survey of Family Growth study of sexual behavior of men and women, 15 to 44 years of age
- The most recent findings of the American College Health Association research on college student sexual behavior

Chapter 3: Female Sexual Anatomy, Physiology, and Response

- New coverage of cosmetic genital surgery
- Expanded discussion of the ovarian cycle
- New research on orgasm and health

Chapter 4: Male Sexual Anatomy, Physiology, and Response

- New coverage of male body modification
- Expanded discussion of sexual practices in other countries
- Updated discussion of testosterone replacement therapy

Chapter 5: Gender and Gender Roles

- Updated nomenclature on disorders of sexual development
- New research on intersex and disorders of sexual development
- New proposed standards of care for those with disorders of sexual development
- New research into the etiology of gender identity disorder

Chapter 6: Sexuality in Childhood and Adolescence

- Expanded coverage of influences on the psychosexual development of children and youth
- New research about social effects on teen sexuality
- Increased coverage of gender differences in rates of masturbation
- New data on prevalence and motivations of sexual behavior
- New research examining the origins of sexual orientation
- Updated discussion and new research on sexuality education

Chapter 7: Sexuality in Adulthood

- Updated discussion of bisexuality
- New Think About It box featuring gender differences and motivations for sex
- New research on cohabiting couples
- New findings on expectations in adult love relationships
- New data on sexual frequency, behaviors, and challenges of older Americans
- Formerly part of a chapter on sexuality and health, the topic of menopause is updated and integrated into this chapter
- New Think About It box on a global perspective on sexual well-being and older adults

Chapter 8: Love and Communication in Intimate Relationships

- New study on love and sexuality activity
- New Think About It box exploring similarities and differences between homosexual couples and heterosexual ones
- Examination of the brain "in love"
- Research questionnaire added: "Passionate Love Scale"
- Deeper exploration into gender differences in communication
- New research on why couples have conflict

Chapter 9: Sexual Expression

- New research about college undergraduate women's view of the sex appeal of muscular men
- New Think About It box on hooking up among college students
- New discussion on college students' desired number of sexual partners
- Expanded discussion of Internet match-making services
- Expanded discussion of gender differences in sexual fantasies
- New research about masturbation among men and women
- New Think About It box on the meanings of kissing
- New research on opinions of what behaviors constitute having had sex
- New research on college students and oral sex
- Updated and expanded art depicting sexual behaviors

Chapter 10: Variations in Sexual Behavior

- Expanded discussion of research on transvestic fetishism
- New Think About It box on college students and voyeurism
- New research on voyeurism and exhibitionism
- New data discussion of how to deal with harassing or obscene phone calls

Chapter 11: Contraception, Birth Control, and Abortion

- New data on unintended pregnancies
- New discussion of family planning clinics and disadvantaged women
- Latest research and updates on all birth control devices
- Update on sterilization
- New data on the prevalence and status of abortion

Chapter 12: Conception, Pregnancy, and Childbirth

- New recommendations for diagnostic testing in pregnancy
- New research on assisted reproductive technologies
- Update on policies and procedures for pregnancy, delivery and new mothers, and families

Chapter 13: The Sexual Body in Health and Illness

- Updated discussion on breast and penis enhancement
- New research on the prevalence and factors related to eating disorders
- New research on anabolic steroid use by college students
- New research on college students and alcohol drinking
- New material on use of drugs as an aphrodisiac
- Updated discussion on breast cancer
- Updated discussion on the HPV vaccine Gardasil
- Updated discussion on prostate cancer
- New material on female genital cutting
- New material on prostatitis

Chapter 14: Sexual Function Difficulties, Dissatisfaction, Enhancement, and Therapy

- Expanded discussion on the prevalence of female orgasm
- New Think About It box on sexual behaviors that enhance female orgasm
- New Think About It box on sexual pleasure
- New material on the sexual response cycle, the Erotic Stimulus Pathway
- Updated discussion on sexual enhancement products
- New material on disparities in sexual desire in a couple
- New material reported by women to facilitate orgasm
- New and refined art depicting sexual behaviors

Chapter 15: Sexually Transmitted Infections

- Updated information on the prevalence and incidence of major STIs
- Updated medical information on the major STIs
- New material on condoms and STI prevention
- Updated discussion of circumcision and STI prevention and sexual pleasure
- Added discussion of cervicitis
- Updated research on condom use errors and problems among college students

Chapter 16: HIV and AIDS

- Updated information on the prevalence and incidence of HIV/AIDS in the United States and worldwide
- Updated medical information on HIV/AIDS
- Updated figure on the infection of a CD4 T cell by HIV
- New research on estimated lifetime risk of HIV diagnosis by race/ethnicity and sex
- New material on sexual risk behaviors
- New material on people's judgment of the HIV risk of a potential sex partner
- New material on the success of HIV prevention efforts

Chapter 17: Sexual Coercion: Harassment, Aggression, and Abuse

- Updated information on the prevalence and outcomes of sexual harassment, aggression, rape, and child sexual abuse
- New public opinion polls on gay and lesbian rights and issues
- Updated coverage of state hate crimes laws
- Updated discussion of date rape drugs
- Expanded discussion of sexual harassing among college students

Chapter 18: Sexually Explicit Materials, Prostitution, and Sex Laws

- New material on Internet sex site use by college students
- New Think About It box on research on college students' viewing of sexually explicit media
- Updated research on the consumption of sexually explicit videos and sexual assault
- Updated discussion of the Child Obscenity and Pornography Act
- Expanded discussion of various types of prostitutes
- New material on court rulings on gay rights

● *Human Sexuality* Teaching and Learning Resources Program

Human Sexuality is the heart of a complete resource program for both students and instructors. The following materials have been carefully developed by a team of experienced human sexuality instructors to support a variety of teaching and learning styles.

Online Learning Center for Instructors This password-protected Web site contains the Test Bank, Instructor's Manual, PowerPoint presentations, CPS questions, and Image Gallery, as well as access to the entire student side of the Web site. To access these resources, please go to www.mhhe.com/yarber7e.

Instructor's Manual prepared by Sandra Pacheco, California State University–Monterey Bay. This guide begins with general concepts and strategies for teaching human sexuality. Each chapter includes a chapter outline, learning objectives, discussion questions, activities, a list of DVDs and videos, a bibliography, worksheets, handouts, and Internet activities. The *Instructor's Manual* can be accessed on the text's Online Learning Center for instructors.

Test Bank prepared by Tori Bovard, American River. The *Test Bank* has been thoroughly revised and updated to support the new edition. Each chapter offers over 100 questions, including multiple choice, true/false, and short answer questions. These test items are available on instructor's Online Learning Center as Word files and in EZ Test, an easy-to-use electronic test bank that allows instructors to easily edit and add their own questions.

PowerPoint Presentations, prepared by Betty Dorr, Fort Lewis College. Available on the Online Learning Center, these slides cover the key points of the chapter and can be used as is or modified to support individual instructors' lectures. Digital versions of many images and figures from the textbook are also available in the Image Gallery.

Classroom Performance System (CPS) The Classroom Performance System (CPS) from **eInstruction** allows instructors to gauge immediately what students are learning during lectures. With CPS, instructors can take attendance, ask questions, take polls, or host classroom demonstrations and get instant feedback.

SexSource **Online** illuminates key concepts in human sexuality with a collection of scientifically based educational videos. Icons appear throughout the text to indicate clips that correspond to specific topics. Each video is accompanied by pre- and post-viewing questions. *SexSource* **Online** content and assessment items are also included in the course cartridge. The site can be accessed from the Online Learning Center or at **www.mhhe.com/sexsource.**

The Online Learning Center for Students includes multiple choice, true/false, and fill-in-the-blank practice quizzes to help the students prepare for exams. To access these resources please go to **www.mhhe.com/yarber7e.**

McGraw-Hill publishes **Annual Editions: Human Sexuality,** a collection of articles on topics related to the latest research and thinking in human sexuality from over 300 public press sources. These editions are updated annually and contain helpful features, including a topic guide, an annotated table of contents, unit overviews, and a topical index. An instructor's guide containing testing materials is also available. ISBN: 0073516341

For information on any component of the teaching and learning package, instructors should contact their McGraw-Hill representative.

● Acknowledgments

Many people contributed to the creation and development of this book. First and foremost, we wish to thank the many students whose voices appear in the introduction of each chapter. The majority of these excerpts come from Bobbi Mitzenmacher's, Barbara Sayad's, and William L. Yarber's undergraduate human sexuality students (California State University, Long Beach and Monterey Bay, and Indiana University), who have courageously agreed to share their experiences. All of these students have given permission to use their experiences and quotations so that others might share and learn from their reflections.

A number of reviewers and adopters were instrumental in directing the authors to needed changes, updates, and resources, and we are most grateful for their insights and contributions. Whenever possible, we have taken their suggestions and integrated them into the text. Special thanks are owed to the following reviewers of the sixth edition:

Michael W. Agopian, Los Angeles Harbor College
Glenn Carter, Austin Peay State University
Ellen Cole, Alaska Pacific University
Sara L. Crawley, University of South Florida
Linda De Villers, Pepperdine University
Betty Dorr, Fort Lewis College
Amanda Emo, University of Cincinnati
Jean Hoth, Rochester Community and Technical College
Mary Meiners, Miramar College
William O'Donohue, University of Nevada
Carlos Sandoval, Cypress College
Mary Ann Watson, Metro State College at Denver
Laurie M. Wagner, Kent State University

Thanks also to the reviewers of the seventh edition:

Stephanie Coday, Sierra College
Jodi Martin deCamilo, St Louis Community College-Meramec-Kirkwood
Dale Doty, Monroe Community College
Duane Dowd, Central Washington University, Ellensburg
Edward Fliss, St. Louis Community College, Florissant Valley
Richard Hardy, Indiana University at Bloomington
Lynne M. Kemen, Hunter College
Nancy King, Western Michigan University, Kalamazoo
Kris Koehne, University of Tennessee–Knoxville
Jennifer Musick, Long Beach City College
Diane Pisacreta, St Louis Community College-Meramec-Kirkwood
Grace Pokorny, Long Beach City College
Michael Rahilly, University of California at Davis
Sally Raskoff, Los Angeles Valley College

Daniel Rubin, Valencia Community College, West Campus
Regine Rucker, University of Illinois, Champaign
Catherine Sherwood-Puzzello, Indiana University at Bloomington
Peggy Skinner, South Plains College

Publishing a textbook is similar to producing a stage show in that even with a clear concept and great writing, there are individuals without whom the production (in this case, of the textbook) would not be possible. Our thanks go to our sponsoring editor, Mike Sugarman, whose vision and energy helped guide the publication of this book. Additional kudos and gratitude go to Dawn Groundwater, director of development, and to Cheri Dellelo, developmental editor, both of whom were intimately involved with all aspects of this publication. Project manager Catherine Morris was a constant in assisting us in finding answers to questions and guiding us through the production process. A special thanks to Margaret Moore, manuscript editor, Ashley Bedell, design manager, Linda Beaupré, text and cover designer, Brian Pecko, photo researcher, Robin Mouat, art editor, Tandra Jorgensen, production supervisor, and Sarah Colwell, supplements editor. Our combined efforts have contributed to a book about which we can all be proud.

Preface to the Student

Being sexual is an essential part of being human. Through our sexuality, we are able to connect with others on the most intimate levels, revealing ourselves and creating strong bonds. Sexuality can be a source of great pleasure and profound satisfaction. Certainly, it is the means by which we reproduce—bringing new life into the world and transforming ourselves into mothers and fathers. Paradoxically, sexuality can also be a source of guilt and confusion, anger and disappointment, a pathway to infection, and a means of exploitation and aggression. Examining the multiple aspects of human sexuality will help you understand, accept, and appreciate your own sexuality and that of others. It will provide the basis for enriching your relationships.

Throughout our lives, we make sexual choices based on our experiences, attitudes, values, and knowledge. The decisions we face include whether to become or remain sexually active; whether to establish, continue, or end a sexual relationship; whether to practice safer sex consistently; and how to resolve conflicts, if they exist, between society's and our own values and our sexual desires, feelings, and behaviors. The choices we make may vary at different times in our lives. Our sexuality evolves as we ourselves change.

● Studying Human Sexuality

Students begin studying sexuality for many reasons: to gain insight into their sexuality and relationships, to become more comfortable with their sexuality, to explore personal sexual issues, to dispel anxieties and doubts, to validate their sexual identity, to resolve traumatic sexual experiences, to learn how to avoid STIs and unintended pregnancy, to increase their knowledge about sexuality, or to prepare for the helping professions. Many students find the study of sexuality empowering; they develop the ability to make intelligent sexual choices based on their own needs, desires, and values rather than on ignorance, pressure, guilt, fear, or conformity.

The study of human sexuality differs from the study of accounting, plant biology, and medieval history, for example, because human sexuality is surrounded by a vast array of taboos, fears, prejudices, and hypocrisy. For many, sexuality creates ambivalent feelings. It is linked not only with intimacy and pleasure but also with shame, guilt, and discomfort. As a result, you may find yourself confronted with society's mixed feelings about sexuality as you study it. You may find, for example, that others perceive you as somehow "unique" or "different" for taking a course in human sexuality. Some may feel threatened in a vague, undefined way. Parents, partners, or spouses (or your own children, if you are a parent) may wonder why you want to take a "sex class"; they may want to know why you don't take something more "serious"—as if sexuality were not one of the most important issues we face as individuals and as a society. Sometimes this uneasiness manifests itself in humor, one of the ways in which we deal with ambivalent feelings: "You mean you have to take a *class* on sex?" "Are there labs?" "Why don't you let me show you?"

Ironically, despite societal ambivalence, you may quickly find that your human sexuality textbook becomes the most popular book in your dormitory or apartment. "I can never find my textbook when I need it," one of our students complained. "My roommates are always reading it. And they're not even taking the course!" Another student observed: "My friends used to kid me about taking the class, but now the first thing they ask when they see me is what we discussed in class." "People borrow my book so often without asking," wrote one student, "that I hide it now."

What these responses signify is simple: Despite their ambivalence, people *want* to learn about human sexuality. On some level, they understand that what they have learned may have been haphazard, unreliable, stereotypical, incomplete, unrealistic, irrelevant—or dishonest. As adults, they are ready to move beyond "sperm meets egg" stories.

As you study human sexuality, you will find yourself exploring areas not ordinarily discussed in other classes. Sometimes they are rarely talked about even among friends. They may be prohibited by parental or religious teaching. The more an area is judged to be in some way "bad," "immoral," or "off-limits" the less likely it is to be discussed. Typical behaviors such as masturbation and sexual fantasies are often the source of considerable guilt and shame. But in your human sexuality course, they will be examined objectively. You may be surprised to discover, in fact, that part of your learning involves *unlearning* myths, factual errors, distortions, biases, and prejudices you learned previously.

You may feel uncomfortable and nervous in your first class meetings. These feelings are not at all uncommon. Sexuality may be the most taboo subject you study as an undergraduate. Your comfort level in class will probably increase as you recognize that you and your fellow students have a common purpose in learning about sexuality. Your sense of ease may also increase as you and your classmates get to know one another and discuss sexuality, both inside and outside of class.

You may find that, as you become accustomed to using the accepted sexual vocabulary, you are more comfortable discussing various topics. For example, your communication with a partner may improve, which will strengthen your relationship and increase sexual satisfaction for both of you. You may never before have used the words "masturbation," "sexual intercourse," "clitoris," or "penis" in a class setting (or any kind of setting, for that matter). But after a while, they may become second nature to you. You may discover that discussing sexuality academically becomes as easy as discussing computer science, astronomy, or literature. You may even find yourself, as many students do, telling your friends what you learned in class while on a bus or in a restaurant, as other passengers or diners gasp in shock or lean toward you to hear better!

Studying sexuality requires respect for your fellow students. You'll discover that the experiences and values of your classmates vary greatly. Some students have little sexual experience, while others have substantial experience; some students hold progressive sexual values, while others hold conservative ones.

Some students are gay, lesbian, or bisexual individuals, while the majority are heterosexual people. Most students are young, others middle-aged, some old—each in a different stage of life and with different developmental tasks before them. Furthermore, the presence of students from any of the numerous ethnic groups in the United States reminds us that there is no single behavioral, attitudinal, value, or sexual norm system that encompasses sexuality in contemporary America. Finally, you will find that you become more accepting of yourself as a sexual being by studying human sexuality. Our culture conveys few positive messages affirming the naturalness of sexuality. Those studying sexuality often report that they become more appreciative of their sexuality and less apologetic, defensive, or shameful about their sexual feelings, attractions, and desires. Accepting one's sexuality also means viewing sexuality as normal and as an integral, beautiful, and joyful part of being human. Accepting one's own sexuality is an important component in owning one's own sexuality.

Because of America's diversity in terms of experience, values, orientation, age, and ethnicity, for example, the study of sexuality calls for us to be open-minded: to be receptive to new ideas and to various perspectives; to seek to understand what we have not understood before; to reexamine old assumptions, ideas, and beliefs; to encompass the humanness and uniqueness in each of us. In our quest for knowledge and understanding, we need to be intellectually curious. As writer Joan Nestle observes, "Curiosity builds bridges. . . . Curiosity is not trivial; it is the respect one life pays to another."

● The Authors' Perspective

We developed this textbook along several themes, which we believe will help you better understand your sexuality and that of others.

Sexuality as a Fundamental Component of Health and Well-Being

As one component of the human condition, sexuality can impact personal well-being. When balanced with other life needs, sexuality contributes positively to personal health and happiness. When expressed in destructive ways, it can impair health and well-being. We believe that studying human sexuality is one way of increasing the healthy lifestyle of our students. Integrated into all chapters are discussions, research, questions, prompts, and Web sites that interrelate students' well-being and their sexuality.

Biopsychosocial Orientation

Although we are creatures rooted in biology, hormones and the desire to reproduce are not the only important factors shaping our sexuality. We believe that the most significant factor is the interplay between biology, individual personalities, and social factors. Therefore, we take a biopsychosocial perspective in explaining human sexuality. This perspective emphasizes the roles of biology (maleness or femaleness, the influence of genetics, the role of hormones), of psychological factors (such as motivation, emotions, and attitudes), and of social learning (the process of learning from others and from society). We look at how sexuality is shaped in our culture; we examine how it varies in different historical periods and between different ethnic groups in our culture. We also examine how sexuality takes different forms in other cultures throughout the world.

In addition, because we want students to apply the concepts presented in this book to their own lives, we present information and ideas in ways that encourage students to become proactive in their own sexual well-being. We highlight sexual health–related topics and prompt revelant questions in boxes called "Think About It"; we ask students to examine their own values and the ways they express their sexuality in boxes called "Practically Speaking"; and we encourage students to probe the subject beyond what the book presents in a feature called "Sex and the Internet" and in the "Discussion Questions."

Sexuality as Intimacy

We believe that sexuality in our culture is basically an expressive and intimate activity. It is a vehicle for expressing feelings, whether positive or negative. Sexuality is also a means for establishing and maintaining intimacy. Sexual expression is important as a means of reproduction as well, but because of the widespread use of birth control, reproduction has increasingly become a matter of choice.

Gender Roles

Gender roles are societal expectations of how women and men should behave in a particular culture. Among other things, gender roles tell us how we are supposed to act sexually. Although women and men differ, we believe most differences are rooted more in social learning than in biology.

Traditionally, our gender roles have viewed men and women as "opposite" sexes. Men were active, women passive; men were sexually aggressive, women sexually receptive; men sought sex, women, love. Research, however, suggests that we are more alike than different as men and women. To reflect our commonalities rather than our differences, we refer not to the "opposite" sex, but to the "other" sex.

Sexuality and Popular Culture

Much of what we learn about sexuality from popular culture and the media—from so-called sex experts, magazine articles, how-to books, the Internet, TV, and the movies—is wrong, half-true, or stereotypical. Prejudice may masquerade as fact. Scholarly research may also be limited or flawed for various reasons. Throughout the textbook, we look at how we can evaluate what we read and see, both in popular culture and in scholarly research. We compare scholarly findings to sexual myths and beliefs, including research about gay men, lesbian women, bisexual individuals, transgender people, and ethnic groups.

The Commonality of Sexual Variation

One of Alfred Kinsey's most important discoveries is that there is wide variation in the sexuality and sexual expression of individuals. As discussed in Chapter 2,

What Students Want to Learn in a Human Sexuality Course: The Personal Dimension

Students begin the study of human sexuality for a **multitude of reasons.** When we asked our students to tell us what they wanted to learn in our class, their answers emphasized the personal dimension of learning. The student responses below are representative.

- My biggest issue is setting my own sexual guidelines, rather than accepting those of others, such as my friends, society, etc.

  —a 20-year-old woman

- I want to know the difference between sex and love. When I have sex with a woman, I think I'm in love with her, or at least want to be. Am I kidding myself?

  —a 21-year-old man

- I have a hard time telling my boyfriend what I want him to do. I get embarrassed and end up not getting what I need.

  —a 19-year-old woman

- I lost my virginity last week. What do you do when you sleep with someone for the first time?

  —an 18-year-old man

- I recently separated from my husband and am beginning to date again. I'd like to know what the proper sexual etiquette is today. Such as, do you kiss or have sex on the first date . . . or what?

  —a 37-year-old woman

- I'm gay, but my family would disown me if they found out. What can I do to make my parents understand that it's OK to be gay?

  —a 20-year-old man

- My parents continue to hassle me about sex. They want me to be a virgin when I marry (which is next to impossible,

since I lost my virginity when I was sixteen). Any suggestions on how to raise parents?

  —a 19-year-old woman

- Is it wrong to masturbate if you have a regular partner?

  —a 22-year-old man

- Why do women get called "sluts" if they have more than one partner, and it doesn't matter for guys? In fact, the more women men "have," the more points they get.

  —an 18-year-old woman

- How do I know if I'm normal? What is normal? And why do I care?

  —a 21-year-old man

- I'm a sexy seventy-year-old. How come young people think sex stops when you're over forty? We don't spend all day just knitting, you know.

  —a 70-year-old woman

Some of these questions relate to facts, some concern attitudes or relationships, and still others concern values. But all of them are within the domain of human sexuality. As you study human sexuality, you may find answers to many of these questions, as well as those of your own. You will also find that your class will raise questions the textbook or instructor cannot answer. Part of the reason we cannot answer all your questions is that there is insufficient research available to give an adequate response. But part of the reason also may be that it is not the domain of social science to answer questions of value. As social scientists, it is our role to provide you with knowledge, analytical skills, and insights for making your own sexual decisions. It is you who are ultimately responsible for determining your sexual value system and sexual code of behavior.

Kinsey also rejected the normal/abnormal dichotomy often used to describe certain sexual behaviors. Throughout the text we examine variation, highlighting its commonality without labeling such behaviors as normal or abnormal. For example, we recognize that gay, lesbian, and bisexual individuals are as capable of achieving happiness and rewarding relationships as heterosexual persons. However, as we know, gay, lesbian, bisexual, and transgender individuals have been subjected to discrimination, prejudice, and injustice for centuries. As society has become more enlightened, it has discovered that these individuals do not differ from heterosexual people in any significant aspect other than their sexual attractions. In 1972 the American Psychiatric Association removed homosexuality from its list of mental disorders, and in 2003 the U.S. Supreme

Court struck down laws against sodomy. Today, the major professional psychological, sociological, and health associations in the United States no longer consider homosexuality an abnormality. In fact, APA repudiates gay-to-straight or so-called "reparative" therapy. We have integrated discussions of lesbian women, gay men, and bisexual people, and other sexual variations throughout the book.

The Significance of Ethnicity

Until recently, Americans have ignored race and ethnicity as a factor in studying human sexuality. We have acted as if being White, African American, Latino, Asian American, or Native American made no difference in terms of sexual attitudes, behaviors, and values. But there are important differences, and we discuss these throughout the book. It is important to examine these differences within their cultural context. Ethnic differences, therefore, should not be interpreted as "good" or "bad," "healthy" or "deficient," but as reflections of the diversity in our culture. Our understanding of the role of race and ethnicity in sexuality, however, is limited because research in this area is still evolving.

• • •

Over the years, we have asked our students to briefly state what they learned or gained in our human sexuality classes. Here are some of their answers:

> I learned to value the exploration of my sexuality much more. I learned that sexuality comes in many forms, and I'm one of them. The class gave me a forum or safe place to explore sexuality, especially since I have not yet had a fully sexual relationship.

> I found the psychological, historical, and anthropological elements of sexuality we discussed to be valuable. I see homosexuality in a totally new light.

> I learned that being sexual is OK, that basically we are all sexual beings and that it is normal to want to have sex. I am no longer afraid to talk about sex with my boyfriend.

> The information about AIDS cleared up many misconceptions and fears I had. I will always practice safer sex from now on.

> The class has helped me come to terms with things that have happened over the last few months that are disturbing to me.

> I have paid more attention to the erotic nature of things, not just the physical aspects of sex.

We believe that the knowledge about sexuality, insights about the role of sexuality in life, and an understanding of the components of a healthy sexuality you gain from studying human sexuality will be something you will carry with you the rest of your life. We hope that studying human sexuality will help you understand and appreciate not only yourself but those who differ from you, and that it will enrich, expand, and enliven your experiences and your relationships, thus contributing to enhanced personal happiness and health.

chapter 1

Perspectives on Human Sexuality

MAIN TOPICS

Sexuality, Popular Culture,
and the Media

Sexuality Across Cultures and Times

Societal Norms and Sexuality

"The media, especially magazines and television, has had an influence on shaping my sexual identity. Ever since I was a little girl, I have watched the women on TV and hoped I would grow up to look sexy and beautiful like them. I feel that because of the constant barrage of images of beautiful women on TV and in magazines young girls like me grow up with unrealistic expectations of what beauty is and are doomed to feel they have not met this exaggerated standard."

—21-year-old female

"The phone, television, and radio became my best friends. I never missed an episode of any of the latest shows, and I knew all the words to every new song. And when they invented three-way calling, you would have thought the phone was glued to my ear. At school, we would talk about the shows: whom we thought was cute and how we wanted houses, cars, and husbands. All of the things we saw on TV were all of the things we fantasized about. Watching music videos and the sexual gestures were always [stereotyped as] male and female. These are the things we would talk about."

—23-year-old female

"Though I firmly believe that we are our own harshest critics, I also believe that the media has a large role in influencing how we think of ourselves. I felt like ripping my hair out every time I saw a skinny model whose stomach was as hard and flat as a board, with their flawless skin and perfectly coifed hair. I cringed when I realized that my legs seemed to have an extra 'wiggle-jiggle' when I walked. All I could do was watch the television and feel abashed at the differences in their bodies compared to mine. When magazines and movies tell me that for my age I should weigh no more than a hundred pounds, I feel like saying, 'Well, gee, it's no wonder I finally turned to laxatives with all these pressures to be thin surrounding me.' I ached to be model-thin and pretty. This fixation to be as beautiful and coveted as these models so preoccupied me that I had no time to even think about anyone or anything else."

—18-year-old female

"I am aware that I may be lacking in certain areas of my sexual self-esteem, but I am cognizant of my shortcomings and am willing to work on them. A person's sexual self-esteem isn't something that is detached from his or her daily life. It is intertwined in every aspect of life and how one views his or her self: emotionally, physically, and mentally. For my own sake, as well as my daughter's, I feel it is important for me to develop and model a healthy sexual self-esteem."

—28-year-old male

Sexuality was once hidden from view in our culture: Fig leaves covered the "private parts" of nudes; poultry breasts were renamed "white meat"; censors prohibited the publication of the works of D. H. Lawrence, James Joyce, and Henry Miller; and homosexuality was called "the love that dares not speak its name." But over the past few generations, sexuality has become more open. In recent years, popular culture and the media have transformed what we "know" about sexuality. Not only is sexuality *not* hidden from view; it often seems to surround us.

In this chapter, we examine popular culture and the media to see how they shape our ideas about sexuality. Then we look at how sexuality has been treated in different cultures and at different times in history. Finally, we examine how society defines various aspects of our sexuality as natural or normal.

● Sexuality, Popular Culture, and the Media

Much of sexuality is influenced and shaped by popular culture, especially the mass media. Popular culture presents us with myriad images of what it means to be sexual. But what kinds of sexuality do the media portray for our consumption?

" Nature is to be reverenced, not blushed at.

—Tertullian,
(c. A.D. 155–c. 220)

Images of sexuality permeate our society, sexualizing our environment. Think about the sexual images you see or hear in a 24-hour period. What messages do they communicate about sexuality?

What messages do the media send about sex to children, adolescents, adults, and older people? To men and women and to those of varied races, ethnicities, and sexual orientations? Perhaps as important as what the media portray sexually is what is not portrayed—masturbation, condom use, and older adults' sexuality, for example.

> One picture is worth more than a thousand words.
>
> —Chinese proverb

Media Portrayals of Sexuality

The media, and television in particular, is one of the sexual socialization agents that has assumed a prominent role in the lives of American youth (Roberts, Foehr, & Rideout, 2005). While television provides sources of information about sex, drugs, AIDS, and violence, as well as about how to behave in relationships (Gruber & Grube, 2000), researchers know almost nothing about the social and physical contexts in which people of any age accept, adopt, or apply television to their lives (Roberts, 2000; Roberts, Foehr, & Rideout, 2005). Given that half the time teens are awake is spent with some form of media (Roberts, Foehr, & Rideout, 2005), American youth devote more time to media than to any other waking activity (see Figure 1.1).

The music industry is awash with sexual images. Contemporary pop music, from rock 'n' roll to rap, is filled with lyrics about sexuality mixed with messages about love, rejection, violence, and loneliness. Popular music is transmitted through CDs and MP3s and through the Internet, television, and radio. MTV, VH1, BET, and music video programs broadcast videos filled with sexually suggestive lyrics, images, and dances. Because of censorship issues, the most overtly sexual music is not played on the radio, except for some college stations.

Magazines, tabloids, and books contribute to the sexualization of our society. Popular novels, romances, and self-help books disseminate ideas and values about sexuality. Supermarket tabloid headlines exploit the unusual ("Woman with Two Vaginas Has Multiple Lovers") or sensational ("Televangelist's Love Tryst Exposed").

● **FIGURE 1.1**

Time U.S. Youth, Ages 8–18, Spend Using Media per Day by Type of Media. (*Source:* Roberts, Foehr, & Rideout, 2005.)

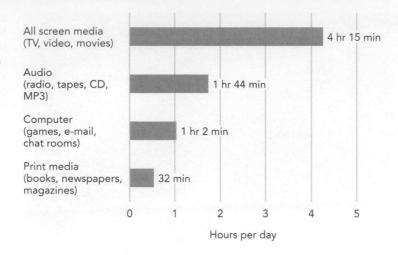

All screen media (TV, video, movies)	4 hr 15 min
Audio (radio, tapes, CD, MP3)	1 hr 44 min
Computer (games, e-mail, chat rooms)	1 hr 2 min
Print media (books, newspapers, magazines)	32 min

Hours per day

Women's magazines such as *Cosmopolitan, Vogue,* and *Glamour* use sex to sell their publications. How do these magazines differ from men's magazines such as *Men's Health, Playboy,* and *Maxim* in their treatment of sexuality?

Men's magazines have been singled out for their sexual emphasis. *Playboy, Penthouse,* and *Maxim,* with their Playmates of the Month, Pets of the Month, and other nude pictorials, are among the most popular magazines in the world. *Sports Illustrated*'s annual swimsuit edition sells more than 5 million copies, twice as many as its other issues. But it would be a mistake to think that only male-oriented magazines focus on sex.

Women's magazines such as *Cosmopolitan* and *Redbook* have their own sexual content. These magazines feature romantic photographs of lovers to illustrate stories with such titles as "Sizzling Sex Secrets of the World's Sexiest Women," "Making Love Last: If Your Partner Is a Premature Ejaculator," and "Turn on Your Man with Your Breasts (Even If They Are Small)." Preadolescents and young teens are not exempt from sexual images and articles in magazines such as *Seventeen* and *YM.* Some of the men's health magazines have followed the lead of women's magazines, featuring sexuality-related issues as a way to sell more copies.

For many, a click on the World Wide Web allows sex on demand. The Internet's contributions to the availability and commercialization of sex include live clips and chats, personalized pages and ads, and links to potential or virtual sex partners. The spread of the Web has made it easy to obtain information, social ties, and sexual gratification.

Telephone sex has become an increasingly popular means of attaining sexual arousal and pleasure. Because the Federal Communications Commission (FCC) has banned obscene communication for commercial purposes in the United States, most calls made for this purpose are to overseas businesses.

Advertising in all media uses the sexual sell, promising sex, romance, popularity, and fulfillment if the consumer will only purchase the right soap, perfume, cigarettes, alcohol, toothpaste, jeans, or automobile. In reality, not only does one *not* become "sexy" or popular by consuming a certain product, but the product may actually be detrimental to one's sexual well-being, as in the case of cigarettes or alcohol.

Media images of sexuality permeate a variety of areas in people's lives (see Figure 1.2). They can produce sexual arousal and emotional reactions, increase sexual behaviors, and be a source of sex information. Summarizing a handful of studies on the relationship between exposure to sexual media and our sexual behavior, professor and writer Jane D. Brown (2002) reports that the media (1) keep sexual behavior visible, (2) reinforce a consistent set of sexual and relationship norms, and (3) rarely include sexually responsible models. No doubt, this form of persuasive

Sexual images are used to sell products. What ideas are conveyed by this advertisement? How does its appeal differ according to whether one is male or female?

We know what makes you feel good.

communication is altering patterns of social communication and interpersonal relationships.

Mass-media depictions of sexuality are meant to entertain and exploit, not to inform. As a result, the media do not present us with "real" depictions of sexuality. Sexual activities, for example, are usually not explicitly acted out or described in mainstream media, nor is interracial dating often portrayed. The social and cultural taboos that are still part of mainstream U.S. culture remain embedded in the media. Thus, the various media present the social *context* of sexuality; that is, the programs, plots, movies, stories, articles, newscasts, and vignettes tell us *what* behaviors are appropriate (e.g., kissing, sexual intercourse), *with whom* they are appropriate (e.g., girlfriend/boyfriend, partner, heterosexual), and *why* they are appropriate (e.g., attraction, love, to avoid loneliness).

● **FIGURE 1.2**

(a) Percentage of Sexual Talk and Displays in the Media. (*Source:* Brown, 2002.) (b) Sexual Content on TV. (*Source:* Kunkel, Eyal, Finnerty, Biely, & Donnerstein, 2005.)

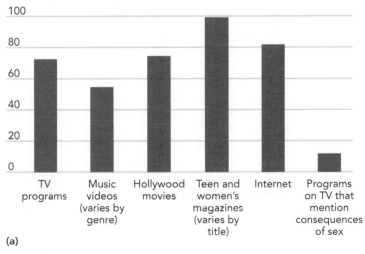

Percentage of the total talk in the media that is sex-related

(a)

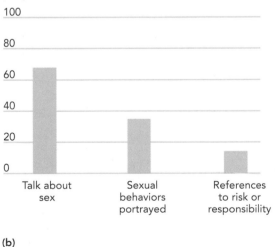

Percentage of different types sexual displays in the TV programs that show sexual content

(b)

Television

Among all types of media, television has been the most prevalent, pervasive, and vexing icon, saturating every corner of public and private space, shaping consciousness, defining reality, and entertaining the masses (American Academy of Pediatrics, 2001; Gerbner, Gross, Morgan, Signorielli, & Shanahan, 2002). Between ages 8 and 18, the average youth spends 3 hours 50 minutes a day watching TV and videos. Though this figure varies across age, gender, race/ethnicity, and socioeconomic status, there is no subgroup of U.S. youth for which average exposure to all media (e.g., Internet, music) drops below 7 hours per day (Roberts, Foehr, & Rideout, 2005). By the time an American teenager finishes high school, he or she will have spent more time in front of a television screen than in the classroom. At the same time, most of the consumption of media leaves the majority of young people outside the purview of adult comment (Roberts, Foehr, & Rideout, 2005) and with few messages or images that demonstrate the risks and responsibilities that accompany sexuality (Kunkel, Eyal, Finnerty, Biely, & Donnerstein, 2005).

While the frequency of TV viewing has been increasing, so has been the number of sexual references in programs. In their study, Kunkel and colleagues (2005) report that television is indeed a major source of information about sex for teenagers. Exposure to sexual content on television is a significant contributor to many aspects of young people's sexual knowledge, beliefs, and behavior. Kunkel et al. conclude by stating:

> Given television's devotion to the topic of sex, there is no more salient context in which to convey sexual risk or responsibility messages. The lack of attention afforded such issues at best reduces the relevance of these concerns for viewers, and misses an opportunity to provide a potentially beneficial perspective on television's treatment of sexual themes and topics.

This study, along with a new wave of empirical evidence (e.g., American Psychological Association [APA], 2007; Pardun, L'Engle, & Brown, 2005; Taylor, 2005) is demonstrating consistent negative impacts of exposure to sexual media content among teens and young adults.

In the accumulated volume of media research, media content does not reflect the realities of the social world; rather, the media images of women and men reflect and reproduce a set of stereotypical and unequal but changing gender roles (Kim, Sorsoli, Collins, et al., 2007). For example, women wearing skimpy clothing and expressing their sexuality to attract attention underscores the objectification of women seen in many genres of media. And men's messages are equally unilateral, which is that they should accumulate sexual experience with women by any means possible. Sexist advertising and stereotypical roles in comedy series and dramas may take subtle (or not so subtle) forms that, over time, may have an effect on the way some women and men view themselves. For example, studies examining the effects of television have shown a positive correlation between television viewing self-image, and healthy development, particularly among girls and young women (APA, 2007). While it is apparent that exposure to television does not affect all people in the same way, it is clear that the sexual double standard that does exist taps into our national ambivalence about sex, equality, morality, and violence.

Unlike the film industry, which uses a single ratings board to regulate all American releases, television has been governed by an informal consensus. In 1997, networks began to rely on watchdog standards and practices departments to rate their shows; however, these divisions have few, if any, hard-and-fast rules (Robson, 2004). While the FCC does not offer clear guidelines about what is and is not permissible on the airwaves, the agency does permit looser interpretations

The vast wasteland of TV is not interested in producing a better mousetrap but in producing a worse mouse.

—Laurence Coughlin

Would you like to come back to my place and do what I'm going to tell my friends we did anyway?

—Spanky

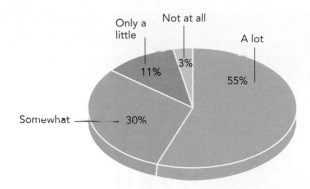

Only a little
Not at all
A lot
11%
3%
55%
Somewhat
30%

● **FIGURE 1.3**

Parents' response to how much, if at all, they felt exposure to sexual content in the media contributed to children becoming involved in sexual situations before they were ready. (*Source:* Victoria Rideout, *Parents, Children & Media: A Kaiser Family Foundation Survey,* (#7638) The Henry J. Kaiser Family Foundation, June 2007. This information was reprinted with permission from the Henry J. Kaiser Family Foundation. The Kaiser Family Foundation is a non-profit private operating foundation based in Menlo Park, California, dedicated to producing and communicating the best possible information, research, and analysis on health issues.)

of its decency standards for broadcasts between 10 P.M. and 6 A.M. Additionally, in 2006, the television industry launched a large campaign to educate parents about TV ratings and the V-chip, technology that allows the blocking of programs based on their rating category. Because of the vulnerability that parents still feel about their children becoming involved in sexual situations before they are ready (see Figure 1.3), the majority (65%) say they "closely" monitor their children's media use (Rideout, 2007).

Reality Shows   Among the shows listed at the top of the Nielsen ratings and most popular among young people are reality shows (Christenson & Ivancin, 2006). On any given day, scores of unscripted and seemingly spontaneous adventures, transformations, and tribulations take place from which viewers may seek and absorb guidance regarding what is normal and natural. Driving this genre are thin, young, and sexually attractive men and women who garner the attention of all ages and sizes. Popular shows like *The Real World, American Idol, Temptation Island,* and *America's Next Top Model* can provide education and ways to escape, but they can also foster unrealistic expectations, inaccurate or unhealthy information, and model behaviors with no consequences. At particular risk are 8- to 15-year-olds who fail to see the contrived nature of this form of entertainment and incorporate these ideals into their sense of personal identity as well as their ideas of familial, fraternal, and sexual relationships. The subtle or not-so-subtle sexualized images of girls and young women depicted in shows such as these are now known to negatively influence the girls' self-image and healthy development (APA, 2007). With these shows filling the airwaves and blurring the boundaries between reality and entertainment, it is crucial that individuals learn as much as they can about humans as sexual beings so that they can both separate truths from lies and distortions and come to accept themselves.

Comedy Series   Sex in comedy series? When asked, most people think there is none. After all, comedy series usually deal with families or familylike relationships, and children are often the main characters. Because they are family oriented, comedy series do not explicitly depict sex. Instead, they deal with sexuality in the form of taboos centering around marital or family issues. The taboos are mild, such as the taboo against a married person flirting with another man or woman. If a comedy series were to deal with a major taboo, such as incest, the program would go beyond the genre's normal boundaries, and most viewers would not be amused.

Soap Operas   Soap operas are one of the most popular TV genres. Although sexual transgressions are soon forgotten in comedy series, they are never forgotten in soap operas. Rather, they are the lifeblood of soaps: jealousy and revenge are

Reality shows such as *Flavor of Love* frequently have sexual themes. What are some of the sexual themes or ideas of the most popular reality shows? Do they differ according to ethnicity?

Soap operas offer distinct visions of sexuality. Sexuality is portrayed as intense and as a cause of jealousy. Women are the primary audience. What do you think the relationship is between these factors?

ever present. Most characters are now, or once were, involved with one another. The ghosts of past loves haunt the mansions and townhouses; each relationship carries a heavy history with it. Whether they are in English or Spanish-language soaps (*telenovelas*), extrarelational sex, pregnancy alarms, betrayals, and jealousy punctuate every episode. Depictions of sexual behavior are frequent.

Crime/Action-Adventure Programs   In crime and action-adventure programs, there are few intimate relationships. Instead, relationships are fundamentally sexual, based on attraction. They are the backdrop to crime and adventure, which form the basis of the plot. The basic theme of a crime program is disorder (a crime) that must be resolved so that order can be restored. Often, the disorder is caused by a sexual episode or a sexually related issue, such as prostitution, sexually explicit materials, rape, cross-dressing, sexual blackmail, or seduction for criminal purposes. As such, we see the underside of sex.

Drama Series   Dramas focus on situational themes that often revolve around a particular setting or issue, such as a singles household or mob family. Topics such as pregnancy, extramarital liaisons, rape, sexual harassment, prostitution, and AIDS are addressed. Because television often seeks to entertain and exploit rather than inform, most of the sexuality that appears in these programs lends itself to sensationalism, humor, or shock.

Commercials   Commercials are a unique genre in TV programming. Although they are not part of the TV program per se, because they are inserted before, after, and during it, they become a free-floating part of it. In these

Click on "Beautiful" to see an award-winning Nike commercial that challenges conventional notions of who is beautiful.

commercials, advertisers may manipulate sexual images to sell products. The most sexually explicit commercials generally advertise jeans, beer, and perfume. Others talk frankly about "erectile dysfunction" while revealing seemingly happy couples in states of sexual bliss.

These commercials tell a story visually through a series of brief scenes or images. They do not pretend to explain the practical benefits of their product, such as cost or effectiveness. Instead, they offer viewers an image or attitude. Directed especially toward adolescents and young adults, these commercials play upon fantasies of attractiveness, sexual success, sexual performance, and fun. They also work to shape our eating styles, appearance, body image, and sense of what is attractive and desirable in ourselves and others. We are led to believe that we can acquire these attributes by using a particular product.

Music and Game Videos   MTV, MTV2, VH1, BET, and music video programs such as *Pussy Cat Dolls,* are very popular among adolescents and young adults. Approximately 8% of young viewers report watching music videos each day (Roberts, Foehr, & Rideout, 2005).

Unlike audio-recorded music, music videos play to the ear and the eye. Young female artists such as Alicia Keys and Beyoncé have brought energy, sexuality, and individualism to the young music audience. They have also objectified and degraded women by stripping them of any sense of power and individualism and focusing strictly on their sexuality. Male artists such as Souja Boy, 50 Cent, and Kanye West provide young audiences with a steady dose of sexuality, power, and rhythm.

Video games that promote sexist and violent attitudes toward women have filled the aisles of stores across the country. Pushing the line between obscenity and amusement, games often provide images of unrealistically shaped and submissive women mouthing sexy dialogues in degrading scenes. Men, in contrast, are often revealed as unrealistic, violent figures whose primary purpose is to destroy and conquer. Though many of these video games are rated "M" (mature) by the Entertainment Software Ratings Board, they are both popular with and accessible to young people.

Feature-Length Films

From their very inception, motion pictures have dealt with sexuality. In 1896, a film titled *The Kiss* outraged moral guardians when it showed a couple stealing a quick kiss. "Absolutely disgusting," complained one critic. "The performance comes near being indecent in its emphasized indecency. Such things call for police action" (quoted in Webb, 1983). Today, in contrast, film critics use "sexy," a word independent of artistic value, to praise a film. "Sexy" films are movies in which the requisite "sex scenes" are sufficiently titillating to overcome their lack of aesthetic merit.

In Hollywood films of the 1990s through today, there has been considerable female nudity, especially above the waist. But men are almost never filmed nude in the same manner as women. Men are generally clothed or partially covered; if they are fully nude, the scene takes place at night, the scene is blurred, or we see only their backsides. Only on rare occasions is the penis shown; if it is visible, it is flaccid (unaroused), not erect.

What is clear is that movies are not that dissimilar from television in their portrayal of the consequences of unprotected sex, such as unplanned pregnancies or sexually transmitted infections (STIs), including HIV/AIDS. In an

Confident female icons such as Queen Latifa reflect mainstream culture's acceptance of assertive women.

" *Of the delights of this world man cares most for is sexual intercourse, yet he has left it out of his heaven.*

—Mark Twain
(1835–1910)

In recent years, mainstream movies such as *Milk* have presented their homosexual characters as fully realized human beings.

analysis of 87 movies, 53 of which had sex episodes, there was only one suggestion of condom use, which was the only reference to any form of birth control (Gunasekera, Chapman, & Campbell, 2005). While one might argue that it is bad art to confuse education with entertainment, it is apparent that the Hollywood film industry may be bad for one's sexual health.

Gay Men, Lesbian Women, Bisexual and Transgendered People in Film and Television

Gay men, lesbian women, and bisexual and transgendered individuals are only minimally represented in mainstream films and television. When gay men and lesbian women do appear, they are frequently defined in terms of their sexual orientation, as if there is nothing more to their lives than sexuality. Gay men are generally stereotyped as effeminate, flighty, or "arty," or they may be closeted. Lesbian women are often stereotyped as super-feminine and stilettoed. In fact, some film critics are now asking, "Where has the butch gone in film?"

In recent years, gay, lesbian, bisexual, and transgendered portrayals in film and television have increasingly integrated their characters' orientation into the plot. Before such television programs as *The L Word* and *Queer as Folk,* interested viewers had to observe either stereotypical characters or search and second-guess a character's sexuality (Glock, 2005). Now there is an entire cable network, LOGO, that has helped pave the way for more gay and lesbian programming. Once cable television produced *The L Word,* the first television program devoted exclusively to the social lives of lesbian women, raw and unbridled sex shifted from the shadows to front and center viewing. While *Queer as Folk* accustomed viewers to gayness, it is unclear whether the networks that promoted kisses between women did so to titillate audiences or to offer positive portrayals of lesbian women living fully engaged lives.

Online Sexual Networks

For millions, surfing the Web has become a major recreational activity and has altered the ways in which they communicate and carry on interpersonal relationships. Though social theorists have long been concerned with the alienating effects of technology, the Internet appears quite different from other communication technologies. Its efficacy, power, and influence, along with the anonymity and depersonalization that accompanies its use, have made it possible for consumers to more easily obtain and distribute sexual materials and information, as well as to interact sexually in different ways.

In place of dance clubs and bars, the Internet and mobile technology are replacing the ways in which people meet and interact with others. With an estimated 420 million adult web pages online (Downs, 2007), which are visited by approximately one-third of U.S. Internet users, viewing online sexual activity (OSA) is a significant part of the sexual practices of the population (Irvine, 2007).

The upside of such a powerful tool is its availability and capacity to educate, particularly youth, who are early adopters of media. While OSA will continue to occupy the bedrooms and gathering places of young people, their counterparts, educational video games, mass texts and instant messages, and online cards, are among the ways in which technology can be used to increase awareness about sexuality-related issues. Given that more than 9 in 10 people ages 12 to 17 are using the Internet, and more than 60% of them use it daily, technology can provide youth with an easily accessible and legitimate way to learn more about themselves and the sexual health of others (Lee, 2008). While some OSAs are visual (e.g., adult movies and photos), others are more interactive (e.g., discussion forums, chatting, blogs, and online dating). Though there are educational and community forums available, the vast majority of OSAs are for recreational sex. In spite of the large numbers of people tapping into OSAs, little is known about their users or their full impact on sexual attitudes and behaviors.

Relative newcomers to the online social networks are such sites as MySpace, Facebook, LinkedIn, and Craigslist, where individuals and members may complete profiles, use message boards, write blogs, and post photos in order to interact with others. Serving millions around the world, these sites often provide social interaction, act as a procrastination tool, or in some cases, provide a graphic and targeted venue for immediate, free, and intimate contact. Since 65% of Americans spend more time with their computers than with their significant others and the average visit to a social network site lasts more than 20 minutes, hanging out with "friends" has never been easier or more available (Kim, 2008). Thus, it's not surprising that such sites are also used to invite "friends" or post invitations for specific sexual behaviors on such boards as "my friends," "men seeking men," "casual encounters," and "erotic services." In 2008, MySpace reached an agreement with legal authorities in 49 states to help prevent sexual predators and others from misusing it. Other sites have initiated similar caveats. In the meantime, the popularity of these sites is causing some to report online networking fatigue as they navigate the plethora of new social sites dedicated to everything from divorce to paganism to firefighting to anime (Kim, 2008).

For anyone with a computer, social networking and pornography are readily accessible.

Cybersex   A subcategory of online sexual activities is cybersex. **Cybersex** is a real-time event involving two persons who are engaging in sexual talk for the purpose of sexual pleasure. In some cases a couple may find or create a chat room in cyberspace or may use a chat client. Typically, persons find each other on the Internet, may exchange pictures or short movies of themselves or use erotic pictures and movies found on the Web to accompany their text-based communication, and/or play different roles that they otherwise couldn't or wouldn't in real life. The popularity of cybersex is rooted in what has been termed the "Triple-A-Engine" (access, affordability, and anonymity). For example, a person

The Web of Cybersex

The lure of a twenty-first-century computerized sex toy is more than some individuals can resist. Just a few years ago, cybersex meant glancing at nude images on the computer screen. It now beckons users to join fantasy-filled chat rooms, observe images of another person, and watch live sex shows. One no longer has to travel across town to a sleazy bar or movie theater and risk being "caught" by a co-worker or fellow student to access explicit, interactive sex or to share a fantasy with another person. Much of this interactive media is different from other sexually explicit material in that the user can manipulate the images and stimulation that he or she receives.

"Compulsive use" of the Internet covers a wide variety of behaviors and impulsive control problems. Though the term "sexual addiction" has been used by a number of researchers, many psychologists question whether the concept of addiction can be applied to nonchemical behaviors (Downs, 2007). Rather, they describe excessive or compulsive Internet sex in terms of behaviors or activities that take precedence over other parts of life and that dominate one's thinking and feelings. Until more empirical research occurs, the question of whether compulsive Internet sex is different from more traditional forms of sexual compulsion cannot be answered. There needs to be more research identifying both the risk factors and protective factors for those who might be susceptible to Internet sexual compulsion.

Psychologist Kimberly Young (1998) has created the Cybersexual Addiction Index to help people recognize potentially unhealthy uses of the Internet. Even though the term "addiction" in the questionnaire title might not be appropriate, completing this questionnaire may help you identify potentially excessive or compulsive cybersex use.

Are You Addicted to Cybersex?

Answer "yes" or "no" to the following statements:

1. Do you routinely spend time in sex chat rooms and instant messaging with the sole purpose of finding cybersex?
2. Do you feel preoccupied with using the Internet for cybersex?
3. Do you frequently use anonymous communication to engage in sexual fantasies not typically carried out in real life?
4. Do you anticipate your next online session with the expectation that you will find sexual arousal or gratification?
5. Do you move from cybersex to phone sex or even real-life meetings?
6. Do you hide your online interactions from your significant other?
7. Do you feel guilt or shame from your online use?
8. Did you accidentally become aroused by cybersex at first, and now find that you actively seek it out when you log online?
9. Do you masturbate when having cybersex or looking at online pornography?
10. Do you feel less interest with your real-life sex partner only to prefer cybersex as a primary form of sexual gratification?

If you answered "yes" to any of the above questions, you *may* be "addicted" to cybersex, to use the label of this questionnaire. With the availability of adult sites and sex chat rooms, more and more people have come to realize their initial curiosity may have become expensive or problematic.

SOURCE: Reprinted with permission of Kimberly Young, Center for Internet Addiction Recovery. Available: http://www.netaddiction.com/resources/cybersex_addiction_test.htm.

called "Hot Dog" can enter a "place" called "Hot Tub" and soak for a couple of hours with "Bubbles," "Sexy Lady" (a transvestite), and others who pop in and out. "Hot Dog" flirts with everyone; he describes himself, tells his fantasies, and has kinky sex with "Sexy Lady" and a dozen others. "Hot Dog" is actually a woman, but she doesn't tell anyone. Every now and then, "Hot Dog" goes private and exchanges fantasies. But none of this happens in the physical world. "Hot Tub" is a chat room on a computer network. People at different locations, linked by the network, type their fantasies on their keyboards, and those fantasies almost immediately appear on the other people's computer screens. With the Internet increasingly being used to meet and communicate with others, many people who believe sexuality to be an important part of a good relationship are increasingly utilizing it to see if their sexual proclivities are compatible with those of a potential partner.

The Internet has brought a new dimension to sexuality by making it a highly desirable commodity online, at school, and at work. By removing many of the emotional and physical attributes of the individual and allowing emotional and physical fulfillment to occur with an electronic partner, one is removed from the social contexts in which sexual expression has previously occurred. Like other forms of media, the Internet does not simply provide sexual culture; it also shapes sexual culture. For the isolated, underrepresented, and disenfranchised whose sexual identities up until now have been hidden, Internet communication may be a lifeline. For others, whether they be cybersex fans or blog users in the dating game, the Internet is a means of sexual discourse, autostimulation, and coupling. For still others, particularly young women, the Internet takes the form of unapologetic exhibitionism.

For most cybersex users, the Internet provides a fascinating venue for experiencing sex. For some users, however, porn consumption gets them in trouble: maxed out credit cards, neglected responsibility, and overlooked loved ones. There are both online and community resources for those who desire counseling. While searching for such sources, however, consumers and professionals must be aware of the differences between therapy, consultation, and entertainment. Additionally, because entrepreneurs can make more money from hype and misinformation than from high-quality therapy and education, consumers must remain vigilant in assessing the background of the therapist and the source of the information.

Because of the high volume of sexual discussions and material available on the Internet, there is an increasing demand for government regulation. In 1996, Congress passed the Communications Decency Act, which made it illegal to use computer networks to transmit "obscene" materials or place "indecent" words or images where children might see or read them. However, courts have declared this legislation as a violation of freedom of speech. (For further discussion of this issue, see Chapter 18.)

● Sexuality Across Cultures and Times

What we see as "natural" in our culture may be viewed as unnatural in other cultures. Few Americans would disagree about the erotic potential of kissing. But other cultures perceive kissing as merely the exchange of saliva. To the Mehinaku of the Amazonian rain forest, for example, kissing is a disgusting sexual abnormality; no Mehinaku engages in it (Gregor, 1985). The fact that others press their lips against each other, salivate, *and* become sexually excited merely confirms their "strangeness" to the Mehinaku.

Culture takes our **sexual interests**—our incitements or inclinations to act sexually—and molds and shapes them, sometimes celebrating sexuality and other times condemning it. Sexuality can be viewed as a means of spiritual enlightenment, as in the Hindu tradition, in which the gods themselves engage in sexual activities; it can also be at war with the divine, as in the Judeo-Christian tradition, in which the flesh is the snare of the devil (Parrinder, 1980).

Among the variety of factors that shape how we feel and behave sexually, culture is possibly the most powerful. A brief exploration of sexual themes across cultures and times will give you a sense of the diverse shapes and meanings humans have given to sexuality.

Birds do it, bees do it. Even educated fleas do it.

—Cole Porter
(1891–1964)

The sensual movements of Latin American dancing have become mainstream in American culture, as can be seen in the popularity of *Dancing with the Stars*.

Sexual Interests

All cultures assume that adults have the *potential* for becoming sexually aroused and for engaging in sexual intercourse for the purpose of reproduction. But cultures differ considerably in terms of how strong they believe sexual interests are. These beliefs, in turn, affect the level of desire expressed in each culture.

The Mangaia   Among the Mangaia of Polynesia, both sexes, beginning in early adolescence, experience high levels of sexual desire (Marshall, 1971). Around age 13 or 14, following a circumcision ritual, boys are given instruction in the ways of pleasing a girl: erotic kissing, cunnilingus, breast fondling and sucking, and techniques for bringing her to multiple orgasms. After 2 weeks, an older, sexually experienced woman has sexual intercourse with the boy to instruct him further on how to sexually satisfy a woman. Girls the same age are instructed by older women on how to be orgasmic: how to thrust their hips and rhythmically move their vulvas in order to have multiple orgasms. A girl finally learns to be orgasmic through the efforts of a "good man." If the woman's partner fails to satisfy her, she is likely to leave him; she may also ruin his reputation with other women by denouncing his lack of skill. Young men and women are expected to have many sexual experiences prior to marriage.

This adolescent paradise, however, does not last forever. The Mangaia believe that sexuality is strongest during adolescence. As a result, when the Mangaia leave young adulthood, they experience a rapid decline in sexual desire and activity, and they cease to be aroused as passionately as they once were. They attribute this swift decline to the workings of nature and settle into a sexually contented adulthood.

The Dani   In contrast to the Mangaia, the New Guinean Dani show little interest in sexuality (Schwimmer, 1997). To them, sex is a relatively unimportant aspect of life. The Dani express no concern about improving sexual techniques or enhancing erotic pleasure. Extrarelational sex and jealousy are rare. As their only sexual concern is reproduction, sexual intercourse is performed quickly, ending with male ejaculation. Female orgasm appears to be unknown to them. Following childbirth, both mothers and fathers go through 5 years of sexual abstinence. The Dani are an extreme example of a case in which culture, rather than biology, shapes sexual attractions.

Victorian Americans   In the nineteenth century, White middle-class Americans believed that women had little sexual desire. If they experienced desire at all, it was "reproductive desire," the wish to have children. Reproduction entailed the unfortunate "necessity" of engaging in sexual intercourse. A leading reformer wrote that in her "natural state" a woman never makes advances based on sexual desires, for the "very plain reason that she does not feel them" (Alcott, 1868). Those women who did feel desire were "a few

> Sex is hardly ever just about sex.
> —Shirley MacLaine
> (1934–)

exceptions amounting in all probability to diseased cases." Such women were classified by a prominent physician as suffering from "Nymphomania, or Furor Uterinus" (Bostwick, 1860).

Whereas women were viewed as asexual, men were believed to have raging sexual appetites. Men, driven by lust, sought to satisfy their desires by ravaging innocent women. Both men and women believed that male sexuality was dangerous, uncontrolled, and animal-like. It was part of a woman's duty to tame unruly male sexual impulses.

The polar beliefs about the nature of male and female sexuality created destructive antagonisms between "angelic" women and "demonic" men. These beliefs provided the rationale for a "war between the sexes." They also led to the separation of sex from love. Intimacy and love had nothing to do with male sexuality. In fact, male lust always lingered in the background of married life, threatening to destroy love by its overbearing demands.

Although a century has passed since the end of the Victorian era, many Victorian sexual beliefs and attitudes continue to influence us. These include the belief that men are "naturally" sexually aggressive and women sexually passive, the sexual double standard, and the value placed on women being sexually "inexperienced."

Like beliefs about sexuality, ideals about body image (and what women are willing to do to achieve it) change over time.

Sexual Orientation

Sexual orientation is the pattern of sexual and emotional attraction based on the gender of one's partner. **Heterosexuality** refers to emotional and sexual attraction between men and women; **homosexuality** refers to emotional and sexual attraction between persons of the same sex; **bisexuality** is an emotional and sexual attraction to both males and females. In contemporary American culture, heterosexuality is still the only sexual orientation receiving full social and legal legitimacy. Although same-sex relationships are common, they do not receive general social acceptance. Some other cultures, however, view same-sex relationships as normal, acceptable, and even preferable. A small number of countries worldwide and a few states in the United States have legalized same-sex marriage. (See Chapter 18 for a list of these countries and states.)

Ancient Greece In ancient Greece, the birthplace of European culture, the Greeks accepted same-sex relationships as naturally as Americans today accept heterosexuality. For the Greeks, same-sex relationships between men represented the highest form of love.

The male-male relationship was based on love and reciprocity; sexuality was only one component of it. In this relationship, the code of conduct called for the older man to initiate the relationship. The youth initially resisted; only after the older man courted the young man with gifts and words of love would he reciprocate. The two men formed a close, emotional bond. The older man was the youth's mentor as well as his lover. He introduced the youth to men who would be useful for his advancement later; he assisted him in learning his duties as a citizen. As the youth entered adulthood, the erotic bond between the two evolved into a deep friendship. After the youth became an adult, he married a woman and later initiated a relationship with an adolescent boy.

In ancient Greece, the highest form of love was that expressed between males.

Greek male-male relationships, however, were not substitutes for male-female marriage. The Greeks discouraged exclusive male-male relationships because marriage and children were required to continue the family and society. Men regarded their wives primarily as domestics and as bearers of children (Keuls, 1985). (The Greek word for woman, *gyne*, translates literally as "childbearer.") Husbands turned for sexual pleasure not to their wives but to *hetaerae* (hi-TIR-ee), highly regarded courtesans who were usually educated slaves.

The Sambians   Among Sambian males of New Guinea, sexual orientation is very malleable (Herdt, 1987). Young boys begin with sexual activities with older boys, move to sexual activities with both sexes during adolescence, and engage in exclusively male-female activities in adulthood. Sambians believe that a boy can grow into a man only by the ingestion of semen, which is, they say, like mother's milk. At age 7 or 8, boys begin their sexual activities with older boys; as they get older, they seek multiple partners to accelerate their growth into manhood. At adolescence, their role changes, and they must provide semen to boys to enable them to develop. At first, they worry about their own loss of semen, but they are taught to drink tree sap, which they believe magically replenishes their supply. During adolescence, boys are betrothed to preadolescent girls, with whom they engage in sexual activities. When the girls mature, the boys give up their sexual involvement with other males. They become fully involved with adult women, losing their desire for men.

Gender

Although sexual interests and orientation may be influenced by culture, it may be difficult for some people to imagine that culture has anything to do with **gender,** the characteristics associated with being male or female. Our sex appears solidly rooted in our biological nature. But is being male or female *really* biological? The answer is yes *and* no. Having male or female genitals is anatomical. But the possession of a penis does not *always* make a person a man, nor does the possession of a clitoris and vagina *always* make a person a woman. Men who consider themselves women, "women with penises," are accepted or honored in many cultures throughout the world (Bullough, 1991). Thus, culture and a host of other factors help to shape masculinity and femininity, while biology defines men and women.

Transsexual and Transgendered People It is difficult to estimate the number of **transsexual** and **transgendered** people in the United States whose genitals and/or identities as men or women are discordant. In transsexuality, a person with a penis, for example, identifies as a woman, or a person with a vulva and vagina identifies as a man. Transgendered individuals have an appearance and behaviors that do not conform to the gender role ascribed for people of a particular sex. These differences often involve cross-dressing; however, unlike transvestites who report achieving sexual arousal when cross-dressing, transgendered people who cross-dress typically do so to obtain psychosocial gratification.

Transsexuality appears in many cultures, crossing age, religion, and status.

To make their genitals congruent with their gender identity, many transsexuals have their genitals surgically altered. If being male or female depends on genitals, then postsurgical transsexuals have changed their sex—men have become women, and women have become men. But defining sex in terms of genitals presents problems, as has been shown in the world of sports. In the 1970s, Renee Richards, whose genitals had been surgically transformed from male to female, began competing on the women's professional tennis circuit. Protests began immediately. Although Richards's genitals were female, her body and musculature were male. Despite the surgery, she remained genetically male because her sex chromosomes were male. Her critics insisted that genetics, not genitals, defines a person's sex; anatomy can be changed, but chromosomes cannot. Richards, however, maintained that she was a woman by any common definition of the word. (Issues of sex, gender, and biology are discussed in Chapter 5.)

Two-Spirits Most Americans consider transsexuality problematic at best. But this is not the case in all regions of the world. In some communities, an anatomical man identifying as a woman might be considered a "man-woman" and be accorded high status and special privileges. He would be identified as a **two-spirit,** a man who assumes female dress, gender role, and status. Two-spirit emphasizes the spiritual aspect of one's life and downplays the homosexual persona (Jacobs, Thomas, & Lang, 1997). It is inclusive of transsexuality, **transvestism** (wearing the clothes of or passing as a member of the other sex), and a form of same-sex relationship (Roscoe, 1991). Two-spirits are found in numerous communities throughout the world, including American Indian, Filipino, Lapp, and Indian communities. In South Asian society, the third gender is known as the *hijra*. Regarded as sacred, they

In some cultures, men who dress or identify as women are considered shamans. We'wha was a Zuni man-woman who lived in the nineteenth century.

perform as dancers or musicians at weddings and religious ceremonies, as well as providing blessings for health, prosperity, and fertility (Nanda, 1990). It is almost always men who become two-spirits, although there are a few cases of women assuming male roles in a similar fashion (Blackwood, 1984). Two-spirits are often considered shamans, individuals who possess great spiritual power.

Among the Zuni of New Mexico, two-spirits are considered a third gender (Roscoe, 1991). Despite the existence of transsexual people and those born with disorders of sexual development (e.g., two testes or two ovaries but an ambiguous genital appearance), Westerners tend to view gender as biological, an incorrect assumption. The Zuni, in contrast, believe that gender is socially acquired.

American Indian two-spirits were suppressed by missionaries and the U.S. government as "unnatural" or "perverted." Their ruthless repression led anthropologists to believe that two-spirits had been driven out of existence in American Indian communities, but there is evidence that two-spirits continue to fill ceremonial and social roles in tribes such as the Lakota Sioux. Understandably, two-spirit activities are kept secret from outsiders for fear of reprisals. Among gay and lesbian American Indians, the two-spirit role provides historical continuity with their traditions (Roscoe, 1991).

● Societal Norms and Sexuality

The immense diversity of sexual behaviors across cultures and times immediately calls into question the appropriateness of labeling these behaviors as *inherently* natural or unnatural, normal or abnormal. Too often, we give such labels to sexual behaviors without thinking about the basis on which we make those judgments. Such categories discourage knowledge and understanding because they are value judgments, evaluations of right and wrong. As such, they are not objective descriptions about behaviors but statements of how we feel about those behaviors.

Natural Sexual Behavior

How do we decide if a sexual behavior is natural or unnatural? To make this decision, we must have some standard of nature against which to compare the behavior. But what is "nature"? On the abstract level, nature is the essence of all things in the universe. Or, personified as nature, it is the force regulating the universe. These definitions, however, do not help us much in trying to establish what is natural or unnatural.

When we asked our students to identify their criteria for determining which sexual behaviors they considered "natural" or "unnatural," we received a variety of responses, including the following:

- "If a person feels something instinctive, I believe it is a natural feeling."
- "Natural and unnatural have to do with the laws of nature. What these parts were intended for."
- "I decide by my gut instincts."

❝ If it makes you happy, it can't be that bad.

—Sheryl Crow (1962–)

think
about it

Am I Normal?

The question "Am I normal?" seems to haunt many people. For some, it causes a great deal of unnecessary fear, guilt, and anxiety. For others, it provides the motivation to study the literature, consult with a trusted friend or therapist, or take a course in sexuality.

What is normal? We commonly use several criteria in deciding whether to label different sexual behaviors "normal" or "abnormal." According to professor and psychologist Leonore Tiefer (2004), these criteria are subjective, statistical, idealistic, cultural, and clinical. Regardless of what criteria we use, they ultimately reflect societal norms.

- *Subjectively "normal" behavior.* According to this definition, normalcy is any behavior that is similar to one's own. Though most of us use this definition, few of us will acknowledge it.

- *Statistically "normal" behavior.* According to this definition, whatever behaviors are more common are normal; less common ones are abnormal. However, the fact that a behavior is not widely practiced does not make it abnormal except in a statistical sense. **Fellatio** (fel-AY-she-o) (oral stimulation of the penis) and **cunnilingus** (cun-i-LIN-gus) (oral stimulation of the female genitals), for example, are widely practiced today because they have become "acceptable" behaviors. But a generation ago, oral sex was tabooed as something "dirty" or "shameful."

- *Idealistically "normal" behavior.* Taking an ideal for a norm, individuals who use this approach measure all deviations against perfection. They may try to model their behavior after Christ or Gandhi, for example. Using idealized behavior as a norm can easily lead to feelings of guilt, shame, and anxiety.

- *Culturally "normal" behavior.* This is probably the standard most of us use most of the time: We accept as normal what our culture defines as normal. This measure explains why our notions of normalcy do not always agree with those of people from other countries, religions, communities, and historical periods. Men who kiss in public may be considered normal in one place but abnormal in another. It is common for deviant behavior to

be perceived as dangerous and frightening in a culture that rejects it.

- *Clinically "normal" behavior.* The clinical standard uses scientific data about health and illness to make judgments. For example, the presence of the syphilis bacterium in body tissues or blood is considered abnormal because it indicates that a person has a sexually transmitted infection. Regardless of time or place, clinical definitions should stand the test of time. The four criteria mentioned above are all somewhat arbitrary—that is, they depend on individual or group opinion—but the clinical criterion has more objectivity.

These five criteria form the basis of what we usually consider normal behavior. Often, the different definitions and interpretations of "normal" conflict with one another. How does a person determine whether he or she is normal if subjectively "normal" behavior—what that person actually does—is inconsistent with his or her ideals? Such dilemmas are commonplace and lead many people to question their normalcy. However, they should not question their normalcy so much as their *concept* of normalcy.

Think Critically

- How do you define normal sexual behavior? What criteria did you use to create this definition?

- How do your sexual attitudes, values, and behaviors compare to what you believe are "normal" sexual behaviors? If they are different, how do you reconcile these? If they are similar, how do you feel about others who may not share them?

- In Nepal, young women are isolated for 1 week during their first menses, whereas in Brazil, it is common to see men embrace or kiss in public. What are your thoughts about how other cultures define normality?

SOURCE: Tiefer, L. (2004). *Sex is not a natural act and other essays* (2nd ed.). Boulder, CO: Westview Press.

- "I think all sexual activity is natural as long as it doesn't hurt you or anyone else."
- "Everything possible is natural. Everything natural is normal. If it is natural and normal, it is moral."

When we label sexual behavior as "natural" or "unnatural," we are typically indicating whether the behavior conforms to our culture's sexual norms. Our sexual norms appear natural because we have internalized them since infancy. These norms are part of the cultural air we breathe, and, like the air, they are invisible. We have learned our culture's rules so well that they have become a "natural" part of our personality, a "second nature" to us. They seem "instinctive."

Normal Sexual Behavior

Closely related to the idea that sexual behavior is natural or unnatural is the belief that sexuality is either normal or abnormal. More often than not, describing behavior as "normal" or "abnormal" is merely another way of making value judgments. Psychologist Sandra Pertot (2007) quips, "Normal today means that a person should have a regular and persistent physical sex drive, easy arousal, strong erections and good control over ejaculation for males, powerful orgasms, and a desire for a variety and experimentation [for women]" (p. 13). Although "normal" has often been used to imply "healthy" or "moral" behavior, social scientists use the word strictly as a statistical term. For them, **normal sexual behavior** is behavior that conforms to a group's average or median patterns of behavior. Normality has nothing to do with moral or psychological deviance.

Ironically, although we may feel pressure to behave like the average person (the statistical norm), most of us don't actually know how others behave sexually. People don't ordinarily reveal much about their sexual activities. If they do, they generally reveal only their most conformist sexual behaviors, such as sexual intercourse. They rarely disclose their masturbatory activities, sexual fantasies, or anxieties or feelings of guilt. All that most people present of themselves—unless we know them well—is the conventional self that masks their actual sexual feelings, attitudes, and behaviors.

The guidelines most of us have for determining our normality are given to us by our friends, partners, and parents (who usually present conventional sexual images of themselves) through stereotypes, media images, religious teachings, customs, and cultural norms. None of these, however, tells us much about how people *actually* behave. Because we don't know how people really behave, it is easy for us to imagine that we are abnormal if we differ from our cultural norms and stereotypes. We wonder if our desires, fantasies, and activities are normal: Is it normal to fantasize? To masturbate? To enjoy erotica? To be attracted to someone of the same sex? Some of us believe that everyone else is "normal" and that only we are "sick" or "abnormal." The challenge, of course, is to put aside our cultural indoctrination and try to understand sexual behaviors objectively (Pertot, 2007).

Because culture determines what is normal, there is a vast range of normal behaviors across different cultures. What is considered the normal sexual urge for the Dani would send most of us into therapy for treatment of low sexual desire. And the idea of teaching sexual skills to early adolescents, as the Mangaia do, would horrify most American parents.

Are there behaviors, however, that are considered essential to sexual functioning and consequently, universally labeled as normal? Not surprisingly, **reproduction,** or the biological process by which individuals are produced, is probably one shared view of normal sexual behavior that most cultures would agree upon (Pertot, 2007). That is, "men should feel desire, achieve an erection, and ejaculate within the vagina, and women would participate in sex" (p. 15). All other beliefs about sexual expression and behavior develop from social context.

The greatest pleasure in life is doing what people say you cannot do.
—Walter Bagehot (1826–1877)

Kissing is "natural" and "normal" in our culture. It is an expression of intimacy, love, and passion for young and old, heterosexual persons, gay men, and lesbian women.

Sexual Behavior and Variations

Sex researchers have generally rejected the traditional sexual dichotomies of natural/unnatural, normal/abnormal, moral/immoral, and good/bad. Regarding the word "abnormal," sociologist Ira Reiss (1989) writes:

> We need to be aware that people will use those labels to put distance between themselves and others they dislike. In doing so, these people are not making a scientific diagnosis but are simply affirming their support of certain shared concepts of proper sexuality.

Instead of classifying behavior into what are essentially moralistic normal/abnormal and natural/unnatural categories, researchers view human sexuality

Declaration of Sexual Rights

Sexuality is an integral part of the personality of every human being. Its full development depends upon the satisfaction of basic human needs such as the desire for contact, intimacy, emotional expression, pleasure, tenderness, and love. Sexuality is constructed through the interaction between the individual and social structures. Full development of sexuality is essential for individual, interpersonal, and social well-being. Sexual rights are universal human rights based on the inherent freedom, dignity, and equality of all human beings. Since health is a fundamental human right, so must sexual health be a basic human right. In order to ensure that human beings and societies develop healthy sexuality, the following sexual rights must be recognized, promoted, respected, and defended by all societies through all means. Sexual health is the result of an environment that recognizes, respects, and exercises these rights.

1. *The right to sexual freedom.* Sexual freedom encompasses the possibility for individuals to express their full sexual potential. However, this excludes all forms of sexual coercion, exploitation, and abuse at any time and situations in life.

2. *The right to sexual autonomy, sexual integrity, and safety of the sexual body.* This right involves the ability to make autonomous decisions about one's sexual life within a context of one's own personal and social ethics. It also encompasses control and enjoyment of our own bodies free from torture, mutilation, and violence of any sort.

3. *The right to sexual privacy.* This involves the right for individual decisions and behaviors about intimacy as long as they do not intrude on the sexual rights of others.

4. *The right to sexual equity.* This refers to freedom from all forms of discrimination regardless of sex, gender, sexual orientation, age, race, social class, religion, or physical and emotional disability.

5. *The right to sexual pleasure.* Sexual pleasure, including autoeroticism, is a source of physical, psychological, intellectual, and spiritual well-being.

6. *The right to emotional sexual expression.* Sexual expression is more than erotic pleasure or sexual acts. Individuals have a right to express their sexuality through communication, touch, emotional expression, and love.

7. *The right to sexually associate freely.* This means the possibility to marry or not, to divorce, and to establish other types of responsible sexual associations.

8. *The right to make free and responsible reproductive choices.* This encompasses the right to decide whether or not to have children, the number and spacing of children, and the right to full access to the means of fertility regulation.

9. *The right to sexual information based upon scientific inquiry.* This right implies that sexual information should be generated through the process of unencumbered and yet scientifically ethical inquiry, and disseminated in appropriate ways at all societal levels.

10. *The right to comprehensive sexuality education.* This is a lifelong process from birth throughout the life cycle and should involve all social institutions.

11. *The right to sexual health care.* Sexual health care should be available for prevention and treatment of all sexual concerns, problems, and disorders.

Think Critically

- What are your immediate reactions to the "Declaration of Sexual Rights"? For whom should these rights be promoted? Would you delete, edit, or add rights to the list?

- Why do you suppose such a declaration is necessary and important?

- What (if any) consequences should there be for governments, cultures, or individuals who do not follow these rights?

SOURCE: "Declaration of Sexual Rights" from World Association for Sexual Health, 1999. http://www.worldsexology.org/about_sexualrights.asp.

as characterized by **sexual variation**—that is, sexual variety and diversity. As humans, we vary enormously in terms of our sexual orientation, our desires, our fantasies, our attitudes, and our behaviors. Alfred Kinsey and his colleagues (1948) succinctly stated the matter: "The world is not to be divided into sheep and goats."

Researchers believe that the best way to understand our sexual diversity is to view our activities as existing on a continuum. On this continuum, the frequency with which individuals engage in different sexual activities (e.g., sexual intercourse, masturbation, and oral sex) ranges from never to always. Significantly, there is no point on the continuum that marks normal or abnormal behavior. In fact, the difference between one individual and the next on the continuum is minimal (Kinsey, Pomeroy, & Martin, 1948; Kinsey, Pomeroy, Martin, & Gebhard, 1953). The most that can be said of a person is that his or her behaviors are more or less typical or atypical of the group average. Furthermore, nothing can be inferred about an individual whose behavior differs significantly from the group average except that his or her behavior is atypical. Except for engaging in sexually atypical behavior, one person may be indistinguishable from any other.

Many activities that are usually thought of as "deviant" or "dysfunctional" sexual behavior—activities diverging from the norm, such as exhibitionism, voyeurism, and fetishism—are engaged in by most of us to some degree. We may delight in displaying our bodies on the beach or in "dirty dancing" in crowded clubs (exhibitionism). We may like watching ourselves make love, viewing erotic videos, or seeing our partner undress (voyeurism). Or we may enjoy kissing our lover's photograph, keeping a lock of his or her hair, or sleeping with an article of his or her clothing (fetishism). Most of the time, these feelings or activities are only one aspect of our sexual selves; they are not especially significant in our overall sexuality. Such atypical behaviors represent nothing more than sexual nonconformity when they occur between mutually consenting adults and do not cause distress.

The rejection of natural/unnatural, normal/abnormal, and moral/immoral categories by sex researchers does not mean that standards for evaluating sexual behavior do not exist. There are many sexual behaviors that are harmful to oneself (e.g., masturbatory asphyxia—suffocating or hanging oneself during masturbation to increase sexual arousal) and to others (e.g., rape, child molestation, and obscene phone calls). Current psychological standards for determining the harmfulness of sexual behaviors center around the issues of coercion, potential harm to oneself or others, and personal distress. (These issues are discussed in greater detail in Chapter 10.)

We, the authors, believe that the basic standard for judging various sexual activities is whether they are between consenting adults and whether they cause harm. "Normality" and "naturalness" are not useful terms for evaluating sexual behavior, especially variations, because they are usually nothing more than moral judgments. What people consider "normal" is often statistically common sexual behavior, which is then defined as good or healthy. But for many forms of sexual behavior, a large percentage of people will not conform to the average. There is a great deal of variation, for example, in the extent to which people eroticize boxer shorts and lacy underwear. Who determines at what point on the continuum that interest in undergarments is no longer acceptable? The individual? Her or his peer group? Religious groups? Society? As sociologists Suzanna Rose and Victoria Sork (1984a) note: "Because everyone's sexuality does not completely overlap with the norm, the only liberating approach to sexuality is to envision it from the perspective of variation."

As social scientists, sex researchers have a mandate to *describe* sexual behavior, not evaluate it as good or bad, moral or immoral. It is up to the individual to evaluate the ethical or moral aspects of sexual behavior in accordance with his or her ethical or religious values. At the same time, however, understanding diverse sexual attitudes, motives, behaviors, and values will help deepen the individual's own value system.

Judge not, that ye be not judged.
—Matthew 7:1
The Bible

My Genes Made Me Do It: Sociobiology, Evolutionary Psychology, and the Mysteries of Love

Do you ever wonder why you do what you do or feel as you feel—especially when it comes to matters like attraction, relationships, and sex? Do you wonder why the object of your affection behaves in such inexplicable ways—why he or she flies into a jealous rage for no reason? Or why your friend always seems to fall for the "wrong" person? Sometimes, the answers may be obvious, but other times, they are obscure. Our motivations come from a variety of sources, including personality traits, past experiences, peer pressure, and familial and cultural influences. Many of our feelings probably result from a complex yet subtle blending of these influences—combined with innate responses programmed into our genes and manifested in our brains.

Our growing understanding of the biological bases of behavior comes from a variety of disciplines: history, psychology, sociology, neurophysiology, and endocrinology. Many scholars base their study of sexuality on Charles Darwin's theory of evolution. According to Darwin's theory, evolution favors certain physical traits that enable a species to survive. To more fully understand the mechanisms through which the brain and body perpetuate mating and survival, MRI brain scans of people in love are helping scientists understand more about the science of love: why it is so powerful and why being rejected is so painful.

From a sociobiological perspective, males, who are consistently fertile from early adolescence on, seek to impregnate as many females as possible to ensure genetic success. Differences in men's and women's brains reveal men's to have more activity in the region that integrates visual stimuli. This is not surprising, considering that from an evolutionary perspective, men have to be able to size up a woman visually to see if she can bear babies (Fisher, 2004). Females, however, ovulate only once a month. For them, a single episode of intercourse can result in pregnancy, childbirth, and years of child rearing. Women's brain activities, though more puzzling, than men's, reveal that their brain has more activity in the areas that govern memories. Dr. Helen Fisher, an anthropologist and author, theorizes that this may be a female mechanism for mate choice—that if a woman really studies a man and remembers things about his behavior, she can try to determine whether he'd make a reliable mate and father. In this way, women can help ensure that the carriers of their genes (their children) will reach adulthood and pass along their parents' genetic legacy. The bonds of love are what keep the male around, or, in other words, females trade sex for love, and males trade love for sex.

Evolutionary psychologists seek to explain the biological bases of love and other emotions such as hope, anger, jealousy, fear, and grief. We may wonder why Mother Nature made us so emotional when emotion so often leads to disaster. But there are good reasons (evolutionarily speaking) for having emotions. Even though in the short term emotions can get us into trouble—if we act impulsively rather than rationally—over the long term our emotions have helped our genes survive and replicate (Kluger, 2008). Emotions exist to motivate us to do things that serve (or once served) the best interests of our genetic material—things like fleeing, fighting, or forming close relationships to protect our "genetic investment" (offspring).

Critics of sociobiology argue that inferences from animal behavior may not be applicable to human beings; they feel that sociobiologists base their assumptions about human behavior (such as men wanting sex versus women wanting love) more on cultural stereotypes than on actual behavior. Sociobiologists reply that they report what they observe in nature and suggest connections to human behavior (humans are part of nature, after all) but do not make judgments about the meaning or morality of their observations.

As you study human sexuality, we hope that the information you gain from this text will help you integrate your own feelings and experiences with the information and advice you get from family, friends, lovers, and society. In the text, we take what might be called a "biopsychosocial" approach to our subject, recognizing that the sexual self is produced by the interconnections of body, mind, spirit, and culture. As you continue your study, remember that, although our culture, beliefs, and cognitive processes (what we might call the "software" of the mind) have been created by humans, our bodies and brains (the "hardware" of the mind) are the products of evolution. They've been developing over a long, long time.

Think Critically

- To what extent do you agree or disagree with the biopsychosocial approach that the authors of this text take toward sexuality? On what do you base this?
- To what do you attribute sexual attraction? On what observations and experiences do you base this?
- How do you feel about the statement "Females trade sex for love, and males trade love for sex"?

Final Thoughts

Popular culture both encourages and discourages sexuality. It promotes stereotypical sexual interactions but fails to touch on the deeper significance sexuality holds for us or the risks and responsibilities that accompany it. Love and sexuality in a committed relationship are infrequently depicted, in contrast to casual sex. (By ignoring sex between committed partners, popular culture implies that partnership is a "sexual wasteland." Yet it is within couples that the overwhelming majority of sexual interactions take place.) The media ignore or disparage the wide array of sexual behaviors and choices—from masturbation to gay, lesbian, bisexual, and transgender relationships—that are significant in many people's lives. They discourage the linking of sex and intimacy, contraceptive responsibility and the acknowledgment of the risk of contracting sexually transmitted infections.

What is clear from examining other cultures is that sexual behaviors and norms vary from culture to culture and, within our own society, from one time to another. The variety of sexual behaviors even within our own culture testifies to diversity not only between cultures but within cultures as well. Understanding diversity allows us to acknowledge that there is no such thing as inherently "normal" or "natural" sexual behavior. Rather, sexual behavior is strongly influenced by culture—including our own.

Summary

Sexuality, Popular Culture, and the Media

- Popular culture, especially the media, is one of the sexual socialization agents that have gained prominence among American youth.

- Each television genre depicts sexuality according to its formula. Both the frequency of watching television and the number of sexual references displayed across all genres of TV have significantly increased. At the same time, the risks and responsibilities that accompany TV programs remain sadly disproportionate to the sexual images that are portrayed.

- Although Hollywood films depict sexual behavior more graphically than television does, sex scenes are often gratuitous. Sexuality tends to be stereotypical. Gay men, lesbian women, and bisexual and transgendered individuals have been increasingly integrated into the plots of both television and movies.

- Computer networks and personalized pages have created *cybersex,* providing new ways of establishing relationships and conveying sexual fantasies. The debate concerning the effects and transmittal of these materials continues.

Sexuality Across Cultures and Times

- One of the most powerful forces shaping human sexuality is culture. Culture molds and shapes our *sexual interests.*

- The Mangaia of Polynesia and the Dani of New Guinea represent cultures at the opposite ends of a continuum, with the Mangaia having an elaborate social and cultural framework for instructing adolescents in sexual technique and the Dani downplaying the importance of sex.

- Middle-class Americans in the nineteenth century believed that men had strong sexual drives but that women had little sexual desire. Because sexuality was considered animalistic, the Victorians separated sex and love.

- *Sexual orientation* is the pattern of sexual and emotional attraction based on the sex of one's partner. In contemporary America, *heterosexuality,* or attraction between men and women, is the only sexual orientation that receives full societal and legal legitimacy. *Homosexuality* refers to same-sex attractions, and *bisexuality* involves attraction to both males and females.

- In ancient Greece, same-sex relationships between men represented the highest form of love. Among the Sambians of New Guinea, boys have sexual contact with older boys, believing that the ingestion of semen is required for growth. When the girls to whom they are betrothed reach puberty, adolescent boys cease these same-sex sexual relations.

- The characteristics associated with being male or female are otherwise called *gender.* While culture helps to shape masculinity or feminity, biology defines men and women.

- A *transsexual person* has the genitals of one sex but identifies as a member of the other sex.

- A *two-spirit* is a person of one sex who identifies with the other sex; in some communities, such as the Zuni, a two-spirit is considered a third gender and is believed to possess great spiritual power.

Societal Norms and Sexuality

- Sexuality tends to be evaluated according to categories of natural/unnatural, normal/abnormal, and moral/immoral. These terms are value judgments, reflecting social norms rather than any quality inherent in the behavior itself.

- There is no commonly accepted definition of natural sexual behavior. *Normal sexual behavior* is what a culture defines as normal. We commonly use five criteria to categorize sexual behavior as normal or abnormal: subjectively normal, statistically normal, idealistically normal, culturally normal, and clinically normal.

- Human sexuality is characterized by *sexual variation.* Researchers believe that the best way to examine sexual behavior is on a continuum. Many activities that are considered deviant sexual behavior exist in most of us to some degree. These include exhibitionism, voyeurism, and fetishism.

- Behaviors are not abnormal or unnatural; rather, they are more or less typical or atypical of the group average. Many of those whose behaviors are atypical may be regarded as sexual nonconformists rather than as abnormal or perverse.

Questions for Discussion

- Should television producers be forced to address in their programming the consequences and/or responsibilities related to sex if they also portray sexual images or messages? If so, how? If not, why not?

- To what extent do you think your peers are influenced by the media? To what extent are you?

- While growing up, what sexual behaviors did you consider to be normal? Abnormal? How have these views changed now that you are older?

Sex and the Internet

Sex and the Media

With hundreds of millions of sex-related Web sites available, you might wonder about the issues and laws associated with access to cyberspace. Though the following sites each deal primarily with intellectual freedom, they also contain information and links to other sites that address issues of sex and the media. Select one of the following:

- Electronic Frontier Foundation: http://www.eff.org

- National Coalition for Sexual Freedom: http://www.ncsfreedom.org

- Kaiser Family Foundation:
  http://kff.org/entmedia/index.cfm
- Sexual Literacy:
  http://sexliteracy.org

Go to the site and answer the following questions:

- What is the mission of the site—if any?
- Who are its supporters and advocates?
- Who is its target audience?
- What is its predominant message?
- What current issue is it highlighting?

Given what you have learned about this site, how do your feelings about sex and the Internet compare with those of the creators of this Web site?

Suggested Web Sites

It's Your (Sex) Life
http://thinkmtv.com/campaigns/iysl
MTV-sponsored Web site on information about sexual health.

The Media Project
http://www.themediaproject.com
Offers the latest facts, research assistance, script consultation, and story ideas on today's sexual and reproductive health issues, including condoms, pregnancy, HIV/AIDS, abstinence, and abortion.

National Gay and Lesbian Task Force
http://thetaskforce.org
Provides information and referrals on gay, lesbian, bisexual, and transsexual issues and rights.

Noah
http://www.noah-health.org/en/healthy/sexuality
Run by the New York Online Access to Health; contains information on various sexual health topics and links.

Suggested Reading

Brown, J. D., Steele, J. R., & Walsh-Childers, K. (Eds.). (2002). *Sexual teens, sexual media: Investigating media's influence on adolescent sexuality.* Mahwah, NJ: Erlbaum. Explores the sexual content of mass media and its impact on adolescents.

Castaneda, L., & Campbell, S. B. (Eds.). (2005). *News and sexuality: Media portrayals of diversity.* Thousand Oaks, CA: Sage. Provides an understanding of issues and perspectives on gender, race, ethnicity, and sexual orientation as addressed in the media.

Fisher, H. (2004). *Why we love.* New York: Henry Holt. Uses neurophysiological research to explore the chemistry of attachment.

Francoeur, R. T., & Noonan, R. (Eds.). (2004). *The continuum complete international encyclopedia of sexuality.* New York: Continuum. The foremost reference work on sexual behavior throughout the world.

Gauntlett, D. (2007). *Media, gender & identity: An Introduction.* New York: Routledge. An introduction to the main themes of popular culture and the ways in which it influences lifestyles and concepts of gender and identity.

Middleton, D. R. (2001). *Exotics and erotics: Human culture and sexual diversity.* Prospect Heights, IL: Waveland Press. Explores universal human sexuality in conjunction with its local manifestations in specific cultural contexts; topics include the body, patterns of sexuality, sexual behavior, romantic passion, marriage, and kinship.

Tiefer, L. (2004). *Sex is not a natural act and other essays* (2nd ed.). Boulder, CO: Westview Press. A revised collection of provocative essays on sex and its many meanings in our culture.

For links, articles, and study material, go to the McGraw-Hill Web site, located at **www.mhhe.com/yarber7e.**

2

Studying Human Sexuality

MAIN TOPICS

Sex, Advice Columnists, and Pop
Psychology

Thinking Critically About Sexuality

Sex Research Methods

The Sex Researchers

Contemporary Research Studies

Emerging Research Perspectives

Ethnicity and Sexuality

"I've heard about those sex surveys, and I wonder how truthful they are. I mean, don't you think that people who volunteer for those studies only admit to behaviors which they deem socially acceptable? I just don't think people who lose their virginity, for instance at age 12 or age 30, would actually report it. Besides, no sex study is going to tell me what I should do or whether I am normal."

—21-year-old male

"I feel that sexual research is a benefit to our society. The human sexuality class I took my sophomore year in college taught me a lot. Without research, many of the topics we learned about would not have been so thoroughly discussed due to lack of information. Sexual research and human sexuality classes help keep the topic of sex from being seen as such a faux pas by society."

—20-year-old female

"I took a sex survey once, during my undergraduate years. I found that the survey was easy to take, and the process of answering the questions actually led me to ask myself more questions about my sexual self. The survey was detailed, and I was encouraged to answer truthfully. Ultimately, every answer I gave was accurate because I knew that the research would benefit science (and it was completely anonymous)."

—22-year-old female

"I think sex research is great because it helps remove the taboo from the topic. Sex, in this country, is on TV all the time, but people do not want to seriously discuss it, especially adults with children. Sex research, when made public, can help ease the tension of discussing sex—especially when it reveals that something considered abnormal actually is normal and that many people practice the specific behavior."

—24-year-old male

"A NEW UNIVERSITY STUDY finds that many college students lie to a new sex partner about their sexual past . . . but first, a message from . . ." So begins a commercial lead-in on the evening news, reminding us that sex research is often part of both news and entertainment. In fact, most of us learn about the results of sex research from television, newspapers, the Internet, and magazines rather than from scholarly journals and books. After all, the mass media are more entertaining than most scholarly works. And unless we are studying human sexuality, few of us have the time or interest to read the scholarly journals in which scientific research is regularly published.

But how accurate is what the mass media tell us about sex and sex research? In this chapter, we discuss the dissemination of sexuality-related information by the various media. Then we look at the critical-thinking skills that help us evaluate how we discuss and think about sexuality. When are we making objective statements? When are we reflecting biases or opinions? Next, we examine sex research methods because they are critical to the scientific study of human sexuality. Then we look at some of the leading sex researchers to see how they have influenced our understanding of sexuality. Next, we discuss four national studies as examples of important research being done. Finally, we examine feminist, gay, lesbian, bisexual, transgender, and ethnic sex research to see how they enrich our knowledge of sexuality.

Ignorance is like a delicate exotic fruit; touch it and the bloom is gone.

—Oscar Wilde
(1854–1900)

● Sex, Advice Columnists, and Pop Psychology

As we saw in Chapter 1, the mass media convey seemingly endless sexual images. In addition to the various television, film, Internet, and advertising genres, there is another genre, which we might call the **sex information/advice genre,** that transmits information and norms, rather than images, about sexuality to a mass audience to both inform and entertain in a simplified manner. For most college students, as well as many other people, the sex information/advice genre is a major source of their knowledge about sex. This genre is ostensibly concerned with transmitting information that is factual and accurate. In addition, on an increasing number of college campuses, sex columns in student-run newspapers have become popular and sometimes controversial.

Information and Advice as Entertainment

Newspaper columns, magazine articles, TV programs, and syndicated radio shows share several features. First, their primary purpose is to sell newspapers and magazines or to raise program ratings. This goal is in marked contrast to that of scholarly research, whose primary purpose is to increase knowledge. Even the inclusion of survey questionnaires in magazines asking readers about their sexual attitudes or behaviors is ultimately designed to promote sales. We fill out the questionnaires for fun, much as we would crossword puzzles or anagrams. Then we buy the subsequent issue or watch a later program to see how we compare to other respondents.

Second, the success of media personalities rests not so much on their expertise as on their ability to present information as entertainment. Because the genre seeks to entertain, sex information and advice must be simplified. Complex explanations and analyses must be avoided because they would interfere with the entertainment purpose. Furthermore, the genre relies on high-interest or bizarre material to attract readers, viewers, and listeners. Consequently, we are more likely to read, hear, or view stories about unusual sexual behaviors or ways to increase sexual attractiveness than stories about new research methods or the negative outcomes of sexual stereotyping.

Third, the genre focuses on how-to information or on morality. Sometimes it mixes information and normative judgments. How-to material tells us how to improve our sex lives. Advice columnists often give advice on issues of sexual morality: "Is it all right to have sex without commitment?" "Yes, if you love him/her" or "No, casual sex is empty," and so on. These columnists act as moral arbiters, much as ministers, priests, and rabbis do.

Fourth, the genre uses the trappings of social science and psychiatry without their substance. Writers and columnists interview social scientists and therapists

> *If you believe everything you read, don't read.*
>
> —Chinese proverb

LUANN: © GEC Inc./Dist. by United Feature Syndicate, Inc.

think
about it

Campus Newspaper Sex Advice Columns: Education or Entertainment?

In response to curious and knowledge-seeking students, the number of college newspapers with sex advice columns has skyrocketed. For generations of Americans, the newspaper advice column has been a daily "must-read." Many cannot wait to find what the advice columnist has to say about sex, dating, love, gender roles, and relationships. The columns have filled a cultural void of open dialogue about sexuality by serving as a venue for public discourse of sexuality-related issues. People read the columns as a way to gauge the normality of their own behavior and to find solutions to their own difficulties, as well as eavesdrop on the problems of their neighbors. But these advice columns are not without their critics. Many health professionals contend that the columns are largely entertainment, treating the topics superficially and frivolously. And some opponents believe that advice columns, by their very nature, discourage persons from seeking professional help (Gudelunas, 2007). Researcher David Gudelunas (2007) argues that advice columns have a greater purpose than just entertainment, in that "they have told the story of sexual practices in America in the last century, and their cultural importance far surpasses a collection of witticisms." He continues by noting:

> Advice columns serve as a moral barometer as much as a source of interpersonal advice, and letter writers are just as anxious to weigh in with their own advice as they are to seek it from the columnist. (p. 4)

The college newspaper sex advice column attempts to provide accurate information and sound advice on topics such as contraception and safer sex and specific issues such as orgasm, oral sex, masturbation, bondage, pleasure, and penis size. Usually, an editor for the newspaper, typically an undergraduate student, is the "sex expert" who answers the questions. Although the columns have become very popular on many campuses, they are not universally liked. Some school administrators are uncomfortable about the columns, worrying that the columns lack taste and might tarnish the college's reputation. And some have even attempted to ban the columns. Critics often state the column's main purpose is entertainment (thus increasing newspaper sales), not

education. Moreover, the "sex expert" columnist may have little or no background in human sexuality or counseling and may provide misinformation or harmful advice. Defenders believe that the columns provide a valuable service—information about relevant issues in a culture that has little healthy discussion about sexuality—to their primary readers: college students.

One newspaper column is Kinsey Confidential, a weekly sex information column and podcast published by the Indiana University (IU) student-run newspaper, the *Indiana Daily Student*. A strength of this column is that it is written by the professional staff of the Kinsey Institute for Research in Sex, Reproduction, and Gender at IU. Undergraduate and graduate students at IU often intern with the Kinsey Institute and help develop the content for the Web site and blog (www.kinseyconfidential.org). These students have access to the Institute's resources, which helps ensure greater accuracy in the information they provide. Questions submitted by IU students are personally answered via e-mail. Questions are also submitted by the general public; but given the large volume of questions received, all questions may not receive personal e-mail replies. However, selected questions for IU students and the general public are confidentially printed in the newspaper and posted on the Kinsey Confidential Web site. Anyone can read past questions and answers online.

Think Critically

- Given the ambivalence about college sex advice columns, what are your thoughts about them?
- Should college student-run newspapers have sex advice columns? If so, should the newspaper be required to get the school administrator's approval for the responses provided in the column?
- Should all types of questions be answered, regardless of how explicit or "risqué"?
- In your view, should these columns be considered as education or simply as entertainment? Why?

to give an aura of scientific authority to their material. They rely especially heavily on therapists, whose background is clinical rather than academic. Because clinicians tend to deal with people with problems, they often see the problematic aspects of sexuality.

The line between media sex experts and advice columnists is often blurred. This line is especially obscure on the Internet, where Web sites dealing with sex

Evaluating Pop Psychology

After you have read several sex books and watched several sex experts on television, you will discover that they tend to be repetitive. There are two main reasons for this. First, the media repeatedly report more or less the same stories because sex research is a small discipline and fewer studies are conducted compared to other academic areas. Scientific research is painstakingly slow, and the results are tedious to produce. Research results often do not change the way we view a topic; instead, they tend to verify what we already know. Although research is seldom revolutionary, the media must nevertheless continually produce new stories to fill their pages and programs. Consequently, they report similar material in different guises— as interviews, survey results, and first-person stories, for example.

Second, the media are repetitive because their scope is narrow. There are only so many ways how-to books can tell you "how to do it." Similarly, the personal and moral dilemmas most of us face are remarkably similar: Am I normal? When should I be sexual with another person? Is sex without love moral?

With the media awash with sex information and advice, how can you evaluate what is presented to you? Here are some guidelines:

1. *Be skeptical.* Remember, much of what you read or see is meant to entertain you. If it seems superficial, it probably is.
2. *Search for biases, stereotypes, and lack of objectivity.* Information is often distorted by points of view. One should assess if there is any reason to suspect bias in the selection of subjects.
3. *Look for moralizing.* Many times, what passes for fact is really disguised moral judgment.
4. *Go to the original source or sources.* The media always simplify. Find out for yourself what the studies really reported. It can be helpful to note the credentials of the researchers and the type of organization that conducted the study, as well as who, if anyone, funded the study. Learning how representative the sample was, the study parameters, and the study strengths and limitations is also important.
5. *Seek additional information.* The whole story is probably not told. Look for additional information in scholarly books and journals, reference books, or textbooks. Do not put too much credence in one study; later studies may contradict the findings.

Keeping these guidelines in mind will help you steer a course between blind acceptance and offhand dismissal of a study.

have proliferated. Most of these sites are purely for entertainment rather than education, and it can be difficult to determine a site's credibility. One way to assess the educational value of a Web site is to investigate its sponsor. Reputable national organizations like the American Psychological Association (http://www.apa.org) and the Sexuality Information and Education Council of the United States (http://www.siecus.org) provide reliable information and links to other, equally reputable, sites.

The Use and Abuse of Research Findings

To reinforce their authority, the media often incorporate statistics from a study's findings, which are key features of social science research. However, as Susan Faludi (1991) notes:

> The statistics that the popular culture chooses to promote most heavily are the very statistics we should view with the most caution. They may well be in wide circulation not because they are true but because they support widely held media preconceptions.

Further, the media may report the results of a study that are contradicted by subsequent research. It is common, particularly in the medical field, for the original results not to be replicated when continued research is conducted (Tanner, 2005). For example, a review of major studies published in three influential medical journals from 1990 to 2003 found that one third of the results do not hold up (Ionannidis, 2005). But, of course, changes in "current knowledge" also happen in behavioral research. For example, research showing a possible relationship between brain anatomy, genes, and sexual orientation was heavily covered by the media. But many reports exaggerated the certainty of the research findings, leading people to conclude that biology, not social influences, causes males to be homosexual. The "nature versus nurture" influence on sexual orientation is still being debated and investigated by **sexologists** (specialists in the study of human sexuality) and remains controversial. Another area that is often presented in the media as definitive is that consumption of alcohol, per se, always leads to sexual risk behaviors. Yet, studies have found that among young people the relationship between alcohol use and risky sexual behaviors is complex and often the research findings are inconsistent or inconclusive. An alternative explanation is that possibly a high proportion of young people take more risks than other young people in several areas such as cigarette use, drug use, alcohol use, driving, and sex. That is, there is a clustering of risk behaviors representing high sensation seeking, and alcohol use alone does not cause risky sex but both are part of the total risk behavior pattern (Coleman, 2001; Coleman & Cater, 2005; Zuckerman, 1994).

The media frequently quote or describe social science research, but they may do so in an oversimplified or distorted manner. An excellent example of distorted representation of sex-related research was some of the media coverage of the research on ram sheep by Charles Roselli, a researcher at the Oregon Health and Science University. Dr. Roselli searched for physiological explanations of why 8% of rams exclusively seek sex with other rams instead of ewes. His research was funded by the National Institutes of Health and published in major scientific journals. Following media coverage of his research, animal-rights activists, gay advocates, and others criticized the studies. A *New York Times* article in January 2007 noted that his research drew outrage based on, according to Dr. Roselli and his colleagues, "bizarre misinterpretation of what the work is about." The researchers contended that discussion of possible human implications of their findings in their reports differed from intentions of carrying the work over to humans. Critics claimed that the research could lead to altering or controlling sexual orientation. According to the *Times* article, *The Sunday Times* in London asserted, incorrectly, that Dr. Roselli found a way to "cure" homosexual rams with hormone treatment, adding that critics feared the research "could pave the way for breeding out homosexuality in humans." John Schwartz, author of the *Times* article, concluded that "the story of the gay sheep became a textbook example of the distortion and vituperation that can result when science meets the global news cycle" (Schwartz, 2007). As this example illustrates, scholars tend to qualify their findings as tentative or limited to a certain group, and they are very cautious about making generalizations. In contrast, the media tend to make results sound generalizable.

Clearly, the media are not always the best place to learn about the latest sex research. As consumers of the findings of sex research, we need to determine whether the report mentions study limitations and whether the researchers are from a reputable university or institution. If the report overgeneralizes the results, beware.

● Thinking Critically About Sexuality

Although each of us has our own perspective, values, and beliefs regarding sexuality, as students, instructors, and researchers, we are committed to the scientific study of sexuality. Basic to any scientific study is a fundamental commitment to **objectivity,** or the observation of things as they exist in reality as opposed to our feelings or beliefs about them. Objectivity calls for us to suspend the beliefs, biases, or prejudices we have about a subject in order to understand it.

Objectivity in the study of sexuality is not always easy to achieve, for sexuality can be the focal point of powerful emotions and moral ambivalence. We experience sex very subjectively. But whether we find it easy or difficult to be objective, objectivity is the foundation for studying sexuality.

Most of us think about sex, but thinking about it critically requires us to be logical and objective. It also requires that we avoid making value judgments; put aside our opinions, biases, and stereotypes; and not fall prey to common fallacies such as egocentric and ethnocentric thinking.

Value Judgments Versus Objectivity

For many of us, objectivity about sex is difficult because our culture has traditionally viewed sexuality in moral terms: Sex is moral or immoral, right or wrong, good or bad, or normal or abnormal. When examining sexuality, we tend, therefore, to make **value judgments,** evaluations based on moral or ethical standards rather than objective ones. Unfortunately, value judgments are often blinders to understanding. They do not tell us about what motivates people, how frequently they behave in a given way, or how they feel. Value judgments do not tell us anything about sexuality except how we ourselves feel. In studying human sexuality, then, we need to put aside value judgments as incompatible with the pursuit of knowledge.

How can we tell the difference between a value judgment and an objective statement? Examine the following two statements. Which is a value judgment? Which is an objective statement?

- College students should be in a committed relationship before they have sex.
- The majority of students have sexual intercourse sometime during their college careers.

The first statement is a value judgment; the second is an objective statement. There is a simple rule of thumb for telling the difference between the two: Value judgments imply how a person *ought* to behave, whereas objective statements describe how people *actually* behave.

There is a second difference between value judgments and objective statements: Value judgments cannot be empirically validated, whereas objective statements can be. That is, the truth or accuracy of an objective statement can be measured and tested.

Opinions, Biases, and Stereotypes

Value judgments obscure our search for understanding. Opinions, biases, and stereotypes also interfere with the pursuit of knowledge.

Opinions   An **opinion** is an unsubstantiated belief or conclusion about what seems to be true according to our thoughts. Opinions are not based on accurate knowledge or concrete evidence. Because opinions are unsubstantiated, they often reflect our personal values or biases.

Biases   A **bias** is a personal leaning or inclination. Biases lead us to select information that supports our views or beliefs while ignoring information that does not. We need not be victims, however, of our biases. We can make a concerted effort to discover what they are and overcome them. To avoid personal bias, scholars apply the objective methods of social science research.

Stereotypes   A **stereotype** is a set of simplistic, rigidly held, overgeneralized beliefs about an individual, a group of people, an idea, and so on. Stereotypical beliefs are resistant to change. Furthermore, stereotypes—especially sexual ones—are often negative.

Common sexual stereotypes include the following:

- Men are always ready for sex.
- "Nice" women are not interested in sex.
- Women need a reason for sex; men need a place.
- Virgins are uptight and asexual.
- The relationships of gay men never last.
- Lesbian women hate men.
- African American men lust after White women.
- Latino men are promiscuous.

Psychologists believe that stereotypes structure knowledge. They affect the ways in which we process information: what we see, what we notice, what we remember, and how we explain things. Or, as humorist Ashleigh Brilliant said, "Seeing is believing. I wouldn't have seen it if I hadn't believed it." A stereotype is a type of **schema,** a way in which we organize knowledge in our thought processes. Schemas help us channel or filter the mass of information we receive so that we can make sense of it. They determine what we will regard as important. Although these mental plans are useful, they can also create blind spots. With stereotypes, we see what we expect to see and ignore what we don't expect or want to see.

Sociologists point out that sexual stereotyping is often used to justify discrimination. Targets of stereotypes are usually members of subordinate social groups or individuals with limited economic resources. As we will see, sexual stereotyping is especially powerful in stigmatizing African Americans, Latinos, Asian Americans, gay men, lesbian women, and bisexual and transgendered individuals.

We all have opinions and biases, and most of us to varying degrees think stereotypically. But the commitment to objectivity requires us to become aware of our opinions, biases, and stereotypes and to put them aside in the pursuit of knowledge.

Common Fallacies: Egocentric and Ethnocentric Thinking

A **fallacy** is an error in reasoning that affects our understanding of a subject. Fallacies distort our thinking, leading us to false or erroneous conclusions. In the field of sexuality, egocentric and ethnocentric fallacies are common.

The Egocentric Fallacy   The **egocentric fallacy** is the mistaken belief that our own personal experience and values generally are held by others. On the basis of

The human understanding when it has once adopted an opinion . . . draws all things else to support and agree with it.

—Francis Bacon
(1561–1626)

No question is so difficult as that to which the answer is obvious.

—George Bernard Shaw
(1856–1950)

Ethnocentrism is the belief that one's own culture or ethnic group is superior to others. Although child marriage is prohibited in our society, it is acceptable in many cultures throughout the world, including India.

our belief in this false consensus, we use our own beliefs and values to explain the **attitudes,** motivations, and **behaviors** of others. Of course, our own experiences and values are important; they are the source of personal strength and knowledge, and they can give us insight into the experiences and values of others. But we cannot necessarily generalize from our own experience to that of others. Our own personal experiences are limited and may be unrepresentative. Sometimes, our generalizations are merely opinions or disguised value judgments.

The Ethnocentric Fallacy   The **ethnocentric fallacy,** also known as **ethnocentrism,** is the belief that our own ethnic group, nation, or culture is innately superior to others. Ethnocentrism is reinforced by opinions, biases, and stereotypes about other groups and cultures. As members of a group, we tend to share similar values and attitudes with other group members. But the mere fact that we share these beliefs is not sufficient proof of their truth.

Ethnocentrism has been increasingly evident as a reaction to the increased awareness of **ethnicity,** or ethnic affiliation or identity. For many Americans, a significant part of their sense of self comes from identification with their ethnic group. An **ethnic group** is a group of people distinct from other groups because of cultural characteristics, such as language, religion, and customs, that are transmitted from one generation to the next.

Although there was little research on ethnicity and sexuality until the 1980s, evidence suggests that there are significant ethnic variations in terms of sexual attitudes and behavior. When data are available, the variations by ethnicity will be presented throughout this book.

Ethnocentrism results when we stereotype other cultures as "primitive," "innocent," "inferior," or "not as advanced." We may view the behavior of other peoples as strange, exotic, unusual, or bizarre, but to them it is normal. Their attitudes, behaviors, values, and beliefs form a unified sexual system that makes sense within their culture. In fact, we engage in many activities that appear peculiar to those outside our culture.

All universal judgments are weak, loose, and dangerous.

—Michel de Montaigne
(1533–1595)

● Sex Research Methods

One of the key factors that distinguishes the findings of social science from beliefs, prejudice, bias, and pop psychology is its commitment to the scientific method. The **scientific method** is the method by which a hypothesis is formed from impartially gathered data and tested empirically. The scientific method relies on **induction**—that is, drawing a general conclusion from specific facts. The scientific method seeks to describe the world rather than evaluate or judge it.

Although sex researchers use the same methodology as other social scientists, they are constrained by ethical concerns and taboos that those in many other fields do not experience. Because of the taboos surrounding sexuality, some traditional research methods are inappropriate.

Sex research, like most social science research, uses different methodological approaches. These include clinical research, survey research (questionnaires and interviews), observational research, and experimental research. And as in many fields, no single research paradigm has emerged in sexual science (Weis, 2002).

Research Concerns

Researchers face two general concerns in conducting their work: (1) ethical concerns centering on the use of human beings as subjects and (2) methodological concerns regarding sampling techniques and their accuracy. Without a representative sample, the conclusions that can be drawn using these methodologies are limited.

Ethical Issues   Ethics are important in any scientific endeavor. They are especially important in such an emotional and value-laden subject as sexuality. Among the most important ethical issues are informed consent, protection from harm, and confidentiality.

Informed consent is the full disclosure to an individual of the purpose, potential risks, and benefits of participating in a research project. Under informed consent, people are free to decide whether to participate in a project without coercion or deceit. Studies involving children and other minors typically require parental consent. Once a study begins, participants have the right to withdraw at any time without penalty.

Each research participant is entitled to **protection from harm.** Some sex research, such as the viewing of explicit films to measure physiological responses, may cause some people emotional distress. The identity of research subjects should be kept confidential. Because of the highly charged nature of sexuality, participants also need to be guaranteed anonymity.

All colleges and universities have review boards or human-subject committees to make sure that researchers follow ethical guidelines. Proposed research is submitted to the committee before the project begins.

Sampling   In each research approach, the choice of a sample—a portion of a larger group of people or population—is critical. To be most useful, a sample should be a **random sample**—that is, a sample collected in an unbiased way, with the selection of each member of the sample based solely on chance. Furthermore, the sample should be a **representative sample,** with a small group

We are the recorders and reporters of facts—not judges of the behavior we describe.

—Alfred C. Kinsey
(1894–1965)

Anything more than truth would be too much.

—Robert Frost
(1874–1963)

A couple is being interviewed by a sex researcher. The face-to-face interview, one method of gathering data about sexuality, has both advantages and disadvantages.

representing the larger group in terms of age, sex, ethnicity, socioeconomic status, sexual orientation, and so on. When a random sample is used, information gathered from a small group can be used to make inferences about the larger group. Samples that are not representative of the larger group are known as **biased samples.**

Using samples is important. It would be impossible, for example, to study the sexual behaviors of all college students in the United States. But we could select a representative sample of college students from various schools and infer from their behavior how other college students behave. Using the same sample to infer the sexual behavior of Americans in general, however, would mean using a biased sample. We cannot generalize the sexual activities of American college students to the larger population because the majority of college students sampled are biased in terms of age (young), education (college), socioeconomic status (middle class), and ethnicity (European American) (Dunne, 2002; Strassberg & Lowe, 1995).

Most samples in sex research are limited for several reasons:

- They depend on volunteers or clients. Because these samples are generally self-selected, we cannot assume that they are representative of the population as a whole. Volunteers for sex research are often more likely to be male, sexually experienced, liberal, and less religious and to have more positive attitudes toward sexuality and less sex guilt and anxiety than those who do not choose to participate (Strassberg & Lowe, 1995; Whitley, 2002; Wiederman, 1999).

- Most sex research takes place in a university or college setting with student volunteers. Is the value they place on emotional intimacy during sex likely to be the same as the value older adults give it?

- Some ethnic groups are generally underrepresented. Representative samples of African Americans, Latinos, American Indians, and some Asian Americans, for example, are not easily found because these groups are underrepresented at the colleges and universities where subjects are generally recruited.

- The study of gay men, lesbian women, and bisexual and transgendered individuals presents unique sampling issues. Are gay men, lesbian women, and bisexual individuals who have **come out**—publicly identified themselves as gay, lesbian, or bisexual—different from those who have not? How do researchers find and recruit subjects who have not come out?

Because these factors limit most studies, we must be careful in making generalizations from studies.

Clinical Research

Clinical research is the in-depth examination of an individual or group that comes to a psychiatrist, psychologist, or social worker for assistance with psychological or medical problems or disorders. Clinical research is descriptive; inferences of cause and effect cannot be drawn from it. The individual is interviewed and treated for a specific problem. At the same time the person is being treated, he or she is being studied. In their evaluations, clinicians attempt to determine what caused the disorder and how it may be treated. They may also try to infer from dysfunctional people how healthy people develop. Clinical research often focuses on atypical, unhealthy behaviors, problems related to sexuality (e.g., feeling trapped in the body of the wrong gender), and sexual function problems (e.g., lack of desire, early ejaculation, erectile difficulties, or lack of orgasm).

A major limitation of clinical research is its emphasis on **pathological behavior,** or unhealthy or diseased behavior. Such an emphasis makes clinical research dependent on cultural definitions of what is "unhealthy" or "pathological." These definitions, however, change over time and in the context of the culture being studied. In the nineteenth century, for example, masturbation was considered pathological. Physicians and clinicians went to great lengths to root it out. In the case of women, surgeons sometimes removed the clitoris. Today, masturbation is viewed more positively.

Survey Research

Survey research is a method that uses questionnaires or interviews to gather information. Questionnaires offer anonymity, can be completed fairly quickly, and are relatively inexpensive to administer; however, they usually do not allow an in-depth response. A person must respond with a short answer or select from a limited number of options. The limited-choices format provides a more objective assessment than the short-answer format and results in a total score. Interview techniques avoid some of the shortcomings of questionnaires, as interviewers are able to probe in greater depth and follow paths suggested by the participant.

Although surveys are important sources of information, the method has several limitations. First, people tend to be poor reporters of their own sexual behavior. For example, some people may exaggerate their number of sexual partners; others may minimize their casual encounters. Respondents generally underreport experiences that might be considered deviant or immoral, such as bondage and same-sex experiences. Second, interviewers may allow their own preconceptions to influence the way in which they frame questions and to bias their interpretations of responses. Third, some respondents may feel uncomfortable about revealing information—such as about masturbation or fetishes—in a face-to-face interview. Fourth, the interviewer's sex may also influence how comfortable respondents are in disclosing information about themselves. Fifth, the accuracy of one's memory may fade as time passes. Sixth, providing an accurate estimation, such as how long sex lasted, may be difficult. Finally, some ethnic groups, because of their cultural values, may be reluctant to reveal sexual information about themselves.

Some researchers use computers to improve interviewing techniques for sensitive topics. With the audio computer-assisted self-interviewing (audio-CASI) method, the respondent hears the questions over headphones or reads them on a computer screen and then enters her or his responses into the computer. Audio-CASI apparently increases feelings of confidentiality and accuracy of

The great tragedy of science—the slaying of a beautiful hypothesis by an ugly fact.

—Thomas Huxley
(1825–1895)

Answering a Sex Research Questionnaire: Sexual Orientation Identity Uncertainty

To measure variables related to sexuality, many sex researchers use standardized (i.e., reliable and valid) questionnaires. One such questionnaire, the Sexual Orientation Identity Uncertainty (SOIU), assesses sexual identity development and can be used by persons of any sexual orientation (Worthington, Navarro, Savoy, & Hampton, 2008). **Sexual identity** refers to one's self-label or self-identification as a heterosexual, homosexual, or bisexual person (Hyde & DeLamater, 2008). The SOIU is a theoretically based questionnaire that contains four components or subscales: exploration (pursuit of a revised and refined sense of self), commitment (choice to adopt a specific identity represented by a unified set of goals, values, and beliefs), synthesis (a state of congruence among all dimensions of individual sexual identity and the broader sense of self), and sexual orientation identity uncertainty (not being sure about one's sexual identity). The SOIU can help sex researchers, for example, understand the relationship between the processes of sexual identity development and sexual risk behavior related to sexually transmitted infections, including HIV, and unintended pregnancy.

The SOIU is presented below. Take it to find out what it is like to complete a sex research questionnaire, as well as get a general idea about your own sexual identity development.

Directions

Refer to these definitions when completing the questionnaire:

Sexual needs   An internal, subjective experience of instinct, desire, appetite, biological necessity, impulses, interest, and/or libido with respect to sex.

Sexual values   Moral evaluations, judgments, and/or standards about what is appropriate, acceptable, desirable, and innate sexual behavior.

Sexual activities   Any behavior that a person might engage in relating to or based on sexual attraction, sexual arousal, sexual gratification, or reproduction (e.g., fantasy to holding hands to kissing to sexual intercourse).

Modes of sexual expression   Any form of communication (verbal or nonverbal) or direct and indirect signals that a person might use to convey her or his sexuality (e.g., flirting, eye contact, touching, vocal quality, compliments, suggestive body movements or postures).

Sexual orientation   An enduring emotional, romantic, sexual, or affectional attraction to other persons that ranges from exclusive heterosexuality to exclusive homosexuality and includes various forms of bisexuality.

Respond to each below item as honestly as you can, using the key 1 = very uncharacteristic of me to 6 = very characteristic of me. Circle your response. There are no right or wrong answers.

	very uncharacteristic of me			very characteristic of me		
1. My sexual orientation is clear to me.	1	2	3	4	5	6
2. I went through a period in my life when I was trying to determine my sexual needs.	1	2	3	4	5	6
3. I am actively trying to learn more about my own sexual needs.	1	2	3	4	5	6
4. My sexual values are consistent with all of the other aspects of my sexuality.	1	2	3	4	5	6
5. I am open to experiment with new types of sexual activities in the future.	1	2	3	4	5	6
6. I am actively trying new ways to express myself sexually.	1	2	3	4	5	6
7. My understanding of my sexual needs coincides with my overall sense of sexual self.	1	2	3	4	5	6
8. I went through a period in my life when I was trying different forms of sexual expression.	1	2	3	4	5	6
9. My sexual values will always be open to sexual exploration.	1	2	3	4	5	6
10. I know what my preferences are for expressing myself sexually.	1	2	3	4	5	6
11. I have a clear sense of the types of sexual activities I prefer.	1	2	3	4	5	6
12. I am actively experimenting with sexual activities that are new to me.	1	2	3	4	5	6

	very uncharacteristic of me				very characteristic of me	
13. The ways I express myself sexually are consistent with all of the other aspects of my sexuality.	1	2	3	4	5	6
14. I sometimes feel uncertain about my sexual orientation.	1	2	3	4	5	6
15. I do not know how to express myself sexually.	1	2	3	4	5	6
16. I have never clearly identified what my sexual values are.	1	2	3	4	5	6
17. The sexual activities I prefer are compatible with all of the other aspects of my sexuality.	1	2	3	4	5	6
18. I have never clearly identified what my sexual needs are.	1	2	3	4	5	6
19. I can see myself trying new ways of expressing myself sexually in the future.	1	2	3	4	5	6
20. I have a firm sense of what my sexual needs are.	1	2	3	4	5	6
21. My sexual orientation is not clear to me.	1	2	3	4	5	6
22. My sexual orientation is compatible with all of the other aspects of my sexuality.	1	2	3	4	5	6

Scoring

Scores for the questionnaire components or subscales are obtained by averaging the ratings on the items for each subscale (this method ensures scores when an item is not answered). Use the below items for an average or mean score for each subscale. *Note:* Items that should be scored in reverse are listed in **bold typeface;** for example, if you marked a 2, give it a 5 score.

Exploration = 2, 3, 5, 6, 8, 9, 12, 19
Commitment = 10, 11, **15, 16, 18,** 20
Synthesis = 4, 7, 13, 17, 22
Sexual orientation identity uncertainty = **1**, 14, 21

What Do Your Scores Mean?

Exploration Higher average scores on this subscale mean that a person has a greater tendency toward self-exploration across the dimensions of sexual identity (e.g., perceived sexual needs, preferred sexual activities, sexual values, recognition and identification of sexual orientation, and preferred modes of sexual expression). Sexual identity exploration is a normal aspect of human development, especially for people in their adolescence and young adulthood. Studies have shown that those who are uncertain about their sexual identity or who identify as a lesbian, gay, or bisexual person tend to score higher on this subscale than heterosexual individuals.

Commitment Higher average scores on this subscale mean that a person has a clear and relatively fixed sense of perceived sexual needs, preferred sexual activities, sexual values, recognition and identification of sexual orientation, and preferred modes of sexual expression. Sexual identity typically becomes stronger as one ages, and high scores can be found in persons of any sexual orientation identity.

Synthesis Higher average scores on this scale mean that the person has expressed greater congruence and correspondence in his/her level of commitment across all dimensions of sexual identity. That is, those who score higher on this subscale tend to perceive their sexual values, needs, activities, modes of sexual expression, and sexual orientation identities as in sync with one another, as well as with their broader sense of self.

Sexual Orientation Uncertainty Higher average scores on this subscale mean that the person has expressed greater uncertainty about his/her sexual orientation as a gay, lesbian, bisexual, or heterosexual individual. Research shows that many people experience sexual orientation uncertainty at some time in their lives, and that uncertainty is often accompanied by lower levels of sexual identity commitment and higher levels of sexual identity exploration. Bisexual persons tend to score higher on this subscale than those of other sexual orientation groups, possibly because of experiencing negative societal biases from heterosexual persons, as well as from lesbian women and gay men, which can result in greater demands for exploration among bisexual persons during the course of sexual identity formation.

Take some time to reflect on your experience in completing this survey:

- Did you learn something about your own sexual identity development?
- How valid do you think the results from a questionnaire such as this are? That is, do you think the questionnaire actually measures what it claims to measure, such as sexual orientation uncertainty?
- Would your responses have been the same if you had been asked these same questions on the telephone, in an interview, or via the computer?

SOURCES: Hyde, J. S., & DeLamater, J. D. (2008). *Understanding human sexuality* (10th ed.). New York: McGraw-Hill; Worthington, R. L., Navarro, R. L., Savoy, H. B., & Hampton, D. (2008). Development, reliability, and validity of the Measure of Sexual Identity Exploration and Commitment (MoSIEC). *Developmental Psychology, 44,* 22–33; (Table 1, p. 26). No further reproduction or distribution is permitted without written permission from the American Psychological Association. R. L. Worthington (personal communication, January 31, 2008).

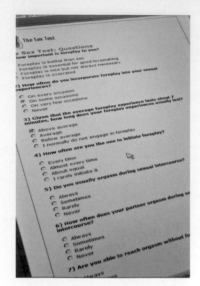

An increasing number of sex researchers are placing their questionnaires on the Internet so that persons at any location or at any time can participate in the study.

Discovery consists of seeing what everybody has seen and thinking what nobody has thought.

—Albert Szent-Györgyi
(1893–1986)

responses. In studies comparing the face-to-face interview with audio-CASI, more respondents reported HIV risk behaviors and stigmatized activities in audio-CASI than in face-to-face interviews (Des Jarlais et al., 1999; Gribble, Miller, Rogers, & Turner, 1999).

Another new technique is the use of the Internet to administer questionnaires and conduct interviews. Respondents to Web-based interviews tend to have a higher income and level of education than those without access to the Internet, making it difficult to generalize from their responses. However, geographically isolated individuals can be reached more easily (Ross, Tikkanen, & Mansson, 2000). Stigmatized groups (e.g., bisexual people) may feel more comfortable participating and much larger samples may be obtained. For example, a British Internet study on sexuality and gender had about 255,000 participants (Reimers, 2007).

Daily data collection, using a **sexual diary,** or personal notes of one's sexual activity, can increase the accuracy of self-report data (Crosby, DiClemente, & Salazar, 2006). Often, research participants make daily diary entries about sexual variables such as interest, fantasies, and behavior. Or they may be requested to make entries only after a certain sexual activity has occurred, such as intercourse. Research suggests that event-specific behaviors such as condom use during sex will be more accurately recalled in diaries than by retrospective methods such as self-report questionnaires and interviews (Fortenberry, Cecil, Zimet, & Orr, 1997; Gilmore et al., 2001; Graham & Bancroft, 1997). The diary may also foster a richer, more conceptualized assessment of sexual behavior. Researcher Paul Okami (2002) states that the diary may also be a superior survey method for assessing sex-related variables because it may reduce problems of recall and because some people seem to prefer diaries to questionnaires. However, Okami notes that diaries require greater participant compliance (e.g., daily entries) and may produce underestimates or overestimates of sexual behavior in ways questionnaires do not.

Observational Research

Observational research is a method by which a researcher unobtrusively observes and makes systematic notes about people's behavior without trying to manipulate it. The observer does not want his or her presence to affect the subject's behavior, although this is rarely possible. Because sexual behavior is regarded as significantly different from other behaviors, there are serious ethical issues involved in observing people's sexual behavior without their knowledge and consent. Researchers cannot observe sexual behavior as they might observe, say, flirting at a party, dance, or bar, so such observations usually take place in a laboratory setting. In such instances, the setting is not a natural environment, and participants are aware that their behavior is under observation.

Participant observation, in which the researcher participates in the behaviors she or he is studying, is an important method of observational research. For example, a researcher may study prostitution by becoming a customer (Snyder, 1974) or anonymous sex between men in public restrooms by posing as a lookout (Humphreys, 1975). There are several questions raised by such participant observation: How does the observer's participation affect the interactions being studied? For example, does a prostitute respond differently to a researcher if she or he tries to obtain information? If the observer participates, how does this affect her or his objectivity? And what are the researcher's ethical responsibilities regarding informing those she or he is studying?

Participant observation is an important means by which anthropologists gain information about other cultures.

Experimental Research

Experimental research is the systematic manipulation of individuals or the environment to learn the effects of such manipulation on behavior. It enables researchers to isolate a single factor under controlled circumstances to determine its influence. Researchers are able to control their experiments by using **variables,** or aspects or factors that can be manipulated in experiments. There are two types of variables: independent and dependent. **Independent variables** are factors that can be manipulated or changed by the experimenter; **dependent variables** are factors that are likely to be affected by changes in the independent variable.

Because it controls variables, experimental research differs from the previous methods we have examined. Clinical studies, surveys, and observational research are correlational in nature. **Correlational studies** measure two or more naturally occurring variables to determine their relationship to each other. Because these studies do not manipulate the variables, they cannot tell us which variable *causes* the other to change. But experimental studies manipulate the independent variables, so researchers *can* reasonably determine what variables cause the other variables to change.

Much experimental research on sexuality depends on measuring physiological responses. These responses are usually measured by **plethysmographs** (pluh-THIZ-muh-grafs)—devices attached to the genitals to measure physiological response. Researchers use either a penile plethysmograph, a **strain gauge** (a device resembling a rubber band), or a Rigiscan™ for men and a vaginal plethysmograph for women. Both the penile plethysmograph and the strain gauge are placed around the penis to measure changes in its circumference during sexual arousal. The Rigiscan, probably the most widely used device to measure male genital response, consists of a recording unit strapped around the waist or the thigh and two loops, one placed around the base of the penis and the other around the shaft just behind the glans. The Rigiscan not only measures penile circumference but also assesses rigidity (Janssen, 2002). The vaginal plethysmograph is about

Click on "The Plethysmograph" to see how a Rigiscan works.

the size of a menstrual tampon and is inserted into the vagina like a tampon. The device measures the amount of blood within the vaginal walls, which increases as a woman becomes sexually aroused.

Suppose researchers want to study the influence of alcohol on sexual response. They can use a plethysmograph to measure sexual response, the dependent variable. In this study, the independent variable is the level of alcohol consumption: no alcohol consumption, moderate alcohol consumption (1–3 drinks), and high alcohol consumption (3+ drinks). In addition, extraneous variables, such as body mass and tolerance for alcohol, need to be controlled. In such an experiment, subjects may view an erotic video. To get a baseline measurement, researchers measure the genitals' physiological patterns in an unaroused state, before participants view the video or take a drink. Then they measure sexual arousal (dependent variable) in response to erotica as they increase the level of alcohol consumption (independent variable).

● The Sex Researchers

It was not until the nineteenth century that Western sexuality began to be studied using a scientific framework. Prior to that time, sexuality was the domain of religion rather than science; sex was the subject of moral rather than scientific scrutiny. From the earliest Christian era, treatises, canon law, and papal bulls, as well as sermons and confessions, catalogued the sins of the flesh. Reflecting this Christian tradition, the early researchers of sexuality were concerned with the supposed excesses and deviances of sexuality rather than its healthy functioning. They were fascinated by what they considered the pathologies of sex, such as fetishism, sadism, masturbation, and homosexuality—the very behaviors that religion condemned as sinful. Alfred Kinsey ironically noted that nineteenth-century researchers created "scientific classifications . . . nearly identical with theological classifications and with moral pronouncements . . . of the fifteenth century" (Kinsey et al., 1948).

As we will see, however, there has been a liberalizing trend in our thinking about sexuality. Both Richard von Krafft-Ebing and Sigmund Freud viewed sexuality as inherently dangerous and needing repression. But Havelock Ellis, Alfred Kinsey, William Masters and Virginia Johnson, and many other more recent researchers have viewed sexuality more positively; in fact, historian Paul Robinson (1976) regards these later researchers as modernists, or "sexual enthusiasts." Three themes are evident in the work of modernists: (1) They believe that sexual expression is essential to an individual's well-being, (2) they seek to broaden the range of legitimate sexual activity, including homosexuality, and (3) they believe that female sexuality is the equal of male sexuality.

As much as possible, sex researchers attempt to examine sexuality objectively. But, as with all of us, many of their views are intertwined with the beliefs and values of their times. This is especially apparent among the early sex researchers, some of the most important of whom are described here.

Richard von Krafft-Ebing

Richard von Krafft-Ebing (1840–1902), a Viennese professor of psychiatry, was probably the most influential of the early researchers. In 1886 he published his most famous work, *Psychopathia Sexualis,* a collection of case histories of fetishists, sadists, masochists, and homosexuals. (He invented the words "sadomasochism" and "transvestite.")

Richard von Krafft-Ebing (1840–1902) viewed most sexual behavior other than marital coitus as a sign of pathology.

Krafft-Ebing traced variations in Victorian sexuality to "hereditary taint," to "moral degeneracy," and, in particular, to masturbation. He intermingled descriptions of fetishists who became sexually excited by certain items of clothing with those of sadists who disemboweled their victims. For Krafft-Ebing, the origins of fetishism and murderous sadism, as well as most variations, lay in masturbation, the prime sexual sin of the nineteenth century. Despite his misguided focus on masturbation, Krafft-Ebing's *Psychopathia Sexualis* brought to public attention and discussion an immense range of sexual behaviors that had never before been documented in a dispassionate, if erroneous, manner. A darkened region of sexual behavior was brought into the open for public examination.

Sigmund Freud

Few people have had as dramatic an impact on the way we think about the world as the Viennese physician Sigmund Freud (1856–1939). In his attempt to understand the **neuroses,** or psychological disorders characterized by anxiety or tension, plaguing his patients, Freud explored the unknown territory of the unconscious. If unconscious motives were brought to consciousness, Freud believed, a person could change his or her behavior. But, he suggested, **repression,** a psychological mechanism that kept people from becoming aware of hidden memories and motives because they aroused guilt, prevents such knowledge.

To explore the unconscious, Freud used various techniques; in particular, he analyzed dreams to discover their meaning. His journeys into the mind led to the development of **psychoanalysis,** a psychological system that ascribes behavior to unconscious desires. He fled Vienna when Hitler annexed Austria in 1938 and died a year later in England.

Freud believed that sexuality begins at birth, a belief that set him apart from other researchers. Freud described five stages in psychosexual development. The first stage is the **oral stage,** lasting from birth to age 1. During this time, the infant's eroticism is focused on the mouth; thumb sucking produces an erotic pleasure. Freud believed that the "most striking character of this sexual activity . . . is that the child gratifies himself on his own body; . . . he is autoerotic" (Freud, 1938). The second stage, between ages 1 and 3, is the **anal stage.** Children's sexual activities continue to be autoerotic, but the region of pleasure shifts to the anus. From age 3 through 5, children are in the **phallic stage,** in which they exhibit interest in the genitals. At age 6, children enter a **latency stage,** in which their sexual impulses are no longer active. At puberty, they enter the **genital stage,** at which point they become interested in genital sexual activities, especially sexual intercourse.

The phallic stage is the critical stage in both male and female development. The boy develops sexual desires for his mother, leading to an **Oedipal complex.** He simultaneously desires his mother and fears his father. This fear leads to **castration anxiety,** the boy's belief that the father will cut off his penis because of jealousy. Girls follow a more complex developmental path, according to Freud. A girl develops an **Electra complex,** desiring her father while fearing her mother. Upon discovering that she does not have a penis, she feels deprived and develops **penis envy.** By age 6, boys and girls resolve their Oedipal and Electra complexes by relinquishing their desires for the parent of the other sex and identifying with their same-sex parent. In this manner, they develop their masculine and feminine identities. But because girls never acquire their "lost penis," Freud believed, they fail to develop an independent character like that of boys.

Sigmund Freud (1856–1939) was the founder of psychoanalysis and one of the most influential European thinkers of the first half of the twentieth century. Freud viewed sexuality with suspicion.

" *The true science and study of man is man.*

—Pierre Charron
(1541–1603)

In many ways, such as in his commitment to science and his explorations of the unconscious, Freud seems the embodiment of twentieth-century thought. But in recent times, his influence among American sex researchers has dwindled. Two of the most important reasons are his lack of empiricism and his inadequate description of female development.

Because of its limitations, Freud's work has become mostly of historical interest to mainstream sex researchers. It continues to exert influence in some fields of psychology but has been greatly modified by other fields. Even among contemporary psychoanalysts, Freud's work has been radically revised.

Havelock Ellis

English physician and psychologist Havelock Ellis (1859–1939) was the earliest important modern sexual thinker. His *Studies in the Psychology of Sex* (the first six volumes of which were published between 1897 and 1910) consisted of case studies, autobiographies, and personal letters. One of his most important contributions was pointing out the relativity of sexual values. In the nineteenth century, Americans and Europeans alike believed that their society's dominant sexual beliefs were the only morally and naturally correct standards. But Ellis demonstrated not only that Western sexual standards were hardly the only moral standards but also that they were not necessarily rooted in nature. In doing so, he was among the first researchers to appeal to studies in animal behavior, anthropology, and history.

Ellis also challenged the view that masturbation was abnormal. He argued that masturbation was widespread and that there was no evidence linking it with any serious mental or physical problems. He recorded countless men and women who masturbated without ill effect. In fact, he argued, masturbation had a positive function: It relieved tension.

In the nineteenth century, women were viewed as essentially "pure beings" who possessed reproductive rather than sexual desires. Men, in contrast, were driven by such strong sexual passions that their sexuality had to be severely controlled and repressed. In countless case studies, Ellis documented that women possessed sexual desires no less intense than those of men.

Ellis asserted that a wide range of behaviors was normal, including much behavior that the Victorians considered abnormal. He argued that both masturbation and female sexuality were normal behaviors and that even the so-called abnormal elements of sexual behavior were simply exaggerations of the normal.

He also reevaluated homosexuality. In the nineteenth century, homosexuality was viewed as the essence of sin and perversion. It was dangerous, lurid, and criminal. Ellis insisted that it was not a disease or a vice, but a congenital condition: A person was *born* homosexual; one did not *become* homosexual. By insisting that homosexuality was congenital, Ellis denied that it could be considered a vice or a form of moral degeneracy, because a person did not *choose* it. If homosexuality were both congenital and harmless, then, Ellis reasoned, it should not be considered immoral or criminal.

Alfred Kinsey

Alfred C. Kinsey (1894–1956), a biologist at Indiana University and America's leading authority on gall wasps, destroyed forever the belief in American sexual innocence and virtue. He accomplished this through two books, *Sexual Behavior*

Havelock Ellis (1859–1939) argued that many behaviors previously labeled as abnormal were actually normal, including masturbation and female sexuality. For example, he found no evidence that masturbation leads to mental disorders, and he documented that women have sexual drives no less intense than those of men.

Alfred C. Kinsey (1894–1956) photographed by William Dellenback, 1953. Kinsey shocked Americans by revealing how they actually behaved sexually. His scientific efforts led to the termination of his research funding because of political pressure.

in the Human Male (Kinsey, Pomeroy, & Martin, 1948) and *Sexual Behavior in the Human Female* (Kinsey, Pomeroy, Martin, & Gebhard, 1953). These two volumes statistically documented the actual sexual behavior of Americans. In massive detail, they demonstrated the great discrepancy between *public* standards of sexual behavior and *actual* sexual behavior. In the firestorm that accompanied the publication of Kinsey's books (popularly known as the *Kinsey Reports*), many Americans protested the destruction of their cherished ideals and illusions.

Kinsey was highly criticized for his work—and that criticism continues even today. Many people believe that his findings are responsible for a moral breakdown in the United States. Eminent sex researcher Vern Bullough (2004) stated that

> few scholars or scientists have lived under the intense firestorm of publicity and criticism that he did but even as the attacks on him increased and as his health failed, he continued to gather his data, and fight for what he believed. He changed sex for all of us.

Not only were Kinsey's scientific findings profound, but his work made it possible to talk about sex. Julia Heiman, director of the Kinsey Institute for Research in Sex, Gender, and Reproduction, noted that "he broke the taboo of silence. He was a visionary" (quoted in Elias, 2004). Not only did he change the way we look at sex, but his findings freed many persons from the stigma of abnormality (Bullough, 2004; Gagnon, 1975).

Sexual Diversity and Variation   What Kinsey discovered in his research was an extraordinary diversity in sexual behaviors. Among men, he found individuals who had orgasms daily and others who went months without orgasms. Among women, he found individuals who had never had orgasms and others who had them several times a day. He discovered one male who had ejaculated only once in 30 years and another who ejaculated 30 times a week on average. "This is the order of variation," he commented dryly, "which may occur between two individuals who live in the same town and who are neighbors, meeting in the same place of business and coming together in common social activities" (Kinsey et al., 1948).

A Reevaluation of Masturbation   Kinsey's work aimed at a reevaluation of the role of masturbation in a person's sexual adjustment. Kinsey made three points about masturbation: (1) It is harmless, (2) it is not a substitute for sexual intercourse but a distinct form of sexual behavior that provides sexual pleasure, and (3) it plays an important role in women's sexuality because it is a more reliable source of orgasm than heterosexual intercourse and because its practice seems to facilitate women's ability to become orgasmic during intercourse. Indeed, Kinsey believed that masturbation is the best way to measure a woman's inherent sexual responsiveness because it does not rely on another person.

Sexual Orientation   Prior to Kinsey's work, an individual was identified as homosexual if he or she had ever engaged in any sexual behavior with a person of the same sex. Kinsey found, however, that many people had sexual experiences with persons of both sexes. He reported that 50% of the men and 28% of the women in his studies had had same-sex experiences and that 38% of the men and 13% of the women had had orgasms during these experiences (Kinsey et al., 1948, 1953). Furthermore, he discovered that sexual attractions

Liam Neeson portrayed Alfred C. Kinsey and Laura Linney played his wife, Clara, in the 2004 movie *Kinsey*.

" *You shall know the truth and the truth shall make you mad.*

—Aldous Huxley
(1894–1963)

Click on "Alfred Kinsey" to hear about Kinsey's research methodology.

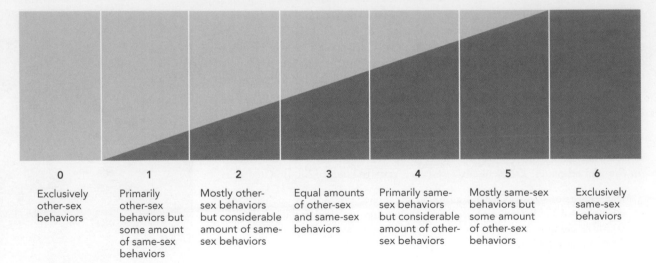

0	1	2	3	4	5	6
Exclusively other-sex behaviors	Primarily other-sex behaviors but some amount of same-sex behaviors	Mostly other-sex behaviors but considerable amount of same-sex behaviors	Equal amounts of other-sex and same-sex behaviors	Primarily same-sex behaviors but considerable amount of other-sex behaviors	Mostly same-sex behaviors but some amount of other-sex behaviors	Exclusively same-sex behaviors

● **FIGURE 2.1**

The Kinsey Scale. This scale illustrates the degree to which a person may engage in other-sex and same-sex behaviors.

could change over the course of a person's lifetime. Kinsey's research led him to conclude that it was erroneous to classify people as either heterosexual or homosexual. A person's sexuality was significantly more complex and fluid.

Kinsey wanted to eliminate the concept of heterosexual and homosexual *identities*. He did not believe that homosexuality, any more than heterosexuality, existed as a fixed psychological identity. Instead, he argued, there were only sexual behaviors, and behaviors alone did not make a person gay, lesbian, bisexual, or heterosexual. It was more important to determine what proportion of behaviors were same-sex and other-sex than to label a person as gay, lesbian, or heterosexual.

He devised the Kinsey scale to represent the proportion of an individual's sexual behaviors with the same or other sex (see Figure 2.1). This scale charted behaviors ranging from no behaviors with the same sex to behaviors exclusively with members of the same sex, with the behaviors existing on a continuum. His scale radicalized the categorization of human sexual behavior (McWhirter, 1990).

> *I don't see much of Alfred anymore since he got so interested in sex.*
> —Clara Kinsey
> (1898–1982)

Rejection of Normal/Abnormal Dichotomy As a result of his research, Kinsey insisted that the distinction between normal and abnormal was meaningless. Like Ellis, he argued that sexual differences were a matter of degree, not kind. Almost any sexual behavior could be placed alongside another that differed from it only slightly. His observations led him to be a leading advocate of the toleration of sexual differences.

William Masters and Virginia Johnson

In the 1950s, William Masters (1915–2001), a St. Louis physician, became interested in treating sexual difficulties—such problems as early ejaculation and erection difficulties in men, and lack of orgasm in women. As a physician, he felt that a systematic study of the human sexual response was necessary, but none existed. To fill this void, he decided to conduct his own research. Masters was joined several years later by Virginia Johnson (1925–), a psychologist.

Masters and Johnson detailed the sexual response cycles of 382 men and 312 women during more than 10,000 episodes of sexual behavior, including masturbation and sexual intercourse. The researchers combined observation

William Masters (1915–2001) and Virginia Johnson (1925–) detailed the sexual response cycle in the 1960s and revolutionized sex therapy in the 1970s.

with direct measurement of changes in male and female genitals using electronic devices. (See Chapter 3 for a detailed discussion of their four-phase sexual response cycle.)

Human Sexual Response (1966), their first book, became an immediate success among both researchers and the public. What made their work significant was not only their detailed descriptions of physiological responses but also the articulation of several key ideas. First, Masters and Johnson discovered that, physiologically, male and female sexual responses are very similar. Second, they demonstrated that women achieve orgasm primarily through clitoral stimulation. Penetration of the vagina is not needed for orgasm to occur. By demonstrating the primacy of the clitoris, Masters and Johnson destroyed once and for all the Freudian distinction between vaginal and clitoral orgasm. (Freud believed that an orgasm a woman experienced through masturbation was somehow physically and psychologically inferior to one experienced through sexual intercourse. He made no such distinction for men.) By destroying the myth of the vaginal orgasm, Masters and Johnson legitimized female masturbation.

In 1970, Masters and Johnson published *Human Sexual Inadequacy,* which revolutionized sex therapy by treating sexual problems simply as difficulties that could be treated using behavioral therapy. They argued that sexual problems were not the result of underlying neuroses or personality disorders. More often than not, problems resulted from a lack of information, poor communication between partners, or marital conflict. Their behavioral approach, which included "homework" exercises such as clitoral or penile stimulation, led to an astounding increase in the rate of successful treatment of sexual problems. Their work made them pioneers in modern sex therapy.

Is there a difference between clitoral and vaginal orgasm? Click on "Studying Female Sexual Response" to hear about various scientists' contributions to research on female sexual response.

Click on "Masters and Johnson" to hear about their study of sexual response and sexual function problems.

● Contemporary Research Studies

Several large, national sexuality-related studies have been conducted in recent years. We briefly describe four national surveys here to illustrate research on the general population of men and women, adolescents, and college students. The studies cited below, largely directed to determine the prevalence of certain behaviors, give little or no attention to factors that help explain the findings. Further, these studies represent only the tip of the sexuality-related research pertinent to the topics covered in this textbook. Sex research continues to be an emerging field of study. Most studies are not national projects but are smaller ones dealing with special populations or issues and focus on examining factors that are related to or influence sexual behavior. Even though these studies may be smaller in scope, they provide valuable information for furthering our understanding of human sexual expression. Throughout the book, we cite numerous studies to provide empirical information about the topic.

Before describing these studies, it is important to note that, just like in the days of Alfred Kinsey, these are difficult times to conduct sex research. Increasingly, members of Congress and some conservative groups are attacking the value of certain sex research topics, even those related to HIV prevention. The result: a chilling effect on sex research. Funding for sex research has become more limited, and sexuality-related grant applications to the National Institutes of Health that have been approved by peer review have been questioned (Clark, 2003; Navarro, 2004). In the midst of this, highly respected scientific organizations such as the American Association of Science and the American Psychological Association have offered support to threatened federally approved projects (Hyde & DeLamater, 2006). Sex research is a relatively young area of study when compared to better-established fields such as psychology, and the number of researchers specializing in sexuality-related study is small. Hopefully, these attacks will not discourage the next generation of researchers from becoming sex researchers.

The National Health and Social Life Survey

In 1994, new figures were released showing us to be in a different place than when Kinsey did his research a half century earlier. Researchers from the University of Chicago published, according to their own description, the "only comprehensive and methodologically sound survey of America's sexual practices and beliefs." Their findings, which were released under two titles—the popular trade book *Sex in America: A Definitive Survey* (Michael, Gagnon, Laumann, & Kolata, 1994) and a more detailed and scholarly version, *The Social Organization of Sexuality* (Laumann, Gagnon, Michael, & Michaels, 1994)—not only raised questions about research methodology in human sexuality but also contradicted many previous findings and beliefs about sex in America.

The study, titled the National Health and Social Life Survey (NHSLS), was originally intended to be federally funded, but because of political opposition, it was completed with private funds. The authors set out to conduct a strong study by randomly sampling 3,432 Americans, ages 18–59, in 90-minute face-to-face interviews. Rigorous training of the interviewers, pretesting of the questionnaire, and built-in checkpoints to test the veracity of the responses were among the methods chosen to help ensure the accuracy and reliability of the test results. Even though this study was conducted several years ago and had some sampling limitations, sexual scientists regard it as one of the most methodologically sound to date; hence, we highlight its findings here and in subsequent chapters of this text.

Released as the first study to explore the social context of sexuality, the NHSLS revealed the following:

- *Americans are largely exclusive.* The median number of sex partners since age 18 for men was six and for women, two.
- *On average, Americans have sex about once a week.* On frequency of sex, adults fell roughly into three groups: Nearly 30% had sex with a partner only a few times a year or not at all, 35% had sex once or several times a month, and about 35% had sex two or more times a week.

Researchers Robert T. Michael, John H. Gagnon, Stuart Michaels, and Edward O. Laumann conducted the National Health and Social Life Survey, a study of sexual behavior involving interviews with over 3,000 adults. Their study is one of the most comprehensive investigations of sexual behavior in the United States since Kinsey's research.

- *Extramarital sex is the exception, not the rule.* Among those who were married, 75% of men and 85% of women said they had been sexually exclusive with their spouse.

- *Most Americans have fairly traditional sexual behaviors.* When respondents were asked to name their preferences from a long list of sexual practices, vaginal intercourse was considered "very appealing" by most of those interviewed. Ranking second, but far behind, was watching a partner undress. Oral sex ranked third.

- *Homosexuality is not as prevalent as originally believed.* Among men, 2.8% described themselves as homosexual or bisexual; among women, 1.4% did so.

- *Orgasms appear to be the rule for men and the exception for women.* Seventy-five percent of men claimed to have orgasms consistently with their partners, whereas only 29% of women did. Married women were most likely to report that they always or usually had orgasms.

- *Forced sex and the misperception of it remain critical problems.* Twenty-two percent of women said they had been forced to do sexual things they didn't want to do, usually by a loved one. Only 3% of men reported ever forcing themselves on women.

- *Three percent of adult Americans claim never to have had sex.*

The National Survey of Family Growth

Periodically, the National Center for Health Statistics (NCHS) conducts the National Survey of Family Growth (NSFG) to collect data related to marriage, divorce, contraception, infertility, and the health of women and infants in the United States. The 2002 study, *Sexual Behavior and Selected Health Measures: Men and Women 15–44 Years of Age, United States, 2000,* focused on determining national estimates of several measures of sexual behavior (National Center for Health Statistics, 2005). In-person, face-to-face interviews were conducted with a national sample of 12,571 males and females (90% of both sexes self-identified as heterosexual) in the household population of the United States. Audio-CASI was used for the sexual behavior questions. This study is one of the most recent comprehensive studies assessing the prevalence of certain sexual behaviors among the general population. The researchers state that the estimates of behaviors can be generalized to the national household population given that a rigorous probability sampling design was used for data collection. This trait makes the study results extraordinary in the sex research field and certainly valuable in determining public health initiatives. Important findings for this sample included the following:

- Among adults 25–44 years of age, 97% of men and 98% of women have had vaginal intercourse; 90% of men and 88% of women have had oral sex with an other-sex partner; and 40% of men and 35% of women have had anal sex with an other-sex partner.

- Counting vaginal intercourse, oral sex, and anal sex, 10% of males and 8% of females, 15–44 years of age, respectively, have never had sex in their lives.

- About 6.5% of men 25–44 years of age have had oral or anal sex with another man. Eleven percent of women 25–44 years of age reported having had a sexual experience with another woman.

- Among men 18–44 years of age, 92% said they were attracted "only to females," and 3.9% said "mostly females." Among women, 86% said they were attracted "only to males" and 10% "mostly to males."

- Men 30–44 years of age reported an average (median) of six to eight female sex partners in their lifetime; among women 30–44 years of age, the median number of male sex partners in their lifetime was about four.

- At ages 15–17, about 13% of males and 11% of females have had other-sex oral sex but not vaginal intercourse. At ages 18–19, about 11% of males and 9% of females have had other-sex oral sex but not vaginal intercourse.

- Among men who ever had male-to-male sexual contact, 17% reported having been treated for a sexually transmitted infection other than HIV, compared with 7% of those who had never had male-to-male sexual contact.

- Among men 15–44 years of age who had at least one sexual partner in the last 12 months, 39% used a condom during their most recent sex (vaginal intercourse, oral sex, and anal sex).

- Among males who had ever had sexual contact with another male, 91% used a condom during their last sexual encounter, compared with 36% of men who never had sex with another male.

For a full copy of the report, see the National Center for Health Statistics Web site: http://www.cdc.gov/nchs/products/pubs/pubd/ad/361-370/ad362/htm.

The Youth Risk Behavior Survey

The Youth Risk Behavior Survey (YRBS), conducted biannually by the Centers for Disease Control and Prevention (CDC), measures the prevalence of six categories of health risk behaviors among youths through representative national, state, and local surveys using a self-report questionnaire. Sexual behaviors that contribute to unintended pregnancy and sexually transmitted infections, including HIV, are among those assessed. The 2007 YRBS includes a national school-based survey of students in grades 9–12, from 157 schools in 39 states, and 22 local surveys, revealing the following (CDC, 2008a):

- Forty-eight percent of students (46% of females and 50% of males) reported ever having had sexual intercourse.

- Fifteen percent of students (12% of females and 18% of males) reported having had sexual intercourse with four or more partners during their life.

- Seven percent of students (4% of females and 10% of males) reported having had sexual intercourse for the first time before age 13.

- Thirty-five percent of students (36% of females and 34% of males) reported having had sexual intercourse with at least one person during the 3 months before the survey.

- Sixty-two percent of students (55% of females and 69% of males) who reported being currently sexually active also reported using a condom during their most recent sexual intercourse.

- Sixteen percent of students (19% of females and 13% of males) who reported being currently sexually active also reported that either they or their partner had used birth control pills before their most recent sexual intercourse.

- Twenty-three percent of students (18% of females and 28% of males) who reported being currently sexually active also reported using alcohol or drugs prior to their most recent sexual intercourse.

- Eight percent of students (11% of females and 5% of males) reported ever being forced to have sexual intercourse.

- Thirteen percent of students (15% of females and 11% of males) reported having been tested for HIV (not counting being done while donating blood).

See http://www.cdc.gov/mmwr/preview/mmwrhtml/ss5704a1.htm for more information on the 2007 YRBS.

Researchers often analyze YRBS data to determine the health risk behaviors of certain groups. For example, analysis of 1999 YRBS data of rural adolescents determined that there were relationships between several health and sexual risk behaviors. In general, the analysis found that rural adolescents who initiated sexual intercourse at an early age (prior to age 15) were at a markedly greater risk for engaging in subsequent sexual risk behaviors, such as having multiple sex partners and not using condoms during intercourse (Yarber, Milhausen, Crosby, & DiClemente, 2002).

The National College Health Assessment

Since year 2000, every fall and spring term the American College Health Association has conducted research at colleges and universities throughout the United States to assess students' health behaviors and their perceptions of the prevalence of these behaviors among their peers. Areas covered are alcohol, tobacco, and other drug use; sexual health, weight, nutrition, and exercise; mental health, injury prevention, personal safety, and violence. For the Spring 2006 survey, 94,357 students at 117 U.S. campuses participated (American College Health Association, 2006). Findings from the sexual health questions include:

- Within the last school year, 70.3% of college men and 71.0% of college women had at least one sexual partner. Most had one sexual partner—42.6% of men and 48.9% of women—although 10.7% of men and 5.6% of women had four or more partners.

- For oral sex in the past 30 days, 45.2% of college men and 45.1% of college women had done this one or more times. Slightly more than one fifth reported that they have never had oral sex.
- For vaginal sex within the past 30 days, 45.6% of college men and 50.5% of college women had done this one or more times. About 3 of every 10 indicated that they have never had vaginal sex.
- For anal sex within the past 30 days, 6.3% of college men and 3.8% of college women had done this one or more times. About 7 of every 10 men and about 8 of every 10 women indicated that they have never had anal sex.
- For using a condom the last time they had sex, 3.2%, 49.7%, and 26.2% of sexually active students reported this behavior for oral, vaginal, and anal sex, respectively.
- Among sexually active students, birth control pills and condoms were the most common (about 40% each) birth control methods used by the students or their partner the last time they had vaginal intercourse.
- Among sexually active students, 11.2% reported using (or reported their partner used) emergency contraception ("morning after pill") within the last school year.
- Among students who had vaginal intercourse within the last school year, 2.1% reported experiencing an unintentional pregnancy or getting someone pregnant.

A copy of the report can be found at the American College Health Association Web site: http://www.acha.org/pubs_rpts.html.

● Emerging Research Perspectives

Although sex research continues to explore diverse aspects of human sexuality, some scholars feel that their particular interests have been given insufficient attention. Feminist, gay, lesbian, bisexual, and transgender research has focused on issues that mainstream research has largely ignored. And ethnic research, only recently undertaken, points to the lack of knowledge about the sexuality of some ethnic groups, such as African Americans, Latinos, Asian Americans, and American Indians. These emerging research perspectives enrich our knowledge of sexuality.

Feminist Scholarship

The initial feminist research generated an immense amount of groundbreaking work on women in almost every field of the social sciences and humanities. Feminists made gender and gender-related issues significant research questions in a multitude of academic disciplines. In the field of sexuality, feminists expanded the scope of research to include the subjective experience and meaning of sexuality for women; sexual pleasure; sex and power; erotic material; risky sexual behavior; and issues of female victimization, such as rape, the sexual abuse of children, and sexual harassment.

There is no single feminist perspective; instead, there are several. For our purposes, **feminism** is "a movement that involves women and men working together for equality" (McCormick, 1996); it cannot be construed more narrowly as only women working toward greater equality for women. Neither is feminism a license for political rigidity, division, or intolerance of diversity (McCormick, 1996). Feminism centers on understanding female experience in cultural and historical context—that is, the social construction of gender asymmetry (Pollis, 1988). **Social construction** is the development of social categories, such as masculinity, femininity, heterosexuality, and homosexuality, by society.

Feminists believe in these basic principles:

- *Gender is significant in all aspects of social life.* Like socioeconomic status and ethnicity, gender influences a person's position in society.

- *The female experience of sex has been devalued.* By emphasizing genital sex and such aspects of it as frequency of sexual intercourse and number of orgasms, both researchers and society ignore other important aspects of sexuality, such as kissing, caressing, love, commitment, and communication. Sexuality in lesbian women's relationships is even more devalued. Until the 1980s, most research on homosexuality centered on gay men, making lesbian women invisible.

- *Power is a critical element in male-female relationships.* Because women are often subordinated to men as a result of our society's beliefs about gender, women generally have less power than men. As a result, feminists believe that men have defined female sexuality to benefit themselves. Not only do men typically decide when to initiate sex, but the man's orgasm often takes precedence over the woman's. The most brutal form of the male expression of sexual power is rape.

- *Ethnic diversity must be addressed.* Women of color, feminists point out, face a double stigma: being female *and* being from a minority group. Although few studies exist on ethnicity and sexuality, feminists are committed to examining the role of ethnicity in female sexuality (Amaro, Raj, & Reed, 2001).

Despite its contributions, feminist research and the feminist approach have often been marginalized and considered subversive in many academic circles (McCormick, 1996). However, the feminist perspective in sex research has expanded in recent years, and many more women are making important contributions to the advancement of sexual science. Women have increasingly assumed leadership roles in professional organizations and societies, and more are earning advanced degrees in sexuality-related fields. As one consequence, the research literature will increase, resulting in an expansion of our understanding of female as well as male sexuality.

Gay, Lesbian, Bisexual, and Transgender Research

During the nineteenth century, sexuality became increasingly perceived as the domain of science, especially medicine. Physicians competed with ministers, priests, and rabbis in defining what was "correct" sexual behavior. However, as noted previously, medicine's so-called scientific conclusions were not scientific; rather, they were morality disguised as science. "Scientific" definitions of healthy sex closely resembled religious definitions of moral sex. In studying sexual activities between men, medical researchers "invented" and popularized the distinction between heterosexuality and homosexuality (Gay, 1986; Weeks, 1986).

Magnus Hirschfeld (1868–1935) was a leading European sex reformer who championed homosexual rights. He founded the first institute for the study of sexuality, which was burned when the Nazis took power in Germany. Hirschfeld fled for his life.

Evelyn Hooker (1907–1996) conducted landmark research on homosexual individuals in the 1950s, finding that "typical" gay men had personalities similar to those of "typical" heterosexual men.

Early Researchers and Reformers Although most physician-moralists condemned same-sex relationships as not only immoral but also pathological, a few individuals stand out in their attempt to understand same-sex sexuality.

Karl Heinrich Ulrichs Karl Ulrichs (1825–1895) was a German poet and political activist who in the 1860s developed the first scientific theory about homosexuality (Kennedy, 1988). As a rationalist, he believed reason was superior to religious belief and therefore rejected religion as superstition. He argued from logic and inference and collected case studies from numerous men to reinforce his beliefs. Ulrichs maintained that men who were attracted to other men represented a third sex, whom he called "Urnings." Urnings were born as Urnings; their sexuality was not the result of immorality or pathology. Ulrichs believed that Urnings had a distinctive feminine quality about them that distinguished them from men who desired women. He fought for Urning rights and the liberalization of sex laws.

Karl Maria Kertbeny Karl Kertbeny (1824–1882), a Hungarian physician, created the terms "heterosexuality" and "homosexuality" in his attempt to understand same-sex relationships (Feray & Herzer, 1990). Kertbeny believed that "homosexuals" were as "manly" as "heterosexuals." For this reason, he broke with Ulrichs's conceptualization of Urnings as inherently "feminine" (Herzer, 1985). Kertbeny argued that homosexuality was inborn and thus not immoral. He also maintained "the rights of man" (quoted in Herzer, 1985):

> The rights of man begin . . . with man himself. And that which is most immediate to man is his own body, with which he can undertake fully and freely, to his advantage or disadvantage, that which he pleases, insofar as in so doing he does not disturb the rights of others.

Magnus Hirschfeld In the first few decades of the twentieth century, there was a great ferment of reform in England and other parts of Europe. While Havelock Ellis was the leading reformer in England, Magnus Hirschfeld (1868–1935) was the leading crusader in Germany, especially for homosexual rights.

Hirschfeld was a homosexual and possibly a transvestite (a person who wears clothing of the other sex). He eloquently presented the case for the humanity of transvestites (Hirschfeld, 1991). And in defense of homosexual rights, he argued that homosexuality was not a perversion but rather the result of the hormonal development of inborn traits. His defense of homosexuality led to the popularization of the word "homosexual." Hirschfeld's importance, however, lies not so much in his theory of homosexuality as in his sexual reform efforts. In Berlin in 1897, he helped found the first organization for homosexual rights. In addition, he founded the first journal devoted to the study of sexuality and the first Institute of Sexual Science, where he gathered a library of more than 20,000 volumes.

Evelyn Hooker As a result of Kinsey's research, Americans learned that same-sex sexual relationships were widespread among both men and women. A few years later, psychologist Evelyn Hooker (1907–1996) startled her colleagues by demonstrating that homosexuality in itself was not a psychological disorder. She found that "typical" gay men did not differ significantly in personality characteristics from "typical" heterosexual men (Hooker, 1957). The reverberations of her work continue to this day.

Earlier studies had erroneously reported psychopathology among gay men and lesbian women for two reasons. First, because most researchers were clinicians, their samples consisted mainly of gay men and lesbian women who were seeking treatment. The researchers failed to compare their results against a control group of similar heterosexual individuals. (A **control group** is a group that is not being treated or experimented on; it controls for any variables that are introduced from outside the experiment, such as a major media report related to the topic of the experiment.) Second, researchers were predisposed to believe that homosexuality was in itself a sickness, reflecting traditional beliefs about homosexuality. Consequently, emotional problems were automatically attributed to the client's homosexuality rather than to other sources.

Later Contributions: Michel Foucault   One of the most influential social theorists in the twentieth century was the French thinker Michel Foucault (1926–1984). A cultural historian and philosopher, Foucault explored how society creates social ideas and how these ideas operate to further the established order. His most important work on sexuality was *The History of Sexuality, Volume I* (1980), a book that gave fresh impetus to scholars interested in the social construction of sex, especially those involved in gender and gay and lesbian studies.

Foucault challenged the belief that our sexuality is rooted in nature. Instead, he argued, it is rooted in society. Society "constructs" sexuality, including homosexuality and heterosexuality. Foucault's critics contend, however, that he underestimated the biological basis of sexual impulses and the role individuals play in creating their own sexuality.

Michel Foucault (1926–1984) of France was one of the most important thinkers who influenced our understanding of how society "constructs" human sexuality.

Contemporary Gay, Lesbian, Bisexual, and Transgender Research   In 1973, the American Psychiatric Association (APA) removed homosexuality from its list of psychological disorders in its *Diagnostic and Statistical Manual of Mental Disorders (DSM-II)*. The APA decision was reinforced by similar resolutions by the American Psychological Association and the American Sociological Association. More recently, in 1997 at its annual meeting, the American Psychological Association overwhelmingly passed a resolution stating that there is no sound scientific evidence on the efficacy of reparative therapies for gay men and lesbian women. This statement reinforced the association's earlier stand that, because there is nothing "wrong" with homosexuality, there is no reason to try to change sexual orientation through therapy. In 1998, the APA issued a statement opposing reparative therapy, thus joining the American Psychological Association, the American Academy of Pediatrics, the American Medical Association, the American Counseling Association, and the National Association of Social Workers.

As a result of the rejection of the psychopathological model, social and behavioral research on gay men, lesbian women, and bisexual individuals has moved in a new direction. Research no longer focuses primarily on the causes and cures of homosexuality, and most of the contemporary research approaches homosexuality in a neutral manner.

Directions for Future Research

Historically, sex research has focused on preventive health, which "prioritizes sexuality as a social problem and behavioral risk" (di Mauro, 1995). In light of the HIV/AIDS pandemic and other social problems, this emphasis is important, but it fails to examine the full spectrum of individuals' behaviors or the social and cultural factors that drive those behaviors.

According to Diane di Mauro (1995) of the Center for Gender, Sexuality, and Health at Columbia University, three priorities of applied and basic research in sexuality need to be recognized: (1) research that integrates an expanded definition of sexuality, one that provides a thorough knowledge of human sexuality, (2) relevant intervention research that is attuned to communication needs and incorporates appropriate evaluative processes, and (3) a more accepting and positive depiction of sexuality.

Sex research, globally, faces several challenges. Few sex researchers and sex research centers exist worldwide, particularly in developing countries. Only a few Western countries have comprehensive statistics, and most of them are about fertility or sexually transmitted infections rather than sexual behaviors of various groups. There is no international depository for sex data. Few standardized terms exist in sex research. Lastly, quantitative data are especially difficult to obtain, and qualitative data are less suitable for international comparisons (MacKay, 2001).

● Ethnicity and Sexuality

Researchers have begun to recognize the significance of ethnicity in various aspects of American life, including sexuality. However, a review of ethnicity in published sexuality research has revealed a deficit in empirical investigation (Wiederman, Maynard, & Fretz, 1996). Though the results indicated modest increases in ethnic diversity of research samples, important questions must still be addressed. These include the differences that socioeconomic status and environment play in sexual behaviors, the way in which questions are posed in research studies, the research methods that are used, and researchers' preconceived notions regarding ethnic differences. Diversity-related bias can be so ingrained in the way research is conducted (Rogler, 1999) that it is difficult to detect. Although limited research is available, we, the authors, attempt to provide some background to assist an understanding of sexuality and ethnicity.

African Americans

Several factors must be considered when studying African American sexuality, including sexual stereotypes, racism, socioeconomic status, and Black subculture.

Sexual stereotypes greatly distort our understanding of Black sexuality. One of the most common stereotypes, strongly rooted in American history, culture, and religion, is the image of Blacks as hypersexual beings (Staples, 2006). This stereotype, which dates back to the fifteenth century, continues to hold considerable strength among non-Blacks. Family sociologist Robert Staples (1991) writes: "Black men are saddled with a number of stereotypes that label them as irresponsible, criminalistic, hypersexual, and lacking in masculine traits." But the reality is, no one has attempted a comprehensive evaluation of the sexuality of Black males (Grimes, 1999). Evelyn Higginbotham (1992), a leading authority on the African American experience, discussed the racialized constructions of African American women's sexuality as primitive, animal-like

In the rich cultural history of African Americans, family life is very important.

and promiscuous, and nonvirtuous. During the days of slavery, this representation of Black sexuality rationalized sexual exploitation of Black women by White masters. The belief that Black women were "promiscuous" by nature was perpetuated by a variety of media, such as theater, art, the press, and literature. From this, historian Darlene Hine (1989) notes that silence arose among women: a "culture of dissemblance." To protect the sanctity of inner aspects of their lives and to combat pervasive negative images and stereotypes about them, Black women (particularly the middle class) began to represent their sexuality through silence, secrecy, and invisibility. For example, they would dress very modestly to remain invisible—hence, not drawing attention that might lead to being sexually assaulted. Efforts to adhere to Victorian ideology and represent pure morality were deemed by Black women to be necessary for protection and upward mobility and to attain respect and justice. These representations continue today for many older African American women. For some younger, "new" African American women, however, the opposite is happening: being more visible and less reserved about their sexuality. These younger women feel more self-assured about themselves and their sexuality. The emphasis on sexuality of the younger African American woman is often depicted, for example, in advertising and rap music videos, particularly Gangsta rap, shown on Black Entertainment Television (BET). Unfortunately, much Gangsta rap is explicit about both sex and violence and rarely illustrates the long-term consequences of sexual risk behaviors; research has shown that these videos lead to increased sexual risk behavior among African American adolescents (Wingood et al., 2002).

Socioeconomic status is a person's ranking in society based on a combination of occupational, educational, and income levels. It is an important element in African American sexual values and behaviors (Staples, 2006; Staples & Johnson, 1993). For example, a study of White and African American women and Latinas who voluntarily sought HIV counseling and testing found that socioeconomic status, not race, was directly related to HIV risk behavior.

In studying Latino sexuality, it is important to remember that Latinos come from diverse ethnic groups, including Mexican American, Cuban American, and Puerto Rican, each with its own unique background and set of cultural values.

Women with lower incomes had riskier (e.g., drug-injecting) sexual partners and higher levels of stress, factors related to risky sexual behaviors (Ickovics et al., 2002).

Values and behaviors are shaped by culture and social class. The subculture of Blacks of low socioeconomic status is deeply influenced by poverty, discrimination, and structural subordination. In contrast to middle-class Whites and Blacks, low-income Blacks are more likely to engage in sexual intercourse at an earlier age and to have children outside of marriage. Because of the poverty, violence, and prejudice of inner-city life, many low-income Black children do not experience a prolonged or "innocent" childhood. They are forced to become adults at an early age.

Although there has been a significant increase in African American research, much still needs to be done. For example, researchers need to (1) explore the sexual attitudes and behaviors of the general African American population, not merely adolescents, (2) examine Black sexuality from an African American cultural viewpoint, and (3) utilize a cultural equivalency perspective that rejects differences between Blacks and Whites as signs of inherent deviance. (The **cultural equivalency perspective** is the view that the attitudes, values, and behaviors of one ethnic group are similar to those of another ethnic group.)

Latinos

Latinos are the fastest-growing ethnic group in the United States. There is very little research, however, about Latino sexuality.

Two common stereotypes depict Latinos as sexually permissive and Latino males as pathologically macho. Like African Americans, Latino males are often stereotyped as being "promiscuous," engaging in excessive and indiscriminate sexual activities. No research, however, validates this stereotype.

The macho stereotype paints Latino males as hypermasculine—swaggering and domineering. But the stereotype of machismo distorts its cultural meaning among Latinos. (The Spanish word "machismo" was originally incorporated into English in the 1960s as a slang term to describe any male who was sexist.) Within its cultural context, however, **machismo** is a positive concept, celebrating the values of courage, strength, generosity, politeness, and respect for others. And in day-to-day functioning, relations between Latino men and women are significantly more egalitarian than the macho stereotype suggests. This is especially true among Latinos who are more acculturated (Sanchez, 1997). (**Acculturation** is the process of adaptation of an ethnic group to the values, attitudes, and behaviors of the dominant culture.)

Another trait of Latino life is **familismo,** a commitment to family and family members. Researcher Rafael Diaz (1998) notes that familismo can be a strong factor in helping heterosexual Latinos reduce rates of unprotected sex with casual partners outside of primary relationships. He warns, however, that for many Latino men who have sex with men, familismo and homophobia can create conflict because families may perceive homosexuality as wrong.

Three important factors must be considered when Latino sexuality is studied: (1) diversity of ethnic groups, (2) significance of socioeconomic status, and (3) degree of acculturation. Latinos comprise numerous ethnic subgroups, the largest of which are Mexican Americans, Puerto Ricans, and Cubans (Vega, 1991). Each group has its own unique background and set of cultural traditions that affect sexual attitudes and behaviors.

Rebellion against the native culture may be expressed through sexual behavior (Sanchez, 1997). Traditional Latinos tend to place a high value on female virginity while encouraging males, beginning in adolescence, to be sexually active (Guerrero Pavich, 1986). Females are viewed according to a virgin/whore dichotomy—"good" girls are virgins and "bad" girls are sexual (Espín, 1984). Females are taught to put the needs of others, especially males, before their own. Among traditional Latinos, fears about American "sexual immorality" produce their own stereotypes of Anglos. Adolescent boys learn about masturbation from peers; girls rarely learn about it because of its tabooed nature. There is little acceptance of gay men and lesbian women, whose relationships are often regarded as "unnatural" or sinful (Bonilla & Porter, 1990; Raffaelli & Ontai, 2004).

In traditional Latino culture, Catholicism plays an important role, especially in the realm of sexuality. The Church advocates premarital virginity and prohibits both contraception and abortion. For traditional Latinas, using contraception may lead to "considerable guilt and confusion on the part of the individual woman who feels she is alone in violating the cultural taboos against contraception" (Guerrero Pavich, 1986). Traditional Latinas are generally negative toward birth control; however, some evidence suggests that women are increasingly approving of and using available contraception (Baca-Zinn, 1994). Abortion is virtually out of the question; only the most acculturated Latinas view abortion as an option.

Among bicultural Latinos, there may be conflict concerning the roles of men and women (Salgado de Snyder, Cervantes, & Padilla, 1990). Researcher Emma Guerrero Pavich (1986) describes the conflicts some Latinas experience: "She observes the freedom and sexual expression 'Americanas' have. At first she may condemn them as 'bad women'; later she may envy their freedom. Still later she may begin to want those freedoms for herself" (Guerrero Pavich, 1986). For bicultural Latinos, sexual values and attitudes appear to lie at different points along the continuum, depending on the degree of acculturation.

There is significantly greater flux among Latinos as a result of continuing high rates of immigration and the acculturation process. Much current research on Latinos focuses on the acculturation of new immigrants. We know less, however, about bicultural Latinos and even less about acculturated Latinos.

Asian Americans and Pacific Islanders

Asian Americans and Pacific Islanders represent one of the fastest-growing and most diverse populations in the United States. Significant differences in attitudes, values, and practices in this population make it difficult to generalize about these groups without stereotyping and oversimplifying. Given this caveat, we can say that many Asian Americans are less individualistic and more relationship oriented than members of other cultures. Individuals are seen as the products of their relationships to nature and other people (Shon & Ja, 1982). Asian Americans are less verbal and expressive in their interactions and often rely on indirection and nonverbal communication, such as silence and avoidance of eye contact as signs of respect (Del Carmen, 1990).

More than half of Chinese Americans are foreign born. In traditional Chinese culture, the in-laws of a married woman were responsible for safeguarding her chastity and keeping her under the ultimate control of her spouse. Where extended families worked and lived in close quarters for extended periods, many spouses found it difficult to experience intimacy with each other. Though not much is known about mate selection among the foreign-born U.S. Chinese population, of those born in the United States, love and compatibility are the basis for marriage partners (Ishii-Kuntz, 1997). As in other Asian American populations, the rate of cross-cultural marriage among younger Chinese Americans is higher than in their parents' and grandparents' generations. Still, Confucian principles, which teach women to be obedient to their spouse's wishes and attentive to their needs and to be sexually loyal, play a part in maintaining exclusivity and holding down the divorce rate among traditional Chinese families (Ishii-Kuntz, 1997). In contrast, men are expected to be sexually experienced, and their engagement in nonmarital sex is frequently accepted. Chinese American parents tend to teach their children to control their emotional expressions; thus, affection is not often displayed openly (Uba, 1994).

For more than a century, Japanese Americans have maintained a significant presence in the United States. Japanese cultural values of loyalty and harmony are strongly embedded in Confucianism and feudalism (loyalty to the ruler), yet Japanese lives are not strongly influenced by religion (Ishii-Kuntz, 1997). Like Chinese Americans born in the United States, Japanese Americans born in the United States base partner selection more on love and individual compatibility than on family concerns (Nakano, 1990). Among the newest generation of Japanese Americans, the incidence of cross-cultural marriage has risen dramatically, to about 50–60% (Kitano, 1994).

Traditional Japanese values allowed sexual freedom for men but not for women. Traditionally, Japanese women were expected to remain pure; sexual

Among Asian Americans (as with other ethnic groups), attitudes toward relationships, family, and sexuality are related to the degree of acculturation.

permissiveness or nonexclusiveness on the part of women was considered socially disruptive and threatening (Ishii-Kuntz, 1997). Over time, attitudes and conditions related to sexuality have changed so that sexual activity is no longer considered solely procreational, and there is increased use of contraceptives. Japanese Americans have one of the lowest divorce rates of any group in the United States. A desire not to shame the family or the community may partially account for this low rate.

As with other groups, the degree of acculturation may be the most important factor affecting sexual attitudes and behaviors of Asian Americans. Compared with those who were raised in the United States, those who were born and raised in their original homeland tend to adhere more closely to their culture's norms, customs, and values. Further, a research study of Asian women attending a large Canadian university found that those who maintained affiliation with traditional Asian heritage became less acculturated with the more liberal, Western sexuality-related attitudes (Brotto, Chik, Ryder, Gorzalka, & Seal, 2005).

Sumie Okazaki (2002) reviewed the scientific literature concerning several aspects of Asian Americans' sexuality: sexual knowledge, attitudes, norms, and behavior. Okazaki reports that she found notable differences in several sexuality-related areas between Asian Americans and other ethnic groups:

> For example, relative to other U.S. ethnic group cohorts, Asian American adolescents and young adults tend to show more sexually conservative attitudes and behavior and initiate intercourse at a later age. There are indications that as Asian Americans become more acculturated to the mainstream American culture, their attitudes and behavior become more consistent with the White American norm. Consistent with their more sexually conservative tendencies in normative sexual behavior, Asian American women also appear more reluctant to obtain sexual and reproductive health care, which in turn places them at greater risk for delay in treatment for breast and cervical cancer as well as other gynecological problems.

As in other areas of social science research, there are gaps concerning the sexuality of Asian Americans and other racial and ethnic groups. Obviously, more empirical work is needed.

Men do not seek truth. It is the truth that pursues men who run away and will not look around.

—Lincoln Steffens
(1866–1936)

Final Thoughts

Popular culture surrounds us with sexual images, disseminated through advertising, music, television, film, video games, and the Internet, that form a backdrop to our daily living. Much of what is conveyed is simplified, overgeneralized, stereotypical, shallow, sometimes misinterpreted—and entertaining. Studying sexuality enables us to understand how research is conducted and to be aware of its strengths and its limitations. Traditional sex research has been expanded in recent years by feminist, gay, lesbian, bisexual, and transgender research, which provides fresh insights and perspectives. Although the study of sexuality and ethnicity has only recently begun, it promises to enlarge our understanding of the diversity of attitudes, behaviors, and values in contemporary America.

Summary

Sex, Advice Columnists, and Pop Psychology

- The *sex information/advice genre* transmits information to both entertain and inform; the information is generally oversimplified and sometimes distorted so that it does not interfere with the genre's primary purpose, entertainment. Much of the information or advice conveys dominant social norms.

Thinking Critically About Sexuality

- *Objective statements* are based on observations of things as they exist in themselves. *Value judgments* are evaluations based on moral or ethical standards. *Opinions* are unsubstantiated beliefs based on an individual's personal thoughts. *Biases* are personal leanings or inclinations. *Stereotypes*—rigidly held beliefs about the personal characteristics of a group of people—are a type of *schema,* which is the organization of knowledge in our thought processes.

- *Fallacies* are errors in reasoning. The *egocentric fallacy* is the belief that others necessarily share one's own values, beliefs, and attitudes. The *ethnocentric fallacy* is the belief that one's own ethnic group, nation, or culture is inherently superior to any other.

Sex Research Methods

- Ethical issues are important concerns in sex research. The most important issues are *informed consent, protection from harm,* and confidentiality.

- In sex research, *sampling* is a particularly acute problem. To be meaningful, samples should be representative of the larger group from which they are drawn. But most samples are limited by volunteer bias, dependence on college students, underrepresentation of ethnic groups, and difficulties in sampling gay men and lesbian women.

- The most important methods in sex research are clinical, survey, observational, and experimental. *Clinical research* relies on in-depth examinations of individuals or groups who come to the clinician seeking treatment for psychological or medical problems. *Survey research* uses questionnaires, interviews, or diaries, for example, to gather information from a representative sample of people. *Observational research* requires the researcher to observe interactions carefully in as unobtrusive a manner as possible. *Experimental research* presents subjects with various stimuli under controlled conditions in which their responses can be measured.

- Experiments are controlled through the use of *independent variables* (which can be changed by the experimenter) and *dependent variables* (which change in relation to changes in the independent variable). Clinical, survey, and observational research efforts, in contrast, are *correlational studies* that reveal relationships between variables without manipulating them. In experimental research, physiological responses are often measured by a *plethysmograph, strain gauge,* or *Rigiscan*™.

The Sex Researchers

- Richard von Krafft-Ebing was one of the earliest sex researchers. His work emphasized the pathological aspects of sexuality.

- Sigmund Freud was one of the most influential thinkers in Western civilization. Freud believed there were five stages in psychosexual development: the *oral stage, anal stage, phallic stage, latency stage,* and *genital stage.*

- Havelock Ellis was the first modern sexual thinker. His ideas included the relativity of sexual values, the normality of masturbation, a belief in the sexual equality of men and women, the redefinition of "normal," and a reevaluation of homosexuality.

- Alfred Kinsey's work documented enormous diversity in sexual behavior, emphasized the role of masturbation in sexual development, and argued that the distinction between normal and abnormal behavior was meaningless. The Kinsey scale charts sexual behaviors along a continuum ranging from exclusively other-sex behaviors to exclusively same-sex behaviors.

- William Masters and Virginia Johnson detailed the physiology of the human sexual response cycle. Their physiological studies revealed the similarity between male and female sexual responses and demonstrated that women achieve orgasm through clitoral stimulation. Their work on sexual inadequacy revolutionized sex therapy through the use of behavioral techniques.

Contemporary Research Studies

- The National Health and Social Life Survey is one of the largest and most comprehensive studies of sexual behavior to date.

- The National Survey of Family Growth (NSFG) is a periodic survey that collects data related to marriage, divorce, contraception, infertility, and the health of women and infants in the United States. A 2005 NSFG is one of the most recent comprehensive surveys of the prevalence of certain sexual behaviors in the general population.

- The Youth Risk Behavior Study is a large, national, school-based study of the health behaviors of adolescents. Behaviors related to sexuality and risk taking are assessed.

- The American College Health Association National College Health Assessment has conducted research on campuses throughout the United States since 2000 to determine students' health behaviors and their perceptions of the prevalence of these behaviors among their peers. Number of sexual partners in the last school year, condom use during vaginal intercourse during the last 30 days, and methods of pregnancy prevention used for last vaginal intercourse are the sexual health items surveyed.

Emerging Research Perspectives

- There is no single feminist perspective in sex research.

- Most feminist research focuses on gender issues, assumes that the female experience of sex has been devalued, believes that power is a critical element in female-male relationships, and explores ethnic diversity.

- Research on homosexuality has rejected the moralistic-pathological approach. Researchers in gay and lesbian issues include Karl Ulrichs, Karl Kertbeny, Magnus Hirschfeld, Evelyn Hooker, and Michel Foucault.

- Contemporary gay, lesbian, bisexual, and transgender research focuses on the psychological and social experience of being other than heterosexual.

Ethnicity and Sexuality

- The role of ethnicity in human sexuality has been largely overlooked until recently.

- *Socioeconomic status* is important in the study of African American sexuality. Other factors to consider include the stereotype of Blacks as hypersexual and "promiscuous," and racism.

- Two common stereotypes about Latinos are that they are sexually permissive and that Latino males are pathologically macho. Factors to consider in studying Latino sexuality include the diversity of national groups, the role of socioeconomic status, and the degree of *acculturation*.

- Significant differences in attitudes, values, and practices make it difficult to generalize about Asian Americans and Pacific Islanders. Degree of acculturation and adherence to traditional Asian heritage are important factors affecting sexual attitudes and behaviors. Religious and cultural values still play an important role in the lives of many Asian Americans and Pacific Islanders.

Questions for Discussion

- Is sex research valuable or necessary? If you feel that it is, what areas of sexuality do you think need special attention? Which, if any, areas of sexuality should be prohibited from being researched?

- Alfred Kinsey was, and continues to be, criticized for his research. Some people even believe that he was responsible for eroding sexual morality. Do you think his research was valuable, or that it led to the sexual revolution in the United States, as many people claim?

- Would you volunteer for a sexual research study? Why or why not? If so, what kind of study?

Suggested Web Sites

Advocates for Youth
http://www.advocatesforyouth.org
Focuses on teen sexual health; provides valuable data on issues related to teen sexual health.

Centers for Disease Control and Prevention
http://www.cdc.gov
A valuable source of research information about sexual behavior and related health issues in the United States.

Gallup Poll
http://www.gallup.com
Provides results of current surveys, including those dealing with sexuality-related issues.

"Go Ask Alice"
http://www.goaskalice.columbia.edu
A credible Internet question-and-answer service dealing with sexual and health issues, directed by the Columbia University Health Education Program.

International Academy of Sex Research
http://www.iasr.org
A scientific society that promotes research in sexual behavior; provides announcements of IASR conferences and abstracts of its journal's recent articles.

Magnus Hirschfeld Archive for Sexology
http://www2.hu-berlin.de/sexology/Entrance_Page/history_of_sexology.html
Has an extensive history of early and contemporary sex researchers as well as other valuable sexology resources.

National Sexuality Resource Center
http://nsrc.sfsu.edu
This center gathers and disseminates the latest accurate information and research on sexual health, education, and rights.

Society for the Scientific Study of Sexuality
http://www.sexscience.org
A nonprofit organization dedicated to the advancement of knowledge about sexuality; provides announcements of the SSSS conferences and other meetings.

Suggested Reading

Bancroft, J. (Ed.). (1997). *Researching sexual behavior.* Bloomington: Indiana University Press. A discussion of the methodological issues of large-scale survey research in studying human sexuality.

Bullough, V. L. (1994). *Science in the bedroom: A history of sex research.* New York: Basic Books. A comprehensive history of sex research of the past twentieth century.

Garton, S. (2004). *Histories of sexuality: Antiquity to sexual revolution.* New York: Routledge. A comprehensive historical review of major figures, from Havelock Ellis to Alfred Kinsey, and exploration of such topics as the "invention" of homosexuality in the nineteenth century to the rise of sexual sciences in the twentieth century.

Meezen, W., & Martin, J. I. (Eds.). (2006). *Research methods with gay, lesbian, bisexual and transgendered populations.* New York: Harrington Park Press. Discusses the unique issues in sexuality-related research among gay, lesbian, bisexual, and transgendered populations and provides suggestions for doing this research.

Staples, R. (2006). *Exploring Black sexuality.* Boulder, CO: Rowman & Littlefield. A distinguished Black sexologist explores the sexual mores, folkways, and values among African Americans.

Wiederman, M., & Whitley, B., Jr. (2002). *Handbook for conducting research on human sexuality.* Mahwah, NJ: Erlbaum. A reference tool for researchers and students interested in research in human sexuality from a variety of disciplines; examines the specific methodological issues inherent in conducting human sexuality research.

Wyatt, G. (1997). *Stolen women: Reclaiming our sexuality and taking back our lives* . New York: Wiley. Discusses sociocultural influences such as slavery and institutionalized racism on the expression of sexuality among African American women.

For links, articles, and study material, go to the McGraw-Hill Web site, located at **www.mhhe.com/yarber7e.**

3

Female Sexual Anatomy, Physiology, and Response

"I identify with the passion [of women], the strength, the calmness, and the flexibility of being a woman. To me being a woman is like being the ocean. The ocean is a powerful thing, even at its calmest moments. It is a beauty that commands respect. It can challenge even the strongest men, and it gives birth to the smallest creatures. It is a provider, and an inspiration; this is a woman and this is what I am."

—20-year-old female

"The more I think about things that annoy me about being a woman, the more I realize that those annoyances are what make it so special. When I get my period, it isn't just a 'monthly curse'; it is a reminder that I can have children."

—19-year-old female

"When I started my period, my father kept a bit of a distance. How could I forget [that day]? The entire family was at my aunt's house, and no one had pads. You would think among 67 or so people one female would have a pad. I remember crying and my grandmother asking me what was wrong. After I told her, she began to laugh and said it was a natural cycle. I knew this from sixth-grade sex education class, but I still didn't want it. I was finally a woman."

—19-year-old female

"I think I am a good sexual partner and enjoy pleasing a woman. I especially love the foreplay that occurs between two people because it gets the body more excited than just going at it. I can go on forever with foreplay because I get to explore my partner's body, whether it is with my hands, lips, or tongue."

—25-year-old male

ALTHOUGH WOMEN AND MEN are similar in many more ways than they are different, we tend to focus on the differences rather than the similarities. Various cultures hold diverse ideas about exactly what it means to be female or male, but virtually the only differences that are consistent are actual physical differences, most of which relate to sexual structure and function. In this chapter and the following one, we discuss both the similarities and the differences in the anatomy (body structures), physiology (body functions), and sexual response of females and males. This chapter introduces the sexual structures and functions of women's bodies, including hormones and the menstrual cycle. We also look at models of sexual arousal and response, the relationship of these to women's experiences of sex, and the role of orgasm. In Chapter 4, we discuss male anatomy and physiology, and in Chapter 5, we move beyond biology to look at gender and the meanings we ascribe to being female and male.

● Female Sex Organs: What Are They For?

Anatomically speaking, all embryos are female when their reproductive structures begin to develop (see Figure 3.1). If it does not receive certain genetic and hormonal signals, the fetus will continue to develop as a female. In humans and most other mammals, the female, in addition to providing half the genetic instructions for the offspring, provides the environment in which it can develop until it becomes capable of surviving as a separate entity. She also nourishes

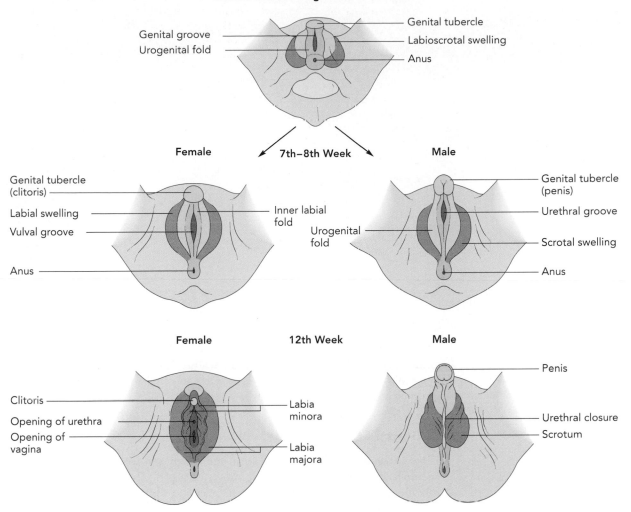

Undifferentiated Stage Prior to 6th Week

Genital groove
Urogenital fold

Genital tubercle
Labioscrotal swelling
Anus

Female · 7th–8th Week · **Male**

Genital tubercle (clitoris)
Labial swelling
Vulval groove
Anus

Inner labial fold

Urogenital fold

Genital tubercle (penis)
Urethral groove
Scrotal swelling
Anus

Female · 12th Week · **Male**

Clitoris
Opening of urethra
Opening of vagina

Labia minora
Labia majora

Penis
Urethral closure
Scrotum

● **FIGURE 3.1**

Embryonic-Fetal Differentiation of the External Reproductive Organs. Female and male reproductive organs are formed from the same embryonic tissues. An embryo's external genitals are female in appearance until certain genetic and hormonal instructions signal the development of male organs. Without such instructions, the genitals continue to develop as female.

the offspring, both during gestation (the period of carrying the young in the uterus) via the placenta and following birth via the breasts through lactation (milk production).

In spite of what we do know, researchers are finding that we haven't yet mapped all of the basic body parts of women, especially as they relate to the microprocesses of sexual response (Leland, 2000). Such issues as the function of the G-spot, the role of orgasm, and the placement of the many nerves that spider through the pelvic cavity still loom large. Add to these puzzles the types, causes, and treatments of sexual function problems and one can quickly see that the new science of sexual response is still emerging.

Clearly, the female sex organs serve a reproductive function. But they perform other functions as well. Significant to nearly all women are the sexual parts that bring them pleasure; they may also serve to attract potential sexual partners. Because of the mutual pleasure partners give each other, we can see that sexual structures also serve an important role in human relationships. People demonstrate their affection for one another by sharing sexual pleasure

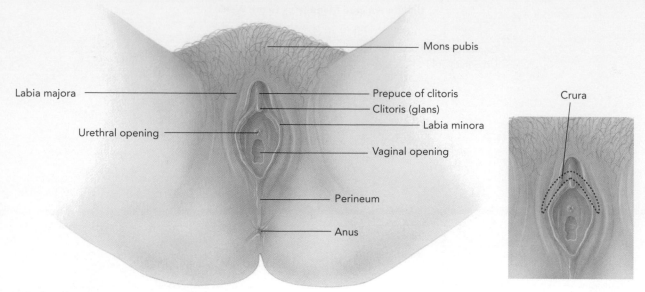

Mons pubis

Labia majora

Prepuce of clitoris

Urethral opening

Clitoris (glans)

Labia minora

Vaginal opening

Perineum

Anus

Crura

● **FIGURE 3.2**
External Female Sexual Structures (Vulva)

and generally form enduring partnerships at least partially on the basis of mutual sexual sharing. Let's look at the features of human female anatomy and physiology that provide pleasure to women and their partners and that enable women to conceive and give birth.

External Structures (the Vulva)

The sexual and reproductive organs of both men and women are usually called **genitals,** or genitalia, from the Latin *genere,* "to beget." The external female genitals are the mons pubis, the clitoris, the labia majora, and the labia minora, collectively known as the **vulva** (see Figure 3.2). (People often use the word "vagina" when they are actually referring to the vulva. The vagina is an internal structure.)

The Mons Pubis   The **mons pubis** (pubic mound), or **mons veneris** (mound of Venus), is a pad of fatty tissue that covers the area of the pubic bone about 6 inches below the navel. Beginning in puberty, the mons is covered with pubic hair. Because there is a rich supply of nerve endings in the mons, caressing it can produce pleasure in most women.

The practice of trimming and shaving the pubic hair appears to have gone mainstream among American women. This practice is not new; many societies have adopted the practice for personal hygiene when access to clean water is restricted. If a woman chooses to shave, wax, or have her genitals pierced, she should use only clean tools and exercise caution, since this is a sensitive area of her body. Usually, the only side effects, besides some discomfort with waxing, are skin irritations and itching during the regrowth of hair.

The Clitoris   The **clitoris** (KLIH-tuh-rus) is considered the center of sexual arousal. It contains a high concentration of nerve endings and is exquisitely

Artwork often imitates anatomy, as can be seen in this painting titled *Black Iris* (Georgia O'Keeffe, 1887–1986)

sensitive to stimulation, especially at the tip of its shaft, the **glans clitoris.** A fold of skin called the **clitoral hood** covers the glans when the clitoris is not engorged. Although the clitoris is structurally analogous to the penis (it is formed from the same embryonic tissue), its sole function is sexual arousal. (The penis serves the additional functions of urine excretion and semen ejaculation.) The shaft of the clitoris is both an external and an internal structure. The external portion is about 1 inch long and a quarter inch wide. Internally, the shaft is divided into two branches called **crura** (KROO-ra; singular, *crus*), each of which is about 3.5 inches long, which are the tips of erectile tissue that attach to the pelvic bones. The crura contain two **corpora cavernosa** (KOR-por-a kav-er-NO-sa), hollow chambers that fill with blood and swell during arousal. The hidden erectile tissue of the clitoris plus the surrounding muscle tissue all contribute to muscle spasms associated with orgasm. When stimulated, the clitoris enlarges initially and then retracts beneath the hood just before and during orgasm. With repeated orgasms, it follows the same pattern of engorgement and retraction, although its swellings may not be as pronounced after the initial orgasm. The role of the clitoris in producing an orgasm is discussed later in the chapter.

The Labia Majora and Labia Minora   The **labia majora** (LAY-be-a ma-JOR-a) (major lips) are two folds of spongy flesh extending from the mons pubis and enclosing the labia minora, clitoris, urethral opening, and vaginal entrance. The **labia minora** (minor lips) are smaller folds within the labia majora that meet above the clitoris to form the clitoral hood. The labia minora also enclose the urethral and vaginal openings. They are smooth and hairless and vary quite a bit in appearance from woman to woman. Another rich source of sexual sensation, the labia are sensitive to the touch and swell during sexual arousal, doubling or tripling in size and changing in color from flesh-toned to a deeper hue. The area enclosed by the labia minora is referred to as the

> *Really that little dealybob is too far away from the hole. It should be built right in.*
>
> —Loretta Lynn (1935–)

vestibule. During sexual arousal, the clitoris becomes erect, the labia minora widen, and the vestibule (vaginal opening) becomes visible. Within the vestibule, on either side of the vaginal opening, are two small ducts from the **Bartholin's glands** (or vestibular glands), which secrete a small amount of moisture during sexual arousal.

Internal Structures

The internal female sexual anatomy and reproductive organs include the vagina; the uterus and its lower opening, the cervix; the ovaries; and the fallopian tubes. (Figure 3.3 provides illustrations of the front and side views of the female internal sexual anatomy.)

● **FIGURE 3.3**
Internal Female Sexual Structures

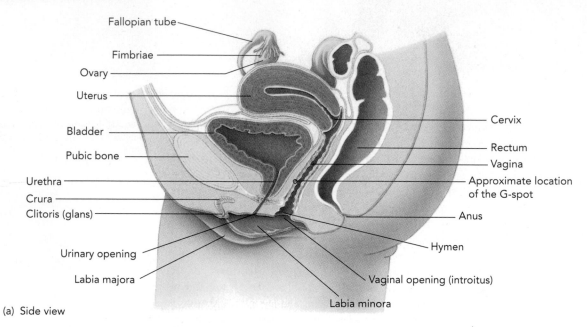

(a) Side view

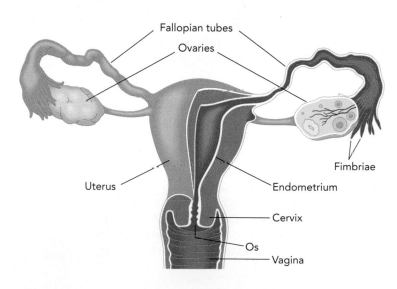

(b) Front view

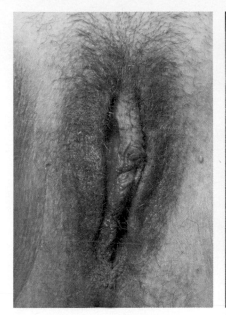 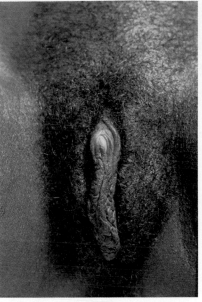 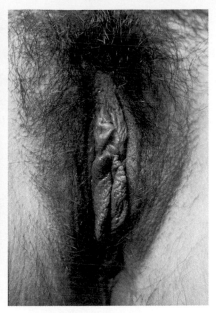

The external female genitalia (vulva) can assume many different colors, shapes, and structures.

The Vagina   The **vagina** (va-JI-na), from the Latin word for sheath, is a flexible, muscular structure that extends 3–5 inches back and upward from the vaginal opening. It is the **birth canal** through which an infant is born, allows menstrual flow to pass from the uterus, and encompasses the penis or other object during sexual expression. Normally, the walls of the vagina are relaxed and collapsed together, but during sexual arousal, the inner two thirds of the vagina expand while pressure from engorgement causes the many small blood vessels that lie in the vaginal wall to produce lubrication. In response to sexual stimulation, lubrication can occur within 10–30 seconds. The majority of sensory nerve endings are concentrated in the lower third of the vagina, or the **introitus** (in-TROY-tus). This part of the vagina is the most sensitive to erotic pressure and touch. In contrast, the inner two thirds of the vagina have virtually no nerve endings, which make it likely that a woman cannot feel a tampon when it is inserted deep in the vagina. Although the vaginal walls are generally moist, the wetness of a woman's vagina can vary by woman, by the stage of her menstrual cycle, and after childbirth or at menopause. Lubrication also increases substantially with sexual excitement. This lubrication serves several purposes. First, it increases the possibility of conception by alkalinizing the normally acidic chemical balance in the vagina, thus making it more hospitable to sperm, which die faster in acid environments. Second, it can make penetration more pleasurable for the woman and her partner by reducing friction in the vaginal walls.

   Prior to first intercourse or other form of penetration, the introitus is partially covered by a thin membrane containing a relatively large number of blood vessels, the **hymen** (named for the Roman god of marriage). The hymen typically has one or several perforations, allowing menstrual blood and mucous secretions to flow out of the vagina (and generally allowing for tampon insertion). In many cultures, it is (or was) important for a woman's hymen to be intact on her wedding day. Blood on the nuptial bedsheets is taken as proof of her virginity. The stretching or tearing of the hymen may produce some pain or discomfort and possibly some bleeding. Usually, the man has little trouble

Performing a Gynecological Self-Examination

While reading this material, female readers may wish to examine their own genitals and discover their own unique features. In a space that is comfortable for you, take time to look at your vulva, or outer genitals, using a mirror and a good light. The large, soft folds of skin with hair on them are the outer lips, or labia majora. The color, texture, and pattern of this hair vary widely among women. Inside the outer lips are the inner lips, or labia minora. These have no hair and vary in size from small to large and protruding. They extend from below the vagina up toward the pubic bone, where they form a hood over the clitoris. The glans may not be visible under the clitoral hood, but it can be seen if a woman separates the labia minor and re-tracts the hood. The size and shape of the clitoris, as well as the hood, also vary widely among women. These variations have nothing to do with a woman's ability to respond sexu-ally. You may also find some cheesy white matter under the hood. This is called smegma and is normal.

Below the clitoris is a smooth area and then a small hole. This is the urinary opening, also called the meatus. Below the urinary opening is the vaginal opening, which is surrounded by rings of tissue. One of these, which you may or may not be able to see, is the hymen. Just inside the vagina, on both sides, are the Bartholin's glands. These may secrete a small amount of mucus during sexual excitement, but little else of their function is known. If they are infected, they will be swol-len, but otherwise you won't notice them. The smooth area between your vagina and anus is called the perineum.

You can also examine your inner genitals, using a specu-lum, flashlight, and mirror. A speculum is an instrument used to hold the vaginal walls apart, allowing a clear view of the vagina and cervix. You should be able to obtain a spec-ulum and information about doing an internal exam from a clinic that specializes in women's health or family planning.

It is a good idea to observe and become aware of what your normal vaginal discharges look and feel like. Colors vary from white to gray, and secretions change in consis-

Examining your genitals can be an enlightening and useful practice that can provide you with information about the health of your body.

tency from thick to thin and clear (similar to egg white that can be stretched between the fingers) over the course of the menstrual cycle. Distinct changes or odors, along with burning, bleeding between menstrual cycles, pain in the pelvic region, itching, or rashes, should be reported to a physician.

By inserting one or two fingers into the vagina and reaching deep into the canal, it is possible to feel the cervix, or tip of the uterus. In contrast to the soft vaginal walls, the cervix feels like the end of a nose: firm and round.

In doing a vaginal self-exam, you may initially experience some fear or uneasiness about touching your body. In the long run, however, your patience and persistence will pay off in increased body awareness and a heightened sense of personal health.

Once you're familiar with the normal appearance of your outer genitals, you can check for unusual rashes, soreness, warts, or parasites, such as crabs.

inserting the penis through the hymen if he is gentle and there is adequate lubrication. Prior to first intercourse, the hymen may be stretched or ruptured by tampon insertion, by the woman's self-manipulation, by a partner during noncoital sexual activity, by accident, or by a health-care provider conducting a routine pelvic examination. Hymenoplasty, a controversial procedure that reattaches the hymen to the vagina, is now sought by some women to create the illusion that they are still virgins. Hymen repair, also referred to as "revir-gination," may also be performed for women who have been abused or those from cultures who risk a violent reaction from their partners. In spite of its

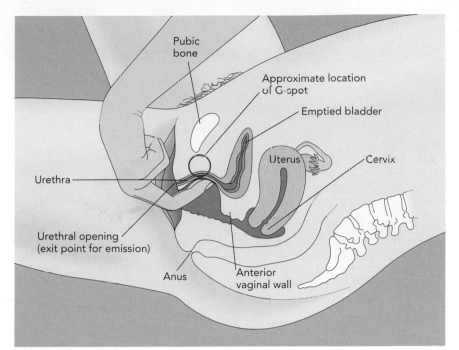

• **FIGURE 3.4**

The Grafenberg Spot
To locate the Grafenbe[rg]
insert two fingers into th[e]
and press deeply into its [anterior]
wall.

Figure labels:
Pubic bone
Approximate location of G-spot
Emptied bladder
Uterus
Cervix
Urethra
Urethral opening (exit point for emission)
Anus
Anterior vaginal wall

availability, the American College of Obstetricians and Gynecologists has issued strong warnings to women that there is no evidence cosmetic genital surgery is safe or effective (ACOG, 2007).

An area inside the body, surrounding the urethra, is what many women report to be an erotically sensitive area, the **Grafenberg spot,** or **G-spot.** The name is derived from Ernest Grafenberg, a gynecologist, who first discussed its erotic significance. Located on the front wall of the vagina midway between the pubic bone and the cervix on the vaginal side of the urethra (see Figure 3.4), this area varies in size from a small bean to a half walnut. It can be located by pressing one or two fingers into the front wall of a woman's vagina. Coital positions such as rear entry, in which the penis makes contact with the spot, may also produce intense erotic pleasure (Ladas, Whipple, & Perry, 1982; Whipple & Komisaruk, 1999). A variety of responses have been reported by women who first locate this spot. Initially, a woman may experience a slight feeling of discomfort or the need to urinate, but shortly thereafter, the tissue may swell and a pleasurable feeling may occur. Women who report orgasms as a result of stimulation of the G-spot describe them as intense and extremely pleasurable (Perry & Whipple, 1981; Whipple, 2002). In some women, an emission of a clear fluid from the urethra, also referred to as female ejaculation or female emission, occurs as well (Ann, 1997; Belzer, 1984). Though an exact gland or site has not been found in all women, nor do all women experience pleasure when the area is massaged, it has been suggested that the Skene's glands, which are located inside the urethra and function in a way similar to that of the prostate in males, may be responsible for the liquid that is sometimes expelled during intense orgasms (Zaviacic, 2002). Women who do experience this phenomenon should know that the fluid they expel is different from urine and some researchers suggest that the fluid resembles male prostate fluid in chemical composition (Cabello Santamaria, 1997).

Click on "G Marks the Spot" for theories and experiences about this erotically sensitive area.

Maintaining Vaginal Health

The mucous membranes lining the walls of the vagina normally produce clear, white, or pale yellow secretions. These secretions pass from the cervix through the vagina and vary in color, consistency, odor, and quantity depending on the phase of the menstrual cycle, the woman's health, and her unique physical characteristics. It is important for you to observe your secretions periodically and note any changes, especially if symptoms accompany them. Because self-diagnosis of unusual discharges is inaccurate over half the time, it is wise to go ahead with self-treatment only after a diagnosis is made by a health-care practitioner. Call a health-care practitioner if you feel uncertain or suspicious and/or think you may have been exposed to a sexually transmitted infection.

Here are some simple guidelines that may help a woman avoid getting vaginitis:

1. Do not use vaginal deodorants, especially deodorant suppositories or tampons. They upset the natural chemical balance of the vagina. Despite what pharmaceutical companies may advertise, a healthy vagina does not have a bad odor. If the vagina does have an unpleasant smell, then something is wrong, and you should check with your doctor or clinic.

2. Avoid douching. Douching is thought to disturb the normal balance of the beneficial bacteria in the vagina, thus raising the risk of bacterial infections and pregnancy complications like preterm birth (Reuters, 2005).

3. Maintain good genital hygiene by washing the labia and clitoris regularly (about once a day) with mild soap. Bubble baths and strongly perfumed soaps may irritate the vulva.

4. After a bowel movement, wipe the anus from front to back, away from the vagina, to prevent contamination with fecal bacteria.

5. Wear cotton underpants and pantyhose with a cotton crotch. Nylon does not "breathe," and it allows heat and moisture to build up, creating an ideal environment for infectious organisms to reproduce.

6. If you use a vaginal lubricant, be sure it is water-soluble. Oil-based lubricants such as Vaseline encourage bacterial growth.

7. Consider drinking unfiltered cranberry juice every day to help keep the vaginal pH balanced.

8. If you have candidiasis (yeast infection), drinking 8 ounces of cranberry juice daily; inserting plain, unsweetened, live-culture yogurt into the vagina; or inserting garlic suppositories may be successful in treating the infection. Reducing sugar in one's diet, getting enough rest, and not using tampons for some of your period may also help.

9. If you are diagnosed with a vaginal infection, particularly trichomoniasis, be sure to have your partner treated as well, to avoid being reinfected.

Vaginal Mucus and Secretions

Color	Consistency	Odor	Other Symptoms	Possible Causes	What to Do
Clear	Slightly rubbery, stretchy	Normal	—	Ovulation, sexual stimulation	Nothing
Milky	Creamy	Normal	—	Preovulation	Nothing
White	Sticky, curdlike	Normal	—	Postovulation, the pill	Nothing
Brownish	Watery and sticky	Normal or slightly different	—	Last day of period, spotting	Nothing
White	Thin, watery, creamy	Normal to foul or fishy	Itching	*Gardnerella* bacteria or nonspecific bacterial infection	See health-care practitioner
White	Curdlike or flecks, slight amount of discharge	Yeasty or foul	Itching or intense itching, inflammation of vaginal walls	Overgrowth of yeast cells, yeast infection	Apply yogurt, vinegar solution, or antifungal medication designed for this purpose
Yellow, yellow-green	Smooth or frothy	Usually foul	Itching, perhaps red dots on cervix	Possible *Trichomonas* infection	See health-care practitioner
Yellow, yellow-green	Thick, mucous	None to foul	Pelvic cramping or pelvic pain	Possible infection of fallopian tubes	See health-care practitioner right away

SOURCE: From B. Strong, C. DeVault, and B. Sayad, *Marriage and Family Experience*, 7th ed. © 1998 Wadsworth, a part of Cengage Learning, Inc. Reproduced by permission. www.cengage.com/permissions.

The Uterus and Cervix   The **uterus** (YU-te-rus), or womb, is a hollow, thick-walled, muscular organ held in the pelvic cavity by a number of flexible ligaments and supported by several muscles. It is pear-shaped, with the tapered end, the **cervix,** extending down and opening into the vagina. If a woman has not given birth, the uterus is about 3 inches long and 3 inches wide at the top; it is somewhat larger in women who have given birth. The uterus expands during pregnancy to the size of a volleyball or larger, to accommodate the developing fetus. The inner lining of the uterine walls, the **endometrium** (en-doe-MEE-tree-um), is filled with tiny blood vessels. As hormonal changes occur during the monthly menstrual cycle, this tissue is built up and then shed and expelled through the cervical **os** (opening), unless fertilization has occurred. In the event of pregnancy, the pre-embryo is embedded in the nourishing endometrium.

In addition to the more or less monthly menstrual discharge, mucous secretions from the cervix also flow out through the vagina. These secretions tend to be somewhat white, thick, and sticky following menstruation, becoming thinner as ovulation approaches. At ovulation, the mucous flow tends to increase and to be clear, slippery, and stretchy, somewhat like egg white. (Birth control using cervical mucus to determine the time of ovulation is discussed in Chapter 11.)

The Ovaries   On each side of the uterus, held in place by several ligaments, is one of a pair of ovaries. The **ovary** is a **gonad,** an organ that produces **gametes** (GA-meets), the sex cells containing the genetic material necessary for reproduction. Female gametes are called **oocytes** (OH-uh-sites), from the Greek words for egg and cell. (Oocytes are commonly referred to as eggs or **ova** [singular, **ovum**]. Technically, however, the cell does not become an egg until it completes its final stages of division following fertilization.) The ovaries are the size and shape of large almonds. In addition to producing oocytes, they serve the important function of producing hormones such as estrogen, progesterone, and testosterone. (These hormones are discussed later in this chapter.)

At birth, the female's ovaries contain about half a million oocytes. During childhood, many of these degenerate; then, beginning in puberty and ending after menopause, a total of about 400 oocytes mature and are released during a woman's reproductive years. The release of an oocyte is called **ovulation.** The immature oocytes are embedded in saclike structures called **ovarian follicles.** The fully ripened follicle is called a vesicular or Graffian follicle. At maturation, the follicle ruptures, releasing the oocyte. After the oocyte emerges, the ruptured follicle becomes the **corpus luteum** (KOR-pus LOO-tee-um) (from the Latin for yellow body), a producer of important hormones; it eventually degenerates. The egg is viable for about 24 hours.

The Fallopian Tubes   At the top of the uterus are two tubes, one on each side, known as **fallopian tubes,** uterine tubes, or oviducts. The tubes are about 4 inches long. They extend toward the ovaries but are not attached to them. Instead, the funnel-shaped end of each tube (the **infundibulum**) fans out into fingerlike **fimbriae** (fim-BREE-ah), which drape over the ovary but may not actually touch it. Tiny, hairlike **cilia** on the fimbriae and ampulla become active during ovulation. Their waving motion, along with contractions of the walls of the tube, transports the oocyte that has been released from the ovary into the fallopian tube. Just within the infundibulum is the **ampulla,** the widened part of the tube in which fertilization normally occurs if sperm and oocyte are there

> Girls got balls. They're just a little higher up, that's all.
>
> —Joan Jett
> (1960–)

Click on "The Ovaries" to gain a deeper understanding of the development of hormones and the ovum.

at the same time. (The process of ovulation and the events leading to fertilization are discussed later in this chapter; fertilization is covered in Chapter 12.)

Other Structures

There are several other important anatomical structures in the genital areas of both men and women. Although they may not serve reproductive functions, they may be involved in sexual activities. Some of these areas may also be affected by sexually transmitted infections. In women, these structures include the urethra, anus, and perineum. The **urethra** (yu-REE-thra) is the tube through which urine passes; the **urethral opening,** or meatus, is located between the clitoris and the vaginal opening. Between the vagina and the **anus**—the opening of the rectum, through which excrement passes—is a diamond-shaped region called the **perineum** (per-e-NEE-um). This area of soft tissue covers the muscles and ligaments of the **pelvic floor,** the underside of the pelvic area extending from the top of the pubic bone (above the clitoris) to the anus. (To learn more about this muscle and Kegel exercises, which can strengthen it, see Chapter 14.)

The anus consists of two sphincters, which are circular muscles that open and close like valves. The anus contains a dense supply of nerve endings that, along with the tender rings at the opening, can respond erotically. (For additional discussion about anal eroticism, see Chapter 9.) In sex play or intercourse involving the anus or rectum, care must be taken not to rupture the delicate tissues. This may occur because of the lack of adequate lubrication or very rough anal sex play. Anal sex, which involves insertion of the penis or other object into the rectum, is potentially unsafe, as is vaginal sex, because abrasions of the tissue provide easy passage for pathogens, such as HIV (the virus that causes AIDS), to the bloodstream (see Chapter 16). To practice safer sex, partners who engage in anal intercourse should use a latex condom with a water-based lubricant.

The Breasts

With the surge of sex hormones that occurs during adolescence, the female breasts begin to develop and enlarge (see Figure 3.5). The reproductive function

● **FIGURE 3.5**
The Female Breast. Front and cross-section views.

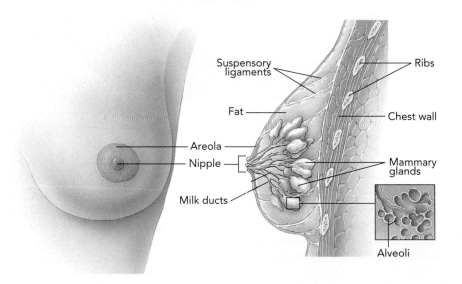

Suspensory ligaments

Ribs

Fat

Chest wall

Areola

Nipple

Mammary glands

Milk ducts

Alveoli

Western culture tends to be ambivalent about breasts and nudity. Many people are comfortable with artistic portrayals of the nude female body, as in this photograph by Imogen Cunningham titled *Triangles*.

of the breasts is to nourish offspring through **lactation,** or milk production. A mature female breast, also known as a **mammary gland,** is composed of fatty tissue and 15–25 lobes that radiate around a central protruding nipple. Around the nipple is a ring of darkened skin called the **areola** (a-REE-o-la). Tiny muscles at the base of the nipple cause it to become erect in response to touch, cold, or sexual arousal.

When a woman is pregnant, the structures within the breast undergo further development. Directly following childbirth, in response to hormonal signals, small glands within the lobes called **alveoli** (al-VEE-a-lee) begin producing milk. The milk passes into ducts, each of which has a dilated region for storage; the ducts open to the outside at the nipple. (Breast-feeding is discussed in Chapter 12.) During lactation, a woman's breasts increase in size from enlarged glandular tissues and stored milk. Because there is little variation in the amount of glandular tissue among women, the amount of milk produced does not vary with breast size. In women who are not lactating, breast size depends mainly on fat content, which is determined by hereditary factors.

In the Western culture, women's breasts capture a significant amount of attention and serve an erotic function. Many, but not all, women find breast stimulation intensely pleasurable, whether it occurs during breast-feeding or sexual contact. Partners tend to be aroused by both the sight and the touch of women's breasts. Although there is no basis in reality, some believe that large breasts denote greater sexual responsiveness than small breasts. (See Chapter 13 for a discussion of breast enhancement.) (Table 3.1 provides a summary of female sexual anatomy.)

" *Uncorsetted, her friendly bust gives promise of pneumatic bliss*

—T. S. Eliot
(1888–1965)

What's the fascination with breasts? Click on "Breasts" to hear women discussing myths and pressures surrounding breast size and perkiness.

Table 3.1 • Summary Table of Female Sexual Anatomy

External Structures (Vulva)

Mons pubis (mons veneris)	Fatty tissue that covers the area of the pubic bone
Clitoris	Center of sexual arousal
Clitoral hood	Covers the glans clitoris when the clitoris is not engorged
Crura (singular, crus)	Tips of erectile tissue that attach to the pelvic bones
Corpora cavernosa	Hollow chambers that fill with blood and swell during sexual arousal
Labia majora (major lips)	Two folds of spongy flesh that extend from the mons pubis and run downward along the sides of the vulva
Labia minora (minor lips)	Smaller, hairless folds within the labia majora that meet above the clitoris to form the clitoral hood
Vestibule (vaginal opening)	Area enclosed by the labia minora
Bartholin's glands	Glands that secrete a small amount of moisture during sexual arousal

Internal Structures

Vagina (birth canal)	Flexible, muscular structure in which menstrual flow and babies pass
Introitus	The lower part of the vagina
Hymen	Thin membrane that partially covers the introitus and contains a relatively large number of blood vessels
Grafenberg spot (G-spot)	Located on the front wall of the vagina, an erotically sensitive area that may produce intense erotic pleasure in some women
Uterus (womb)	Hollow, thick-walled muscular organ in which a fertilized ovum implants and develops until birth
Cervix	Lower end of the uterus that extends down and opens to the vagina
Endometrium	Inner lining of the uterine wall to which the fertilized egg attaches; partly discharged (if pregnancy does not occur) with the menstrual flow
Os	Opening to the cervix
Ovary (gonad)	Organ that produces gametes (see below)
Gametes	Sex cells containing the genetic material necessary for reproduction; also referred to as oocytes, eggs, ova (singular, ovum)
Ovarian follicles	Saclike structures that contain the immature oocytes
Corpus luteum	Tissue formed from a ruptured ovarian follicle that produces important hormones after the oocyte emerges
Fallopian tubes (oviducts)	Uterine tubes that transport the oocyte from the ovary to the uterus
Infundibulum	Funnel-shaped end of each fallopian tube
Fimbriae	Fingerlike projections that drape over the ovary and help transport the occyte from the ovary into the fallopian tube
Cilia	Tiny, hairlike structures that provide waving motion to help transport the oocyte within the fallopian tube to the ovary
Ampulla	Widened part of the fallopian tube in which fertilization normally occurs

Other Structures

Urethra	Tube through which urine passes
Urethral opening (meatus)	Opening in the urethra, through which urine is expelled
Anus	Opening in the rectum, through which excrement passes
Perineum	Area that lies between the vaginal opening and the anus
Pelvic floor	Underside of the pelvic area, extending from the top of the pubic bone (above the clitoris) to the anus

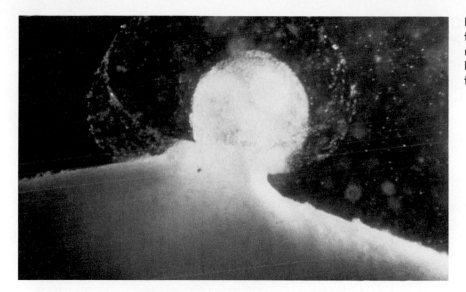

During ovulation, the ovarian follicle swells and ruptures, releasing the mature oocyte to begin its journey through the fallopian tube.

• Female Sexual Physiology

Just how do the various structures of the female anatomy function to produce the menstrual cycle? The female reproductive cycle can be viewed as having two components (although, of course, multiple biological processes are involved): (1) the ovarian cycle, in which eggs develop, and (2) the menstrual, or uterine, cycle, in which the womb is prepared for pregnancy. These cycles repeat approximately every month for about 35 or 40 years. The task of directing these processes belongs to a class of chemicals called hormones.

Reproductive Hormones

Hormones are chemical substances that serve as messengers, traveling within the body through the bloodstream. Most hormones are composed of either amino acids (building blocks of proteins) or steroids (derived from cholesterol). They are produced by the ovaries and the endocrine glands—the adrenals, pituitary, and hypothalamus. Hormones assist in a variety of tasks, including development of the reproductive organs and secondary sex characteristics during puberty, regulation of the menstrual cycle, maintenance of pregnancy, initiation and regulation of childbirth, initiation of lactation, and, to some degree, the regulation of **libido** (li-BEE-doh; sex drive or interest). Hormones that act directly on the gonads are known as **gonadotropins** (go-nad-a-TRO-pins). Among the most important of the female hormones are the **estrogens,** which affect the maturation of the reproductive organs, menstruation, and pregnancy, and **progesterone,** which helps to maintain the uterine lining until menstruation occurs. (The principal hormones involved in a woman's reproductive and sexual life and their functions are described in Table 3.2.) (Testosterone is discussed later in this chapter.)

The Ovarian Cycle

The development of female gametes is a complex process that begins even before a woman is born. In infancy and childhood, the cells develop into ova (eggs). During puberty, hormones trigger the completion of the process of **oogenesis**

Table 3.2 • Female Sex Hormones

Hormone	Where Produced	Functions
Estrogen (including estradiol, estrone, estriol)	Ovaries, adrenal glands, placenta (during pregnancy)	Promotes maturation of reproductive organs, development of secondary sex characteristics, and growth spurt at puberty; regulates menstrual cycle; sustains pregnancy; may maintain libido
Progesterone	Ovaries, adrenal glands, placenta	Promotes breast development, maintains uterine lining, regulates menstrual cycle, sustains pregnancy
Gonadotropin-releasing hormone (GnRH)	Hypothalamus	Promotes maturation of gonads, regulates menstrual cycle
Follicle-stimulating hormone (FSH)	Pituitary	Regulates ovarian function and maturation of ovarian follicles
Luteinizing hormone (LH)	Pituitary	Assists in production of estrogen and progesterone, regulates maturation of ovarian follicles, triggers ovulation
Human chorionic gonadotropin (HCG)	Embryo and placenta	Helps sustain pregnancy
Testosterone	Adrenal glands and ovaries	Helps stimulate sexual desire
Oxytocin	Hypothalamus	Stimulates uterine contractions during childbirth and possibly during orgasm, promotes milk let-down
Prolactin	Pituitary	Stimulates milk production
Prostaglandins	All body cells	Mediates hormone response, stimulates muscle contractions

(oh-uh-JEN-uh-sis), literally, "egg beginning" (see Figure 3.6). The oocyte, otherwise referred to as germ cell or immature ovum, marks the start of mitosis, the process by which a cell duplicates the chromosome in its cell nucleus. Oogenesis results in the formation of both primary oocytes, before birth, and as secondary oocytes after it and as part of ovulation. This process, called the **ovarian cycle** (or menstrual cycle), continues until a woman reaches menopause.

The ovarian cycle averages 28 days in length, although there is considerable variation among women, ranging from 21 to 40 days. In their own particular cycle length after puberty, however, most women experience little variation. Generally, ovulation occurs in only one ovary each month, alternating between the right and left sides with each successive cycle. If a single ovary is removed, the remaining one begins to ovulate every month. The ovarian cycle has three phases: follicular (fo-LIK-u-lar), ovulatory (ov-UL-a-tor-ee), and luteal (LOO-tee-ul) (see Figure 3.7). As an ovary undergoes its changes, corresponding changes occur in the uterus. Menstruation marks the end of this sequence of hormonal and physical changes in the ovaries and uterus.

The Follicular Phase On the first day of the cycle, **gonadotropin-releasing hormone (GnRH)** is released from the hypothalamus. GnRH begins to stimulate the pituitary to release **follicle-stimulating hormone (FSH) and luteinizing hormone (LH),** initiating the **follicular phase.** During the first 10 days,

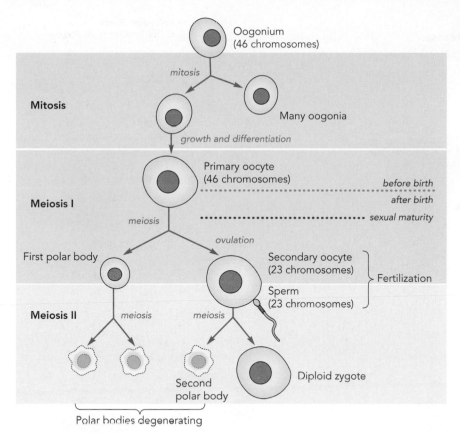

Oogenesis. This diagram charts the development of an ovum, beginning with embryonic development of the oogonium and ending with fertilization of the secondary oocyte, which then becomes the diploid zygote. Primary oocytes are present in a female at birth; at puberty, hormones stimulate the oocyte to undergo meiosis.

10–20 ovarian follicles begin to grow, stimulated by FSH and LH. In 98–99% of cases, only one of the follicles will mature completely during this period. (The maturation of more than one oocyte is one factor in multiple births.) All the developing follicles begin secreting estrogen. Under the influence of FSH and estrogen, the oocyte matures, bulging from the surface of the ovary. This may also be referred to as the proliferative phase.

Ovulatory Phase   The **ovulatory phase** begins at about day 11 of the cycle and culminates with ovulation at about day 14. Stimulated by an increase of LH from the pituitary, the primary oocyte undergoes cell division and becomes ready for ovulation. The ballooning follicle wall thins and ruptures, and the oocyte enters the abdominal cavity near the beckoning fimbriae. Ovulation is now complete. Some women experience a sharp twinge, called **Mittelschmerz,** on one side of the lower abdomen during ovulation. A very slight bloody discharge from the vagina may also occur. Occasionally, more than one ovum is released. If two ova are fertilized, nonidentical twins will result. If one egg is fertilized and divides into two separate zygotes, identical twins will develop.

The Luteal Phase   Following ovulation, estrogen levels drop rapidly, and the ruptured follicle, still under the influence of increased LH, becomes a corpus luteum, which secretes progesterone and small amounts of estrogen. Increasing levels of these hormones serve to inhibit pituitary release of FSH and LH. Unless fertilization has occurred, the corpus luteum deteriorates. In the event of pregnancy, the corpus luteum maintains its hormonal output, helping to

Menstrual Phase

(Menstruation)

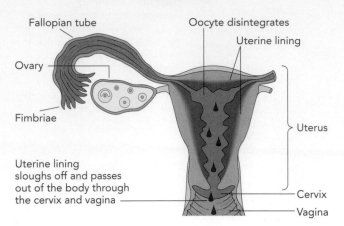

Fallopian tube

Ovary

Fimbriae

Oocyte disintegrates

Uterine lining

Uterus

Uterine lining sloughs off and passes out of the body through the cervix and vagina

Cervix

Vagina

Follicular Phase
(also called the Proliferative Phase)

(Follicle development)

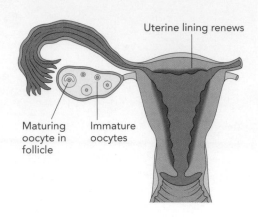

Uterine lining renews

Maturing oocyte in follicle

Immature oocytes

Ovulatory Phase

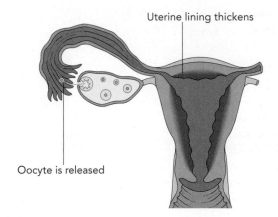

Uterine lining thickens

Oocyte is released

Luteal Phase

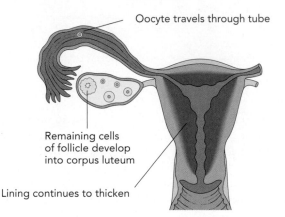

Oocyte travels through tube

Remaining cells of follicle develop into corpus luteum

Lining continues to thicken

● FIGURE 3.7

Ovarian and Menstrual Cycles.
The ovarian cycle consists of the activities within the ovaries and the development of oocytes; it includes the follicular, ovulatory, and luteal phases. The menstrual cycle consists of processes occurring in the uterus. Hormones regulate these cycles.

sustain the pregnancy. The hormone human chorionic gonadotropin (HCG)—similar to LH—is secreted by the embryo and signals the corpus luteum to continue until the placenta has developed sufficiently to take over hormone production.

The **luteal phase** typically lasts from day 14 (immediately after ovulation) through day 28 of the ovarian cycle. Even when cycles are more or less than 28 days, the duration of the luteal phase remains the same; the time between ovulation and the end of the cycle is always 14 days. At this point, the ovarian hormone levels are at their lowest, GnRH is released, and FSH and LH levels begin to rise.

The Menstrual Cycle

As hormone levels decrease following the degeneration of the corpus luteum, the uterine lining (endometrium) is shed because it will not be needed to help sustain the fertilized ovum. The shedding of endometrial tissue and the bleeding

Sexual Health Care: What Do Women Need?

Women have unique sexual and reproductive needs and may face difficulties in the health-care system. There are a number of things that women can do in order to be aware and proactive in their medical care. This means learning as much as possible about their bodies and acknowledging their accompanying feelings and sensations. Much information can also be obtained by doing research on the Internet. Additionally and in order to maximize outcomes, it is advisable to

- Interview a new physician before seeking his or her care and be sure that the physician's attitude about women's health is similar to your own.
- Ask in advance if the doctor or clinic accepts your medical insurance and how billing and payment for services occur.
- Keep a diary or journal of your health history and bring it with you to your doctor visit. This may involve asking relatives about their health status and maladies in order that you and the doctor can watch for potential hereditary health problems.
- It might be helpful for you to bring along an advocate, such as a friend or relative who will help support you while listening to and inquiring about the doctor's explanation.
- List all questions and make sure that you understand the answers. Acknowledging that doctors have limited time,

it is advisable to list those questions in order of their importance to you.

- Bring to the visit a list of the dosages and names of any medicines, vitamins or minerals, herbal treatments, and over-the-counter medications that you take.
- Ask your doctor for an explanation of anything you do not understand. Obtain a written statement of the diagnosis and treatment plan so that you can follow up, seek a second opinion if you need it, or have it available in case there is a medical emergency.
- Request a printed copy of the results of any test results or lab work that you may have, along with an explanation of any abnormal findings.
- Obtain a second opinion if you have a diagnosis of a serious disease, the doctor suggests surgery or other invasive procedure, or if you are unsure about the diagnosis or treatment.

The best option for care is for women to have both a gynecologist (a doctor who specializes in women's reproductive health) and a primary-care physician and to be sure that they communicate with each other. Though either one can fulfill a woman's health-care needs, the combination ensures that each doctor's specialization can be maximized and that there is a broader range of input about her well-being.

that accompanies it are, collectively, a monthly event in the lives of women from puberty through menopause. Cultural and religious attitudes, as well as personal experience, influence our feelings about this phenomenon. (The physical and emotional effects of menstruation are discussed later in this section. The onset of menstruation and its effect on a woman's psychosexual development are discussed in Chapter 6. Menopause is discussed in Chapter 7.)

Most American women who menstruate use sanitary pads, panty liners, or tampons to help absorb the flow of menstrual blood. While pads and panty liners are used outside the body, tampons are placed inside the vagina. For a wide variety of reasons, including environmental concerns, comfort, chemical residues, and **toxic shock syndrome** (a bacterial infection that can occur in menstruating women and cause a person to go into shock; discussed in Chapter 13), women are turning to alternative means for catching menstrual flow. These products include all-cotton, organic, chlorine-free tampons; washable cloth pads; and devices, such as a reusable silicon cup, to collect the menstrual flow. Whether a woman chooses to wear a product on the outside of her body or use one on the inside is a matter of personal choice.

While some Americans may question the use of alternative products, across time and culture a wide variety of methods have been used to absorb the flow

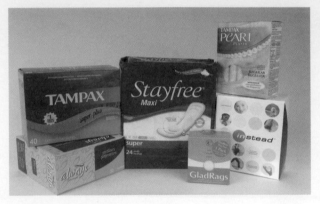

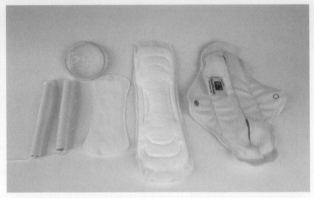

An array of choices that collect and absorb menstrual flow are now available to women.

of blood. Cloth menstrual pads, also referred to as Glad Rags, are organic, reusable, washable, and quite comfortable. For those desiring to wear something internally, other products, called The Keeper, DivaCup™, or Instead, consist of a menstrual cup that is held in place by suction in the lower vagina and acts to collect menstrual fluid. Some women have used the diaphragm or cervical cap in a similar manner. Reusable sea sponges can work like tampons in absorbing blood. Boiling the sponge before and between uses can help to rid it of possible ocean pollutants and help to keep it sanitary. Sewing or tying a piece of cotton string on the sponge for easy retrieval is suggested. Most likely, the majority of American women will continue to rely on more widely available and advertised commercial tampons or sanitary pads; however, alternatives provide women with an opportunity to take charge of how they respond to their menstrual flow and the environmental impacts of that decision.

The **menstrual cycle** (or uterine cycle), is divided into three phases: menstrual, proliferative, and secretory. What occurs within the uterus is inextricably related to what is happening in the ovaries, but only in their final phases do the two cycles actually coincide (see Figure 3.8).

The Menstrual Phase   With hormone levels low because of the degeneration of the corpus luteum, the outer layer of the endometrium becomes detached from the uterine wall. The shedding of the endometrium marks the beginning of the **menstrual phase.** This endometrial tissue, along with mucus, other cervical and vaginal secretions, and a small amount of blood (2–5 ounces per cycle), is expelled through the vagina. The menstrual flow, or **menses** (MEN-seez), generally occurs over a period of 3–5 days. FSH and LH begin increasing around day 5, marking the end of this phase. A girl's first menstruation is known as **menarche** (MEH-nar-kee).

The Proliferative Phase   The **proliferative phase** lasts about 9 days. During this time, the endometrium thickens in response to increased estrogen. The mucous membranes of the cervix secrete a clear, thin mucus with a crystalline structure that facilitates the passage of sperm. The proliferative phase ends with ovulation.

The Secretory Phase   During the first part of the **secretory phase,** with the help of progesterone, the endometrium begins to prepare for the arrival of a fertilized ovum. Glands within the uterus enlarge and begin secreting glycogen,

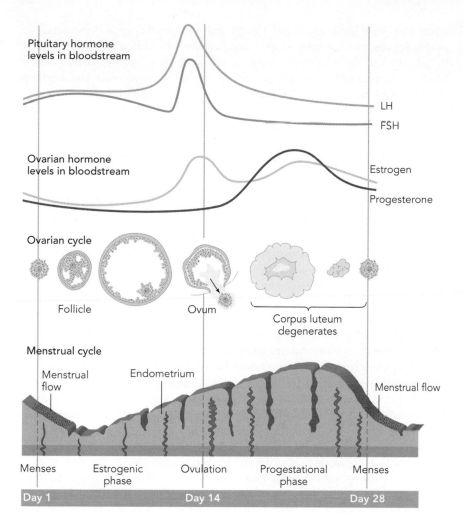

● **FIGURE 3.8**

The Menstrual Cycle, Ovarian Cycle, and Hormone Levels. This chart compares the activities of the ovaries and uterus and shows the relationship of hormone levels to these activities.

Pituitary hormone levels in bloodstream

LH
FSH

Ovarian hormone levels in bloodstream

Estrogen
Progesterone

Ovarian cycle

Follicle Ovum Corpus luteum degenerates

Menstrual cycle

Menstrual flow Endometrium Menstrual flow

Menses Estrogenic phase Ovulation Progestational phase Menses

Day 1 Day 14 Day 28

a cell nutrient. The cervical mucus thickens and starts forming a plug to seal off the uterus in the event of pregnancy. If fertilization does not occur, the corpus luteum begins to degenerate, as LH levels decline. Progesterone levels then fall, and the endometrial cells begin to die. The secretory phase lasts 14 days, corresponding with the luteal phase of the ovarian cycle. It ends with the shedding of the endometrium.

Menstrual Synchrony Women who live or work together often report developing similarly timed menstrual cycles (Cutler, 1999). Termed **menstrual synchrony,** this phenomenon appears to be related to the sense of smell—more specifically, a response to **pheromones,** chemical substances secreted into the air. Though there is considerable controversy among researchers as to whether the phenomenon actually exists, if it does, there could be implications for birth control, sexual attraction, and other aspects of women's lives. (Pheromones are discussed later in the chapter.)

Menstrual Effects American women have divergent attitudes toward menstruation. For some women, menstruation is a problem; for others, it is simply a fact of life that creates little disruption. For individual women, the problems

Menstrual Period Slang
that time of the month
monthlies
the curse
female troubles
a visit from my friend
a visit from Aunt Flo
a visit from George
on the rag
on a losing streak
falling off the roof

associated with their menstrual period may be physiological, emotional, or practical. The vast majority of menstruating women notice at least one emotional, physical, or behavioral change in the week or so prior to menstruation. Most women describe the changes negatively: breast tenderness and swelling, abdominal bloating, irritability, cramping, depression, or fatigue. Some women also report positive changes such as increased energy, heightened sexual arousal, or a general feeling of well-being. For most women, changes during the menstrual cycle are usually mild to moderate; they appear to have little impact on their lives. The most common problems associated with menstruation are discussed below.

Premenstrual Syndrome   A collection of physical, emotional, and psychological symptoms that many women experience 7–14 days before their menstrual period is known as **premenstrual syndrome (PMS).** These symptoms disappear soon after the start of menstrual bleeding. Though no one knows for sure what causes PMS, it seems to be linked to alterations in the levels of sex hormones and brain chemicals, or neutrotransmitters.

Controversy exists over the difference between premenstrual discomfort and true PMS. Premenstrual discomfort is a common occurrence, affecting about 75% of all menstruating women (InteliHealth, 2005). Only about 3–8% of women, however, have symptoms that are severe enough to be labeled PMS. While some doctors equate **premenstrual dysphoric disorder** to PMS, others use a less stringent definition for PMS, which includes mild to moderate symptoms. Symptoms of PMS fall into two categories: physical symptoms, which may include bloating, breast tenderness, swelling and weight gain, headaches, cramping, migraine headaches, and food cravings; and psychological and emotional symptoms, which include fatigue, depression, irritability, crying, and changes in libido. For many, symptoms may be worse some months and better other ones.

Although there is no singular finding that will confirm a diagnosis of PMS, a physical exam and a Pap smear can check for other medical problems and rule out medical disorders. After reviewing a history of symptoms, and if there are no abnormal lab results, the doctor can make a diagnosis of PMS. Though there is no way to prevent PMS, there may be some ways to treat and alleviate some symptoms. Most of these involve leading a healthier lifestyle. For more severe symptoms, the doctor may prescribe a variety of medications, depending on the symptoms. It may also be comforting to know that in most women, PMS symptoms begin to subside after the age of 35 and at menopause.

Menorrhagia   At some point in her menstrual life, nearly every woman experiences heavy or prolonged bleeding during her menstrual cycle, also known as **menorrhagia.** Although heavy menstrual bleeding is common among most women, only a few experience blood loss severe enough for it to be defined as menorrhagia. Signs and symptoms may include a menstrual flow that soaks through one or more sanitary pads or tampons every hour for several consecutive hours, the need to use double sanitary protection throughout the menstrual flow, menstrual flow that includes large blood clots, and/or heavy menstrual flow that interferes with the regular lifestyle ("Menorrhagia," 2005). Though the cause of heavy menstrual bleeding is unknown, a number of conditions may cause menorrhagia, including hormonal imbalances, uterine fibroids, having an IUD, cancer, or certain medications. The combined effect of hormonal imbalances and uterine fibroids accounts for 80% of all cases of menorrhagia. Excessive or prolonged menstrual bleeding can lead to iron deficiency anemia and other medical conditions; thus, it is advisable for women with this problem to seek medical care and treatment.

Dysmenorrhea While menstrual cramps are experienced by some women before or during their periods, a more persistent, aching, and serious pain sufficient to limit a woman's activities is called **dysmenorrhea.** There are two types of dysmenorrhea. Primary dysmenorrhea is not associated with any diagnosable pelvic condition. It is characterized by pain that begins with (or just before) uterine bleeding when there is an absence of pain at other times in the cycle. It can be very severe and may be accompanied by nausea, weakness, or other physical symptoms. In secondary dysmenorrhea, the symptoms may be the same, but there is an underlying condition or disease causing them; pain may not be limited to the menstrual phase alone. Secondary dysmenorrhea may be caused by pelvic inflammatory disease (PID), endometriosis, endometrial cancer, or other conditions that should be treated. (See Chapters 13 and 15.)

The effects of dysmenorrhea can totally incapacitate a woman for several hours or even days. Once believed to be a psychological condition, primary dysmenorrhea is now known to be caused by high levels of **prostaglandins** (pros-ta-GLAN-dins), a type of hormone with a fatty-acid base that is found throughout the body. Drugs like ibuprofen (Motrin and Advil) relieve symptoms by inhibiting the production of prostaglandins. Some doctors may prescribe birth control pills.

Amenorrhea When women do not menstruate for reasons other than aging, the condition is called **amenorrhea** (ay-meh-neh-REE-a). Principal causes of amenorrhea are pregnancy and breast-feeding. Lack of menstruation, if not a result of pregnancy or nursing, is categorized as either primary or secondary amenorrhea. Women who have passed the age of 16 and never menstruated are diagnosed as having primary amenorrhea. It may be that they have not yet reached their critical weight (when an increased ratio of body fat triggers menstrual cycle–inducing hormones) or that they are hereditarily late maturers. But it can also signal hormonal deficiencies, abnormal body structure, or an intersex condition or other genital anomaly that makes menstruation impossible. Most primary amenorrhea can be treated with hormone therapy.

Secondary amenorrhea exists when a previously menstruating woman stops menstruating for several months. If it is not due to pregnancy, breast-feeding, or the use of hormonal contraceptives, the source of secondary amenorrhea may be found in stress, lowered body fat, heavy physical training, or hormonal irregularities. Anorexia (discussed in Chapter 13) is a frequent cause of amenorrhea. If a woman is not pregnant, is not breast-feeding, and can rule out hormonal contraceptives as a cause, she should see her health-care practitioner if she has gone 3 months without menstruating.

Lifestyle changes or treatment of the underlying condition can almost always correct amenorrhea, unless it is caused by a congenital anomaly. Because there is no known harm associated with amenorrhea, the condition is corrected when an underlying problem presents itself or it causes a woman psychological distress.

Menstrual Health Care

Many factors can influence the way we experience and feel about menstruation, including culture, religion, traditions, and the ways in which we experienced our first cycle. While the vast majority of women feel few and minor changes, others experience changes that are uncomfortable and debilitating. The variations can be significant in any one woman and from month to month. Some of the more negative experiences can be addressed by lifestyle changes and modifications, including managing stress, reducing caffeine and salt, eliminating nicotine, eating a well-balanced diet, and exercising. For women, recognizing their menstrual patterns, learning about their bodies, and recognizing and dealing with existing difficulties can be useful in heading off or easing potential problems. Different remedies work for different women. We suggest that you try varying combinations of them and keep a record of your response to each. Following are suggestions for relieving the more common premenstrual and menstrual changes; both self-help and medical treatments are included.

For Premenstrual Changes

1. *Modify your diet.* Moderate amounts of protein and substantial amounts of carbohydrates (such as fresh fruits, some vegetables, whole-grain breads and cereals, beans, rice, and pasta) are recommended. A diet rich in vitamin A and calcium will also lower the chances of experiencing PMS (Bertone-Johnson et al., 2005). Reduce or avoid salt, sugar, and caffeine products such as coffee and colas. Although you may crave chocolate, it can have a negative effect on you; try fruit or popcorn instead, and see how you feel. Frequent small meals may be better than two or three large meals.

2. *Avoid alcohol and tobacco and get sufficient sleep.*

3. *Exercise.* Moderate exercise is suggested, but be sure to include a daily regimen of at least 30–45 minutes of movement. Aerobic exercise brings oxygen to body tissues and stimulates the production of endorphins, chemical substances that help promote feelings of well-being. Yoga may also be helpful, especially the "cobra" position.

4. *Seek medical advice.* When symptoms are severe enough to impair work performance and relationships, you should seek medical attention. However, there is much controversy within the medical profession about treatment for PMS. Progesterone therapy, once advocated as a treatment, is now considered ineffective. Selective serotonin-reuptake inhibitors, such as Prozac and Zoloft, have been found to be effective in treating

Sexuality and the Menstrual Cycle Although studies have tried to determine whether there is a biologically based cycle of sexual interest and activity in women that correlates with the menstrual cycle (such as higher interest around ovulation), the results have been varied. There is also variation in how people feel about sexual activity during different phases of the menstrual cycle. If a woman believes she is ovulating, and if she and her partner do not want a pregnancy, they may feel negative or ambivalent about intercourse. If a woman is menstruating, she, her partner, or both of them may not wish to engage in intercourse or cunnilingus, for a number of reasons.

There is a general taboo in our culture, as in many others, against sexual intercourse during menstruation. This taboo may be based on religious or cultural beliefs. Among Orthodox Jews, for example, women are required to refrain from intercourse for 7 days following the end of menstruation. They may then resume sexual activity after a ritual bath, the *mikvah.* Contact with blood may make some people squeamish. Some women, especially at the beginning of their period, feel bloated or uncomfortable; they may experience breast tenderness or a general feeling of not wanting to be touched. Others may find that sexual activity helps relieve menstrual discomfort.

For some couples, merely having to deal with the logistics of bloodstains, bathing, and laundry may be enough to discourage them from intercourse at this

PMS in some women (Saks, 2000). No medication for PMS has yet received FDA approval.

5. *Join a support group.* Therapy or support groups may help you deal with the ways PMS affects your life. They may also help you deal with issues that may be exacerbated by the stress of coping with PMS.

For Cramps

1. *Relax.* Rest, sleep, and relaxation exercises can help reduce pain from uterine and abdominal cramping, especially in combination with one or more of the remedies listed below.

2. *Apply heat.* A heating pad or hot-water bottle (or, in a pinch, a cat) applied to the abdominal area may help relieve cramps; a warm bath may also help.

3. *Get a massage.* Lower back massage or other forms of massage, such as acupressure, Shiatsu, or polarity therapy, are quite helpful for many women.

4. *Try herbal remedies.* Herbal teas, especially raspberry leaf, are helpful for some women. Health food stores carry a variety of teas, tablets, and other preparations. Use them as directed, but stop using them if you experience additional discomfort or problems.

5. *Take prostaglandin inhibitors.* Antiprostaglandins reduce cramping of the uterine and abdominal muscles. Aspirin is a mild prostaglandin inhibitor. Ibuprofen, a highly effective prostaglandin inhibitor, was often prescribed for menstrual cramps (as Motrin) before it became available over the counter. Aspirin increases menstrual flow slightly, whereas ibuprofen reduces it. Stronger antiprostaglandins may be prescribed. Taking medication at the first sign of cramping—as opposed to waiting until the pain is severe—increases its effectiveness greatly.

6. *Have an orgasm.* Some women report relief of menstrual congestion and cramping during orgasm (with or without a partner).

If pain cannot be managed with these methods, further medical evaluation is needed. The symptoms may indicate an underlying problem, such as endometriosis or pelvic inflammatory disease (PID).

time. For many people, however, menstrual blood holds no special connotation. It is important to note that although it is unusual, conception *can* occur during menstruation, especially if the woman has short or irregular cycles. Some women find that a diaphragm or menstrual cup can collect the menstrual flow. Menstrual cups, however, are not a contraceptive. It is not recommended that women engage in intercourse while a tampon is inserted because of possible injury to the cervix. And inventive lovers can, of course, find many ways to give each other pleasure that do not require putting the penis into the vagina.

● Female Sexual Response

The ways in which individuals respond to sexual arousal are highly varied. Women's sexuality, though typically thought of as personal and individual, is significantly influenced by the social groups to which women belong. Sociocultural variables include gender, religious preference, class, educational attainment, age, marital status, race, and ethnicity. For many women, gender—the social and cultural characteristics associated with being male or female—is probably the most influential variable in shaping their sexual desires, behaviors, and partnerships. Because gender is largely defined by cultural expectations, women's sexual experiences must be understood in terms of cultural, political, and relational forces. New research into the anatomy and physiology of sexuality has helped us to increase our understanding of orgasm. By looking beyond the genitals to the central nervous system, where electrical impulses travel from the brain to the spinal cord, researchers are examining nerves and pathways to better understand the biology of the orgasm. What is probably most critical to all of these functions are the ways we interpret sexual cues.

Though scientific research has contributed much to our understanding of sexual arousal and response, there is still much to be learned. One way in which researchers investigate and describe phenomena is through the creation of models, hypothetical descriptions used to study or explain something. Although models are useful for promoting general understanding or for assisting in the treatment of specific clinical problems, we should remember that they are only models. It may be helpful to think of sexual functioning as interconnected, linking desire, arousal, orgasm, and satisfaction. Turbulence or distraction at any one point affects the functioning of the others.

Sexual Response Models

> *Passion, though a bad regulator, is a powerful spring.*
>
> —Ralph Waldo Emerson
> (1803–1882)

A number of sexologists have attempted to outline the various physiological changes that both men and women undergo when they are sexually stimulated. Three important models are described here. The sequence of changes and patterns that take place in the body during sexual arousal is referred to as the **sexual response cycle. Masters and Johnson's four-phase model of sexual response** identifies the significant stages of response as excitement, plateau, orgasm, and resolution (see Figure 3.9). Helen Singer Kaplan (1979) collapses the excitement and plateau phases into one, eliminates the resolution phase, and adds a phase to the beginning of the process. **Kaplan's tri-phasic model of sexual response** includes the desire, excitement, and orgasm phases. Though Masters and Johnson's and Kaplan's are the most widely cited models used to describe the phases of the sexual response cycle, they do little to acknowledge the affective parts of human response. A third but much less known pattern is **Loulan's sexual response model,** which incorporates both the biological and affective components into a six-stage cycle. Beyond any questions of similarities and differences in the female and male sexual response cycle is the more significant issue of variation in how individuals experience each phase. The diversity of experiences can be described only by the individual. (These models are described and compared in Table 3.3.)

Desire: Mind or Matter?

> *Some desire is necessary to keep life in motion.*
>
> —Samuel Johnson
> (1709–1784)

Desire is the psychological component of sexual arousal. Although we can experience desire without becoming aroused, and in some cases become aroused without feeling desire, some form of erotic thought or feeling is usually involved in our sexual behavior. The physical manifestations of sexual arousal involve a complex interaction of thoughts and feelings, sensory organs, neural responses, and hormonal reactions involving various parts of the body, including the nucleus accumbens, cerebellum, and hypothalamus of the brain, the nervous system, the circulatory system, and the endocrine glands—as well as the genitals.

A study of women found that lubrication was only one of the physiological changes that occurred when they were sexually aroused, and not a necessary condition for women to report that they were sexually aroused (Graham et al.,

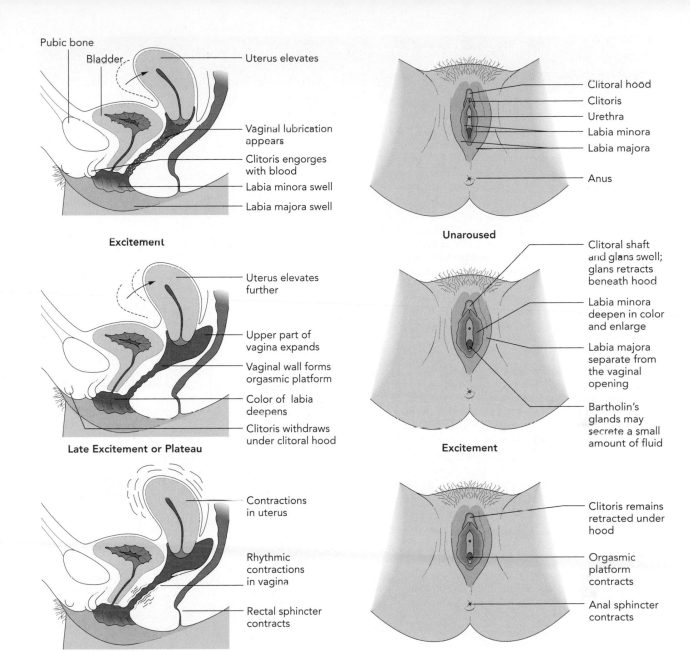

Excitement

- Pubic bone
- Bladder
- Uterus elevates
- Vaginal lubrication appears
- Clitoris engorges with blood
- Labia minora swell
- Labia majora swell

Late Excitement or Plateau

- Uterus elevates further
- Upper part of vagina expands
- Vaginal wall forms orgasmic platform
- Color of labia deepens
- Clitoris withdraws under clitoral hood

Orgasm

- Contractions in uterus
- Rhythmic contractions in vagina
- Rectal sphincter contracts

Unaroused

- Clitoral hood
- Clitoris
- Urethra
- Labia minora
- Labia majora
- Anus

Excitement

- Clitoral shaft and glans swell; glans retracts beneath hood
- Labia minora deepen in color and enlarge
- Labia majora separate from the vaginal opening
- Bartholin's glands may secrete a small amount of fluid

Orgasm

- Clitoris remains retracted under hood
- Orgasmic platform contracts
- Anal sphincter contracts

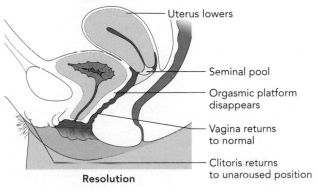

Resolution

- Uterus lowers
- Seminal pool
- Orgasmic platform disappears
- Vagina returns to normal
- Clitoris returns to unaroused position

● **FIGURE 3.9**

Masters and Johnson Stages of Female Sexual Response (internal, left; and external, right)

Table 3.3 • Sexual Response Models Compared: Masters/Johnson, Kaplan, and Loulan

Psychological/Physiological Process	Name of Phase
Two people make a conscious decision to have sex even if there might not be emotional or physical desire.	Willingness (Loulan)
Some form of thought, fantasy, or erotic feeling causes individuals to seek sexual gratification. (An inability to become sexually aroused may be due to a lack of desire, although some people have reported that they acquire sexual desire after being sexually aroused.)	Desire (Kaplan, Loulan)
Physical and/or psychological stimulation produces characteristic physical changes. In men, increased amounts of blood flow to the genitals produce erection of the penis; the scrotal skin begins to smooth out, and the testicles draw up toward the body. Later in this phase, the testes increase slightly in size. In women, vaginal lubrication begins, the upper vagina expands, the uterus is pulled upward, and the clitoris becomes engorged. In both women and men, the breasts enlarge slightly, and the nipples may become erect. Both men and women experience increasing muscular contractions.	Excitement (Masters/Johnson, Loulan) — Excitement (Kaplan)
Sexual tension levels off. In men, the testes swell and continue to elevate. The head of the penis swells slightly and may deepen in color. In women, the outer third of the vagina swells, lubrication may slow down, and the clitoris pulls back. Coloring and swelling of the labia increase. In both men and women, muscular tension, breathing, and heart rate increase.	Plateau (Masters/Johnson) — Engorgement (Loulan)
Increased tension peaks and discharges, affecting the whole body. Rhythmic muscular contractions affect the uterus and outer vagina in women. In men, there are contractions of the tubes that produce and carry semen, the prostate gland, and the urethral bulb, resulting in the expulsion of semen (ejaculation).	Orgasm (Masters/Johnson, Kaplan, and Loulan)
The body returns to its unaroused state. In some women, this does not occur until after repeated orgasms.	Resolution (Masters/Johnson) — Pleasure (Loulan)
Pleasure is one purpose of sexuality and can be defined only by the individual. One can experience pleasure during all or only some of the above stages, or one can leave out any of the stages and still have pleasure.	

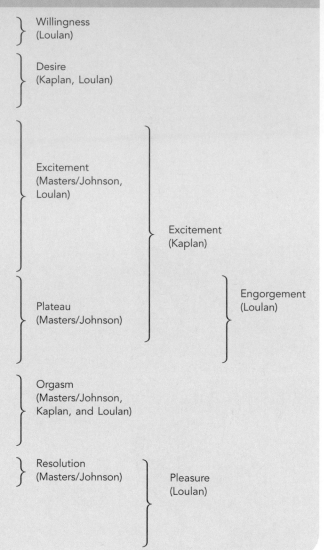

2004). This finding points to the possibility that women's ratings of arousal, unlike men's, are more influenced by their state of general arousal than by their genital response. It is still unclear whether this is a result of learning or biology.

The Neural System and Sexual Stimuli The brain is crucial to sexual response and is currently a focus of research to understanding how we respond to sexual stimulation. Through the neural system, the brain receives stimuli from the five senses plus one: sight, smell, touch, hearing, taste, *and* the imagination.

The Brain The brain, of course, plays a major role in all of our body's functions. Nowhere is its role more apparent than in our sexual functioning. The relationship between our thoughts and feelings and our actual behavior is not well understood (and what is known would require a course in neurophysiology to satisfactorily explain it). Relational factors and cultural influences, as well as expectations, fantasies, hopes, and fears, combine with sensory inputs and neurotransmitters (chemicals that transmit messages in the nervous system) to bring us to where we are ready, willing, and able to be sexual. Even then, potentially erotic messages may be short-circuited by the brain itself, which can inhibit as well as incite sexual responses. It is not known how the inhibitory mechanism works, but negative conditioning and emotions will prevent the brain from sending messages to the genitals. In fact, the reason moderate amounts of alcohol and marijuana appear to enhance sexuality is that they reduce the control mechanisms of the brain that act as inhibitors. Conversely, women who feel persistent sexual arousal and no relief from orgasm reveal unusually high activation in regions of the brain that respond to genital stimulation (Komisaruk, Beyer-Flores, & Whipple, 2006). (See Chapter 14 for a discussion of persistent sexual arousal syndrome.)

Anatomically speaking, the part of the body that appears to be involved most in sexual behaviors of both men and women is the vast highway of nerves called the vagus nerve network that stretches to all the major organs, including the brain. Using MRI scans to map the brain, researchers have found increases in brain activity during sexual arousal (Holstege et al., 2003; Komisaruk, Beyer-Flores, & Whipple, 2006). Since specific parts of the brain send their sensory signals via specific nerves, the different quality of orgasms that result from clitoral or anal stimulation, for example, is divided among the different genital sensory nerves.

Researchers and professors Barry Komisaruk, Carlos Beyer-Flores, and Beverly Whipple have recently discovered that orgasms elicit strong activity in the nucleus accumbens, the reward center; the cerebellus, which helps to coordinate muscle tension; and the hypothalamus, which releases oxytocin—all of which work in concert to produce strong physical and emotional sensations (2006). The amygdala, the brain's emotional center, and the hippocampus, the memory center, also show involvement. Interestingly, the same region that is activated during orgasm, the accumbens, also lights up in response to chocolate, nicotine, cocaine, and music. Additionally, the authors found that as a woman orgasms, an area of the brain governing emotional control and pain is largely deactivated. No comparable results were found in men.

The Senses   An attractive person (sight), a body fragrance or odor (smell), a lick or kiss (taste), a loving caress (touch), and erotic whispers (hearing) are all capable of sending sexual signals to the brain. Preferences for each of these sensory inputs are largely determined by culture and are very individualized. Many of the connections we experience between sensory data and emotional responses are probably products of the **limbic system,** or those structures of the brain that are associated with emotions and feelings and involved in sexual arousal. Some sensory inputs may evoke sexual arousal without a lot of conscious thought or emotion. Certain areas of the skin, called **erogenous zones,** are highly sensitive to touch. These areas may include the genitals, breasts, mouth, ears, neck, inner thighs, and buttocks; erotic associations with these areas vary from culture to culture and from individual to individual. Our olfactory sense (smell) may bring us sexual messages below the level of our conscious awareness. Scientists have isolated chemical substances, called pheromones, that are secreted into the air by many kinds of animals, including humans, ants, moths, pigs, deer, dogs, and monkeys. One function of pheromones, in animals at least, appears to be to arouse the libido.

> *Women might be able to fake orgasms. But men can fake whole relationships.*
>
> —Sharon Stone
> (1958–)

Sensory inputs, such as the sight, touch, or smell of someone we love or the sound of his or her voice, may evoke desire and sexual arousal.

think
about it

The Role of Orgasm

Many of us measure both our sexuality and ourselves in terms of orgasm: Did we have one? Did our partner have one? Was it good? Did we have simultaneous orgasms? When we measure our sexuality by orgasm, however, we discount activities that do not necessarily lead to orgasm, such as touching, caressing, and kissing. We discount erotic pleasure as an end in itself. Our culture tends to identify sex with sexual intercourse, and the end of sexual intercourse is literally orgasm (especially male orgasm).

An Anthropological and Evolutionary Perspective

A fundamental, biological fact about orgasm is that male orgasm and ejaculation are required for reproduction, whereas the female orgasm is not. The male orgasm is universal in both animal and human species, but sociobiologists and anthropologists have found immense variation in the experience of female orgasm. Anthropologists such as Margaret Mead (1975) found that some societies, such as the Mundugumor, emphasize the female orgasm but that it is virtually nonexistent in other societies, such as the Arapesh.

In our culture, women most consistently experience orgasm through a combination of vaginal intercourse and manual and oral stimulation of the clitoris (Richters, de Visser, Rissel, & Smith, 2006). In cultures that cultivate female orgasm, according to sociobiologist Donald Symons (1979), there is, in addition to an absence of sexual repression, an emphasis on men's skill in arousing women. In our own culture, among men who consider themselves

(and are considered) "good lovers," great emphasis is placed on their abilities to arouse their partners and bring them to orgasm. These skills include not only penile penetration but also, often more importantly, clitoral or G-spot stimulation. This, of course, is based on the sexual script that men are to "give orgasms to women," a message that places pressure on men and that tells women they are not responsible for their own sexual response. According to this script, the woman is "erotically dependent" on the man. The woman can, of course, also stimulate her own clitoris to experience orgasm.

Because it is closely tied to reproduction, evolutionary scientists have never had difficulty explaining the male orgasm; it ensures reproduction. In the same vein, scientists have for decades insisted on finding an evolutionary function for female orgasm but have not been as successful. Since women can have sexual intercourse and become pregnant without experiencing orgasm, perhaps there is no evolutionary function for orgasm (Lloyd, 2005). However, philosopher and professor Elisabeth Lloyd acknowledges, evolution does not dictate what is culturally important. In reviewing 32 studies conducted over 74 years, Lloyd found that when intercourse was unassisted—that is, not accompanied by stimulation of the clitoris—just one quarter of the women studied experienced orgasms often or very often and a full one third never do; the rest sometimes do and sometimes don't. Without a link to fertility or reproduction, it is argued that orgasm is not adaptive; that is, women who are orgasmic would have had to have contributed more genes to future generations. This would imply

Hormones The libido in both men and women is biologically influenced by the hormone **testosterone.** In men, testosterone is produced mainly in the testes; in women, it is produced in the adrenal glands and the ovaries. Growing evidence suggests that testosterone may play an important role in the maintenance of women's bodies ("Women's Hormones," 2002). Although it does not play a large part in a woman's hormonal makeup, it is present in the blood vessels, brain, skin, bone, and vagina. Testosterone is believed to contribute to bone density, blood flow, hair growth, energy and strength, and libido.

Although women produce much less testosterone than men, this does not mean that they have less sexual interest; apparently, women are much more sensitive than men to testosterone's effects. Though testosterone decreases in women as they age, the ovaries manufacture it throughout life. Symptoms produced by the decrease of testosterone can be similar to those related to estrogen loss, including fatigue, vaginal dryness, and bone loss. Signs specific

that over time all women would be orgasmic. This obviously isn't the case.

The Tyranny of the Orgasm

Sociologist Philip Slater (1974) suggests that our preoccupation with orgasm is an extension of the Protestant work ethic, in which nothing is enjoyed for its own sake; everything is work, including sex. Thus, we "achieve" orgasm much as we achieve success. Those who achieve orgasm are the "successful workers" of sex; those who do not are the "failures."

As we look at our sexuality, we can see pressure to be successful lovers. Men talk of performance anxiety. We tend to evaluate a woman's sexual self-worth in terms of her being orgasmic (able to have orgasms). For men, the significant question about women's sexuality has shifted from "Is she a virgin?" to "Is she orgasmic?"

Faking Orgasm

Although during sexual intercourse women are not as consistently orgasmic as men, there is considerable pressure on them to be so. In one study, college students were asked whether they had faked orgasm; 60% of heterosexual women and 71% of lesbian or bisexual women said yes, while only 17% of heterosexual men and 27% of gay or bisexual men acknowledged doing so (Elliott & Brantley, 1997). The reason most women fake orgasm is not to protect their own feelings as much as to protect those of their partner. They want to please and avoid hurting or disappointing their partners. Other reasons include fear of their own sexual inadequacy and a desire to prevent their partner from seeking another partner and to end boring or painful intercourse (Darling & Davidson, 1986; Ellison, 2000).

"Was It Good for You?"

A question often asked following intercourse is "Was it good for you?" or its variation, "Did you come?"

Such questions are often asked by men rather than women, and women tend to resent them. Part of the pressure to pretend to have an orgasm is caused by these questions. What is really being asked? If the woman enjoyed intercourse? If she thinks the man is a good lover? Or is the question merely a signal that the lovemaking is over?

While the question "Was it good for you?" may initiate a dialogue, the statement "Orgasm is good for us" acknowledges a fact. Though it's apparent that orgasm feels good, some of us may not recognize that orgasm is indeed good for our health. Sexual activity not only burns quite a few calories and boosts the metabolism, it also improves immune function, helps you sleep better, and relieves menstrual cramps and stress (Chia & Abrams, 2005). Though we don't yet understand all of the benefits of sex and orgasm, there is mounting evidence that the enjoyment we receive from sex moderates our hormones and improves our emotional state.

Think Critically

- How important is it that each partner experience orgasm? What (if anything) would you say to a sexual partner who never or rarely experienced one?
- Do you believe there are differences in the amount of emphasis that men and women give to orgasm? If so, why? If not, why not?
- How would you feel about your partner faking an orgasm? Would you like to know or not whether your partner actually experienced an orgasm?

to testosterone deficiency in both men and women include decreases in sexual desire, arousability, and orgasmic capacity; diminished motivation; increased fat mass; thinning of body hair; and decreases in muscle mass and strength (Kingsberg, 2002; McNicholas et al., 2003). In spite of widespread claims of testosterone's effect in treating low sex desire in women, in December 2004, the Food and Drug Administration voted against approval of a testosterone patch, citing concerns about the safety of long-term use of the patch and use by groups that have not been adequately studied. Though research has shown that women whose ovaries have been removed and/or who take estrogen could benefit from testosterone therapy, the long-term effects on women's health are not yet known (Allina, 2005a). Regardless, many gynecologists recommend off-label uses of testosterone therapy (Warner, n.d.). Though sexual problems, including low libido and/or sexual dissatisfaction, may have physiological causes, they may also be caused by relationship issues, work fatigue, past experiences, or financial problems. It is necessary to look beyond medical solutions when assisting women who have the courage to confront their sexual dissatisfaction. (Testosterone replacement therapy is discussed in Chapter 7.)

Estrogen also plays a role in sexual functioning, though its effects on sexual desire are not completely understood. In women, estrogen helps to maintain the vaginal lining and lubrication, which can make sex more pleasurable. However, when a woman is given oral estrogen replacement, her serum levels of testosterone are decreased (Johnson, 2002). Men also produce small amounts of estrogen, whose functions are to facilitate the maturation of sperm and maintain bone density. Too much estrogen, however, can cause erection difficulties. Like testosterone replacement, some doctors are also promoting estrogens and bioidentical or natural estrogen supplements to treat conditions caused by estrogen deficiency. The most significant push is aimed at menopausal women. Because no risk-free hormone has ever been identified, claims that human estrogens will protect against cardiovascular effects and other maladies are misleading (Fugh-Berman, 2004). While a number of estrogens are effective treatments for hot flashes and vaginal dryness, any health-promotion claims for these drugs are clearly wrong.

Oxytocin is a hormone more commonly associated with contractions during labor and breast-feeding. It is also increased by nipple stimulation in men and women. This neurotransmitter, which has also been linked to bonding, is released in variable amounts among women during orgasm. It helps us feel connected and promotes touch, affection, and relaxation. Interestingly, oxytocin is important in stimulating the release of all the other sex hormones and, since it peaks during orgasm, is also responsible for the desire to touch or cuddle after orgasm occurs (Chia & Abrams, 2005).

Additionally, a natural form of amphetamine called phenylethylmine (PEA) is produced during early courtship and orgasm (Chia & Abrams, 2005). This substance is associated with excitement and giddiness and may be one reason why so many crave the feelings associated with early romance. Not surprising, low levels are associated with depression but can be artificially stimulated with chocolate.

In spite of what we do know about the importance of biological influences on sexual desire and performance, when biological determinants or evolutionary accounts are given undue weight and psychosocial forces are ignored or minimized, a medical model that negates the significance of culture, relationships, and equality can emerge (Lloyd, 2007; Wood, Koch, & Mansfield, 2006).

Experiencing Sexual Arousal

Those who restrain desire do so because theirs is weak enough to be restrained.

—William Blake
(1757–1827)

For both males and females, physiological changes during sexual excitement depend on two processes: vasocongestion and myotonia. **Vasocongestion** is the concentration of blood in body tissues. For example, blood fills the genital regions of both males and females, causing the penis to become erect and the clitoris to swell. **Myotonia** is increased muscle tension accompanying the approach of orgasm; upon orgasm, the body undergoes involuntary muscle contractions and then relaxes. The sexual response pattern remains the same for all forms of sexual behavior, whether autoerotic or sex with a partner, heterosexual or homosexual. Nevertheless, approximately 14% of women report problems related to arousal (Leland, 2000).

Sexual Excitement   Some women do not separate sexual desire from arousal (Tiefer, 2004). Additionally, many seem to care less about physical arousal but rather place more emphasis on the relational and emotional aspects of intimacy. In any case, for women, one of the first signs of sexual excitement is the moistening of the vaginal walls through a process called **sweating.** Some women also report "tingling" in the genital area. Caused by lymphatic fluids pushing through the vaginal walls during vasocongestion, these secretions lubricate the vagina, enabling it to encompass the penis or other object easily. The upper two thirds of the vagina expands in a process called **tenting;** the vagina expands about an inch in length and doubles its width. The labia minora begin to protrude outside the labia majora during sexual excitement, and breathing and heart rate increase. These signs do not occur on a specific timetable; each woman has her own pattern of arousal, which may vary under different conditions, with different partners, and so on.

Contractions raise the uterus, but the clitoris remains virtually unchanged during this early phase. Although the clitoris responds more slowly than the penis to vasocongestion, it is still affected. The initial changes, however, are minor. Clitoral tumescence (swelling) occurs simultaneously with engorgement of the labia minora. During masturbation and oral sex, the clitoris is generally stimulated directly. During intercourse, clitoral stimulation is mostly indirect, caused by the clitoral hood being pulled over the clitoris or by pressure in the general clitoral area. At the same time that these changes are occurring in the genitals, the breasts are also responding. The nipples become erect, and the breasts may enlarge somewhat because of the engorgement of blood vessels; the areolae may also enlarge. Many women (and men) experience a **scx flush,** a darkening of the skin or rash that temporarily appears as a result of blood rushing to the skin's surface during sexual excitement.

As excitement increases, the clitoris retracts beneath the clitoral hood and virtually disappears. The labia minora become progressively larger until they double or triple in size. They deepen in color, becoming pink, bright red, or a deep wine-red color, depending on the woman's skin color. This intense coloring is sometimes referred to as the "sex skin." When it appears, orgasm is imminent. Meanwhile, the vaginal opening and lower third of the vagina decrease in size as they become more congested with blood. This thickening of the walls, which occurs in the plateau stage of the sexual response cycle, is known as the **orgasmic platform.** The upper two thirds of the vagina continues to expand, but lubrication decreases or may even stop. The uterus becomes fully elevated through muscular contractions.

Changes in the breasts continue. The areolae become larger even as the nipples decrease in relative size. If the woman has not breast-fed, her breasts may increase by up to 25% of their unaroused size; women who have breast-fed may have little change in size.

Orgasm   Continued stimulation brings **orgasm,** a peak sensation of intense pleasure that creates an altered state of consciousness and is accompanied by involuntary, rhythmic uterine and anal contractions, myotonia, and a state of well-being and contentment (Meston, Levin, Spiski, Hull, & Heiman, 2004). The upper two thirds of the vagina does not contract; instead, it continues its tenting effect. The labia do not change during orgasm, nor do the breasts. Heart and respiratory rates and blood pressure reach their peak during orgasm. (For a review of the literature related to the nature of orgasm, see Meston et al., 2004.)

The reason so many women fake orgasms is that so many men fake foreplay.

—Graffito

What is the earth? What are the body and soul without satisfaction?

—Walt Whitman
(1819–1892)

After orgasm, the orgasmic platform rapidly subsides. The clitoris reemerges from beneath the clitoral hood. If a woman does not have an orgasm once she is sexually aroused, the clitoris may remain engorged for several hours, possibly creating a feeling of frustration. A similar reaction can occur among men and is commonly called "blue balls." The labia slowly return to their unaroused state, and the sex flush gradually disappears. About 30–40% of women perspire as the body begins to cool.

Interestingly, when women and men are asked to use adjectives to describe their experience of orgasm, data suggest that, beyond the awareness of ejaculation that men report, their sensations bear more similarities than differences (Mah & Binik, 2002).

Following ejaculation, men experience a refractory period, in which they are unable to ejaculate again. In contrast, women are often physiologically able to be orgasmic immediately following the previous orgasm. As a result, women can have repeated orgasms, also called multiple orgasms, if they continue to be stimulated. Though findings vary on the percentage of women who experience multiple orgasms (estimates range from 14% to 40%), what is clear is that wide variability exists among women and within any one woman from one time to another.

Final Thoughts

In the next chapter, we discuss the anatomical features and physiological functions that characterize men's sexuality and sexual response. The information in these two chapters should serve as a comprehensive basis for understanding the material that follows.

Summary

Female Sex Organs: What Are They For?

- All embryos appear as female at first. Genetic and hormonal signals trigger the development of male organs in those embryos destined to be male.

- Sex organs serve a reproductive purpose, but they perform other functions also: giving pleasure, attracting sex partners, and bonding in relationships.

- The external female *genitals* are known collectively as the *vulva*. The *mons pubis* is a pad of fatty tissue that covers the area of the pubic bone. The *clitoris* is the center of sexual arousal. The *labia majora* are two folds of spongy flesh extending from the mons pubis and enclosing the other external genitals. The *labia minora* are smooth, hairless folds within the labia majora that meet above the clitoris.

- The internal female sexual structures and reproductive organs include the *vagina,* the *uterus,* the *cervix,* the *ovaries,* and the *fallopian tubes.* The vagina is a flexible muscular organ that encompasses the penis or other object during sexual expression and is the *birth canal* through which an infant is born. The opening of the vagina, the *introitus,* is partially covered by a thin, perforated membrane, the *hymen,* prior to first intercourse or other intrusion.

- Many women report the existence of an erotically sensitive area, the *Grafenberg spot (G-spot),* on the front wall of the vagina midway between the introitus and the cervix.

- The *uterus,* or womb, is a hollow, thick-walled, muscular organ; the tapered end, the *cervix,* extends downward and opens into the vagina. The lining of the uterine walls, the *endometrium,* is built up and then shed and expelled through the cervical *os* (opening) during menstruation. In the event of pregnancy, the pre-embryo is embedded in the nourishing endometrium. On each side of the uterus is one of a pair of *ovaries,* the female *gonads* (organs that produce *gametes,* sex cells containing the genetic material necessary for reproduction). At the top of the uterus are the *fallopian tubes,* or uterine tubes. They extend toward the ovaries but are not attached to them. The funnel-shaped end of each tube (the *infundibulum*) fans out into fingerlike *fimbriae,* which drape over the ovary. Hairlike *cilia* on the fimbriae transport the ovulated *oocyte* (egg) into the fallopian tube. The *ampulla* is the widened part of the tube in which fertilization normally occurs. Other important structures in the area of the genitals include the *urethra, anus,* and *perineum.*

- The reproductive function of the female breasts, or *mammary glands,* is to nourish the offspring through *lactation,* or milk production. A breast is composed of fatty tissue and 15–25 lobes that radiate around a central protruding nipple. *Alveoli* within the lobes produce milk. Around the nipple is a ring of darkened skin called the *areola.*

Female Sexual Physiology

- *Hormones* are chemical substances that serve as messengers, traveling through the bloodstream. Important hormones that act directly on the gonads (*gonadotropins*) are *follicle-stimulating hormone (FSH)* and *luteinizing hormone (LH).* Hormones produced in the ovaries are *estrogen,* which helps regulate the menstrual cycle, and *progesterone,*

which helps maintain the uterine lining, until menstruation occurs.

- At birth, the human female's ovaries contain approximately half a million *oocytes,* or female gametes. During childhood, many of these degenerate. In a woman's lifetime, about 400 oocytes will mature and be released, beginning in puberty when hormones trigger the completion of *oogenesis,* the production of oocytes, commonly called eggs or ova.

- The activities of the ovaries and the development of oocytes for ovulation, the expulsion of the oocyte, are described as the three-phase *ovarian cycle,* which is usually about 28 days long. The phases are *follicular* (maturation of the oocyte), *ovulatory* (expulsion of the oocyte), and *luteal* (hormone production by the corpus luteum).

- The *menstrual cycle* (or uterine cycle), like the ovarian cycle, is divided into three phases. The shedding of the endometrium marks the beginning of the *menstrual phase.* The menstrual flow, or *menses,* generally occurs over a period of 3–5 days. Endometrial tissue builds up during the *proliferative phase;* it produces nutrients to sustain an embryo in the *secretory phase.*

- Women who live or work together often develop similarly timed menstrual cycles, called *menstrual synchrony.*

- The most severe menstrual problems have been attributed to *premenstrual syndrome (PMS),* a cluster of physical, psychological, and emotional symptoms that many women experience 7–14 days before their menstrual period. Some women experience very heavy bleeding (*menorrhagia*), while others have pelvic cramping and pain during the menstrual cycle (*dysmenorrhea*). When women do not menstruate for reasons other than aging, the condition is called *amenorrhea.* Principal causes of amenorrhea are pregnancy and nursing.

Female Sexual Response

- *Masters and Johnson's four-phase model of sexual response* identifies the significant stages of response as excitement, plateau, orgasm, and resolution. *Kaplan's tri-phasic model of sexual response* consists of three phases: desire, excitement, and orgasm. *Loulan's sexual response model* includes both biological and affective components in a six-stage cycle.

- The physical manifestations of sexual arousal involve a complex interaction of thoughts and feelings, sensory perceptions, neural responses, and hormonal reactions occurring in many parts of the body. For both males and females, physiological changes during sexual excitement depend on two processes: *vasocongestion,* the concentration of blood in body tissues; and *myotonia,* increased muscle tension with approaching orgasm.

- For women, an early sign of sexual excitement is the moistening, or *sweating,* of the vaginal walls. The upper two thirds of the vagina expands in a process called *tenting;* the labia may enlarge or flatten and separate; the clitoris swells. Breathing and heart rate increase. The nipples become erect, and the breasts may enlarge somewhat. The uterus elevates. As excitement increases, the clitoris retracts beneath the clitoral hood. The vaginal opening decreases by about one third, and its outer third becomes more congested, forming the *orgasmic platform.*

- Continued stimulation brings *orgasm,* a peak sensation of intense pleasure that creates an altered state of consciousness and is accompanied by contractions, myotonia, and a state of well-being and contentment. Women are often able to be orgasmic following a previous orgasm if they continue to be stimulated.

Questions for Discussion

- Are changes in mood that may occur during a woman's menstrual cycle caused by biological factors, or are they learned? What evidence supports your response?

- Given the choice between the environmentally friendly menstruation products and commercial products, which would you choose for yourself (or recommend to a woman), and why?

- If another adult were to ask you, "What is an orgasm?", how would you reply? If the person were to proceed to ask you how to induce one in a woman, what would you say?

- What are your thoughts and reactions to learning about the Grafenberg spot? Do you believe it is an invented erotic spot for some women or a genuine gland or erogenous zone?

- Do you believe that it is nature or nurture that contributes to a woman's response to sexual stimulation? What evidence supports your response?

- For women only: What is your response to looking at your genitals? For men only: What is your response to viewing photos of women's genitals? Why is it that women are discouraged from touching or looking at their genitals?

- How do you feel about the idea of having sex during a woman's menstrual period? Why do you feel this way?

Sex and the Internet

Sexuality and Ethnicity

Of the 304 million people living in the United States, over 154 million are women. Many of these women are in poor health, use fewer reproductive health services, and continue to suffer disproportionately from premature death, disease, and disabilities. In addition, there are tremendous economic, cultural, and social barriers to achieving optimal health. To find out more about the reproductive health risks of special concern to women of color, go to the National Women's Health Information Center Web site: http://www.womenshealth.gov/minority. From the menu, select one ethnic group of women and report on the following:

- One reproductive health concern

- Obstacles women may encounter that would prevent them from obtaining services

- Potential solutions to this problem

Suggested Web Sites

Centers for Disease Control and Prevention
http://www.cdc.gov/health/womensmenu.htm
Provides a wide variety of specific information and links related to all aspects of women's well-being.

Guttmacher Institute
http://www.guttmacher.org
A global research institute that explores aspects of sexuality and relationships.

National Institute of Child Health and Human Development (part of the National Institutes of Health)
http://www.nichd.nih.gov/womenshealth/womenshealth.cfm
Provides a wide-ranging research portfolio on women's health.

National Organization for Women (NOW)
http://www.now.org
An organization of women and men who support full equality for women in truly equal partnerships.

National Women's Health Network
http://www.womenshealthnetwork.org
Provides clear and well-researched information about a variety of women's health- and sexuality-related issues.

North American Menopause Society
http://www.menopause.org
Promotes women's health during midlife and beyond through an understanding of menopause.

Our Bodies, Ourselves
http://www.ourbodiesourselves.org
Provides a multicultural perspective on women's physical and sexual health.

The Women's Sexual Health Foundation
http://www.twshf.org
Focuses on medical treatment and provides a multidisciplinary approach to sexual problems and health.

Suggested Reading

Angier, N. (1999). *Women: An intimate geography*. Boston: Houghton Mifflin. A study that draws on science, medicine, mythology, history, and art to expand the definitions of female geography.

Boston Women's Health Book Collective. (2005). *Our bodies, ourselves: For the new century*. New York: Touchstone. A thorough, accurate, and proactive women's text covering a broad range of health, and sexuality-related issues.

Daniluk, J. C. (2003). *Women's sexuality across the life span*. New York: Guilford Press. Explores how women express their sexuality and the meanings they ascribe to it.

Komisaruk, B. R., Beyer-Flores, C., & Whipple, B. (2006). *The science of orgasm*. Baltimore: Johns Hopkins University Press. Explores the complex biological process behind orgasm.

Lloyd, E. (2005). *The case of the female orgasm*. Cambridge, MA: Harvard University Press. Argues that female orgasms are simply artifacts.

Ogden, G. (2006). *Heart and soul of sex: Making the ISIS connection*. Boston: Trumpter. Explores women's sexual experiences, holistically and with academic rigor.

Wingood, G., & DiClemente, R. (Eds.). (2002). *Handbook of women's sexual and reproductive health*. New York: Kluwer Academic/Plenum. A sourcebook for women's sexuality.

For links, articles, and study material, go to the McGraw-Hill Web site, located at **www.mhhe.com/yarber7e.**

chapter 4

Male Sexual Anatomy, Physiology, and Response

MAIN TOPICS

Male Sex Organs: What Are They For?

Male Sexual Physiology

Male Sexual Response

Student Voices

C LEARLY, MALE SEXUAL STRUCTURES and functions differ in many ways from those of females. What may not be as apparent, however, is that there are also a number of similarities in the functions of the sex organs and the sexual response patterns of men and women. In the previous chapter, we learned that the sexual structures of both females and males derive from the same embryonic tissue. But when this tissue receives the signals to begin differentiation into a male, the embryonic reproductive organs begin to change their appearance dramatically.

" Behold—the penis mightier than the sword.

—Mark Twain
(1835–1910)

● Male Sex Organs: What Are They For?

Like female sex organs, male sex organs serve several functions. In their reproductive role, a man's sex organs manufacture and store gametes and can deliver them to a woman's reproductive tract. Some of the organs, especially the penis, provide a source of physical pleasure for both the man and his partner.

External Structures

The external male sexual structures are the penis and the scrotum.

The Penis The **penis** (from the Latin word for tail) is the organ through which both sperm and urine pass. It is attached to the male perineum, the diamond-shaped region extending from the base of the scrotum to the anus.

• FIGURE 4.1
External Male Sexual Structures

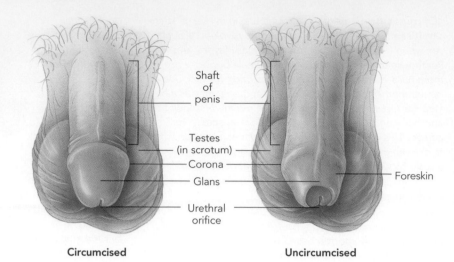

Circumcised   Uncircumcised

Is size important? Click on "Male Anatomy" to hear men talking honestly about penis size.

The penis consists of three main sections: the root, the shaft, and the head (see Figure 4.1). The **root** attaches the penis within the pelvic cavity; the body of the penis, the **shaft,** hangs free. At the end of the shaft is the head of the penis, the **glans penis,** and at its tip is the **urethral orifice,** for semen ejaculation or urine excretion. The rim at the base of the glans is known as the **corona** (Spanish for crown). On the underside of the penis is a triangular area of sensitive skin called the **frenulum** (FREN-you-lem), which attaches the glans to the foreskin. The glans penis is particularly important in sexual arousal because it contains a relatively high concentration of nerve endings, making it especially responsive to stimulation.

A loose skin covers the shaft of the penis and extends to cover the glans penis; this sleevelike covering is known as the **foreskin** or **prepuce** (PREE-pews). It can be pulled back easily to expose the glans. In the United States, the foreskins of male infants are often surgically removed by a procedure called **circumcision.** As a result of this procedure, the glans penis is left exposed. The reasons for circumcision seem to be rooted more in tradition and religious beliefs (it is an important ritual in Judaism and Islam) than in any firmly established health principles. Beneath the foreskin are several small glands that produce a cheesy substance called **smegma.** If smegma accumulates, it thickens, produces a foul odor, and can become granular and irritate the penis, causing discomfort and infection. It is important for uncircumcised adult males to observe good hygiene by periodically retracting the skin and washing the glans to remove the smegma. (For further discussion of circumcision, see Chapters 12 and 15.)

The shaft of the penis contains three parallel columns of erectile tissue. The two that extend along the front surface are known as the **corpora cavernosa** (KOR-por-a kav-er-NO-sa; cavernous bodies), and the third, which runs beneath them, is called the **corpus spongiosum** (KOR-pus spun-gee-OH-sum; spongy body), which also forms the glans (see Figure 4.2). At the root of the penis, the corpora cavernosa form the **crura** (KROO-ra), which are anchored by muscle to the pubic bone. The **urethra,** a tube that transports both urine and semen, runs from the bladder (where it expands to form the **urethral bulb**), through the spongy body, to the tip of the penis, where it opens to the outside. Inside the three chambers are a large number of blood vessels through which blood freely circulates when the penis is flaccid (relaxed). During sexual arousal, these vessels fill with blood and expand, causing the penis to become erect. (Sexual arousal, including erection, is discussed in greater detail later in the chapter.)

(Top of penis)

Corpora cavernosa

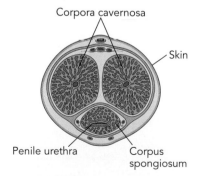

Skin

Penile urethra

Corpus spongiosum

• **FIGURE 4.2**

Cross Section of the Shaft of the Penis

The Penis: More Than Meets the Eye

Man's preoccupation with his "generative organ" extends far back into history and appears in diverse cultures all over the world. The penis is an almost universal symbol of power and fertility. It may also be a source of considerable pleasure and anxiety for the individuals who happen to possess one.

Power to the Penis

Earthenware figurines from ancient Peru, ink drawings from medieval Japan, painted walls in the villas of Pompeii—in the art and artifacts from every corner of the world, we find a common theme: penises! And not just any old penises, but organs of such length, girth, and weight that they can barely be supported by their possessors. Whether as an object of worship or an object of jest, the giant penis has been (and continues to be) a symbol that holds deep cultural significance, especially in societies in which men are dominant over women. Although it seems reasonable for the erect penis to be used as a symbol of love, or at least lust, many of its associations appear to be as an instrument of aggression and power. In New Guinea, Kiwai hunters pressed their penises against the trees from which they would make their harpoons, thereby ensuring the strength and straightness of their weapons. Maori warriors in New Zealand crawled under the legs of their chief so that the power of his penis would descend onto them (Strage, 1980).

In many cultures, the penis has also represented fertility and prosperity. In India, large stone phalluses (*lingams*), associated with the Hindu god Shiva, are adorned with flowers and propitiated with offerings. Ancient peoples as diverse as the Maya in Central America and the Egyptians in North Africa believed that the blood from the penises of their rulers was especially powerful. Mayan kings ceremonially pierced their penises with stingray spines, and the pharaohs and high priests of Egypt underwent ritual circumcision. In other places, men have ritually offered their semen to ensure a plentiful harvest.

"Phallic Phallacies"

It is interesting (but perhaps not surprising) that the responsibility of owning an instrument of great power can carry with it an equally great burden of anxiety. In some ways, the choice of the penis as a symbol of domination seems rather unwise. Any man (and a good many women) can tell you that a penis can be disturbingly unreliable and appear to have a mind of its own. For men who are already insecure about their abilities on the job or in the bedroom, the penis can take on meanings quite beyond those of procreation, elimination, or sensual pleasure. How can a man be expected to control his employees or his children when he can't control the behavior of his own penis?

As discussed in Chapter 2, Sigmund Freud believed that women are unconsciously jealous of men's penises (penis envy). In reality, those who appear to suffer the most from penis envy are men, who indeed possess a penis but often seem to long for a bigger one. The idea that "the larger the penis, the more effective the male in coital connection" is referred to by Masters and Johnson as a "phallic phallacy" (Masters & Johnson, 1966). Perhaps not surprising, girth, as opposed to length, has been judged as being more important to women in one study (Stulhofer, 2006).

Another manifestation of penile anxiety, also named by Freud, is castration anxiety (see Chapter 2). This term is misleading, for it does not describe what the actual fear is about. Castration is the removal of the testes, but castration anxiety is fear of losing the penis. In China and other parts of Asia, there have been documented epidemics of *koro* (a Japanese term), the conviction that one's penis is shrinking and is going to disappear. Otherwise known as genital retraction syndrome, this malady has no physiological basis and appears to be most common in anxiety-prone men (Dzokoto & Adams, 2005).

For his own psyche's sake, as well as the sake of his partner and that of society, a man would do well to consider how his feelings about his penis and his masculinity affect his well-being. Additionally, he might consider learning that there is a wide variation in penis size—and understanding that he is in that range. At this point, we can only speculate, but perhaps there will come a time when men allow themselves to focus less on the size and performance of their "equipment" and more on acceptance, communication, and the mutual sharing of pleasure.

Think Critically

- What type of symbolism, if any, do you attribute to the penis?
- How would you describe the significance of the penis in U.S. culture to a person from another culture?
- Do you feel that men's preoccupation with their penis size is comparable to a preoccupation of women with their breast size? Explain.

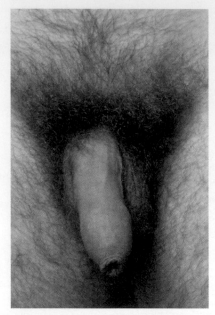
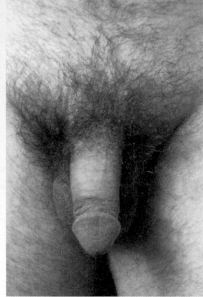
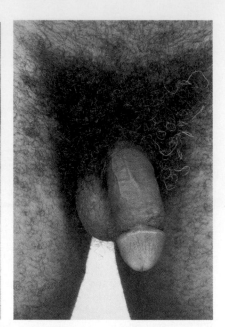

There is great variation in the appearance, size, and shape of the male genitalia. Note that the penis on the left is not circumcised.

It can safely be said that the adult male population suffers an almost universal anxiety in regard to penile size.

—James F. Glenn, MD

In men, the urethra serves as the passageway for both urine and semen. Because the urinary opening is at the tip of the penis, it is vulnerable to injury and infection. The sensitive mucous membranes around the opening may be subject to abrasion and can provide an entrance into the body for infectious organisms. Condoms, properly used, can provide an effective barrier between this vulnerable area and potentially infectious secretions or other substances.

In an unaroused state, the *average* penis is slightly under 3 inches long, although there is a great deal of individual variation. When erect, penises become more uniform in size, as the percentage of volume increase is greater with smaller penises than with larger ones. Cold air or water, fear, and anxiety, for example, often cause the penis to temporarily be pulled closer to the body and to decrease in size. When the penis is erect, the urinary duct is temporarily blocked, allowing for the ejaculation of semen. But erection does not necessarily mean sexual excitement. A man may have erections at night during REM sleep, the phase of the sleep cycle when dreaming occurs, or when he is anxious.

Myths and misconceptions about the penis abound, especially among men. Many people believe that the size of a man's penis is directly related to his masculinity, aggressiveness, sexual ability, or sexual attractiveness. Others believe that there is a relationship between the size of a man's penis and the size of his hands, feet, thumbs, or nose. In fact, the size of the penis is not specifically related to body size or weight, muscular structure, race or ethnicity, or sexual orientation; it is determined by individual hereditary factors. Except in very rare and extreme cases, there is no relationship between penis size and a man's ability to have sexual intercourse or to satisfy his partner.

The Scrotum   Hanging loosely at the root of the penis is the **scrotum,** a pouch of skin that holds the two testicles. The skin of the scrotum is more heavily pigmented than the skin elsewhere on the body; it is sparsely covered with hair and divided in the middle by a ridge of skin. The skin of the scrotum varies in appearance under different conditions. When a man is sexually aroused, for example, or

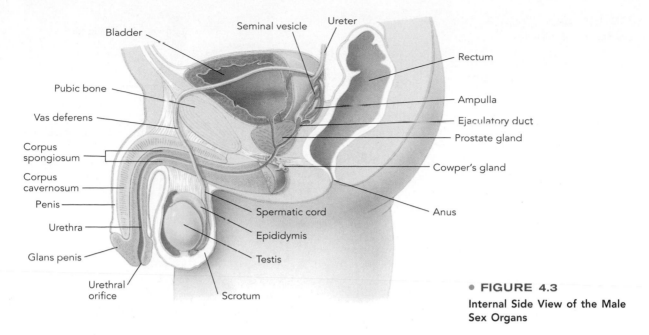

FIGURE 4.3
Internal Side View of the Male Sex Organs

Labels: Bladder, Seminal vesicle, Ureter, Rectum, Pubic bone, Ampulla, Vas deferens, Ejaculatory duct, Prostate gland, Corpus spongiosum, Cowper's gland, Corpus cavernosum, Penis, Anus, Urethra, Spermatic cord, Epididymis, Glans penis, Testis, Urethral orifice, Scrotum

when he is cold, the testicles are pulled close to the body, causing the skin to wrinkle and become more compact. The changes in the surface of the scrotum help maintain a fairly constant temperature within the testicles (about 93°F). Two sets of muscles control these changes: (1) the dartos muscle, a smooth muscle under the skin that contracts and causes the surface to wrinkle, and (2) the fibrous cremaster muscle within the scrotal sac that causes the testes to elevate.

Internal Structures

Male internal reproductive organs and structures include the testes (testicles), seminiferous tubules, epididymis, vas deferens, ejaculatory ducts, seminal vesicles, prostate gland, and Cowper's (bulbourethral) glands (see Figure 4.3).

The Testes   Inside the scrotum are the male reproductive glands or gonads, which are called **testicles** or **testes** (singular, *testis*). The testes have two major functions: sperm production and hormone production. Each olive-shaped testis is about 1.5 inches long and 1 inch in diameter and weighs about 1 ounce; in adulthood and as a male ages, the testes decrease in size and weight. The testicles are usually not symmetrical; the left testicle generally hangs slightly lower than the right one. Within the scrotal sac, each testicle is suspended by a **spermatic cord** containing nerves, blood vessels, and a vas deferens (see Figure 4.4). Within each testicle are around 1,000 **seminiferous tubules,** tiny, tightly compressed tubes 1–3 feet long (they would extend several hundred yards if laid end to end). Within these tubes, spermatogenesis—the production of sperm—takes place.

As a male fetus grows, the testes develop within the pelvic cavity; toward the end of the gestation period, the testes usually descend into the scrotum. In about 3–4% of cases and up to 30% of premature male infants, one or both of the testes fail to descend, a condition known as cryptorchidism. This usually corrects itself within a year or two (Ferrer & McKenna, 2000). If this condition is not corrected before puberty, usually by surgery or hormones, sperm will be less likely to mature because of the higher temperatures in the abdomen.

Nowhere does one read of a penis that quietly moseyed out for a look at what was going on before springing and crashing into action.

—Bernie Zilbergeld
(1939–2002)

Click on "The Testes" to see microscopic views of human sperm and the tubules in the testes.

• FIGURE 4.4
Cross Section of a Testicle

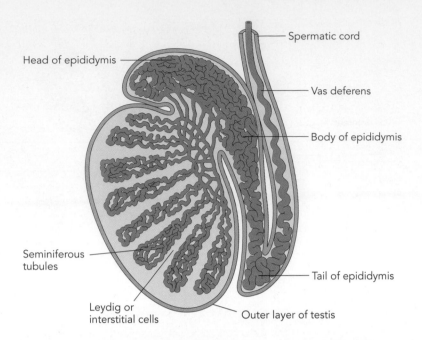

Spermatic cord

Head of epididymis

Vas deferens

Body of epididymis

Seminiferous tubules

Tail of epididymis

Leydig or interstitial cells

Outer layer of testis

Click on "Vasectomy" for a look at male genitals, and to see a vasectomy performed.

> My brain. It's my second favorite organ.
>
> —Woody Allen
> (1935–)

The Epididymis and Vas Deferens The epididymis and vas deferens (or ductus deferens) are the ducts that carry sperm from the testicles to the urethra for ejaculation. The seminiferous tubules merge to form the **epididymis** (ep-e-DID-i-mes), a comma-shaped structure consisting of a coiled tube about 20 feet long, where the sperm finally mature. Each epididymis merges into a **vas deferens,** a tube about 18 inches long, extending into the abdominal cavity, over the bladder, and then downward, widening into the flask-shaped **ampulla.** The vas deferens joins the **ejaculatory duct** within the prostate gland. The vas deferens can be felt easily in the scrotal sac. Because it is easily accessible and is crucial for sperm transport, it is usually the point of sterilization for men. The operation is called a vasectomy (discussed fully in Chapter 11). A vasectomy does not affect the libido or the ability to ejaculate because only the sperm are transported through the vas deferens. Most of the semen that is ejaculated comes from the prostate gland and the seminal vesicles.

The Seminal Vesicles, Prostate Gland, and Cowper's Glands At the back of the bladder lie two glands, each about the size and shape of a finger. These **seminal vesicles** secrete a fluid that makes up about 60% of the seminal fluid. Encircling the urethra just below the bladder is a small muscular gland about the size and shape of a chestnut called the **prostate gland,** which produces about 30–35% of the seminal fluid in the ejaculated semen. These secretions flow into the urethra through a system of tiny ducts. Some men who enjoy receiving anal sex experience erotic sensations when the prostate is gently stroked; others find that contact with the prostate is uncomfortable. Men, especially if they are older, may be troubled by a variety of prostate problems, ranging from relatively benign conditions to more serious inflammations and prostate cancer. (Problems and diseases of the prostate are covered in Chapter 13.)

Below the prostate gland are two pea-sized glands connected to the urethra by tiny ducts. These are **Cowper's** or **bulbourethral** (bul-bo-you-REE-thrul) **glands,** which secrete a thick, clear mucus prior to **ejaculation,** the process by which semen is forcefully expelled from the penis. This fluid may appear at the tip of the erect penis; its alkaline content may help buffer the acidity within the urethra and provide

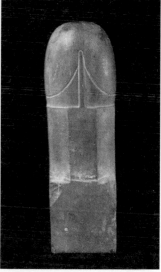

a more hospitable environment for sperm. Fluid from the Cowper's glands may contain sperm that have remained in the urethra since a previous ejaculation or that have leaked in from the ampullae. Consequently, it is possible for a pregnancy to occur from sperm left over even if the penis is withdrawn before ejaculation.

The penis is a prominent symbol in both ancient and modern art. Here we see a contemporary phallic sculpture in Frogner Park, Oslo, Norway, and a stone *lingam* from Thailand.

The Breasts and Anus

Male anatomical structures that do not serve a reproductive function but that may be involved in or affected by sexual activities include the breasts, urethra, buttocks, rectum, and anus.

Although the male breast contains the same basic structures as the female breast—nipple, areola, fat, and glandular tissue—the amounts of underlying fatty and glandular tissues are much smaller in men. Our culture appears to be ambivalent about the erotic function of men's breasts, but it does appear to place emphasis on their appearance. We usually do not even call them breasts, but refer to the general area as the chest or "pecs." Some men find stimulation of their breasts to be sexually arousing; others do not. **Gynecomastia** (gine-a-ko-MAS-tee-a), the swelling or enlargement of the male breast, caused by an estrogen imbalance, can occur during adolescence or adulthood. In puberty, gynecomastia is a normal response to hormonal changes (see Chapter 6). In adulthood, its causes may include alcoholism, liver or thyroid disease, and cancer. Probably not surprising in this perfection-driven society is the rise in pectoral implants among men who wish to have sculpted chests (Guthmann, 2008). Though still a niche market, some men are finding these semisolid silicon implants to be a confidence booster. The risks of the procedure are similar to those of female implant procedures (migration, infection, loss of feelings around the nipple) and the costs, ranging from $7,000 to $12,000 per pair, should be seriously considered before a man elects to have this surgery.

An organ used primarily for excretion, the anus can also be used by both men and women for sexual purposes. Because the anus is kept tightly closed by the external and internal anal sphincters, most of the erotic sensation that occurs during anal sex is derived from the penetration of the anal opening. Beyond the sphincters lies a larger space, the rectum. In men, the prostate gland is located in front of the rectum, and stimulation of this and nearby structures

Male breasts, which are usually referred to euphemistically as "the chest" or "pecs," may or may not be considered erotic areas. Men are allowed to display their naked breasts in certain public settings. Whether the sight is sexually arousing depends on the viewer and the context.

Table 4.1 • Summary Table of Male Sexual Anatomy	
External Structures	
Penis	Organ through which both sperm and urine pass
Root of penis	Attaches the penis within the pelvic cavity
Shaft	Body of the penis that hangs free
Glans penis	Enlarged head of the penis
Corona	Rim at the base of the glans
Frenulum	A triangular area of sensitive skin that attaches the glans to the foreskin
Foreskin (prepuce)	Loose skin or sleevelike covering of the glans. The removal of the foreskin in male infants is called circumcision.
Corpora cavernosa	Two parallel columns of erectile tissue that extend along the front surface of the penis
Corpus spongiosum	One of three parallel columns of erectile tissue that runs beneath the corpora cavernosa, surrounds the urethra, and forms the glans
Crura	Root of the penis that is anchored by muscle to the pubic bone
Urethra	Tube that transports both urine and semen and runs from the bladder
Scrotum	Pouch of loose skin that holds the two testicles
Internal Structures	
Testes (testicles)	Male reproductive glands or gonads whose major functions are sperm and hormone production
Spermatic cord	Located within the scrotal sac; suspends each testicle and contains nerves, blood vessels, and a vas deferens
Seminiferous tubules	Tiny, highly compressed tubes where the production of sperm takes place
Epididymis	Merged from the seminiferous tubules, a comma-shaped structure where the sperm mature
Vas deferens	A tube that extends into the abdominal cavity and carries the sperm from the testicles to the urethra for ejaculation
Ampulla	Widened section of the vas deferens
Ejaculatory duct	One of two structures within the prostate gland connecting to the vas deferens
Seminal vesicle	One of two glands at the back of the bladder that together secrete about 60% of the seminal fluid
Prostate gland	Produces about 30–35% of the seminal fluid in the ejaculated semen
Cowper's glands	Also called bulbourethral glands; secrete a clear, thick, alkaline mucus prior to ejaculation

can be very pleasing. Because the anus and rectum do not provide significant amounts of lubrication, most people use some sort of water-based lubricant for penetrative sexual activity. Both men and women may enjoy oral stimulation of the anus ("rimming"); the insertion of fingers, a hand ("fisting"), a dildo, or a penis into the rectum may bring erotic pleasure to both the receiver and the giver. (Anal sex is discussed more fully in Chapter 9; safer sex guidelines appear in Chapter 15. Table 4.1 provides a summary of male sexual anatomy.)

● Male Sexual Physiology

The reproductive processes of the male body include the manufacture of hormones and the production and delivery of sperm. Although men do not have a monthly reproductive cycle comparable to that of women, they do experience

Table 4.2 ● **Male Reproductive Hormones**

Hormone	Where Produced	Functions
Testosterone	Testes, adrenal glands	Stimulates sperm production in testes, triggers development of secondary sex characteristics, regulates sex drive
GnRH	Hypothalamus	Stimulates pituitary during sperm production
FSH	Pituitary	Stimulates sperm production in testes
ICSH (LH)	Pituitary	Stimulates testosterone production in interstitial cells within testes
Inhibin	Testes	Regulates sperm production by inhibiting release of FSH
Oxytocin	Hypothalamus, testes	Stimulates contractions in the internal reproductive organs to move the contents of the tubules forward; influences sexual response and emotional attraction
Relaxin	Prostate	Increases sperm motility

regular fluctuations of hormone levels; there is also some evidence that men's moods follow a cyclical pattern.

Sex Hormones

Within the connective tissues of a man's testes are **Leydig cells** (also called interstitial cells), which secrete **androgens** (male hormones). The most important of these is testosterone, which triggers sperm production and regulates the sex drive. Other important hormones in male reproductive physiology are GnRH, FSH, and LH. In addition, men produce the protein hormone inhibin, oxytocin, and small amounts of estrogen. (Table 4.2 describes the principal hormones involved in sperm production and their functions.)

Testosterone Testosterone is a steroid hormone synthesized from cholesterol. Testosterone is made by both sexes—by women mostly in the adrenal glands (located above the kidneys) and ovaries and by men primarily in the testes. Furthermore, the brain converts testosterone to estradiol (a female hormone). This flexibility of the hormone makes the link between testosterone and behavior precarious.

During puberty, besides acting on the seminiferous tubules to produce sperm, testosterone targets other areas of the body. It causes the penis, testicles, and other reproductive organs to grow and is responsible for the development of **secondary sex characteristics,** those changes to parts of the body other than the genitals that indicate sexual maturity. In men, these changes include the growth of pubic, facial, underarm, and other body hair and the deepening of the voice. (In women, estrogen and progesterone combine to develop secondary sex characteristics such as breast development, growth of pubic and underarm hair, and the onset of vaginal mucous secretions.) Testosterone also influences the growth of bones and increase of muscle mass and causes the skin to thicken and become oilier (leading to acne in many teenage boys).

Many researchers do see a correlation between testosterone and personality. It has been found to correspond with energy, confidence, and sexual drive (Sullivan, 2000). What complicates this equation, however, is the fact that testosterone levels vary according to what specific components of the hormone testosterone were measured and the fact that levels are rarely stable; they appear to respond positively

> *Women say it's not how much men have, but what we do with it. How many things can we do with it? What is it, a Cuisinart? It's got two speeds: forward and reverse.*
>
> —Richard Jeni

Sexual Health Care: What Do Men Need?

Because men do not get pregnant or bear children, and because condom use is possible without medical intervention, men's sexual and reproductive health needs are not as obvious as women's and often are ignored. In recent years, however, the high incidence of HIV and sexually transmitted infections and concerns regarding the role of males in teenage pregnancies and births have begun to alter this trend. Clearly, a movement toward a more holistic and broad-based approach to sexual and reproductive health care for men is still needed.

Here are some facts you may or may not know about the sexual health of men (Alan Guttmacher Institute, 2005a):

- Men in the United States spend an average of 10 years being sexually active and unmarried.
- Only about 14% of men ages 15–49 make a sexual and reproductive health visit each year; young men are the least likely to make this visit.
- Most men who have had more than one sex partner did not use a condom the first time they had sex.

From adolescence on, most men need information and referrals for their sexual and reproductive concerns. Unfortunately, health insurance often does not cover the services men need, and a high proportion of men, particularly low-income men, do not have health insurance. Thus, there are significant gaps between needs and services. Furthermore, few health professionals are specifically trained to provide men with sexual and reproductive health education and services. Men's reproductive health involves both their own well-being and their ability to engage in healthy, fulfilling relationships. To achieve this, men need the following:

- Information and education about contraceptive use, pregnancy, and childbearing
- Education about and access to routine screening and treatment for sexually transmitted infections
- Information about where to obtain and how to use condoms correctly
- Counseling and support regarding how to talk about these issues with partners
- Surgical services for vasectomies, screening and treatment for reproductive cancers (particularly prostate and testicular cancer), sexual problems, and infertility treatment

Additionally, skills development related to self-advocacy, risk assessment and avoidance, resistance to peer pressure, communication with partners, fatherhood skills, and role expectations are both needed and desired.

The complex relationships between poverty, high-risk behaviors, and poor health outcomes are undeniable for both men and women. Helping men lead healthier sexual and reproductive lives is a goal that is garnering attention and legitimacy. What is increasingly seen as good for men in their own right should turn out to be just as good for their partners—to the ultimate benefit of society as a whole.

(For more on men's health, see *In Their Own Right: Addressing the Sexual and Reproductive Health Needs of American Men* (2002) at the Alan Guttmacher Institute Web site: http://guttmacher.org/pubs/summaries/exs_men.pdf.)

or negatively to almost every challenge, and not necessarily in a way we might predict. Consequently, if a man suspects he has a testosterone deficiency, he would be wise to have his bioavailable testosterone levels assessed (Tunuguntla, 2005).

The increasing research about testosterone and its derivatives, the anabolic-androgenic steroids, has fueled a market for those seeking anti-aging therapies, desiring athletic bodies and performance, and feeling entitled to unfailing and lifelong sexual prowess and fulfillment (Hoberman, 2005). The complex interaction of hormonal, psychological, situational, and physical factors that men experience with age can result in erectile problems, decreased bone density, heart disease, changes in moods, difficulty in thinking, and weakness (Khaw, Dowsett, Folkerd, et al., 2007; Meier, Nguyen, Handelsman, et al., 2008). Some of these symptoms can be reversed with **testosterone replacement therapy;** however, research also indicates that testosterone replacement is associated with increased prostate cancer (DeNoon, 2007). Because of lack of solid evidence, testosterone replacement therapy is recommended only for those who prove to have a deficiency of testosterone, which is common among men with metabolic syndrome—a

The sex organ has a poetic power, like a comet.

—Joan Miró
(1893–1983)

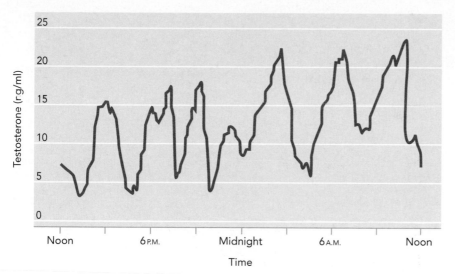

● **FIGURE 4.5**

Testosterone Cycles. Every 2–4 hours, testosterone levels in the blood peak. (*Source: Human Sexuality*, 3rd ed., by LeVay, S., and Baldwin, J. Copyright © 2008 by Sinauer Associates, Inc. Reprinted with permission.)

constellation of risk factors including abdominal fat, high blood sugar, and high blood-fat levels. (For a discussion of male menopause, see Chapter 7.)

Male Cycles   Studies comparing men and women have found that both sexes are subject to changes in mood and behavior patterns (Lips, 2004). Whereas such changes in women are often attributed (rightly or wrongly) to menstrual cycle fluctuations, it is not clear that male changes are related to levels of testosterone or other hormones. Men do appear to undergo cyclic changes, although their testosterone levels do not fluctuate as dramatically as do women's estrogen and progesterone levels. On a daily basis, men's testosterone levels appear to be lowest in the evening and highest in the morning (midnight to noon) (see Figure 4.5) (Winters et al., 2001). Moreover, their overall levels appear to be relatively lower in the spring and higher in the fall.

Throughout the night, specifically during REM sleep, men experience spontaneous penile erections. (Women experience labial, vaginal, and clitoral engorgement.) These erections are sometimes referred to as "battery-recharging mechanisms" for the penis, because they increase blood flow and bring fresh oxygen to the penis. Four or five times a night, both men and women experience this type of engorgement (Goldstein, 2000). If a man has erectile difficulties while he is awake, it is important to determine whether he has normal erections during sleep. If so, his problems may have to do with something other than the physiology of erection. Approximately 90% of men and nearly 40% of women experience **nocturnal orgasms;** for men, these are often referred to as "wet dreams" (Kinsey, Pomeroy, & Martin, 1948; Wells, 1986).

> *Men always want to be a woman's first love—women like to be a man's last romance.*
>
> —Oscar Wilde
> (1854–1900)

Spermatogenesis

Within the testes, from puberty on, **spermatogenesis,** the production of **sperm,** is an ongoing process. Every day, a healthy, fertile man produces several hundred million sperm within the seminiferous tubules of his testicles (see Figure 4.6). After they are formed in the seminiferous tubules, which takes 64–72 days, immature sperm are stored in the epididymis. It then takes about 20 days for the sperm to travel the length of the epididymis, during which time they become fertile and motile (able to move) (see Figure 4.7). Upon ejaculation, sperm in

Spermatogenesis. This diagram shows the development of spermatozoa, beginning with a single spermatogonium and ending with four complete sperm cells. Spermatogenesis is an ongoing process that begins in puberty. Several hundred million sperm are produced every day within the seminiferous tubules of a healthy man.

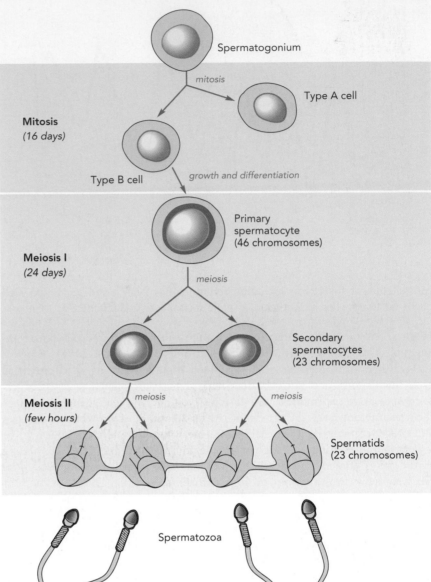

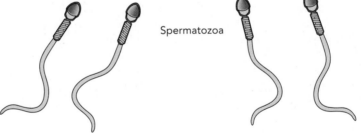

Spermatozoa

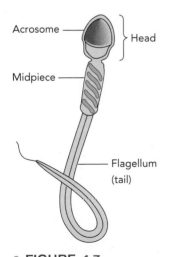

Acrosome — Head
Midpiece
Flagellum (tail)

● FIGURE 4.7

The Human Spermatozoon (Sperm Cell). The head contains the sperm's nucleus, including the chromosomes, and is encased in the helmetlike acrosome.

the tail section of the epididymis are expelled by muscular contractions of its walls into the vas deferens; similar contractions within the vas deferens propel the sperm into the urethra, where they are mixed with semen, also called seminal fluid, and then expelled, or ejaculated, through the urethral orifice.

The sex of the zygote produced by the union of egg and sperm is determined by the chromosomes of the sperm. The ovum always contributes a female sex chromosome (X), whereas the sperm may contribute either a female or a male sex chromosome (Y). The combination of two X chromosomes (XX) means that the zygote will develop as a female; with an X and a Y chromosome (XY), it will develop as a male. In some cases, combinations of sex chromosomes other than XX or XY occur, causing sexual development to proceed differently. (These variations are discussed in Chapter 5.)

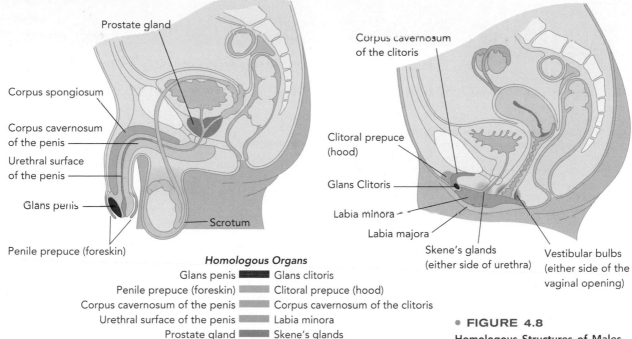

Homologous Organs

Glans penis	Glans clitoris
Penile prepuce (foreskin)	Clitoral prepuce (hood)
Corpus cavernosum of the penis	Corpus cavernosum of the clitoris
Urethral surface of the penis	Labia minora
Prostate gland	Skene's glands
Scrotum	Labia majora
Corpus spongiosum	Vestibular bulbs

● **FIGURE 4.8**

Homologous Structures of Males and Females. Note that males and females share many of the same structures since they developed from the same cells during fetal development.

Semen Production

Semen, or **seminal fluid,** is the ejaculated liquid that contains sperm. The function of semen is to nourish sperm and provide them with a hospitable environment and means of transport if they are deposited within the vagina. Semen is mainly made up of secretions from the seminal vesicles and prostate gland, which mix together in the urethra during ejaculation. Immediately after ejaculation, the semen is somewhat thick and sticky from clotting factors in the fluid. This consistency keeps the sperm together initially; then the semen becomes liquefied, allowing the sperm to swim out. Semen ranges in color from opalescent or milky white to yellowish or grayish in tone upon ejaculation, but it becomes clearer as it liquefies. Normally, about 2–6 milliliters (about 1 teaspoonful) of semen are ejaculated at one time; this amount of semen generally contains between 100 million and 600 million sperm. In spite of their significance, sperm occupy only about 1% of the total volume of semen; the remainder comes primarily from the seminal vesicles (70%) and the prostate gland (30%). Fewer than 1,000 sperm will reach the fallopian tubes. Most causes of male infertility are related to low sperm count and/or motility. When the sperm count is low, the optimal frequency for intercourse with ejaculation is every other day. (For more information about infertility, see Chapter 12.)

Homologous Organs

Interestingly, each of the male sexual structures has a **homologous structure,** or similar characteristic, that is developed from the same cells in the developing female fetus. The presence of a Y chromosome in a male produces testosterone in greater amounts. Without this Y chromosome, the fetus would become a female. (See Figure 4.8 for the homologous structures of males and females.)

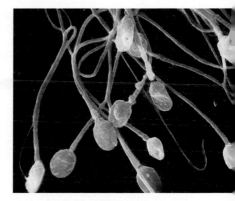

Between 100 million and 600 million sperm are present in the semen from a single ejaculation. Typically, following ejaculation during intercourse, fewer than 1,000 sperm will get as far as a fallopian tube, where an ovulated oocyte may be present. Though many sperm assist in helping to dissolve the egg cell membrane, typically only one sperm ultimately achieves fertilization.

think
about it

The Sexual and Reproductive Health Needs of Men: A Global Perspective

The sexual and reproductive health needs of men beyond their role as partners have received little attention. Important goals for most men worldwide are sexual and intimate relationships and a stable family life. Coupled with these goals are risks of sexually transmitted infections and unplanned pregnancies that can have devastating effects on men, their partners, and communities.

Though men have many similarities in their health behavior, desires, outcomes, and needs, statistics about them demonstrate distinct differences among them by country and world region (Sonfield, 2004). In 2003, the Alan Guttmacher Institute surveyed men from 23 countries in 5 regions to present a profile of the sexual, marital, and fathering behavior of men in 39 developing countries and 6 industrialized countries that represent each major world region.

Sexual Behavior

Men's sexual and reproductive lives do not occur in a vacuum. A wide range of individual and societal factors shape and constrain men's desires and behaviors as partners and undermine their traditional roles. These factors include income, access to resources such as clean water and sanitation, changing labor market conditions, and life expectancy. Reduced prospects for a long and healthy life—a by-product of not only the AIDS epidemic but of persistent poverty, violence, poor health, and malnutrition—can affect men's attitudes toward how they plan and live their lives.

As can be seen in the first graph, the median ages at which men reach the four milestones in their sexual and reproductive lives vary by region.

Men's Unmet Needs

The number of men having had more than one sex partner during the past year and not having used a condom at last intercourse underscores the need for preventing

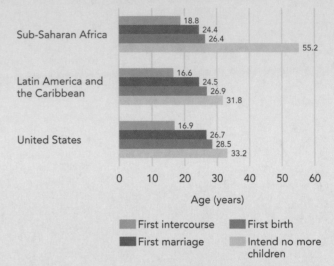

Global Look at Men's Ages at Which Key Milestones Are Met. The median ages at which men reach key milestones in their sexual and reproductive lives depend in part on where men live. (*Source:* Guttmacher Institute, *In Their Own Right: Addressing the Sexual and Reproductive Health Needs of Men Worldwide*, New York, 2004, http://www.guttmacher.org/pubs/itor_intl.pdf, accessed 3/2/09.)

sexually transmitted infections (STIs) among men. Qualitative studies from many parts of the world suggest that most young men who lack exposure to clear and unbiased information about sexuality and protective sexual behavior are not prepared to navigate their sexual lives without risk. More than ever, young men are facing influential factors that affect their sexual behavior, such as urbanization, a decline in traditional and multigenerational families, and increasing pressure to demonstrate their sexual prowess. The graph on the following page demonstrates the

● Male Sexual Response

> Bring me to my bow of burning gold. Bring me my arrow of desire.
> —William Blake
> (1757–1827)

At this point, it might be useful to review the material on sexual arousal and response in Chapter 3, including the models of Masters and Johnson, Kaplan, and Loulan. Even though their sexual anatomy is quite different, women and men follow roughly the same pattern of excitement and orgasm, with two exceptions: (1) Generally (but certainly not always), men become fully aroused and ready for penetration in a shorter amount of time than women do; and

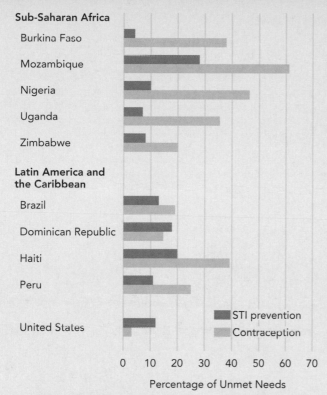

Sub-Saharan Africa

Burkina Faso

Mozambique

Nigeria

Uganda

Zimbabwe

Latin America and the Caribbean

Brazil

Dominican Republic

Haiti

Peru

United States

■ STI prevention
■ Contraception

0 10 20 30 40 50 60 70

Percentage of Unmet Needs

Global Look at Unmet Needs in Men for STI Prevention and Contraception. (*Source:* Guttmacher Institute, *In Their Own Right: Addressing the Sexual and Reproductive Health Needs of Men Worldwide,* New York, 2004, http://www.guttmacher.org/pubs/itor_intl.pdf, accessed 3/2/09.)

men's sexual and reproductive health needs. Among them is a growing consensus and numerous recommendations about what men need. Services should be accessible, welcoming, sensitive to men's needs, and consonant with existing community values; programs should seek men out where they congregate; and projects must be tailored to meet the special needs of younger, poor and minority men, older men, and gay and bisexual men.

By making men's sexual and reproductive health practices evident, researchers have quickly made clear the links between their sexual and reproductive behavior and the cultural, social, and economic factors associated with it. In spite of the fact that men need better information and health services, the political will to translate advocacy into action has so far been seriously absent.

Think Critically

- How might an inadequacy of resources affect the reproductive health-care needs of men?
- Why, in your opinion, is it important to recognize and understand global data as it relates to sexual health?
- If you had unlimited resources, what would you do to improve the sexual and reproductive health needs of men?

SOURCE: The Alan Guttmacher Institute (AGI), *In Their Own Right: Addressing the Sexual and Reproductive Health Needs of Men Worldwide.* New York: AGI, 2004, http://www.guttmacher.org/pubs/itor_intl.pdf, accessed 3/2/09.

proportion of men who have unmet needs for STI prevention or contraception.

Meeting Men's Needs

In both developed and developing countries, a number of national and international organizations are addressing

---

(2) once men experience ejaculation, they usually cannot do so again for some time, whereas women may experience repeated orgasms.

Probably one of the most controversial topics in the field of sexuality theory is whether sexual desire is shaped more by nature or culture. As suggested in Chapter 3, societal expectations, health, education, class, politics, and relational factors are thought to influence both men's and women's sexual desire and functioning. Combined, these influence sexual desire and response in profound ways. (See Chapter 14 for further discussion of sexual desire.)

Sexual arousal in men includes the processes of myotonia (increased muscle tension) and vasocongestion (engorgement of the tissues with blood). Vasocongestion in men is most apparent in the erection of the penis.

Erection

When a male becomes aroused, the blood circulation within the penis changes dramatically (see Figure 4.9). During the process of **erection,** the blood vessels expand, increasing the volume of blood, especially within the corpora cavernosa. At the same time, expansion of the penis compresses the veins that normally carry blood out, so the penis becomes further engorged. (There are no muscles in the penis that make it erect, nor is there a bone in it.) Secretions from the Cowper's glands appear at the tip of the penis during erection.

> An erection at will is the moral equivalent of a valid credit card.
>
> —Alex Comfort MD (1920–2000)

● **FIGURE 4.9**

Masters and Johnson Stages in Male Sexual Response

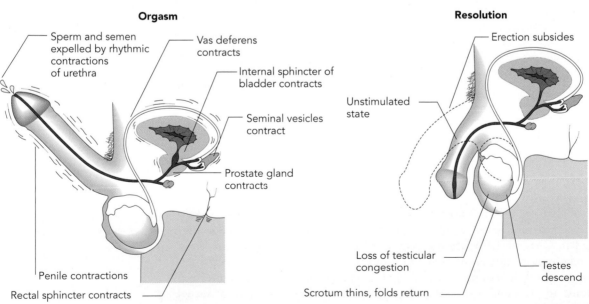
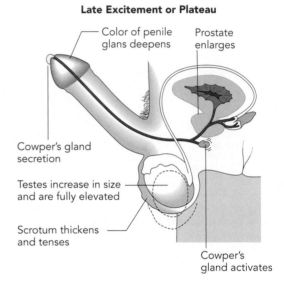

Excitement

Vasocongestion of penis results in erection

Partial erection

Unstimulated state

Testes elevate toward perineum

Skin of scrotum tenses, thickens, and elevates

Late Excitement or Plateau

Color of penile glans deepens

Prostate enlarges

Cowper's gland secretion

Testes increase in size and are fully elevated

Scrotum thickens and tenses

Cowper's gland activates

Orgasm

Sperm and semen expelled by rhythmic contractions of urethra

Vas deferens contracts

Internal sphincter of bladder contracts

Seminal vesicles contract

Prostate gland contracts

Penile contractions

Rectal sphincter contracts

Resolution

Erection subsides

Unstimulated state

Loss of testicular congestion

Testes descend

Scrotum thins, folds return

Ejaculation and Orgasm

What triggers the events that lead to ejaculation are undetermined, but it appears that it may be the result of a critical level of excitation in the brain or spinal cord (Komisaruk, Beyer-Flores, & Whipple, 2006). Regardless, increasing stimulation of the penis generally leads to ejaculation. Orgasm occurs when the impulses that cause erection reach a critical point and a spinal reflex sets off a massive discharge of nerve impulses to the ducts, glands, and muscles of the reproductive system. Ejaculation then occurs in two stages.

Emission   In the first stage, **emission,** contractions of the walls of the tail portion of the epididymis send sperm into the vasa deferentia (plural for vas deferens). Rhythmic contractions also occur in the vasa deferentia, ampullae, seminal vesicles, and ejaculatory ducts, which spill their contents into the urethra. The bladder's sphincter muscle closes to prevent urine from mixing with the semen and semen from entering the bladder, and another sphincter below the prostate also closes, trapping the semen in the expanded urethral bulb. At this point, the man feels a distinct sensation of **ejaculatory inevitability,** the point at which ejaculation *must* occur even if stimulation ceases. These events are accompanied by increased heart rate and respiration, elevated blood pressure, and general muscular tension. About 25% of men experience a sex flush.

> When the prick stands up, the brain goes to sleep.
>
> —Yiddish proverb

Expulsion   In the second stage of ejaculation, **expulsion,** there are rapid, rhythmic contractions of the urethra, the prostate, and the muscles at the base of the penis. The first few contractions are the most forceful, causing semen to spurt from the urethral opening. Gradually, the intensity of the contractions decreases and the interval between them lengthens. Breathing rate and heart rate may reach their peak at expulsion. When the sensations of orgasm were compared among college-age women and men, the only significant gender difference involved the "shooting" sensations reported by men. This variation most likely reflects ejaculation (Mah & Binik, 2002).

Some men experience **retrograde ejaculation,** the "backward" expulsion of semen into the bladder rather than out of the urethral opening. This unusual malfunctioning of the urethral sphincters may be temporary (e.g., induced by tranquilizers), but if it persists, the man should seek medical counsel to determine if there is an underlying problem. Retrograde ejaculation is not normally harmful; the semen is simply collected in the bladder and eliminated during urination.

Orgasm   The intensely pleasurable physical sensations and general release of tension that typically accompany ejaculation constitute the experience of orgasm. Orgasm is a series of muscular contractions of the pelvis that occurs at the height of sexual arousal. Orgasm does not always occur with ejaculation, however. It is possible to ejaculate without having an orgasm and to experience orgasm without ejaculating. Some men have reported having more than one orgasm without ejaculation ("dry orgasm") prior to a final, ejaculatory, orgasm. Following ejaculation, men experience a **refractory period,** during which they are not capable of having an ejaculation again. This is the time in which nerves cannot respond to additional stimulation. Refractory periods vary greatly in length, ranging from a few minutes to many hours (or even days, in some older men). Other changes

> When the appetite arises in the liver, the heart generates a spirit which descends through the arteries, fills the hollow of the penis and makes it hard and stiff. The delightful movements of intercourse give warmth to all the members, and hence to the humor which is in the brain; this liquid is drawn through the veins which lead from behind the ears to the testicles and from them it is squirted by the penis into the vulva.
>
> —Constantinus Africanus (c. 1070)

Can an Erection Be Willed?

The erection reflex can be triggered by various sexual and nonsexual stimuli, including tactile stimulation (touching) of the penis or other erogenous areas; sights, smells, or sounds (usually words or sexual vocalizations); and emotions or thoughts. Even negative emotions such as fear can produce an erection. Conversely, emotions and thoughts can also inhibit erections, as can unpleasant or painful physical sensations. The erectile response is controlled by the parasympathetic nervous system, a component of the involuntary or "autonomic" nervous system, and therefore cannot be consciously willed.

The length of time an erection lasts varies greatly from individual to individual and from situation to situation. With experience, most men are able to gauge the amount of stimulation that will either maintain the erection without causing orgasm or cause orgasm to occur too soon. Failure to attain an erection when one is desired is something most men experience at one time or another. (Erectile difficulties are discussed further in Chapter 14.)

There are, however, some things you can do to maximize your chances of producing viable erections. Because you need a steady flow of blood to your penis, you should get enough aerobic exercise and refrain from smoking to maintain your circulation. A diet low in fat and cholesterol and high in fiber and complex carbohydrates may also prevent hardening of the arteries, which restricts blood flow. Also, learning to relax during sexual activity with a partner can help with erections.

Some conditions, including diabetes, tension, depression, and abnormalities in blood pressure, and some medications that treat the abnormalities may have an adverse effect on blood flow and erectile capacity. If any of these conditions are present, or if the failure to attain an erection is persistent, see your physician.

What can you do about unwanted erections at inappropriate times? Distract yourself or stop your thoughts or images. Remember, the brain is the most erotic (and unerotic) organ of the body.

occur immediately following ejaculation. The erection diminishes as blood flow returns to normal, the sex flush (if there was one) disappears, and fairly heavy perspiration may occur. Men who experience intense sexual arousal without ejaculation may feel some heaviness or discomfort in the testicles; this is generally not as painful as the common term "blue balls" implies. If discomfort persists, however, it may be relieved by a period of rest or by ejaculation. When the seminal vesicles are full, feedback mechanisms diminish the quantity of sperm produced. Excess sperm die and are absorbed by the body. For some men, the benefits of strengthening the muscles that surround the penis by doing what are called **Kegel exercises** can produce more intense orgasms and ejaculations. (For a description of Kegel exercises, see Chapter 14.)

Final Thoughts

In this chapter and the previous one, we have looked primarily at the *physical* characteristics that designate us as female or male. But, as we discover in the following chapter, there's more to gender than mere chromosomes or reproductive organs. How we feel about our physical selves (our male or female anatomy) and how we act (our gender roles) also determine our identities as men or women.

Summary

Male Sex Organs: What Are They For?

- In their reproductive role, a man's sex organs produce and store gametes and can deliver them to a woman's reproductive tract. The *penis* is the organ through which both sperm and urine pass. The *shaft* of the penis contains two *corpora cavernosa* and a *corpus spongiosum,* which fill with blood during arousal, causing an erection. The head is called the *glans penis;* in uncircumcised men, it is covered by the *foreskin.* Myths about the penis equate its size with masculinity and sexual prowess. The *scrotum* is a pouch of skin that hangs at the root of the penis. It holds the *testes.*

- The paired testes or testicles have two major functions: sperm production and hormone production. Within each testicle are about 1,000 *seminiferous tubules,* where the production of sperm takes place. The seminiferous tubules merge to form the *epididymis,* a coiled tube where the sperm finally mature, and each epididymis merges into a *vas deferens,* which joins the *ejaculatory duct* within the *prostate gland.* The *seminal vesicles* and prostate gland produce *semen,* or *seminal fluid,* which nourishes and transports the sperm. Two tiny glands called *Cowper's* or *bulbourethral glands* secrete a thick, clear mucus prior to *ejaculation,* whereby semen is forcefully expelled from the penis.

- Male anatomical structures that do not serve a reproductive function but that may be involved in or affected by sexual activities include the breasts, *urethra,* buttocks, rectum, and anus.

Male Sexual Physiology

- The reproductive processes of the male body include the manufacture of hormones and the production and delivery of *sperm,* the male gametes. Although men do not have a monthly reproductive cycle comparable to that of women, they do experience regular fluctuations of hormone levels; there is also some evidence that men's moods follow a cyclical pattern. The most important male hormone is *testosterone,* which triggers sperm production and regulates the sex drive. Other important hormones in male reproductive physiology are GnRH, FSH, LH, inhibin, and oxytocin.

- Sperm carry either an X chromosome, which will produce a female zygote, or a Y chromosome, which will produce a male.

- Semen is the ejaculated liquid that contains sperm. The function of semen is to nourish sperm and provide them with a hospitable environment and means of transport if they are deposited within the vagina. It is mainly made up of secretions from the seminal vesicles and prostate gland. The semen from a single ejaculation generally contains between 100 million and 600 million sperm, yet only about 1,000 make it to the fallopian tubes.

Male Sexual Response

- Male sexual response, like that of females, involves the processes of vasocongestion and myotonia. *Erection* of the penis occurs when sexual or tactile stimuli cause its chambers to become engorged with blood. Continuing stimulation leads to ejaculation, which occurs in two stages. In the first stage, *emission,* semen mixes with sperm in the urethral bulb. In the second stage, *expulsion,* semen is forcibly expelled from the penis. Ejaculation and orgasm, a series of contractions of the pelvic muscles occurring at the height of sexual arousal, typically happen simultaneously. However, they can also occur separately. Following orgasm is a *refractory period,* during which ejaculation is not possible.

Questions for Discussion

- Make a list of anything you have heard about men's sexuality. Identify the myths and compare them with information from the text.

- If you had a son, would you get him circumcised? Why or why not? Do you think that the decision to circumcise a boy should be postponed until the child is old enough to decide for himself?

- Do you believe that men have cycles, similar to women's menstrual cycles? If so, what might contribute to this phenomena? If not, why not?

Sex and the Internet

Men's Sexuality

Try to locate Internet sites about men's sexuality. You'll find that, apart from those relating to erectile dysfunction, AIDS, and sexually explicit materials, few sites address this topic. What does this say about men? About the topic of men and sex? Because of this absence of content-specific sites, it is necessary to search a broader topic: men's health. Go to the Men's Health Network (http://www.menshealthnetwork.org) and, in the Library section, scroll down to one of the health links. If you don't find a topic there that interests you, go to "Links" and search for a relevant subject. When you find a topic that interests you, see if you can find the following:

- Background information about the topic

- The incidence or prevalence of the issue/problem

- Whom it impacts or affects

- The causes and potential solutions

- A related link that might broaden your understanding of this topic

Last, what recommendation might you make to someone who identified with this issue?

Suggested Web Sites

American Urological Association
http://www.urologyhealth.org/adult/index.cfm
Provides a variety of information on adult sexual functioning and infertility.

Male Health Center
http://www.malehealthcenter.com
Provides information on a wide variety of issues related to male genital health, birth control, and sexual functioning, from the male perspective.

Men's Health Resource Guide
http://www.menshealth.com/cda/homepage.do
A resource guide from *Men's Health* magazine that offers links to many topics in men's health and to discussions of relationship and family issues.

Men's Issues Page
http://www.menweb.org
Provides discussions on a wide variety of men's issues.

National Organization of Circumcision Information Resources
http://www.nocirc.org
Contains information and resources about male and female circumcision.

Suggested Reading

Bordo, S. (2000). *The male body: A new look at men in public and private.* New York: Farrar, Straus, & Giroux. An examination of the presentation of maleness in everyday life; rejects rigid categories in favor of an honest vision of men as flesh-and-blood human beings.

Friedman, D. (2001). *A mind of its own: A cultural history of the penis.* New York: Free Press.

Hoberman, J. (2005). *Testosterone dreams: Rejuvenation, aphrodisia, doping.* Berkeley: University of California Press. Investigates the history of synthetic testosterone and other male hormone therapies and their implications and dangers.

McCarthy, B., & Metz, M. E. (2008). *Men's sexual health: Fitness for satisfying sex.* New York: Routledge. Aimed to help men and women overcome sexual problems with the goal of greater acceptance and satisfaction.

McLaren, A. (2007). *Impotence: A cultural history.* Chicago: University of Chicago Press. By investigating the history of impotence, the author reveals the enormous pains a culture and society take in goading men in the painful pursuit of what is normal and natural.

Peate, I. (2005). *Men's sexual health.* New York: Wiley. For nurses and others who need to consider the often complex sexual health-care needs of men.

Zilbergeld, B. (1999). *The new male sexuality* (Rev. ed.). New York: Bantam Books. An explanation of both male and female anatomy and sexual response, plus communication, sexual problem solving, and much more; authoritative, interesting, and readable; written for men (but recommended for women as well).

For links, articles, and study material, go to the McGraw-Hill Web site, located at **www.mhhe.com/yarber7e.**

5

Gender and Gender Roles

MAIN TOPICS

Studying Gender and Gender Roles

Gender-Role Learning

Contemporary Gender Roles

Gender Variations

"As early as pre-school I learned the difference between boy and girl toys, games, and colors. The boys played with trucks while the girls played with dolls. If a boy were to play with a doll, he would be laughed at and even teased. In the make-believe area, once again, you have limitations of your dreams. Girls could not be police, truck drivers, firemen, or construction workers. We had to be people that were cute, such as models, housewives, dancers, or nurses. We would sometimes model ourselves after our parents or family members."

—23-year-old female

"I grew up with the question of 'why?' dangling from the tip of my tongue. Why am I supposed to marry a certain person? Why do I have to learn how to cook meat for my husband when I am a vegetarian? Why can't I go out on dates or to school formals? The answer was the same every time:

'Because you're a girl.' Being that she is such a strong woman, I know it tore a bit of my grandmother's heart every time she had to say it."

—19-year-old female

"My stepfather and I did not get along. I viewed him as an outsider, and I did not want a replacement father. Looking back, I feel like I overcompensated for the lack of a male figure in my life. I enlisted in the Navy at 18, have a huge firearm collection, and play ice hockey on the weekends. All of these activities seem to be macho, even to me. I guess it's to prove that even though a woman raised me I'm still a man's man."

—27-year-old male

"I was in fifth grade, and my parents put me on restriction. My mom inquired where I got the [Playboy] magazine. I told her we found it on the way home from school. She wanted to know where. I lied and said it was just sitting in somebody's trashcan and I happened to see it. She wanted to know where. I said I forgot. My sexual identity was being founded on concealment, repression, and lies. Within my family, my sexual identity was repressed."

—27-year-old male

> There is no essential sexuality. Maleness and femaleness are something we are dressed in.
>
> —Naomi Wallace
> (1960–)

How can we tell the difference between a man and a woman? Everyone knows that women and men, at a basic level, are distinguished by their genitals. However, as accurate as this answer may be academically, it is not particularly useful in social situations. In most social situations—except in nudist colonies or while sunbathing au naturel—our genitals are not visible to the casual observer. We do not expose ourselves (or ask another person to do so) for gender verification. We are more likely to rely on secondary sex characteristics, such as breasts and body hair, or on bone structure, musculature, and height. But even these characteristics are not always reliable, given the great variety of shapes and sizes we come in as human beings. And from farther away than a few yards, we cannot always distinguish these characteristics. Instead of relying entirely on physical characteristics to identify individuals as male and female, we often look for other clues.

Culture provides us with an important clue for recognizing whether a person is female or male in most situations: dress. In almost all cultures, male and female clothing differs to varying degrees so that we can easily identify a person's gender. Some cultures, such as our own, may accentuate secondary sex characteristics, especially for females. Traditional feminine clothing, for example, emphasizes a woman's gender: dress or skirt, a form-fitting or low-cut top revealing the breasts, high heels, and so on. Most clothing, in fact, that emphasizes or exaggerates secondary sex characteristics is female. Makeup (lipstick, blush, eyeliner) and hairstyles also serve to mark or exaggerate the differences between females and males. Even smells (perfume for women, cologne for men) and colors (blue for boys, pink for girls) help distinguish females and males.

Clothing and other aspects of appearance even further exaggerate the physical differences between women and men. And culture encourages us to accentuate (or invent) psychological, emotional, mental, and behavioral differences. But what happens when these lines are blurred, especially in young children who defy gender norms? Should parents and their doctors be permitted to block puberty medically in order to buy time and figure out who these children are? While a biological understanding of gender identity remains somewhat of a mystery, medical, ethical, and parental maps are being created to respond to the growing number of individuals who see gender variance as a normal occurring phenomenon rather than a disorder.

In this chapter, we examine some of the critical ways being male or female affects us both as human beings and as sexual beings. We look at the connection between our genitals, our identity as female or male, and our feelings of being feminine or masculine. We also examine the relationship between femininity, masculinity, and sexual orientation. Then we discuss how masculine and feminine traits result from both biological and social influences. Next, we focus on theories of socialization and how we learn to act masculine and feminine in our culture. Then we look at traditional, contemporary, and androgynous gender roles. Finally, we examine gender variations: disorders of sexual development/intersex, gender identity disorder, and transsexuality—phenomena that involve complex issues pertaining to gender, gender variance, and gender identity.

● Studying Gender and Gender Roles

Let's start by defining some key terms, to establish a common terminology. Keeping these definitions in mind will make the discussion clearer.

Sex, Gender, and Gender Roles: What's the Difference?

The word **sex** refers to whether one is biologically female or male, based on genetic and anatomical sex. **Genetic sex** refers to one's chromosomal and hormonal sex characteristics, such as whether one's chromosomes are XY or XX and whether estrogen or testosterone dominates the hormonal system. **Anatomical sex** refers to physical sex: gonads, uterus, vulva, vagina, penis, and so on.

Although "sex" and "gender" are often used interchangeably, gender is not the same as biological sex. As noted in Chapter 3, gender relates to femininity or masculinity, the social and cultural characteristics associated with biological sex. Whereas sex is rooted in biology, gender is rooted in culture. **Assigned gender** is the gender given by others, usually at birth. When a baby is born, someone looks at the genitals and exclaims, "It's a boy!" or "It's a girl!" With that single utterance, the baby is transformed from an "it" into a "male" or a "female." **Gender identity** is a person's internal sense of being male or female.

Gender roles are the attitudes, behaviors, rights, and responsibilities that particular cultural groups associate with each sex. Age, race, and a variety of other factors further define and influence these. The term "gender role" is gradually replacing the traditional term "sex role" because "sex role" continues to suggest a connection between biological sex and behavior. Biological males are expected

Whatever women do they must do twice as well as men to be thought half as good. Luckily, this is not difficult.

—Charlotte Whitton
(1896–1975)

The interaction of biological and psychological factors contributes to the development of gender. (Lisa Lyon, 1981. Copyright © 1981 The Estate of Robert Mapplethorpe.)

to act out masculine gender roles; biological females are expected to act out feminine gender roles. A **gender-role stereotype** is a rigidly held, oversimplified, and overgeneralized belief about how each gender should behave. Stereotypes tend to be false or misleading, not only for the group as a whole (e.g., women are more interested in relationships than sex) but also for any individual in the group (e.g., Peter may be more interested in sex than relationships). Even if a generalization is statistically valid in describing a group average (e.g., males are generally taller than females), such generalizations do not necessarily predict the facts (e.g., whether Roberto will be taller than Andrea). **Gender-role attitude** refers to the beliefs a person has about him- or herself and others regarding appropriate female and male personality traits and activities. **Gender-role behavior** refers to the actual activities or behaviors a person engages in as a female or a male. **Gender presentation,** either through bodily habits or personality, is what is perceived by others.

Sex and Gender Identity

We develop our gender through the interaction of its biological and psychosocial components. The biological component includes genetic and anatomical sex; the psychosocial component includes assigned gender and gender identity. Because these dimensions are learned together, they may seem to be natural. For example, if a person looks like a girl (biological), believes she should be feminine (cultural), feels as if she is a girl (psychological), and acts like a girl (social), then her gender identity and role are congruent with her anatomical sex. Our culture emphasizes that there are only two genders and that there should be coherence among the biological, social, cultural, and psychological dimensions of each gender. Deviations, still often stigmatized, are now being reexamined, evaluated, and viewed as **gender variations.** Those individuals who cannot or choose not to conform to societal gender norms associated with their biological sex are gender variant. Other terms for this variation include gender identity disorder or gender dysphoria. Many experts are now finding that molding a child's gender identity is not as important as allowing them to be who they are and accepting that person, regardless of what their genitals may tell them (Brown, 2006).

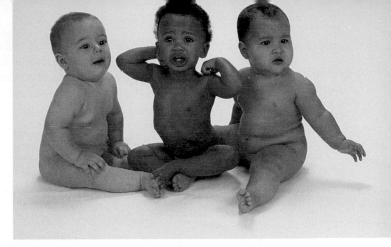

Although strangers can't always readily tell the sex of a baby, once they learn the sex, they often respond with gender stereotypes and expectations.

Assigned Gender When we are born, we are assigned a gender based on anatomical appearance. Assigned gender is significant because it tells *others* how to respond to us. As youngsters, we have no sense of ourselves as female or male. We *learn* that we are a girl or a boy from the verbal responses of others. "What a pretty *girl*" or "What a good *boy*," our parents and others say. We are constantly given signals about our gender. Our birth certificate states our sex; our name, such as Jarrod or Felicia, is most likely gender-coded. Our clothes, even in infancy, reveal our gender.

By the time we are 2 years old, we are probably able to identify ourself as a girl or a boy based on what we have internalized from what others have told us coupled with factors not yet understood. We might also be able to identify strangers as "mommies" or "daddies." But we don't really know *why* we are a girl or a boy. We don't associate our gender with our genitals. In fact, until the age of 3 or so, most children identify girls or boys by hairstyles, clothing, or other nonanatomical signs. At around age 3, we begin to learn that the genitals are what make a person male or female.

By age 4 or 5, children have learned a wide array of social stereotypes about how boys and girls should behave. Consequently, they tend to react approvingly or disapprovingly toward each other according to their choice of sex-appropriate play patterns and toys. Fixed ideas about adult roles and careers are also established by this time in their lives.

> Roles came with costumes and speeches and stage directions. In a role, we don't have to think.
>
> —Ellen Goodman
> (1948–)

Gender Identity By about age 2, we internalize and identify with our gender. We *think* we are a girl or a boy. This feeling of our femaleness or maleness is our gender identity. For most people, gender identity is permanent and is congruent with their sexual anatomy and assigned gender.

Some cultures, however, put off instilling gender identity in males until later. People in these cultures believe in a latent or dormant femaleness in males. As a consequence, such cultures institute rituals or ceremonies in childhood to ensure that males will identify themselves as males. In some East African societies, for example, a male child is referred to as a "woman-child"; there are few social differences between young boys and girls. Around age 7, the boy undergoes male initiation rites, such as circumcision, whose avowed purpose is to "make" him into a man. Such ceremonies may serve as a kind of "brainwashing," helping the young male make the transition to a new gender identity with new role expectations. Other cultures allow older males to act out a latent female identity with such practices as the couvade, in which husbands mimic their wives giving birth. And in our own society, into the early twentieth century, boys were dressed in gowns and wore their hair in long curls until age 2. At age 2 or 3, their dresses were replaced by pants, their hair was cut, and children were socialized to conform to their anatomical sex. Children who deviated from this expected conformity were referred to as sissies (boys) or tomboys (girls) and ridiculed to conform to gender stereotypes. More recently, a new brand of thinking supported by advocates of gender-identity rights has sparked debate among professionals over how to best counsel families whose child does not conform to gender norms in either clothing or behavior and has identified intensely with the other sex. **Transgendered** is currently the umbrella term for those who do not conform to traditional notions of gender expression.

Masculinity and Femininity: Opposites or Similar?

Each culture determines the content of gender roles in its own way. Among the Arapesh of New Guinea, for example, members of both sexes possess what we consider feminine traits. Both men and women tend to be passive, cooperative, peaceful, and nurturing. The father as well as the mother is said to "bear a child"; only the father's continual care can make the child grow healthily, both in the womb and in childhood. Eighty miles away, the Mundugumor live in remarkable contrast to the peaceful Arapesh. "Both men and women," Margaret Mead (1975) observed, "are expected to be violent, competitive, aggressively sexed, jealous, and ready to see and avenge insult, delighting in display, in action, in fighting." Biology creates males and females, but it is culture that creates our concepts of masculinity and femininity.

In the traditional Western view of masculinity and femininity, men and women are seen as polar opposites. Our popular terminology, in fact, reflects this view. Women and men refer to each other as the "opposite sex." But this implies that women and men are indeed opposites, that they have little in common. (We use "other sex" in this book.) Our gender stereotypes fit this pattern of polar differences: Men are aggressive, whereas women are passive; men embody **instrumentality** and are task-oriented, whereas women embody **expressiveness** and are emotion-oriented; men are rational, whereas women are irrational; men want sex, whereas women want love; and so on.

It is important to recognize that gender stereotypes, despite their depiction of men and women as opposites, are usually not all-or-nothing notions. Most of us do not think that only men are assertive or only women are nurturing. Stereotypes merely reflect *probabilities* that a woman or a man will have a certain characteristic based on her or his gender. When we say that men are more independent than women, we simply mean that there is a greater probability that a man will be more independent than a woman.

Sexism, discrimination against people based on their sex rather than their individual merits, is often associated with gender stereotypes and may prevent individuals from expressing their full range of emotions or seeking certain vocations. For example, sexism may discourage a woman from pursuing a career in math or inhibit a man from choosing nursing as a profession. Children may develop stereotypes about differences between men and women and carry these into their adult lives.

> " One half the world cannot understand the pleasures of the other.
> —Jane Austen
> (1775–1817)

> " The main difference between men and women is that men are lunatics and women are idiots.
> —Rebecca West
> (1892–1983)

Many gay and lesbian couples do not conform to stereotypical characteristics or roles.

As technology becomes more advanced, we learn more about what contributes to making the sexes different. We are already getting hints that our identities as men and women are a combination of nature and nurture. It is through new technology that researchers can observe brains in the act of cogitating, feeling, or remembering. Other research has revealed that some differences between men and women may be due to differences in the part of the brain that controls emotional processing. In men, the part thought to control action-oriented responses appears to be more active; in women, the part thought to control more symbolic emotional responses is more active (Gur, Mozley, Mozley, et al., 1995). Women's more active emotional processing may be explained by neurological responses interacting with hormonal surges that fluctuate throughout life. In fact, many differences and similarities that we once attributed to learning or culture have been found to be biologically based (Brizendine, 2006). Add to this our individual choices, sense of identities, and life experiences, and we can begin to get a picture of what contributes to making each person unique.

Gender and Sexual Orientation

Gender, gender identity, and gender role are conceptually independent of sexual orientation. But, in many people's minds, these concepts are closely related to sexual orientation (discussed at greater length in Chapter 6). Our traditional notion of gender roles assumes that heterosexuality is a critical component of masculinity and femininity. That is, a "masculine" man is attracted to women and a "feminine" woman is attracted to men. From this assumption follow two beliefs about homosexuality: (1) If a man is gay, he cannot be masculine, and if a woman is lesbian, she cannot be feminine; and (2) if a man is gay, he must have some feminine characteristics, and if a woman is lesbian, she must have some masculine characteristics. What these beliefs imply is that homosexuality is somehow associated with a failure to fill traditional gender roles. A "real" man is not gay; therefore, gay men are not "real" men. Similarly, a "real" woman is not a lesbian; therefore, lesbian women are not "real" women. These negative stereotypes have merely fueled homophobia.

Stereotypes fall in the face of humanity . . . this is how the world will change for gay men and lesbians.

—Anna Quindlen
(1953–)

Gender Theory

To really understand gender, we must look at social explanations as well as biological ones. Traditionally, the social sciences have not paid much attention to *why* a culture develops its particular gender roles. They have been more interested in such topics as the process of socialization and male/female differences. In the 1980s, however, gender theory was developed to explore the role of gender in society. According to **gender theory,** a society may be best understood by how it is organized according to gender. Gender is viewed as a basic element in social relationships, based on the socially perceived differences between the sexes that justify unequal power relationships. Imagine, for example, an infant crying in the night. Which parent gets up to take care of the baby—the father or the mother? In most cases, the mother does because women are perceived to be nurturing, and it is the woman's "responsibility" as mother (even if she hasn't had a full night's sleep in a week and is employed full-time). Yet the father could just as easily care for the crying infant. He may not, because caregiving is socially perceived as "natural" to women.

In psychology, gender theory focuses on (1) how gender is created and what its purposes are and (2) how specific traits, behaviors, and roles are defined as male or female and how they create advantages for males and disadvantages for females. Gender theorists reject the idea that biology creates male/female differences and believe, rather, that gender differences are largely, if not entirely, created by society.

The key to the creation of gender inequality lies in the belief that men and women are, indeed, "opposite" sexes—that they are opposite each other in personalities, abilities, skills, and traits. Furthermore, the differences between the sexes are unequally valued: Reason and aggressiveness (defined as male traits) are considered to be more valuable than emotion and passivity (defined as female traits). In reality, however, men and women are more like each other than they are different. Both are reasonable and emotional, aggressive and passive.

> " The war between the sexes is the only one in which both sides regularly sleep with the enemy.
>
> —Quentin Crisp
> (1908–1999)

● Gender-Role Learning

As we have seen, gender roles are socially constructed and rooted in culture. So how do individuals learn what their society expects of them as males or females?

Theories of Socialization

It is important to recognize that definitions and concepts of how gender emerges come from a wide variety of theoretical perspectives. Theories influence how we approach sexuality research, practice, education, and policy. Two of the most prominent theories are cognitive social learning theory and cognitive development theory. In the study of sexuality, a growing body of literature uses a social constructionist perspective on gender (Tolman, Striepe, & Harmon, 2003).

Cognitive social learning theory is derived from behavioral psychology. In explaining our actions, behaviorists emphasize observable events and their consequences, rather than internal feelings and drives. According to behaviorists, we learn attitudes and behaviors as a result of social interactions with others—hence the term "social learning" (Bandura, 1977).

The cornerstone of cognitive social learning theory is the belief that consequences control behavior. Behaviors that are regularly followed by a reward are likely to occur again; behaviors that are regularly followed by a punishment are less likely to recur. Thus, girls are rewarded for playing with dolls ("What a nice mommy!"), but boys are not ("What a sissy!").

This behaviorist approach has been modified to include cognition—mental processes that intervene between stimulus and response, such as evaluation and reflection. The cognitive processes involved in social learning include our ability to (1) use language, (2) anticipate consequences, and (3) make observations. By using language, we can tell our daughter that we like it when she does well in school and that we don't like it when she hits someone. A person's ability to anticipate consequences affects behavior. A boy doesn't need to wear lace stockings in public to know that such dressing will lead to negative consequences. Finally, children observe what others do. A girl may learn that she "shouldn't" play video games by seeing that the players in video arcades are mostly boys.

We also learn gender roles by imitation, through a process called modeling. Most of us are not even aware of the many subtle behaviors that make up gender roles—the ways in which men and women use different mannerisms and gestures, speak differently, use different body language, and so on. We don't "teach" these behaviors by reinforcement. Children tend to model friendly, warm, and nurturing adults; they also tend to imitate adults who are powerful in their eyes—that is, adults who control access to food, toys, or privileges. Initially, the most powerful models that children have are their parents. As children grow older and their social world expands, so does the number of people who may act as their role models: siblings, friends, teachers, athletes, media figures, and so on. Children sift through the various demands and expectations associated with the different models to create their own unique selves.

In contrast to social learning theory, **cognitive development theory** (Kohlberg, 1966) focuses on children's active interpretation of the messages they receive from the environment. Whereas social learning assumes that children and adults learn in fundamentally the same way, cognitive development theory stresses that we learn differently depending on our age. At age 2, children can correctly identify themselves and others as boys or girls, but they tend to base this identification on superficial features such as hair and clothing: Girls have long hair and wear dresses; boys have short hair and wear pants. Some children even believe they can change their gender by changing their clothes or hair length.

Cognitive development theory recognizes gender as a characteristic people use to understand their social environment and interact with it (Cross & Markus, 1993). Thus, children compare themselves to others, including parents, and develop and attach to masculine or feminine values. When children are 6 or 7, they begin to understand that gender is permanent; it is not something they can alter in the same way they can change their clothes. They acquire this understanding because they are capable of grasping the idea that basic characteristics do not change. A woman can be a woman even if she has short hair and wears pants. Children not only understand the permanence of gender but also tend to insist on rigid adherence to gender-role stereotypes.

According to cognitive social learning theory, boys and girls learn appropriate gender-role behavior through reinforcement and modeling (Perry & Bussey, 1979). But, according to cognitive development theory, once children learn that gender is permanent, they independently strive to act like "proper" girls or boys. They do this on their own because of an internal need for congruence, or agreement between

Science magazine came out with a report on the difference between men's and women's brains. Apparently, women are more controlled by a part of the brain called singletgyrus, and men are controlled by a part of the brain known as the penis.

—Jay leno
(1950–)

what they know and how they act. Also, children find performing the appropriate gender-role activities to be rewarding in itself. Models and reinforcement help show them how well they are doing, but the primary motivation is internal.

Social construction theory views gender as a set of practices and performances that occur through language and a political system (Bartky, 1990; Butler, 1993; Connell, 1995; Gergen, 1985). This perspective acknowledges the relationships that exist among meaning, power, and gender and suggests that language mediates and deploys how each will be expressed. Inspired by feminist and **queer theories,** which identify sexuality as a system that cannot be understood as gender neutral or by the actions of heterosexual males and females (Parker & Gagnon, 1995), social constructionists suggest that gendered meanings are only one vehicle through which sexuality is constituted. Feminist researchers purport that the meanings and realities associated with sexuality are socially constructed to serve political systems that perpetuate White, heterosexual, middle- and upper-class male privilege. Thus, a social constructionist approach to gender would inquire about ways in which males and females make meaning out of their experiences with their bodies, their relationships, and their sexual choices.

Gender-Role Learning in Childhood and Adolescence

It is difficult to analyze the relationship between biology and personality because learning begins at birth. In our culture, infant girls are usually held more gently and treated more tenderly than boys, who are ordinarily subjected to rougher forms of play. The first day after birth, parents characterize their daughters as soft, fine-featured, and small and their sons as strong, large-featured, big, and bold. When children do not measure up to these expectations, they may stop trying to express their authentic feelings and emotions. Evidence of the continued existence of **sexual double standards**—different standards of behavior and permissiveness—still exists (Crawford & Popp, 2003). (See Chapter 6 for a discussion of socializing agents of children and adolescents.)

Parents as Socializing Agents   During infancy and early childhood, children's most important source of learning is the primary caregiver, whether the mother, father, grandmother, or someone else. Many parents are not aware that their words and actions contribute to their children's gender-role socialization. Nor are they aware that they treat their daughters and sons differently because of their gender. Although parents may recognize that they respond differently to sons than to daughters, they usually have a ready explanation: the "natural" differences in the temperament and behavior of girls and boys.

Children are socialized in gender roles through several very subtle processes (Oakley, 1985):

- *Manipulation.* Parents manipulate their children from infancy onward. They treat a daughter gently, tell her she is pretty, and advise her that nice girls do not fight. They treat a son roughly, tell him he is strong, and advise him that big boys do not cry. Eventually, children incorporate their parents' views in such matters as integral parts of their personalities.

- *Channeling.* Children are channeled by directing their attention to specific objects. Toys, for example, are differentiated by sex. Dolls are considered appropriate for girls, and cars for boys.

What are little girls made of?
Sugar and spice
And everything nice.
That's what little girls are made of.
What are little boys made of?
Snips and snails
And puppy dogs' tails.
That's what little boys are made of.

—Nursery rhyme

- *Verbal appellation.* Parents use different words with boys and girls to describe the same behavior. A boy who pushes others may be described as "active," whereas a girl who does the same is usually called "aggressive."
- *Activity exposure.* The activity exposure of girls and boys differs markedly. Although both are usually exposed to a variety of activities early in life, boys are discouraged from imitating their mothers, whereas girls are encouraged to be "mother's little helper."

It is generally accepted that parents socialize their children in outmoded and different ways according to gender. This occurs in spite of the fact that everything we've learned about the need for bonding and connecting for girls is also true for boys. In fact, noted researcher and author Michael Gurian (1999) recommends more connection between sons and mothers. His studies show that such closeness with a mother (as well as with a father) leads to a more successful and satisfying adulthood. Fathers, more than mothers, pressure their children to behave in "gender-appropriate" ways. Fathers set higher standards of achievement for their sons than for their daughters; with their daughters, fathers emphasize the interpersonal aspects of their relationship. But mothers also reinforce the interpersonal aspects of the parent-daughter relationship. Both parents tend to be more restrictive with their daughters and to allow their sons more freedom and to provide less intervention.

Parents' influence on children cannot be overemphasized.

Although hundreds of studies have examined gender roles and their importance, few have compared ethnic groups to explore differences in gender roles (Konrad & Harris, 2002). The idea that women's roles should be centered around the home and family generally reflects the traditions of White, middle-class, heterosexual men in the United States (Blee & Tickamyer, 1995). African Americans have been found to have more fluid gender roles (McCollum, 1997), evidently to accommodate the stresses of racism and the relatively greater importance that race plays in African American identity (Shelton & Sellers, 2000). There is also evidence that African American families socialize their daughters to be more independent than White families do. Indeed, among African Americans, the "traditional" female role model may never have existed. The African American female role model in which the woman is both wage-earner and homemaker is more common and more accurately reflects the African American experience than does the traditional female role model.

As children grow older, their social world expands, and so do their sources of learning. Around the time children enter day care or kindergarten, teachers and peers become important influences.

Teachers as Socializing Agents Day-care centers, nursery schools, and kindergartens are often children's first experience in the world outside the family. Teachers become important role models for their students. Because most

Among African Americans, the traditional female gender role includes strength and independence.

day-care workers and kindergarten and elementary school teachers are women, children tend to think of child-adult interactions as primarily the province of women. In this sense, schools reinforce the idea that women are concerned with children and men are not. Teachers may also tend to be conventional in the gender-role messages they convey to children (Sadker & Zittleman, 2005). They may encourage different activities and abilities in boys and girls such as contact sports for boys and gymnastics or dance for girls. Academically, teachers tend to encourage boys more than girls in math and science and girls more than boys in language skills. Consequently, beginning in adolescence there is evidence of a downward spiral in test scores in math and science among girls who previously scored equal to or even higher than boys on nearly every standardized test, except when math is taught by female math instructors (Keiser, Wilkins, Meier, & Holland, 2000). No such downward spiral is observed for boys. It has also been observed that teachers and parents may shame boys into conforming to the traditional image of masculinity. For example, boys are taught to hide their emotions, act brave, and demonstrate independence. Even though boys may get good grades and be considered normal, healthy, and well-adjusted by peers, parents, and teachers, they may also report feeling deeply troubled about the roles and goals of their gender.

Gender bias often follows students into the college arena. Though little research is available on the effects of a college education on women, there is evidence that undergraduate women tend to report more discrimination and sexual bias in their academic departments than do male students (Fischer & Good, 1994).

Peers as Socializing Agents   Children's age-mates, or peers, become especially important when they enter school. By granting or withholding approval, friends and playmates influence what games children play, what they wear, what music they listen to, what TV programs they watch, and even what cereal they eat. Peers

When boys and girls participate in sports together, they develop comparable athletic skills. Segregation of boys and girls encourages the development of differences that otherwise might not occur.

provide standards for gender-role behavior in several ways (Absi-Semaan, Crombie, & Freeman, 1993; Moller, Hymel, & Rubin, 1992):

- Peers provide information about gender-role norms through play activities and toys. Girls play with dolls that cry and wet themselves or with glamorous dolls with well-developed figures and expensive tastes. Boys play with video games in which they kill and maim in order to dominate and win.

- Peers influence the adoption of gender-role norms through verbal approval or disapproval. "That's for boys!" or "Only girls do that!" is a strong negative message to the girl playing with a football or the boy playing with dolls.

- Children's perceptions of their friends' gender-role attitudes, behaviors, and beliefs encourage them to adopt similar ones to be accepted. If a girl's same-sex friends play soccer, she is more likely to play soccer. If a boy's same-sex friends display feelings, he is more likely to display feelings.

Even though parents tend to fear the worst in general from peers, peers provide important positive influences. It is within their peer groups, for example, that adolescents learn to develop intimate relationships.

Media Influences   Though much of television programming promotes or condones negative stereotypes about gender, ethnicity, age, ability, and sexual orientation, media and the public benefit when a broad range of voices are included. Female characters on television typically are under age 40, well groomed, attractive, and excessively concerned with their appearance. In contrast, male characters are more aggressive and constructive; they solve problems and rescue others from danger. Thus, boys must grapple daily with exaggerated images of men. Indeed, all forms of media glorify the enforcers and protectors, the ones who win by brute force, intimidation, and anger. Only in recent years on prime-time series have men been shown in emotional, nurturing roles.

That's not me you're in love with. That's my image. You don't even know me.

—Kelly McGillis (1957–)

Gender Schemas: Exaggerating Differences

Actual differences between females and males are minimal or nonexistent, except in levels of aggressiveness and visual/spatial skills, yet culture exaggerates these differences or creates differences where none otherwise exist. One way that culture does this is by creating a schema. Recall from Chapter 2 that a schema is a set of interrelated ideas that helps us process information by categorizing it in a variety of ways. We often categorize people by age, ethnicity, nationality, physical characteristics, and so on. Gender is one such way of categorizing.

Psychologist Sandra Bem (1983) observes that, although gender is not inherent in inanimate objects or in behaviors, we treat many objects and behaviors as if they were masculine or feminine. These gender divisions form a complex structure of associations that affects our perceptions of reality. Bem refers to this cognitive organization of the world according to gender as a **gender schema.** We use gender schemas in many dimensions of life, including activities (nurturing, fighting), emotions (compassion, anger), behavior (playing with dolls or action figures), clothing (dresses or pants), and even colors (pink or blue), considering some appropriate for one gender and some appropriate for the other.

Children are taught the significance of gender differences. They learn that "the dichotomy between male and female has intensive and extensive relevance to virtually every domain of human experience" (Bem, 1983). Thus, children learn very early that it is important whether someone is female or male; they begin thinking in terms of gender schemas at a young age (Liben & Signorella, 1993).

Processing information by gender is important in cultures such as ours, for several reasons. First, gender-schema cultures make multiple associations between gender and other non-sex-linked qualities such as affection and strength. Our culture regards affection as a feminine trait and strength as a masculine one. Second, such cultures make gender distinctions important, using them as a basis for norms, status, taboos, and privileges. Men are assigned leadership positions, for example, whereas women are placed in the rank and file (if not at home). Men are sexually assertive; women are sexually passive. These associations, however, often undermine and undervalue the uniqueness of individuals.

● Contemporary Gender Roles

In recent decades, there has been a significant shift toward more egalitarian gender roles. Although women's roles have changed more than men's, men's are also changing. These changes seem to affect all socioeconomic classes. Members of conservative religious groups, such as Mormons, Catholics, and fundamentalist and evangelical Protestants, adhere most strongly to traditional gender roles (Eitzen & Zinn, 1994). Despite the ongoing disagreement, it is likely that the egalitarian trend will continue.

Traditional Gender Roles

In social science research, those who are studied have defined the norms against which all other experience has been evaluated (Stevenson, 2002). Consequently, much of what we know about sexuality is confined to a limited sector of society: White and middle class, many of whom are also college students. It is important to consider the relationships between the participants in sexuality research and the limitations regarding whom a study actually describes.

The Traditional Male Gender Role   What does it mean to be a "real" man in America? One can simply go online to find stereotypical jokes ranging from "Men are like animals: messy, insensitive, and potentially violent but they make great pets" to the top ten Chuck Norris facts, including "Chuck Norris's tears cure cancer; too bad he never cries!"

Central personality traits associated with the traditional male role—no matter the race or ethnicity—are instrumental, or involve practical or task-oriented traits that may include aggressiveness, emotional toughness, independence, feelings of superiority, and decisiveness. Males are generally regarded as being more power-oriented than females, and they exhibit higher levels of aggression, especially violent aggression (such as assault, homicide, and rape), dominance, and competitiveness. Although these tough, aggressive traits may be useful in the corporate world, politics, and the military (or in hunting saber-toothed tigers), they are rarely helpful to a man in his intimate relationships, which require understanding, cooperation, communication, and nurturing.

Who perpetuates the image of the dominance of men, and what role does it serve in a society that no longer needs or respects such an image? It may be that a man's task is not to define masculinity but rather to redefine what it means to be human.

Men of color move between dominant and ethnic cultures with different role requirements. They are expected to conform not only to the gender-role norms of the dominant group but to those of their own group as well. Black males, for example, must conform to both stereotypical expectations related to success, competition, and aggression and expectations of the African American community—most notably, those regarding cooperation and the promotion of ethnic survival. They must also confront negative stereotypes about Black masculinity, such as hypersexuality and violence.

> " A man is by nature a sexual animal. I've always had my share of pets.
>
> —Mae West
> (1893–1980)

Male Sexual Scripts   In sociology, a **script** refers to the acts, rules, and expectations associated with a particular role. It is like the script handed out to an actor. Unlike dramatic scripts, however, social scripts allow for considerable improvisation within their general boundaries. We are given many scripts in life according to the various roles we play. Among them are sexual scripts that outline how we are to behave sexually when acting out our gender roles. Sexual scripts and gender roles for heterosexuals may be different from those for gay, lesbian, bisexual, or transgendered people. Perceptions and patterns in sexual behavior are shaped by sexual scripts. (See Chapter 9 for further discussion of sexual scripts.)

Psychologist Bernie Zilbergeld (1992) suggested that the male sexual script includes the following elements:

- *Men should not have (or at least should not express) certain feelings.* Men should not express doubts; they should be assertive, confident, and aggressive. Tenderness and compassion are not masculine emotions.

- *Performance is the thing that counts.* Sex is something to be achieved, to win at. Feelings only get in the way of the job to be done. Sex is not for intimacy but for orgasm.

- *The man is in charge.* As in other realms, the man is the leader, the person who knows what is best. The man initiates sex and gives the woman her orgasm. A real man doesn't need a woman to tell him what women like; he already knows.

- *A man always wants sex and is ready for it.* No matter what else is going on, a man wants sex; he is always able to become erect. He is a machine.

- *All physical contact leads to sex.* Because men are basically sexual machines, any physical contact is a sign for sex. Touching is seen as the first step toward sexual intercourse, not an end in itself. There is no physical pleasure other than sexual pleasure.

- *Sex equals intercourse.* All erotic contact leads to sexual intercourse. Foreplay is just that: warming up, getting one's partner ready for penetration. Kissing, hugging, erotic touching, and oral sex are only preliminaries to intercourse.

- *Sexual intercourse leads to orgasm.* The orgasm is the "proof in the pudding." The more orgasms, the better the sex. If a woman does not have an orgasm, she is not sexual. The male feels that he is a failure because he was not good enough to give her an orgasm. If she requires clitoral stimulation to have an orgasm, she has a problem.

Common to all these myths is a separation of sex from love and attachment. Sex is seen as performance.

The Traditional Female Gender Role   Although many of the features of the traditional male gender role, such as being in control, are shared by both sexes, there are striking ethnic and individual differences in the female gender role. Traditional female roles are expressive, or assume emotional or supportive characterics. They emphasize passivity, compliance, physical attractiveness, and being a wife and mother.

Among Whites, the traditional female gender role centers around women as wives and mothers. When this woman leaves adolescence, she is expected to get married and have children. Although the traditional woman may work prior to marriage, she is not expected to defer marriage for career goals.

In recent years, the traditional role has been modified to include work and marriage. Work roles, however, are clearly subordinated to marital and family roles. Upon the birth of the first child, the woman is expected to both work and parent or, if economically feasible, to become a full-time mother.

The traditional White female gender role does not extend to African American women. This may be attributed to a combination of the African heritage; slavery, which subjugated women to the same labor and hardships as men; and economic discrimination, which forced these women into the labor force. African American men are generally more supportive than White or Latino men of egalitarian gender roles for both women and men.

Among traditional Latinas, stereotypical gender roles are characterized by *marianismo,* which involves being faithful and subordinate to husbands and maintaining family traditions and culture (McNeill et al., 2001). Though not all Latinas strive to maintain these gender-role stereotypes, those who do may experience conflict and stress as they try to balance these expectations with work-related and family demands.

According to available data, Asian Americans are relatively conservative in their attitudes about sexual behavior and norms. These attitudes, however, often change with increased exposure to the American culture (Okazaki, 2002). Asian Americans appear to share Asian cultural characteristics such as the central role of the family, the appropriateness of sexuality only within the context of marriage, and sexual restraint and modesty.

Female Sexual Scripts   Whereas the traditional male sexual script focuses on sex over feelings, the traditional female sexual script focuses on feelings over sex, on love over passion. The traditional female sexual script cited by psychologist and sex therapist Lonnie Barbach (2001) includes the following ideas:

- *Sex is good and bad.* Women are taught that sex is both good and bad. What makes sex good? Sex in marriage or a committed relationship. What makes sex bad? Sex in a casual or uncommitted relationship. Sex is "so good" that a woman needs to save it for her husband (or for someone with whom she is deeply in love). Sex is bad—if it is not sanctioned by love or marriage, a woman will get a bad reputation.

- *It's not OK to touch themselves "down there."* Girls are taught not to look at their genitals, not to touch them, and especially not to explore them. As a result, some women know very little about their genitals. They are often concerned about vaginal odors and labia size, making them uncomfortable about cunnilingus.

- *Sex is for men.* Men want sex; women want love. Women are sexually passive, waiting to be aroused. Sex is not a pleasurable activity as an end in itself; it is something performed *by* women *for* men.

- *Men should know what women want.* This script tells women that men know what they want even if women don't tell them. The woman is supposed to remain pure and sexually innocent. It is up to the man to arouse the woman even if he doesn't know what she finds arousing. To keep her image of sexual innocence, she does not tell him what she wants.

- *Women shouldn't talk about sex.* Many women are uncomfortable talking about sex because they are not expected to have strong sexual feelings. Some women may know their partners well enough to have sex with them but not well enough to communicate their needs to them.

- *Women should look like models.* The media present ideally attractive women as beautiful models with slender hips, supple breasts, and no fat or cellulite; they are always young, with never a pimple, wrinkle, or gray hair in sight. As a result of these cultural images, many women are self-conscious about their physical appearance. They worry that they are too fat, too plain, or too old. They often feel awkward without clothes on trying to hide their imagined flaws.

- *Women are nurturers.* Women give; men receive. Women give themselves, their bodies, their pleasures to men. Everyone else's needs come first: his desire over hers, his orgasm over hers.

- *There is only one right way to have an orgasm.* Women often "learn" that there is only one "right" way to have an orgasm: during sexual intercourse as a result of penile stimulation.

Changing Gender Roles

Contemporary gender roles are evolving from traditional hierarchical gender roles (in which one sex is subordinate to the other) to egalitarian roles (in which both sexes are treated equally) and to androgynous roles (in which both sexes display the instrumental and expressive traits previously associated with one sex). Thus, contemporary gender roles often display both traditional elements and egalitarian and androgynous ones.

Women are made, not born.
—Simone de Beauvoir
(1908–1986)

The beautiful bird gets caged.
—Chinese proverb

If men knew all that women think, they'd be twenty times more audacious.
—Alphonse Kerr
(1808–1890)

Men have traditionally coached women's and men's sports teams without ever being questioned or challenged. Changing gender roles are now supporting women in a wider array of fields and occupations.

> I don't know why people are afraid of new ideas. I am terrified of the old ones.
>
> —John Cage
> (1912–1992)

Contemporary female sexual scripts: Click on "Women Talk Sex" to hear what women have to say about how they like to be sexually stimulated.

Contemporary Sexual Scripts As gender roles change, so do sexual scripts. Traditional sexual scripts have been challenged by more egalitarian ones, and sexual attitudes and behaviors have become increasingly balanced for males and females. Many college-age women have made an explicit break with the more traditional scripts, especially the good girl/bad girl dichotomy and the belief that "nice" girls don't enjoy sex. Older professional women who are single also appear to reject outdated images.

Contemporary sexual scripts include the following elements for both sexes:

- Sexual expression is positive.
- Sexual activities involve a mutual exchange of erotic pleasure.
- Sexuality is equally involving, and both partners are equally responsible.
- Legitimate sexual activities are not limited to sexual intercourse but include a wide variety of sexual expression.
- Sexual activities may be initiated by either partner.
- Both partners have a right to experience orgasm, no matter from what type of stimulation.
- Sex is acceptable within a relationship context.

These contemporary scripts give more recognition to female sexuality and are increasingly relationship-centered rather than male-centered. Women, however, are still not granted full sexual equality with males. Only when men and women begin to recognize and free themselves from ineffectual and limiting stereotypes can they fully embrace their humanity.

Androgyny

> Once made equal to man, woman becomes his superior.
>
> —Socrates
> (c. 469–399 B.C.)

Some scholars have challenged the traditional masculine/feminine gender-role dichotomy, arguing that such models are unhealthy and fail to reflect the real world. Instead of looking at gender roles in terms of polar opposites, they suggest examining them in terms of androgyny. **Androgyny** refers to flexibility in gender roles and the unique combination of instrumental and expressive traits as influenced by individual differences, situations, and stages in the life cycle (Bem, 1975; A. Kaplan, 1979). (The term "androgyny" is derived from the Greek *andros,* man, and *gyne,* woman.) An androgynous person combines both the instrumental traits traditionally associated with masculinity and the expressive traits traditionally associated with femininity. An androgynous lifestyle allows men and women to choose from the full range of emotions and behaviors, according to their temperament, situation, and common humanity, rather than their gender. Thus, men can cry and display tenderness; they can touch, feel, and nurture. Women can be aggressive or career-oriented; they can seek leadership and can be mechanical or physical.

Flexibility and adaptability are important aspects of androgyny. Individuals who are rigidly instrumental or expressive, despite the situation, are not considered androgynous. A woman who is always aggressive at work and passive at home, for example, would not be considered androgynous, as work may call for compassion and home life for assertion.

Filling an androgynous gender role, however, may be just as stultifying to an individual as trying to be traditionally feminine or masculine. In advocating the expression of both feminine and masculine traits, perhaps we are imposing a new form of gender-role rigidity on ourselves.

> Throughout history the more complex activities have been defined and redefined, now as male, now as female—sometimes as drawing equally on the gifts of both sexes. When an activity to which each sex could have contributed is limited to one sex, a rich, differentiated quality is lost from the activity itself.
>
> —Margaret Mead
> (1901–1978)

Gender Variations

For most of us, there is no question about our gender: We *know* we are female or male. We may question our femininity or masculinity, but rarely do we question being female or male. For gender-variant individuals, or those who see themselves as part of a normal phenomenon with a right to self-definition and actualization in regard to sexual identity, "What sex am I?" is a real dilemma (Gijs & Brewaeys, 2007). Their answer to this question reinforces the fact that psychosexual development is influenced by multiple factors including exposure to androgens, sex chromosome genes, and brain structure, as well as social circumstance and family dynamics (Hughes, Houk, Ahmed, et al., 2006).

Because our culture views sexual anatomy as a male/female dichotomy, it is difficult for many people to accept the more recent view of gender variation (Figure 5.1) and the ways in which oppression impacts social identities. Most people still think of genetic sex—XX or XY—as a person's "true sex." Because gender is related to biological sex for most people, one of the primary challenges facing the public is to place the transgendered experience into a context by which

Boy or Girl? Click on "First Do No Harm" to get a glimpse of the issues surrounding sex assignment of intersexed children.

● FIGURE 5.1

Gender Variations: The Gender Continuum. In contrast to the traditional binary view, the concept of gender is on a continuum with a multitude of gender-variant identities.

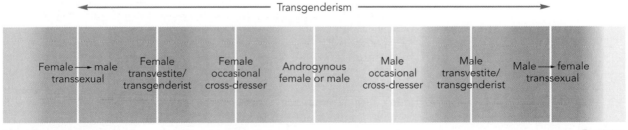

Transgenderism

Female → male transsexual | Female transvestite/transgenderist | Female occasional cross-dresser | Androgynous female or male | Male occasional cross-dresser | Male transvestite/transgenderist | Male → female transsexual

Masculine   Feminine

it can be readily understood. Transgender people are the most stigmatized and misunderstood of the larger sexual minorities (gay, lesbian, bisexual, transgender individuals) (Gender Education & Advocacy, 2001). While transgender people are most familiar with gender-variant expressions and cross-gender identities, there are many other forms of gender variance exhibited by all kinds of people, including cross-dressers, feminine gay men, "butch" lesbians, androgynes, transsexuals, and intersex people (Lev, 2007). Revealing these other forms of gender variance can provide an important context to understand transgender people. At the same time, it is important to recognize that none of the forms of gender variance necessarily makes anyone a transgender, gay, lesbian, or bisexual individual.

The Transgender Phenomenon

In recent years, there has been a major shift in the gender world. Upsetting old definitions and classification systems, a new transgender community, one that embraces the possibility of numerous genders and multiple social identities, has emerged.

Transgenderism is an inclusive category. The term "transgenderist" was first coined by Virginia Prince, the founding mother of the U.S. contemporary cross-dressing community, to describe someone who lives full-time in a gender role different from the gender role presumed by society to match the person's genetic sex (Richards, 1997).

In past decades, those who were transgendered could escape from the traditional male and female categories only if they were "diagnosed" as transvestite or transsexual (Denny, 1997). This resulted in a larger number of "heterosexual" cross-dressers who were actually gay or bisexual or who had transsexual issues. It also involved diagnosis on the part of the psychiatric community and subsequent labeling and stigma. In North America, a paradigm shift has occurred that challenges the male/female dichotomy of gender, thereby making it more acceptable to live in a permanent preoperative state without the threat of "cure." This acceptance has "opened the door for political and scientific activism and the realization that being preoperative is not inevitably a way-station on the road to surgery" (Denny, 1997).

Transgenderist Sky Renfro describes his gender identity (quoted in Feinberg, 1996):

> My identity, like everything else in my life, is a journey. It is a process and an adventure that in some ways brings me back to myself, back into the grand circle of living. . . . My sense of who I am at any given time is somewhere on that wheel and the place that I occupy there can change depending on the season and life events as well as a number of other influences. Trying to envision masculine at one end of a line and feminine on the other, with the rest of us somewhere on that line, is a difficult concept for me to grasp. Male and female—they're so close to each other, they sit next to each other on that wheel. They are not at opposite ends as far as I can tell. In fact, they are so close that they're sometimes not distinguishable.

This paradigm shift in thinking regarding gender has implications for the clinical management of gender identity disorder. Treatment is no longer aimed at identifying the "true transsexual" but is open instead to the possibility of affirming a unique transgender identity and role.

A growing number of major employers are posting first-of-a-kind policies covering transgender employees. Advocacy groups such as the Human Rights

The fact that we are all human beings is infinitely more important than all the peculiarities that distinguish humans from one another.

—Simone de Beauvoir
(1908–1986)

Campaign (HRC) are pushing to get transgender issues raised and their success is noted in the fact that in 2002, 15 Fortune 500 companies had protections for employees based on gender identity. Today, there are more than 60 that do. At the same time, transgender workers have little legal protection. In most states, it is legal to fire employees because they are transgendered.

Disorders of Sexual Development/Intersex

Researchers have long recognized the existence of individuals who are born with a variety of conditions other than a "standard" male or female anatomy. In the recent past, terms such as intersex, pseudohermaphroditism, hermaphroditism, sex reversal, and gender-based diagnostic labels have been used to describe the existence of atypical anatomy. However, these labels are now recognized by some individuals as controversial and confusing (Hughes, Houk, Ahmed, et al., 2006). The term **intersex** has been used to refer to a variety of conditions in which a person is born with a reproductive or sexual anatomy that doesn't fit the typical definitions of female or male (Intersex Society of North America [ISNA], 2008). As such, intersex conditions may or may not include atypical genital appearance. More recently, a proposed change in terminology is reflected in the term **disorders of sex development (DSD),** defined by congenital conditions in which development of chromosomal, gonadal, or anatomical sex is atypical. (We shall utilize both terms interchangeably.) It is estimated that genital anomalies occur in 1 in 4,500 births. With progress in diagnosis, surgical techniques, and understanding of psychosexual development, better management of DSD is evolving in a more positive direction.

What causes DSD? Despite the immediate definition of genetic sex at conception, the chromosome that carries the gene responsible for sexual differentiation will, by week 7 or 8, usually dictate which sex the child will be born. If the genetic or hormonal process that causes this fetal tissue to become male or female is disrupted, ambiguous genitalia can develop. Even if genetic sexual determinations occur normally, abnormal sexual differentiation can occur. Thus, a person is born with sex chromosomes, external genitalia, or an internal reproductive system that is not considered "standard" for either male or female, thereby making the person's sex unclear (ISNA, 2005). Sometimes, a child is born with an underdeveloped penis or an enlarged clitoris, making it uncertain whether the child is male or female. Such a child may look nearly male but have a small penis or hypospadias (discussed later in this section). (The most common DSDs are discussed below and summarized in Table 5.1.)

Disorders of Gonadal Differentiation Chromosomal anomalies are common. Disorders of sex development occur when an individual has fewer or more X or Y chromosomes than normal. Approximately 25% of all conceptions have a chromosomal abnormality ("Chromosomal Anomalies," 2004). Two syndromes resulting from erroneous chromosomal patterns may result in gender confusion: Turner syndrome and Klinefelter syndrome. In both of these, the body develops with some marked physical characteristics of the other sex.

> Treat people as if they were what they ought to be and you help them become what they are capable of being.
>
> Johann Goethe
> (1749–1832)

> Each time a person stands up for an ideal, or acts to improve the lot of others, or strikes out against injustice, he sends forth a tiny ripple of hope.
> That ripple builds others.
> Those ripples—crossing each other from a million different centers of energy—build a current that can sweep down the mightiest walls of oppression and injustice.
>
> —Senator Robert F. Kennedy
> (1925–1968)

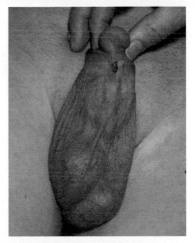

The genitals of a fetally androgenized female may resemble those of a male.

Table 5.1 • Disorders of Sexual Development

	Chromosomal Sex[a]	Gonads	Internal Reproductive Structures	External Reproductive Structures	Secondary Sex Characteristics	Fertility	Gender Identity
Disorders of Gonadal Differentiation							
Turner syndrome	Female (45, X)	Nonfunctioning or absent ovaries	Normal female except for ovaries	Underdeveloped genitals	No breast development or menstruation at puberty	Sterile	Usually female
Klinefelter syndrome	Male (47, XXY)	Testes	Normal male	Small penis and testes, gynecomastia (breast development)	Female secondary sex characteristics develop at puberty	Sterile	Usually male, but there may be gender confusion at puberty
Androgen-insensitivity syndrome	Male (46, XY)	Testes, but body unable to utilize androgen (testosterone)	Shallow vagina, lacks normal male structures	Labia	Female secondary sex characteristics develop at puberty; no menstruation	Sterile	Usually female
Congenital adrenal hyperplasia (pseudohermaphroditism)	Female (46, XX)	Ovaries	Normal female	Ambiguous tending toward male appearance; fused vagina and enlarged clitoris may be mistaken for empty scrotal sac and micropenis	Female secondary sex characteristics develop at puberty; abnormal growth for both sexes	Fertile	Usually male unless condition discovered at birth and altered by hormonal therapy
DHT deficiency	Male (46, XY)	Testes undescended until puberty	Partially formed internal structures but no prostate	Ambiguous; clitoral appearing micropenis; phallus enlarges and testes descend at puberty	Male secondary sex characteristics develop at puberty	Viable sperm but unable to inseminate	Female identity until puberty; majority assume male identity later
Unclassified Form of Abnormal Development							
Hypospadias	Male (46, XY)	Normal	Normal	Opening of penis located on underside rather than tip of penis; penis may also be twisted and small	Male secondary sex characteristics develop at puberty	Fertile	Male

[a]Chromosomal sex refers to 46, XX (female) or 46, XY (male). Sometimes a chromosome will be missing, as in 45, X, or there will be an extra chromosome, as in 47, XXY. In these notations, the number refers to the number of chromosomes (46, in 23 pairs, is normal); the letters X and Y refer to chromosomes.

A New Approach to Addressing Disorders of Sexual Development or Intersex

Disorders of sexual development occur in as much as 1% of the population. Sexually ambiguous infants have historically been given a gender assignment (usually female) along with treatment to support the assignment, including surgery, and, later, hormones and psychotherapy. Physicians have defended the practice of "correcting" ambiguous genitals, citing the success of current technology. Recently, however, this practice has undergone scrutiny by researchers and patients who point to the lack of evidence supporting its long-term success.

Endocrinologists, physicians, ethicists, and gender activists began in the 1990s to seriously challenge the traditional pediatric postulates for sex assignment/reassignment (Diamond, 1996; Diamond & Sigmundson, 1997a). Their research and that of others suggest that one's sexual identity is not fixed by the gender one is reared in, that atypical as well as typical individuals undergo psychosexual development, and that sexual orientation develops independent of rearing (Hughes, Houk, Ahmed, et al., 2006; ISNA, 2005; Reiner & Gearhart, 2004).

Many individuals consider whether or not to have surgery a decision best delayed unless medically urgent (as when a genetic anomaly interferes with urination or creates a risk of infection) or requested by the individual. They believe that letting well enough alone is the better course and that the erotic and reproductive needs of the adult should take precedence over the cosmetic needs of the child. Pointing to their own dissatisfaction, as well as to the lack of research supporting the long-term success of surgical treatment, those affected recommend that the professional community offer support and information to parents and families and empower the intersexed individual to understand his or her status and choose (or reject) medical intervention (Diamond & Sigmundson, 1997a). In cases where puberty may be psychologically traumatic, hormones may be used to delay its onset.

With children as young as 5 displaying predispositions to dress and behave like the other sex, the consensus to let children be "who they are" has finally emerged in a handful of school districts that have laws which respect parents' decisions about the gender of their child. Targeted to protect transgender students, some public schools are actively engaged in dismantling gender stereotypes by creating situations where students are no longer "boxed in." They do this,

for example, by encouraging a gender-neutral vocabulary, lining up students by sneaker color, and providing locker rooms that correspond to a student's chosen gender.

Though there is no one agreed-upon standard of care for those with disorders of sexual development, clinicians and other professionals can adopt general concepts of care that include (Hughes, Houk, Ahmed, et al., 2006):

- Avoid gender assignment before expert evaluation of newborns;
- Carry out evaluation and long-term management at a center with an experienced multidisciplinary team;
- Encourage patients and families to communicate openly and participate in decision making; and
- Address and respect patient and family concerns in strict confidence.

While there is no history to monitor the success for such proposed standards, Edgardo Menvielle, a child-adolescent psychiatrist, states: "We know that sexually marginalized children have a higher rate of depression and suicide attempts. The goal is for the child to be well-adjusted, healthy, and have good self-esteem. What's not important is molding their gender" (quoted in Brown, 2006). Such thinking, though still controversial, will no doubt alter the gender-identity landscape.

Think Critically

- Imagine you are the parent of a newborn and the doctor approaches you with the diagnosis that your child's sex is ambiguous. What, if anything, would you do? Whom might you consult? What might you tell your family and others?

- Of the two ways to address disorders of sexual development—immediate sexual assignment or waiting until the child identifies himself or herself as a particular sex—which would you choose and why?

- What are your thoughts about cosmetic genital surgeries performed on intersexed infants being compared to the practice of female genital cutting performed in some African and Asian countries? Which, if any, is more acceptable?

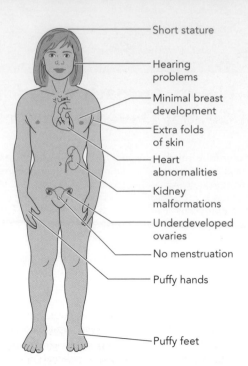

• FIGURE 5.2
Characteristics of Turner Syndrome

Short stature

Hearing problems

Minimal breast development

Extra folds of skin

Heart abnormalities

Kidney malformations

Underdeveloped ovaries

No menstruation

Puffy hands

Puffy feet

Turner Syndrome Females with **45, X,** or **Turner syndrome** are not XX and not XY. It is one of the most common chromosomal DSDs among females, occurring in an estimated 1 in 2,500 live female births (Fennell, 2003; ISNA, 2005). Infants and young girls with Turner syndrome appear normal externally, but they have no ovaries. At puberty, changes initiated by ovarian hormones cannot take place. The body does not gain a mature look or height, and menstruation cannot occur. The adolescent girl may question her femaleness because she does not menstruate or develop breasts or pubic hair like her peers. (See Figure 5.2.) Girls with Turner syndrome may have academic problems and poor memory and attention (Sybert & McCauley, 2004). Hormonal therapy, including androgen (testosterone) therapy, estrogen therapy, and human growth hormone (HGH) therapy, replaces the hormones necessary to produce normal adolescent changes, such as growth and secondary sex characteristics. Even with ongoing hormonal therapy, women with Turner syndrome will likely remain infertile, although they may successfully give birth through embryo transfer following in vitro fertilization with donated ova.

Klinefelter Syndrome Males with **Klinefelter syndrome** have one or more extra X chromosomes (47, XXY; 48, XXXY; or 49, XXXXY) (Zurenda & Sandberg, 2003a). Klinefelter syndrome is quite common, occurring in 1 in 1,000 live births (Blackless et al., 2000; ISNA, 2005). The effects of Klinefelter syndrome are variable, and many men with the syndrome are never diagnosed. The presence of the Y chromosome designates a person as male. It causes the formation of small, firm testes and ensures a masculine physical appearance. However, the presence of a double X chromosome pattern, which is a female trait, adds some female physical traits. At puberty, traits may vary:

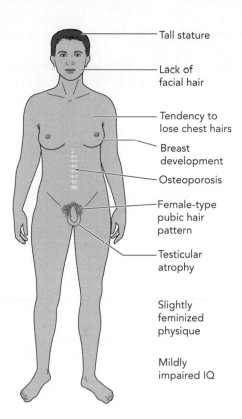

Tall stature

Lack of facial hair

Tendency to lose chest hairs

Breast development

Osteoporosis

Female-type pubic hair pattern

Testicular atrophy

Slightly feminized physique

Mildly impaired IQ

• FIGURE 5.3
Characteristics of Klinefelter Syndrome

tallness, gynecomastia (breast development in men), sparse body hair, and/or small penis and testes. (See Figure 5.3.) XXY boys also tend to exhibit some degree of learning disability. Long-term treatment with testosterone can alleviate some aspects of Klinefelter syndrome. Because of low testosterone levels, there may be a low sex drive, inability to experience erections, and infertility. Consequently, individuals will need testosterone replacement to prevent osteoporosis and maintain physical energy, sexual functioning, and well-being (Zurenda & Sandberg, 2003a). In vitro techniques can allow some men to become biological fathers.

Hormonal Disorders   Hormonal imbalances may cause males or females to develop physical characteristics associated with the other sex.

Androgen-Insensitivity Syndrome   **Androgen-insensitivity syndrome,** or **testicular feminization,** is a genetic, inherited condition passed through X chromosomes (except for occasional spontaneous mutations) (Mazur, Colsman, & Sandberg, 2007). It occurs in 1 in 13,000 individuals (Blackless et al., 2000; ISNA, 2005). A genetic male (XY) is born with testes, but because of the body's inability to absorb testosterone, the estrogen influence prevails. From the earliest stages, therefore, the body tends toward a female appearance while not developing male internal and external reproductive structures. Externally, the infant is female, with labia and vagina, but the internal female structures are not present. At puberty, the body develops breasts, hips, and other secondary female sex characteristics but does not grow pubic hair. The testes remain in the abdomen

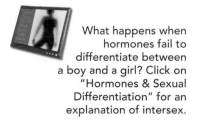

What happens when hormones fail to differentiate between a boy and a girl? Click on "Hormones & Sexual Differentiation" for an explanation of intersex.

and are sterile. People with androgen insensitivity are usually assigned female gender status at birth.

Physically, individuals with androgen-insensitivity syndrome develop as females, except for their inability to menstruate. It is often not until puberty that the physical anomaly is discovered. There has been controversy over the stability of gender identity and gender-role behavior among these individuals, especially as they transition through puberty (Cohen-Kettenis, 2005). Medical treatment may involve removal of the undescended testes (to reduce the risk of cancer) and estrogen replacement therapy (to prevent osteoporosis).

Congenital Adrenal Hyperplasia   In **congenital adrenal hyperplasia** (also known as pseudohermaphroditism), a genetic female (XX) with ovaries and a vagina develops externally as a male, the result of a malfunctioning adrenal gland. This condition is the most prevalent cause of intersex among females, with a frequency of about 1 in 13,000 births (Blackless et al., 2000; ISNA, 2005). It occurs when the adrenal gland produces androgen instead of androgen-inhibiting cortisone.

At birth, the child appears to be a male with a penis and an empty scrotum. The appearance, however, may be ambiguous. Some of these children have an enlarged clitoris, with or without a vaginal opening, some a micropenis, and some a complete penis and scrotum. When the condition is discovered at birth, the child is usually assigned female status, and treatment is given to promote female development. Though gender development is normally female, gender-role behavior is often masculine and there is a higher likelihood of females experiencing homoerotic dreams and sexual attraction (Zurenda & Sandberg, 2003b).

DHT Deficiency   Because of a genetic disorder, some males are unable to convert testosterone to the hormone dihydrotestosterone (DHT). This disorder is known as **DHT deficiency** but sometimes is also referred to as 5-alpha reductase syndrome. There is no available estimate on how often this condition occurs. DHT is required for the normal development of external male genitals. At birth, children with DHT deficiency have internal male organs but a clitoris-like penis, undescended testes, a labia-like scrotum, and a closed vaginal cavity. They may be assigned either a male or female gender at birth. At puberty, a virilization occurs when their testes descend and their phallus enlarges to resemble a penis. There is also an increase in muscle size, deepening of the voice, and no breast development.

Unclassified Form of Abnormal Development

Of unknown origin is a condition called **hypospadias** (hi-puh-SPAY-dee-as), in which the opening of the penis, rather than being at the tip, is located somewhere on the underside, glans, or shaft or at the junction of the scrotum. In addition, the foreskin may form a hood over the top of the glans, and there may be a twist in the shaft. In mild cases, the condition will form a slit in the underside of the glans. In more extreme cases, the urethra may be open from midshaft out to the glans, or the urethra may be entirely absent so that the urine exits the bladder behind the penis (Kappy, Blizzard, & Migeon, 1994). As many as 1 in every 100 boys are born with this condition each year in the

United States (CDC, 2004b). A variety of techniques are available to repair hypospadias when it is severe.

Gender Identity Disorder

According to the American Psychiatric Association, **gender identity disorder (GID)** consists of a strong and persistent cross-gender identification and persistent discomfort about one's assigned sex (American Psychiatric Association [APA], 2000). This diagnosis is not made if the individual has a concurrent physical disorder of sexual development or intersex condition. Furthermore, there must be clinically significant distress or impairment in social, occupational, or other important areas of functioning.

Investigations into the etiology of GID have not been able to reveal whether it is biological, psychological/environmental, or both. However, it has been suggested that there are unique factors that differentiate persons with intersex or disorders of sexual development and non-intersex conditions (Mazur, Colsman, & Sandberg, 2007). For example, among those with GID, gender problems appear before age 6, whereas, among those with intersex, gender problems occur during adolescence. Additionally, those with disorders of sexual development need monitoring by health-care professionals, beginning with the first few days of life (Meyer-Bahlburg, 1994). The final explanations in both groups await further research.

Boys with GID might be preoccupied with traditionally feminine activities. For example, they may prefer to dress in girls' or women's clothes, be attracted to stereotypical games and pastimes of girls, and express a wish to be a girl. They may insist on sitting to urinate and, more rarely, find their penis or testes disgusting. Girls with GID might display intense negative reactions to parental expectations or attempts to have them dress in feminine attire. Their fantasy heroes are often powerful male figures. Furthermore, they often prefer boys as playmates and show little interest in dolls or any form of feminine dress-up or role-play activity. They may claim that they will grow a penis and may not want to grow breasts or to menstruate. They may assert as well that they will grow up to be a man.

Adults with GID are preoccupied with their wish to live as a member of the other sex. This preoccupation may be manifested as an intense desire to adopt the social role of the other sex or to acquire the physical appearance of the other sex through hormonal or surgical correction. There is no diagnostic test specific for GID, nor are there data on its prevalence. However, there is counseling available for gender-variant individuals (Bieschke, Perez, & Debord, 2007).

Traditional medical treatment for GID has included three phases: (1) a real-life experience in the desired role, (2) hormones of the desired gender, and (3) surgery to change the genitalia and other sex characteristics. However, the diagnosis of GID invites the consideration of a broader spectrum of therapeutic options because the goal of treatment for people with GID is lasting comfort with the gendered self ("Standards of Care," 2001). The Harry Benjamin International Gender Dysphoria Association, a professional organization dedicated to the treatment of individuals with gender identity problems and dysphoria, has articulated a variety of factors and issues in treating those with GID. Though there are limitations to the knowledge in this area, there is an emerging thesis that the genitals are not the basis of

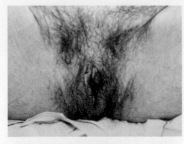

The genitals of a postoperative male-to-female transsexual, above, and the genitals of a postoperative female-to-male transsexual, below.

To hear Denise, a transsexual person, talk about her transgender experience, click on "Videocase: Denise."

Following hormone treatment and surgery, most transsexual individuals cannot be identified or differentiated from others.

the gendered self nor is assigned gender effective in establishing a gender identity (Vitale, 2005).

Transsexuality

In transsexuality, a person's gender identity and sexual anatomy are not compatible. Transsexual individuals are convinced that by some strange quirk of fate they have been given the body of the wrong sex. They generally want to change their sex, not their personality.

Transsexuality revolves around issues of gender identity; it is a distinctly different phenomenon from homosexuality. Gay men and lesbian women are not transsexuals. Rather, lesbian women and gay men feel confident of their female or male identity. Being a lesbian or gay person reflects sexual orientation rather than gender questioning. Furthermore, following surgery, transsexual individuals may or may not change their sexual orientation, whether it is toward members of the same, the other, or both sexes.

As mentioned, transsexual people often seek **sex reassignment surgery (SRS)** to bring their genitals in line with their gender identity and to diminish the serious suffering they experience. Male-to-female operations outnumber female-to-male by a ratio of 5 to 1 (Gijs & Brewaeys, 2007). Some transsexual individuals forgo the surgery but still identify themselves as transsexual, or transgendered, or gender variant.

The prevalence of transsexuality is unknown, though it is estimated that there may be 1 transsexual per 50,000 people over age 15 in the United States. There are also no known statistics on the number of postoperative transsexuals. Some cultures accept a gender identity that is not congruent with sexual anatomy and create an alternative third sex, as we saw in Chapter 1. "Men-women"— Native American two-spirits, Indian *hijras,* and Burmese *acaults*—are considered a third gender (Bullough, 1991; Coleman, Colgan, & Gooren, 1992; Roscoe, 1991). Members of this third gender are often believed to possess spiritual powers because of their "specialness."

think
about it

Sex Reassignment

Many transsexual people view their condition not as a psychological problem but as a medical one. As a result, they tend to seek surgeons to change their genitals rather than therapists to help them examine and then match their gender identity with their physical body. Gender reassignment is not about sex but about matching one's gender identity to one's physiological status.

Psychotherapy

Many individuals with gender identity disorder (GID) find that psychotherapy can be helpful in coming to an acceptance of themselves; however, not every adult gender patient requests therapy. Though effective for many, psychotherapy is not an absolute requirement prior to hormone therapy, real-life experience, or surgery (Gijs & Brewaeys, 2007).

Hormone Therapy

Hormonal treatments play an important role in the anatomical and psychological gender transition process and are often medically necessary for successful living in the new gender. When physicians administer androgens to biological females and estrogens, progesterone, and testosterone-blocking agents to biological males, patients feel and appear more like members of their preferred gender.

The Real-Life Experience

Living as a member of the preferred gender is essential. This is not an easy task, for such subtle gender clues as mannerisms, voice inflections, and body movement, learned in childhood, must be altered.

Sex Reassignment Surgery

Sex reassignment surgery (SRS), along with hormone therapy and real-life experience, is a treatment that has proved to be effective. Breast augmentation and removal are common operations. For the female-to-male patient, a mastectomy is usually the first surgery performed, sometimes when the individual begins hormones. For the male-to-female patient, augmentation may be performed if hormone treatment for 18 months is not sufficient.

Genital surgery for the male-to-female patient involves a penile inversion technique, in which doctors create a vaginal cavity with inverted penile skin, a rectosigmoid transplant, in which tissue is cut from the sigmoid section of the colon and used to create a vaginal cavity, or a free-skin graft to line the neovagina. A clitoris is formed from penile corpus spongiosum, and inner and outer lips are crafted from scrotal tissue. Other cosmetic procedures, such as nose surgery, tracheal shave, and electrolysis, may be performed. Though there may be some decline in orgasmic capacity, most postoperative transsexuals report an enjoyment of sexual activities.

In female-to-male patients, the ovaries, uterus, and breasts are removed. The clitoris, which has been enlarged by testosterone therapy, is refashioned into a penis, and the labia are formed into a scrotum. Several techniques may be used to simulate penile erection, ranging from the insertion of a semierect rod to the surgical implantation of an inflatable device. According to studies, orgasmic capacity and/or sexual satisfaction among postoperative transsexuals varies (Gijs, 2007). Parenthood is a choice for many transsexuals, and reproductive options are discussed with them in detail.

Follow-Up and Prognosis

Long-term postoperative follow-up is encouraged, from both a physical and psychological perspective. Research suggests that the majority of people who have undergone gender reassignment procedures report that sexual reassignment is the most appropriate treatment to alleviate the suffering of extremely gender dysphoric individuals (Gijs & Brewaeys, 2007).

Think Critically

- What would you say to another person who confided in you that he or she was experiencing gender dysphoria? To whom might you refer this person?

- What are your thoughts about psychotherapy as a requirement prior to hormone treatment or before sex reassignment surgery?

- How might you feel or react if it was revealed to you that your good friend, fellow student, or coworker had undergone sex reassignment surgery? Would it make any difference if this was a close or a distant friend? Lover?

SOURCE: Harry Benjamin International Gender Dysphoria Association. (2001). *Standards of Care for Gender Identity Disorders, Sixth Edition*. Available: http://www.wpath.org/Documents2/socv6.pdf.

Final Thoughts

We ordinarily take our gender as female or male for granted. The making of gender, however, is a complex process involving both biological and psychological elements. Biologically, we are male or female in terms of genetic and anatomical makeup. Psychologically, we are male or female in terms of our assigned gender and our gender identity. Only in rare cases, as with chromosomal and hormonal anomalies or gender dysphoria, can our gender identity be problematic. For most of us, gender identity is rarely a source of concern. More often, what concerns us is related to our gender roles: Am I sufficiently masculine? Feminine? What it means to be feminine or masculine differs from culture to culture. Although femininity and masculinity are generally regarded as opposites in our culture, there are relatively few significant inherent differences between the sexes aside from males impregnating and females giving birth and lactating. The majority of social and psychological differences are exaggerated or culturally encouraged. All in all, women and men are more similar than different.

Summary

Studying Gender and Gender Roles

- *Sex* is the biological aspect of being female or male. Gender encompasses the social and cultural characteristics associated with biological sex. Normal gender development depends on both biological and psychological factors. Psychological factors include *assigned gender* and *gender identity*. *Gender roles* tell us how we are to act as men and women in a particular culture. *Gender variations* occur among those who cannot or choose not to conform to societal gender norms.

- Although our culture encourages us to think that men and women are "opposite" sexes, they are more similar than dissimilar. Innate gender differences are generally minimal; differences are primarily encouraged by socialization.

- Masculine and feminine stereotypes assume heterosexuality. If men or women do not fit the stereotypes, they are likely to be considered gay or lesbian. Gay men and lesbian women, however, are as likely as heterosexuals to be masculine or feminine.

- *Gender theory* examines gender as a basic element in society and social arrangements. It focuses on how gender is created and how and why specific traits, behaviors, and roles benefit or cost women and men. In general, gender theorists believe gender differences are socially created to benefit men.

Gender-Role Learning

- *Cognitive social learning theory* emphasizes learning behaviors from others through cognition and modeling. *Cognitive development theory* asserts that once children learn gender is permanent they independently strive to act like "proper" girls and boys because of an internal need for congruence.

- *Social construction theory* views gender as a set of practices and performances that occur through language and a political system. *Queer theories* view sexuality as a system that cannot be understood as gender neutral or by the actions of heterosexuals.

- Though the stereotypes are somewhat outmoded, children still learn their gender roles from parents through manipulation, channeling, verbal appellation, and activity exposure. Parents, teachers, peers, and the media are the most important agents of socialization during childhood and adolescence.

- A *gender schema* is a set of interrelated ideas used to organize information about the world on the basis of gender. We use our gender schemas to classify many non-gender-related objects, behaviors, and activities as male or female.

Contemporary Gender Roles

- The traditional male gender role is *instrumental*. It emphasizes aggression, independence, and sexual prowess. Traditional male sexual *scripts* include the denial of the expression of feelings, an emphasis on performance and being in charge, the belief that men always want sex and that all physical contact leads to sex, and assumptions that sex equals intercourse and that sexual intercourse always leads to orgasm.

- Traditional female roles are *expressive*. They emphasize passivity, compliance, physical attractiveness, and being a wife and mother. Female sexual scripts suggest that sex is good and bad (depending on the context); genitals should not be touched; sex is for men; men should know what women want; women shouldn't talk about sex; women should look like models; women are nurturers; and there is only one "right" way to experience an orgasm.

- Important changes affecting today's gender roles and sexual scripts include increasing questioning of values and expectations around parenting, dating, and careers.

- Contemporary sexual scripts are more egalitarian than traditional ones and include the belief that sex is positive, that it involves a mutual exchange, and that it may be initiated by either partner.

- *Androgyny* combines traditional female and male characteristics into a more flexible pattern of behavior, rather than seeing them as opposites.

Gender Variations

- A number of atypical hormonal and chromosomal conditions can affect gender development. Some of these can result in people who are referred to as having *disorders of sexual development* or being *intersexed.* Disorders of gonadal differentiation include *Turner syndrome* and *Klinefelter syndrome, androgen-insensitivity syndrome, congenital adrenal hyperplasia,* and *DHT deficiency.* An unclassified form of abnormal development is *hypospadias.*

- A transgender community, one that embraces the possibility of numerous genders and multiple social identities, has emerged. A *transgender* individual is one who lives full-time in a gender role different from the gender role presumed by society to match that person's genetic sex.

- *Gender identity disorder* is the state of dissatisfaction individuals may experience about their gender. People who plan to or do transition to the "other" gender are known as transsexuals. This transition is known as *sex reassignment.* The causes of transsexuality are not known.

Questions for Discussion

- How have gender stereotypes and roles influenced your views of your sexuality and the ways in which you relate to others?

- If you had an infant born with ambiguous genitalia, would you opt for surgery? Inhibit the onset of puberty with drugs? What gender would you raise the child? If surgery were chosen, when the child was old enough, would you inform him or her about this treatment? Or would you not choose surgery, and instead leave the decision to the individual at a later time?

- Do you believe that your gender identity was biologically or socially determined? Who or what most influenced your gender identity? In what ways?

Sex and the Internet

Gender Studies

The number of gender studies has increased tremendously in recent years. Now, both men and women can learn more about the history and politics of gender by simply clicking onto a Web site. Go to the Voice of the Shuttle Gender Studies Page, based at the University of California at Santa Barbara (http://vos.ucsb.edu). Select one of these areas: "Women's Studies and Feminist Theories"; "Gay, Lesbian, and Queer Studies"; or "Men's Movement and Men's Studies." Click on three related links and read what they have to offer. Once you have read three articles, answer the following questions:

- What is the history of this subject area?

- How does the new information you have gathered influence the way you think about gender and/or sexual orientation?

- What was one specific aspect of this subject that most interested you?

- What is one point you still have questions about?

- What have you learned as a result of this research?

Suggested Web Sites

Bodies Like Ours
http:/www.bodieslikeours.org/forums
Information and peer support for the intersex community.

Disorders of Sexual Development
www.dsdguidelines.org
Handbooks for clinicians and parents about the diagnosis, treatment, education, and support of those children with disorders of sexual development.

Intersex Society of North America
http://www.isna.org
Information, referrals, and support for those who are seeking information and advice about atypical reproductive anatomies and disorders of sexual development.

Johns Hopkins Children's Center
http://hopkinschildrens.org
Training programs, research, and services related to variations in gender and sex differentiation.

National Center for Transgender Equity
http://nctequality.org
Dedicated to advancing the equality of transgender people through advocacy, collaboration, and empowerment.

United Nations Inter-Agency Network on Women and Gender
http://www.un.org/womenwatch
Gateway to information and resources on the promotion of gender equality.

World Professional Association for Transgender Health (WPATH)
http://www.wpath.org
A professional organization that provides standards of care and is devoted to the understanding and treatment of gender identity disorders.

Suggested Reading

Bieschke, K. J., Perez, R. M., & Debord, K. A. (Eds.). (2007). *Handbook of counseling and psychotherapy with lesbian, gay, bisexual and transgender clients.* Washington, DC: American Psychological Association. An authoritative guide to assist and support counselors treating sexual orientation and identity.

Brizendine, L. (2006). *The female brain.* Northridge, CA: Morgan Road. Argues that it is nature, not nurture, that creates behavioral and emotional differences between men and women.

Brill, S. & Pepper, R. (2008). *The transgender child. A guide for families and professionals.* Provides an extensive understanding of gender-variant and transgender youth.

Dreger, A. D. (2004). *One of us: Conjoined twins and the future of normal.* Cambridge, MA: Harvard University Press. An analysis of children born with anatomical anomalies and the lives they lead.

Fausto-Sterling A. (2000). *Sexing the body: Gender politics and the construction of sexuality.* New York: Basic Books. An examination of the cultural biases underlying scientific thought on gender.

Lips, H. (2007). *Sex and gender: An introduction* (6th ed.). Burr Ridge, IL: McGraw-Hill. Gender theories, research, and issues examined and discussed in light of their similarities and differences.

Meyer, I. H., & Northridge, M. E. (Eds.). (2006) *The health of sexual minorities. Public health perspectives on lesbian, gay, bisexual and transgender populations.* New York: Springer. Challenges assumptions about how people manage their identities at various stages of their lives.

For links, articles, and study material, go to the McGraw-Hill Web site, located at **www.mhhe.com/yarber7e.**

Sexuality in Childhood and Adolescence

6

chapter

"I cannot say that I am sexually attracted to females, but I get lost in their looks and their angelic energy. I love to kiss girls and have close relationships with them. There is a liberating and beautiful trust that I find between certain women and myself that I have not shared with a man. I am, however, sexually attracted to men and love to be affectionate and have relationships with them."

—22-year-old female

"I discovered that White and Latino men find me attractive, but I'm still hurt that I don't fit in completely with my own people. I'm sure most of it has to do with my baggage and me. I sometimes see Black men's heads turn, and some speak to me. But it's when that one or two don't; it's like a stab in the heart again. I believe that I reject those who show interest because of what Black guys in my past have put me through. Perhaps I think if I'm myself around them they may think I talk White and I'm stuck up. Because they have never wanted me, my preference is now Latino men."

—19-year-old Black female

"For most of college, I dated several women, but I never found the right one. Sex is special to me, and although at times I feel like just doing it with anyone, like all my friends, I don't. However, the first time that I did have actual intercourse was in my sophomore year with a random person. I was almost 20 years old and living in my fraternity house. Constantly, I was bombarded with stories of the conquests of my fraternity brothers. Why was I different? I had remained a virgin for so long, and up until then I was pretty secure about it. But during that time, not only did I give up my virginity, but I also slipped in life. This represented a major down time for me."

—25-year-old male

As we consider the human life cycle from birth to death, we cannot help but be struck by how profoundly sexuality weaves its way through our lives. From the moment we are born, we are rich in sexual and erotic potential, which begins to take shape in our sexual curiosity and experimentations in childhood. As children, we are only partly formed, but the world around us helps shape our sexuality. In adolescence, our education continues as a random mixture of learning, yearning, and experimenting with new behaviors.

In this chapter, we discuss both the innate and the learned aspects of sexuality, from infancy through adolescence. We examine both physical development and **psychosexual development,** which involves the psychological aspects of sexuality. We see how culture, family, media, and other factors affect children's feelings about their bodies and influence their sexual feelings and activities. We look at how the physical changes experienced by teenagers affect their sexual awareness and sexual identity as heterosexual, gay, lesbian, bisexual, or transgendered individuals. And we discuss adolescent sexual behaviors, teenage pregnancy, teenage parenthood, and sexuality education.

● Sexuality in Infancy and Childhood (Ages 0 to 11)

Our understanding of infant sexuality is based on observation and inference. It is obvious that babies derive sensual pleasure from stroking, cuddling, bathing, and other tactile stimulation. Ernest Borneman, a researcher of children's sexuality in the 1950s, suggested that the first phase of sexual development be called the cutaneous phase (from the Greek *kytos,* skin). During this period, an infant's skin can be considered a "single erogenous zone" (Borneman, 1983).

The young child's healthy psychosexual development lays the foundation for further stages of growth. Psychosexual maturity, including the ability to love, begins to develop in infancy, when babies are lovingly touched all over their bodies (which appear to be designed to attract the caresses of their elders).

Infants and young children communicate by smiling, gesturing, crying, and so on. Before they understand the language, they learn to interpret movements, facial expressions, body language, and tone of voice. Humans' earliest lessons are conveyed in these ways. Infants begin to learn how they "should" feel about their bodies. If a parent frowns, speaks sharply, or slaps an exploring hand, the infant quickly learns that a particular activity—touching the genitals, for example—is wrong. The infant may or may not continue the activity, but if he or she does, it will be in secret, probably accompanied by feelings of guilt and shame.

Infants also learn about the gender role they are expected to fulfill (Bussey & Bandura, 1999). In our culture, baby girls are often handled more gently than baby boys, are dressed up more, and are given soft toys and dolls to play with. Baby boys, in contrast, are expected to be "tough." Their dads may rough-house with them and speak more loudly to them than to baby girls. They are given "boy toys"—blocks, cars, and action figures. This gender-role learning is reinforced as the child grows older (see Chapter 5).

Conscience is the inner voice which warns us that someone may be looking.
—H. L. Mencken
(1880–1956)

Infancy and Sexual Response (Ages 0 to 2)

Infants can be observed discovering the pleasure of genital stimulation soon after they are born. However, the body actually begins its first sexual response even earlier, in utero, when sonograms have shown that boys have erections. This begins a pattern of erections that will occur throughout their lives. Signs of sexual arousal in girls, though less easily detected, begin soon after birth and include vaginal lubrication and genital swelling. In some cases, both male and female infants have been observed experiencing what appears to be an orgasm. Obviously, an infant is unable to differentiate sexual pleasure from other types of enjoyment, so viewing these as sexual responses are adult interpretations of these normal reflexes and do not necessarily signify the infant's desire or interest. What it does reveal is that the capacity for sexual response is present soon after conception (DeLamater & Friedrich, 2002).

Childhood Sexuality (Ages 3 to 11)

Children become aware of sex and sexuality much earlier than many people realize. They generally learn to disguise their interest rather than risk the disapproval of their elders, but they continue as small scientists—collecting data, performing experiments, and attending conferences with their colleagues.

Curiosity and Sex Play   Starting as early as age 3, when they start interacting with their peers, children begin to explore their bodies together. They may masturbate or play "mommy and daddy" and hug and kiss and lie on top of each other; they may play "doctor" so that they can look at each other's genitals. Author and social justice activist Letty Cottin Pogrebin (1983) suggests that we think of children as "students" rather than "voyeurs." It is important for them to know what others look like in order to feel comfortable about themselves.

I do not think that there is even one good reason for denying children the information which their thirst for knowledge demands.
—Sigmund Freud
(1856–1939)

Kissing and cuddling are essential to an infant's healthy psychosexual development.

Children are naturally curious about bodies. It is important that these kinds of explorations are seen as normal and not be labeled "bad."

Physician and noted sexuality educator Mary Calderone (1983) stressed that children's sexual interest should never be labeled "bad" but that it may be deemed inappropriate for certain times, places, or persons. According to Calderone, "The attitude of the parents should be to socialize for privacy rather than to punish or forbid." If children's natural curiosity about their sexuality is satisfied, they are likely to feel comfortable with their own bodies as adults.

Children who participate in sex play generally do so with their own sex. In fact, same-sex activity is probably more common during the childhood years when the separation of the sexes is particularly strong (DeLamater & Friedrich, 2002).

Most go on to develop heterosexual orientations; some do not. But whatever a person's sexual orientation, childhood sex play clearly does not *create* the orientation. The origins of sexual orientation are not well understood; in some cases, there may indeed be a biological basis. Many gay men and lesbian women say that they first became aware of their attraction to the same sex during childhood, but many heterosexual people also report attraction to the same sex. These feelings and behaviors appear to be quite common and congruent with healthy psychological development in heterosexual, lesbian, and gay individuals (DeLamater & Friedrich, 2002).

Masturbation and Permission to Feel Pleasure   Most of us masturbate; most of us also were raised to feel guilty about it. When college students were asked to recall when they first masturbated, about 40% of the women and 38% of the men remember masturbating before puberty (Bancroft, Herbenick, & Reynolds, 2003). But the message "If it feels good, it's bad" is often internalized at an early age, leading to psychological and sexual difficulties in later life. Virtually all psychologists, physicians, child development specialists, and other professionals agree that masturbation is healthy. Negative responses from adults only magnify the guilt and anxiety that a child is taught to associate with this behavior.

> *A good thing about masturbation is that you don't have to dress up for it.*
> —Truman Capote
> (1924–1984)

Children often accidentally discover that playing with their genitals is pleasurable and continue this activity until reprimanded by an adult. Male infants have been observed with erect penises a few hours after birth. A baby boy may laugh in his crib while playing with his erect penis. Baby girls sometimes move their bodies rhythmically, almost violently, appearing to experience orgasm. By the time they are 4 or 5, children have usually learned that adults consider this form of behavior "nasty." Parents generally react negatively to masturbation, regardless of the age and sex of the child. Later, this negative attitude becomes generalized to include the sexual pleasure that accompanies the behavior. Children thus learn to conceal their masturbatory play.

When boys and girls reach adolescence, they no longer regard masturbation as ambiguous play; they know that it is sexual. This is a period of intense change, emotionally and biologically. Complex emotions are often involved in adolescent masturbation. Teenagers may feel guilt and shame for engaging in a practice that their parents and other adults indicate is wrong or bad, and they may be fearful of discovery. A girl who feels vaginal lubrication or finds stains on her underwear for the first time may be frightened, as may a boy who sees the semen of his first ejaculation. Yet, many find masturbation very pleasurable. Although open discussion could alleviate fears, frank talk is not always possible in a setting that involves shame. (Masturbation is discussed further in Chapter 9.)

Children need to understand that pleasure from self-stimulation is normal and acceptable. But they also need to know that self-stimulation is something that we do in private, yet something that some people are uncomfortable with.

When Children "Act Out": Red Flags for Problematic Sexual Behavior
Distinguishing between normal and problematic childhood sexual behaviors is a matter of degree and context of the behavior and may be difficult for many parents and adults to recognize. When a child exhibits persistence and intensity with a sexual activity and it can be tied to other troubling behaviors, there may be broader issues that need to be addressed. For example, if a child appears preoccupied with touching himself or herself or others in public or appears to know "too much" about sexual behaviors, there may be cause for concern for

parents or caregivers. It is important, at the same time, to know that the expression of sexuality is only one component of many factors to consider before designating a behavior as a sexual problem. If, however, sexual abuse or an emotional problem is suspected, professional help should be sought. (Child sexual abuse is discussed further in Chapter 17.)

The Family Context

Family styles of physical expression and feelings about modesty, privacy, and nudity vary considerably.

Family Nudity   Some families are comfortable with nudity in a variety of contexts: bathing, swimming, sunbathing, dressing, undressing. Others are comfortable with partial nudity from time to time: when sharing the bathroom, changing clothes, and so on. Still others are more modest and carefully guard their privacy. Most researchers and therapists would agree that all these styles can be compatible with the creation of sexually well-adjusted children, as long as some basic guidelines are observed:

- *Accept and respect a child's body (and nudity).* If 4-year-old Chantel runs naked into her parents' dinner party, she should be greeted with friendliness, not horror or harsh words. If her parents are truly uncomfortable, they can help her get dressed matter-of-factly, without recrimination.

- *Do not punish or humiliate a child for seeing his or her parents naked, going to the bathroom, or being sexual with each other.* If the parent screams or lunges for a towel, little Robbie will think he has witnessed something wicked or frightening. He can be gently reminded that mommy or daddy wants privacy at the moment.

- *Respect a child's need for privacy.* Many children, especially as they approach puberty, become quite modest. It is a violation of the child's developing sense of self not to respect his or her need for privacy. If 9-year-old Jeremy starts routinely locking the bathroom door or 11-year-old Sarah covers her chest when a parent interrupts her while she is dressing, it is most likely a sign of normal development. Children whose privacy and modesty are respected will learn to respect those of others.

Expressing Affection   Families also vary in the amount and type of physical contact in which they engage. Some families hug and kiss, give back rubs, sit and lean on each other, and generally maintain a high degree of physical closeness. Some parents extend this closeness to their sleeping habits, allowing their infants and small children in their beds each night. (In many cultures, this is the rule rather than the exception.) Other families limit their contact to hugs and tickles. Variations of this kind are normal. Concerning children's needs for physical contact, we can make the following generalizations:

- *All children (and adults) need freely given physical affection from those they love.* Although there is no prescription for the right amount or form of such expression, its quantity and quality affect both children's emotional well-being and the emotional and sexual health of the adults they will become.

- *Children should be told, in a nonthreatening way, what kind of touching by adults is "good" and what is "bad."* Children need to feel that they are in charge of their own bodies, that parts of their bodies are "private property," and that no one has the right to touch them with sexual intent.

- *It is not necessary to frighten a child by going into great detail about the kinds of things that might happen.* A better strategy is to instill a sense of self-worth and confidence in children so that they will not allow themselves to be victimized.
- *We should listen to children and trust them.* Children need to know that if they are sexually abused it is not their fault. They need to feel that they can tell about it and still be worthy of love.

Sexuality in Adolescence (Ages 12 to 19)

Puberty is the stage of human development when the body becomes capable of reproduction. For legal purposes (e.g., laws relating to child abuse), puberty is considered to begin at age 12 for girls and age 14 for boys. **Adolescence** is the social and psychological state that occurs between the beginning of puberty and acceptance into full adulthood.

Psychosexual Development

Adolescents are sexually mature (or close to it) in a physical sense, but they are still learning about their gender and social roles, and they still have much to learn about their sexual scripts (see Chapter 5). They may also be struggling to understand the meaning of their sexual feelings for others and their sexual orientation.

Physical Changes During Puberty   Though the mechanisms that activate the chain of development that occurs during puberty are not fully understood, researchers have observed that as the child approaches puberty, beginning about age 9 or 10, the levels of hormones begin to increase. This period of rapid physical changes is triggered by the hypothalamus, which plays a central role in increasing secretions that cause the pituitary gland to release large amounts of hormones into the bloodstream. The hormones, called gonadotropins, stimulate activity in the gonads and are chemically identical in boys and girls. In girls, they act on the ovaries to produce estrogen; in boys, they cause the testes to increase testosterone production. These higher levels of male and female hormones result in the development of specific external signs of male and female sexual maturation, known as secondary sex characteristics, including the onset of menstruation (in girls) and ejaculation (in boys). (See Figure 6.1.)

In girls, physical changes usually begin between ages 7 and 14. These include a rapid increase in height (called the growth spurt), the development of breasts, the growth of pubic and underarm hair, and the onset of vaginal mucous secretions. Menarche, the onset of menstruation, follows within a year or two. The average age of menstruation is 12 years 4 months, although girls may begin menstruating as early as 9 or as late as 17 (Anderson & Must, 2005).

Given the fact that girls are undergoing sexual maturation at a younger age than previous studies had indicated, parents would be advised to read about the wide variety of changes and behaviors that exist among adolescents and discuss these changes with their children prior to the onset of puberty. Early puberty is now occurring in girls as young as 8 and is more often seen in young Black girls. No one is quite sure what is causing this early sexual development. A number of potential factors, including weight gain, a protein called leptin (produced by body fat), hormones in meat and milk, and exposure to chemicals that act as hormone disrupters, such as PCBs and certain pesticides, have been implicated (Anderson & Must, 2005; Lee, Appugliese, Kaciroti, et al., 2007; Steingraber,

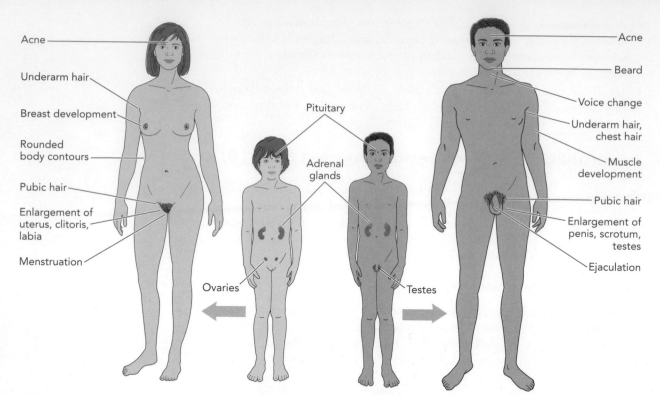

Acne

Underarm hair

Breast development

Rounded
body contours

Pubic hair

Enlargement of
uterus, clitoris,
labia

Menstruation

Ovaries

Pituitary

Adrenal
glands

Testes

Acne

Beard

Voice change

Underarm hair,
chest hair

Muscle
development

Pubic hair

Enlargement of
penis, scrotum,
testes

Ejaculation

● **FIGURE 6.1**

**Physical and Hormonal Changes
During Puberty**

Click on "Period
Piece" to hear ways
that women plan to
celebrate the next generation of
menstruating girls.

2007). Experts find early menarche concerning for a number of reasons, including a possible increase in the risk of breast and uterine cancers later in life. One explanation for this is a greater lifetime exposure to estrogen. Biologist Sandra Steingraber (2007), herself a cancer survivor, concludes in her review of literature on early puberty that it is an ecological disorder resulting from a variety of environmental hits.

Perhaps as troubling as the early physical changes that are occurring are the potential psychological effects of premature sexual development. The concern, of course, is that young girls who *look* older than they are, are being pressured to *act* older. Unfortunately, when children are bombarded by sexual images and their bodies push them toward adulthood before they are ready psychologically, they lose the freedom to be a child. The cultural pressure to short-circuit the time when a young girl is developing her sense of self and her place in the world can set a dangerous precedent for later behavior. Because hormonal changes often stoke the fires of sexual curiosity and behavior in young people, early dating and possible progression toward sexual intercourse may begin at a young age. Given the many psychological motives that are involved in sexual activity, if a young person is not prepared for the outcomes and responsibilities that accompany sexual behavior, social, psychological, and emotional problems can result.

How are boys responding to this phenomenon? There has been less research on the issue, and that which does exist is controversial and inconclusive. The growth spurt in boys typically begins around age 13, with earlier changes less noticed and reported than in girls. How boys are reacting to the younger girls' earlier maturation apparently hasn't changed much, however. According to Glenn Elliott, director of child and adolescent psychiatry at the University of California Medical Center in San Francisco, "They really don't have much concept of sex" (quoted in Greenwald, 2000).

In boys, physical changes include a growth spurt; hand and foot growth; muscle-mass growth; voice deepening; and hair growth on the face, the underarms, and the pubic area, and sometimes on other parts of the body. The penis and testicles also grow larger. Some boys reach puberty around age 12; others, not until their later teens. Generally, however, they lag about 2 years behind girls in pubertal development.

The scarcity of research on early orgasm is apparent in contemporary sexology (Janssen, 2007). However, we do know that at puberty, boys begin to ejaculate semen, which accompanies the experience of orgasm they may have been having for some time. Just as girls often do not know what is happening when they begin to menstruate, many boys are unnerved by the first appearance of semen as a result of masturbation or **nocturnal emissions** during sleep ("wet dreams"). Like menstruation for girls, the onset of ejaculation is a sexual milestone for boys: It is the beginning of their fertility. Alfred Kinsey called first ejaculation the most important psychosexual event in male adolescence (Kinsey, Pomeroy, & Martin, 1948).

What can parents do when these early changes occur? As always, they should try to maintain open lines of communication, assuring girls that the changes they are going through are natural and normal and continuing to love them for who they are. At the same time, boys should know that girls naturally mature earlier than they do and should be made to feel OK about their own (slower) development. Preparing young adolescents for these changes might help to alleviate the emotional roller coaster that many experience.

Influences on Psychosexual Development Besides biological forces, numerous factors are known to increase or decrease teen sexual behavior (Kirby, 2007). Though teens' behaviors cannot necessarily be controlled, parents and other concerned adults can attempt to affect the factors that influence teens' sexual decisions in order to facilitate the development of a healthy sexuality.

Parental Influence Children learn a great deal about sexuality from their parents. For the most part, however, they learn, not because their parents set out to teach them, but because they are avid observers of their parents behavior and family dynamics and characteristics. Much of what they learn involves the connection (or lack of) they have with their parents.

As they enter adolescence, young people are especially concerned about their own sexuality, but they are often too embarrassed to ask their parents directly about these "secret" matters. And most parents are ambivalent about their children's developing sexual nature. Parents often underestimate their children's involvement in sexual activities, even as their children progress through adolescence, and so perceive less need to discuss sexuality with them. They are often fearful that their children (daughters especially) will become sexually active if they have "too much" information. They tend to indulge in wishful thinking: "I'm sure Jenny's not really interested in boys yet"; "I know Jose would never do anything like that." Parents may put off talking seriously with their children about sex, waiting for the "right time." Or they may bring up the subject once, make their points, breathe a sigh of relief, and never mention it again. Consequently, college students have reported that they rarely if ever discussed sex with their parents, and, if they did, those conversations were with same-sex parents (Sprecher, Harris, & Meyers, 2008). Sociologist John Gagnon calls this the "inoculation" theory of sexuality education: "Once is enough" (Roberts, 1983). But children need frequent "boosters" of sexual knowledge. Not talking about sex-related issues

> *Most mothers think that to keep young people from love making it is enough not to speak of it in their presence.*
>
> —Marie Madeline de la Fayette (1634–1693)

Rites of passage are built into the traditions of most cultures. Among them are the Jewish Bar Mitzvah, Indian Navjote ritual, and South African Xhosa initiation rite.

can have serious consequences, leaving adolescents vulnerable to other sources of information and opinions, such as media and peers.

Family characteristics and dynamics exhibit a strong influence on teens' sexual attitudes and behaviors, most notably living with and experiencing close relationships with both parents, having parents who are more educated and have adequate family income, feeling parental support and connection, having no family abuse of alcohol or drugs, and having parents who identify sexual risk-taking and early childbearing as inconsistent with their own values (Kirby, 2007). When parents have early and consistent conversations in an open and comfortable manner with their children, many of the risk factors associated with teen sexuality can be reduced.

Parents can also contribute to their children's feelings of self-worth through ongoing demonstrations of acceptance and affection. Adolescents need to know that their sexuality is OK and that they are loved in spite of the changes they are going through. Whereas low self-esteem increases vulnerability to peer pressure, high self-esteem increases adolescents' confidence and can enhance their sense of responsibility regarding their sexual behavior.

● **FIGURE 6.2**

Percentage of U.S. Men and Women Aged 18–19 Who Talked With a Parent About "How to Say No to Sex," "Methods of Birth Control," and "Sexually Transmitted Diseases."
(*Source:* Abma, Martinez, Mosher, & Dawson, 2004.)

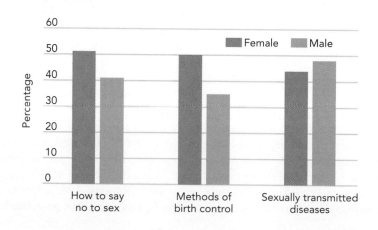

Peer Influence Consistent in most research findings is that adolescents receive more information about sex from peers (especially if they are same-sex) than from any other source (Sprecher, Harris, & Meyers, 2008). Additionally, they may put pressure on each other to carry out traditional gender roles. Boys encourage other boys to be sexually active even if they are unprepared or uninterested. They must camouflage their inexperience with bravado, which increases misinformation; they cannot reveal sexual ignorance. Bill Cosby (1968) recalled the pressure to have sexual intercourse as an adolescent: "But how do you find out how to do it without blowin' the fact that you don't know how to do it?" On his way to his first sexual encounter, he realized that he didn't have the faintest idea of how to proceed:

> So now I'm walkin', and I'm trying to figure out what to do. And when I get there, the most embarrassing thing is gonna be when I have to take my pants down. See, right away, then, I'm buck naked . . . buck naked in front of this girl. Now, what happens then? Do . . . do you just . . . I don't even know what to do . . . I'm gonna just stand there and she's gonna say, "You don't know how to do it." And I'm gonna say, "Yes, I do, but I forgot." I never thought of her showing me, because I'm a man and I don't want her to show me. I don't want nobody to show me, but I wish somebody would kinda slip me a note.

Even though many teenagers find their early sexual experiences less than satisfying, they still seem to feel a great deal of pressure to conform, which means becoming or continuing to be sexually active. The social effects on teen sexuality are strong. Teens are more likely to be sexually active if their best friends and peers are sexually active and are older, use alcohol or drugs, or engage in other risky behaviors (Kirby, 2007). Similarly, simply having a romantic partner increases the chances of sexual activity, especially if that partner is older.

What may not seem apparent but is consistent with the impact of peers on sexual behavior is the role of peer rejection, especially for girls. Rejection by peers in childhood is associated, at least indirectly, with the early onset of sexual intercourse (Brendgen, Wanner, & Vitaro, 2007). More specifically, peer rejection is related to low self-esteem, which is related to an increased risk of early sexual intercourse. Interestingly, and for unknown reasons among boys, it is higher self-esteem that is related to early onset of sexual intercourse.

Young people's ability to communicate their sexual beliefs and desires is a necessary step toward their development of healthy sexual intimacy. In this society, where traditional gender roles establish expectations that men will initiate sexual activity and women will respond with permission or denial, it is especially critical that girls and young women be able to clearly communicate their sexual beliefs and desires in order to protect their sexual health and autonomy. If, for

In addition to biological factors, social forces strongly influence young teenagers. Because certain types of violence and aggression are considered "manly" in our culture, the boys in this photograph (top) take great pleasure in a video game featuring simulated violence. For adolescent girls, the physical and social changes of puberty often result in a great deal of interest (some would say obsession) with personal appearance, including the selection of makeup, clothing, and shoes.

example, a young woman does not believe that she has the right to be sexually assertive, her risk of pregnancy and STIs is increased. In a study of 904 sexually active women aged 14–26, almost 20% believed that they did not have the right to communicate about or control aspects of their sexual behavior, including the right to refuse to have sexual intercourse, to ask their partner if he has been examined for STIs, or to say when their partner was being too rough (Rickert, Sanghvi, & Wiemann, 2002). Given that an important part of adolescence is the development of a healthy sexuality and sexual self-esteem, parents, teachers, and the rest of us need to communicate with both boys and girls about their desires, needs, and boundaries and provide the tools and support they need to navigate them.

For boys, especially those with working-class backgrounds, adolescence is characterized by relationships in which self-esteem and status are more closely linked to evaluations from people of the same sex than of the other sex. This characterization has important consequences in terms of relationships with girls. To a boy, his girlfriend's importance may lie in giving him status among other boys; his relationship with her may be secondary. The generalized role expectations of males—that they must be competitive, aggressive, and achievement-oriented—carry over into sexual activities. They receive recognition for "scoring" with a girl, much as they would for scoring a touchdown or hitting a home run. Girls, in contrast, run the risk of being labeled as "sluts" by both male and female peers if they have sex in any context other than a committed relationship.

The Media   As discussed in Chapter 1, erotic portrayals—nudity, sexually provocative language, and displays of sexual passion—are of great interest to the American viewing public. This public includes many curious and malleable children and adolescents who don't just absorb mass media representations but respond to them in various ways (Couch, Dowsett, Dutertrc, et al., 2006). In an era in which we are bombarded with sexual images, the challenge of making healthy choices about sex is substantial. Given that teens watch about 3 hours of television every day, of which 70% contains sexual content, it is not surprising that the pervasive and explicit exposure increases teens' willingness to experiment with sex. The growing influence of the media on teens' attitudes and behaviors makes it apparent how important it is for parents to understand and discuss with their children the nature and extent of the information being conveyed (Kunkel, Eyal, Finnerty, et al., 2005).

Although some people would protect young viewers by censoring what is shown on television or the Internet, or played on the radio or CDs, a more viable solution to sexual hype in the media is to balance it with information about real life. Parents can help their children understand that sexuality occurs in a context, that it involves several psychological and physical components, and that it entails a great deal of personal responsibility. Themes from television can be used by parents to initiate discussions about sex, love, and desire (including the goal of advertisers to sell their products) and encourage their children to think for themselves. It's also important to remember that the media also offer positive and informative sexual messages and outcomes that can be instrumental in educating young people about sex.

Gay, Lesbian, and Questioning Adolescents

During adolescence and early adulthood, sexual orientation becomes a very salient issue. In fact, few adolescents experience this as a trouble- or anxiety-free time. Many young people experience sexual fantasies involving others of their own sex; some engage in same-sex play. For many, these feelings of sexual attraction are a normal stage of sexual

Lesbian and gay teenagers often have an especially difficult time coming to terms with their sexuality because some sectors of society disapprove of their orientation.

development, but for 2–10% of the population, the realization of a romantic attraction to members of their own sex will begin to grow (Ellis, Robb, & Burke, 2005; Laumann, Gagnon, Michael, & Michaels, 1994). Some gay men and lesbian women report that they began to be aware of their "difference" in middle or late childhood. Thus, the term "questioning" is used to describe those individuals who are examining their sexual orientation during this time of life. Gay and lesbian adolescents usually have heterosexual dating experiences, and some engage in intercourse during their teens, but they often report ambivalent feelings about them.

Society in general has difficulty dealing with adolescent sexuality. Accepting the fact of gay and lesbian (or bisexual) adolescent sexuality has been especially problematic. Although there is more understanding of homosexuality now than in decades past, and more counseling and support services are available in some areas, gay, lesbian, bisexual, and transgendered individuals are still subject to ridicule and rejection. The assumed heterosexuality of society has resulted in a collective homophobia such that the phrase "That's so gay" (used as a derogatory statement) is part of mainstream and youth vernacular. Teachers, parents, and administrators also perpetuate homophobia by ignoring and/or contributing to the harassment of sexual minorities (Finz, 2000). While over 80% of gay and lesbian youth report feeling "very good" or "OK" about their sexuality, about 5% hate or would do anything to change their sexual orientation (Savin-Williams, 2005). Teens who identify themselves as gay, lesbian, or bisexual are more likely than heterosexual teens to have an unusually high incidence of depression, substance abuse, and attempted suicide (Harrison, 2003). Homophobia is also a major factor in precipitating homelessness, a state that renders young people especially vulnerable to sexual harm, including exploitation and abuse (Couch, Dowsett, Dutertrc, et al., 2006).

Very few gay and lesbian teens feel that they can talk to their parents about their sexual orientation. Many (especially boys) leave home or are kicked out because their parents cannot accept their sexuality. It is sobering to think that a significant number of our children are forced into lives of secrecy, suffering, and shame because of parents' and society's reluctance to openly acknowledge the existence of homosexual orientations.

Nowadays the polite form of homophobia is expressed in safeguarding the family, as if homosexuals somehow came into existence independent of families and without family ties.

—Dennis Altman
(1943–)

Corey Johnson, co-captain of his high school football team, made history when he came out to his teammates and they rallied around him. Click on "Corey Johnson" for more of his story.

What kinds of events validate heterosexuality? Click on "Learning to Be Straight" to learn about heterosexism.

" Sex is a holy thing, and one of the most marvelous revelations of the divine.

—Alan Watts
(1915–1973)

Nevertheless, evidence suggests a positive association between coming out to oneself and feelings of self-worth. Those who are "out" to themselves and have integrated a sexual identity with their overall personal identity are usually more psychologically well-adjusted than individuals who have not moved through this process (Savin-Williams, 2005). Support groups such as the Gay/ Straight Alliance are one means by which homosexual adolescents can deal with the discrimination and other difficulties they face. For those who do not want their sexuality to define them, an option is to shun their gay label. Nineteen-year-old Simone Sneed of Albany, New York (self-described as a "full-fledged" lesbian when she was 13), states:

> Over the years I have met an ever-expanding population of queers, polyamorous people, flexuals, gender queers, bois, boy-girl wonders, tranny fags, tranny chasers, hetero boys who used to be lesbians, and lesbians who used to be hetero bio boys. . . . The gay community has bought into consumerism, and "gay" no longer appears to be an identity that my peers and I are comfortable with. . . . So please don't call me a lesbian. (Matarazzo, 2004)

Developing a mature identity is a more formidable task for gay, lesbian, bisexual, and transgendered individuals who also face issues of color. The racial or ethnic background of a youth may be both an impediment and an advantage in forming a sexual identity. Though racial, ethnic, and cultural communities can provide identification, support, and affirmation, all too often families and peer groups within the community present youths with biases and prejudices that undermine the process of self-acceptance as a lesbian, gay, bisexual, or transgendered person. The individual may have to struggle with the question of whether sexual orientation or ethnic identification is more important; he or she may even have to choose one identity over the other.

Adolescent Sexual Behavior

Hormonal changes during puberty bring about a dramatic increase in sexual interest. Whether this results in sexual activity is individually determined.

Masturbation   If children have not begun masturbating before adolescence, they likely will begin once the hormonal and physical changes of puberty start. Masturbation is less common among women than men and more common among Whites than Blacks, Hispanics, or Asians (Laumann et al., 1994). Among college students, it has been found that 78% of males and 43% of females masturbate at least once a month (Elliott & Brantley, 1997). Rates of masturbation appear to be affected by a wide range of complex factors. In addition to providing release from sexual tension, masturbation gives us the opportunity to learn about our sexual functioning, knowledge that can later be shared with a sex partner.

When boys reach adolescence, they no longer regard masturbation as ambiguous play; they know that it is sexual. Data reveal that many males begin masturbating between ages 13 and 15, whereas among females it occurs more gradually (Bancroft, Herbenick, and Reynolds, 2003). Additionally, among those adolescents who do masturbate, boys do so about 3 times more frequently than girls (Leitenberg, Detzer, & Srebnik, 1993).

Gender differences may be the result of social conditioning and communication. Though both boys and girls may feel guilt and shame for engaging in a practice that their parents and other adults indicate is wrong or bad, most

Table 6.1 ● **Prevalence of Sexual Behaviors, Students in Grades 9–12, 2007**

	Female	Male
Ever had sexual intercourse	45.9%	49.8%
Had intercourse with 4 or more partners during life	11.8	17.9
Had sexual intercourse before age 13	4.0	10.1
Currently sexually active	35.6	34.3
Used a condom during last sexual intercourse	54.9	68.5
Used birth control pills before last sexual intercourse	18.7	13.1
Drank alcohol or used drugs before last sexual intercourse	17.7	27.5
Ever taught in school about AIDS or HIV infection	90.2	88.7

SOURCE: Centers for Disease Control and Prevention (2007). Youth risk behavior surveillance—United States, 2007. Available: http://www.cdc.gov/yrbs

boys discuss masturbatory experiences openly with one another, whereas girls seldom talk about their own sexuality, including masturbatory activities.

First Intercourse With the advent of the "sexual revolution" in the 1960s, adolescent sexual behavior began to change. The average age for first intercourse has dropped sharply in the past four decades, to 16.7 years, with a significant percentage of teens being sexually active by the time they graduate high school (see Table 6.1). Even with some important differences, though, men and women both experience similar events.

For most teens, increased commitment to the relationship is accompanied by increased likelihood of sexual intimacy.

think
about it

The "Origins" of Homosexuality

What causes homosexuality? What causes heterosexuality? Many have asked the first question, but few have asked the second. Although researchers don't understand the origins of sexual orientation in general, they have nevertheless focused almost exclusively on homosexuality, and their explanations generally fall into either biological or psychological categories.

Biological Theories

In genetic studies of homosexuality, researchers found a strong link between both gay men and lesbian women and their identical twins (Bailey, Dunne, & Martin, 2000; Bailey & Pillard, 1991; Bailey, Pillard, Neale, & Agyei, 1993). (As you might recall, identical twins are genetic clones, having developed from a single egg that split after fertilization; fraternal twins develop simultaneously from two separate eggs and two sperm.) The researchers matched identical and fraternal twins and adopted siblings of the same age to determine if there was a genetic component in homosexuality. The results from both studies were similar in that, among both gay men and lesbian women, a genetic marker for homosexuality was identified in identical twins (depending on the study, there was between a 20% and 50% chance that the identical sibling would also be homosexual), less prevalent among fraternal twins (0–22%) and found only to a small degree among genetically unrelated (adopted) siblings (0–10%).

Researchers have found a statistically significant association in the number of older brothers a man has and his likelihood of being gay, regardless of the brothers' sexual orientation; this is known as the "big brother effect" (Motluk, 2003). It has been found across cultures that each additional older brother increases the odds of a gay sexual orientation by one third (Cantor, Blanchard, Paterson, & Bogaert, 2002).

In another study, scientists studied genetic material from 40 pairs of gay brothers and discovered that 33 of the pairs had identical pieces of the end tip of the X chromosome (Hamer, Hu, Magnuson, & Pattatucci, 1993). Ordinarily, only half the pairs should have shared the same region. (The odds, in fact, of such an occurrence randomly happening were less than half of 1%.) This finding indicates that there may be one or more genes that play a role in predisposing some men to homosexuality. Researchers caution, however, that they have not identified a specific gene linked to homosexuality. Furthermore, because their findings have not been replicated, additional studies are necessary to validate their hypothesis.

Other researchers have explored the possibility that homosexuality could have a hormonal basis. Because hormonal levels are sensitive to such factors as general health,

Though attitudes and behaviors of teenagers about sex and childbearing have changed over time, there is still much work to do to reduce adolescent sexual risk-taking. According to Dr. Robert Blum, chair of the Department of Population and Family Health at the Johns Hopkins Bloomberg School of Public Health (quoted in Jossi, 2005):

> The factors that lead young people to be sexually active are complex and they do not lend themselves to any simple or slogan-based approach. We should not underestimate young people's ability to see some of the complexities in a range of issues including sexual behaviors.

Before she said, "I do . . ." she did.

—Bill Margold
(1943–)

Why do some emerging adults (aged 13–19) have sexual intercourse while others do not? As most of us know, the motivations for sexual experimentation and activity are numerous and complex: curiosity, appetite, and desire, to name a few. Though these may not be articulated or lend themselves to scientific analysis or quantification, sexuality researchers have been able to, nevertheless, target and cluster several important factors that are beneficial to the understanding of sexual behavior and that predispose individuals to sexual behavior: social/environmental factors (which include community,

diet, smoking, and stress, it is very difficult to control studies measuring sexual orientation. There are some relevant studies, however. It has been found that women who took the synthetic estrogen DES when pregnant were more likely to have daughters with bisexual or same-sex attraction (Fagin, 1995). No such increase was found in males. Suggesting biological influences in the development of some homosexual people, additional research has found a correlation between homosexuality and handedness in that homosexual participants had a 39% greater chance of being left-handed than heterosexuals (Lalumiere, Blanchard, & Zucker, 2000). More recently, findings have shown that lesbian women and gay men are more likely to be left-handed than heterosexual people (Blanchard, Cantor, Bogaert, et al., 2006). Other indicators of prenatal influences on the brain come as a result of studying age of onset of puberty (Bogaert, Friesen, & Klentrou, 2002), birth order of siblings (Blanchard & Bogaert, 2004), and finger-length patterns (Williams, Pepitone, Christensen, & Cooke, 2000). Collectively, these studies suggest the influence of biology on sexual orientation.

Social Constructionism and Psychological Theories

A different school of thought, known as social constructionism, regards sexual orientation as a malleable concept that varies from one culture to another. Daryl Bem, a social psychologist from Cornell University, states in a theory he refers to as "exotic becomes erotic," that children who infrequently view members of the other sex (and in a minority of the cases, members of the same sex) see them as exotic. Exotic peers elicit physiological tingles and jolts that seem offensive at first but that fire up sexual desire later in life (Bem, 1996, 2000).

Because research on the origins of sexual orientation focuses on homosexuality and not heterosexuality, there tends to be an underlying bias that homosexuality is not an acceptable or normal sexual variation. This bias has skewed research studies, especially psychoanalytic studies. Research should examine the origins of sexual orientation in general, not the origins of one type of orientation. As homosexuality has become increasingly accepted by researchers and psychologists as one type of sexual variation, scholars have shifted their research from determining the "causes" of homosexuality to understanding the nature of gay men and lesbian women in relationships.

Think Critically

- What, in your opinion, causes a person to have a heterosexual orientation? A homosexual one? How do your thoughts about this compare and contrast with those presented in this box?
- How important is it to understand the causes or factors that lead to homosexuality? Would conclusive evidence alter your opinion about sexual orientation?
- Who in your family would be most accepting and most rejecting of homosexuality? Why? How do these attitudes impact you and your feelings about sexual orientation?

family structure, peers, and romantic partners) and individual characteristics. Particularly influential are the individual's characteristics, including biology (age, physical development, and gender); race and ethnicity; connection to family, school, church, and community; alcohol and drug use; levels of aggression; and involvement in sports, to name a few (Kirby, 2007). Those characteristics which influence sexual behaviors among American youth don't appear to be significantly different than those that influence youth in other countries. Using worldwide data, researchers cite environmental factors that are consistent in having an impact on sexual vulnerability, including the community in which a teen lives (including whether he or she is homeless or part of a gang and the norms of the social environment), his or her family, peers and best friends, romantic partnerships, level of access to services, and notions of gender and sexuality (Couch, Dowsett, Dutertrc, et al., 2006). Solutions to address the well-being of youth are complex but involve health education, more comprehensive health services, and policies that support both of these (Centers for Disease Control and Prevention [CDC], 2007). (See Figure 6.3 for percentages of teens who have engaged in selected sexual behaviors.)

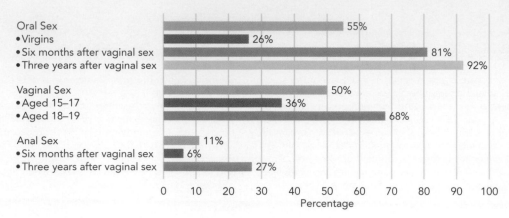

FIGURE 6.3

Percentage of Teens Aged 15–19 Who Engaged in Selected Sexual Behaviors With the Other Gender. (*Source:* Lindberg, Jones, & Santelli, 2008.)

Teenage Pregnancy

After a 15-year period of steady decline, the birth rate among teens aged 15–17 increased from 21 births per 1,000 girls in 2005 to 22 per 1,000 in 2006 (Forum on Child and Family Statistics, 2008). "This is only a single-year increase, but we believe it bears watching," says Edward J. Sondik, director of the National Center for Health Statistics (2008). Between 1991 and 2005, the birth rate of babies born to both Black and White non-Hispanic teenagers had dropped. However, rates for both groups increased in 2006. The rate for Hispanic teens did not change. These data have taken on political implications, with the opponents of abstinence-based programs using it as evidence against the "effectiveness" of these programs. (See Figure 6.4 for teen birth rates.)

It's not surprising that the vast majority (81%) of these pregnancies are unplanned, but what is interesting is that the majority (57%) result in live births (National Campaign to Prevent Teen and Unplanned Pregnancy, 2007).

FIGURE 6.4

Birth Rates for Teenagers by Age: United States, Final 1980–2005 and Preliminary 2006. (*Source:* CDC/NCHS, National Vital Statistics System.)

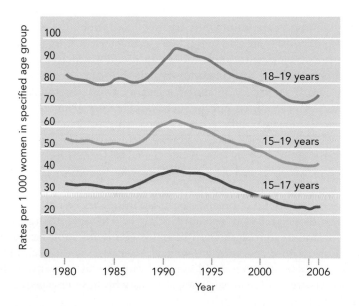

(See Figure 6.5.) Teen pregnancies trap most of the young mothers and fathers and their children in a downward spiral of lowered expectations, economic hardship, and poverty. Because of poor nutrition and inadequate medical care during pregnancy, babies born to teenagers have twice the normal risk of low birth weight, which is responsible for numerous physical and developmental problems. Also, many of these children will have disrupted family lives, absent fathers, and the attendant problems of poverty, such as poor diet, violent neighborhoods, limited health care, and limited access to education. They are also at higher risk for being abused than children born to older parents. Monetary costs are also high. Teenage childbearing cost taxpayers $9.1 billion in 2004 (Kirby, 2007).

Contraception can fail or not be available or used. But not all teen pregnancies are unintended; about 22% of them are planned (Abma et al., 2004). This compares with a 50% rate for all women (Alan Guttmacher Institute [AGI], 2005c). The idea of having someone to love them exclusively and unconditionally is a strong incentive for some teenage girls. Others see having a baby as a way to escape from an oppressive home environment. Both teen males and females may see parenthood as a way to enhance their status, to give them an aura of maturity, or to enhance their masculinity or femininity. Some believe a baby will cement a shaky relationship. (Many adult women and men choose to have babies for these same less-than-sensible reasons.) Unfortunately, for many expectant teens, parenthood may turn out to be as much a disaster as a blessing.

Teenage Mothers   More than 30% of teenage girls in the United States become pregnant at least once by the age of 20. Of those who have children, most feel that they are "good" girls and that they became pregnant in a moment of unguarded passion. The reality of the *boy + girl = baby* equation often doesn't sink in until pregnancy is well advanced. This lack of awareness makes it difficult (emotionally and physically), if not impossible, for those who might otherwise choose to do so to have an abortion. Teenage mothers are far more likely than other mothers to live below the poverty level and to receive welfare. Teenage mothers also are significantly less likely to go on to college compared with women who delay childbearing.

Not only are African American and Hispanic teens more likely to be sexually active than Whites, but their birth rates are also higher (see Figure 6.6). This is partly explained by the way in which the forces of racism and poverty combine to limit the options of young people of color. (Poor Whites also have disproportionately high teenage birth rates.) But additional factors contribute to pregnancy and childbirth among Black and Hispanic teens. For one thing, African American communities are far more accepting of births to unmarried women than their White counterparts; among Hispanics and African Americans, three-generation families are much more common, with the result that grandparents often play an active role in child rearing. Additionally, there is often a great deal of pressure among young men of color (especially in communities with lower socioeconomic status) to prove their masculinity by engaging in sexual activity (Staples & Johnson, 1993; Yawn & Yawn, 1997).

Teenage mothers have special needs. The most pressing that can be provided for within the community are health care and education. Improving preconception

Pregnancy rate = 75.4
  Miscarriage rate* = 16
  Birth rate = 57
  Abortion rate = 27
*Rates are per 1,000 women.

● **FIGURE 6.5**
Pregnancy Outcomes Among Teen Girls Aged 15–19, 2004.
Data Source: *The National Campaign to Prevent Teen and Unplanned Pregnancy (2008). Science Says. www.thenationalcampaign.org/resources/pdf/ss/ss38_saywhat.pdf, accessed 6/9/09.*

Click on "Baby Love" to hear teenage mothers talk about when they became sexually active.

● **FIGURE 6.6**

**U.S. Birth Rates by Race,
15–19-Year-Olds.** (*Source:* Hamilton,
Martin, & Ventura, 2007.)

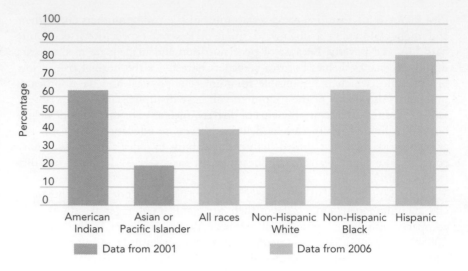

health and regular prenatal care are essential to monitor fetal growth and the mother's health, including diet, possible STIs, and possible alcohol or drug use (CDC, 2006). Nevertheless, 15.4% of births to girls under age 15 and 7.6% of births to teens aged 15 to 17 are to those receiving late or no prenatal care (Martin, Hamilton, Sutton, et al., 2005). Babies born to young mothers are more likely to have childhood health problems and to be hospitalized than those born to older mothers. After the birth, both mother and child need continuing care. The mother may need contraceptive counseling and services, and the child needs regular physical checkups and immunizations. Graduation from high school is an important goal of education programs for teenage mothers because it directly influences their employability and ability to support (or help support) themselves and their children. Some teenage mothers need financial assistance, at least until they complete their education. Government programs such as food stamps, Medicaid, and WIC (Women, Infants, and Children, which provides coupons for essential foods) are often crucial to the survival of young mothers and their children. Such programs are often underfunded and are periodically threatened with termination. Even with programs such as these in place, most families need additional income to survive.

Coordination of health, educational, and social services is important because it reduces costs and provides the most comprehensive support for both mothers and fathers who, as a result of an unplanned pregnancy, are at greater risk for depression and relationship conflict (Child Trends Inc., 2007). School-based health clinics, which offer prenatal and postnatal care, contraception, and counseling, and teenage parent education programs, which provide general education and teach job and life skills, are examples of coordinated care. Such programs may be costly, but the costs of *not* providing them are far greater.

Teenage Fathers   The incidence of teenage fatherhood is lower than that of teenage motherhood. Teen fatherhood is not a function of any single risk factor. Living in an inner city, having certain expectations and values about early childbearing, having poor school achievement, and engaging in delinquent behavior seem to be pathways leading to adolescent fatherhood. Other risk

Though fewer than 1% of unmarried pregnant women relinquish their infants for adoption, movies like *Juno* portray teen pregnancy and adoption in a humorous and supportive manner.

factors include a minority ethnic background and socioeconomic disadvantages. Such circumstances may prompt some men to react by avoiding marriage or rejecting the responsibilities of fatherhood (AGI, 2004b).

Adolescent fathers typically remain physically or psychologically involved throughout the pregnancy and for at least some time after the birth. It is usually difficult for teenage fathers to contribute much to the support of their children, although most express the intention of doing so during the pregnancy. Most have a lower income, less education, and more children than men who

Abstinence-Only Versus Comprehensive Sexuality Programs

Though trends in the prevalence of sexual intercourse and pregnancy among teens have occurred over time and sexuality education programs have attempted to address these changes, until now little evidence has been available to assess their long-term effectiveness on teens' behaviors, attitudes, or beliefs. After analyzing hundreds of program evaluations, scientist and researcher Douglas Kirby (2007, 2008) stated that there is strong evidence that comprehensive sexuality education can effectively delay sexual intercourse among young people and increase condom and contraceptive use among sexually active youth. This contrasts with a recent, congressionally mandated evaluation of federally funded abstinence-only programs by Mathematica Policy Research, which found that these programs have no beneficial impact on young people's sexual behavior. In spite of this, we still know that the sexual risk behaviors that lead to high pregnancy, birth, and STI rates among American teens and the factors that influence them remain very high, both in relation to other developed countries and in terms of the costs to those involved, their children, and society (Kirby, 2007).

Abstinence-only-until-marriage programs have been the cornerstone of the previous two administrations and the answer to addressing the U.S. teen pregnancy and STI rates. In 2008, for example, the spending on abstinence-only-until-marriage programs was $204 million, $27 million more than the previous year (Boonstra, 2007). Counter to the current federal policies, most Americans believe that sexuality education should promote abstinence and provide information about the effectiveness and benefits of contraception (Boonstra, 2007; Kirby, 2007). Overall, 82% support a comprehensive approach and 68% favor instruction on how to use a condom, while only 36% support abstinence-only education.

The support of the public has been acknowledged by public school districts, more than two thirds of which have a policy about teaching sexuality education (Alan Guttmacher, 2005a). Of those school districts with a policy, all require that abstinence be taught, yet only 14% have a policy of teaching abstinence as part of a comprehensive sexuality program. Particularly troubling is the fact that 1 in 4 teachers are prevented from teaching about contraception and that 4 in 10 teachers do not teach about contraceptive methods (including condoms) or they teach that they are ineffective. Consequently, some states have found the rules that govern the abstinence program so restrictive that they have turned down the funding.

What Does the Research Reveal?

The good news is that comprehensive sexuality education can indeed delay sexual intercourse, improve contraceptive use, and/or prevent teen pregnancy. Douglas Kirby (2007, 2008), at the nonprofit National Campaign to Prevent Teen and Unplanned Pregnancy, has identified numerous risk and protective factors that influence teens' sexual behavior. About two thirds of them showed evidence that they positively affected young people's sexual behavior, including both delaying initiation of sex and increasing condom and contraceptive use. More specifically, of the 48 comprehensive sexuality programs studied (Kirby, 2008):

- over 40% delayed the initiation of sex, reduced the number of sexual partners, and increased condom or contraceptive use;
- almost 30% reduced the frequency of sex (including a return to abstinence);

postpone having children until age 20 or older. They may feel overwhelmed by the responsibility and may doubt their ability to be good providers. Though many teenage fathers are the sons of absent fathers, most do want to learn to be fathers. Teen fathers are a seriously neglected group who face many hardships. Policies and interventions directed at reducing teen fatherhood will have to take into consideration the many factors that influence it and focus efforts throughout the life cycle.

Sexuality Education

Sexuality education is a lifelong process. From the time that we are born, we learn about love, touch, affection, and our bodies. As we grow, the messages

- more than 60% reduced unprotected sex; and
- nearly 40% had positive effects on more than one of these behaviors.

No comprehensive program was found to hasten the initiation of sex or increase the frequency of sex—results that a minority of voices have feared. Comprehensive programs work for both genders, for all major ethnic groups, for sexually inexperienced and experienced teens, in different settings, and in different communities.

Though there are no easy answers, just as there is no specific program that provides a complete solution to getting young people to delay having sex or to use protection against pregnancy and STIs, the more effective programs may reduce one or more types of risky behavior by roughly one third. If adopted, the results from these findings can lay the groundwork for significant changes and positive outcomes in comprehensive sexuality education programs across the country.

What Do We Know About Abstinence-Only-Until-Marriage Programs?

The verdict is in about the effectiveness of abstinence-only programs: None have a statistically beneficial impact on young people's sexual behavior (Boonstra, 2007; Kirby, 2007, 2008). More specifically, the results from a large-scale, $8 million study of 8 abstinence programs revealed that none of them delayed initiation of sex and only 3 of 9 had any significant effects on any sexual behavior. In fact, during the time that the number of abstinence-only programs more than doubled, instruction on birth control dramatically declined. Underscoring this evidence is Heather Boonstra (2007), researcher with the Alan Guttmacher Institute, a nonprofit and independent organization that studies trends and public policy in sexuality, who concludes: "Since 1996, the federal government has poured more than a billion dollars into abstinence-only-until-marriage education programs, even though there is clear evidence that they are not effective in stopping or even delaying teen sex."

Although the opposition to comprehensive sexuality education may be small, it is very vocal. The coalition, led by conservative political groups and parents, teachers, and religious groups, argues that to instruct children in birth control or abortion is confusing and can lead them down the path of self-destruction. Evidence to support this has not been found.

So, What Have We Learned?

Because there is no evidence that any one abstinence program is effective at delaying the initiation of sex or reducing sexual behaviors, there is little justification from a public health perspective for their widespread use or dissemination. Thus, the challenge is for families, schools, communities, and policy makers to build on the knowledge and successes that comprehensive programs have demonstrated and for the federal government to allocate the dollars and support necessary to build on what we now know.

Think Critically

- What are your reactions to these findings? What might you tell others who inquire about your thoughts and feelings about sexuality education in the schools?
- While in school, what exactly were you taught about sex? What impact do you feel this curriculum had on you? On other students? What aspects of your sexuality education would you support and which would you change?
- What do you feel is the role of the federal government in guiding states and communities in the teaching of sexuality education?

continue from both our families and the social environment, with school-based programs complementing and augmenting these primary sources of information.

It is the responsibility of schools and communities to develop their own curricula and pedagogy regarding sexuality education. Though programs vary widely, four types of sexuality education programs are currently offered in schools and communities (Sexuality Information and Education Council of the United States [SIECUS], 2001):

- *Comprehensive.* These programs start in kindergarten and continue through 12th grade. They include information on a broad range of topics, including STI/HIV and pregnancy prevention, and provide opportunities for students to develop relationship and interpersonal skills, as well as to exercise responsibility regarding sexual relationships.

■ *Abstinence-based.* These programs emphasize the benefits of abstinence. They also include information about noncoital sexual behavior, contraception, and disease prevention methods.

■ *Abstinence-only.* These programs emphasize abstinence from all sexual behaviors. They do not include any information about contraception or disease prevention methods.

■ *Abstinence-only-until-marriage.* These programs emphasize abstinence from all sexual behaviors outside of marriage. They do not include any information about contraception or disease prevention methods. Marriage is presented as the only morally acceptable context for all sexual activity.

Different Values, Different Goals Among parents, teachers, and school administrators, there is substantial disagreement about what a "comprehensive" course in sexuality education should include. Some believe that only basic reproductive biology should be taught. Others see the prevention (or at least the reduction) of sexually transmitted infections (STIs) as a legitimate goal of sexuality education. Still others would like the emphasis to be on the prevention of sexual activity among adolescents. Many think it's also important to address other issues, such as the role of pleasure and desire, sexual orientations, and the development of skills for making healthful, responsible decisions regarding sexual behavior.

The Sexuality Information and Education Council of the United States (SIECUS) developed the *Guidelines for Comprehensive Sexuality Education* (SIECUS, 2004), the first national model for comprehensive sexuality education. The guidelines, the most widely recognized and implemented framework for comprehensive sexuality education in the United States and several countries worldwide, address four developmental levels—early childhood, preadolescence, early adolescence, and adolescence—and six main topics—human development, relationships, personal skills, sexual behavior, sexual health, and society and culture. (See page 187 in Chapter 7 for the behaviors of a sexually healthy adult that are listed in the SIECUS guidelines.)

In response to the increased attention and funding that abstinence-only-until-marriage programs have been receiving, 35 organizations, including the American Psychological Association, American College of Obstetricians and Gynecologists, and Planned Parenthood Federation of America, have joined together to urge the federal government to reconsider funding only abstinence-only education and to reexamine scientific evidence that demonstrates that responsible sexuality education works ("SSSS Signs Letter," 2002).

Although much more research needs to be done on sexuality education and its impact on young people, most professionals agree that it is one of the most important preventive means we have. Young people, guided by their parents and armed with knowledge and self-confidence, can make informed decisions and direct their own sexual destinies.

Final Thoughts

From birth, humans are rich in sexual and erotic potential. As children, the world around us begins to shape our sexuality and the ways that we ultimately express it. As adolescents, our education continues as a random mixture of learning and yearning. With sexual maturity, the gap between physiological development and psychological development begins to narrow and emotional and intellectual capabilities begin to expand. Responses to and decisions about sexuality education, sexual activity, sexual orientation, and pregnancy begin to emerge. Each of these presents a challenge and an opportunity to more fully evolve into the sexual beings that we are.

Summary

Sexuality in Infancy and Childhood

- *Psychosexual development* begins in infancy, when we begin to learn how we "should" feel about our bodies and our gender roles. Infants need stroking and cuddling to ensure healthy psychosexual development.

- Children learn about their bodies through various forms of sex play. Their sexual interest should not be labeled "bad" but may be deemed inappropriate for certain times, places, or persons. Children need to experience acts of physical affection and to be told nonthreateningly about "good" and "bad" touching by adults.

Sexuality in Adolescence

- *Puberty* is the biological stage when reproduction becomes possible. The psychological state of puberty is *adolescence,* a time of growth and often confusion as the body matures faster than the emotional and intellectual abilities. The traits of adolescence are culturally determined.

- Pubertal changes that result in secondary sex characteristics in girls begin between ages 7 and 14. They include a growth spurt, breast development, pubic and underarm hair, vaginal secretions, and menarche (first menstruation). Pubertal changes in boys generally begin about 2 years later than in girls. They include a growth spurt, a deepening voice, hair growth, development of external genitals, and ejaculation of semen. Preparing young people for these changes is helpful.

- Children and adolescents often learn a great deal about sexuality from their family dynamics and characteristics. A strong bond between parent and child reduces the risk of early sexual involvement and pregnancy.

- Peers provide a strong influence on the values, attitudes, and behavior of adolescents. They are also a source of much misinformation regarding sex.

- The media present highly charged images of sexuality that are often out of context. Parents can counteract media distortions by discussing the context of sexuality with their children and controlling access to television and the Internet.

- Young gay and lesbian individuals are largely invisible because of society's assumption of heterosexuality. They may begin to come to terms with their homosexuality during their teenage years. Because of society's reluctance to acknowledge homosexuality openly, most gay, lesbian, and bisexual teens suffer a great deal of emotional pain.

- Most adolescents engage in masturbation. Gender differences in rates of masturbation may be the result of social conditioning and communication.
- In spite of a 15-year decline, the birth rate among teens aged 15–17 recently increased. These data, combined with data from abstinence-only programs, have taken on political implications in the arena of sexuality education.

- Most teenagers have pressing concerns about sexuality, and most parents and the public favor sexuality education for their children. Yet the subject remains controversial in many school districts. This is mainly the result of opposition from a vocal minority. Areas of controversy include homosexuality, contraception (versus abstinence), and condom availability.

Questions for Discussion

- Who or what taught you the most about sexuality when you were a child and teenager? What lessons did you learn? What would have made the transition from childhood to adolescence easier?

- Should masturbation in young children be ignored, discouraged, or encouraged? What effect might each of these responses have on a child who is just beginning to learn about herself or himself?

- After reviewing the literature on abstinence-only-until-marriage versus comprehensive sexuality education, what are your thoughts on each? Which do you advocate and why?

- What are some ways to reduce the rates of unintended teenage pregnancy?

Access this site and see if you can find each of the following:

- The age of first intercourse among teens
- The most common type of contraceptive used
- The risk of acquiring a specific STI with one act of intercourse
- The percentage of teen mothers who complete high school
- The number of pregnancies that are terminated by abortion

Now answer the following questions:

- Which fact was the most surprising to you?
- Which fact was the least surprising?
- If you had unlimited resources, how might you go about solving the problem of teen pregnancy?

Suggested Web Sites

American Academy of Pediatrics
http://www.aap.org
A wealth of information about the physical, mental, and social health and well-being of infants, children, adolescents, and young adults.

Child Trends
http://www.childtrends.org
A nonprofit, nonpartisan research center that studies developmental stages of children and uses evidence-based data to provide guidance on policy and practice.

Mayo Clinic Foundation for Medical Education and Research
http://www.mayoclinic.org
Resources to help individuals and families stay healthy.

Midwest Teen Sex Show
http://www.midwestteensexshow.com
Uses broadcast media to provide sex information to teens.

Sex and the Internet

Sexual Activity and Teens
Data on teen STI rates and unplanned pregnancy have recently appeared in the headlines of our newspapers, not to remind us of the dismal figures, but to inform us that the rates are unacceptably high. One of the most helpful and thorough sites that report on this and other adolescent sexuality issues is the Alan Guttmacher Institute: http://www.guttmacher.org.

The National Campaign to Prevent Teen Pregnancy
http://www.thenationalcampaign.org
Dedicated to providing information, resources, and support for parents and teens. It specifically seeks to help ensure that children are born into stable, two-parent families.

National Federation of Parents and Friends of Lesbians and Gays (PFLAG)
http://www.pflag.org
Provides information and support for those who care about gay and lesbian individuals.

Scarleteen
http://www.scarleteen.com
Staffed by volunteers, some of whom are young adults. Provides sexuality information for a young adult population.

Society for Research on Adolescence (SRA)
http://www.s-r-a.org
A multidisciplinary, international organization dedicated to understanding adolescence through research and dissemination.

Youth Resource: A Project of Advocates for Youth
http://www.youthresource.com
A Web site for gay, lesbian, bisexual, transgender, and questioning young people aged 13 to 24 that offers support, community resources, advocacy, and peer-to-peer education about issues of concern.

Suggested Reading

Bancroft, J. (2003). *Sexual development in childhood*. Bloomington: Indiana University Press. Scholarly and well-researched edited text by one of the leaders in the field; also, one of the few books available on this subject.

Gurian, M. (2006). *The wonder of boys*. New York: Penguin Putnam. With emphasis on the importance of family and community support, describes what boys need to become responsible, sensitive, and strong men.

Haffner, D. W. (2008). *What every 21st-century parent needs to know: Facing today's challenges with wisdom and heart*. New York: New Market Press. A practical and reassuring book for parents.

Richardson, J., & Schuster, M. A. (2004). *Everything you never wanted your kids to know about sex (but were afraid they'd ask)*. New York: Three Rivers Press. Written by a physician and a psychiatrist, a survival guide that may help parents unravel and explain every stage of sexual development to their children.

Savin-Williams, R. C. (2006). *The new gay teenager (adolescent lives)*. Boston: Harvard University Press. Contains real-world case studies that reveal that being young and homosexual is not the identity crisis we might expect.

Steinberg, L. D. (2007). *Adolescence* (8th ed.). Boston: McGraw-Hill. A comprehensive, research-based examination of adolescent development within the context of environmental and social relationships.

For links, articles, and study material, go to the McGraw-Hill Web sites, located at **www.mhhe.com/yarber7e.**

MAIN TOPICS

Sexuality in Early Adulthood

Sexuality in Middle Adulthood

Sexuality in Late Adulthood

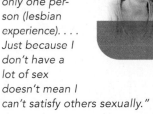
"By looking at me, no one would know that I am as sexual as I am. I see many interesting things out there and when the time is right, I will try them. I think it's fine for a virgin (like me) to be sexual and be with someone without sex, until they become familiar and comfortable with one another."

—19-year-old female

"Sexuality has to have a place in my life because it is how I connect with a person and show her that I am a human who has feelings, whether it be giving affection or receiving it. Sexuality allows me to be free with my feelings, thereby allowing myself to open up and become a better partner for my mate."

—25-year-old male

"My skills and experience as a sexual person are limited compared to other people my age. I got married young and the fact that I was practically brainwashed as a child has greatly reduced my sexual partners. I have had intercourse with three people and oral sex with only one person (lesbian experience). . . . Just because I don't have a lot of sex doesn't mean I can't satisfy others sexually."

—23-year-old female

"Staying happily married isn't easy. Children, workload, financial issues, and a host of other factors create difficult circumstances that often put my relationship on the back burner. If someone came along with a magic panacea that would help to ignite our marriage and our sexuality, I would take it."

—51-year-old female

As we enter adulthood, with greater experience and understanding, we develop a potentially mature sexuality. We establish our sexual orientation; we integrate love and sexuality; we forge intimate connections and make commitments; we make decisions regarding our fertility; and we develop a coherent sexual philosophy. Then, in our middle years, we redefine the role of sex in our intimate relationships, accept our aging, and reevaluate our sexual philosophy. Finally, in later adulthood we reinterpret the meaning of sexuality in accordance with the erotic capabilities of our bodies. We come to terms with the possible loss of our partner and our own eventual decline. In all these stages, sexuality weaves its bright and dark threads through our lives.

In this chapter, we continue the exploration and discussion of sexuality over the human life cycle. We begin with an examination of the developmental concerns of young adults, further explore the establishment of sexual orientation, turn to singlehood and cohabitation, then to middle adulthood, continuing to focus on developmental concerns, relational and nonrelational sexuality, and divorce. Next, we look at sexuality in late adulthood, examining developmental issues, stereotypes, and differences and similarities in aging and sex between men and women. Finally, we examine the role of the partner in sustaining health.

" *The good life is one inspired by love and guided by knowledge.*

—Bertrand Russell
(1872–1970)

● Sexuality in Early Adulthood

Like other life passages, the one from adolescence to early adulthood offers potential for growth if one is aware of and remains open to the opportunities this period brings (see Figure 7.1).

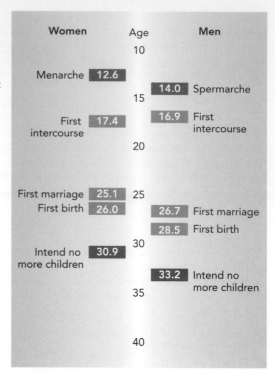

• FIGURE 7.1

Sexual and Reproductive Time Line: Mean Age of Major Events (*Source:* Guttmacher Institute, *Sex education: Needs, programs and policies.* New York: Guttmacher Institute, 2006.)

Developmental Concerns

Several tasks challenge young adults as they develop their sexuality (Gagnon & Simon, 1973):

- *Establishing sexual orientation.* Children and adolescents may engage in sexual experimentation, such as playing doctor, kissing, and fondling, with members of both sexes, but they do not necessarily associate these activities with sexual orientation. Instead, their orientation as heterosexual, gay, lesbian, bisexual, or transgendered is in the process of emerging.

- *Integrating love and sex.* Traditional gender roles call for men to be sex-oriented and women to be love-oriented. In adulthood, this sex-versus-love conflict needs to be addressed. Instead of polarizing love and sex, people need to develop ways of uniting them.

- *Forging intimacy and making commitments.* Young adulthood is characterized by increasing sexual experience. Through dating, courtship, and cohabitation, individuals gain knowledge of themselves and others as potential partners. As relationships become more meaningful, the degree of intimacy and interdependence increases. Sexuality can be a means of enhancing intimacy and self-disclosure, as well as a source of physical pleasure. As adults become more intimate, most desire to develop their ability to make commitments.

- *Making fertility/childbearing decisions.* Becoming a parent is socially discouraged during adolescence, but it becomes increasingly legitimate when people reach their twenties, especially if they are married. Fertility issues are often critical but unacknowledged, especially for single young adults.

> " *Let's face it, a date is like a job interview that lasts all night.*
>
> —Jerry Seinfeld
> (1954–)

Life Behaviors of a Sexually Healthy Adult

In 1996, the Sexuality Information and Education Council of the United States (SIECUS) published the first national guidelines for comprehensive sexuality education in kindergarten through 12th grade. These guidelines covered the life behaviors of a sexually healthy adult in six areas and were updated in 2004.

Behaviors of the Sexually Healthy Adult

1. Human development:
   a. Appreciate one's own body.
   b. Seek further information about reproduction as needed.
   c. Affirm that human development includes sexual development, which may or may not include reproduction or sexual experience.
   d. Interact with all genders in respectful and appropriate ways.
   e. Affirm one's own sexual orientation and respect the sexual orientation of others.
   f. Affirm one's own gender identities and respect the gender identities of others.

2. Relationships:
   a. Express love and intimacy in appropriate ways.
   b. Develop and maintain meaningful relationships.
   c. Avoid exploitative or manipulative relationships.
   d. Make informed choices about family options and relationships.
   e. Exhibit skills that enhance personal relationships.

3. Personal skills:
   a. Identify and live according to one's own values.
   b. Take responsibility for one's own behavior.
   c. Practice effective decision making.
   d. Develop critical thinking skills.
   e. Communicate effectively with family, peers, and romantic partners.

4. Sexual behavior:
   a. Enjoy and express one's sexuality throughout life.
   b. Express one's sexuality in ways congruent with one's values.
   c. Enjoy sexual feelings without necessarily acting on them.
   d. Discriminate between life-enhancing sexual behaviors and those that are harmful to oneself and/or others.
   e. Express one's sexuality while respecting the rights of others.
   f. Seek new information to enhance one's sexuality.
   g. Engage in sexual relationships that are consensual, nonexploitative, honest, pleasurable, and protected.

5. Sexual health:
   a. Practice health-promoting behaviors, such as regular checkups, breast and testicular self-exams, and early identification of potential problems.
   b. Use contraception effectively to avoid unintended pregnancy.
   c. Avoid contracting or transmitting an STI, including HIV.
   d. Act consistent with one's values in dealing with an unintended pregnancy.
   e. Seek early prenatal care.
   f. Help prevent sexual abuse.

6. Society and culture:
   a. Demonstrate respect for people with different sexual values.
   b. Exercise democratic responsibility to influence legislation dealing with sexual issues.
   c. Assess the impact of family, cultural, religious, media, and societal messages on one's thoughts, feelings, values, and behaviors related to sexuality.
   d. Critically examine the world around them for biases based on gender, sexual orientation, culture, ethnicity, and race.
   e. Promote the rights of all people to have access to accurate sexuality information.
   f. Avoid behaviors that exhibit prejudice and bigotry.
   g. Reject stereotypes about the sexuality of different populations.
   h. Educate others about sexuality.

Think Critically

- Is it possible for young people to enact or achieve all of the behaviors?
- Which of the behaviors would seem to be the most difficult to achieve? Why?
- Would some of the behaviors change over the life span?
- Are there life behaviors related to sexuality that are missing from the list?

SOURCE: National Guidelines Task Force. (2004). *Guidelines for comprehensive sexuality education: Kindergarten–12th grade* (3rd ed.). New York: Sexuality Information and Education Council of the United States. 130 W. 42nd St., Suite 350, New York, NY 10036. Reprinted with permission.

Critical life questions, such as those involving relationships, personal skills, sexual behavior, and health, often arise during the college-age years when young people begin to live independently and away from their parents.

> Somewhere in the mounting and mating, rutting and butting is the very secret of nature itself.
>
> —Graham Swift
> (1949–)

- *Practicing safer sex to protect against sexually transmitted infections (STIs).* An awareness of the various STIs and ways to best protect against them must be integrated into the communication, values, and behaviors of all young adults.

- *Evolving a sexual philosophy.* As individuals move from adolescence to adulthood, they reevaluate their moral standards, moving from moral decision making based on authority to standards based on their personal principles of right and wrong, caring, and responsibility. They become responsible for developing their own moral code, which includes sexual issues. In doing so, they need to evolve a personal philosophical perspective to give coherence to sexual attitudes, behaviors, beliefs, and values. They need to place sexuality within the larger framework of their lives and relationships. They need to integrate their personal, religious, spiritual, and humanistic values with their sexuality.

Establishing Sexual Orientation

A critical task of adulthood is establishing one's sexual orientation as heterosexual, gay, lesbian, bisexual, or transgendered. As mentioned previously, in childhood and early adolescence, there is often sex play or sexual experimentation with members of the other sex and same sex. These exploratory experiences are tentative in terms of sexual orientation. But in late adolescence and young adulthood, men and women are confronted with the important developmental task of establishing intimacy. And part of the task of establishing intimate relationships is solidifying one's sexual orientation.

Most people develop a heterosexual identity by adolescence or young adulthood. Their task is simplified because their development as heterosexuals is approved by society. But for those who are lesbian, gay, bisexual, or unsure, their development features more doubt and anxiety. Because those who are attracted to members of the same sex are aware that they are violating deep societal taboos, it can take them longer to confirm and accept their sexual orientation. It may also be difficult and dangerous for them to establish a relationship. In fact, fewer

• FIGURE 7.2

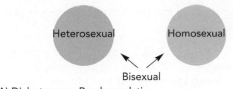
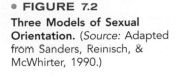

(A) Dichotomous-Psychoanalytic

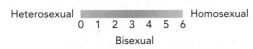

(B) Unidimensional-Bipolar (Kinsey)

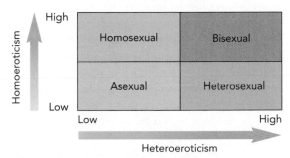

(C) Two-Dimensional—Orthogonal (Storms)

than 1 in 5 gay and lesbian adolescents had their first sexual experience in the context of a relationship (Diamond, Savin-Williams, & Dube, 1999). This compares to one half of male and three fourths of female adolescent heterosexuals (Jessor & Jessor, 1997).

Models of Sexual Orientation Sexual orientation is an area of human sexuality that has been clouded by misunderstanding, myth, and confusion. To help explain the complex nature of sexual orientation, psychologists and researchers in sexuality have developed various models (Figure 7.2). Much as our views of gender, masculinity, and femininity have changed, so have conceptualizations of sexual orientation, although these are different phenomena.

Until the research of Alfred C. Kinsey and his colleagues, sexual orientation was dichotomized into "heterosexual" and "homosexual"—that is, a person could be one or the other. As shown in Model A in Figure 7.2, some researchers considered a third category, bisexuality, although others believed that a bisexual was a homosexual person trying to be heterosexual. One of Kinsey's most significant contributions was his challenge to this traditional model. Research by Kinsey and others showed that homosexuality was not uncommon and that engaging in same-sex behaviors did not necessarily make a person homosexual. They also found that participation in both same- and other-sex behavior was not uncommon. This led them to conclude that sexual orientation is a continuum from exclusively heterosexual to exclusively homosexual, as depicted in Model B, and that a person's sexual behavior pattern could change across a lifetime. This continuum has been widely utilized in sexuality research, education, and therapy since it was developed by Kinsey.

Sex lies at the root of life, and we can never learn to revere life until we know how to understand sex.

—Havelock Ellis
(1859–1939)

Kinsey rejected the traditional explanation of sexual orientation and sexuality in general by saying:

> The world is not divided into sheep and goats. Not all things are black nor all things white. . . . Nature rarely deals with discrete categories. Only the human mind invents categories and tries to force facts into separated pigeonholes. The living world is a continuum in each and every one of its aspects. The sooner we learn this concerning human sexual behavior the sooner we shall reach a sound understanding of the realities of sex. (Kinsey, Pomeroy, & Martin, 1948)

The Kinsey continuum has been criticized for its implication that the more heterosexual a person is the less homosexual he or she must be, and vice versa. Sex researchers Sanders, Reinisch, and McWhirter (1990) note that some researchers have modified the Kinsey scale by using bipolar ratings of heterosexuality and homosexuality; that is, indicators such as sexual behavior, sexual fantasies, the person one loves, and feelings about which sex is more "attractive" can each be assessed independently. Storms (1980, 1981) suggested that homoeroticism and heteroeroticism are independent continua (Model C). A bisexual individual is high on both homoeroticism and heteroeroticism dimensions, a heterosexual is high on heteroeroticism and low on homoeroticism, and a homosexual is high on homoeroticism and low on heteroeroticism. A person low on both dimensions would be considered asexual.

Statistics on Sexual Orientation

We do not know the numbers of men and women who identify as a heterosexual, gay, lesbian, bisexual, or transgendered person. In large part, this is because homosexuality is stigmatized. Gay men and lesbian women are often reluctant to reveal their identities in research surveys for reasons of personal hesitancy as well as conceptual problems surrounding what constitutes sexual orientation (Ellis, Robb, & Burke, 2005).

The majority of studies on the prevalence of people's variations in sexual orientation have been conducted in the United States and suggest that about 1–4% of males and females consider themselves to be something other than heterosexual (either homosexual or bisexual) (Ellis, 1996; Laumann, Gagnon, Michael, & Michaels, 1994). Additionally, 10–15% report at least occasional sexual attraction to or sexual fantasy about their same sex (Ellis, 1996). (For additional data on same-sex behavior, see the National Survey of Family Growth, Chapter 2.)

What are we to make of these findings? In part, the variances that exist in the literature regarding the rates of homosexuality may be explained by different methodologies, interviewing techniques, sampling procedures, definitions of homosexuality, or random response errors. Furthermore, sexuality is more than simply sexual behaviors; it also includes attraction and desire. One can be a virgin or celibate and still be gay, lesbian, or heterosexual. One can also participate in sexual behavior with a person of the other or same sex, but not label oneself as heterosexual or homosexual. Finally, because sexuality is varied and changes over time, its expression at any one time is not necessarily the same as at another time or for all time.

The Gay/Lesbian/Bisexual Identity Process

Identifying oneself as a lesbian, gay, or bisexual person takes considerable time and, for some, may involve moving back and forth among these categories (Diamond, 2005). The most intense phase in the development of one's sexual identity is during late adolescence and early adulthood. Researchers have found that college graduates are more likely

Love is sacred, and sex is sacred too. The two things are not a part; they belong together.

—Lame Deer, Lakota Indian holy man (1903–1976)

Bisexuality: The Nature of Dual Attraction

"**H**eterosexuality" and "homosexuality" are terms used to categorize people according to the sex of their sex partners. But, as noted in the discussion of Kinsey's work in Chapter 2, such categories do not always adequately reflect the complexity of sexual orientation or of human sexuality in general.

Most individuals view bisexuality as a pattern of erotic responsiveness to both sexes (Rust, 2002). This broad thinking leaves some questions unanswered: Do short-term sexual experiences with both sexes qualify one to be labeled bisexual? Does everyone have the potential to be bisexual? Does attraction to the same or both sexes mean one is bisexual? Though some may suggest that love has no sexual orientation, others may desire a category for the feelings they experience. Regardless, researchers still wonder whether bisexuality is (1) a temporary stage of denial, transition, or experimentation; (2) a third type of sexual orientation, characterized by fixed patterns of attraction to both sexes; or (3) a strong form of all individuals' capacity for sexual fluidity (Diamond, 2008).

Bisexual Identity Formation

In contrast to homosexuality, there is little research on bisexuality. The process of bisexual identity formation appears to be complex, requiring the rejection of the two recognized categories of sexual orientation. Consequently, bisexual people often find themselves stigmatized by gay men and lesbian women, as well as by heterosexual individuals, a kind of discrimination called biphobia.

Those people who do identify as bisexual have partners of both sexes. Sometimes, they have had only one or two same-sex experiences; nevertheless, they identify themselves as bisexual. They believe they can love and enjoy sex with both women and men. In other instances, those with predominately same-sex experience and only limited other-sex experience consider themselves bisexual. In most cases, bisexual people do not have sex with men one night and women the next. Rather, their bisexuality is sequential. That

is, they are involved in other-sex relationships for certain periods, ranging from a few weeks to years; later, they are involved in same-sex relations for another period of time.

The Nature of Bisexuality

As discussed in Chapter 5, sexuality runs along a continuum, with bisexuality falling midway between exclusive heterosexuality and exclusive homosexuality. Given this, one might ask whether bisexual people are merely in transition toward one or the other end of the continuum or whether bisexuality is a sexual ordination in its own right. Recent research among women reveals some interesting findings that are inconsistent with the long-debated belief that bisexuality is a transitional stage or "phase" (Diamond, 2008). Longitudinal data collected from 79 lesbian, bisexual, and "unlabeled" women reveal that there are, in fact, boundaries between the long-term development stages of lesbian, bisexual, and unlabeled women, but these boundaries are rather fluid. More specifically, over time, it was found that more women appeared to have adopted bisexual/unlabeled identities rather than relinquish them. Hence, bisexuality is seen as a third type of sexual orientation and, as such, has a capacity for flexibility in erotic response. Whether this finding is applicable to men remains unknown. Ultimately, accepting bisexuality as a legitimate orientation reflects acknowledging our diversity.

Think Critically

- What are your thoughts about bisexuality: a legitimate sexual orientation or one that is uncertain or temporary?
- Would you agree to taking a questionnaire on sexual orientation? If so, how might you feel if the results were different from what you expected?
- What might your reaction be if a dating partner revealed that he or she was bisexual?

to identify themselves as gay, lesbian, or bisexual while they are attending college because postsecondary education tends to engage students with issues of pluralism, diversity, and self-evaluation (Green, 1998). **Homoeroticism**—feelings of sexual attraction to members of the same sex—almost always precedes lesbian or gay activity by several years (Bell, Weinberg, & Hammersmith, 1981).

How does one arrive at his or her sexual orientation? Does it really matter if one is born heterosexual or homosexual, whether it comes later, or whether one chooses? Would you be willing to complete a questionnaire that would measure your sexual orientation? One such measuring tool, the Klein Sexual Orientation Grid (Klein, 1993), measures seven different aspects of sexual orientation as they relate to past, present, and an ideal future. Tools like this and the Sexual Orientation Identity Uncertain scale (Worthington, Navarro, Savoy, & Hampton, 2008), included in Chapter 2, can provide one with a greater awareness and acceptance of sexual identity, the self-labeling or self-identification as a heterosexual, homosexual, or bisexual person. For some, the awareness of being or feeling something other than heterosexual appears in phases, marked first by fear and suspicion that somehow one's desires are different, a feeling that some find difficult to label. This may or may not be followed by a labeling of feelings of attraction, love, or desire as gay or lesbian. These categories may be difficult for some and not important for others, but for most of us it means accepting one's sexual orientation. For those who identify as gay, lesbian, or bisexual, this means accepting an identity that society generally regards as deviant. Questions often arise about whether to tell parents or friends or whether to hide one's identity (stay in the closet) or make it known (come out of the closet). However, the categorization of individuals as gay, straight, or bisexual does not allow for the fact that some may move back and forth among sexual identities, and it is this fluidity that is a crucial variable in sexual development (Diamond, 2005).

> "Bisexuality immediately doubles your chances for a date on a Saturday night.
>
> —Rodney Dangerfield
> (1921–2004)

For many, being a lesbian or gay person is associated with a total lifestyle and way of thinking. Publicly acknowledging one's homosexuality (coming out) has become especially important. Coming out is a major decision because it may jeopardize many relationships, but it is also an important means of self-validation and self-affirmation. By publicly acknowledging a lesbian, gay, or bisexual orientation, a person begins to reject the stigma and condemnation associated with it. Generally, coming out to heterosexual people occurs in stages involving friends and family members.

Lesbian women, gay men, and bisexual individuals are often "out" to varying degrees. Some are out to no one, not even themselves, while others are out only to selected individuals lovers, and others to close friends and lovers but not to their families, employers. Because of fear of reprisal, dismissal, or public reaction, many gay, lesbian, and bisexual professionals are not out to their employers, co-workers, or the public.

Contradicting many assumptions about sexual orientation as being early developing and unstable, **sexual fluidity** is situation-dependent flexibility in the gender of a woman's sexual attraction (Diamond, 2008). Regardless of their sexual orientation, this flexibility makes it possible for some women under unique circumstances to experience same-sex or other-sex desires. While men appear more likely to regard their sexual orientation as fixed and innate, women are more likely to acknowledge choice and change, depending on the circumstances.

Many gay men and lesbian women experience some of the same negative attitudes toward homosexuality as their heterosexual counterparts. **Internalized homophobia** is a set of negative attitudes and affects toward homosexuality in other persons and toward same-sex attraction in oneself. Growing up in a heterosexual world that condones only one way of sexual expression and reproduction, many gay men and lesbian women learn to believe that heterosexuality is the only option and that homosexuality is a perversion. Such self-hatred can significantly impede the self-acceptance process that many gay men and lesbian women must go through in order to come out and embrace their sexuality.

Gay pride has taken root throughout the country.

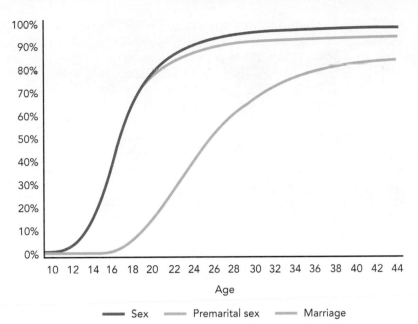

● **FIGURE 7.3**

Percentage of Individuals Who Had Had Sex, Had Premarital Sex, and Married by Specific Ages, 2002 National Survey of Family Growth. (*Source:* Figure 1 (p. 75) from Finer, L. B. (2007). Trends in premarital sex in the United States, 1954–2003. *Public Health Reports*, 122: 73–78. © 2007 Association of Schools of Public Health. Reprinted with permission.)

Being Single

In recent decades, there has been a staggering increase in the numbers of unmarried adults (never married, divorced, or widowed). Most of this increase has been the result of men and women, especially young adults, marrying later.

The New Social Context of Singlehood   The outcomes of this dramatic increase in unmarried young adults include the following:

- *Greater sexual experience.* Men and women who marry later are more likely to have had more sexual experience and sex partners than earlier generations. Nonmarital sex has become the norm among many adults. (See Figure 7.3.)

- *Widespread acceptance of cohabitation.* As young adults are deferring marriage longer and cohabitation is seen as a viable living arrangement, it has also become an integral part of young adult life. Because gay men and lesbian women are not legally permitted to marry in nearly all states, domestic partnerships have become for many of them a form of marriage.

- *Unintended pregnancies.* Because greater numbers of women are single and sexually active, they are more likely to become unintentionally pregnant as a result of unprotected sexual intercourse or contraceptive failure.

- *Increased numbers of abortions and births to single women.* The increased number of unintended pregnancies has led to more abortions and births to single mothers. Birth to unmarried couples now rivals birth to married ones as a pathway by which children enter family structures.

- *Greater numbers of separated and divorced men and women.* Approximately 20% of all new marriages are likely to end in divorce in any one year (U.S. Bureau of the Census, 2006). Because of their previous marital experience, separated and divorced men and women tend to have different expectations about relationships than never-married young adults. Nearly half of all marriages are now remarriages for at least one partner.

The college social setting provides opportunities for students to meet others and establish relationships.

■ *A rise in the number of single-parent families.* Today, nearly one third of all family groups with children are headed by single parents, with the vast majority being single mothers (U.S. Census Bureau, 2008).

The world that unmarried young adults inhabit is one in which greater opportunities than ever before exist for exploring intimate relationships.

The College Environment The college environment is important not only for intellectual development but also for social development. The social aspects of the college setting—classes, dormitories, fraternities and sororities, parties, clubs, and athletic events—provide opportunities for meeting others. For many, college is a place to search for or find mates.

Dating in college is similar to high school dating in many ways. It may be formal or informal ("getting together" or "hooking up"); it may be for recreation or for finding a mate. Features that distinguish college dating from high school dating, however, include the more independent setting (away from home, with diminished parental influence), the increased maturity of partners, more role flexibility, and the increased legitimacy of sexual interactions. For most college students, love and dating become qualitatively different during emerging adulthood, with more focus on sexuality as it relates to developing one's own identity. (See Chapter 2 for the prevalence of sexual behaviors among college students.)

Sociologist Ira Reiss (1967) describes four moral standards of nonmarital sexuality among college students. The first is the abstinence standard, which was the official sexual ideology in American culture until the early 1960s. According to this belief, it is wrong for either men or women to engage in sexual intercourse before marriage regardless of the circumstances or their feelings for each other. The second is the double standard, widely practiced but rarely approved publicly. This permits men to engage in nonmarital intercourse, but women are considered immoral if they do so. Permissiveness with emotional affection represents a third standard. It describes sex between men and women who have a stable, loving relationship. Though these standards were put forth over 40 years ago, they are still widely held today. Permissiveness without affection, the fourth standard and the type of sexual expression that usually occurs in "hooking up" on college campuses, holds that people may have sexual relationships with each other even if there is no affection or commitment.

Although acceptance of sex outside of marriage is widespread among college students, there are more baudaries placed on woman. If a woman has sexual intercourse, most people believe it should take place in the context of a committed relationship. Women who "sleep around" are morally censured. Reflecting the continuing sexual double standard, men are not usually condemned as harshly as women for having sex without commitment.

For the nearly 4% of college males and nearly 2% of college females who identify themselves as being predominately nonheterosexual (Ellis, Robb, & Burke, 2005), along with others who are transgendered or questioning their sexual orientation, the college environment is often liberating because campuses tend to be more accepting of sexual diversity than society at large is. College campuses often have lesbian, gay, bisexual, and transgender organizations that sponsor social events and get-togethers. There, individuals can freely meet others in open circumstances that permit meaningful relationships to develop and mature. Although prejudice against those who are different continues to exist in colleges and universities, college life has been an important haven for many.

The Singles World Men and women involved in the singles world tend to be older than college students, typically ranging in age from 25 to 40. They have never been married, or, if they are divorced, they usually do not have primary responsibility for children. Single adults are generally working rather than attending school.

Although dating in the singles world is somewhat different from dating in high school and college, there are similarities. Singles, like their counterparts in school, emphasize recreation and entertainment, sociability, and physical attractiveness.

The problem of meeting other single people is very often central. In college, students meet each other in classes or dormitories, at school events, or through friends. There are many meeting places and large numbers of eligibles. Singles who are working may have less opportunity than college students to meet available people. For single adults, the most frequent means of meeting others are introductions by friends, common interests, parties, the Internet, and social or religious groups.

Sexual experimentation and activity are important for many singles. Although individuals may derive personal satisfaction from sexual activity, they must also manage the stress of conflicting commitments, loneliness, and a lack of connectedness. To fill the demand for meeting others, the singles world has spawned a multibillion-dollar industry—bars, resorts, clubs, housing, and the Internet sites dedicated solely to them. In fact, of the 33 million U.S. adult singles who go online, about 6% of them subscribe to a dating Web site (Marcotty, 2007). Singles increasingly rely on personal classified ads, Internet sites such as MySpace, dating sites such as eHarmony.com or Chemistry.com, or chat rooms, in which men advertise themselves as "success objects" and women advertise themselves as "sex objects." These ads, postings, and messages tend to reflect stereotypical gender

> " *I must paint you.*
> —Paul Gauguin, pick-up line
> (1848–1903)

> " *Wherever there are rich men trying not to feel old, there will be young girls trying not to feel poor.*
> —Julie Burchill
> (1959–)

Why College Students Have Sex: Gender Differences, or Not?

The reasons why people have sex may appear obvious and simple when, in fact, they are actually quite complex and diverse. Add gender differences to this mix, and the reasons for having sex begin to mount. Researchers Cindy Meston and David Buss (2007), in a 5-year study, sought to identify an array of potential reasons that motivate people to engage in sexual intercourse and to classify reasons by gender. Meston suggests these findings have "refuted a lot of gender stereotypes that men only want sex for the physical pleasure and women want love." What they found is that college-age men and women seek sex for mostly the same reason: lust in the body more than a love connection in the heart. In fact, both sexes agree that their primary reason for having sex was attraction; they wanted to experience physical pleasure. Men and women were not found to be very different on many counts: 20 of the top 25 reasons given for having sex were the same for men and women. Though expressing love and showing affection were in the top 10 for both men and women, the clear number-one reason was "I was attracted to the person."

The researchers began with 444 men and women—ranging in age from 17 to 52—and a list of 237 reasons why people have sex. Among the top 10 reasons for having sex (for all ages and both genders) were to experience physical pleasure, to express love, and to show affection. From the same list of reasons, the researchers asked 1,549 college students to rank the reasons and collected some interesting data:

- What motivated college-age students most of the time included attraction, pleasure, affection, love, romance, emotional closeness, arousal, the desire to please, adventure, excitement, experience, connection, celebration, curiosity, and opportunity.

- The less frequently endorsed reasons for having sex included giving someone else an STI, wanting to break up a rival's relationship by having sex with his/her partner, or wanting to get a promotion.

- Men, significantly more than women, cited reasons for having sex centered on the physical appearance and physical desirability of a partner. Additionally, they indicated experience-seeking and mere opportunity as factors.

- Women exceeded men in endorsing certain emotional motivations for sex, such as wanting to express love and realizing they were in love.

- Interestingly, among both the college students and older individuals, none of the gender differences for why humans had sex were that significant.

When examining the psychological motivations for having sex, the researchers noted that what constituted a rare reason for the population as a whole might constitute a major motivation for individuals. For example, though most people are not motivated by the desire to humiliate another or to feel humiliated through sex, for others who practice sadism or masochism, this is their principal sexual motivation.

Think Critically

- Can you relate to any of these data? What are the reasons you have or do not have sex?
- Do you feel the data found in this study can be replicated across cultures?
- To what extent do the reasons for having sex change across the life span?

roles. Men frequently advertise for women who are attractive, de-emphasizing intellectual, professional, and financial considerations. Women often advertise for men who hold jobs and who are financially secure, intelligent, emotionally expressive, and interested in commitment. Men are twice as likely as women to place ads. Additional forms of people meeting others include video dating services, introduction services, and 1-900 party-line phone services.

Single men and women often rely on their religious organization to meet other singles. About 8% of married couples meet in church (Laumann et al., 1994). Churches are especially important for middle-class African Americans. African Americans also attend Black-oriented concerts, plays, film festivals, and other social gatherings to meet other singles.

As a result of the wide acceptance of sexuality outside of marriage, single people are presented with various sexual options. Some choose celibacy for religious or moral reasons. Others choose celibacy over casual sex; when they are involved in a committed nonmarital relationship, they may become sexually intimate. Some are temporarily celibate "taking a vacation from sex," and may utilize their celibate time to clarify the meaning of sexuality in their relationships.

In the late nineteenth century, as a result of the stigmatization of homosexuality, groups of gay men and lesbian women began congregating in their own secret clubs and bars. There, in relative safety, they could find acceptance and support, meet others, and socialize. Today, some neighborhoods in large cities are identified with gay, lesbian, bisexual, and transgendered people. These neighborhoods feature not only openly gay and/or lesbian bookstores, restaurants, coffeehouses, and bars but also churches, clothing stores, medical and legal offices, hair salons, and so on.

While many gay men and lesbian women choose to affirm their commitment in a marriage ceremony, states across the country continue to argue its place in society.

African American gay men and lesbian women often experience a conflict between their Black and gay identities. African Americans are less likely to disclose their gay identity because the Black community is less accepting of homosexuality than is the White community (Edozien, 2003). Several factors contribute to this phenomenon. Although there is some support for gay civil rights among Black leaders, strong fundamentalist Christian beliefs influence some African Americans to be unaccepting of lesbian women and gay men. Additionally, because homosexuality is sometimes thought of as having originated from slavery or imprisonment, these beliefs result in openly gay Black individuals being considered traitors to their own race. The internalization of the dominant culture's stereotyping of African Americans as highly sexual beings may also prompt many African Americans to feel a need to assert and express their sexuality in ways that are considered "normal."

For gay Latinos and lesbian Latinas living in cities with large Latino populations, there is usually at least one gay bar. Such places specialize in dancing or female impersonation. The extent to which a gay Latino man participates in the Anglo or Latino gay world depends on the individual's degree of acculturation (Carrier, 1992). While traditional standards of Latino and Latina culture expect men to support and defend the family and women to be submissive to men and maintain their virginity until married, it is not uncommon for many Latinos and Latinas to engage in same-sex behavior without considering themselves gay (Greene, 1994). Additionally, lesbian Latinas are doubly stigmatized because they may be seen as defying expectations of women's roles and challenging the traditional male dominance of the culture (Trujillo, 1997).

Traditional Asian cultures place significance on respecting elders, conforming to one's family's expectations, and assuming distinct gender roles with less regard for individual needs and desires (Chan, 1992). As in strict traditional Latino(a) cultures, traditional Asian American culture de-emphasizes the importance of sex to women. Open acknowledgment of lesbian or gay

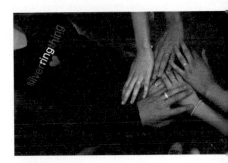

A rising number of single people are committing to celibacy before marriage by the wearing of "celibacy vow" or "promise" rings.

think about it

Common Misconceptions About Homosexuality

Just as there are myths about bisexuality, there are also numerous misconceptions about being a gay man or a lesbian woman. These continue to circulate, fueling the fires of prejudice. The misconceptions include the following:

- *Misconception 1: Men and women are gay or lesbian because they can't get a heterosexual partner.* This belief is reflected in such remarks about lesbian women as "All she needs is a good lay" (implying a man). Similar remarks about men include "He just needs to meet the right woman." In fact, studies comparing partners from same-sex couples to heterosexuals have found same-sex couples to be equivalent to heterosexuals in the quality of their relationship (Peplau & Beals, 2004; Peplau & Spaulding, 2000).

- *Misconception 2: Lesbian women and gay men "recruit" heterosexuals to become gay.* People are not recruited or seduced into being gay any more than they are recruited into being heterosexual. Most gay men and lesbian women have their first gay experience with a peer, either a friend or an acquaintance. They report having had same-sex feelings prior to their first experience.

- *Misconception 3: Gay men are child molesters.* This is a corollary to the recruitment misconception. The overwhelming majority of child molesters are heterosexual males who molest girls; these men include fathers, stepfathers, uncles, and brothers. A large percentage of men who molest boys identify themselves as heterosexual (Arndt, 1991).

- *Misconception 4: Homosexuality can be "caught" or "taught."* Homosexuality is not the flu. Some parents express fear about having their children taught by homosexual teachers. They fear that their children will model themselves after the teacher or be seduced by him or her. But a child's sexual orientation is often established by the time he or she enters school, and a teacher would not have an impact on that child's orientation. Neither do parents teach children to be straight or gay.

- *Misconception 5: Gay men and lesbian women could change if they wanted to.* Many gay men and lesbian women believe that they cannot change their sexual orientation. The belief that they should reflects assumptions that homosexuality is abnormal or sinful.

Most psychotherapy with gay men and lesbian women who are unhappy about their orientation aims at helping them adjust to it. So-called reparative therapy, which has not been scientifically shown to be effective, is based on the belief that orientation can be changed.

- *Misconception 6: All gay men are effeminate; all lesbian women are butch.* Empirical research has demonstrated that these perceptions of gay men and of lesbian women have been shaped more by cultural ideologies about homosexuality than by individuals' own unbiased observations (cited in Herek, 1995).

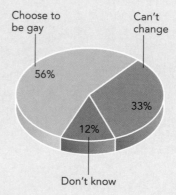

Choose to be gay — 56%
Can't change — 33%
Don't know — 12%

● FIGURE 7.4

Percentage of Adults Who Believe Homosexuality Is Chosen or Can't Be Changed. (*Source:* "Can Gays Convert?," 2000.)

Think Critically

- What were you taught about homosexuality? How much of what you learned while growing up do you still hold to be true? What, if anything, altered or reinforced your thoughts and opinions?

- If you were told that you had to go to therapy in order to change your sexual orientation, how successful do you believe it would be?

- If you were to compile your own list of misconceptions about homosexuality, what would they be? On what do you base your knowledge?

identity is seen by mainstream Asian society as a rejection of traditional cultural roles and a threat to the continuity of family life. If, however, family expectations can be met, then secretly engaging in same-sex behavior may not cause the individual to feel guilty or bring embarrassment to the family (Matteson, 1997).

An exception to the negativity experienced by many gay and lesbian people of color is experienced among Native American cultures, whose traditions place high value on individual differences. Based on the belief of the Great Spirit, who acknowledges the sacredness of each person's sexual orientation and gender role, tolerance of individual differences has persisted despite long-standing assaults on the Native American culture (Epstein, 1997).

Cohabitation

In 2005, of the more than 111 million households in the United States, nearly 6 million of them consisted of unmarried couples (U.S. Census Bureau, 2008). Most of these were younger adults, who tend to attach far less moral stigma than do their elders to cohabitation and out-of-wedlock births (Pew Research Center, 2007). These numbers were in sharp contrast to those gathered in 1969 when only 400,000 heterosexual couples reported cohabitating. Though marriage remains an ideal for most, albeit a more elusive one, cohabitation is the lifestyle choice for a vast number of adults in this country. (See Figure 7.5 for the percentage of cohabiting couples by race.)

A New Norm   **Cohabitation** is increasingly accepted at almost every level of society. Also referred to as POSSLQ, *People of Opposite Sex Sharing Living Quarters*, the U.S. Census Bureau now keeps track of this rising demographic. By age 30, half of all people will have cohabited. In fact, cohabitation perhaps is becoming institutionalized as part of the normal mate selection process. The

Lesbian women and gay celebrities, such as Ellen DeGeneres and her wife, Portia de Rossi, are increasingly being accepted into mainstream media.

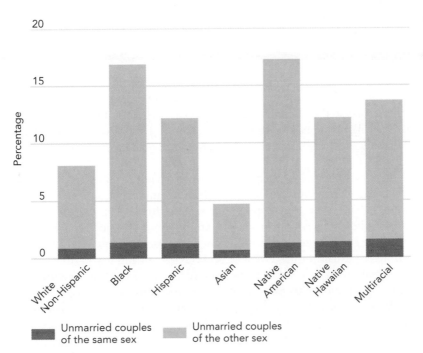

● **FIGURE 7.5**
Percent of Cohabitating Couples, by Race and Sexual Orientation, 2002. (*Source:* U.S. Census Bureau, 2003.)

concept of **domestic partnership** has led to laws granting some of the protections of marriage to men and women, including gay men and lesbian women, who cohabit in committed relationships.

Cohabitation has become more widespread and accepted in recent years for several reasons. First, the general climate regarding sexuality is more liberal than it was a generation ago. Sexuality is more widely considered to be an important part of people's lives, whether or not they are married. The moral criterion for judging sexual intercourse has shifted; love rather than marriage is now widely regarded as making sex with another person moral. Second, divorce is seen now as more preferable than an unhappy marriage. Because of the dramatic increase in divorce rates in recent decades, marriage is no longer thought of as necessarily a permanent commitment. Permanence is increasingly replaced by **serial monogamy,** a succession of marriages, whereby the average marriage now lasts approximately 7 years. Third, young adults are continuing to defer marriage. At the same time, they want the companionship found in living intimately with another person.

For young adults, there are a number of advantages to cohabitation. First, because their lives are often in transition—as they finish school, establish careers, or become more secure financially—cohabitation represents a tentatively committed relationship. Second, in cohabiting relationships, partners tend to be more egalitarian. They do not have to deal with the more traditionally structured roles of husband and wife and are freer to develop their own individuality independent of marital roles. Third, the partners know they are together because they want to be, not because of the pressure of marital obligations. With the increased acceptance of cohabitation, more than half of the Fortune 500 companies have extended domestic partner benefits to both homosexual and heterosexual partners. This change has helped employers hire and keep qualified employees while providing employees with partners the same health benefits as married couples.

Although there are a number of advantages to cohabitation, there can also be disadvantages. Hence, cohabiting couples also may find that they cannot easily buy a house together because some banks may not view their income as joint. If one partner has children, the other partner is usually not as involved as if the couple were married. Cohabiting couples may find themselves socially stigmatized if they have a child. Extrarelational sex is more likely to occur in cohabiting relationships than in married ones. Finally, cohabiting relationships generally don't last more than 5 years; couples either break up or get married (Tolson, 2000).

In 2005, about 1 in 8 couples who were living together had partners of the same sex (U.S. Census Bureau, 2008). The relationships of gay men and lesbian women have been stereotyped as less committed than those of heterosexual couples because (1) lesbian women and gay men cannot legally marry in the vast majority of states (2) they may not appear to emphasize sexual exclusiveness, (3) heterosexuals misperceive love between lesbian and gay partners as somehow less "real" than love between heterosexuals, and (4) some heterosexuals view same-sex relationships as a threat to the institution of marriage. Regardless of their sexual orientation, most people want a close, loving relationship with another person.

" *The censor believes that he can hold back the mighty traffic of life with a tin whistle and a raised hand. For after all, it is life with which he quarrels.*

—Heywood Broun
(1888–1939)

With the increased acceptance of cohabitation, many couples are postponing decisions about marriage and children until their thirties.

For gay men, lesbian women, and heterosexual individuals, intimate relationships provide love, romance, satisfaction, and security. There is one important difference, however: Many lesbian and gay relationships resist the traditional heterosexual provider/homemaker roles. Among heterosexual couples, these divisions are often gender-linked as male or female. In same-sex couples, however, tasks are often divided pragmatically, according to considerations such as who likes cooking more (or dislikes it less) and who works when. Most gay couples are dual-worker couples; neither partner supports or depends on the other economically. And because partners in gay and lesbian couples are the same sex, the economic discrepancies based on greater male earning power are absent. Although gay couples emphasize egalitarianism, if there are differences in power, they are attributed to personality; if there is an age difference, the older partner is usually more powerful.

● Sexuality in Middle Adulthood

In the middle-adulthood years, family and work become especially important. Personal time is spent increasingly on marital and family matters, especially if a couple have children. Sexual expression often decreases in frequency, intensity, and significance, to be replaced by family and work concerns. Sometimes, the change reflects a higher value placed on family intimacy; other times, it may reflect habit, boredom, or conflict.

Developmental Concerns

In the middle-adulthood years, some of the psychosexual developmental tasks begun in young adulthood may be continuing. These tasks, such as ones related to intimacy issues or parenting decisions, may have been deferred or only partly completed in young adulthood. Because of separation or divorce, people may find themselves facing the same intimacy and commitment tasks at age 40 that they thought they had completed 15 years earlier (Cate & Lloyd, 1992). But life does not stand still; it moves steadily forward, and other developmental issues appear, including the following:

- *Redefining sex in marital or other long-term relationships.* In new relationships, sex is often passionate and intense; it may be the central focus. But in long-term marital or cohabiting relationships, habit, competing family and work obligations, fatigue, and unresolved conflicts often erode the passionate intensity associated with sex. Sex may need to be redefined as an expression of intimacy and caring. Individuals may also need to decide how to deal with the possibility, reality, and meaning of extramarital or extrarelational sex.

- *Reevaluating one's sexuality.* Single women and single men may need to weigh the costs and benefits of sex in casual or lightly committed relationships. In long-term relationships, sexuality often becomes less than central to relationship satisfaction, as nonsexual elements such as communication, intimacy, and shared interests and activities become increasingly important. Women who desire children and who have deferred their childbearing begin to reappraise their decision: Should they remain child-free, race against their biological clock, or adopt a child? Some people may redefine their sexual orientation. One's sexual philosophy continues to evolve.

- *Accepting the biological aging process.* As people age, their skin wrinkles, their flesh sags, their hair turns gray (or falls out), their vision blurs—and they become, in the eyes of society, less attractive and less sexual. By their forties, their physiological responses have begun to slow. By their fifties, society begins to "neuter" them, especially women who have been through menopause. The challenge of aging is to come to terms with its biological changes and challenges.

Sexuality in Established Relationships

When people marry, they may discover that their sex lives are very different from what they were before marriage. Sex is now morally and socially sanctioned. It is in marriage that the great majority of heterosexual interactions take place, yet as a culture, we feel ambivalent about marital sex. On the one hand, marriage is the only relationship in which sexuality is legitimized. On the other, marital sex is an endless source of humor and ridicule.

Frequency of Sexual Interactions   Sexual intercourse tends to diminish in frequency the longer a couple is married. For newly married couples, the average

Seldom, or perhaps never, does a marriage develop into an individual relationship smoothly and without crisis; there is no coming to consciousness without pain.

—Carl Jung
(1875–1961)

Setting a good example for your children takes all the fun out of middle age.

—William Feather
(1889–1981)

frequency of sexual intercourse is about 3 times a week. As couples get older, the frequency drops. In early middle age, married couples have sexual intercourse an average of 1–2 times a week. After age 50, the rate is about once a week or less (American Association of Retired Persons [AARP], 2005). Decreased frequency, however, does not necessarily mean that sex is no longer important or that the marriage is unsatisfactory. It may be the result of biological aging and declining sexual drive, or it could be the way our brains adapt, from the initial surge of dopamine that prompts romance and desire to the relative quiet of an oxytocin-induced attachment (Slater, 2006). Oxytocin is a hormone that produces a feeling of connectedness and bonding. But decreasing frequency of sexual interaction may, for example, simply mean that one or both partners are too tired. For dual-worker families and families with children, fatigue and lack of private time may be the most significant factors in the decline of frequency.

The demands of parenting may diminish a couple's ability to be sexually spontaneous.

Ask any married couple about their patterns of lust over time, and you'll no doubt find wide variations, from no lust to large fluctuations in desire and activity from day to day. Such patterns were evidenced in a study of married individuals who reported about the role of emotions in the way they negotiated sexuality in their relationships (Ridley, Cate, Ressing, et al., 2006). The researchers found that power and closeness were implicated in these negotiations and provided the desire for bonding and sexual desire. When partners treated each other well (e.g., were close and equal in power), the link between emotions and lust became stronger.

Most married couples don't seem to feel that declining frequency in sexual intercourse is a major problem if their overall relationship is good (Cupach & Comstock, 1990; Sprecher & McKinney, 1993). Sexual intercourse is only one erotic bond among many in marriage. There are also kisses, caresses, nibbles, massages, candlelight dinners, hand-in-hand walks, intimate words, and so on.

Sexual Satisfaction and Pleasure   Higher levels of sexual satisfaction and pleasure seem to be found in marriage than in singlehood or extramarital relationships (Laumann et al., 1994). More than 50% of married men report that they are extremely satisfied physically and emotionally with their partner, while 40–45% of married women report similar levels of satisfaction ("Global Study," 2002; Laumann et al., 1994). The lowest rates of satisfaction were among those who were neither married nor living with someone, a group thought to have the most frequent sex.

About 75% of single, married, and cohabiting men always have an orgasm with their partner, but those who are married report the highest rates of physical and emotional satisfaction with their partner. Among women, the rate of always having an orgasm varies. The highest rate of orgasm—34%—is found among divorced women living alone, followed by married women, 30% of whom report always having an orgasm.

Adult love relationships often have complex expectations: emotional stabilization, shared time and values, personal enrichment, security, and support, to name

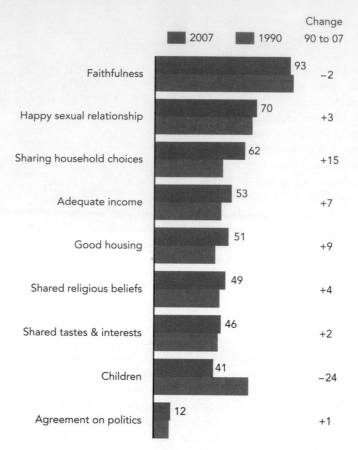

● **FIGURE 7.6**

What Makes a Marriage Work?
Percentage who say each
expectation is very important
for a successful marriage.
(*Source:* From *As Marriage and
Parenthood Drift Apart, Public Is
Concerned about Social Impact.*
Washington, DC: Pew Research
Center, July 1, 2007, p. 2.
Reprinted with permission. http://
pewresearch.org/assets/social/
pdf/Marriage.pdf)

	2007	1990	Change 90 to 07
Faithfulness	93		−2
Happy sexual relationship	70		+3
Sharing household choices	62		+15
Adequate income	53		+7
Good housing	51		+9
Shared religious beliefs	49		+4
Shared tastes & interests	46		+2
Children	41		−24
Agreement on politics	12		+1

a few (see Figure 7.6). What are some of the ways that the public views marriage, and how important in this mix are children? Findings from a telephone survey conducted among a randomly selected, nationally representative sample of 2,020 adults reveal several interesting findings (Pew Research Center, 2007):

- Even though a decreasing percentage of the adult population is married, most unmarried adults say they want to marry. Of those married, more are satisfied with their lives than their unmarried counterparts.

- Only 41% of those surveyed view having children as "very important" to a successful marriage, down from 65% in 1990.

- While the vast majority of Americans endorse two-parent families, a similar majority view divorce as preferable to an unhappy marriage.

Married partners have a commitment to learning each other's likes and dislikes and being sensitive to the other's needs. The longer the partnership lasts, the greater the commitment is likely to be to making its various aspects—including the sexual component—work.

Divorce and After

Divorce has become a major force in American life. A quick observation of demographics in this country points to a growing way of life: postdivorce single-hood. Contrary to divorce trends in the twentieth century, in recent decades, the divorce rate has actually dropped. In 1990, the divorce rate was 4.7 per

1,000; in 2000, it was 4.2; and in 2004, the rate dropped to 3.6 (U.S. Census Bureau, 2008). And since more couples now live together without marrying, the divorce rate is down, especially among those who are college-educated.

Scholars suggest that divorce represents, not a devaluation of marriage, but, oddly enough, an idealization of it. We would not divorce if we did not have such high expectations for marriage's ability to fulfill various needs. Our divorce rate further tells us that we may no longer believe in the permanence of marriage. Instead, we remain married only as long as we are in love or until a potentially better partner comes along.

Consequences of Divorce   Because divorce is so prevalent, many studies have focused on its effects on partners and children. From these studies, a number of consequences of divorce have been identified (Amato, 2000; Thables, 1997):

- There is often stigmatization by family, friends, and co-workers.
- There is a change of income (usually a substantial decline for women and their children).
- There is a higher incidence of physical and emotional problems among both men and women, including depression, injury, and illness.
- There are significantly more problems with children, including criminality, substance abuse, lower academic performance, earlier sexual activity, and a higher rate of divorce.
- Children are twice as likely as those in two-parent families to develop serious psychiatric problems and addictions later in life (Whitehead & Holland, 2003).

Slightly over half of all divorces involve children. Our understanding about the long-term impact of divorce on children is, at best, mixed. Impressive and influential research by psychologists Judith Wallerstein and her colleagues (2000) demonstrates fairly extensive, long-term trauma and distress that appeared to stay with and impact children of divorce well into their adulthood. Specifically, more than a third of the children at the 5-year mark of divorce struggled in school, experienced depression, had difficulty with friendships, and had a higher than average rate of marriage before age 25 and consequent divorce. More moderate and encouraging views emerge from other studies (see Ahrons, 2004; Amato, 2003; and Hetherington & Kelly, 2002) that demonstrate the majority of children whose parents have divorced do not suffer long-term consequences. In most cases, the way the children think and feel about the important relationships in their families are not significantly altered. In fact, these same children grow up to be well-adjusted adults who sustain family connections and commitments.

Although there are several theories about how to maintain stability in a child's life following divorce, experts cite the economic circumstances, quality of the parenting, timing of the divorce, level of respect between the parents, and quality of the social network, which includes teachers, parents, and other role models, as being significant in a child's ability to cope with the divorce.

While our understanding of the long-term impact of divorce on children is still limited, there are some positive outcomes from divorce that may offset or even provide relief from the negative ones. Divorce offers options for individuals in unhappy marriages. Divorce also may eliminate the stressful and frustrating experience of marriage and improve the family's mental and emotional well-being. And divorce can provide both parents and children with a

To hear Mike's views on marriage and divorce, click on "Mike on Marriage."

less idealized view of marriage, an opportunity for growth, and a more harmonious family situation. Obviously, most individuals would not opt for divorce if a viable alternative were available. However, when it is not, acknowledging that the process of divorce will involve change may help prepare the people involved for the transition that lies ahead.

Dating Again A first date after years of marriage and subsequent months of singlehood evokes some of the same emotions felt by inexperienced adolescents. Separated or divorced men and women who are beginning to date again may be excited and nervous; worry about how they look; and wonder whether it's OK to hold hands, kiss, or make love. They may believe that dating is incongruous with their former selves, or they may be annoyed with themselves for feeling excited and awkward. Furthermore, they may know little about the norms of postmarital dating.

Dating serves several important purposes for separated and divorced people. Primarily, it is a statement to both the former spouse and the world at large that the person is available to become someone else's partner. Also, dating is an opportunity to enhance one's self-esteem. Free from the stress of an unhappy marriage, people may discover, for example, that they are more interesting and charming than either they or (especially) their former spouses had imagined. And dating initiates people into the singles subculture, where they can experiment with the freedom about which they may have fantasized when they were married.

Sexual activity is an important component in the lives of separated and divorced men and women. Engaging in sexual behavior with someone for the first time following separation helps people accept their newly acquired single status. Because sexual exclusivity is usually an important element in marriage, becoming sexually active with someone other than one's spouse is a dramatic symbol that the old marriage vows are no longer valid.

Single Parenting In 2006, nearly 30% of all families were headed by single parents, the vast majority of which were single mothers (U.S. Census Bureau, 2008). Several demographic trends have affected the shift from two-parent to

You have to accept the fact that part of the sizzle of sex comes from the danger of sex.

—Camille Paglia
(1947–)

The bed: A place where marriages are decided.

—Anonymous

Because of their child-rearing responsibilities, single parents are usually not part of the singles world.

one-parent families, including a larger proportion of births to unmarried women, the delay of marriage, and the increase in divorce among couples with children. White single mothers are more likely to be divorced than their African American or Latina counterparts, who are more likely to be unmarried at the time of birth or to be widowed.

Single parents are not often a part of the singles world, which involves more than simply not being married. It requires leisure and money, both of which single parents, especially women, generally lack because of their family responsibilities.

The presence of children affects a divorced woman's sexual activity. Single divorced parents are less likely than divorced women without children to be sexually active (Stack & Gundlach, 1992). Children enormously complicate a single parent's sexual decision making. A single mother must decide, for example, whether to permit a potential partner to spend the night with her when her children are present. This is often an important symbolic act for a woman, for several reasons. First, it involves her children in her romantic relationships. Women are often hesitant to again expose their children to the distress associated with the initial parental separation and divorce, which is often seared into everyone's mind. Second, it reveals to her children that their mother is sexual, which may make her feel uncomfortable. Third, it opens her up to moral judgments from her children regarding her sexuality. Single parents are often fearful that their children will lose respect for them, which can happen when children reach middle childhood (approximately ages 10–14).

● Sexuality in Late Adulthood

Sexual feelings and desires continue throughout the life cycle. Though many of the standards of activity or attraction are constant, it may be necessary for each of us to overcome the taboos and stereotypes associated with sex and aging in order to create a place for its expression in our lives.

Developmental Concerns

Many of the psychosexual tasks older Americans must undertake are directly related to the aging process, including the following (DeLamater & Sill, 2005):

- *Biological changes.* As older men's and women's physical abilities change with age, their sexual responses change as well. A 70-year-old person, though still sexual, is not sexual in the same manner as an 18-year-old individual. As men and women continue to age, their sexuality tends to be more diffuse, less genitally oriented, and less insistent. Chronic illness, hormonal changes, vascular changes, and increasing frailty understandably result in diminished sexual activity. These considerations contribute to the ongoing evolution of the individual's sexual philosophy.

- *Death of a partner.* One of the most critical life events is the loss of a partner. After age 60, there is a significant increase in spousal deaths. Because having a partner is the single most important factor determining an older person's sexual interactions, the absence of a sexual partner signals a dramatic change in the survivor's sexual interactions.

- *Psychological influences.* Given America's obsession with youth and sexuality, it is not surprising that many people consider it inappropriate for older men and women to continue to be sexually active. Such factors as lack of sexual information, negative attitudes toward sexual expression, and mental health problems including depression (along with the treatments that remedy it) may interfere with older individuals' ability or willingness to see themselves as sexual beings.

Older adults negotiate these issues within the context of continuing aging. Resolving them as we age helps us to accept the eventuality of our death.

Stereotypes of Aging

Our society stereotypes aging as a lonely and depressing time, but most studies of older adults find that, relative to younger people, they express high levels of satisfaction and well-being. It is poverty, loneliness, and poor health that make old age difficult. But, even so, older people have lower levels of poverty than most Americans, including young adults, women, and children. More importantly, until their mid-seventies, most older people report few, if any, restrictions on their activities because of health.

The sexuality of older Americans tends to be invisible, as society discounts their sexuality. Several factors account for this in our culture (Barrow & Smith, 1992). First, we associate sexuality with young people, assuming that sexual attraction

One of the most famous twentieth-century sculptures is Auguste Rodin's *The Kiss*, which depicts young lovers embracing. Here, the aging model Antoni Nordone sits before the statue that immortalized his youth.

exists only between those with youthful bodies. Interest in sex is considered normal in 25-year-old men, but in 75-year-old men, it is considered lecherous. Second, we associate the idea of romance and love with the young; many of us find it difficult to believe that older adults can fall in love or love intensely. Third, we continue to associate sex with procreation, measuring a woman's femininity by her childbearing and maternal role and a man's masculinity by the children he has. Finally, older people do not have sexual desires as strong as those of younger people, and they do not express them as openly. Intimacy is especially valued and important for an older person's well-being.

Aging gay men and lesbian women face a double stigma: Stigmas related to their sexual orientation and to their age, which paint them as undesirable and target them for ostracism. But, like other stigmas of aging Americans, these reflect myths rather than realities. Targeted educational programs can help to reduce fears and discomfort related to both aging and sexual orientation.

Stereotypes and myths about aging are not the only factors that affect the sexuality of older Americans. The narrow definition of sexuality contributes to the problem. Sexual behavior is defined by researchers and the general population in terms of masturbation, sexual intercourse, and orgasm. The continued focus on physical and hormonal changes highlights the general trend toward the medicalization of sexual functioning rather than the emotional, sensual, and relationship aspects that are enjoyed by all people, regardless of age (Tiefer, 2004).

Sexuality and Aging

Sexuality remains an essential element in the lives of individuals 45 and over (AARP, 2005), although men and women tend to view aging differently. As men approach their fifties, they generally fear the loss of their sexual capacity but not their attractiveness; in contrast, women generally fear the loss of their attractiveness but not their sexuality.

Cultural attitudes toward sexuality and aging appear to influence whether sex among older individuals is encouraged or discouraged. Sexual expression has historically been viewed in the United States as an activity reserved for young and newly married people. Fortunately, this viewpoint is not universally accepted. Cross-cultural studies show that in many countries sexual activity is not only accepted but also expected among older adults.

Despite conventional wisdom, recent studies conducted in the United States have revealed that older Americans continue to be sexual beings. This comes from the most comprehensive sex survey ever done among 57–85-year-olds in the United States (Lindau, Schumm, Laumann, et al., 2007). Based on interviews with more than 3,000 Americans, who gave detailed descriptions of their sexual activities, it was found that most Americans remain regularly sexually active into their seventies, and a quarter of those up to age 85 report having had sex in the previous year. For varied reasons, women were significantly less likely than men to report being sexually active; however the drop-off appeared to have a lot to do with health or lack of a partner. (For highlights of this study, see Figure 7.7.)

Why conduct this type of research? Sex is an important indicator of health. The findings of this research give people a way to gauge their own experiences and might prompt those with questions or problems to discuss them with their doctors.

Among older lesbian and gay couples, as well as heterosexual couples, the happiest are those with a strong commitment to the relationship. The need for intimacy, companionship, and purpose transcends issues of sexual orientation.

You only possess what will not be lost in a shipwreck.

—Al Ghazali
(1058–1111)

Old age has its pleasures, which, though different, are not less than the pleasures of youth.

—W. Somerset Maugham
(1874–1965)

How many older Americans have been sexually active with a partner in the last month? Decisively more men than women. How many are sexually active with a partner at least 2–3 times per month? Nearly equal numbers of men and women.

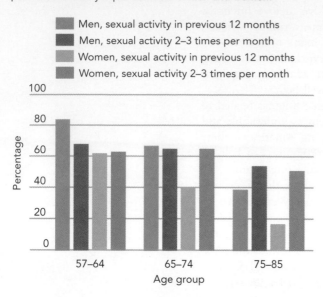

- Men, sexual activity in previous 12 months
- Men, sexual activity 2–3 times per month
- Women, sexual activity in previous 12 months
- Women, sexual activity 2–3 times per month

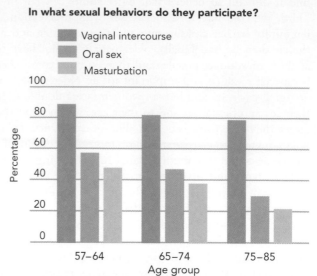

In what sexual behaviors do they participate?

- Vaginal intercourse
- Oral sex
- Masturbation

What problems do they have?
At least half of both men and women reported having at least one bothersome sexual problem and almost one third reported having at least two. Here are some of the most commonly reported difficulties.

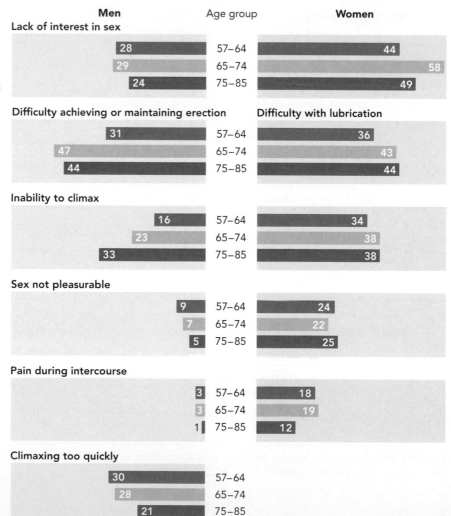

	Men	Age group	Women
Lack of interest in sex	28	57–64	44
	29	65–74	58
	24	75–85	49
Difficulty achieving or maintaining erection / **Difficulty with lubrication**	31	57–64	36
	47	65–74	43
	44	75–85	44
Inability to climax	16	57–64	34
	23	65–74	38
	33	75–85	38
Sex not pleasurable	9	57–64	24
	7	65–74	22
	5	75–85	25
Pain during intercourse	3	57–64	18
	3	65–74	19
	1	75–85	12
Climaxing too quickly	30	57–64	
	28	65–74	
	21	75–85	

● **FIGURE 7.7**

Sexual Frequency, Behaviors, and Problems of Older Americans.
(*Source:* Lindau, Schumm, Laumann, et al., 2007.)

Marital satisfaction and emotional health foster the desire for sexual intimacy in lasting relationships. The greatest determinants of an older person's sexual activity are the availability of a partner and health.

Because our society tends to desexualize the old, aging people may interpret their slower responses as signaling the end of their sexuality. Sexuality education programs for older people, in which they learn about anatomy, physiology, STIs, and sexual response, have been shown to be helpful in dispelling myths, building confidence, and giving permission to be sexual (Davila, 2008).

Women's Issues   Beginning sometime in their forties, most women start to experience a normal biological process resulting in a decline in fertility. Many women are relieved when they no longer have to worry about getting pregnant and pleased when they no longer have to deal with a monthly menstrual flow. This period of gradual change and adjustment is referred to as **perimenopause.** During this time, the ovaries produce less and less estrogen and progesterone, and ovulation becomes less regular. Over a few years' time, menstrual periods become irregular and eventually stop, usually between the ages of 45 and 55, but it can happen anytime from the thirties to mid-fifties or later. The average age of **menopause,** the complete cessation of menstruation for at least one year, is 51, although about 10% of women complete it before age 40 (National Institute on Aging, 2005a). A woman can also undergo menopause as a result of a hysterectomy, the surgical removal of the uterus, if both ovaries are also removed. In postmenopausal women, estrogen levels are about one tenth those in premenopausal women, and progesterone is nearly absent (National Cancer Institute, 2002a). Most women experience some physiological or psychological symptoms during menopause, but for only about 5–15% of women are the effects severe enough to cause them to seek medical assistance.

Physical Effects of Menopause   Whether a woman goes through menopause naturally or surgically, symptoms can appear as the woman's body attempts to adjust to the drop in estrogen levels. The symptoms vary from one woman to the next: Some may breeze through menopause with few symptoms, whereas others may experience many discomforting symptoms for several months or even years. The most common symptoms of menopause are hot flashes or flushes, sweating, and sleeping disturbances (National Institutes of Health, 2005). Another symptom, thinning of the vaginal walls, can result in the length and width of the vagina decreasing and the vagina not being able to expand during penile-vaginal intercourse as it once could. Intercourse can be painful, bleeding can occur, and the vagina can be more susceptible to infection. These effects may begin while a woman is still menstruating and may continue after menstruation has ceased. As many as 75% of women experience some degree of hot flashes, which usually diminish within 2 years following the end of menopause. A **hot flash** is a period of intense warmth, flushing, and (often) perspiration, typically lasting for a minute or two, but ranging anywhere from 15 seconds to 1 hour in length. A hot flash occurs when falling estrogen levels cause the body's "thermostat" in the brain to trigger dilation (expansion) of blood vessels near the skin's surface, producing a sensation of heat. Hot flashes that occur with severe sweating during sleep are called night sweats. Some women who are going through menopause experience insomnia (which can be related to hot flashes), changes in sexual interest (more commonly a decrease), urinary incontinence, weakening of pelvic floor muscles, headaches, or weight gain. Some women also report depression, irritability, and other emotional problems.

Long-term effects related to lowered estrogen levels may be experienced by some women. Osteoporosis, the loss of bone mass, leads to problems such as wrist and hip fractures. Lowered estrogen can also contribute to diseases of the heart and arteries related to rising levels of LDL (low-density lipoprotein, or "bad" cholesterol) and falling levels of HDL (high-density lipoprotein, or "good" cholesterol). Hereditary factors also play a part in cardiovascular disease.

Changes that may reduce the physical effects of menopause may include low-cholesterol, high-fiber diets, weight-bearing exercise and nutritional supplements to lower cholesterol, maintenance of a healthy weight, topical lubricants to counteract vaginal dryness, and Kegel exercises to strengthen pelvic floor muscles. Frequent sexual stimulation (by self or partner) may help maintain vaginal moistness. For women who smoke, quitting provides benefits in many areas, including reducing the risk of osteoporosis, diminishing the intensity of hot flashes, and establishing an improved sense of well-being (North American Menopause Society, 2006).

Menopausal Hormone Therapy   To relieve the symptoms of menopause, a physician may prescribe **menopausal hormone therapy (MHT),** a new name for **hormone replacement therapy (HRT).** The National Institutes of Health (NIH) recently began using the term "menopausal hormone therapy," believing that it is more accurate (other federal government health agencies use other terms such as "menopausal hormone use," "hormone therapy for menopause," and "postmenopause hormone therapy"). This therapy involves the use of the hormone estrogen or a combination of estrogen with another hormone, progesterone, or progestin in its synthetic form.

Estrogen and progestin normally help regulate a woman's menstrual cycle. In MHT, progestin is added to estrogen to prevent the overgrowth of cells in the lining of the uterus, which can lead to uterine cancer. If a woman is going through menopause and is experiencing symptoms that are interfering with her quality of life, she might be prescribed estrogen-plus-progestin therapy; a woman who has had a hysterectomy would receive estrogen-only therapy. The hormones can be taken daily or only on certain days of the month. Depending on their purpose, the hormones can be taken orally, applied as a patch on the skin, used as a cream or gel, or absorbed via an intrauterine device (IUD) or vaginal ring. A vaginal estrogen ring or cream can minimize vaginal dryness, urinary leakage, and vaginal or urinary infection, but it does not ease hot flashes. MHT may cause side effects such as bloating, breast tenderness or enlargement, bleeding, headaches, irritability,

You can take no credit for beauty at sixteen. But if you are beautiful at sixty, it will be your soul's own doing.

—Marie Stopes
(1880–1958)

depression, nausea, and sometimes having spotting or a return of monthly periods for a few months or years (National Institute on Aging, 2006).

Menopause is a normal part of life, not a disease that must be treated. Still, some women may be bothered enough by attendant symptoms to seek medical advice or assistance. Some women may be concerned about the possibility of future problems such as osteoporosis. Others may be concerned about changes in their sexual feelings or patterns or about the implications of fertility loss, aging, and changing standards of attractiveness. Because physicians have a tendency to treat menopause as a medical "problem," women may find themselves subjected to treatments they don't understand or would not choose if they were better informed. It's important that women seek out health-care practitioners who will work with them to meet their needs.

Though there are benefits associated with taking menopausal hormone therapy, a clear understanding of the benefits versus the more significant risks should be understood by any woman considering treatment (see Table 7.1). In a recent follow-up report on the results of a 3-year study conducted by the

Generally by the time you become real, most of your hair has been loved off and your eyes drop out and you get loose in the joints and very shabby. But these things don't matter at all, because once you are real you can't be ugly, except to people who don't understand.

—from *The Velveteen Rabbit*
by Margery Williams
(1881–1944)

Table 7.1 ● Benefits and Risks of Menopausal Hormone Therapy, July 2006	Women with a Uterus: Estrogen + Progestin	Women Without a Uterus[a]: Estrogen Only
Benefits		
Relieves hot flashes/night sweats	Yes	Yes
Relieves vaginal dryness	Yes	Yes
Reduces risk of bone fractures	Only when drug is taken	Yes
Improves cholesterol levels	Yes	Yes
Reduces risk of colon cancer	Only when drug is taken	Don't know
Risks		
Increases risk of stroke	Yes	Yes
Increases risk of serious blood clots	Yes	Yes
Increases risk of heart attack	Yes	No
Increases risk of breast cancer	Yes	Possibly
Increases risk of dementia, when begun by women age 65 and older	Yes	Yes
Unpleasant side effects, such as bloating and tender breasts	Yes	Yes
Pill form can raise level of triglycerides (a type of fat in the blood)	Yes	Yes

[a]Women who have had a hysterectomy have had their uterus but not their ovaries removed.

SOURCES: Heiss, G., Wallace, R., Anderson, G. L., Aragaki, A., Beresford, S., et al. (2008). Health risks and benefits 3 years after stopping randomized treatment with estrogen and progestin. *Journal of the American Medical Association, 299*(9), 1036–1045; National Institute on Aging. (2006). Hormones and menopause: Tips from the National Institute on Aging. Available: http://niapublications.org/tipsheets/hormones.asp

Sexual Well-Being and Older Adults: A Global Study

In spite of debate about the nature, predictors, and outcomes of sexual behaviors, little is known about what constitutes perceived sexual health and well-being and its importance to older men and women around the globe. One recent large-scale study, however, investigated subjective sexual well-being, particularly as it related to judgments about sexual satisfaction. Using existing data from an investigation of 27,500 people aged 40 to 80, in 29 countries, this study was the first to examine global data, attitudinal beliefs, and health in sexual relationships among middle-aged and older adults (Laumann, Nicolosi, Glasser, et al., 2005; Laumann, Paik, Glasser, et al., 2006; Nicolosi, Laumann, Glasser, et al., 2004). By concentrating on sexual well-being, the researchers examined emotional and physical aspects of relationships, satisfaction with sexual functioning, and the relative importance of sexuality in one's overall life.

To help recognize patterns of what people from various countries thought about these domains, the researchers made a cluster analysis of shared responses. After data were analyzed, three prominent clusters emerged: physical pleasure, emotional pleasure, and the importance of sex (see Figure 7.8). The results and discussion were rich with data, and some interesting findings from the analysis emerged: In addition to finding that respondents from Western societies were happiest with their sex lives, researchers found a strong gendered response to subjective well-being, whereby men reported higher levels of satisfaction than women. This finding was in sharp contrast to previous studies that report women experiencing greater happiness and more intense positive emotions than men. Compared with their male counterparts, those women with the lowest average subjective sexual well-being were much more negatively affected by their emotional satisfaction with their sexual partners than by their physical satisfaction. Additionally, it was found that in male-centered cultures, where sexual behavior was more oriented toward reproduction, men tended to discount the relational meaning of sex and the importance of sexual pleasure for women. In spite of this finding, true parity in sexual well-being remained an ideal for both genders, even in countries where beliefs about gender equality vary. The consistently low level of sexual well-being for men and women in many Asian countries suggests that future research should be focused on finding the causes of this variation.

From the findings, the researchers drew the following conclusions:

- Despite cultural variation, predictors of subjective sexual well-being—physical and mental health, sexual practices, and relationship context—were consistent across world regions.

- Strong evidence existed for a gendered response to subjective sexual well-being.

- Subjective sexual well-being was correlated with overall happiness in both men and women.

Women's Health Initiative, a study of 15,730 postmenopausal women with an intact uterus aged 50 to 79, it was concluded that the health risks of long-term use of combination (estrogen plus progestin) HRT to healthy, postmenopausal women persist even a few years after stopping the drugs and clearly outweigh the benefits (Heiss, Wallace, Anderson, et al., 2008). About 3 years after women stopped taking combination HRT, many of the health effects of the hormones, such as increased risk of heart disease, were diminished; however, overall risks, including risk of stroke, blood clots, and cancer, remained high. As a result, the FDA now recommends that HRT never be used to prevent heart disease and that, when it is used for menopausal symptoms, it should only be taken in the smallest dose and for the shortest time possible. What are the exceptions to this? If the ovaries were surgically removed before age 45 or if the woman is at very low risk of breast cancer and very high risk of

Below, a sampling from a sex-satisfaction survey of 27,500 people, aged 40–80, in 29 countries.

On the whole, respondents from Western societies were happiest with sex.

	United States	Canada	Mexico	Germany	France	Britain	Italy	South Africa	Brazil	Israel	Turkey	South Korea	Philippines	Egypt	China	Indonesia	Japan	Thailand
Physical Pleasure																		
Men	73%	71	69	63	61	61	40	61	59	52	51	47	47	36	25	22	18	38
Women	65	68	57	57	52	56	32	47	47	48	25	36	40	24	24	20	11	21
Emotional Pleasure																		
Men	77	74	72	69	60	71	49	65	61	69	56	54	49	44	36	19	24	43
Women	68	63	62	60	55	68	41	47	41	55	33	47	39	29	33	20	16	23
Importance of Sex																		
Men	37	45	59	41	56	45	56	55	75	64	70	73	57	53	29	35	28	24
Women	28	34	37	33	39	30	33	26	43	53	29	46	30	40	18	17	12	10

● **FIGURE 7.8**

Survey on Enjoying Sex Finds Geography Matters.
This cross-national study of subjective well-being among older women and men (27,500 people aged 40–80, in 29 countries) found that, on the whole, respondents from Western societies were happiest with sex. (*Source:* Laumann, E. O., Paik, A., Glasser, D. B., et al. [2006]. Findings from the global study of sexual attitudes and behaviors. *Archives of Sexual Behavior, 35*[2], 145.)

Think Critically

- What factors might influence the ways in which men and women perceive their sexuality? Do you believe that younger people might view pleasure in the same ways as those cited in this study?
- Was there anything in this study that surprised you? If so, what?
- What questions would you ask of someone if you were trying to assess his or her sexual well-being?

fracture, hormones may be considered for a few years, provided that severe hot flashes or night sweats resurface when she stops therapy (Weingert & Kantrowitz, 2007). To assist with the problematic symptoms often associated with menopause, it is recommended that women adopt and maintain a healthy lifestyle; that is, engage in regular physical activity, maintain a healthy body weight, consume a diet low in saturated fat, and do not smoke (Heiss, Wallace, Anderson, et al., 2008).

Men's Issues   Changes in male sexual responsiveness begin to become apparent when men are in their forties and fifties, a period of change sometimes referred to as the male climacteric. For about 5% of men, these physical changes of aging are accompanied by experiences such as fatigue, an inability to concentrate, depression, loss of appetite, and a decreased interest in sex (Kolodny,

Click on "The Personals" to hear the challenges one older man faced in staying sexually active.

Masters, & Johnson, 1979). As a man ages, his frequency of sexual activity declines, achieving erection requires more stimulation and time, and the erection may not be as firm. Ejaculation takes longer and may not occur every time the penis is stimulated; also, the force of the ejaculation is less than before, as is the amount of ejaculate; and the refractory period is extended (up to 24 hours or longer in older men). However, sexual interest and enjoyment generally do not decrease, as witnessed by the frequency and variety of sexual activity reported by older adults. Although some of the changes are related directly to age and a normal decrease in testosterone production, others may be the result of diseases associated with aging. Poor general health, diabetes, atherosclerosis, urinary incontinence, and some medications can contribute to sexual function problems.

It is important for older men to understand that slower responses are a normal function of aging and are unrelated to the ability to give or receive sexual pleasure. "The senior penis," wrote Bernie Zilbergeld (1999), "can still give and take pleasure, even though it's not the same as it was decades ago." Prescription drugs have become available to aid men in achieving erections. In fact, 1 in 7 men over age 57 report having used Viagra or other substances to improve their sexual performance (Lindau, Schumm, Laumann, et al., 2007).

About half of men over age 50 are affected to some degree by **benign prostatic hypertrophy (BPH),** an enlargement of the prostate gland. The prostate starts out about the size of a walnut. By age 40, it may have grown slightly larger, to the size of an apricot. By age 60, it may be the size of a lemon. By age 70, almost all men have some prostate enlargement. BPH is not linked to cancer and does not raise a man's chance of getting prostate cancer, yet the symptoms of BPH and prostate cancer can be similar. The enlarged prostate may put pressure on the urethra, resulting in difficulty urinating and the frequent and urgent need to urinate. It does not affect sexual functioning. About half the men with BPH eventually have symptoms that are bothersome enough to need treatment, although many men with mild symptoms choose to live with the symptoms while getting annual checkups. BPH symptoms do not always get worse. At the same time, BPH cannot be cured, but drugs can often relieve its symptoms. If the blockage of the urethra is too severe, surgery can correct the problem. The surgery may lead to retrograde ejaculation, in which the ejaculate is released into the bladder instead of the urethra upon orgasm (see Chapter 4). Retrograde ejaculation is not dangerous, and the sensations of orgasm are generally unchanged (National Cancer Institute, 2004).

Testosterone Supplement As you may recall from your reading in Chapter 4, testosterone plays an important role in puberty and throughout a man's life. Although it is the main sex hormone of men, women produce small amounts of it as well. Testosterone production is the highest in adolescence and early adulthood and declines as a man ages. However, an estimated 2 million to 4 million men in the United States suffer from low levels of testosterone (Hartman, Metter, Tobin, Pearson, & Blackman, 2001; Morley et al., 1997). But the chance that a man will ever experience a major shutdown of hormone production similar to a woman's menopause is remote (National Institute on Aging, 2008). Most older men maintain a sufficient amount for normal functioning.

As men age, changes such as less energy and strength, decreased bone density, and erectile difficulties occur; these changes are often erroneously blamed on decreasing testosterone levels. Because of changes like these—particularly sexual declines—a rapidly growing number of older men are taking supplemental testosterone. Testosterone is currently available in deep muscle injections, patches, and topical gels. However, despite the fact that some older men who have tried these supplements report feeling more energetic, experts are inconclusive about whether testosterone supplements should be prescribed. The National Institute on Aging (2008a) states that supplemental testosterone remains a scientifically unproven method for preventing or relieving any physical or psychological changes that men with normal testosterone levels may experience as they age. Potential side effects include prostate problems and sleep apnea (Weingert & Kantrowitz, 2007).

Final Thoughts

As this chapter has shown, psychosexual development occurs on a continuum rather than as a series of discrete stages. Each person develops in his or her own way, according to personal and social circumstances and the dictates of biology. In early adulthood, tasks that define adult sexuality include establishing sexual orientation, making commitments, entering long-term intimate relationships, and deciding whether or not to have children. None of these challenges is accomplished overnight. Nor does a task necessarily end as a person moves into a new stage of life.

In middle adulthood, individuals face new tasks involving the nature of their long-term relationships. Often, these tasks involve reevaluating these relationships. As people enter late adulthood, they need to adjust to the aging process—to changed sexual responses and needs, declining physical health, the loss of a partner, and their own eventual death. Each stage is filled with its own unique meaning, which gives shape and significance to life and to sexuality.

Summary

Sexuality in Early Adulthood

- The two most widely held standards regarding non-marital sexual intercourse are permissiveness with affection and the double standard. For gay men, lesbian women, and bisexual and transgendered individuals, the college environment is often liberating because of greater acceptance and tolerance.

- Among single men and women not or no longer attending college, meeting others can be a problem.

Singles often meet via the Internet and at work, clubs, resorts, housing complexes, and churches.

- Internalization of a culture's stereotyping about homosexuality may be among the issues that prevent gay men and lesbian women of color from coming out.

- *Cohabitation* has become more widespread and accepted in recent years. By age 30, half of all people will have cohabited. *Domestic partnerships* provide some legal protection for cohabiting couples in committed relationships.

Sexuality in Middle Adulthood

- Developmental issues of sexuality in middle adulthood include redefining sex in long-term relationships, reevaluating one's sexuality, and accepting the biological aging process.

- In marriage, sex tends to diminish in frequency the longer a couple is married. Most married couples don't feel that declining frequency is a major problem if their overall relationship is good.

- Divorce has become a major force in American life. Sexual experiences following divorce are linked to well-being, especially for men. Single parents are usually not a part of the singles world because the presence of children constrains their freedom.

Sexuality in Late Adulthood

- Many of the psychosexual tasks older Americans must undertake are directly related to the aging process, including changing sexuality and the loss of a partner. Most studies of older adults find that they express relatively high levels of satisfaction and well-being. Older adults' sexuality tends to be invisible because society associates sexuality and romance with youthfulness and procreation.

- For many, sexual behavior in late adulthood is both intimacy-based, involving touching and holding, and genital. Physiologically, men are less responsive. Women's concerns are more social than physical.

- Although some physical functions may be slowed by aging, sexual interest and activity remain high for many older people. Diminished sexual activity for both men and women is primarily due to health issues and/or loss of a partner.

- In their forties, women's fertility begins to decline. Generally, between ages 45 and 55, *menopause*, cessation of menstrual periods, occurs. Other physical changes occur, which may or may not present problems. *Menopausal hormone therapy (MHT)* is sometimes used to treat these symptoms.

- Men need to understand that slower responses are a normal part of aging and are not related to the ability to give or receive sexual pleasure. About half of men experience some degree of prostate enlargement after age 50.

Questions for Discussion

- The text describes some of the challenges faced by people who choose to live together without marrying. Should society support cohabitation, such as by providing tax benefits or acknowledging domestic partnerships? If so, how? If not, why not?

- Many changes have taken place in marriage policies, and there has been liberalization of divorce laws. Has divorce become too easy? What factors do you feel contribute to long-term partnerships?

- Given the three models of sexual orientation previously referred to in the text, which model do you think is most accurate? Can you find a place for yourself within each model?

Sex and the Internet

Sexuality in Early Adulthood

Go Ask Alice! is the health question-and-answer Internet service produced by Alice!, Columbia University's Health Promotion Program, a division of Health Services. This site has three primary features: It provides recently published inquiries and responses, lets you find health information by subject via a search of the ever-growing Go Ask Alice! Archives, and gives you the chance to ask and submit a question to Alice!

To access the site, go to http://www.goaskalice.columbia.edu and select two categories. In each one of these, investigate three responses to the options provided and prepare a summary of what you have learned. Would you recommend this site to others? Why or why not? Did you feel comfortable entering your own response? What position did you take on the issue that you investigated? Do you feel that diversity in sexual attitudes and behaviors was represented by this site?

Suggested Web Sites

American College Health Association
http://www.acha.org
Provides information and resources for and about college-age students.

American Institute of Bisexuality
http://www.bisexual.org
Encourages, supports, and assists research and education about bisexuality.

American Psychological Association
http://www.apa.org
A source of information on a broad range of psychological problems and concerns.

Men's Web, Men's Voices
http://www.menweb.org
Provides discussions on a wide variety of issues for and about men.

National Institutes of Health—Menopausal Hormone Therapy Information
http://www.nih.gov/PHTindex.htm
New findings from large studies offer important information about the risks and benefits of long-term menopausal hormone therapy.

National Institute on Aging
http://www.nia.nih.gov
Leads the federal government's efforts on aging research.

Suggested Reading

Diamond, L. M. (2008). *Sexual fluidity: Understanding women's love and desire.* Cambridge, MA: Harvard University Press. Delving into brain science on lust and love, offers a new understanding of women's sexual attraction.

Gott, M. (2005). *Sexuality, sexual health & ageing.* New York: Open University Press. Solid information on the sociological issues associated with sex and aging, including an examination of the myth of asexual old age, what we know across cultures, and the importance of sex to older people.

Harvey, J. H., Wenzel, A., & Sprecher, S. (Eds.). (2004). *The handbook of sexuality in close relationships.* Mahwah, NJ: Lawrence Erlbaum Associates. The handbook brings together major scholars from diverse fields working on close relations topics to explore past contributions and new directions in sexuality.

Ince, J. (2005). *The politics of lust.* Amherst, NY: Prometheus Books. The author examines the sociocultural ambivalences and contradictions surrounding human sexuality and people's erotophobic conditioning toward sexual expression.

Sheehy, G. (2006). *Sex and the seasoned woman.* New York: Random House. For women (and their partners) who are willing to embrace their "second adulthood" as a period of reawakening.

Wallerstein, J. S., Lewis, J., & Blakeslee, S. (2001). *The unexpected legacy of divorce.* New York: Hyperion. A long-term study assessing the effects of divorce on children as they grow into adulthood and pursue relationships of their own.

For links, articles, and study material, go to the McGraw-Hill Web sites, located at **www.mhhe.com/yarber7e.**

chapter 8

Love and Communication in Intimate Relationships

MAIN TOPICS

"Because my father was both a raving drug addict and a loving warm father, I grew up with a very dualistic look at men. I can be madly in love with them and bitterly hate them at the same time. This affects all of my relationships with men. I truly love them and can feel so connected to them one day, but other days I am so distant from them that I begin to wonder if I am there myself."

—22-year-old female

"My grandfather, being a Hindustani priest, talks to me a lot about love. It was not through a lecture but through stories he told from the Gita [somewhat like an Indian Bible]. Spending time with him, I learned to respect sex, even though he never plain-out meant it; he described how marriage is a love bond between two people who share mind, body, and soul with each other and no one else. These stories like Kama Sutra and Ramayan sound so beautiful. Because of his influence, I want to try my best to wait to have sex until I meet my soul mate."

—19-year-old female

"I have difficulty trusting women. Getting close to my girlfriend has been difficult. My first reaction in most instances is to wonder what her ulterior motive is. Being intimate is tough for me because those I have trusted most have betrayed me. Sometimes I feel like I am alone for the simple fact that I don't know how to act when I am with people."

—23-year-old male

"Through high school and college, my relationship with my father grew. . . . During the time I lived with my father, I noticed his inability to express his emotions and his closed relationships with others. Thankfully, I have not yet noticed this rubbing off on my relationships or me."

—20-year-old male

LOVE IS ONE of the most profound human emotions, and it manifests itself in various forms across all cultures. In our culture, love binds us together as partners, parents, children, and friends. It is a powerful force in the intimate relationships of almost all individuals, regardless of their sexual orientation, and it crosses all ethnic boundaries. We make major life decisions, such as whom we marry, based on love. We make sacrifices for it, sometimes giving up even our lives for those we love. Sometimes, we even become obsessed with love. Popular culture in America glorifies it in music, films, television, and print. Individuals equate romantic love with marriage and often assess the quality of their partnerships by what they consider love to be.

Love is both a feeling and an activity. We can feel love for someone and act in a loving manner. But we can also be angry with the person we love, or feel frustrated, bored, or indifferent. This is the paradox of love: It encompasses opposites. A loving relationship includes affection and anger, excitement and boredom, stability and change, bonds and freedom. Its paradoxical quality makes some ask whether they are really in love when they are not feeling "perfectly" in love or when their relationship is not going smoothly. Love does not give us perfection, however; it gives us meaning. In fact, as sociologist Ira Reiss (1980) suggests, a more important question to ask is not if one is feeling love, but "Is the love I feel the kind of love on which I can build a lasting relationship or marriage?"

Communication is the thread that connects sexuality and intimacy. The quality of the communication affects the quality of the relationship, and the quality

> *Love doesn't make the world go round. Love is what makes the ride worthwhile.*
>
> —Franklin P. Jones
> (1853–1935)

At the start of a relationship, it is often impossible to tell whether one's feelings are infatuation or the beginning of love.

of the relationship affects the quality of the sex. Good relationships tend to feature good sex; bad relationships often feature bad sex. Sex, in fact, frequently serves as a barometer for the quality of the relationship. The ability to communicate about sex is important in developing and maintaining both sexual and relationship satisfaction. People who are satisfied with their sexual communication also tend to be satisfied with their relationships as a whole. Effective communication skills do not necessarily appear when a person falls in love; they can, however, be learned with practice.

Most of the time, we don't think about our ability to communicate. Only when problems arise do we consciously think about it. Then we become aware of our limitations in communicating or, more often, our perceptions of the limitations of others: "You just don't get it, do you?" or "You're not listening to me." And as we know, communication failures are marked by frustration.

In this chapter, we examine the relationship between sex, love, and communication and look at the always perplexing question of the nature of love. Next, we explore sex outside of committed relationships and examine the ways that social scientists study love to gain new insights into it. We then turn to the darker side of love—jealousy—to understand its dynamics. We see how love transforms itself from passion to intimacy, providing the basis for long-lasting relationships. We then examine the characteristics of communication and the way different contexts affect it. We discuss forms of nonverbal communication, such as touch, which are especially important in sexual relationships. Then we look at the different ways we communicate about sex in intimate relationships, and explore ways we can develop our communication skills in order to enhance our relationships. Finally, we look at the different types of conflicts in intimate relationships and at methods for resolving them.

● Friendship and Love

Friendship and love breathe life into humanity. They bind us together, provide emotional sustenance, buffer us against stress, and help to preserve our physical and mental well-being.

What distinguishes love from friendship? Research has found that, although love and friendship are alike in many ways, some crucial differences make love relationships both more rewarding and more vulnerable (Davis & Todd, 1985). Best-friend relationships are similar to spouse/lover relationships in several ways: levels of acceptance, trust, and respect; and levels of confiding, understanding, spontaneity, and mutual acceptance. Levels of satisfaction and happiness with the relationship were also found to be similar for both groups. What separates friends from lovers is that lovers have much more fascination and a greater sense of exclusiveness with their partners than do friends. Though love has a greater potential for distress, conflict, and mutual criticism, it runs deeper and stronger than friendship.

Friendship appears to be the foundation for a strong love relationship. Shared interests and values, acceptance, trust, understanding, and enjoyment are at the root of friendship and a basis for love. Adding the dimensions of passion and emotional intimacy alters the nature of the friendship and creates new expectations and possibilities.

Although some believe that marriage should satisfy all their needs, it is important to remember that when people marry they do not cease to be separate individuals. Friendships and patterns of social behavior continue, so the mix of friendship and love must be understood as it affects marital satisfaction.

With men and women marrying later than ever before and women being an integral part of the workforce, close friendships are more likely to be a part of the tapestry of relationships in people's lives. The support of good friends is, in fact, a more significant factor in determining longevity than close family ties (Giles, Glonek, Luszcz, & Andrew, 2005). Partners need to communicate and seek understanding regarding the nature of activities and degree of emotional closeness they find acceptable in their partner's friendships. Boundaries should be clarified and opinions shared. Many couples find friendships acceptable and even desirable. Like other significant issues involving partnerships, success in balancing a love relationship and other friendships depends on the ability to communicate concerns and on the maturity of the people involved.

> A friend may well be reckoned a masterpiece of nature.
> —Ralph Waldo Emerson
> (1803–1882)

● Love and Sexuality

Love and sexuality are intimately intertwined. Although marriage was once the only acceptable context for sexual intercourse, for most people today, love legitimizes sex outside of marriage. With the "sex with affection" standard of sexual expression with others, we use individualistic rather than social norms to legitimize sexual relations. Our sexual standards may have become personal rather than institutional. This shift to personal responsibility makes love even more important in sexual relationships.

We can even see this connection between love and sex in our everyday use of words. Think of the words we use to describe sexual interactions. When we say that we "make love," are "lovers," or are "intimate" with someone, we generally

> Sex is a momentary itch. Love never lets you go.
> —Kingsley Amis
> (1922–1995)

mean that we are sexually involved. But this involvement has overtones of caring or love. Such potential meanings are absent in such technically correct words as "sexual intercourse," "fellatio," and "cunnilingus," as well as in such slang words as "fuck," "screw," and "hook up."

There is considerable evidence that demonstrates that love, in combination with a variety of factors including social rewards, intimacy, commitment, and equity, is an important determinant of sexual satisfaction (Harvey, Wenzel, & Sprecher, 2004; Sprecher, 2002). Two of the most important factors in sexual activity, however, are the level of intimacy in the relationship and the length of time the couple has been together. Even those who are less permissive in their sexual attitudes tend to accept sexual involvement if the relationship is emotionally intimate and long-standing. People who are less committed (or not committed) to a relationship are less likely to be sexually involved. A nationally representative sample of 6,421 young adults in the United States, aged 18–26, found that those reporting mutually high levels of love between partners also reported a wide range of sexual activities, including oral sex for both males and females. Thus, both mutual love and varied sexual behaviors appeared to be major features of long-term, committed relationships. The researchers concluded that these findings may indicate that, as the amount of time the couple has been sexually active grows, their comfort level with varied sexual activities increases (Kaestle & Halpern, 2007). Finally, people in relationships who share power equally are more likely to be sexually involved than those in inequitable relationships.

Environmental factors involving both the physical and the cultural setting play a role in the level of sexual activity. In the most basic sense, the physical environment affects the opportunity for sex. Because sex is a private activity, the opportunity for it may be precluded by the presence of parents, friends, roommates, or children. The cultural environment also affects the decision of whether to have sex. The values of one's parents or peers may encourage or discourage sexual involvement. Furthermore, a person's subculture—such as the university or religious environment, the singles world, or the gay and lesbian community—exerts an important influence on sexual decision making.

Among the most important factors associated with nonmarital sex for both men and women are their attraction and feelings for each other, willingness, amount of preplanning, and sexual arousal prior to their encounter.

A factor that heterosexual men see as evidence of sexual interest and intensity in the context of an ongoing, romantic relationship is assertive, forceful, and even aggressive behavior on the part of the woman. Rather than viewing this behavior as inappropriate or threatening, men more often find it to be desirable. This contrasts with the perceptions of heterosexual women, who more often perceive forceful behavior by men as related to power; these overtures may seem threatening and dangerous rather than sexually arousing. Women see sexual activity as being more appropriate and desirable when their romantic partner engages in behavior that inspires trust and confidence (Hill, 2002).

Sex Outside of Committed Relationships

A little more than a generation ago, virginity until marriage was the norm. Sex outside of marriage was considered sinful and immoral. Today, however, values have shifted. Nonmarital sex among young adults (but not adolescents) in a relational context has become the norm. However, older Americans and groups with conservative religious backgrounds continue to view all nonmarital sex as morally wrong.

This shift from sin to acceptance is the result of several factors. Effective contraception, legal abortion, and changing gender roles legitimizing female sexuality have had major impacts. But one of the most significant factors may be traced to demography. Over the past 30 or so years, there has been a dramatic increase in the number of unmarried men and women over age 18. It is this group that has traditionally looked the most favorably on nonmarital intercourse. In 2006, the median age for first marriage for men was 27.5 years, compared with 23.5 years in 1975. For women, the median age in 2006 was 25.9 years, compared with 21.1 years in 1975. Men spend a slightly longer time after first coitus being sexually active before getting married—nearly 10 years, compared with nearly 8 years for women (Alan Guttmacher Institute, 2004b).

Men, Women, Sex, and Love

Though men and women share more similarities than differences, they tend to have somewhat different perspectives on love and sex (see Chapter 6). For example, men are more likely than women to separate sex from affection. Studies consistently show that, for the majority of men, sex and love can be easily separated (Blumstein & Schwartz, 1983; Carroll, Volk, & Hyde, 1985; Laumann, Gagnon, Michael, & Michaels, 1994).

Although men are more likely than women to separate sex and love, authors and sex therapists Linda Levine and Lonnie Barbach (1983) found that men indicated that their most erotic sexual experiences took place in a relational context. Most men in the study reported that it was primarily the emotional quality of the relationship that made their sexual experiences special.

Researchers suggest that heterosexual men are not as different from gay men in terms of their acceptance of casual sex. Heterosexual men, they maintain, would be as likely as gay men to engage in casual sex if women were equally interested. Women, however, are not as interested in casual sex; as a result, heterosexual men do not have as many willing partners as gay men do (Blum, 1997; Foa, Anderson, Converse, & Urbansky, 1987).

Gay men are especially likely to separate love and sex. Although gay men value love, many also value sex as an end in itself. Furthermore, they place less

Click on "Men Talk Sex" to see the role of sex and intimacy in men's lives.

> There is hardly any activity, any enterprise, which is started with such tremendous hopes and expectations and yet fails so regularly as love.
>
> —Erich Fromm
> (1900–1980)

> Of course heaven forbids certain pleasures, but one finds means of compromise.
>
> —Molière, Tartuffe
> (1622–1673)

> Love is the irresistible desire to be irresistibly desired.
>
> —Robert Frost
> (1874–1963)

See "What Women Want" out of a good sexual relationship.

Familiar acts are beautiful through love.

—Percy Bysshe Shelley (1792–1822)

For lesbian women, gay men, and bisexual individuals, love is an important component in the formation and acceptance of their sexual orientation. The public declaration of love and commitment is a milestone in the lives of many couples.

emphasis on sexual exclusiveness in their relationships. Many gay men appear to successfully negotiate sexually open relationships. Keeping the sexual agreements they make seems to matter most to these men. Data from 560 self-selected gay couples indicate that the pursuit of outside sex should not be taken as evidence that sex between the partners is lacking (Demian, 1994).

Though we have seen women report having sex for lust, they generally view sex from a relational perspective. They often seek emotional relationships; some men initially seek physical relationships. Whereas most men value independence and self-sufficiency (Buss & Schmitt, 1993), there is evidence that women derive their self-worth from the quality of their relationships (Cross & Madson, 1997). Traditionally, women were labeled "good" or "bad" based on their sexual experience and values. "Good" women were virginal, sexually naive, and passive, whereas "bad" women were sexually experienced, independent, and passionate. According to researcher Lillian Rubin (1990), this attitude has not entirely changed. In spite of changing gender norms, society remains ambivalent about sexually active and experienced women. During an interview, one exasperated woman leaped out of her chair and began to pace the floor, exclaiming to Rubin, "I sometimes think what men really want is a sexually experienced virgin. They want you to know the tricks, but they don't like to think you did those things with anyone else."

Lesbian women share sex less often than gay male or heterosexual couples. They tend to postpone sexual involvement until they have developed emotional intimacy with a partner, to be more satisfied with their sexual lives, and to have a greater sense of intimacy with their partners (Schureurs, 1993). For many, caresses, nongenital stimulation, and affectionate foreplay are the preferred expressions of sexuality and love.

Love is equally important for heterosexuals, gay men, lesbian women, and bisexual individuals. Many heterosexual individuals perceive lesbians' and gay persons' love relationships as less satisfying and less loving than heterosexual ones. However, it is well documented that love is important for gay men and lesbian women too; their relationships have multiple emotional dimensions and are not based solely on sex (Zak & McDonald, 1997).

Love Without Sex: Celibacy and Asexuality

In a society that often seems obsessed with sexuality, it may be surprising to find individuals who choose to be celibate as a lifestyle. **Celibacy**—abstention from sexual activity—is not necessarily a symptom of a problem or disorder. It is important to note that though some researchers may blur the definitions of celibacy with **asexuality,** the absence of a traditional sexual orientation in which there is little or no sexual attraction to males or females, differences do in fact exist. Implicit in this discussion is consideration about what constitutes a "normal" level of sexual desire. The term "asexuality" implies an assumption that *some* level of sexual desire is normal.

While celibacy is considered by most to be a choice of refraining from sexual activity with a partner, asexuality is best predicted by low sexual desire. In fact, recent research has found that there are no gender or relationship status differences between asexuals and non-asexuals, that a higher percentage of asexuals had completed at least a college degree, and that asexuals and non-asexuals had an equal number of lifetime sexual partners (Prause & Graham, 2007). Celibacy may be a choice for some, such as those who have taken religious vows or are in relationships in which nonsexual affection and respect provide adequate fulfillment. For

Are Gay/Lesbian Couples Any Different From Heterosexual Ones?

What impact does sexual orientation have on the longevity and quality of relationships? Are those qualities that help to sustain heterosexual couples any different for homosexual ones? Two recently published studies that examine the quality of same- and other-sex relationships finally provide a little more evidence to assist in helping us understand what, if anything, makes gay and straight couples different. What the researchers found may have implications for all of us who desire healthy relationships and longevity with that person we love.

The lack of societal support has been among the many challenges facing same-sex couples and their families even though marriage is now legal in a few states and domestic partnerships or civil unions acknowledged in some. Though some progress has been made over the years in advancing the cause of civil rights for lesbian, gay, and bisexual people in the United States, research is still young when it comes to studying the impact that commitment has on the quality of same-sex relationships. We know that, over a 12-year period, 21% of gay and lesbian couples break up, compared with 14% of heterosexual married couples (Kurdek, 2004). And we know that among married couples, for example, stability in marriage over time is related to the couple's ability to resolve conflict, including validation of the partner's feelings and the ability of both members to adapt to a current style of conflict (Gottman & Levenson, 1992).

It appears that the level and type of communication that partners share underscores much of the success (or lack of success) of the relationship. For example, same-sex couples are significantly less belligerent, less domineering, less fearful, and use more humor and show greater affection than heterosexual married couples (Gottman & Levenson, 1992; Gottman, Levenson, Gross, et al., 2003). However, when gay men initiated difficult discussions with their partners, they were less likely to make up afterward. Further evaluation of similarities and differences in communication and behavioral styles may provide important links to the success in human relationships.

Assessing the influence that stability has in partnerships by comparing same-sex couples in civil unions, same-sex cohabiting couples, and a group of married heterosexual couples over a 3-year period, researchers found (Balsam, Beauchaine, Rothblum, & Solomon, 2008):

- *Cross-group differences.* Despite the legalized nature of the relationships, civil union couples did not differ on any measure from same-sex couples who were not in civil unions. However, same-sex couples not in civil unions were more likely to have ended their relationships than same-sex civil union or heterosexual married couples.
- *Relationship quality.* Compared with heterosexual married participants, both types of same-sex couples reported greater relationship quality, compatibility, and intimacy and lower levels of conflict.
- *Predictors of relationship quality.* Outness was a predictor of relationship quality, particularly for gay men, who experience greater obstacles to being out than do lesbian women. For men in same-sex relationships, having a relationship of shorter duration was a predictor of relationship quality. For lesbian women, frequency of sex was an important predictor.

Added to this body of evidence was another study that investigated whether committed same-sex couples differed from engaged and married ones on their level of attachment (Roisman, Clausell, Holland, et al., 2008). The authors of that study concluded that individuals in committed same-sex relationships were generally not distinguishable from their committed heterosexual counterparts, with one exception: Lesbian women were especially effective at working together harmoniously.

The two most recent studies share the same conclusion: Gay and lesbian couples are not all that different from heterosexual ones. In fact, in their desire to achieve healthy and long-term involvement, both groups have a lot to learn from each other.

Think Critically

- What characteristics are important for you in maintaining a committed relationship with another person? Do you feel that sexual orientation can alter these characteristics? How?
- What advantages and disadvantages do you anticipate a committed gay or lesbian couple might have in this society?
- How might the presence or absence of children influence the longevity of a same-sex relationship?

others, it is a result of life circumstances, such as the absence of a partner or imprisonment. Still others report very low interest in sex or express concern over the spread of HIV or other sexually transmitted infections. Less common and with little known about it, asexuality appears to occur in approximately 1% of a sample population (Bogaert, 2004). According to the National Social Life Survey, 4% of men and 14% of women rarely or never think about sex (Laumann, Gagnon, Michael, & Michaels, 1994).

Individuals who choose celibacy may report a better appreciation of the nature of friendship. In giving up their sexual pursuits, celibate individuals may learn to relate to others without sexual tension. Although these traits may also be developed within a sexual relationship, those who choose celibacy as a lifestyle may feel that it frees up energy for personal growth or other kinds of relationships.

How Do I Love Thee? Approaches and Attitudes Related to Love

Love and you shall be loved. All love is mathematically just, as much as two sides of an algebraic equation.

—Ralph Waldo Emerson
(1803–1882)

For most people, love and sex are closely linked in the ideal intimate relationship. Love reflects the positive factors—such as caring—that draw people together and sustain them in a relationship. Sex reflects both emotional and physical elements, such as closeness and sexual excitement, and differentiates romantic love from other forms of love, such as parental love. Although the two are related, they are not necessarily connected. One can exist without the other; that is, it is possible to love someone without being sexually involved, and it is possible to be sexually involved without love.

Styles of Love

Sociologist John Lee describes six basic styles of love (Borrello & Thompson, 1990; Lee, 1973, 1988). These styles of love, he cautions, reflect relationship styles, not individual styles. The style of love may change as the relationship changes or when individuals enter different relationships.

If you love somebody, let them go. If they return, they were always yours. If they don't, they never were.

—Anonymous

Eros was the ancient Greek god of love, the son of Aphrodite, the goddess of love and fertility. (The Romans called him Cupid.) As a style of love, **eros** is the love of beauty. Erotic lovers are passionate and delight in the tactile, the sensual, the immediate; they are attracted to beauty (though beauty is in the eye of the beholder). They love the lines of the body, its feel and touch. They are fascinated by every physical detail of their beloved. Their love burns brightly and is idealized but soon flickers and dies.

Mania, from the Greek word for madness, is obsessive and possessive love. For manic lovers, nights are marked by sleeplessness and days by pain and anxiety. The slightest sign of affection brings ecstasy for a short while, only to disappear. Satisfactions last for but a moment before they must be renewed. Manic love is roller-coaster love.

Ludus, from the Latin word for play, is playful love. For ludic lovers, love is a game, something to play at rather than to become deeply involved in. Love is ultimately "*ludic*rous"; encounters are casual, carefree, and often careless. "Nothing serious" is the motto of ludic lovers. Those with a ludus style thrive on attention and are often willing to take risks (Paul et al., 2000).

Love never dies a natural death. It dies because we don't know how to replenish its source.

—Anaïs Nin
(1903–1977)

Storge (STOR-gay), from the Greek word for natural affection, is the love between companions. It is, wrote Lee, "love without fever, tumult, or folly, a peaceful and enchanting affection." It usually begins as friendship and gradually deepens into love. If the love ends, that also occurs gradually, and the people often become friends once again.

Agape (AH ga pay), from the Greek word for brotherly love, is the traditional Christian love that is chaste, patient, undemanding, and altruistic; there is no expectation of reciprocation. It is the love of saints and martyrs. Agape is more abstract and ideal than concrete and real. It is easier to love all of humankind than an individual in this way.

Pragma, from the Greek word for business, is practical love. Pragmatic lovers are, first and foremost, businesslike in their approach to looking for someone who meets their needs. They use logic in their search for a partner, seeking background, education, personality, religion, and interests that are compatible with their own. If they meet a person who satisfies their criteria, erotic, manic, or other feelings may develop. In addition to these pure forms, there are mixtures of the basic types: storge-eros, ludus-eros, and storge-ludus.

Lee believes that, to have a mutually satisfying relationship, people have to find a partner who shares the same style and definition of love. The more different two people are in their styles of love, the less likely they are to understand each other's love.

One could expect there to be some consistency between love styles and sexual attitudes, since beliefs about sexuality could help determine the choice and maintenance of a romantic relationship. But are there gender differences in the ways men and women express their love style? Research reports the presence of significant gender differences in love styles and attraction criteria among college students (Grello, Welsh, & Harper, 2006; Lacey, et al., 2004). Surveying the love styles of college students, researchers have found that men were more likely to have a ludus style while others who endorsed an eros style were more likely to either be virgins or engage in sexual activity with only a romantic partner (Grello, Welsh, & Harper, 2006).

According to sociologist John Lee, there are six styles of love: eros, mania, ludus, storge, agape, and pragma. What style do you believe this couple illustrates? Why?

The Triangular Theory of Love

The **triangular theory of love,** developed by psychologist and educator Robert Sternberg (1986), emphasizes the dynamic quality of love relationships. According to this theory, love is composed of three elements, as in the points of a triangle: intimacy, passion, and decision/commitment (see Figure 8.1). Each can be enlarged or diminished in the course of a love relationship, which will affect the quality of the relationship. They can also be combined in different ways. Each combination produces a different type of love, such as romantic love, infatuation, empty love, and liking. Partners may combine the components differently at different times in the same love relationship.

When you are courting a nice girl an hour seems like a second. When you sit on a red-hot cinder a second seems like an hour. That's relativity.

—Albert Einstein
(1879–1955)

The Components of Love Intimacy refers to the warm, close, bonding feelings we get when we love someone. According to Sternberg and Grajek (1984), there are 10 signs of intimacy:

1. Wanting to promote your partner's welfare

2. Feeling happiness with your partner

3. Holding your partner in high regard

4. Being able to count on your partner in times of need

5. Being able to understand your partner

6. Sharing yourself and your possessions with your partner

• FIGURE 8.1

Sternberg's Triangular Theory of Love. The three elements of love are intimacy, passion, and decision/commitment. (*Source:* From Sternberg, R. J. (1988). *The Triangle of Love: Intimacy, Passion, Commitment.* New York: Basic Books, 1988. Used by permission of Robert J. Sternberg.)

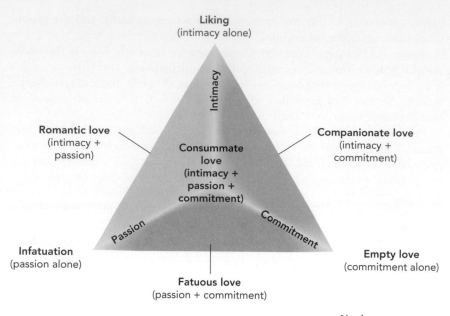

If love does not know how to give and take without restrictions, it is not love, but a transaction that never fails to lay stress on a plus and a minus.

—Emma Goldman
(1869–1940)

Don't threaten me with love, baby.

—Billie Holiday
(1915–1959)

7. Receiving emotional support from your partner

8. Giving emotional support to your partner

9. Being able to communicate with your partner about intimate things

10. Valuing your partner's presence in your life

The passion component refers to the elements of romance, attraction, and sexuality in the relationship. These may be fueled by a desire to increase self-esteem, to be sexually active or fulfilled, to affiliate with others, to dominate, or to subordinate.

The decision/commitment component consists of two separate parts—a short-term part and a long-term part. The short-term part refers to an individual's decision that he or she loves someone. People may or may not make the decision consciously. But it usually occurs before they decide to make a commitment to the other person. The commitment represents the long-term part; it is the maintenance of love. But a decision to love someone does not necessarily entail a commitment to maintaining that love.

Kinds of Love   The intimacy, passion, and decision/commitment components can be combined in eight basic ways, according to Sternberg:

1. Liking (intimacy only)

2. Infatuation (passion only)

3. Romantic love (intimacy and passion)

4. Companionate love (intimacy and commitment)

5. Fatuous love (passion and commitment)

6. Consummate love (intimacy, passion, and commitment)

7. Empty love (decision/commitment only)

8. Nonlove (absence of intimacy, passion, and commitment)

These types represent extremes that few of us are likely to experience. Not many of us, for example, experience infatuation in its purest form, in which there is absolutely *no* intimacy. And empty love is not really love at all. These categories are nevertheless useful for examining the nature of love.

Liking: Intimacy Only   Liking represents the intimacy component alone. It forms the basis for close friendships but is neither passionate nor committed. As such, liking is often an enduring kind of love. Boyfriends and girlfriends may come and go, but good friends remain.

Infatuation: Passion Only   Infatuation is "love at first sight." It is the kind of love that idealizes its object; the infatuated individual rarely sees the other as a "real" person with normal human foibles. Infatuation is marked by sudden passion and a high degree of physical and emotional arousal. It tends to be obsessive and all-consuming; one has no time, energy, or desire for anything or anyone but the beloved (or thoughts of him or her). To the dismay of the infatuated individual, infatuations are usually asymmetrical: The passion (or obsession) is rarely returned equally. And the greater the asymmetry, the greater the distress in the relationship.

Romantic Love: Intimacy and Passion   Romantic love combines intimacy and passion. It is similar to liking except that it is more intense as a result of physical or emotional attraction. It may begin with an immediate union of the two components, with friendship that intensifies into passion, or with passion that also develops intimacy. Although commitment is not an essential element of romantic love, it may develop.

Companionate Love: Intimacy and Commitment   Companionate love is essential to a committed friendship. It often begins as romantic love, but as the passion diminishes and the intimacy increases, it is transformed into companionate love. Some couples are satisfied with such love; others are not. Those who are dissatisfied in companionate love relationships may seek extrarelational partners to maintain passion in their lives. They may also end the relationship to seek a new romantic relationship that they hope will remain romantic.

Fatuous Love: Passion and Commitment   Fatuous or deceptive love is whirlwind love; it begins the day two people meet and quickly results in cohabitation or engagement, and then marriage. It develops so quickly that they hardly know what happened. Often, nothing much really did happen that will permit the relationship to endure. As Sternberg and Barnes (1989) observe, "It is fatuous in the sense that a commitment is made on the basis of passion without the stabilizing element of intimate involvement—which takes time to develop." Passion fades soon enough, and all that remains is commitment. But commitment that has had

> " Being deeply loved by someone gives you strength; loving someone deeply gives you courage.
>
> —Lao Tzu
> (sixth century B.C.)

> " We are never so defenseless against suffering as when we love.
>
> —Sigmund Freud
> (1856–1939)

| YOU TWO HAVE BEEN MARRIED 30 YEARS. WHAT'S YOUR SECRET? | BE YOUR OWN PERSON... HAVE YOUR OWN INTERESTS, GIVE EACH OTHER SPACE, AND STAY OUT OF EACH OTHER'S WAY | WHY DID YOU GET MARRIED? | COMPANIONSHIP |

BEETLE BAILEY © King Features Syndicate.

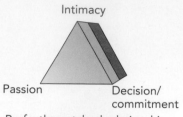

Intimacy

Passion   Decision/
commitment

Perfectly matched relationship

Closely matched relationship

Moderately mismatched
relationship

Severely mismatched
relationship

 Self   Other

● **FIGURE 8.2**

The Geometry of Love. According to the triangular theory of love, the shape and size of each person's triangle indicates how well each is matched to the other. (*Source:* From Sternberg, R. J. (1988). *The Triangle of Love: Intimacy, Passion, Commitment.* New York: Basic Books, 1988, p. 79. Used by permission of Robert J. Sternberg.)

relatively little time to deepen is a poor foundation on which to build an enduring relationship. With neither passion nor intimacy, the commitment wanes.

Consummate Love: Intimacy, Passion, and Commitment Consummate love results when intimacy, passion, and commitment combine to form their unique constellation. It is the kind of love we dream about but do not expect in all our love relationships. Many of us can achieve it, but it is difficult to sustain over time. To sustain it, we must nourish its different components, for each is subject to the stress of time.

Empty Love: Decision/Commitment Only This is love that lacks intimacy or passion. Empty love involves staying together solely for the sake of appearances or the children, for example.

Nonlove: Absence of Intimacy, Passion, and Commitment Nonlove can take many forms, such as attachment for financial reasons, fear, or the fulfillment of neurotic needs.

The Geometry of Love The shape of the love triangle depends on the intensity of the love and the balance of the parts. Intense love relationships lead to triangles with greater area; such triangles occupy more of one's life. Just as love relationships can be balanced or unbalanced, so can love triangles. The balance determines the shape of the triangle (see Figure 8.2). A relationship in which the intimacy, passion, and commitment components are equal results in an equilateral triangle. But if the components are not equal, unbalanced triangles form. The size and shape of a person's triangle give a good pictorial sense of how that person feels about another. The greater the match between the triangles of the two partners in a relationship, the more likely each is to experience satisfaction in the relationship.

Love as Attachment

Humans need to bond with other people. At the same time, many people fear bonding. Where do these contradictory impulses and emotions come from? Can they ever be resolved?

Attachment theory, the most prominent approach to the study of love, helps us understand how adult relationships develop, what can go wrong in them, and what to do when things do go wrong. In this theory, love is seen as a form of **attachment,** a close, enduring emotional bond that finds its roots in infancy (Hazan & Shaver, 1987; Shaver, 1984; Shaver, Hazan, & Bradshaw, 1988). Research suggests that romantic love and infant-caregiver attachment have similar emotional dynamics.

Infant-Caregiver Attachment

- The attachment bond's formation and quality depend on the attachment object's (AO) responsiveness and sensitivity.
- When the AO is present, the infant is happier.
- The infant shares toys, discoveries, and objects with the AO.
- The infant coos, talks baby talk, and "sings."
- The infant shares feelings of oneness with the AO.

Romantic Love

- Feelings of love are related to the lover's interest and reciprocation.
- When the lover is present, the person feels happier.
- Lovers share experiences and goods and give gifts.
- Lovers coo, sing, and talk baby talk.
- Lovers share feelings of oneness.

According to attachment theory, the holding and cuddling behaviors between parents and babies resemble those of adult lovers.

The implications of attachment theory are far-reaching. Attachment affects the way we process information, interact with others, and view the world. Basically, it influences our ability to love and to see ourselves as lovable. One study showed that we can carry an attachment style with us for life; this style predisposes us to behave in certain ways in love relationships (Shaver et al., 1988). In a later study, researchers found a significant association between attachment styles and relationship satisfaction (Brennan & Shaver, 1995).

The core elements of love appear to be the same for children as for adults: the need to feel emotionally safe and secure. When a partner responds to a need, for instance, adults view the world as a safe place. In this respect, we don't differ greatly from children.

The most basic concept of attachment theory is that to be whole adults we need to accept the fact that we are also vulnerable children. In a secure, intimate adult relationship, it is neither demeaning nor diminishing nor pathological to share honest emotions. It is the capacity to be vulnerable and open and accepting of others' giving that makes us lovable and human.

Based on observations made by Mary Ainsworth and colleagues (1978, cited in Shaver et al., 1988), Phillip Shaver and colleagues (1988) hypothesized that the styles of attachment developed in childhood—secure, anxious/ambivalent, and avoidant—continue through adulthood. Their surveys revealed similar styles in adult relationships.

Adults with **secure attachments** found it relatively easy to get close to other people. They felt comfortable depending on others and having others

Adults with secure attachments find it easy to get close to others.

think
about it

The Science of Love

Throughout history there have been poems and stories, plays and pictures that have attempted to explain love. Each has provided some insight into the ways that passion grabs us and, almost as quickly, leaves us. More recently, science has explored the complexities involved in love by examining the parts of the brain linked to reward and pleasure and providing us with particulars of its chemical components.

The scientific tale of love begins with the reward and pleasure part of the brain: the ventral tegmental area (the part of the midbrain that is rich in dopamine and seratonin) and the caudate nucleus (located deep within the brain and involved with the control of involuntary movement). Anthropologist Helen Fisher, a professor at Rutgers University, has studied the biochemical pathways of love with the aid of an MRI machine. Fisher found that love lights up the caudate nucleus because it is home to a dense spread of receptors for a neurotransmitter called dopamine, the chemical in the brain that stimulates feelings of attraction and accompanies passion. This is the same chemical that is produced in response to the ingestion of cocaine. Following the flooding of dopamine, the caudate then sends signals for more dopamine. "The more dopamine you get, the more high you feel," says Dr. Lucy Brown, neurologist at the Albert Einstein College of Medicine in New York. In the right proportions, dopamine creates intense energy, focused attention, exhilaration, and desire. It is why a newly-in-love person can live passionately without sleep, feel bold and bright, and run risks.

The simple act of kissing triggers a flood of chemicals and neural messages that transmit tactile sensations, sexual excitement, feelings of closeness, and euphoria (Walter, 2008). Since lips are among the most densely populated with sensory neurons of any body region, when we kiss, these neurons along with those in the tongue and mouth send messages to the brain and body that intensify emotions and physical reactions. Kissing also unleashes a cocktail of chemicals that govern stress, motivation, social bonding, and sexual stimulation.

Because the brain adapts to the excessive influx of dopamine as the neurons become desensitized over time, it needs more of the drug to produce the same high. Similarly, the chemically altered state induced by romantic love cannot sustain itself forever, and so it changes into something else (e.g., intimacy), or one moves on to another partner for a new surge. "We now have physiological data that suggests there are different brain systems for sex and love," says Fisher (2007). At some point, however, the two systems become linked. People in love have elevated levels of dopamine, which in turn triggers the production of testosterone, responsible for the sex drive in men and women. This explains why falling in love can make someone seem sexy all of a sudden.

Interestingly, the brains of love-struck men and women also seem to differ: More activity exists for men in the brain region that integrates visual stimuli; whereas, for women, the areas of the brain that govern memories are more active. Women's brain activity is different than men's, but it may be that when a woman really studies a man, she can remember things about his behavior in order to determine whether he'd make a reliable mate and father.

In studying romance and passion historically and globally, scientists now believe that romance is universal and has been embedded in our brains since prehistoric times. It has been observed that, in all societies, passion usually diminishes. From a physiological perspective, this makes sense. The dopamine-drenched state of romantic love adapts and changes into a relatively quiet one that is explained by the presence of oxytocin, a hormone that promotes feelings of connectedness and bonding. This is the same chemical that is released when a mother nurses her infant and when we hug our children and others whom we love.

What researchers have learned from lovers' brains is that romantic love isn't really an emotion—it's a drive that is based deep within our brains and that helps to explain why we might do crazy things for love.

Think Critically

- How important is it that science investigates the "brain in love"? What impact might this information have on you or others?
- How much validity do you give to the various changes in chemicals that the brain undergoes in its response to love? Have you experienced these chemical surges and drops?
- What gender differences do you see, if any, between how men and women respond to love?

SOURCES: Cohen, E. (2007, February 15). Loving with all your . . . brain. Available: http://www.cnn.com/2007/HEALTH/02/14/love.science/index.html; Slater, L. (2006, February). Love: The chemical reaction. *National Geographic*, pp. 34–49.

depend on them. They didn't frequently worry about being abandoned or having someone get too close to them. More than anxious/ambivalent and avoidant adults, they felt that others usually liked them; they believed that people were generally well intentioned and good-hearted. Their love experiences tended to be happy, friendly, and trusting. They accepted and supported their partners. On average, their relationships lasted 10 years. About 56% of the adults in the study were secure.

Adults with **anxious/ambivalent attachments** believed that other people did not get as close as they themselves wanted. They worried that their partners didn't really love them or would leave them. They also wanted to merge completely with another person, which sometimes scared others away. More than others, they felt that it is easy to fall in love. Their experiences in love were often obsessive and marked by desire for union, high degrees of sexual attraction, and jealousy. Their love relationships lasted an average of 5 years. Approximately 19–20% of the adults were identified as anxious/ambivalent.

Adults with **avoidant attachments** felt discomfort in being close to other people; they were distrustful and fearful of being dependent. More than others, they believed that romance seldom lasts but that at times it can be as intense as it was at the beginning. Their partners wanted more closeness than they did. Avoidant lovers feared intimacy and experienced emotional highs and lows and jealousy. Their relationships lasted an average of 6 years. Approximately 23–25% of the adults in the study were avoidant.

In adulthood, the attachment style developed in infancy combines with sexual desire and caring behaviors to give rise to romantic love. However, it is also important to know that an individual's past does not necessarily determine the future course of his or her relationships (Simpson, Collins, Tran, & Haydon, 2007).

Unrequited Love

As most of us know from painful experience, love is not always returned. People may suffer tremendous anguish when they feel they have been rejected or ignored, even if the relationship was imagined. Several researchers (Baumeister, Wotman, & Stillwell, 1993) accurately captured some of the feelings associated with **unrequited love**—love that is not returned—in the title of their study: "Unrequited Love: On Heartbreak, Anger, Guilt, Scriptlessness, and Humiliation." They found that unrequited love is distressing for both the would-be lover and the rejecting person. Would-be lovers had both positive and intensely negative feelings about their failed relationship. The rejectors, however, felt uniformly negative about the experience. Unlike the rejectors, the would-be lovers felt that the attraction was mutual, that they had been led on, and that the rejection had never been clearly communicated. Rejectors, in contrast, felt that they had not led the other person on; moreover, they felt guilty about hurting him or her. Nevertheless, many found the other person's persistence intrusive and annoying; they wished he or she would have simply gotten the hint and gone away. Rejectors saw would-be lovers as self-deceiving and unreasonable; would-be lovers saw their rejectors as inconsistent and mysterious.

'Tis better to have loved and lost Than never to have loved at all.

—Alfred, Lord Tennyson (1809–1892)

● Jealousy

Many of us think that the existence of jealousy proves the existence of love. We may try to test someone's interest or affection by attempting to make him or her jealous by flirting with another person. If our date or partner becomes jealous, the jealousy is taken as a sign of love. But provoking jealousy proves only that the other person can be made jealous. Making jealousy a litmus test of love is dangerous, for jealousy and love are not necessarily companions. Jealousy may be a more accurate yardstick for measuring insecurity or immaturity than for measuring love (Pistole, 1995).

It is important to understand jealousy for several reasons. First, jealousy is a painful emotion associated with anger, hurt, and loss. If we can understand jealousy, especially when it is irrational, then we can eliminate some of its pain. Second, jealousy can help cement or destroy a relationship. Jealousy helps maintain a relationship by guarding its exclusiveness. But in its irrational or extreme forms, it can destroy a relationship by its insistent demands and attempts at control. We need to understand when and how jealousy is functional and when it is not. Third, jealousy is often linked to violence in marriages and dating relationships (Buss, 1999; Puente & Cohen, 2003). Furthermore, marital violence and rape are often provoked by jealousy. Rather than being directed at a rival, jealous aggression is often used against the partner.

Defining Jealousy

Jealousy is an aversive response that occurs because of a partner's real, imagined, or likely involvement with a third person. Jealousy sets boundaries for the behaviors that are acceptable in relationships; the boundaries cannot be crossed without evoking jealousy. Though a certain amount of jealousy can be expected in any loving relationship, it is important that partners communicate openly about their fears and boundaries. Jealousy is a paradox; it doesn't necessarily signal difficulty between partners, nor does it have to threaten the relationship.

The Psychological Dimension   As most of us know, jealousy is a painful emotion. It is an agonizing compound of hurt, anger, depression, fear, and doubt. When we are jealous, we may feel less attractive and acceptable to our partner. Jealousy can also enrich relationships and spark passion by increasing the attention individuals pay to their partner. According to David Buss (2000), psychology professor at the University of Texas–Austin, the total absence of jealousy is a more ominous sign than its presence for romantic partners because it signifies emotional bankruptcy. Though both sexes may elicit jealousy intentionally as an assessment tool to gauge the strength of a partner's commitment, they seem to use it unequally. Buss (2000) found that 31% of women and 17% of men had intentionally elicited jealousy in their relationship.

Jealous responses are most intense in committed or marital relationships because both assume "specialness." This specialness occurs because our intimate partner is different from everyone else. With him or her, we are our most confiding, revealing, vulnerable, caring, and trusting. There is a sense of exclusiveness. Being intimate outside the relationship violates that sense of exclusiveness because intimacy (especially sexual intimacy) symbolizes specialness. Words such as "disloyalty," "cheating," and "infidelity" reflect the sense that an unspoken

think
about it

The Passionate Love Scale

Are you in love with someone right now? Have you ever been in love? How intense are your feelings compared to those of other lovers? Researchers have suggested that almost everyone is capable of loving passionately. Social psychologists Hatfield and Walster (1978) described a kind of love, passionate love, as "a state of intense longing for union with another. Reciprocated love (union with the other) is associated with fulfillment and ecstasy while unrequited love (separation) is associated with emptiness, anxiety, or despair. Both involve a state of profound physiological arousal" (p. 9). Sometimes labeled "puppy love," "infatuation," or "lovesickness," passionate love often includes sexual desire. The Passionate Love Scale (PLS), which follows, is a measure of these emotions. (Hatfield & Sprecher, 1986)

Directions:
For each of the 15 sentences below, choose a number from 1 (not at all true) to 9 (definitely true) that most accurately describes your feelings toward the person you love. Indicate your answer by circling the number in the corresponding row.

	Not at all true		Moderately true			Definitely true		
1. I would feel deep despair if _____ left me.	1 2	3	4 5	6	7	8	9
2. Sometimes I feel I can't control my thoughts; they are obsessively about _____.	1 2	3	4 5	6	7	8	9
3. I feel happy when I am doing something to make _____ happy.	1 2	3	4 5	6	7	8	9
4. I would rather be with _____ than anyone else.	1 2	3	4 5	6	7	8	9
5. I'd get jealous if I thought _____ were falling in love with someone else.	1 2	3	4 5	6	7	8	9
6. I yearn to know all about _____.	1 2	3	4 5	6	7	8	9
7. I want _____ physically, emotionally, mentally.	1 2	3	4 5	6	7	8	9
8. I have an endless appetite for affection from _____.	1 2	3	4 5	6	7	8	9
9. For me, _____ is the perfect romantic partner.	1 2	3	4 5	6	7	8	9
10. I sense my body responding when _____ touches me.	1 2	3	4 5	6	7	8	9
11. _____ always seems to be on my mind.	1 2	3	4 5	6	7	8	9
12. I want _____ to know me—my thoughts, fears and hopes.	1 2	3	4 5	6	7	8	9
13. I eagerly look for signs indicating _____'s desire for me.	1 2	3	4 5	6	7	8	9
14. I possess a powerful attraction for _____.	1 2	3	4 5	6	7	8	9
15. I get extremely depressed when things don't go right in my relationship with _____.	1 2	3	4 5	6	7	8	9

Passionate Love Scale Scores

Extremely passionate = 106–135 (wildly, recklessly in love)
Passionate = 86–105 (passionate, but less intense)
Average = 66–85 (occasional bursts of passion)
Cool = 45–65 (tepid, infrequent passion)
Extremely cool = 15–44 (the thrill is gone)

Think Critically

- How does your score compare to the PLS scores with any other persons you have loved passionately? How reliable do you believe this instrument to be?

- Do you believe that love changes over time? If so, in a long-term relationship, can passionate love be maintained? If it can, how?

- What steps might you consider if you felt that the passion in your relationship was waning?

SOURCE: The Passionate Love Scale (shorter version) reprinted by permission of Elaine Hatfield. From Hatfield, E. (1998). The Passionate Love Scale. In C. M. Davis, W. L. Yarber, R. Bauserman, G. Schreer, & S. L. Davis (Eds.). *Handbook of Sexuality-Related Measures*. Thousand Oaks, CA: Sage Publications, p. 451.

pledge has been broken. This unspoken pledge is the normative expectation that serious relationships will be sexually exclusive.

Managing Jealousy

Jealousy can be unreasonable, based on fears and fantasies, or realistic, in reaction to genuine threats or events. Unreasonable jealousy can become a problem when it interferes with an individual's well-being or that of the relationship. Dealing with irrational suspicions can often be very difficult, for such feelings touch deep recesses in ourselves. As noted previously, jealousy is often related to personal feelings of insecurity and inadequacy. The source of such jealousy lies within ourselves, not within the relationship.

If we can work on the underlying causes of our insecurity, then we can deal effectively with our irrational jealousy. Excessively jealous people may need considerable reassurance, but at some point, they must also confront their own irrationality and insecurity. If they do not, they emotionally imprison their partner. Their jealousy may destroy the very relationship they have been desperately trying to preserve.

But jealousy is not always irrational. Sometimes, there are valid reasons, such as the relationship boundaries being violated. In this case, the cause lies not within ourselves but within the relationship. If the jealousy is well-founded, the partner may need to modify or end the relationship with the third party whose presence initiated the jealousy. Modifying the third-party relationship reduces the jealous response and, more importantly, symbolizes the partner's commitment to the primary relationship. If the partner is unwilling to do this, because of a lack of commitment, unsatisfied personal needs, or problems in the primary relationship, the relationship is likely to reach a crisis point. In such cases, jealousy may be the agent for profound change.

There are no set rules for dealing with jealousy. Each person must deal with it using his or her own understanding and insights. As with many of life's problems, jealousy has no simple answers.

Extradyadic Involvement

A fundamental assumption in our culture is that committed relationships are sexually exclusive. Each person remains the other's exclusive intimate partner, in terms of both emotional and sexual intimacy. **Extradyadic involvement (EDI),** sexual or romantic relationships outside of a primary or dating couple, alters that assumption.

According to the NSFG, 7.6% of married men and 5.8% of married women aged 15–44 report having more than one sexual partner in the previous 12 months (Mosher, Chandra, & Jones, 2005). Although we tend to think of EDI involvements as being sexual, they actually assume several forms. They may be (1) sexual but not emotional, (2) sexual and emotional, or (3) emotional but not sexual. In a series of experiments in which participants were forced to choose between emotional nonexclusiveness and sexual nonexclusiveness as more distressing, women were found to choose emotional nonexclusiveness, whereas men were more likely to choose sexual nonexclusiveness (Buss, 1999; Cann, Mangum, & Wells, 2001). These results are consistent with findings reported across many cultures (Buss, 1999). This gender difference can partly be explained using an evolutionary model, which proposes that men, because they cannot be completely confident about the paternity of any offspring from a relationship, will be more upset by sexual nonexclusiveness. Women, in

Jealousy is not a barometer by which the depth of love can be read. It merely records the depth of the lover's insecurity.

—Margaret Mead
(1901–1978)

Love withers under constraints: its very essence is liberty: it is not compatible either with obedience, jealousy, nor fear: it is there most pure, perfect, and unlimited where its votaries live in confidence, equality and unreserve.

—Percy Bysshe Shelley
(1792–1822)

What I have seen of the love affairs of other people has not led me to regret that deficiency in my experience.

—George Bernard Shaw
(1856–1950)

When extradyadic sex occurs, a crisis in the primary relationship usually results.

contrast, should be more upset by emotional nonexclusiveness, which might signal the man's lack of commitment to the long-term success of the relationship and any offspring. No differences have been found among men or women, dating or married, in their level of emotional closeness with the extradyadic partner, (Allen & Baucom, 2006).

Research into why people get involved in extradyadic relationships has been piecemeal and based on small samples that have limited generalizability. In spite of this, studies have shown that there is a higher likelihood of sexual activity outside the marriage among those with stronger sexual interests, more permissive sexual values, greater sexual opportunities, and weaker marital relationships (Treas & Giesen, 2000). This suggests that sexual behavior is positively correlated with social factors.

Extradyadic Involvements in Dating and Cohabiting Relationships Both cohabiting couples and those in committed relationships usually have expectations of sexual exclusiveness. But, like some married men and women who take vows of exclusivity, these couples do not always remain sexually and/or emotionally exclusive. Research has revealed that cohabitors are more likely to have relationships outside their primary one, suggesting that perhaps they have lower investments in their unions (Treas & Giesen, 2000) or concerns about their sexual health (Allen, Atkins, Baucom, et al., 2005). Gay men had more partners than cohabiting and married men, while lesbian women had fewer partners than any other group.

Extradyadic Involvement in Exclusive Marriages In marriages that assume emotional and sexual exclusivity, mutuality and sharing are emphasized. Extradyadic sexual relationships are assumed to be destructive of the marriage; nonsexual heterosexual relationships may also be judged threatening. The possibility of infecting one's spouse with an STI must also be considered.

As a result of marital assumptions, both sexual and nonsexual extradyadic relationships take place without the knowledge or permission of the other partner. If the extradyadic sex is discovered, a marital crisis often ensues. Many married people feel that the spouse who is not exclusive has violated a basic trust. Sexual accessibility implies emotional accessibility. When a person learns that his or her spouse is having another relationship, the emotional commitment

There is one thing I would break up over, and that is if she caught me with another woman. I won't stand for that.
—Steve Martin
(1945–)

of that spouse is brought into question. How can the person prove that he or she still has a commitment? He or she cannot—commitment is assumed; it can never be proved. Furthermore, the extradyadic sex may imply to the partner (rightly or wrongly) that he or she is sexually inadequate or uninteresting.

Extradyadic Involvement in Nonexclusive Marriages   There are several types of nonexclusive marriage: (1) open marriage in which intimate but non-sexual friendships with others are encouraged, (2) open marriage in which outside sexual relationships are allowed, and (3) group marriage/multiple relationships. In **open marriage,** partners may mutually agree to allow sexual contact with others. Other terms used to describe these individuals are **swingers** or **polyamorists.** The marriage relationship is considered the primary relationship in both nonsexual extradyadic relationships and open marriages. Only the group marriage/multiple relationships model rejects the primacy of the married relationship. Group marriage is the equal sharing of partners, as in polygamy; it may consist of one man and two women, one woman and two men, or two couples. Open marriages are more common than group marriages.

● Making Love Last: From Passion to Intimacy

Ultimately, passionate or romantic love may be transformed or replaced by a quieter, more lasting love. Otherwise, the relationship will likely end, and each person will search for another who will once again ignite her or his passion.

Although love is one of the most important elements of our humanity, it seems to come and go. The kind of love that lasts is what we might call **intimate love.** In intimate love, each person knows he or she can count on the other. The excitement comes from the achievement of other goals—from creativity, from work, from child rearing, from friendships—as well as from the relationship. The key to making love endure seems to be, not maintaining love's passionate intensity, but transforming it into intimate love. Intimate love is based on commitment, caring, and self-disclosure.

Commitment is an important component of intimate love. It reflects a determination to continue a relationship or marriage in the face of bad times as well as good. It is based on conscious choices rather than on feelings, which, by their very nature, are transitory. Commitment involves a promise of a shared future, a promise to be together, come what may. We seem to be as much in search of commitment as we are in search of love or marriage. We speak of "making a commitment" to someone or to a relationship. A "committed" relationship has become almost a stage of courtship, somewhere between dating and being engaged or living together.

Caring involves the making of another person's needs as important as your own. It requires what the philosopher Martin Buber called an "I-Thou" relationship. Buber described two fundamental ways of relating to people: I-Thou and I-It. In an I-Thou relationship, each person is treated as a Thou—that is, as a person whose life is valued as an end in itself. In an I-It relationship, each person is treated as an It; the person has worth only as someone who can be used. When a person is treated as a Thou, his or her humanity and uniqueness are paramount.

Self-disclosure is the revelation of personal information that others would not ordinarily know because of its riskiness. When we self-disclose, we reveal

To be faithful to one is to be cruel to all the others.

—Wolfgang Amadeus Mozart (1756–1791)

Thou shalt not commit adultery . . . unless in the mood.

—W. C. Fields (1879–1946)

What determines whether a relationship will last? Click on "Staying in Love" to see a couple working to save their marriage.

Lessons From the Love Lab

For many people, forming a new relationship appears to be a lot easier (and a lot more fun) than maintaining one. If this were not the case, then marital therapy and how-to articles and books on keeping love alive would not be so prevalent. One person who has spent a significant part of his career investigating the quandaries of partnerships is John M. Gottman, professor emeritus of psychology at the University of Washington–Seattle's Family Research Lab, better known as the "Love Lab." Over the past quarter century, Gottman and his colleagues have video-recorded thousands of conversations between couples, scoring words and sentences based on facial expressions such as disgust, affection, and contempt. Though most of his work has involved married couples, applications can be made to any couple interested in improving their relationship.

Gottman believes that in order to resolve difficulties in communication partners must learn new approaches to settling conflict. By studying what couples both overtly and covertly communicate, Gottman has arrived at what he considers to be a new model for resolving conflict in a loving relationship. His model entails the following steps:

1. *Soften up your startup.* Perhaps the most important aspect of this step is the avoidance of the "Four Horsemen of the Apocalypse"—criticism, contempt, defensiveness, and stonewalling. Only 40% of marriages end because of frequent, devastating fights. More often, partners end up distancing themselves so much that their friendship and sense of connection are lost.

2. *Learn to make and receive repair attempts.* What seems to separate stable, emotionally intelligent partnerships from others is not that the partners' repair attempts are more skillful but that the attempts focus on getting through to each other. This is because the air between them hasn't been clouded by negativity. To assess the effectiveness of repair attempts in your own relationship, consider how you might resolve conflict:

   - We are good at taking breaks when we need them.
   - My partner usually accepts my apologies.
   - I can say that I am wrong.
   - We can maintain our sense of humor.
   - We can be affectionate even when we are disagreeing.

   Note that the more you agree with the statements, the stronger your partnership is.

3. *Soothe yourself and each other.* To discover whether distress is a problem in your relationship, consider the following statements:

   - Our discussions get too heated.
   - After a fight, I want to keep my distance.
   - I can't think straight when my partner gets hostile.

   The more you agree with the statements, the greater the tendency to get overwhelmed during arguments. Calming the body through meditative techniques can help to prevent feelings of righteous indignation and innocent victimhood.

4. *Compromise.* Gottman puts it this way: "Like it or not, the only solution to marital problems is to find a compromise." Negotiation begins with softening the startup, repairing the discussion, and keeping calm. Deciding which solvable problem to tackle, looking for common bases of agreement, and sharing these with each other helps couples develop a common way of thinking about the issue. In this way, partners can work together to construct a real plan that both can live with. Asking yourself the following questions may be helpful:

   - What do we agree about?
   - What are our common feelings, or what is the most important feeling here?
   - What common goals do we have and how can they be accomplished?
   - How can we understand this situation or issue?

   If you are grappling with a solvable problem, finding the aspects of the problem that you can and cannot compromise on can help you develop a reasonable solution.

5. *Be tolerant of each other's faults.* As long as someone does not accept a partner's flaws and foibles, he or she will not be able to compromise successfully. Conflict resolution is not about one person changing; it's about negotiating, finding common ground, and identifying ways to accommodate each other.

SOURCE: Adapted from Gottman, J., & Silver, N. (1999). *The seven principles for making marriage work.* New York: Crown.

ourselves—our hopes, our fears, our everyday thoughts—to others. Self-disclosure deepens others' understanding of us. It also deepens our own understanding, for we discover unknown aspects as we open up to others.

Without self-disclosure, we remain opaque and hidden. If others love us, such love makes us anxious: Are we loved for ourselves or for the image we present to the world?

Together, these elements help transform love. But in the final analysis, perhaps the most important means of sustaining love are our words and actions; caring words and deeds provide the setting for maintaining and expanding love.

Being able to sustain love in the day-to-day world involves commitment, compassion, and most importantly, communication. Researchers have found that positive outcomes for relationships can be often predicted by the ways in which couples communicate to resolve conflict (Holman & Jarvis, 2003). Clear communication can take the guesswork out of relationships, subdue jealousy, increase general satisfaction, and possibly put couple therapists out of business.

● The Nature of Communication

Communication is a transactional process by which we use symbols, such as words, gestures, and movements, to establish human contact, exchange information, and reinforce or change our own attitudes and behaviors and those of others. Communication takes place simultaneously within cultural, social, and psychological contexts. These contexts affect our ability to communicate clearly by prescribing rules (usually unwritten or unconscious) for communicating about various subjects, including sexuality.

The Cultural Context

The cultural context of communication refers to the language that is used and to the values, beliefs, and customs associated with it. Traditionally, reflecting our Judeo-Christian heritage, our culture has viewed sexuality negatively. Thus, sexual topics are often taboo. Children and adolescents are discouraged from obtaining sexual knowledge; they learn that they are not supposed to talk about sex. Censorship abounds in the media, with the ever-present "bleep" on television or the "f—k" in newspapers and magazines to indicate a "forbidden" word. Our language has a variety of words for describing sex, including scientific or impersonal ones ("sexual intercourse," "coitus," "copulation"), moralistic ones ("fornication"), euphemistic ones ("doing it," "being intimate," "sleeping with"), and taboo ones ("fucking," "screwing," "banging"). A few terms place sexual interactions in a relational category, such as "making love." But love is not always involved, and the term does not capture the erotic quality of sex. Furthermore, the gay, lesbian, bisexual, and transgender subcultures have developed their own sexual argot, or slang, because society suppresses the open discussion or expression of same-sex behavior.

Different ethnic groups within our culture also have different language patterns that affect the way they communicate about sex and sexuality. African American culture, for example, creates distinct communication patterns. Among African Americans, language and expressive patterns are characterized by, among other things, emotional vitality, realness, confrontation, and a focus on direct

> *Everyone has experienced that truth: that love, like a running brook, is disregarded, taken for granted; but when the brook freezes over, then people begin to remember how it was when it ran, and they want it to run again.*
>
> —Kahlil Gibran
> (1883–1931)

> *The greatest science in the world, in heaven and on earth, is love.*
>
> —Mother Teresa
> (1910–1997)

experience (Mackey & O'Brien, 1999). Emotional vitality is communicated through the animated, expressive use of words. Realness refers to "telling it like it is," using concrete, nonabstract language.

Among Latinos, especially traditional Latinos, there may be power imbalances that are potentially more significant for women than men. This may be due to the cultural values of a traditionally *machista* society in which men are defined by their ability to maintain control and to assert dominance by being the active sexual partner (Melhuus, 1996). Among traditional Latinos, the type and frequency of sexual behaviors are most often determined by men (Wood & Price, 1997). Although most Latinos agree that men tend to be the initiators of sexual activity and women are more likely to suggest condom use, they report that couples share responsibility for decisions regarding sexual activities and contraceptive use.

Asian Americans constitute a population group that defies simple characterizations; it includes a variety of demographic, historical, and cultural factors and traditions. At the same time, Asian Americans share many cultural characteristics, such as the primacy of the family and of collective goals over individual wishes, an emphasis on propriety and social roles, the appropriateness of sex only within the context of marriage, and sexual restraint and modesty (Okazaki, 2002). Because harmonious relationships are highly valued, Asian Americans have a greater tendency to avoid direct confrontation if possible. Despite significant steps in modernization and sexual liberation in recent decades, many Asian Americans' views of sexuality are still rooted in cultural heritage and traditional beliefs (So & Cheung, 2005). To avoid conflict, their verbal communication is often indirect or ambiguous; it skirts issues rather than confronting them. As a consequence, Asian Americans rely on each other to interpret the meaning of conversations or nonverbal cues.

Among those from the Middle East, sexual relations are often rooted in power and based on dominant and subordinate positions (Rathus, Nevid, & Fichner-Rathus, 2005). The family is the backbone of Islamic society; Islam is the dominant religion in the Middle East. Because Muhammad decreed that marriage represents the only road to virtue, celibacy is frowned on while homosexuality is condemned.

The Social Context

The social context of communication refers to the roles we play in society as members of different groups. For instance, as men and women, we play out masculine and feminine roles. As members of marital units, we act out roles of husband and wife. As members of cohabiting units, we perform heterosexual, gay, or lesbian cohabiting roles.

Roles exist in relationship to other people. Without a female role, there would be no male role; without a wife role, there would be no husband role. Because roles exist in relationship to others, **status**—a person's position or ranking in a group—is important. In traditional gender roles, men are accorded higher status than women; in traditional marital roles, husbands are superior in status to wives. And in terms of sexual orientation, society awards higher status to heterosexual people than to gay men, lesbian women, or bisexual or transgender people. Because of this male/female disparity, heterosexual couples tend to have a greater power imbalance than do gay and lesbian couples (Lips, 2004).

The Psychological Context

Although the cultural and social contexts are important factors in communication, they do not *determine* how people communicate. The psychological context of communication does that. We are not prisoners of culture and society; we are unique individuals. We may accept some cultural or social aspects, such as language taboos, but reject, ignore, or modify others, such as traditional gender roles. Because we have distinct personalities, we express our uniqueness by the way we communicate: We may be assertive or submissive, rigid or flexible, and sensitive or insensitive; we may exhibit high or low self-esteem.

Our personality characteristics affect our ability to communicate, change, or manage conflict. Rigid people, for example, are less likely to change than are flexible ones, regardless of the quality of communication. People with high self-esteem may be more open to change because they do not necessarily interpret conflict as an attack on themselves. Personality characteristics such as negative or positive feelings about sexuality affect our sexual communication more directly.

Nonverbal Communication

> " *The cruelest lies are often told in silence.*
>
> —Robert Louis Stevenson (1850–1894)

There is no such thing as not communicating. Even when we are not talking, we are communicating by our silence (an awkward silence, a hostile silence, a tender silence). We are communicating by our body movements, our head positions, our facial expressions, our physical distance from another person, and so on. We can make sounds that aren't words to communicate nonverbally; screams, moans, grunts, sighs, and so on communicate a range of feelings and reactions. Look around you: How are the people in your presence communicating nonverbally?

Most of our communication of feeling is nonverbal. We radiate our moods: A happy mood invites companionship; a solemn mood pushes people away.

Proximity, eye contact, and touching are important components of nonverbal communication. What do you think this man and woman are "saying" to each other?

Joy infects; depression distances—all without a word being said. Nonverbal expressions of love are particularly effective—a gentle touch, a loving glance, or the gift of a flower.

One of the problems with nonverbal communication, however, is the imprecision of its messages. Is a person frowning or squinting? Does the smile indicate friendliness or nervousness? Is the silence reflective, or does it express disapproval or remoteness?

Three of the most important forms of nonverbal communication are proximity, eye contact, and touching.

Proximity   Nearness in physical space and time is called **proximity.** Where we sit or stand in relation to another person signifies a level of intimacy. Many of our words that convey emotion relate to proximity, such as feeling "distant" or "close" or being "moved" by someone. We also "make the first move," "move in" on someone else's partner, or "move in together."

In a social gathering, the distances between individuals when they start a conversation are clues to how they wish to define the relationship. All cultures have an intermediate distance in face-to-face interactions that is neutral. In most cultures, decreasing the distance signifies either an invitation to greater intimacy or a threat. Moving away denotes the desire to terminate the interaction. When we stand at an intermediate distance from someone at a party, we send the message "Intimacy is not encouraged." If we move closer, however, we risk rejection.

Eye Contact   Much can be discovered about a relationship by watching how the two people look at each other. Making eye contact with another person, if only for a split second longer than usual, is a signal of interest. Brief and extended glances, in fact, play a significant role in women's expression of initial interest. When we can't take our eyes off another person, we probably have a strong attraction to him or her. In addition to eye contact, dilated pupils may be an indication of sexual interest. (They may also indicate fear, anger, and other strong emotions.)

The amount of eye contact between partners in conversation can reveal couples who have high levels of conflict and those who don't. Those with the greatest degree of agreement have the most eye contact with each other. Those in conflict tend to avoid eye contact (unless it is a daggerlike stare). As with proximity, however, the level of eye contact may differ by culture.

Touching   It is difficult to overestimate the significance of touch and its significance to human development, health, and sexuality. Touch is the most basic of all senses. The skin contains receptors for pleasure and pain, heat and cold, roughness and smoothness. "Touch is the mother sense and out of it, all the other senses have been derived," writes anthropologist Ashley Montagu (1986). Touch is a life-giving force for infants. If babies are not touched, they can fail to thrive and even die. We hold hands and cuddle with small children and with people we love. Levels of touching differ among cultures and ethnic groups. Although the value placed on nonverbal expression may vary across groups and cultures, the ability to communicate and understand nonverbally remains important in all cultures.

But touch can also be a violation. Strangers or acquaintances may touch inappropriately, presuming a level of familiarity that does not actually exist. A date

> " Touch is a language that can communicate more love in five seconds than words can in five minutes.
>
> —Ashley Montagu
> (1905–1999)

Married couples who love each other tell each other a thousand things without talking.

—Chinese proverb

Healing touch belongs to all of us.

—Dolores Kreiger
(1935–)

or partner may touch the other person in a manner she or he doesn't like or want. And sexual harassment includes unwelcome touching (see Chapter 17).

Touch often signals intimacy, immediacy, and emotional closeness. In fact, touch may very well be the *closest* form of nonverbal communication. One researcher writes: "If intimacy is proximity, then nothing comes closer than touch, the most intimate knowledge of another" (Thayer, 1986). And touching seems to go hand in hand with self-disclosure. Those who touch appear to self-disclose more; in fact, touch seems to be an important factor in prompting others to talk more about themselves.

If touching is an issue in your relationship, discussing what it means to each of you can begin to unravel and expose existing patterns of behavior. Also, experiment with nonsexual touching. Learn to enjoy giving and receiving touch. Give and accept feedback nondefensively. Give feedback, especially verbal cues, about what does and does not feel good. Initiate touch when it is appropriate, even though it may be awkward at first. Don't be afraid to be adventurous in learning and utilizing methods that are pleasing to both you and your partner.

At the same time, be prepared to accept individual differences. In spite of forthright and ongoing communication, people still have unique comfort levels. Again, honest feedback will help you and your partner find a mutually acceptable level. If you are both able to understand and enjoy the rich and powerful messages that touch sends, then your relationship can be enriched by yet another dimension.

● Sexual Communication

Communication is important in developing and maintaining sexual relationships. In childhood and adolescence, communication is critical for transmitting sexual knowledge and values and forming our sexual identities. As we establish our relationships, communication enables us to signal sexual interest and initiate sexual interactions. In developed relationships, communication allows us to explore and maintain our sexuality as couples.

Sexual Communication in Beginning Relationships

Our interpersonal sexual scripts provide us with "instructions" on how to behave sexually, including the initiation of potentially sexual relationships. Because as a culture we share our interpersonal sexual scripts, we know how we are supposed to act at the beginning of a relationship. But how do we begin relationships? What is it that attracts us to certain individuals?

The Halo Effect   Imagine yourself unattached at a party. You notice someone standing next to you as you reach for some chips. In a split second, you decide whether you are interested in her or him. On what basis do you make that decision? Is it looks, personality, style, sensitivity, intelligence, smell, or what?

If you're like most people, you base this decision, consciously or unconsciously, on appearance. Physical attractiveness is particularly important during the initial meeting and early stages of a relationship. If you don't know anything else about a person, you tend to judge on appearance.

Most people would deny that they are attracted to others simply because of their looks. We like to think we are deeper than that. But looks are important, in part because we tend to infer qualities based on looks. This inference is based on what is known as the **halo effect,** the assumption that attractive or charismatic people also possess more desirable social characteristics.

One of the most primal means of assessment is smell. Humans, like all animals, assign values to scents, recognizing those that affect them in powerful ways (Fisher, 2004). Scent lets both sexes narrow their choices of potential partners by identifying those unspoken characteristics, such as level of testosterone and ovulation, that may lead toward mating. (See Chapter 3 for the discussion on pheromones and menstrual synchrony.)

Interest and Opening Lines After sizing someone up based on his or her appearance, what happens next in interactions between men and women? (Gay men's and lesbian women's beginning relationships are discussed later.) Does the man initiate the encounter? On the surface, yes, but in reality, the woman often "covertly initiates . . . by sending nonverbal signals of availability and interest" (Metts & Cupach, 1989). The woman will "glance" at the man once or twice and "catch" his eye; she may smile or flip her hair. If the man moves into her physical space, the woman then communicates interest by nodding, leaning close, smiling, or laughing.

If the man believes the woman is interested, he then initiates a conversation with an opening line, which tests the woman's interest and availability. Men use an array of opening lines. According to women, the most effective ones are innocuous, such as "I feel a little embarrassed, but I'd like to meet you" or "Are you a student here?" The least effective lines are sexually blunt ones, such as "You really turn me on."

Fascinating to many is the digital world of dating where words alone capture (or repel) the potential love object. Since this method of communication can occur without having to make eye contact or interpret facial cues, it is safer, bolder, and uncensored. Consequently, individuals may be inclined to reveal themselves more quickly and intimately over the Internet, which can result in relationships that escalate more than those that begin face-to-face.

The First Move and Beyond When we first meet someone, we weigh his or her attitudes, values, and philosophy to see if we are compatible. We evaluate his or her sense of humor, intelligence, "partner" potential, ability to function in a relationship, sex appeal, and so on. Based on our overall judgment, we may pursue the relationship. If the relationship continues in a romantic vein, we may decide to move into one that includes some kind of physical intimacy. To signal this transition from nonphysical to physical intimacy, one of us must "make the first move." Making the first move marks the transition from a potentially sexual relationship to one that is actually sexual.

If the relationship develops along traditional gender-role lines, one of the partners, usually the man, will make the first move to initiate sexual intimacy, whether it is kissing, fondling, or engaging in sexual intercourse. The point at which this occurs generally depends on two factors: the level of intimacy and the length of the relationship. The more emotionally involved the two people are, the more likely they will be sexually involved as well. Similarly, the longer the relationship, the more likely there is sexual involvement (Christopher & Sprecher, 2000).

Nontraditional roles are changing the ways in which couples make contact and initiate conversation. What appear to be the roles of each person in this photograph?

Whereas a lot of men used to ask for conversation when they really wanted sex, nowadays they often feel obliged to ask for sex even when they really want conversation.

—Katherine Whitehorn
(1926–)

Regardless of our sexual orientation, age, gender, or ethnicity, much of our sexual communication is nonverbal.

In new relationships, we communicate *indirectly* about sex because, although we may want to become sexually involved with the other person, we also want to avoid rejection. By using indirect strategies, such as turning down the lights, moving closer, and touching the other person's face or hair, we can test his or her interest in sexual involvement. If he or she responds positively to our cues, we can initiate a sexual encounter.

Because so much of our sexual communication is indirect, ambiguous, or nonverbal, there is a high risk of misinterpretation. Both men and women may say "no" to sex while actually desiring it (Sprecher et al., 1994).

Gay men and lesbian women, like heterosexual persons, rely on both non-verbal and verbal communication in expressing sexual interest in others. Unlike heterosexual people, however, they cannot necessarily assume that the person in whom they are interested is of the same sexual orientation. Instead, they must rely on specific identifying factors, such as meeting at a gay or lesbian bar, wearing a gay/lesbian pride button, participating in gay/lesbian events, or being introduced by friends to others identified as lesbian or gay. In situations in which sexual orientation is not clear, some gay men and lesbian women use "gaydar" (gay radar), in which they look for clues as to orientation. They give ambiguous cues regarding their own orientation while looking for cues from the other person. These cues can include mannerisms, speech patterns, slang, and lingering glances. They may also include the mention of specific places for entertainment or recreation that are frequented mainly by lesbian women or gay men, songs that can be interpreted as having "gay" meanings, or movies with gay or lesbian themes. Once a like orientation is established, lesbian women and gay men often use nonverbal communication to express interest.

Directing Sexual Activity   As we begin a sexual involvement, we have several tasks to accomplish. First and foremost, we must practice safer sex (see Chapters 15 and 16). We should gather information about our partner's sexual history, determine whether she or he knows how to practice safer sex, and use condoms. Unlike much of our sexual communication, which is nonverbal or ambiguous, practicing safer sex requires direct verbal communication. Second, heterosexual couples must discuss birth control (unless both partners have

If you don't risk anything, you risk even more.

—Erica Jong
(1942–)

agreed to try for pregnancy). Contraceptive responsibility, like safer sex, requires verbal communication (see Chapter 11).

In addition to communicating about safer sex and contraception, we need to communicate about what we like and need sexually. What kind of touching do we like? For example, do we like to be orally or manually stimulated? If so, how? What stimulation does each partner need to be orgasmic? Many of our needs and desires can be communicated nonverbally by movements or physical cues. But if our partner does not pick up our nonverbal signals or cues, we need to discuss them directly and clearly to avoid ambiguity.

Sexual Communication in Established Relationships

In developing relationships, partners begin modifying their individual sexual scripts as they interact with each other. The scripts become less rigid and conventional as each partner adapts to the uniqueness of the other. Partners develop a shared sexual script. Through their sexual interactions, they learn what each other likes, dislikes, wants, and needs. Much of this learning takes place non-verbally: Partners in established relationships, like those in emerging relationships, tend to be indirect and ambiguous in their sexual communication. Like partners in new relationships, they want to avoid rejection. Indirection allows them to express sexual interest and, at the same time, protect themselves from embarrassment or loss of face.

Past research has demonstrated that intimate communication is associated with both sexual satisfaction and relationship satisfaction (Cupach & Comstock, 1990; Fowers & Olson, 1989). More recently, researchers have found that over time, communication is also associated with changes in both relationship satisfaction and sexual satisfaction (Byers, 2005). That is, poor communicators are more likely to report decreases in both relationship satisfaction and sexual satisfaction whereas good communicators are more likely to report increases in satisfaction. Not surprisingly, communication accounts in part for increases and decreases in sexual satisfaction.

When in doubt, tell the truth.
—Mark Twain
(1835–1910)

Click on "Communicating About Sex" to see how one couple learned to discuss their sexual expression.

Initiating Sexual Activity Within established heterosexual relationships, men continue to overtly initiate sexual encounters more frequently than women. But women continue to signal their willingness. They show their interest in intercourse with nonverbal cues, such as giving a "certain look" or lighting candles by the bed. (They may also overtly suggest "making love.") Their partners pick up on the cues and "initiate" sexual interactions. In established relationships, many women feel more comfortable with overtly initiating sex. In part, this may be related to the decreasing significance of the double standard as relationships develop. In a new relationship, the woman's initiation of intercourse may be viewed negatively, as a sign of a "loose" sexual standard. But in an established relationship, the woman's initiation may be viewed positively, as an expression of love. This shift may also be the result of couples becoming more egalitarian in their gender-role attitudes. Not surprisingly, sexual initiations are more often successful in long-term relationships than in new or dating relationships.

In both lesbian and gay relationships, the more emotionally expressive partner is likely to initiate sexual interaction. The gay or lesbian individual who talks more about feelings and who spontaneously gives his or her partner hugs or kisses is the one who most often begins sexual activity.

Charm is a way of getting the answer without having asked any question.
—Albert Camus
(1913–1960)

Gender Differences in Partner Communication Though men and women speak about the same number of words each day, gender differences lie in the topics they discuss. Men tend to talk about technology, sports, and money, while women tend to talk about fashion and relationships (Mehl, Vazire, Ramírez-Esparza, et al., 2007). Specific gender differences in communication between sexual partners also seem to occur such that some men may avoid talking about feelings and personal issues, while some women may be inclined to show more interest and seek agreement and acceptance in the context of the sexual relationship (Gottman & Carrere, 2000; Klinetob & Smith, 1996).

● Developing Communication Skills

Generally, poor communication skills precede the onset of relationship problems. The material that follows will help you understand and develop your skills in communicating about sexual matters.

Talking About Sex

Good communication is central to a healthy intimate relationship. Unfortunately, it is not always easy to establish or maintain.

Obstacles to Sexual Discussions The process of articulating our feelings about sex can be very difficult, for several reasons. First, we rarely have models for talking about sex. As children and adolescents, we probably never discussed sex with our parents, let alone heard them talking about sex. Second, talking about sexual matters defines us as being interested in sex, and interest in sex is often identified with being sexually obsessive, immoral, prurient, or "bad." If the topic of sex is tabooed, we further risk being labeled "bad." Third, we may believe that talking about sex will threaten our relationships. We don't talk about tabooed sexual feelings, fantasies, or desires because we fear that our partners may be repelled or disgusted. We also are reluctant to discuss sexual difficulties or problems because doing so may bring attention to our own role in them.

Keys to Good Communication Being aware of communication skills and actually using them are two separate matters. Furthermore, even though we may be comfortable sharing our feelings with another, we may find it more difficult to discuss our sexual preferences and needs. Self-disclosure, trust, and feedback are three keys to good communication.

Self-Disclosure Self-disclosure creates the environment for mutual understanding. Most people know us only through the conventional roles we play as female/male, wife/husband, parent/child, and so on. These roles, however, do not necessarily reflect our deepest selves. If we act as if we are nothing more than our roles, we may reach a point at which we no longer know who we are.

Through the process of **self-disclosure,** we not only reveal ourselves to others but also find out who we are. We discover feelings we have hidden, repressed, or ignored. We nurture forgotten aspects of ourselves by bringing them to the surface. Moreover, self-disclosure is reciprocal: In the process of our sharing, others share themselves with us. The ability to disclose or reveal

think
about it

Communication Patterns and Partner Satisfaction

Researchers studying relationship satisfaction have found a number of communication patterns that offer clues to enhancing our intimate relationships (Byers, 2005; Gottman & Carrere, 2000; Noller & Fitzpatrick, 1991). They found that men and women in satisfying heterosexual relationships tend to have the following common characteristics regarding communication:

- *The ability to disclose or reveal private thoughts and feelings, especially positive ones.* Dissatisfied partners tend to disclose mostly negative thoughts. Satisfied partners say such things as "I love you," "You're sexy," or "I feel vulnerable; please hold me." Unhappy partners may also say that they love each other, but more often they say things like "Don't touch me; I can't stand you," "You turn me off," or "This relationship makes me miserable and frustrated."

- *The expression of more or less equal levels of affective disclosures.* Both partners in satisfied couples are likely to say things like "You make me feel happy," "I love you more than I can ever say," or "I love the way you touch me."

- *More time spent talking, discussing personal topics, and expressing feelings in positive ways.* Satisfied couples talk about their sexual feelings and the fun they have in bed together.

- *A willingness to accept conflict but to engage in conflict in nondestructive ways.* Satisfied couples view conflict as a natural part of intimate relationships. When partners have sexual disagreements, they do not accuse or blame; instead, they exchange viewpoints, seek common ground, and compromise.

- *Less frequent conflict and less time spent in conflict.* Both satisfied and unsatisfied couples, however, experience perpetual problems surrounding the same issues, especially communication, sex, and personality characteristics.

- *The ability to accurately encode (send) verbal and non-verbal messages and accurately decode (understand) such messages.* This ability to send and understand non-verbal messages is especially important for men. In satisfied couples, for example, if a man wants his partner to initiate sex more often, he can say, "I'd like you to initiate sex more often," and she will understand the message correctly. In dissatisfied couples, the man may stop initiating sex, hoping his partner will be forced to initiate more often in order to have sex. Or he may ask her to initiate sex more often, but she may mistakenly interpret the request as a personal attack.

Many of these communication patterns appear to hold true for gay and lesbian relationships as well.

Think Critically

- What characteristics regarding communication are important to you?
- What are your thoughts and feelings about the role of conflict in a relationship?
- What are some ways of developing good communication?

---

private thoughts and feelings, especially positive ones, can contribute to enhancing relationships. Men are less likely than women, however, to disclose intimate aspects of themselves (Lips, 2004). Because they have been taught to be "strong and silent," they are more reluctant to express feelings of tenderness or vulnerability. Women find it easier to disclose their feelings because they have been conditioned from childhood to express themselves (Tannen, 1990). These differences can drive wedges between men and women. Even when people cohabit or are married, they can feel lonely because there is little or no interpersonal contact. And the worst kind of loneliness is feeling alone when we are with someone to whom we want to feel close.

Trust When we talk about intimate relationships, the two words that most frequently pop up are "love" and "trust." Trust is the primary characteristic we

> *The other night I said to my wife, Ruth: "Do you feel that the sex and excitement has gone out of our marriage?" Ruth said: "I'll discuss it with you during the next commercial."*
>
> —Milton Berle (1908–2002)

associate with love. But what, exactly, is trust? **Trust** is a belief in the reliability and integrity of a person. When someone says, "Trust me," he or she is asking for something that does not easily occur.

Trust is critical in close relationships for two reasons. First, self-disclosure requires trust because it makes us vulnerable. A person will not self-disclose if he or she believes the information may be misused—by mocking or revealing a secret, for example. Second, the degree to which we trust a person influences how we interpret ambiguous or unexpected messages from him or her. If our partner says that he or she wants to study alone tonight, we are likely to take the statement at face value if we have a high level of trust. But if we have a low level of trust, we may believe that he or she actually will be meeting someone else.

Self-disclosure is reciprocal. If we self-disclose, we expect our partner to self-disclose as well. As we self-disclose, we build trust; as we withhold self-disclosure, we erode trust. To withhold ourselves is to imply that we don't trust the other person, and if we don't, she or he will not trust us.

Feedback A third critical element in communication is **feedback,** the ongoing process of restating, checking the accuracy of, questioning, and clarifying messages. If someone self-discloses to a partner, his or her response to that self-disclosure is feedback, and the partner's response is feedback to that feedback. It is a continuous process (see Figure 8.3). The most important form of feedback for improving relationships is constructive feedback. Constructive feedback focuses

● **FIGURE 8.3**

Communication Loop. In successful communication, feedback between the sender and the receiver ensures that both understand (or are trying to understand) what is being communicated. For communication to be clear, the message and the intent behind the message must be congruent. Nonverbal and verbal components must also support the intended message. Communication includes not just language and word choice but also nonverbal characteristics such as tone, volume, pitch, rate, and silence.

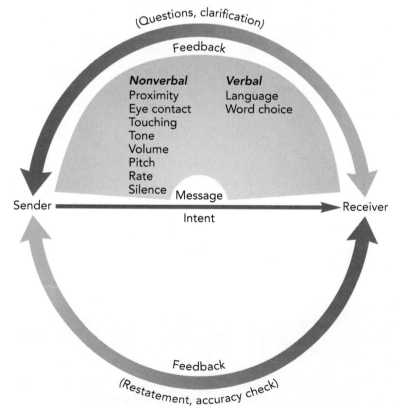

on self-disclosing information that will help part-ners understand the consequences of their actions—for each other and for the relationship. For example, if your partner discloses her or his doubts about the relationship, you can respond in a number of ways. Among these are remaining silent, venting anger, expressing indifference, and giving constructive feedback. Of these responses, con-structive feedback is the most likely to encourage positive change.

● Conflict and Intimacy

Conflict is the process in which people perceive incompatible goals and interference from others in achieving their goals. Conflict is a special type of communication.

We expect love to unify us, but sometimes it doesn't. Two people do not become one when they love each other, although at first they may have this feeling or expectation. Their love may not be an illusion, but their sense of ultimate oneness is. In reality, we retain our individual identities, needs, wants, and pasts—even while loving each other. It is a paradox that, the more intimate two people become, the more likely they are to experience conflict. In fact, a lack of arguing can signal trouble in a relationship because it may mean that issues are not being resolved or that there is indifference. Conflict itself is not dangerous to intimate relationships; it is the manner in which the conflict is handled. The presence of conflict does not necessarily indicate that love is wan-ing or has disappeared. It may mean that love is *growing*. A willingness to accept and engage in conflict in nondestructive ways can assist couples in enhancing their relationship.

Conflict in relationships is expressed differently by different ethnic groups. Whites tend to seek either dominance, which is confrontational and controlling, or integration, which is solution-oriented. They seem to believe that conflict is natural in a relationship, perhaps because of the high cultural value placed on individualism. Both African Americans and Mexican Americans view conflict less positively; they believe that conflict has both short- and long-term negative effects. Whites tend to be more solution-oriented than African Americans, who tend to be more controlling. In interpersonal relationships, both groups tend to identify conflict in terms of issues and goals. In contrast, Mexican Americans view conflict more in relationship terms; conflict occurs when a relationship is out of balance or harmony (Collier, 1991).

Gender differences separate not only what couples fight about (see Figure 8.4), but also how arguing can take a toll on their health. A recent study revealed that, for women, whether a husband's arguing style was warm or hostile had the most significant effect on her heart health, whereas, for a man, heart risk increased if disagreements with his wife involved a battle for control (Smith, Uchino, Berg, et al., 2007).

Conflict is natural in intimate relationships because each person has her or his own unique identity, values, needs, and history.

	Women	Men
Children	9.7%	5.6%
Sex	7.1	9.1
Housework	8.7	4.2
Money	8.5	6.2
Leisure	8.1	6.2
Alcohol	7.2	4.4

● **FIGURE 8.4**

Why Couples Fight: The Percent Indicating Various Reasons. Here are the top reasons men and women listed for why they argue. (*Source:* From Eaker, E. D., et al. (2007). Marital status, marital strain, and risk of coronary heart disease or total mortality: The Framingham Offspring Study. *Psychosomatic Medicine*, 69, 509–513. Copyright © 2007 by the American Psychosomatic Society. Reprinted by permission of Lippincott Williams & Wilkins. http://lww.com)

These differing views of conflict and conflict resolution affect each group's willingness to deal with sexual conflicts. Understanding these differences will help in resolving sexual problems and issues.

Sexual Conflicts

Common practices such as using sex as a scapegoat for nonsexual problems and using arguments as a cover-up for other problems frequently lead to additional disagreements and misunderstandings. Clinging to these patterns can interfere with problem solving and inhibit conflict resolution.

Fighting About Sex Fighting and sex can be intertwined in several ways. A couple may have a disagreement about sex that leads to a fight. For example, if one person wants to be sexual and the other does not, they may fight.

Sex can also be used as a scapegoat for nonsexual problems. If a man is angry because his partner has called him a lousy communicator, he may take it out on her sexually by calling her a lousy lover. They fight about their lovemaking rather than about the real issue, his communication role.

Finally, a fight can be a cover-up. If a man feels sexually inadequate and does not want to have sex as often as his partner, he may pick a fight and make her so angry that the last thing she would want to do is to be sexual with him.

For couples with children, relationships tend to follow a predictable pattern of satisfaction in the early years, a decrease in satisfaction during the child-rearing years, and a return to a higher level after the children are grown. An awareness of this pattern can be helpful to couples whose levels of conflict are escalating. Acknowledging a relationship's changing nature and focusing on strengths that each person brings to the relationship are ways to adapt to the inevitable changes that occur over time.

Conflict Resolution

The way in which couples deal with conflict reflects and perhaps contributes to their relationship happiness. Partners who communicate with affection and interest and who integrate humor when appropriate can use such positive affect to defuse conflict (Gottman & Carrere, 2000).

Strategies for Resolving Conflicts There are several ways to end conflicts. We can give in, but unless we believe that the conflict ended fairly, we are likely to feel resentful. We can try to impose our will through the use of power, force, or the threat of force. But using power to end conflict leaves the partner with the bitter taste of injustice. Or we can end the conflict through negotiation. In negotiations, the partners discuss their differences until they come to a mutually acceptable agreement.

Sometimes, even if we sincerely commit ourselves to working out our problems, it is difficult to see our own role in sustaining a pattern of interaction. If partners are unable to resolve their conflicts, they should consider entering relationship counseling. A therapist or other professional can often help identify underlying problems, as well as help couples develop negotiating skills.

Negotiating Conflicts Conflicts can be solved through negotiation in three major ways: agreement as a gift, bargaining, and coexistence.

" *For a marriage to be peaceful, the husband should be deaf and the wife blind.*

—Spanish proverb

" *Hatred does not cease by hatred at any time. Hatred ceases by love. This is an unalterable law.*

—Siddhartha Gautama, the Buddha (c. 563–483 B.C.)

Agreement as a Gift   If partners disagree on an issue, one can freely agree with the other as a gift. For example, if a woman wants her partner to stimulate her clitoris, and he doesn't want to because he feels it reflects badly on him, he can agree to try it because he cares about his partner. Similarly, a woman who does not want to perform oral sex can do so as a gift of caring. Neither, however, needs to continue if the activity remains objectionable.

Agreement as a gift is different from giving in. When we give in, we do something we don't want to do. But when we agree without coercion or threats, the agreement is a gift of love. It's acceptance in its best form—loving a partner not in spite of the differences but because of them. As in all exchanges of gifts, there will be reciprocation: Our partner will be more likely to give us a gift of agreement in return.

Bargaining   Bargaining means making compromises. But bargaining in relationships is different from bargaining in the marketplace or in politics. In relationships, partners want not the best deal for themselves but the most equitable deal for *both* partners. At all points during the bargaining process, they need to keep in mind what is best for the relationship, as well as for themselves, and to trust each other to do the same. In a relationship, both partners need to win. The purpose of conflict resolution in a relationship is to solidify the relationship, not to make one partner the winner and the other the loser. Achieving our ends by exercising coercive power or withholding love, affection, or sex is a destructive form of bargaining. If we get what we want, how will that affect our partner and the relationship? Will he or she feel that we're being unfair and become resentful? A solution has to be fair to both partners, or it won't enhance the relationship.

Coexistence   Sometimes, differences can't be resolved, but they can be lived with. If a relationship is sound, differences can be absorbed without undermining the basic ties. All too often, we regard differences as threatening rather than as the unique expression of two personalities. If one person likes to masturbate, the partner can accept it as an expression of her or his unique sexuality. Coexistence focuses on the person we have the most power over—ourself.

Final Thoughts

The study of love is only beginning, but it is already helping us to understand the various components that make up this complex emotion. Although there is something to be said for the mystery of love, understanding how it works in the day-to-day world may help us keep our love vital and growing.

If we can't talk about what we like and what we want, there is a good chance we won't get either one. Communication is the basis for good sex and good relationships. Communication and intimacy are reciprocal: Communication creates intimacy, and intimacy, in turn, creates good communication. But communication is learned behavior. If we have learned *not* to communicate, we can learn *how* to communicate. Communication allows us to expand ourselves and to feel more connected to and intimate with another person.

Summary

Friendship and Love

- Close friend relationships are similar to spouse/lover relationships in many ways. But lovers/spouses have more fascination and a greater sense of exclusiveness with their partners.

Love and Sexuality

- Sexuality and love are intimately related in our culture. Sex is most highly valued in loving relationships. A loving relationship rivals marriage as an acceptable moral standard for intercourse.

- Nonmarital sex among young adults (but not adolescents) in a relational context has become the norm. An important factor in this shift is the surge in the numbers of unmarried men and women.

- Men and women tend to have different ideas about how they view love, sex, and attraction. Love, however, is equally important for heterosexual people, gay men, lesbian women, and bisexual individuals.

- For a variety of reasons, some people choose *celibacy* as a lifestyle. These individuals may have a better appreciation of the nature of friendship and an increased respect for the bonds of long-term partnerships. Fewer people may be *asexual,* or not attracted to either sex.

How Do I Love Thee? Approaches and Attitudes Related to Love

- According to sociologist John Lee, there are six basic styles of love: *eros, mania, ludus, storge, agape,* and *pragma.*

- The *triangular theory of love* views love as consisting of three components: intimacy, passion, and decision/commitment.

- The *attachment* theory of love views love as being similar in nature to the attachments we form as infants. The attachment (or love) styles of both infants and adults are *secure, anxious/ambivalent,* and *avoidant.*

- *Unrequited love*—love that is not returned—is distressing for both the would-be lover and the rejecting partner.

Jealousy

- *Jealousy* is an aversive response to a partner's real, imagined, or likely involvement with a third person. Jealous responses are most likely in committed or marital relationships because of the presumed "specialness" of the relationship, symbolized by sexual exclusiveness.

- As individuals become more interdependent, there is a greater fear of loss. There is some evidence that jealousy may serve to ignite the passion in a relationship.

- *Extradyadic involvement* exists in dating, cohabiting, and marital relationships. In exclusive marriages, extradyadic involvement is assumed to be destructive to the marriage and is kept secret. In nonexclusive marriages, extradyadic involvement is permitted. In *open marriage,* partners mutually agree to allow sexual relationships with others.

- Extradyadic involvement appears to be related to three factors: values, opportunities, and the quality of the relationship.

Making Love Last: From Passion to Intimacy

- Time affects romantic relationships, potentially transforming it, with words and actions, into something that sustains and expands. *Intimate love* is based on *commitment, caring,* and *self-disclosure,* the revelation of information not normally known by others.

The Nature of Communication

- The ability to communicate is important in developing and maintaining relationships. Partners satisfied with their sexual communication tend to be satisfied with their relationship as a whole.

- *Communication* is a transactional process by which we use symbols, such as words, gestures, and movements, to establish human contact, exchange information, and reinforce or change the attitudes and behaviors of ourselves and others.
- Communication takes place within cultural, social, and psychological contexts. The cultural context refers to the language that is used and to the values, beliefs, and customs associated with it. Ethnic groups communicate about sex differently, depending on their language patterns and values. The social context refers to the roles we play in society that influence our communication. The most important roles affecting sexuality are those relating to gender and sexual orientation. The psychological context refers to our personality characteristics, such as having positive or negative feelings about sex.
- Communication is both verbal and nonverbal. The ability to correctly interpret nonverbal messages is important in successful relationships. *Proximity,* eye contact, and touching are especially important forms of nonverbal communication.

Sexual Communication

- In initial encounters, physical appearance is especially important. Because of the *halo effect,* we infer positive qualities about people based on their appearance. Women typically send nonverbal cues to men indicating interest; men often begin a conversation with an opening line.
- The "first move" marks the transition to physical intimacy. In initiating the first sexual interaction, people generally keep their communication nonverbal, ambiguous, and indirect. Sexual disinterest is usually communicated nonverbally. With sexual involvement, the couple must communicate verbally about contraception, STI prevention, and sexual likes and dislikes.
- Unless there are definite clues as to sexual orientation, gay men and lesbian women try to determine through nonverbal cues whether others are appropriate partners.
- In established heterosexual relationships, many women feel more comfortable in initiating sexual interactions than in newer relationships. Sexual initiations are more likely to be accepted in established relationships; sexual disinterest is communicated verbally. Women do not restrict sexual activities any more than do men.
- There are gender differences in partner communication. Women send clearer messages; men tend to send negative messages or withdraw; and women tend to set the emotional tone and escalate arguments more than men.

Developing Communication Skills

- The keys to effective communication are self-disclosure, trust, and feedback. *Self-disclosure* is the revelation of intimate information about ourselves. *Trust* is the belief in the reliability and integrity of another person. *Feedback* is a constructive response to another's self-disclosure.

Conflict and Intimacy

- *Conflict* is natural in intimate relationships. Conflicts about sex can be specific disagreements about sex, arguments that are ostensibly about sex but that are really about nonsexual issues, or disagreements about the wrong sexual issue.
- Conflict resolution may be achieved through negotiation in three ways: agreement as a freely given gift, bargaining, and coexistence.

Questions for Discussion

- Using Sternberg's triangular theory of love, identify one significant past or a current relationship and draw triangles for yourself and your partner. Compare the components of each. Have you coupled with someone who shares the same view of love as you? Why or why not is/was this person your "ideal match"? What characteristics in a relationship are important to you?

- What has been your experience when friends ask, "Are you two attracted to each other?" Can individuals be "just friends"? What are the meanings and implications of engaging in sex with a friend? What are the reasons underlying the decision to have sex?

- Do you think sexual activity implies sexual exclusiveness? Do you feel that it is important for you and your partner to agree on this? If not, how might you address this?

- How comfortable are you about sharing your sexual history with your partner? Do you feel that individuals should be selective in what they share, or do you find it beneficial to discuss your likes, dislikes, and past partners? How does this type of disclosure influence the nature of a relationship (dating, cohabiting, or married)?

Sex and the Internet

Sexual Intelligence

Sex therapist and licensed marriage and family therapist Marty Klein has established an online newsletter of sexuality-related information, updates, and political commentaries available at http://www.sexual intelligence.org. Go to the site and select and read one recent publication and article, then answer these questions:

- Why did you select this article?
- What was the main point?
- How was your thinking influenced by the viewpoint of the author?

Suggested Web Sites

Advocate
http://www.advocate.com
A comprehensive lesbian, gay, bisexual, and transgender news and resource site.

American Association for Marriage and Family Therapy
http://aamft.org/index_nm.asp
Provides referrals to therapists, books, and articles that address family and relationship problems and issues.

Psychology Today Relationship Center
http://psychologytoday.com/topics/relationships.html
Articles on friendship, relationship stages, sex, moods, and behavior, to name a few.

Sex and Communication
http://www.health.arizona.webfiles/main htm
Answers questions about sexuality and communication in the "Sexual Health" section of the Health Education On-Line Library.

Suggested Reading

Ackerman, D. (1995). *A natural history of love.* New York: Random House. A historical and cultural perspective on love.

Buss, D. M. (2003). *Evolution of desire.* New York: Basic Books. A study encompassing more than 10,000 people, which resulted in a unified theory of human mating behavior.

Fisher, H. (2004). *Why we love: The nature and chemistry of romantic love.* New York: Henry Holt. The author challenges traditional beliefs about love and romance and demonstrates how love is a chemical state with genetic roots and environmental influences.

Fletcher, G. (2002). *The new science of intimate relationships.* Oxford, UK: Blackwell. By showcasing scientific work on intimate relationships, counters many of the stereotypes and misperceptions fostered by popular psychology books.

Gottman, J. (2002). *The seven principles for making marriage work.* Waltham, MA: Adobe Systems. The results of a 10-year study of couples' patterns of communication.

Peck, M. S. (2003). *The road less traveled: A new psychology of love, traditional values, and spiritual growth.* New York: Touchstone. A psychological/spiritual approach to love that sees love's goal as spiritual growth.

Sternberg, R., & Barnes, M. (Eds.). (1989). *The psychology of love.* New Haven, CT: Yale University Press. An excellent collection of essays by some of the leading researchers in the area of love.

Tannen, D. (2001). *You just don't understand: Women and men in conversation.* New York: Harper-Collins. A best-selling, intelligent, and lively discussion of how women use communication to achieve intimacy and men use communication to achieve independence.

Tepper, M., & Owens, A. F. (Eds.). (2007). *Sexual health* (Vols. 1–4). Westport, CT: Praeger Perspectives. A comprehensive text that explores sex, love, and psychology.

Ting-Toomey, S., & Chung, L. C. (2004). *Understanding intercultural communication.* New York: Roxbury Publishing Co. Addresses communication and relationships among different ethnic and cultural groups, including African American, Latino, Korean, and Chinese ethnic groups and cultures.

For links, articles, and study material, go to the McGraw-Hill Web site, located at **www.mhhe.com/yarber7e.**

MAIN TOPICS

"I grew up thinking that I would wait until I got married before having sex. It was not just a religious or moral issue—it was more about being a 'good' girl. When I went away to college, some of my new friends were sexually active and had more open thoughts about having sex. I did have sex with someone during my first year in college, but afterwards I felt really embarrassed about it. When some of my friends at home found out, they were really shocked as well. Even though my first sexual relationship was one full of love and commitment, these feelings of shame and embarrassment and shock kept me from sleeping with my boyfriend for the next four months. I really struggled with the 'good girl' versus 'slut' extreme images I had grown up with."

—29-year-old female

I remember the first time one of my girlfriends told me she went down on a guy. I was seventeen and she was eighteen.

We were still in high school. I thought it was the grossest thing and couldn't imagine doing it. I'm embarrassed to admit that I kind of thought she was a slut. Then, a few months later, I tried it with my boyfriend. Then I began to feel like a slut."

—20-year-old female

"It's funny now how easy it is to talk about masturbation. When you get to college, some of the taboo is lifted from the subject, at least between the guys, I think. When someone brings up masturbating, we all kind of have that uncomfortable moment, but then we get into talking about when our last time was, how often, how we administer clean-up, techniques. It has become a normal subject with us. Considering how many males I have spoken to about masturbation, I think it is less taboo than thought."

—20-year-old male

"It bothers me as a woman that other women, or at least several I have come in contact with, feel that it is nasty for their partners to please them orally but have no problem pleasing their partners that way. That's crazy!"

—21-year-old female

Sex is as important as eating or drinking and we ought to allow one appetite to be satisfied with as little restraint or false modesty as the other.

—Marquis de Sade
(1740–1814)

For different perspectives on sex, click on "Mother and Daughter Discussing Sex."

SEXUAL EXPRESSION is a complex process through which we reveal our sexual selves. Sexual expression involves more than simply sexual behaviors; it involves our feelings as well. "Behavior can never be unemotional," one scholar observes (Blechman, 1990). As human beings, we do not separate feelings from behavior, including sexual behavior. Our sexual behaviors are rich with emotions, ranging from love to anxiety and from desire to antipathy.

To fully understand our sexuality, we need to examine our sexual behaviors *and* the emotions we experience along with them. If we studied sexual activities apart from our emotions, we would distort the meaning of human sexuality. It would make our sexual behaviors appear mechanistic, nothing more than genitals rubbing against each other.

In this chapter, we first discuss sexual attractiveness. Next, we turn to sexual scripts that give form to our sexual drives. Finally, we examine the most common sexual behaviors, both autoerotic, such as fantasies and masturbation, and interpersonal, such as oral-genital sex, sexual intercourse, and anal eroticism. When we discuss sexual behaviors, we cite results from numerous studies to illustrate the prevalence of those behaviors in our society. These results most often represent self-reports of a certain group of people. As discussed in Chapter 2, self-reporting of sexual behavior is not always exact or unbiased. The research data provide only a general idea of what behaviors actually occur and do not indicate how people should express their sexuality or what "normal" behavior is. Sexuality is one of the most individualistic aspects of life; each of us has our own sexual values, needs, and preferences.

● Sexual Attractiveness

Sexual attractiveness is an important component in sexual expression. As we shall see, however, there are few universals in what people from different cultures consider attractive.

A Cross-Cultural Analysis

In a landmark cross-cultural survey, anthropologists Clelland Ford and Frank Beach (1951) discovered that there appear to be only two characteristics that women and men universally consider important in terms of sexual attractiveness: youthfulness and good health. All other aspects may vary significantly from culture to culture. Even though this large survey was conducted a half century ago, subsequent smaller and more-local studies support the importance of youthfulness and good health in sexual attraction, as well as the significance of culture in determining sexual attractiveness. One might ask why youthfulness and health were the only universals identified by Ford and Beach. Why not other body traits, such as a certain facial feature or body type?

Although we may never find an answer, sociobiologists offer a possible (but untestable) explanation. They theorize, as we saw in Chapter 1, that all animals instinctively want to reproduce their own genes. Consequently, both humans and other animals adopt certain reproductive strategies. One of these strategies is choosing a mate capable of reproducing one's offspring. Men prefer women who are young because young women are the most likely to be fertile. Good health is also related to reproductive potential, because healthy women are more likely to be both fertile and capable of rearing their children. Evolutionary psychologist David Buss (1994) notes that our ancestors looked for certain physical characteristics that indicated a woman's health and youthfulness. Buss identifies certain physical features that are cross-culturally associated with beauty: good muscle tone; full lips; clear, smooth skin; lustrous hair; and clear eyes. Our ancestors also looked for behavioral cues such as animated facial expressions; a bouncy, youthful gait; and a high energy level. These observable physical cues to youthfulness and health (and hence to reproductive capacity) constitute the standards of beauty in many cultures.

Vitality and health are important to human females as well. Women prefer men who are slightly older than they are, because an older man is likely to be more stable and mature and to have greater resources to invest in children. Similarly, in the animal kingdom, females choose mates who provide resources, such as food and protection. Among American women, Buss (1994) points out, countless studies indicate that economic security and employment are much more important for women than for men. If you look in the personal ads on Internet dating sites or in any newspaper, you'll find this gender difference readily confirmed. A woman's ad typically reads: "Lively, intelligent woman seeks professional, responsible gentleman for committed relationship." A man's ad typically reads: "Financially secure, fit man looking for attractive woman interested in having a good time. Send photo."

Women also prefer men who are in good health and physically fit so as to be good providers. If a woman chooses someone with hereditary health problems, she risks passing on his poor genes to her children. Furthermore, an unhealthy partner is more likely to die sooner, cutting the woman and her children off from resources. Ford and Beach (1951) found that signs of ill health are universally considered unattractive.

You can't control whom you are attracted to and who is attracted to you.
—Carol Cassell
(1936–)

After people are clothed and fed, then they think about sex.
—K'ung-Fu-tzu (Confucius)
(551–479 B.C.)

What constitutes physical attractiveness may vary among cultures.

Aside from youthfulness and good health, however, Ford and Beach found no universal standards of physical sexual attractiveness. In fact, they noted considerable variation from culture to culture in what parts of the body are considered erotic. In some cultures, the eyes are the key to sexual attractiveness; in others, it is height and weight; and in still others, the size and shape of the genitals matter most. In our culture, female breasts, for example, are considered erotic; in other cultures, they are not.

Cultures that agree on which body parts are erotic may still disagree on what constitutes attractiveness. In terms of female beauty, American culture considers a slim body attractive. But worldwide, Americans are in the minority, for the type of female body most desired cross-culturally is plump. Similarly, Americans prefer slim hips, but in the majority of cultures in Ford and Beach's study, wide hips were most attractive. In our culture, large breasts are ideal, but other cultures prefer small breasts or long and pendulous breasts. In recent years, well-defined pectoral, arm, and abdominal muscles have become part of the ideal male body. Interestingly, a recent study of college undergraduate women rated muscular men as sexier than nonmuscular and very muscular men, but men with moderate muscularity were considered most attractive and more desirable for long-term relationships (Frederick & Haselton, 2007; Jayson, 2007). Participants thought that the more brawny men would be more domineering, volatile, and less committed to their partners, whereas the moderately muscular man would be more sexually exclusive and romantic.

Evolutionary Mating Perspectives

One prominent theoretical explanation for human mating is the **sexual strategies theory** (Buss, 2003; Buss & Schmitt, 1993). An important component of this theory addresses gender differences in short-term and long-term heterosexual relationships from an evolutionary mating perspective. This theory posits that males and females face different adaptive problems in "casual" or short-term mating and long-term, reproductive mating, leading to different strategies or behaviors for solving these problems. A woman may select a partner who offers immediate resources, such as food or money, for short-term mating, whereas for long-term mating, more substantial resources are important. For males, a sexually available female may be chosen for a short-term liaison, but this type of woman would be avoided when selecting a long-term mate (Hyde & DeLamater, 2008).

David Geary and colleagues (2004) reviewed the evolutionary theory and empirical research on mating and identified the potential costs and benefits of short-term and long-term sexual relationships in both men and women (see Table 9.1). The most fundamental difference is that women are predicted to be most selective in mate choices for both short-term and long-term relationships given the costs of reproduction. Even in selecting a short-term mate, a woman may be more choosy than a man because she is evaluating him as a potential long-term mate. But, in general, women are predicted to avoid short-term relationships given that the

To see what evolutionary psychology says about mate choices, click on "Evolutionary Psychology and Mate Selection."

Table 9.1 ●	Examples of Costs and Benefits of Short-Term and Long-Term Sexual Relationships	
Costs	**Benefits**
Women's short-term mating	
Risk of STD	Some resources from mate
Risk of pregnancy	Good genes from mate
Reduced value as a long-term mate	
Women's long-term mating	
Restricted sexual opportunity	Significant resources from mate
Sexual obligation to mate	Paternal investment
Men's short-term mating	
Risk of STD	Potential to reproduce
Some resource investment	No parental investment[a]
Men's long-term mating	
Restricted sexual opportunity	Increased reproductive certainty
Heavy parental investment	Higher quality children
Heavy relationship investment	Sexual and social companionship

Note: STD = sexually transmitted disease.
[a]Low paternal investment may result in lower quality children, but this is not a cost to the man because it does not lower his ability to invest in other relationships.
SOURCE: From Geary, D. C., Vigil, J., & Byrd-Craven, J. (2004). Evolution of human mate choice. *Journal of Sex Research, 41*(1), 29. Reprinted by permission of The Society for the Scientific Study of Sexuality.

think
about it

"Hooking Up" Among College Students

"**H**ooking up," a term used by some college students to describe being sexual with others, has replaced traditional dating rituals—in fact, many have never gone out on a date—and is as ambiguous as the term "having sex." It may mean anything from kissing to engaging in sexual intercourse. After several weeks of intimacy with another person, some college students aren't sure if they are in a relationship or simply "hooking up." For many college-age students, marriage no longer comes on the heels of graduation. Hooking up for "casual sex" allows them to put off serious romance yet be sexual with another person and free to pursue personal and economic goals.

Although hooking up may sound like a good idea with few problems, casual sex itself may not be as simple as one might think. Sociologist Kathleen Bogle (2008), who studied hooking up by interviewing undergraduates and alumni of two colleges, found that this form of casual sex gives both men and women more sexual options, although arguably it may favor men's interest in "playing the field" but not support women's interest in hooking up evolving into a relationship. Bogle's study revealed that there are no clear rules for hooking up for women, meaning that they must learn as they go along, which limits their options in seeking sexual relationships.

Another study of college students also found that casual sex is not without "strings attached" (Grello, Welsh, & Harper, 2006). Just over 400 female and male undergraduate students (limited to only those reporting other-gender partners) at a large public university in the southeastern United States filled out a questionnaire designed to identify factors and circumstances associated with being sexual with a casual sex partner. More than one half of the sexually experienced students reported that they had engaged in sex with partners, usually friends, with whom they were not involved romantically. More males than females (52% vs. 36%) reported engaging in casual sex.

Here are the study's major findings:

- Most students indicated that they knew that their casual sex encounters were not going to develop into romantic relationships.
- No matter whether the student was female or male, the casual sex often occurred with drug and alcohol use. Most students reported that they met most of their recent casual sex partners in places that promote or condone alcohol and drug use, such as bars and parties.
- Depressive symptoms were associated with casual sex, but more so for the female students.
- When casual sex occurred with a friend, the students reported that they engaged in more affectionate sexual

behaviors (kissing, hugging, holding hands, massage) and genital sexual behaviors (intimate touching, oral sex, and intercourse) than with partners who were acquaintances or strangers.

- Students reporting casual sex reported having begun sex with others at earlier ages than those not reporting casual sex. If their first sexual encounter was not with a romantic partner, they were more likely to report more recent casual sexual partners.
- Students reporting casual sex also indicated having had more sexual partners than those who engaged in sex only with romantic partners.

In discussing the results, Grello and colleagues noted that "an important finding in this study is that sexual behavior in a romantic context was not associated with symptoms of depression." They continue by stating that college students may have different reasons for engaging in sexual behavior with a casual partner and that the casual sex may be a symptom of pathology for some or a way to promote status for others. The researchers recommend that students need education concerning the emotional and physical risks of casual sex to help them make better decisions about sexual behavior with others. They also note that informing students about the relationship between casual sex and drug and alcohol use needs particular emphasis, hopefully to prepare them to be aware of environments such as parties and bars where substances are involved if they want to avoid casual sex.

Think Critically

- If you know of people who have hooked up, have they talked about it positively or negatively?
- Have you ever engaged in sexual behavior with a casual sex partner? If so, did you have similar experiences as found in the research studies reported here?
- Is casual sex more socially acceptable for males than females?
- Why do you think depression was associated more with casual sex for the females than for the males in the study by Grello and colleagues reported here?

SOURCES: Bogle, K. A. (2008). *Hooking up: Sex, dating, and relationships on campus.* New York: New York University Press; Grello, C. M., Welsh, D. P., & Harper, M. S. (2006). No strings attached: The nature of casual sex in college students. *Journal of Sex Research, 43,* 255–267.

possible costs outweigh the possible benefits. In contrast, the opposite is evident for men given that the potential benefits outweigh the potential costs. In choosing a short-term partner, the man may want to minimize commitment. Once a man commits to a long-term relationship, the costs increase and the level of choosiness is also predicted to increase. In their research on short-term sexual relationships, Todd Shackelford and colleagues (2004) found women prefer short-term partners who are not involved in other relationships to present a greater potential as a long-term partner and that men were more likely to pursue short-term, or casual, sexual relationships than women. (To find out the results of studies on casual sex among college students, see the "Think About It" box on the previous page.)

Evolutionary biologists have hypothesized that men's short-term mating strategy is rooted in the desire for sexual variety, and a massive cross-cultural study of 16,288 people across 10 major world regions seems to demonstrate this (Schmitt, 2003). This study on whether the sexes differ in the desire for sexual variety found strong and conclusive differences that appear to be universal across the world regions: Men possess more desire than women for a variety of sexual partners and were more likely to seek short-term relationships than women. This was true regardless of the participant's relationship status or sexual orientation. The researchers concluded that these findings confirm that men's short-term sexual strategy is based on the desire for numerous partners. This behavior, from an evolutionary perspective, would maximize reproductive success. Interestingly, the study also found that men required less time to elapse than women before consenting to intercourse.

A study of undergraduate college students examined gender differences in an imagined desired number of sex partners during the next year (Fenigstein & Preston, 2007). In this imaginary scenario, the sex would be either safe from STIs and pregnancy or dangerous and relatively unavailable. The study found that over the next year, the majority of women desired one sex partner. In contrast, the men indicated a desire for numerous partners, especially when they imagined less negative sexual concerns. The researchers concluded that the results can be explained by the sexual strategies theory, discussed earlier in this section, and social role theory (Eagly, 1987), which contends that men are socialized toward the pleasurable components of sexual interaction and that women are more concerned with the relational components of sex.

A promiscuous person is someone who is getting more sex than you are.
—Victor Lownes
(1928–)

Views of College Students

Although attractiveness is important, looks certainly aren't everything. In a study spanning an amazing nearly six decades, undergraduate male and female college students rated the importance of 18 mate characteristics, including "good looks" (Buss, Shackelford, Kirkpatrick, & Larsen, 2001). Ratings were obtained using a questionnaire at one college in 1939 and 1956, four colleges in 1967 and 1977, and three colleges in 1996 in various locations across the United States. This longitudinal comparison allowed the researchers to determine which important characteristics in a mate had changed and if there were gender differences in ratings during the half century of dramatic cultural changes. One cultural change the researchers noted was the proliferation of visual images of physically attractive models and actors via television, movies, and the Internet. The researchers explain: "From an evolutionary psychological perspective, such images may 'trick' our evolved mating mechanisms, deluding us into believing that we are surrounded by hundreds of attractive partners, as well as hundreds of potential intrasexual

Sex is one of the nine reasons for reincarnation. . . . The other eight are unimportant.
—Henry Miller
(1891–1980)

• FIGURE 9.1

Rank Ordering of Mate Characteristics by College Undergraduates Across Six Decades, by Gender. (*Source:* Adapted from Buss, Shackelford, Kirkpatrick, & Larsen, 2001.)

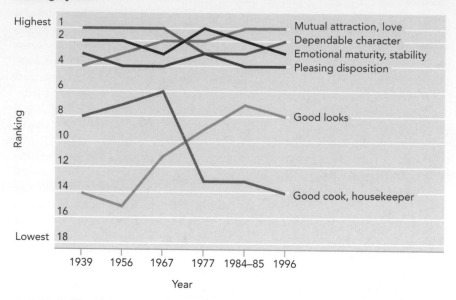

Ranking by Men

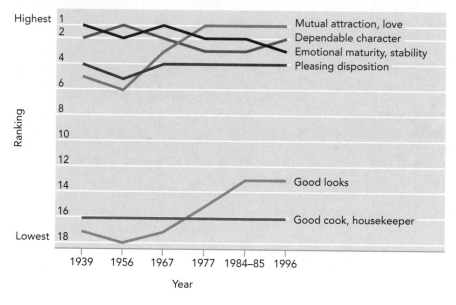

Ranking by Women

competitors." They ask whether this profusion of visual images in the twentieth century elevated the ranking of physical attractiveness relative to other traits.

Several patterns were identified across the 57-year span (see Figure 9.1). Mutual attraction and love, dependable character, emotional maturity and stability, and pleasing disposition were rated highly at all times, suggesting that physical attractiveness is not the most important trait in mate selection. However, over the years, a large shift occurred in the importance of good looks for both genders. For men, it jumped from 14th in 1939 to 8th in 1996; for women, it increased from 17th in 1939 to 13th in 1996. The surge of media images of attractive people may have contributed to this shift. Certainly, the popularity of cosmetics, diet, cosmetic surgery, exercise programs, and muscle-enhancing products reflects this increasing value of physical attractiveness.

Interestingly, the researchers note that the order of importance for both the male and female college students converged during the five decades, with the ordering showing maximum similarity in 1996. Also, domestic skills plummeted in importance for male students over the decades.

Some Internet matchmaking services use information similar to the 18 mate characteristics of the study by Buss and colleagues (2001) discussed in this section to match persons wanting to find partners. These services believe that finding "lasting love" is based on compatibility and shared interests. While they have successfully matched plenty of people, Carol Cassell, a nationally recognized leader in human sexuality, presents an interesting caveat to this type of search for compatibility. In her book *Put Passion First* (2008), Cassell states that, although compatibility is certainly important in long-term relationships, it is not the only or most valuable component. She contends that "if you have a comfortable, compatible love without sexual sparks, you don't have enough." She continues by noting that matchmaking that does not account for sexual chemistry rarely ignites fire in a couple.

Women's Body Ratios

Adam Cohen and Hara Tannenbaum (2001) investigated physical attraction among nonheterosexual women by asking samples of lesbian and bisexual women to rate the figures of women according to weight (slender or heavy), waist-to-hip ratio (0.7 or 1.0), and breast size (small or large). The researchers found that the subjects preferred a heavy figure with the 0.7 waist-to-hip ratio and large breasts, rather than the low waist-to-hip ratio, large breasts, and slender figure preferred by most heterosexual females and males. In interpreting the results, the researchers note that lesbian women are heavier on average than heterosexual women and are more comfortable with their body weight, and that their preference for heavy body weight may be a rejection of an inappropriate societal fixation on thinness.

> " A pair of powerful spectacles has sometimes sufficed to cure a person in love.
>
> —Friedrich Nietzsche (1844–1900)

Click on "Waist-to-Hip Ratio" to hear a discussion of a current cultural value of sexual attractiveness.

Sexual Desire

Desire can exist separately from overtly physical sexual expression. As discussed in Chapter 3, desire is the psychobiological component that motivates sexual behavior. But little scientific research exists on sexual desire. One of the most important reasons researchers have avoided studying it is that desire is difficult to define and quantify.

Sexual desire is affected by physical, emotional, and sexual relationship issues, as discussed throughout this book. Life events can have both positive and negative impacts on sexual desire. (See Chapter 14 for a discussion of sexual desire discrepancies within a couple.) Two factors affecting sexual desire are **erotophilia** and erotophobia. Erotophilia is a positive emotional response to sexuality, and **erotophobia** is a negative emotional response to sexuality. Researchers have hypothesized that where someone falls on the erotophilic/erotophobic continuum strongly influences his or her overt sexual behavior (Fisher, 1986, 1998). In contrast to erotophobic individuals, for example, erotophilic men and women accept and enjoy their sexuality, experience less guilt about engaging in sex, seek out sexual situations, engage in more autoerotic and interpersonal sexual activities, enjoy talking about sex, and are more likely to engage in certain sexual health practices, such as obtaining and using contraception. Furthermore, erotophilic people are more likely to have positive sexual attitudes, to engage in more involved

> " The degree and kind of a person's sexuality reaches up into the ultimate pinnacle of his spirit.
>
> —Friedrich Nietzsche (1844–1900)

sexual fantasies, to be less homophobic, and to have seen more erotica than erotophobic people. A person's emotional response to sex is also linked to how she or he evaluates other aspects of sex. Erotophilic individuals, for example, tend to evaluate sexually explicit material more positively.

Erotophilic and erotophobic traits are not fixed. Positive experiences can alter erotophobic responses over time. In fact, some therapy programs work on the assumption that consistent positive behaviors, such as loving, affirming, caring, touching, and communicating, can do much to diminish sexual fears and anxieties. Positive sexual experiences can help dissolve much of the anxiety that underlies erotophobia.

● Sexual Scripts

Click on "The Dance of Life" for a discussion of why men and women may have varying sexual appetites.

As you will recall from Chapter 5, gender roles have a significant impact on how we behave sexually, for sexual behaviors and feelings depend more on learning than on biological drives. Our sexual drives can be molded into almost any form. What is "natural" is what society says is natural; there is very little spontaneous, unlearned behavior. Sexual behavior, like all other forms of social behavior (such as courtship, classroom behavior, and sports), relies on scripts.

As you will also recall from Chapter 5, scripts are like plans that organize and give direction to our behavior. The **sexual scripts** we receive strongly influence our sexual activities as men and women in our culture. Our sexual scripts have several distinct components:

- *Cultural.* The cultural component provides the general pattern that sexual behaviors are expected to take. Our cultural script, for example, emphasizes heterosexuality, gives primacy to sexual intercourse, and discourages masturbation.

- *Intrapersonal.* The intrapersonal component deals with the internal and physiological states that lead to, accompany, or identify sexual arousal, such as a pounding heart and an erection or vaginal lubrication.

- *Interpersonal.* The interpersonal component involves the shared conventions and signals that enable two people to engage in sexual behaviors, such as body language, words, and erotic touching.

Cultural Scripting

Many are saved from sin by being inept at it.

—Mignon McLaughlin
(1913–1983)

Our culture sets the general contours of our sexual scripts. It tells us which behaviors are acceptable ("moral" or "normal") and which are unacceptable ("immoral" or "abnormal"). For example, a norm may have a sequence of sexual events consisting of kissing, genital caressing, and sexual intercourse. Imagine a scenario in which two people from different cultures try to initiate a sexual encounter. One person follows the script described above, while the one from a different culture follows a sequence beginning with sexual intercourse, moving to genital caressing, and ending with passionate kissing. At least initially, such a couple might experience frustration and confusion as one partner tries to initiate the sexual encounter with kissing and the other with sexual intercourse.

Yet this kind of confusion occurs fairly often because there is not necessarily a direct correlation between what our culture calls erotic and what any particular individual calls erotic. Culture sets the general pattern, but there is too much diversity in terms of individual personality, socioeconomic status, and ethnicity for everybody to have exactly the same erotic script. Thus, sexual scripts can be highly ambiguous and varied.

We may believe that everyone shares our own particular script, projecting our experiences onto others and assuming that they share our erotic definitions of objects, gestures, and situations. But often, they initially do not. Our partner may have come from a different socioeconomic or ethnic group or religious background and may have had different learning experiences about sexuality. Each of us has to learn the other's sexual script and be able to complement and adjust to it. If our scripts are to be integrated, we must make our needs known through open and honest communication involving words, gestures, and movements. This is the reason many people view their first intercourse as something of a comedy or tragedy—or perhaps a little of both.

In our society, passionate kissing is part of the cultural script for sexual interactions.

Intrapersonal Scripting

On the intrapersonal level, sexual scripts enable people to give meaning to their physiological responses. The meaning depends largely on the situation. An erection, for example, does not always mean sexual excitement. Young boys sometimes have erections when they are frightened, anxious, or worried. Upon awakening in the morning, men may experience erections that are unaccompanied by arousal. Adolescent girls sometimes experience sexual arousal without knowing what these sensations mean. They report them as funny, weird kinds of feelings, or as anxiety, fear, or an upset stomach. The sensations are not linked to a sexual script until the girl becomes older and her physiological states acquire a definite erotic meaning.

Intrapersonal scripts provide a sequence of body movements by acting as mechanisms that activate biological events and release tension. We learn, for example, that we may create an orgasm by manipulating the penis or clitoris during masturbation.

Interpersonal Scripting

The interpersonal level is the area of shared conventions, which make sexual activities possible. Very little of our public life is sexual. Yet there are signs and gestures—verbal and nonverbal—that define encounters as sexual. We make our sexual motives clear by the looks we exchange, the tone of our voices, the movements of our bodies, and other culturally shared phenomena. A bedroom or a hotel room, for example, is a potentially erotic location; a classroom or an office may not be. The movements we use in arousing ourselves or others are erotic activators. Within a culture, there are normative scripts leading to intimate sexual behavior.

People with little sexual experience, especially young adolescents, are often unfamiliar with sexual scripts. What do they do after kissing? Do they embrace? Caress above the waist? Below? Eventually, they learn a comfortable sequence based on cultural inputs and personal and partner preferences. For gay men and lesbian women, learning the sexual script is more difficult because it is socially stigmatized. The sexual script is also related to age. Older children and young adolescents often limit their scripts to kissing, holding hands, and embracing, and they may feel completely satisfied. Kissing for them may be as exciting as intercourse for more experienced people. When the range of their scripts increases, they lose some of the sexual intensity of the earlier stages.

The concept of sexual scripts has been used often in research to further explain sexual expression among individuals and couples. To illustrate with a study pertinent to college students, Columbia University researchers Sheri Dworkin and Lucia O'Sullivan (2005) note that research on men's sexuality has tended to disregard looking at sexual scripts (e.g., aggressive initiators and orchestrators of sexual activity) or culturally dominant scripts. By interviewing 32 college-age men, they found that indeed these men wished to share initiation of sex, enjoyed being a desired sex object, and wanted egalitarian scripts. Dworkin and O'Sullivan conclude that these findings may "mean shifts in broader gender relations towards more companionate norms, a stretching of traditional scripts, a desire for egalitarian relationships, or social structural shifts in women's or men's power that may make sexual scripts more flexible."

● Autoeroticism

Autoeroticism consists of sexual activities that involve only the self. Autoeroticism is an *intrapersonal* activity rather than an *interpersonal* one. It includes sexual fantasies, erotic dreams, and self-**masturbation** (stimulating one's genitals for pleasure). A universal phenomenon in one form or another (Ford & Beach, 1951), autoeroticism is one of our earliest expressions of sexual stirrings. It is also one that traditionally has been condemned in our society. (Figure 9.2 shows one device created to curb masturbation.) By condemning it, however, our culture sets the stage for the development of deeply negative and inhibitory attitudes toward sexuality.

Many people purchase or seek out materials and activities for their autoerotic behaviors. In the National Health and Social Life Survey (NHSLS), researchers found that 41% of men and 16% of women had engaged in an autoerotic activity in the past year. The most common activities for men were viewing X-rated videos (23%) and visiting clubs with nude or seminude dancers (22%). The most common activity among women was also viewing videos (11%), followed by visiting clubs and viewing sexually explicit books or magazines (4% each). Sixteen percent of men reported purchasing explicit books or magazines. Other activities included using vibrators and other sex toys and calling sex phone lines (Laumann, Gagnon, Michael, & Michaels, 1994).

Do people participate in autoerotic activities because they do not have a sex partner? The same survey found the opposite to be true (Laumann et al., 1994):

> Those who engage in relatively little autoerotic activity are less likely to prefer a wider range of sexual techniques, are less likely to have a partner, and if they have a partner, are less likely to have sex frequently or engage in oral or anal sex. Similarly, individuals who engage in different kinds of autoerotic activity more often find a wider range of practices appealing and are more likely to have had at least one partner with

● **FIGURE 9.2**

Devices Designed to Curb Masturbation. Because of the widespread belief in the nineteenth century that masturbation was harmful, various devices were introduced to prevent the behavior. (*Sources:* Crooks & Baur, 2005; Rathus, Nevid, & Fichner-Rathus, 2002.)

whom they have sex frequently. Individuals who frequently think about sex, masturbate, and have used some type of pornography/erotica within the last year are much more likely to report enacting more elaborate interpersonal sexual scripts.

Sexual Fantasies and Dreams

Men and women, but especially men, think about sex often. According to the NHSLS, 54% of men and 19% of women think about sex at least once a day; 43% of men and 67% of women think about sex a few times per week or per month (Laumann et al., 1994). According to sex researchers Harold Leitenberg and Kris Henning (1995), about 95% of men and women say that they have had sexual fantasies in one context or another. And a *Details* magazine study of more than 1,700 college students reported that 94% of men and 76% of women think about sex at least once a day (Elliott & Brantley, 1997).

Erotic fantasy is probably the most universal of all sexual behaviors. Nearly everyone has experienced such fantasies, but because they touch on feelings or desires considered personally or socially unacceptable, they are not widely discussed. Furthermore, many people have "forbidden" sexual fantasies that they never act on.

Whether occurring spontaneously or resulting from outside stimuli, fantasies are part of the body's regular healthy functioning. Research indicates that sexual fantasies are related to sexual drives: the higher the sexual drive, the higher the frequency of sexual fantasies and level of satisfaction in one's sex life (Leitenberg & Henning, 1995). Fantasies help create an equilibrium between our environment and our inner selves, as we seek a balance between the two. We use them to enhance our masturbatory experiences, as well as oral-genital sex, sexual intercourse, and other interpersonal experiences.

In their review of the research on sexual fantasies, Leitenberg and Henning (1995) found notable differences in the fantasies of men and women, reflecting the different gender-role stereotypes and sexual scripts taught to men and women:

- Men's fantasies are more active and focus more on women's bodies and on what they want to do with them, whereas women's fantasies are more passive and focus more on men's interest in their bodies.

- Men's sexual fantasies focus more on explicit sexual behaviors, nude bodies, and physical gratification, whereas women use more emotional content and romance in their sexual fantasies.

- Men are more likely to fantasize about multiple partners and group sex than are women.

- Men are more likely to have dominance fantasies, whereas women are more likely to have submission fantasies.

Relative to types of fantasies based on sexual orientation, Leitenberg and Henning (1995) found that the content of sexual fantasies for gay men and lesbian women tends to be the same as for their heterosexual counterparts, except that homosexuals imagine same-sex partners and heterosexuals imagine other-sex partners.

In another study, Thomas Hicks and Harold Leitenberg (2001) found gender differences in the proportion of sexual fantasies that involved someone other than a current partner (extradyadic fantasies). In a sample of 349 university students and employees in heterosexual relationships, 98% of men and 80% of women reported having extradyadic fantasies in the past 2 months.

Grant yourself and your lover freedom of fantasy. Sexual fantasies are normal, healthy and sex enhancing.

—Michael Castleman
(1950–)

Another study that examined gender differences in sexual fantasies found that, among adults aged 21–45, men mentioned sexual desire and pleasure of both themselves and their partners, but women tended to mention just their own desire and pleasure (Zurbriggen & Yost, 2004). The researchers of the study concluded that "pleasure and desire may serve different purposes in men's and women's fantasies, with men using fantasy to imagine female partners who are clearly aroused and easily pleased and women using fantasy to focus on their own desire and pleasure."

The Function of Sexual Fantasies Sexual fantasies have a number of important functions. First, they help direct and define our erotic goals. They take our generalized sexual drives and give them concrete images and specific content. We fantasize about certain types of men or women and reinforce our attraction through fantasy involvement. Unfortunately, our fantasy model may be unreasonable or unattainable, which is one of the pitfalls of fantasy; we can imagine perfection, but we rarely find it in real life.

Second, sexual fantasies allow us to plan for or anticipate situations that may arise. They provide a form of rehearsal, allowing us to practice in our minds how to act in various situations. Our fantasies of what *might* take place on a date, after a party, or in bed with our partner serve as a form of preparation.

Third, sexual fantasies provide escape from a dull or oppressive environment. Routine or repetitive labor often gives rise to fantasies as a way of coping with boredom.

Fourth, even if our sex lives are satisfactory, we may indulge in sexual fantasies to bring novelty and excitement into the relationship. Fantasy offers a safe outlet for sexual curiosity. One study found that some women are capable of experiencing orgasm solely through fantasy (Whipple, Ogden, & Komisaruk, 1992).

Fifth, sexual fantasies have an expressive function in somewhat the same manner that dreams do. Our sexual fantasies may offer a clue to our current interests, pleasures, anxieties, fears, or problems. Because fantasies use only a few details from the stream of reality, what we select is significant, expressing feelings that often lie beneath the surface of our consciousness (Sue, 1979). Repeated fantasies of extradyadic relationships, for example, may signify deep dissatisfaction with a marriage, whereas mental images centering around erectile difficulties may represent fears about sexuality or a particular relationship.

Fantasies During Sexual Expression A sizable number of people fantasize during sex. The fantasies are usually a continuation of daydreams or masturbatory fantasies, transforming one's partner into a famous, attractive Hollywood star, for example. Couples often believe that they should be totally focused on each other during sex and not have any thoughts about others, particularly sexual thoughts. However, during the passion of sex, many people have thoughts not only about their partner but also about others such as past lovers, acquaintances, and movie stars. Many people feel guilty about such thoughts, feeling that they are being "mentally unfaithful" to their partner. Yet, sex therapists consider fantasies of other lovers to be quite normal and certainly typical.

Women who fantasize about being forced into sexual activity or about being victimized do not necessarily want this to actually occur. Rather, these women tend to be more interested in a variety of sexual activities and to be more sexually experienced than women who don't have these fantasies.

Erotic Dreams   Almost all of the men and two thirds of the women in Alfred Kinsey's studies reported having had overtly erotic or sexual dreams (Kinsey, Pomeroy, & Martin, 1948; Kinsey, Pomeroy, Martin, & Gebhard, 1953). Sexual images in dreams are frequently very intense. Although people tend to feel responsible for their fantasies, which occur when they are awake, they are usually less troubled by sexual dreams.

Overtly sexual dreams are not necessarily exciting, although dreams that are apparently nonsexual may cause arousal. It is not unusual for individuals to awaken in the middle of the night and notice an erection or vaginal lubrication or to find their bodies moving as if they were making love. They may also experience nocturnal orgasm (or emission). About 2–3% of women's total orgasms may be nocturnal, whereas for men the number may be around 8% (Kinsey et al., 1948, 1953). About 50% of the men interviewed by Kinsey had more than five nocturnal orgasms a year; less than 10% of the women experienced them that frequently.

Dreams almost always accompany nocturnal orgasm. The dreamer may awaken, and men usually ejaculate. Although the dream content may not be overtly sexual, it is always accompanied by sensual sensations. Erotic dreams run the gamut of sexual possibilities: other-sex, same-sex, or autoerotic behavior; incestuous, dominant and submissive, bestial, or fetishistic behavior. Women seem to feel less guilty or fearful about nocturnal orgasms than men do, accepting them more easily as pleasurable experiences.

Masturbation

People report that they masturbate for several reasons: for relaxation, for relief of sexual tension, because a partner is not available or does not want sex, for physical pleasure, as an aid to falling asleep, and as a means to avoid STIs (Laumann et al., 1994). They may masturbate during particular periods or throughout their entire lives. For older adults, often after the loss of their

MASTURBATION, n. An extremely disgusting act performed on a regular basis by everyone else.

—Robert Tefton

Female masturbation: Many people "discover" their sexual potential through masturbation. Sometimes, women learn to be orgasmic through masturbation and then bring this ability to their relationships.

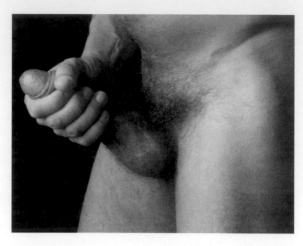

Male masturbation: Masturbation is an important form of sexual behavior in which individuals explore their erotic capacities and bring pleasure to themselves.

partners, masturbation regains much of the primacy of their earlier years and is often the most common sexual activity.

Masturbation is an important means of learning about our bodies. Through masturbation, children and adolescents learn what is sexually pleasing, how to move their bodies, and what their natural rhythms are. The activity has no harmful physical effects. Although masturbation often decreases when individuals are regularly sexual with another person, it is not necessarily a temporary substitute for sexual intercourse but rather is a legitimate form of sexual activity in its own right. Sex therapists may encourage clients to masturbate as a means of overcoming specific sexual problems and discovering their personal sexual potential. Masturbation, whether practiced alone or mutually with a partner (see Figure 9.3), is also a form of safer sex. (See Chapter 6 for more information about masturbation and children and adolescents.)

Masturbation is an intrinsically and seriously disordered act.

—Vatican Declaration on Sexual Ethics

● **FIGURE 9.3**

Mutual Masturbation. Many couples enjoy mutual masturbation, one form of safer sex.

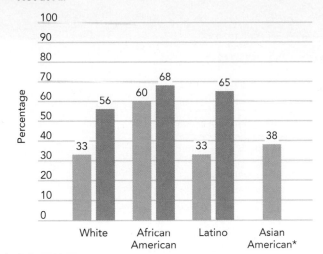

Not at All

Female data not available.

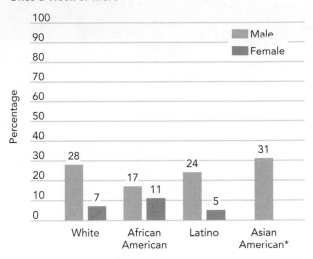

Once a Week or More

Male
Female

● **FIGURE 9.4**

Frequency of Masturbation by Ethnicity in One Year. (*Source:* Adapted from Laumann et al., 1994.)

> Masturbation is the primary sexual activity of [human] kind. In the nineteenth century it was a disease; in the twentieth, it's a cure.
>
> —Thomas Szasz (1920–)

Ethnicity and Masturbation   Behavior and attitudes toward masturbation vary along ethnic lines (see Figure 9.4). For example, data from a nationally representative sample of the British population aged 16 to 44 years found that both men and women who reported their ethnicity as White were significantly more likely to report masturbation in the past 4 weeks than those of other ethnic groups (Gerressu, Mercer, Graham, Wellings, & Johnson, 2008). Other studies also show that Whites are quite accepting of masturbation, for example, whereas African Americans are less so. The differences can be explained culturally. Because Whites tend to begin coital activities later than Blacks, most Whites regard masturbation as an acceptable alternative to sexual intercourse. Much of Black culture, in contrast, accepts sexual intercourse at an earlier age. In this context, Blacks may view masturbation as a sign of personal and sexual inadequacy. As a result, many Blacks tend to view sexual intercourse as normal and masturbation as deviant (Cortese, 1989; Kinsey et al., 1948; Wilson, 1986). However, masturbation is becoming more accepted within the African American community as a legitimate sexual activity.

Latinos, like African Americans, are more conservative than Anglos in their attitudes toward masturbation (Cortese, 1989; Padilla & O'Grady, 1987). For many, masturbation is not considered an acceptable sexual option, particularly for women. In part, this is because of the cultural emphasis on sexual intercourse and the influence of Catholicism, which regards masturbation as sinful. As with other forms of sexual behavior, however, acceptance becomes more likely as Latinos become more assimilated.

Even though masturbation is becoming more accepted in our culture, many people still have negative feelings about it. A large-scale survey (Laumann et al., 1994) reported that nearly an equal percentage—about 50%—of adult White and Latino males and females felt guilty after masturbating. For Blacks, about 50% of the males felt guilty afterward, but only about 36% of the females felt guilty. (To assess your attitude toward masturbation, take the questionnaire in the "Practically Speaking" box beginning on the next page.)

Assessing Your Attitude Toward Masturbation

Masturbation guilt is a learned script in which the negative affects of guilt, disgust, shame, and fear are related to masturbation (Abramson & Mosher, 1975). As discussed in this chapter, feelings of shame and guilt have long been associated with masturbation, and a more positive attitude has emerged only recently. Still, many people continue to feel guilty about their own masturbatory activity. Take this inventory to determine how much you have been affected by negative messages about masturbation.

Directions

Indicate how true each of the following statements is for you, on a scale from "Not at all true" to "Very true," by circling the appropriate number.

	Not at all true				Very true
1. People masturbate to escape feelings of tension and anxiety.	1	2	3	4	5
2. People who masturbate will not enjoy sexual intercourse as much as those who refrain from masturbation.	1	2	3	4	5
3. Masturbation is a private matter which neither harms nor concerns anyone else.	1	2	3	4	5
4. Masturbation is a sin against yourself.	1	2	3	4	5
5. Masturbation in childhood can help a person develop a natural, healthy attitude toward sex.	1	2	3	4	5
6. Masturbation in an adult is juvenile and immature.	1	2	3	4	5
7. Masturbation can lead to deviant sexual behavior.	1	2	3	4	5
8. Excessive masturbation is physically impossible, so it is needless to worry.	1	2	3	4	5
9. If you enjoy masturbating too much, you may never learn to relate to a sex partner.	1	2	3	4	5
10. After masturbating, a person feels degraded.	1	2	3	4	5
11. Experience with masturbation can potentially help a woman become orgasmic for sexual intercourse.	1	2	3	4	5
12. I feel guilt about masturbating.	1	2	3	4	5
13. Masturbation can be a "friend in need" when there is no "friend indeed."	1	2	3	4	5
14. Masturbation can provide an outlet for sex fantasies without harming anyone else or endangering oneself.	1	2	3	4	5

> *Masturbation! The amazing availability of it!*
>
> —James Joyce
> (1882–1941)

Prevalence of Masturbation   Kinsey and his colleagues (1953) reported that 92% of the men and 58% of the women they interviewed said they had masturbated. Today, there appears to be a slight increase in both incidence and frequency. Nevertheless, gender differences continue to be significant. A *Details* magazine survey reported that 50% of college males and 31% of college females reported masturbating at least two or three times a week (Elliott & Brantley, 1997). Another study of college undergraduates (78 men, 145 women) found that almost all of the men (98%) and the majority of women (64%) reported that they had masturbated in the past. Both indicated frequent masturbation: men averaging 36 times and women 14 times in the past 3 months. The study also examined factors that would predict frequent masturbation. For the college men, higher frequency of masturbation occurred in men who believed that their peers masturbated frequently. And men who believed that masturbation was pleasurable also reported more frequent masturbation. For women, masturbation frequency was most associated with perceived pleasure and somewhat with the frequency of intercourse. The researchers concluded that, for this sample, perceived social norms,

15. Excessive masturbation can lead to problems with erections in men and women not being able to have an orgasm. 1 2 3 4 5

16. Masturbation is an escape mechanism which prevents a person from developing a mature sexual outlook. 1 2 3 4 5

17. Masturbation can provide harmless relief from sexual tension. 1 2 3 4 5

18. Playing with your own genitals is disgusting. 1 2 3 4 5

19. Excessive masturbation is associated with neurosis, depression, and behavioral problems. 1 2 3 4 5

20. Any masturbation is too much. 1 2 3 4 5

21. Masturbation is a compulsive, addictive habit which once begun is almost impossible to stop. 1 2 3 4 5

22. Masturbation is fun. 1 2 3 4 5

23. When I masturbate, I am disgusted with myself. 1 2 3 4 5

24. A pattern of frequent masturbation is associated with introversion and withdrawal from social contacts. 1 2 3 4 5

25. I would be ashamed to admit publicly that I have masturbated. 1 2 3 4 5

26. Excessive masturbation leads to mental dullness and fatigue. 1 2 3 4 5

27. Masturbation is a normal sexual outlet. 1 2 3 4 5

28. Masturbation is caused by an excessive preoccupation with thoughts about sex. 1 2 3 4 5

29. Masturbation can teach you to enjoy the sensuousness of your own body. 1 2 3 4 5

30. After I masturbate, I am disgusted with myself for losing control of my body. 1 2 3 4 5

Scoring

To obtain an index of masturbation guilt, sum the circled numbers to yield a score from 30 to 150. Before summing, reverse the scoring for these ten items: 3, 5, 8, 11, 13, 14, 17, 22, 27. That is, a 1 would be converted to a 5, a 2 to a 4, a 4 to a 2, and 5 to a 1. The lower your score, the lower your guilt about and negative attitude toward masturbation.

SOURCE: Adapted from Abramson, P. R., & Mosher, D. L. (1975). The development of a measure of negative attitudes toward masturbation. *Journal of Consulting and Clinical Psychology, 43,* 485–490. (Table 1, p. 487). Copyright © 1975 by the American Psychological Association. Adapted with permission. No further reproduction or distribution is permitted without written permission from the American Psychological Association.

perceived pleasure, and sexual behaviors helped explain and understand masturbation among college students (Pinkerton, Bogart, Cecil, & Abramson, 2002).

Masturbatory behavior is influenced by education, ethnicity, religion, and age, with education a particularly strong factor. The more educated one becomes, the more frequently he or she masturbates. The British study of masturbation among the general population found that masturbation frequency was greater for both men and women with higher levels of education, in higher social classes, and at younger ages (Gerressu et al., 2008).

Masturbation in Adulthood Masturbation continues after adolescence, although the frequency often declines among men and increases among women.

Women and Masturbation One way in which women become familiar with their own sexual responsiveness is through masturbation. According to the National Health and Social Life Survey (NHSLS), 42% of women surveyed had masturbated in the preceding year (Laumann et al., 1994). The British study of masturbation among the general population found that 37% of the women reported masturbating in the past 4 weeks. Masturbation was more common among those who reported more frequent vaginal intercourse in the past 4 weeks, who had the greater repertoire of sexual behaviors such as oral and anal sex, who had the most sexual partners in the past year, who reported same-sex partners, and who were less religiously devout (Gerressu et al., 2008). Women who masturbate appear to hold more positive sexual attitudes and are more likely to be orgasmic than those who don't (Kelly, Strassberg, & Kircher, 1990; Schnarch, 2002). Among women who experience multiple orgasms, about one fifth do so through masturbation (Darling, Davidson, & Jennings, 1991). Although the majority of women believe that orgasms experienced through masturbation differ from those experienced in sexual intercourse, they feel the same levels of sexual satisfaction (Davidson & Darling, 1986).

Though no two women masturbate in exactly the same manner, a number of common methods are used to achieve orgasm. Most involve some type of clitoral stimulation, by using the fingers, rubbing against an object, or using a vibrator. The rubbing or stimulation tends to increase just prior to orgasm and to continue during orgasm.

Because the glans clitoris is often too sensitive for prolonged direct stimulation, women tend to stroke gently on the shaft of the clitoris. Another common method, which exerts less direct pressure on the clitoris, is to stroke the mons areas or the minor lips. Individual preferences play a key role in what method is chosen, how rigorous the stimulation is, how often masturbation occurs, and whether it is accompanied by erotic aids such as a vibrator or sensual oils. A number of women, for instance, may find that running a stream of warm water over the vulva or sitting near the jet stream in a hot tub is sexually arousing. Stimulation of the breasts and nipples is also very common, as is stroking the anal region. Some women enjoy inserting a finger or other object into their vagina; however, this is less common than clitoral stimulation. Some women apply deep pressure in the region of the G-spot to give themselves a different type of orgasm. Using common sense in relation to cleanliness, such as not inserting an object or finger from the anus into the vagina and keeping vibrators and other objects used for insertion clean, helps to prevent infection.

Men and Masturbation   According to the NHSLS, 62% of men surveyed had masturbated in the preceding year (Laumann et al., 1994). The study of masturbation of the British general population found that 73% of the men reported masturbating in the past 4 weeks. The prevalence of masturbation was higher among men reporting less frequent vaginal intercourse and among those reporting same-sex partners (Gerressu et al., 2008).

Like women, men have individual preferences and patterns in masturbating. Nearly all methods involve some type of direct stimulation of the penis with the hand. Typically, the penis is grasped and stroked at the shaft, with up-and-down or circular movements of the hand, so that the edge of the corona around the glans and the frenulum on the underside are stimulated. How much pressure is applied, how rapid the strokes are, how many fingers are used, where the fingers are placed, and how far up and down the hands move vary from one man to another. Whether the breasts, testicles, anus, or other parts of the body are stimulated also depends on the individual, but it appears to be the up-and-down stroking or rubbing of the penis that triggers orgasm. The stroking tends to increase just prior to ejaculation and then to slow or stop during ejaculation.

What I like about masturbation is that you don't have to talk afterwards.
—Milos Forman
(1932–)

To add variety or stimulation, some men may elect to use lubricants, visual or written erotic materials, artificial vaginas, inflatable dolls, or rubber pouches in which to insert their penis. Regardless of the aid or technique, it is important to pay attention to cleanliness to prevent bacterial infections.

Masturbation in Sexual Relationships   Most people continue to masturbate after they marry or are in a steady relationship, although the rate is significantly lower. Actually, the NHSLS found that married people are less likely to have masturbated during the preceding 12 months than those never-married or formerly married. About 57% and 37% of married men and women, respectively, reported having masturbated in the preceding year, as opposed to about 69% and 48% of never-married and formerly married men and women, respectively (Laumann et al., 1994).

There are many reasons for continuing the activity during marriage or other sexual relationships; for example, masturbation is pleasurable, a partner is away or unwilling, sexual intercourse is not satisfying, the partner(s) fear(s) sexual inadequacy, the individual acts out fantasies, or he or she seeks to release tension. During times of relationship conflict, masturbation may act as a distancing device, with the masturbating partner choosing masturbation over sexual interaction as a means of emotional protection.

● Sexual Behavior With Others

We often think that sex is sexual intercourse, but sex is not limited to sexual intercourse. Heterosexuals engage in a wide variety of sexual activities, which may include erotic touching, kissing, and oral and anal sex. Except for vaginal intercourse, gay and lesbian couples engage in basically the same sexual activities as do heterosexuals. Which of these "sexual" activities actually constitute sex? This topic has been publicly debated recently, largely fueled by former president Clinton's declaration that he did not have sex with Monica Lewinsky despite the fact that she performed fellatio on him. (To find out what a representative sample of young adults believed constituted having "had sex," see the "Think About It" box starting on the next page.)

In one study, American adults were asked to rank how appealing certain sexual activities are to them (Laumann et al., 1994). For all the ethnic groups studied, overwhelmingly, vaginal intercourse was the most appealing activity, with watching the partner undress and giving and receiving oral sex next. Only a small minority found other activities, such as anal sex or use of a vibrator or dildo, very appealing. Apparently, Americans are more traditional in their sexual interests than previously believed.

One caution about sexual behavior with others: Sexually transmitted infections (STIs), including HIV, can be transmitted and acquired during intimate sexual behavior, such as penile-vaginal intercourse, penile-anal intercourse, and oral sex, if at least one of the partners is infected. Strategies for reducing STI risk during sex with others will be discussed in Chapters 15 and 16.

Touching

Whether sex begins with the heart or the genitals, touch is the fire that melds the two into one. Touching is both a sign of caring and a signal for arousal.

Love is the self-delusion we manufacture to justify the trouble we take to have sex.

—Dan Greenberg

think
about it

You Would Say You "Had Sex" If You . . .

When people say they "had sex," "hooked up," or "did some things" but did not have sex, what do they mean? Many people have different ideas about what it means to have sex; it all depends on the behavioral criteria they use. Social and legal definitions of "sex" and crimes related to "having sex" vary and are sometimes vague, depending on the source. Some definitions may be used by couples or individuals to justify a wide range of intimate behaviors other than penile-vaginal intercourse or penile-anal intercourse in order to, for example, preserve

Percentage of 18–29-year-old Indiana residents (31 females, 31 males) answering "yes" to the question "Would you say you 'had sex' with someone if the most intimate behavior you engaged in was . . . ?

Behavior	% of Women	% of Men
You touched, fondled, or manually stimulated a partner's genitals	29.0	9.7
A partner touched, fondled, or manually stimulated your genitals	32.3	16.7
You had oral (mouth) contact with a partner's genitals	61.3	33.3
A partner had oral (mouth) contact with your genitals	67.7	40.0
Penile-vaginal intercourse	93.5	96.7
Penile-vaginal intercourse with no ejaculation; that is, the man did not "come"	93.5	90.0
Penile-vaginal intercourse with no female orgasm; that is, the woman did not "come"	90.3	96.7
Penile-vaginal intercourse, but very brief	96.8	96.7
Penile-vaginal intercourse with a condom	93.5	100
Penile-anal intercourse	83.9	76.7
Penile-anal intercourse with no male ejaculation	83.9	76.7
Penile-anal intercourse with no female orgasm	83.9	76.7
Penile-anal intercourse, but very brief	83.9	76.2
Penile-anal intercourse with a condom	83.9	83.3

SOURCE: Yarber, W. L., Sanders, S. A., Graham, C. A., Crosby, R. A., & Milhausen, R. R. (2007, November). *Public opinion about what behaviors constitute "having sex": A state-wide telephone survey in Indiana.* Paper presented at the annual meeting of The Society for the Scientific Study of Sexuality, Indianapolis, IN.

Touching does not need to be directed solely toward the genitals or erogenous zones. The entire body is responsive to a touch or a caress. Even handholding can be sensual for two people sexually attracted to each other. Women appear to be especially responsive to touch, but traditional male gender roles give little significance to touching. Some men regard touching as simply a prelude to intercourse. When this occurs, touch is transformed into a demand for intercourse rather than an expression of intimacy or erotic play. The man's partner may become reluctant to touch or show affection for fear her gestures will be misinterpreted as a sexual invitation.

William Masters and Virginia Johnson (1970) suggest a form of touching they call "pleasuring." **Pleasuring** is nongenital touching and caressing. Neither partner tries to sexually stimulate the other; they simply explore, discovering how their bodies respond to touching. One partner guides the other partner's

I scarcely seem to be able to keep my hands off you.

—Ovid
(43 B.C.–A.D. 17)

or lose their virginity, not to "have cheated" on another person, or to believe they had sex. Without a universal definition of "having sex," confusion or false assumptions can result (Sanders & Reinisch, 1999).

Researchers at The Kinsey Institute for Research in Sex, Gender, and Reproduction and the Rural Center for AIDS/STD Prevention at Indiana University conducted a public opinion study of a representative sample of adults to determine if certain sexual behaviors, as well as whether male ejaculation, female orgasm, condom use, or brevity during penile-vaginal intercourse or penile-anal intercourse, are considered "having sex." The opinions of 482 adult residents of Indiana of varying ages were obtained by telephone, using random digital dialing. (Results of the participants ages 18–29 are shown in the table on the previous page.)

Not surprisingly, nearly all of the participants considered penile-vaginal intercourse—even under the specific circumstances listed—as having "had sex." This was basically true for penile-anal intercourse, although the percentage indicating "yes" was not quite as high. As expected, the percentage indicating "yes" to oral sex and manual stimulation of the genitals was less than intercourse; interestingly, the responses varied considerably by gender with a much greater percentage of women than men indicating "yes" to these two behaviors.

Two additional studies of college students further our understanding of young adults' definition of "having sex." A study of 164 heterosexual Canadian university students not only asked their views of what constitutes "having sex," but also examined what constitutes a sexual partner and

what they consider to be "unfaithful" in a sexual partner. The results showed discrepancies in the students' opinions on these three issues. For example, although 25% of the students considered oral-genital behaviors as having sex, more than 60% thought that the giver or receiver of oral sex was a sex partner, and more than 97% considered a sex partner who had oral sex with someone else to have been unfaithful (Randall & Byers, 2003). Further, while masturbating to orgasm in the presence of another person was considered as having sex by less than 4% of the students, 34% reported that this behavior would make that person a sexual partner and 95% considered it to be unfaithful if done with someone else.

Think Critically

- Do any of the results of the research studies on the definition of "having sex, surprise you? Do you agree or disagree with the findings?
- Does it make any difference how "having sex, is defined?
- How do you define "having sex,? Has your definition changed over time?

SOURCES: Randall, H. E., & Byers, E. S. (2003). What is sex? Students' definitions of having sex, sexual partner, and unfaithful sexual behavior. *Canadian Journal of Human Sexuality, 12,* 87–96; Sanders, S., & Reinisch, J. (1999). Would you say you "had sex" if...? *Journal of the American Medical Association, 281,* 275–277.

hand over her or his body, telling her or him what feels good; the roles are then reversed.

Such sharing gives each a sense of his or her own responses; it also allows each to discover what the other likes and dislikes. We can't assume we know what a particular person likes, for there is too much variation among people: Watching a partner masturbate can provide clues on how he or she likes to be stimulated. Pleasuring opens the door to communication; couples discover that the entire body, not just the genitals, is erogenous. Actually, Masters and Johnson (1970) noted that women tend to prefer genital touching after general body contact, whereas many men prefer stroking of their genitals early.

Nude or clothed massages, back rubs, foot rubs, scalp massages—all are soothing and loving forms of touch. The sensuousness of touching may be enhanced by the use of lubricating oils. Such erotic touching is a form of safer sex.

> " Sex, indeed, has been called the highest form of touch. In the profoundest sense, touch is the true language of sex.
>
> —Ashley Montagu
> (1905–1999)

Touching can increase relaxation and enhance intimacy.

Some forms of touching are directly sexual, such as caressing, fondling, or rubbing our own or our partner's genitals or breasts. Sucking or licking earlobes, the neck, toes, or the insides of thighs, palms, or arms can be highly stimulating. Oral stimulation of a woman's or man's breasts or nipples is often exciting. Moving one's genitals or breasts over a partner's face, chest, breasts, or genitals is very erotic for some people. The pressing together of bodies with genital thrusting is called **tribidism,** or "dry humping" among heterosexual couples. Many lesbian women enjoy the overall body contact and eroticism of this form of genital stimulation; sometimes, the partners place their pelvic areas together to provide mutual clitoral stimulation (Figure 9.5). Rubbing the penis between the thighs of a partner is a type of touching called **interfemoral intercourse.** Heterosexual couples who do not use contraception must be sure the man does not ejaculate near the vaginal opening so as to avoid conception, however unlikely it may be.

Stimulating a partner's clitoris or penis with the hand or fingers can increase excitement and lead to orgasm. A word of caution: Direct stimulation of the clitoral glans may be painful for some women at specific stages of arousal, so stimulation of either side of the clitoris may work better. Certainly, the clitoris and surrounding areas should be moist before much touching is done. Inserting a finger or fingers into a partner's wet vagina and rhythmically moving it at the pace she likes can also be pleasing. Some women like to have their clitoris licked or stimulated with one hand while their vagina is being penetrated with the other. Men like having their penises lubricated so that their partner's hand glides smoothly over the shaft and glans penis. (Be sure to use a water-based lubricant if you plan to use a condom later, because oil-based lubricants may cause the

● **FIGURE 9.5**
Tribidism

condom to deteriorate.) Masturbating while one partner is holding the other can be highly erotic for both people. Mutual masturbation can also be intensely sexual. Some people use sex toys such as dildos, vibrators, or ben-wah balls to enhance sexual touching. (These are discussed in Chapter 14.)

As we enter old age, touching becomes increasingly significant as a primary form of erotic expression. Touching in all its myriad forms—from holding hands to caressing, from massaging to hugging, and from walking with arms around each other to fondling—becomes the touchstone of eroticism for the elderly.

The Advocate, a magazine focusing on gay and lesbian issues, conducted a survey of its readers concerning relationships and sexuality. A strong majority of the lesbian women said they loved many nongenital, touching activities: 91% loved hugging, caressing, and cuddling; 82% loved French kissing; 74% loved simply holding hands. Three quarters loved both touching a woman's genitals and having their own touched. About 80% enjoyed caressing another woman's breasts or sucking her nipples; 68% enjoyed receiving such attention (Lever, 1995). For 85% of gay men, hugging, kissing, and snuggling were also the favorite activities (Lever, 1994).

Kissing

Kissing is usually our earliest interpersonal sexual experience, and its primal intensity may be traced back to our suckling as infants. The kiss is magic: Fairy tales keep alive the ancient belief that a kiss can undo spells and bring a prince or princess back to life. Parental kisses show love and often remedy the small hurts and injuries of childhood.

Kissing is probably the most acceptable of all sexual activities. The tender lover's kiss symbolizes love, and the erotic lover's kiss, of course, simultaneously represents and *is* passion. Both men and women regard kissing as a romantic expression, a symbol of affection as well as desire.

The lips and mouth are highly sensitive to touch and are exquisitely erotic parts of our bodies. Kisses discover, explore, and excite the body. They also involve the senses of taste and smell, which are especially important because they activate unconscious memories and associations. Often, we are aroused by familiar smells associated with particular sexual memories, such as a person's body scent or a perfume or fragrance. In some languages—among the Borneans, for example—the word "kiss" literally translates as "smell." In fact, among the Eskimos and the Maoris of New Zealand, there is no mouth kissing, only the touching of noses to facilitate smelling.

Although kissing may appear innocent, it is in many ways the height of intimacy. The adolescent's first kiss is often regarded as a milestone, a rite of passage, the beginning of adult sexuality. It is an important developmental step, marking the beginning of a young person's sexuality. (To find out the meanings of kissing, including their first kiss, among a sample of college students, see the "Think About It" box on the next page.)

The amount of kissing differs according to sexual orientation. Lesbian women couples tend to engage in more kissing than heterosexual couples, while gay men couples kiss less than heterosexual couples (Blumstein & Schwartz, 1983).

Ordinary kissing is considered safer sex. French kissing is probably safe, unless the kiss is hard and draws blood or either partner has open sores or cuts in or around the mouth.

> The kiss originated when the first male reptile licked the first female reptile, implying in a subtle, complimentary way that she was as succulent as the small reptile he had for dinner the night before.
>
> —F. Scott Fitzgerald
> (1896–1940)

> If it's uplift you're after, if it's that thrust, stop talking, put lips and tongue to other use.
>
> —Horace
> (65–8 B.C.)

think
about it

The First Kiss: A Deal-Breaker?

Is there more to kissing than just lips touching? Surprisingly, there has been little scientific research on this topic, although philosophers have written about "the kiss" for centuries. However, a seminal study on college students and kissing published recently in the scientific journal *Evolutionary Psychology* revealed that a lot of information is exchanged during kissing (Hughes, Harrison, & Gallup, 2007). The study, involving in-depth interviews, provided a descriptive account of kissing behavior in a sample of 1,041 undergraduate students (limited to those indicating kissing preference only or mostly with the other sex) at a large university in the eastern United States. About 70% of the students reported kissing six or more people, and 20% estimated to have kissed more than 20 people; no differences were found between men and women in the number of kissing partners nor the age of first romantic kiss.

An intriguing finding of the study was that a nearly equal number of men and women noted that a bad kiss is a "deal-breaker," often leading to the ending of a potential new relationship. Fifty-nine percent of men and 66% of women said they were attracted to someone until they kissed the person; then, they were no longer interested. One of the study's researchers, Gordon Gallup, stated that while a kiss may not make a relationship, it can kill one and that "there may be unconscious mechanisms that would make people make an assessment of genetic compatibility through a kiss" (Gordon, quoted in Best, 2007).

The research by Hughes and colleagues (2007) suggests that the meanings associated with kissing vary considerably between men and women. Women placed more significance on kissing as a way of assessing the person as a potential mating partner and as a means of initiating, bonding, maintaining, and monitoring the current status of a long-term relationship. Men, on the other hand, placed less emphasis on kissing, especially with short-term partners, and appeared to use kissing as a means to an end—that is, to gain sexual access. About one half of the men, in contrast to one third of the women, assumed that kissing would lead to sex whether they were in a short-term or long-term relationship. Gallup notes that kissing for males is one way of keeping their partners physically interested, stating that "as a consequence of male saliva exchange extending over a long period of time, it's conceivable that the testosterone in male saliva can stimulate female sex hormones and make females more receptive to sex" (Gordon, quoted in Best, 2007).

Other notable gender differences found in the study:

- Taste and smell of the person was more important to women.
- Women were more likely to rebuff sex with a partner unless they kissed first.

- More women indicated that they would refuse to have sex with a bad kisser.
- Men were more likely to desire exchanging saliva during a kiss, showing greater preference for tongue contact and open-mouth kissing.
- Men were more likely to believe that kissing could stop a fight.
- More men felt that it was OK to kiss on the first date and it was OK for the female partner to make the move for the first kiss.

The first kiss is a memorable, once-in-lifetime experience. A study of 356 heterosexual students at a large university in the western United States examined the emotional responses that commonly accompany the first kiss (Regan, Shen, De La Pena, & Gosset, 2007). The researchers found that most reported an array of emotions—dread, nervousness, fright, awkwardness, and confusion—as they approached their first kiss. They found that emotions shifted during the kiss. For men, their anxiety and fear was replaced with elation, happiness, sexual arousal, enjoyment, and other positive feelings. Women experienced a more mixed reaction: disgust, uncertainty, boredom, enjoyment, tenderness, and excitement. Following the first kiss, most men continued to feel positive responses, but some experienced embarrassment and other negative feelings. For women, although many reported positive feelings, negative responses such as disappointment, regret, and distress were more commonly experienced.

Think Critically

- Do you agree that a bad first kiss can be a potentially new relationship "deal-breaker"? Has this happened to you?
- How important is kissing to you in a relationship?
- What is a good kiss? Should a kiss lead to sexual intercourse?
- What were your experiences with your first kiss?

SOURCES: Best, K. (2007, December 17). Kiss and tell: Smooches make or break a relationship. *Indianapolis Star*, p. E1; Hughes, S. M., Harrison, M. A., & Gallup, G. G. (2007). Sex differences in romantic kissing among college students: An evolutionary perspective. *Evolutionary Psychology, 5*, 612–631; Regan, P. C., Shen, W., De La Pena, E., & Gossett, E. (2007). "Fireworks exploded in my mouth": Affective responses before, during, and after the very first kiss. *International Journal of Sexual Health, 19*(2), 1–16; Stein, R. On this you can rely: A kiss is fundamental. *Indianapolis Star*, p. A4.

Oral-Genital Sex

In recent years, oral sex has become a part of many people's sexual scripts. The two types of **oral-genital sex** are cunnilingus and fellatio, which may be performed singly or simultaneously. Recall from Chapter 1 that cunnilingus is the erotic stimulation of a woman's vulva and/or clitoris by her partner's mouth and tongue. Recall, too, that fellatio is the oral stimulation of a man's penis by his partner's sucking and licking. When two people orally stimulate each other simultaneously, their activity is sometimes called "sixty-nine." The term comes from the configuration "69," which visually suggests the activity.

For people of every orientation (especially among high school and college students), oral sex is an increasingly important aspect of their sexual selves. Of the men and women in various studies, 70–90% report that they have engaged in oral sex (Billy et al., 1993; Janus & Janus, 1993; Laumann et al., 1994; Mosher, Chandra, & Jones, 2005). Sociologists Philip Blumstein and Pepper Schwartz (1983) found that 50% of gay couples, 39% of lesbian couples, and 30% of heterosexual couples usually or always had oral sex as part of their lovemaking routine.

Although oral-genital sex is increasingly accepted, this change has historically been the greatest among White, middle-class Americans. The National Survey of Family Growth (NSFG) study (see Chapter 2) of selected sexual behaviors of 12,571 males and females aged 15–44 throughout the United States (90% of those 18–44 years considered themselves heterosexual) shows not only that the vast majority of persons in the United States have experienced oral-genital sex but also that the percentages of Whites, African Americans, and Hispanics are fairly similar, although oral-genital sex continues to be more prevalent among Whites (see Figure 9.6). The percentages of males aged 25–44 who have ever had oral-genital sex with a female are the same as those for the 15–44-year-old males (White, 87%; African American, 79%; Hispanic, 74%). However, for females the variance by race/ethnicity is greater: 88% of White females reported ever having had oral-genital sex with a male compared with 79% for African American females and 74% for Hispanic females (Mosher et al., 2005). The NSFG data illustrate some continuing of variance of oral-genital sex prevalence among the three races/ethnicities, although the gap could be considered small.

> As for the topsy turvy tangle known as soixante-neuf, personally I have always felt it to be madly confusing, like trying to pat your head and rub your stomach at the same time.
>
> —Helen Lawrenson
> (1904–1982)

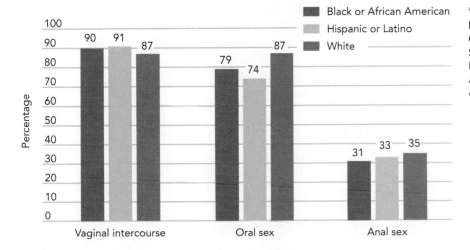

● **FIGURE 9.6**

Percentage of U.S. 15–44-Year-Olds Who Have Ever Had Specified Sexual Behavior, by Race/Ethnicity, 2002. (*Source:* Adapted from Mosher, Chandra, & Jones, 2005.)

A study of university students of both sexes revealed that a person's attitudes toward his or her genitals may be an important facet of sexual interaction (Reinholtz & Muehlenhard, 1995). Someone who believes his or her genitals are attractive and sexy may be more comfortable during sexual interaction than someone who feels self-conscious about them. Furthermore, this same study found that the vast majority of participants who had engaged in oral sex had both performed and received it. According to a study of nearly 2,000 college students, nearly all of the students who ever had sexual intercourse had also engaged in oral sex, in contrast to only about 1 in 4 virgins having had oral sex (Chambers, 2007). In comparing both sexes, significantly more women than men indicated that they gave more oral sex, and men reported more pleasure in receiving and giving oral sex than women. Nearly all of the sample cited the pleasure of their partner as the most important reason they gave or received oral sex. The study also found that the students, particularly the women, perceived oral sex as less intimate than intercourse. Most study participants noted that they felt comfortable engaging in oral sex in a committed relationship. According to a survey of lesbian and gay sexuality, about 7 in 10 lesbian women and gay men enjoy giving and receiving oral sex (Lever, 1994).

Cunnilingus   In cunnilingus, a woman's genitals are stimulated by her partner's tongue and mouth, which gently and rhythmically caress and lick her clitoris and the surrounding area (Figure 9.7). During arousal, the mouth and lips can nibble, lick, and kiss the inner thighs, stomach, and mons pubis and then move to the sensitive labia minora clitoral area. Orgasm may be brought on by rhythmically stimulating the clitoris. During cunnilingus, some women also enjoy insertion of a finger into the vagina or anus for extra stimulation. Many women find cunnilingus to be the easiest way to reach orgasm because it provides such intense stimulation.

● **FIGURE 9.7**
Cunnilingus

Among lesbian women, cunnilingus is a common activity for achieving orgasm. According to one study, however, as many as 25% of the lesbian women rarely or never engaged in cunnilingus (Blumstein & Schwartz, 1983). Instead, they relied on holding, kissing, manual stimulation, and pressing themselves erotically against each other. Nevertheless, the more often the women in the study had oral sex, the more likely they were to be satisfied with their sex lives and partners.

Some women, however, have concerns regarding cunnilingus. The most common worries revolve around whether the other person is enjoying it and, especially, whether the vulva has an unpleasant odor. Concerns about vaginal odors may be eased by washing. Undeodorized white soap will wash away unpleasant smells without disturbing the vagina's natural erotic scent. If an unpleasant odor arises from the genitals, it may be because the woman has a vaginal infection.

A woman may also worry that her partner is not enjoying the experience because she or he is giving pleasure rather than receiving it. What she may not recognize is that such sexual excitement is often mutual. Because our mouths and tongues are erotically sensitive, the giver finds erotic excitement in arousing her or his partner.

Fellatio   In fellatio, a man's penis is taken into his partner's mouth. The partner licks the glans penis and gently stimulates the shaft (Figure 9.8). Also, the scrotum may be gently licked. If the penis is not erect, it usually will become erect within a short time. The partner sucks more vigorously as excitement increases, down toward the base of the penis and then back up, in a rhythmical motion, being careful not to bite hard or scrape the penis with the teeth. While the man is being stimulated by mouth, his partner can also stroke

● **FIGURE 9.8**
Fellatio

the shaft of the penis by hand. Gently playing with the testicles is also arousing as long as they are not held too tightly. As in cunnilingus, the couple should experiment to discover what is most stimulating and exciting. The man should be careful not to thrust his penis too deeply into his partner's throat, for that may cause a gag reflex. He should let his partner control how deeply the penis goes into the mouth. The partner can do this by grasping the penis below his or her lips so that the depth of insertion can be controlled. Furthermore, gagging is less likely when the one performing fellatio is on top. The gag reflex can also be reconditioned by slowly inserting the penis into the mouth at increasing depth over time. Some women feel that fellatio is more intimate than sexual intercourse; others feel that it is less intimate. It is the most common form of sexual activity performed on men by prostitutes (Monto, 2001). Most men find fellatio to be highly arousing.

For gay men, fellatio is an important component of their sexuality. As with sexual intercourse for heterosexual men, however, fellatio is only one activity in their sexual repertoire. Generally, the more often gay couples engage in giving and receiving oral sex, the more satisfied they are (Blumstein & Schwartz, 1983). Because oral sex often involves power symbolism, reciprocity is important. If one partner always performs oral sex, he may feel he is subordinate to the other. The most satisfied gay couples alternate between giving and receiving oral sex.

A common concern about fellatio centers around ejaculation. Should a man ejaculate into his partner's mouth? Some people find semen to be slightly bitter, but others like it. Some find it exciting to suck even harder on the penis during or following ejaculation; others do not like the idea of semen in the mouth. For many, a key issue is whether to swallow the semen. Some swallow it; others spit it out. It is simply a matter of personal preference, and the man who is receiving fellatio should accept his partner's feelings about it and avoid equating a dislike for swallowing semen with a personal rejection.

Some men try to provide oral stimulation to their own penis, a practice called **autofellatio.** Kinsey and his colleagues (Kinsey, Pomeroy, & Martin, 1948) found that many males try this behavior, but less than 1% of their sample were actually able to achieve it.

Sexual Intercourse

Sexual intercourse is the more common, less technical name for vaginal intercourse, penile-vaginal intercourse, or **coitus.** Sometimes, sexual intercourse is also used to describe penile-anal sex. But, for our discussion here, we mean penile-vaginal intercourse when we use the term "sexual intercourse." Sexual intercourse has intense personal meaning; it is a source of pleasure, communication, and love. If forced, however, it becomes an instrument of aggression and pain. Its meaning changes depending on the context in which we engage in it. How we feel about sexual intercourse may depend as much on the feelings and motives we bring to it as on the techniques we use or the orgasms we experience. Being the most valued and sought-after sexual behavior among persons desiring sex with the other sex, the prevalence of sexual intercourse is very high: About 9 out of every 10 participants in the NSFG study (Mosher et al., 2005) reported ever having had sexual intercourse (Figure 9.6). There were few differences in prevalence of sexual intercourse in the NSFG among Whites, African Americans, and Hispanics or Latinos.

" The sexual act is in time what the tiger is in space.

—Georges Bataille
(1897–1962)

" Sex is the great amateur art.

—David Cort

The Significance of Sexual Intercourse   Although sexual intercourse is important for most sexually involved couples, the significance of it often differs between men and women. For men, sexual intercourse is only one of several sexual activities that they enjoy. For many heterosexual women, however, intercourse is central to their sexual satisfaction. More than any other heterosexual sexual activity, sexual intercourse can involve equal participation by both partners. Both partners equally and simultaneously give and receive. As a result, a woman may feel greater shared intimacy than she does in other sexual activities.

The Positions   The playfulness of the couple, their movement from one bodily configuration to another, and their ingenuity can provide an infinite variety of sexual intercourse positions. The same positions played out in different settings can cause an intensity that transforms the ordinary into the extraordinary.

The most common position is face-to-face with the man on top (Figure 9.9). Many people prefer this position, for several reasons. First, it is the traditional, correct, or "official" position in our culture, which many people find reassuring and validating in terms of their sexuality. (The man-on-top position is commonly known as the missionary position because it was the position missionaries traditionally encouraged people to use.) Second, it can allow the man maximum activity, movement, and control of coitus. Third, it allows the woman freedom to stimulate her clitoris to assist in her orgasm. The primary disadvantages are that it makes it difficult for the man to caress his partner or to stimulate her clitoris while supporting himself with his hands and for the woman to control the angle, rate, and depth of penetration. Furthermore, some men have difficulty controlling ejaculation in this position, because the penis is highly stimulated.

Another common position is face-to-face with the woman on top (Figure 9.10). The woman either lies on top of her partner or sits astride him. This position allows the woman maximum activity, movement, and control. She can control the depth to which the penis penetrates. Additionally, when the woman sits astride her partner, either of them can caress or stimulate her labia and clitoris, thus facilitating orgasm in the woman. As with the man-on-top position, kissing is easy. A disadvantage is that some men or women may feel uneasy about the woman assuming a position that signifies an active role in coitus. This position tends to be less stimulating for the man, thus making it easier for him to control ejaculation.

Intercourse can also be performed with the man positioned behind the woman. There are several variations on the rear-entry position. The woman may kneel supported on her arms and receive the penis in her vagina from behind. The

> The sexual embrace can only be compared with music and prayer.
> —Havelock Ellis
> (1859–1939)

couple may lie on their sides, with the woman's back to her partner (Figure 9.11). This position offers variety and may be particularly suitable during pregnancy because it minimizes pressure on the woman's abdomen. This position facilitates clitoral stimulation by the woman. Generally, it is also possible for the man to stimulate her during intercourse. Some people object to the rear-entry position as "animal-like," or they may feel it inhibits intimacy or resembles anal intercourse. Furthermore, it is sometimes difficult to keep the penis inside the vagina.

In the face-to-face side position, both partners lie on their sides facing each other (Figure 9.12). Each partner has greater freedom to caress and stimulate the other. As with the rear-entry position, a major drawback is that keeping the penis in the vagina may be difficult.

Tantric sex is a type of sexual intimacy based on Eastern religious beliefs beginning in India around 5000 B.C. The tantric sex technique of sexual intercourse involves the couple sharing their "energies" by initially thrusting minimally, generating energy via subtle, inner movements. They visualize the energy of the genitals moving upward in their bodies (Figure 9.13). The couple may harmonize their breathing and achieve intimacy (often looking into each other's eyes), ecstasy, and abandon. Many books have been written on tantric sex, and numerous Web sites are devoted to it.

Anal Eroticism

Anal eroticism refers to sexual activities involving the anus, whose delicate membranes (as well as taboo nature) make it erotically arousing for many people. These activities include **analingus,** the licking of the anal region (colloquially

● **FIGURE 9.11**
Rear Entry

● **FIGURE 9.13**
Tantric Sex

known as "rimming" or "tossing salad"). Anal-manual contact consists of stimulating the anal region with the fingers; sometimes, an entire fist may be inserted (known as "fisting" among gay White males and "fingering" among gay African American males). Many couples engage in this activity along with fellatio or sexual intercourse. Though little is known about the prevalence of this activity, many report it to be highly arousing because of the sensitivity of the skin around the anus. Keeping this area clean is extremely important because the intestinal tract, which extends to the anus, carries a variety of microorganisms.

Anal intercourse refers to the male's inserting his erect penis into his partner's anus (Figure 9.14). Both heterosexual people and gay men participate in anal intercourse. According to the NHSLS, 26% of heterosexual men and 20% of heterosexual women have engaged in anal sex in their lifetime (Laumann et al., 1994). However, only 10% of sexually active heterosexual couples reported engaging in anal intercourse during the preceding year; it is not a common practice after it has been experienced once. For many heterosexuals, it is more of an experimental activity, but for others, it is a regular and pleasurable activity. Interestingly, the NHSLS found anal sex to be more common among the well educated (Laumann et al., 1994). The NSFG study found that 40% of the men and 35% of the women reported ever having had anal sex with an other-sex partner. For those 15–44 years old, the prevalence of anal sex is about one third: 31%, 33%, and 35% for African Americans, Hispanics, and Whites, respectively (Mosher et al., 2005). As you can see, the prevalence is highest among Whites, but variance between the three races/ethnicities is small.

Anal intercourse is a major mode of sexual interaction for gay men. In fact, there are more colloquial terms for anal eroticism among gay men than for any other form of sexual activity (Mays, Cochran, Bellinger, & Smith, 1992). The *Advocate* magazine survey found that 46% of gay men loved insertive anal intercourse and 43% loved receptive anal intercourse (Lever, 1994).

Among gay men, anal intercourse is less common than oral sex, but it is, nevertheless, an important ingredient to the sexual satisfaction of many gays (Berger, 1991; Blumstein & Schwartz, 1983). Although heterosexual imagery portrays the person who penetrates as "masculine" and the penetrated person as "feminine," this imagery does not generally reflect gay reality. For both partners, anal intercourse is regarded as masculine.

Although anal sex may heighten eroticism for those who engage in it, from a health perspective, it is riskier than most other forms of sexual interaction. The

rectum is particularly susceptible to STIs. If the penis or a foreign object is inserted into the anus, it must be washed before insertion into the vagina because it may cause a bacterial infection. Other health hazards associated with anal erotic practices include rupturing the rectum with foreign objects and lacerating the anus or rectal wall through the use of enemas. Licking the anus puts individuals at risk for acquiring HIV, hepatitis, and other STIs (see Chapters 15 and 16).

Final Thoughts

As we have seen, sexual behaviors cannot be separated from attraction and desire. Our autoerotic activities are as important to our sexuality as are our interpersonal ones. Although the sexual behaviors we have examined in this chapter are the most common ones in our society, many people engage in other, less typical, activities. We discuss these atypical behaviors in Chapter 10.

Summary

Sexual Attractiveness

- The characteristics that constitute sexual attractiveness vary across cultures. Youthfulness and good health appear to be the only universals. Our culture prefers slender women with large breasts and men who are muscular, but not too brawny. A study of college students over five decades found that "good looks" of a potential partner have increased in importance for both men and women.

- Casual sex is not without "strings attached." A study of college students found that depressive symptoms are associated with casual sex, particularly for females.

- Sexual desire is affected by *erotophilia,* a positive emotional response to sex, and by *erotophobia,* a negative response to sex.

Sexual Scripts

- Sexual scripts organize our sexual expression. They have three major components: cultural, intrapersonal, and interpersonal. The cultural script provides the general forms sexual behaviors are expected to take in a particular society. The intrapersonal script interprets our physiological responses as sexual or not. The interpersonal script is the shared conventions and signals that make sexual activities between two people possible.

Autoeroticism

- *Autoeroticism* refers to sexual activities that involve only oneself. These activities include sexual fantasies, erotic dreams and *nocturnal orgasm,* and *masturbation,* or stimulation of the genitals for pleasure. Persons practicing various types of autoerotic activity are also more likely to report enacting more elaborate interpersonal sexual scripts.

- Sexual fantasies and dreams are probably the most universal of all sexual behaviors; they are normal aspects of our sexuality. Erotic fantasies have several functions: They take our generalized sexual drives and help define and direct them, they allow us to plan or anticipate erotic situations, they provide pleasurable escape from routine, they introduce novelty, and they offer clues to our unconscious.

- Most men and women masturbate. Masturbation may begin as early as infancy and continue throughout old age. Attitudes toward masturbation vary across ethnic groups.

Sexual Behavior With Others

- Sexual intercourse is the most appealing sexual activity for both female and male heterosexuals.

- The erotic potential of touching has been undervalued, especially among males, because our culture tends to be orgasm oriented.

- Lesbian women and gay men report that hugging, kissing, and cuddling are their favorite erotic activities.

- Erotic kissing is usually our earliest interpersonal sexual experience and is regarded as a rite of passage into adult sexuality.

- *Oral-genital sex* is becoming increasingly accepted, especially among young adults. Cunnilingus is the stimulation of the vulva with the tongue and mouth. It is engaged in by both men and women. Fellatio is the stimulation of the penis with the mouth; it is engaged in by both men and women.

- *Sexual intercourse* can be an intimate and rewarding interaction between two people. It is both a means of reproduction and a pleasurable form of communication.

- *Anal eroticism* refers to sexual activities involving the anus. It is engaged in by heterosexuals, gay men, and lesbian women.

 ## Questions for Discussion

- What is your sexual script relative to initiating sexual behavior with another person? Do you always want to take the lead, or are you comfortable with the other person doing that or sharing in initiating the sexual behavior?

- How often do you fantasize about sex? Are you comfortable about your fantasies? Have you ever shared them with anyone?

- Do you consider oral sex more or less intimate than sexual intercourse? What do you consider to be the primary reason for giving and receiving oral sex?

Sex and the Internet

Sexual Health InfoCenter

A well-done and comprehensive Web site, the Sexual Health InfoCenter has many features, including "channels" on better sex, masturbation, sex health videos, STIs, birth control, safe sex, sexual problems, and "Sex Tip of the Week." The Web site also has featured articles on a variety of sexuality topics as well as "Frequently Asked Questions," "Our Community," and a shopping section (videos, sex toys, etc.). Visit this Web site (http://www.sexhealth.org) and find out the following:

- What are the options of the site?
- How did the site begin?
- What is the sex tip of the week?
- For one sexual expression topic, such as masturbation or oral sex, what information does the site provide?

Suggested Web Sites

JackinWorld
http://www.jackinworld.com
Provides honest, straightforward, nonexplicit information on masturbation.

Sex Coach at iVillage
http://www.ivillage.com
Provides information on a broad range of sexuality and relationship issues, including suggestions for enhancing sexual pleasure. Click on the "Love" section.

Tantra.com
http://tantra.com
An online resource for tantric sex, tantra, and the Kama Sutra as well as numerous commercial products for enhancing sexual expression.

Yahoo! Directory on Masturbation
http://www.yahoo.com/society_and_culture/sexuality/activities_and_practices/masturbation
Gives the names of and links to many Web sites concerning masturbation.

Suggested Reading

Bogle, K. (2008). *Hooking up: Sex, dating, and relationships on campus.* New York: New York University Press. A sociologist employed in-depth interviews with students and graduates of two universities to identify the culture of hooking up in a historical and current context.

Cornog, M. (2003). *The big book of masturbation: From angst to zeal.* San Francisco: Down There Press. An interdisciplinary examination of the history, evolution, psychology, literature, modern culture, and humor of masturbation.

Giles, J. (2008). *The nature of sexual desire.* Lanham, MD: University Press of America. Sexual desire is explored from a psychological, philosophical, and anthropological perspective and in relation to sexual interaction, erotic pleasure, the experience of gender, and romantic love.

Joannides, P. (2009). *Guide to getting it on* (6th ed.). Waldport, OR: Goofy Foot Press. A very popular and thorough sex manual that has been translated into over 10 languages. Has superb anatomical and sexual behavior drawings.

Klein, M. (2002). *Beyond orgasm: Dare to be honest about the sex you really want.* Berkeley, CA: Ten Speed Press. Designed to help readers accept their own sexuality, approach partners with confidence, and become involved in a wider range of erotic activities.

Kouth, M. R. (Ed.). (2006). *Handbook of the evolution of human sexuality.* Binghamton, NY: Haworth Press. Leading experts examine various aspects of evolutionary theory and sexuality.

Millner, D., & Chiles, N. (1999). *What brothers think, what sistahs think: The real deal on love and relationships.* New York: Morrow. A study of sexuality-related issues written from a Black perspective and using the question-answer format.

Newman, F. (2004). *The whole lesbian sex book* (revised and expanded). San Francisco: Cleis Press. A comprehensive lesbian sex guide including guidance and practical suggestions based on the experiences of over 200 women.

Ochs, R., & Rowley, S. E. (Eds.). (2005). *Getting bi: Voices of bisexuals around the world.* Boston: Bisexual Resource Center. A collection of numerous stories about their bisexuality from persons around the world.

Silverstein, C., & Picano, F. (2003). *The new joy of gay sex* (3rd ed.). New York: HarperCollins. An illustrated guide to gay male sexuality.

For links, articles, and study material, go to the McGraw-Hill Web site, located at **www.mhhe.com/yarber7e.**

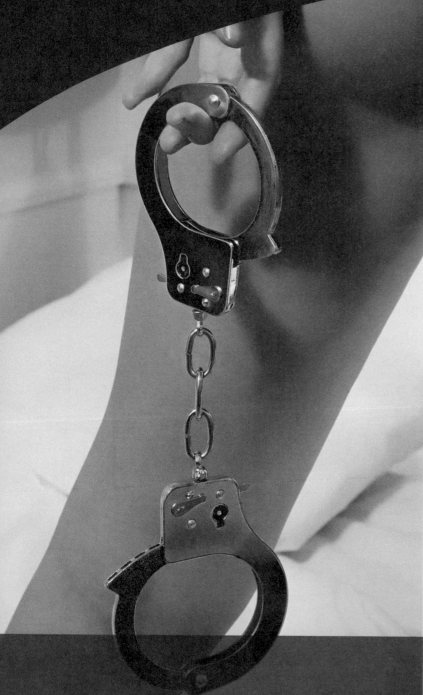

Variations in Sexual Behavior

10 chapter

CHAPTER OUTLINE

Sexual Variations and Paraphilic Behavior

Sexual Variation: Domination and Submission

Noncoercive Paraphilias

Coercive Paraphilias

Origins and Treatment of Paraphilias

"I do like sex a lot, but I wouldn't call myself addicted. I think an addiction to sex would only be a bad thing in the event that it's interfering with other parts of a person's life."

—27-year-old male

"I think that some fetishes are good and healthy. I really don't think that someone who is turned on by feet or a pair of shoes is wrong. I do have a major problem with those who are into bondage because that is just sick."

—21-year-old female

"I really don't think that atypical sex exists. Everyone should find what feels good and natural for them; others' opinions and statistics shouldn't matter."

—20-year-old male

"From my point of view, fetishism misses the main point of sex: physical pleasure and emotional closeness. This sort of "erotic communion" of sensation and emotion can be wholly fulfilling without the bells and whistles of whips, diapers, or anything else. To me, fetishism brings psychological incompleteness to the bedroom. It carries childhood problems, unresolved conflicts, and past trauma into an arena best suited for the psychologist's couch."

—23-year-old female

"My boyfriend always thought that having his feet licked would be weird and gross. I'd never tried it or had it done to me, but I'd heard a lot of people really love it, so on Valentine's day, I tried it. Now he likes it almost as much as oral sex. In fact, he gets excited when he hears me walking around barefoot!"

—20-year-old female

SEXUALITY CAN BE EXPRESSED in a variety of ways, some more common than others. Many of the less common behaviors have been negatively labeled by the public, often implying that the behavior is unnatural or "perverted." In this chapter, we examine variations in sexual behavior, such as cross-dressing and domination and submission, which are not within the range of sexual behaviors in which people typically engage. Then we turn to sexual behaviors that are classified by the American Psychiatric Association as noncoercive paraphilias, including fetishism and transvestism. Finally, we examine the coercive paraphilias, which include zoophilia, pedophilia, sexual sadism, sexual masochism, and necrophilia.

There is hardly anyone whose sexual life, if it were broadcast, would not fill the world at large with surprise and horror.

—Somerset Maugham
(1874–1965)

• Sexual Variations and Paraphilic Behavior

The range of human sexual behavior is almost infinite. Yet most of our activities and fantasies, such as intercourse, oral-genital sex, and masturbation, and our orientation as a heterosexual, gay, lesbian, or bisexual person cluster within a general range of behaviors and desires. Those behaviors and fantasies that do not fall within this general range are considered variations. In this chapter, we use the term **sexual variations** to refer to those behaviors that are not *statistically* typical of American sexual behaviors.

What Are Sexual Variations?

Of all the sexual aberrations, the most peculiar is chastity.

—Remy de Gourmont (1858–1915)

"Sexual variation" is the most common term used, although **atypical sexual behavior** is sometimes used. It is important to remember, however, that atypical does not necessarily mean abnormal; it simply means that the majority of people do not engage in that particular behavior. Even though today's society is less judgmental about sex, resulting in people who engage in sexual variations feeling less shame and guilt, some sexual variations are considered to be so extreme by the American Psychiatric Association (APA) that they are classified as mental disorders, or paraphilias. Paraphilic behaviors tend to be compulsive, long-standing, and distressing to the individual. Having a diagnostic category like paraphilic may indicate that our culture continues to find some sexual behaviors unacceptable and needing treatment.

What Is Paraphilia?

According to the fourth edition (text revision) of the APA's *Diagnostic and Statistical Manual of Mental Disorders (DSM-IV-TR)* (2000), a **paraphilia** is a mental disorder characterized by recurrent, intense sexually arousing fantasies, sexual urges, or sexual behaviors lasting at least 6 months and involving (1) nonhuman objects, (2) the suffering or humiliation of oneself or one's partner, or (3) children or other nonconsenting people. The *DSM-IV-TR* lists eight paraphilias, along with a "not otherwise specified" category, of which six examples are given (see Table 10.1). The "not specified" category actually contains many behaviors, though, which suggests that almost any behavior can take on erotic significance. To minimize the negative message of labeling and to recognize individuals' many components, it seems more appropriate to use the term "person with paraphilia" than "paraphiliacs." This is the term we will use in this textbook.

For people with a paraphilia, the paraphilic behavior is the predominant sexual behavior, although they may engage in other sexual activities as well. They may engage in the paraphilic behavior every day or several times a day, or they may participate in a variety of paraphilic behaviors. Even though the behavior may lead to legal or interpersonal difficulties, it may be so rewarding and irresistible that they continue to practice it. Mild versions of paraphilias may manifest only in disturbing fantasies, often occurring during masturbation. Severe versions can include sexual victimization of children and the use of threats or force with other adults (Seligman & Hardenberg, 2000).

The overwhelming majority of people with paraphilia are males (McConaghy, 1998); they are most likely to engage in paraphilic activities between the ages of 15 and 25. One of the most common paraphilias, sexual masochism, is diagnosed much less frequently in women; the ratio is estimated to be 20 males for each female (APA, 2000). Paraphilias are diagnosed in all ethnic and socioeconomic groups and among all sexual orientations. All people with paraphilia share one common trait: Their sexual behavior has been disconnected from a loving, consensual relationship with another adult (Schwartz, 2000).

The distinction between sexual variations and behavior that might be classified as paraphilic behavior is sometimes more a difference of degree than kind. For example, many men find that certain objects, such as black lingerie, intensify their sexual arousal; for other men, these objects are necessary for arousal. In the first case, there is nothing particularly unusual. But if a man

Table 10.1 • The *DSM-IV-TR* Paraphilias

Specified Paraphilias	Sexual Arousal Activity
Exhibitionism	Exposing one's genitals to an unsuspecting person
Fetishism	Using a nonliving object
Frotteurism	Touching or rubbing one's genitals against a nonconsenting person
Pedophilia	Having sexual activity with a prepubescent child
Sexual masochism	Being humiliated, beaten, bound, or otherwise made to suffer
Sexual sadism	Inflicting psychological or physical suffering
Transvestic fetishism	Cross-dressing
Voyeurism	Observing an unsuspecting person who is disrobing or having sex

Paraphilias Not Otherwise Specified	Sexual Arousal Activity
Telephone scatologia	Making obscene phone calls
Necrophilia	Having sexual activity with corpses
Zoophilia	Having sexual activity with animals (bestiality)
Coprophilia	Being sexually aroused in response to feces
Klismaphilia	Being sexually aroused in response to enemas
Urophilia	Being sexually aroused in response to urine

SOURCE: Reprinted with permission from the *Diagnostic and Statistical Manual of Mental Disorders,* Fourth Edition, Text Revision (Copyright 2000). American Psychiatric Association.

is unable to become sexually aroused without the lingerie and the purpose of sex is to bring him in contact with it, the behavior is considered paraphilic by the APA (2000).

It is also important to recognize that seemingly scientific or clinical terms may not be scientific at all. Instead, they may be pseudoscientific terms hiding moral judgments, as in the case of "nymphomania" and "satyriasis." **Nymphomania** is a pejorative term referring to "abnormal or excessive" sexual desire in a woman and is usually applied to sexually active single women. But what is "abnormal" or "excessive" is often defined moralistically rather than scientifically. Nymphomania is not recognized as a clinical condition by the APA (2000). Although the term "nymphomania" dates back to the seventeenth century, it was popularized in the nineteenth century by Richard von Krafft-Ebing and others. Physicians and psychiatrists used the term to pathologize women's sexual behavior if it deviated from nineteenth-century moral standards (see Chapter 2). Even today, "nymphomania," "nymphomaniac," and "nympho" retain pathological connotations.

Very few studies have been conducted on women, or men, who might be considered "highly sexual" by cultural norms. American women with very strong sexual desire have been both largely ignored by researchers and stigmatized by society. However, an interview study of 44 highly sexual women aged 20–82

"Sexual Interest Disorder": A Viable Alternative to Paraphilia or a Radical Departure?

Since the APA began listing certain variant sexual behaviors as "paraphilia" in its 1980 edition of *Diagnostic and Statistical Manual of Mental Disorders (DSM),* the paraphilia construct has been widely critiqued. Critics of the *DSM* paraphilias contend that the listing of behaviors as paraphilic is merely an attempt to pathologize sexual behaviors not approved of by society. Physician and sexologist Charles Moser (2001) concurs with this stance and has suggested an alternative classification.

Moser notes that the term "paraphilia" was popularized by sexologist John Money (1980, 1984), as a way of describing nonstandard or unusual sexual behavior in a nonjudgmental manner. He indicates that paraphilias, unfortunately, were assimilated into the *DSM* as a classification of pathology. The *DSM* is the standard, worldwide resource for defining psychopathology (mental illness)—that is, for determining which behaviors and desires are healthy and unhealthy.

Moser notes that each person has a unique sexual pattern, which has led to variations in sexual behaviors and to differences in acceptance by society. He explains:

Simplistically, the general public finds some sexual interests acceptable (heterosexual coitus within marriage), some possibly acceptable (homosexual attraction), some odd (shoe fetishes), and some disgusting (pedophilia). Acceptable sexual interests vary cross-culturally and change transhistorically. Over the last century, we have seen a relative reversal in North American societal and scientific views of masturbation, oral-genital contact, and homosexuality. Each of these was thought to be the cause, sign, or result of mental illness and all were seen as particularly dangerous to children; these behaviors are now relatively accepted.

Nevertheless, society continues to classify certain sexual behaviors as unacceptable, resulting in imprisonment, executions, personal distress, and/or family dissolutions among individuals expressing these behaviors.

Moser has proposed a new classification—"sexual interest disorder (SID)"—to replace the paraphilias. This new classification would emphasize the effect of the sexual interest on the individual rather than implying that participants in certain sexual behaviors are inherently "sick"; it would also avoid naming specific sexual behaviors. To quality as an SID, a behavior would have to meet two criteria:

- Specific fantasies, sexual urges, or behaviors that cause clinically significant distress or impairment in social, occupational, or other important areas of functioning
- The sexual interest not better accounted for in another Axis I disorder (e.g., schizophrenia disorder, mood disorder, or anxiety disorder), not due to the effects of a general medical disorder, and not the result of substance use, misuse, or abuse

This new classification does not suggest that all sexual interests are acceptable, nor that any interest should be afforded special rights or protections. As an example, Moser discusses pedophilia. He says, "To be perfectly clear, adult-child sexual contact should not be condoned under any circumstances." However, he says that the punishment of adults who have sexual contact with children "should not be mitigated by claims of mental illness." Moser further states that having sexual interest in prepubescent children is not a problem, but acting on it is and should be dealt with in the criminal justice system.

Think Critically

- Do you believe that the *DSM*'s classification of certain variant sexual behaviors as paraphilia is "an attempt to pathologize sexual behaviors not approved by society" or a necessary way to address sexual behaviors that indeed represent mental illness?
- Is Moser's alternative classification—SID—a viable alternative to or a radical departure from the *DSM* category of paraphilia?

provided insights into their sexual lives and how their sexuality has affected them (Blumberg, 2003). "Highly sexual" was defined as a woman who either (1) typically desired sexual stimulation, usually to the point of orgasm, by herself or a partner six to seven times per week or more and acted upon the desire whenever possible, or (2) thought of herself as a highly sexual person with sex often on her mind and considered her sexuality as an aspect that strongly and frequently affected her behavior, life choices, and quality of life satisfaction. The women reported that their lives had been strongly affected by their sexuality, that their sexual appetite was too intense to be ignored, and for some, it was a major factor impacting their time and energy. Many reported struggles and challenges in their lives because of their sexuality including being labeled with historically pathologizing terms such as "nymphomaniac" and "sex addict," although the researcher conducting the interview concluded that neither the term "addiction" nor "compulsion" is applicable in describing these women. However, the women reported that their experiences as highly sexual women were filled with satisfactions and pleasure—in fact, each would not permanently change her sexuality if she had that option. The researcher also noted that many of the women indicated they wanted to participate in the study in hope that society would become more understanding and accepting of them and that other highly sexual women would become more accepting of themselves with less internal distress about their sexuality.

Satyriasis, referring to "abnormal" or "uncontrollable" sexual desire in men, is less commonly used than "nymphomania" because society has come to believe and expect men to be more sexual than women. For this reason, definitions of satyriasis infrequently include the adjective "excessive." Instead, reflecting ideas of male sexuality as a powerful drive, "uncontrollable" becomes the significant adjective. Satyriasis is not recognized as a clinical condition by the APA (2000).

As you read this chapter, remember to distinguish clearly between the clinical, judgmental, or casual connotations of the various terms. It can be tempting to define a behavior you don't like or approve of as paraphilic. But, unless you are clinically trained, you cannot diagnose someone (including yourself) as having a mental disorder.

As touched on previously, the line between a sexual variation and a paraphilia is often not exact, and the "labeling" of specific behaviors as either may be open to debate and void of scientific justification. However, for the sake of discussion, several variations in sexual behaviors are presented in the context of the *DSM-IV-TR* classifications. Some mental health professionals believe that classifying some sexual behaviors as paraphilias is flawed and reflects a pseudo-scientific attempt to control sexuality (see the "Think About It" box on the previous page).

> Through me forbidden voices.
> Voices of sexes and lusts . . .
> Voices veiled, and I remove the veil,
> Voices indecent by me clarified and
>   transfigured.
>
> —Walt Whitman
> (1819–1892)

Sexual Variations Among College Students

We have no reliable estimates of the number of individuals with paraphilias, although various studies have produced some clues. For example, a *Details* magazine survey of college students reported the prevalence of some variant and paraphilic behaviors among the sample (Elliott & Brantley, 1997). (See Figure 10.1.) Except for one behavior, "talked dirty," only a minority of the students reported ever having engaged in any of the behaviors listed. Note that the percentages of female and male students who had participated in a behavior were often nearly equal; for example, 6% of both female and male students indicated that they had engaged in sadomasochism. These findings of nearly similar behaviors seem to refute societal beliefs that women, in contrast to men, are more reserved or unconventional in their sexual expression.

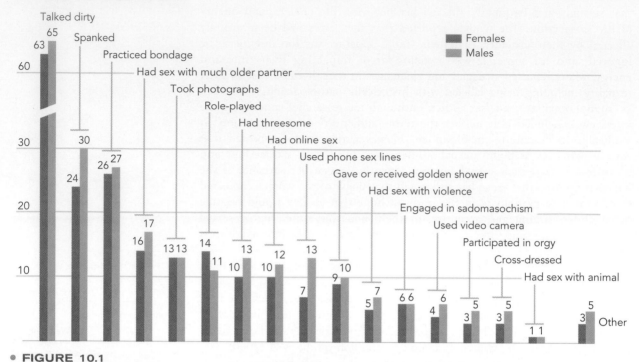

Percentage reporting participation

● **FIGURE 10.1**

Percentage of College Students Who Report Ever Having Engaged in Variations of Sexual Behavior. (*Source:* Adapted from Elliott & Brantley, 1997.)

Click on "Whipsmart: A Beginner's Guide to S/M" to meet a couple experimenting with domination and submission.

● Sexual Variation: Domination and Submission

Variations in sexual behavior are not rare. Although the majority of people do not engage in these activities, they are not necessarily uncommon. One of the more widespread forms of sexual variation is domination and submission.

Sexual arousal derived from the *consensual* acting out of sexual scenes in which one person dominates and the other submits is called **domination and submission (D/S).** The term **sadomasochism (S&M)** is also used by the general public to describe domination and submission, but it is no longer used as a clinical term in psychiatry and psychology to describe consensual domination and submission.

Domination and submission are forms of fantasy sex, and the D/S behaviors are carefully controlled by elaborate shared scripts. The critical element is not pain, but power. The dominant partner is perceived as all-powerful, and the submissive partner as powerless. Significantly, the amount or degree of "pain," which is usually feigned or slight, is controlled by the submissive partner, typically by subtle nonverbal signals. As such, fantasy plays a central role, especially for the submissive person (Arndt, 1991). As two people enact the agreed-upon master-slave script, the control is not complete. Rather, it is the *illusion* of total control that is fundamental to D/S (Hyde & DeLamater, 2008).

A large-scale study of a nonclinical population revealed that the majority of people who engage in domination and submission do so as "a form of sexual enhancement which they voluntarily and mutually choose to explore" (Weinberg, Williams, & Moser, 1984). As such, domination and submission are not paraphilic since the behavior is consensual and without pain. To be considered paraphilic,

Bondage and discipline, or B&D, often involves leather straps, handcuffs, and other restraints as part of its scripting.

Click on "Shannon: A Private Club Dancer Discusses S&M" to hear Shannon talk about her dominance-submission fantasy performances.

such behavior requires that the suffering or humiliation of oneself or one's partner be real, not merely simulated (APA, 2000). (Sexual sadism and sexual masochism, which are considered coercive paraphilias, are discussed later in the chapter.)

Domination and submission take many forms. The participants generally assume both dominant and submissive roles at different times; few are interested only in being on "top" or "bottom." Probably the most widely known form is **bondage and discipline (B&D).** B&D is a fairly common practice in which a person is bound with scarves, leather straps, underwear, handcuffs, chains, or other such devices while another simulates or engages in light-to-moderate discipline activities such as spanking or whipping. The bound person may be blindfolded or gagged. A woman specializing in disciplining a person is known as a **dominatrix,** and her submissive partner is called a slave.

Bondage and discipline may take place in specialized settings called "dungeons" furnished with restraints, body suspension devices, racks, whips, and chains. Eleven percent of both men and women have had experience with bondage, according to one study (Janus & Janus, 1993).

Another common form of domination and submission is humiliation, in which the person is debased or degraded. In the Janus study, 5% of the men and 7% of the women had engaged in verbal humiliation (Janus & Janus, 1993). One third of the submission respondents in another study received enemas ("water treatment"), were urinated on ("golden showers"), or were defecated on ("scat") (Breslow, Evans, & Langley, 1985). In the Janus study, 6% of the men and 4% of the women had participated in golden showers (Janus &

Ah beautiful, passionate body,
That never has ached with a heart!
On the mouth though the kisses are bloody,
Though they sting till it shudder and smart
More kind than the love we adore is
They hurt not the heart nor the brain
Oh bitter and tender Dolores
Our Lady of Pain.

—Algernon Swinburne
(1837–1909)

Bettie Page, who has become a cult figure among those interested in domination and submission, was one of the most photographed women in the 1950s.

Janus, 1993). (According to the *DSM-IV-TR,* sexual pleasure derived from receiving enemas is known as **klismaphilia** [klis-muh-FIL-ee-uh], that derived from contact with urine is called **urophilia** [yore-oh-FIL-ee-uh], and that derived from contact with feces is called **coprophilia** [cop-ro-FIL-ee-uh].) Humiliation activities may include servilism, infantilism (also known as babyism), kennelism, and tongue-lashing. In servilism, the person desires to be treated as a servant or slave. In infantilism, the person acts in a babyish manner—using baby talk, wearing diapers, and being pampered, scolded, or spanked by his or her "mommy" or "daddy." Kennelism refers to being treated like a dog (wearing a studded dog collar and being tied to a leash) or ridden like a horse while the dominant partner applies whips or spurs. Tongue-lashing is verbal abuse by a dominant partner who uses language that humiliates and degrades the other person.

People engage in domination and submission in private or as part of an organized subculture complete with clubs and businesses catering to the acting out of D/S fantasies. This subculture is sometimes known as "the velvet underground." There are scores of noncommercial D/S clubs throughout the United States. The clubs are often specialized: lesbian S&M, dominant men/submissive women, submissive men/dominant women, gay men's S&M, and transvestite S&M. Leather sex bars are meeting places for gay men who are interested in domination and submission. The D/S subculture includes D/S videos, Web sites, books, newspapers, and magazines.

> Do not do unto others as you would that they should do unto you. Their tastes may not be the same.
>
> —George Bernard Shaw (1856–1950)

● Noncoercive Paraphilias

An important aspect of paraphilias is whether they involve coercion. **Noncoercive paraphilias** are regarded as relatively benign or harmless because they are victimless. Noncoercive paraphilias include fetishism and transvestism.

Fetishism

We attribute special or magical powers to many things: a lucky number, a saint's relic, an heirloom, a lock of hair, or an automobile. These objects possess a kind of symbolic magic. We will carry our boyfriend's or girlfriend's photograph (and sometimes talk to it or kiss it), ask for a keepsake if we part, and become nostalgic for a former love when we hear a particular song. All these behaviors are common, but they point to the symbolic power of objects, or fetishes.

Fetishism is sexual attraction to objects that become, for the person with the fetish, sexual symbols. The fetish is usually required or strongly preferred for sexual arousal, and its absence may cause erectile problems in males (APA, 2000). Instead of relating to another person, a fetishist gains sexual gratification from kissing a shoe, caressing a glove, drawing a lock of hair against his or her cheek, or masturbating with a piece of underwear. But the focus of a person with fetishism is not necessarily an inanimate object; he may be attracted to a woman's feet, ears, breasts, legs, or elbows or to any other part of her body. (Exclusive attraction to body parts is known as **partialism.**) However, using objects for sexual stimulation, such as vibrators, or using articles of female clothing for cross-dressing is not a sign of fetishism (APA, 2000). According to the Janus study, 11% of the men and 6% of the women had engaged in fetishistic behaviors (Janus & Janus, 1993).

Fetishistic behavior may be viewed as existing on a continuum, or existing in degrees, moving from a slight preference for an object, to a strong preference for it, to the necessity of the object for arousal, and, finally, to the object as a substitute for a sexual partner (McConaghy, 1993). Most people have slight fetishistic traits. For example, some men describe themselves as "leg men" or "breast men"; they prefer dark-haired or light-haired partners. Some women

> *It is very disturbing indeed when you can't think of any new perversions that you would like to practice.*
>
> —James Pickey
> (1923–1997)

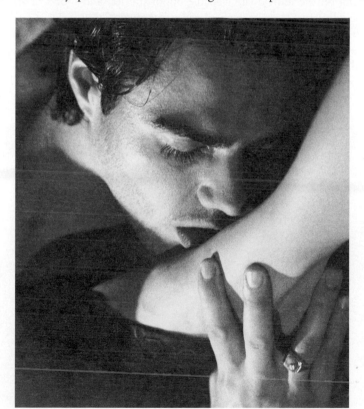

Inanimate objects or parts of the body, such as the foot, may be sexualized by some people.

are attracted to muscular men, others to hairy chests, and still others to shapely buttocks. However, to meet the APA definition of fetishism, a person must not be able to have sex without that fetish (Schwartz, 2000). Most fetishes and partialisms rarely cause harm, although, on rare occasions, individuals have committed burglary to acquire the fetish object (Lowenstein, 2002).

Transvestism

Transvestism ("trans" means cross, "vest" means dress) is the wearing of clothing of the other sex, usually for sexual arousal. In one study, 6% of the men and 3% of the women reported cross-dressing (Janus & Janus, 1993). Although the literature indicates that cross-dressing occurs almost exclusively in males, there are studies of women who have erotic attachment to men's garments (Bullough & Bullough, 1993; Stoller, 1982). The rarity of transvestism may have several reasons. One may be that our society is more accepting of women wearing "men's" clothing, such as ties, than men wearing "women's" clothes. So, women are not perceived as cross-dressing and men are less likely to report engaging in it because of negative social repercussions.

Transvestism covers a broad range of behaviors. Some persons with transvestism prefer to wear only one article of clothing (usually a brassiere or panties) of the other sex in the privacy of their home; others choose to don an entire outfit in public. The distinction between fetishism and transvestism involves the wearing of the garment versus the viewing or fondling of it. The frequency of cross-dressing ranges from a momentary activity that produces sexual excitement, usually through masturbation, to more frequent and long-lasting behavior, depending on the individual, available opportunities, and mood or stressors.

Some who cross-dress are considered psychologically disordered, as in **transvestic fetishism.** Research on the prevalence of transvestic fetishism is limited, but one random sample study of 2,450 persons from the general population of Sweden revealed that 2.8% of men and 0.4% of women reported at least one episode of transvestic fetishism (Langstrom & Zucker, 2005). The study found separation from parents, same-sex experiences, being sexually aroused

Cross-dressing is not necessarily a paraphilia. It may be a source of humor and parody, as the traditional boundaries of gender are explored and challenged.

think
about it

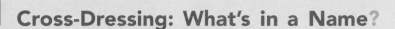

Cross-Dressing: What's in a Name?

Each year, vast numbers of ordinary men dress as women during Halloween, Mardi Gras, and Carnival. **Cross-dressing** is a staple of television shows such as *Saturday Night Live* and has been the focus of many movies, recently including *Kinky Boots, She's the Man*, and *Sorority Boys*. Rock culture includes cross-dressed performances by Marilyn Manson, Alice Cooper, Mick Jagger, David Bowie, Blondie, and Madonna. In the gay subculture, cross-dressing (or **drag**) is a source of humor and parody. In all these cases, cross-dressing represents a loosening of traditional boundaries. Behind masks and costumes, men and women play out fantasies that are forbidden to them in their daily lives.

According to a study of 1,032 cross-dressing men, excluding female impersonators and drag queens, 87% were heterosexual, 60% were married, and 65% were college educated. Sixty percent reported that sexual excitement and orgasm often or almost always occurred with cross-dressing (Docter & Prince, 1997). (**Female impersonators** are men who dress as women and **male impersonators** are women who dress as men, often as part of their job in entertainment. Gay men who cross-dress to entertain are often referred to as **drag queens.** Because neither female impersonators nor drag queens typically cross-dress for sexual arousal, they are not considered transvestites.)

As can readily be seen, people cross-dress for a variety of reasons. Some cross-dress to relieve the pressure associated with traditional gender roles. Others are satirizing or parodying social conventions. Still others want to challenge what they see as narrow views of gender and sexuality.

Given the humor, playfulness, and sense of relaxation apparent in many cases of cross-dressing, how do we distinguish this phenomenon from transvestic fetishism, which is considered a paraphilia? If those who cross-dress are labeled as having a paraphilia, what effect does it have on them? Does such labeling create mental distress in an otherwise relatively well-adjusted person?

Questions like these lead us to consider the effect of labeling in general and to ask, "What's in a name?" Although clinical labels and definitions help professionals to diagnose illnesses and create treatment plans, labeling can also cause problems. Consider the difference between someone said to have a strong libido and someone labeled a sex addict. The label adds a clinical dimension and stigma to the person's behavior. Labeling can have a profound effect both on an individual's self-concept and on the perceptions and behaviors of those involved with the person.

Among those who cross-dress, being labeled a person with a paraphilia can contribute to maladaptation by fostering unnecessary shame and guilt and may become a self-fulfilling prophecy. Although cross-dressing is variant, the majority of people who cross-dress are not maladapted or mentally disordered, nor is their behavior pathological. Therefore, to label all those who cross-dress as individuals with paraphilias is inaccurate and potentially harmful.

Think Critically

- Have you ever been to an event in which people cross-dressed? If so, how did you feel about the individuals who cross-dressed?
- What impact does labeling a certain sexual behavior have on a person?
- Why do you think our culture labels sexual behaviors, particularly those that are variant?
- Have you ever thought about cross-dressing yourself?

---

easily, use of sexually explicit materials, and higher frequency of masturbation to be related to the transvestic fetishism behavior.

According to the APA (2000), people with this label are heterosexual men who, over a period of at least 6 months, act upon intense, usually distressful, sexual urges and fantasies involving the wearing of women's clothes. Because many people with transvestism contend that they are not abnormal but are merely revealing a legitimate source of sexual expression and arousal, they resist and shun this diagnosis. Transvestic fetishism usually begins prior to adulthood. Some men report childhood experiences of being humiliated or punished by women and forced to dress in female attire (Maxmen & Ward, 1995).

Men with transvestism are usually quite conventional in their masculine dress and attitudes. Dressed as women or wearing only one women's garment, they

Those hot pants of hers were so damned tight, I could hardly breathe.

—Benny Hill
(1924–1992)

Cross-dressing has been important in popular culture, including comedy and Hollywood. A scene from the movie *Anger Management* shows Jack Nicholson with Woody Harrelson as Galaxia/Gary the Guard.

> I don't think painting my fingernails is a big deal. It's not like I'm sitting home by myself trying on lingerie. . . . When I cross-dress now, it's just another way I can show all the sides of Dennis Rodman.
>
> —Dennis Rodman (1961–)

> I don't mind drag—women have been female impersonators for some time.
>
> —Gloria Steinem (1934–)

may become sexually aroused and masturbate or have sex with a woman. As time passes, however, the erotic element of the female garment may decrease and the comfort level increase. The majority of people with transvestism have no desire to undergo a sex-change operation. If they do, there may be an accompanying diagnosis of gender dysphoria. Transvestism should not be confused with transsexualism. Most people with transvestism have no desire to change their anatomical sex, whereas transsexuals often do. Men with transvestism are rarely attracted to other men (Brown, 1995). They believe they have both masculine and feminine personalities within them; research shows that transvestites strongly prefer both their masculine and feminine selves equally (Docter & Prince, 1997). "TV" is the acronym for "transvestism" and often appears in personal ads in underground newspapers and in Internet dating services.

Many people with transvestism marry in hopes of "curing" their desire to cross-dress. Of those who marry, about two thirds have children. Some voluntarily reveal their cross-dressing to their spouse after marriage, but the majority have it discovered. Invariably, the partners are distressed and blame themselves for somehow "emasculating" their partners. Some people with transvestism and their spouses and families are able to adjust to the cross-dressing. Data suggest, however, that women merely tolerate rather than support their partner's cross-dressing, and many feel betrayed, angry, and scared that outsiders will find out about their partner's behavior (Reynolds & Caron, 2000). Sometimes, however, the stress is too great, and separation follows soon after the transvestism is discovered.

As transvestism is neither dangerous nor reversible (Wise & Meyer, 1980), the preferred clinical treatment is to help the person and those close to her or him accept the cross-dressing. Many transvestites seek counseling, often to deal with their feelings of guilt and shame.

● Coercive Paraphilias

Few noncoercive paraphilias are brought to public attention because of their private, victimless nature. But **coercive paraphilias,** which involve victimization, are a source of concern for society because of the harm they cause others. All of these paraphilias involve some kind of coercive or nonconsensual relationship with another person or with an animal.

Zoophilia

Zoophilia, sometimes referred to as "bestiality," involves deriving sexual pleasure from animals (APA, 2000). True zoophilia occurs only when animals are the preferred sexual contact regardless of what other sexual outlets are available. Zoophilia is classified as a coercive paraphilia based on the assumption that the animal is an unwilling participant. Alfred Kinsey and his colleagues reported that about 8% of the men and 4% of the women they surveyed had experienced at least one sexual contact with animals. Seventeen percent of the men who had been reared on farms had had such contact, but these activities accounted for less than 1% of their total sexual activity (Kinsey, Pomeroy, & Martin, 1948; Kinsey, Pomeroy, Martin, & Gebhard, 1953). Sexual contact with animals usually takes place among adolescents and is a transitory phenomenon. Males are likely to have intercourse with the animal or to have their genitals licked by the animal. Females are more likely to have contact with a household pet, such as having intercourse, having the animal lick their genitals, or masturbating the animal. Among adults, such contact usually occurs when human partners are not available (Money, 1981).

A research study of 114 self-identified men with zoophilia examined sexual interest in animals. The participants were primarily acquired through the use of an online questionnaire, and those who volunteered were asked to refer others who had similar interests. More than 9 of every 10 men who self-identified as "zoophiles" indicated that they were concerned with the welfare of the animals. They emphasized the importance of consensual sexual activity in contrast to persons they labeled as "**bestialists,**" those who have sex with animals but are not concerned with the animals' welfare. The men listed desire for affection and pleasurable sex as the most important reasons for sexual interest in animals. Many of the men had not had sex with a human partner of either sex in the past year. The researchers suggest that sexual activity with animals is usually immediate, easy, and intense, thus reinforcing the behavior (Williams & Weinberg, 2003).

Voyeurism

Viewing sexual activities is a commonplace activity. Many individuals have used mirrors to view themselves during sexual behavior, watched their partners masturbate, videotaped themselves and their partner having sex for later viewing, or watched others having intercourse. Americans' interest in viewing sexual activities has spawned a multibillion-dollar sex industry devoted to fulfilling those desires. Sexually explicit magazines, books, and Web sites and X-rated DVDs are widely available. Topless bars, live sex clubs, strip and peep shows, and erotic dancing attest to the attraction of visual erotica. These activities are not considered voyeurism because the observed person is willing and these activities typically do not replace interpersonal sexuality.

Voyeurism involves recurring, intense sexual urges and fantasies related to secretly observing an unsuspecting person who is nude, disrobing, or engaging in sexual activity (APA, 2000). To be considered paraphilic behavior, voyeurism must be preferred over sexual expression with another person or entail some risk. In order to become aroused, people with voyeurism must hide and remain unseen, and the person or couple being watched must be unaware of their

Would You Watch?
College Students and Voyeurism

Most research on voyeurism has focused on males in clinical and criminal settings. To investigate aspects of voyeurism in a relatively "normal" group of individuals, a sample of Canadian university students (232 women and 82 men) enrolled in a human sexuality class were asked to indicate whether they would watch an attractive person undressing or two attractive persons having sex in a hypothetical situation (Rye & Meaney, 2007). Students responded to the scenario below using a 0 to 100% scale with 0% meaning "extremely unlikely to watch" to 100% being "extremely likely to watch." They were also asked if their responses would be different if there was a possibility of being caught and punished for their behavior.

Students were presented with the following scenario:

You see someone whom you find *very* attractive. The person does not suspect that you can see him or her. He/she begins undressing.

Two questions were then posed:

1. If there were no chance of getting caught, how likely would it be that you would watch the person undressing?
2. He or she begins to have sex with another attractive person. How likely is it that you would watch the two people having sex?

Here is what the study found:

- With both men and women combined, the self-reported likelihood of watching an attractive person undress was significantly higher (67% on the 0-to-100% scale) than watching two attractive people having sex (45%).
- Men and women were not significantly different in their reported likelihood of watching an attractive person undress (73% men, 65% women).
- Men were significantly more likely than women (64% men, 39% women) to be willing to watch two attractive people having sex.
- When there was no possibility of being caught, the students were much more likely to be willing to watch an attractive person undress.

- When there was no possibility of being caught, the students were only slightly more likely to be willing to watch two attractive people having sex.

In discussing the results, the researchers noted that the students may have considered watching a couple having sex as more invasive than watching a person undress. They note that there are many more opportunities to observe others, covertly, in the different stages of undress (e.g., at the gym, at the beach) than seeing people having sex (usually limited to sex clubs or accidently walking in on a roommate or exhibitionistic, thrill-seeking couples in the college library stacks). The researchers also state that voyeuristic behavior may be acquired in several ways, such as evolutionary adaptations and social learning, then modified by social constraints, and that this perspective "fits well with Buss's (1998) sexual strategies theory—evolution may contribute to a psychological disposition toward voyeurism (probably higher for men than women), but actual behavior is influenced heavily by the environment. Similarly, women may have less desire for sexual viewing, but may still engage in such behavior when social constraints are relaxed." The researchers also conclude that the study results support contentions that social constraints are a regulator of voyeurism. (See Chapter 9 for a discussion of Buss's sexual strategies theory.)

Think Critically

- How would you have answered the questions presented in this research study? Were there any responses that surprised you? Would the possibility of being caught alter your responses?
- How would you feel if you found out you had been watched while undressing or having sex with someone?
- If you have had sex, did you enjoy watching him or her undress? If so, what impact did this have on your sexual interaction?

SOURCE: Rye, B. J., & Meaney, G. J. (2007). Voyeurism: It is good as long as we do not get caught. *International Journal of Sexual Health, 19,* 47–56.

presence. The excitement is intensified by the possibility of being discovered. Sometimes, the person with voyeurism will masturbate or imagine having sex with the observed person. People with voyeurism are sometimes called "peepers" or "peeping Toms." (Watching others who know they are being observed, such as a sex partner, stripper, or actor in a sexually explicit film, is not classified as voyeurism.) Voyeurism appeals primarily to heterosexual men (Arndt, 1991), most of whom are content to keep their distance from their victim. Many lack social and sexual skills and may fear rejection.

In a more recent type of voyeurism, labeled "video voyeurism," video cameras are used to take pictures of persons in private places as they change their clothes, shower, or engage in sexual activities. For example, video cameras have been hidden in places that are considered private, such as in health clubs and gyms. Cell phones with cameras have made it even easier to take pictures of nude persons and send them to others, a practice referred to as "sexting." A study conducted in 2008 found that 20% of teens and 33% of young adults ages 20–26 years have sent or posted nude or semi-nude images of themselves (The National Campaign to Prevent Teen and Unplanned Pregnancy, n.d.).

Very little research on voyeurism has been conducted, although the same nationally representative study of 2,450 persons in Sweden cited earlier in the discussion of transvestic fetishism also examined the prevalence of voyeurism, as well as exhibitionism (discussed in the next section of this chapter). Nearly 8% (7.7%) reported at least one incident of being sexually aroused by spying on others having sex (Langstrom & Seto, 2006). Like their study on transvestic fetishism, the researchers found that voyeurism and exhibitionism were associated with several variables; that is, those reporting voyeuristic and exhibitionistic behaviors were more likely to be male, to have more psychological problems, to have lower life satisfaction, to have greater substance abuse problems, to masturbate and use sexually explicit material more frequently, and to have had a same-sex partner. Further, they had greater odds of reporting other variant sexual behaviors, such as transvestic fetishism and sadomasochism. In their discussion of these findings, the researchers cautioned that the study found only an association, not a causation, between voyeurism and exhibitionism and lower psychological health and lower life satisfaction. (See the "Think About It" box on the previous page and consider how you would answer the research questions about voyeurism that were posed to a sample of college students.)

Exhibitionism

Also known as "indecent exposure," **exhibitionism** is the recurring, intense urge or fantasy to display one's genitals to an unsuspecting stranger (APA, 2000). The individual, who is almost always male and is sometimes called a "flasher," has acted on these urges or is greatly disturbed by them. People with exhibitionism may derive sexual gratification from the exposure of their genitals: The general population study in Sweden on voyeurism and exhibitionism found that 3.1% of the study participants reported at least one episode of being aroused by exposing their genitals to a stranger (Langstrom & Seto, 2006). However, exposure is not a prelude or invitation to intercourse. Instead, it is an escape from intercourse, for the man never exposes himself to a willing woman—only to strangers or near-strangers. Typically, he obtains sexual gratification after exposing himself as he fantasizes about the shock and horror he caused his victim. Other people with exhibitionism experience orgasm as they expose themselves; still others may masturbate during or after the exhibitionism (APA, 2000). These men generally expose themselves to children, adolescents, and young women; they rarely expose themselves to older women. In those few instances in which a woman shows interest, the person with exhibitionism immediately flees. Usually, there is no physical contact. Exotic dancers and nude sunbathers are not considered people with exhibitionism because they typically do not derive sexual arousal from the

Some people like to exhibit their bodies within public settings that are "legitimized," such as Mardi Gras. Such displays may be exhibitionistic, but they are not considered exhibitionism in the clinical sense.

behavior, nor do they expose themselves to unwilling people. Furthermore, stripping for a sex partner to arouse him or her involves willing participants.

Exhibitionism is a fairly common paraphilia; more than one third of all males arrested for sexual offenses are arrested for exhibitionism. According to one study, 7% of college men expressed interest in exhibiting themselves; 2% actually had (Templeman & Stinnett, 1991). Because of the widespread incidence of exhibitionism, at least half of adult women may have witnessed exhibitionism at least once in their lives (Arndt, 1991).

The stereotype of the person with exhibitionism as a dirty old man, lurking in parks or building entryways, dressed only in a raincoat and sneakers, is erroneous. Fewer than 10% of these individuals are over 50 years old, although a few may be in their eighties when they first begin (Arndt, 1991; Kenyon, 1989). Sometimes, the term "exhibitionist" is used in a pejorative way to describe a woman who dresses provocatively. These women, however, do not fit the American Psychiatric Association (2000) definition of exhibitionism described above. For example, they do not expose their genitals, nor does the provocative dressing cause marked distress or interpersonal behavior. Labeling women who dress provocatively as "exhibitionists" is more a case of a moral judgment than a scientific assessment.

A clinical interview study of 25 males with exhibitionism in which data were collected from 2003 to 2005 added further understanding of the features of males with exhibitionism. Most of the participants were heterosexual, and all reported urges to expose themselves with little control of the urges. For this sample of exhibitionists, exposing oneself while driving was the most common expression of this paraphilia. Over 90% suffered from depression, personality disorders, or substance abuse disorders, and suicidal thoughts were common (Grant, 2005). Exhibitionists often feel powerless as men, and their sexual relations with their wives or partners usually are poor. This sense of powerlessness gives rise to anger and hostility, which they direct toward other women by exhibiting themselves. However, they

Dealing With a Harassing or Obscene Phone Call

A **harassing or obscene phone call can be shocking and even traumatizing.** A person who receives such a call may feel attacked, singled out, or victimized. Many who have received such calls consider them a very frightening invasion of their privacy. If you have had this experience, it may be helpful to know that the obscene phone caller often picks the victim at random and is merely trying to elicit a response. Obscene phone callers rarely follow up their verbal intrusions with physical attacks on their victims. Horror, anger, and shock are the reactions the caller anticipates and finds arousing; thus, your initial response is critical.

If you receive a harassing or obscene phone call, the best thing to do is not to overreact and to quietly hang up the telephone. Banging down the receiver or trying to retaliate by screaming or scolding gives the caller the desired response. Keep cool. Don't engage in a conversation with the caller, such as trying to determine why the person is calling or why the person won't stop calling. Remember, the caller wants an audience. You should not give out personal information such as your name or phone number to anyone who is a stranger nor respond to any questions if you do not know the caller.

If the phone immediately rings again, don't answer it. If obscene calls are repeated, the telephone company suggests changing your number (many companies will do this at no charge), keeping a log of the calls, or, in more serious cases, working with law enforcement officials to trace the calls. A service available through many telephone companies is "call trace." When the recipient of a call enters a designated code, the telephone company can trace the call. After a certain number of traces to the same telephone number, the offender will receive a warning that the unlawful behavior must stop. Ignoring this warning results in police or civil legal intervention. Other solutions include getting an unlisted phone number, screening calls with an answering machine, and obtaining caller ID. By the way, don't include your name, phone number, or other personal information such as when you will be away and returning in the outgoing message on your answering service. Furthermore, when listing a number in the telephone book, many women use initials for their first (and middle) names to help disguise their gender. One final suggestion—be cautious in placing ads in newspapers or on electronic media or allowing strangers access to personal information on social networking sites. Obscene phone callers are frequent readers of the classified ads. Use a post office number or e-mail address. If you feel you must give your phone number, don't give the address of your residence.

rarely are violent. If confronted with a person with exhibitionism, it is best to ignore and distance oneself from the person and then report the incident to the police. Reacting strongly, though a natural response, only reinforces the behavior.

Telephone Scatologia

Telephone scatologia—the making of obscene phone calls to unsuspecting people—is considered a paraphilia because the acts are compulsive and repetitive or because the associated fantasies cause distress to the individual.

Those who engage in this behavior typically get sexually aroused when their victim reacts in a shocked or horrified manner. Obscene phone calls are generally made randomly, by chance dialing or phone book listings. Some people with this paraphilia repeatedly make these calls.

The overwhelming majority of callers are male, but there are female obscene callers as well (Price, Kafka, Commons, Gutheil, & Simpson, 2002; Saunders & Awad, 1991). Male callers frequently make their female victims feel annoyed, frightened, anxious, upset, or angry, while the callers themselves often suffer from feelings of inadequacy and insecurity. They may use obscenities, breathe heavily into the phone, or say they are conducting sex research. Also, they usually masturbate during the call or immediately afterward. The victims of male callers often

...

"Sexual Addiction": Repressive Morality in a New Guise?

Are you a sex addict? As you read descriptions of sexual addiction, you may begin to think that you are. But don't believe everything you read. Consider the following: "The moment comes for every addict," writes psychologist Patrick Carnes (1983, 1991), who developed and marketed the idea of sexual addiction, "when the consequences are so great or the pain so bad that the addict admits life is out of control because of his or her sexual behavior." Money is spent on pornography, affairs threaten a marriage, masturbation replaces jogging, and fantasies interrupt studying. Sex, sex, sex is on the addict's mind. And he or she has no choice but to engage in these activities.

Sex addicts' lives are filled with guilt or remorse, according to Carnes. They cannot make a commitment; instead, they move from one affair to another. They make promises to themselves, to their partners, and to a supreme being to stop, but they cannot. Like all addicts, they are powerless before their addiction (Butts, 1992; Carnes, 1983, 1991). Their addiction is rooted in deep-seated feelings of worthlessness, despair, anxiety, and loneliness. These feelings are temporarily allayed by the "high" obtained from sexual arousal and orgasm. According to Carnes, sexual addiction is viewed in the same light as alcoholism and drug addiction; it is an activity over which the addict has no control. And, as for alcoholism, a 12-step treatment program for sex addiction has been established by the National Council on Sexual Addiction/Compulsivity.

Are you wondering, "Am I a sex addict?" Don't worry; you're probably not. The reason you might think you're suffering from sexual addiction is that its definition taps into many of the underlying anxieties and uncertainties we feel about sexuality in our culture. The problem lies not in you but in the concept of sexual addiction.

Although the idea of sexual addiction has found some adherents among clinical psychologists, they are clearly a minority. The influence of the sexual addiction concept is not the result of its impact on therapy, psychology, and social work. Its influence is due mainly to its popularity with the media, where talk-show hosts interview so-called sex addicts and advice columnists caution their readers about the signs of sexual addiction. The popularity of an idea is no guarantee of its validity, however. The sexual addiction concept has been rejected by a number of sex researchers as nothing more than pop psychology. These researchers suggest that the idea of sexual addiction is really repressive morality in a new guise.

Attempts to describe certain sexual behaviors by labeling them as sexual addictions continue to be problematic for the professional sexuality community. Different terms have been used in attempts to describe certain behavioral patterns. For example, Eli Coleman (1991; 1996; cited in Tepper & Owens, 2007), director of the human sexuality program at the University of Minnesota Medical School, favors "sexual compulsivity" over "sexual addiction" and

feel violated, but female callers have a different effect on male recipients, who generally do not feel violated or who may find the call titillating (Matek, 1988).

Frotteurism

Frotteurism (also known as "mashing" or "frottage") involves recurrent, intense urges or fantasies—lasting over a period of at least 6 months—to touch or rub against a nonconsenting person for the purpose of sexual arousal and gratification (APA, 2000). It is not known how many people practice frotteurism, but 21% of college males in one study reported engaging in at least one episode of frotteurism (Templeman & Stinnett, 1991).

The person with frotteurism, most often a male, usually carries out his touching or rubbing in crowded subways or buses or at large sporting events or rock concerts. When he enters a crowd, his initial rubbing can be disguised by the crush of people. He usually rubs against his victim's buttocks or thighs with his erect penis inside his pants. Other times, he may use his hands to rub a woman's buttocks, pubic region, thighs, or breasts. Generally, he rubs against the woman for 60–90 seconds. If he ejaculates, he stops; if he doesn't, he usually moves on to find another victim (Abel, 1989). The frotteurism may be so

goes further by distinguishing between compulsive and problematic sexual behavior:

> There has been a long tradition of pathologizing behavior which is not mainstream and which some might find distasteful. Behaviors which are in conflict with someone's value system may be problematic but not obsessive-compulsive. Having sexual problems is common. Problems are caused by a number of nonpathological factors. People make mistakes. They can at times act impulsively. Their behavior can cause problems in a relationship. Some people will use sex as a coping mechanism similar to the use of alcohol, drugs, or eating. This pattern of sexual behavior is problematic. Problematic sexual behavior is often remedied by time, experience, education, or brief counseling. Obsessive and compulsive behavior, by its nature, is much more resistant to change.

Coleman and colleagues (1987; Coleman, Raymond, & McBean, 2003) consider compulsive sexual behavior as a clinical syndrome in which the person experiences sexual urges, fantasies, and behaviors that are recurrent and intense and interfere with daily functioning. Persons with compulsive sexual behavior often perceive their sexual behavior as being excessive and uncontrollable.

The term "hypersexuality" has sometimes been used as a less prejorative term for sexual addiction. Because of the limitations of the sexual addiction concept, the APA chose not to include "hypersexuality" in its most recent edition of the *DSM*. John Bancroft, senior research fellow and former director of The Kinsey Institute for Research in Sex, Gender, and Reproduction, and colleague Zoran Vukadinovic (2004) add even another perspective. After reviewing the concepts and theoretical bases of sexual addition, sexual compulsivity, and sexual impulsivity (another labeling term), they concluded that it is premature to attempt an overriding definition because patterns of such behavior are varied in both their causes and how they are best treated. They continue by noting that until there is better understanding of this type of sexual expression, they prefer the general descriptive term "out-of-control sexual behavior."

All of this discussion has challenged us to consider what is "excessive sexual behavior" and how culture shapes norms and our reactions and thoughts surrounding it. Certainly, it has caused mental health professionals to consider ways to address highly sexual persons.

If your sexual fantasies and activities are distressing to you, or your behaviors are emotionally or physically harmful to yourself or others, you should consult a therapist. The chances are, however, that your sexuality and your unique expression of it are healthy.

Think Critically

- What are your thoughts about the term "sexual addiction"? Do you like the term "sexual compulsivity" or "out-of-control sexual behavior" better?
- Do you agree or disagree that the idea of sexual addiction is really repressive morality in a new guise?
- Have you ever wondered if you are a sex addict or that your sexual behavior is out of control? On what did you base this label?

surreptitious that the woman may not know what is happening. If she discovers it, the man will usually run away. Hence, nearly all escape. While mashing, the male may fantasize about having consensual sex with the women, and he may recall the mashing episode when masturbating in the future.

Frotteurism often occurs with other paraphilias, especially exhibitionism, voyeurism, pedophilia, and sadism. It is also associated with rape.

Necrophilia

Necrophilia is sexual activity with a corpse. It is regarded as nonconsensual because a corpse is obviously unable to give consent. There are relatively few instances of necrophilia, yet it retains a fascination in horror literature, especially vampire stories and legends, and in gothic novels. It is also associated with ritual cannibalism in other cultures. Within our own culture, *Sleeping Beauty* features a necrophilic theme, as does the crypt scene in Shakespeare's *Romeo and Juliet*.

In a review of 122 cases of supposed necrophilia or necrophilic fantasies, researchers found only 54 instances of true necrophilia (Rosman & Resnick, 1989). The study found that neither sadism, psychosis, nor mental impairment was inherent in necrophilia. Instead, the most common motive for necrophilia

> The dead person who loves will love forever and will never be weary of giving and receiving caresses.
>
> —Ernest Jones
> (1879–1958)

was the possession of a partner who neither resisted nor rejected. Clearly, many people with necrophilia are severely mentally disturbed.

Pedophilia

Pedophilia refers to "recurrent intense sexual urges and sexually arousing fantasies involving sexual activity with a prepubescent child or children" that the individual has acted upon or finds distressing or that results in interpersonal difficulty (APA, 2000). However, acting upon fantasies without personal distress is still considered a pedophilia by the APA. According to the APA, the children are aged 13 or younger and a person with pedophilia must be at least 16 and at least 5 years older than the child. (A late adolescent is not considered to have pedophilia if he or she is involved in an ongoing sexual relationship with a 12-year-old or older child.) Almost all people with pedophilia are males. In this section, we discuss only pedophilia. Pedophilia is different from "child sexual abuse," "child molestation," and "incest," although all denote sex with minors, which is a criminal action. Pedophilia, as defined by the APA, is a psychiatric disorder. Not all of those who sexually abuse minors would be considered people with pedophilia unless the APA criteria are met. Sexual contact with a minor is not, in itself, a determination of pedophilia (Fagan, Wise, Schmidt, & Berlin, 2002). It is, however, illegal. Nonpedophilic child sexual abuse and incest, their impact on the victims, and prevention of child sexual abuse are discussed in Chapter 17. Child sexual abuse is illegal in every state.

Some individuals with pedophilia prefer only one sex, whereas others are aroused by both male and female children. Those attracted to females usually seek 8–10-year-olds, and those attracted to males usually seek slightly older children. Some people with pedophilia are sexually attracted to children only, and some are aroused by both children and adults (APA, 2000).

Other-Sex Pedophilia   Other-sex pedophilia is more common than same-sex pedophilia. About half of people with pedophilia report stressful events, such as marital or work conflict, personal loss, or rejection, preceding the sexual assault. Many are fearful that their sexual abilities are decreasing or that they are unable to perform sexually with their partners.

People with pedophilia often use seduction and enticement to manipulate children—their own children, stepchildren, relatives, or children outside the family (APA, 2000). The Internet provides a way for a person with pedophilia to make contact with unsuspecting children. A man sometimes cruises chat rooms designed for children, and he may convince a girl to agree to e-mail, postal, or telephone contact. He may befriend the girl, talking to her, giving her candy, taking her to the store, going for walks with her, and letting her watch TV or use a computer at his house. Gradually, he initiates visual and/or tactile contact with her such as watching pornographic sites with her, having her sit on his lap, rough-housing with her, or giving her a back rub. Eventually, he may attempt to fondle her. If she resists, he will stop and try again later. He will resort to added inducements or pressure but will rarely use force. The perpetrator is more likely to be a relative or someone else the victim knows. Even though these latter cases are far more common, they are much less likely to be reported because of the pressures and consequences the molester threatens the child with.

Pedophilic behaviors rarely involve sexual intercourse. The person with pedophilia usually seeks to fondle or touch the child, usually on the genitals, legs, and buttocks. Sometimes, he exposes himself and has the child touch his penis.

He may masturbate in the presence of the child. Occasionally, oral or anal stimulation is involved (Arndt, 1991).

About half of people with pedophilia are or have been married. Most who are married claim that their marriages are happy, although many describe their wives as controlling and sexually distant. Their frequency of marital intercourse does not differ from that of people without pedophilia, but many report a low sex drive and erectile difficulties. Few have serious mental disorders, such as psychosis (Arndt, 1991).

Same-Sex Pedophilia Same-sex pedophilia is a complicated phenomenon. It does not appear to be as closely linked to homosexuality as other-sex pedophilia is to heterosexuality. A different kind of psychosexual dynamic seems to be at work for a large number of same-sex pedophiles. Although most people with same-sex pedophilia have little interest in other-sex relationships, a significant number do not identify themselves as gay. In fact, many reject a gay identity or are homophobic. Although some people believe that pedophilia is the means by which the gay community "recruits" boys into homosexuality, pedophiles are strongly rejected by the gay subculture (Peters, 1992).

The mean age of the victim is between 10 and 12. A large number of men with same-sex pedophilia describe feelings of love, friendship, or caring for the boy. Others blatantly entice or exploit their victims. Force is rarely used. Voluntary interviews with 27 men with same-sex pedophilia reveal four themes to explain their involvement with children: (1) their pedophilic desire feels "natural" to them, (2) children are appealing because they are gentle and truthful, (3) adult-child sexual involvement can be positive for the child, and (4) the relationship is characterized by romantic love, not casual sex (Li, 1990). Such views are generally regarded as cognitive distortions or rationalizations. Adult-child sexual relationships are by definition exploitive. The majority of children report feelings of victimization (Finkelhor, 1990).

The most common same-sex pedophilia activities are fondling and masturbation, usually with the man masturbating the boy. Other behaviors include oral-genital sex, with the man fellating the boy, and anal sex, with the man assuming the active role.

Female Pedophilia Although there are relatively few reports of females with pedophilia, they do exist (Arndt, 1991; Rowan, 1988). Female pedophilia appears to be underreported for two reasons (Rowan, 1988). First, women are viewed as maternal and nurturing. Because of these stereotypes, women are given greater freedom than men in touching children and expressing feelings for them. As a consequence, when a female with pedophilia embraces, kisses, or caresses a child, her behavior may be viewed as nurturing rather than sexual. But when a male not having pedophilia does the same thing, his behavior may be misinterpreted as sexual. Second, the majority of male children who have sexual contact with adult women generally view the experience positively rather than negatively. As a consequence, they do not report the contact (Condy, Templer, Brown, & Veaco, 1987).

Sexual Sadism and Sexual Masochism

Sadism and masochism are separate but sometimes related phenomena. People with sadism do not necessarily practice masochism, and vice versa. In order to

I had to give up masochism—I was enjoying it too much.

—Mel Calman
(1931–1994)

make this distinction clear, the APA (2000) has created separate categories: sexual sadism and sexual masochism.

Often, there is no clear dividing line between sexual sadism/sexual masochism and domination and submission. In the case of sadism, coercion separates sexual sadism from domination. But for consensual behaviors, there is no clear distinction. A rule of thumb for separating consensual sexual sadism and masochism from domination and submission may be that acts of sadism and masochism are extreme, compulsive, and dangerous. Sadomasochistic sex partners often make specific agreements ahead of time concerning the amount of pain and punishment that will occur during sexual activity. Nevertheless, the acting-out of fantasies involves risk, such as physical injury (e.g., a deep cut); thus, it is important that individuals communicate their preferences and limits before they engage in any new activity.

A questionnaire study of 184 Finnish men and women who were members of two sadomasochistic-oriented clubs identified 29 sexual behaviors that were grouped in four different sexual scripts: hypermasculinity (e.g., using a dildo, an enema), administration and receipt of pain (e.g., hot wax, clothespins attached to nipples), physical restriction (e.g., using handcuffs), and psychological humiliation (e.g., face slapping and using knives to make surface wounds) (Alison, Santtila, Sandnabba, & Nordling, 2001; Santilla, Sandnabba, Alison, & Nordling, 2002).

Sexual Sadism According to the *DSM-IV-TR*, a person may be diagnosed with **sexual sadism** if, over a period of at least 6 months, she or he experiences intense, recurring sexual urges or fantasies involving real (not simulated) behaviors in which physical or psychological harm (including humiliation) is inflicted upon a victim for purposes of sexual arousal. The individual either has acted on these urges with a nonconsenting person or finds them extremely distressful (APA, 2000). Characteristic symptoms include sexual thoughts and fantasies involving dominating behaviors centering on a victim's physical suffering, which is sexually arousing. The victim may be a consenting person with masochism or someone abducted by a person with sadism. The victim may be tortured, raped, mutilated,

I would love to be whipped by you, Nora, love!

—James Joyce (1882–1941), from a love letter to his wife

The movie *Lies* (also called *Gojitmal*) explores the "fantasy and flesh" of sexual sadism.

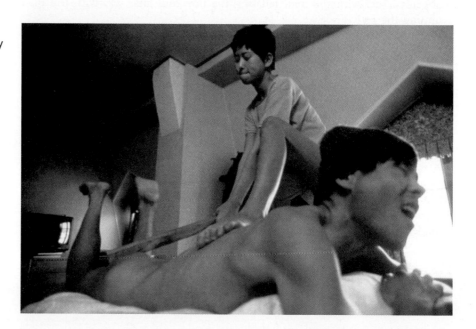

or killed; often, the victim is physically restrained and blindfolded or gagged (Money, 1990). However, most rapes are not committed by sexual sadists.

Sexual Masochism According to the *DSM-IV-TR,* for a diagnosis of **sexual masochism** to be made, a person must experience for a period of at least 6 months intense, recurring sexual urges or fantasies involving real (not simulated) behaviors of being "humiliated, beaten, bound, or otherwise made to suffer." These fantasies, sexual urges, or behaviors must result in significant distress or social impairment. Some individuals express the sexual urges by themselves (e.g., through self-mutilation or by binding themselves); others act with partners. Masochistic behaviors expressed with a partner may include being restrained, blindfolded, paddled, spanked, whipped, beaten, shocked, cut, "pinned and pierced," and humiliated (e.g., being urinated or defecated on or forced to crawl and bark like a dog). The individual may desire to be treated as an infant and be forced to wear diapers ("infantilism"). The degree of pain one must experience to achieve sexual arousal varies from symbolic gestures to severe mutilations. As noted previously, sexual masochism is the only paraphilia that occurs with some frequency in women.

> Ouch! That felt good.
> —Karen E. Gordon

> It's been so long since I made love I can't even remember who gets tied up.
> —Joan Rivers
> (1933–)

Autoerotic Asphyxia A form of sexual masochism called **autoerotic asphyxia** (also called hypoxphilia or asphyxiphilia) links strangulation with masturbation. Those who participate in this activity seek to heighten their masturbatory arousal and orgasm by cutting off the oxygen supply to the brain. A person may engage in this practice either alone or with a partner. If death occurs, it is usually accidental. Autoerotic asphyxiation is an increasing phenomenon, with more than 1,000 fatalities in the United States per year and the ratio of male to female accidental deaths being more than 50 to 1 (Gosink & Jumbelic, 2000). Because of the secrecy and shame that accompany this and other masturbatory activities, it is difficult to estimate the number of individuals who find this practice arousing. Reports by survivors are extremely rare or are masked by another cause of death.

Individuals often use ropes, cords, or chains along with padding around the neck to prevent telltale signs. Others may place bags or blankets over their heads. Still others inhale asphyxiating gases such as aerosol sprays or amyl nitrate ("poppers"), a drug used to treat heart pain. The corpses are usually found either naked or partially clothed, often in women's clothing. Various forms of bondage have also been observed (Blanchard & Hucker, 1991). A review of all published cases of autoerotic deaths from 1954 to 2004 found 408 deaths reported in 57 articles. The review revealed that autoerotic practitioners were predominantly White males ranging in age from 9 to 77 years. Most cases of asphyxia involved hanging, use of ligature, plastic bags, chemical substances, or a combination of these. Atypical methods accounted for about 10% of the cases and included electrocution, overdressing/body wrapping, foreign-body insertion, and chest compression (Sauvageau & Racette, 2006). The possibility of suicide should always be considered even in cases that initially appear to be accidental (Byard & Botterill, 1998).

Although researchers have some understanding of why people participate in this practice, it is more important that medical personnel, parents, and other adults recognize signs of it and respond with strategies commensurate with its seriousness. Those who engage in such sexual practices rarely realize the potential consequences of their behavior; therefore, parents and others must be alert to physical and other telltale signs. An unusual neck bruise; bloodshot eyes; disoriented behavior, especially after the person has been alone for a while; and unexplained possession of or fascination with ropes or chains are the key signs. Until we as a society can educate about, recognize, and respond to autoerotic asphyxia assertively and compassionately, we can expect to see more deaths as a result of this practice.

● Origins and Treatment of Paraphilias

How do people develop paraphilias? As with many other behaviors, paraphilias probably result from some type of interaction among biology, sociocultural norms, and life experiences. Because most people with paraphilia are male, biological factors may be particularly significant. Some researchers have postulated that males with paraphilia may have higher testosterone levels than those without paraphilias, that they have had brain damage, or that the paraphilia may be inherited. Because the data are inconclusive, however, it has not been possible to identify a specific biological cause of paraphilia. People with paraphilia seem to have grown up in dysfunctional environments and to have had early experiences that limited their ability to be sexually stimulated by consensual sexual activity; as a result, they obtain arousal through varied means. They may have low self-esteem, poor social skills, and feelings of anger and loneliness; be self-critical; and lack a clear sense of self (Fisher & Howells, 1993; Goodman, 1993; Marshall, 1993). Another factor may be a limited ability to empathize with the victims of their behavior. The psychological outcomes of these behaviors serve to direct sexual attraction and response away from intimate relationships in later life (Schwartz, 2000).

Therapists have found paraphilias to be difficult to treat (McConaghy, 1998). Most people who are treated are convicted sex offenders, who have the most severe paraphilias, while those with milder paraphilias go untreated. Multifaceted treatments, such as psychodynamic therapy, aversive conditioning, cognitive-behavioral programs, relapse prevention, and medical intervention, have been tried to reduce or eliminate the symptoms of the paraphilia. Enhancing social and sexual skills, developing self-management plans, modifying sexual interests, and providing sexuality and relationship education may help people with paraphilia engage in more appropriate behavior (Marshall, Marshall, & Serran, 2006; Seligman & Hardenberg, 2000). However, even when the client desires to change, treatments may not be effective, and relapses often occur. Hence, some experts believe that prevention is the best approach, although prevention programs are currently very limited.

Final Thoughts

Studying variations in sexual behaviors reveals the variety and complexity of sexual behavior. It also underlines the limits of tolerance. Mental health professionals believe unconventional sexual behaviors, undertaken in private between consenting adults as the source of erotic pleasure, should be of concern only to the people involved. As long as physical or psychological harm is not done to oneself or others, is it anyone's place to judge? Coercive paraphilic behavior, however, may be injurious and should be treated.

Summary

Sexual Variations and Paraphilic Behavior

- *Sexual variation* is behavior in which less than the majority of individuals engage. Variant sexual behavior is not abnormal behavior, the definition of which varies from culture to culture and from one historical period to another.

- Recurring, intense, sexually arousing fantasies, urges, or behaviors involving nonhuman objects, suffering or humiliation, or children or other nonconsenting individuals or animals are known as *paraphilias.* Paraphilias tend to be injurious, compulsive, and long-standing. They may be noncoercive or coercive.

Sexual Variation: Domination and Submission

- *Domination and submission (D/S)* is a form of consensual fantasy sex involving no pain with perceived power as the central element.

Noncoercive Paraphilias

- Although there are no reliable data on the number of individuals involved, paraphilic activities are widespread in the nonoffender population.

- *Fetishism* is sexual attraction to objects. The fetishism is usually required or strongly preferred for sexual arousal.

- *Transvestism* is the wearing of clothes of a member of the other sex, usually for sexual arousal.

Coercive Paraphilias

- *Zoophilia* involves animals as the preferred sexual outlet even when other outlets are available.

- *Voyeurism* is the nonconsensual and secret observation of others for the purpose of sexual arousal.

- *Exhibitionism* is the exposure of the genitals to a nonconsenting stranger.

- *Telephone scatologia* is the nonconsensual telephoning of strangers and often involves the use of obscene language.

- *Frotteurism* involves touching or rubbing against a nonconsenting person for the purpose of sexual arousal.

- *Necrophilia* is sexual activity with a corpse.

- *Pedophilia* refers to sexual arousal and contact with children aged 13 or younger by adults. A person with pedophilia must be at least 16 and at least 5 years older than the child. Child sexual abuse is illegal in every state. For many people with pedophilia, the fact that a child is a child is more important than gender. Heterosexual and gay men may both be pedophilically attracted to boys; gay men with pedophilia are less attracted to girls.

- The Internet is a place for people with pedophilia to contact unsuspecting children.

- The majority of people with pedophilia know their victim. About half of pedophiles have been married. The most common activities are fondling and masturbation.

- There are relatively few reported cases of females with pedophilia, but it may be underreported for two reasons: because of stereotypes of female nurturance, pedophilic activities may not be recognized and the majority of male children apparently view the event positively or neutrally.

- *Sexual sadism* refers to sexual urges or fantasies of intentionally inflicting real physical or psychological pain or suffering on a person.

- *Sexual masochism* is the recurring sexual urge or fantasy of being humiliated or made to suffer through real behaviors, not simulated ones.

- *Autoerotic asphyxia* is a form of sexual masochism linking strangulation with masturbatory activities.

Origins and Treatment of Paraphilias

- Paraphilias are likely the result of social/environmental, psychological, and biological factors.

- Paraphilias are difficult to treat, and relapses often occur.

- Prevention programs may be the most effective way to address paraphilias.

Questions for Discussion

- Do you consider certain sexual behaviors to be "deviant," "abnormal," or "perverted"? If so, how did you come to believe this?

- From the types of paraphilias discussed in this chapter, do you find any of them to be repulsive or even "pathological"?

- Do you think that labeling certain sexual behaviors as paraphilic is a reflection of efforts to control and discourage behaviors that society does not want expressed? If yes, should any sexual behaviors, such as pedophilia, be controlled? If no, why do you think certain sexual behaviors are labeled a paraphilia?

- Are you comfortable with the term "sexual variations"? If yes, why is it a good term for you? If no, which term do you like to describe "unusual" sexual behavior? Explain.

Sex and the Internet

Paraphilias

The Web is one resource for locating information about paraphilias. Go to the Google Web site (http://www.google.com) and type "paraphilias" in the Google Search box. As you can see, there are a wide range of different sites posted. Look over the posted sites and answer the following questions:

- What types of Web sites are listed?
- Are the sites from medical and academic organizations, individuals, or commercial groups?
- Are there sites for specific paraphilias?
- Which sites provide the most valuable information to you? Why?
- Did you learn anything new about paraphilias from the Web sites? If so, what?
- Do you believe that any of the sites contain inaccurate or harmful information? Explain.

Suggested Web Sites

AllPsych Online
http://allpsych.com/disorders/paraphilias
Offers information on numerous psychiatric disorders, including symptoms, etiology, treatment, and prognosis for paraphilias and sexual disorders.

Discovery Health Channel, Sexual Health Center
http://health.discovery.com/centers/sex/sexpedia/sexpedia.html
Provides comprehensive information about sexuality, including paraphilias.

Mental-Health-Matters.com
http://www.mental-health-matters.com/disorders
Provides information, help sources, and advocacy suggestions concerning mental health issues, including paraphilias, sexual addiction, and gender identity disorder.

Suggested Reading

Arndt, W. B., Jr. (1991). *Gender disorders and the paraphilias.* Madison, CT: International Universities Press. A comprehensive look at transvestism, transsexuality, and the paraphilias.

Boyd, H. (2007). *She's not the man I married: My life with a transgender husband.* Emeryville, CA: Seal Press. Explores the impact of the author's husband becoming a transgender person.

Brame, G. G. (2000). *Come hither: A commonsense guide to kinky sex.* New York: Fireside Books. More than a "how-to-do" book, this straightforward book includes anecdotes and a useful, sex-positive message about kinky sex.

Laws, D. R., & O'Donohue, W. (Eds.). (1997). *Sexual deviance: Theory, assessment and treatment.* New York: Guilford Press. A collection of papers that examine the theories, assessment procedures, and treatment techniques for a spectrum of sexually variant behaviors.

Money, J. (1989). *Lovemaps.* Buffalo, NY: Prometheus Books. A description of variant and paraphilic behavior.

Moser, C., & Madeson, J. J. (1996). *Bound to be free: The SM experience.* New York: Continuum. A collaborative personal view of S&M by a sexologist and a practitioner of S&M.

Tyler, A., & Bussel, R. K. (Eds.). (2006). *Caught looking: Erotic tales of voyeurs and exhibitionists.* San Francisco: Cleis Press. A collection of 20 short fiction stories with the theme being voyeurism and exhibitionism.

For links, articles, and study material, go to the McGraw-Hill Web site, located at **www.mhhe.com/yarber7e.**

Contraception, Birth Control, and Abortion

"My parents and I never talked about sex until I had to ask them questions for one of my high school classes. They got so excited about the topic. I guess they were just waiting for me to ask. I remember my mom throwing a pack of condoms on the bed. She said, 'Just in case!' We just all laughed."

—20-year-old male

"During the summer before my sophomore year, things started to change. My father came into my room much as he had done the first time. It was 'The Talk, Part Two.' He asked me if I knew what a condom was and told me about abstinence. I told him I wasn't planning on having sex for a while, but I was lying; it was all I thought about. I felt awkward and embarrassed. Nevertheless, he made his point, and before he left he said, 'I love you.'"

—20-year-old male

"Mom gave me an important sense that my body was mine, that it was my responsibility and under my control. Birth control was always discussed whenever sex was mentioned, but when it was, it was treated like a joke. The message was that sex can be a magical thing as long as you are being responsible—responsible for not getting yourself or anyone else pregnant. Back then, sexually transmitted diseases were not discussed, so it was the pill or a diaphragm for me and condoms for my brothers."

—26-year-old female

TODAY, MORE THAN EVER BEFORE, we are aware of the impact of fertility on our own lives, as well as on the world. Reproduction, once considered strictly a personal matter, is now a subject of open debate and political action. Yet, regardless of our public views, we must each confront fertility on a personal level. In taking charge of our reproductive potential, we must be informed about the available methods of birth control, as well as ways to protect ourselves against sexually transmitted infections (STIs). But information is only part of the picture. We also need to understand our own personal needs, values, and habits so that we can choose methods we will use consistently, thereby minimizing our risks.

In this chapter, we begin by examining the psychology of risk taking and the role of individual responsibility in contraception. We then describe in detail the numerous contraceptive devices and techniques that are used today: methods of use, effectiveness rates, advantages, and possible problems. Finally, we look at abortion, its effect on individuals and society, and research issues.

> The command 'be fruitful and multiply' was promulgated according to our authorities, when the population of the world consisted of two people.
>
> —Dean Inge
> (1860–1954)

• Risk and Responsibility

A typical woman in the United States spends about 39 years—almost half of her life span of 80 years—with the biological ability to become pregnant (Hatcher et al., 2007). Over the course of this time, her contraceptive needs will change; however, the most important factor in her choice of a method of contraception will often be its effectiveness.

In the United States nearly half of all pregnancies each year are intended (49%) and half of unintended pregnancies (51%) are terminated by abortion (Guttmacher Institute, 2008c). (See Figure 11.1 for the outcomes of unintended

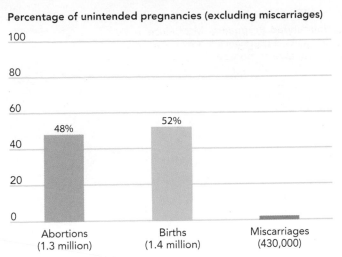

Percentage of unintended pregnancies (excluding miscarriages)

Abortions (1.3 million): 48%
Births (1.4 million): 52%
Miscarriages (430,000)

Outcomes of Unintended Pregnancies in the United States, 2002. Each year, 6.4 million of the 60 million American women of childbearing age (15–44) become pregnant. Approximately 3.1 million of these pregnancies are unintended. (*Source:* Finer, 2006.)

pregnancies in the United States.) Although on average a woman has only about a 2–4% chance of becoming pregnant during intercourse without contraception, timing affects the odds. For example, if intercourse occurs during ovulation, the chance of conception is about 25%. Over a period of a year, sexually active couples who do not use contraception have a 90% chance of conception.

Because the potential for getting pregnant is so high for a sexually active, childbearing-age couple, it would seem reasonable that sexually active couples would use contraception to avoid unintended pregnancy. Unfortunately, all too often, this is not the case. Of the 60 million women in the United States of childbearing age (15–44), one third do not need contraceptives because they are sterile, pregnant, postpartum, trying to become pregnant, or abstinent (Foster-Rosales & Stewart, 2002). Approximately 90% of the remaining women at risk for unintended pregnancy use some method of contraception (see Figure 11.2). Not surprisingly, the nonusers of contraception account for about half of unintended pregnancies; those who used contraception report that the method either failed or was not used correctly or consistently (see Figure 11.3).

Numerous studies have indicated that the most consistent users of contraception are men and women who explicitly communicate about the subject.

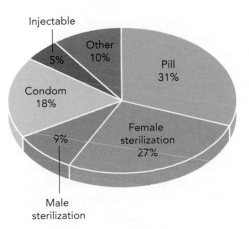

Injectable 5%
Other 10%
Pill 31%
Condom 18%
Female sterilization 27%
Male sterilization 9%

Percentage of Current Contraceptive Users Using Each Method: United States, 2002. (*Source:* CDC/NCHS, National Survey of Family Growth, 2002.)

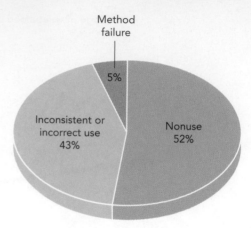

• **FIGURE 11.3**

Unintended Pregnancy. Most unintended pregnancies are attributable to nonuse, inconsistent use, or incorrect use of contraceptives. (*Sources:* Finer, 2006; Guttmacher Institute, Improving Contraceptive Use in the United States, In Brief. 2008 Series, No. 1. New York: Guttmacher Institute, 2008. Kost et al., 2008; Trussell, 2007.)

3.1 million unintended pregnancies

People at greatest risk for not using contraceptives are those in casual dating relationships and those who infrequently discuss contraception with their partners or others.

Women, Men, and Birth Control: Who Is Responsible?

If oral contraceptives for men became available, how many women would trust their partner to use them? Because women bear children and have most of the responsibility for raising them, they may have a greater interest than their partners in controlling their fertility. Also, it is generally easier to keep one egg from being fertilized once a month than to stop millions of sperm during each episode of intercourse. For these and other reasons, birth control has traditionally been seen as the woman's responsibility, but attitudes and practices are changing. The more schooling couples have, the more likely they are to talk about and utilize family planning (Frost & Darroch, 2008; Guttmacher Institute, 2008a). Education appears to instill confidence in both partners to discuss intended family size and birth control methods. Regardless of the motive or level of education, society no longer views the responsibility for birth control to lie solely with women. Rather, the majority of men (as well as women) perceive that there is gender equality in sexual decision making and equal responsibility for decisions about contraception. Male methods now account for approximately one-fifth of all reversible contraceptive use (Guttmacher Institute, 2008e). In fact, male methods of contraception (e.g., condoms and withdrawal) predominate among men 25–39 in all industrialized countries of the world except the United States. Although withdrawal, a common method in most countries around the world, is not considered a reliable method of birth control, the condom is quite effective when used consistently and correctly, especially in combination with a spermicide.

In addition to using a condom, a man can take contraceptive responsibility by (1) exploring ways of being sexual without intercourse; (2) helping to pay doctor or clinic bills and sharing the cost of pills, injections, or other birth control methods; (3) checking on supplies, helping to keep track of his partner's menstrual cycle, and helping her with her part in the birth control routine; and (4) in a long-term relationship, if no (or no more) children are planned, having a vasectomy.

think
about it

Risky Business: Why Couples Fail to Use Contraception

Most people know they are taking a chance when they don't use contraception. But the more frequently a person takes chances with unprotected intercourse without resultant pregnancy, the more likely he or she is to do so again. Eventually, the woman or couple will feel almost magically invulnerable to pregnancy. Each time they are lucky, their risk taking is reinforced.

The consequences of an unintended pregnancy—economic hardships, adoption, or abortion—may be overwhelming. So, why do people take chances in the first place? Part of the reason is faulty knowledge. People often underestimate how easy it is to get pregnant, or they may not know how to use a contraceptive method correctly.

Perceived Costs of Contraceptive Planning

One reason people avoid taking steps to prevent pregnancy is that they don't want to acknowledge their own sexuality. Acknowledging our sexuality is not necessarily easy, for it may be accompanied by feelings of guilt, conflict, and shame. The younger or less experienced we are, the more difficult it is for us to acknowledge our sexuality.

Planning contraception requires us to acknowledge not only that we are sexual but also that we plan to be sexually active. Without such planning, men and women can pretend that their sexual intercourse "just happens"—when a moment of passion occurs, when they have been drinking, or when the moon is full—even though it may happen frequently.

Another reason people don't use contraception is difficulty in obtaining it. It is often embarrassing for sexually inexperienced people to be seen in contexts that identify them as sexual beings. The cost of contraceptives is also a problem for some. Although free or low-cost contraceptives may be obtained through family planning clinics or other agencies, people may have transportation or work considerations that keep them away.

Because it is women who get pregnant, men tend to be unaware of their responsibility or to downplay their role in conception, although with the popularity of the condom, responsibility may become more balanced (especially if women insist on it). Nevertheless, males, especially adolescents, often lack the awareness that supports contraceptive planning.

Many people, especially women using the pill, practice birth control consistently and effectively within an ongoing relationship but may give up their contraceptive practices if the relationship breaks up. They define themselves as sexual only within the context of a relationship. When men or women begin a new relationship, they may not use contraception because the relationship has not yet become established. They do not expect to have sexual intercourse or to have it often, so they are willing to take chances.

Using contraception such as a condom or spermicide may destroy the feeling of "spontaneity" in sex. For those who justify their sexual behavior by romantic impulsiveness, using these devices seems cold and mechanical.

Anticipated Benefits of Pregnancy

Ambivalence about pregnancy is a powerful incentive *not* to use contraception. For many people, being pregnant proves that a woman is indeed feminine on the most fundamental biological level. Getting a woman pregnant provides similar proof of masculinity for a man.

Pregnancy also proves beyond any doubt that a person is fertile. Many men and women have lingering doubts about whether they can have children. This is especially true for partners who have used contraception for a long time, but it is also true for those who constantly take chances.

Another anticipated benefit of pregnancy is that it requires the partners to define their relationship and level of commitment to each other. It is a form of testing, albeit often an unconscious one. Many men and women unconsciously expect their partners to be pleased, but this is not always the reaction they get.

Finally, pregnancy involves not only two partners but may involve their parents as well (especially the woman's). Pregnancy may force a young person's parents to pay attention to and deal with him or her as an adult. Pregnancy may mean many things with regard to the parent-child relationship: a sign of rebellion, a form of punishment for a parental lack of caring, a plea for help and understanding, or an insistence on autonomy, independence, or adulthood.

Think Critically

- If sexually active, do you take risks relative to not adequately protecting yourself or your partner from conception? If so, what kinds? Why?
- When do you believe a person is more inclined to take risks?
- What would you say to a sexual partner who hesitates in using a condom because he or she doesn't like the way it feels?

Planning contraception requires us to acknowledge our sexuality. One way a responsible couple can reduce the risk of unintended pregnancy is by visiting a family planning clinic—together.

Family Planning Clinics

Reproductive health care reflects a deep commitment to supporting the family and makes an essential contribution to the human infrastructure in which our society thrives (Hatcher et al., 2007). Since more than 17 million women in the United States cannot afford reproductive health care, low-income women are far more likely to take advantage of publicly funded family planning clinics than those who have the means to seek out private care. Title X is the nation's only federal program dedicated to providing family planning services for those in need, giving funding for contraceptive services to approximately 7 million women each year. It is estimated that publicly funded family planning clinics result in a yearly savings of $4.3 billion in public funds (Guttmacher Institute, 2008a).

Among the poor are youth who either lack insurance or are afraid to ask their parents for help in gaining access to preventive doctor visits or contraception. Over the past 30 years, some states have acknowledged this by providing laws that expand minors' ability to consent to their own health care, including services related to family planning. This movement reflects the recognition that many minors will remain sexually active but not seek services if they have to tell their parents beforehand. In seeking to reduce unintended pregnancies and STIs, and with support of the majority of parents, about one fourth of student health centers that serve adolescents aged 11 and older currently dispense some form of contraception (Fram, 2007; "Middle School," 2007). School districts are also opting to provide birth control and condoms to their students. Still, creative strategies and broad-based changes aimed at both service providers and policy makers are still needed to improve access to and use of contraceptives among women, especially those who are disadvantaged (Guttmacher Institute, 2008a).

Adolescents and Contraception Condoms are the method of choice among sexually active teens. We know that among 15–19-year-olds, condom use at first intercourse was at 71%. However, fewer than half of sexually

What is the message of these posters? What myths or stereotypes do they challenge? By the way, there is no such thing as safe sex, only safer sex.

active men aged 15–19 reported using condoms 100% of the time during the previous year (Guttmacher Institute, 2008b). Teens appear to have conflicting views when it comes to condoms and the implications of carrying them. This ambivalence related to condom use seems to apply to both young women and men.

Methods of Contraception and Birth Control

The methods we use to prevent pregnancy or to keep it from progressing vary widely. Thus, the best method of contraception is one that will be used consistently and correctly. Hopefully, this method is also one that is available and in harmony with one's preferences, fears, and expectations.

Birth Control and Contraception: What's the Difference?

Although the terms "birth control" and "contraception" are often used interchangeably, there is actually a subtle difference in meaning. **Birth control** is any means of preventing a birth from taking place. Thus, methods that prevent a fertilized egg from implanting in the uterine wall (such as the IUD in some instances and emergency contraceptive pills) and methods that remove the **conceptus**—the fertilized egg, embryo, or fetus—from the uterus (such as nonsurgical and surgical abortions) are forms of birth control. These are not, however, true contraceptive methods. **Contraception**—the prevention of conception altogether—is the category of birth control in which the sperm and egg are prevented from uniting. This is done in a variety of ways, including (1) barrier methods, such as condoms and diaphragms, which place a physical barrier between the sperm and the egg; (2) spermicides, which kill the sperm before they can get to the egg; (3) hormonal methods, such as the pill, the shot, and the patch, which inhibit the release of the oocyte from the ovary; and (4) intrauterine devices, which prevent the sperm from fertilizing the egg.

Choosing a Method

To be fully responsible in using birth control, individuals must know what options they have, how reliable these methods are, and what advantages and disadvantages (including possible side effects) each has. Thus, it is important to be aware of both personal health issues and the specifics of the methods themselves.

Most women who are not currently using contraception go to a clinic or doctor's office knowing exactly what method they want. However, many of these women are not aware of other options available to them. In some instances, the method they think they want may not be medically appropriate or may not be one they will use correctly and consistently. Knowing the facts about the methods gives you a solid basis from which to make decisions, as well as more security once you reach a decision.

To help make an informed decision about which method of birth control is medically appropriate and will be used every time, consider these questions (Hatcher et al., 2007):

- Do you have any particular preferences or biases related to birth control?
- Do you know the advantages and disadvantages of each of the contraceptive methods?
- How convenient and easy is it to use this method?
- If you or your partner is at risk, does this method provide protection against STIs, including HIV?
- What are the effects of this method on menses?
- Is it important that you negotiate with your partner to help determine the method?
- What other influences (e.g., religion, privacy, past experience, friends' advice, and frequency of intercourse) might affect your decision?
- Have you discussed potential methods with your health practitioner?

In the following discussion of method effectiveness, "perfect use" refers to the percentage of women who become pregnant during their first year of use when they use the method *correctly and consistently.* "Typical use" refers to the percentage of women who become pregnant during their first year of use; this number includes both couples who use the method correctly and consistently and those who do not (see Table 11.1). Thus, typical use is the more significant number to use when considering a method of contraception. In spite of very effective contraceptive options, about one half of all pregnancies in the United States are unintended.

Sexual Abstinence

Before we begin our discussion of devices and techniques for preventing conception, we must acknowledge the oldest and most reliable birth control method of all: abstinence. There is a wide variety of opinion about what constitutes sexual activity. However, from a family planning perspective, **abstinence** is the absence of genital contact that could lead to a pregnancy (i.e., penile penetration of the vagina). The term "celibacy" is sometimes used interchangeably with "abstinence." We prefer "abstinence" because "celibacy" often implies the

Table 11.1 • Failure Rates of Contraceptives During First Year of Use

Method	% of Women Experiencing an Unintended Pregnancy Within the First Year of Use		% of Women Continuing Use at One Year
	Typical Use (%)[a]	Perfect Use (%)[b]	
No method	85	85	
Spermicides	29	18	42
Withdrawal	27	4	43
Fertility awareness-based methods	25		51
Sponge			
Parous women (given birth)	32	20	46
Nulliparous women (never given birth)	16	9	57
Diaphragm	16	6	57
Condom			
Female (Reality)	21	5	49
Male	15	2	53
Combined pill and progestin-only pill	8	0.3	68
Evra patch	8	0.3	68
NuvaRing	8	0.3	68
Depo-Provera	3	0.3	56
IUD			
ParaGard	0.8	0.6	78
Mirena	0.2	0.2	80
Implanon	0.05	0.05	84
Female sterilization	0.5	0.5	100
Male sterilization	0.15	0.10	100

[a]The percentage of typical users who become pregnant within 1 year while using the method.
[b]The percentage of women who become pregnant within 1 year using the method *perfectly* every time.

SOURCE: Adapted from Hatcher, R. A., et al. (2007). *Contraceptive technology* (19th rev. ed.). New York: Reprinted by permission of Ardent Media.

avoidance of *all* forms of sexual activity and, often, the religious commitment to not marry or to maintain a nonsexual life.

Individuals who choose not to have intercourse are still free to express affection (and to give and receive sexual pleasure if they so desire) in a variety of ways that include talking, hugging, massaging, kissing, petting, and manually and orally stimulating the genitals. Those who choose sexual abstinence from sexual intercourse as their method of birth control need to communicate this clearly to their dates or partners. They should also be informed about other forms of contraception. And, in the event that either partner experiences a change of mind, it can't hurt to have a condom handy. An advantage of abstinence is that refraining from sexual intercourse in a new relationship may allow two people to get to know and trust each other more before experiencing greater intimacy and it is nearly 100% effective at preventing pregnancy.

Hormonal Methods

In addition to the tried-and-true birth control pill, several varieties of hormonal contraception are also available. These include a pill that causes menstrual suppression, injectable hormones, a vaginal ring, and a patch.

The Pill **Oral contraceptives (OCs),** popularly called "the pill," are the most popular form of reversible contraception in the United States (see Figure 11.4). The pill is actually a series of pills (various numbers to a package) containing synthetic estrogen and/or progesterone that regulates egg production and the menstrual cycle. When taken for birth control, oral contraceptives accomplish some or all of the following:

- Suppress ovulation (90–95% of the time).
- Thicken cervical mucus (preventing sperm penetration into the woman's upper genital tract).
- Thin the lining of the uterus to inhibit implantation of the fertilized ovum.
- Slow the rate of ovum transport.
- Disrupt transport of the fertilized egg.
- Inhibit capacitation of the sperm, which limits the sperm's ability to fertilize the egg.

The pill produces basically the same chemical conditions that would exist in a woman's body if she were pregnant.

Types and Usage   Oral contraceptives must be prescribed by a physician or family planning clinic. More than 70 combinations are available, containing

● **FIGURE 11.4**
Percentage of Women Aged 18–44 Using the Pill, 2004.
(*Source:* Frost & Darroch, 2008.)

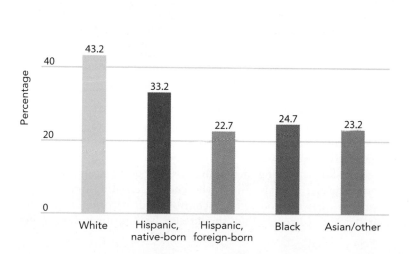

various amounts of hormones. Most commonly prescribed are the combination pills, which contain a fairly standard amount of estrogen (usually about 35 micrograms) and different doses of progestin according to the pill type. In the triphasic pill, the amount of progestin is altered during the cycle, purportedly to approximate the normal hormonal pattern. There is also a "minipill" containing progestin only, but it has been generally prescribed only for women who should not take estrogen such as those who are breastfeeding and older women. It is considered slightly less effective than the combined pill, and it must be taken with precise, unfailing regularity to be effective.

A woman can begin taking oral contraceptives on the same day as her office visit, providing she is not pregnant and not in need of emergency contraception. This "quick start" practice may be preferred by women because other approaches generally leave a time gap between the time the pills are prescribed and the time one starts taking them.

The pill is considered the most effective birth control method available (except for sterilization) when used correctly. But the pill is *not* effective when taken inconsistently. It must be taken every day, as close as possible to the same time each day. If one pill is missed, it should be taken as soon as the woman remembers, and the next one taken on schedule. If two are missed, the method cannot be relied on, and an additional form of contraception should be used for the rest of the cycle. A year's supply of birth control pills may be free from a public clinic or cost more than $500 at a private doctor's office or pharmacy. More than half of the states require insurers that provide prescription drug coverage to also cover contraceptives (Planned Parenthood, 2008).

A recent shift to extended-use oral contraceptives acknowledges a little known fact: Women don't need to have monthly periods. Extended-cycle oral contraceptives provide women with a safe, acceptable, and effective form of contraception (Hatcher et al., 2007) while also eliminating many of the pill's side effects (headache, bloating, cramping, breast tenderness) that occur when they are not taking hormone pills (Sulak, Scow, Preece, Riggs, & Kuehl, 2000). Though researchers may not yet have enough data to recommend one particular extended-cycle regimen over another, the use of these new regimens provides women with more options and almost certainly improves the acceptability and efficacy of hormonal contraception (Steinauer & Autry, 2007). Women for whom extended use would be attractive include those with dysmenorrheal or menstrual migraines and those who are on military duty or have other active jobs.

Since none of the hormonal methods of birth control offer protection against STIs, women on the pill should consider the additional use of a condom.

Effectiveness The combination pill is more than 99.7% effective if used correctly. The typical-use rate is 92%. Progestin-only pills are somewhat less effective and may contribute to irregular bleeding. However, they have fewer side effects and health risks than the combination pill.

Advantages The benefits of combined oral contraceptives (COCs) generally far outweigh any significant negative effects. Pills are easy to take. They are dependable. No applications or interruptions are necessary before or during intercourse. In fact, millions of women use the pill with moderate to high degrees of satisfaction. For many women, if personal health or family history does not contraindicate it, the pill is both effective and safe. Some women

Although oral contraceptives are effective in preventing pregnancy, they do not provide protection against STIs, including HIV infection.

experience side effects that please them, such as more regular or reduced menstrual flow, less menstrual cramping, enlarged breasts, or less acne. The pill may offer some protection against osteoporosis and rheumatoid arthritis. In addition, new evidence has revealed that women on the birth control pill are protected from ovarian cancer, even decades after they stop taking it. According to one study, women who had taken the pill for 15 years halved their chances of developing ovarian cancer, one of the most common types of cancer among women in the West, and the risk remained low more than 30 years later (Beral, 2007).

Possible Problems There are many possible side effects, which may or may not prevent the user from taking the pill. Those most often reported are spotting, breast tenderness, nausea or vomiting, and weight gain or loss. Other side effects include spotty darkening of the skin, nervousness and dizziness, loss of scalp hair, headaches, and changes in appetite, sex drive, and moods. Studies that have examined the effect of the pill on the libido are mixed (Doheny, 2006).

These side effects can sometimes be eliminated by changing the prescription, but not always. Certain women react unfavorably to the pill because of existing health factors or extrasensitivity to female hormones. Women with heart or kidney diseases, asthma, high blood pressure, diabetes, epilepsy, gall bladder disease, or sickle-cell disease and those prone to migraine headaches or depression are usually considered poor candidates for the pill. Certain medications may react differently or unfavorably with the pill, either diminishing in their therapeutic effect or interfering with oral contraceptive effectiveness. Thus, it is important to check with your doctor before starting any new prescriptions if you are taking the pill.

The pill also creates certain health risks, but to what extent is a matter of controversy. Though the pill has been studied extensively and is very safe, in rare instances hormonal methods can lead to serious problems. Some of the warning signs to look for spell out the word **"ACHES."** If you experience any of these, you need to check with your clinician as soon as possible:

- **A**bdominal pain (severe)
- **C**hest pain
- **H**eadaches (severe)
- **E**ye problems (including blurred vision, spots, or a change in shape of the cornea)
- **S**evere leg pain

You should also consult your clinician if you develop severe mood swings or depression, become jaundiced (yellow-colored skin), miss two periods, or have signs of pregnancy.

Researchers have found that current and past users of combined oral contraceptives aged 35 to 64 were at no higher risk for developing breast cancer than nonusers (Marchbanks, McDonald, Wilson, et al., 2002). Doctors say that the type of hormones and the stage of life when they are used may be what make them helpful at one point and harmful at another.

The health risks for taking the pill are low for the young, but they increase with age. The risk for smokers, women over 35, and those with certain other health disorders is considered high. Current literature on the pill especially emphasizes the risks for women who smoke. Definite risks of cardiovascular

Literature is mostly about sex and not much about having children and life is the other way round.

—David Lodge
(1921–2003)

complications and various forms of cancer exist because of the synergistic action of the ingredients in cigarettes and oral contraceptives.

Certain other factors may need to be taken into account in determining if oral contraceptives are appropriate. Nursing mothers cannot use pills containing estrogen because the hormone inhibits milk production, although some lactating women use the minipill successfully once lactation has been established.

Once a woman stops taking the pill, her menstrual cycle will usually resume the next month, though it may take several months before it becomes regular. If a woman wants to become pregnant, it is recommended that she change to another method of contraception for 2–3 months after she stops taking the pill and then start efforts to conceive.

Injectable Contraceptive The injectable contraceptive reformulated in 2004 to provide lower doses of hormone, medroxyprogesterone acetate, or Depo-Provera (DMPA), provides protection from pregnancy for 12 weeks. The newer formulation is injected four times a year under the skin instead of in the muscle. Generally, this progestin-only method has been considered to have few serious side effects and complications. In approximately half the women taking DMPA, menstruation stops completely after a year of use. Menstrual spotting, weight gain, headaches, breast tenderness, dizziness, loss of libido, and depression have also been reported. Consequently, continuation of use rates vary from 26% to 53% at one year of use (Hatcher et al., 2007).

Effectiveness The perfect-use effectiveness rate is 99.7% while the typical-use rate is slightly less at 97%.

Advantages Because DMPA injections contain no estrogen, they do not appear to cause the rare but potentially serious problems associated with estrogen. Additionally, DMPA is highly effective for 3 months, causes women to have very light or missed periods (women vary in their reactions to this), decreased menstrual symptoms, and less pain from endometriosis.

Disadvantages Menstrual cycle disturbances may occur, including unpredictable or prolonged episodes of bleeding or spotting, weight gain, depression, and temporary and reversible decrease in bone density.

Serious health problems are rarely associated with DMPA use; however, if a woman develops very painful headaches, heavy bleeding, serious depression, severe lower abdominal pain (may be a sign of pregnancy), or pus or pain at the site of the injection, she should see her clinician. Because Depo-Provera lowers estrogen levels, it may cause women to lose calcium stored in their bones.

A woman should get her first injection of DMPA within 5 days of the start of her menstrual period. The drug is effective immediately. In addition to an examination, which may cost from $35 to $250, each injection costs between $30 and $75.

Contraceptive Patch In 2002, the FDA approved a transdermal **contraceptive patch.** Called Ortho Evra, this reversible method of birth control releases synthetic estrogen and progestin to protect against pregnancy for 1 month. Consisting of three layers, the 4.5-centimeter beige patch may be applied to the lower abdomen, buttocks, upper arm, or upper torso (excluding

The contraceptive patch, also called Ortho Evra, is prescribed by a physician and protects against pregnancy for one month.

the breasts). After 7 days, the woman removes the patch and applies a new one to another site. Three consecutive 7-day patches are typically followed by a patch-free week to allow for menstruation to occur. The combination of hormones works the same way that oral contraceptives do. The patch is most effective when it is changed on the same day of the week for 3 weeks in a row. Pregnancy can happen if an error is made in using the patch, especially if it becomes loose for longer than 24 hours or falls off or if the same patch is left on for more than 1 week.

If the patch has partially or completely detached for less than 24 hours, the woman should try to reapply it; however, if it does not stick well, a replacement should be applied. Two groups of women that may need additional counseling about the use of the contraceptive patch are obese women and adolescents. Obese women, or those who weigh more than 198 pounds, should be aware that they have a slightly increased risk of pregnancy due to lower levels of blood hormones.

Since 2005, the patch has been under the scrutiny of the FDA, which has added a warning label to indicate that this product exposes women to higher levels of estrogen than most birth control pills (FDA News, 2005). In general, increased estrogen exposure may increase the risk of blood clots. Women taking or considering using this product should work with their health-care practitioner to balance the potential risks related to increased estrogen exposure against the risk of pregnancy.

Like other hormonal methods of contraception, the patch requires a prescription. A 1-month supply costs between $15 and $50.

Effectiveness   Overall, contraceptive efficacy of the patch is similar to that of oral contraceptives; if used perfectly, the patch is more than 99% effective. Typical use results in a success rate of 92%.

Advantages   Like those who take OCs, many women who use the patch report the same benefits, including more-regular, lighter, and shorter periods. Furthermore, a woman's ability to become pregnant returns quickly when the patch is discontinued. Ortho Evra is safe, simple, and convenient, and it does not interfere with sex. Additionally, a woman does not have to remember to take a pill each day.

Disadvantages   The most common side effects reported by users of the patch include mild skin reactions, breast tenderness (mainly in cycles 1 and 2), headaches, and nausea. The risk of stroke or heart attack is similar to that of combined oral contraceptives. Adolescents, on the other hand, appear to experience more problems with patch compliance and unintended pregnancy, probably due to site reactions and patch detachments.

The Vaginal Ring   In 2001, the FDA approved a **vaginal ring,** commonly referred to as NuvaRing, the vaginal form of a reversible, hormonal method of birth control. It is a small, flexible ring inserted high into the vagina once every 28 days. The ring is kept in place for 21 days and removed for a 7-day break to allow a withdrawal bleed. The ring releases synthetic estrogen and progestin, preventing ovulation in a manner similar to that of other combined hormonal contraceptives. The vaginal ring is prescribed by a doctor and costs between $20 and $50 per 1-month supply.

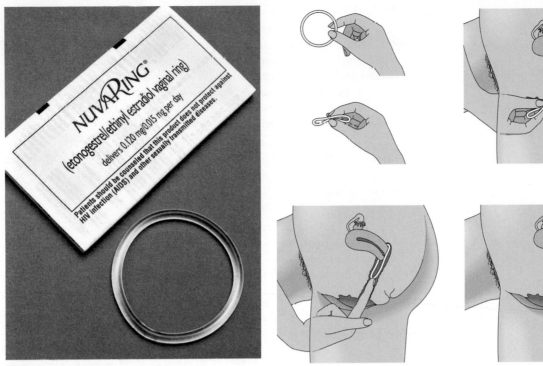

Effectiveness   Like the other methods of hormonal contraception, if used perfectly, the vaginal ring is more than 99% effective. Typical use results in a success rate of 92%.

Advantages   The ring protects against pregnancy for 1 month and is easy to use. Many women who use the ring have more regular, lighter, and shorter periods. A woman can stop using NuvaRing at any time, offering her more control over contraception than with some other hormonal methods of birth control. The ring provides a consistent release of hormones, does not usually cause weight gain, and can be removed for up to 3 hours without compromising effectiveness.

Disadvantages   The side effects of the ring are similar to those associated with oral contraceptives. Additionally, there may be an increased risk of blood clots possibly due to the hormone desogesterel. Vaginal wetness, sensation of a foreign body, expulsion, and headaches may also occur.

Like a tampon, the ring can be placed anywhere in the vagina that is comfortable. There is no specific fit or need to check the position of the ring. If it causes pressure, the user may just push it farther into the vagina. (*Source:* "Contraception Online," 2003.)

Implants   A variety of contraceptive implants have come and gone. One that has been approved and made available in the United States is Implanon. Implanon, a contraceptive **implant,** is a thin, flexible plastic rod about the size of a cardboard matchstick that is inserted under the skin of the upper arm and protects against pregnancy for up to 3 years. Like several other progestin-containing methods of birth control, Implanon prevents the ovaries from releasing eggs and thickens the cervical mucus to block sperm.

Implants are among the most effective of the available contraceptives, similar in effectiveness to intrauterine devices (IUDs) and sterilization (Hatcher et al., 2007). However, because Implanon was only approved by the FDA in 2006, it is possible that it can cause problems we do not yet understand. Implanon requires a doctor to insert and remove it, along with the use of local anesthesia. If a woman desires to become pregnant within the 3 years following insertion, the device can be removed.

The cost of the exam, Implanon, and insertion ranges from $400 to $800. Removal costs between $75 and $150. The total costs pay for pregnancy protection (but not STI protection) for 3 years.

Advantages The device is highly effective, easy to insert, discrete, does not interrupt sex or require maintenance, has no estrogen-related side effects, and is easily reversible.

Disadvantages Like all progestin-only methods, implants may cause unpredictable bleeding and weight gain, may have insertion complications, and may increase the risk of blood clots. The implant is also clinician-dependent, so that once it is inserted, women have little control over their contraceptive choices.

Barrier Methods

Barrier methods are designed to keep sperm and egg from uniting. The barrier device used by men is the condom. Barrier methods available to women include the diaphragm, the cervical cap, the female condom, and the contraceptive sponge. These methods of birth control have become increasingly popular because, in addition to preventing conception, they can reduce the risk of STIs. The effectiveness of all barrier methods is increased by use with spermicides, which are discussed later in this chapter.

The Condom A **condom** (or **male condom**) is a thin, soft, flexible sheath of latex rubber, polyurethane, or processed animal tissue that fits over the erect

Male condoms come in a variety of sizes, colors, and textures; some are lubricated, and many have a reservoir tip designed to collect semen.

Tips for Effective Condom Use

Condoms can be very effective contraceptive devices **when used properly.** They also can protect against STIs, including HIV. Here are some tips for their use:

1. Use condoms every time you have sexual intercourse; this is the key to successful contraception and disease prevention.

2. Carefully open the condom package—teeth or finger-nails can tear the condom.

3. If the penis is uncircumcised, pull back the foreskin before putting on the condom.

4. Do not use a condom lubricated with nonoxynol-9 (N-9) for vaginal or anal intercourse; N-9 can damage the cells lining the vagina and rectum and can provide a portal of entry for HIV and other STIs.

5. Put on the condom before it touches any part of a partner's body.

6. If you accidentally put the condom on wrong-side up, discard the condom and use another.

7. Leave about a half inch of space at the condom tip, and roll the condom all the way down the erect penis to the base. Push out any air bubbles.

8. Withdraw the penis soon after ejaculation. Make sure someone holds the base of the condom firmly against the penis as it is withdrawn.

9. After use, check the condom for possible tears. If you find a tear or hole, consider the use of emergency contraception (see the section "Emergency Contraception" later in the chapter). If torn condoms are a persistent problem, use a water-based lubricant such as K-Y jelly.

10. Do not reuse a condom.

11. Keep condoms in a cool, dry, and convenient place.

12. To help protect against HIV and other STIs, always use a latex rubber or polyurethane condom, *not* one made of animal tissue.

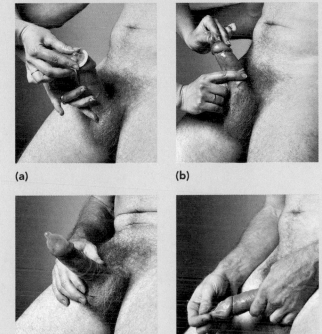

(a) Place the rolled condom on the erect penis, leaving about a half inch of space at the tip (first, squeeze any air out of the condom tip). (b) Roll the condom down, smoothing out any air bubbles. (c) Roll the condom to the base of the penis. (d) After ejaculation, hold the condom base while withdrawing the penis.

penis to help prevent semen from being transmitted. Condoms prevent infections by covering the portals of entry and exit for many STI organisms.

Condoms are the third most widely used form of birth control in the United States (after sterilization and the pill). Their use has increased significantly since the late 1980s, due in large part to their effectiveness in helping prevent the spread of STIs, including HIV, when they are used properly. (For a further discussion of the use of condoms, see Chapter 15.) A condom costs anywhere from about 50¢ (for "plain") to $2.50 (for textured). Condoms should be checked for their expiration date.

Condoms are available in a wide variety of shapes, sizes, and colors. Some are lubricated with a small amount of spermicide, **nonoxynol-9 (N-9);** however, despite their higher cost and shorter shelf life, their use is not recommended because spermicidal condoms are no more effective than other lubricated condoms (CDC, 2008e). In addition and because the frequent use of N-9 has been associated with genital ulceration and irritation, products with this ingredient may have the potential to actually facilitate transmission of STIs, including HIV (Hatcher et al., 2007).

A small proportion of condoms are made of polyurethane and other synthetic materials. These condoms are more resistant to deterioration than latex condoms, may provide a more comfortable fit, may enhance sensitivity, and can provide an alternative if a person is allergic to latex. Unlike latex condoms, oil-based lubricants can be used with condoms made from synthetic materials. Evidence for protection against STIs is not available; however, they are believed to provide protection similar to that of latex condoms (Hatcher et al., 2007).

Many of the newer condoms are very thin (but also strong); they conduct heat well and allow quite a bit of sensation to be experienced. Latex condoms that are flavored, glow in the dark, or are brightly colored should not be used for vaginal or anal intercourse. Latex condoms should be used with water-based lubricants (like K-Y Jelly) or glycerine only because oil-based lubricants such as Vaseline can weaken the rubber. If a condom breaks, slips, or leaks, there are some things a person can do (see the section "Emergency Contraception" later in the chapter).

Women and Condom Use Today, nearly half of male condoms are purchased by women, and condom advertising and packaging increasingly reflect this trend. Several key points are relevant to the issue of women and condom use:

- Women experience more health consequences than men from STIs; they can suffer permanent infertility, for example. Condoms, when used consistently and correctly, are an effective means of protection against these.

- Since women are far more likely to contract an STI from intercourse with a male partner than vice versa, it is in the woman's best interest to use or have her partner use a condom.

- Condoms help protect women against unplanned pregnancy, ectopic pregnancy, bacterial infections such as vaginitis and pelvic inflammatory disease (PID), viral infections such as herpes and HIV, cervical cancer, and infections that may harm a fetus or an infant during delivery.

- A woman can protect herself by insisting on condom use. Even if a woman regularly uses another form of birth control, such as the pill or an IUD, she may want to have the added protection provided by a condom.

It is now vitally important that we find a way of making the condom a cult object of youth.

—Germaine Greer
(1939–)

Effectiveness With perfect use, condoms are 98% effective in preventing conception, but user effectiveness is about 85%. Failures sometimes occur from mishandling the condom, but they are usually the result of not putting it on until after some semen has leaked into the vagina or simply not putting it on at all. When used in anal sex, a male condom is more likely to break and slip than when used for vaginal sex if adequate lubrication is not used.

Advantages   Condoms are easy to obtain and do not cause harmful side effects. They are easy to carry and are inexpensive or even free. Latex condoms help protect against STIs, including HIV infection. Some men appreciate the slightly reduced sensitivity they experience when using a condom because it helps prolong intercourse.

Possible Problems   Condoms can reduce but cannot eliminate the risks of STIs, nor are they 100% effective in preventing pregnancy. The chief drawback of a condom is that it should be put on after the penis has become erect but before penetration. This interruption is the major reason users neglect to put them on. Some men and women complain that sensation is dulled, and (very rarely) cases of allergy to rubber are reported. Couples who experience significant loss of feeling with one type of condom are advised to try other kinds.

The Female Condom

Currently, there is one **female condom** available for women. Called Reality, it is a disposable, soft, loose-fitting polyurethane pouch with a diaphragm-like ring at each end. It is designed to line the inner walls of the vagina and to protect women against sperm. If used correctly and consistently, the female condom reduces the risk of contracting many STIs, including HIV. One ring, which is sealed shut, is inside the sheath and is used to insert and anchor the condom against the cervix. The larger outer ring remains outside the vagina and acts as a barrier, protecting the vulva and the base of the penis (see Figure 11.5). This condom can also be inserted into the rectum to provide protection during anal intercourse. The pouch is lubricated both inside and out with a nonspermicidal lubricant and is meant for one-time use. It can be inserted up to 8 hours before intercourse and can be used without additional spermicide. Female and male condoms should not be used together because they can adhere to each other and cause one or both to slip out of position. The cost of a female condom, which can be purchased without a prescription, is about $3.50.

● **FIGURE 11.5**

The Female Condom in Position (left). The female condom, a sheath of soft polyurethane, is anchored around the cervix with a flexible ring (much like a diaphragm). A larger ring secures the sheath outside the vagina and also helps protect the vulva.

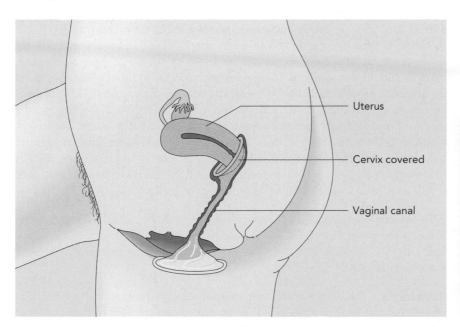

Uterus

Cervix covered

Vaginal canal

Effectiveness The perfect-use contraceptive effectiveness rate for female condoms is 95%, similar to that for other barrier methods in protecting against pregnancy. The typical-use effectiveness rate is 79%.

Advantages One advantage of the female condom over the male condom is that it not only protects the vagina and cervix from sperm and microbes but also is designed so that the open end covers the woman's external genitals and the base of her partner's penis, thus offering both people excellent protection against disease. Because polyurethane is stronger than latex, the device is less likely than the male latex condom to break and can be used with both water- and oil-based lubricants. Female condoms may prove advantageous for women whose partners are reluctant to use a male condom, in part because they do not constrict the penis as do male latex condoms. They also give women an additional way to control their fertility, do not require a prescription, and transport heat.

Possible Problems The female condom is relatively problem-free. The major complaint is aesthetic: Some women dislike the complete coverage of the female genitals provided by the condom (one of its chief health advantages) and don't want to use it for this reason. Sometimes, the female condom may slip into the vagina or anus during intercourse. Noise made during intercourse may be distracting; however, additional lubricant can quiet this.

The Diaphragm A **diaphragm** is a rubber cup with a flexible rim that is placed deep inside the vagina, blocking the cervix, to prevent sperm from entering the uterus and fallopian tubes. Different women require different sizes, and a woman's size may change, especially after a pregnancy; the size must be determined by an experienced practitioner. Diaphragms are available by prescription from doctors and family planning clinics. Somewhat effective by itself, the diaphragm is highly effective when used with a spermicidal cream or jelly. (Creams and jellies are considered more effective than foam for use with a diaphragm.) Diaphragm users should be sure to use an adequate amount of spermicide and to follow their practitioner's instructions carefully. Diaphragms are relatively inexpensive—about $30 to $50, plus the cost of spermicide and the initial exam and fitting.

Once inserted, the diaphragm provides effective contraceptive protection for 6 hours. After intercourse, it should be left in place for at least 6 hours. A woman should not dislodge it or douche before it is time to remove it. If intercourse is repeated within 6 hours, the diaphragm should be left in place and more spermicide inserted with an applicator. To remove a diaphragm, the woman inserts a finger into her vagina and under the front of the diaphragm rim and then gently pulls it out. The diaphragm should be washed in mild soap and water and patted dry before being put away in its storage case. A diaphragm is available by prescription only and should be replaced about once a year at a cost of about $60 to $75 plus spermicide.

Effectiveness Studies of diaphragm effectiveness have yielded varying results. Though the perfect-use effectiveness rate is quite high at 94%, the typical-use rate falls considerably, to 84%. Consistent, correct use is essential to achieve maximum effectiveness.

Advantages The diaphragm is safe, is relatively inexpensive, has limited side effects, and can be discretely used. It helps protect against STIs of the cervix and PID (see Chapter 15) but does not protect against HIV.

When used correctly and consistently and with a spermicide, the diaphragm can be an effective method of contraception.

Possible Problems   Some women dislike the process of inserting a diaphragm, or the mess or smell of the chemical contraceptives used with them. Some men complain of rubbing or other discomfort caused by the diaphragm. Occasionally, a woman will be allergic to rubber. Some women have a slightly increased risk of repeated urinary tract infections (see Chapter 15). Because there is a small risk of toxic shock syndrome (see Chapter 3), associated with its use, a woman should not leave a diaphragm in her vagina for more than 24 hours.

The Sponge   After being taken off the market in 1994, the **sponge,** otherwise called Today Sponge, has finally returned. This round plastic foam shield measures about 2 inches in diameter and has a pouch in the center that fits over the cervix. The sponge is filled with the spermicide nonoxynol-9 (N-9). Because N-9 does not reduce the risk of HIV infection, women should always use a latex condom—just as they should with all other contraceptive methods. The insertion and removal of the sponge is similar to that of the diaphragm and, with a little practice, is easy to do. An advantage of the sponge is that it can be left in place for up to 24 hours without reinsertion or the application of more spermicide. The perfect-use effectiveness rate is similar to that of a diaphragm—94%; for typical use, and for those who have delivered a child vaginally, the rate drops to 84%. This lowered effectiveness rate may be because the one size in which the sponge is available may not adequately cover the cervix after childbirth. Shelf life of the sponge is limited. The cost is approximately $9 to $15 per three-pack and they are available without a prescription.

FemCap and Lea's Shield   Both FemCap and Lea's Shield are vaginal barriers that prevent pregnancy in ways similar to those of the diaphragm. Made from silicon rubber shaped like a sailor's cap, FemCap comes in three sizes and can be worn for up to 48 hours, double the time recommended for similar birth control devices. Lea's Shield is a one-size, cup-shaped silicon device that contains a central valve that allows passage of cervical secretions and air. Both devices are held in place by suction, must be used with a spermicide, and must be obtained through a health-care provider. The effectiveness ranges from 80% to 91%.

Advantages   The cervical cap may be more comfortable and convenient than the diaphragm for some women. Much less spermicide is used than with the diaphragm, and spermicide need not be reapplied if intercourse is repeated. The cap can be inserted many hours before intercourse and can be worn for as long as 48 hours. It does not interfere with the body physically or hormonally. It may also protect against some STIs, but not HIV.

Possible Problems   Some users are bothered by an odor that may develop from the interaction of the cap's rubber with either vaginal secretions or the spermicide. There is some concern that the cap may contribute to erosion of the cervix. If a partner's penis touches the rim of the cap, it can become displaced during intercourse. Theoretically, the same risk of toxic shock syndrome exists for the cervical cap as for the diaphragm. (See also possible problems associated with the diaphragm.)

The sponge is easy to use, relatively effective, and safe, but does not protect against HIV.

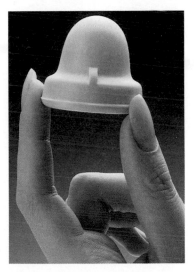

The cervical cap is smaller than a diaphragm and covers only the cervix.

Spermicides

A **spermicide** is a substance that is toxic to sperm. The most commonly used spermicide in products sold in the United States is the chemical nonoxynol-9 (N-9). Originally developed as a detergent, N-9 has been used for nearly 50 years as a vaginal cream that rapidly kills sperm cells. Cautions about N-9 have been suggested for several years, and it is now known that frequent spermicidal use can result in a breakdown of vaginal tissue that could increase susceptibility to HIV (Hatcher et al., 2007). Spermicidal preparations are available in a variety of forms: foam, film, cream, jelly, and suppository and are considered most effective when used in combination with a barrier method of contraception. Spermicides are sold in tubes, packets, or other containers that hold 12–20 applications. The cost per use ranges from about 50¢ to $2.50. The perfect-use effectiveness is 82% while the typical use effectiveness is 71%.

Contraceptive Foam

Contraceptive foam is a chemical spermicide sold in aerosol containers. It is a practical form of spermicide for use with a condom. Methods of application vary with each brand, but foam is usually released deep in the vagina either directly from the container or with an applicator. The foam forms a physical barrier to the uterus, and its chemicals kill sperm in the vagina. It is most effective if inserted no more than half an hour before intercourse. Shaking the container before applying the foam increases its foaminess so that it spreads farther. The foam begins to go flat after about half an hour. It must be reapplied when intercourse is repeated.

Some women dislike applying foam, complaining of messiness, leakage, odor, or stinging sensations. Occasionally, a woman or a man may have an allergic reaction to the foam. Because it is impossible to know how much remains in a container of foam, it is wise to keep a backup can available at all times.

Contraceptive Film

Contraceptive film (also called vaginal contraceptive film [VCF]) consists of a paper-thin tissue that contains nonoxynol-9, which dissolves into a sticky gel when inserted into the vagina. The film is placed directly over the cervix at least 15 minutes before intercourse to allow time for the sheet to dissolve and disperse. Like other spermicides, contraceptive film works effectively in conjunction with the male condom.

Many women find film easy to use. It can be obtained from a drugstore and carried in a purse, wallet, or pocket. However, some women may not like inserting the film into the vagina, and others may be allergic to it. Some women report increased vaginal discharge and temporary skin irritation to be a problem.

Creams, Jellies, and Vaginal Suppositories

Spermicidal creams and jellies come in tubes and are inserted with applicators or placed inside diaphragms or cervical caps. These chemical spermicides can be bought without a prescription at most drugstores. They work in a manner similar to that of foams but are considered less effective when used alone.

Suppositories are chemical spermicides inserted into the vagina before intercourse. Body heat and fluids dissolve the ingredients, which will kill sperm in the vagina. Suppositories must be inserted early enough to dissolve completely before intercourse.

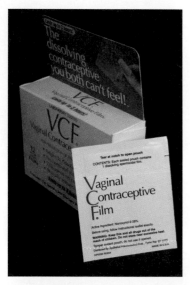

Contraceptive film is among the types of spermicides that are available without a prescription.

Spermicidal creams, jellies, and suppositories are simple to use and easy to obtain. They may reduce the danger of acquiring pelvic inflammatory disease (see Chapter 13). The use of spermicides does not affect any pregnancy that may follow.

Some people have allergic reactions to spermicides. Some women dislike the messiness or odor involved or the necessity of touching their own genitals. Others experience irritation or inflammation, especially if they use any of the methods frequently. A few women lack the vaginal lubrication to dissolve the suppositories in a reasonable amount of time. And a few women complain of being anxious about the effectiveness of these methods during intercourse.

The IUD (Intrauterine Device)

The **intrauterine device,** or **IUD,** is a tiny flexible plastic device that is inserted into the uterus through the cervical os (opening) to prevent sperm from fertilizing ova (see Figure 11.6). The type of device inserted determines how long it may be left in place; the range is 5–12 years.

The two IUDs currently available in the United States are the Copper T 380A (TCu380A), marketed as ParaGard®, and a hormone-releasing intrauterine system, marketed as Mirena®. ParaGard is made of polyethylene; the stem of the T is wrapped with fine copper wire. It can be left in place for 10–12 years. Mirena is also in the form of a T. It is made of a polymer plastic with a hollow stem containing levonorgestrel, a progestin, which is continually released. This device is effective for at least 5 years. At the time an IUD is removed, a new one can be inserted. The cost of an IUD, including insertion, ranges from $300 to $500, making it the most inexpensive long-term and reversible form of birth control. IUDs must be inserted and removed by a trained practitioner.

Current evidence does not support the common belief that the IUD is an **abortifacient,** a device or substance that causes an abortion. Rather, it primarily prevents pregnancy by preventing fertilization. Both types of IUDs alter the lining of the uterus. Additionally, the progestin in Mirena prevents ovulation and thickens cervical mucus.

IUDs are 99% effective with perfect use; the typical user effectiveness rate is 98%. Mirena has the lowest failure rate of any IUD developed to date.

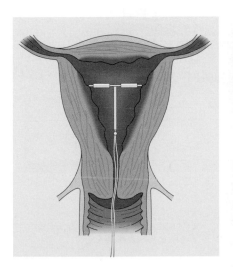
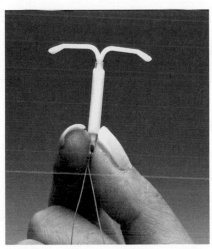

● **FIGURE 11.6**

An IUD (Copper T 380A or ParaGard®) in Position (left) and the Progestin-Releasing IUD (Mirena) (right). Once the IUD is inserted, the threads attached to the IUD will extend into the vagina through the cervical opening.

Once inserted, IUDs require little care and don't interfere with spontaneity during intercourse; however, insertion may be uncomfortable. Also, heavy cramping typically follows and sometimes persists. Menstrual flow usually increases, often significantly, with the use of ParaGard but decreases after 3–6 months of using Mirena. An estimated 2–10% of IUD users, especially women who have never borne children, expel the device within the first year. This usually happens during the first 3 months after insertion. Another IUD can be inserted, however, and many women retain it the second time.

Few methods of contraception are as convenient, effective, and as low a daily cost as the IUD. Additionally, fertility rebounds quickly upon discontinuation, users are at low risk for side effects, and the device has been shown to provide some protection against ectopic pregnancy, or one that occurs outside the uterus. An IUD is also an excellent alternative for women who cannot use oral contraceptives because of medical disorders (Hatcher et al., 2007).

Fertility Awareness–Based Methods

Fertility awareness–based (FAB) methods of family planning require substantial education, training, and diligence. They are based on a woman's knowledge of her body's reproductive cycle. Requiring a high degree of motivation and self-control, these methods are not for everyone. FAB methods are also referred to as "natural family planning." Some people make the following distinction between the two: With fertility awareness, the couple may use an alternative method (such as a diaphragm with jelly or a male condom with foam) during the fertile part of the woman's cycle. Natural family planning does not include the use of any contraceptive device and is thus considered to be more natural; it is approved by the Catholic Church.

Fertility awareness–based methods include the calendar (rhythm) method, the basal body temperature (BBT) method, the ovulation method, and the symptothermal method, which combines the latter two (see Figure 11.7). These methods are free and pose no health risks. If a woman wishes to become pregnant, awareness of her own fertility cycles is useful. But these methods are not

● **FIGURE 11.7**

Fertility Awareness Calendar. To use the calendar method or other fertility awareness methods, a woman must keep track of her menstrual cycles. (a) This chart shows probable safe and unsafe days for a woman with a regular 28-day cycle. (b) This chart shows safe and unsafe days for a woman whose cycles range from 25 to 31 days. Note that the woman with an irregular cycle has significantly more unsafe days. The calendar method is most effective when combined with the basal body temperature (BBT) and cervical mucus methods.

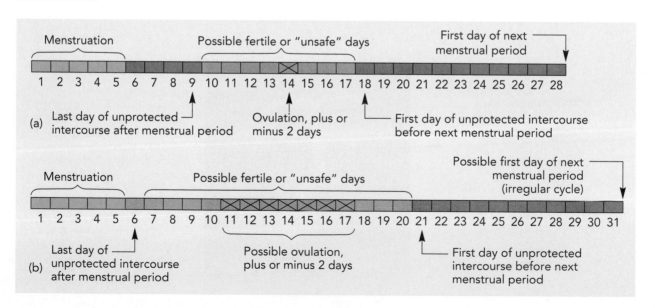

suitable for women with irregular menstrual cycles or for couples not highly motivated to use them. Certain conditions or circumstances, such as recent menarche, approaching menopause, recent childbirth, breastfeeding, and recent discontinuation of hormonal contraceptives, make fertility awareness methods more difficult to use and require more extensive monitoring. Couples practicing abstinence during fertile periods may begin to take risks out of frustration. These couples can benefit from exploring other forms of sexual expression, and counseling can help. Among typical users of fertility awareness, about 25% of women experience unintended pregnancy during the first year of use because it is difficult to predict when ovulation will occur.

The Calendar (Rhythm) Method   The **calendar (rhythm) method** is based on calculating "safer" days, which depends on the range of a woman's longest and shortest menstrual cycles. It may not be practical or safe for women with irregular cycles. Because sperm generally live 2–4 days, the maximum period of time in which fertilization could be expected to occur may be calculated with the assistance of a calendar. To prevent pregnancy, a woman should not rely on this method alone.

Ovulation generally occurs 14 (plus or minus 2) days before a woman's menstrual period. (However, ovulation can occur anytime during the cycle, including the menstrual period.) Taking this into account, and charting her menstrual cycles for a minimum of 8 months to determine the longest and shortest cycles, a woman can determine her expected fertile period. (Figure 11.7 shows the interval of fertility calculated in this way.) Thus, women who monitor their fertility to prevent pregnancy need to avoid unprotected vaginal intercourse or use an alternative method of contraception for at least one third of each menstrual cycle.

> Women who miscalculate are called mothers.
>
> —Abigail Van Buren
> (1918–)

The Basal Body Temperature (BBT) Method   A woman's temperature tends to be slightly lower during menstruation and for about a week afterward. Just before ovulation, it dips a few tenths of a degree; it then rises sharply (one half to nearly one whole degree) at the time of ovulation. It stays high until just before the next menstrual period.

A woman practicing the **basal body temperature (BBT) method** must record her temperature every morning upon waking for 6–12 months to gain an accurate idea of her temperature pattern. This change can best be noted using a BBT thermometer, before getting out of bed. When she can recognize the rise in her temperature and predict when in her cycle ovulation will occur, she can begin using the method. She should abstain from intercourse or use an alternative contraceptive method for 3–4 days before the expected rise and for 4 days after it has taken place.

Cervical Mucus Method   Women who use the **cervical mucus method** determine their stage in the menstrual cycle by examining the mucus secretions of the cervix. In many women, there is a noticeable change in the appearance and character of cervical mucus prior to ovulation. After menstruation, most women experience a moderate discharge of cloudy, yellowish or white mucus. Then, for a day or two, a clear, stretchy mucus is secreted. Ovulation occurs immediately after the clear, stretchy mucus secretions appear. The preovulatory mucus is elastic in consistency, rather like raw egg white, and a drop can be stretched into a thin strand. Following ovulation, the amount of discharge decreases markedly. The 4 days before and 4 days after these secretions are considered the unsafe days. Fewer pregnancies occur when intercourse takes place only on the dry days following ovulation ("Fertility Awareness," 2005).

The Symptothermal Method When two or more fertility indicators are used together, the approach is called the **symptothermal method.** Additional signs that may be useful in determining ovulation are midcycle pain in the lower abdomen on either side, a slight discharge of blood from the cervix ("spotting"), breast tenderness, feelings of heaviness, and/or abdominal swelling.

Sterilization

Sterilization is the most widely used method of contraception in the world, in both developing and developed countries (Landry, 2003). Among men and women in the United States, sterilization is the most common form of birth control, with females accounting for nearly three times the rate of surgery (Mosher et al., 2004). Couples and individuals choose sterilization because they want to limit or end childbearing. **Sterilization** involves surgical intervention that makes the reproductive organs incapable of producing or delivering viable gametes (sperm and eggs). The sterilization procedure is simpler, safer, and cheaper when performed on men than when performed on women.

Sterilization for Women Female sterilization is now a relatively safe, simple, and common procedure. Most female sterilizations are **tubal ligations,** familiarly known as "tying the tubes" (Figure 11.8). The two most common operations are laparoscopy and minilaparotomy. Less commonly performed types of sterilization for women are laparotomy and culpotomy or culdoscopy. Generally, this surgery is not reversible; only women who are

• **FIGURE 11.8**

Types of Female Sterilization. A variety of techniques are used to render a woman sterile.

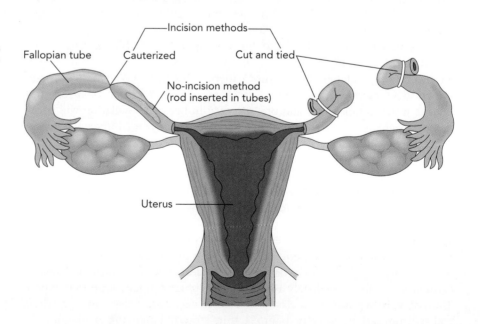

Incision methods

Fallopian tube   Cauterized   Cut and tied

No-incision method
(rod inserted in tubes)

Uterus

completely certain that they want no (or no more) children should choose this method.

Sterilization for women is quite expensive. Surgeon, anesthesiologist, and hospital fees are substantial. Costs may range from $2,000 to $6,000, depending on whether it is performed in the public or the private sector. Most health insurance policies will cover all or part of the cost of sterilization for both men and women. In some states, Medicaid pays for certain patients.

Laparoscopy   There are a variety of techniques used to sterilize women, and all seem to provide the same effectiveness. Sterilization by **laparoscopy** is the most frequently used method. This procedure is performed on an outpatient basis and takes 20–30 minutes. The woman's abdomen is inflated with gas to make the organs more visible. The surgeon inserts a rodlike instrument with a viewing lens (the laparoscope) through a small incision at the edge of the navel and locates the fallopian tubes. Through this incision or a second one, the surgeon inserts another instrument that closes the tubes, usually by electrocauterization (burning). Special small forceps that carry an electric current clamp the tubes and cauterize them. The tubes may also be closed off or blocked with tiny rings, clips, or plugs; no stitches are required. There is a recovery period of up to a week. During this time, the woman will experience some tenderness, cramping, and vaginal bleeding. Rest is important.

Click on "Tubal Ligation" to see what's involved in an actual laparoscopy.

Essure   In 2002, the U.S. FDA approved a permanent method of birth control called Essure®, a soft, flexible micro-insert placed into each fallopian tube in a 35-minute procedure that uses local anesthesia. For 3 months following insertion, the body and the device work together to form a tissue barrier that prevents sperm from reaching the egg. During that time, it is recommended that a woman use another method of birth control. By 6 months, the device is considered 100% effective. The number of providers placing Essure is increasing because of its safety, convenience, and cost benefit.

The Essure® procedure involves inserting a micro-rod into each fallopian tube. Tissue growth (causing sterilization) takes about 12 weeks.

Evaluating the Sterilization Methods for Women   Once sterilization has been done, no other method of birth control will ever be necessary. (A woman who risks exposure to STIs, however, should protect herself with a condom.)

Sterilization does not reduce or change a woman's hormone levels. It is not the same as menopause, nor does it hasten the onset of menopause, as some people believe. A woman still has her menstrual periods until whatever age menopause naturally occurs for her. The regularity of menstrual cycles is also not affected. A woman's ovaries, uterus (except in the case of hysterectomy), and hormonal system have not been changed. The only difference is that sperm cannot now reach her eggs. (The eggs, which are released every month as before, are reabsorbed by the body.) Sexual enjoyment is not diminished. In fact, a high percentage of women report that they feel more relaxed during intercourse because anxiety about pregnancy has been eliminated. There seem to be no harmful side effects associated with female sterilization. Sterilization should be considered irreversible.

Sterilization for Men   A **vasectomy** is a minor surgical procedure that can be performed in a doctor's office under a local anesthetic. It takes approximately

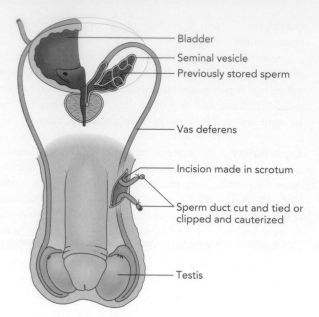

● **FIGURE 11.9**

Male Sterilization, or Vasectomy. This is a relatively simple procedure that involves local anesthesia and results in permanent sterilization.

Bladder

Seminal vesicle

Previously stored sperm

Vas deferens

Incision made in scrotum

Sperm duct cut and tied or clipped and cauterized

Testis

half an hour. In this procedure, the physician makes a small incision (or two incisions) in the skin of the scrotum. Through the incision, each vas deferens (sperm-carrying tube) is lifted, cut, tied, and often cauterized with electricity (Figure 11.9). After a brief rest, the man is able to walk out of the office; complete recuperation takes only a few days.

A man may retain some viable sperm in his system for days or weeks following a vasectomy. Because it takes about 15–20 ejaculations to get rid of these sperm, a couple should use other birth control until his semen has been checked.

Vasectomies are 99.9% effective. In very rare cases, the ends of a vas deferens may rejoin, but this is virtually impossible if the operation is correctly performed. Thus, following a vasectomy, no birth control method will ever be needed again. However, the man may still wish to use a condom to prevent acquiring or transmitting STIs. Sexual enjoyment will not be diminished; the man will still have erections and orgasms and ejaculate semen. A vasectomy is relatively inexpensive compared with female sterilization. Depending on where the surgery is performed, it costs from $350 to $1,000.

Compared with other birth control methods, the complication rates for vasectomy are very low. Most problems occur when proper antiseptic measures are not taken during the operation or when the man exercises too strenuously in the few days after.

Men who equate fertility with virility and potency may experience psychological problems following a vasectomy. However, most men experience no adverse psychological reactions if they understand what to expect and have the opportunity to express their concerns and ask questions. Vasectomy should be considered permanent.

Emergency Contraception (EC)

No birth control device is 100% effective: Condoms can break or slip, spermicides can expire, and devices can be used inconsistently and incorrectly.

Furthermore, intercourse sometimes occurs unexpectedly, and rape is, unfortunately, always a possibility. **Emergency contraception (EC),** also known as the "morning-after pill" or **Plan B,** is a safe and effective way to prevent pregnancy following unprotected intercourse. It can be taken within 3–5 days (120 hours) after unprotected intercourse and is 89% effective when taken within 72 hours, or 3 days, after unprotected intercourse ("Emergency Contraception," 2008). EC is not the "abortion pill" (RU-486), and it will not terminate an established pregnancy, in which the fertilized egg has already attached itself to the wall of the uterus, nor will it cause any harm to the developing fetus. Rather, EC inhibits ovulation and thickens cervical mucus, which prevents the sperm from joining the egg. Capping a contentious 3-year effort to ease access to the emergency contraception, the Food and Drug Administration ruled in 2006 to allow women aged 18 and older to buy the morning-after pill without a prescription. Those younger than 18 will still need a doctor's note to buy the pills.

Plan B is a brand of hormone pills that is specially packaged as emergency contraception. It contains the progestin levonorgestrel, the same hormone found in birth control pills. Thus, certain brands of birth control pills may still be used as backup birth control. Plan B does not, however, have the same risks as taking hormonal contraceptives because the hormones in Plan B do not stay in a woman's body as long as they do with ongoing birth control. Emergency contraception should not be used as a form of ongoing birth control because it is less effective. Plan B can be taken in one or two doses and is both cost-effective, usually about $10 to $45, and relatively safe. Though many women use Plan B with few or no problems, nausea and vomiting are among the most common side effects. Other side effects may include breast tenderness, irregular bleeding, dizziness, and headaches.

The ParaGard IUD can be used as EC when inserted by a health-care practitioner within 5 days after unprotected sexual intercourse. The mechanism interferes with implantation and may act as a contraceptive if inserted prior to ovulation. Because this method is most appropriate for women who plan to continue using an IUD as their contraceptive method, it is not widely utilized.

● Abortion

When most people hear the word "abortion," they think of a medical procedure. But **abortion,** or expulsion of the conceptus, can happen naturally or can be made to happen in one of several ways. Many abortions occur spontaneously—because a woman suffers a physical trauma, because the conceptus is not properly developed, or, more commonly, because physical conditions within the uterus break down and end the development of the conceptus. Approximately one third of all abortions reported annually in the United States are **spontaneous abortions,** or death of a fetus before it can survive on its own, otherwise referred to as **miscarriage** (see Chapter 12). In this section, however, we examine *induced* abortions, or intentionally terminated pregnancies. Unless otherwise noted, when we refer to abortion, we mean induced abortion.

Abortions cannot be viewed as if they are all the same. Distinctions must be made, for example, among wanted, unintended, and unwanted pregnancies.

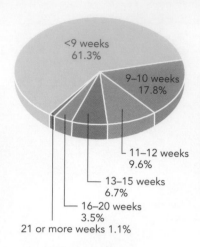

<9 weeks
61.3%

9–10 weeks
17.8%

11–12 weeks
9.6%

13–15 weeks
6.7%

16–20 weeks
3.5%

21 or more weeks 1.1%

● **FIGURE 11.10**

Weeks of Pregnancy When Women Have Abortions. In 2004, 88% of abortions occurred in the first 12 weeks of pregnancy. (*Source:* Guttmacher Institute, Facts on induced abortion in the United States, *In Brief*, New York: Guttmacher Institute, 2008, http://www.guttmacher.org/pubs/fb_induced_abortion.html, accessed 9/18/2008.)

● **FIGURE 11.11**

Medical Abortion With Mifepristone and Misoprostol. (*Source: Human Sexuality*, 3rd ed., by LeVay, S. and Baldwin, J. Copyright © 2008 by Sinauer Associates, Inc. Reprinted with permission.)

The duration of pregnancy, more than any other factor, determines which abortion method is performed.

Methods of Abortion

An abortion can be induced in several ways. Surgical methods are most common in this country, but the use of medications is also possible, as is suction. Methods for early abortions (those performed in the first 3 months of pregnancy) differ from those for late abortions (those performed after the third month). Nearly 90% of all abortions occur in the first 3 months of pregnancy, and 61% occur in the first 8 weeks (Guttmacher Institute, 2008c) (see Figure 11.10).

Medication Abortion (RU-486) After a decade of controversy, **medication abortion** (long known as **RU-486** and marketed as Mifeprex, or "miffy") became available in the United States in 2000. Widely used in several European countries for over two decades, it has been shown to be safe, effective, and acceptable (Hatcher et al., 2007) and has become an increasingly common alternative to surgical procedures. In fact, RU-486 induced abortions now account for 13% of all abortions (Jones et al., 2008).

Doctors can now prescribe the two-drug regimen (mifepristone and misoprostol) to terminate early pregnancy, provided they have some surgical backup arrangement should the treatment fail or side effects result. Mifepristone prevents the cells of the uterine lining from getting the progesterone they need to support a blastocyst (fertilized ovum); the embryo therefore cannot survive and is expelled from the uterus. Depending on the regimen used, this method is most effective when used during the first 7–9 weeks of pregnancy (see Figure 11.11).

Surgical Methods Surgical methods include vacuum aspiration, dilation and evacuation (D&E), and hysterotomy.

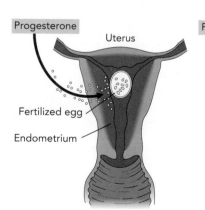

(a) In normal pregnancy, the endometrium is sustained by progesterone.

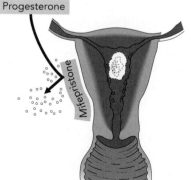

(b) Mifepristone blocks the action of progesterone, leading to breakdown of the endometrium and disruption of the embryo.

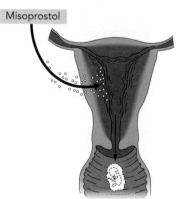

(c) Misoprostol, given 2 days later, causes myometrial contractions and expulsion of the fetal remains.

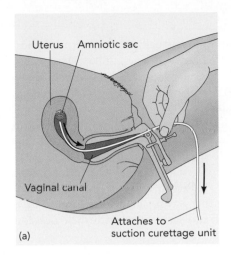

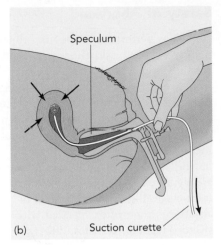

Vacuum Aspiration. (a) The vagina is opened with a speculum, and a thin vacuum tube is inserted through the cervix into the uterus. (b) The uterus is gently vacuumed, and the conceptus and other contents of the uterus are suctioned out.

Vacuum Aspiration (First-Trimester Method) **Vacuum aspiration,** sometimes called vacuum curettage or suction curettage, is performed under local anesthesia. The first step involves the rinsing of the vagina with an antiseptic solution. Next, the cervix is dilated with a series of graduated rods. Then a small tube attached to a vacuum is inserted through the cervix. The uterus is gently vacuumed, removing the conceptus, placenta, and endometrial tissue (see Figure 11.12). The most widely used abortion procedure used in the United States today, vacuum aspiration, which takes approximately 10–15 minutes to perform, can be used up to 14 weeks' gestation. There is no evidence of childbearing problems among women who have had vacuum aspiration abortion (Guttmacher Institute, 2008c).

Dilation and Evacuation (D&E) (Second-Trimester Method) **Dilation and evacuation (D&E)** is usually performed during the second trimester (weeks 13 to 24) of pregnancy, but it can be performed beyond week 24. Local or general anesthesia is used. The cervix is slowly dilated, and the fetus is removed by alternating curettage and other procedures. Because it is a second-trimester procedure, a D&E is somewhat riskier and often more traumatic than a first-trimester abortion.

Late-Term Abortions In rare cases during the late part of the second trimester, abortion can be achieved by inducing labor by use of either saline or prostaglandin. This procedure involves injecting a needle into the amniotic sac and removing a portion of the amniotic fluid. An equal amount of saline or prostaglandin (a hormone-like substance that causes contractions) is then injected into the amniotic sac, which causes labor to begin. The drug misoprostol can also be used to induce labor in second-trimester abortions.

If any of the above methods are contraindicated or if a woman's life is in imminent danger, a **hysterotomy** can be performed. This surgical method of abortion requires an incision in the woman's stomach, similar to a cesarean section, whereby the fetus is removed. This procedure is rarely performed, requires general anesthesia and hospitalization, and involves greater risks than other methods of abortion.

Safety of Abortion

Abortions performed in the first trimester pose virtually no long-term physical or psychological risks (Boonstra, Gold, Richards, & Finer, 2006; Major, Cozzarelli, Cooper, et al., 2000). In fact, the overall physical risk of complications from abortion is minimal: Fewer than 0.3% of women experience a complication that requires hospitalization (Henshaw, 1999). Regardless of the method performed, however, almost all women have some bleeding after the procedure that lasts from several days to several weeks, and the risks of complications increase with the length of pregnancy. Teenagers are the most likely to delay having an abortion until after 15 weeks of gestation, when the medical risks are significantly higher (Strauss, Gamble, & Parker, 2007). For most women, transient feelings of loss, sadness, or stress that accompany the decision to have an abortion are often replaced with relief and satisfaction with their decision (Kero, Hogberg, & Lalos, 2004).

Women and Abortion

Click on "The Secret Club" to hear women who have had abortions discuss what was most helpful to them.

Many women are reluctant to talk openly about their abortion experiences, but accurate information about women who have abortions may help dispel their possible feelings of isolation or rejection.

A broad cross section of U.S. women have abortions (Physicians for Reproductive Choice and Health & Guttmacher Institute, 2008):

- 56% of women having abortions are in their 20s;
- 66% have never married;
- 57% are economically disadvantaged;
- 41% are non-Hispanic White women; and
- 78% report a religious affiliation.

With an estimated 1.2 million procedures performed in 2005, abortion is a common experience among women in the United States (Guttmacher Institute, 2008c). (See Figure 11.13.) It is important to remember that women who have abortions are as diverse as their reasons for doing so. The high levels of unintended

● **FIGURE 11.13**

Rate of Abortions in Women Aged 15fi44 by Year. (*Source:* Guttmacher Institute, Facts on induced abortion in the United States, In Brief, New York: Guttmacher Institute, 2008, http://www.guttmacher.org/pubs/fb_induced_abortion.pdf, accessed 9/18/08.)

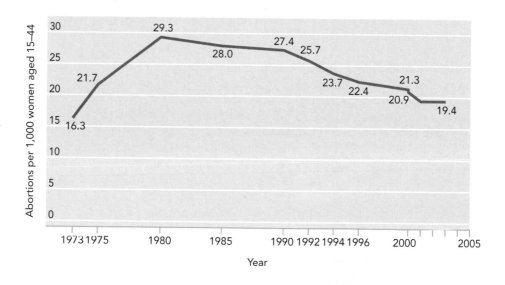

pregnancy and subsequent abortion can be attributed to three factors: (1) the failure of couples to practice contraception, (2) incorrect or inconsistent use of contraceptive methods, and (3) method failure among those practicing contraception correctly and consistently (Jones, Darroch, & Henshaw, 2002b).

Making an abortion decision, regardless of the ultimate outcome, raises many emotional issues for women. There are few painless ways of dealing with an unintended pregnancy. For many women, such a decision requires a reevaluation of their relationships, an examination of their childbearing plans, a search to understand the role of sexuality in their lives, and an attempt to clarify their life goals. Clearly, women *and* men need accurate information about fertility cycles and the risk of pregnancy when a contraceptive is not used consistently or correctly, as well as access to contraceptive and abortion services.

Men and Abortion

In the abortion decision-making process, the man is often forgotten. Attention is usually focused on the woman, who is making an agonizing decision. If the man is thought of, it is often with hostility. And yet the man, like the woman, may be experiencing his own personal guilt and anxiety, feeling ambivalent about the possibility of parenthood.

A common feeling men experience is powerlessness. They may try to remain cool and rational, believing that if they reveal their feelings they will be unable to give their partners emotional support. Because the drama is within the woman and her body, a man may feel he must not influence her decision.

There is the lure of fatherhood, all the same. A pregnancy forces a man to confront his own feelings about parenting. Parenthood for males, as for females, can be a profound right. For young men, there is a mixture of pride and fear about potential fatherhood and adulthood.

After an abortion, many men feel residual guilt, sadness, and remorse. It is also fairly common for couples to split up after an abortion; the stress, conflict, and guilt can be overwhelming. Many clinics now provide counseling for men, as well as women, involved in an abortion.

The Abortion Debate

In the abortion debate, those who believe abortion should be prohibited generally identify themselves as "pro-life." Those who support a woman's right to choose for herself whether to have an abortion generally identify themselves as "pro-choice."

The Pro-Life Stance
For those who oppose abortion, there is a basic principle from which their stance follows: The moment an egg is fertilized, it becomes a human being, with the full rights and dignity afforded other humans. An embryo is no less human than a fetus, and a fetus is no less human than a baby. Morally, aborting an embryo is the equivalent of murder.

Even though the majority of those opposing abortion would consider rape and incest (and sometimes a defective embryo or fetus) to be exceptions, the pro-life leadership generally opposes any justification for an abortion other than to save the life of the pregnant woman. To abort the embryo of a rape or incest survivor, they reason, is still to take an innocent human life.

In addition, pro-life advocates argue that abortion is the first step toward a society that eliminates undesirable human beings. If we allow the elimination

> I have noticed that all the people who favor abortion have already been born.
>
> —Ronald Reagan
> (1911–2004)

of embryos, they argue, what is to stop the killing of people who are disabled or elderly, or merely inconvenient? Finally, pro-life advocates argue that there are thousands of couples who want to adopt children but are unable to do so because so many pregnant women choose to abort rather than to give birth.

The Pro-Choice Argument   Under safe, clean, and legal conditions, abortion is a very safe medical procedure. Self-administered or illegal, clandestine abortions, however, can be very dangerous. The continued availability of legal abortion is considered by most physicians, psychologists, and public health professionals to be critical to the public's physical and mental well-being. Those who believe that abortion should continue to be legal present a number of arguments. First, for pro-choice men and women, the fundamental issue is who decides whether a woman will bear children: the woman or the government. Because women continue to bear the primary responsibility for rearing children, pro-choice advocates believe that women should not be forced to give birth to unwanted children. Becoming a mother alters a woman's role more profoundly than almost any other event in her life. When women have the *choice* of becoming mothers, they are able to decide the timing and direction of their lives.

Second, in addition to supporting comprehensive sexuality education and contraception to eliminate much of the need for abortion, pro-choice advocates believe that abortion should continue to be available as birth control backup. Because no contraceptive method is 100% effective, unintended pregnancies occur even among the most conscientious contraceptive users.

Third, if abortion is made illegal, large numbers of women nevertheless will have illegal abortions, substantially increasing the likelihood of procedural complications, infections, and death. Those who are unable to have an abortion may be forced to give birth to and raise a child they did not want or cannot afford to raise.

Constitutional Issues   In 1969 in Texas, 21-year-old Norma McCorvey, a single mother, discovered she was pregnant. In the hope of obtaining a legal abortion, she lied to her doctor, saying that she had been raped. Her physician informed her, however, that Texas prohibited all abortions except those to save the life of the mother. He suggested that she travel to California, where she could obtain a legal abortion, but she had no money. Two lawyers heard of her situation and took her case in order to challenge abortion restrictions as an unconstitutional invasion of the individual's right to privacy. For the case, McCorvey was given "Roe" as a pseudonym. In 1970, a court in Texas declared the law unconstitutional, but the state appealed the decision. Meanwhile, McCorvey had her baby and gave it up for adoption. Ultimately, the case reached the U.S. Supreme Court, which issued its famous *Roe v. Wade* decision in 1973. Under the 1973 *Roe* decision, a woman's right to abortion is guaranteed as a fundamental right, part of the constitutional right to privacy. At the time, only four states permitted abortion at the woman's discretion.

The *Roe* decision created a firestorm of opposition among political and religious conservatives and fueled a right-wing political resurgence. But because abortion was determined a fundamental right by the *Roe* decision, efforts by the states to curtail it failed.

Since the 1973 Supreme Court decision in *Roe v. Wade,* states have been undergoing rigorous debate about how best to interpret, regulate, limit, and define under what circumstances a woman may obtain an abortion. Though a host of legislative challenges have occurred and a variety of abortion laws are

> *There are few absolutes left in the age after Einstein, and the case of abortion, like almost everything else, is a case of relative goods and ills to be evaluated one against the other.*
>
> —Germaine Greer
> (1939–)

> *If men could get pregnant, abortion would be a sacrament.*
>
> —Florynce Kennedy (attributed)
> (1916–2000)

on the books, many laws may not be enforced. A few highlights of the laws at the time of printing of this book include (Guttmacher Institute, 2008d):

- 38 states require an abortion to be performed only by a licensed physician;
- 36 states prohibit abortions, except when necessary to protect the woman's life or health, most often after fetal viability is determined;
- 14 states prohibit "partial-birth" abortions, in spite of the fact that a definition for this term is not yet sufficiently precise or agreed upon;
- 24 states require a woman seeking an abortion to wait a specified period of time, usually 24 hours, between abortion counseling and the procedure;
- 35 states require some type of parental involvement in a minor's decision to have an abortion.

The shared objective between the pro-life and pro-choice camps is the reduction in the number of abortions performed each year in this country. Research both in this country and abroad has demonstrated that education about effective and safe sexual choices and access to contraceptive services can decrease abortion rates (Marston & Cleland, 2003; Rahman, DaVanzo, & Razzaque, 2001). While each state will continue to define and enforce laws according to the ideological standpoints of its leaders, the protection of legal abortion is in the hands of the Supreme Court. The votes of these justices will be critical in influencing access to abortion in this country.

● Research Issues

Most users of contraception find some drawback to whatever method they choose. Hormonal methods may be costly or have undesirable side effects. Putting on a condom or inserting a sponge may seem to interrupt lovemaking too much. The inconveniences, the side effects, the lack of 100% effectiveness—all point to the need for more effective and more diverse forms of contraception than we have now.

High developmental costs, government regulations, social issues, political constraints, and marketing priorities all play a role in restricting contraceptive research. The biggest barrier to developing new contraceptive techniques may be the fear of lawsuits. Pharmaceutical manufacturers will not easily forget that the IUD market was virtually destroyed in the 1970s and 1980s by numerous costly lawsuits.

Another reason for limited contraceptive research is extensive government regulation, which requires exhaustive product testing. Although no one wants to be poisoned by medicines, perhaps it wouldn't hurt to take a closer look at the process by which new drugs become available to the public. Approval by the FDA takes an average of 7.5 years. Drug patents are in effect for only 17 years, so the pharmaceutical companies have less than 10 years to recover their developmental costs once a medication is approved for sale. Furthermore, pharmaceutical companies are not willing to expend millions in research only to have the FDA refuse to approve the marketing of new products. According to chemist Carl Djerassi (1981), the "father" of the birth control pill, safety is a relative, not an absolute, concept. We may need to reexamine the question "How safe is safe?" and weigh potential benefits along with possible problems.

Though research has investigated a number of contraceptives for men, none have been found to adequately eliminate sperm production while maintaining the libido.

A lily pond, so the French riddle goes, contains a single leaf. Each day the number of leaves doubles—two leaves the second day, four the third, eight the fourth, and so on. Question: If the pond is completely full on the thirtieth day, when is it half full? Answer: On the twenty-ninth day. The global lily pond in which [six] billion of us live may already be half full.

—Lester Brown
(1934–)

Final Thoughts

Control over our fertility helps us control our lives. It also allows the human species to survive and, at least in parts of the world, to prosper. The topic of birth control provokes much emotional controversy. Individuals and institutions alike are inclined to believe in the moral rightness of their particular stance on the subject, whatever that stance may be. As each of us tries to find his or her own path through the quagmire of controversy, we can be guided by what we learn. We need to arm ourselves with knowledge—not only about the methods and mechanics of contraception and birth control but also about our own motivations, needs, weaknesses, and strengths.

Summary

Risk and Responsibility

- Over the period of 1 year, sexually active couples who do not use contraception have a 90% chance of getting pregnant. Not surprising, the nonusers of contraception account for about half of unintended pregnancies.

- Many people knowingly risk pregnancy by having unprotected intercourse. The more "successful" they are at risk taking, the more likely they are to take chances again. People also take risks because of faulty knowledge, denial of their sexuality, or a subconscious desire for a child.

- Because women are the ones who get pregnant, they may have a greater interest than men in controlling their fertility. However, more men are now sharing the responsibility.

Methods of Contraception and Birth Control

- *Birth control* is any means of preventing a birth from taking place. *Contraception* is birth control that works specifically by preventing the union of sperm and egg.

- The most reliable method of birth control is *abstinence*— refraining from sexual intercourse.

- *Oral contraceptives* are the most widely used form of reversible birth control in the United States. The majority of birth control pills contain synthetic hormones: progestin and (usually) estrogen. The pill is highly effective if taken regularly. There are side effects and possible problems for some users. The greatest risks are to smokers, women over 35, and women with certain health disorders, such as cardiovascular problems. Other methods of hormonal contraception include the *patch;* the *vaginal ring;* the injectable hormone, Depo-Provera; and the **implant,** Implanon.

- A *condom* (or *male condom*) is a thin sheath of latex, rubber, polyurethane, or processed animal tissue that fits over the erect penis and prevents semen from being transmitted. It is the third most widely used birth control method in the United States. Condoms are very effective for contraception when used correctly. Latex and polyurethane condoms also help provide protection against STIs.

- The *female condom, diaphragm, sponge,* Lea's Shield, and FemCap are barrier methods used by women. Each covers the cervical opening and is used with spermicidal jelly or cream. Female condoms, in addition to lining the vagina, cover much of the vulva, providing more protection against disease organisms.

- *Spermicides* are chemicals that are toxic to sperm. Though *nonoxynol-9* is the most common ingredient in spermicides, it is no longer recommended for use on condoms. *Contraceptive foam* provides fairly good protection when used alone, but other chemicals are more effective if combined with a barrier method. Other spermicidal products are *film,* cream, jelly, and vaginal suppositories.

- An *intrauterine device (IUD)* is a tiny flexible plastic device that is inserted through the cervical os into the uterus. It disrupts the fertilization and implantation processes.

- *Fertility awareness–based methods* (or natural family planning) involve a woman's awareness of her body's reproductive cycles. These include the *calendar (rhythm), basal body temperature (BBT), cervical mucus,* and *symptothermal methods.* These methods are suitable only for women with regular menstrual cycles and for couples with high motivation.

- *Sterilization* is the most widely used method of contraception in the world. The most common form for women is *tubal ligation,* closing off the fallopian tubes. Another female sterilization device, called Essure, does not require surgical incision. The surgical procedure that sterilizes men is a *vasectomy,* in which each vas deferens (sperm-carrying tube) is closed off. These methods of birth control are very effective.

- The use of *emergency contraception* prevents pregnancy by keeping a fertilized egg from implanting into the uterus. When used within 3–5 days of unprotected intercourse, it can be quite effective. The ParaGard IUD can also be used as a postcoital form of birth control.

Abortion

- *Abortion,* the expulsion of the conceptus from the uterus, can be spontaneous or induced. *Medication abortion* (also known as *RU-486*) is now available in the United States to terminate early pregnancy. Surgical methods of abortion are *vacuum aspiration, dilation and evacuation (D&E),* and *hysterotomy.* Nonsurgical methods utilize injections of prostaglandins or saline solution. Abortion is generally safe if done in the first trimester. Second-trimester abortions are riskier.

- In the United States, there are about 1.2 million abortions annually. The abortion rate has declined slightly in recent years.

- For women, the abortion decision is complex and raises many emotional issues. Men often feel powerless and ambivalent when their partner has an abortion, and many feel residual guilt and sadness following the abortion.

- In the abortion controversy, pro-life advocates argue that life begins at conception, that abortion leads to euthanasia, and that many who want to adopt are unable to because fewer babies are born as a result of abortion. Pro-choice advocates stance that women have the right to decide whether to continue a pregnancy, that abortion is needed as a birth control alternative because contraceptives are not 100% effective, and that if abortion is not legal women will have unsafe illegal abortions. A key issue in the debate is when the embryo or fetus becomes human life.

- The current constitutional doctrine on abortion is evolving and dependent upon decisions of the U.S. Supreme Court and interpretations of state governments.

Research Issues

- High developmental costs, government regulations, political agendas, and marketing priorities all play a part in restricting contraceptive research. The biggest barrier, however, is the fear of lawsuits.

Questions for Discussion

- Who, in your opinion, should have access to birth control? Should the parent(s) of individuals younger than age 18 be informed that the child has obtained birth control? Why or why not?

- What considerations do you have before you would use a method of birth control? With whom would you discuss these? What sources of information might you use to verify your concerns or issues?

- If you or your partner experienced an unplanned pregnancy, what would you do? What resources do you have that would support your decision?

The Emergency Contraception Website
http://ec.princeton.edu
Operated by the Office of Population Research at Princeton University, this project is designed to provide accurate information about emergency contraception derived from the medical literature.

National Abortion and Reproductive Rights Action League
http://www.naral.org
Advocates for comprehensive reproductive health policies to secure reproductive *choice* for all Americans.

National Right to Life
http://www.nrlc.org
Goal is to provide legal protection to human life.

Population Council
http://www.popcouncil.org
An international, nonprofit, nongovernmental organization that conducts biomedical, social science, and public health research.

United Nations Population Fund
http://www.unfpa.org/about/index.htm
An international development agency that promotes well-being by providing countries with population data for policies and programs.

Suggested Web Sites

Association of Reproductive Health Professionals (ARHP)
http://www.arhp.org
A site for health-care providers, as well as those interested in reproductive health news.

Centers for Disease Control and Prevention Reproductive Health Information Source
http://www.cdc.gov/reproductivehealth/index.htm
Provides information, research, and scientific reports on men's and women's reproductive health.

The Contraception Report
http://www.contraceptiononline.org
Aimed primarily at physicians and sponsored by Baylor College of Medicine; a peer-reviewed journal that provides up-to-date findings concerning all forms of contraception.

Suggested Reading

Hatcher, R. A., et al. (2007). *Contraceptive technology* (19th rev. ed.) New York: Ardent Media. This updated book provides recent information on all methods of contraception.

Schoen, J. (2005). *Choice and coercion: Birth control, sterilization, & abortion in public health and welfare.* Chapel Hill: University of North Carolina Press. Provides an understanding of the modern welfare state as it relates to reproductive choices of women.

Tone, A. (2002). *Devices and desires: A history of contraceptives in America.* Provides a social history of birth control, from the beginning use of condoms through the controversy surrounding the pill.

For links, articles, and study material, go to the McGraw-Hill Web site, located at **www.mhhe.com/yarber7e.**

Conception, Pregnancy, and Childbirth

MAIN TOPICS

Fertilization and Fetal Development

Being Pregnant

Infertility

Giving Birth

Becoming a Parent

"When I was in my teens, I moved from my home [Guatemala] to the states and found things turned upside [down] from my traditional background. Take, for example, breastfeeding. In my country, it is a normal thing to breastfeed; you would not think twice about seeing a nurturing mother breastfeeding her child in public. Here, it seems to upset people's sensibilities when a nursing mother feeds her child in public. I wonder, that which is so natural and necessary, how can we debate whether a woman has a right to feed her child in public?"

—20-year-old female

"Pregnancy and childbirth have changed my life. As the mother of three young children, I look back at my pregnancies as probably three of the best periods of my life. Oh, sure, there were the days of exhaustion and nausea, pelvic heaviness, the large cumbersome breasts, and lost sleep, but in retrospect, they were overshadowed by the life growing inside of me. In giving life, I celebrate my womanhood."

—43-year-old female

"After getting married and having a daughter, things changed. While I was pregnant we, maybe, had sex 10 times. I was really sick during the first trimester and on bed rest during the second and third trimesters. At the time, it wasn't that big of a deal since we were so preoccupied with my health and our daughter. After she was born, it seemed that we were just out of practice and had a hard time initiating sex. When we did have sex we would both say, 'WOW, we should do this more often,' but then life would get in the way and 2 weeks would go by before we had sex again."

—28-year-old female

THE BIRTH OF A CHILD is considered by many parents to be the happiest event of their lives. For most American women, pregnancy is relatively comfortable and the outcome predictably joyful. Yet, for increasing numbers of others, especially among the poor, the prospect of having children raises the specters of drugs, disease, malnutrition, and familial chaos. And there are those couples who have dreamed of and planned for families for years, only to find that they are unable to conceive.

In this chapter, we view pregnancy and childbirth from biological, social, and psychological perspectives. We consider pregnancy loss, infertility, and reproductive technology. And we look at the challenges of the transition to parenthood.

• Fertilization and Fetal Development

If your parents didn't have any children, there's a good chance that you won't have any.

—Clarence Day
(1874–1935)

As you will recall from Chapter 3, once the ovum has been released from the ovary, it drifts into the fallopian tube, where it may be fertilized if live sperm are present (see Figure 12.1). If the pregnancy proceeds without interruption, the birth will occur in approximately 266 days. (Traditionally, physicians count the first day of the pregnancy as the day on which the woman began her last menstrual period; they calculate the due date to be 280 days, which is also 10 lunar months, from that day.)

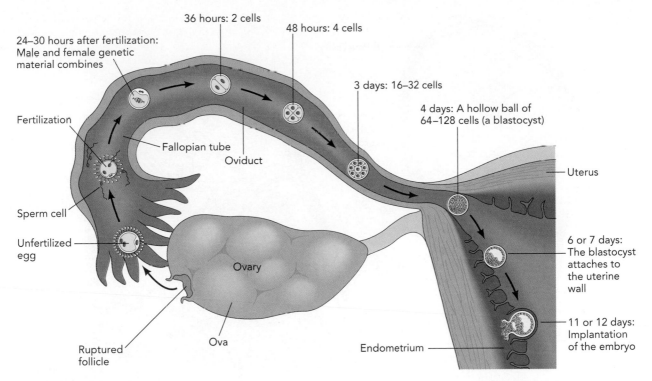

24–30 hours after fertilization:
Male and female genetic
material combines

36 hours: 2 cells

48 hours: 4 cells

3 days: 16–32 cells

4 days: A hollow ball of
64–128 cells (a blastocyst)

Fertilization

Fallopian tube

Oviduct

Uterus

Sperm cell

Unfertilized
egg

Ovary

6 or 7 days:
The blastocyst
attaches to
the uterine
wall

11 or 12 days:
Implantation
of the embryo

Ruptured
follicle

Ova

Endometrium

● **FIGURE 12.1**

**Ovulation, Fertilization, and
Development of the Blastocyst.**
This drawing charts the progress
of the released ovum (unfertilized
egg) through fertilization and
pre-embryonic development.

The Fertilization Process

The **oocyte** (ovum, or unfertilized egg) remains viable for 12–24 hours after ovulation; most sperm are viable in the female reproductive tract for 12–48 hours, although some may be viable for up to 5 days. Therefore, for fertilization to occur, intercourse must take place within 5 days before and 1 day after ovulation.

Of the millions of sperm ejaculated into the vagina, only a few thousand (or even a few hundred) actually reach the fallopian tubes. The others leak from the vagina or are destroyed within its acidic environment. Those that make it into the cervix (which is easier during ovulation, when the cervical mucus becomes more fluid) may still be destroyed by white blood cells within the uterus. Furthermore, the sperm that actually reach the oocyte within a few minutes of ejaculation are not yet capable of getting through its outer layers. They must first undergo **capacitation,** the process by which their membranes become fragile enough to release the enzymes from their acrosomes (the helmet-like coverings of the sperm's nuclei). It takes 6–8 hours for this acrosomal reaction to occur. It has been observed that sperm have receptor molecules that are attracted to a chemical released by the egg. Furthermore, the membrane of the sperm cell contains a chemical that helps the sperm adhere to, and eventually penetrate, the outer layer of the egg.

Once a single sperm is inside the oocyte cytoplasm, an electrical reaction occurs that prevents any other sperm from entering the oocyte. Immediately, the oocyte begins to swell, detaching the sperm that still cling to its outer layer. Next, it completes the final stage of cell division and becomes a mature ovum by forming the ovum nucleus. The nuclei of sperm and ovum then release their chromosomes, which combine to form the diploid zygote, containing 23 pairs of chromosomes. (Each parent contributes one chromosome to each of the

*Expectant parents who want a boy
will get a girl, and vice versa; those who
practice birth control will get twins.*

—John Rush

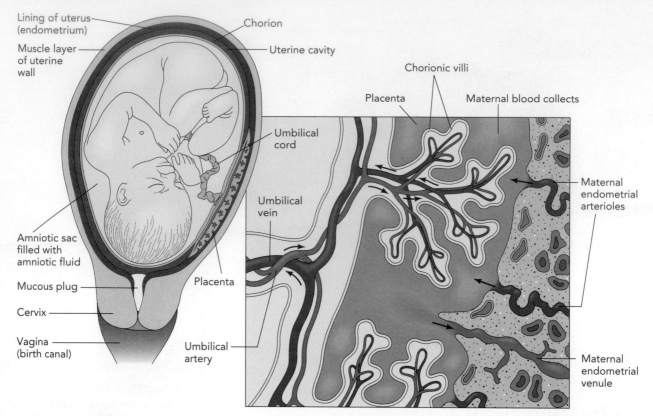

FIGURE 12.2

The Fetus in the Uterus and a Cross Section of the Placenta. The placenta is the organ of exchange between mother and fetus. Nutrients and oxygen pass from the mother to the fetus, and waste products pass from the fetus to the mother via blood vessels within the umbilical cord.

pairs.) Fertilization is now complete, and pre-embryonic development begins. Within 9 months, this single cell, the zygote, may become the 600 trillion cells that constitute a human being.

Development of the Conceptus

Following fertilization, the zygote undergoes a series of divisions, during which the cells replicate. After 4 or 5 days, there are about 100 cells, now called a **blastocyst.** On about the 5th day, the blastocyst arrives in the uterine cavity, where it floats for a day or two before implanting in the soft, blood-rich uterine lining (endometrium), which has spent the past 3 weeks preparing for its arrival. The process of **implantation** takes about 1 week. Human chorionic gonadotropin (HCG) secreted by the blastocyst maintains the uterine environment in an "embryo-friendly" condition and prevents the shedding of the endometrium, which would normally occur during menstruation.

The blastocyst, or pre-embryo, rapidly grows into an **embryo,** which will, in turn, be referred to as a **fetus** after the 8th week of **gestation** (pregnancy). During the first 2 or 3 weeks of development, the **embryonic membranes** are formed. These include the **amnion** (amniotic sac), a membranous sac that will contain the embryo and **amniotic fluid;** the **yolk sac,** producer of the embryo's first blood cells and the germ cells that will develop into gonads; and the **chorion,** the embryo's outermost membrane (see Figure 12.2).

During the 3rd week, extensive cell migration occurs, and the stage is set for the development of the organs. The first body segments and the brain begin to form. The digestive and circulatory systems begin to develop in the 4th week,

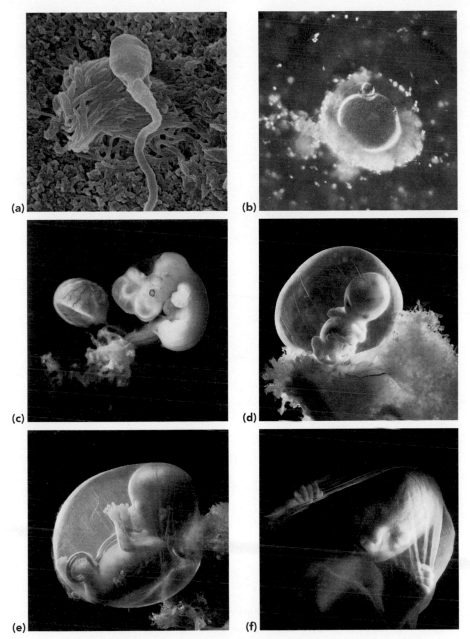

(a) After ejaculation, several million sperm move through the cervical mucus toward the fallopian tubes; an ovum has moved into one of the tubes. On their way to the ovum, millions of sperm are destroyed in the vagina, uterus, or fallopian tubes. Some go the wrong direction in the vagina, and others swim into the wrong tube. (b) The woman's and man's chromosomes have united, and the fertilized ovum has divided for the first time. After about 1 week, the blastocyst will implant itself in the uterine lining. (c) The embryo is 5 weeks old and is ²/₅ of an inch long. It floats in the embryonic sac. The major divisions of the brain can be seen, as well as an eye, hands, arms, and a long tail. (d) The embryo is now 7 weeks old and is almost 1 inch long and is connected to its umbilical cord. Its external and internal organs are developing. It has eyes, nose, mouth, lips, and tongue. (e) At 12 weeks, the fetus is over 3 inches long and weighs almost 1 ounce. (f) At 16 weeks, the fetus is more than 6 inches long and weighs about 7 ounces. All its organs have been formed. The time that follows is now one of simple growth.

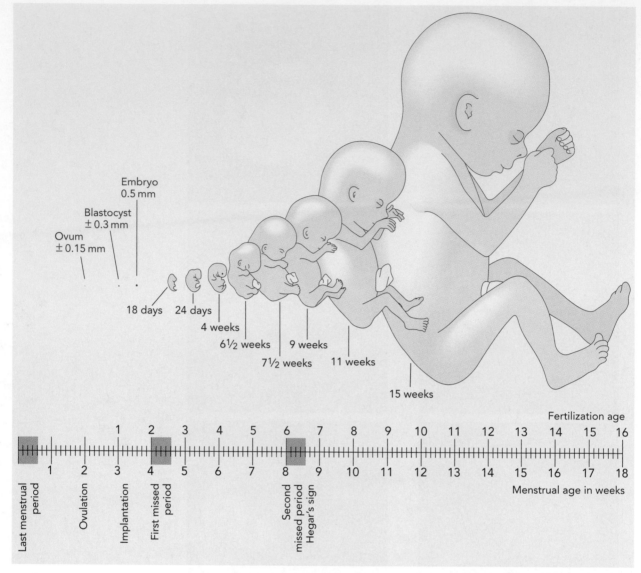

Embryo
0.5 mm

Blastocyst
± 0.3 mm

Ovum
± 0.15 mm

18 days 24 days

4 weeks

6½ weeks   9 weeks

7½ weeks   11 weeks

15 weeks

Fertilization age

| 1 | 2 | 3 | 4 | 5 | 6 | 7 | 8 | 9 | 10 | 11 | 12 | 13 | 14 | 15 | 16 |

| 1 | 2 | 3 | 4 | 5 | 6 | 7 | 8 | 9 | 10 | 11 | 12 | 13 | 14 | 15 | 16 | 17 | 18 |

Menstrual age in weeks

Last menstrual period

Ovulation

Implantation

First missed period

Second missed period
Hegar's sign

● **FIGURE 12.3**

Growth of the Embryo and Fetus. In this drawing, the actual sizes of the developing embryo and fetus are shown, from conception through the first 15 weeks.

What was your original face before you were born?

—Zen koan (riddle)

and the heart begins to pump blood. By the end of the 4th week, the spinal cord and nervous system have also begun to develop. The 5th week sees the formation of arms and legs. In the 6th week, the eyes and ears form. At 7 weeks, the reproductive organs begin to differentiate in males; female reproductive organs continue to develop. At 8 weeks, the fetus is about the size of a thumb, although the head is nearly as large as the body. The brain begins to function to coordinate the development of the internal organs. Facial features begin to form, and bones begin to develop. Arms, hands, fingers, legs, feet, toes, and eyes are almost fully developed at 12 weeks. At 15 weeks, the fetus has a strong heartbeat, some digestive functioning, and active muscles. Most bones are developed by then, and the eyebrows appear. At this stage, the fetus is covered with a fine, downy hair called **lanugo** (see Figure 12.3).

Throughout its development, the fetus is nourished through the **placenta.** The placenta begins to develop from part of the blastocyst following implantation.

A Matter of Choice

Parenthood is now a matter of choice, thanks to the widespread use of contraception and changing perceptions of child-free couples. For the most part, women and men who want to have children can decide not only how many children they want but when to have them. Among women of childbearing age, approximately 6.6% have chosen not to have children ("Childless by Choice," 2001). This translates to over 4 million women. In the past, couples without children were referred to as "childless," conveying the sense that they were missing something they wanted or were supposed to have. But this term has been replaced with **child-free,** as we have experienced a cultural shift and demographic trend in the direction of increasing numbers of women who expect and intend to remain nonparents. The term "child-free" suggests that couples who do not choose to have children need no longer be seen as sympathetic figures, lacking something considered essential for personal and relationship fulfillment.

Even with less familial and social pressure to reproduce, the decision not to have children can be a difficult one. Factors include timing, divorce, ambivalence on the part of one partner, lack of desire to conceive or adopt a child when single, and career ambitions and promotions. Couples usually have some idea that they will or will not have children before they marry. If the intent isn't clear from the start or if one partner's mind changes, the couple may have serious problems ahead.

Think Critically

- Do you want to have children? Why or why not?
- What are your feelings about those who choose to remain child-free?
- Do you believe that the government should provide tax incentives to couples who are child-free?

It grows larger as the fetus does, passing nutrients from the mother's bloodstream to the fetus, to which it is attached by the **umbilical cord.** The placenta serves as a biochemical barrier, allowing dissolved substances to pass to the fetus but blocking blood cells and large molecules.

By 5 months, the fetus is 10–12 inches long and weighs between $1/2$ and 1 pound. The internal organs are well developed, although the lungs cannot function well outside the uterus. At 6 months, the fetus is 11–14 inches long and weighs more than 1 pound. At 7 months, it is 13–17 inches long and weighs about 3 pounds. At this point, most healthy fetuses are viable—that is, capable of surviving outside the womb. (Although some fetuses are viable at 5 or 6 months, they require specialized care to survive.) The fetus spends the final 2 months of gestation growing rapidly. At term (9 months), it will be about 20 inches long and will weigh about 7 pounds. The mean gestational age for single-child births is 38.7 weeks (Centers for Disease Control and Prevention, 2005a).

● Being Pregnant

From the moment it is discovered, a pregnancy affects people's feelings about themselves, their relationships with their partners, as well as the interrelationships of other family members. There were 4.3 million births in the United States in 2008, nearly 3% more than in 2005 (Tejada-Vera & Sutton, 2008). Births to Hispanic women accounted for nearly one quarter of all U.S. births, but non-Hispanic White women and other racial and ethnic groups were having more babies too (Ventura, Abma, Mosher, & Henshaw, 2008). The fertility rate, now 2.1 children, is at the highest level since 1971. Accounting for the rise in this rate are declines in contraceptive use, limited access to abortion in some states, low levels of education, and poverty. It is also more common for American women to have babies out of wedlock and terminate unintended pregnancies than it was even a decade ago. While fertility rates are increasing in some segments of the population, they tend to decline as women become better educated and gain career opportunities and as they postpone childbearing until they are older. Interestingly, these reported trends seem to be at odds with those reported in many other industrialized countries (Stobbe, 2008).

Pregnancy Detection

Chemical tests designed to detect the presence of **human chorionic gonadotropin (HCG),** secreted by the developing placenta, can usually determine pregnancy approximately 2 weeks following a missed (or spotty) menstrual period. Pregnancy testing may be done in a doctor's office or family planning clinic, or home pregnancy tests may be purchased in most drugstores. The directions must be followed closely. Blood analysis can also be done to determine if a pregnancy exists. Although such tests diagnose pregnancy within 7 days after conception and with better than 95% accuracy, no absolute certainty exists until fetal heartbeat and movements can be detected or ultrasound is performed.

The first reliable physical sign of pregnancy can be observed about 4 weeks after a woman misses her period. By this point, changes in her cervix and pelvis are apparent during a pelvic examination. At this stage, the woman is considered to be 8 weeks pregnant, according to medical terminology; physicians calculate pregnancy as beginning at the time of the woman's last menstrual period rather than at the time of actual fertilization (because that date is often difficult to determine). Another signal of pregnancy, called **Hegar's sign,** is a softening of the uterus just above the cervix, which can be felt during a vaginal examination. In addition, a slight purple hue colors the labia minora; the vagina and cervix also take on a purplish color rather than the usual pink.

Changes in Women During Pregnancy

A woman's early response to pregnancy will vary dramatically according to who she is, how she feels about pregnancy and motherhood, whether the pregnancy was planned, whether she has a secure home situation, and many other factors. Her feelings may be ambivalent, and they will probably change over the course of the pregnancy.

A woman's first pregnancy is especially important because it has traditionally symbolized her transition to maturity. Even as social norms change and it becomes more common and "acceptable" for women to defer childbearing until they've established a career or to choose not to have children, the significance of a first pregnancy should not be underestimated. It is a major developmental milestone in the lives of mothers—and of fathers as well.

A couple's relationship is likely to undergo changes during pregnancy. It can be a stressful time, especially if the pregnancy was unanticipated. Women with supportive partners have fewer health problems in pregnancy and more positive feelings about their changing bodies ("Especially for Fathers," n.d.). Communication is especially important during this period, because each partner may

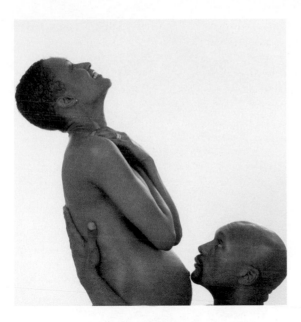

The physical and psychological changes that accompany pregnancy can have a ripple effect on a woman's relationship with her partner and family.

have preconceived ideas about what the other is feeling. Both partners may have fears about the baby's well-being, the approaching birth, their ability to parent, and the ways in which the baby will interfere with their own relationship. All of these concerns are normal. Sharing them, perhaps in the setting of a prenatal group, can strengthen the relationship. If the pregnant woman's partner is not supportive or if she does not have a partner, it is important that she find other sources of support—family, friends, women's groups—and that she not be reluctant to ask for help.

A pregnant woman's relationship with her own mother may also undergo changes. In a certain sense, becoming a mother makes a woman the equal of her own mother. She can now lay claim to co-equal status as an adult. Women who have depended on their mother tend to become more independent and assertive as their pregnancy progresses. Women who have been distant from, hostile to, or alienated from their mother may begin to identify with their mother's experience of pregnancy. Even women who have delayed childbearing until their thirties may be surprised to find their relationships with their mother changing and becoming more "adult." Working through these changing relationships is a kind of "psychological gestation" that accompanies the physiological gestation of the fetus.

The first trimester (3 months) of pregnancy may be difficult physically for the expectant mother. Approximately two thirds of women experience nausea, vomiting, fatigue, and painful swelling of the breasts. The nausea and vomiting that often occur during the first trimester of pregnancy usually subside with time. The pregnant woman may have fears that she will miscarry or that the child will not be normal. Her sexuality may undergo changes, resulting in unfamiliar needs (for more, less, or differently expressed sexual behaviors), which may, in turn, cause anxiety. (Sexuality during pregnancy is discussed further in the "Think About It" box on page 371.) Education about the birth process and her own body's functioning and support from partner, friends, relatives, and health-care professionals are the best antidotes to fear.

During the second trimester, most of the nausea and fatigue disappear, and the pregnant woman can feel the fetus move within her. Worries about miscarriage

> Only through sexual union are new beings capable of existing. This union, therefore, represents a place between two worlds, a point of contact between being and nonbeing, where life manifests itself and incarnates the divine spirit.
>
> —Alan Daniélou

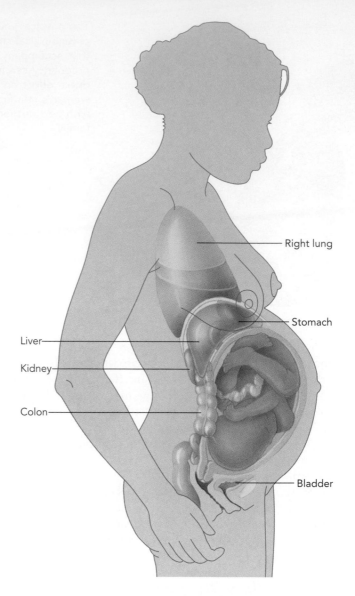

• FIGURE 12.4

Mother and Fetus in Third Trimester of Pregnancy. The expanding uterus affects the mother's internal organs, causing feelings of pressure and possible discomfort.

Right lung

Stomach

Liver

Kidney

Colon

Bladder

will probably begin to diminish, too, for the riskiest part of fetal development has passed. The pregnant woman may look and feel radiant. She will very likely be proud of her accomplishment and be delighted as her pregnancy begins to show. She may feel in harmony with life's natural rhythms. Some women, however, may be concerned about their increasing size, fearing that they are becoming unattractive. A partner's attention and reassurance will ease these fears.

The third trimester may be the time of the greatest difficulties in daily living. The uterus, originally about the size of the woman's fist, enlarges to fill the pelvic cavity and push up into the abdominal cavity, exerting increasing pressure on the other internal organs (see Figure 12.4). Water retention (edema) is a fairly common problem during late pregnancy. Edema may cause swelling in the face, hands, ankles, and feet, but it can often be controlled by cutting down on the intake of salt and carbohydrates. If dietary changes do not help this condition, the woman should consult her physician. Her physical abilities also are limited by her size, and she may need to cut back or stop her work.

Sexuality During Pregnancy

It is not unusual for a woman's sexual feelings and actions to change during pregnancy, although there is great variation among women in these expressions of sexuality. Some women feel beautiful, energetic, and sensual and are very much interested in sex; others feel awkward and decidedly unsexy. It is also quite possible for a woman's sexual feelings to fluctuate during this time. Men may also feel confusion or conflicts about sexual activity.

Although there are no "rules" governing sexual behavior during pregnancy, a few basic precautions should be observed:

- If the woman has had a prior miscarriage, she should check with her health-care practitioner before having intercourse, masturbating, or engaging in other activities that might lead to orgasm. Powerful uterine contractions could induce a spontaneous abortion in some women, especially during the first trimester.

- If the woman has vaginal bleeding, she should refrain from all sexual activity and consult her physician or midwife at once.

- If the insertion of the penis or other object into the vagina causes pain that is not easily remedied by a change of position, the couple should refrain from penetration.

- Pressure on the woman's abdomen should be avoided, especially during the final months of pregnancy.

- Late in pregnancy, an orgasm is likely to induce uterine contractions. Generally, this is not considered harmful, but the pregnant woman may want to discuss it with her practitioner. (Occasionally, labor begins when the waters break as the result of orgasmic contractions.)

A couple may be uncertain as to how to express their sexual feelings, especially if it is their first pregnancy. The following guidelines may be helpful:

- Even during a normal pregnancy, sexual intercourse may be uncomfortable. The couple may want to try such positions as side by side or rear entry to avoid pressure on the woman's abdomen and to facilitate more shallow penetration. (See the illustrations of different sexual positions in Chapter 9.)

- Even if intercourse is not comfortable for the woman, orgasm may still be intensely pleasurable. She may wish to consider masturbating (alone or with her partner) or engaging in cunnilingus. It is important to note that air should *not* be blown into the vagina during cunnilingus.

Once the baby has been born, a couple can resume intercourse after the bleeding has stopped and the vaginal walls have healed. This may take anywhere from 4 to 8 weeks.

Think Critically

- What are your views about having sex during pregnancy?
- What new information did you learn as a result of reading this box?

The woman and her partner may become increasingly concerned about the upcoming birth. Some women experience periods of depression in the weeks preceding delivery; they may feel physically awkward and sexually unattractive. Many feel a sense of exhilaration and anticipation marked by bursts of industriousness. They feel that the fetus already is a member of the family. Both parents may begin talking to the fetus and "playing" with it by patting and rubbing the mother's belly. (The principal developmental tasks for the expectant mother and father are summarized in Table 12.1.)

Complications of Pregnancy and Dangers to the Fetus

Usually, pregnancy proceeds without major complications. Good nutrition, a moderate amount of exercise, and manageable levels of stress are among the most significant factors in a complication-free pregnancy. In addition, early and ongoing prenatal care is important.

Table 12.1 • Principal Tasks of Expectant Parents	
Mothers	**Fathers**
Development of an emotional attachment to the fetus	Acceptance of the pregnancy and attachment to the fetus
Differentiation of the self from the fetus	Acceptance and resolution of the relationship with his own father
Acceptance and resolution of the relationship with her own mother	Resolution of dependency issues (involving parents or wife/partner)
Resolution of dependency issues (involving parents or husband/partner)	Evaluation of practical and financial responsibilities
Evaluation of practical and financial responsibilities	

Effects of Teratogens   Substances other than nutrients may reach the developing embryo or fetus through the placenta. Although few extensive studies have been done on the subject, toxic substances in the environment can also affect the health of the fetus. Whatever a woman breathes, eats, or drinks is eventually received by the conceptus in some proportion. A fetus's blood-alcohol level, for example, is equal to that of the mother. **Teratogens** are substances that cause defects (e.g., brain damage or physical deformities) in developing embryos or fetuses.

Chemicals and environmental pollutants are also potentially threatening. Continuous exposure to lead, most commonly in paint products or water from lead pipes, has been implicated in a variety of learning disorders. Mercury, from fish contaminated by industrial wastes, is a known cause of physical deformities. Solvents, pesticides, and certain chemical fertilizers should be avoided or used with extreme caution both at home and in the workplace. X-rays should also be avoided if possible during pregnancy.

Infectious Diseases   Infectious diseases can also damage the fetus. If a woman contracts German measles (rubella) during the first 3 months of pregnancy, her child may be born with physical or mental disabilities. Immunization against rubella is available, but it must be done before the woman is pregnant; otherwise, the injection will be as harmful to the fetus as the disease itself. Group B streptococcus, a bacterium carried by 15–40% of pregnant women, is harmless to adults but can be fatal to newborns. The American Academy of Pediatrics recommends that all pregnant women be screened for strep B. Antibiotics administered to the newborn during labor can greatly reduce the danger.

Sexually Transmitted Infections   STIs can be transmitted from a pregnant woman to the fetus, newborn, or infant before, during, or after birth. The Centers for Disease Control and Prevention (CDC) recommends that all pregnant women be screened for chlamydia, gonorrhea, hepatitis B, HIV, and syphilis. If she has contracted any of these or other STIs, she should discuss with her doctor potential effects on the baby, delivery procedures, treatment, and breastfeeding.

Women who are pregnant can acquire an STI from their own risky behavior or from an infected partner. Because avoidance of STIs is critical throughout a woman's pregnancy, she may want to consider consistent and correct use of latex condoms for each episode of sexual intercourse.

Pregnancy and Drugs: A Bad Mix

Among the lessons most of us learn from our parents is to be good to our children. This lesson is crucial during pregnancy, when the unborn child is most vulnerable to substances ingested by the mother.

Because the placenta does not block all substances from entering the fetus's bloodstream, it is prudent to assume that there is no safe drug during pregnancy. Sometimes, the effect of a drug depends on when in the pregnancy it is used. All drugs—including alcohol, tobacco, street drugs, and many over-the-counter medications, including aspirin, ibuprofen, and antihistamines—can cause physical damage, malformation, and miscarriage.

The following is a partial list of categories of drugs and their effects on the fetus. Not well understood or studied are the effects of the father's drug use on the health of the fetus. Regardless, it is prudent for both partners to assume healthy lifestyles before considering pregnancy.

Alcohol

When it comes to alcohol and pregnancy, how much is too much? The short answer is that we really don't know. Moderate drinking—that is, as little as one drink a day—has been shown to retard the growth of the infant (Mills & England, 2001), and a single drinking binge can permanently damage the brain of the fetus. Studies have linked chronic ingestion of alcohol during pregnancy to **fetal alcohol syndrome (FAS),** which can include unusual facial characteristics, small head and body size, congenital heart defects, defective joints, and intellectual and behavioral impairment. About half of all FAS children are developmentally disabled. Lower levels of alcohol consumption (7–14 drinks per week) may result in **fetal alcohol effect (FAE).** Children affected by FAE often experience moderate intellectual and behavioral deficits that resemble those of FAS children but at a less severe level.

Opiates and Cocaine

Mothers who regularly use opiates (heroin, morphine, codeine, and opium) are likely to have infants who are addicted to opiates at birth. In addition, there can be neonatal intoxication, spontaneous abortion, respiratory depression, low birth weight, and lower IQ scores (Bada et al., 2005; Bauer et al., 2005).

Tobacco

Both maternal and paternal cigarette smoking is associated with spontaneous abortion, persistent breathing problems, and a variety of complications during pregnancy and birth

(Venners et al., 2004). Babies born to women who smoke during pregnancy may be low birth weight, have increased risk of asthma, and are more likely to smoke as adults (Gilliland et al., 2000; Jaakkola & Gissler, 2004).

Prescription and Over-the-Counter Drugs

Prescription drugs should be used only under careful medical supervision because some may cause serious harm to the fetus. Additionally, over-the-counter drugs, including vitamins and aspirin, as well as large quantities of caffeine-containing food and beverages should be avoided or used only under medical supervision. The Food and Drug Administration has initiated a pregnancy safety coding system for both prescription and over-the-counter medications. By using the codes A (safest), B, C, D, and X (harmful), the danger of a substance to a fetus can be identified in hopes that pregnant women will be cautious before taking any medication.

A Legal Approach

Women may be exposed at work to agents that could disable them and harm the fetus. Your employer can tell you about health-care benefits, disability benefits, and maternity leave. The federal Pregnancy Discrimination Act requires employers that have at least 15 employees to treat workers disabled by pregnancy or childbirth the same as workers disabled by illness or accident. The Occupational Safety and Health Administration requires employers to provide a workplace free from known hazards that cause, or are likely to cause, serious physical harm or death.

Though no state specifically criminalizes drug use during pregnancy, prosecutors have attempted to rely on a host of criminal laws already on the books to prosecute women for prenatal substance abuse.

Think Critically

- How do you feel about testing, reporting, and prosecuting pregnant women who use drugs?
- How might you assess whether a drug is safe during pregnancy?
- If you were in a situation with a pregnant woman who wished to consume a drug, what (if anything) might you do or say?
- Do you feel that pregnant women who use drugs should be charged with child endangerment? Why or why not?

Pregnancy After Age 35 Delaying pregnancy until after age 35 has become a more common reality for many women. While men can father children late into their life, the quality and quantity of a woman's eggs begin to decline in her late 20s and fall off rapidly after age 35 so that by age 40, her odds of conceiving decrease and her risk of pregnancy-related complications and having a live baby with a chromosomal abnormality significantly increases (American College of Obstetricians and Gynecologists, 2006a). While the chromosomal abnormality Down syndrome affects 2.6 in 1,000 births at maternal age 30, the rate gradually increases to 47.6 in 1,000 births at maternal age 45. Paternal age also increases the likelihood of Down syndrome, but only if the mother is over 35 (Fisch et al., 2003). Women who give birth at age 40 or older are also at a slightly higher risk for maternal death, premature delivery, Cesarean sections, and low-birth-weight babies (London, 2004). As women age, chronic illnesses such as high blood pressure and diabetes may also present pregnancy- and birth-related complications. Genetic counseling may help a woman and her partner assess their risks, make an informed choice about pregnancy, and decide whether or not to have testing for chromosomal abnormalities.

Ectopic Pregnancy In **ectopic pregnancy** (tubal pregnancy), which occurs in about 1% of all pregnancies, the fertilized egg grows outside the uterus, usually in the fallopian tube. Any sexually active woman of childbearing age is at risk for ectopic pregnancy. Women who have abnormal fallopian tubes are at higher risk for ectopic pregnancy. Generally, this occurs because the tube is obstructed, most often as a result of pelvic inflammatory disease due to chlamydia and gonorrhea infections. Factors such as a previous ectopic pregnancy and **endometriosis** (growth of tissue outside the uterus) can also increase the risk. The pregnancy will never come to term. The embryo may spontaneously abort, or the embryo and placenta will continue to expand until they rupture the fallopian tube. If the pregnancy is early and has not ruptured, drugs may be used instead of surgery to remove the conceptus. A ruptured ectopic pregnancy, however, is a true medical emergency that can endanger the mother's life.

Pregnancy-Induced Hypertension Previously referred to as toxemia or eclampsia, **pregnancy-induced hypertension** is characterized by high blood pressure and edema along with protein in the urine. It occurs in less than 10% of pregnancies and can usually be treated by diet, bed rest, and medication. If untreated, it can progress to maternal convulsions that pose a threat to mother and child. It is important for a pregnant woman to have her blood pressure checked regularly.

Premature Births Births that take place prior to 37 weeks of gestation are considered to be **premature births.** About 10% of all pregnancies in the United States result in premature births. A consequence of this is **low-birth-weight infants** (those who weigh less than 2,500 grams, or 5.5 pounds, at birth). About three fourths of infant deaths in the United States are associated with prematurity. The fundamental problem of prematurity is that many of the infant's vital organs are insufficiently developed. Most premature infants will grow normally, but many will experience disabilities and health problems, including cranial abnormalities, various respiratory problems, and infections. Feeding, too, is a problem because the infants may be too small to suck a breast or bottle, and their swallowing mechanisms may be too underdeveloped to permit them to drink. As premature infants get older, problems such as low

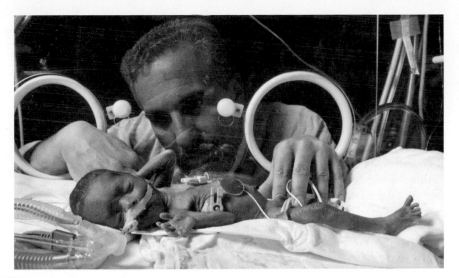

Low birth weight affects about 7% of newborns in the United States. Adequate prenatal care significantly reduces the risk of low birth weight.

intelligence, learning difficulties, poor hearing and vision, and physical awkwardness may become apparent. Nevertheless, the majority of preterm babies eventually catch up with their peers and thrive.

Premature delivery is one of the greatest problems confronting obstetrics today; most of the cases are related to teenage pregnancy, smoking, poor nutrition, and poor health in the mother. Prenatal care is extremely important as a means of preventing prematurity. We need to understand that if children's needs are not met today we will all face the consequences of their deprivation tomorrow. The social and economic costs are bound to be very high. (Table 12.2 lists various demographic "facts of life" for the United States and the rest of the world.)

Table 12.2 • The Demographic Facts of Life		
	United States	**World**
Population, mid-2008	308.8 million	6.9 billion
Population per square mile	84	115
Births per 1,000 population	12	21
Deaths per 1,000 population	10	8
Population change, 2008–2050	5	39
Projected population, 2025	1269 million	8 billion
Total fertility rate per 100,000	1.6	2.6
Percentage of population under age 15	17	28
Percentage of population over age 65	16	7
Life expectancy in years	75 (male), 81 (female)	67 (male), 70 (female)
Maternal deaths per 100,000	9	400
Infant deaths per 1,000 live births	6	49
Percentage of married women using contraception	69	62
Births per 1,000 population	12	21

SOURCE: *The Demographic Facts of Life*. Population Connection. Reprinted by permission.

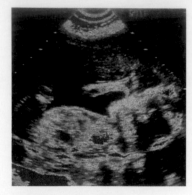

The pictures produced by ultrasound are called sonograms. They are used to determine fetal age, position of the fetus and placenta, and possible developmental problems.

Delayed Labor About 10% of women have **delayed labor,** or pregnancies that go longer than 2 weeks after the expected delivery date. The primary risks associated with this are the fetus growing too large to pass through the birth canal and the placenta ceasing to nourish the child. Because postterm babies are about three times more likely to die neonatally than babies born at term, labor is often induced with drugs such as prostaglandins and oxytocin.

Diagnosing Abnormalities of the Fetus

Both the desire to bear children and the wish to ensure that those children are healthy have encouraged the use of diagnostic technologies. The American College of Obstetricians and Gynecologists (ACOG) now recommends that all pregnant women, regardless of their age, be offered screening for Down syndrome (ACOG, 2007). Previously, women were automatically offered genetic counseling and diagnostic testing for Down syndrome if they were 35 years and older. Because of the number of screening tests available, guidelines are now available that discuss the advantages and disadvantages of each test and some of the factors that determine which screening test should be offered and when. Along with specific training, standardization, and use of appropriate equipment and quality assessment, ACOG (2007) recommends the following:

- Late first-trimester screening can use an **ultrasound,** consisting of high-frequency sound waves that create a computer-generated picture, to measure the thickness at the back of the neck of the fetus.

- Women found to be at increased risk of having a baby with Down syndrome should be offered genetic counseling and the option of **chorionic villus sampling (CVS),** the removal of a small sample of cells taken from the placenta sometime between 10 and 12 weeks of gestation; **amniocentesis,** whereby a small amount of amniotic fluid is withdrawn from the uterus at 15–20 weeks of gestation and tested for chromosomal defects (see Figure 12.5). The pregnancy loss rates for both amniocentesis and CVS do not differ between the two procedures (Caughey, Hopkins, & Norton, 2006).

● **FIGURE 12.5**

Diagnosing fetal abnormalities via (a) Amniocentesis and (b) Chorionic Villus Sampling

Amniocentesis

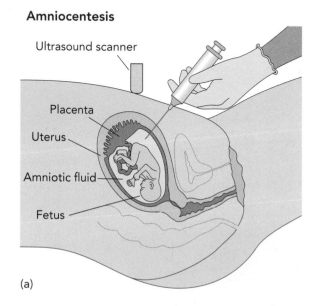

(a)

Chorionic villus sampling

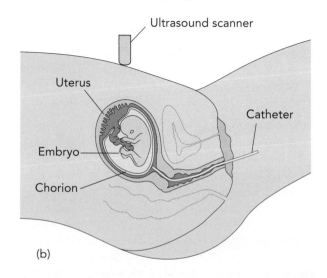

(b)

- **Neural tube defect screening,** performed on the mother's blood to measure the level of alpha-fetoprotein, reveals possible defects of the spine, spinal cord, skull, and brain. This test should be offered during the second trimester to women who elect only first-trimester screening (CVS) for Down syndrome.

- Other tests can be performed to provide further information.

Regardless of the kind of prenatal diagnostic procedure done, there may be complications or risks for pregnancy loss associated with the tests, so the cost-benefit ratio of the procedure should be discussed with one's doctor.

Pregnancy Loss

A normal pregnancy lasts about 40 weeks. The death of a fetus before 20 weeks is called early pregnancy loss. Often, the death is a miscarriage (spontaneous loss of a fetus before it can survive on its own), stillbirth, or death during early infancy—a devastating experience that has been largely ignored in our society. The death of a baby at any stage in the pregnancy is as emotional as it is physical. The statement "You can always have another one" may be meant as consolation, but it can be particularly chilling to a grieving mother or father. In the past few years, however, the medical community has begun to respond better to the emotional needs of parents who have lost a fetus or an infant.

Miscarriage   Spontaneous abortion, or miscarriage, is a powerful natural selective force in bringing healthy babies into the world. Between 30% and 50% of all pregnancies end before women are aware that they have conceived, and at least 1 in 7 known pregnancies ends in miscarriage. Most of these—up to 80%—happen because of chromosomal abnormalities (Springen, 2005). The first sign that a pregnant woman may miscarry is vaginal bleeding (spotting). If a woman's symptoms of pregnancy disappear and she develops pelvic cramps, she may be miscarrying; the fetus is usually expelled by uterine contractions. Most miscarriages occur between the 6th and 8th weeks of pregnancy and are caused by an abnormal number of chromosomes and usually occur before the end of the first trimester. Sometimes the embryos are healthy, but women miscarry for other reasons: for example, a misshapen or scarred uterus, insulin or hormonal imbalances, or chronic infections in the uterus. Women can take steps to lessen the likelihood of pregnancy loss, beginning with taking a multivitamin with folic acid, not smoking or using drugs, exercising, and maintaining a healthy weight.

Infant Mortality   The U.S. infant mortality rate, although at its lowest point ever, remains far higher than that of most of the developed world: an estimated 6.3 deaths for every 1,000 live births (Central Intelligence Agency, 2008). The United States ranks 29th worldwide in infant mortality, tying Slovakia and Poland but lagging behind Cuba (DeNoon, 2008).

Although many infants die of poverty-related conditions, including lack of prenatal care, others die from congenital problems (conditions appearing at birth) or from infectious diseases, accidents, or other causes. Sometimes, the causes of death are not apparent; more than 3,000 infant deaths per year are attributed to **sudden infant death syndrome (SIDS),** a perplexing phenomenon wherein an apparently healthy infant dies suddenly while sleeping. Sleeping position may be one variable contributing to SIDS in vulnerable infants. The American Academy of Pediatrics recommends that infants be placed on their backs for sleeping. Maternal smoking during pregnancy and exposure of the baby to secondhand smoke are also implicated in SIDS. No one knows what all the factors are that contribute to this unpredictable event.

Coping With Loss   The feelings of shock and grief felt by individuals whose child dies before or during birth can be difficult to understand for those who have not had a similar experience. What they may not realize is that most women form a deep attachment to their children even before birth. At first, the attachment may be to a fantasy image of the unborn child. During the course of the pregnancy, the mother forms an acquaintance with her infant through the physical sensations she feels within her. Thus, the death of the fetus can also represent the loss of a dream and of a hope for the future. This loss must be acknowledged and felt before psychological healing can take place.

The healing process takes time—months, a year, perhaps more for some women. Support groups and counseling often are helpful, especially if healing does not seem to be progressing—if, for example, depression and physical symptoms don't appear to be diminishing.

● Infertility

Some couples experience the pain of loss when they plan to have a child and then discover that they cannot get pregnant. **Infertility** is defined as the inability to conceive a child after a year of unprotected intercourse or the inability to carry a fetus to term. Infertility affects over 6.1 million women aged 15–44 and 1 in 6 couples each year (Planned Parenthood, 2008). Fertility problems are equally likely to be caused by a disorder on the man's side, the woman's side, or both; but in 20% of cases, the cause is unexplained. The most common risk factors for infertility are advancing age, smoking, high body weight, STIs, and consumption of alcohol and caffeine (MayoClinic.com, 2008a). The good news is that the American Society for Reproductive Medicine (2008) reports that 85–90% of infertile couples can now be successfully treated using conventional fertility treatments, such as medications to trigger ovulation or surgical procedures to correct problems with the reproductive tract. For the remaining couples, assisted reproductive technologies offer the greatest possibility of pregnancy. In 2005, almost 39,000 live births occurred as a result of these technologies (Centers for Disease Control and Prevention, 2008b).

Female Infertility

Most cases of infertility among women are due to physical factors. Hormones, stress, immunological factors, and environmental factors may also be involved.

Physical Causes   About 20% of infertility cases occur as a result of abnormalities in the woman's reproductive tract. One of the leading causes of female infertility is blocked, scarred, or obstructed fallopian tubes, generally the result of **pelvic inflammatory disease (PID),** an infection of the fallopian tubes or uterus that is usually the result of an STI such as chlamydia (see Chapter 15). About 1 million cases of PID are treated each year; doctors

> Dear Auntie will come with presents and will ask, "Where is our baby, sister?" And, Mother, you will tell her softly, "He is in the pupils of my eyes. He is in my bones and in my soul."
>
> —Rabindranath Tagore
> (1864–1941)

estimate that about half of the cases go untreated because PID is often symptomless, especially in the early stages. Other causes include endometriosis, fibroids, a tilted uterus, diabetes, and hypertension. Smoking may also influence a woman's ability to conceive. The greatest increase in infertility is found among women aged 35–44.

A below-normal or high amount of body fat may inhibit ovulation and delay pregnancy. Once normal body fat is restored, fertility is likely to occur. In addition, benign growths such as fibroids and polyps on the uterus, ovaries, or fallopian tubes may affect a woman's fertility. Surgery can restore fertility in many of these cases.

Hormonal and Psychological Causes   Another 20% of infertility cases are caused by problems related to ovulation. The pituitary gland may fail to produce sufficient hormones (follicle-stimulating hormone, or FSH, and luteinizing hormone, or LH) to stimulate ovulation, or it may release them at the wrong time. Stress, which may be increased by the anxiety associated with trying to become pregnant, may also contribute to lowered fertility. Occasionally, immunological causes may be present, the most important of which is the production of sperm antibodies by the woman. For some unknown reason, a woman may be allergic to her partner's sperm, and her immune system will produce antibodies to destroy them.

Environmental Factors   Toxic chemicals, such as those found in paint, solvents, and insecticides, or exposure to radiation therapy can threaten a woman's reproductive capacity. Excessive drug and alcohol use can also affect fertility. Evidence indicates that the daughters of mothers who took DES, a drug once thought to increase fertility and reduce the risk of miscarriage, have a significantly higher infertility rate. As mentioned earlier, mercury contained in certain fish can be toxic.

Male Infertility

The primary causes of male infertility are low sperm count, decrease of sperm motility, and poor sperm morphology (misshapen sperm). Sperm ducts may become blocked, or for some reason, the male may not ejaculate. Sperm-related problems account for about 25% of all infertility problems. Insufficient or defective sperm affect a man's ability to impregnate his partner. Though sperm morphology is the best indicator of fertility, since sperm counts are easy to perform, this parameter is more often studied.

Men are more at risk than women from environmental factors because they are constantly producing new sperm cells; for the same reason, men may also recover faster once the affecting factor has been removed. Increasing evidence suggests that toxic substances, such as lead or chemicals found in some solvents and herbicides, are responsible for decreased sperm counts. Alcohol, tobacco, and marijuana use may produce reduced sperm counts or abnormal sperm. Some prescription drugs have also been shown to affect the number of sperm a man produces.

Sons of mothers who took DES may have increased sperm abnormalities and fertility problems. Also, too much heat may temporarily reduce a man's sperm count (the male of a couple trying to conceive may want to stay out of the hot tub for a while). A fairly common problem is the presence of a varicose vein called a **varicocele** above the testicle. Because it impairs circulation to the testicle, the varicocele causes an elevated scrotal temperature and thus interferes with sperm development. The varicocele may be surgically removed, but unless the man has a fairly good sperm count to begin with, his fertility may not improve.

Emotional Responses to Infertility

By the time partners seek medical advice about their fertility problems, they may have already experienced a crisis in confronting the possibility of not being able to become biological parents. Many such couples feel they have lost control over a major area of their lives. Coming to a joint decision with one's partner about goals, acceptable therapies, and an endpoint for therapy is important and advisable.

Infertility Treatment

Rarely is moral queasiness a match for the onslaught of science.

—Sharon Begley

Almost without exception, fertility problems are physical, not emotional, despite myths to the contrary. The two most popular myths are that anxiety over becoming pregnant leads to infertility and that if an infertile couple adopt a child the couple will then be able to conceive on their own. Neither has any basis in medical fact, although some presumably infertile couples have conceived following an adoption. (This does not mean, however, that one should adopt a child to remedy infertility.) In some cases, fertility is restored for no discernible reason; in others, the infertility remains a mystery.

Enhancing Fertility There are many ways that fertility can be enhanced, the most important of which involves the timing of coitus with respect to the woman's menstrual cycle. Because an ovum is viable for about 24 hours after ovulation, a pregnancy is most likely to occur when intercourse takes place at the same time as ovulation. If a man wears tight underwear, he might switch to boxer-type shorts to allow his testicles to descend from his body. Having the woman lie on her back for an hour after coitus can aid sperm in traveling up the vagina, and more frequent intercourse near the time of ovulation can increase the chances of conception. Following intercourse, a pillow can be placed under the woman's buttocks to help sperm swim into the uterus. Since women retain more sperm if coital orgasm occurs after rather than before male ejaculation, fertilization can be enhanced if women can regulate coital orgasm timing (Singh, Meyer, Zambarano, & Hurlbert, 1998). However, for many couples, these techniques are not enough; they may seek medical intervention to diagnose and treat infertility.

Medical Intervention Medical technology now offers more treatment options to men and to women trying to conceive a child. The techniques and technologies developed to promote conception include the following:

- *Fertility medications.* A variety of medications can be used to treat infertility, so it is important to understand each one and its purpose.
- *Surgery.* This is a treatment option for both male and female infertility. Used to correct a structural problem, surgery can often return normal fertility.

- *Artificial insemination.* Used if sperm numbers are too low, **artificial insemination (AI)** involves injecting the woman with sperm from her partner or a donor. This procedure may be performed in conjunction with ovulation-stimulating medications.

- *Assisted reproductive technology (ART).* All fertility treatments in which both eggs and sperm are handled are known as **assisted reproductive technology (ART).** In general, ART procedures involve surgically removing eggs from a woman's ovaries, combining them with sperm in the laboratory, and returning them to the woman's body or donating them to another woman. The types of ART include the following (American Society for Reproductive Medicine, 2008).

  - **IVF (in vitro fertilization).** This involves extracting a woman's eggs, fertilizing the eggs in the laboratory, and then transferring the resulting embryos into the woman's uterus through the cervix. Sometimes, a technique known as intracytoplasmic sperm injection (ICSI) may occur by injecting a single sperm directly into the woman's egg. Excess embryos may be frozen for future use.

  - **GIFT (gamete intrafallopian transfer).** This involves the use of a fiber-optic instrument to guide the transfer of unfertilized eggs and sperm (gametes) into the woman's fallopian tubes through small incisions in her abdomen.

  - **ZIFT (zygote intrafallopian transfer).** A woman's eggs are fertilized in the laboratory and then transferred to her fallopian tubes.

  ART is often categorized according to whether the procedure uses a woman's own eggs (nondonor) or eggs from another woman (donor) and according to whether the embryos used were newly fertilized (fresh) or previously fertilized, frozen, and then thawed (frozen).

- *Surrogate motherhood.* In this case, one woman, a surrogate mother, bears a child for another.

Click on "The Surrogate Motherhood Debate" to hear women discuss their experiences as surrogate mothers.

The most important factor for success of these procedures is the age of the woman. When a woman is using her own egg, success rates decline as she ages and drop off even more dramatically after about age 37. Other factors to consider are whether the woman is using her own eggs and the number of embryos transferred. These procedures are also quite costly. For example, a single cycle of in vitro fertilization typically costs around $12,500, and the procedure usually needs to be repeated a number of times before a viable pregnancy results (see Figure 12.6). Nearly 12% of women in the United States have undergone infertility procedures. Of those children who are conceived through these procedures, the risk for having certain types of birth defects, including heart problems, cleft lip, cleft palate, and abnormalities in the esophagus or rectum, is two to four times greater than among children conceived naturally (Reefhuis, Honein, Schieve, et al., 2008). Nevertheless, it appears that patients are accepting of this risk because the alternative is even more daunting: not having a child.

Cloning is the reproduction of an individual from a single cell taken from a donor or parent. Specifically, this technique involves replacing the nucleus from a donor to produce an embryo that is genetically identical to it. The success of reproductive cloning depends on the species. For example, plant cloning

A loud noise at one end and no sense of responsibility at the other.

—Father Ronald Knox (1888–1957)

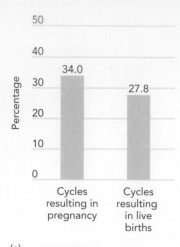

(a)

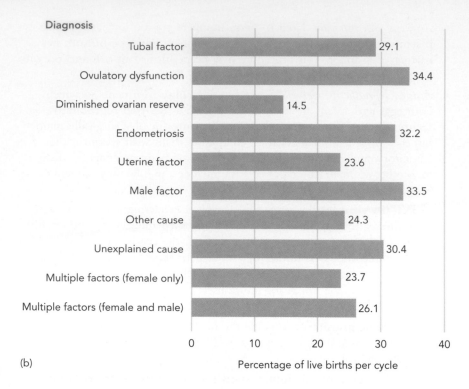

Diagnosis

Tubal factor	29.1
Ovulatory dysfunction	34.4
Diminished ovarian reserve	14.5
Endometriosis	32.2
Uterine factor	23.6
Male factor	33.5
Other cause	24.3
Unexplained cause	30.4
Multiple factors (female only)	23.7
Multiple factors (female and male)	26.1

(b)

Percentage of live births per cycle

● **FIGURE 12.6**

Results of Assisted Reproductive Technology (ART) Cycles. (a) This graph represents the success rates for ART cycles using fresh nondonor eggs or embryos in 2005. (b) This graph represents the live-birth percentages among women who had ART cycles using fresh nondonor eggs or embryos, by infertility diagnosis, in 2005. (*Source:* CDC, Division of Reproductive Health, National Center for Chronic Disease and Prevention, 2007b.)

For a discussion of how technology will enable us to design children in new and different ways, click on "Designer Babies."

occurs every day, as when an apple grows from a cloned fruit tree. Cloning in small animal species has been somewhat successful, though the spontaneous abortion rate is high, as are the rates of fetal mortality and genetic anomalies. What has caught the attention of the public is the potential for human reproductive cloning and the questions that accompany this procedure: When does human life begin, and what is the moral and legal status of the human embryo? Human embryonic stem cells, which are extracted from embryos when they are still tiny clusters of no more than 300 cells, are generating great excitement in science because they can, in theory, grow into any of the body's cell types. Scientists hope someday to use them for replacement tissue and organs for patients with a variety of diseases, including diabetes and Parkinson's. Cloning has huge potential as a source of organs for implantation or as an alternative in cases of infertility.

Sex selection, also marketed under the title "family balancing," is a technology that allows couples to choose whether to have a boy or a girl. It can be accomplished via both pre- and post-implantation of an embryo. By creating embryos outside the womb, then testing them for gender, pre-implantation genetic diagnosis can guarantee the sex of a baby. Price tag: $20,000. Controversy arises, however, over potential sex imbalances in our population and cases in which the sex selection results do not match the parents' expectations.

Each of these techniques raises questions. For example, some lesbian women, especially those in committed relationships, are choosing to create families through artificial insemination. To date, there are no reliable data on the number of such births, but experts in the field estimate that at least 5% of lesbian women have used infertility clinics (Hall, 2007). In part, the increasing acceptance of nontraditional families is providing this boom in biological parenthood. Many questions are raised when a lesbian couple contemplate having a

When assisted reproductive technology is used to treat infertility, there is about a 1 in 2 chance of a multiple birth.

baby in this way: Who will be the birth mother? What will the role status of the other mother be? Will the donor be known or unknown? If known, will the child have a relationship with him? Will the child have a relationship with the donor's parents? Who gets custody if the couple breaks up? Will there be a legal contract between the parenting parties? There are few precedents to learn from or role models to follow in these cases. Another issue that such couples face is that the nonbiological parent may have no legal tie to the child (in some states, the nonbiological parent may adopt the child as a "second parent"). Furthermore, society may not recognize a nonbiological parent as a "real" parent, because children are expected to have only one real mother and one real father.

Increasingly, gay and lesbian couples are creating families that are diverse along dimensions of social class, gender, and race.

● Giving Birth

Throughout pregnancy, numerous physiological changes occur to prepare the woman's body for childbirth. Hormones secreted by the placenta regulate the growth of the fetus, stimulate maturation of the breasts for lactation, and ready the uterus and other parts of the body for labor. During the later months of pregnancy, the placenta produces the hormone **relaxin,** which increases flexibility in the ligaments and joints of the pelvic area. In the last trimester, most women occasionally feel uterine contractions that are strong but generally not painful. These **Braxton-Hicks contractions** exercise the uterus, preparing it for labor.

Labor and Delivery

During labor, contractions begin the **effacement** (thinning) and **dilation** (gradual opening) of the cervix. It is difficult to say exactly when labor starts, which helps explain the great differences reported in lengths of labor for different women. True labor begins when the uterine contractions are regularly spaced, thinning and dilation of the cervix occurs, and the fetus presents a part of itself into the vagina. During the contractions, the lengthwise muscles of the uterus involuntarily pull open the circular muscles around the cervix. This process generally takes 2–36 hours. Its duration depends on the size of the baby, the baby's position in the uterus, the size of the mother's pelvis, and the condition of the uterus. The length of labor tends to shorten after the first birth experience.

Labor can generally be divided into three stages. The first stage is usually the longest, lasting 4–16 hours or longer. An early sign of first-stage labor is the expulsion of a plug of slightly bloody mucus that has blocked the opening of the cervix during pregnancy. At the same time or later on, there is a second fluid discharge from the vagina. This discharge, often referred to as the "breaking of the waters," is the amniotic fluid, which comes from the ruptured amnion. (Because the baby is subject to infection after the protective membrane breaks, the woman should receive medical attention soon thereafter, if she has not already.)

The hormone oxytocin produced by the fetus, along with prostaglandins from the placenta, stimulate strong uterine contractions. At the end of the first stage of labor, which is called the **transition,** the contractions come more quickly and are much more intense than at the beginning of labor. Most women report that transition is the most difficult part of labor. During the last part of first-stage labor, the baby's head enters the birth canal. This marks the shift from dilation of the cervix to expulsion of the infant. The cervical opening is now almost fully dilated (about 10 centimeters [4 inches] in diameter), but the baby is not yet completely in position to be pushed out. Transition is usually briefs half to one hour.

Second-stage labor begins when the baby's head moves into the birth canal and ends when the baby is born. During this time, many women experience a great force in their bodies. Some women find this the most difficult part of labor; others find that the contractions and bearing down bring a sense of euphoria.

The baby is usually born gradually. With each of the final few contractions, a new part of the infant emerges (see Figure 12.7). The baby may even cry before he or she is completely born, especially if the mother did not have medication.

The baby will still be attached to the umbilical cord connected to the mother, which is not cut until it stops pulsating. He or she will appear wet and often be covered by a waxy substance called **vernix.** The head may look oddly shaped at first, from the molding of the soft plates of bone during birth. This shape is temporary; the baby's head usually achieves a normal appearance within 24 hours.

> *If men had to have babies, they would only ever have one each.*
>
> —Princess Diana
> (1961–1997)

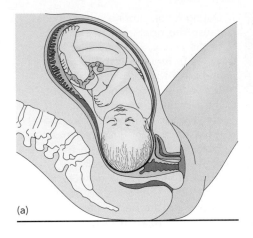

(a)

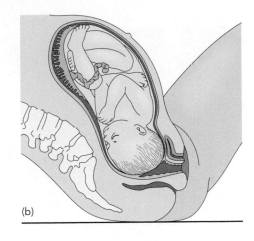

(b)

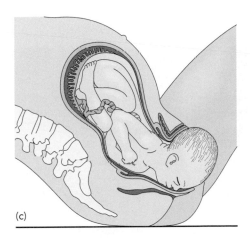

(c)

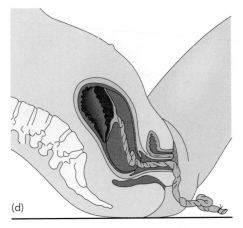

(d)

● **FIGURE 12.7**

The Birth Process: Labor and Delivery. (a) In the first stage, the cervix begins to efface (thin out) and dilate. (b) In the transition stage, the cervix dilates from 8 to 10 centimeters. (c) In the second stage, the infant is delivered. (d) In the third stage, the placenta (afterbirth) is delivered.

After the baby has been delivered, the uterus continues to contract, expelling the placenta, the remaining section of the umbilical cord, and the fetal membranes. Completing the third and final stage of labor, these tissues are collectively referred to as the **afterbirth.** The doctor or midwife examines the placenta to make sure it is whole. If the practitioner has any doubt that the entire placenta has been expelled, he or she may examine the uterus to make sure no parts of the placenta remain to cause adhesions or hemorrhaging. Immediately following birth, the attendants assess the physical condition of the **neonate,** or newborn. Heart rate, respiration, skin color, reflexes, and muscle tone are individually rated with a score of 0 to 2. The total, called an **Apgar score,** will be at least 8 if the baby is healthy. For a few days following labor (especially if it is a second or subsequent birth), the mother will probably feel strong contractions as the uterus begins to return to its prebirth size and shape. This process takes about 6 weeks. She will also have a bloody discharge called **lochia,** which continues for several weeks.

Following birth, if the mother did not receive pain medication, the baby will probably be alert and ready to nurse. Breastfeeding (discussed later) provides benefits for both mother and child. If the infant is a boy, the parents will need to decide about circumcision, the surgical removal of the foreskin of the penis.

❝ *Wash, don't amputate.*
—Alex Comfort, MD
(1920–2000)

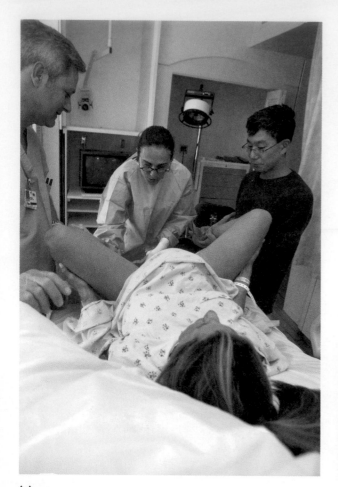

(a)

During labor, uterine contractions cause the opening and thinning of the cervix. The length of labor varies from woman to woman and birth to birth; it is usually between 4 and 16 hours. During the transition, the end of first-stage labor, contractions are the most intense. (a) Encouragement from her partner can help the mother relax. (b) The second stage of labor is the delivery of the infant. The mother is coached to push as the baby's head begins to crown. (c) The baby may be ready to nurse following delivery. Medical staff can give advice for getting started.

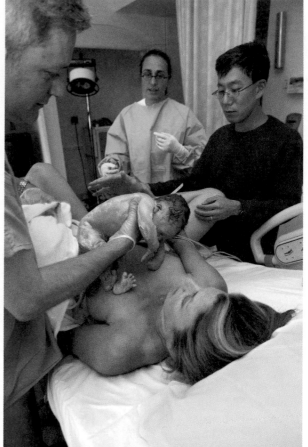

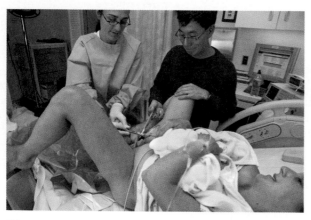

(b)

(c)

The Question of Male Circumcision

In 1975, when about 93% of newborn boys were circumcised, the American Academy of Pediatrics and the American College of Obstetricians and Gynecologists issued a statement declaring that there is "no absolute medical indication" for routine circumcision. This procedure, which involves slicing and removing the sleeve of skin (foreskin) that covers the glans penis, has been performed routinely on newborn boys in the United States since the 1930s. Parents should discuss with their pediatrician the use of an anesthetic cream or medication. Circumcision carries medical risks, including excessive bleeding, infection, and faulty surgery.

In 1999 and again in 2005, the American Academy of Pediatrics (AAP) changed from a neutral stance on circumcision to say that the data was insufficient to recommend routine neonatal male circumcision (AAP, 2007).

The Centers for Disease Control and Prevention (2008c) states that research shows that circumcision has been associated with lower risk of HIV infection. CDC notes that an individual man may want to consider circumcision as an additional HIV preventive measure, but realize that circumcision has risks and that it has only been proven effective in reducing HIV risk through insertive vaginal sex. Research on the effectiveness of circumcision on reducing STI prevalence has found conflicting results. (Further discussion on this topic is found in Chapter 15.)

Today, about 57% of male newborns delivered in hospitals are circumcised. With the exception of Israel, this places the United States far ahead of other developed countries. In Judaism, the ritual circumcising, the *brit milah* or *bris,* is an important religious event. Circumcision has religious significance for Muslims as well.

Aside from religious considerations, the other common reasons given by parents for circumcising their infants are "cleanliness" and "so he'll look like his dad." A circumcised penis is not necessarily any cleaner than an uncircumcised one. Infants do not require cleaning under their foreskins; adults do. If reasonable cleanliness is observed, an intact penis poses no more threat of disease to a man's sex partner than a circumcised one would. As for "looking like dad," there is no evidence to suggest that little boys are seriously traumatized if dad's penis doesn't look exactly like theirs.

Think Critically

- Given the information we have about circumcision, would you have your son circumcised? Why or why not?
- How important would the data be in deciding whether to have your son circumcised?

Choices in Childbirth

Women and couples planning the birth of a child have decisions to make in a variety of areas: place of birth, birth attendant(s), medications, preparedness classes, circumcision, breastfeeding—to name just a few. The "childbirth market" has responded to consumer concerns, so it's important for prospective consumers to fully understand their options.

Hospital Birth   Because of the traditional and seemingly impersonal care provided in some hospitals, in recent decades, many people have recognized the need for family-centered childbirth. Fathers and other relatives or close friends often participate today. Most hospitals permit rooming-in, in which the baby stays with the mother rather than in the nursery, or a modified form of rooming-in.

Some form of pain relief is administered during most hospital deliveries, as are various hormones to intensify the contractions and to shrink the uterus after delivery. There are two types of pain-relieving drugs—analgesics, which provide pain relief without loss of feeling or muscle movement; and anesthetics, which block all feelings, including pain. The most common form of analgesic administration is the **epidural,** which is administered through a tiny catheter placed in the woman's lower back. When administered properly, an epidural diminishes the

Making a Birth Plan

Prospective parents must make many important decisions. The more informed they are, the better able they will be to decide what is right for them. If you were planning a birth, how would you answer the following questions?

- Who will be the birth attendant—a physician or a nurse-midwife? Do you already have someone in mind? If not, what criteria are important to you in choosing a birth attendant? Have you considered hiring a labor assistant (sometimes called a *doula,* a professional childbirth companion employed to guide the mother during labor)?

- Who will be present at the birth—your spouse or partner? Other relatives or friends? Children? How will these people participate?

- Where will the birth take place—in a hospital, in a birthing center, or at home? If in a hospital, is there a choice of rooms?

- What kind of environment will you create in terms of lighting, room furnishings, and sounds? Is there special music you would like to hear?

- What kinds of medication, if any, would you feel comfortable being given to you? Do you know what the options are for pain-reducing drugs? What about hormones to speed up or slow down labor?

- What about fetal monitoring? Will there be machines attached to the mother or the baby?

- What is your attendant's policy regarding food and drink during labor?

- What about freedom of movement during labor? Will you (or your partner) want the option of walking around during labor? Will there be a shower or bath available? Will the baby be delivered with the mother lying on her back with her feet in stirrups, or will she be free to choose her position, such as squatting or lying on her side?

- What do you know about having an episiotomy? Under what conditions would it be acceptable?

- Under what conditions is a cesarean section acceptable? Who will decide?

- Who will "catch" the baby as she or he is born? Who will cut the umbilical cord, and at what point will it be cut?

- What will be done with the baby immediately after birth? What kinds of tests will be done on the baby, and when? What other kinds of procedures, such as shots and medicated eyedrops, will be given, and when?

- Will the baby stay in the nursery, or is rooming-in available? Is there a visiting schedule?

- How will the baby be fed—by breast or by bottle? Will feeding be on a schedule or "on demand"? Is there someone with breastfeeding experience available to answer questions if necessary? Will the baby have a pacifier between feedings?

- If the baby is boy, will he be circumcised? When? Will anesthesia be used during the procedure to decrease pain?

---

sensations of labor in the lower areas of the body. Drugs have been used successfully and safely during labor. However, the mother isn't the only recipient of the drug; it travels through the placenta to the baby, in whom it may reduce heart and respiration rates. The use of an epidural entails a slightly higher risk of vacuum or forceps delivery and cesarean section than does a drug-free birth.

Until recently, during delivery, the mother was given an **episiotomy,** an incision that enlarges the vaginal opening by cutting through the perineum toward the anus. Contradicting the long-accepted rationale for the operation—to make childbirth less damaging—a comprehensive analysis has concluded that having an episiotomy has no benefits and actually causes more complications than not having one (American College of Obstetricians and Gynecologists, 2006b). As a result, the researchers concluded that routine use of this procedure, undergone by more than 1 million U.S. women each year, should be discontinued and the incision should be considered only to speed delivery when the health of the baby is at risk.

The baby is usually delivered on a table. If such factors as medication or exhaustion slow labor, he or she may be pulled from the womb with a vacuum extractor (which has a small suction cup that fits onto the baby's head) or

Minor surgery is one that is performed on someone else.

—Eugene Robin, MD

Childbirth classes enable both partners to understand and share the birth process.

forceps. (In some cases of acute fetal distress, these instruments may be crucial in order to save the infant's life.)

Cesarean Section   **Cesarean section,** or **C-section,** involves the delivery of a baby through an incision in the mother's abdominal wall and uterus. In 1970, 5.5% of American births were done by C-section. Today, 1 in 3 births are cesareans, a record high for the surgical method that is a controversial subject among both obstetricians and mothers (March of Dimes, 2008).

There are many reasons to deliver a baby by C-section, such as abnormalities of the placenta and umbilical cord, and/or prolonged or ineffective labor. Although there is a lower mortality rate for infants born by C-sections, the mother's mortality rate is higher. As with all major surgeries, there are possible complications, and recovery can be slow and difficult.

The fact that a woman has had a previous cesarean delivery does not mean that subsequent deliveries must be C-sections. In fact, 60–80% of women who attempt a vaginal delivery after cesarean (VBAC) have successful vaginal deliveries (MayoClinic.com, 2008b). Many times the condition that made a C-section necessary in one birth will not exist in the next; thus a VBAC is safer than a scheduled repeat C-section.

Prepared Childbirth   Increasingly, Americans are choosing among such childbirth alternatives as prepared childbirth, rooming-in birthing centers, home birth, and midwifery.

Prepared childbirth (or natural childbirth) was popularized by English gynecologist Grantly Dick-Read (1972), who observed that fear causes muscles to tense, which, in turn, increases pain and stress during childbirth. He taught both partners about childbirth and gave them physical exercises to ease muscle tension. In the 1950s, French obstetrician Fernand Lamaze (1970) developed a method of

The Huichol people of Mexico traditionally practiced couvade. The father squatted in the rafters above the laboring mother. When the mother experienced a contraction, she would pull the ropes that had been attached to his scrotum so that he could "share" the experience of childbirth.

prepared childbirth based on knowledge of conditioned reflexes. Women learn to mentally separate the physical stimulus of uterine contractions from the conditioned response of pain. With the help of a partner, women perform breathing and other exercises throughout labor and delivery. Prepared childbirth, then, is not so much a matter of controlling the birth process as of understanding it and having confidence in nature's plan. Prepared mothers (who usually attend classes with the father or another partner) handle pain better, use fewer pain-relieving drugs, express greater satisfaction with the childbirth process, and experience less postpartum depression than women who undergo routine hospital births.

Birthing Rooms and Centers Birthing (or maternity) centers, institutions of long standing in England and other European countries, have now been developed in the United States. Although they vary in size, organization, and orientation, birthing centers share the view that childbirth is a normal, healthy process that can be assisted by skilled practitioners (midwives or physicians) in a homelike setting. Some centers provide emergency care; all have procedures for transfer to a hospital if necessary.

Home Birth Home births have increased during the past three decades, although they still constitute a small fraction of total births. Careful medical screening and planning that eliminate all but the lowest-risk pregnancies can make this a viable alternative for some couples.

Midwifery and Doulas In most countries, midwives attend the majority of births. The United States has an increasing number of certified nurse-midwives who are registered nurses trained in obstetrical techniques. They are qualified for routine deliveries and minor medical emergencies. They also often operate as part of a medical team that includes a backup physician. Their fees are generally considerably less than a doctor's.

Unlike midwives, who are medical professionals, *doulas* do not make clinical decisions. Rather, they offer emotional support and manage pain using massage, acupressure, and birthing positions.

If a woman decides she wants to give birth with the aid of a midwife outside a hospital setting, she should have a thorough medical screening to make sure she and her infant will not be at risk during delivery. She should investigate the midwife's or doula's training and experience, the backup services available in the event of complications or emergencies, and the procedures for a transfer to a hospital if necessary.

Breastfeeding

About 3 days after childbirth, lactation—the production of milk—begins. Before lactation, sometimes as early as the second trimester, a yellowish liquid called **colostrum** is secreted by the nipples. It is what nourishes the newborn infant before the mother's milk comes in. Colostrum is high in protein and contains antibodies that help protect the baby from infectious diseases. Hormonal changes during labor trigger the changeover from colostrum to milk, but unless a mother nurses her child, her breasts will soon stop producing milk. If she chooses not to breastfeed, she is usually given an injection of estrogen soon after delivery to stop lactation. It is not certain, however, whether estrogen is actually effective; furthermore, it may increase the risk of blood clotting.

Breastfeeding provides the best nutrition for infants. It also helps protect against many infectious diseases and gives both mother and child a sense of well-being.

Breast Versus Bottle: Which Is Better for You and Your Child?

If you are a woman who plans to have children, you will have to decide whether to breastfeed or bottlefeed. Perhaps you already have an idea that breastfeeding is healthier for the baby but are not sure why.

The following list of benefits and advantages should help you understand why mother's milk is the ideal food for most infants. The American Academy of Pediatrics now recommends breastfeeding for an infant's first year, however, only 21% of mothers in the United States reach this ideal (Centers for Disease Control and Prevention, 2008d).

Physical Benefits of Breastfeeding

- Breast milk contains antibodies that protect the baby from many infectious diseases, ear infections, diarrhea, and other maladies for at least 6 months.
- Breast milk forms softer curds in the infant's stomach, making digestion and elimination easier.
- Breast milk puts less stress on the infant's immature liver and kidneys because its total protein is lower than that of other mammalian milk.
- Breast milk is high in cholesterol, which is needed for proper development of the nervous tissue.
- Breast milk causes fewer allergic reactions because of its concentration and type of protein.
- Breast milk is a better source of nutrition for low-birth-weight babies because nature adapts the content of the mother's milk to meet the infant's needs.
- Babies who have been breastfed have fewer problems with tooth decay.
- Breastfeeding is thought to encourage the development of the dental arch, helping prevent the need for orthodontia later on.
- Breastfed babies have a 30% reduction in obesity rates (Severson, 2003).

- Breastfed children attain higher IQ scores than children not fed breast milk (Caspi, Williams, Kim-Cohen, et al., 2007).
- For mothers, hormonal changes stimulated by breastfeeding cause the uterus to contract and return to its normal size.
- Breastfeeding mothers reduce their risk of ovarian cancer, early breast cancer, and postmenopausal hip fractures due to osteoporosis.
- The longer a woman nurses, the lower her risk for developing type 2 diabetes (Wilson, Murphy, & Aguirre, 2008).

Psychological Benefits of Breastfeeding

- The close physical contact of breastfeeding provides a sense of emotional well-being for mother and baby.
- Sustaining the life of another through her milk may affirm a woman's sense of self and ability to give.

Health and Logistical Advantages of Breastfeeding

- Breastfeeding requires no buying, mixing, or preparing of formulas.
- Breast milk is not subject to incorrect mixing or spoilage.
- Breast milk is clean and is not easily contaminated.
- Breastfeeding provides some protection against pregnancy (if the woman is breastfeeding exclusively).
- The breast is always available.

Bottlefeeding

For those women whose work schedules, health problems, or other demands prohibit them from breastfeeding, holding and cuddling the baby while bottlefeeding can contribute to the sense of emotional well-being that comes from a close parent-baby relationship. Bottlefeeding affords a greater opportunity for fathers to become involved in the feeding of the baby.

Widespread research into the properties of breast milk has repeatedly shown that breastfeeding is best for babies as well as for mothers, families, and society (Brenner, 2005). Benefits for babies range from preventing infectious diseases and chronic conditions to improved neurodevelopment and psychosocial adaptation. For parents, the price and availability of breastfeeding cannot be beat and, environmentally, there are no negative impacts. The American Academy of Pediatrics provides "enthusiastic support and involvement of pediatricians in the promotion and practice of breastfeeding (as) essential to the achievement of optimal infant and child health, growth, and development" (American Academy of Pediatrics, 2003).

● Becoming a Parent

Click on "That's a Family" to hear children of gay and lesbian parents talk about their families.

Men and women who become parents enter a new phase of their lives. Even more than marriage, parenthood signifies adulthood—the final, irreversible end of childhood. A person can become an ex-spouse but never an ex-parent. The irrevocable nature of parenthood may make the first-time parent doubtful and apprehensive, especially during the pregnancy. Yet, for the most part, parenthood has to be learned experientially, although ideas can modify practices. A person may receive assistance from more experienced parents, but ultimately, each new parent has to learn on his or her own.

Many of the stresses felt by new parents closely reflect gender roles. Overall, mothers seem to experience greater stress than fathers. When we speak of "mothering" a child, everyone knows what we mean: nurturing, caring for, diapering, soothing, loving. Mothers generally "mother" their children almost every day of the year for at least 18 years. For some, the meaning of "fathering" may be different. However, because the lines between roles are becoming increasingly blurred as fathers play a more active part in raising their children, the verb "to parent" has been used to describe the caregiving behaviors of both mothers and fathers.

The time immediately following birth is a critical period for family adjustment. No amount of reading, classes, and expert advice can prepare expectant parents for the "real thing." The 3 months or so following childbirth (the "fourth trimester") constitute the **postpartum period.** This time is one of physical stabilization and emotional adjustment. The abrupt transition from being a nonparent to being a parent may create considerable stress. Parents take on parental roles literally overnight, and the job goes on without relief around the clock. Many parents express concern about their ability to meet all the responsibilities of child rearing.

To support couples in the adjustment and care of their newborn child, the **Family and Medical Leave Act (FMLA)** assures eligible employees up to a total of 12 workweeks of unpaid leave for the birth and care of the newborn child of the employee (U.S. Department of Labor, 2005). If the employee has to use some of that leave for another reason, including a difficult pregnancy, it may be counted as part of the 12-week FMLA leave entitlement. (For more information about this law, go to http://www.dol.gov/esa/whd/fmla.)

Sexual desire in the majority of women generally decreases during pregnancy and following delivery (De Judicibus & McCabe, 2002). Though 83% of couples in one study reported reduced frequency of sexual intercourse at 6 months postpartum, enjoyment of sensual activity and sexual intercourse tends to return gradually after childbirth (Ahlborg, Dahlof, & Hallberg, 2005). By 12 weeks postpartum, the majority of women have resumed sexual intercourse; however, many experience sexual difficulties, particularly dyspareunia (genital pain) and lowered sexual desire. At 6 months, when the baby's presence and the demands of parenting intrude on the sex lives of the parents, some women continue to report significantly lowered sexual desire. Depending on a couple's ability to adjust to the physical and psychological changes that occur during this time and the depth and range of their communication, most new parents experience a fulfilling sexual relationship. Information about what changes to expect may help new parents avoid making unfounded and harmful assumptions about their relationship.

The postpartum period may be a time of significant emotional upheaval. Even women who had easy and uneventful pregnancies may experience the "baby blues." On the third or fourth day postpartum, 80% of women notice a brief period of mild weepiness, irritability, and depressed mood (Tam, 2001). New mothers often have irregular sleep patterns because of the needs of their newborn,

Gay and Lesbian Parents

Because of the nontraditional nature of gay and lesbian families, it is difficult to determine both the number of children in the United States with at least one parent who is a gay man or lesbian woman or the choices or circumstances that these parents have engaged in order to become a family.

In 2002, the American Academy of Pediatrics endorsed same-sex adoptions, saying gay couples can provide the loving, stable, and emotionally healthy family life that children need (American Academy of Pediatrics, 2002). This policy is important for several reasons. First, same-sex parents are often the primary caregivers, but if they do not have parental rights, they have no legal say in matters. Second, children in gay households may lack health insurance if the family's only breadwinner is a gay parent without parental rights. In addition, gay parents lacking parental rights may lose visitation or custody battles if the couple separate or if one partner dies (Tanner, 2002).

Heterosexual fears about gay men and lesbian women as parents center around concerns about parenting abilities, fears of sexual abuse, and worries that the children will "catch" the homosexual orientation. All of these fears are unwarranted.

Fears that gay and lesbian parents may reject children of the other sex also appear unfounded. Such fears reflect two common misconceptions: that being gay or lesbian is a rejection of members of the other sex and that people are able to choose their sexual orientation. Research on children of lesbian women and gay men has shown that the parents' orientation has no impact on the children's sexual orientation or their feelings about their gender (Flaks, Ficher, Masterpasqua, & Joseph, 1995).

Despite the abundance of research and cases to support the above conclusion, gay men and lesbian women still fight for the legal rights and protections they deserve. Because in the vast majority of states they cannot legally marry and because of pervasive anti-gay prejudices, such issues as custody, visitation, and adoption remain legal dilemmas or obstacles for many contemplating becoming or trying to become parents.

A number of services and programs have been established to assist prospective gay and lesbian parents in sorting through the myriad questions and issues they face. In the end, it is the welfare of the child that society should support. This can best be achieved with loving, caring, responsible parents, regardless of sexual orientation.

Think Critically

- What are your thoughts and feelings about this issue?
- Why does society perpetuate fears about gay men and lesbian women as parents?
- What would you say to a gay or lesbian friend who desired to have children?

the discomfort of childbirth, or the strangeness of the hospital environment. Some mothers may feel isolated from their familiar world. These are considered normal, self-limiting postpartum symptoms and generally go away within a week or two.

Postpartum depression occurs in 10–15% of new mothers and can have its onset at any time in the first year postpartum. Like the blues, postpartum depression is thought to be related to hormonal changes brought on by sleep deprivation, weaning, and the resumption of the menstrual cycle. A prior history of depression also increases a woman's risk. It is common as well for anxiety disorders to arise or recur in the postpartum period, when some women may feel hypervigilant about possible harm to their baby. The most serious and rarest postpartum mental illness is **postpartum psychosis.** Unlike the other disorders, postpartum psychosis is thought to be exclusively biologically based and related to hormonal changes. Affected women tend to have difficulty sleeping, be prone to agitation or hyperactivity, and intermittently experience delusions, hallucinations, and paranoia. This behavior represents a medical emergency and usually requires hospitalization. Interestingly, the incidence of postpartum psychosis is the same the world over, suggesting little cultural difference (Tam, 2001). Depression rates, in comparison, vary from industrialized cultures (more) to nonindustrialized ones (less), suggesting that psychological, cultural, and social factors have a more significant effect on whether a woman experiences postpartum depression.

As a result of rare but highly publicized instances in which infants have been abandoned and sometimes left to die, every state has enacted a provision to provide a safe and confidential means of relinquishing an unwanted infant (Guttmacher Institute, 2008f). Under certain circumstances and without the threat of prosecution for child abandonment, these policies, also called "safe haven" or "safe surrender," typically allow a parent or other specified person to relinquish an infant at specific locations or to personnel authorized to accept the child.

> Cleaning and scrubbing can wait till tomorrow.
> For babies grow up we've learned to our sorrow.
> So quiet down cobwebs, dust go to sleep.
> I'm rocking my baby and babies don't keep.
>
> —Anonymous

Final Thoughts

For many people, the arrival of a child is one of life's most significant events. It signifies adulthood and conveys social status for those who are now parents. It creates the lifelong bonds of family. And it can fill the new parents with a deep sense of accomplishment and well-being.

Summary

Fertilization and Fetal Development

- Fertilization of the oocyte by a sperm usually takes place in the fallopian tube. The chromosomes of the ovum combine with those of the sperm to form the diploid zygote; it divides many times to form a *blastocyst,* which *implants* itself in the uterine wall.

- The blastocyst becomes an *embryo* and then a *fetus,* which is nourished through the *placenta* via the *umbilical cord.*

- Parenthood is now a matter of choice. Increasing numbers of individuals and couples are choosing to remain *child-free.*

Being Pregnant

- The most commonly used chemical pregnancy test can be taken 2–4 weeks after a woman misses her menstrual period. *Hegar's sign* can be detected by a trained examiner. Pregnancy is confirmed by the detection of the fetal heartbeat and movements or through examination by ultrasound.

- A woman's feelings vary greatly during pregnancy. It is important for her to share her concerns and to have support from her partner, friends, relatives, and health-care practitioners. Her feelings about sexuality are likely to change during pregnancy. Men may also have conflicting feelings. Sexual activity is generally safe unless there is pain, bleeding, or a history of miscarriage.

- Harmful substances may be passed to the embryo or fetus through the placenta. Substances that cause birth defects are called *teratogens;* these include alcohol, tobacco, certain drugs, and environmental pollutants. Infectious diseases such as rubella may damage the fetus. Sexually transmitted infections may be passed to the infant through the placenta or the birth canal during childbirth.

- *Ectopic pregnancy, pregnancy-induced hypertension,* and *premature birth* are the most common complications of pregnancy.

- Abnormalities of the fetus may be diagnosed using *ultrasound, amniocentesis, chorionic villus sampling (CVS),* or *neural tube defect screening.*

- Some pregnancies end in miscarriage. Infant mortality rates in the United States are extremely high compared with those in other industrialized nations. Loss of a pregnancy or death of a young infant is a serious life event.

Infertility

- *Infertility* is the inability to conceive a child after a year of unprotected intercourse or the inability to carry a child to term. The most common risk factors for infertility are body weight, age, sexually transmitted infections, smoking, and alcohol. Couples with fertility problems often feel they have lost control over an important area of their lives.

- Techniques for combating infertility include fertility medications, surgery, and *assisted reproductive technology. Surrogate motherhood* is also an option for childless couples. *Cloning,* the most controversial of reproductive technologies, is still in its infancy.

Giving Birth

- In the last trimester of pregnancy, a woman feels *Braxton-Hicks contractions.* These contractions also begin the *effacement* and *dilation* of the cervix to permit delivery.

- Labor can be divided into three stages. First-stage labor begins when uterine contractions become regular. When the cervix has dilated approximately 10 centimeters, the baby's head enters the birth canal; this is called *transition.* In second-stage labor, the baby emerges from the birth canal. In third-stage labor, the *afterbirth* is expelled.

- *Cesarean section,* or *C-section,* is the delivery of a baby through an incision in the mother's abdominal wall and uterus.

- *Prepared childbirth* encompasses a variety of methods that stress the importance of understanding the birth process, teaching the mother to relax, and giving her emotional support during childbirth.

- Birthing centers and birthing rooms in hospitals provide viable alternatives to traditional hospital birth settings for normal births. Instead of medical doctors, many women now choose trained nurse-midwives or doulas.

- *Male circumcision* has been performed routinely in this country for many years. The American Academy of Pediatrics says that the evidence is not sufficient to recommend that boys be circumcised. Circumcision holds religious meaning for Jews and Muslims.

- Mother's milk is more nutritious than formula or cow's milk and provides immunity to many diseases. Breastfeeding also offers benefits to mother, family, society, and the environment.

Becoming a Parent

- Because the roles involving "mothering" and "fathering" are becoming blurred, the term "to parent" has been used to describe caregiving behaviors.

- A critical adjustment period—the *postpartum period*—follows the birth of a child. The mother may experience feelings of depression (sometimes called "baby blues") that are a result of biological, psychological, and social factors. The majority of women also experience a decrease in sexual desire.

Questions for Discussion

- Most likely, you have a strong opinion about pregnancy and how one would affect your life. If you or your partner became pregnant today, what would you do? Where would you go in order to receive support for your decision?

- If you (or your partner) were to have a child, where and how would you prefer to deliver the baby? Whom would you want present? What steps would you be willing to take in order to ensure that your wishes were granted?

- After trying and failing to conceive for one year, you now realize that you or your partner may have a fertility problem. What measures would you consider in order to have a child? How much would you be willing to pay?

- Like many issues related to sexual orientation, adoption by same-sex couples is a controversial issue. What are your views on this, and do you feel that enacting laws is the best way to support your point of view?

Sex and the Internet

Pregnancy and Childbirth

Even though pregnancy is a natural and normal process, there are still myriad issues, questions, and concerns surrounding it. This is especially true when couples are considering pregnancy, are trying to become pregnant, or find out that the woman is pregnant. Fortunately, there is help and support on the Internet. One Web site was established specifically to educate men and women about pregnancy: http://www.childbirth.org. Go to this site and select two topics you wish to learn more about. You might choose "Signs of Pregnancy," "Cesareans," "Episiotomy," "Birth Plans," or "Fertility." After you have investigated the topics and perhaps linked them to another resource, answer these questions for each:

- What topics did you choose? Why?
- What three new facts did you learn about each?
- How might you integrate this information into your own choices and decisions around pregnancy or parenthood?
- What additional link did you follow, and what did you learn as a result?

Suggested Web Sites

American College of Nurse-Midwives
http://www.midwife.org
Provides a directory of certified nurse-midwives in your area.

American College of Obstetricians and Gynecologists
http://www.acog.org
A professional association with information for the lay public about pregnancy and childbirth.

Dad's Rights
http://www.dadsrights.org
Dedicated to the premise that parenting is a 50-50 proposition; it works to ensure that both parents are allowed to be involved with their children.

La Leche League International
http://www.llli.org
Provides advice and support for nursing mothers.

Population Connection
http://www.populationconnection.org
Grassroots population organization that educates and advocates for action to stabilize world population.

Resolve: The National Infertility Association
http://www.resolve.org/site/PageServer
Dedicated to providing education, advocacy, and support for men and women facing the crisis of infertility.

Share: Pregnancy & Infant Loss Support
http://nationalshareoffice.com
Serves those whose lives are touched by the death of a baby.

Society for Assisted Reproductive Technology
http://www.sart.org
Promotes and advances the standards for the practice of assisted reproductive technology.

Suggested Reading

For the most current research findings in obstetrics, see *Obstetrics and Gynecology, The New England Journal of Medicine,* and *JAMA: Journal of the American Medical Association.*

American College of Obstetricians and Gynecologists. (2005). *Planning your pregnancy and birth* (4th ed.). Washington, DC: Author. A comprehensive and scientifically accurate guide to pregnancy and birth.

Brott, A. A., & Ash, J. (2004). *Father knows best: The expectant father.* New York: Abbeville Press. A guide to the emotional, physical, and financial changes the father-to-be may experience during the course of his partner's pregnancy.

Gotsch, G., Fazal, A., & Torgas, J. (2004). *The womanly art of breastfeeding* (7th ed.). New York: La Leche League International. A comprehensive and supportive guide to breastfeeding.

Jana, L. A., & Shu, J. (2005). *Heading home with your newborn.* American Academy of Pediatrics. Offers parent-tested, pediatrician-approved advice.

Nilsson, L. & Hamburger, L. (2004). *A child is born* (4th ed.). New York: Delacourt/Seymour Lawrence. The study of birth, beginning with fertilization, told in stunning photographs with text.

Sher, G., Davis, V., & Stoess, J. (2005). *In-vitro fertilization: The A.R.T. of making babies* (Rev. ed.). New York: Checkmark Books. A comprehensive guide to the increasingly common and successful practice of in vitro fertilization.

For links, articles, and study material, go to the McGraw-Hill Web site, located at **www.mhhe.com/yarber7e.**

The Sexual Body in Health and Illness

MAIN TOPICS

"I have learned not to take the media or anyone else's opinion as the gospel. Now when I look in the mirror, I see the strong, beautiful, Black woman that I am. I no longer see the woman who wanted breast implants and other superficial aspects of beauty. My beauty now flows from within, and all I had to acquire was love for myself and knowledge of myself, and it did not cost me anything."

—21-year-old female

"It was never about food; it was always about the way I felt inside. The day that changed my life forever was January 29, 2007. It was the mortifying reflection of myself off the porcelain toilet I hovered over that made me see the truth. At that moment, I knew I could no longer go on living or dying like a parched skeleton. I had to hit rock bottom before I realized that what I was doing was wrong. I feel that, even if twenty people had sat me down at that time and told me I had an eating disorder, I would have laughed. I was blind."

—20-year-old female

"Interestingly, I am writing this paper with a bald head. I used to have long, beautiful blonde hair. Chemotherapy took care of that little social/sexual status symbol. I was not at all prepared for losing my looks along with that much of my sexual identity. It has taken me by surprise to realize how much the way you look influences how people react to you, especially the opposite sex. The real lesson comes from the betrayal I feel from my body. I was healthy before, and now that I am sick, I feel as if my identity has changed. I always saw my body as sexual. Now after surgery, which left a large scar where my cleavage used to be, and with chemotherapy, which left me bald, I feel like my body is a medical experiment. My sexual desire has been very low, and I think it is all related to not feeling good about the way I look. Amazing how much of our identities are wrapped around the way we feel about the way we look. The good news for me is that my foundation is strong: I am not just what is on the outside."

—26-year-old female

"On the weekend, I like to go out with my friend. When I drink alcohol in excessive amounts, I never have any problems performing sexually. But when I smoke marijuana, I have a major problem performing up to my standards."

—19-year-old male

THE INTERRELATEDNESS OF OUR PHYSICAL HEALTH, our psychological well-being, and our sexuality is complex. It's not something that most of us even think about, especially as long as we remain in good health. We may encounter physical and emotional problems and limitations, many of which may profoundly influence our sexual lives. We need to inform ourselves about these problems so that we can deal with them effectively.

In this chapter, we examine our attitudes and feelings about our bodies, in addition to looking at specific health issues. We begin with a discussion of body image and eating disorders. Next we look at the relationship between alcohol and other drugs and our sexuality. Then we turn to issues of sexuality and disability. We also discuss the physical and emotional effects of specific diseases such as diabetes, heart disease, arthritis, and cancer as they influence our sexual functioning. Finally, we address other issues specific to women or men.

As we grow emotionally and physically, we may also develop new perceptions of what it means to be healthy. We may discover new dimensions in ourselves to lead us to a more fulfilled and healthier sex life.

Contrary to popular stereotypes, people of all shapes, sizes, and ages can lead healthy and happy sexual lives.

● Living in Our Bodies: The Quest for Physical Perfection

Health is more than the absence of disease, and sexual health is more than the presence of healthy sexual parts. According to the World Health Organization (2006):

> **Sexual health** is a state of physical, emotional, mental and social well-being related to sexuality; it is not merely the absence of disease, dysfunction or infirmity. Sexual health requires a positive and respectful approach to sexuality and sexual relationships, as well as the possibility of having pleasurable and safe sexual experiences, free of coercion, discrimination and violence. For sexual health to be attained and maintained, the sexual rights of all persons must be respected, protected and fulfilled.

Sexual health has to do with how we function biologically, but it is also a function of our behavior and our awareness and acceptance of our bodies. In terms of sexuality, good health requires us to know and understand our bodies, to feel comfortable with them. It requires a woman to feel at ease with the sight, feel, and smell of her vulva, and to be comfortable with and aware of her breasts—their shape, size, and contours. Sexual health requires a man to accept his body, including his genitals, and to be aware of physical sensations such as lower back pain or a feeling of congestion in his bladder. A sexually healthy man abandons the idea that masculinity means he should ignore his body's pains, endure stress, and suffer in silence.

Our general health affects our sexual functioning. Fatigue, stress, and minor ailments all affect our sexual interactions. If we ignore these aspects of our health, we are likely to experience a decline in our sexual drive, as well as suffer physical and psychological distress. A person who always feels tired or stressed or who is constantly ill or debilitated is likely to feel less sexual than a healthy, rested person. Health and sexuality are gifts we must care for and respect, not use and abuse.

I wouldn't sue anyone for saying I had a big prick. No man would. In fact, I might pay them to do it.

—Joe Orton
(1933–1967)

think
about it

"Oh to Be Bigger": Breast and Penis Enhancement

In their search for the "perfect" body, many people try to achieve what they consider to be the cultural ideal for breast and penis size. Our culture, more than most, places emphasis on breast and penis size: Bigger is better. In our preoccupation with size, many of us have come to believe that a larger penis or breasts will make us more alluring, a better lover, and more self-confident. Amazingly, some women have even had surgery (usually augmentation) on their labia to make them the supposedly "ideal" size.

Both men and women believe that size is more important to their partners than it actually is. Women are often more unhappy than their partner about their own breasts. One study of 52,227 adults found that most women (70%) were dissatisfied with the size and shape of their breasts, whereas most men (56%) were satisfied with their partner's breasts (Frederick, Peplau, & Lever, 2008). At the same time, men sometimes worry that their partners will think that their penis is too small, yet a study of 52,031 heterosexual men and women found that 85% of women were satisfied with their partner's penis size (only 55% of men were satisfied with their penis size and 45% wanted it larger) (Lever, Frederick, & Peplau, 2006).

The desire to be bigger has led to ads in newspapers, magazines, and spam e-mails and to Web sites that try to make people feel inadequate or embarrassed if they are not "large." The ads promote methods such as special pills or drugs to increase size and promise quick and easy results. What they may not address, however, are questions of safety, functioning, erotic pleasure, and necessity. Rarely, if ever, have the products been approved by the Food and Drug Administration (FDA) or been shown to be effective in clinical tests.

In 2007, according to the American Society of Plastic Surgeons, 347,524 women had breast augmentation (65% were saline solution and 35% silicone gel), an increase of 64% since 2000, making breast implantation the most popular cosmetic surgery performed in this country (American Society of Plastic Surgeons, 2008). Breast implants can cause serious and costly complications, such as pain, infection, and hardening of the area around the implant. Furthermore, all women with breast implants will likely need to have their implants replaced or removed sometime during their lifetime. The FDA recommends that women who get the silicone gel implant have an MRI 3 years after the implant surgery and every 2 years thereafter to check for "silent ruptures" (U.S. Food and Drug Administration, 2006).

Only rarely is a man's penis actually too small; a more common problem is a partner's complaint that it is too large. Nevertheless, a variety of products and techniques promise penis enlargement, including vacuum pumps, exercises, pills, and surgical procedures such as suctioning fat from the abdomen and injecting it into the penis. The short- and long-term effectiveness and safety of these methods has not been well established, and the degree of patient satisfaction varies. Many men who have had penis augmentation surgery report that they regret having the surgery (Wessells, Lue, & McAninch, 1996).

If you are unhappy with your breast or penis size, talk to a professional health-care provider such as a physician or mental health counselor. If you are in a relationship, talk to your partner; in most cases, you will learn that size is usually not an important issue. Intimacy, communication, mutual respect, and acceptance of your own body and sexuality are the most important aspects of a rewarding sexual relationship. Each person's body is special and capable of giving and receiving erotic pleasure in its unique way.

Think Critically

- How do you feel about the size of your penis, breasts, or genitals? If you are uncomfortable, what might help you feel satisfied?
- Have you ever been rejected by a sexual partner because he or she was dissatisfied with your breast or penis size? Have you ever rejected a sexual partner for the same reason?
- What could you do to help a sexual partner feel more comfortable about accepting his or her body?

Eating Disorders

Click on "The Inner Voice" to hear the experiences of young people who have struggled with food issues.

Many of us are willing to pay high costs—physical, emotional, and financial—to meet the expectations of our culture and to feel worthy, lovable, and sexually attractive. Although having these desires is clearly a normal human characteristic, the means by which we try to fulfill them can be extreme and even self-destructive. Many American women and some men try to control their weight by dieting, but some people's fear and loathing of fat (often combined with fear or disgust regarding sexual functions) impels them to extreme eating behaviors. Compulsive overeating (binge eating) and compulsive overdieting (which may include self-starvation and binge eating and purging)—and combinations thereof—are the behaviors classified as **eating disorders.**

Most people with eating disorders have certain traits, such as low self-esteem, perfectionism, difficulty dealing with emotions, unreasonable demands for self-control, negative perceptions of self in relation to others, and, of course, a fear of becoming fat. Often, the person lacks adequate skills for dealing with stress. The American Psychiatric Association Work Group on Eating Disorders (2006) states that eating disorders are real, treatable medical illnesses in which certain maladaptive patterns of eating take on a life of their own and are not due to lack of will or behavior. Eating disorders are frequently present with other psychiatric disorders, such as depression, substance abuse, and anxiety disorders (National Institute of Mental Health [NIMH], 2007).

Although many studies of eating disorders have singled out White middle-class and upper-class women, these problems transcend ethnic, socioeconomic, and gender boundaries. Most research suggests that eating disorders are equally common among White females and Latinas, more frequent among American Indian females, and not as common among African American and Asian American females. Among minority racial/ethnic groups, the females who are younger, have more body weight, are better educated, and identify with middle-class values are at higher risk for eating disorders than their peers (Insel & Roth, 2008). Yet Warren and colleagues (2005) speculated that ethnicity may protect against the development of eating disorders. Their study of European American women and Spanish/Mexican American women found that the strongest relationship between the personal internalization of the "thin body" ideal and body dissatisfaction occurred among the European American women.

Anorexia Nervosa **Anorexia** is the medical term for loss of appetite. The term **anorexia nervosa** is a misnomer for the condition it purports to describe; the "relentless pursuit of excessive, thinness" (American Psychiatric Association [APA], 2000). Those with anorexia are, in fact, obsessively preoccupied with food; they live in a perpetual struggle with the pangs of hunger. Loss of appetite is rare (APA, 2000). Anorexia usually develops between the ages of 10 and 18. The percentages of men and women from the National Comorbidity Survey Replication (NCS-R) reporting anorexia nervosa at one point in their lives are presented in Figure 13.1.

Most people with anorexia are ruled by a desire for thinness, the conviction that their bodies are too large (even in the face of evidence to the contrary), and the "grim determination" to sustain weight loss (Levine, 1987). The individual refuses to maintain a minimally normal body weight and has a significant disturbance in perception of body shape or size, perceiving himself or herself as overweight although dangerously thin. Typically, a person with anorexia has a body weight at least 15% below normal. The process of eating becomes an obsession. The person's behavior can be depicted as self-starvation. Unusual eating habits develop, such as avoiding food and meals, picking out a few foods and eating these in small quantities, or carefully weighing and portioning food. According to some studies, people with anorexia are up to 10 times more likely to die as a result of their disorder compared to those without the disorder (APA 2000; American Psychiatric Association Work Group on Eating Disorders, 2006; NIMH, 2007).

" Muscles I don't care about—my husband likes me to be squishy when he hugs me.

—Dixie Carter
(1939–)

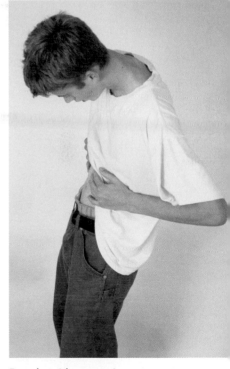

People with anorexia are obsessed by a desire to be thin.

● **FIGURE** 13.1

Percentage of U.S. Men and Women Reporting Eating Disorder's at One Point in Their Lives. (*Source:* Hudson, Hiripi, Pope, & Kessler, 2007.)

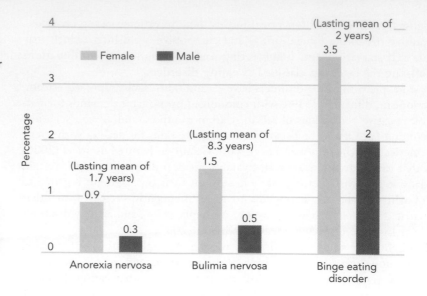

Physiologically, those with anorexia suffer from amenorrhea, delay of menarche or cessation of menstrual periods for at least three menstrual cycles (see Chapter 3); they may also suffer from hypothermia, the body's inability to maintain heat. Hormone levels decline in both men and women. Adolescents with this disorder may not achieve the secondary sex characteristics that are normal for this stage, such as breast development and a growth spurt.

The American Psychiatric Association (2000) identifies two types of anorexia nervosa: restricting and binge eating/purging. The restricting type involves weight loss that occurs as a result of dieting, fasting, or excessive exercise but no regular binge eating or purging. The binge eating/purging type occurs as a result of binge eating or purging (or both) at least weekly. A person may purge by self-induced vomiting or misuse of laxatives, diuretics, or enemas. Some persons with anorexia do not binge eat but regularly purge after consuming small amounts of food.

> *The essence of beauty is the unity of variety.*
>
> —William Somerset Maugham (1874–1965)

Bulimia **Bulimia** is characterized by episodes of uncontrolled, often secret, overeating (binge eating), which the person then tries to counteract by purging—vomiting, fasting, excessive exercising or dieting, or using laxatives or diuretics. People with bulimia usually weigh within the normal range for their age and height, but they may fear gaining weight, desire to lose weight, and feel intensely dissatisfied with their bodies (NIMH, 2007). Differentiating between anorexia nervosa, binge eating/purging, and bulimia is often a matter of clinical judgment; however, the "sense of lack of control" is more characteristic of bulimia (APA, 2000).

Traits that may distinguish the individual with bulimia from people without an eating disorder include childhood physical and sexual abuse, severe physical health problems, perfectionism, and/or parental depression. Bulimia has also been shown to develop more frequently in women who began to menstruate by age 12 than in those who began later. Early changes in body shape associated with puberty may be seen as another incentive to diet. Other characteristics associated with bulimia are dramatic weight fluctuations, major life changes, emotional instability, and a high need for approval (APA, 2000). The percentages of men and women from the NCS-R reporting bulimia nervosa at one point in their lives are presented in Figure 13.1.

think
about it

Body Modification: Tattooing, Piercing, and Branding

It's nearly impossible to watch MTV, televised sports, or fashion events these days without seeing someone with a tattoo or ring discreetly (or not so discreetly) displayed on his or her body. As the latest expressions of individuality, piercing and tattooing have attracted a diverse set of enthusiasts and have moved into mainstream culture.

A study of 454 students at one college found that body modification (body piercing and tattooing) was common. Half said that they had nontraditional body piercings (other than for women's earrings) and just under a quarter reported having tattoos. The most common "nontraditional" piercing sites among women were the navel (29%), upper ear (27%), tongue (12%), nipple (5%), and genitals (2%). Piercing other than in the ears was rare among the male students: 2% had pierced tongues, and 1% reported pierced eyebrows, nipples, or genitals. Male athletes were more likely to be tattooed than male nonathletes, with the hand/arm (12%), back (7%), and shoulder (6%) the most common sites. The most common tattoo body sites for the female students were the back (14%), foot/leg (5%), and shoulder and abdomen (4% each) (Mayers, Judelson, Moriarty, & Rundell, 2002).

Tattooing in our culture has become widespread and nearly routine, with tattoo "studios" presenting their services as art (Petrecca, 2007). The tattooing procedure involves injecting dye into the skin, resulting in a permanent marking. Potential problems associated with the dye-injecting procedure include the risk of infection, including hepatitis and HIV.

Like tattooing, body piercing has become increasingly popular as a dramatic way to help define oneself. What keeps piercing exotic is not only the look but also the pain factor that accompanies it. For some, the pain is viewed as a drug, a way of releasing anxiety or aggression, and/or a means of erotic stimulation (Stirn & Hinz, 2008). Psychologists report that cutting and other self-injury provide relief by releasing endorphins, which can actually boost one's mood (Ryan, 1997). Piercing capitalizes on a fascination with the look of deviance and its sadomasochistic undertones.

A third practice is branding, now becoming more common in the mainstream, with some clubs offering branding as a stage show. Hot-iron branding leaves a scar that may be treated with steroid injections but that can never be totally removed.

One study found that tattoos and body piercings among college students were associated with significantly more risk-taking behavior, greater use of alcohol and marijuana, and less social conformity (Forbes, 2001). However, this study as well as a more recent one (Armstrong et al., 2004) found that even though college students with tattoos and body piercings were risk takers, the traditional negative stereotype that body modifications are indicators of social or personal pathology was not found.

Because all these markings are considered permanent and potentially dangerous, as medical complications can occur, the procedures should be performed only by professionals. Keys to safety and satisfaction include basic aftercare, which involves keeping the site clean and avoiding contact with dirty hands, saliva, or other body fluids; an awareness of anatomy and knowledge of proper healing procedures on the part of the person providing the services; proper placement of the marks or piercings; and the use of sterile tools ("Piercing Exquisite," 1998).

Think Critically

- What are your views about individuals who have tattooing, piercing, or branding done?
- Do you think that people who get body modifications done are different in some way than those who have not?
- Have you had any type of body modification done? If not, why? If so, why?

Binge Eating Disorder Another recognized eating disorder, **binge eating disorder,** more commonly known as compulsive overeating, is similar to bulimia except that there is no purging, excessive exercise, or fasting. Loss of control may be accompanied by a variety of symptoms, including rapid eating, eating to the point of discomfort or beyond, continual eating throughout the day, eating alone to hide the binge eating, and eating large amounts when not hungry. Compulsive overeaters rarely eat because of hunger; rather, they use food to cope with stress, conflict, and other difficult emotions (Insel & Roth, 2008; NIMH, 2007). Obsessive thinking, embarrassment, depression, and feelings of guilt and disgust often accompany the overeating. Those with binge eating disorder are often overweight or obese; many are dieters. Evidence indicates that 25–45% of obese dieters, most of whom are women, may have binge eating disorder (APA, 2000). The percentages of men and women from the NCS-R reporting binge eating disorder at one point in their lives are presented in Figure 13.1.

Treatment Strategies According to the National Institute of Mental Health (2007), eating disorders are very complex, and consequently researchers are unsure of the underlying biological, behavioral, and social causes of them. Scientists and physicians are increasingly thinking of them as medical illnesses with certain biological causes. Researchers are investigating behavioral questions, along with genetic and brain systems information, to understand risk factors, identify biological markers, and develop medications that can target specific pathways that control eating behavior. Eating disorders are frequently undertreated (Hudson, Hiripi, Pope, & Kessler, 2007), although treatments for many eating disorders are effective. Early diagnosis and treatment enhances the chances of successful treatment. Because of their complexity, eating disorders often require a comprehensive treatment plan that involves medical care and monitoring, psychosocial intervention, nutritional counseling, and possible medication. Since many people with eating disorders do not recognize that they have an illness, they often strongly resist getting and staying in treatment; hence, family members and trusted individuals are valuable in ensuring that the person with an eating disorder receives treatment.

> O, that this too too solid flesh would melt Thaw and resolve itself into a dew!
>
> —William Shakespeare, *Hamlet* (1564–1616)

Retreating From Sexuality

Clinicians who work with people with eating disorders often find that they have histories of abuse, including incest or other sexual abuse (Simpson & Ramberg, 1992). They may also have been raised to be fearful of sex and to view the body as dirty or sinful. According to a review of studies dealing with eating disorders and sexuality, women with anorexia are relatively less likely to have sexually intimate relationships, are relatively self-critical of their sexual attractiveness to others, report lower interest in sex, and have more sexual function problems than women with normal eating patterns. Women with bulimia, however, are as likely as, and sometimes more likely than, women without an eating disorder to engage in sexual relationships and a variety of sexual activities (Wiederman, 1996). The results of a study of 3,627 women provide further evidence of the role of dissatisfaction with one's body image (e.g., perceiving or actually being overweight) in sexual behavior. This study found that women who are satisfied with their body image engage in more sexual activity, have more orgasms, and are more likely to initiate sex, feel comfortable taking off their clothes in the presence of their partner, have sex with the lights on, try new sexual behaviors, and aim to please their partners sexually than women who are dissatisfied with their body image (Ackard, Kearney-Cooke, & Peterson, 2000). Little research has been published on the relationship of eating disorders and sexual expression in males. However, males with the disorders, like females, have a warped sense of body image and often have an extreme concern with becoming more muscular. One would think that a poor concept of one's body would impact male's sexuality as it often does for females. However, research has yet to draw this conclusion.

The body type that is idealized by ultrathin fashion models is impossible for most women to obtain without imperiling their health.

Anabolic Steroids: A Dangerous Means to an End

Athletes and body-builders often embrace the goal of great success at their activity and optimal body composition. However, in their quest for enhanced performance, many of them reach the limits of their genetic endowment and training and turn to substances known as ergogenic aids. Among these is a synthetic version of the hormone testosterone, otherwise referred to as **anabolic steroids.** These drugs are used by body-builders and other athletes to enhance their strength and add bulk to their bodies. In addition, they may produce a state of euphoria, diminished fatigue, and increased sense of power in both sexes, which gives them an addictive quality. A large study involving 199 nationally representative U.S. colleges found that the prevalence of lifetime, past-year, and past-month use of anabolic steroids by the college students who were interviewed was less than 1%, occurring more frequently among male intercollegiate athletes (McCabe, Brower, West, Nelson, & Wechsler, 2007).

Anabolic steroids can also have serious adverse effects, some of which are irreversible. These include sterility, heart attacks, strokes, liver damage, and personality changes, the most common being pathological aggressiveness (Ahrendt, 2001). When taken by healthy men, anabolic steroids can cause the body to shut down its production of testosterone, causing their breasts to grow and testicles to atrophy. In women, the drugs can cause hirsutism (excessive hair growth), acne, reproductive problems, and voice change, which can be permanent. Anabolic steroids such as testosterone and its derivatives are prescription medications with clearly defined uses. Procuring and using them without a prescription is both illegal and dangerous.

● Alcohol, Drugs, and Sexuality

In the minds of many Americans, sex and alcohol (or sex and "recreational" drugs) go together. Although experience shows us that sexual performance and enjoyment generally decrease as alcohol or drug consumption levels increase, many people cling to the age-old myths.

Alcohol Use and Sexuality

The belief that alcohol and sex go together, although not new, is certainly reinforced by popular culture. Alcohol advertising often features beautiful, scantily clad women. Beer drinkers are portrayed as young, healthy, and fun-loving. Wine drinkers are romantics, surrounded by candlelight and roses. Those who choose Scotch are the epitome of sophistication. These images reinforce long-held cultural myths associating alcohol with social prestige and sexual enhancement.

It is well known that alcohol use among college students is very common. When the results of five large studies of alcohol use among college students were analyzed, it was found that about 2 in 5 American college students were heavy drinkers, defined as having had five or more drinks in a row in the past 2 weeks. As reported in *Details* magazine, 68% of college males and 69% of college females reported that they had consumed alcohol before having sex (Elliott & Brantley, 1997). Drinking is associated with sexual risks. Studies examining the association between drinking and risky sex in samples of college students and youth over a 10-year period found that drinking was strongly related to the decision to have sex and to engage in indiscriminate forms of risky sex such as having numerous or casual partners, but was inconsistently related to protective behaviors such as condom use (Cooper, 2002). Other researchers have found that college males who reported alcohol use during their last sexual encounter were more likely not to discuss HIV/STIs, birth control, or emotional commitment with their female partners before having sex with them than men who reported little or no alcohol use (Koch, Palmer, Vicary, & Wood, 1999).

Because of the ambivalence we often have about sex ("It's good but it's bad"), many people feel more comfortable about initiating or participating in sexual activities if they have had a drink or two. This phenomenon of activating behaviors that would normally be suppressed is known as **disinhibition.** Although a small amount of alcohol may have a small disinhibiting, or relaxing, effect, greater quantities can result in aggression, loss of judgment, poor coordination, and loss of consciousness.

Alcohol affects the ability of both men and women to become sexually aroused. Men may have difficulty achieving or maintaining an erection, and women may not experience vaginal lubrication. Physical sensations are likely to be dulled. Chronic users of alcohol typically experience desire and arousal difficulties (Bacon et al., 2003; Schiavi, Schreiner-Engle, Mandeli, Schanzer, & Cohen, 1990). Researchers have determined that drinking a six-pack of beer in less than 2 hours can affect testosterone and sperm production for up to 12 hours. This does not mean, however, that no sperm are present; production is slowed,

Researchers are not sure if alcohol use leads to risky sexual behavior, but it is possibly part of a risky health behavior pattern.

but most men will remain fertile when drinking alcohol. However, ingestion of large amounts of alcohol by both men and women can contribute to infertility and birth defects (see Chapter 12).

Alcohol use has also been found to be associated with numerous dangerous consequences such as unwanted sexual intercourse and sexual violence. The disinhibiting effect of alcohol allows some men to justify various types of sexual violence they would not otherwise commit. Men may expect that alcohol will make them sexually aggressive and act accordingly. In drinking situations, women are viewed as more sexually available and impaired. Thus, males may participate in drinking situations expecting to find a sex partner. Additionally, a woman who has been drinking may have difficulty in sending and receiving cues about expected behavior and in resisting assault. Alcohol use is often a significant factor in sexual violence of all types. According to data from 119 schools participating in three of the Harvard School of Public Health College Alcohol Study surveys, about 1 in 20 women reported being raped and nearly three quarters of the victims reported being raped while intoxicated (Mohler-Kuo, Dowdall, Koss, & Wechsler, 2004). Studies of college students have shown that alcohol consumption by either the perpetrator or the victim, or both, increases the chance of sexual assault (Abbey, 2002) and that the higher the amount of alcohol consumption by either person, the more likely the sexual victimization to the woman will be severe (Abbey, Clinton-Sherrod, McAussian, Zawacki, & Buck, 2003).

Drinking alcohol has long been assumed in both the scientific and popular literature to lead to sexual risk taking. However, recently some researchers have begun to find that alcohol use among young people is just one component of an overall risk behavior pattern and not the cause of sexual risk behavior. For example, a recent study of 219 college students found no evidence indicating that condom use was less prevalent during intercourse when alcohol was consumed in contrast to when it was not, regardless of whether intercourse occurred with a casual or romantic partner. The study concluded that stable and behavioral dimensions, such as impulsivity/sensation seeking, sociability, and usual drinking pattern, provided a better explanation for sexual risk taking than acute alcohol effects (Velez-Blasini, 2008).

Other Drug Use and Sexuality

Substances that purport to increase sexual desire or improve sexual function are called **aphrodisiacs.** In addition to drugs, aphrodisiacs can include perfumes and certain foods, particularly those that resemble genitals, such as bananas and oysters (Sandroni, 2001). Ground rhinoceros horn has been considered an aphrodisiac in Asia, possibly giving rise to the term "horny" (Taberner, 1985). Painstaking research, both personal and professional, inevitably leads to the same conclusion: One's inner fantasy life and a positive image of the sexual self, coupled with an interested and responsive partner, are the most powerful aphrodisiacs. Nevertheless, the search continues for this elusive magic potion, and many people take a variety of drugs in an attempt to enhance their sexual experiences.

Studies have examined the prevalence of the use of drugs as an aphrodisiac. A sample of 1,114 sexually experienced individuals aged 18 to 39 years was studied to determine if the participants had ever used a drug to enhance their sexual experience. Among the 28% who reported ever using a drug to improve sex, several drugs were commonly cited (see Figure 13.2). When considering

Most Commonly Cited Drugs Used by a Sample of 18–39-Year-Olds Who Reported Ever Using a Drug to Improve Sex. (*Source:* Foxman, Sevgi, & Holmes, 2006.)

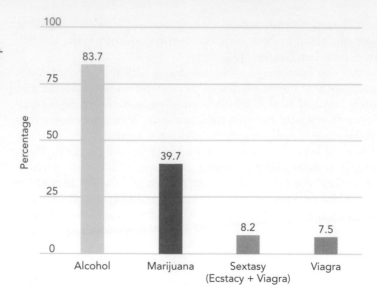

this self-report, it is important to realize that the "placebo effect," of aphrodisiacs has been estimated at 50% (Yates & Wolman, 1991).

Most recreational drugs, although perceived as increasing sexual enjoyment, actually have the opposite effect. (Many prescribed medications have negative effects on sexual desire and functioning as well, and users should read the information accompanying the prescription or ask the pharmacist about any sexual side effects.) Although recreational drugs may reduce inhibitions and appear to enhance the sexual experience, many also have the capacity to interfere with the libido and sexual functioning. They also have the potential to interfere with fertility and have a serious impact on overall health and well-being.

The effects of marijuana are in large part determined by the expectations of its users; therefore, no definitive statement can be made about how marijuana affects sexual encounters. Specific information about its effects in a relationship can be found by looking at the role it plays in a couple's life. In some cases, marijuana (or any drug) can become a crutch to help people deal with situations or behaviors they find uncomfortable. Long-term marijuana use can also cause or contribute to low motivation to achieve and to low sex drive.

The substance amyl nitrate, also known as "poppers," is a fast-acting muscle relaxant and coronary vasodilator, meaning it expands the blood vessels around the heart. Medically, it is used to relieve attacks of angina. Some people attempt to intensify their orgasms by "popping" an amyl nitrate vial and inhaling the vapor. The drug causes engorgement of the blood vessels in the penis, vagina, and anus. It also causes a drop in blood pressure, which may result in feelings of dizziness and giddiness. The most common side effects are severe headaches and fainting, and, if allowed to touch the skin, the drug can cause burns.

Another drug widely considered to be an aphrodisiac is cantharides, or "Spanish fly." This substance is produced by drying and heating certain beetles' bodies until they disintegrate into a powder. There have not yet been controlled studies to confirm its aphrodisiac effect. Taken internally, the substance causes acute irritation and inflammation of the genitourinary tract, including the kidneys, bladder, and urethra, and it can result in permanent tissue damage and death. This substance is banned in the United States.

LSD and other psychedelic drugs (including mescaline and psilocybin) have no positive effects on sexual ability. They may actually cause constant and painful erections, a condition called priapism (see Chapter 14).

Cocaine, a central nervous system stimulant, reduces inhibitions and enhances feelings of well-being. But regular use nearly always leads to sexual difficulties in both men and women, as well as an inability to achieve erection or orgasm. Male cocaine users also have a lower sperm count, less active sperm, and more abnormal sperm than nonusers. The same levels of sexual impairment occur among those who snort the drug and those who smoke or "freebase" it. Those who inject cocaine experience the greatest dysfunction.

Ecstasy (MDMA) is a hallucinogenic amphetamine that produces heightened arousal, a mellowing effect, and an enhanced sense of self. It is an illegal drug with no legitimate use. Rates of ecstasy use among college students vary from nearly 5% to 10%, depending on the study (Boyd, McCabe, & d'Arcy, 2003; Strote, Lee, & Wechsler, 2002), and, unlike other drugs whose use peaked in the 1970s, the use of ecstasy has been climbing consistently over the past 20-plus years (Pope, Ionescu-Pioggia, & Pope, 2001). It has been associated with dehydration due to physical exertion without breaks for water; heavy use has been linked to paranoia, liver damage, and heart attacks. Because users feel increased empathy, ecstasy can lower sexual inhibitions. However, men generally cannot get erections when they are high but are often very sexual when the effects of the drug begin to fade. Men who use ecstasy are 2.8 times more likely to have unprotected sex than nonusers ("Ecstasy: Happiness Is," 2000).

Some young men, in an attempt to enhance sexual functioning, are mixing recreational drugs such as cocaine, poppers, and ecstasy with Viagra, a prescription medication for erectile problems (see Chapter 14). The combination of ecstasy and Viagra, often called "Sextasy," "Trail Mix," and "Hammerheading," has gotten the attention of public health officials worldwide, resulting in increased efforts to warn about the dangers of drug use and the combining of drugs. This mixing is very dangerous; lowered blood pressure, heart attacks, or death may occur.

The use of methamphetamine, often referred to as "crystal," "Christina," or "Tina," is increasingly becoming associated with casual sex (Carey & O'Connor, 2005). In New York, for instance, methamphetamine has gained popularity among gay club-hoppers. A study of gay men who had attended a circuit party in the past year found that over one third had used methamphetamine during circuit-party weekends (Mansergh et al., 2001). A study of 1,011 heterosexual men found that recent meth users were more likely to have a casual or anonymous sex partner, have a female partner who injected drugs, or have ever received money or drugs for sex from a male or female partner (Centers for Disease Control and Prevention, 2006b). Prized as an aphrodisiac and a long-lasting stimulant, methamphetamine can be snorted, inhaled, swallowed, or injected. The sharp increase in sexual interest caused by crystal use can lead to dangerous behavior. And methamphetamine use may increase the user's susceptibility to HIV infection by suppressing the immune system (Casey & O'Connor, 2005).

Aside from the adverse physical effects of drugs themselves, their use has begun to be associated with greater risk for acquiring STIs, including HIV infection (Foxman, Sevgi, & Holmes, 2006). Addiction to cocaine, especially crack cocaine, has led to the widespread practice of bartering sex for cocaine. This practice, as well as the practice of injecting cocaine or heroin, combined with the low rate of condom use, has led to epidemics of STIs, including AIDS, in many urban areas. (For additional information on drugs and HIV, see Chapter 16.)

The use of recreational drugs has become an all too common part of the party scene.

Sexuality and Disability

A wide range of disabilities and physically limiting conditions affect human sexuality, yet the sexual needs and desires of those with disabilities have generally been overlooked and ignored. Certainly, a disability or chronic condition does not inevitably mean the end of a person's sexual life (Owens & Tepper, 2007). In 1987, Ellen Stohl, a young woman who uses a wheelchair, created a controversy by posing seminude in an eight-page layout in *Playboy*. Some people (including some editors at *Playboy*) felt that the feature could be construed as exploitive of people with disabilities. Others, Stohl among them, believed that it would help normalize society's perception of individuals who are disabled. She said, "I realized I was still a woman. But the world didn't accept me as that. Here I am a senior in college [with] a 3.5 average, and people treat me like I'm a 3-year-old" (quoted in Cummings, 1987). Though Stohl's layout in *Playboy* occurred over two decades ago, even today we rarely see media depictions of people living with disabilities or chronic illness as having sex lives (Kaufman, Silverberg, & Odette, 2003).

A study involving 367 men and 381 women (average age 36 years) who had a physical disability investigated the association between the severity and duration of physical disability and sexual esteem, sexual depression, sexual satisfaction, and the frequency of sexual activity. Researchers found that people with more severe physical impairments experienced less sexual esteem and sexual satisfaction and more sexual depression than those having a mild impairment or no impairment. Individuals having the more severe physical disabilities engaged less frequently in sexual experiences with others. Women with physical disabilities had more positive feelings about their sexuality and more frequent sexual episodes with others than their male counterparts (McCabe & Taleporos, 2003).

Physical Limitations and Changing Expectations

"I get the feeling people think that because I am in a chair there is just a blank space down there."

—Anonymous quote in the book *The Ultimate Guide to Sex and Disability*

Many people are subject to sexually limiting conditions for some or all of their lives. These conditions may be congenital, appearing at birth, such as cerebral palsy (a neuromuscular disorder) and Down syndrome (a developmentally disabling condition). They may be caused by a disease such as diabetes, arthritis, or cancer or be the result of an accident, as in the case of spinal cord injuries.

In cases in which the spinal cord is completely severed, for example, there is no feeling in the genitals, but that does not eliminate sexual desires or exclude other possible sexual behaviors. Many men with spinal cord damage are able to have full or partial erections; some may ejaculate, although the orgasmic feelings accompanying ejaculation are generally absent. Nearly 40% of quadriplegic men are able to experience orgasm and ejaculation (Ducharme & Gill, 1997). Those who are not capable of ejaculation may be able to father a child through electroejaculation sperm retrieval and intrauterine insemination of the man's partner. In this procedure, the prostate gland is electrically stimulated through the rectum, causing erection and ejaculation. Many women with spinal cord damage injuries are able to have painless childbirth, although forceps delivery, vacuum extraction, or cesarean section may be necessary.

Women with spinal cord injuries generally do not experience orgasm, although they are able to experience sensuous feelings in other parts of their

All individuals, including those with physical limitations, have a need for touch and intimacy.

bodies. People with spinal cord injuries (and anyone else, for that matter) may engage in oral or manual sex—anything, in fact, they and their partners find pleasurable and acceptable. They may discover new erogenous areas of their bodies, such as their thighs, necks, ears, or underarms. A study by The Kinsey Institute for Research in Sex, Gender, and Reproduction at Indiana University of 186 people (140 men and 46 women) with spinal cord injuries revealed that the injury affected masturbation, coitus, noncoital sex, sexual response during sleep, and fertility (Donohue & Gebhard, 1995). Within 3 years of the injury, however, 95% of the women (excluding three who were virgins) and 90% of the men had resumed sexual intercourse.

To establish sexual health, people with disabilities must overcome previous sexual function expectations and realign them with their actual sexual capacities. A major problem for many people with disabilities is overcoming the anger or disappointment they feel because their bodies don't meet the cultural "ideal." They often live in dread of rejection, which may or may not be realistic, depending on whom they seek as partners. Many people with disabilities have rich fantasy lives. This is fortuitous because imagination is a key ingredient to developing a full sex life. Robert Lenz, a consultant in the field of sexuality and disability, received a quadriplegic (paralyzed from the neck down) spinal cord injury when he was 16 (Lenz & Chaves, 1981). In the film *Active Partners,* he says:

> One thing I do know is that I'm a much better lover now than I ever was before. There are a lot of reasons for that, but one of the biggest is that I'm more relaxed. I don't have a list of do's and don'ts, a timetable or a proper sequence of moves to follow, or the need to "give" my partner an orgasm every time we make love. Sex isn't just orgasm for me; it's pleasuring, playing, laughing, and sharing.

Educating people with physical limitations about their sexuality and providing a holistic approach that includes counseling to build self-esteem and combat negative stereotypes are increasingly being recognized as crucial issues by the medical community. Important tasks of therapists working with people with disabilities are to give their clients "permission" to engage in sexual activities that are appropriate to their capacities and to suggest new activities or techniques (Kaufman, Silverberg, & Odette, 2003; Kolodny, Masters, & Johnson, 1979). Researchers suggest that nonpenetrative sexual behaviors should be affirmed as valid and healthy expressions of the individual's or couple's sexuality, recognizing that the men might feel a stronger desire than women for genitally focused activities such as oral sex or nude cuddling and that women may have a stronger desire for deep kissing (McCabe & Taleporos, 2003). Clients should also be advised about the use of vibrators, artificial penises and vaginas, and other aids to sexual excitement. Certainly, with proper information and sexual self-esteem, people with disabilities can have full and satisfying sex lives.

Vision and Hearing Impairment

Loss of sight or hearing, especially if it is total and has existed from infancy, presents many difficulties in both the theoretical and the practical understanding of sexuality. A young person who has been blind from birth is unlikely to know what a person of the other sex actually "looks" (or feels) like. Children who are deaf often do not have parents who communicate well in sign language; as a result, they may not receive much instruction about sexuality at home, nor are they likely to understand abstract concepts such as "intimacy." Older individuals who experience significant losses of sight or hearing may become depressed, develop low self-esteem, and withdraw from contact with others. Because they don't receive the visual or auditory cues that most of us take for granted, people with hearing or vision impairments may have communication difficulties within their sexual relationships. These difficulties often can be overcome with education or counseling, depending on the circumstances. Schools and programs for children who are sight- and hearing-impaired offer specially designed curricula for teaching about sexuality.

Chronic Illness

Diabetes, cardiovascular disease, and arthritis are three of the most prevalent diseases in America. Although these conditions are not always described as disabilities, they may require considerable adjustments in a person's sexuality because they (or the medications or treatments given to control them) may affect libido, sexual capability or responsiveness, and body image. Many older partners find themselves dealing with issues of disease and disability in addition to those of aging.

There may be other disabling conditions, too numerous to discuss here, that affect our lives or those of people we know. Some of the information presented here may be applicable to conditions not specifically dealt with, such as multiple sclerosis or postpolio syndrome. We encourage readers with specific questions regarding sexuality and chronic diseases to seek out networks, organizations, and self-help groups that specialize in those issues.

Diabetes **Diabetes mellitus,** commonly referred to simply as diabetes, is a chronic disease characterized by an excess of sugar in the blood and urine, due to a deficiency of insulin, a protein hormone. About 24 million people in the United States, or nearly 8% of the population, have diabetes (Centers for Disease Control and Prevention, 2007c). Nerve damage or circulatory problems caused by diabetes can cause sexual problems. Men with diabetes are often more affected sexually by the disease than are women. Some men with diabetes experience erectile problems, although there is apparently little or no relationship between the severity of the diabetes and the erectile difficulty. Heavy alcohol use and poor blood-sugar control also increase the risk of erectile problems.

Diabetes can affect a woman's sexuality as well. Some women with diabetes may have less interest in being sexual because of frequent yeast infections. High blood-sugar levels can make some women feel tired, resulting in reduced sexual interest. Also, intercourse may be painful because of vaginal dryness (American Diabetes Association, 2001).

Cardiovascular Disease   Obviously, a heart attack or stroke is a major event in a person's life, affecting important aspects of daily living. Following an attack, a person often enters a period of depression in which the appetite declines, sleep habits change, and there is fatigue and a loss of libido. There is often an overwhelming fear of sex based on the belief that sexual activity might provoke another heart attack or stroke. The partners of male heart attack patients also express great concern about sexuality. They are fearful of the risks, concerned over sexual difficulties, and apprehensive about the possibility of another attack during intercourse. Most people can start having sex again 3 to 6 weeks after their condition becomes stable following an attack, if the physician agrees (National Institute on Aging, 2008a). In general, the chance of a person with a prior heart attack having another one during sex is no greater than that of anyone else.

Arthritis   About 1 in 5 Americans has some type of arthritis, most of them older women, but the disease may afflict and disable children and adolescents as well. Arthritis is a painful inflammation and swelling of the joints, usually of the knees, hips, and lower back, which may lead to deformity of the limbs. Sometimes, the joints can be moved only with great difficulty and pain; sometimes, they cannot be moved at all. Arthritis is a leading cause of disability in Americans and the third leading cause of work limitation in the United States (Lethbridge-Cejku, Schiller, & Bernadel, 2004; National Institutes of Health, 1997). The cause of arthritis is not known.

Sexual intimacy may be difficult for people with arthritis because of the pain. Oral sex, general pleasuring of the body, and creative sexual positioning have definite advantages for those with arthritis. Applying moist heat to the joints prior to sexual activity with a partner can help.

Developmental Disabilities

Developmental disabilities are severe, lifelong chronic conditions attributable to mental and/or physical impairments that manifest themselves before the age of 22 years and result in major lifestyle limitations. People with developmental disabilities most often have problems with major life activities such as language, mobility, learning, self-help, and independent living (U.S. Department of Health & Human Services, 2008a). The sexuality of those who are developmentally disabled has only recently been widely acknowledged by those who work with them. The capabilities of individuals with developmental disabilities vary widely. People with mild or moderate disabilities may be able to learn to behave appropriately, protect themselves from abuse, and understand the basics of reproduction. Some may manage to marry, work, and raise families with little assistance.

Sexuality education is extremely important for adolescents who have developmental disabilities. Some parents may fear that this will "put ideas into their

LAMENT OF A CORONARY
My doctor has made a prognosis
That intercourse fosters thrombosis,
But I'd rather expire fulfilling desire
Than abstain, and suffer neurosis.

—Anonymous

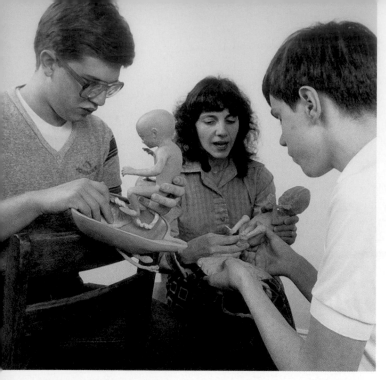

heads," but it is more likely, given the combination of explicit media and Internet images and the effects of increased hormonal output, that the ideas are already there. It may be difficult or impossible to teach more severely affected people how to engage in safe sexual behaviors. There is ongoing debate about the ethics of mandatory birth control or sterilization for those who are developmentally disabled. These issues are especially salient in cases in which there is the chance of passing the disability genetically to a child.

The Sexual Rights of People With Disabilities

Although many of the concerns of people with disabilities are becoming more visible through the courageous efforts of certain groups and individuals, much of their lives still remains hidden. By refusing to recognize the existence and concerns of those with physical and developmental limitations, the rest of us do a profound disservice

Children with physical or developmental disabilities may have special needs when it comes to sexuality education. Here, students with visual impairments take a hands-on approach to learning about pregnancy and childbirth with the help of lifelike models.

to our fellow human beings—and, ultimately, to ourselves. The United Nations General Assembly (1993) noted that states "should promote their [persons with disabilities] rights to personal integrity and ensure that laws do not discriminate against persons with disabilities with respect to sexual relationships, marriage, and parenthood." The federal Developmental Disabilities Assistance and Bill of Rights Act of 2000 explicitly states that individuals with intellectual disability have the fundamental right to engage in meaningful relationships with others (Matich-Maroney, Boyle, & Crocker, 2007; U.S. Department of Health and Human Services, 2000).

Though the majority supports the right of consenting adults to have access to sexuality education and a sexual life, few acknowledge the needs and rights of those with disabilities to have the same.

The sexual rights of persons with disabilities should be the same as those for persons without disabilities and include the following:

- The right to sexual expression
- The right to privacy
- The right to be informed about and have access to needed services, such as contraceptive counseling, medical care, genetic counseling, and sex counseling
- The right to choose one's marital status
- The right to have or not have children
- The right to make one's own decisions and develop to one's full potential

Sexuality and Cancer

Cancer is not a single disease; it is more than 300 distinct illnesses that can affect any organ of the body. These various cancers grow at different speeds and have different treatment success and failure rates. Most cancers, but not all (e.g., leukemia), form solid tumors.

All cancers have one thing in common: They are the result of the aberrant behavior of cells. Cancer-causing agents (carcinogens) are believed to jumble up the messages of the DNA within cells, causing the cell to abandon its normal functions. Tumors are either benign or malignant. **Benign tumors** usually are slow growing and remain localized. **Malignant tumors,** however, are cancerous. Instead of remaining localized, they invade nearby tissues and disrupt the normal functioning of vital organs. The process by which the disease spreads from one part of the body to another, unrelated, part is called **metastasis.** This metastatic process, not the original tumor, accounts for the vast majority of cancer deaths.

Women and Cancer

Because of their fear of breast cancer and cancer of the reproductive organs, some women avoid having regular breast examinations or Pap tests. If a woman feels a lump in her breast or her doctor tells her she has a growth in her uterus, she may plunge into despair or panic. These reactions are understandable, but they are also counterproductive. Most lumps and bumps are benign conditions, such as uterine fibroids, ovarian cysts, and fibroadenomas of the breast.

Breast Cancer Excluding cancers of the skin, breast cancer is the most common cancer among women, accounting for slightly more than 1 out of every 4 cancers diagnosed in American women (National Cancer Institute, 2007). After lung cancer, breast cancer is the second leading cause of death in women. About 182,460 women were found to have invasive breast cancer in 2008, with about 40,000 dying from the disease. The chance of dying from breast cancer is about 1 in 35 (American Cancer Society, 2008a). The chance of a woman having invasive breast cancer sometime during her life is about 1 in 8. There are about 2.5 million breast cancer survivors in the United States. Even though the incidence of breast cancer has increased over the past decade, breast cancer deaths have declined probably because of earlier cancer detection, improved treatment, and decreased use of menopausal hormone therapy in older women. Nearly 89% of women diagnosed with cancer survive at least 5 years after diagnosis, 81% at least 10 years, and 73% at least 15 years (American Cancer Society, 2007a, 2008a; Brewster et al., 2008).

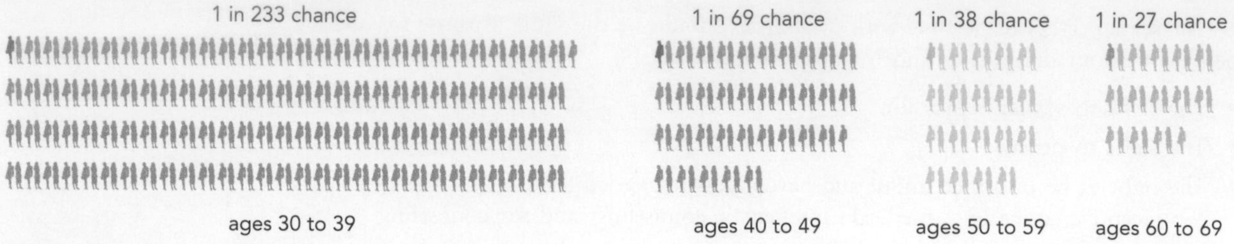

| 1 in 233 chance | 1 in 69 chance | 1 in 38 chance | 1 in 27 chance |
| ages 30 to 39 | ages 40 to 49 | ages 50 to 59 | ages 60 to 69 |

● **FIGURE 13.3**

Chance of Women Developing Breast Cancer by Age. (*Source:* "Breast Cancer Risk" by Marcy E. Mullins, *USA Today*, January 27, 2007. Reprinted by permission.)

Breast cancer is about 100 times more common in women than in men. Several factors increase a woman's risk for developing breast cancer. Some of these factors cannot be altered, while others can be affected by changes in lifestyle. Simply being a woman who is aging increases the risk, and two thirds of breast cancer in women occurs in those aged 55 and older; the disease is not common before menopause. The risk of breast cancer in women gradually increases with age, as shown in Figure 13.3 (National Cancer Institute, 2007; Rubin, 2007). Women who have had breast cancer have an increased risk of getting breast cancer again.

About 20–30% of women with breast cancer have a family history of breast cancer. White women have a slightly greater risk for developing breast cancer than African American women, although African American women are more likely to die from breast cancer. Asian, Hispanic, and American Indian women have a lower risk of both developing and dying from breast cancer than White women. The risk is higher when the biological relationship of the affected relative is closer—that is, a woman's risk of breast cancer is higher if her mother, sister, or daughter had breast cancer, particularly if the family member got breast cancer before age 40. Within the group of women with a family history of breast and/or ovarian cancer, a relatively small subset have inherited two genetic mutations. About 5–10% of breast cancer cases result from these gene changes. However, women with these gene changes have up to an 80% chance of breast cancer during their lives (American Cancer Society, 2008a; National Cancer Institute, 2007).

Having had certain types of abnormal biopsy results may increase a woman's risk of developing breast cancer. Women who had cancer in one breast have an increased chance of getting cancer in the other breast or in a different part of the same breast. Women who have had no children, had fewer children, or had their first child after age 30 have a slightly greater chance of developing breast cancer than women who had children at a younger age. Higher risk also is associated with an increased amount of time a woman's body is exposed to estrogen, such as for women who started menstruating at an early age (before age 12) or experienced menopause late (after age 55). Other factors implicated in increased risk for breast cancer include long-term estrogen-plus-progestin hormone therapy (see Chapter 7 on menopausal hormone therapy), not breastfeeding, alcohol use, obesity and dense breast tissue, earlier breast radiation, physical inactivity, and environmental pollution. Studies have shown that current users of oral contraceptives have a slightly higher risk than women who have never used them, but women who stopped using them more than 10 years ago do not seem to have the increased risk (American Cancer Society, 2008a). Studies have failed to show a link between breast cancer and breast implants, previous abortions, stillbirths, smoking, night work, or bruising, bumping, or touching the breast (American Cancer Society, 2008a; Bardia, 2006; Michels, Xue, Colditz, & Willet, 2007; National Cancer Institute, 2007). Of course, having a risk factor does not always indicate that a woman will develop breast cancer.

Table 13.1 ● **American Cancer Society Guidelines for the Early Detection of Breast Cancer in Average-Risk, Asymptomatic Women**

Ages 40 and older

- Annual mammogram
- Annual clinical breast examination
- Monthly breast self-examination (optional)

Ages 20–39

- Clinical breast examination every 3 years
- Monthly breast self-examination (optional)

SOURCE: American Cancer Society. (2007). *Breast cancer facts and figures 2007–2008*. Atlanta, GA: ACS.

Lesbian Women and Breast Cancer   No epidemiological data exist indicating that lesbian women are at increased risk for breast cancers (or other cancers). Studies, however, have shown a greater prevalence of certain risk factors in lesbian women, such as higher rates of alcohol usage, increased chances of being overweight, lower rates of breast cancer screening, and less likelihood of having children (Cochran et al., 2001; Institute of Medicine, 1999; Kavanaugh-Lynch, White, Daling, & Bower, 2002), suggesting that lesbian women may be at greater risk of breast cancer than women who are not lesbian. One study comparing lesbian and heterosexual women found that slightly more than twice as many of the heterosexual women regularly practiced breast self-examination (BSE) (45% to 21%), with about one third of both groups never or rarely practicing BSE. Heterosexual women were found to get gynecological examinations more regularly. Having an annual gynecological examination may be an important motivator to practice BSE because of the reminder and encouragement to perform BSE that occurs during the examination (Ellingson & Yarber, 1997).

Detection   The American Cancer Society (ACS) provides guidelines for early detection of breast cancer (American Cancer Society, 2007a). The screening recommendations, listed in Table 13.1, present guidelines for average-risk, asymptomatic women ages 40 or older and 20–39. Women at increased risk (e.g., having family history, genetic tendency, past breast cancer) should talk with their doctors about the benefits and limitations of starting **mammography** screening earlier, having additional tests (i.e., breast ultrasound and magnetic resonance imaging), or having more frequent exams. Mammography is the use of X-rays to detects breast tumors before they can be seen or felt.

Early detection is an important part of preventive care. The earlier breast cancer is found, the better the chances that treatment will be effective and the breast can be saved. The goal is to discover cancer prior to symptoms appearing. Most physicians believe that early detection of breast cancer saves thousands of lives yearly (American Cancer Society, 2008a). Mammography-screened breast cancers are associated with reduced morbidity and mortality, and most women who participate in screening will not develop breast cancer in their lifetime. Harm may occur in women who undergo a biopsy for abnormalities that are not breast cancer. This is why the American College of Physicians recommends that women aged 40 to 49 consult with their doctors before undergoing routine mammography. The group

Breast Self-Examination

Breast lumps are often discovered by a woman or her sex partner. You should become familiar with the way your breasts normally look and feel. That way you will be more likely to notice any changes.

Some women use breast self-exams (BSEs) to get to know their breasts. If you would like to learn how to do a BSE, your clinician can teach you. The best time for a BSE is a few days after your period, when your breasts are not swollen or tender. Lumps are also noticed during day-to-day activities such as showering or sex play. Most lumps are not cancerous. But report anything unusual to your clinician as soon as possible.

Three Positions for Breast Self-Exam

1. Lying down with a pillow or folded towel under your right shoulder, place your hand behind your head. Examine every part of your right breast using the pads of three middle fingers of your left hand to feel for lumps, bumps, or thickening. Move from spot to spot on your breast using a straight up-and-down pattern. Press each spot using a small, circular motion. Use three levels of pressure on each spot: light for the breast tissue near the surface, medium for the tissue underneath, and firm for the tissue closest to the ribs. Switch positions and feel the left breast with your right hand, making sure to examine all parts using the up-and-down pattern.

2. Standing up in front of a mirror, place your hands on your hips. Look at each breast for changes in size, shape, and form.

3. Standing up, raise your right arm slightly to the side and examine the underarm with your left hand. Feel for lumps, bumps, or thickening in the same way as you examined your breasts. Repeat with the other underarm.

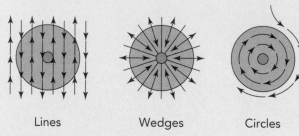

Lines   Wedges   Circles

Using any one of these patterns, be sure to check the entire breast, underarm area, and upper chest.

SOURCE: Reprinted with permission from Planned Parenthood® Federation of America, Inc. © 2009 PPFA. All rights reserved.

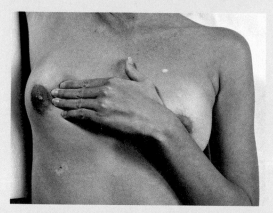

Breast examination is more effective when specific steps are followed. Any new symptoms should be promptly reported to a health-care provider.

says that the benefits of mammography have to be weighed against the risk of false-positives, which often lead to repeated exams and biopsies causing anxiety and possible disfigurement (Qaseem et al., 2007). The ACS made the new recommendations in consideration of the benefits, limitations, and harms associated with screening.

A few studies have questioned the value of screening mammography, but the ACS report presents data showing that mammograms save lives, thus strengthening the ACS's stance that mammograms reduce the risk of dying from breast cancer by one fourth (Rubin, 2003b). A report in the *New England Journal of Medicine* (Berry et al., 2005) concluded that, on average, nearly one half of the sharp decrease in breast cancer deaths from 1990 to 2000 was due to mammogram screening; the rest of the decrease was attributed to new powerful drugs for breast cancer treatment. Mammography is the single most effective method of early detection (American Cancer Society, 2007a). However, a recent study found declining use of mammography among women aged 40 and older, possibly because an increasing number of women are uninsured, lack access to adequate screening facilities, or are complacent (Centers for Disease Control and Prevention, 2007d).

Because a large majority of tumors are detected by women themselves, a heightened awareness of her normal breast composition can help a woman to notice changes and, when necessary, seek early medical attention. **Breast self-examination (BSE)** is an option for women in their 20s and 30s. The American Cancer Society (2008a) says that it is alright for women not to do BSE or to do it once in a while. Research has shown that BSE plays a slight role in discovering breast cancer compared with finding a breast lump by chance or just being aware of what is normal for each woman. (The steps in doing BSE are described in the "Practically Speaking" box on the previous page.) Women who have breast implants can also do BSE. These women should have their surgeon help them identify the edges of the implant so that they can know what they are feeling (American Cancer Society, 2008a).

It is important to recognize that most breast lumps—75–80%—are *not* cancerous. Many disappear on their own. Of lumps that are surgically removed for diagnostic purposes (biopsied), 80% prove to be benign. Most are related to **fibrocystic disease** (a common and generally harmless breast condition, not really a disease at all), or they are fibroadenomas (round, movable growths, also harmless, that occur in young women). Because some benign breast lumps can increase a woman's chance of developing breast cancer, it is important that any breast lumps be checked by a health-care provider.

Treatment   Most women with breast cancer undergo some type of surgery to remove the primary tumor. Other reasons for surgery include finding out whether the cancer has spread to the lymph nodes under the arm, restoring the breast's appearance, and relieving symptoms of advanced cancer. Common breast cancer surgeries described by the American Cancer Society (2008a) include the following (see Figure 13.4):

- *Lumpectomy.* This procedure involves the removal of only the breast lump and some normal tissue around it.
- *Partial (segmental) mastectomy.* This surgery involves the removal of more of the breast tissue than with a lumpectomy.

Christina Applegate, an award-winning actress, became an advocate for breast cancer education and research after being diagnosed with breast cancer.

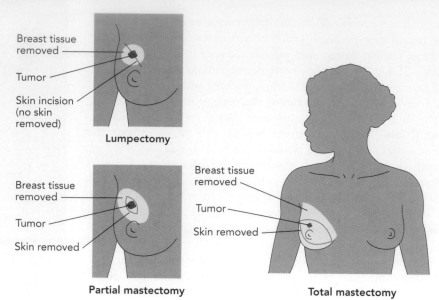

- *Simple or total mastectomy.* This operation involves the removal of the entire breast, but not the lymph nodes from under the arm or muscle tissue from beneath the breast.
- *Modified radical mastectomy.* This surgery involves the removal of the entire breast and some of the lymph nodes under the arm. This is the most common breast cancer surgery.
- *Radical mastectomy.* This operation involves the removal of the entire breast, lymph nodes, and chest wall muscles under the breast. Because the modified radical mastectomy has proved to be just as effective, with less disfigurement and fewer side effects, radical mastectomy is rarely done now.

Surgery may also be combined with other treatments such as chemotherapy, hormone therapy, or radiation therapy.

Sometimes, women must choose between lumpectomy and mastectomy. The American Cancer Society (2007a) suggests that, for most women with stage I or stage II breast cancer (stages are I–IV, from least to most serious), lumpectomy or partial mastectomy is as effective as mastectomy; the survival rates of women treated with these two approaches are no different. An advantage of lumpectomy is that it preserves the way the breast looks. A downside is the need for many weeks of radiation treatment after the surgery. However, some women who have a mastectomy will still need radiation treatment (American Cancer Society, 2008a). Lumpectomy is not an option for all women. A woman's physician can provide information on which surgery is best (American Cancer Society, 2008a).

For women choosing mastectomy, research has found that more women with cancer in one breast are choosing to have both breasts removed. In 2003, 11% of women having a mastectomy in one breast opted to also have the unaffected breast removed; this more than doubles the rate from 1998 (Tuttle, Habermann, Grund, Morris, & Virnig, 2007). Knowledge of one's inherited risk and of the increased chance of getting a separate occurrence of cancer in the unaffected breast may contribute to this trend. In addition, many women may feel reassured knowing that breast reconstructive surgery has improved.

Surviving cancer can deepen one's appreciation of life. Notice the tattoo along this woman's mastectomy scar.

Other treatments for cancer are external radiation and chemotherapy. The female hormone, estrogen, promotes the growth of breast cancer cells in some women. For these women, several methods, including the use of the drug tamoxifen, can block the effects of estrogen or lower its levels (American Cancer Society, 2008a).

An analysis of 194 studies involving 145,000 women in two dozen countries provided good news about long-term survival for women with breast cancer, finding that standard chemotherapy and treatment that blocks the effects of estrogen worked better in reducing death rates from breast cancer than expected (Early Breast Cancer Trialists' Collaborative Group, 2005). The analysis found that for middle-aged women with an early-stage breast cancer, combining the treatments can halve the risk of death for at least 15 years. Another finding may help allay a common fear of drug treatment: The delayed side effects of tamoxifen or chemotherapy might be so deadly that the woman would be trading breast cancer for another cause of death. The research found this not to be the case; the increased risk of death linked to the drugs was only 0.2% (Grady, 2005).

Sexual Adjustment After Treatment Sexuality is one aspect of life that may be profoundly altered by cancer. Women with breast cancer often have worrisome concerns about sexuality. Psychologically, the loss of a breast may symbolize for her the loss of sexuality; she may feel scarred and be fearful of rejection because breasts in America are such primary sexual symbols. Besides affecting her body image, some breast cancer treatments can change a woman's hormone levels and may affect sexual interest and response. Some women continue to enjoy being touched around the area of surgery, whereas others do not and even may not enjoy being touched on the unaffected breast. However, breast surgery or radiation does not physically decrease sexual desire in a woman, nor does it decrease her ability to have sexual intercourse and orgasm. Many women with early-stage breast cancer have adjusted well within their first year (American Cancer Society, 2008a). Realizing that there are alternative ways of expressing one's sexuality can be valuable. The woman and her partner can decide what is satisfying and pleasurable. Being comfortable with her sexuality can enhance self-esteem, improve personal comfort, and make coping with cancer easier.

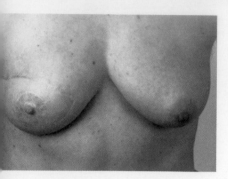

For some women, breast reconstruction is chosen as one step in recovering from a mastectomy.

The American Cancer Society (2008a) provides several suggestions for staying sexually healthy after being treated for cancer. To learn these suggestions, go to the "How About My Sexuality" page at http://cancer.org.

Breast Reconstruction and Breast Implant Surgery   Because breast cancer is sometimes treated by surgical removal of the breast, the subject of breast reconstruction—literally, building a new breast—is one of paramount interest to many women (and those who care about them).

In 1978, the total number of American women who had undergone breast reconstruction was 15,000. Today, due to sophisticated plastic surgery and the fact that most insurance companies are willing to provide coverage for it, breast reconstruction is undertaken by more than 57,000 women annually, typically after mastectomies. Most women who have had a mastectomy can have breast reconstruction therapy. However, women who have had a lumpectomy usually do not need reconstruction. No studies have shown that reconstruction causes a recurrence of breast cancer (American Cancer Society, 2007b; American Society of Plastic Surgeons, 2008).

For some women, reconstruction is an important step in recovering from breast cancer. Depending on a woman's age, general health, type of tumor, and individual preference, breast reconstruction may be performed at the same time as mastectomy or several months (or longer) afterward. A saline-filled implant that has an external silicone shell filled with sterile saline (salt water) is the most common implant. Silicone gel-filled implants are also an option, although they are not used as frequently as saline implants because of past concerns that silicone leakage might cause immune system disease. However, most recent research has found that implants do not increase the risk of immune system diseases (American Cancer Society, 2007b).

During reconstructive surgery or in a subsequent operation, the surgeon may also attach a nipple fashioned out of skin from the labia, inner thigh, inside of the mouth, or other tissue. If there are no cancerous cells in it, the woman's own nipple sometimes can be saved ("banked") by temporarily attaching it to another part of the body, such as the inner thigh, and moving it to the new breast after reconstruction. Other times, a tattoo can be used to create the illusion of a nipple.

Deciding about breast reconstruction involves many issues, and a woman should become fully informed about the procedure. For example, the feeling of pleasure from fondling the breast and nipple is typically decreased, but the reconstruction may provide the woman with increased feelings of wholeness and attractiveness. A woman should be realistic about what to expect from reconstruction—it does not fix things that the person was unhappy with before the surgery.

Cervical Cancer and Cervical Dysplasia   **Cervical dysplasia,** also called **cervical intraepithelial neoplasia (CIN),** squamous intraepithelial lesion (SIL), and dysplasia, is a condition of the cervical epithelium (covering membrane) that *may* lead to cancer if not treated. If cancer develops, it usually takes several years, but sometimes it happens in less than a year. For most women, CIN will remain unchanged and will go away without treatment (American Cancer Society, 2008b). Because cervical dysplasia is confined to the cervix, it is nearly 100% treatable. However, recent research highlights the need to go for continuing screening following treatment for CIN (Kalliala, Anttila, Pukkala, & Nieminen, 2005). Approximately 15% of sexually active teenage girls show evidence of CIN (Strider, 1997).

The more advanced and dangerous malignancy is invasive cancer of the cervix (ICC), also called **cervical cancer.** The American Cancer Society (2008b) estimated over 10,000 new cases of invasive cervical cancer in 2008 and that nearly 3,900 women would die from this disease. The most important risk factor for cervical cancer is infection by the sexually transmitted human papillomavirus (HPV), although most women with HPV do not get cervical cancer as the infection usually goes away without any treatment. Additional risk factors include age (the average age for cervical cancer diagnosis is 50–55), HIV infection (which makes women more vulnerable to HPV), chlamydia infection, poor diet, many sex partners, a mother who was given diethylstilbestrol (DES) during pregnancy, sexual intercourse before age 18, long-term use of birth control pills, cigarette smoking, family history, and low socioeconomic status. Some lesbian women are at risk for cervical cancer, as many report a history of having had heterosexual intercourse (Institute of Medicine, 1999). When detected and treated in its early stages, the disease is both prevented from spreading to other organs and cured. Unusual discharge or bleeding from the vagina may be a sign of cervical cancer (American Cancer Society, 2008b).

In June 2006, the U.S. Food and Drug Administration approved a vaccine that would protect thousands of women each year from cervical cancer. The vaccine, the world's first cancer vaccine and a major medical advance toward protecting women's health, works by preventing infection by four of the numerous strains of the human papillomavirus, or HPV, the most common sexually transmitted infection (see Chapter 15). Two of the strains the vaccine blocks cause 70% of cervical cancers, and the other two strains cause 90% of genital warts. The vaccine also protects against vaginal and vulvar cancers linked to the four strains of HPV. The vaccine, called Gardasil, has been approved for girls and women, but not boys. It works best when given before girls begin having sex, although girls and women aged 9 to 26 are the target recipients. The vaccine does not protect those already infected; hence, public health officials want the vaccine given to girls prior to their first sexual intercourse. The vaccine requires three injections in a 6-month period. However, because it does not protect against all cancer-causing types of HPV, Pap tests are still important (American Cancer Society, 2008b; Bridges, 2006; Harris, 2006). Not all people approve of this vaccination for young people. For example, a recent study of public opinion of adults in a midwestern state showed that only one quarter favored requiring the HPV vaccination for both middle school girls and boys. (The HPV vaccination has not yet been approved for boys.) Study participants believing that the vaccination would encourage sex were nearly three times more likely to oppose requiring HPV vaccination in middle schools (Milhausen, Crosby, & Yarber, 2008).

Detection: The Pap Test   The most reliable means of early detection of cervical cancer is the **Pap test** (or Pap smear). This is a simple procedure that can not only detect cancer but also reveal changes in cells that make them precancerous. A Pap test can warn against cancer even before it begins, and the use of the Pap test has resulted in dramatic decreases in cervical cancer deaths in the United States. The importance of the Pap test is shown by the fact that 60–80% of American women with newly diagnosed invasive cervical cancer have not had a Pap test in the past 5 years, and many have never had a Pap test, particularly older, African American, and low-income women (American Cancer Society, 2005c). Analysis of cervical screening records of 348,419 British women found that, for every 100,000 women, 10 deaths could be avoided by annual Pap tests (Raffle, Alden, Quinn, Babb, & Brett, 2003).

The Pap test is usually done during a pelvic exam and takes about a minute. Cell samples and mucus are lightly scraped from the cervix and examined under a microscope. If anything unusual is found, the physician will do further tests. Women should have a Pap test annually unless their physician recommends otherwise. Unfortunately, the test is not as effective in detecting cancer in the body of the uterus, which occurs in women most frequently during or after menopause.

The American Cancer Society (2008b) offers the following guidelines for early detection of precancerous changes of the cervix:

- All women should begin screening for cervical cancer about 3 years after they begin having penile-vaginal intercourse, but no later than age 21. Screening should be done every year using the regular Pap test and every 2 years using the newer, liquid-based Pap test.

- Starting at age 30, women having 3 normal Pap test results in a row may get screened every 2–3 years. Women having certain risk factors, such as HIV infection or a weakened immune system, should have a Pap test each year.

- Another option for women over age 30 is to get screened every 3 years with a Pap test and the HPV DNA test. Health-care professionals can now test for certain types of HPV that are most likely to cause cervical cancer by searching for pieces of their DNA in cervical cells. The sample is collected in a way similar to the one used with the Pap test.

- Women aged 70 and older who have had 3 or more normal Pap tests in a row and no abnormal Pap test results in the previous 10 years may choose to stop having cervical cancer screening. Women with a history of cervical cancer, or who have certain other risk factors, should continue screening.

- Women who have had their uterus and cervix removed (total hysterectomy) may also choose to stop having cervical cancer screening unless the surgery was done as a treatment for cervical cancer or precancerous lesion. Women who have had a simple hysterectomy without the cervix being removed should continue to follow the preceding guidelines.

To make the Pap test more accurate, women should not schedule the appointment for a time during their menstrual period, and for 48 hours prior to the test, they should not douche, have intercourse, or use tampons, birth control foams, jellies, or other vaginal creams or vaginal medications.

Treatment   Cervical dysplasia is very responsive to treatment in its early stages. With an abnormal Pap smear, a **biopsy**—surgical removal of tissue for diagnosis— may be performed. Some abnormalities clear up on their own, so the physician may not do the biopsy right away but do a follow-up smear in several months. The British study cited previously also concluded that there is only a 1-in-80 chance that a woman will develop cervical cancer following an abnormal cervical screening (Raffle et al., 2003). There may be some risk in delaying treatment, however. If the cervix shows visible signs of abnormality, a biopsy should be performed at once. Sometimes, conization, the removal of a cone of tissue from the center of the cervix, is performed. This procedure is time-consuming and requires hospitalization. Depending on the extent and severity of the dysplasia and whether it has progressed to cancer, other treatment options range from electrocauterization (or cryosurgery) to laser surgery, radiotherapy, or hysterectomy. The 5-year survival rate for the earliest stage of cervical cancer is 92%; for all stages combined, it's 72% (American Cancer Society, 2008b).

Ovarian Cancer Ovarian cancer is the eighth most common cancer in women (excluding skin cancer) and is the fourth-ranked cause of cancer death in women. The American Cancer Society (2008c) estimated that there were about 22,430 new cases of ovarian cancer in the United States in 2007 and that about 15,280 women will die from the disease. Ovarian cancer is slightly more common in White women than African American women. The odds of a woman getting ovarian cancer during her lifetime are about 1 in 71. The risk of getting ovarian cancer and dying is 1 in 95. Evidence links pregnancy, breastfeeding, tubal ligation or hysterectomy, and use of oral contraceptives with a lower risk of ovarian cancer, perhaps because each gives the woman a rest from ovulation and eases wear and tear on the ovaries. Factors that increase risk include age (about two thirds of all ovarian cancers are found in women over 55), use of the fertility drug clomiphene citrate, more monthly periods, a family history of ovarian cancer, not having children, estrogen replacement therapy, smoking and alcohol use, breast cancer, obesity, and poor diet. Ovarian cancer is hard to diagnose because there are no symptoms in the early stages; it is not usually detectable by a Pap test. Diagnosis is done by pelvic examination and needle aspiration (removal of fluid) or biopsy. Treatment involves surgical removal of the tumor and ovary, often followed by radiation or chemotherapy. Follow-up care is especially important. If ovarian cancer is found early, the chances of survival are much greater. Though ninety percent of women will survive at least 5 years if the cancer is found and treated before it has spread outside the ovary, only one quarter of ovarian cancers are found at this stage (American Cancer Society, 2008c). Because many lesbian women are not likely to have children, they may be at increased risk for ovarian cancer (Institute of Medicine, 1999).

Uterine Cancer Slightly more than 40,000 new cases of cancers of the uterus were estimated for 2008, with about 7,400 women in the United States dying from uterine cancer. More than 95% of cancers of the uterus involve the endometrium, the lining of the uterus. Certain women appear more at risk for developing endometrial cancer than others. Obesity, certain types of estrogen replacement therapy, treatment with tamoxifen, infertility, diabetes, menstruation before age 12, and menopause after age 52 are risk factors for endometrial cancer (American Cancer Society, 2008d).

Hysterectomy The surgical removal of the uterus is known as a **hysterectomy.** Hysterectomy is the second most frequent major surgical procedure among reproductive-age women, with about 600,000 performed each year. An estimated 20 million U.S. women have had a hysterectomy. Hysterectomy rates are the highest in women aged 40–44 years. More than one fourth of U.S. women will have a hysterectomy by the time they are 60 years old (Whiteman et al., 2008). A simple hysterectomy removes the uterus and the vagina remains entirely intact, and a radical hysterectomy involves the removal of the upper part of the vagina and adjacent tissues. The ovaries and fallopian tubes are not removed unless there is some other medical reason to do so (American Cancer Society, 2008d). Certain conditions make a hysterectomy necessary: (1) when a cancerous or precancerous growth cannot be treated otherwise, (2) when noncancerous growths on the uterus become so large that they interfere with other organs (such as when they hinder bladder or bowel functions) or cause pain or pressure, (3) when bleeding is so heavy that it cannot be controlled or when it leads to anemia, and/or (4) when severe infection cannot be controlled in any other way. If a woman's physician recommends a hysterectomy, she should have the opinion confirmed by a second physician. A hysterectomy is performed by removing the uterus surgically through the vagina or through an abdominal incision. At the same time, there may be an **oophorectomy,** removal of one or both ovaries, because of endometriosis, cysts, or tumors. If both ovaries are removed from a premenopausal woman, she may begin hormone supplement therapy to control the symptoms caused by the lack of estrogen.

A radical hysterectomy does not alter a woman's ability to feel sexual pleasure. A woman does not need a uterus or cervix to have an orgasm. Actually, in a study of more than 1,100 Maryland women aged 35–49 who had a hysterectomy, the women reported increased libido; sexual activity, enjoyment, and orgasm; and relief from painful intercourse (Rhodes, Kjerulff, Langenberg, & Guzinski, 1999).

Removal of the ovaries can result in lowered libido because testosterone (the sex-drive hormone) is mainly produced there. Furthermore, the absence of ovarian estrogen can cause menopausal symptoms such as vaginal dryness and thinning of the vaginal walls. Therapy and self-help groups for posthysterectomy patients can be very useful for women who wish to increase sexual desire and pleasure. Most women who have had a hysterectomy are satisfied with the results.

Vaginal Cancer   Vaginal cancer is rare, accounting for only about 2–3% of the cancers of the female reproductive system, although some cancers start in other organs (such as the uterus or bladder) and spread to the vagina. The American Cancer Society (2008e) estimated that there were about 2,210 new cases of vaginal cancer in the United States in 2008, with about 760 women dying from this cancer. Although the exact cause of most vaginal cancers is not known, established risk factors include age (over two thirds of women are 60 or older at the time of diagnosis), mother's use of DES when pregnant, HPV infection, previous cervical cancer, and smoking. Symptoms include abnormal vaginal bleeding, vaginal discharge, a mass that can be felt, and pain during intercourse. Treatment options, based on the type of cancer and the stage of the disease when diagnosed, are surgery, radiation, and chemotherapy in combination with radiation for advanced disease. New surgical operations for repairing the vagina after radical surgery are being developed (American Cancer Society, 2008e).

In September 2008, the U.S. Food and Drug Administration approved the HPV vaccine Gardasil to also protect against vaginal and vulvar cancers (Barclay, 2008). Vaginal and vulvar cancers in young women are often linked to HPV infection (see the cervical cancer section of this chapter). Research involving over 18,000 women found that Gardasil was as effective in preventing vaginal and vulvar cancers as it is in protecting against cervical cancer (Joura et al., 2007).

Men and Cancer

Generally, men are less likely than women to get regular checkups and to seek help at the onset of symptoms. This tendency can have unfortunate consequences where reproductive cancers are concerned, because early detection can often mean the difference between life and death. Men should pay attention to what goes on in their genital and urinary organs.

Prostate Cancer   Prostate cancer is the most common form of cancer (excluding skin cancer) among American men; it causes the second highest number of deaths among men diagnosed with cancer (lung cancer is first). Of all men diagnosed with cancer each year, more than one fourth have prostate cancer. The American Cancer Society (2008f) estimated that there were about 186,320 new cases of prostate cancer in the United States in 2008, with about 28,660 deaths. About 10% of cancer-related deaths in men are from prostate cancer. One man in 6 will get prostate cancer during his lifetime, but only 1 man in 35 will die from this disease. The mortality rate from prostate cancer is decreasing. More than 2 million men in the United States are survivors of prostate cancer.

Risk factors for prostate cancer include aging, a family history, being African American, a high-fat diet, obesity, and nationality; prostate cancer is more common in North America and northwestern Europe than in Asia, Africa, Central America, and South America. For reasons still unknown, African American men are more likely to have prostate cancer, have a more advanced disease when it is found, and die from it than men of other races. Prostate cancer occurs less frequently in Asian American and Hispanic/Latino men than in non-Hispanic White men. About two thirds of prostate cancers are found in men over age 65. Some research suggests that high levels of testosterone may increase a man's chance of having prostate cancer. Some early studies suggested that men who had a vasectomy were at a slightly greater risk for prostate cancer. However, more recent studies have not shown any increased risk among men who have had this procedure (American Cancer Society, 2005g, 2008f).

Some researchers have tried to find a relationship between risk for prostate cancer and ejaculation frequency. A longitudinal study of 29,342 men from the National Cancer Institute revealed that high ejaculations frequency—21 or more ejaculations per month—was related to decreased risk of prostate cancer. Each increment of an increase of 3 ejaculations per week across a lifetime was associated with a 15% decrease in risk of prostate cancer. The study also found that ejaculation frequency was not related to increased risk of prostate cancer (Leitzmann, Platz, Stampfer, Willet, & Giovannucci, 2004). For example, lower ejaculation frequency was not related to increased risk. Interestingly, high ejaculation frequency may actually decrease the concentration of carcinogens that accumulate in prostate fluid. Frequent ejaculations are, however, associated with lower sperm counts (but not sperm motility or morphology), one factor in male infertility (Carlsen, Petersen, Anderson, & Shakkebaek, 2004).

Detection Various symptoms may point to prostate cancer, a slow-growing disease, but often there are no symptoms or symptoms may not appear for many years. Although the symptoms listed below are more likely to indicate prostatic enlargement or benign tumors than cancer, they should never be ignored. By the time symptoms do occur, the cancer may have spread beyond the prostate. When symptoms do occur, they may include

- Weak or interrupted flow of urine
- Inability to urinate or difficulty in beginning to urinate
- Difficulty holding back urine
- Frequent need to urinate, especially at night; bed-wetting
- Urine flow that is not easily stopped
- Painful or burning urination
- Difficulty in having an erection
- Painful ejaculation

- Blood in urine or semen
- Continuing pain in lower back, pelvis, or upper thighs

Most often, these symptoms are not due to cancer, but they may be caused by cancer or less serious health problems (National Cancer Institute, 2005).

One step in diagnosing prostate cancer is to have a physician conduct a digital rectal exam (DRE). By inserting a gloved, lubricated finger into the rectum, the physician can usually feel an irregular or unusually firm area on the prostate that may indicate a tumor. If the physician discovers a suspicious area, he or she will then run a battery of tests, including X-rays, urine and blood analyses, and biopsy.

A blood test, called the **prostate-specific antigen (PSA) test,** can be used to help diagnose prostate cancer although research shows that PSA misses some early prostate cancers (Thompson et al., 2004). This test is more accurate than previous methods in detecting prostate cancer, but levels of PSA can be elevated in men with a benign condition called prostatic hyperplasia. Ultrasound is often used as a follow-up to the PSA test to detect lumps too small to be felt. A needle biopsy of suspicious lumps can be performed to determine if the cells are benign or malignant. The DRE and PSA tests together are better than either test alone in detecting prostate cancer. Health-care providers should offer both the DRE and PSA yearly, beginning at age 50 to men who have at least a 10-year life expectancy. Men at high risk for prostate cancer should have tests before age 50 (American Cancer Society, 2008f).

Since the use of early-detection tests became more common beginning in about 1990, the prostate cancer death rate has decreased. But it has not been proved that this drop was the direct result of screening. Some research has shown that many, and probably most, tumors discovered during the screenings are so small and slow growing that they are unlikely to do any harm to patients. Prostate cancer develops slowly over many years, and most cases are not life threatening. Other research has shown that when dangerous tumors are found, the mortality rates are usually the same among men who had regular screenings and those who did not see a physician until they developed symptoms. However, if a young man gets prostate cancer it will probably shorten his life if it is not caught early. For an older man or one in poor health, prostate cancer may never become a major problem because it often grows so slowly. No major scientific or medical organizations in the United States (including the American Cancer Society) advocate routine testing for prostate cancer at this time. Actually, the U.S. Preventive Services Task Force recommended in August 2008 that men aged 75 and older not be screened for prostate cancer because the risks of screening cause more harm than good. Men diagnosed with prostate cancer after age 75 more often die of other causes, and treatment can cause complications such as erectile problems and urinary incontinence (U.S. Preventive Services Task Force, 2008). Health-care providers should discuss the option of testing with their male patients, pointing out the potential benefits, side effects, and unresolved issues regarding early prostate cancer detection and treatment (American Cancer Society 2008f).

Treatment   Ninety-one percent of all prostate cancers are detected while they are still in the prostate or nearby area, and the 5-year survival rate for these cancers is nearly 100%. Including all stages and grades of prostate cancer, about 99% of men diagnosed with prostate cancer survive at least 5 years, 92% survive at least 10 years, and 61% survive at least 15 years. The death rates in men with localized prostate cancer are nearly the same as the 5- and 10-year survival rates in men without prostate cancer. For the 6% of men whose cancer has already spread to other parts of the body, the 5-year survival rate is 34% (American Cancer Society, 2003, 2008f).

Depending on the stage of the cancer, treatment may include surgery, hormone therapy, radiation therapy, and chemotherapy. If the cancer has not spread beyond the prostate gland, all or part of the gland is removed by surgery. Radical surgery has a high cure rate, but it often results in incontinence and erectile difficulties. An alternative to removal of the prostate is "watchful waiting," in which men do not have any treatment, such as surgery or radiation therapy, immediately after cancer diagnosis but are closely followed by their physicians to see if their tumors begin to grow and advance. Because prostate cancer often spreads slowly, some men may never need treatment. The premise of watchful waiting is that cases of localized cancer may advance so slowly that they are unlikely to cause men, especially older men, any health problems during their lifetime. Hence, the best candidates for watchful waiting are older men whose tumors are small and slow growing. A study of 900 older men with early-stage prostate cancer found that they were not taking a big risk by keeping an eye on their disease rather than immediately treating it. Ten years later, only 10% of the men who chose to delay or skip treatment had died of prostate cancer. The vast majority of men were alive without significant worsening symptoms or had died of other causes. Further, 30% who were eventually treated were able to delay the treatment for an average of 11 years (Marchione, 2008). Therefore, the American Cancer Society (2008f) said that at this time "watchful waiting is a reasonable option for some men with slow-growing cancers because it is not known if active treatment helps them live longer."

Sensitive sex counseling should be an integral part of treatment for men who have had prostrate cancer surgery. The American Cancer Society (2006b) also recommends the use of erection-enhancing drugs—Viagra, Levitra, or Cialis—for those who experience erection difficulties after surgery. These drugs will not work, however, if important nerves are removed or damaged during surgery. Further, some men who retain the ability to become erect on their own experience retrograde ejaculation (see Chapter 4) and are infertile because semen does not pass out of the urethra.

Since the exact cause of prostate cancer is unknown, it is not possible to prevent most cases of the disease. But some cases might be prevented. The American Cancer Society (2008f) suggests eating less red meat and fat and eating more vegetables, fruits, and whole grains, which may also lower one's risk for some other types of cancer and diseases. Recent research found that men taking the drug finasteride (Proscar) were 25% less likely to get prostate cancer than men taking a placebo. However, the men taking the drug who did get prostate cancer were more likely to have cancers that looked like they might grow and spread. Further, the men taking the drug were more likely to have side effects, including decreased sex drive and erection difficulties, yet have fewer urinary problems. The American Cancer Society (2008f) states that at this time it is unknown if taking finasteride to lower risk of prostate cancer is wise or not. The ACS says that the results of the study will become more clear over the next few years.

Testicular Cancer According to the American Cancer Society (2008g), about 8,090 new cases of testicular cancer were estimated to be diagnosed in 2008, with an estimated 380 deaths. The chance of a man developing testicular cancer in his lifetime is about 1 in 300. Because treatment is very successful, the risk

> *Oh, to be seventy again [at the age of 91, upon seeing a young woman].*
>
> —Oliver Wendell Holmes, Sr. (1809–1894)

Testicular Self-Examination

Some doctors believe that a man increases the chances of early cancer detection by performing a monthly testicular self-exam. It is important that you know what your own testicles feel like normally so that you'll recognize any changes. The best time to perform the examination is after a warm shower or bath, when the scrotum is relaxed.

1. Stand in front of a mirror and look for any swelling on the scrotum.

2. Hold the penis out of the way and examine each testicle separately. With your thumb on top of the testicle and two fingers underneath, gently roll the testicle to check for lumps or areas of particular firmness. A normal testicle is smooth, oval, and uniformly firm to the touch. Don't worry if your testicles differ slightly in size; this is common. And don't mistake the epididymis, the sperm-carrying tube at the rear of the testicle, for an abnormality.

3. If you find any hard lumps or nodules, or if there has been any change in shape, size, or texture of the testicles, consult a physician. These signs may not indicate a malignancy, but only your physician can make a diagnosis.

Testicular self-examination can enhance a man's familiarity with his genitals.

SOURCE: From Fahey, T., Insel, P., & Roth, W. (2000). *Fit and well: Core concepts and labs in physical fitness and wellness.* Copyright © 2000 by The McGraw-Hill Companies, Inc. Reprinted with permission.

of dying from this cancer is 1 in 5,000. The exact cause of most cases of testicular cancer is unknown, but risk factors include age (9 out of 10 cases occur between the ages of 20 and 54), undescended testicle(s), a family history of testicular cancer, HIV infection, cancer of the other testicle, and ethnicity. A man who has had cancer in one testicle has about a 3% chance of developing cancer in the other testicle. This is usually a new cancer. The risk of developing testicular cancer in the United States is 5 times greater for White men than for African American men and more than 3 times that for Asian American and American Indian men. The risk for Hispanics is between the risks for Asians and non-Hispanic Whites (American Cancer Society, 2008g).

Detection Most cases of testicular cancer can be found at an early stage. The first sign of testicular cancer is usually a painless lump or slight enlargement and a change in the consistency of the testicle. In 90% of testicular cancer cases, the man has a lump on a testicle or notices that the testicle is swollen. Some types of testicular cancers have no symptoms until the advanced stage. Although the tumors that grow on the testes are generally painless, there is often a dull ache in the lower abdomen and groin, accompanied by a sensation of dragging and heaviness. If the tumor is growing rapidly, there may be severe pain in the testicles. Because of the lack of symptoms and pain in the early stage, men often do not go to a doctor for several months after discovering a slightly enlarged testicle.

The examination of a man's testicles is a valuable part of a general physical examination, and the American Cancer Society includes testicular examination in its recommendations for routine cancer-related checkups. Whether a man should perform a regular testicular self-examination is debated, though. The American Cancer Society believes that it is important to make men aware of testicular cancer and to remind them that any testicular mass should be immediately evaluated by a physician. Some doctors recommend monthly testicular self-examination by all men after puberty. The American Cancer Society believes that for men with average testicular cancer risk there is no medical evidence to suggest that monthly examination is any more effective than simple awareness and prompt medical attention. However, whether to perform this examination is a decision best made by each man. Men with certain risk factors, such as previous testicular cancer or a family history, should consider monthly self-examinations and discuss the issue with their doctor (American Cancer Society, 2008g). Sometimes, ultrasound and blood tests are used as diagnostic tools for testicular cancer.

Treatment   Testicular cancer is a highly treatable form of cancer. The three main methods of treatment are surgery, radiation therapy, and chemotherapy. After the affected testicle is removed, an artificial one may be inserted in the scrotal sac. Radiation treatment or chemotherapy may follow. The success of treatment for testicular cancer has been highlighted by the athletic achievements of Lance Armstrong. Following treatment for testicular cancer, he won more Tour de France bicycle races than anyone else—a record-breaking seven consecutive years, 1999 to 2005.

The success rate of testicular cancer treatment is highlighted by the achievements of Lance Armstrong. Following treatment for testicular cancer he won the Tour de France a record-breaking seven years in a row.

Although the cure rate for all types of testicular cancer is very high (provided the disease has not widely metastasized), the man's fertility is often a major concern. Researchers in Norway examined 1,433 men living in Norway diagnosed with testicular cancer between 1980 and 1994 to assess paternity among longtime survivors of testicular cancer. After receiving cancer treatment, 554 had attempted conception: 15% were successful within 15 years without the use of frozen semen and 76% were successful within 20 years. Of men who had the affected testicle removed, 92% fathered a child, but only 48% of the men who received high doses of chemotherapy had fathered a child. Despite these findings, the researchers noted that sperm preservation still should be offered to all patients who will have testicular cancer treatment (Brydoy et al., 2005). Sperm banks and support groups may be helpful resources for some men and their partners when the man's own sperm cannot be preserved before he receives cancer treatment.

Penile Cancer   Cancer of the penis affects only 1 out of every 100,000 men in the United States. The American Cancer Society (2008h) estimated that about 1,250 new cases of penile cancer were diagnosed in 2008, with an estimated 290 deaths from it. Although it is very rare in North America and Europe, it is more common in parts of Africa and South America, where it accounts for up to 10% of cancers in men. Risk factors include HPV infection, smoking, having AIDS, being treated for psoriasis with ultraviolet light and a drug called psoralen, and age (nearly two thirds of cases are diagnosed in men over 65). For reasons not entirely clear, men who are circumcised as babies have less than half the chance of getting cancer of the penis than those who were not. Being circumcised later, as an adult, does not lower the risk of penile cancer.

Many cases of penile cancer can be detected early on. Men should be alert to any unusual growths on or other abnormalities of the penis. If such changes occur, men should promptly consult a physician. Treatment options include surgery, radiation, and chemotherapy. Most early-stage penile cancers can be completely cured by fairly minor surgery: with little or no damage to the penis. Removal of all or part of the penis is rare, except for late-stage cancer. Adult

Female Genital Cutting: Mutilation or Important Custom?

In nearly 30 African countries, some parts of Asia, and the Middle East, and among certain immigrant communities in North American and Europe, female infants, girls, or young women may undergo female genital cutting (FGC). An estimated 100 to 140 million girls and women in the world are estimated to have undergone FGC, 3 million each year, or 6,000 each day. In the late 1970s, several international organizations, including the World Health Organization, began using the term "female genital mutilation" to refer to this act, emphasizing that the act violates girls' and women's human rights. The United Nations Children's Fund and the United Nations Population Fund use the less judgmental expression "female genital mutilation/cutting" (World Health Organization, 2008). For the sake of this discussion, we will use the less judgmental female genital cutting as well.

One type of FGC is clitoridectomy, or female circumcision: having their clitoris slit or cut out entirely and all or part of their labia sliced off. The sides of their vulvas or their vaginal openings may be stitched together—a process called infibulation—leaving only a tiny opening for the passage of urine and menstrual blood. These surgeries are generally performed in unsanitary conditions, with a knife, a razor, or even a tin can lid or piece of broken glass, without medical anesthesia; antiseptic powder or concocted pastes may be applied. FGC has no known health benefits. On the contrary, the effects of the devastatingly painful operations include bleeding, infections, infertility, scarring, the inability to enjoy sex, and, not uncommonly, death. Upon marriage, a young woman may experience considerable pain and bleeding as the entry to the vagina is reopened by tearing her flesh. In childbirth, the old wounds must be reopened surgically, or tearing will result. Women who have undergone FGC and their babies are more likely to die during childbirth (Eke & Nkanginieme, 2006; World Health Organization, 2008).

This ancient custom, practiced mainly in Africa, is difficult for outsiders to understand. Why would loving parents allow this to be done to their defenseless daughter, and even hold her down during the procedure? As with many other practices (including male circumcision in our own culture), the answer is "tradition." The surgery is practiced for several reasons including as a way of controlling women's sexuality, and for many women, FGC does impair sexual enjoyment. Yet a study of 1,836 Nigerian women found no

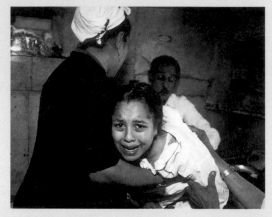

Female genital cutting is common in many African, Asian, and Middle Eastern countries.

difference in the frequency of sex and coital orgasm in women having undergone female genital cutting and those not having done so (Okonofua, Larsen, Oronsaye, Snow, & Slanger, 2002).

Progress has been made in curtailing FGC throughout the world. For example, it has been banned in at least 16 African countries. However, strongly held customs are hard to change, and there are still many places where it continues. In 2008, ten United Nations agencies called for the global elimination of FGC within a generation and a major reduction by 2015 (World Health Organization, 2008).

Think Critically

- Should female genital cutting be eliminated worldwide, or should it be permitted in countries where it is an important custom?
- Which is the better term: female genital cutting or female genital mutilation? Why?
- Does FGC violate the human rights of girls and women? If so, in what ways? If not, why not?

men can lower their risk of penile cancer by avoiding the things that are known to increase the risk. However, the American Academy of Pediatrics does not recommend routine circumcision of newborns for medical reasons. Decisions about circumcision are highly personal, often depending more on social and religious factors than on medical evidence (American Cancer Society, 2008h).

Male Breast Cancer Breast cancer is about 100 times less common among men than among women. The lifetime risk of a man getting breast cancer is 1 in 1,000. However, an estimated 1,990 new cases of breast cancer were diagnosed in men in the United States in 2008, with about 450 deaths (American Cancer Society, 2008i). As is the case for women, most breast disorders in men are benign. Known risk factors include aging (the average age is about 67 at diagnosis), family history of breast cancer for both male and female blood relatives, heavy alcohol use, inheritance of BRCA2 gene mutation (responsible for some breast cancers in women), Klinefelter's syndrome, radiation exposure, liver disease, physical inactivity and obesity, and estrogen treatment (for prostate cancer, for example). Symptoms of possible breast cancer include a lump or swelling of the breast, skin dimpling or puckering, nipple retraction (turning inward), redness or scaling of the nipple or breast skin, and discharge from the nipple. Diagnosis involves clinical breast examination, mammography, ultrasound, nipple discharge examination, and biopsy. Male breast cancer is treated with surgery, radiation therapy, and chemotherapy. The survival rate is very high following early-stage detection. Survival rates are about the same for both men and women when looking at each stage of breast cancer (American Cancer Society, 2008i).

Anal Cancer in Men and Women

Anal cancer is fairly uncommon, although the number of cases has been increasing for many years. The American Cancer Society (2008j) estimated that about 5,070 new cases of anal cancer were diagnosed in 2008, with about 680 deaths. Women get anal cancer slightly more often than men. Anal cancer is mainly found in adults older than 50. Risk factors include HPV infection, having numerous lifetime sex partners, history of receptive anal intercourse particularly under age 30, HIV infection, and smoking. Pain in the anal area, change in the diameter of the stool, abnormal discharge from the anus, and swollen lymph glands in the anal or groin areas are the major symptoms of anal cancer. Bleeding occurs in more than half of the cases of anal cancer and is usually the first sign of the disease. The digital rectal examination for prostate cancer will find some cases of rectal cancer. Like many other cancers, surgery, radiation therapy, and chemotherapy are the major treatments for anal cancer (American Cancer Society, 2008j).

● Additional Sexual Health Issues

In this section, we discuss two disorders of the female reproductive system, toxic shock syndrome and endometriosis, as well as some other sexual health issues. Sexually transmitted infections and related problems are discussed in Chapters 15 and 16.

Toxic Shock Syndrome

Toxic shock syndrome (TSS) is caused by the *Staphylococcus aureus* bacterium, a common agent of infection. This organism is normally present in the body

Vulvodynia: A Little-Known Condition

- Remains an unrecognized and underresearched medical condition among women.
- The incidence and prevalence have been understudied.
- Is often misdiagnosed as a chronic yeast infection, sexually transmitted infection, or a psychological problem.
- Pain may last for weeks and months.
- Intercourse may be uncomfortable at times, although many women with this condition maintain active sex lives.
- The genitals itch, burn, and are sore—nothing seems to relieve the pain for long.

These descriptions may characterize genital pain called **vulvodynia**—a condition that many women have, yet they are often reluctant to mention to their doctors. Among women who see gynecologists, the prevalence of vulvodynia may be as high as 15%. Many women with chronic vulvar pain do not seek medical help (Harlow & Steward, 2003).

The International Society for the Study of Vulvovaginal Disease defines vulvodynia as "discomfort or pain, characterized by burning, stinging, irritation or rawness of the female genitalia of which there is no infection or skin disease of the vulva or vagina causing these symptoms." The unexplained vulvar pain makes this condition particularly frustrating for the woman and her health-care provider, and any sexual partner. The pain may be continuous or occasional and may last for months and years; but the pain can vanish as suddenly or mysteriously as it started. The causes of vulvodynia are still unknown. Sexual risk taking is rare in patients who have vulvodynia, and few patients have a history of STIs. Vulvodynia is not a sign of cancer.

A woman experiencing pain in her genital area should discuss it with her doctor and consider asking for a referral to a gynecologist or dermatologist. At this time, there is no "cure" for vulvodynia. There are treatments that can partially or totally alleviate symptoms, but no single treatment works all the time or is best for every woman.

Vulvodynia can have a major impact on a woman's quality of life, often affecting her ability to engage in sexual activity and daily functioning such as sitting, walking, exercising, and participating in social activities (Ayling & Ussher, 2008; National Vulvodynia Association, 2008). Often, women experience anger and anxiety because of these problems and because of the lack of a definitive cause. One way to help cope with the condition is to find out more information, such as checking out the Web site of the National Vulvodynia Association (http://www.nva.org) and reading books that discuss vulvodynia such as *The Vulvodynia Survival Guide* (Glazer and Gae, New Harbinger Publishers, 2002) and *The V Book: A Doctor's Guide to Complete Vulvovaginal Health* (Stewart and Spencer, Bantam Books, 2002). Also, some women with vulvodynia have found a support group valuable (e.g., http://www.vulvodyniasupport.com).

and usually does not pose a threat. Tampons, especially the superabsorbent type, or other devices that block the vagina or cervix during menstruation apparently lead to the creation of an ideal culture medium for the overgrowth of staph bacteria. Women of all ages can get TSS, but teenage girls and women under age 30 are at higher risk because they may not have developed antibodies to the disease. TSS can occur in men—for example, from skin wounds and surgery—but it is uncommon.

The risk of developing TSS is quite low; after the initial epidemic in the late 1970s and early 1980s, the number of reported cases decreased significantly. The rate is estimated to be 3 to 4 cases per 100,000 menstruating women (Schlievert, cited in Roan, 2005). The U.S. Food and Drug Administration (2003) advises all women who use tampons to reduce the already low risk by carefully following the directions for insertion, choosing the lowest-absorbing one for their flow, changing the tampon at least every 4 to 8 hours, alternating pads with tampons, and not using tampons between periods.

TSS can be treated effectively if it is detected. The warning signs are sudden fever (102°F or higher), diarrhea, vomiting, fainting or nearly fainting when standing up, and/or a sunburnlike rash. Early detection is critical; otherwise,

TSS can be fatal. Women should talk with their health-care provider about any new information regarding prevention.

Endometriosis

Endometriosis is one of the most common gynecological diseases; it affects at least 5.5 million women in the United States. Endometriosis involves the growth of endometrial tissue (uterine lining) outward into the organs surrounding the uterus. Between 2% and 10% of women of reproductive age are estimated to have endometriosis. Endometriosis can affect any menstruating woman from the time of her first period to menopause, regardless of whether she has had children, her race or ethnicity, and her socioeconomic status. The exact cause of endometriosis has not been identified. About 30–40% of women with endometriosis are infertile, making it among the top three causes of infertility in women.

Symptoms of endometriosis include pain (usually pelvic pain, which can be very intense), very painful cramps or periods, heavy periods, intestinal pain, pain during or after sex, and infertility. Some women do not have symptoms and may not find out they have the disease until they have trouble getting pregnant. It is usually diagnosed by imaging tests (e.g., ultrasound) to produce a picture of the inside of the body or by laparoscopic examination. Prompt treatment is crucial if endometriosis is suspected. There is currently no cure for endometriosis, but there are ways to minimize the symptoms caused by the condition, and endometriosis-related fertility often can be treated successfully using hormones and surgery (National Institute of Child Health and Human Development, 2007).

Lesbian Women's Health Issues

Research specifically focused on lesbian women did not begin until the 1950s. Then the origins of sexual orientation and the psychological functioning of lesbian women were major topics of study. During the 1970s, studies on lesbian women as psychologically healthy individuals emerged, and some of the research of the 1980s examined issues related to the development of lesbian women across their life span (Tully, 1995). It was found that lesbian women may be at higher risk than other women for uterine, breast, cervical, endometrial, and ovarian cancers because they are less likely to bear children; have higher rates of alcohol use, obesity, and poor nutrition; and are less likely to visit a health-care provider for routine screenings, such as a Pap test. And, as discussed in Chapter 15, some lesbian women are at risk for many of the same STIs as heterosexual women (National Women's Health Information Center, 2005).

In addition to many of the medical concerns shared by all women, lesbian women face other challenges. Several studies have shown that lesbian women encounter prejudice and discrimination when seeking health care (Mautner Project, 2005; Rankow, 1997). First, it may be assumed that they are heterosexual, leading to the inclusion of inappropriate questions, comments, or procedures and the exclusion of appropriate measures. Second, if they do disclose their orientation, they are likely to be treated with hostility—lesbian woman are more than twice as likely as heterosexual women to say they had bad experiences with health-care providers. As a result of these experiences, lesbian women are less likely than heterosexuals to seek health care. Thus, they may put themselves at higher risk for diseases that could be detected early on. Further, research has shown that lesbian and bisexual women report much lower rates of recent preventive health behaviors, rates that compare unfavorably to national rates for all women (Wells, Bimbi, Tider, Van Ora, & Parsons, 2006).

Prostatitis

Many of men's sexual health problems are related to STIs. One condition affecting men that is not sexually transmitted is **prostatitis,** the inflammation of the prostate gland. Researchers estimate that 10–12% of men experience prostatitis-like symptoms (McNaughton-Collins, Joyce, Wise, & Pontari, 2007). Men are more likely to develop prostatitis when they are young, even prior to age 40 (Mayo Clinic, 2007a).

Prostatitis is usually caused by bacteria found in the large intestines. Most often, acute prostatitis originates in the prostate, but occasionally the infection can spread from a bladder or urethral infection. Men infected with HIV are at greater risk for bacterial prostatitis, although it is not clear why. Symptoms of prostatitis include frequent and urgent need to urinate and pain or burning when urinating, often accompanied by pelvic, groin, or low-back pain. Prostatitis can be difficult to diagnose because the symptoms often are similar to those of other medical conditions such as bladder infections, bladder cancer, or prostate enlargement. No evidence exists indicating that having prostatitis increases the risk of prostate cancer. Digital rectal exam and urine and semen tests are used to diagnose prostatitis. Antibiotics and pain relievers are the main treatment for prostatitis; acute prostatitis may require a short hospital stay.

Prostatitis can affect fertility as it interferes with movement of sperm cells and may interfere with ejaculation. However, a man does not necessarily need to avoid sexual intercourse if he has prostatitis. Prostatitis is usually not made worse by sexual activity although, sometimes, men with prostatitis will experience pain during ejaculation or sexual intercourse. If sex is too painful, a man may consider abstaining from sexual activity until the prostatitis symptoms improve (Mayo Clinic, 2007a, 2007b).

Final Thoughts

In this chapter, we've explored issues of self-image and body image as they interact with our society's ideas about beauty and sexuality. We've considered the effects of alcohol and certain drugs on our sexuality. We've looked at physical limitations and disabilities and cancer and other health issues. Our intent is to give you information to assist you in personal health issues and to stimulate thinking about how society deals with certain aspects of sexual health. We encourage you to learn more about your own body and your own sexual functioning. If things don't seem to work right, if you don't feel well, or if you have questions, consult your physician or other health-care practitioner. If you're not satisfied, get a second opinion. Read about health issues that apply to you and the people you're close to. Because we live in our bodies, we need to appreciate and respect them. By taking care of ourselves physically and mentally, we can maximize our pleasures in sexuality and in life.

Summary

Living in Our Bodies: The Quest for Physical Perfection

- Our society is preoccupied with bodily perfection. As a result, *eating disorders* have become common, especially among young women. Eating disorders reduce a person's health and vigor; are carried out in secrecy; are accompanied by obsessions, depression, anxiety, and guilt; lead to self-absorption and emotional instability; and are characterized by a lack of control. Those with eating disorders may have a history of psychological or sexual abuse in childhood.

- *Anorexia nervosa* is characterized by an all-controlling desire for thinness. Those with anorexia, usually female teenagers, are convinced that their bodies are too large, no matter how thin they actually are. Sexual difficulties often accompany anorexia. Those with anorexia diet (and often exercise) obsessively. Anorexia is potentially fatal.

- *Bulimia nervosa* is characterized by episodes of un-controlled overeating (binge eating), counteracted by purging—vomiting, dieting, exercising excessively, or taking laxatives or diuretics.

- *Binge eating disorder* is similar to bulimia except that the purging does not occur.

- *Anabolic steroids,* used to enhance body appearance and athletic performance, can cause serious and permanent body damage.

Alcohol, Drugs, and Sexuality

- Drugs and alcohol are commonly perceived as enhancers of sexuality, although in reality this is rarely the case.

- Researchers are beginning to believe that alcohol use among young people is just one component of an overall risky health behavior pattern—not the cause of sexual risk behavior—and that other factors are powerful causes of risk.

- Some people use alcohol to give themselves permission to be sexual. Some men may use alcohol to justify sexual violence. People under the influence of alcohol or drugs tend to place themselves in risky sexual situations, such as exposing themselves to sexually transmitted infections.

Sexuality and Disability

- A wide range of disabilities and physical limitations can affect sexuality. People with these limitations need support and education so that they can enjoy their full sexual potential. Society as a whole needs to be aware of the concerns of people with disabilities and to allow them the same sexual rights as others have.

- Chronic illnesses such as diabetes, cardiovascular disease, and arthritis pose special problems with regard to sexuality. People with these diseases (and their partners) can learn what to expect of themselves sexually and how to best cope with their particular conditions.

Sexuality and Cancer

- Cancer (in its many forms) occurs when cells begin to grow aberrantly. Most cancers form tumors. *Benign tumors* grow slowly and remain localized. *Malignant tumors* can spread throughout the body. When malignant cells are released into the blood or lymph system, they begin to grow away from the original tumor; this process is called *metastasis.*

- Other than cancers of the skin, breast cancer is the most common cancer among women. Although the survival rate is improving, those who survive it may still suffer psychologically. *Mammograms* (low-dose X-ray screenings) are the principal methods of detection. Surgical removal of the breast is called *mastectomy;* surgery that removes only the tumor and surrounding lymph nodes is called *lumpectomy.* Radiation and chemotherapy are also used to fight breast cancer. The decision to undertake breast reconstruction involves many issues.

- *Cervical dysplasia,* or *cervical intraepithelial neoplasia (CIN),* the appearance of certain abnormal cells on the cervix, can be diagnosed by a *Pap test.* It may then be treated by *biopsy,* cauterization, cryosurgery, or other surgery. If untreated, it may lead to cervical cancer.

- New cases of ovarian cancer have been slowly decreasing since 1991. Pregnancy, breastfeeding, tubal ligation, and hysterectomy are considered factors that lower the risk of ovarian cancer.

- A new vaccine that guards against four strains of the STI human papillomavirus (HPV) that cause 70% of cervical cancer and 90% of genital warts is now available for girls and women. This vaccine works only if the girl or woman is not already infected with any of the four specific strains of HPV. The HPV vaccine was recently approved to also protect against vaginal and cervical cancers.

- Nearly all cancers of the uterus involve the endometrium, the lining of the uterus. Uterine cancer is treated with surgery (hysterectomy), radiation, or both.

- *Hysterectomy* is the surgical removal of the uterus. A hysterectomy is required when cancerous or precancerous growths cannot be treated with less invasive procedures, when noncancerous growths interfere with other organs, when heavy bleeding cannot be otherwise controlled, and when severe infection cannot be otherwise controlled. Other problems may sometimes require a hysterectomy. The removal of the ovaries *(oophorectomy)* will precipitate menopausal symptoms because the estrogen supply stops.

- Vaginal cancer represents only 2–3% of the cancers of the female reproductive system.

- Prostate cancer is the most common form of cancer among men, excluding skin cancer. If detected early, it has a high cure rate. One useful test is the *prostate-specific antigen (PSA) test.* Surgery, radiation, hormone therapy, and chemotherapy are possible treatments. If the entire prostate is removed, sterility results, and erectile difficulties may occur.

- Testicular cancer primarily affects young men aged 20–54. If caught early, it is curable; if not, it may be deadly. Self-examination is the key to detection; even slight symptoms should be reported at once.

- Penile cancer affects only 1 in 100,000 men in the United States, with most early-stage cancers being completely cured. Men can develop breast cancer, but this cancer is 100 times more common among women.

- Anal cancer is uncommon, although it has been increasing in both men and women in recent years.

Additional Sexual Health Issues

- *Toxic shock syndrome (TSS)* is a potentially fatal disease caused by the *Staphylococcus aureus* bacterium. The disease is easily cured with antibiotics if caught early.

- *Endometriosis* is the growth of endometrial tissue outside the uterus. It is a major cause of infertility. Symptoms include intense pelvic pain and abnormal menstrual bleeding. Treatment depends on a number of factors. Various hormone treatments and types of surgery are employed.

- Lesbian women are less likely to seek health care than heterosexual women, partly because they face hostility from health-care practitioners. Fear of discrimination may keep them from getting early diagnosis of serious diseases, such as breast cancer.

- *Prostatitis* is the inflammation of the prostate gland. Antibiotics and pain medications are the primary treatment for prostatitis. No evidence has been found that prostatitis increases the risk of prostate cancer. Prostatitis is usually not made worse by sexual activity.

Questions for Discussion

- Is there too much emphasis on body perfection in our society? Have you had friends who took extreme measures to make their body fit the cultural ideal? How have you dealt with pressure to have a certain body?

- Women, how comfortable are you in doing monthly breast self-examinations? Men, how comfortable are you doing monthly testicular examinations? If you feel uncomfortable, why do you think you feel that way? Have you ever discussed the need for self-examination with a friend or partner?

- Do many of your peers use alcohol as a "sexual lubricant" hoping that its use will lead to sexual activity? Do you know of individuals who regret being sexual because they were not able to make responsible decisions after drinking alcohol? What, in your opinion, is the role of alcohol in dating?

Sex and the Internet

Cancer and Sexuality

The American Cancer Society (ACS) has an extensive Web site that provides detailed information on prevention of and risk factors for, detection and symptoms of, and treatment for the various cancers, including those of the reproductive system. The impact of cancer of the reproductive structures on sexuality also is discussed. Go to the ACS Web site (http://www.cancer.org) to research this issue. After getting on the Web site, answer the following questions concerning a specific cancer:

- What are the risk factors for the cancer?
- How can the cancer be prevented?
- What are some of the methods used to treat this form of cancer?
- What are the sexuality-related outcomes of the cancer and its treatment?

Suggested Web Sites

Mautner Project
http://www.mautnerproject.org
Mautner Project, part of the National Lesbian Health Organization, educates lesbian women about their health and trains health-care providers about their lesbian women patients, providing tools and insights on how to achieve better health outcomes for lesbian women.

National Breast Cancer Coalition
http://www.stopbreastcancer.org
A grassroots advocacy organization that provides information on breast cancer and supports research, medical access, and influence.

National Eating Disorders Association
http://www.nationaleatingdisorders.org
An organization that is dedicated to providing education, resources, and support to those affected by eating disorders.

National Institutes of Health
http://www.nih.gov
Offers information on an array of health topics, including cancer.

National Women's Health Network
http://www.nwhn.org
Offers evidence-based, independent information about women's health issues online, by mail, and through an information clearinghouse.

ZERO—The Project to End Prostate Cancer
http://www.zerocancer.org
Contains information on prostate cancer, as well as outreach and advocacy information.

Suggested Reading

Journals with articles relevant to sexual health include *JAMA: Journal of the American Medical Association, New England Journal of Medicine,* and the British journal *Lancet.*

Elson, J. (2004). *Am I still a woman? Hysterectomy and gender issues.* Philadelphia: Temple University Press. A discussion of the interviews of 44 women who have had hysterectomies.

Kaufman, M., Silverberg, C., & Odette, F. (2007). *The ultimate guide to sexuality and disability* (2nd ed.). San Francisco: Cleis Press. A sex guide for people living with disabilities, chronic pain, and illness.

Kuczynski, A. (2006). *Beauty junkies: Inside our $15 billion obsession with cosmetic surgery.* New York: Doubleday. An analysis of the cosmetic surgery industry and its trends. The author talks of some of her own experiences.

Link, J. (2007). *The breast cancer survival guide: A step-by-step guide for the woman with newly diagnosed breast cancer* (4th ed.). New York: Holt Paperbacks. Written by a practicing internist and oncologist, a valuable guide for a woman who has just been diagnosed with breast cancer.

Newman, F. (2004). *The whole lesbian sex book.* San Francisco: Cleis Press. A comprehensive lesbian sex guide that provides information on sexuality as well as sexual health.

Silver, M. (2004). *Breast cancer husband: How to help your wife (and yourself) through diagnosis, treatment, and beyond.* New York: Rodale. A practical guide for men and women that combines information, wit, humor, and empathy.

For links, articles, and study material, go to the McGraw-Hill Web site, located at **www.mhhe.com/yarber7e.**

Sexual Function Difficulties, Dissatisfaction, Enhancement, and Therapy

14 chapter

MAIN TOPICS

Sexual Function Difficulties:
Definitions, Types, and Prevalence

Physical Causes of Sexual Function
Difficulties and Dissatisfaction

Psychological Causes of Sexual
Function Difficulties and
Dissatisfaction

Sexual Function Enhancement

Treating Sexual Function
Difficulties

"Sometimes my sexual desire gets so low that I will not be intimate with my girlfriend for a few weeks. And then there are times when sexual desire is so high that I can't control myself. Why is this?"

—19-year-old male

"My friend has a problem that seems to occur once every few months. He suddenly becomes not able to get erect. It seems like it happens very suddenly."

—18-year-old male

"I have not experienced any sexual dysfunctions. On the other hand, I have been with my boyfriend for three years and I only had two orgasms. I enjoy having sex with him even though I don't have an orgasm every time. Sometimes I'm really into it, but sometimes I'm not. I do sometimes feel like something is wrong, but I do feel it is normal and okay as long as I enjoy it. I guess I may be thinking about it too hard, but like I said, I enjoy it either way."

—21-year-old female

"When having a sexual experience with a new partner, I sometimes have a sense of guilt about past relationships. This can make performing in the new situation really difficult."

—21-year-old male

"I always had a really low sex drive with past boyfriends. I never understood why until I started dating my current boyfriend. The key is communication! We're open with each other and honest about what we like and dislike. Now my sex drive is through the roof!"

—20-year-old female

T HE QUALITY OF OUR SEXUALITY is intimately connected to the quality of our lives and relationships. Because our sexuality is an integral part of ourselves, it reflects our excitement and boredom, intimacy and distance, emotional well-being and distress, and health and illness. As a consequence, our sexual desires and activities ebb and flow. Sometimes, they are highly erotic; other times, they may be boring. Furthermore, many of us who are sexually active may sometimes experience sexual function difficulties or problems, often resulting in disappointment in ourselves, our partners, or both. Studies indicate that many men and women report occasional or frequent lack of desire, problems in arousal or orgasm, and pain during intercourse or noncoital sex. Even among well-functioning couples, less than one half of their sexual experiences have similar desire, arousal, and orgasm and up to 15% would be considered mediocre, unsatisfying, or failures. Yet, this is considered "normal" (McCarthy & McCarthy, 2003). (Later in this chapter, we discuss the prevalence and predictions of sexual function difficulties found in three nationally representative studies to illustrate the commonality of sexual problems.) The widespread variability in our sexual functioning suggests how "normal" at least occasional sexual difficulties are. Sex therapist Bernie Zilbergeld (1999) writes:

> Sex problems are normal and typical. I know, I know, all of your buddies are functioning perfectly and never have a problem. If you really believe that, I have a nice piece of oceanfront property in Kansas I'd like to talk to you about.

In this chapter, we look at several common sexual function difficulties, their causes, and ways to enhance your sexuality to bring greater pleasure and intimacy.

When sex is good, it's 10% of the relationship. When it is bad, it's 90%.

—Charles Muir

Sexual Function Difficulties: Definitions, Types, and Prevalence

Nearly all of the literature concerning sexual difficulties or problems with sexual functioning deals with heterosexual couples; thus, most of the discussion in this chapter reflects that bias. Unfortunately, too little research has been done on the sexual function difficulties of gay, lesbian, bisexual, or transgender individuals and couples. One study a number of years ago did find that heterosexual individuals, gay men, and lesbian women experience similar kinds of sexual function problems (Margolies, Becher, & Jackson-Brewer, 1988). However, further research is needed on sexual function difficulties among varied populations.

Defining Sexual Function Difficulties: Different Perspectives

The line between "normal" sexual functioning and a sexual difficulty or problem is not always clear. Enormous variation exists in levels of sexual desire and forms of expression, and these differences do not necessarily indicate any sexual function difficulty. It can be difficult to determine exactly when something is a sexual function problem, and so we must be careful in defining a particular sexual function difficulty as a problem. Some people have rigid and possibly unrealistic expectations for their own or their partner's sexual expression and may perceive something wrong with their behavior that need not be considered a "sexual function problem." Still, people sometimes experience difficulties in sexual function that are so persistent that they would benefit from sex therapy.

Health-care providers, including sex therapists, need to be aware of different types of sexual function difficulties that can interfere with sexual satisfaction and intimacy. Therefore, a structure to diagnose and address difficulties can be valuable. However, there has been some debate among sexuality and mental health professionals about which terms accurately describe sexual function difficulties and how to classify sexual function difficulties (West, Vinikoor, & Zolnoun, 2004). Though categories such as "dysfunction," "disorder," "difficulty," and "problem" have been used, this chapter presents alternate classification models.

The standard medical diagnostic classification of sexual function difficulties is found in the American Psychiatric Association's *Diagnostic and Statistical Manual of Mental Disorders* (2000), which uses the terms "dysfunction" and "disorders." Because the *DSM*'s is the most widely used classification system, the discussion of various sexual function difficulties in the professional literature is largely based on the *DSM* and uses the terms "sexual dysfunction" and "sexual disorders." Thus, the *DSM* terminology is quoted often in this chapter, particularly in the context of the *DSM* categories of sexual dysfunction.

An alternative term to "sexual dysfunction" is **sexual function dissatisfaction.** Sexual dissatisfaction is a common outcome of a difficulty in sexual functioning. In contrast to the broad medical focus of the *DSM* term, this term reflects an individual perception. That is, a person or couple could experience some of the *DSM* dysfunctions yet be satisfied with their sex lives. The difficulty in functioning might be considered a "dysfunction" only when the two people are dissatisfied and decide they may have a problem. The "dissatisfaction" concept is a fundamental tenet of the classification system for women's sexual problems of the Working Group for a New View of Women's Sexual Problems (2001). The system begins with a woman-centered definition of sexual function problems as "discontent or dissatisfaction with any emotional, physical, or relational aspects of sexual experience"—a definition that could also be applied to men. Furthermore, according to the World Health Organization's (1992) International Classification of Diseases (ICD-10), "sexual dysfunction" includes "the various ways in which an individual is unable to participate in a sexual relationship as he or she would wish."

An advantage of the term "sexual function dissatisfaction" is that it acknowledges sexual scripts as individual and avoids an overarching definition of what is "normal" versus what is dysfunctional (i.e., pathological). Adopting this subjective and personal view might help people be more comfortable with their own sexuality and less likely to feel "sexually flawed." We favor the terms "sexual function difficulties" and "sexual function dissatisfaction" and use them in this chapter whenever possible. However, in citing reports or research related to sexual difficulties, we often utilize the terms used therein.

Couples can experience sexual function difficulties that may lead to dissatisfaction, as well as frustration, with their sex lives.

Three alternate classifications of sexual function difficulties and dissatisfaction, based on medical and feminist models, illustrate different perspectives on the origins and causes of sexual problems: the *DSM;* the International Definitions Committee (on women's sexual problems), organized by the American Foundation of Urological Disease; and the Working Group for a New View of Women's Sexual Problems.

The *Diagnostic and Statistical Manual of Mental Disorders* The fourth edition (text revision) of the American Psychiatric Association's *Diagnostic and Statistical Manual of Mental Disorders (DSM-IV-TR)* (2000) labels sexual function difficulties as disorders and characterizes them according to the four phases of Masters and Johnson's sexual response cycle. The *DSM-IV-TR* defines **sexual dysfunctions** as "disturbance in sexual desire and in the psychophysiological changes that characterize the sexual response cycle and cause marked distress and interpersonal difficulty" (see Table 14.1). For any clinical diagnosis of sexual disorders, the term "persistent or recurrent" must also apply. The disorders could occur at one or more of the response cycle stages, meaning that a person could have more than one disorder, as often occurs. The *DSM-IV-TR* notes that other factors—such as age, psychological problems, sexual desires and expectations, ethnic and sociocultural background, the adequacy of sexual stimulation during sexual encounters, and drug use—should be considered in making any diagnosis of sexual disorders. The *DSM-IV-TR* contains disorders associated with sexual pain and includes a category called "sexual dysfunction due to general medical concern." The essential feature of the later category is the presence of a clinically significant sexual dysfunction that is judged to be due exclusively to the direct physiological effects of a general medical condition.

For each sexual dysfunction, the *DSM-IV-TR* has subtypes based on the onset of the dysfunction and the context in which it occurs. Lifelong dysfunctions are those present since the beginning of sexual functioning; acquired patterns develop only after a period of normal functioning. A generalized pattern of dysfunction is one that occurs in practically all sexual situations; a situational

Table 14.1 • *DSM-IV-TR* Categories of Sexual Dysfunctions

Disorder	Symptoms or Characteristics
Sexual Desire Disorders	
Hypoactive sexual desire disorder	Persistent or recurrent absence or deficiency of sexual fantasies and desire for sexual activity, causing marked or interpersonal difficulty
Sexual aversion disorder	Aversion to and active avoidance of genital sexual contact with a sex partner, causing marked or interpersonal difficulty
Sexual Arousal Disorders	
Female sexual arousal disorder	Inability to attain and maintain an adequate lubrication-swelling response to sexual excitement until completion of sexual activity, causing marked or interpersonal difficulty
Male erectile disorder	Inability to attain or maintain an adequate erection until completion of sexual activity, causing marked or interpersonal difficulty
Orgasmic Disorders	
Female orgasmic disorder	Delay or absence of orgasm following normal sexual excitement, causing marked or interpersonal difficulty
Male orgasmic disorder	Delay or absence of orgasm following normal sexual excitement, causing marked or interpersonal difficulty
Premature ejaculation	Ejaculation with minimal sexual stimulation, before the person or partner desires it, causing marked or interpersonal difficulty
Sexual Pain Disorders	
Dyspareunia	Persistent or recurrent pain associated with intercourse in either the female or male, causing marked or interpersonal difficulty
Vaginismus	Involuntary spasms of the vaginal muscles that interfere with penetration, causing marked or interpersonal difficulty

SOURCE: American Psychiatric Association. (2000). *Diagnostic and statistical manual of mental disorders* (4th ed., text revision). Washington, DC: Author.

type of dysfunction is limited to certain types of situations, stimulation, or partners. In most instances, the dysfunction whether generalized or situational, occurs during sexual activity with a partner. The acquired and situational dysfunctions typically are more successfully addressed in sex therapy.

Although the *DSM-IV-TR* is the most widely used categorization of sexual disorders, it largely reflects a psychiatric medical model and has been criticized. Further, it generally presents problems only in the heterosexual context.

The International Definitions Committee   In recent years, more attention has been directed to increasing our understanding of female sexual desire and sexual function difficulties (Wood, Koch, & Mansfield, 2006). The Consensus Development Panel on Female Sexual Dysfunction (Basson et al., 2001) noted that "in contrast to the widespread interest in research and treatment of male sexual dysfunctions, less attention has been paid to the sexual problems of women" and asserted the need for new definitions and classifications of female sexual function difficulties, as well as a set of new diagnostic criteria. Physician and sex researcher Rosemary Basson and colleagues (2004) stated that existing definitions of women's sexual disorders are grounded on genitally focused events in a linear sequence of desire, arousal, orgasm, and so on. Further, an extensive review of the professional literature on female sexual dysfunction since the early 1990s to the present found inconsistent definitions of female sexual dysfunction; the reviewers noted that there is an urgent need to determine measurable outcomes (West et al., 2004).

Given contentions that there are shortcomings in the traditional conceptualization of female sexual function difficulties, an international multidisciplinary group of 13 experts from seven countries, called the International Definitions Committee, proposed new definitions "based on an alternative model reflecting women's reasons/incentives for sexual activity beyond any initial awareness of sexual desire" (Basson et al., 2003, 2004). The committee notes that for many women fulfillment of sexual desire is not an infrequent reason for sexual activity and that sexual desire is often experienced only following sexual stimuli that have resulted in subjective sexual arousal (e.g., the woman does not feel aroused). Common complaints are lack of subjective arousal even though normal genital vasocongestion has apparently occurred. Further, the committee stated that "dysfunction may be largely related to contextual factors—evidence of something psychologically or biologically amiss with the woman herself, being absent."

Based on their review of the facets of women's sexual function and dysfunction that vary with traditional perspectives of women's sexual response, the committee proposed the following definitions of women's sexual function difficulties (Basson et al., 2003). As you can see, the definitions still reflect some of the components of the traditional Masters and Johnson model of sexual response (arousal followed by orgasm), which some researchers believe reflect males' experiences with sex more than those of females.

- *Women's sexual interest/desire disorder:* Absent or diminished sexual interest or desire beyond normal lessening with life cycle and relationship duration. Motivations for attempting to experience sexual desire are lacking or rare.

- *Subjective sexual arousal disorder:* Absence or markedly diminished feelings of sexual arousal (sexual excitement and sexual pleasure) from sexual stimulation although vaginal lubrication or other physical responses still occur.

- *Combined genital and subjective arousal disorder:* Absence or markedly diminished feelings of sexual arousal (sexual excitement and sexual pleasure) from sexual stimulation in combination with complaints of absence or impaired genital arousal, such as vulval swelling and lubrication.

- *Genital sexual arousal disorder:* Complaints of absent or impaired genital sexual arousal from any type of sexual stimulation.

- *Persistent sexual arousal disorder:* Spontaneous and unwanted arousal of genitals (e.g., tingling, throbbing, pulsating) without sexual interest and desire persisting for hours or days. The arousal is not relieved by one or more orgasms. Previously considered rare, this disorder is increasingly encountered in clinical practice.

- *Women's orgasmic disorder:* Despite reporting high sexual arousal and excitement, there is lack of orgasms, or markedly low orgasmic sensations, or marked delay of orgasm resulting from any type of stimulation.

- *Vaginismus:* Continuous or frequent difficulties of vaginal entry of a penis, a finger, and/or any object despite the woman's expressed desire for the entry. Involuntary pelvic muscle contraction; fear, anticipation, and/or experience of pain; and avoidance often occur. Difficulty is not caused by physical or structural abnormalities.

- *Dyspareunia:* Continuous or frequent pain with attempted or complete vaginal entry and/or penile-vaginal intercourse.

A New View of Women's Sexual Problems The Working Group for a New View of Women's Sexual Problems (2001), a group of clinicians and social scientists, offers a new classification system called "A New View of Women's Sexual Problems." This system classifies women's sexual function difficulties based on women's own needs and sexual realities.

The Working Group believes that a fundamental barrier to understanding women's sexuality is the *DSM* medical classification system. It contends that the *DSM* framework has shortcomings as applied to women, which include the following:

- *A false notion of sexual equivalency between men and women.* Early researchers emphasized similarities in men's and women's physiological responses during sexual activities and concluded that their sexual problems must also be similar. The few studies that asked women to describe their own experiences found significant differences.

- *The unacknowledged role of relationships in sexuality.* The Working Group states that the *DSM* does not address the relational aspects of women's sexuality, which are often fundamental to sexual function satisfaction and problems. It contends that the *DSM* reduction of "normal sexual functioning" to physiology implies, incorrectly, that sexual dissatisfaction can be treated without considering the relationship in which sex occurs.

- *The leveling of differences among women.* The Working Group contends that women are dissimilar, and the varied components of their sexuality do not fit neatly into the categories of desire, arousal, orgasm, or pain.

The Working Group suggests a women-centered definition of sexual function problems "as discontent or dissatisfaction with any emotional, physical, or relational aspect of sexual experience," which may arise in one or more of four categories underlying the dissatisfaction.

- *Sociocultural, political, or economic factors.* These include inadequate sexuality education, lack of access to health services, a perceived inability to meet cultural norms regarding correct or ideal sexuality, inhibitions due to conflict between the sexual norms of the subculture or culture of origin and those of the dominant culture, and a lack of interest, time, or energy due to family and work obligations.

- *Partner and relationship problems.* These include discrepancies in desire for sexual activity or in preferences for various sexual activities, inhibitions about communicating preferences, loss of interest due to conflicts over commonplace issues, and inhibitions due to a partner's health status or sexual problems.

- *Psychological problems.* These include past abuse; problems with attachment, rejection, cooperation, or entitlement; fear of pregnancy and sexually transmitted infections (STIs); and loss of partner or reputation.

- *Medical factors.* These include numerous local or systemic medical conditions, pregnancy, STIs, and side effects of drugs, medications, and medical treatments, including surgery.

Prevalence and Cofactors

Local and national studies have been conducted concerning the prevalence of sexual function difficulties. Two national studies of samples in the United States—the National Health and Social Life Survey and The Kinsey Institute's survey of women in heterosexual relationships—and a population study in the United Kingdom, the 2000 National Survey of Sexual Attitudes and Lifestyles, are featured here.

The National Health and Social Life Survey: Sexual Dysfunction Findings
The National Health and Social Life Survey (NHSLS), according to the authors, "provides the first population-based assessment of sexual dysfunction in the half-century since Kinsey et al" (Laumann, Paik, & Rosen, 1999). Using a national sample of 1,749 women and 1,410 men aged 18–59, the researchers found that self-reported sexual dysfunctions are widespread and are influenced by both health-related and psychosocial factors. According to the NHSLS, sexual dysfunctions were more prevalent among women (43%) than men (31%) (Figure 14.1) and were generally most common among young women and older men (Figure 14.2). For both genders, African Americans are more likely to have sexual dysfunctions, and Latinos are less likely to. Sexual dysfunctions are associated with poor quality of life, although females appear to be impacted by this factor more than males. Those who experienced emotional or stress-related problems had more difficulties. Those having had an STI, reporting moderate to high consumption of alcohol, or (for men) having been circumcised generally were not any more likely to have had a sexual dysfunction. Having had more than five lifetime partners or regularly masturbating did not generally increase the relative risk for sexual dysfunction for either women or men. Other important findings by gender include the following:

Females

- The prevalence of sexual function problems for women tends to decrease with increasing age except for those who report trouble lubricating.
- Nonmarried women are about 1.5 times more likely to have orgasm problems and sexual anxiety as married women.
- Women who have graduated from college are about half as likely to experience low sexual desire, difficulties achieving orgasm, sexual pain, and sexual anxiety as women who have not graduated from high school. Overall, women with lower educational attainment report less pleasure with sex and greater levels of sexual anxiety.
- African American women have higher rates of low sexual desire and derive less sexual pleasure than White women, and Whites are more likely to have sexual pain. Overall, Latinas experience lower rates of sexual function problems than other women, and African American women appear more likely to have sexual function problems.
- Poor health is associated with sexual pain for women.

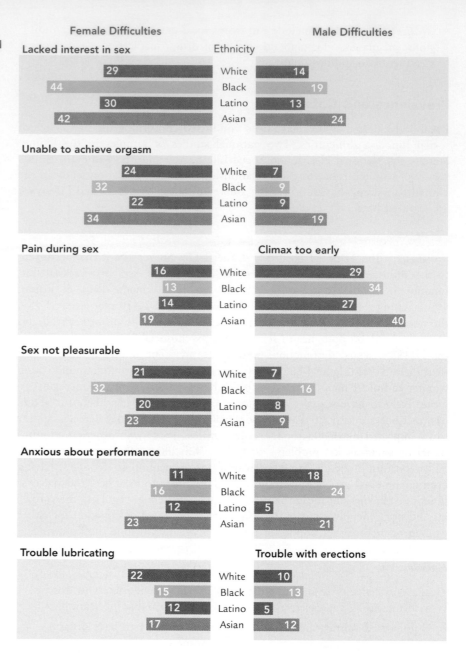

● FIGURE 14.1

Percentage of Self-Reported Sexual Function Difficulties in the Past 12 Months, by Gender and Ethnicity. (*Source:* Adapted from Laumann, Paik, & Rosen, 1999.)

Female Difficulties   **Male Difficulties**

Lacked interest in sex   Ethnicity
| | | |
White — 29 / 14
Black — 44 / 19
Latino — 30 / 13
Asian — 42 / 24

Unable to achieve orgasm
White — 24 / 7
Black — 32 / 9
Latino — 22 / 9
Asian — 34 / 19

Pain during sex   **Climax too early**
White — 16 / 29
Black — 13 / 34
Latino — 14 / 27
Asian — 19 / 40

Sex not pleasurable
White — 21 / 7
Black — 32 / 16
Latino — 20 / 8
Asian — 23 / 9

Anxious about performance
White — 11 / 18
Black — 16 / 24
Latino — 12 / 5
Asian — 23 / 21

Trouble lubricating   **Trouble with erections**
White — 22 / 10
Black — 15 / 13
Latino — 12 / 5
Asian — 17 / 12

- Deterioration in economic status is associated with a moderate increase in sexual function difficulties for women.

- Women with low sexual activity or interests are at higher risk for low sexual desire and arousal problems.

- Rates of sexual problems are the same for women who report any same-sex activity and those who do not.

- Sexual arousal problems appear to be more common among women who have experienced sexual victimization through adult-child or forced sexual contact.

- All types of sexual function difficulties are correlated with levels of physical and emotional satisfaction and happiness.

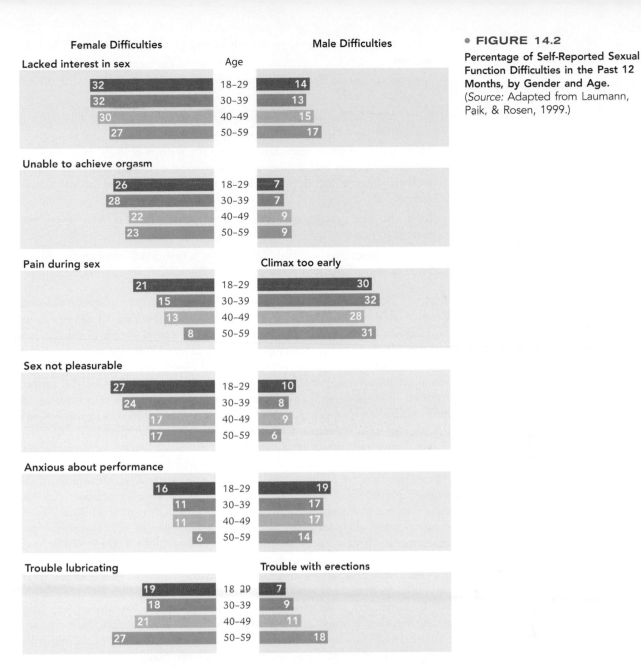

Female Difficulties

Lacked interest in sex

	Age	
32	18–29	14
32	30–39	13
30	40–49	15
27	50–59	17

Male Difficulties

Unable to achieve orgasm

	Age	
26	18–29	7
28	30–39	7
22	40–49	9
23	50–59	9

Pain during sex / **Climax too early**

	Age	
21	18–29	30
15	30–39	32
13	40–49	28
8	50–59	31

Sex not pleasurable

	Age	
27	18–29	10
24	30–39	8
17	40–49	9
17	50–59	6

Anxious about performance

	Age	
16	18–29	19
11	30–39	17
11	40–49	17
6	50–59	14

Trouble lubricating / **Trouble with erections**

	Age	
19	18–29	7
18	30–39	9
21	40–49	11
27	50–59	18

● **FIGURE 14.2**

Percentage of Self-Reported Sexual Function Difficulties in the Past 12 Months, by Gender and Age.
(*Source:* Adapted from Laumann, Paik, & Rosen, 1999.)

Males

- The prevalence of erectile problems and lack of sexual desire increases with age for men.
- Nonmarried men report higher rates for most sexual function difficulties than married men.
- Male college graduates are only two thirds as likely to report early orgasm and half as likely to report nonpleasurable sex and sexual anxiety as men who have not graduated from high school.
- Men with poor health have an elevated risk for all types of sexual function difficulties.

- Deterioration in economic position is generally related to erectile difficulties in men.

- Low sexual activity or interest is not related to low sexual desire and arousal problems in men.

- Men reporting any same-sex activity are more than 2 times as likely to experience early ejaculation and low sexual desire.

- Male victims of adult-child sexual contact are 3 times as likely to experience erectile difficulties and 2 times as likely to experience early ejaculation and low sexual desire than those who have not been victims of adult-child sexual contact.

- Men who have sexually assaulted women are $3\frac{1}{2}$ times as likely to report erectile difficulty.

- Men reporting erectile difficulties and low sexual desire experience diminished quality of life, but those with early ejaculation are not affected.

Distress About Sex: A National Survey of Women in Heterosexual Relationships   The Kinsey Institute studied the prevalence of distress about sexuality and predictors of such distress among a national sample of women in a random telephone survey (Bancroft, Loftus, & Long, 2003). The sample included 835 White and African American women aged 20–65 who had been in a heterosexual relationship for at least 6 months. In the study, 24.4% of the women reported "marked distress" about their sexual relationship, their own sexuality, or both, within the previous month. This figure is much lower than the NHSLS finding that 43% of women have one or more sexual dysfunctions.

The best predictors of sexual distress in the Kinsey study were markers of general emotional well-being and the emotional relationship with the partner during sexual activity. That is, women with good mental health who felt close to their partner during sex were most likely to be sexually satisfied. Physical aspects of sexual response in women, including arousal, vaginal lubrication, and orgasm, were poor predictors. The Kinsey report also stated, "In general, the predictors of distress about sex did not fit well with the *DSM-IV-TR* criteria for the diagnosis of sexual dysfunction in women." Dr. John Bancroft, senior research fellow and former director of The Kinsey Institute and lead author of the study, notes that a woman who is distressed or has children and a job might put sex aside for a while as an adaptive behavior, not because there is anything wrong with her or she is dysfunctional (Elias, 2003). The report also cautioned that treatment for "sexual dysfunction" should consider whether the difficulty is the primary problem or a "reaction to circumstances."

The 2000 National Survey of Sexual Attitudes and Lifestyles   The 2000 National Survey of Sexual Attitudes and Lifestyles (Natsal 2000) is a nationally representative survey of 11,161 men and women aged 16–44 who resided in private households in Britain (Mercer et al., 2003, 2005). All participants reported at least one heterosexual partnership in the year before the interview. We highlight this study because of its similarity to the United States NHSLS; that is, both are large population-based studies of sexual function difficulties. In general similarity to the NHSLS, the Natsal study found that sexual function problems were common more so for women than men. About one half of the women (53.8%) and about one third of the men (34.8%) from the Natsal 2000 study reported experiencing any sexual function difficulty for at least one month in the past year. Smaller proportions—15.6% of women and 6.2% of men—reported any sexual function problem lasting at least 6 months of the past year. Also like the NHSLS, the Natsal study discovered that the reported sexual function problems were significantly associated with socio-demographic, health-related sexual behaviors and attitude factors.

The Natsal researchers observed that many of the participants avoided sex because of their sexual function problems and few sought help for their problems. They also noted that the results "highlight how, in some cases, sexual function problems are often not an individual's problem but that they may be partnership specific, such that it may be important to consider an individual's partnership(s) in the 'treatment' or 'management' of sexual function problems." A note of caution in interpreting the findings: Like the NHSLS, the Natsal 2000 is a cross-sectional survey in which it is not possible to determine causality—some of the factors identified in the study (e.g., marital status, communication) may have caused the sexual function problems, whereas other factors may be the consequence of sexual function problems.

Disorders of Sexual Desire

Hypoactive Sexual Desire Disorder

The persistent or recurrent deficiency or lack of sexual fantasies and desire for sexual activity that causes marked distress or interpersonal difficulty is called **hypoactive sexual desire (HSD)** in the *DSM-IV-TR* (2000). It is sometimes called "inhibited sexual desire" or "low sexual desire." This disorder may encompass all types of sexual behavior or may be limited to one partner or to a specific problem such as arousal or orgasm difficulties. In the NHSLS, about 3 in 10 women report a lack of interest in sex, although the number decreases slightly with age; fewer men (about 1 in 7) report HSD disorder, with a very slight increase with age (see Figure 14.2). The number-one sexual function problem of American couples is inhibited sexual desire. (Discrepancies in sexual desire, which will be discussed later in this chapter, is the second most common problem.) More than one half of married couples experience inhibited sexual desire or desire discrepancy at some time in their marriage. Inhibited sexual desire causes more stress in a marriage than any other sexual function problem (McCarthy & McCarthy, 2003).

Defining low desire is tricky, often subjective, as there is no norm level for sexual desire, and based on an assumption that there is an optimal level of sexual desire (Hall, 2004). Certainly, sexually "normal" people vary considerably in their sexual fantasies and desires and occasionally experience a lack of desire. Low sexual desire is most often acquired; that is, the person felt sexual previously, but no longer experiences desire. The good news: It is often transitory. People with HSD disorder reluctantly participate in sex when it is initiated by a partner. Most often, the disorder develops in adulthood in association with psychological distress resulting from depression, stressful life events, or interpersonal difficulties. The loss of desire, whether ongoing or situational, can negatively affect a relationship (American Psychiatric Association [APA], 2000). Anger within a relationship can also diminish sexual desire. Over time, if the anger is not resolved, it may develop into resentment or hatred that colors every aspect of the relationship. Most people cannot experience sexual desire for someone with whom they are angry or whom they deeply resent. Drugs, hormone deficiency, and illness can also decrease desire.

> Sexual desire is a fragile, mysterious appetite.
>
> —Michael Castleman
> (1950–)

> If you have a comfortable compatible love without sexual sparks, you don't have enough. If you have sexual heat but not friendship, you don't have enough. Neither lust nor love by itself is enough. You have to have passion.
>
> —Carol Cassell
> (1936–)

Gay men and lesbian women may experience HSD disorder if they are having difficulty with their sexual orientation (Margolies, Becher, & Jackson-Brewer, 1988; Reece, 1988).

Sexual Aversion Disorder   According to the *DSM-IV-TR*, persistent and recurrent aversion to and avoidance of genital contact with a partner that causes marked distress is called **sexual aversion disorder.** The possibility of sexual contact may cause anxiety, disgust, or fear in a person with this disorder, and some sufferers create covert strategies (e.g., traveling, sleeping, or being heavily involved with work) to avoid sex (APA, 2000). A mere kiss, touch, or caress may cause a phobic response out of fear that it might lead to something sexual. Sometimes, these responses are internalized; other times, they can lead to panic attacks and physiological responses such as sweating, nausea, vomiting, and diarrhea. For people with this disorder, the frequency of sexual contact with a partner is rare and can lead to severe relationship stress. Sexual aversion often results from severely negative parental attitudes during childhood; sexual trauma, such as rape or sexual abuse, especially in women; consistent sexual pressure from a long-term partner; a history of erectile difficulties in men; and/ or gender identity confusion (Masters, Johnson, & Kolodny, 1992).

Barry McCarthy and Emily McCarthy, in their book *Rekindling Desire: A Step-by-Step Program to Help Low-Sex and No-Sex Marriages* (2003), write about what they call "no-sex marriages," the extreme of desire problems which they define as having sex less than 10 times a year. They state that couples in a no-sex marriage experience a cycle of anticipatory anxiety, negative experiences, and eventually, avoidance of sex—a cycle that they did not plan for in their marriage. According to the McCarthys, about 1 in 5 marriages is a no-sex marriage. The longer the couple avoids sexual contact, the more difficult it is to break the cycle and the more they blame each other. Further, the more shameful they feel, the harder it is to break the cycle. The McCarthys note, however, that motivated couples can reestablish desire through self-help and therapy.

As with heterosexuals, gay men and lesbian women may enjoy certain activities, such as kissing or mutual masturbation, but feel aversion to other activities. For gay men, sexual aversion often focuses on issues of anal eroticism (Reece, 1988). For lesbian women, it may focus on cunnilingus (Nichols, 1987), which is often their preferred activity for reaching orgasm.

Interestingly, the *DSM-IV-TR* does not include a "hyperactive sexual desire disorder," implying that its authors, mental health professionals, do not believe that high sexual desire is a mental disorder. This is contrary to the view of the general public and some professionals who espouse the concept of sexual addiction (see Chapter 10). Sexual desire exists on a continuum, with some people having very low desire and others having very high desire. Most people seem to be somewhere in the middle, however.

Sexual Arousal Disorders

Female Sexual Arousal Disorder   The persistent or recurring inability to attain or maintain the level of vaginal lubrication and swelling associated with sexual excitement, causing marked distress or interpersonal difficulty, is called **female sexual arousal disorder** by the *DSM-IV-TR*. This disorder may be accompanied by sexual desire disorder and female orgasmic disorder. The term "frigid" was once used to describe this problem, but this pejorative and value-laden term is no longer used by professionals. This difficulty can occur when a woman desires sex but has difficulty maintaining arousal, resulting in vaginal dryness and tightness and subsequent discomfort if intercourse is attempted. About one fifth to one quarter of women in the NHSLS report poor lubrication, with increasing difficulty as they age (see Figure 14.2). Female sexual arousal disorder is often accompanied by sexual desire and orgasm disorders, as well as sexual avoidance and stress in sexual relationships. If there are no physiological or substance use reasons for poor lubrication, this disorder is diagnosed as psychological in origin (APA, 2000). However, the lack of vaginal lubrication may be misleading, as some women reporting dryness indicate the presence of sexual excitement and arousal. These women often use artificial lubricants. Further, some women report their clitoris engorged and their vagina lubricated, but that they do not feel psychologically aroused. Given these experiences, many sex therapists believe that sexual arousal is much more of a psychological process in women than in men and that the *DSM-IV-TR* fails to account for this difference (Keesling, 2006).

Male Erectile Disorder The persistent or recurring inability to attain or maintain an adequate erection until completion of sexual activity, causing marked distress or interpersonal difficulty, is called **male erectile disorder,** or **erectile dysfunction,** by the *DSM-IV-TR*. At one time, this disorder was called "impotence," but like "frigid," this value-laden and pejorative term is no longer used. This was a very common male sexual difficulty treated by therapists before the introduction of Viagra. Sexual anxiety, fear of failure, high performance standards, concerns about sexual performance, and low sexual excitement, as well as specific medical conditions and medications, are often associated with male erectile disorder (APA, 2000).

The prevalence of male erectile disorder increases with age, with more than twice as many men 50–59 reporting problems with erections as men 18–29 in the NHSLS (see Figure 14.2). However, it is important to note that, like female arousal disorders, male erectile disorders are not an inevitable consequence of aging. But the health problems that often accompany aging increase the disorder's prevalence. The prevalence of erectile difficulty has been directly correlated with certain diseases, such as hypertension, diabetes mellitus, and heart disease; certain medications, such as cardiac drugs and antihypertensives; cigarette smoking in association with treated heart disease and treated hypertension; excessive alcohol consumption; suppression and expression of anger; obesity; and depression (Feldman et al., 1994; Nusbaum, 2002).

The diagnosis of male erectile disorder is usually psychologically based. Men who have erections while sleeping or masturbating obviously are physically able to have erections, meaning that an erectile disorder during two-person sexual activity has a psychological origin. As with the other *DSM-IV-TR* sexual dysfunctions, male erectile disorder is typically diagnosed only when the man or his partner is dissatisfied and distressed by the occurrence (Schwartz, 2000).

Sex therapist and author Barbara Keesling (2006) gives some cautions relative to expectations of erections. She notes that men's concept of an adequate erection varies considerably from person to person, and that a man does not necessarily have an erection problem if he doesn't have reflex or spontaneous erections from viewing a partner's body, for example. Many men, even young men, always need direct stimulation to have an erection. Also, she says that "it's probably also unrealistic to expect that your erection will maintain the

> Thou treacherous, base deserter of my flame,
> False to my passion, fatal to my fame,
> Through what mistaken magic dost thou prove
> So true to lewdness, so untrue to love?
>
> —John Wilmot, Earl of Rochester (1647–1680)

same level of rigidity throughout the course of a sexual encounter." During any particular sexual encounter, a man's erection can vacillate between several levels of rigidity depending on the amount of stimulation.

Persistent Sexual Arousal Syndrome A sexual function problem not included in the *DSM-IV-TR* and only recently described in the professional literature is **persistent sexual arousal syndrome (PSAS).** Sex therapists Sandra Leiblum and Sharon Nathan note several cases of women reporting that their sexual arousal does not resolve in ordinary ways and continues for hours, days, or even weeks (Leiblum & Nathan, 2001). Sexual stimulation, masturbation, stress, and anxiety often trigger the symptoms (Leiblum, Brown, Wan, & Rawlinson, 2005). The therapists state that the women came to them for therapy because of distress about their symptoms, but they point out that other women may not find the symptoms to be upsetting. To date, no obvious hormonal, vascular, neurological, or psychological causative factors have been linked to PSAS. The number of women experiencing PSAS is unknown, because some women may be embarrassed to report it to their health-care provider or not be distressed by it. Leiblum and Nathan hope that their report will stimulate further efforts to investigate PSAS. The recent identification of PSAS highlights the fact that female sexuality is underinvestigated and not adequately understood.

Orgasmic Disorders

Female Orgasmic Disorder According to the *DSM-IV-TR*, the persistent and recurrent absence of or delay in orgasm for women following normal sexual excitement is called **female orgasmic disorder.** It is the second most common sexual function difficulty (after low sexual desire) treated by therapists (Keesling, 2006). This disorder has also been called anorgasmia, inorgasmia, pre-orgasmia, inhibited female orgasm, and the pejorative "frigidity." Most female orgasmic disorders are lifelong rather than acquired problems; once a woman learns how to have an orgasm, it is uncommon for her to lose that capacity (APA, 2000).

Female orgasm is not universal, a slight minority never or rarely have them. In the NHSLS, about one quarter of women report they were able to experience orgasm with a partner in the past 12 months, although the percentage decreases with age (see Figure 14.2). No relationships were found between certain personality traits or psychopathology and orgasm. A study of a nationally represented sample of Australians aged 16 to 59 found that about 7 in 10 women reported orgasm during the last sexual encounter, but only one half of those reporting intercourse only experienced orgasm (Richters, de Visser, Rissel, & Smith, 2006).

Some women who enjoy sexual activity with a partner have difficulty achieving orgasm with them, thereby sometimes causing dissatisfaction or distress within the relationship. Many women with female orgasmic disorder have negative or guilty attitudes about their sexuality, as well as relationship difficulties. Inadequate sexual stimulation is also a factor in this disorder (APA, 2000). Keesling (2006) states that "the number-one reason why some women have difficulty with orgasm is lack of experience with self-touch." As shown in Table 14.2, one study found that "lack of foreplay" as the most prominent factor that inhibited orgasm in the women. Also, as described in the box "Is Intercourse Enough? The Big 'O' and Sexual Behaviors," an Australian study of men and women found that women were more likely to experience orgasm during sexual encounters that included a wider variety of sexual behaviors than intercourse.

Table 14.2 • Factors Inhibiting Women's Orgasm During Coitus	
Factors	**Percentage Affected**
Lack of foreplay	63.8
Fatigue	53.6
Preoccupation with nonsexual thoughts	45.5
Ejaculation too soon after intromission[a]	43.1
Conflicts between partners unrelated to intromission	34.6
Lack of interest or foreplay by partner	24.3
Lack of adequate vaginal lubrication	23.7
Lack of tenderness by partner	22.7
Lack of privacy for intromission	20.3
Overindulgence in alcohol	16.3
Desire to perform well after intromission	14.9
Difficulty with sexual arousal with partner	14.3
Painful sexual intercourse	12.0
Overeating	10.3

[a]Insertion of the penis into the vagina.

SOURCE: Darling, C. A., Davidson, J. K., & Cox, R. P. (1991). Female sexual response and the timing of partner orgasm. *Journal of Sex and Marital Therapy, 17*(1), 11.

Some women have wondered "Why all this fuss about having orgasm during sex?" and have questioned whether women need to have orgasms during partner sex to feel sexually satisfied. As described in the box on the next page, many women surveyed for the NHSLS reported that they do not need to have an orgasm to be physically and emotionally satisfied with sex.

Male Orgasmic Disorder   The *DSM-IV-TR* defines **male orgasmic disorder** as the persistent or recurrent delay in or absence of orgasm following a normal sexual excitement phase of Masters and Johnson's sexual response cycle that causes marked distress or interpersonal difficulty. Because ejaculation and orgasm are two separate events (see Chapter 4), the delay or absence of ejaculation is a more accurate description of the disorder; that is, these men may have an orgasm (the full-body response) but either do not have the genital response of ejaculation or have a delayed response. A component of this disorder is **inhibited ejaculation,** in which the man is unable to ejaculate no matter how long stimulation is maintained. In **delayed ejaculation,** the man is not able to ejaculate easily; it may take 40 minutes or more of concentrated thrusting before ejaculation occurs. In the NHSLS, only a small percentage of men were unable to achieve orgasm (i.e., unable to ejaculate) (see Figure 14.2).

In the most common form of male orgasm disorder, the man cannot ejaculate during intercourse but can ejaculate from a partner's manual or oral stimulation. To be considered a disorder, the lack of ejaculation cannot be caused by substance abuse or illness (APA, 2000). Anxiety-provoking sexual situations can interfere with a man's ejaculatory reflex, or he may not be able to have an orgasm in situations in which he feels guilty or conflicted. Often, the man can overcome this disorder when the situation or partner changes or when he engages in a fantasy or receives additional stimulation.

Is Intercourse Enough? The Big "O" and Sexual Behaviors

In sexual encounters between men and women, is penile-vaginal intercourse sufficient stimulation for orgasm to occur? As we know, men almost always have orgasms during sexual encounters with women, and that is not considered a sexual function problem unless he experiences early or delayed ejaculation. However, women are less likely to have orgasms during sex with men, and that *is* viewed as problematic by some sex therapists and disappointing to many women and their partners. Several personal and relationship factors, such as anxiety and shame about one's sexuality and lack of trust of one's partner, can keep women from experiencing orgasms. However, a more proximal cause, such as the type of sexual stimulation received during a sexual encounter with a male partner, also plays an important role. Actually, research involving over 2,000 nurses found that the most desired change in their sexual lives regardless of marital status, was more foreplay prior to vaginal intercourse (Davidson & Darling, 1989).

Researchers, noting that there has been little study of predictors or factors associated with orgasm at any one sexual encounter, analyzed data from the Australian Study of Health and Relationships, a national telephone sexuality study of a representative sample of Australians aged 16–59 (Richters, de Visser, Rissel, & Smith, 2006). Respondents in the survey were to indicate whether at their last sexual encounter they gave or received manual stimulation and oral sex, had vaginal or anal intercourse, and whether or not they had orgasm. Only those participants (5,118 men and women) who were sexually active in the past year and who reported that their most recent sexual encounter was with another-sex partner were used in this analysis. For this last sexual encounter, 95% of the men and women reported having vaginal intercourse, about 8 in 10 reported manual stimulation of the woman by the man, about 7 in 10 reported manual stimulation of the man by the woman, about one quarter reported cunnilingus and fellatio, and less than 1 in 10 reported anal intercourse.

The data helped answer the question of whether vaginal intercourse is enough or other sexual behaviors are necessary for men and women to achieve orgasm during sex with each other. Here is what the researchers found:

- At their last sexual encounter, 95% of men and 69% of women had an orgasm.

- Almost all men (95%) experienced orgasm in encounters that included vaginal intercourse, whereas orgasm for women was less likely (50%) among those who reported only having vaginal intercourse.

- For women, the rate of orgasm (about 70%) was higher among those reporting intercourse plus receiving manual stimulation or intercourse plus cunnilingus, although orgasm did not necessarily occur during these practices; orgasm was even more likely for those who had intercourse and had received both manual and oral stimulation.

- Over 80% of the men who did not have vaginal intercourse experienced orgasm from receiving oral and/or manual stimulation.

Premature Ejaculation   The persistent and recurrent ejaculation with minimal sexual stimulation, before or shortly after penetration, that causes marked distress or interpersonal difficulty is called **premature ejaculation** by the *DSM-IV-TR*. This disorder is fairly common, with about 3 out of every 10 men in the NHSLS reporting it (see Figure 14.2). Some professionals use the term "early ejaculation" or "rapid ejaculation," believing it is less pejorative than "premature ejaculation," whereas others use **"involuntary ejaculation"** (see below).

Couples often are confused, bewildered, and unhappy when the man consistently ejaculates too early, although the woman often seems to be more disturbed by the disorder than the man is. The woman may be sexually dissatisfied, while her partner may feel that she is too demanding. He may also feel considerable guilt and anxiety. They may begin to avoid sexual contact with each other. The man may experience erectile problems because of his anxieties over early ejaculation, and he may withdraw from sexual activity completely. Other factors may contribute to early or involuntary ejaculation in men, such as inexperience in negotiating with a sex partner, inadequate understanding of sexual response in both women and men, unwittingly training themselves to

- Women were less likely to experience orgasm (less than 50%) during their most recent sexual encounter if the sex was with a nonregular sexual partner; women in relationships of 1 to 2 years were more likely to experience an orgasm.

The researchers concluded that men were highly likely to experience an orgasm in any sexual encounter that included vaginal intercourse, but women who had vaginal intercourse only had only about a 50% chance of experiencing orgasm. Women were more likely to experience orgasm during sexual encounters that included more sexual practices, particularly cunnilingus.

The researchers cautioned that we should not assume that everyone having a sexual encounter wants to experience an orgasm; that is, it may not matter to everyone. They note that one possible reason for the lower orgasm rate for women is that on occasion a woman may have an intercourse-only encounter (a "quickie" or "freebie") with their male partner to oblige the man. Further, some of the no-intercourse episodes reported by the participants may have been the man obliging the woman; that is, the man might have provided manual and oral stimulation of the woman although he was not interested in experiencing orgasm himself. The National Health and Social Life Survey (NHSLS) found that only 29% of females reported always having had an orgasm with their partner during the preceding year, yet 41% said that they were "extremely physically satisfied" by sex and 39% reported "extreme emotional satisfaction" (Lauman, Gagnon, Michael, & Michaels, 1994). In other words, many of the females of the study did not have to have an orgasm to be physically and emotionally satisfied with sex. Possibly, tenderness, intimacy, and affection were more important determinants of gratification than having an orgasm. The results for males in the NHSLS were intriguing as well. Seventy-five percent claimed to always have had an orgasm while having sex with their partner during the preceding year, more than twice the percentage for females. On the other hand, only 47% of the males reported being "extremely physically satisfied" by sex, yet 42% reported "extreme emotional" satisfaction—rates very similar to those of the females in the study.

Think Critically

- Are men interested in providing manual and oral stimulation to their women partners, and are women comfortable and willing to request these behaviors?
- For most women of your age, how important is experiencing an orgasm during a sexual encounter?
- Can a person experience physical satisfaction and not experience an orgasm during sex? Why or why not?
- Is emotional satisfaction more a matter of expressing tender feelings than achieving an orgasm? Explain your answer.

SOURCE: Richters, J., de Visser, R., Rissel, C., & Smith, A. (2006). Sexual practices at last heterosexual encounter and occurrence of orgasm in a national survey. *Journal of Sex Research, 43*, 217–226.

ejaculate quickly during masturbation, inability to relax deeply during sexual intercourse, nonsensual lovemaking, and a narrow focus on the penis and a partner's genitals during sex (Castleman, 2004).

Most men with this disorder can delay ejaculation during self-masturbation for a longer period of time than during coitus. With sexual experience and aging, many males learn to delay ejaculation, but others continue to ejaculate early and may seek professional help (APA, 2000). This disorder often occurs in young and sexually inexperienced males, especially those who have primarily been in situations in which speed of ejaculation was important so as for example, to avoid being discovered. It is the number-one sexual function complaint of young men.

As with many sexual difficulties, there is a problem with definitions: What is premature ejaculation? Some sex therapists have defined it according to how long intercourse lasts, how many pelvic thrusts there are, and how often the woman achieves orgasm. Therapist Helen Singer Kaplan (1974) suggested that the absence of voluntary control at orgasm is the key to defining premature ejaculation. Some sex therapists suggest that the term "involuntary ejaculation" is the more accurate term, given that the treatment focuses on acquiring voluntary control over something that has been involuntary (Castleman, 2004). Early ejaculation is a problem when the man or his partner is dissatisfied by the amount of time it takes him to ejaculate. Some couples want intercourse to last a long time, but others are not concerned about that.

Interestingly, the *DSM-IV-TR* does not have a premature or rapid orgasm category for women. Some women do have orgasms very quickly and may not be interested in continuing sexual activity; others, however, are open to continued stimulation and may have repeated orgasms.

Sexual Pain Disorders

Vaginismus   According to the *DSM-IV-TR*, the persistent or recurrent involuntary spasm of the muscles of the outer third of the vagina (pubococcygeus) that interferes with sexual intercourse and causes marked distress or interpersonal difficulties is called **vaginismus.** In vaginismus, the muscles around the vaginal opening go into involuntary spasmodic contractions, preventing the insertion of the penis, finger, tampon, or speculum. Vaginismus occurs in some women during sexual activity or during a pelvic examination; it is found more often in younger than older women (APA, 2000). In rare cases, the vaginal entrance becomes so tight that the penis or another object cannot penetrate it (Leiblum & Nathan, 2001). Vaginismus may occur in conjunction with other sexual function difficulties, such as hyposexual disorder or dyspareunia, or sexual function difficulties in the partner such as problems with erections or ejaculation.

During the nineteenth century, vaginismus was one of the most common complaints among women, who were taught to dread intercourse or to perform it perfunctorily. Currently an estimated 2% of women experience vaginismus (Renshaw, 1988a). It is a common reason for unconsummated marriage. Vaginismus is essentially a conditioned response that reflects fear, anxiety, or pain. It may result from negative attitudes about sexuality, harsh early sexual experiences, sexual abuse or rape, or painful pelvic examinations (Vandeweil, Jaspers, Schultz, & Gal, 1990). An inability to look at one's own genitals, touch one's own genitals, masturbate, receive manual or oral sex from a partner, or experience an orgasm often accompanies vaginismus (Keesling, 2006).

Dyspareunia   Persistent or recurrent genital pain, ranging from mild to severe, that is associated with intercourse and that causes marked distress or interpersonal difficulty is called **dyspareunia** by the *DSM-IV-TR*. A key to the *DSM-IV-TR* definition is that the pain must be persistent or recurrent. Occasional pain in the vagina or penis that is experienced during sex and is temporary is not part of this definition. This disorder can occur in both men and women, although it most often is considered to occur in women. The NHSLS, for example, reported pain during sex only for women. In that study, about one fifth of the women aged 18–29 reported pain during sex, decreasing to 8% for women 50–59 (Laumann, Paik, & Rosen, 1999) (see Figure 14.2). Many women experience occasional pain during intercourse, but persistent dyspareunia may indicate difficulties that need to be addressed. When the pain occurs exclusively as a result of a medical or physiological condition, such as an STI, acute infections in the pelvic area, or menopause, the person has, not dyspareunia, but "sexual dysfunction due to a general medical condition" or "substance-induced sexual dysfunction" (APA, 2000). This disturbance is not

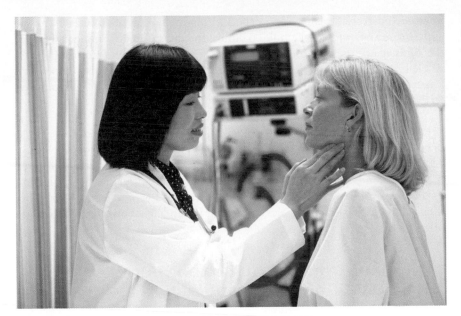

Discussing sexuality and becoming educated about one's sexual functioning with a qualified health-care professional can sometimes help resolve questions, issues, or problems.

caused exclusively by vaginismus or lack of lubrication. The diagnosis of dyspareunia usually has a strong psychological component.

Inadequate sexuality education, fear of the genitals, sexual trauma such as rape, sexual guilt over perceived sexual transgressions by oneself or one's partner, sexual inhibitions, a poor relationship with her partner, and hormonal imbalances may contribute to a woman's pain associated with intercourse (Keesling, 2006). If longer stimulation or the use of lubricants does not relieve the dyspareunia, a woman should consult her physician or health-care practitioner to determine the cause.

A type of pain associated with sex that is not included in the *DSM-IV-TR* is **anodyspareunia,** pain occurring during anal intercourse. Gay men sometimes experience this, often due to lack of adequate lubrication. The depth of penile penetration into the anus, the rate of thrusting, and anxiety or embarrassment about the situation often are associated with anodyspareunia (Rosser, Short, Thurmes, & Coleman, 1998). A study of 404 men who have sex with men found that 55 (14%) experienced anodyspareunia; these men reported their pain as lifelong, experienced psychological distress as a result, and avoided anal sex for periods of time (Damon & Rosser, 2005). The men with anodyspareunia also reported their beliefs that psychological factors were the primary causes of the pain. The researchers noted that "the findings contradict the myth that pain is a necessary consequence of receptive anal sex and show that anodyspareunia is similar to dyspareunia in women in terms of prevalence, mental health consequences, and contributing factors."

Other Disorders

Two other disorders not mentioned in the *DSM-IV-TR* because they are based on physical conditions are Peyronie's disease and priapism. These conditions can also cause other difficulties in sexual functioning.

Peyronie's Disease A condition in which calcium deposits and tough fibrous tissue develop in the corpora cavernosa within the penis is known as

Peyronie's disease. This problem occurs primarily in older men (usually for no apparent reason) and can be quite painful. The disease results in a curvature of the penis that, in severe cases, interferes with erection and intercourse (Wilson & Delk, 1994). Medical treatments can alleviate the source of discomfort, and sometimes the condition disappears without treatment. Rarely are penises perfectly straight; most curve to one side or the other.

Priapism Prolonged and painful erection, occurring when blood is unable to drain from the penis, is called **priapism.** Lasting from several hours to a few days, this problem is not associated with sexual thoughts or activities. Rather, it results from certain medications, including some antidepressants, erection medications, and excessive doses of penile injections for producing an erection. Medical conditions such as sickle-cell disease and leukemia may also cause priapism ("What Is Priapism?," 1997).

● Physical Causes of Sexual Function Difficulties and Dissatisfaction

Until recently, researchers believed that most sexual function problems were almost exclusively psychological in origin. Current research challenges this view as more is learned about the intricacies of sexual physiology, such as the subtle influences of hormones. Our vascular, neurological, and endocrine systems are sensitive to changes and disruptions. As a result, various illnesses or disturbances to these systems may have an adverse effect on our sexual functioning (Nusbaum, Hamilton, & Lenahan, 2003). Some prescription drugs, such as medication for hypertension or for depression, may affect sexual responsiveness. Chemotherapy and radiation treatment for cancer, and pain from cancer, affect sexual desire and responsiveness (Fleming & Pace, 2001). More research has been conducted on male sexual function; hence, more is known about the impact of physical causes of male sexual functioning than female sexual functioning (Bancroft, 2002).

Although sexual dissatisfaction often reflects conflict and discord within a relationship or disrupts a relationship, if the problem is due to a medical problem, there may be less relationship strain. If the relationship was stable before the onset of the illness or condition, a couple may have a satisfactory relationship without sexual intercourse. Other forms of sexual interaction may also provide sexual intimacy and pleasure.

Physical Causes in Men

Diabetes and alcoholism are leading causes of male erectile difficulties; together, they account for several million cases. Diabetes damages blood vessels and nerves, including those within the penis. Other causes of sexual function difficulties include lumbar disc disease and multiple sclerosis, which interfere with the nerve impulses regulating erection. In addition, atherosclerosis causes blockage of the arteries, including the blood flow necessary for erection. Spinal cord injuries and prostate-cancer treatment may affect erectile abilities as well. Alcoholism and drug use are widely associated with sexual difficulties. Smoking may also contribute to sexual difficulties. One study found that men who are heavy smokers are 50% more likely to experience erectile problems than nonsmokers (National Center for Environmental Health, 1995). Bicycle-induced sexual difficulties can occur as a result of a flattening of the main penile artery, thereby temporarily blocking the blood flow required for erections. Diseases of the heart and circulatory system may be associated with erectile difficulty. A four-country study of 2,400 men found that "erectile dysfunction was associated with diabetes, heart disease, lower urinary tract symptoms, heavy smoking and depression and increased by 10 percent per year of age" (Nicolosi, Moreiba, Shirai, Bin Mohd Tambi, & Glasser, 2003).

Physical Causes in Women

Organic causes of female orgasmic disorder include medical conditions such as diabetes and heart disease, hormone deficiencies, and neurological disorders, as well as general poor health, extreme fatigue, drug use, and alcoholism. Spinal cord injuries may affect sexual responsiveness (Jackson & Wadley, 1999). Multiple sclerosis can decrease vaginal lubrication and sexual response.

Dyspareunia may result from an obstructed or thickened hymen, clitoral adhesions, infections, painful scars, a constrictive clitoral hood, vulvodynia (see Chapter 13), or a weak **pubococcygeus** (pew-bo-kawk-SEE-gee-us), or P.C., the pelvic floor muscle surrounding the urethra and the vagina. Antihistamines used to treat colds and allergies can reduce vaginal lubrication, as can marijuana. Endometriosis and ovarian and uterine tumors and cysts may affect a woman's sexual response.

The skin covering the clitoris can become infected. Women who masturbate too vigorously can irritate their clitoris, making intercourse painful. A partner can also stimulate a woman too roughly, causing soreness in the vagina, urethra, or clitoral area. And dirty hands may cause a vaginal or urinary tract infection.

● Psychological Causes of Sexual Function Difficulties and Dissatisfaction

Sexual function difficulties may have their origin in any number of psychological causes. Some difficulties originate from immediate causes, others from conflict within the self, and still others from a particular sexual relationship. Gay men and lesbian women often have unique issues affecting their sexual functioning.

Immediate Causes

The immediate causes of sexual function difficulties include fatigue, stress, ineffective sexual behavior, and sexual anxieties.

Fatigue and Stress   Many difficulties have fairly simple causes. Men and women may find themselves physically exhausted from the demands of daily life. They may bring their fatigue into the bedroom in the form of sexual apathy or disinterest. "I'm too tired to make love tonight" can be a truthful description of a person's feelings. What these couples may need is not therapy or counseling but temporary relief from their daily routines.

Long-term stress can also contribute to lowered sexual drive and reduced responsiveness. A man or woman preoccupied with making financial ends meet, raising children, or coping with prolonged illness can temporarily lose sexual desire.

Ineffective Sexual Behavior   Ignorance, ineffective sexual communication, and misinformation prevent partners from being effectively sexual with each

The demands of work and child rearing may create fatigue and stress, which can create sexual apathy for one or both partners.

other. Ineffective sexual stimulation is especially relevant in explaining why some women do not experience orgasm in sexual interactions, as discussed earlier and in the box "Is Intercourse Enough? The Big 'O' and Sexual Behaviors."

Some gay men and lesbian women have not learned effective sexual stimulation behaviors because they are inexperienced. They have grown up without easily accessible sexual information or positive role models.

Sexual Anxieties   A number of anxieties, such as performance anxiety, can lead to sexual function dissatisfaction. If a man fails to experience an erection or a woman is not orgasmic, he or she may feel anxious and fearful. And the anxiety may block the very response the man or woman desires.

Performance anxieties may give rise to **spectatoring,** in which a person becomes a spectator of her or his own sexual performance (Masters & Johnson, 1970). When people become spectators of their sexual activities, they critically evaluate and judge whether they are "performing" well or whether they are doing everything "right." Kaplan and Horwith (1983) suggest that spectatoring is involved in most orgasmic difficulties.

Performance anxiety may be even more widespread among gay men. Sex researcher Rex Reece (1988) writes: "Many gay men move in a social, sexual milieu where sexual arousal is expected immediately or soon after meeting someone. If response is not rapidly forthcoming, rejection is very likely."

Excessive Need to Please a Partner   Another source of anxiety is an excessive need to please a partner. A man who feels this need, sometimes labeled as trying to be the "delivery boy," may want a speedy erection to please (or impress) his partner (Castleman, 2004). He may feel that he must "give her orgasms" through his expert lovemaking or always delay his orgasm until after his partner's. A woman who experiences this anxiety may want to have an orgasm quickly to please her partner. She may worry that she is not sufficiently attractive to her partner or that she is sexually inadequate.

One result of the need to please is that men and women may pretend to have orgasms. (Meg Ryan famously demonstrated faking an orgasm in a deli in the film *When Harry Met Sally*.) One study found that two thirds of the women and one third of the men reported faking orgasm (Darling & Davidson, 1986). Women fake orgasm most often to avoid disappointing their partner or hurting his feelings and, according to sex therapist Kathryn Hall (2004), "are buying into the myth that men are really concerned only with satisfying their own ego." Both men and women also fake orgasm to present a false image of their sexual performance. Unfortunately, faking orgasm miscommunicates to the partner that a person is equally satisfied. Because the orgasmic problem is not addressed, negative emotions may simmer. The wisest decision is never to pretend to experience feelings, interests, or pleasures that do not happen (Hall, 2004).

Conflict Within the Self

Negative parental attitudes toward sex are frequently associated with subsequent sexual function difficulties. Much of the process of growing up is a casting off of the sexual guilt and negativity instilled in childhood. Some people fear becoming emotionally intimate with another person. They may enjoy the sex but fear the accompanying feelings of vulnerability and so withdraw from the sexual relationship before they become emotionally close to their partner (Hyde & DeLamater, 2008). And among gay men and lesbian women, **internalized homophobia**— self-hatred because of one's homosexuality—is a major source of conflict that can be traced to a number of factors including conservative religious upbringing (Nichols, 1988; Reece, 1988).

Sources of severe sexual function difficulties include childhood sexual abuse, adult sexual assault, and rape. Guilt and conflict do not usually eliminate a person's sex drive; rather, they inhibit the drive and alienate the individual from his or her sexuality. He or she may come to see sexuality as something bad or "dirty," rather than something to happily affirm.

Therapists Robert Firestone, Lisa Firestone, and Joyce Catlett (2006) provide an alternative perspective on the decline of sexual passion in long-term relationships and marriage. They believe that the decline cannot be attributed to the usual given reasons such as familiarity, gender differences, economic hardships, and other stressors but rather to changes in the relationship dynamics, emergence of painful feelings from childhood, and fears of rejection that cause partners to retreat to a more defended posture. Many men and women have difficulty in maintaining sexually satisfying relationships "because in their earlier relationships, hurt and frustration caused them to turn away from love and closeness and to become suspicious and self-protective." In advising couples in longer-term relationships, the therapists note:

> To sustain a loving sexual relationship, individuals must be willing to face the threats to the defense system that loving another person and being loved for oneself evoke. To be able to accept genuine affection, tenderness, love, and fulfilling sexual experiences as part of an ongoing relationship, they must be willing to challenge their negative voices, modify the image of themselves formed in the family, and give up well-entrenched defenses, which would cause them a great deal of anxiety.

Relationship Causes

Sexual function difficulties do not exist in a vacuum, but usually within the context of a relationship. All couples at some point experience difficulties in

In the 1990s a feminist joke asked, "Why do women fake orgasm?" and answered "Because men fake foreplay." In the masculinist version, the question was "Why do women fake orgasm?" and the answer, "Because they think men care."

—Angus McLaren

Pleasure is the object, duty, and the goal of all rational creatures.

—Voltaire
(1694–1770)

think
about it

Surrendering to Sexual Pleasure

Sexual pleasure is considered an innate trait of human sexuality that permeates the human experience. Given the frequency of which sexual pleasure is the topic of song, art, literature, daily conversation and fantasies, it seems to be a universal human trait, one that we humans are driven to seek. Evolutionary theory contends that sexual pleasure is a by-product of motivation to propagate one's genes as reflected in sexual strategies theory (Buss, 2003; Buss & Schmitt, 1993), which is discussed in Chapter 9. But, for the vast majority of us, sexual pleasure, not procreation, is the guiding beacon for how our sexuality is defined and experienced.

Given historical stances that the primary role of human sexuality is reproduction, sexual pleasure has been projected as inappropriate and unworthy, particularly by social regulation, religious groups and cultural expression. Hence, its expression and experience has been regulated, altered, and even criminalized by social regulation and cultural expression. The capacity for sexual pleasure is physiologically determined, but for both men and women, particularly women, guilt, shame, fear, and embarrassment, for example, hinder the "surrender to sexual pleasure" (Garza-Mercer, 2006). Sex therapist Esther Perel (2006) contends that we are socialized to control ourselves, to restrain and edit ourselves and mask our ravenous appetites. She states that "Because loss of control is almost exclusively seen in a negative light, we don't even entertain the idea that surrender can be emotionally or spiritually enlightening."

Dr. David Reed of the Medical College of Philadelphia has developed a schematic model, called the erotic stimulus Pathway (ESP), to represent the psychological nature of sexual response, as shown on the next page (Reed, cited in Stayton, 1996). It helps us to understand the importance of sexual pleasure. Reed uses the terms seduction, sensations, surrender, and reflection as alternative descriptions to the traditional sexual response components of desire, excitement, plateau, orgasm, and so on, of the Masters and Johnson (1966) and Kaplan (1979) models that are discussed in Chapter 3. According to the ESP model, one must "surrender" for orgasm to occur as a pleasurable experience.

All persons are capable of sexual desire and experiencing sexual pleasure. However, roadblocks keep many people from claiming their right to sexual pleasure. Mantak Chia and Rachel Abrams, in their book *The Multi-Orgasmic Woman* (2007), state that the situation may be perfect for very pleasurable sex, but it may not happen if the person likes to "be in control" and cannot surrender to orgasm. They note that knowing how to help one's body surrender to the ecstatic rush of pleasures that is orgasm is a necessary part of gaining mastery and fulfillment in one's sexual repertoire.

Human sexuality authors and instructors Vera Bodansky and Steve Bodansky (2006) believe that if one is going to pursue sexual pleasure, it is best to pursue it with all of one's capability. They contend that many women surrender only partially to sexual pleasure. But, if the woman feels safe with a trusted person and is relaxed, surrender most likely

their sexual relationship. Sex therapist David Schnarch (2002) writes that "sexual problems are common among healthy couples who are normal in every other way—so common, in fact, that they are arguably a sign of normality." Most frequently, married couples go into therapy because they have a greater investment in the relationship than couples who are dating or cohabiting. Sexual function difficulties in a dating or cohabiting relationship often do not surface; it is sometimes easier for couples to break up than to change the behaviors that contribute to their sexual function problems.

Sex therapist Esther Perel, in her book *Mating in Captivity* (2006), presents a provocative view of desire difficulties in marriage, one that is counter to often-held perspectives among sex therapists. She contends that eroticism thrives on the unpredictable and that increased intimacy often leads to a decrease in sexual desire. Perel states that love is fed by knowing everything about one's partner while desire needs mystery, and that love wants to shrink the distance between the two people while desire is energized by it. She continues by declaring that "as an expression of longing, desire requires

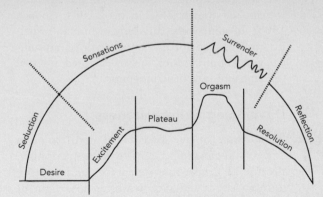

The Erotic Stimulus Pathway. (*Source:* Reed, cited in Stayton, 1996.)

will happen gradually. So, there is no need to rush to total surrender. Bodansky and Bodansky state:

> To surrender one's nervous system, one has to trust that the person they are surrendering with (notice that we did not say "surrendering to," as the surrender is actually to one's own greater pleasure) knows what he or she is doing and isn't going to cause any physical, emotional, or mental harm. To surrender is to make oneself vulnerable. Therefore, doing so can be a challenge, especially the first few times.

Part of owning one's sexuality is freeing oneself from shame, fear, and guilt, and believing that it is OK to be a fully sexual being. Being a fully sexual human being means having the freedom and ability to surrender to sexual pleasure and to

cultivate sexual passion. Carrol Cassell, a nationally recognized leader in human sexuality, states that passionate sex dissolves boundaries, bonds one in a primal form of intimacy, and allows a couple to surrender to the experience of pleasure (2008). Cassell continues by noting that "what counts is to let yourself have fun in bed, to sometimes be very nice and sometimes be very naughty." Barriers to experiencing sexual pleasure and ways to enhance pleasure are discussed in more detail in later sections of this chapter.

Think Critically

- Do you like the expression "surrender to sexual pleasure" as a way to convey what must occur to be fully sexual? Why or why not?
- Do you believe that sexual pleasure is an innate capability of all humans? Explain.
- Why do you think it is more difficult for women, in general, in our culture to surrender to sexual pleasure?
- What personal and relationship conditions make it easier to surrender to sexual pleasure?

SOURCES: Cassell, C. (2008). *Put passion first: Why sexual chemistry is the key to finding and keeping lasting love.* New York: McGraw-Hill; Chia, M., & Abrams, R. C. (2007). *The multi-orgasmic woman.* London: Rodale International; Garza-Mercer, F. D. (2006). The evolution of sexual pleasure. In M. R. Kurth (Ed.), *Handbook of the evolution of human sexuality.* New York: Haworth; Perel, E. (2006). *Mating in captivity.* New York: Harper. Stayton, W. R. (1996). A theology of sexual pleasure. In E. Stuart & A. Thatcher (Eds.), *Christian perspectives on sexuality and gender.* Grand Rapids, MI: Eerdmans, and Herefordshire, UK: Gracewing.

elusiveness." Perel contends that couples may be more successful in maintaining and cultivating sexual desire by enriching their separate lives instead of always striving for closeness. The challenge for many couples is balancing separateness with togetherness as both are important components of a loving relationship.

If sexual function problems are left unresolved, disappointment, rage, anger, resentment, power conflicts, and hostility often become a permanent part of couple interaction.

> As with singers in a harmony, a harmonious sex life is not necessarily one in which you are both wanting and doing exactly the same things in the same way, but one that is characterized by blending the strengths that you each have to create an agreeable and pleasant sex life.
>
> —Sandra Pertot
> (1950–)

● Sexual Function Enhancement

Improving the quality of a sexual relationship is referred to as **sexual function enhancement.** There are several sexual function–enhancement programs for people who function well sexually but who nevertheless want to improve the quality of their sexual interactions and relationships. The programs generally

Good sex involves the ability to communicate nonverbally—through laughter and good times—as well as verbally.

seek to provide accurate information about sexuality, develop communication skills, foster positive attitudes, provide sexual homework for practicing techniques discussed in therapy, and increase self-awareness (Castleman, 2004; Cooper, 1985). In some ways, the study of human sexuality involves many of the same cognitive, attitudinal, and communication themes explored in sexual function–enhancement programs.

Developing Self-Awareness

Being aware of our own sexual needs is often critical to enhancing our sexual functioning. Because of gender-role stereotypes and negative learning about sexuality, we often lose sight of our own sexual needs.

What Is Good Sex?   Sexual stereotypes present us with images of how we are supposed to behave sexually. Images of the "sexually in charge" man and the "sexual but not too sexual" woman may interfere with our ability to express our own sexual feelings, needs, and desires. We follow the scripts and stereotypes we have been socialized to accept, rather than our own unique responses. Following these cultural images may impede our ability to have what therapist Carol Ellison calls "good sex." In an essay about intimacy-based sex therapy, Ellison (1985) writes that we will know we are having good sex if we feel good about ourselves, our partners, our relationships, and our sexual behaviors. Further, we will feel good about sex before, during, and after being sexual with our partners (Hall, 2004). Good sex does not necessarily include orgasm or intercourse. It can be kissing, cuddling, masturbating, performing oral or anal sex, and so on; it can be other-sex or same-sex sexual expression.

Discovering Your Conditions for Good Sex   Zilbergeld (1999) has suggested that to fully enjoy our sexuality we need to explore our "conditions for good sex." There is nothing unusual about requiring conditions for any activity. Of conditions for good sex, Zilbergeld (1999) writes:

> In a sexual situation, a condition is anything that makes you more relaxed, more comfortable, more confident, more excited, more open to your experience. Put differently, a condition is something that clears your nervous system of unnecessary clutter, leaving it open to receive and transmit sexual messages in ways that will result in a good time for you.

Some common conditions, according to Zilbergeld (1999), include the following:

■ *Feeling intimate with your partner.* Intimacy is often important for both men and women. Partners who are feeling distant from each other may need to talk about their feelings before becoming sexual. Emotional distance can take the heart out of sex.

" *When our innermost desires are revealed and are met by our loved one with acceptance and validation, the shame dissolves.*

—Esther Perel
(1958–)

Sexual Turn-Ons and Turn-Offs: What College Students Report

What turns college men and women on and off sexually? Are there gender differences and similarities? Sex researcher Robin R. Milhausen conducted an online study of 822 heterosexual students (440 women and 382 men) between ages 18 and 37 from Indiana University who were randomly selected to participate. She contends that a greater understanding of factors that turn on and turn off men and women can be valuable in increasing sexual well-being and improving sexual relationships. Here are the study's major findings.

Some Important Factors Men and Women Agreed On

Factors that *enhance sexual arousal* for both men and women:

- A good sense of humor, self-confidence, and intelligence
- Feeling desired as a partner
- Spontaneous and varied sex (e.g., not the same activities every time, having sex in a different setting)
- Fantasizing about and anticipating a sexual encounter
- Doing something fun together

Turn-offs for both men and women:

- A lack of balance in giving and receiving during sex
- A partner who is self-conscious about his or her body
- Worrying about getting a bad reputation
- Worrying about STIs
- Using condoms

Some Important Factors Men and Women Disagreed On

- Women were more concerned about their sexual functioning (e.g., being a good lover, worrying about taking too long to become aroused, feeling shy or self-conscious).
- Being in a relationship characterized by trust and emotional safety was considered more important to sexual arousal for women than for men.

- More women than men indicated that "feeling used" was a big turn-off.
- Men more often considered a variety of sexual stimuli (e.g., thinking about someone they find sexually attractive, "talking dirty," thinking and talking about sex, being physically close to a partner) as enhancers to sexual arousal.
- Women more often considered partner characteristics and behaviors (e.g., partner showing talent, interacting well with others, doing chores) as enhancers to sexual arousal.
- Women more often considered elements of the sexual setting (e.g., a setting where they might be seen or heard while having sex) as inhibitors to sexual arousal.
- Women were more aware of the role of hormones in sexual arousal.
- Women more often considered elements of the sexual interaction (e.g., partner not sensitive to the signals being given and received during sex, being uncertain how her partner feels) as inhibitors of sexual arousal.
- More men than women *disagreed* that "going right to the genitals" during sex would be a turn-off during sex.

Think Critically

- Were you surprised by any of the findings?
- Are some of the results similar to what you would consider sexual turn-ons and turn-offs?
- Have you learned anything from this study that you might use in your future sexual encounters?
- Do you think the results would be similar for gay men couples and lesbian women couples?

SOURCES: Milhausen, R. R. (2004). *Factors that inhibit and enhance sexual arousal in college men and women.* Doctoral dissertation. Indiana University, Bloomington, IN; Milhausen, R. R., Yarber, W., Sanders, S., & Graham, C. (2004, November). *Factors that inhibit and enhance sexual arousal in college men and women.* Paper presented at the annual meeting of the Society for the Scientific Study of Sexuality, Orlando, FL.

- *Feeling sexually capable.* Generally, feeling sexually capable relates to an absence of anxieties about sexual functioning. For men, these include anxiety about becoming erect or ejaculating too soon. For women, these include anxiety about painful intercourse or lack of orgasm. For both men and women, they include worry about whether one is a good lover.

- *Feeling trust.* Both men and women may need to know that they are emotionally safe with their partner. They need to feel confident that they will not be judged, ridiculed, or talked about.

- *Feeling physically and mentally alert.* This condition requires that partners not feel particularly tired, ill, stressed, or preoccupied, as well as not be excessively under the influence of alcohol or drugs.

- *Feeling positive about the environment and situation.* A partner may need privacy, to be in a place where he or she feels protected from intrusion. Each needs to feel that the other is sexually interested and wants to be sexually involved.

Each individual has his or her own unique conditions for good sex. If you are or have been sexually active, to discover your conditions for good sex, think about the last few times you were sexual and were highly aroused. Then compare those times with other times when you were much less aroused (Zilbergeld, 1999). Identify the needs that underlie these factors and communicate these needs to your partner.

Doing Homework Exercises   We are often unaware of our body and our erotic responses. Sexual function–enhancement programs often specify exercises for couples to undertake in private. Such "homework" exercises require individuals to make a time commitment to themselves or their partner. Typical assignments include the following exercises. If you feel comfortable with any of the assignments, you might want to try one or more.

Click on "Self-Awareness" to see a woman doing a mirror examination and other "homework" exercises.

- *Mirror examination.* Use a full-length mirror to examine your nude body. Use a hand mirror to view your genitals. Look at all your features in an uncritical manner; view yourself with acceptance.

- *Body relaxation and exploration.* Take 30–60 minutes to fully relax. Begin with a leisurely shower or bath; then, remaining nude, find a comfortable place to touch and explore your body and genitals.

- *Masturbation.* In a relaxed situation, with body oils or lotions to enhance your sensations, explore ways of touching your body and genitals that bring you pleasure. Do this exercise for several sessions without having an orgasm; experiencing erotic pleasure without orgasm is the goal. If you are about to have an orgasm, decrease stimulation. After several sessions without having an orgasm, continue pleasuring yourself until you have an orgasm.

- *Erotic aids.* Products designed to enhance erotic responsiveness, such as vibrators, dildos, G-spot stimulators, artificial vaginas and mouths, clitoral stimulators, vibrating nipple clips, explicit videos, oils, and lotions, are referred to as **erotic aids.** They are also called **sex toys,** emphasizing their playful quality. Vibrators and dildos seem to be the most common sex toys and are usually considered "women's toys." But, of course, they can be for either gender and can be used alone or with a partner. Two recent national studies of men and women in the U.S., ages 18–60 years, assessed lifetime use of vibrators: 44.8% of men had incorporated a vibrator into their sexual activities during their lives and 52.5% of women had ever used a vibrator (Reece et al., 2009; Herbenick et al., 2009). You may wish to try using a sex toy or shower massage as you masturbate with

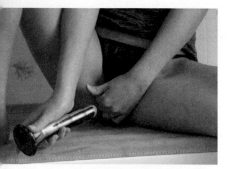

A vibrator can be a valuable aid in increasing sexual arousal and experiencing an orgasm.

Some individuals and couples use erotic aids like vibrators, dildos, videos, oils, and lotions to enhance their sexual pleasure and responsiveness.

your partner or by yourself. You may also want to view videos at home or read erotic poetry or stories to yourself or your partner. Recently, there has been a dramatic increase in natural herbal sexual enhancers that promise terrific sex. Do they work? See the accompanying box to find out.

Intensifying Erotic Pleasure

One of the most significant elements in enhancing our physical experience of sex is intensifying arousal. In intensifying arousal, the focus is on erotic pleasure rather than on sexual functioning. This can be done in a number of ways.

Sexual Arousal   Sexual arousal refers to the physiological responses, fantasies, and desires associated with sexual anticipation and activity. We have different levels of arousal, and they are not necessarily associated with particular types of sexual activities. Sometimes, we feel more sexually aroused when we kiss or masturbate than when we have sexual intercourse or oral sex.

The first element in increasing sexual arousal is having your conditions for good sex met. If you need privacy, find a place to be alone; if you need a romantic setting, go for a relaxing walk or listen to music by candlelight; if you want limits on your sexual activities, tell your partner; if you need a certain kind of physical stimulation, show or tell your partner what you like.

Natural Sexual Enhancers in a Bottle: The "Magic Bullet" for Spicing Up Your Sex Life?

Preying on people's insecurities and distorted images of perfect sex, "natural sexual enhancers" promise to "spice up your sex life," "rekindle desire," "improve sexual performance," and "enhance the body's own natural sexual health."** The number of homeopathic products sold on the Internet and in grocery stores, convenience stores, health food stores, and drugstores surged following the Food and Drug Administration's approval of Viagra in 1998 (Schardt, 2004). Supported by unsubstantiated claims and personal testimonials, these "magic bullet" capsules, herbal erection pills, creams, sprays, lubricants, gels, and tonics promise greater sexual arousal and rock-hard erections and are promoted widely. Apparently, a lot of people have been persuaded by the advertising campaigns, as sales have increased dramatically (Riscol, 2003), reaching nearly $400 million in 2006.

Most, but not all, of the natural sexual enhancement products focus on men's erections. Not surprisingly, very few of these erection-enhancing products, such as Stamina-RX® and Vigor-25, have demonstrated the effectiveness of their claims. Actually, the labels of "all natural" products, as well as others, include disclaimers as required by law: "These statements have not been evaluated by the Food and Drug Administration" and "This product is not intended to diagnose, treat, cure, or prevent any disease." Since these products are unregulated by the FDA, they may or may not contain the ingredients listed on the label. Further, they may contain unregulated versions of the pharmaceuticals they are marketed to replace. This is what is becoming a major concern of public health officials.

An analysis of the "natural" male sexual enhancers has found that the vast majority of the products contained forms of patented pharmaceuticals, such as sildenafil citrate, the main ingredient in Viagra, for treating erectile dysfunction. The danger of this is that, for the 5.5 million American men who take nitrates prescribed to lower blood pressure and regulate heart disease, taking one of these products could lead

to a stroke or death. When used together, nitrates and erectile dysfunction drugs can slow blood flow, which can lead to a stroke or heart attack. Hospital emergency rooms and poison-control hotlines have had an increase in visits and inquiries from men who used the all-natural sex pills. The pills that claim immediate results seem to exhibit more danger than some legitimate herbal mixtures that claim they work gradually over weeks (Pritchard, 2007).

A Tufts University, Health and Nutrition Letter (2002) titled "Better Sex Life Not Found Over the Counter" commented on any possible effectiveness of natural sexual enhancers:

> Granted, there is some weak, preliminary evidence of a few substances. But that's all. For instance, yohimbe, an herb derived from the bark of a West African evergreen tree, contains the chemical yohimbine, a drug used for such things as pupil dilation. However, there is no support for yohimbe as an effective treatment for impotence. The amino acid L-Arginine, or arginine, is another popular sexual aid supplement. It is typically combined with other ingredients (including yohimbe), but again clinical proof for the efficacy of the substance is lacking. These findings don't mean there's no evidence, but it is much too fragile for consumers to invest money and hopes in any of these products.

Herbs, such as Asian ginseng and *Ginkgo biloba*, and antioxidants such as vitamins E and C have been touted as improving sexual function, but the research is not conclusive. In short, there aren't any natural "magic bullets" that will "transform you into an instant lovemaking machine" (Riscol, 2003). Conclusive evidence of the effectiveness of the natural sexual enhancers for treating male and female, sexual function problems has not been established. As suggested throughout this book, enhancing your emotional and physical health, as well as your relationship with your partner, is usually the best path to sexual pleasure.

A second element in increasing arousal is focusing on the sensations you are experiencing. Once you begin an erotic activity such as massaging or kissing, do not let yourself be distracted. When you're kissing, don't think about what you're going to do next or about an upcoming test. Instead, focus on the sensual experience of your lips and heart. Zilbergeld (1999) writes:

> Focusing on sensations means exactly that. You put your attention in your body where the action is. When you're kissing, keep your mind on your lips. This is *not* the

same as thinking about your lips or the kiss; just put your attention in your lips. As you focus on your sensations, you may want to convey your pleasure to your partner. Let him or her know through your sounds and movements that you are excited.

Alternatives to Intercourse Waiting, delaying, and facing obstacles may intensify arousal. This is one of the pleasures of sexual abstinence that may get lost soon after you begin intercourse. Lonnie Barbach (2001) suggests that sexually active people may intensify arousal by placing a ban on sexual intercourse for a period of time. If you are a gay or lesbian person, you may place a comparable ban on your preferred activity. During this time, explore other ways of being erotic or sexual, such as showering together, giving or receiving an erotic massage without genital stimulation, sharing one's sexual fantasies, or dancing together sexually.

Changing a Sexual Relationship

In his book *Resurrecting Sex* (2002), David Schnarch, a prominent sex therapist and clinical psychologist, discusses common sexual function difficulties of couples and provides practical suggestions for addressing them. Schnarch says that every couple has sexual function problems at some point, although most couples do not anticipate that they will end up being bedeviled by sexual dissatisfaction. In a statement that might seem surprising, Schnarch notes, "If your sexual relationship stays the same, you are more likely to have sexual dysfunctions (and be bored to death)." He suggests that we "think of medical-related sexual problems as 'problems given the way we usually have sex,' as opposed to 'intractable problems you'll have no matter what you do.'"

Schnarch declares that changing the sexual relationship is necessary for couples having sexual function problems:

> Expect to shake up your sexual relationship every once in a while. I know that's exactly opposite what couples want to do. People usually like stability in their sexual relationships. Just incorporate episodic shake-ups into your notion of long-term stability. You have a dormant sexual potential that's ready and waiting to be developed.

Schnarch suggests 22 ways to "resurrect sex." His concepts and strategies for resolving sexual function difficulties include the following:

1. Put some effort into the nonsexual aspects of the relationship. Focus on the daily things.

2. Expand your repertoire of sexual behaviors, "tones," styles, and meanings. Push yourself to try sexual behaviors that might seem to be a stretch. Resurrecting sex means doing things differently.

3. Address any issues you and your partner have swept under the carpet. Trying to be intimate and sexual when you are angry, frustrated, or resentful often does not work.

4. Deal with unresolved personal issues. They can hinder your arousal and make you vulnerable to sexual difficulties.

5. Do not become overly concerned with possible unconscious meanings of your sexual problems, and don't get sidetracked playing amateur psychoanalyst. No personality traits or life experiences invariably result in sexual function difficulties. Pay attention to your specific situation, and focus on what is actually happening to you.

License my roving hands, and let them go,
Behind, before, above, between, below.

—John Donne
(1572–1631)

Surprising how the most common sexual problem is not low libido, rapid ejaculation, or difficulty with orgasm: it is that people are not prepared for the extent of individual differences in human sexuality.

—Sandra Pertot
(1950–)

6. Recognize that changing a sexual relationship typically involves embracing a deeper connection. Given that many couples do not achieve much emotional connection through sex, this can be a challenge. Intimate, deep connection during sex requires a sensory and emotional bond with your partner.

Schnarch guarantees one thing: To resurrect or improve an intimate relationship, you have to change the current relationship. He notes that this is no small task. Rather, it involves raising your level of stimulation, growing up, accepting new truths, becoming closer, and changing yourself in the process. Resurrecting sex requires becoming unstuck without taking out frustrations on your partner, even if you think she or he deserves it.

Disparities in Sexual Desire

Among the sexual problems a couple may experience and desire to change, disparities in sexual desire ranks at the top. Actually, difference in sexual desire is the most common complaint among couples (Schnarch, 2002). This is why we are giving special attention to this particular issue.

According to Schnarch (2002), one person of a couple often gets blamed for having low sexual desire, but, actually, the issue is the difference in sexual desire between both partners. For most long-term relationships, sexual passion subsides but not always at the same rate for each partner. Most sex therapists believe that differences arise because, for example, one or both partners may be fatigued, ill, under the influence of alcohol or other drugs, or consumed with the tasks of daily living. Or there may be problems with the sexual relationship of the couple, such as anger or imbalance of power between the partners. Clinical psychologist and sex therapist Sandra Pertot, in her book *When Your Sex Drives Don't Match* (2007), presents another perspective on why couples experience variation in sexual desire. She contends that the sexual issues, including very common desire discrepancies, typically do not represent individual pathology or relationship problems, but, instead, reflect the fact that there are different sexual types, which she labels "libido types," such as sensual, erotic, stressed, detached, and disinterested. Interestingly, she states that "people are different just because they are, not because there is anything wrong with them" and encourages an acceptance of different libido types as one way of minimizing misinterpreting each other's sexuality.

Michael Castleman, an award-winning medical writer, notes in his book *Great Sex: A Man's Guide to the Secret Principles of Total-Body Sex* (2004) that there is no magic formula for resolving sexual desire discrepancies. But he does offer some suggestions for dealing with desire differences in couples:

- *Count your blessings.* The higher desire partner may want sex more often than the lower desire partner. But at least the lower desire person wants sex sometimes. Isn't some sex better than none? Because differences in sexual desire occur in most long-term relationships, adapting to the change is the key.

- *Don't try to change your partner's libido.* In a couple with desire discrepancy, each partner may hope that the other person will change and acquire a compatible level of desire. But it is difficult for a lover to do that. Sexual desire can change, but this must come from within the person.

- *Consider your choices and negotiate.* A couple having chronic difficulties with sexual desire has three choices: (1) break up, (2) do nothing and live in misery, or (3) negotiate a mutually agreed compromise. Couples wanting to live comfortably with each other have no choice other than to compromise by being flexible, showing good faith, and being willing to invest in the happiness of the relationship.

- *Schedule sex dates.* Certainly there is some excitement when sex occurs spontaneously. But scheduling has an advantage of eliminating sexual uncertainty for couples facing major desire differences. Both partners know when sex will occur. The higher desire person then may not make as many sexual advances and the lower desire person will not have to experience repeated requests.

- *Cultivate nonsexual affection.* Once sex dates are scheduled, nonsexual affection has less chance of being misconstrued as having sexual expectations. Being held and touched is one of the most important ways to nurture a relationship, and knowing that it has no sexual connotations may provide a great relief.

- *Savor your solution.* Once a couple negotiates a mutual compromise, the relationship often improves and resentments slowly fade. The lower desire person may become more comfortable, which often improves that person's responsiveness. There may still be some desire differences; the ability to compromise means that the couple has found a workable solution for their relationship.

Because fluctuations in individual sexual desire are a normal part of life, as are differences in desire between partners, individuals may choose masturbation as an acceptable and pleasurable outlet for sexual desire. As is true for all areas of sexual functioning, the important thing to remember, when sexual appetites differ, is that communicating openly and honestly and appreciating what a person brings to the relationship pave the way to resolution and fulfillment. Cultivating sexuality by planning for sex, using one's imagination, learning to play, recognizing your partner's mystery, and respecting his or her privacy can all increase desire. If given sufficient attention, desire often returns (Perel, 2006; Pertot, 2007).

● Treating Sexual Function Difficulties

There are several psychologically based approaches to sex therapy, the most important ones being behavior modification and psychosexual therapy. William Masters and Virginia Johnson were the pioneers in the cognitive-behavioral approach; one of the most influential psychosexual therapist is Helen Singer Kaplan. Medical approaches may also be effective with some sexual function problems.

Click on "Taking a Sexual History" to see a urologist taking a sexual history from a man with erectile dysfunction.

Masters and Johnson: A Cognitive-Behavioral Approach

The program developed by Masters and Johnson for the treatment of sexual function difficulties was the starting point for contemporary sex therapy. Not only did they reject the Freudian approach of tracing sexual function problems to childhood; they relabeled sexual function problems as sexual dysfunctions rather than aspects of neuroses. Masters and Johnson (1970) argued that the majority of sexual function problems are the result of sexual ignorance, faulty techniques, or relationship problems. They treated difficulties using a combination of cognitive and behavioral techniques, and they treated couples rather than individuals.

Couples With Difficulties Cognitive-behavioral therapists approach the problems of erectile and orgasmic difficulties by dealing with the couple rather than the individual. They regard sexuality as an interpersonal phenomenon rather than an individual one. In fact, they tell their clients that there are no individuals with sexual function difficulties, only couples with sexual function difficulties. Sex therapist Sandra Pertot (2007) states that "even people with secure, happy personal histories can end up with unsatisfying sexual relationships, because it is how your individual sexuality interacts with your partner's that defines what is a problem and what isn't." In this model, neither individual is to blame for any sexual dissatisfaction; rather, it is their mutual interaction that sustains a difficulty or resolves a problem. Masters and Johnson called this principle "neutrality and mutuality" (Masters & Johnson, 1974).

Therapists using this approach prefer to treat only those couples who are genuinely committed to their relationship. The partners are told not to attempt sexual intercourse or other intimate sexual behavior until they are given permission by their therapist or team of two therapists (both sexes for heterosexual couples). In this way, each partner is immediately relieved of any pressure to perform, thus easing anxieties and allowing the development of a more relaxed attitude toward sex.

Case Histories During the first session, each individual is interviewed separately. Blame is not assigned to either partner, for it is the couple, rather than the individuals, who are being treated.

After the interviews and the case histories have been completed, the couple meets with the therapist(s) to discuss what has been learned so far. The therapists explain what they have learned about the couple's personal and sexual interaction, encouraging each individual to expand on or correct what they are saying. Then, any sexual myths and fallacies the partners hold that may interfere with their sexual interaction are discussed.

Sensate Focus Early in the therapy sessions, the therapists introduce **sensate focus,** focusing on touch and the giving and receiving of pleasure (see Figure 14.3). The other senses—smell, sight, hearing, and taste—are worked on indirectly as a means of reinforcing the touch experience. To increase their sensate focus, the couple are given "homework" assignments. In the privacy of their own room, the partners are to take off their clothes so that nothing will restrict their sensations. One partner must give pleasure and the other receive it. The giver touches, caresses, massages, and strokes his or her partner's body everywhere except the genitals and breasts. The purpose is not sexual arousal but simply sense awareness.

For subsequent sessions, therapy is basically the same for any type of sexual problem. Thereafter, the therapists begin to focus on the particular problem affecting the couple.

Treating Male Function Difficulties The therapy utilizes different techniques for treating the specific problem.

Full nakedness! All joys are due to thee,
As souls unbodied, bodies unclothed must be,
To taste whole joys.

—John Donne
(1572–1631)

Erection Difficulties When the problem is erection difficulties, the couple are taught that fears and anxieties are largely responsible and that the removal of these fears is the first step in therapy. Once the fear is removed, the man is less likely to be an observer of his sexuality; he can become an actor rather than a spectator or judge.

After the sensate focus exercises have been integrated into the couple's behavior, the partners are told to play with each other's genitals, but not to attempt an erection. Often, erections may occur because there is no demand on the man; but he is encouraged to let his penis become flaccid again, then erect, then flaccid, as reassurance that he can successfully have erections. This builds his confidence, as well as his partner's, by letting her know that she can excite him.

During this time, the partners are counseled on other aspects of their relationship that contribute to their sexual function difficulties. Then they attempt their first intercourse, if the man has had erections with some success. Eventually, in the final session, the man will most likely have an orgasm.

Therapists also try to dispel many of the erection myths. Although the majority of difficulties with erections are caused by a combination of factors, such as relationship difficulties, cardiovascular problems, and depression, becoming more knowledgeable and realistic about erections is an important step to overcoming difficulties. Common myths include (Castleman, 2004):

- *Erection is something that is achieved.* Penises don't become erect through work, but from just the opposite. The more sensual the lovemaking, the more likely an erection will occur.

- *Men are sex machines, always ready, always hard.* A man can really enjoy sex, but if certain conditions are not met, his penis might not become aroused. Instead of thinking of sex as performance, think about it as play that occurs best when both partners are able to relax.

- *During a sexual encounter, you get only one shot at an erection.* Erection changes during a sexual encounter are very common. If an erection subsides during sex, the man shouldn't tense up and decide it is over, but breathe deeply, keep the faith, and request the partner to provide stimulation that is sensual.

- *I blew it last time; I will never get it up again.* It's a mistake to overgeneralize from a single sexual episode to a lifetime of erection difficulties.

 *The penis, far from being an impenetrable knight in armor, in fact bears its heart on its sleeve.*

—Susan Bordo
(1947–)

• FIGURE 14.4
The Squeeze and Start-Stop Techniques

Overgeneralizing can cause stress, sometimes resulting in a self-fulfilling prophecy.

■ *If I can't have an erection, my partner can't be sexually satisfied.* Certainly there are numerous ways of providing sexual stimulation to a partner without an erection. How many people who care about their partners would leave him if he has erection problems? Most would want to help him resolve them.

Early Ejaculation Cognitive-behavioral therapists treat early or rapid ejaculation by using initially the same pattern as in treating erectile difficulties. They concentrate especially on reducing fears and anxieties and increasing sensate focus and communication. Then they use a simple exercise called the **squeeze technique** (see Figure 14.4). The penis is brought manually to a full erection. Just before he is about to ejaculate, his partner squeezes his penis with thumb and forefinger just below the corona. After 30 seconds of inactivity, the partner arouses him again and, just prior to ejaculation, squeezes again. Using this technique, the couple can continue for 15–20 minutes before the man ejaculates.

Some sex therapists suggest that a man can learn ejaculatory control by increasing his ability to extend the plateau phase of his sexual response cycle, largely through learning to delay ejaculation during masturbation. They encourage men to learn their plateau phase well and, when the "point of no return" is reached during masturbation, the man should stop stroking his penis but not cease caressing completely. This "start-stop" technique can be done by the man himself or during intercourse with his partner (see Figure 14.4). He should also strengthen his P.C. muscle so that he can squeeze it to delay ejaculation at the point of no return. Then he returns to masturbation and repeats the cycle several times. For a man to learn ejaculatory control, sex therapists recommend masturbation several times a week for about 30–60 minutes per session. After several weeks, many men are able to hold themselves in the plateau phase for as long as they want. Further, if a man can learn to last 15 minutes, he can probably last as long as he'd like (Castleman, 2004; Keesling, 2006).

Male Orgasmic Disorder This condition, also referred to as delayed ejaculation, is treated by having the man's partner manipulate his penis. The partner asks for verbal and physical directions to bring him the most pleasure possible. It may take a few sessions before the man has his first ejaculation. The idea is to identify his partner with sexual pleasure and desire. He is encouraged to feel stimulated, not only by his partner but also by her erotic responses to him. After the man has reached orgasm through manual stimulation, he then proceeds to vaginal or anal intercourse. With further instruction and feedback, the man should be able to function sexually without fear of delayed ejaculation.

Sex therapist Barbara Keesling (2006) cautions men trying to overcome delayed ejaculation never to pressure themselves during the exercises, nor do anything to try to ejaculate. The goal should be to learn the sensations of high arousal, breathe deeply, relax, and keep the P.C. muscle from tightening. Keesling states, "Ejaculation will happen when it happens," and it will happen when the man focuses on the sensations that allow ejaculation to occur rather than trying to make it happen.

Treating Female Function Difficulties Each female difficulty is treated differently in behavior modification therapy.

Female Orgasmic Disorder After the sensate focus sessions, the woman's partner begins to touch and caress her vulva; she guides the partner's hand to show what she likes. The partner is told, however, not to stimulate the clitoris directly because it may be extremely sensitive and stimulation may cause pain rather than pleasure. Instead, the partner caresses and stimulates the area around the clitoris, the labia, and the upper thighs. During this time, the partners are told not to attempt to achieve orgasm because it would place undue performance pressure on the woman. They are simply to explore the woman's erotic potential and discover what brings her the greatest pleasure.

Here is a special message to partners of women who have difficulty experiencing orgasm during sex: Support her to have an orgasm any way it happens for her. Sex partners do not give each other orgasms—lovers are traveling companions experiencing their own erotic journey (Castleman, 2004). Sex therapist and author Marty Klein, speaking to partners of women with orgasmic difficulties, states that "you can create the environment in which your lover feels relaxed enough and turned on enough to have one [orgasm]. But, she creates her own orgasm. You don't *give* it to her" (quoted in Castleman, 2004). In support of Klein's contention that a woman creates her own orgasm, a study of 2,371 women revealed that many women do things during sex beyond getting specific physical stimulation to aid them in experiencing orgasm (Ellison, 2000). The most frequent activities of these women are shown in Table 14.3. For example, 9 in 10 women indicated that they positioned their body in a way to get the stimulation they needed.

Vaginismus Vaginismus is one of the easiest sexual problems to overcome. The woman uses a set of vaginal dilators (plastic, penile-shaped rods) graduated in diameter. She inserts one before going to bed at night and takes it out in the morning. As soon as the woman is able to receive a dilator of one size without having vaginal spasms, a larger one is used. In most cases, the vaginismus disappears.

Table 14.3 ● Women's Most Frequent Activities to Facilitate Orgasm During Intercourse[a]	
Activity	**Percentage**
Positioned my body to get the stimulation I needed	90
Paid attention to my physical sensations	83
Tightened and released my pelvic muscles	75
Synchronized the rhythm of my movements to my partner's	75
Asked or encouraged my partner to do what I needed	74
Got myself in a sexy mood beforehand	71
Focused on my partner's pleasure	68
Felt/thought how much I love my partner	65
Engaged in a fantasy of my own	56

[a]From a list of 14 possible answers, the answers that were chosen by at least one half of the women who responded to their sentence "In addition to getting specific physical stimulation, I often have done the following to help me reach orgasm during sex with a partner."

SOURCE: Ellison, C. R. (2006). *Women's Sexualities: Generations of Women Share Intimate Secrets of Sexual Self-Acceptance*. Read File Publications, 2006. Reprinted by permission of the author.

Kaplan: Psychosexual Therapy

Helen Singer Kaplan (1974, 1979, 1983) modified Masters and Johnson's behavioral treatment program to include psychosexual therapy. The cognitive-behavioral approach works well for arousal and orgasmic difficulties resulting from mild to midlevel sexual anxieties. But if the individual experiences severe anxieties resulting from intense relationship or psychic conflicts or from childhood sexual abuse or rape, a behavioral approach alone frequently does not work. Such severe anxieties usually manifest themselves in sexual aversion disorder or hypoactive sexual desire.

Other Nonmedical Approaches

Both cognitive-behavioral and psychosexual therapy are expensive and take a considerable amount of time. In response to these limitations, "brief" sex therapy and self-help and group therapy have developed.

PLISSIT Model of Therapy   One of the most common approaches used by sex therapists is based on the **PLISSIT model** (Annon, 1974, 1976). "PLISSIT" is an acronym for the four progressive levels of sex therapy: **p**ermission, **l**imited **i**nformation, **s**pecific **s**uggestions, and **i**ntensive **t**herapy. About 90% of sexual function difficulties can be successfully addressed in the first three levels; only about 10% of patients require extensive therapy.

The first level in the PLISSIT model involves giving permission. At one time or another, most sexual behaviors were prohibited by important figures in our lives. Because desires and activities such as fantasies or masturbation were not validated, we often question their "normality" or "morality." We shroud them in secrecy or drape them with shame. Without permission to be sexual, we may experience sexual disorders and dysfunctions.

Sex therapists act as "permission givers" for us to be sexual. They become authority figures who validate our sexuality by helping us accept our sexual feelings and behaviors. They reassure us and help us clarify our sexual values. They also validate our ability to say no to activities with which we are uncomfortable.

The second level involves giving limited information. This information is restricted to the specific area of sexual function difficulties. If a woman has an orgasmic disorder, for example, the therapist might explain that not all women are orgasmic in coitus without additional manual stimulation before, during, or after penetration. The therapist might discuss the effects of drugs such as alcohol, marijuana, and cocaine on sexual responsiveness.

The third level involves making specific suggestions. If permission giving and limited information are not sufficient, the therapist next suggests specific "homework" exercises. For example, if a man experiences early or involuntary ejaculation, the therapist may suggest that he and his partner try the squeeze technique. A woman with orgasmic disorder might be instructed to masturbate with or without her partner to discover the best way for her partner to assist her in experiencing orgasm.

The fourth level involves undergoing intensive therapy. If the individual continues to experience a sexual function problem, he or she will need to enter intensive therapy, such as psychosexual therapy.

Self-Help and Group Therapy   The PLISSIT model provides a sound basis for understanding how partners, friends, books, sex education videos, self-help exercises, and group therapy can be useful in helping us deal with the first three levels of therapy: permission, limited information, and specific suggestions. Partners, friends, books, sex education videos, and group therapy sessions under a therapist's guidance, for example, may provide "permission" for us to engage in sexual exploration and discovery. From these sources, we may learn that many of our sexual fantasies and behaviors are very common. Such methods are most effective when sexual function difficulties arise from a lack of knowledge or mild sexual anxieties.

The first step in dealing with a sexual function difficulty can be to tap your own immediate resources. Begin by discussing the problem with your partner; find out what she or he thinks. Discuss specific strategies that might be useful. Sometimes, simply communicating your feelings and thoughts will resolve the dissatisfaction. Seek out friends with whom you can share your feelings and anxieties. Find out what they think; ask them whether they have had similar experiences and how they handled them. Try to keep your perspective—and your sense of humor.

Group therapy may be particularly valuable in providing an open, safe forum in which people can discuss their sexual feelings. It is an opportunity to experience and discover that many of their sexual behaviors, fantasies, and problems are very common. The therapist leading these sessions can also provide valuable insight and direction. Another benefit of group therapy is that it is often less expensive than most other types of therapy.

Medical Approaches

Sexual function difficulties are often a combination of physical and psychological problems (LoPiccolo, 1991). Even people whose difficulties are physical may develop psychological or relationship problems as they try to cope with

Three prescription drugs—Viagra, Cialis, and Levitra—have revolutionized the treatment of male erectile disorder.

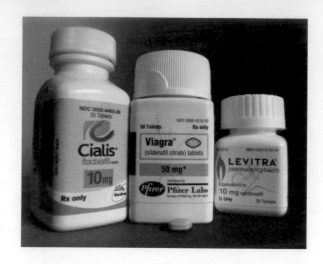

Click on "Viagra and Sexual Pharmacology" to see a discussion of the "accidental" discovery of Viagra.

their difficulties. Thus, treatment for organically based problems may need to include psychological counseling.

Vaginal pain caused by inadequate lubrication and thinning vaginal walls often occurs as a result of the decreased estrogen associated with menopause. A lubricating jelly or estrogen therapy may help. Vaginitis, endometriosis, and pelvic inflammatory disease may also make intercourse painful. Lubricants or menopausal hormone therapy (discussed in Chapter 7) often resolves difficulties. Loss of sex drive and function, low energy and strength, depressed mood, and low self-esteem may sometimes occur from testosterone deficiency (see Chapters 3 and 13). The sex lives of people with significant testosterone deficiencies may be helped by testosterone supplements (see Chapter 4).

The FDA has approved an apparatus called EROS-CTD, a clitoral stimulation device the size of a computer mouse. This device creates a gentle suction over the clitoris, increasing blood flow and sensation (Leland, 2000). The device is quite expensive and available only by prescription.

Most medical and surgical treatment for men has centered on erectile difficulties. Such approaches include microsurgery to improve a blood flow problem, suction devices to induce and maintain an erection, a prosthesis implanted in the penis and abdomen, and drugs injected into the penis. Even though these methods have been used with many men, they are not very practical or pleasant, and they became virtually obsolete with the introduction of Viagra in 1998 by Pfizer. Viagra, the trade name for sildenafil citrate, is the first effective and safe oral drug for the treatment of male erectile difficulty, whether caused by psychological or medical conditions. Viagra revolutionized the treatment of erection difficulties, representing the beginning of a pharmacological approach to treating sexual difficulties. Medical literature shows that Viagra is an effective and well-tolerated treatment for erection difficulties, even for men who have taken the drug for a long period of time, and can improve the sexual satisfaction of both the man and his partner in couples with male erection difficulties (Heiman et al., 2007; Padma-Nathan, Eardley, Kloner, Laties, & Montorsi, 2002). In 2003, two other drugs were approved by the FDA for treatment of erection problems: GlaxoSmithKline and Bayer's Levitra (vardenafil HCI) and Eli Lilly's Cialis (tadalafil). These three drugs are one of the most popular group of drugs in the history of the pharmaceutical industry. Viagra and Levitra are effective for a few hours, whereas Cialis is effective for 24 to 36 hours. Among

Kegel Exercises for Women and Men

Kegel exercises were originally developed by Dr. Arnold Kegel (KAY-gul) to help women with problems controlling urination. They were designed to strengthen and give women voluntary control of a muscle called the pubococcygeus, or P.C. for short. The P.C. muscle is part of the sling of muscle stretching from the pubic bone in front to the tailbone in back, also called the pelvic floor. Because the muscle encircles not only the urinary opening but also the outside of the vagina, some of Kegel's patients discovered a pleasant side effect—increased sexual awareness. Many report that the sensations are similar for men and women. If you are a man reading this, the exercises can be valuable to you, for improving erectile function and in learning ejaculatory control. In fact, a British study found that erection function improved significantly in men after 3 months of Kegel exercises (Dorey, Speakman, Feneley, Swinkels, & Dunn, 2005). So, men, when reading the directions, just substitute your genitals in places where the directions talk about "vagina," and so on.

Why Do Kegel Exercises?

- They can help you be more aware of feelings in your genital area.
- They can increase circulation in the genital area.
- They may help increase sexual arousal started by other kinds of stimulation.
- They can be useful during childbirth to help control the strength and duration of pushing.
- They can be helpful after childbirth to restore muscle tone in the vagina.
- They can help men improve erection function and control the timing of ejaculation.
- If urinary incontinence is a problem, strengthing these muscles may improve urinary control.

Identifying Your P.C. Muscle

Sit on the toilet. Spread your legs apart. See if you can stop and start the flow of urine without moving your legs. That's your P.C. muscle, the one that turns the flow on and off. If you don't find it the first time, don't give up; try again the next time you have to urinate. (For the British study cited above, the researchers instructed the men to tighten their pelvic floor as if they were trying to prevent intestinal gas from escaping or to try retracting the penis and lifting the scrotum and testicles.)

How to Do the Exercises

- *Slow Kegels:* Tighten the P.C. muscle as you did to stop the urine. Hold it for a slow count of three. Relax it.
- *Quick Kegels:* Tighten and relax the P.C. muscle as rapidly as you can.
- *Pull in—push out:* Pull up the entire pelvic floor as though trying to suck water into your vagina. Then push or bear down as if trying to push the imaginary water out. (This exercise will use a number of stomach or abdominal muscles as well as the P.C. muscle.)

At first, do 10 of each of these three exercises (one set) five times every day. Each week, increase the number of times you do each exercise by five (15, 20, 25, etc.). Keep doing five "sets" each day.

Exercise Guidelines

- You can do these exercises anytime during daily activities that don't require a lot of moving around—for example, while driving your car, watching television, sitting in school or at your computer, or lying in bed.
- When you start, you will probably notice that the muscle doesn't want to stay "contracted" during "slow Kegels" and that you can't do "quick Kegels" very rapidly or evenly. Keep at it. In a week or two, you will probably notice that you can control the muscle quite well.
- Sometimes, the muscle will start to feel a little tired. This is not surprising—you probably haven't used it very much before. Take a few seconds' rest and start again.
- A good way to check on how you are doing is to insert one or two lubricated fingers into your vagina. Men can place a finger in their rectum to feel the anus contract. Because it may be a month or so before you notice results, be patient.

Finally, always remember to keep breathing naturally and evenly while doing your Kegels.

the several benefits of the erection drugs is that they are often effective in treating erection difficulties that occur as a result of prostate-cancer treatment and surgery, including complete removal of the prostate (American Cancer Society, 2007c; Brock et al., 2003).

Erection drugs allow the muscles in the penis to relax and penile arteries to dilate, thus expanding the erectile tissues that squeeze shut the veins in the penis. They are taken before sex; the amount of time the effects last varies depending on the drug. The drugs do not increase sexual desire, nor do they produce an erection itself; the man still must be sexually excited. After sex is over, the erection goes away. The primary psychological role of the erection drugs is to eliminate the anticipatory and performance anxiety surrounding intercourse which will usually, in itself, result in erections and increased confidence (McCarthy, 1998). Some men take the drugs as a "quick fix" for a temporary problem or as "insurance" even though they may not really need the drug. Because Viagra increases pelvic blood flow, many women began using it when it was first released in hopes of increasing sensation and orgasm. These experiences, and the results of medical research, though, have yielded mixed results as insufficient vasocongestion probably does not solely account for orgasm difficulties in women. Subsequently, Pfizer discontinued research on Viagra and women in 2004. Efforts to create an effective drug for female sexual difficulties, particularly low sex desire, continue but to no avail (Angier, 2007).

The U.S. Food and Drug Administration notes that these drugs are safe for most men if used according to directions, except for men taking nitrates (often prescribed for chest pain), and those having poor cardiovascular health. Headaches, visual disturbances, and flushing sometimes occur, and in rare cases extended and painful erections occur (Ashton, 2007; Reitman, 2004).

Some men are using the erection drugs casually, as party drugs or as insurance against the effects of alcohol and for a desired increase in "prowess." The erection drugs are sometimes used in combination with other drugs, like crystal methamphetamine, which stimulates sexual desire but interferes with erections (Kirby, 2004). Using ecstasy and Viagra can cause heart problems and erections lasting more than 4 hours, which might lead to anatomical damage (Leinwand, 2002). Certainly, the mixing of street drugs and an erection drug is dangerous. And people should never use someone else's erection drug; they should always get their own prescription from a doctor.

Some experts caution people not to over-rely on medical approaches to solve sexual function difficulties (see the box "The Medicalization of Sexual Function Problems"). Sex therapist and clinical psychologist Julian Slowinski (2007) states that "a man's sexual functioning is determined and affected by the health of his body and lifestyle, his personal emotional state, the quality of his relationship, and the influence of life and environmental stress." Most sexual function difficulties can be resolved through individual and couple therapy. The optimal approach in the use of drugs is in concert with psychotherapy.

Gay, Lesbian, and Bisexual Sex Therapy

Until recently, sex therapists treated sexual function difficulties as implicitly heterosexual. The model for sexual functioning, in fact, was generally orgasmic heterosexual intercourse. There was virtually no mention of gay, lesbian, bisexual, or transgender sexual concerns.

think
about it

The Medicalization of Sexual Function Problems

Since the early 1980s, a number of pharmacological therapies have been introduced for treatment of men's sexual function problems. The erection drugs—Viagra, Levitra, and Cialis—enable some men suffering from hypertension, diabetes, and prostate problems to get an erection by increasing the flow of blood to the penis, provided there is sexual stimulation. However, the pills do not cure fractured relationships, make people more sensual lovers, enlarge penises, or address the complexity of all sexual problems (Reitman, 2004; Slowinski, 2007). One problem with the erection drugs is that they reinforce the widespread, but mistaken, belief that an erection equals a satisfying sexual experience for both men and women. It perpetuates the notion, fed by many erotic videos, that sticking an erection into an erotic opening is the only thing sex is about (Castleman, 2004). Sex therapist Marty Klein says that "it's possible to have a rock-hard erection and still have lousy sex" (quoted in Castleman, 2004). The pills often help individuals postpone or avoid self and couple analysis. Some experts contend that the erection pills have, thus, medicalized sexual problems, resulting in the prevailing medical model that promotes a specific norm of sexual functioning: correct genital performance (Tiefer, 2001). The medical solution would be to take a pill for an erection problem, thus taking the focus off the individual and the dynamics of the relationship (Tiefer, 2001, 2004). However, the best use of Viagra (and Levitra and Cialis) is in the context of a comprehensive assessment and intervention by a sex therapist that focuses on the physical, emotional, and relational aspects of the male (McCarthy, 1998; Slowinski, 2007).

The "Viagra phenomenon," the most recent event in the medicalization of male sexuality, has both positive and negative consequences: It enables millions of men to have reliable erections, but it also calls for a similar pill that would increase female sexual response. Dr. John Bancroft, senior research fellow at The Kinsey Institute, in speaking about pharmacological approaches to female sexual function problems, contends that the term "sexual dysfunction" commonly used in medicine is misleading and dangerous; portraying sexual difficulties as dysfunctions "encourages physicians to prescribe drugs to change sexual function when the attention should be paid to other aspects of the woman's life" (quoted in Moynihan, 2000). Bancroft (2000) stated that a Viagra-type drug might influence female sexual response and enjoyment but treatment should not separate sexual expression from other factors that influence sexual functioning in women such as fatigue, stress, or threatening behavior from their partners.

Leonore Tiefer (2004), a sex therapist and psychiatry faculty member at New York University School of Medicine, says that innumerable professional and scientific conferences have been held on female sexual dysfunction, enthusiastically backed by drug companies. She contends that this is an effort to sell "female sexual dysfunction" as a new medical disorder solvable by medical treatments. In response to this, she and other experts developed a perspective of female sexuality, "The New View of Women's Sexual Problems," described earlier in this chapter, to challenge the medicalization of women's sexuality.

Think Critically

- Do you think that the sexuality of men and women is being medicalized?
- Do you think it would be easier to take an erection drug than seek therapy for erection difficulties?
- Should a drug like Viagra be developed for women?
- Are people over-relying on drugs to solve their sexual function problems?

For gay men, lesbian women, and bisexual individuals, sexual issues differ from those of heterosexuals in several ways. First, although gay men and lesbian women may have arousal, desire, erectile, or orgasmic difficulties, the context in which they occur may differ significantly from that of heterosexual individuals. Problems among heterosexuals most often focus on sexual intercourse, whereas the sexual dissatisfaction of gay men, lesbian women, and bisexual people focuses on other behaviors. Gay men in sex therapy, for example, most often experience aversion toward anal eroticism (Reece, 1988). Lesbian women in sex therapy frequently complain about aversive feelings toward cunnilingus. Female orgasmic difficulty, however, is not frequently viewed as a problem (Margolies et al., 1988). Heterosexual women, in contrast, frequently complain about lack of orgasm.

It is important for gay, lesbian, and bisexual people with sexual difficulties to choose a therapist who affirms their orientation and understands the special issues confronting them.

Second, lesbian women, gay men, and bisexual individuals must deal with both societal homophobia and internalized homophobia. Fear of violence makes it difficult for gay men, bisexual individuals, and lesbian women to openly express their affection in the same manner as heterosexuals. As a consequence, lesbian women, bisexual individuals, and gay men learn to repress their expressions of feelings in public; this repression may carry over into the private realm as well. Internalized homophobia may result in diminished sexual desire, creating sexual aversion and fostering guilt and negative feelings about sexual activity.

Third, gay men must deal with the association between sex and HIV infection that has cut a deadly swath through the gay community. The death of friends, lovers, and partners has left many depressed, which, in turn, affects sexual desire and creates high levels of sexual anxiety. Many gay men are fearful of contracting HIV even if they practice safer sex. And HIV-positive men, even if they are practicing safer sex, are often afraid of transmitting the infection to their loved ones.

These unique lesbian, bisexual, and gay concerns require that sex therapists expand their understanding and treatment of sexual problems. If the therapist is not a gay man or a lesbian woman, he or she needs to have a thorough knowledge of sexual orientation issues and the gay and lesbian world. Therapists further need to be aware of their own assumptions and feelings about homosexuality and be free of bias and value judgments. Therapists working with gay, bisexual, or lesbian clients need to develop inclusive models of sexual treatment that are positive for varied sexual orientations. For therapists who work with clients of varied sexual orientations, the American Psychological Association has developed a valuable resource, *Guidelines for Psychotherapy with Lesbian, Gay, and Bisexual Clients* (American Psychological Association, 2000). These guidelines encourage therapists to examine ways their own attitudes toward sexual minorities may impact their therapeutic approach and to be open to making referrals or seeking outside consultation if appropriate.

Impulse arrested spills over, and the flood is feeling, the flood is passion, the flood is even madness: It depends on the force of the current, the height and strength of the barrier. . . . Feeling lurks in that interval of time between desire and its consummation.

—Aldous Huxley
(1894–1963)

Seeking Professional Assistance

Because something is not "functioning" according to a therapist's model does not necessarily mean that something is wrong. You need to evaluate your sexuality in terms of your own and your partner's satisfaction and the meanings you give to your sexuality. If, after doing this, you are unable to resolve your sexual function difficulties yourself, seek professional assistance. It is important to realize that seeking such assistance is not a sign of personal weakness or failure. Rather, it is a sign of strength, for it demonstrates an ability to reach out and a willingness to change. It is a sign that you care for your partner, your relationship, and yourself. As you think about therapy, consider the following:

- What are your goals in therapy? Are you willing to make changes in your relationship to achieve your goals?

- Do you want individual, couple, or group therapy? If you are in a relationship, is your partner willing to participate in therapy?

- What characteristics are important for you in a therapist? Do you prefer a female or a male therapist? Is the therapist's age, religion, or ethnic background important to you?

- What are the therapist's professional qualifications? There are few certified sex therapy programs; most therapists who treat sexual function difficulties come from various professional backgrounds, such as psychiatry, clinical psychology, psychoanalysis, marriage and family counseling, and social work. Because there is no licensing in the field of sex therapy, it is important to seek out those trained therapists who have licenses in their gener-

alized field. This way, you have recourse if questionable practices arise. It is worth noting that professionals view sexual contact between themselves and their clients as unethical and unlawful.

- What is the therapist's approach? Is it behavioral, psychosexual, psychoanalytic, medical, religious, spiritual, feminist, or something else? Do you feel comfortable with the approach?

- If necessary, does the therapist offer a sliding-scale fee, based on your level of income?

- If you are a lesbian, gay, or bisexual person, does the therapist affirm your sexual orientation? Does the therapist understand the special problems gay men, bisexual individuals, and lesbian women face?

- After a session or two with the therapist, do you have confidence in him or her? If not, discuss your feelings with the therapist. If you believe your dissatisfaction is not a defense mechanism, change therapists.

Just how successful is sex therapy? What constitutes success or failure is subjective and open to interpretation. Most sex therapists believe that their work results in considerable success. Not all problems can be resolved completely, but some—and often great—improvement usually occurs. Much of therapy's success depends on a person's willingness to confront painful feelings and to change. This entails time, effort, and often considerable amounts of money. But, ultimately, the difficult work may reward partners with greater satisfaction and a deeper relationship.

Final Thoughts

As we consider our sexuality, it is important to realize that sexual function difficulties and dissatisfaction are commonplace. But sex is more than orgasms or certain kinds of activities. Even if we have function difficulties in some areas, there are other areas in which we may be fully sexual. If we have erectile or orgasmic problems, we can use our imagination to expand our repertoire of erotic activities. We can touch each other sensually, masturbate alone or with our partner, and caress, kiss, eroticize, and explore our bodies with fingers and tongues. We can enhance our sexuality if we look at sex as the mutual giving and receiving of erotic pleasure, rather than a command performance. By paying attention to our conditions for good sex, maintaining intimacy, and focusing on our own erotic sensations and those of our partner, we can transform our sexual relationships.

Summary

Sexual Function Difficulties: Definitions, Types, and Prevalence

- The line between "normal" sexual functioning and a sexual function difficulty is often not definitive.

- Difficulties in sexual functioning are often called sexual problems, sexual disorders, or *sexual dysfunctions.*

- The *Diagnostic and Statistical Manual of Mental Disorders* classifies four types of sexual dysfunction: disorders of desire, sexual arousal disorders, orgasmic disorders, and sexual pain disorders. According to a newer, woman-centered classification system, sexual function difficulties arise from cultural and relational factors, not medical problems.

- A sexual function difficulty can be defined as a disappointment on the part of one or both partners.

- The NHSLS found that sexual function difficulties are more common in women (43%) than men (31%) and are associated with health-related and psychosocial factors. A Kinsey Institute study of women found that 24% reported marked distress in their sexual relationship.

- *Hypoactive sexual desire (HSD)* is low sexual desire. This disorder usually develops in adulthood and is associated with psychologically stressful life situations. *Sexual aversion disorder* is a consistently phobic response to sexual activities or the idea of such activities.

- *Female sexual arousal disorder* is an inability to attain or maintain the normal vaginal lubrication and swelling that accompany sexual excitement. It is usually accompanied by desire and orgasmic disorders.

- Male sexual problems typically focus on the excitement stage. *Male erectile disorder* is the inability to have or maintain an erection until completion of sexual activity. Erectile difficulties may occur because of fatigue, too much alcohol, smoking, depression, conflict, certain medical conditions, or a host of other transitory reasons.

- *Persistent sexual arousal syndrome,* a newly reported difficulty in women, is persistent arousal that does not resolve itself in ordinary ways and continues for hours, days, and even weeks.

- *Female orgasmic disorder* refers to the condition of not being orgasmic. Negative or guilty sexual attitudes, inadequate sexual stimulation, and relationship difficulties contribute to this disorder. Women are more likely to experience orgasm during sexual encounters that include more sexual behaviors than intercourse.

- *Male orgasmic disorder* is the delay or absence of ejaculation following normal sexual excitement. Psychosocial factors contribute to this condition. In *inhibited ejaculation,* the penis is erect, but the man is unable to ejaculate. In *delayed ejaculation,* the man is not able to ejaculate easily during intercourse.

- *Involuntary ejaculation,* also called *early* or *rapid ejaculation,* is the inability to control or delay ejaculation as long as desired, causing personal or interpersonal distress.

- In *vaginismus,* the muscles around the vaginal entrance go into spasmodic contractions. Vaginismus is essentially a conditioned response that reflects fear, anxiety, or pain. *Dyspareunia,* painful intercourse, often occurs because a woman is not entirely aroused before her partner attempts intercourse. Sexual inhibitions, a poor relationship with her partner, or hormonal imbalances may contribute to dyspareunia.

Physical Causes of Sexual Function Difficulties and Dissatisfaction

- Health problems such as diabetes and alcoholism can cause erectile difficulties. Some prescription drugs affect sexual responsiveness.

- Coital pain caused by inadequate lubrication and thinning vaginal walls often occurs as a result of decreased estrogen associated with menopause. Lubricants can resolve the difficulties.

Psychological Causes of Sexual Function Difficulties and Dissatisfaction

- Sexual function difficulties may have their origin in any number of psychological causes. The immediate causes of sexual function difficulties lie in the current situation, including fatigue and stress, ineffective sexual behavior, sexual anxieties, and an excessive need to please a partner. Internal conflict, caused by religious teachings, guilt, negative learning, and internalized homophobia, can contribute to dissatisfaction, as can relationship conflicts.

Sexual Function Enhancement

- Many people and all couples experience sexual function difficulties and dissatisfaction at one time or another. Discrepancies in sexual desire are the most common complaint among couples. The widespread variability of sexual functioning suggests the "normality" of at least occasional sexual function difficulties.

- *Sexual function enhancement* refers to improving the quality of one's sexual relationship. Sexual function–enhancement programs generally provide accurate information about sexuality, develop communication skills, foster positive attitudes, and increase self-awareness. Awareness of your own sexual needs is often critical to enhancing your sexuality. Enhancement of sex includes the intensification of arousal.

- There has been a dramatic increase in over-the-counter, natural sexual enhancers, but none have been scientifically shown to be effective.

Treating Sexual Function Difficulties

- Masters and Johnson developed a cognitive-behavioral approach to sexual function difficulties. They relabeled sexual problems as dysfunctions rather than neuroses or diseases, used direct behavior modification practices, and treated couples rather than individuals. Treatment includes *sensate focus* exercises without intercourse, "homework" exercises, and, finally, "permission" to engage in sexual intercourse. Kaplan's psychosexual therapy program combines behavioral exercises with insight therapy.

- The *PLISSIT model* of sex therapy refers to four progressive levels: *p*ermission, *l*imited *i*nformation, *s*pecific *s*uggestions, and *i*ntensive *t*herapy. Individuals and couples can often resolve their difficulties by talking over their problems with their partners or friends, reading self-help books, and attending sex therapy groups. If they are unable to resolve their difficulties in these ways, they should consider intensive sex therapy.

- Viagra was introduced in the United States in 1998 and is the first effective and safe oral drug for treatment of male erectile difficulty. Subsequently, two other prescription drugs, Levitra and Cialis, have become available. These drugs do not increase sexual excitement but rather facilitate blood engorgement in the penis.

- Some sexuality professionals claim that drug companies have exaggerated and "medicalized" sexual function difficulties to promote sales.

- There are three significant concerns for gay men, bisexual individuals, and lesbian women in sex therapy. First, the context in which problems occur may differ significantly from that of a heterosexual person; there may be issues revolving around anal eroticism and cunnilingus. Second, they must deal with both societal homophobia and internalized homophobia. Third, gay men must deal with the association between sex and HIV/AIDS.

- In seeking professional assistance for a sexual problem, it is important to realize that seeking help is not a sign of personal weakness or failure, but rather a sign of strength.

 ## Questions for Discussion

- Do you think that sexual function difficulties should be determined by a medical group such as the American Psychiatric Association or by what the individual and/or couple decides is dissatisfying?

- If you have been sexual with another person, have you ever experienced sexual function dissatisfaction or difficulty? After reading this chapter, do you think that this experience is actually a "sexual dysfunction" or possibly a dissatisfaction based on an unrealistic expectation of what sex should be like? Did you talk to your partner about the disappointment?

- What do you consider to be a satisfying sexual experience with a partner? Did the information in this chapter cause you to reevaluate what you consider "good sex" for you and a partner?

- If you had a sexual function difficulty, how comfortable would you be in seeking help from a sex therapist?

- If you or your male partner were having difficulties with erections, would you seek prescription drugs (Viagra, Levitra, or Cialis) to deal with the problem? Is it possible for a man and his partner to have good sex without an erection?

Sex and the Internet

Sexual Difficulties

The Web site WebMD provides information on various health issues, including sexual function difficulties. Go to this site (http://www.webmd.com) and find the "Search" box. Type in various sexual function difficulty terms, such as "sexual dysfunction," "erectile dysfunction," "premature ejaculation," "female orgasmic disorder," and "dyspareunia." Review the information for each topic.

- Is the information given appropriate for nonmedical people?
- What new information is provided?
- Are there links to other sites that provide sexuality information?

Suggested Web Sites

American Family Physician
http://www.aafp.org
Provides information about both female and male sexual function difficulties.

Merck Manual Online Library
http://www.merck.com/mmhe/index
Provides information about various health topics, including sexual function difficulties.

New View Campaign
http://www.newviewcampaign.org
Promotes an alternative view of female sexual function difficulties, challenges the pharmaceutical industry, and calls for further research on women's sexual function difficulties.

Women's Sexual Health
http://www.womenssexualhealth.com
Addresses the questions and concerns of women and their partners concerning female sexual function difficulties and includes a "Physician Locator" to help them find local physicians who treat female sexual function difficulties.

Suggested Reading

Berman, J., Berman, L., & Bumiller, E. (2001). *For women only: A revolutionary guide to overcoming sexual dysfunction and reclaiming your sex life.* New York: Henry Holt. A woman-centered approach to understanding and addressing sexual difficulties.

Cassell, C. (2008). *Put passion first: Why sexual chemistry is the key to finding and keeping lasting love.* New York: McGraw-Hill. Written for women (but can be valuable to men, too), this book helps the reader understand the significance and role of sexual passion within a relationship with emphasis on increasing couple intimacy.

Castleman, M. (2004). *Great sex: A man's guide to the secret principles of total body sex.* New York: Rodale. An exceptionally easy-to-read and practical book for men in which the author quotes well-respected sex therapists throughout the book to show therapists' suggestions for various sexual function problems.

Keesling, B. (2006). *Sexual healing: The complete guide to overcoming common sexual problems* (3rd ed.). Alameda, CA: Hunter House. A greatly expanded edition of the classic book on the healing power of sex that offers more than 125 exercises that help with a wide range of sexual function difficulties.

McCarthy, B. W., & McCarthy, E. (2009). *Discovering your couple sexual style.* New York: Routledge. Focuses on helping couples enhance intimacy and sexual satisfaction by providing relevant sexual information, exercises, and practical tools.

McLaren, A. (2007). *Impotence: A cultural history.* Chicago: University of Chicago Press. A serious, but entertaining, cultural history of how male sexuality was and is constructed around erections.

Perel, E. (2006). *Mating in captivity.* New York: Harper. Presents a provocative perspective on intimacy and sex in exploring the paradoxical union of domesticity and sexual desire.

Pertot, S. (2007). *When sex drives don't match.* New York: Marlow & Company. Presents 10 libido types and how they affect a couple along with rational ways for couples to work through differing sex drives.

Schnarch, D. (2002). *Resurrecting sex.* New York: HarperCollins. Deals with the sexual problems of couples and offers straight talk about sex, intimacy, and relationships.

Zilbergeld, B. (1999). *The new male sexuality* (Rev. ed.). New York: Bantam Books. The book most widely recommended by therapists for men on enhancing sexual relationships. Women can profit equally from it, not only for themselves but also as insight into male sexuality.

For links, articles, and study material, go to the McGraw-Hill Web site, located at
www.mhhe.com/yarber7e.

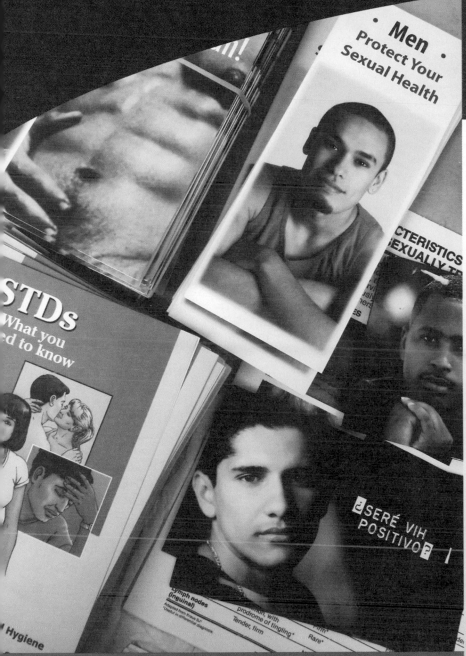

Sexually Transmitted Infections

15 chapter

MAIN TOPICS

The STI Epidemic

Principal Bacterial STIs

Principal Viral STIs

Vaginal Infections

Other STIs

Ectoparasitic Infestations

STIs and Women

Preventing STIs

"Up to this date, I have slept with about thirteen men. My most recent 'wake-up call' was from a threat from a prospective partner and from a human sexuality course. I took a test for HIV; the result was negative. However, I did get infected and passed on genital warts to my ex-boyfriend. I simply pretended that I had never slept with anyone else and that if anyone had cheated it was him. It never fazed me that I was at such a risk for contracting HIV. My new resolutions are to educate my family, friends, and peers about sex, take a proactive approach toward sex with prospective partners, and discuss sex openly and honestly with my mother."

.23-year-old female

"My partner and I want to use a condom to protect ourselves from STIs. But I feel inadequate when we are intimate and he cannot keep an erection to put a condom on. I feel too embarrassed for him to discuss the situation. So, we both walk away a bit disappointed—him because he could not stay erect and me because I did not take the time or have the courage to help him. I think if he masturbated with a condom on it would help him with his performance anxiety problem."

.22-year-old female

"STIs and HIV are precisely the reason I exercise caution when engaging in sexual activity. I don't want to ever get an STI, and I'd rather never have sex again than have HIV."

.24-year-old male

"Why do males often convince women to have sex without proper protection? I don't understand this because there is always a risk of getting an STI. I know that women think about this just as often as men do, but why is it that men do not seem to care?"

.21-year-old female

"I am usually very careful when it comes to my sexual relations and protecting myself from STIs, but there have been a couple of times when I've drunk a lot and have not practiced safe sex. It scares me that I have done things like that and have tried to make sure it doesn't happen again. STIs are just a very uncomfortable subject."

.27-year-old male

O rose, thou art sick!
The invisible worm
That flies in the night,
In the howling storm,
Has found thy bed
Of crimson joy,
And his dark secret love
Does thy life destroy.

—William Blake
(1757–1827)

THE TERM "SEXUALLY TRANSMITTED INFECTIONS" (STIs) refers to more than 25 infectious organisms passed from person to person primarily through sexual contact. STIs were once called venereal diseases (VDs), a term derived from Venus, the Roman goddess of love. More recently, the term "sexually transmitted diseases" (STDs) replaced "venereal diseases." Actually, many health professionals continue to use "STD." However, some believe that "STI" is a more accurate and less judgmental term. That is, a person can be infected with an STI organism but not have developed the illness or disease associated with the organism. So, in this book, we use "STI," although "STD" may appear when other sources are cited.

There are two general types of STIs: (1) those that are bacterial and curable, such as chlamydia and gonorrhea, and (2) those that are viral and incurable— but treatable—such as HIV infection and genital herpes. STIs are a serious health problem in our country, resulting in considerable human suffering.

In this chapter and the next, we discuss the **incidence** (number of new cases) and **prevalence** (total number of cases) of STIs in our country particularly among youth, the disparate impact of STIs on certain population groups, the factors that contribute to the STI epidemic, and the consequences of STIs. We also discuss the incidence, transmission, symptoms, and treatment of the principal STIs that affect Americans, with the exception of HIV/AIDS, which is the subject of Chapter 16. The prevention of STIs, including protective health behaviors, safer sex practices, and communication skills, are also addressed in this chapter.

● The STI Epidemic

The federal Institute of Medicine (IOM) characterizes STIs as "hidden epidemics of tremendous health and economic consequences in the United States," adding that "STDs represent a growing threat to the nation's health and national action is urgently needed." The IOM notes that STIs are a challenging public health problem because of their "hidden" nature. The IOM adds that "the sociocultural taboos related to sexuality are a barrier to STD prevention" (Eng & Butler, 1997). The "silent" infections of STIs make them a serious public threat requiring greater personal attention and increased health-care resources.

STIs: The Most Common Reportable Infectious Diseases

STIs are common in the United States, but identifying exactly how many cases there are is impossible, and even estimating the total number is difficult. Often, an STI is "silent"—that is, it goes undiagnosed because it has no early symptoms or the symptoms are ignored and untreated, especially among people with limited access to health care. Asymptomatic infections can be diagnosed through testing, but routine screening programs are not widespread, and social stigmas and the lack of public awareness about STIs may result in no testing during visits to health-care professionals. And even when STIs are diagnosed, reporting regulations vary. Only a few STIs—gonorrhea, syphilis, chlamydia, hepatitis A and B, and HIV/AIDS—must be reported by health-care providers to health departments in *each* state and to the federal Centers for Disease Control and Prevention (CDC). But no such reporting requirement exists for other major STIs, such as genital herpes, human papillomavirus (HPV), and trichomoniasis. In addition, the reporting of STI diagnoses is inconsistent. For example, some private physicians do not report STI cases to their state health departments (American Social Health Association [ASHA], 1998a, 2006a; CDC, 2002b). In spite of the underreporting and undiagnosed cases, several significant indicators illustrate the STI problem in the United States:

- STIs are the most common reported infectious diseases in the United States. In 2005, STIs represented four of the five most frequently reported infectious diseases (CDC, 2008g; National Center for Health Statistics, 2007) (see Figure 15.1).

- An estimated 19 million new STI cases occur each year (Weinstock, Berman, & Cates, 2004).

- STIs negatively impact the lives of more than 65 million Americans (CDC, 2008g).

- By age 25, 1 in 2 young persons will acquire an STI (Cates, Herndon, Schulz, & Darroch, 2004).

- One in four teenage girls (3.2 million) in the United States are infected with at least one of the most common STIs: HPV, chlamydia, genital herpes, or trichomoniasis (CDC, 2008h).

Who Is Affected: Disparities Among Groups

Anyone, regardless of gender, race/ethnicity, social status, or sexual orientation, can get an STI. What people do—not who they are—exposes them to the organisms that cause STIs. Nevertheless, some population groups are disproportionately

Click on "STDs: The Silent Epidemic" to hear about a peer education program designed to reach those at highest risk for contracting sexually transmitted infections.

Selected Notifiable Diseases, United States, 2005. (*Sources:* Centers for Disease Control and Prevention, 2008f; National Center for Health Statistics, 2007.)

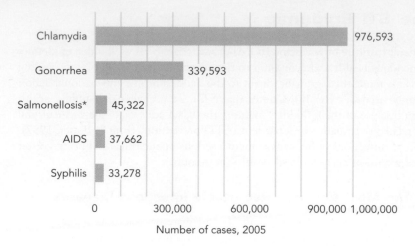

Number of cases, 2005

*Infection with the *Salmonella* bacterium that causes diarrheal illness.

affected by STIs; this disparity reflects gender, age, and racial and ethnic differences (CDC, 2007e).

Gender Disparities Overall, the consequences of STIs for women often are more serious than those for men. Generally, women contract STIs more easily than men and suffer greater damage to their health and reproductive functioning. STIs often are transmitted more easily from a man to a woman than vice versa. Women's increased likelihood of having an asymptomatic infection results in a delay in diagnosis and treatment (ASHA, 1998a; CDC, 2007e).

A kind of "biological sexism" means that women are biologically more susceptible to infection than men when exposed to an STI organism. This is partly a result of the "fluid dynamics of intercourse [wherein] women are apparently more likely than men to acquire an STD infection from any single sexual encounter" (Hatcher et al., 1998). A woman's anatomy may increase her susceptibility to STIs. The warm, moist interior of the vagina and uterus is an ideal environment for many organisms. The thin, sensitive skin inside the labia and the mucous membranes lining the vagina may also be more receptive to infectious organisms than the skin covering a man's genitals. The symptoms of STIs in women are often very mild or absent, and STIs are more difficult to diagnose in women due to the physiology of the female reproductive system (U.S. Department of Health and Human Services, 2000b). The long-term effects of STIs for women may include pelvic inflammatory disease (PID), ectopic pregnancy, infertility, cervical cancer, and chronic pelvic pain, as well as possible severe damage to a fetus or newborn, including spontaneous abortion, stillbirth, low birth weight, neurological damage, and death (CDC, 2007e).

Lesbian and bisexual women may also be at risk for STIs. A study of lesbian and bisexual women found that many underestimated their risk for STIs, had limited knowledge of potential STI transmission, and reported little use of preventive behaviors with female partners, such as washing hands, using rubber gloves, and cleaning sex toys (Marrazzo, Coffey, & Bingham, 2005).

According to a study conducted in Sydney, Australia, women who had sex with other women had a higher rate of bacterial vaginosis than heterosexual women. For both groups, genital herpes and genital warts were common, while the incidence of gonorrhea and chlamydia was low. Among the women who had sex with other women, 93% reported previous sexual contact with men; they had a median of 12 lifetime male sex partners, compared with 6 lifetime partners for the heterosexual women. Thus, lesbian women may not be free of STI risk because many women who have sex with other women and self-identify as lesbian also have sex with men during their lifetime (Fetters, Marks, Mindel, & Estcourt, 2000). Studies have found that women who had sex with both men and women had more HIV/STI behavioral risk factors, such as having multiple male sex partners, having sex with men who have sex with men, and having sex with an injection drug user, than women who had sex only with men (Gonzales et al., 1999; Mercer et al., 2007; Scheer et al., 2002). A case study found that female-to-female transmission of syphilis occurred through oral sex (Campos-Outcalt & Hurwitz, 2002).

Surveillance data on several STIs suggest that an increasing number of men who have sex with men (MSM) are acquiring STIs. For example, in recent years, MSM have accounted for an increasing number of estimated syphilis cases in the United States. In 2006, 64% of syphilis cases in the U.S. were among MSM (CDC, 2007e). (HIV/AIDS data for men who have sex with men will be presented in Chapter 16.) Increases in STIs are consistent with data indicating an increasing number of men who have sex with men are participating in sexual behaviors that place them at risk for STIs (Stall, Hays, Waldo, Ekstrand, & McFarland, 2000).

Age Disparities   Compared to older adults, sexually active young adolescents, 10 to 19 years old, and young adults, 20 to 24 years of age, are at higher risk for acquiring an STI. About one half of new STI cases are among individuals aged 15–24 although they comprise only about one quarter of the sexually active population (CDC, 2007e; Weinstock, Berman, & Cates, 2004). Young people are at greater risk because they are, for example, more likely to have multiple sex partners, to engage in risky behavior, to select higher-risk partners, and face barriers to accessing quality STI prevention services. Infants, like women, disproportionately bear the long-term consequences of STIs. For example, when a woman has a syphilis infection during pregnancy, she may transmit the infection to the fetus in utero, resulting in potential fetal death or an infant born with physical and mental disabilities (CDC, 2007e).

Racial and Ethnic Disparities   Race and ethnicity in the United States are STI risk markers that correlate with other basic determinants of health status, such as poverty, access to quality health care, health-care-seeking behavior, illegal drug use, and communities with high prevalence of STIs. STI rates are higher among racial and ethnic minorities. (See Figures 15.2 and 15.3 for rates of two STIs—chlamydia and gonorrhea—by race/ethnicity, 1997–2006.) Social

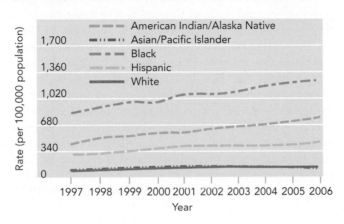

● **FIGURE 15.2**
Rates of Chlamydia by Race/Ethnicity, United States, 1997–2006. (*Source:* CDC, 2008g.)

● **FIGURE** 15.3

Rates of Gonorrhea by Race/
Ethnicity, United States, 1997–2006.
(*Source:* CDC, 2008g.)

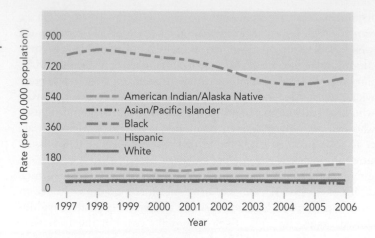

factors, such as poverty and lack of access to health care, in contrast to inherent factors, account for this discrepancy.

Factors Contributing to the Spread of STIs

According to the Institute of Medicine, "STDs are behavioral-linked diseases that result from unprotected sex," and behavioral, social, and biological factors contribute to their spread (Eng & Butler, 1997). These factors are obstacles to the control of STIs in the United States.

Behavioral Factors

Early Initiation of Intimate Sexual Activity People who are sexually active at an early age are at greater risk for STIs because this early initiation increases the total time they are sexually active and because they are more likely to have nonvoluntary intercourse, to have a greater number of sex partners, and to use condoms less consistently (Aral, 1994; Manlove, Ryan, & Franzetta, 2003). For example, a nationally representative sample of 9,844 respondents found that the odds of contracting an STI for an 18-year-old who first had intercourse at age 13 were more than twice those of an 18-year-old who first had intercourse at age 17 (Kaestle, Halpern, Miller, & Ford, 2005).

Numerous Sex Partners The more sex partners an individual has, the greater the chance of acquiring an STI. For example, according to one national study, 1% of respondents with 1 sex partner within the past year, 4.5% of those with 2–4 partners, and 5.9% of those with 5 or more partners became infected with an STI (Laumann, Gagnon, Michael, & Michaels, 1994). In addition, the more sex partners respondents had, the more likely it was that each of those partners was unfamiliar and nonexclusive. Being unfamiliar with partners, especially knowing the person for less than 1 month before first having sex, and having nonexclusive partners were both strongly associated with higher STI incidence. Another study found that 34% of sexually active women aged 15–44 were at risk for STIs because either they had more than 1 sex partner (21%) or their partners had 2 or more sex partners (23%). Interestingly, 20% of the women who had partners who had multiple sex partners thought that they were in mutually exclusive sexual relationships. Among men aged 18–24, 24% were at risk for STIs because of having 2 or more sex partners (Finer, Darroch, & Singh, 1999).

High-Risk Sex Partners Having sex with a person who has had many partners increases the risk of acquiring an STI. One example of this is a female who has a bisexual male partner. Often, the female does not know that her male partner also has sex with men. One study of 415 men who reported having sex with men revealed that 87% also reported having sex with women. These men were more than 2 times as likely as heterosexuals to be HIV-positive, and 29% were married or had been married (Lehner & Chiasson, 1998). Another example is when an older, sexually experienced person has sex with a younger and less experienced partner (Boyer et al., 2000). People often select new sex partners from their social network. If a person acquires an STI, then the social network could be considered a high-prevalence group, thus increasing a person's chance of future STI infections. Research has shown that selecting new partners from outside one's social network is associated with reduced risk for repeat STIs (Ellen et al., 2006).

High-Risk Sexual Behavior Certain sexual behaviors with a partner put individuals at higher risk for acquiring an STI than other behaviors. For example, studies have shown that men and women who have engaged in anal intercourse, have paid for sex, or have had "one-night stands" are more likely to report an STI than those who did not participate in those behaviors (Foxman, Aral, & Holmes, 1998; Tanfer, Cubbins, & Billy, 1995). A study of southern rural women found that those who reported engaging in more high-risk behaviors in the past 12 months were more likely to report having an STI during that same time (Yarber, Crosby, & Sanders, 2000).

Inconsistent and Incorrect Condom Use Correctly using a latex male condom during each sexual encounter and at any time the penis comes into contact with the partner significantly reduces the risk of STIs. Several studies have shown that both correct and consistent condom use is associated with lower STI rates in both men and women and lower rates of PID outcomes in women (Grimley, Annang, Houser, & Chen, 2005; Hutchinson, Kip, & Ness, 2007; Paz-Bailey et al., 2005; Shlay, McClung, Patnaik, & Douglas, 2004; Wald et al., 2005). (See the box "'Do You Know What You Are Doing?' Common Condom-Use Mistakes Among College Students" later in the chapter for a review of recent studies of college students and condom-use errors and problems.)

Substance Abuse The abuse of alcohol and drugs is associated with high-risk sexual behavior, although researchers are not certain if there is a cause-and-effect relationship between alcohol/drug use and risky sexual behavior. Substances may affect cognitive and negotiating skills before and during sex, lowering the likelihood that partners will protect themselves from STIs and pregnancy (U.S. Department of Health and Human Services, 2000b). A recent review of 11 studies of problem drinking and STIs showed an overall association between problematic alcohol use and STI infection (Cook & Clark, 2005).

Sexual Coercion Not all people enter sexual relationships as willing partners, particularly women. The 2007 Youth Risk Behavior Survey (CDC, 2008a) revealed that 9% of the adolescents surveyed had experienced forced sexual intercourse, with a greater percentage of females (11%) being coerced than males (5%). Individuals experiencing violence are less able to protect themselves from STIs.

Lack of Knowledge of and Concern About STIs Studies sponsored by the Kaiser Family Foundation revealed that many Americans are uninformed about STIs. When asked to name STIs they had heard of, only 2% named HPV, the

Preventing STIs: The Role of Male Condoms, Female Condoms, and Nonoxynol-9

For decades, the male condom has been promoted by public health officials as an important STI prevention device for sexually active individuals. However, there has been much discussion about how effective condoms really are in preventing HIV and other STIs. Some skeptics argue that condoms fail too often and that claims of condom effectiveness are misleading and exaggerated. Interestingly, despite these claims and denunciations by skeptics, a random telephone survey of 517 Indiana residents in 2003 found that nearly 92% considered condoms at least somewhat effective in preventing HIV and STIs (Yarber, Milhausen, Crosby, & Torabi, 2005).

The Centers for Disease Control and Prevention (CDC) has issued statements and recommendations on male condoms, female condoms, nonoxynol-9 (N-9), and STI prevention for public health personnel.

Male Condoms

The CDC's (2007f, 2009a) recommendations about the male latex condom and the prevention of STIs, including HIV, are based on information about the ways the various STIs are transmitted, the physical nature of condoms, the coverage or protection that condoms provide, and epidemiological studies of condom use and STIs. About STI prevention and condoms, the CDC has this to say:

> For persons whose sexual behaviors place them at risk for STDs, correct and consistent use of the male latex condom can reduce the risk of STD transmission. However, no protective method is 100 percent effective, and condom use cannot guarantee absolute protection against any STD. Furthermore, condoms lubricated with spermicides are no more effective than other lubricated condoms in protecting against the transmission of HIV and other STDs. In order to achieve the protective effect of condoms, they must be used correctly and consistently. Incorrect use can lead to condom slippage or breakage, thus diminishing their protective effect. Inconsistent use (e.g. failure to use condoms with every act of intercourse) can lead to STD transmission because transmission can occur with a single act of intercourse. While condom use has been associated with a lower risk of cervical cancer, the use of condoms should not be a substitute for routine screening with Pap smears to detect and prevent cancer.

In addressing specific STIs, the CDC has stated that latex condoms, when used consistently and correctly, are highly effective in preventing transmission of HIV and reduce the risk of transmission of gonorrhea, chlamydia, and trichomoniasis. Correct and consistent use of latex condoms reduces the risk of genital herpes, syphilis, and chancroid only when the infected area or site of potential exposure is protected as sometimes the ulcers of these diseases appear on the genital areas not covered by condoms. Condom use may reduce the risk for HPV infection and HPV-associated diseases such as genital warts and cervical cancer (CDC, 2007f, 2009a).

Female Condoms

The CDC (2007g) indicates that the female condom (Reality™) is an effective mechanical barrier to viruses, including HIV. Actually, research has shown that female condoms, when used properly, are as effective as barriers to semen during intercourse as male condoms (Macaluso et al., 2007). When used consistently and correctly, the female condom might substantially reduce the risk for STIs. The CDC recommends that when a male condom cannot be used properly, sex partners should consider using a female condom. The female condom has also been used for STI/HIV protection during receptive anal intercourse (Gross et al., 1999).

Nonoxynol-9

At one time, public health officials recommended the use of nonoxynol-9 (N-9) to help prevent STIs. Tests indicated that it killed many STIs, but, because of its high toxicity, frequent use of N-9 can disrupt the genital epithelium, which might be associated with an increased risk for HIV transmission. The danger in anal sex is especially significant because the rectum has only a single-cell wall; the vagina has a wall that is about 40 cells thick (Zimmerman, 2002). Therefore, the CDC (2007g) does not recommend N-9 for STI/HIV prevention.

SOURCES: Centers for Disease Control and Prevention. (2007). Male latex condoms and sexually transmitted diseases. Available: http://www.cdc.gov/condomeffectivness/latex.htm (Last visited 10/12/08); Centers for Disease Control and Prevention. (2007). Sexually transmitted diseases treatment guidelines 2006. Available: http://www.cdc.gov/std/treatment/2006/clinical.htm (Last visited 10/20/08); Centers for Disease Control and Prevention. (2009a). Condoms and STDs: Fact sheet for public health personnel. Available: http://www.cdc.gov/condomeffectiveness/latex.htm (Last visited 4/19/09). Gross, M., et al. (1999). Use of Reality "female condoms" for anal sex by US men who have sex with men. *American Journal of Public Health, 89,* 1739–1741; Zimmerman, R. (2002, September 25). Some makers, vendors drop N-9 spermicide on HIV risk. *The Wall Street Journal Online.*

most common STI, and only 11% named genital warts (Kaiser Family Foundation/ Harvard School of Public Health, 2000). About one third (36%) were not aware that having an STI increases one's risk of becoming infected with HIV, and almost 70% thought that only 1 in 10 Americans would get an STI in their lifetime (the actual figure is more than 1 in 2 by age 25) (Cates, Herndon, Schulz, & Darroch, 2004; Kaiser Family Foundation/*Glamour*, 1998). A study of 1,101 women aged 18–25 found that 75% believed they were at low risk of acquiring an STI in the next year even though most were having unprotected sex. Some of the women did not perceive STIs as a "big deal" and were desensitized to the risk of STIs (Yarnall et al., 2003).

Erroneous Perception of Partner's Risk   People also often do not have an adequate perception of their partners' risk. In one study of STI clinic patients in Southern California, participants indicated that they did not use condoms when they perceived new sex partners to be STI-free. Instead of directly discussing their partners' sexual history, they relied on both visual and verbal cues to judge whether their partners were disease-free. This assessment reflected serious error in judgment because most of the study participants had, in fact, contracted an STI (Hoffman & Cohen, 1999). Another study found that HIV-infected people had poor knowledge regarding their sex partner's HIV infection status. Sixty-four percent of partners thought to be infected were actually uninfected, and 42% of partners thought to be uninfected were actually infected (Niccolai, Farley, Ayoub, Magnus, & Kissinger, 2002). A recent study found that people perceive attractive partners to be at less risk for contracting on STI or HIV than unattractive partners (Hennessy, Fishbein, Curtis, & Barrett, 2007). This kind of information underscores the need for communication and honesty as part of STI prevention.

Social Factors

Poverty and Marginalization   Disenfranchised individuals and those in social networks in which high-risk behavior is common and access to health care is limited are disproportionately affected by STIs. These groups include sex workers (people who exchange sex for money, drugs, or other goods), adolescents, migrant workers, and incarcerated individuals. STIs, substance abuse, and sex work are closely connected (Eng & Butler, 1997; U.S. Department of Health and Human Services, 2000b).

Access to Health Care   Access to high-quality and culturally sensitive health care is imperative for early detection, treatment, and prevention counseling for STIs. Unfortunately, health services for STIs are limited in many low-income areas where STIs are common, and funds for public health programs are scarce. Without such programs, many people in high-risk social networks have no access to STI care.

Secrecy and Moral Conflict About Sexuality   One factor that separates the United States from other countries with lower rates of STIs is the cultural stigma associated with STIs and our general discomfort with sexuality issues. Historically, a moralistic, judgmental stance on STIs has hindered public health efforts to control STIs. For example, significant funding for AIDS research did not begin until it was clear that heterosexual individuals as well as gay men were threatened (Altman, 1985; Shilts, 1987). Also, the federal government continues to fund school and community adolescent abstinence-only educational programs in which the use of condoms for STI/HIV prevention cannot be mentioned. Educational efforts related to STIs

Social factors contributing to the spread of STIs include situations that support risky sexual behavior.

in particular and to sexuality in general often are hampered by vocal minorities who feel that knowledge about sex is what causes people to engage in it.

Biological Factors

Asymptomatic Nature of STIs   Most STIs either do not produce any symptoms or cause symptoms so mild that they go unnoticed or disregarded. A long time lag—sometimes years—often exists between the contracting of an STI and the onset of significant health problems. During the time in which the STI is asymptomatic, a person can unknowingly infect others. The individual may not seek treatment, allowing the STI to do damage to the reproductive system.

Resistance to Treatment or Lack of a Cure Because resistant strains of viruses, bacteria, and other pathogens are continually developing, antibiotics that have worked in the past may no longer be effective in treating STIs. Infected people may continue to transmit the STI, either because they believe they have been cured or because they currently show no symptoms. And some STIs, such as genital herpes, genital warts, and HIV, cannot be cured. The individual who has any of these viruses is always theoretically able to transmit them to others.

Susceptibility in Women Adolescent women are highly susceptible to acquiring chlamydia and gonorrhea because of an immature cervix (ASHA, 1998c). Women who practice vaginal douching are also at greater risk for PID and STIs (National Women's Health Information Center, 2002b).

Other Biological Factors For males, an uncircumcised penis has been linked to an increased risk for STIs such as HPV, gonorrhea, HIV, and syphilis (Bailey, 2007; Weiss, Thomas, Munabi, & Hayes, 2006; Xavier et al., 2002). Yet, other studies have found that circumcision was not related to greater prevalence of genital herpes (Dickerson, Van Roode, & Paul, 2005; Xu, Markowitz, Sternberg, & Aral, 2007) and one study found that early childhood circumcision does not markedly reduce the risk of genital herpes in the general population (Dickson, van Roode, Herbison, & Paul, 2008). Further, research on male circumcision and STI infection in women found that women with circumcised partners had similar risk of chlamydia, gonorrhea, and trichomoniasis (Turner et al., 2008). Male circumcision has been associated with lower risk of HIV infection in international observational studies and in three randomized controlled clinical trials in Africa. The Centers for Disease Control and Prevention states that it is possible, but not yet adequately assessed, that male circumcision might reduce male-to-female transmission of HIV, but probably to a lesser extent than female-to-male transmission. The CDC notes that male circumcision could be an important part of HIV prevention efforts in settings like those of the clinical trials (CDC, 2008c). The World Health Organization (2007) recommends that male circumcision be made available in countries highly affected by HIV/AIDS to help reduce HIV transmission during heterosexual sex.

For men who have sex with men, little evidence supports circumcision for HIV/STD prevention. A review of 15 studies involving 53,567 gay and bisexual men in eight countries worldwide failed to show any benefit for HIV protection for those who were circumcised (Millett, Flores, Marks, Reed, & Herbst, 2008). Given these mixed findings, in 2008, the CDC (2008e) stated that individual men may wish to consider circumcision as another method to prevent HIV but they should recognize that circumcision has been proven effective only in reducing the risk of HIV infection through insertive penile-vaginal intercourse.

As you can see, further research is needed on the effectiveness of male circumcision for preventing HIV/STI transmission. Whether male circumcision should be routinely done as an HIV/STI prevention strategy is still debated and remains controversial at the time of the printing of this book. On a side note, some males worry that being circumcised will decrease their sexual pleasure; most studies have found little difference in sexual sensation and sexual function between those circumcised and those not (CDC, 2008c; Kigozi et al., 2008).

Consequences of STIs

The list of problems caused by STIs seems almost endless. Women and infants suffer more serious health damage than men from all STIs. Without medical attention, some STIs can lead to blindness, cancer, heart disease, infertility,

STI Attitude Scale

This scale was developed by William L. Yarber, Mohammad Torabi, and C. Harold Veenker to measure the attitudes of young adults to determine whether they may be predisposed to high or low risk for contracting a sexually transmitted infection. The scale presented here is an updated version of the originally published scale. Follow the directions, and mark your responses to the statements below. Then calculate your risk as indicated.

Directions

Read each statement carefully. Indicate your first reaction by writing the letter that corresponds to your answer.

Key

SA = Strongly agree
A = Agree
U = Undecided
D = Disagree
SD = Strongly disagree

1. How I express my sexuality has nothing to do with STIs.
2. It is easy to use the prevention methods that reduce my chances of getting an STI.
3. Responsible sex is one of the best ways of reducing the risk of STIs.
4. Getting early medical care is the main key to preventing the harmful effects of STIs.
5. Choosing the right sex partner is important in reducing my risk of getting an STI.
6. A high prevalence of STIs should be a concern for all people.
7. If I have an STI, I have a duty to get my sex partners to seek medical treatment.
8. The best way to get my sex partner to STI treatment is to take him or her to the doctor with me.
9. Changing my sexual behaviors is necessary once the presence of an STI is known.
10. I would dislike having to follow the medical steps for treating an STI.
11. If I were sexually active, I would feel uneasy doing things before and after sex to prevent getting an STI.
12. If I were sexually active, it would be insulting if a sex partner suggested we use a condom to avoid getting an STI.
13. I dislike talking about STIs with my peers.
14. I would be uncertain about going to the doctor unless I was sure I really had an STI.

15. I would feel that I should take my sex partner with me to a clinic if I thought I had an STI.
16. It would be embarrassing to discuss STIs with my sex partner if I were sexually active.
17. If I were to have sex, the chance of getting an STI makes me uneasy about having sex with more than one partner.
18. I like the idea of sexual abstinence (not having sex) as the best way of avoiding STIs.
19. If I had an STI, I would cooperate with public health people to find the source of my infection.
20. If I had an STI, I would avoid exposing others while I was being treated.
21. I would have regular STI checkups if I were having sex with more than one partner.
22. I intend to look for STI signs before deciding to have sex with anyone.
23. I will limit my sexual activity to just one partner because of the chances of getting an STI.
24. I will avoid sexual contact any time I think there is even a slight chance of getting an STI.
25. The chance of getting an STI will not stop me from having sex.
26. If I had a chance, I would support community efforts to control STIs.
27. I would be willing to work with others to make people aware of STI problems in my town.

Scoring

Calculate points as follows:

Items 1, 10–14, 16, and 25: Strongly agree = 5, Agree = 4, Undecided = 3, Disagree = 2, Strongly disagree = 1
Items 2–9, 15, 17–24, 26, and 27: Strongly Agree = 1, Agree = 2, Undecided = 3, Disagree = 4, Strongly disagree = 5

The higher the score, the stronger the attitude that may predispose a person toward risky sexual behaviors. You may also calculate your points within three subscales: items 1–9 represent the "belief subscale," items 10–18 the "feeling subscale," and items 19–27 the "intention to act" subscale.

SOURCE: Adapted from Yarber, W. L., Torabi, M. R., & Veenker, C. H. (1989). Development of a three-component sexually transmitted diseases attitude scale. *Journal of Sex Education and Therapy, 15,* 36–49. With permission from the authors.

ectopic pregnancy, miscarriage, and even death (CDC, 2004c; Eng & Butler, 1997; Yarber, 2003).

A serious outcome of STI infection is that the presence of other STIs increases the likelihood of both transmitting and acquiring HIV. When someone who is infected with another STI is exposed to HIV through sexual contact, the likelihood of acquiring HIV infection is at least 2–5 times higher than when he or she is not infected with an STI. Research has also shown that the likelihood of a dually infected person (one with both HIV and another STI) infecting other people with HIV through sexual contact also is increased (CDC, 2008i; U.S. Department of Health and Human Services, 2000b; Wasserheit & Gayle, 1997).

Besides having human costs, the direct cost of STI treatment within the U.S. health-care system is at least $15 billion annually. This cost does not include indirect, nonmedical costs such as lost wages and productivity due to illness, out-of-pocket expenses, and costs related to STI transmission to infants (Chesson et al., 2004).

● Principal Bacterial STIs

In this section we discuss chlamydia, gonorrhea, urinary tract infections, and syphilis, the major bacterial STIs. As indicated earlier, bacterial STIs are curable. Table 15.1 summarizes information about all of the principal STIs, including bacterial STIs, viral STIs, vaginal infections, other STIs, and **ectoparasitic infestations** (parasites that live on the outer skin surfaces).

Chlamydia

The most common bacterial STI in the United States is caused by an organism called *Chlamydia trachomatis,* commonly known as **chlamydia.** In 2006, 1,030,911 cases of chlamydia were reported to the CDC, representing a nearly 6% increase over the 2005 total. The national rate of chlamydia was 348 cases per 100,000. An estimated 2.3 million individuals aged 14–39 are infected with chlamydia. Rates of reported chlamydia infections among women have been increasing annually since the late 1980s, and adolescent and young women remain the population most affected by chlamydia (CDC, 2008g; Datta et al., 2007).

Chlamydia is so common in young women that, by age 30, 50% of sexually experienced women show evidence that they had chlamydia sometime during their lives (CDC, 2001a). A study of 789 male and female students from ten southern colleges asymptomatic for chlamydia who volunteered for a urine screening found that 9.7%—nearly 1 in 10—were infected with chlamydia. Students under age 20 were nearly two thirds more likely to be infected than older students, and younger female students were 92% more likely to be infected than older female students (James, Simpson, & Chamberlain, 2008). Women who develop the infection 3 or more times have as great as a 75% chance of becoming infertile. Pelvic inflammatory disease (PID) occurs in up to 40% of women with untreated chlamydia. Also, research shows that women infected with chlamydia have a 5 times greater chance of acquiring HIV if exposed (CDC, 2005c). Untreated chlamydia can be quite painful and can lead to conditions requiring hospitalization, including acute arthritis. Infants of mothers infected with chlamydia may develop dangerous eye, ear, and lung infections.

Table 15.1 • Principal Sexually Transmitted Infections

STI and Infecting Organism	Symptoms	Time from Exposure to Occurrence	Medical Treatment	Comments
Bacterial STIs				
Chlamydia (*Chlamydia trachomatis*)	*Women:* 75% asymptomatic; others may have abnormal vaginal discharge or pain with urination. *Men:* One third to one half asymptomatic; others may have discharge from penis, burning or itching around urethral opening, or persistent low fever.	7–21 days.	Antibiotics	If untreated, may lead to pelvic inflammatory disease (PID) and subsequent infertility in women. By age 30, one half of sexually active women have evidence of previous chlamydial infection.
Gonorrhea (*Neisseria gonorrhoeae*)	*Women:* Up to 80% asymptomatic; others may have symptoms similar to chlamydia. *Men:* Some asymptomatic; others may have itching, burning or pain with urination, discharge from penis ("drip").	*Women:* Often no noticeable symptoms. *Men:* Usually 2–5 days, but possibly 30 days or more.	Antibiotics	If untreated, may lead to pelvic inflammatory disease (PID) and subsequent infertility in women. People with gonorrhea can more easily contract HIV.
Urethritis (various organisms)	Painful and/or frequent urination; discharge from penis; women may be asymptomatic. Can have discharge from vagina and painful urination.	1–3 weeks.	Antibiotics	Laboratory testing is important to determine appropriate treatment.
Syphilis (*Treponema pallidum*)	*Stage 1:* Red, painless sore (chancre) at bacterium's point of entry. *Stage 2:* Skin rash over body, including palms of hands and soles of feet.	*Stage 1:* 1–12 weeks. *Stage 2:* 6 weeks after chancre appears.	Antibiotics	Easily cured, but untreated syphilis can lead to damage of internal organs. There is a two- to fivefold increase of acquiring HIV when infected with syphilis.
Viral STIs				
HIV infection and AIDS (human immunodeficiency virus)*	Possible flulike symptoms but often no symptoms during early phase. Variety of later symptoms, including weight loss, persistent fever, night sweats, diarrhea, swollen lymph nodes, bruise-like rash, persistent cough.	Several months to several years.	No cure available, although new treatment drugs have improved the health and lengthened the lives of many HIV-infected individuals.	HIV infection is usually diagnosed by tests for antibodies against HIV. One in five people living with it are unaware of their infections.

*HIV infection and AIDS are discussed in detail in Chapter 16.

Any sexually active person can become infected with chlamydia. This is particularly true for adolescent girls and young women since their cervix is not fully matured and is probably more susceptible to infection. Chlamydia can be transmitted during vaginal, anal, or oral sex and from an infected mother to her baby during vaginal childbirth. Men who have sex with men are at risk for chlamydial infections since chlamydia can be transmitted during oral or anal sex. Chlamydia is known as a "silent" disease; about three fourths of infected women and about one half of infected men have no

STI and Infecting Organism	Symptoms	Time from Exposure to Occurrence	Medical Treatment	Comments
Genital herpes (herpes simplex virus)	Small sore or itchy bumps on genitals or rectum, becoming blisters that may rupture, forming painful sores; flulike symptoms with first outbreak.	Within 2 weeks	No cure, although antiviral medications may relieve pain and shorten duration of sores.	Virus remains in body, and outbreaks of contagious sores may recur. Most people diagnosed with first episode have four to five symptomatic recurrences a year, although recurrences are most noticeable in first year.
Genital human papillomavirus infection (group of viruses)	Over 40 HPV types, including genital warts, infect the genitals or rectum.	Most people with genital HPV infection do not know they are infected; some get visible genital warts. Most infections are temporary.	Surgical removal by freezing or laser therapy if warts are large or cause problems.	Some HPV types can cause cervical cancer. HPV usually disappears on its own without causing health problems. Most people who have sex acquire HPV at some time in their lifetime. Four strains of HPV can be prevented by a vaccine.
Viral hepatitis (hepatitis A or B virus)	Fatigue, diarrhea, nausea, abdominal pain, jaundice, darkened urine due to impaired liver function.	1–4 months	No medical treatment available; rest and fluids are prescribed until disease runs its course.	Hepatitis B is more commonly spread through sexual contact. Both A and B can be prevented by vaccinations.

Vaginal Infections

STI and Infecting Organism	Symptoms	Time from Exposure to Occurrence	Medical Treatment	Comments
Vaginitis (*Gardnerella vaginalis*, *Trichomonas vaginalis*, or *Candida albicans*)	Intense itching of vagina and/or vulva, unusual discharge with foul or fishy odor, painful intercourse. Men who carry organisms may be asymptomatic.	Within a few days up to 4 weeks.	Depends on organism; oral, topical, and vaginal medications are available.	Not always acquired sexually. Other causes include stress, birth control pills, pregnancy, tight pants or underwear, antibiotics, douching, and diet.

Ectoparasitic Infestations

STI and Infecting Organism	Symptoms	Time from Exposure to Occurrence	Medical Treatment	Comments
Pubic lice, crabs (*Pediculosis pubis*)	Itching, blue and gray spots, and insects or nits (eggs) in pubic area; some people may have no symptoms.	Hatching of eggs in 5–10 days.	Creams, lotions, or shampoos—both over-the-counter and prescription.	Avoid sexual contact with people having unusual spots or insects or nits in the genital area. Also avoid contaminated clothing, sheets, and towels.

symptoms. If symptoms do occur, they usually appear within 1–3 weeks after exposure.

When early symptoms occur in women, they are likely to include the following:

- Unusual vaginal discharge
- A burning sensation when urinating and frequent urination
- Unexplained vaginal bleeding between menstrual periods

Later symptoms, when the infection spreads from the cervix to the fallopian tubes, are these:

- Low abdominal pain
- Lower back pain
- Bleeding between menstrual periods
- A low-grade fever
- Pain during intercourse

One third to one half of men are asymptomatic when first infected. Men's symptoms may include these:

- Unusual discharge from the penis
- A burning sensation when urinating
- Itching and burning around the urethral opening (urethritis)
- Pain and swelling of the testicles
- A low-grade fever

The last two symptoms may indicate the presence of chlamydia-related **epididymitis,** inflammation of the epididymis. Untreated epididymitis can lead to infertility. Chlamydia responds well to antibiotic therapy. Rectal pain, discharge, or bleeding may occur in men or women who acquired chlamydia during receptive anal intercourse. Chlamydia can also be found in the throats of men and women engaging in oral sex with an infected person (CDC, 2005c).

The CDC (2007h) recommends yearly chlamydia testing for all sexually active women aged 25 or younger, older women with risk factors (new sex partner or multiple sex partners), and all pregnant women. Two types of laboratory tests can be used to detect chlamydia. One kind tests a urine sample; another tests fluid from a man's penis or a woman's cervix. A Pap smear does not test for chlamydia (CDC, 2005b).

Gonorrhea

Gonorrhea is the second most commonly reported notifiable disease in the United States. The CDC estimates that more than 700,000 persons in the United States become infected with gonorrhea each year. Only about half of these infections are reported to the CDC. In 2006, 358,366 cases of gonorrhea in the U.S. were reported to the CDC, a rate of 120.9 per 100,000 (CDC, 2008g, 2008j). Popularly referred to as "the clap" or "the drip," gonorrhea is caused by the *Neisseria gonorrhoeae* bacterium. The organism thrives in the warm, moist environment provided by the mucous membranes lining the mouth, throat, vagina, cervix, urethra, and rectum. Gonorrhea is transmitted during vaginal, anal, or oral sex with an infected person. Ejaculation does not have to occur for gonorrhea to be transmitted or acquired.

Men tend to experience the symptoms of gonorrhea more readily than women, notably as a watery discharge ("drip") from the penis, the first sign of urethritis. ("Gonorrhea" is from the Greek, meaning "flow of seed.") Some men infected with gonorrhea may have no symptoms at all. Other men have signs and symptoms that appear 2–5 days after infection. But symptoms can take as long as 30 days to appear (CDC, 2008j). Besides a watery discharge, symptoms in men may include the following:

- Itching or burning at the urethral opening
- Pain when urinating

If untreated, the disease soon produces these other symptoms:

- Thick yellow or greenish discharge
- Increasing discomfort or pain with urination
- Painful or swollen testicles

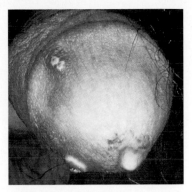

Gonorrhea infection in men is often characterized by a discharge from the penis.

Although most men seek treatment by this stage, some do not. Even if the symptoms diminish, the bacteria are still present. Those who do not get treatment can still infect their partners and may develop serious complications such as abscesses of the prostate gland and epididymitis.

Up to 80% of women with gonorrhea show no symptoms or very mild symptoms, which they tend to ignore. Because untreated gonorrhea, like untreated chlamydia, can lead to PID, it is important for women to be on guard for symptoms and to be treated if they think they may have been exposed to gonorrhea (e.g., if they have had numerous sex partners). Symptoms a woman may experience include the following:

- Thick yellow or white vaginal discharge, which might be bloody
- A burning sensation when urinating
- Unusual pain during menstruation
- Severe lower abdominal pain

Both females and males may have mucous discharge from the anus, blood and pus in feces, irritation of the anus, and mild sore throat (CDC, 2005d).

Gonorrhea is curable with several antibiotics. However, drug-resistant strains of gonorrhea are increasing in many parts of the United States and the world, making successful treatment more difficult (CDC, 2008j).

Untreated gonorrhea can cause sterility in both sexes, ectopic pregnancy, prostate damage, scarring of the urethra in men, and testicular pain. Gonorrhea may be passed to an infant during childbirth, causing conjunctivitis (an eye infection) and even blindness if not treated. People with gonorrhea can more easily contract HIV. People with HIV infection and gonorrhea are more likely than people with HIV infection alone to transmit HIV to others.

Urinary Tract Infections

Urethritis, the inflammation of the urethra, can result from sexual exposure and noninfectious conditions. Among the several organisms that cause these infections, the most common and most serious is chlamydia. Urinary tract infections are sometimes referred to as **nongonococcal urethritis (NGU).** The diagnosis of NGU occurs more frequently in men, largely due to their anatomy. In men, urethritis may produce these symptoms:

- A burning sensation when urinating
- Burning or itching around the opening of the penis
- White or yellowish discharge from the penis
- Underwear stain

*I had the honor
To receive, worse luck!
From a certain empress
A boiling hot piss.*

—Frederick the Great
(1712–1786)

Women are likely to be asymptomatic. They may not realize they are infected until a male partner is diagnosed. If a woman does have symptoms, they are likely to include these:

- Itching or burning while urinating
- Unusual vaginal discharge

It is important to have a laboratory test for an unusual discharge from the penis or vagina so that the appropriate antibiotic can be prescribed. Antibiotics are usually effective against NGU. Untreated NGU may result in permanent damage to the reproductive organs of both men and women and problems in pregnancy. The organisms that cause NGU in men may cause other infections in women, such as cervicitis, which is discussed later in this chapter (ASHA, 2008; CDC, 2007g). The most common urinary tract infection among women, cystitis, is briefly discussed later in this chapter.

Syphilis

Syphilis, a genital ulcerative disease, is caused by the bacterium *Treponema pallidum*. In the United States, health officials reported 36,935 cases of syphilis in 2006, including 9,756 cases of primary and secondary syphilis (see below for explanation of primary and secondary syphilis). Most syphilis cases in 2006 occurred in individuals aged 20–36. Although syphilis rates decreased steadily in the United States during 1900–2000, rates have been increasing since 2001, with the 2006 rate being 12% greater than the 2005 rate. Primary and secondary (P&S) syphilis rates (per 100,000 population) increased each year between 2000 and 2006 from 2.6 to 5.7 and among females between 2004 and 2006. In 2006, 64% of the reported P&S syphilis cases were among MSM, largely because of high rates of HIV coinfection and high-risk sexual behavior. Syphilis continues to be a serious problem in the south and in urban areas in other parts of the U.S. (CDC, 2007e, 2008g, 2008h).

Treponema pallidum is a spiral-shaped bacterium (a **spirochete**) that requires a warm, moist environment such as the genitals or the mucous membranes inside the mouth to survive. It is spread by direct contact with a syphilis sore during vaginal, anal, and oral sexual behavior. The syphilis bacterium of an infected mother can infect the baby during the pregnancy. Depending on how long the woman has been infected, she may have a high risk of having a stillborn baby or giving birth to a baby who dies soon after birth. An infected baby may be born and not have any signs or symptoms, but if not treated immediately, the baby may develop serious health problems within a few weeks. Untreated infants may become developmentally delayed, have seizures, or die (CDC, 2005e). Untreated syphilis in adults may lead to brain damage, heart disease, blindness, and death.

Syphilis has often been called "the great imitator" since many of its signs and symptoms are indistinguishable from those of other diseases. Yet, many people infected with syphilis do not have any symptoms for years but remain at risk for complications if they are not treated. Although transmission occurs from individuals with sores who are in the primary and secondary stages, many of these sores are unrecognized. Thus, transmission may occur from people who are unaware of their infection. Syphilis progresses through three discrete stages, although it is most often treated during the first two:

- *Stage 1: Primary syphilis.* The first symptom of syphilis appears from 10 to 90 days (average 21 days) after contact with an infected partner. It is a small,

And he died in the year fourteen-twenty.
Of the syphilis, which he had a-plenty.

—François Rabelais
(1490–1553).

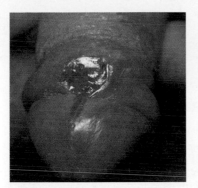 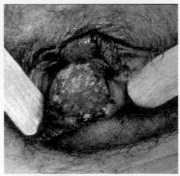

The first symptom of syphilis is a red, pea-sized bump called a chancre at the site where the bacterium originally entered the body.

red, pea-sized bump that soon develops into a round, painless sore called a **chancre** (SHANK-er). The person's lymph nodes may also be swollen. The chancre may appear on the labia, the shaft of the penis, the testicles, or the rectum; within the vagina; within the mouth; or on the lips. Unless it is in a visible area, it may not be noticed. Without treatment, it will disappear in 3–6 weeks, but the bacterium remains in the body, and the person is still highly contagious.

- *Stage 2: Secondary syphilis.* Untreated primary syphilis develops into secondary syphilis about 6 weeks after the chancre has disappeared. The principal symptom at this stage is a skin rash that neither itches nor hurts. The rash is likely to occur on the palms of the hands and the soles of the feet, as well as on other areas of the body. The individual may also experience fever, swollen lymph nodes, patchy hair loss, headaches, weight loss, muscle aches, and fatigue. The rash or other symptoms may be very mild or may pass unnoticed. The person is still contagious.

- *Stage 3: Latency.* If secondary syphilis is not treated, the symptoms disappear within 2–6 weeks, and the latent stage begins. The infected person may experience no further symptoms for years or perhaps never. After about a year, the bacterium can no longer be spread to sex partners, although a pregnant woman can still transmit the disease to her fetus. The late stages of syphilis can develop in about 15% of people who have not been treated for syphilis and can appear 10–20 years after infection was acquired. In the late stages, damage may occur many years later in internal organs, such as the brain, nerves, eyes, heart, blood vessels, liver, bones, and joints. Damage could also include difficulty coordinating muscle movements, paralysis, numbness, gradual blindness, dementia, and even death.

In the primary, secondary, and early latent stages, syphilis can be successfully treated with antibiotics. There is an estimated two- to fivefold increase in the chances of acquiring HIV if exposed to that infection when syphilis is present (CDC, 2008k).

● Principal Viral STIs

Four principal viral STIs—HIV and AIDS, genital human papillomavirus infection, genital herpes, and hepatitis—are discussed here. Recall that diseases caused by viruses are treatable, but not curable.

The Tuskegee Syphilis Study: "A Tragedy of Race and Medicine"

In 1932 in Macon County, Alabama, the U.S. Public Health Service, with the assistance of the Tuskegee Institute, a prestigious Black college, recruited 600 African American men to participate in an experiment involving the effects of untreated syphilis on Blacks. Of this group, 399 men had been diagnosed with syphilis and 201 were controls. The study was originally meant to last 6–9 months, but "the drive to satisfy scientific curiosity resulted in a 40-year experiment that followed the men to 'end point' (autopsy)" (Thomas & Quinn, 1991). The history of this experiment—the racial biases that created it, the cynicism that fueled it, and the callousness that allowed it to continue—is chillingly chronicled by James Jones (1993) in *Bad Blood: The Tuskegee Syphilis Experiment.*

The purpose of the study was to determine if there were racial differences in the developmental course of syphilis. The racial prejudice behind this motivation may seem hard to fathom today, yet, as we shall see, the repercussions still reverberate strongly through African American communities (Ross, James, & Torres, 2006).

Much of the original funding for the study came from the Julius Rosenwald Foundation (a philanthropic organization dedicated to improving conditions within African American communities), with the understanding that treatment was to be a part of the study. Although Alabama law required prompt treatment of diagnosed venereal diseases, the state Public Health Service managed to ensure that treatment was withheld from the participants. Even after 1951, when penicillin became the standard treatment for syphilis, the Public Health Service refused to treat the Tuskegee "subjects" on the grounds that the experiment was a "never-again-to-be-repeated opportunity" (Jones, 1993).

The Tuskegee participants were never informed that they had syphilis. The Public Health Service, assuming they would not understand medical terminology, referred to it as "bad blood," a term used to describe a variety of ailments in the rural South. The participants were not told their disease was sexually transmitted, nor were they told it could be passed from mother to fetus.

It was not until 1966 that anyone within the public health system expressed any moral concern over the study. A congressional subcommittee headed by Senator Edward Kennedy began hearings in 1973. The results included the rewriting of the Department of Health, Education, and Welfare's regulations on the use of human subjects in scientific experiments. A $1.8-billion class-action suit was filed on behalf of the Tuskegee participants and their heirs. A settlement of $10 million was reached out of court. Each survivor received $37,500 in damages, and the heirs of the deceased each received $15,000. Also, a congressionally mandated program, the Tuskegee Health Benefit Program, provides comprehensive lifetime medical benefits to the affected widows and offspring of participants in the Tuskegee syphilis study.

Current public health efforts to control the spread of HIV infection, AIDS, and other STIs raise the specter of genocide and beliefs of conspiracy among many members of the African American community. A random telephone survey of 500 African Americans aged 15–44 years living in the contiguous United States that was conducted in 2002 and 2003 found that a significant proportion of respondents endorsed HIV/AIDS conspiracy beliefs; that is, HIV/AIDS was created by the federal government to kill

HIV and AIDS

On June 5, 1981, the United States federal government published a report warning about a rare disease, eventually named as acquired immunodeficiency syndrome, or AIDS (CDC, 1981). Since that time, this disease has become an enormous public health challenge nationally and globally. Human immuno-deficiency virus (HIV)—the virus that causes AIDS—and AIDS have claimed millions of lives worldwide, becoming one of the deadliest epidemics in human history. Despite advances in medical testing and treatment, and prevention efforts, HIV/AIDS remains a potentially deadly disease. Because of its major global impact and continued medical and prevention challenge, we have decided to devote an entire chapter to HIV and AIDS, which follows this chapter.

and wipe out African Americans. Among men, stronger conspiracy beliefs were significantly associated with negative attitudes about condoms and inconsistent condom use (Bogart & Thornton, 2005).

Many of the current beliefs of African Americans about HIV/AIDS as a form of genocide is attributed to the Tuskegee syphilis study. On both physiological and psychological levels, there is much healing to be done. Even though it is unthinkable that such a study would be done today, efforts must still be made to ensure that all people are protected against such tragedies.

For reflections on the legacy of the Tuskegee study, see Caplan, 1992; Jones, 1993; and King, 1992. Several Internet sites provide further information about this terrible experiment, including the transcript of President Clinton's 1997 formal apology to study participants.

Think Critically

- Is it possible for another medical experiment like the Tuskegee syphilis study to happen in America today? Explain your view.
- What can be done to prevent another Tuskegee syphilis study?
- What can the medical and scientific community do to gain the trust of all Americans?

'NOW can we give him penicillin?'

Genital Human Papillomavirus Infection

Genital human papillomavirus infection, or genital HPV infection, is a group of viruses that includes more than 100 different strains; over 40 are sexually transmitted and can infect the genital and rectal area. Currently, at least 20 million people in the U.S. are infected with HPV, with 6.2 million new infections each year. HPV is the most common STI among young, sexually active people, particularly women. Of U.S. girls and women aged 14–59, about 27% (about 24.9 million) have HPV (Dunne et al., 2007). At least one half of sexually experienced men and women acquire genital HPV infection at some point in their lives. By age 50, at least 80% of women will have acquired genital HPV infection (CDC, 2005g, 2008l).

The type of HPV that infects the genital area is spread primarily through sexual contact with an infected person. In rare instances, a pregnant woman can pass HPV to her baby during vaginal delivery. The incubation period (the period between the time a person is first exposed to a disease and the time the symptoms appear) is usually 6 weeks to 8 months. You cannot see HPV. Most people who have a genital HPV infection do not know they are infected, and most infections are temporary.

Sometimes, certain types of HPV can cause **genital warts** in men and women. Other HPV types can cause cervical cancer and less common cancers of the vulva, vagina, anus, and penis. The types of HPV that can cause genital warts are not the same as the types that can cause cancer. HPV types are referred to as "low risk" (wart causing) or "high risk" (cancer causing). In 90% of the cases, the body's immune system clears the HPV—both high-risk and low-risk types—naturally within 2 years. If a high-risk HPV infection is not cleared by the immune system, it can linger for many years and turn abnormal cells into cancer over time. About 10% of women with high-risk HPV on their cervix will develop long-lasting HPV infections that will put them at risk for cervical cancer (CDC, 2008l).

The Pap test can identify abnormal or precancerous tissue in the cervix so that it can be removed before cancer develops. An HPV DNA test, which can find high-risk HPV on a women's cervix, may also be used with a Pap test in certain cases. There is no general test for men and women to check one's over-all "HPV status." HPV usually goes away on its own, without causing health problems. So an HPV infection that is found today will most likely not be there a year or two from now. Hence, there is no reason to be tested just to find out if you have HPV now. But you should get tested for signs of diseases that HPV can cause, such as cervical cancer (CDC, 2008l).

Click on "HPV" to hear about the experience of a woman with human papillomavirus.

The genital-wart history of a national sample of 8,849 men and women found that 7% of women and 4% of men reported ever being diagnosed with genital warts (Dinh, Sternberg, Dunne, & Markowitz, 2008). Genital warts usually appear as soft, moist, pink, or flesh-colored swellings, usually in the genital area. They can also be flat, single or multiple, small or large, and sometimes cauliflower shaped. They can appear on the penis or scrotum, in or around the vagina or anus, on the cervix, or on the groin or thigh (CDC, 2005g). If the warts cause discomfort or problems (such as interfering with urination), they can be removed by cryosurgery (freezing) or laser surgery. Removal of the warts does not eliminate HPV from the person's system. Because the virus can lie dormant in the cells, in some cases warts can return months or even years after treatment. The extent to which a person can still transmit HPV after the visible warts have been removed is unknown.

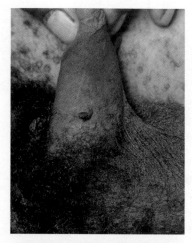

As stated in Chapter 13, the U.S. Food and Drug Administration approved a vaccine Gardasil in June 2006 that would protect thousands of women each year from cervical cancer. The vaccine, approved for girls but not boys, prevents infection by four of the numerous strains of the human papillomavirus—two of the strains the vaccine blocks cause 70% of cervical cancers, and the other two strains cause 90% of genital warts. The vaccine also protects against vaginal and vulvar cancers linked to the four strains of HPV. The vaccine does not protect those already infected; hence, public health officials want the vaccine given to girls prior to their first sexual intercourse (Bridges, 2006; Harris, 2006). No association has been established between genital HPV infection and miscarriage, early delivery or other complications during pregnancy. Very rarely, a pregnant woman with HPV can pass HPV to her baby during vaginal delivery. In these cases, the child may develop warts in the throat or voice box (CDC, 2008l).

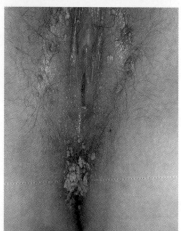

Genital warts appear in a variety of forms.

ASHA has developed a support service for people with HPV called the National HPV and Cervical Cancer Prevention Resource Center (http://www.ashastd.org). It provides information about HPV and its link to cervical cancer, support for emotional issues surrounding HPV, and an Internet chat room (http://www.ashastd.org/hpv/hpv-community_chat.cfn).

If you have HPV, don't blame your current sexual partner or assume that your partner is not sexually exclusive with you. Remember, most people who have sex will have HPV at some time in their lifetimes, and they may have HPV for a very long time before it is detected. Sex partners usually share HPV, particularly those who are together for a long time. There should be no shame or blame involved with having genital HPV; the virus is very common.

Genital Herpes

Genital herpes is an STI caused by the **herpes simplex virus (HSV)** type 1 (HSV-1) and type 2 (HSV-2). Most genital herpes is caused by HSV-2. At least 45 million people in the United States aged 12 and older, or 1 in 5 adolescents and adults, have had genital HSV infection. Over the past decade, the percentage of Americans with genital herpes in the United States has decreased. Genital HSV-2 infection is more common in women (about 1 in 4 are infected) than men (almost 1 in 8). This may be due to male-to-female transmission being more likely than female-to-male transmission. Herpes can make people more susceptible to HIV infection, and it can make HIV-infected individuals more infectious.

HSV-1 and HSV-2 can be found and released from the sores that the viruses cause, but also can be released between outbreaks from skin that does not appear to be broken or have a sore. Generally, a person can get HSV-2 infection only during sexual contact with someone who has a genital HSV-2 infection. It is important to know that transmission can occur from an infected partner who does not have a visible sore and may not know that he or she is infected. HSV-1 can cause genital herpes, but it more often causes infections of the mouth and lips, so-called fever blisters. HSV-1 infection of the genitals can be caused by oral-genital or genital-genital contact with a person infected with HSV-1. Genital HSV-1 outbreaks recur less regularly than genital HSV-2 outbreaks.

Most infected people have no or minimal signs or symptoms from HSV-1 and HSV-2 infection. When signs appear, they typically occur within 2 weeks after the virus is transmitted and appear as one or more blisters on or around the genitals or rectum. The blister breaks, leaving tender ulcers (sores) that may take 2–4 weeks to heal the first time they occur. Most people diagnosed with a first episode of genital herpes can expect to have several (typically four or five) outbreaks within a year, but they are almost always less severe and shorter than the first outbreak. Even though the infection can stay in the body indefinitely, the number of outbreaks tends to decrease over a period of years (CDC, 2008m).

Click on "Herpes" to meet a man with genital herpes.

Managing HSV There is no cure for herpes, but there are medications that can help to keep the virus in check (Handsfield, Warren, Werner, & Phillips, 2007). Antiviral medications can relieve pain, shorten the duration of sores, prevent bacterial infections at the open sores, and prevent outbreaks while the person is taking the medications. Other actions that may be useful in preventing, shortening the duration of, or lessening the severity of recurrent outbreaks include getting plenty of rest, maintaining a balanced diet, avoiding tight clothes, keeping the area cool and dry, taking aspirin or other painkillers, and reducing stress.

Individuals with herpes should inform their partners and together decide what precautions are right for them. Because having sex during a recognized outbreak puts an uninfected partner at risk, people should abstain from sex when signs and symptoms of either oral or genital herpes are present. The male

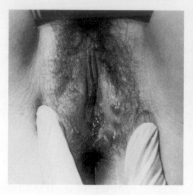 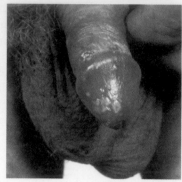

latex condom can help prevent infections, but only when the condom covers the ulcer. Condoms should be used between outbreaks of the ulcers. Also, daily suppressive therapy for symptomatic herpes can reduce transmission to partners. Pregnant women or their partners who have HSV should be sure to discuss precautionary procedures with their medical practitioners.

Genital herpes often causes psychological distress in people who know they are infected. ASHA has developed a support service for people with herpes infections called the Herpes Resource Center (http://www.ashastd.org). It provides current information about herpes, such as the STI Resource Center Hotline (1-800-227-8922), and referrals to local support groups.

Viral Hepatitis

Hepatitis is a viral disease meaning inflammation of the liver. The most common types of the virus that can be sexually transmitted are hepatitis A and hepatitis B. A third type, hepatitis C, is a common virus passed on primarily through contact with infected blood; risk of transmittal from sex partners or from mothers to newborns during birth is low.

Hepatitis A is transmitted primarily through oral contact with contaminated food or water or through sexual contact, especially oral-anal sex. In the United States, there were an estimated 32,000 new hepatitis A infections in 2006. The rates of hepatitis A in the U.S. have been their lowest in the past 40 years. A highly effective vaccine can prevent hepatitis A, and immune serum globulin injections provide some immunity. Although the symptoms of hepatitis A are similar to those of hepatitis B, the disease is not considered as dangerous. Individuals infected with hepatitis A usually experience short-term illness, recover completely, and develop immunity against reinfection (CDC, 2008n).

Hepatitis B is 50–100 times more infectious than HIV. It is commonly spread through sexual contact, in blood, semen, saliva, vaginal secretions, and urine. In the United States, two thirds of acute hepatitis cases resulted from sexual contact with the virus. It can also be contracted by using contaminated needles and syringes, including those used in ear piercing, acupuncture, and tattooing, and by sharing the toothbrush or razor of an infected person. An estimated 800,000 to 1.4 million Americans are chronically infected with hepatitis B. The number of new infections per year has declined dramatically from an average of 260,000 per year in the 1980s to about 46,000 in 2006 (CDC, 2008o). Anyone can get hepatitis B, but individuals in their teens and twenties are at greater risk. Because hepatitis B spreads "silently"—that is, without easily noticeable symptoms—many people are not aware it is in their communities. Chronic hepatitis B is a serious disease that can result in long-term health problems and even death.

Hepatitis B can be prevented by a simple, widely available vaccine. The CDC (2008o) recommends routine vaccination for those most at risk, including sexually active people not in a long-term, exclusive relationship, men who have sex with men, people who share drug-injection equipment, people whose sex partner has hepatitis B, and people with HIV. Screening for hepatitis B is also recommended for pregnant women so that their newborns can be immediately vaccinated if necessary. The vaccine is safe and effective and provides lasting protection. Tattoos and body piercings should be done at parlors that thoroughly sterilize the instruments used to penetrate the skin.

In 2006 there were an estimated 19,000 new hepatitis C virus infections in the United States. An estimated 3.2 million individuals in the U.S. have chronic hepatitis C, and about 75–85% of people who become infected with hepatitis C will develop a chronic infection. About 8,000 to 10,000 people die every year from hepatitis C–related liver disease (CDC, 2008p). Risk of infection from sexual activity is low unless it involves blood contact; numerous sex partners, failure to use condoms, a history of STIs, and sexual activities involving trauma (e.g., "rough" sex) increase the risk. Most cases of hepatitis C can be traced to blood transfusions before 1992, the sharing of needles during injection drug use, and accidental needle-sticks. Known as the "silent epidemic," the disease damages the liver over the course of many years, and even decades, before symptoms appear. To date, there is no vaccine.

The symptoms of all forms of hepatitis include fatigue, diarrhea, nausea, abdominal pain, jaundice, darkened urine, and an enlarged liver. About 15–25% of people who get hepatitis C will clear the virus from their bodies without treatment and will not get a chronic infection. There is no medical treatment for hepatitis C. Occasionally, serious liver damage or death results.

● Vaginal Infections

Vaginal infections, or **vaginitis,** affect 3 out of 4 women at least once in their lives. These infections are often, though not always, sexually transmitted. They may also be induced by an upset in the normal balance of vaginal organisms by such things as stress, birth control pills, antibiotics, nylon panty hose, and douching. The three principal types of vaginitis are bacterial vaginosis, candidiasis, and trichomoniasis.

Bacterial Vaginosis

Bacterial vaginal infections, referred to as **bacterial vaginosis (BV),** may be caused by a number of different organisms, most commonly *Gardnerella vaginalis,* often a normal inhabitant of the healthy vagina. An overabundance of *Gardnerella,* however, can result in vaginal discharge, odor, pain, itching, or burning. Bacterial vaginosis is the most common vaginal infection in women of childbearing age and, in the United States, is common among pregnant women. An estimated 29% of American women (21 million) have BV now (CDC, 2008q; Koumans et al., 2007). Not much is known about how women get bacterial vaginosis, and there are many unanswered questions about the role that harmful bacteria play in causing it and what role sexual activity plays in its development. Any woman can get BV, although some activities can upset the normal balance of bacteria in the vagina and put women at risk, including having a new sex partner or numerous sex partners and douching (Hutchinson, Kip, & Ness, 2007). Bacterial vaginosis may also be spread between female sex partners (Bailey, Farquhar, & Owen, 2004). Women who never had sexual intercourse may get BV (Tabrizi, Fairley, Bradshaw, & Garland, 2006). Most often this infection causes no complications, although having it can increase a woman's susceptibility to HIV infection and other STIs such as chlamydia and gonorrhea and can increase the chances that an HIV-infected woman can pass HIV to her sex partner. BV may also put a woman at increased risk for some complications during pregnancy.

Even though bacterial vaginosis sometimes clears up without treatment, all women with symptoms of BV should be treated with antibiotics so that the bacteria that cause BV do not infect the uterus and fallopian tubes, an infection called pelvic inflammatory disease, or PID. Male partners generally do not need to be treated (CDC, 2008q). A study of women at high risk for STI found that consistent condom users had a 45% decreased risk for BV than women not using condoms consistently (Hutchinson, Kip, & Ness, 2007).

Genital Candidiasis

Sex is a pleasurable exercise in plumbing, but be careful or you'll get yeast in your drainpipe.

—Rita Mae Brown
(1944–)

Genital candidiasis, also known as a "yeast infection," is a common fungal infection that occurs when there is an overgrowth of the fungus called *Candida albicans. Candida* is always present in the body (e.g., vagina, mouth, gastrointestinal tract) in a small amount; however, when an imbalance occurs, such as when the normal acidity of the vagina changes or when hormonal balance changes, *Candida* can multiply. Women with a vaginal yeast infection usually experience itching or burning, with or without a "cottage cheese–like" vaginal discharge. Males with genital candidiasis may have an itchy rash on the penis. Nearly 75% of all adult women have had at least one vaginal yeast infection in their lifetime. Vaginal yeast infections are rarely transmitted during sexual activity. While most cases are caused by the person's own *Candida* organisms, the use of birth control pills or antibiotics, frequent douching, pregnancy, and diabetes can promote yeast infections. Genital candidiasis occurs more often and with more severe symptoms in people with weakened immune systems.

Antifungal drugs, taken orally, applied directly to the affected area, or used vaginally, are the drug of choice for vaginal yeast infections and are effective 80–90% of the time. Because over-the-counter (OTC) treatments are becoming more available, more women are diagnosing themselves with vaginal yeast infections and using one of a family of drugs called "azoles" for therapy. However, studies show that as many as two thirds of OTC drugs sold to treat vaginal yeast infections are used by women *without* the disease, which may lead to resistant infections. Therefore, it is important to be sure of the diagnosis before treating with OTC or other antifungal medications (CDC, 2008r).

Trichomoniasis

Trichomoniasis is caused by a single-celled protozoan parasite, *Trichomonas vaginalis.* Trichomoniasis is the most common curable STI in young, sexually active women. An estimated 7.4 million new cases occur each year in women and men. One study of 1,209 women attending three STI clinics found that trichomoniasis, unlike other STIs, was found more often in older compared to younger women (Helms et al., 2008). In women, the vagina is the most common site of infection; in men, it is the urethra. The parasite is sexually transmitted during penile-vagina intercourse or vulva-to-vulva contact with an infected person. Women can acquire the disease from infected men or women, but men usually contract it only from infected women. Symptoms are more common in women than men, although up to one half of infected women are asymptomatic. Some women have signs and symptoms usually within 5–28 days after exposure, which include frothy, yellow-green vaginal discharge with a strong odor. The infection may also cause discomfort during intercourse and urination, as well as itching and irritation of the female genital area, and, rarely, lower abdominal pain. Some men may temporarily have an irritation inside the penis, mild discharge, or slight burning after urination or ejaculation. For both women and men, a physical examination and a laboratory test are used to diagnose trichomoniasis, although it is harder to detect in men (CDC, 2007i).

Trichomoniasis can cause preterm delivery in pregnant women. Women having the genital inflammation caused by trichomoniasis may have an increased risk of acquiring HIV if exposed to it. Women who have both trichomoniasis infection and HIV infection also have an increased chance of transmitting HIV to a sex partner.

Prescription drugs are effective in treating trichomoniasis. To prevent reinfection, both partners must be treated, even if the man is asymptomatic.

● Other STIs

A number of other STIs appear in the United States, but with less frequency than they do in some developing countries. Among these other STIs are the following:

- Chancroid is a painful sore or group of sores on the penis, caused by the bacterium *Hemophilus ducreyi*. Women may carry the bacterium but are generally asymptomatic for chancroid.
- Cytomegalovirus (CMV) is a virus of the herpes group that affects people with depressed immune systems. A fetus may be infected with CMV in the uterus.
- Enteric infections are intestinal infections caused by bacteria, viruses, protozoans, or other organisms that are normally carried in the intestinal tract. Amebiasis, giardiasis, and shigellosis are typical enteric infections. They often result from anal sex or oral-anal contact.
- Granuloma inguinale appears as single or multiple nodules, usually on the genitals, that become lumpy but painless ulcers that bleed on contact.
- Lymphogranuloma venereum (LGV) begins as a small, painless lesion at the site of infection and then develops into a painful abscess, accompanied by pain and swelling in the groin.
- Molluscum contagiosum, caused by a relatively large virus, is characterized by smooth, round, shiny lesions that appear on the trunk, on the genitals, or around the anus.

● Ectoparasitic Infestations

Although they are not infections per se, parasites such as scabies and pubic lice can be spread by sexual contact. Scabies and pubic lice are considered ectoparasitic parasites or infestations since they live on the outer surfaces of the skin.

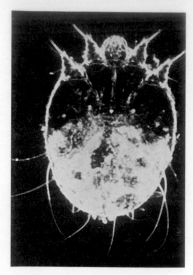

Pubic lice, or "crabs," are easily spread during intimate contact; they may also be transmitted via bedding, towels, or underwear.

Scabies

The red, intensely itchy rash caused by the barely visible mite *Sarcoptes scabiei* is called **scabies.** It usually appears on the genitals, buttocks, feet, wrists, knuckles, abdomen, armpits, or scalp as a result of the mites' tunneling beneath the skin to lay their eggs and the baby mites' making their way back to the surface. It is highly contagious and spreads quickly among people who have close contact, both sexual and nonsexual. The mites can also be transferred during prolonged contact with infested linens, furniture, or clothing. Scabies is usually treated with a prescribed lotion, applied at bedtime and washed off in the morning. Clothing, towels, and bedding of people who have scabies should be disinfected by washing in hot water and drying in high heat or by dry cleaning.

Pubic Lice

The tiny *Phthirus pubis,* commonly known as a "crab," moves easily from the hair of one person to that of another (probably along with several of its relatives). **Pubic lice** usually are found in the genital area on pubic hair, although they can be found on other coarse body hair such as hair on the legs, armpits, mustache, and beard. When pubic lice mate, the male and female grasp adjacent hairs; the female soon begins producing eggs (nits), which she attaches to the hairs at the rate of about three eggs a day for 7–10 days. The nits hatch within 5–10 days and begin reproducing in about 2–3 weeks, creating a very ticklish (or itchy) situation. Pubic lice can be transmitted during sexual contact with a person who has crabs, moving from the pubic hair of one person to the pubic hair of another. They may fall into underwear, sheets, or towels, where they can survive up to a day *and* lay eggs that hatch in about a week. Thus, it is possible to get crabs simply by sleeping in an infected person's bed, wearing his or her clothes, or sharing a towel.

People can usually tell when they have pubic lice. There is intense itching, and upon inspection, they discover a tiny, pale, crablike louse or its minuscule, pearly nits attached near the base of a pubic hair. There are both prescription and over-the-counter treatments for pubic lice. An infected person does not have to shave off his or her pubic hair to get rid of crabs. In addition to killing all the lice and nits on the body, infected individuals must wash all infected linen and clothing in hot water and dry it in high heat, or the crabs may survive (ASHA, 2006; CDC, 2008s).

● STIs and Women

In addition to the direct effects that STIs have on the body, women are vulnerable to complications from STIs that threaten their fertility. These are related to the biological factors, discussed earlier, that make women more susceptible to STIs and make STIs more difficult to detect in women than in men.

Pelvic Inflammatory Disease (PID)

As discussed in Chapter 12, pelvic inflammatory disease (PID), also known as salpingitis, is one of the leading causes of female infertility. Approximately 1 million cases of acute PID occur annually, resulting in more than 100,000 women becoming infertile each year due to the consequences of PID.

PID occurs when bacteria move upward from a woman's vagina or cervix into her uterus, fallopian tubes, and other reproductive organs. Several organisms can cause PID, but many cases are associated with gonorrhea and chlamydia. A prior episode of PID increases the risk of another episode because the reproductive organs may have been damaged during the initial episode. Sexually active women in their childbearing years are at most risk, and those under age 25 are more likely to develop PID than those older than 25. Because the cervix of teenage girls and young women is not fully mature, their susceptibility to the STIs that are linked to PID are increased. Women with repeated episodes of PID are more likely to suffer infertility, ectopic pregnancy, or chronic pelvic pain than those who have had just one episode.

Risk behaviors for PID include having numerous sex partners, having a partner who has more than one sex partner, and douching. Also, women who have an IUD may have a slightly increased risk of PID near the time of insertion as compared with women using other contraceptives or no contraceptive. However, the risk is greatly reduced if a women is tested and, if necessary, treated for STIs before an IUD is inserted.

Symptoms of PID vary from none, to subtle and mild, to severe. PID is difficult to diagnose because of the absent or mild symptoms, and many episodes go undetected. PID goes unrecognized by women and their health-care providers about two thirds of the time. Because there is no precise test for PID, a diagnosis is usually based on clinical findings. Symptoms of PID include lower abdominal pain, fever, unusual vaginal discharge that may have a foul order, painful intercourse, painful urination, irregular menstrual bleeding, and, rarely, pain in the upper right abdomen. A health-care provider may order tests to identify the infection-causing organism (e.g., chlamydial or gonorrheal infection) or to distinguish between PID and other problems with similar symptoms. Sometimes, a pelvic ultrasound is helpful and, in some cases, a laparoscopy may be necessary to confirm the diagnosis. PID can be cured with several types of antibiotics (CDC, 2008t).

Cervicitis

Cervicitis is an inflammation of the cervix, the lower end of the uterus. Cervicitis might be a sign of upper genital infection, most often caused by a sexually transmitted infection such as gonorrhea or chlamydia. Frequently there are no signs of cervicitis, but some women complain of abnormal vaginal discharge, painful urination, and vaginal bleeding between menstrual periods, such as after sexual intercourse. A woman is at greater risk for cervicitis associated with STIs if she engages in high-risk sexual behavior, such as not using condoms or having sex with numerous partners, and if she began having sex at an early age. Having a history of STIs is also a risk factor. Since the signs of cervicitis are not often noticed, the infection may be discovered only in the course of a routine Pap test. This is one important reason to have regular pelvic exams and Pap tests. A woman may not need treatment for cervicitis if it is not caused by an STI. If it is caused by an STI, both the woman and her partner are likely to need treatment. Prescription medications often are effective in clearing up the inflammation of cervicitis (CDC, 2007g; Mayo Clinic, 2007c).

Cystitis

A bladder infection that affects mainly women, **cystitis** is often related to sexual activity, although it is not transmitted from one partner to another. Cystitis is characterized by painful, burning urination and a nearly constant need to urinate.

Cystitis occurs when a bacterium such as *Escherichia coli,* normally present in the lower intestine and in fecal material, is introduced into the urinary tract. This can occur when continuous friction (from intercourse or manual stimulation) in the area of the urethra traumatizes the tissue and allows nearby bacteria to enter the urinary tract. It often occurs at the beginning of a sexual relationship, when sexual activity is high (hence the nickname "honeymoon cystitis"). If cystitis is not treated promptly with antibiotics, more serious symptoms such as lower abdominal pain, fever, and kidney pain will occur. Damage to the kidneys may occur if treatment is delayed.

● Preventing STIs

It seems that STIs should be easy to prevent, at least in theory. But in reality, STI prevention involves a subtle interplay of knowledge, psychological factors, couple dynamics, and behaviors. Earlier in the chapter, you read the facts. Now let's think about the psychological and behavioral components of preventing STIs and some important individual health behaviors you can adapt to prevent STIs.

Avoiding STIs

STIs can be transmitted by sexual contact with an infected partner, by infected blood in injection-drug equipment, and from an infected mother to her child. Because we know that STIs are transmitted by certain behaviors, we know exactly how to keep from getting them. Those behaviors are particularly important because many young people underestimate their risk of becoming infected with an STI and the risk behavior of potential sex partners (Kaiser Family Foundation, 2001b).

1. *Practice abstinence.* The closest thing to a foolproof method of STI prevention is abstaining from intimate sexual contact, especially penile-vaginal intercourse, anal intercourse, and oral sex. Hugging, kissing, caressing, and mutual masturbation are all ways of sharing intimacy that are extremely unlikely to transmit STIs. Freely

An important part of controlling the spread of STIs is having free access to condoms and relevant information.

think
about it

"Do You Know What You Are Doing?" Common Condom-Use Mistakes Among College Students

For those wanting to prevent STIs and pregnancy, condom use is necessary for *all* sexual episodes. But consistent use is only part of the answer—the condom must be used correctly if it is to be effective.

Very little research has been conducted on correct condom use, but the first comprehensive study of college male students produced some startling and alarming results. Researchers at The Kinsey Institute for Research in Sex, Gender, and Reproduction and the Rural Center for HIV/STD Prevention at Indiana University determined the prevalence of male condom–use errors and problems among samples of undergraduate, single, self-identified heterosexual men (N = 158) who applied the condom to themselves and single, self-identified heterosexual women (N = 102) who applied a condom to their male partner at a large, public midwestern university. Participants were asked to indicate if the error or problem occurred at least once during the past 3 months during sex, defined as when the male put his penis in a partner's mouth, vagina, or rectum. The percentage of the errors and problems that occurred at least once in the past 3 months were remarkably similar whether or not the male applied the condom to himself or whether his female partner applied the condom to him. The table indicates some of the most important errors and problems.

Error/Problem	Male Appliers	Female Appliers
Put condom on after starting sex	42.8%*	51.1%*
Did not hold tip and leave space	40.4%	45.7%
Put condom on the wrong side up (had to flip it over)	30.4%	29.6%
Used condom without lubricant	19.2%	25.8%
Took condom off before sex was over	15.3%	14.8%
Did not change to new condoms when switching between vaginal, oral, and anal sex (for those switching)	81.2%	75.0%
Condom broke	29.0%	19.3%
Condom slipped off during sex	13.1%	19.3%
Lost erection before condom was put on	21.6%	14.3%
Lost erection after condom was on and sex had begun	19.6%	20.2%

*Percentage reporting that the error or problem occurred at least once in the past 3 months.

A subsequent focus group study of undergraduates who reported male condom use for other-sex behavior in the previous month found that they had concerns about male condoms, including mistrust of each gender in supplying and properly using condoms, inadequate lubrication during condom use, condoms partially or fully slipping off during sex, "losing" part or all of the condom in the vagina, delayed applications, and irritation and reduced sensation (Yarber et al., 2007).

The researchers concluded that the condom-use errors and problems reported in these studies indicate a possible high risk of exposure of the participants to HIV/STIs and unintended pregnancy. They also stated that the effectiveness of condom use against HIV/STIs and unintended pregnancy is contingent upon correct condom use.

Think Critically

- Did the types and frequency of condom-use errors and problems found in these studies surprise you? Explain.
- Why do you think these errors and problems occurred?
- Is it really that difficult to use condoms correctly— why or why not?
- What can be done to promote correct condom use?

SOURCES: Crosby, R. A., Sanders, S. A., Yarber, W. L., Graham, C. A., & Dodge, B. (2002). Condom use errors and problems among college men. *Sexually Transmitted Diseases, 29,* 552–557; Sanders, S. A., Graham, C. A., Yarber, W. L., & Crosby, R. A. (2003). Condom use errors and problems among young women who put condoms on their male partners. *Journal of the American Medical Women's Association, 58,* 95–98; Yarber, W. L., Graham, C. A., Sanders, S. A., Crosby, R. A., Butler, S. M., & Hartzell, R. M. (2007). "Do you know what you are doing?" College students' experiences with male condoms. *American Journal of Health Education, 39,* 322–331.

adopted, abstinence is a legitimate personal choice regarding sexuality. If you wish to remain abstinent, you need to communicate your preferences clearly and unambiguously to your dates or partners. You also need to learn to avoid high-pressure situations. Interestingly, research on the success rate of individuals practicing abstinence has revealed failure rates between 26% and 86% (Haignere, Gold, & McDaniel, 1999). Apparently, people find it very difficult to maintain abstinence.

2. *Practice sexual exclusivity.* Uninfected partners who practice sexual exclusivity in a long-term relationship or marriage will not contract an STI through sexual contact unless one partner had an STI when they started having sexual contact. Certainly, it is not always possible to know if someone is infected or if she or he is exclusive. This is one reason it is wise to refrain from sexual activity until you can form a trusting relationship with an uninfected partner.

3. *Reduce risk during sexual intimacy.* Unless you are certain that your partner is not infected, you should not allow blood, semen, or vaginal fluids to touch your genitals, mouth, or anus. One of the best ways to prevent these fluids from entering your body is to properly use the male latex condom (or polyurethane condom if allergic to latex). (Guidelines on proper use of the condom are provided in Chapter 11.) Studies have shown that adolescent couples who use condoms at the beginning of their sexual relationship often stop using them and turn to hormonal contraception. For some of these couples, their cessation of condom use is associated with perception of low STI risk (Ott, Adler, Millstein, Tschann, & Ellen, 2002; Royce, 1998; Sieving, Bearinger, Remafedi, Taylor, & Harmon, 1997). Certainly, the lack of condom use for these couples makes them vulnerable to STI transmission if one of the partners is not sexually exclusive. Douching, washing, and urinating after sex have been suggested as possible ways of reducing STI risk, but their effectiveness has not been proved.

4. *Select partners carefully.* Knowing whether a partner might be infected with an STI can be tricky. Thus, this strategy is often not reliable. Certainly, you should avoid sexual contact with someone at high risk for having an STI, such as an individual who has had numerous partners and/or who injects drugs. A person may not be honest about his or her sexual partners or drug use. It is usually impossible to determine who is infected by merely looking at the person or by his or her reputation. Actually, according to one study, the participants had used visual and verbal cues to judge if their partners were disease-free. But in this case, their judgment was wrong, as most of their partners had contracted an STI (Hoffman & Cohen, 1999). A focus group study of young people of various ethnicities found that they mistakenly believed that if they could determine the "cleanliness" of sexual partners by visual or behavioral cues, then they could accurately assess whether that person had obvious symptoms of an STI (Connell, McKevitt, & Low, 2004). If you do not know each other well, you would be wise to exchange phone numbers in the event of an STI infection or other problem or, better yet, wait until you know each other better before initiating sexual activity.

5. *Avoid numerous partners.* As noted in this chapter, having numerous sex partners increases the risk for STIs.

6. *Avoid injection and other drugs.* Another way to avoid HIV and hepatitis B is to not inject drugs and to not share needles and syringes if drugs are injected. Certainly, the drug equipment should be cleaned if sharing occurs. Not only can drugs harm your health, but they can also alter your judgment. Alcohol and/or drugs are often involved in date rapes; people who drink beverages laced with "date-rape drugs" become vulnerable to having sex against their will.

7. *Get vaccinated.* Unfortunately, only HPV and hepatitis A and hepatitis B have vaccines. The vaccine for HPV was approved by the FDA in June 2006.

8. *Protect babies.* Most STIs can be transmitted from mother to child during pregnancy or childbirth. Most often, proper medical treatment can protect the baby from permanent damage. HIV-infected mothers should not breast-feed

Discussing safer sex with a new sex partner can help reduce the risk of contracting an STI.

Safer and Unsafe Sex Practices

Safer sex practices are an integral part of good health practices. (Many people prefer the term "safer sex" to "safe sex" because all sexual contact carries at least a slight risk—a condom breaking, perhaps—no matter how careful we try to be.)

Safer Practices

- Hugging
- Kissing (but possibly not deep, French kissing)
- Massaging
- Petting
- Masturbation (solo or mutual, unless there are sores or abrasions on the genitals or hands)
- Erotic videos, books, and so on

Possibly Safe Practices

- Deep, French kissing, unless there are sores in the mouth
- Vaginal intercourse with a latex condom (or polyurethane condom if allergic to latex)
- Fellatio with a latex condom
- Cunnilingus, if the woman is not menstruating or does not have a vaginal infection (a latex dental dam provides extra protection)
- Anal intercourse with a latex condom (experts disagree about whether this should be considered "possibly safe" even with a condom because it is the riskiest sexual behavior without one)

Unsafe Practices

- Vaginal or anal intercourse without a latex condom
- Fellatio without a latex condom
- Cunnilingus, if the woman is menstruating or has a vaginal infection and a dental dam is not used
- Oral-anal contact without a dental dam
- Contact with blood, including menstrual blood
- Semen in the mouth
- Use of vibrators, dildos, and other "toys" without washing them between uses

their babies. A woman who has an STI and becomes pregnant should inform her doctor, and any pregnant woman should be checked for STIs.

9. *Be a good communicator.* Acquiring an STI requires that you have been sexually intimate with another person. Avoiding an STI demands even more intimacy because it frequently means having to talk. Putting aside embarrassment and learning to communicate isn't always easy. You need to learn how best to discuss prevention with potential sex partners and to communicate your thoughts, feelings, values, needs, and sexual code of behavior. Good communicators are less likely to do things against their values or beliefs. You should be clear about your beliefs and values and should stand by them. And you should never have sex with someone who will not talk about STI prevention.

Treating STIs

If you contract an STI, you can infect others. Practicing health-promoting behaviors will prevent others from acquiring an STI.

1. *Recognize STI symptoms.* People practicing risky sexual behaviors or injecting drugs should be alert to possible STI symptoms, especially if they have sex with partners at risk for STIs. To help avoid STIs, you should know what symptoms to look for, in yourself and others. Changes in the genitals may indicate an infection, although symptoms of some STIs can appear anywhere, and some changes may indicate a health problem other than an STI. If you suspect an

infection, you should not try to diagnose the condition yourself, but should consult a physician or health-care provider. In general, the symptoms of STIs are genital or rectal discharge, abdominal pain, painful urination, skin changes, genital itching, and flulike conditions. However, some STIs do not have any symptoms until the disease is well advanced, symptoms often disappear and then come back, and most STIs can still be passed on to someone even when the symptoms are not visible, are absent, or disappear. Actually, most people who are infected with an STI have no noticeable symptoms. Males are likely to notice symptoms earlier and more frequently than females. If you suspect an infection, you should stop having sex, stop injecting drugs, promptly see a health-care provider, and have sex partners go to a doctor or clinic.

2. *Seek treatment.* If you suspect that you might have an STI, you should seek medical care immediately. Public STI and HIV/AIDS clinics, private doctors, family planning clinics, and hospitals are all places to get treatment. Put aside any feelings of guilt or shame. The important concern is to get treatment promptly. Do not use home remedies, products bought in the mail or through the Internet, or drugs obtained from friends. Only qualified professionals can give proper care. People suspecting an STI shouldn't gamble that it might be something else or that it will go away.

3. *Get partners to treatment.* People who get treatment for an STI are doing the right thing, but they also need to encourage sex and injection-drug-use partners to seek professional care quickly. This helps prevent serious illness in the partner, prevents reinfection, and helps control the STI epidemic. Because the first sign that a woman has an STI is often when her male partner shows symptoms, female partners especially should be advised. And even if a partner has no symptoms of an STI, he or she should still see a health-care provider.

> We kill our selves, to propagate our kinde.
>
> —John Donne
> (1572–1631)

Final Thoughts

A national panel of public health officials and youth, in its 2004 report addressing the STI problem among youth aged 15–24, *Our Voices, Our Lives, Our Futures: Youth and Sexually Transmitted Diseases* (Cates, Herndon, Schulz, & Darroch, 2004), emphasized in the conclusion the importance and role of youth in stemming the STI problem in America:

> In conclusion, young people need to participate in protecting their health, talking with their partners and others about sexual issues, pursuing how and when to get medical testing, and making wise choices as they grow up. It is the responsibility of the larger community to support young people with adequate and easy access to STD information and services. Young people are not mere statistical victims of this country's STD epidemic, and they are not unique in acquiring sexually transmitted infections. They have a crucial role to play in designing, running, and evaluating programs aimed at protecting youth from STDs. In partnership with parents, policy makers, health-care providers, religious leaders, educators, and others, youth hold the key to conquering this epidemic in American society. When youth are able to prevent STDs and make healthy choices for themselves, the results benefit not only youth, but society at large and potentially future generations.

Summary

The STI Epidemic

- STIs are a "hidden" epidemic in the United States, representing four of the five most frequently reported infectious diseases. STIs negatively affect more than 65 million Americans. Women, teens and young adults, and minority racial and ethnic groups are disproportionately affected by STIs.

- STIs are behavior-linked diseases resulting largely from unprotected sexual contact. Behavioral, social, and biological factors contribute to the spread of STIs. The behavioral risk factors include early initiation of intimate sexual activity, numerous and high-risk sex partners, high-risk sexual behavior, inconsistent and incorrect condom use, substance abuse, sexual coercion, lack of personal knowledge and concern about STIs, and erroneous perception of partner's risk. Social risk factors include poverty and marginalization, lack of access to health care, and secrecy and moral conflict about sexuality. Biological factors include the asymptomatic nature of STIs, resistance to treatment, and lack of cures.

- Without medical attention, STIs can lead to serious health problems, including sterility, cancer, heart disease, blindness, ectopic pregnancy, miscarriage, and death. The presence of an STI increases the risk of acquiring an HIV infection if exposed. The direct cost of STIs is at least $15 billion annually.

Principal Bacterial STIs

- Bacterial STIs are curable and include chlamydia, gonorrhea, urinary tract infections (NGU), and syphilis.

- *Chlamydia* is the most common bacterial STI in the United States and very common in young women in whom repeated chlamydial infections can lead to infertility.

- *Gonorrhea* is the second most commonly notifiable disease in the United States. Men tend to experience the symptoms of gonorrhea more readily than women. Untreated gonorrhea can lead to pelvic inflammatory disease.

- *Urinary tract infections* can occur in both men and women and are sometimes referred to as nongonococcal urethritis. Untreated NGU can lead to damage of the reproductive organs of both men and women.

- *Syphilis,* a genital ulcerative disease, declined dramatically in the United States during 1990–2000 but has recently increased.

Principal Viral STIs

- Viral STIs are incurable, but treatable, and include HIV and AIDS, genital human papillomavirus infection, genital herpes, and hepatitis.

- *HIV and AIDS* has become one of the deadliest epidemics in human history. Because this disease remains an enormous medical and public health challenge, an entire chapter (16) is devoted to it.

- *Genital human papillomavirus* infection, or *HPV,* is the most common STI among sexually active young people, particularly women. Some people infected with HPV get genital warts. Persistent HPV infection is a key risk factor for cervical cancer. A vaccine has been approved that protects against HPV strains that can result in cervical cancer and genital warts.

- One in five adolescents and adults have *genital herpes.* Genital herpes can make people more susceptible to HIV infection, and it can make HIV-infected individuals more infectious.

- *Hepatitis* is a viral disease affecting the liver. The most common types that can be sexually transmitted are hepatitis A and hepatitis B.

Vaginal Infections

- Vaginal infections, or *vaginitis,* are often, though not always, sexually transmitted and include bacterial vaginosis, candidiasis, and trichomoniasis.

- *Bacterial vaginosis (BV)* is the most common vaginal infection in women of childbearing age. Any woman can get BV, even women who never have had sexual intercourse.

- *Candidiasis,* also known as a "yeast infection," is an overgrowth of a normally present fungus in the body.

Nearly 75% of all adult women have at least one vaginal yeast infection in their lifetime.

- *Trichomoniasis* is the most common curable STI in young, sexually active women. There are an estimated 7.4 million new cases in the United States each year in women and men.

Other STIs

- Several STIs that do not appear in the United States as often as in developing countries include chancroid, cytomegalovirus, enteric infections, granuloma inguinale, lynphogranuloma, and molluscum contagiosum.

Ectoparasitic Infestations

- Ectoparasitic infestations are parasites that live on the outer surface of the skin and can be spread sexually. They include scabies and pubic lice.
- *Scabies* is caused by a barely visible mite and is highly contagious. It spreads quickly among people who have close contact, sexually or nonsexually (e.g., prolonged contact with infested bedding).

- *Pubic lice,* commonly known as "crabs," can move easily from the pubic hair of one person to that of another.

STIs and Women

- Women tend to be more susceptible than men to STIs and to experience graver consequences, such as pelvic inflammatory disease (PID), an infection of the fallopian tubes that can lead to infertility, and ectopic pregnancy. *Cervicitis* is the inflammation of the cervix, most commonly caused by an STI. Intense stimulation of the vulva can irritate the urethra, leading to *cystitis* (bladder infection).

Preventing STIs

- STI prevention involves the interaction of knowledge, psychological factors, couple dynamics, and risk-avoiding behaviors. Ways to avoid STIs include abstinence, sexual exclusivity, careful partner selection, male condom use, and avoidance of numerous partners and injection drugs. People practicing risky behavior should be alert to possible STI symptoms, seek treatment promptly if an STI is suspected, and inform partners.

Questions for Discussion

- Given that condoms are one of the most important measures for reducing the risk of STI transmission and that many young people do not like condoms, what can be done to make condom use more appealing?
- What would be your most important concern if you just learned you had an STI? What resources would you need? And where could you go to get help?
- Would it be difficult for you to inform a past sexual partner that you have an STI and that he or she might have it too? What would be your "opening line" to get the discussion started?

Sex and the Internet

The American Social Health Association

The American Social Health Association (ASHA), founded in 1914, is a nonprofit organization focusing on STI prevention. ASHA publishes a variety of educational materials, provides direct patient support through national telephone hotlines, and advocates increased federal funding for STI programs and sound public policies on STI control. ASHA also operates a Web site: http://www.ashastd.org. Go to it and then answer the following questions:

- What programs does ASHA offer?
- What services are provided on its Web site?
- What are the current ASHA headlines?
- What is the STI Action Plan?

If you were diagnosed with an STI, would you seek more information from this site? Why or why not?

Suggested Web Sites

CDC National Prevention Information Network
http://www.cdcnpin.org
The nation's largest collection of information resources on HIV/AIDS, STI, and TB prevention.

Centers for Disease Control and Prevention
http://www.cdc.gov/hiv/dhap
Provides information on HIV/AIDS.
http://www.cdc.gov/std
Provides information on STIs.

Joint United Nations Programme on HIV/AIDS
http://www.unaids.org
Contains epidemiological information on HIV/AIDS worldwide, as well as perspectives on HIV/AIDS-related issues.

Kaiser Family Foundation
http://www.kff.org
Offers fact sheets and news releases on STI and HIV/AIDS.

Rural Center for AIDS/STD Prevention
http://www.indiana.edu/~aids
Provides information about issues related to HIV/STI prevention in rural communities.

Suggested Reading

American Social Health Association. (2008). *HPV in perspective: A patient guide* (3rd ed.). Research Triangle Park, NC: Author. Summarizes the latest information about HPV and genital warts in clear, easy-to-understand terms.

Brandt, A. M. (1987). *No magic bullet: A social history of venereal disease in the United States since 1880.* New York: Oxford University Press. An informative and highly readable history of the social and political aspects of STIs.

Ebel, C., & Wald, A. (2007). *Managing herpes: Living and loving with HSV.* Research Triangle Park, NC: American Social Health Association. An essential resource for anyone looking for more information about topics such as transmission, treatment, and telling a partner about one's genital herpes infection.

Hayden, D. (2003). *Pox: Genius, madness, and the mysteries of syphilis.* Boulder, CO: Basic Books. From Beethoven to Oscar Wilde, from Van Gogh to Hitler, this book describes the effects of syphilis on the lives and works of seminal figures from the fifteenth to twentieth centuries.

Jones, J. (1993). *Bad blood: The Tuskegee syphilis experiment—a tragedy of race and medicine* (Rev. ed.). New York: Free Press. A fascinating—and chilling—account of a 40-year experiment by the Public Health Service, using African Americans in the rural South as human guinea pigs; discusses the experiment's impact on current HIV/AIDS prevention efforts in the Black community.

Lowry, T. P. (2005). *Venereal disease and the Lewis and Clark expedition.* Lincoln: University of Nebraska Press. Describes how sex and venereal disease affected the men and mission of the Lewis and Clark expedition.

Marr, L. (2007). *Sexually transmitted diseases: A physician tells you what you need to know.* Baltimore, MD: The Johns Hopkins University Press. A comprehensive guide on the prevention, diagnosis, and treatment of STIs for both gays and straights.

For links, articles, and study material, go to the McGraw-Hill Web site, located at **www.mhhe.com/yarber7e.**

HIV and AIDS

MAIN TOPICS

"I am aware of HIV and STDs, and they are not something I take lightly. In my relationship, trust and honesty are key points, and we discussed our histories ahead of time. We then made educated decisions."

—20-year-old female

"I no longer hate you or feel angry with you [AIDS]. I realize now that you have become a positive force in my life. You are a messenger who has brought me a new understanding of my life and myself. So for that I thank you, forgive you, and release you. Because of you I have learned to love myself."

—21-year-old male

"My father had AIDS. When he found out, I was only four years old. My parents chose to keep it a secret from me and my brothers. I lived with my dad then. Though he felt sick sometimes, we did the normal things that a family would do throughout the rest of my childhood. When I turned twelve Dad became very sick and was hospitalized. I went to live with my mother. When Dad came out of the hospital, he went to live with my grandparents. Still, no one told me what was wrong with him. Two years later, my mom finally told me that Dad had AIDS and was going to die soon. I was shocked and mad at both of my parents for not telling me earlier. My mom wouldn't let me go see

Dad because he looked really bad and was in a lot of pain. I didn't get to see him or talk to him before he died. If I had known he was going to die so soon, I would have found a way to see him."

—19-year-old female

"You have to deal not only with the illness [AIDS] but with the prejudices that you encounter every day."

—19-year-old male

"I think HIV and STDs are the biggest reasons why I'm not promiscuous. I'd love to have sex with multiple partners and experiment, but even if I used a condom every time, I would still feel very much at risk. That is why I am monogamous in my relationship."

—20-year-old female

Few phenomena have changed the face of sexuality as dramatically as the appearance nearly 30 years ago of the microscopic virus known as **HIV,** or **human immunodeficiency virus.** In the early 1980s, physicians in San Francisco, New York, and Los Angeles began noticing repeated occurrences of formerly rare diseases among young and relatively healthy men. Kaposi's sarcoma, a cancer of the blood vessels, and *Pneumocystis carinii* pneumonia, a lung infection that is usually not dangerous, had become killer diseases because of the breakdown of the immune system of the men in whom these diseases were being seen (Centers for Disease Control [CDC], 1981). Even before the virus responsible for the immune system breakdown was discovered, the disease was given a name: acquired immunodeficiency syndrome, or AIDS. In the mid-1980s, the causative agent of AIDS, HIV, was discovered.

At first, AIDS within the United States seemed to be confined principally to three groups: gay men, Haitians, and people with hemophilia. Soon, however, it became apparent that AIDS was not confined to just a few groups; the disease spread into communities with high rates of injection drug use and into the general population, including heterosexual men and women (and their children) at all socioeconomic levels. The far-reaching consequences of the AIDS epidemic, in addition to the pain and loss directly caused by the illness, have included widespread fear, superstition, stigmatization, prejudice, and hatred. Ignorance of its modes of transmission has fueled the flames of homophobia among some people. Among others, it has kindled a general fear of sexual expression.

AIDS has changed us forever. It has brought out the best of us, and the worst.

—Michael Gottlieb, MD
(1948–)

By now, most of us know how HIV is spread. And yet, for a variety of reasons, people continue to engage in behaviors that put them at risk. We hope that the material in this chapter will help you make healthy, informed choices for yourself and become an advocate for education and positive change in the community. Because of the tremendous amount of AIDS research being conducted, some of the information presented here, particularly HIV/AIDS incidence and prevalence, could be outdated by the time this book appears in print. For updates on HIV/AIDS research findings and news, contact the U.S. Centers for Disease Control and Prevention (CDC) (the Web address is given in the "Sex and the Internet" section) or one of the agencies or Web sites listed at the end of this chapter.

We begin the chapter by describing the biology of the disease and the immune system. We next discuss the epidemiology and transmission of HIV and the demographic aspects of the epidemic; i.e. the effect of HIV/AIDS on various groups and communities. Then we address HIV prevention, testing and current treatment. Finally, we discuss living with HIV or AIDS.

> " What we learn in times of pestilence [is] that there are more things to admire in men than to despise.
>
> —Albert Camus
> (1913–1960)

● What Is AIDS?

AIDS is an acronym for **acquired immunodeficiency syndrome.** This medical condition was so named because HIV is acquired (not inherited) and subsequently affects the body's immune system to the point where it often becomes deficient in combating disease-causing organisms, resulting in a group of symptoms that collectively indicate or characterize a disease or syndrome.

To monitor the spread of AIDS through a national surveillance system, the CDC has established a definition of AIDS. To receive an AIDS diagnosis under the CDC's classification system (and thus be eligible for treatments, programs, and insurance funds that would not otherwise be available), a person must, in most cases, have a positive blood test indicating the presence of HIV antibodies and a T-cell count (discussed later) below 200. If the T-cell count is higher, AIDS can still be diagnosed if the person has one or more of the diseases or conditions associated with AIDS (discussed shortly). If a person has HIV antibodies, as measured by a blood test, but does not meet the other criteria, he or she is said to "have HIV," "be HIV-positive," "be HIV-infected," or "be living with HIV." Infection with HIV produces a spectrum of diseases that progress from a latent or asymptomatic state to AIDS as a late manifestation. The rate of this progression varies (CDC, 1992, 2007j).

In 1993, T-cell count, along with cervical cancer/cervical intraepithelial neoplasia (CIN), pulmonary tuberculosis, and recurrent bacterial pneumonia, was added to the CDC definition of AIDS (CDC, 1992). These additions led to a dramatic increase in the number of people who "officially" have AIDS.

Conditions Associated With AIDS

The CDC lists over 20 clinical conditions to be used in diagnosing AIDS along with HIV-positive status (CDC, 1996b). These conditions fall into several categories: opportunistic infections, cancers, conditions associated specifically with AIDS, and conditions that *may* be diagnosed as AIDS under certain circumstances.

Opportunistic Infections Diseases that take advantage of a weakened immune system are known as **opportunistic infections (OIs).** Normally, these

The Stigmatization of HIV and Other STIs

The deep ambivalence our society feels about sexuality is clearly brought to light by the way in which we deal with HIV and other STIs. If we think we have strep throat, we waste no time getting ourselves to a health center or doctor to obtain the appropriate medication. But let's say we're experiencing some discomfort when we urinate, and there's an unusual discharge. We may disregard the symptoms at first. Soon, we're feeling some pain, and we know something is definitely not right. With fear and trepidation, we slink into the clinic or doctor's office, hoping we don't see anyone we know so we won't have to explain why we're there. When we pick up our prescription, we can't look the pharmacist in the eye. And then there's the whole problem of telling our partner—or, worse yet, partners—about our predicament.

Why all this emotion over an STI but not over strep throat? Where does all the fear, denial, embarrassment, guilt, shame, and humiliation come from? Why are STIs the only class of illnesses we categorize by their *mode of transmission* rather than by the type of organism that causes them? All these questions stem from a common source: the stigmatization of persons who contract HIV or another STI. The Joint United Nations Programme on HIV/AIDS (UNAIDS) (2005) describes the origin of HIV stigmatization and some of its negative outcomes:

> HIV stigma stems from fear as well as associations of AIDS with sex, disease and death, and with behaviours that may be illegal, forbidden or taboo, such as pre- and extramarital sex, sex work, sex between men, and injecting drug use. Stigma also stems from lack of awareness and knowledge about HIV. Such stigma can fuel the urge to make scapegoats of, and blame and punish, certain people or groups. Stigma taps into existing prejudices and patterns of exclusion and further marginalizes people who might already be more vulnerable to HIV infection.

Fear of stigmatization and feelings of shame are among the principal factors contributing to the spread of HIV and other STIs. For example, in a sample of clinic patients and others at high risk for gonorrhea and HIV in seven cities, both shame and stigma were related to seeking STI-related care, but stigma may have been a more powerful barrier to obtaining such care (Fortenberry et al., 2002). A study of stigma at public health clinics in west and central Alabama reported that "patient spotting"—neighbors in the nearby housing complex viewing patients entering and leaving the STI clinic and then humiliating them by gossip—was considered a local sport at the small-town clinic. To avoid being discovered by "patient spotting," many men pursued alternative treatments, delayed seeking care, or failed to keep appointments for follow-up care (Lichtenstein, 2003).

The UNAIDS (2008a) says that stigma and other societal causes of HIV risk and vulnerability are present worldwide to some degree and need to be addressed as a "rights-based" response to the epidemic. The organization states that "long-term success in responding to the epidemic will require sustained progress in reducing human rights violations associated with it, including gender inequality, stigma and discrimination."

Think Critically

- How have you observed HIV/STI stigma among your friends or others in our society? How were these stigmas demonstrated?
- In your view, what can be done to eliminate the cultural stigma of HIV/STI?
- If you became infected with HIV or another STI, would stigma and shame be an issue for you? If so, how would you deal with it? From what resources would you seek help and support?

---

infections do not develop in healthy people or are not life-threatening. Common OIs associated with HIV include certain types of tuberculosis, a parasitic disease of the brain and central nervous system, and certain types of pneumonia, including ***Pneumocystis carinii* pneumonia (PCP),** caused by a common organism (probably a protozoan or fungus) that is not usually harmful.

Cancers   Certain types of cancer are commonly associated with AIDS, including cancer of the lymphatic system, invasive cervical cancer, and a cancer of the blood vessels called **Kaposi's sarcoma.** Cervical cancer and CIN are more common in women who are HIV-positive than in women who are not. Kaposi's sarcoma, rare in healthy people, causes red or purple blotches to appear under the skin.

> The fear of stigma leads to silence, and when it comes to fighting AIDS, silence is death.
>
> —Kofi Annan, former Secretary General, United Nations (1938–)

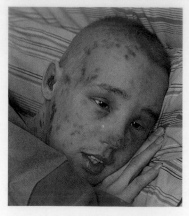

Kaposi's sarcoma is a cancer of the blood vessels commonly associated with AIDS. It causes red or purple blotches to appear under the skin's surface.

Clinical Conditions   Conditions specifically linked to AIDS include wasting syndrome, symptoms of which include severe weight loss with weakness and persistent diarrhea, and AIDS dementia, characterized by impairment of mental and physical functioning and changes in mood and behavior.

Other Infections   Infections that may lead to an AIDS diagnosis under certain circumstances include candidiasis (thrush), a fungal infection that affects the respiratory system and vagina; genital herpes; and cytomegalovirus, a virus of the herpes family that is often sexually transmitted.

Because the immune systems of people with HIV may not be functioning well (and those of people with advanced AIDS certainly are not), they may be subject to numerous other infections that would not normally be much of a problem, such as colds, flus, and intestinal infections. Health precautions for people living with HIV are discussed later in the chapter.

Symptoms of HIV Infection and AIDS

A person infected with HIV may feel fine; many people with HIV do not have symptoms at all for 10 years or more. Or a person may experience one or more of the symptoms listed here. However, no one should assume he or she is infected if any of these symptoms are present. Each symptom can be related to other illnesses. The only way to determine whether a person is infected is to be tested for HIV infection. The following may be warning signs of advanced HIV infection:

- Rapid weight loss
- Dry cough
- Recurring fever or profuse night sweats
- Profound and unexplained fatigue
- Swollen lymph glands in the armpits, groin, or neck
- Diarrhea that lasts more than a week
- White spots or unusual blemishes on the tongue, in the mouth, or in the throat
- Red, brown, pink or purplish blotches on or under the skin or inside the mouth, nose, or eyelids
- Memory loss, depression, and other neurological disorders

A person also cannot rely on symptoms to establish that he or she has AIDS. Remember, AIDS is a medical diagnosis made by a physician using the specific CDC criteria (CDC, 2007k).

Understanding AIDS: The Immune System and HIV

The principal components of blood are plasma (the fluid base), red blood cells, white blood cells, and platelets.

Leukocytes   There are several kinds of **leukocytes,** or white blood cells, all of which play major roles in defending the body against invading organisms or mutant (cancerous) cells. Because HIV invades and eventually kills some kinds of leukocytes, it impairs the body's ability to ward off infections and other harmful conditions that ordinarily would not be threatening. The principal type of leukocyte we discuss is the lymphocyte.

Macrophages, Antigens, and Antibodies White blood cells called **macrophages** engulf foreign particles and display the invader's antigen (*anti*body *gen*erator) like a signal flag on their own surfaces. **Antigens** are large molecules that are capable of stimulating the immune system and then reacting with the antibodies that are released to fight them. **Antibodies** bind to antigens, inactivate them, and mark them for destruction by killer cells. If the body has been previously exposed to the organism (by fighting it off or being vaccinated), the response is much quicker because memory cells are already biochemically programmed to respond.

B Cells and T Cells The **lymphocytes** (a type of leukocyte) crucial to the immune system's functioning are **B cells** and several types of **T cells.** Like macrophages, **helper T cells** are programmed to "read" the antigens and then begin directing the immune system's response. They send chemical signals to B cells, which begin making antibodies specific to the presented antigen. Helper T cells also stimulate the proliferation of B cells and T cells (which are genetically programmed to replicate, or make copies of themselves) and activate both macrophages and **killer T cells,** transforming them into agents of destruction whose only purpose is to attack and obliterate the enemy. Helper T cells display a type of protein receptor called CD4. The number of helper T cells in an individual's body is an important indicator of how well the immune system is functioning, as we discuss later.

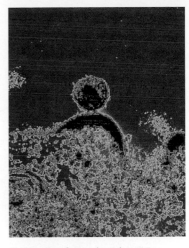

A T cell infected with HIV begins to replicate the virus, which buds from the cell wall, eventually killing the host cell.

The Virus

A **virus** is a protein-coated package of genes that invades a cell and alters the way in which the cell reproduces itself. Viruses can't propel themselves independently, and they can't reproduce unless they are inside a host cell. It would take 16,000 human immunodeficiency viruses to cover the head of a pin in a single layer. Under strong magnification, HIV resembles a spherical pincushion, bristling with tiny pinheadlike knobs (see Figure 16.1). These knobs are the antigens, which contain a protein called GP 120; the CD4 receptors on a helper T cell are attracted (fatally, as it turns out) to GP 120. Within the virus's protein core is the genetic material (RNA) that carries the information the virus needs to replicate itself. Also in the core is an enzyme called **reverse transcriptase,** which enables the virus to "write" its RNA (the genetic software or program) into a cell's DNA. Viruses with the ability to reverse the normal genetic writing process are known as **retroviruses.** There are numerous variant strains of HIV as a result of mutations. The virus begins undergoing genetic variation as soon as it has infected a person, even before antibodies develop. This tendency to mutate is one factor that makes HIV difficult to destroy.

Effect on T Cells When HIV enters the bloodstream, helper T cells rush to the invading viruses, as if they were specifically designed for them. Normally at this stage, a T cell reads the antigen, stimulating antibody production in the B cells and beginning the process of eliminating the invading organism. In the case of HIV, however, although antibody production does begin, the immune process starts to break down almost at once. HIV injects its contents into the host T cell and copies its own genetic code into the cell's genetic material (DNA). As a result, when the immune system is activated, the T cell begins producing HIV instead of replicating itself. The T cell is killed in the process.

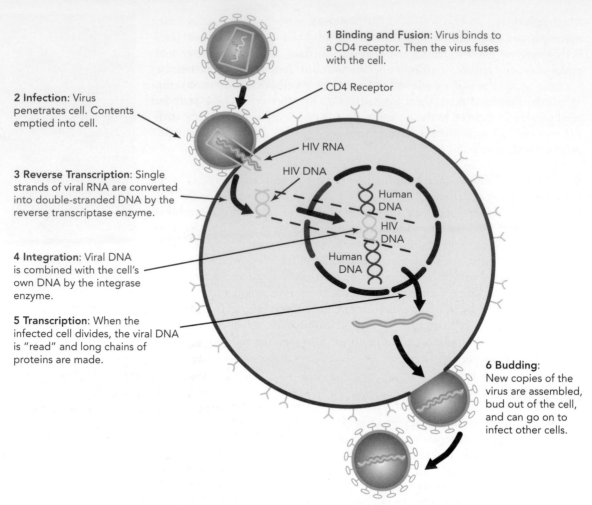

1 Binding and Fusion: Virus binds to a CD4 receptor. Then the virus fuses with the cell.

CD4 Receptor

2 Infection: Virus penetrates cell. Contents emptied into cell.

HIV RNA

HIV DNA

3 Reverse Transcription: Single strands of viral RNA are converted into double-stranded DNA by the reverse transcriptase enzyme.

Human DNA

HIV DNA

Human DNA

4 Integration: Viral DNA is combined with the cell's own DNA by the integrase enzyme.

5 Transcription: When the infected cell divides, the viral DNA is "read" and long chains of proteins are made.

6 Budding: New copies of the virus are assembled, bud out of the cell, and can go on to infect other cells.

● **FIGURE 16.1**

The Infection of a CD4 Cell by HIV. (*Source:* Adapted from *HIV Lifecycle.* Fact Sheet 106. University of New Mexico, Health Sciences Center, April 18, 2008. www.aidsinfonet.org/fact_sheets/view/106. Used with permission.)

HIV also targets other types of cells, including macrophages, dendritic cells (leukocytes found in the skin, lymph nodes, and intestinal mucous membranes), and brain cells.

HIV-1 and HIV-2   Almost all cases of HIV in the United States involve the type of the virus known as HIV-1. Another type, HIV-2, has been found to exist mainly in West Africa. Both HIV-1 and HIV-2 have the same mode of transmission and are associated with similar OIs and AIDS.

AIDS Pathogenesis: How the Disease Progresses

As discussed earlier, when viruses are introduced into the body, they are immediately snatched up by helper T cells and whisked off to the lymph nodes. Although HIV begins replication right away within the host cells, the virus itself may not be detectable in the blood for some time. Most people will develop detectable antibodies within 2–8 weeks after exposure (the average is 25 days). The process by which a person develops antibodies is called **seroconversion.** A person's **serostatus** is HIV-negative if antibodies to HIV are not detected and HIV-positive if antibodies are detected.

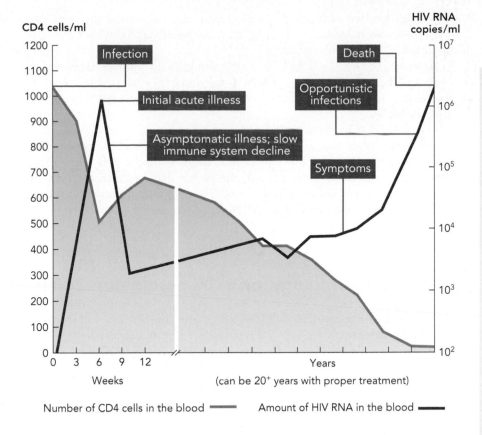

CD4 cells/ml

HIV RNA
copies/ml

Infection

Death

Initial acute illness

Opportunistic
infections

Asymptomatic illness; slow
immune system decline

Symptoms

Number of CD4 cells in the blood ————	Amount of HIV RNA in the blood ————

0   3   6   9   12   Years
Weeks   (can be 20⁺ years with proper treatment)

• FIGURE 16.2
The General Pattern of HIV
Infection.

During the initial acute illness,
CD4 levels (green line) fall
sharply and HIV RNA levels (red
line) increase; many infected
people experience flulike
symptoms during this period.
Antibodies to HIV usually
appear 2–8 weeks after the
initial infection. During the
asymptomatic phase that
follows, CD4 levels (a marker
for the status of the immune
system) gradually decline, and
HIV RNA levels again increase.
Due to declines in immunity,
infected individ-uals eventually
begin to experi-ence
symptoms; when CD4 levels
drop very low, people become
vulnerable to serious
opportunistic infections characteristic of AIDS. Modern
treatment delays or slows the
decline of the CD4 level.
Chronic or recurrent illnesses
continue until the immune
system fails and death results.

(*Source:* From Fauci, A. S., et al.
(1996). Immunopathogenic
mechanisms of HIV infection.
Annals of Internal Medicine, 124,
654–63. Copyright ©1996 by
American College of Physicians—
Journals. Reproduced with
permission of American College
of Physicians—Journals in the
format Textbook via Copyright
Clearance Center.)

T-Cell (CD4) Count   T-cell count—also called CD4 count—refers to the number of helper T cells that are present in a cubic milliliter of blood. A healthy person's T-cell count averages about 1,000, but it can range from 500 to 1,600, depending on a person's general health and whether she or he is fighting off an illness.

Phases of Infection   The pace of disease progression is variable, with the time between infection with HIV and development of AIDS ranging from a few months to many years, depending on several factors including treatment regimes and the person's genetic makeup and health status (see Figure 16.2). Fortunately, people living with HIV who are taking proper medication can go a long time before their immune system is damaged enough for AIDS to develop. When a person is first infected with HIV, he or she may experience severe flulike symptoms as the immune system goes into high gear to fight off the invader. These symptoms usually disappear within a week to a month and are often mistaken for those of another viral infection. More persistent and severe symptoms may not appear for 10 years or more after HIV first enters the body in adults (National Institute of Allergy and Infectious Diseases, 2008). His or her T-cell count may temporarily plunge as the virus begins rapid rep-lication. During this period, the virus is dispersed throughout the lymph nodes, where it replicates, a process called "seeding." The virus may stay localized for years, but it continues to replicate and destroy T cells. One study has shown that viral load is the chief predictor of transmission of HIV; the HIV-infected person is most infectious when the viral load is the highest (Quinn et al., 2000).

Detecting infection early and beginning treatment can reduce the viral load, and possibly an individual's infectiousness, and boost survival (Cates, Chesney, & Cohen, 1997; Sternberg, 2008).

As time goes by, the T cells gradually diminish in number, destroyed by newly created HIV. During this phase, as the number of infected cells goes up, the number of T cells goes down, generally to between 200 and 500 per milliliter of blood.

When AIDS is in the advanced phase, the T cells and other fighter cells of the immune system are no longer able to trap foreign invaders. Infected cells continue to increase, and the T-cell count drops to under 200. The virus is detectable in the blood. At this point, the person may be fairly ill to very ill, although some may not have symptoms. The T-cell count may continue to plummet to zero. The person with AIDS dies from one or more of the opportunistic infections.

• The Epidemiology and Transmission of HIV

Epidemiology is the study of the incidence, process, distribution, and control of diseases. An **epidemic** is the wide and rapid spread of a contagious disease. Worldwide, the Joint United Nations Programme on HIV/AIDS (UNAIDS) and the

• **FIGURE 16.3**
Percentage of Adults (Prevalence) for Each Country, Worldwide, Who Are Living With HIV in 2007. (*Source:* UNAIDS, Joint United Nations Programme on HIV/AIDS. (2008). *08 Report on the Global AIDS Epidemic,* Figure 2.2 (p. 33). © Joint United Nations Programme on HIV/AIDS (UNAIDS) 2008. http://www.unaids.org/en/KnowledgeCentre/HIVData/GlobalReport/2008/2008_Global_report.asp. Reprinted with permission.)

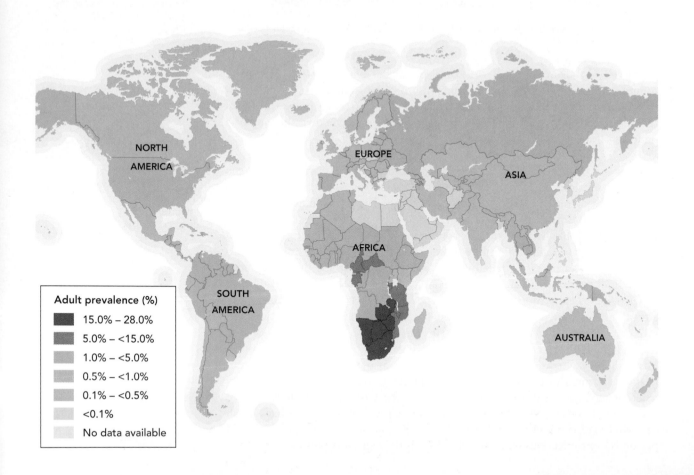

Adult prevalence (%)
15.0% – 28.0%
5.0% – <15.0%
1.0% – <5.0%
0.5% – <1.0%
0.1% – <0.5%
<0.1%
No data available

World Health Organization report that more than 25 million people have died from AIDS, making this epidemic one of the most destructive in recorded history. In 2007, an estimated 2 million people died from AIDS. The UNAIDS notes that an estimated 33 million people are now living with HIV and 2.7 million individuals were newly infected with HIV in 2007 (UNAIDS 2008a, 2008b).

The UNAIDS states that the percentage of people living with HIV worldwide has stabilized since 2000 but is still at an unacceptably high level. However, the overall number of people living with HIV has increased because of newer and more widely available medical therapy. Sub-Saharan Africa remains the region most affected by the HIV epidemic, accounting for 67% of all people living with HIV, 72% of AIDS deaths in 2007, and the greatest prevalence of adults infected with HIV (see Figure 16.3). Worldwide, one half of people living with HIV are women, although women's proportion of infections is increasing in several countries. In nearly all regions outside of sub-Saharan Africa, HIV disproportionately impacts injection drug users, men who have sex with men (MSM), and sex workers. Recent studies indicate high infection levels among these groups in parts of sub-Saharan Africa. HIV infections among MSM are increasing dramatically in some parts of Asia (UNAIDS, 2008a).

The Epidemiology of HIV/AIDS in the United States

In the United States, since the diagnosis of the first AIDS case nearly three decades ago, the number of adults and adolescents living with diagnosed and undiagnosed HIV infection has grown from a few dozen to 1.1 million, with more than 500,000 deaths cumulative through 2006 (CDC, 2008u). Annually, more than 56,000 new HIV infections are estimated to occur, meaning that every 9½ minutes someone becomes infected with HIV (CDC, 2009b; Hall et al., 2008). The proportion of HIV cases differs by sex: In 2006, males accounted for 75% of prevalent HIV cases. The transmission category for each sex also varies (see Figure 16.4). Two thirds of the adult and adolescent male HIV/AIDS cases were attributed to male-to-male sexual contact and 80% of the adult and adolescent female HIV/AIDS cases were attributed to high-risk heterosexual contact (CDC, 2008v).

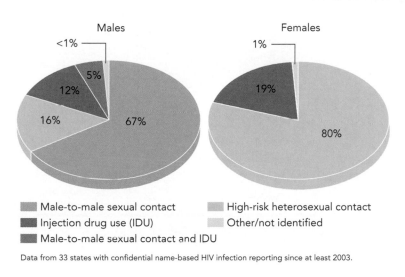

Males

<1%
5%
12%
16%
67%

Females

1%
19%
80%

Male-to-male sexual contact
Injection drug use (IDU)
Male-to-male sexual contact and IDU
High-risk heterosexual contact
Other/not identified

Data from 33 states with confidential name-based HIV infection reporting since at least 2003.

● **FIGURE 16.4**
Proportion of HIV/AIDS Cases Among U.S. Adults and Adolescents by Sex and Transmission Category, in 33 States, 2006. (*Source:* Centers for Disease Control and Prevention. [2008v]. HIV/AIDS statistics and surveillance: Slide sets.)

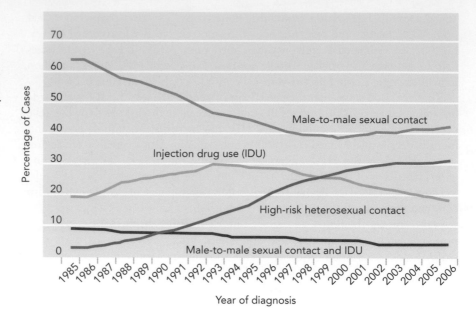

The proportional distribution of AIDS cases by transmission category has shifted since the beginning of the epidemic (see Figure 16.5), with the percentage of cases for male-to-male sexual contact decreasing and for high-risk heterosexual contact increasing. The proportional distribution of AIDS diagnosis among races/ethnicities has changed since the beginning of the epidemic (see Figure 16.6). The proportion of AIDS diagnoses among non-Hispanic Whites has decreased; the proportions among non-Hispanic Blacks and Hispanics have increased. The pie charts in Figure 16.7 illustrate the distribution of AIDS cases reported during 2006 among races/ethnicities and the racial/ethnic distribution in the U.S. population in 2005. Non-Hispanic Blacks and Hispanics are

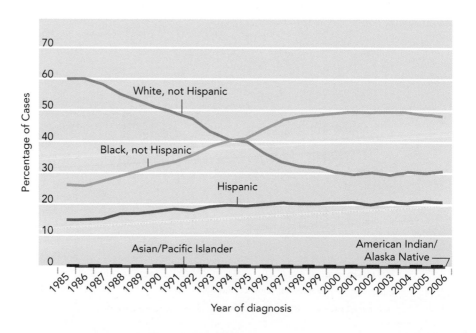

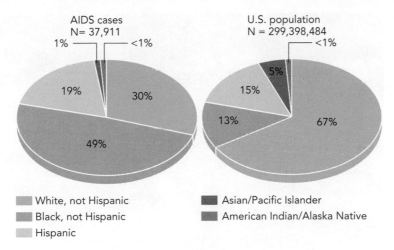

AIDS cases
N= 37,911

1% — <1%
19%
30%
49%

U.S. population
N = 299,398,484

— <1%
5%
15%
13%
67%

White, not Hispanic
Black, not Hispanic
Hispanic
Asian/Pacific Islander
American Indian/Alaska Native

● **FIGURE 16.7**

Proportion of AIDS Cases and Population by Race/Ethnicity, 2006. (*Source:* Centers for Disease Control and Prevention. [2008v]. HIV/AIDS statistics and surveillance: Slide sets.)

disproportionately affected by the AIDS epidemic in comparison to their proportional distribution in the general population (CDC, 2008v).

Using HIV surveillance data and vital statistics from the 33 states in the United States that have confidential, name-based HIV reporting to the Centers for Disease Control and Prevention, researchers have estimated lifetime risk of being diagnosed with HIV (see Table 16.1). Lifetime risk estimates are often reported in the popular press and in scientific literature for cancer and other diseases, but until recently no such estimates have been generated for HIV. **Lifetime risk** is typically considered to be the number of people who would need to be followed throughout their lives to observe one occurrence of the disease. As shown in Table 16.1, in 2004–2005, the estimated lifetime risk of being diagnosed with HIV was 1.9% for males, or 1 in 53 males, and 0.7% for females, or 1 in 141 females. These estimates varied by race/ethnicity. The researchers also found that the highest risk of HIV diagnosis was observed among people in their 30s. These estimates can help strengthen prevention education by highlighting the risk of contracting HIV (Hall, Qian, Hutchinson, & Sansom, 2008).

Table 16.1 ●	Estimated Lifetime Risk of HIV Diagnosis, by Sex, 33 States,[a] 2004–2005	
Race/Ethnicity	**Male**	**Female**
All combined	1.9% (1 in 53)	0.7% (1 in 141)
White	1.0% (1 in 104)	0.2% (1 in 588)
Black	6.2% (1 in 16)	3.3% (1 in 30)
Hispanic	2.9% (1 in 103)	0.9% (1 in 114)
American Indian/Alaska Native	1.0% (1 in 103)	0.4% (1 in 278)
Asian American/Pacific Islander	0.6% (1 in 169)	0.2% (1 in 500)

[a]Based on surveillance data and vital statistics in 33 states in the United States that have confidential, name-based HIV reporting to the Centers for Disease Control and Prevention.

SOURCE: Adapted from Hall, H. I., Qian, N., Hutchinson, A. B., & Sansom, S. (2008). Estimating the lifetime risk of a diagnosis of the HIV infection in 33 states, 2004–2005. *Journal of Acquired Immune Deficiencies Syndromes, 49,* 294–297.

Sharing needles and other injection drug equipment is a common mode of HIV transmission via infected blood. Some organizations provide clean needles for injection drug users.

Myths and Modes of Transmission

Research has revealed a great deal of valuable medical, scientific, and public health information about HIV transmission, and the ways HIV is transmitted have been clearly identified. However, false information not supported by scientific findings is still being shared. Because of this, the CDC has described the ways HIV is transmitted and has corrected misconceptions about HIV. The CDC states that HIV is spread by sexual contact with an infected person, by sharing drug injection needles and/or syringes with someone infected, or, less commonly (and now very rarely in countries where blood is screened for HIV antibodies), by transfusions of infected blood or blood clotting factors. These modes of transmission are the most common and involve transmission of HIV-infected semen, vaginal secretions, or blood. The CDC also says that babies born to HIV-infected women may become infected before or during birth or through breastfeeding after birth. (A more detailed description of these transmission routes is presented later in this chapter.)

Early in the HIV/AIDS epidemic there were a lot of myths about how HIV is transmitted. For example, people feared that HIV could be transmitted via nonsexual contact, also called casual contact, resulting in an unreasonable fear of people with HIV. Sometimes, people refused to be near HIV-infected individuals. However, no scientific evidence to support methods of HIV transmission other than those listed above have been found. All reported cases alleging new or potentially unknown routes of transmission are thoroughly investigated by public health officials, and no additional routes of transmission have been confirmed.

By now, most people have a more accurate understanding of HIV/AIDS and know the difference between actual transmission routes and transmission myths. But, just to briefly review: Scientific and epidemiological evidence shows that the chances are essentially zero of acquiring HIV from an environmental surface (e.g., toilet seat), from nonsexual household or other-settings contact with an HIV-infected person, from typical social contact, from food-serving establishments, from kissing, from insect bites, from sport-participation accidents involving blood, or from donating blood. Contact with the saliva, tears, or sweat from an HIV-infected person has never been shown to result in transmission of the virus. The CDC knows of no instances of HIV being transmitted through tattooing or body piercing, although hepatitis B virus has been transmitted during some of these procedures. Also, biting is not a common method of transmitting HIV. Of the few reports in the medical literature in which HIV appeared to be transmitted by a bite, severe trauma with extensive tissue tearing and damage and the presence of blood were reported (CDC, 2007l).

Some people have been concerned about the possibility of acquiring HIV from a blood transfusion and organ donations. Theoretically, donated blood, plasma, body organs, and semen are all capable of sustaining HIV. Because of this, medical procedures involving these materials now include screening for HIV or destroying the virus, and the chance of acquiring HIV from these procedures is extremely low. To be absolutely safe, some people who know they will have surgery donate their own blood a few weeks before the operation so that it will be available during surgery if needed. Donated organs are screened for HIV, and there are guidelines regarding semen donation for artificial insemination.

Sexual Transmission

HIV can be found in the semen, pre-seminal fluid, vaginal fluid, or blood of a person infected with the virus. Latex barriers, condoms, dental dams, and surgical gloves, if used properly, can provide good protection against the transmission of HIV.

Anal Intercourse   Unprotected anal sex (no condom use) is considered to be very risky behavior, and either sex partner can become infected with HIV during anal sex. In general, the partner receiving the semen is at greater risk of getting HIV because the lining of the rectum is thin and may allow the virus to enter the body during anal sex. However, a person who inserts his penis into an infected partner is also at risk since HIV can enter through the urethra or through small cuts, abrasions, or open sores on the penis. Some people mistakenly believe that only men who have sex with men are at risk of HIV through anal sex. However, a national study of men and women 15–44 years of age found that 35% of women have had anal sex with an other-sex partner (National Center for Health Statistics, 2005). A nationally representative study showed that 9% of heterosexual couples had anal intercourse in the past year (Laumann, Gagnon, Michael, & Michaels, 1994). Lastly, a study of at-risk adolescents and young adults aged 15–21 in three U.S. cities found that 16% reported heterosexual anal intercourse in the past 90 days (Lescano et al., 2009).

Vaginal Intercourse   Vaginal sex is also quite risky as an HIV transmission route, especially for women, and is the most common way HIV is transmitted in much of the world. In women, the lining of the vagina can tear and possibly allow HIV to enter the body. HIV can also be directly absorbed through the mucous membranes that line the vagina and cervix. Adolescent females are

Wake up. Don't let someone feed you a line and don't be afraid to ask questions. Find out yourself.

—Ryan White
(1971–1990)

biologically more susceptible to HIV than older women because their immature cervixes may be more easily infected (Braverman & Strasburger, 1994). However, the virus can enter the bloodstream through the urethra or through small cuts or open sores on the penis. Menstrual blood containing HIV can also facilitate transmission of the virus to a sex partner.

Oral Sex HIV may be transmitted during fellatio, cunnilingus, or analingus (oral-anal contact), although evidence suggests that the risk is less than that from unprotected anal or vaginal sex. There have been a few cases of HIV transmission from performing oral sex on a person infected with HIV (CDC, 2006c). Either partner can become infected with HIV through performing or receiving oral sex. The risk of HIV transmission increases if the person performing oral sex has cuts or sores around or in the mouth or throat, if the male receiving oral sex ejaculates in the mouth of the person performing oral sex, or if the person receiving oral sex has another STI. If the person performing oral sex has HIV, blood from the mouth may enter the body of the person receiving oral sex through the lining of the urethra, vagina, cervix, or anus or directly into the body through small cuts or open sores. If the person receiving oral sex has HIV, the blood, semen, pre-seminal fluid, or vaginal fluid may contain the virus. Cells lining the mouth of the person performing oral sex may allow HIV to enter the body.

Kissing Kissing, because it involves saliva, is a frequent concern. As we said, HIV is not transmitted casually, so kissing on the cheek is very safe. No one has become infected from dry kissing. Open-mouth kissing is considered a very low-risk activity for the transmission of HIV. However, prolonged open-mouth kissing could damage the mouth or lips and allow HIV to pass from an infected person to a partner and then enter the body through cuts or sores in the mouth. Because of this possible risk, the CDC (2006d) recommends against open-mouth kissing with an infected partner.

Sex Toys Although unlikely, HIV can be transmitted in vaginal secretions on such objects as dildos and vibrators; therefore, it is very important that these objects not be shared or that they be washed thoroughly before use.

Injection Drug Use

Sharing needles or other paraphernalia used to inject drugs provides an ideal pathway for HIV. An injection drug user (IDU) may have an immune system that has already been weakened by poor health, poor nutrition, or an STI. IDUs who become infected often pass the virus sexually to their partners.

At the beginning of every drug injection, blood is introduced into the needle and syringe. The reuse of a blood-contaminated needle or syringe by another drug injector (sometimes called "direct syringe sharing") is a high risk of HIV transmission because infected blood can be injected directly into the bloodstream. Infected blood can be introduced into drug solutions by using blood-contaminated syringes to prepare the drugs, reusing water, and reusing bottle caps, spoons, or other containers ("spoons" and "cookers") used to dissolve drugs in water and to heat drugs solutions. Also, infected blood can be introduced by the reusing of pieces of cotton filters ("cottons") used to filter out small particles that could block the needle. "Street sellers" of syringes may repackage used syringes and sell them as sterile needles. For this reason, people who continue to inject drugs should obtain syringes from reliable sources of sterile syringes, such as pharmacies or needle exchange programs. Sharing a needle or syringe for any use, including skin popping and injecting steroids, can put one at risk for HIV and other blood-borne infections.

When we think of injection drug use, we usually think in terms of psychotropic (mind-affecting) drugs such as heroin or cocaine. We may conjure up images of run-down tenement rooms or "shooting galleries," where needles are passed around. But these are not the only settings for sharing drugs. HIV transmission in connection with the recreational use of injection drugs also occurs among people from the middle or upper class. Moreover, injection drug use exists among athletes and bodybuilders, who may share needles to inject steroids. HIV can be transmitted just as easily in a brightly lit locker room or upscale living room as in a dark alley.

Mother-to-Child Transmission

Women can transmit HIV to their babies during pregnancy or labor and delivery. Called **perinatal HIV transmission (mother-to-child),** this mode of transmission is the most common route of HIV infection in children and is the source of almost all of the AIDS cases of children in the United States. Most of the children with AIDS are members of minority races/ethnicities. About one quarter to one third of all untreated pregnant women infected with HIV will pass the infection to their babies. HIV can also be transmitted to babies through the breast milk of mothers infected with the virus. If an HIV-infected woman is treated with certain drugs during pregnancy, she can greatly reduce the chances that her baby will get infected with HIV. If she is treated and her baby is delivered by cesarean section, the chances of the baby being infected can be reduced to a rate of 1%. HIV infection of newborns has been almost eradicated in the United States because of voluntary prenatal HIV testing and medical treatment, yet 100 to 200 infants are still infected with HIV annually. Many of these infections involve women who were not tested early enough in pregnancy or who did not receive prevention services (CDC, 2007m).

Factors Contributing to Infection

Researchers have found that certain physiological or behavioral factors increase one's risk of contracting HIV. For people of both sexes, these include behaviors already discussed, such as anal intercourse, numerous sex partners, and injection drug use. There is considerable biological evidence that the presence of other STIs increases the likelihood of both transmitting and acquiring HIV (Fleming & Wasserheit, 1999). This is true whether the STI causes open sores (e.g., syphilis, herpes) or does not cause breaks in the skin (e.g., chlamydia, gonorrhea). People are 2–5 times more likely to become infected with HIV when they have other STIs. In addition, an HIV-infected person also infected with an STI is 3–5 times more likely than other HIV-infected people to transmit HIV through sexual contact. Although HIV can be transmitted in a single encounter, it usually takes several exposures for a person to contract the virus. Moreover, the probability of HIV transmission is greater when the viral load is the highest, particularly in the early stage of the infection (Cates et al., 1997; Gray et al., 2001; Keele et al., 2008).

● AIDS Demographics

The statistical characteristics of populations are called **demographics.** Public health researchers often look at groups of people in terms of age, socioeconomic status, living area, ethnicity, sex, and so on in order to understand the dynamics of disease transmission and prevention. When STIs are involved, they naturally look at sexual behaviors as well. No one is exempt from HIV exposure by virtue of belonging or not belonging to a specific group. But certain groups appear *as a whole* to be at greater risk than others or to face special difficulties where HIV is concerned. Many individuals within these groups may not be at risk, however, because they do not engage in risky behaviors.

Minority Races/Ethnicities and HIV

In the early 1980s in the United States, HIV/AIDS was primarily considered a gay White disease. Today, however, the epidemic has expanded, and the proportional distribution of AIDS cases among minority racial and ethnic groups has shifted, and, as mentioned earlier, Blacks and Hispanics are disproportionately affected (Figure 16.7). Being of a minority race/ethnic group is not, in itself, a risk factor for HIV infection and other STIs. However, race/ethnicity in the United States is a risk marker that correlates with other, more fundamental determinants of health status, such as poverty, homelessness, lack of access to quality health care, avoiding seeking health care, substance abuse, and residence in communities with a high prevalence of HIV and other STIs.

Although poverty itself is not a risk factor, studies have found a direct relationship between higher AIDS incidence and lower income (CDC, 2000b). A study of a diverse sample of women from urban health clinics found that socioeconomic status, not race/ethnicity, had both direct and indirect associations with HIV risk behaviors; the women with lower income had riskier sexual behaviors (Ickovics et al., 2002). Several socioeconomic problems associated with poverty directly or indirectly raise HIV risk, including limited access to health care. Some minority race/ethnic communities are reluctant to acknowledge sensitive issues such as homosexuality and substance use.

African Americans   Of all racial and ethnic groups in the United States, African Americans have been impacted by HIV and AIDS the most (Figure 16.7). The United States' HIV/AIDS epidemic is a health crisis for African Americans. At all stages of HIV/AIDS—from infection with HIV to death from AIDS—Blacks are disproportionately affected compared to other racial/ethnic groups.

The HIV epidemic has dramatically and disproportionally affected African Americans. The disease poses a serious threat to the future health and well-being of many African American communities.

The reasons for this are not directly related to race or ethnicity, but, rather, to the barriers faced by many African Americans, including poverty, high incidence of another STI, and the stigma of HIV/AIDS. Another barrier to HIV prevention is homophobia and concealment of homosexual behavior. Homophobia and stigmatization can cause some African American men who have sex with men to identify themselves as heterosexual or not to disclose their same-sex behaviors. Black men are more likely than other MSM not to identify themselves as a gay man. This absence of disclosure of self-identification may make it more difficult to present appropriate HIV prevention education, although research has shown that these men are not at greater risk for HIV infection than Black MSM who identify as a gay man (Hart & Peterson, 2004). Additionally, many African Americans may postpone getting tested or treated for HIV because they distrust the medical system (see Chapter 15).

Compared to other races/ethnicities, African Americans account for more HIV/AIDS cases (49%) and those living with HIV/AIDS often do not live as long and die more frequently. Blacks have a much greater lifetime estimated risk of being diagnosed with HIV than Whites and Hispanics: 6.2%, or 1 in 16, for Black males and 0.9%, or 1 in 30, for Black females (Table 16.1). Among all Black men living with HIV/AIDS, sexual contact with other men was the primary transmission category, followed by injection drug use and high-risk heterosexual contact. For all Black women living with HIV/AIDS, the primary transmission category was high-risk heterosexual contact, followed by injection drug use.

The Centers for Disease Control and Prevention has established the African American HIV/AIDS Work Group to increase and strengthen HIV prevention and intervention directed toward African Americans (CDC, 2008w). A nationally representative survey of Americans found that among Whites, Blacks, and Hispanics, Blacks were the only racial/ethnic group to name HIV/AIDS as the number-one health problem in the United States. Half of the Blacks surveyed said that HIV/AIDS is a more urgent problem in their community now than a few years ago. Also, personal concern about becoming infected with HIV was highest among Blacks, and many were concerned about their children contracting HIV (Kaiser Family Foundation, 2006).

Hispanics/Latinos The Hispanic/Latino community, which includes a diverse mixture of ethnic groups and cultures, is the fastest growing and largest ethnic group in the United States, and the HIV/AIDS epidemic is a serious threat to that community. Injection drug use, STIs, poverty, education, and cultural beliefs are some of the HIV prevention challenges that face them.

In 2007, Hispanics/Latinos accounted for 19% of the AIDS cases (see Figure 16.7). During the same year, the rate of new infections among Hispanics/Latinos was three times that of Whites. In 2005, HIV/AIDS was the fourth leading cause of deaths among Hispanic/Latino men and women aged 35–44. The estimated lifetime risk of a HIV diagnosis for Hispanic males is 2.9%, or 1 in 103; for females, 0.9%, or 1 in 114 (see Table 16.1) For Hispanic/Latino males living with HIV/AIDS, the most common methods of HIV transmission were, from most to least common, sexual contact with other males, injection drug use, and high-risk heterosexual contact. For Hispanic/Latina females living with HIV/AIDS, the most common methods of transmission were high-risk heterosexual contact and injection drug use (CDC, 2008x).

Hispanics/Latinos rank AIDS or HIV as the second most urgent problem facing the nation. Like African American parents, many Hispanic/Latino parents express high levels of concern about their children's risk for HIV infection (Kaiser Family Foundation, 2006). Given the growth of the Hispanic/Latino community in the United States, the prevalence of HIV/AIDS among this group will increasingly affect the health status of the nation. Prevention programs must give special attention to the cultural diversity that exists within this community (National Association of People with AIDS, 2002).

Asian Americans/Pacific Islanders   The number of AIDS diagnoses among Asians and Pacific Islanders has increased steadily. Even though only about 1% of the total number of HIV/AIDS cases are among Asians and Pacific Islanders, the percentage may rise because this population group is increasing in the United States. Because of language and cultural barriers, lack of access to care, and other issues, many Asians and Pacific Islanders underuse health-care and prevention services. The low number of HIV/AIDS cases may not accurately reflect the true burden of the epidemic on this population because of under-reporting or misclassification of Asians and Pacific Islanders.

Among Asians and Pacific Islanders, there are many nationalities—Chinese, Filipinos, Koreans, Hawaiians, Indians, Japanese, Samoans, Vietnamese, and others—and more than 100 languages and dialects. Because many Asians and Pacific Islanders living in the United States are foreign born, they experience cultural and language barriers to receiving public health messages, making prevention education very challenging (CDC, 2008y). Most of the Asian and Pacific Islanders who are infected with HIV are men who have sex with men. Methamphetamine and other drug use is a significant factor associated with unprotected anal intercourse among Asian and Pacific Islander MSM. High-risk heterosexual contact is the primary way Asian and Pacific Islander women become infected with HIV.

American Indians and Alaska Natives   Among American Indians and Alaska Natives, HIV/AIDS is a growing problem. The number of HIV and AIDS diagnoses for this population group is less than 1% of the total number of HIV/AIDS cases reported in the United States. Yet, when population size is taken into account, in 2005 American Indians and Alaska Natives ranked third in rates of HIV/AIDS diagnosis, after African Americans and Hispanics. The rate of AIDS diagnosis for this population group has been higher than that for Whites since 1995. Poverty, lower levels of education, and less access to health care coexist as risk factors for HIV infection among American Indians and Alaska Natives. Illicit drug use is higher among American Indians and Alaska Natives than among people of other races or ethnicities. These indicators increase the vulnerability of American Indians and Alaska Natives to additional health stress, including HIV infection.

To be effective, HIV/AIDS prevention education must account for the numerous populations of American Indians and Alaska Natives by tailoring programs to individual tribal cultures and beliefs. The American Indian and Alaska Native population makes up 562 federally recognized tribes plus at least 50 state-recognized tribes. Because each tribe has its own culture, beliefs, and practices and these tribes may be subdivided into language groups, it can be challenging to create effective programs for each group (CDC, 2008z).

The Gay Community

"AIDS has given a human face to an invisible minority," says Robert Bray of the National Gay and Lesbian Task Force. From the beginning of the HIV/AIDS epidemic in the United States, the most disproportionate impact has been among the MSM group. Men who have sex with men is a behavioral description of a diverse population, many of whom identify themselves either privately or publicly as a gay man or bisexual person. Others may engage in sex with men but not think of themselves as a gay man or bisexual person. Even though the numbers of AIDS cases for MSM decreased during the 1980s and 1990s, recent surveillance data show an increase in HIV diagnoses for this group (Figure 16.5). MSM still represent the largest transmission category, accounting for 67% of the AIDS cases among adult and adolescent men (Figure 16.4) even though only about 5–7% of men in the United States identify themselves as gay men (Binson et al., 1995).

Racial disparities exist with regard to HIV diagnoses within the MSM population. A study conducted in five large cities in the United States found that HIV prevalence among Black MSM (48%) was more than twice that among White MSM (21%) (CDC, 2005f). Certainly not all MSM are at risk for HIV even though MSM constitute a group at risk for HIV. A study of more than 5,000 HIV-negative MSM found that older men with a large number of sex partners, young men who used "party" drugs, and older men who used nitrite inhalants were most likely to contract HIV (Bartholow et al., 2006).

Although epidemiologists do not know for certain how HIV first arrived in the gay community, they do know that it spread like wildfire, mainly because anal sex is such an efficient mode of transmission. Furthermore, initial research, education, and prevention efforts were severely hampered by a lack of government and public interest in what was perceived to be a "gay disease" (Shilts, 1987). Now, nearly 30 years after the virus first appeared, the gay community continues to reel from the repeated blows dealt by AIDS.

Sexual risk behaviors account for most HIV infections in MSM. Anal sex without a condom continues to be a major health threat to MSM, particularly having unprotected anal sex (barebacking) with casual partners. The reasons for unprotected sex are not completely understood, but research points to several factors, including optimism about improved HIV treatment, substance use, complex sexual decision making, seeking partners on the Internet, and failure to practice safer sex (Wolitski, 2005). Some of these men may be **serosorting,** or having sex or unprotected sex with a partner whose HIV serostatus, they believe, is the same as their own. For men with casual partners, serosorting alone is likely to be less effective than always and correctly using condoms because some men do not know or disclose their HIV serostatus (Truong et al., 2006).

Nearly three decades into the HIV epidemic, evidence points to an underestimation of risk and difficulty in maintaining safer sex practices among gay and bisexual men. The success of newer medical treatments may have had the unintended consequence of increasing risk behaviors among MSM, because some gay men seem to have abandoned safer sex practices. Research has shown several outcomes of improved treatment, such as minimizing the negative aspects of HIV infection, believing that their partners who take the new treatments are not infectious, and being more willing to have unprotected anal sex (Crepaz, Hart, & Marks, 2004; Ostrow et al., 2002; Suarez, & Miller, 2001).

The Internet has become a popular social network for gay men and is associated with higher-risk sexual behavior. A study of 609 gay men found that 75% used the Internet to access gay-oriented Web sites and 34% reported having met a partner via the Internet. Men meeting partners online, compared with those not meeting partners in this manner, reported higher methamphetamine use, sex with more partners in the previous 6 months, and higher rates

> I think God did send AIDS for a reason. It was to show how mean and sinful a healthy man can be toward a sick man.
>
> —Joe Bob Briggs
> (1953–)

Activism continues to focus public attention on the need for greater resources to control the HIV/AIDS epidemic.

of sexual risk behaviors, including unprotected receptive and insertive anal intercourse (Benotsch, Kalichman, Lawrence, & Nordling, 2002).

The use of alcohol and illegal drugs continues to be prevalent among MSM, increasing the risk of HIV transmission through the tendency toward risky sexual behaviors while under the influence and through sharing needles and other drug equipment. Use of methamphetamine and other "party" drugs such as ecstasy, ketamine, GHB (gamma hydroxy butyrate), and nitrites and the erection drug Viagra decreases social inhibitions and enhances sexual experiences and is often associated with risky sexual practices among MSM (Crosby & DiClemente, 2004; Paul, Pollack, Osmond, & Catania, 2005; Worth & Rawstorne, 2005).

Other factors that increase HIV risk among MSM are high rates of other STIs, social discrimination, poverty, lack of access to health care, stigmatization, concurrent psychosocial problems, lack of risk assessment, being unaware of infection, childhood sexual abuse, and partner violence. A study of more than 573 HIV-infected MSM from six cities found that over three quarters did not recognize their infection yet participated in several high-risk behaviors. The study concluded that the HIV epidemic among MSM in the United States remains a serious problem because many young HIV-infected MSM do not know they are infected and unknowingly expose their partners to HIV infection (MacKellar et al., 2002).

Women and HIV

Early in the epidemic, HIV infection and AIDS were diagnosed for relatively few women and female adolescents. Now, we know that many women were infected with HIV resulting from injection drug use but their infections were not diagnosed. Today, women account for more than one quarter of new HIV/AIDS diagnoses. High-risk heterosexual contact was the source of 80% of these newly diagnosed infections (Figure 16.4). Women of color are especially affected by HIV infection and AIDS. In 2004, HIV infection was the sixth leading cause of death among women aged 25–34, but it was the first leading cause of death for Black women aged 25–34. Further, Black and Hispanic women accounted for 81% of the women living with HIV/AIDS in 2005 who acquired HIV through high-risk heterosexual contact (CDC, 2008aa).

Several factors place women at risk for HIV infection. A woman is significantly more likely than a man to contract HIV infection during vaginal intercourse (Padian, Shiboski, & Jewell, 1991). Some women may be unaware of their male partner's risk factors for HIV infection, such as unprotected sex with numerous partners, sex with men, and injection drug use (Hader, Smith, Moore, & Holmberg, 2001; Montgomery, Mokotoff, Gentry, & Blair, 2003). A study of young men in six U.S. cities who had ever had sex with men found that 65% also reported sex with women (Valleroy, MacKellar, Behel, Secura, and Young Men's Survey, 2003). An estimated 1 in 5 new HIV diagnoses for women is related to injection drug use. Some women infected with HIV report more than one risk factor such as those cited here plus inequity in relationships, socioeconomic stresses, and psychological distress. For example, a study of Black women from North Carolina who were infected with HIV found that their most commonly cited reasons for risky behavior were financial dependence on male partners, feeling invincible, low self-esteem coupled with the need to feel loved by a male figure, and alcohol and drug use (CDC, 2004d).

An HIV diagnosis can have a dramatic negative impact on a woman's sexual interest and activity, sense of sexual attractiveness, and appeal to a sexual partner. In a sample of HIV-infected women, many reported that sex had become too plagued with anxiety, worry, danger, and stress to still be enjoyable. The loss of their sense of themselves as desirable, attractive, and enticing women was very painful for the women. Many would have liked the companionship of men rather than a sexual relationship (Siegel & Schrimshaw, 2006).

To date, there are no confirmed cases of female-to-female sexual transmission of HIV in the United States database. However, case reports of female-to-female transmission of HIV and the well-documented risk of female-to-female transmission indicate that vaginal secretions and menstrual blood are potentially infectious and that mucous membrane (e.g., oral, vaginal) exposure to these secretions has the potential to lead to HIV infection. Through December 2004, a total of 246,461 women were reported as HIV-infected; 7,381 of them had sex with women. However, most had other risk factors such as injection drug use and sex with men who were infected or who had risk factors for infection. Of the 534 (of 7,381) women who were reported to have had sex only with women, 91% also had another risk factor, typically injection drug use (CDC, 2006e).

One study found that the risk for HIV infection may be underestimated in some subgroups of women who have sex with women. The sexual and drug behaviors associated with HIV and STIs among women aged 18–29 were studied. Eighty-eight percent reported having sex exclusively with men, 7% reported having sex with both men and women, and 1% reported having sex only with women. Compared with women who had sex exclusively with men, women who had sex with both women and men were more likely to report having sex with an HIV-positive man, sex with a man who had sex with a man, and sex with an injection drug user, as well as numerous sex partners. They were also more likely to report trading sex for drugs or money, having anal sex, and injecting drugs (Scheer et al., 2002).

Children and HIV

Through 2006, a total of 9,156 children (those under 13 years of age) in the United States were reported as having AIDS. During 2006, 38 new cases of AIDS in children were reported. Of these 38 cases, 30 involved Black children, and 4 involved White children, 3 involved Hispanic children, and 1 involved an Asian/Pacific Islander child (CDC, 2008bb).

The incidence of AIDS among children has been dramatically reduced by recommendations by the CDC, which suggests routine counseling and voluntary prenatal HIV testing for women and the use of medical treatment to prevent perinatal transmission (CDC, 2007m).

HIV/AIDS Among Young People

I have never shared needles. And obviously I'm not a gay man. The only thing I did was something every single one of you has already done or will do.

—Krista Blake, infected with HIV as a teenager

Young people in the United States—defined by the CDC as individuals aged 13–24—are at persistent risk for HIV infection (see Figure 16.8). An estimated 5,394 young people were diagnosed with HIV or AIDS in 2006, representing about 15% of those given a diagnosis during that year (CDC, 2008cc). Cumulatively through 2006, about 16% of cases of HIV infection were youth, with more males than females being diagnosed (see Figure 16.8). However, because HIV may not be diagnosed for several months or years after contracting HIV, the number of young people with HIV is actually higher than that 16%. About 7 in 10 AIDS cases among male youth were from male-to-male sexual contact, with about 8 in 10 AIDS cases among female youth being from high-risk heterosexual contact. The HIV risk is especially notable for youth of minority races and ethnicities. For example, 55% of all HIV infections reported for young people are African Americans (CDC, 2008dd).

Risk factors accounting for the AIDS problem among youth included heterosexual contact, poverty, out-of-school youth, having an STI other than HIV, substance abuse, lack of awareness or concern about HIV, and simply being MSM. According to a CDC study of 5,589 MSM, 55% of young men aged

● **FIGURE 16.8**

U.S. Cases of HIV Infection (Not AIDS) by Age Group and Sex, 2006. (*Source:* Centers for Disease Control and Prevention. [2008v]. HIV/AIDS surveillance in adolescents and young adults [through 2006].)

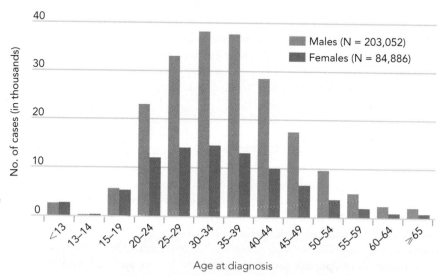

Note. Data from 45 states and 5 U.S. dependent areas with confidential name-based HIV infection reporting as of December 2006.

15–22 did not let other people know they were sexually attracted to men. Men who have sex with men who do not disclose their sexual orientation are less likely to seek HIV testing, so if they become infected, they are less likely to know it. Because MSM who do not disclose their sexual orientation are likely to also have one or more female sex partners, MSM who become infected may transmit the virus to women as well as to men. Young women are at risk for sexually transmitted HIV for several reasons, including biologic vulnerability, lack of recognition of their partner's risk factors, and having sex with older men, who are more likely to be infected with HIV (CDC, 2003e, 2008dd).

Click on "Just Like Me" to hear young people with AIDS talk about risk factors for becoming infected with HIV.

Older Adults and HIV

By the end of 2006, 124,474 AIDS cases had been diagnosed among adults aged 50 and older, representing over 12% of the total AIDS cases (see Figure 16.8). In 2006, 7,548 AIDS cases were diagnosed among those aged 50 and older (CDC, 2008bb). The proportion of individuals aged 50 and older living with HIV/AIDS has increased in recent years, partly due to more effective medical treatments that make it possible for HIV-infected people to live longer and to newly diagnosed infections in those over age 50 (CDC, 2008ee).

Compared with the early days of the epidemic, when most cases among older adults were contracted through a blood transfusion, more cases are now the result of unprotected sex and injection drug use. Contributing to the higher rates among both older men and older women are the similarity of symptoms of AIDS with other age-related diseases, increasing population of sexually-active divorced singles, a lack of awareness on the part of physicians, and a sense among older people that they are not vulnerable to AIDS. Because of an increasingly aging society and the recent availability of sexual performance enhancement prescription drugs (e.g., Viagra), focus on HIV and other STIs among older adults has increased.

Geographic Region and HIV

The distribution of AIDS cases in 2006 shows that most of the adults and adolescents (aged 13 years and older) reported with AIDS (82%) resided in metropolitan areas with populations of more than 500,000 at the time of diagnosis. In 2006, nearly 11% of cases were reported from metropolitan areas with populations of 50,000 to 500,000; 7% were reported from nonmetropolitan areas. Smaller metropolitan and nonmetropolitan areas, especially in the South, share a significant burden of the AIDS epidemic (CDC, 2008ff). Several factors may contribute to AIDS cases in rural communities: lack of availability of and access to health-care services, poverty, sexual risk behavior, injection drug use, and stigmatization. These barriers are particularly difficult to overcome in the rural areas (Rural HIV/STD Prevention Work Group, 2009).

Few studies have compared the sexual risk behavior of rural and urban residents. Analysis of national probability data indicates that rural residents are at greater risk for health problems compared to residents of metropolitan areas (Auchincloss & Hadden, 2002). However, because rural areas often have more conservative values, rural residence has been viewed as protective of sexual risk that might lead to HIV/STIs in contrast to urban areas. Data from a nationally represented survey of adults in the United States were analyzed to compare coital risk behaviors of single, young adult rural men and women to those of their nonrural counterparts. No significant differences were found between rural and nonrural men and women relative to lifetime number of penile-vaginal intercourse

HIV Prevention Attitude Scale

Mohammad Torabi and William L. Yarber developed a scale to measure attitudes toward HIV and its prevention. Completing this scale can help you determine which behaviors you might need to improve your HIV prevention attitude.

Directions

Read each statement carefully. Record your immediate reaction to each statement by writing the letter that corresponds to your answer. There is no right or wrong answer for each statement.

Key

A = Strongly agree
B = Agree
C = Undecided
D = Disagree
E = Strongly disagree

1. I am certain that I could be supportive of a friend infected with HIV.
2. I feel that people infected with HIV got what they deserve.
3. I am comfortable with the idea of using condoms for sex.
4. I would dislike the idea of limiting sex to just one partner to avoid HIV infection.
5. It would be embarrassing to get the HIV antibody test.
6. It is meant for some people to get HIV.
7. Using condoms to avoid HIV is too much trouble.
8. I believe that AIDS is a preventable disease.
9. The chance of getting HIV makes using injection drugs stupid.
10. People can influence their friends to practice safe behavior.
11. I would shake hands with a person infected with HIV.
12. I will avoid sex if there is a slight chance that my partner might have HIV.
13. If I were to have sex, I would insist that a condom be used.
14. If I used injection drugs, I would not share the needles.
15. I intend to share HIV facts with my friends.

Scoring

Calculate the total points for each statement using the following point values:

Items 1, 3, 8–15: Strongly agree = 5, Agree = 4, Undecided = 3, Disagree = 2, Strongly disagree = 1

Items 2, 4–7: Strongly agree = 1, Agree = 2, Undecided = 3, Disagree = 4, Strongly disagree = 5

The higher the score, the more positive the prevention attitude. Higher prevention attitudes are often associated with lower HIV risk behaviors.

SOURCE: Adapted from Torabi, Mohammad R., & Yarber, William L. (1992) Alternate Forms of the HIV Prevention Attitude Scale for Teenagers. *AIDS Education and Therapy, 4,* 172–182. With permission from the authors.

partners, number of penile-vaginal intercourse partners in the past 3 months, frequency of unprotected sex during the previous 4 weeks, condom use at last sexual contact, ever having had an HIV test, and discussing correct condom use with a health professional during the last HIV test. This suggests that effective HIV prevention education must be provided in rural as well as urban areas of the United States (Yarber, Milhausen, Huang, & Crosby, 2008).

● Prevention and Treatment

As a whole, our society remains ambivalent about the realities of HIV risk. Many people assume that their partners are not HIV-infected because they look healthy, "clean," and/or attractive. In addition, some believe that the federal government has failed to provide enough resources to combat the HIV/AIDS epidemic. With tens of thousands of Americans—many of them teenagers and young adults— becoming infected with HIV each year, inactivity and apathy become enemies

Health Protective Sexual Communication Scale

The Health Protective Sexual Communication Scale (HPSCS) assesses how often people discuss health protection, safer sex, sexual histories, and condom/contraception use with a first-time partner. High scores on the HPSCS are strongly linked to high-risk sexual behaviors, including multiple partners, incorrect or inconsistent condom use, and alcohol use before sex. An adapted form of the HPSCS follows.

The HPSCS is designed for individuals who have had a new sex partner in the past 12 months. If this is not the case for you, it might be in the future. The scale can alert you to health protection issues that are important to discuss, so go ahead and look at the questions.

Directions

Read each question carefully, and record your immediate reaction by writing the number that best applies.

Key

1 = Always
2 = Almost always
3 = Sometimes
4 = Never
5 = Don't know
6 = Decline to answer

Note: Questions 9 and 10 are excluded for gay men and lesbian women.

How often in the past 12 months have you:

1. Asked a new sex partner how he/she felt about using condoms before you had intercourse?
2. Asked a new sex partner about the number of past sex partners he/she had?
3. Told a new sex partner about the number of sex partners you have had?
4. Told a new sex partner that you won't have sex unless a condom is used?
5. Discussed with a new sex partner the need for both of you to get tested for HIV before having sex?
6. Talked with a new sex partner about not having sex until you have known each other longer?
7. Asked a new sex partner if he/she has ever had some type of STD, like genital herpes, genital warts, syphilis, chlamydia, or gonorrhea?
8. Asked a new sex partner if he/she has ever shot drugs like heroin, cocaine, or speed?
9. Talked about whether you or a new sex partner has ever had homosexual experiences?
10. Talked with a new sex partner about birth control before having sex for the first time?

Scoring

To obtain your score, add up the points for all items. The lower your score, the more health protective sexual communication occurred with a new partner.

SOURCE: Catania, Joseph A. (1998). Health Protective Sexual Communication Scale. In Clive M. Davis, William L. Yarber, Robert Bauserman, George Schreer, & Sandra L. Davis (Eds.), *Handbook of sexuality related measures* (pp. 544–557). Copyright ©1998 by Sage Publications Inc Books. Reproduced with permission of Sage Publications Inc Books in the format Textbook via Copyright Clearance Center.

in the fight against this disease. To assess your own attitudes toward HIV prevention, see the box "HIV Prevention Attitude Scale" on the previous page.

Protecting Ourselves

To protect ourselves and those we care about from HIV infection, there are some things we should know in addition to the basic facts about transmission and prevention. First, to protect ourselves, we need to assess our risks when we are clearheaded and act to protect ourselves. Second, we need to develop our communication skills so that we can discuss risks and prevention with our partner or potential partner. (To assess how often you discuss health protective concerns related to safer sex, sexual histories, and condom or contraception use with a new partner, see the above box "Health Protective Sexual Communication Scale.") If we want our partner to disclose information about past high-risk behavior, we have to be willing to do the same. One study of 203 HIV-positive hospital patients found that 40% did not tell their sex partners about their HIV status (Stein et al., 1998). A study of 55 HIV-infected men who have sex with men who reported recent STI or unprotected anal intercourse with an HIV-negative or HIV-status-unknown partner found that only 16 (29%) indicated that they either always disclosed or had a consistent pattern of disclosing their HIV status to their partner. However, a study of 322 HIV-infected women found that the majority disclosed their HIV-positive status to some sex partners: 75% disclosed to their current sex partner, and 67% disclosed to all of their partners (Sowell, Seals, Phillips, & Julious, 2003).

Disclosure of HIV-positive status is critical, as research has shown that people poorly judge their sex partner's HIV status (Niccolai, Farley, Ayoub, Magnus, & Kissinger, 2002). One study found that attractive romantic sex partners are perceived as less likely to have HIV/AIDS or another STI. Studies have shown that many people engage in risky sexual behavior with partners perceived to be "safe," but have "safer" sex with those judged to be riskier (Hennessy, Fishbein, Curtis, & Barrett, 2007). Another study showed that many people are relying on partner attributes and relationship characteristics when assessing the HIV/STI status of a sexual partner. Partners who were known well and trusted were evaluated as safe, yet these assessments of partners' sexual risk were shown to be inaccurate when compared to partners' self-reported risk. The researchers concluded that when trust has been "established" in a relationship, some people assume their partner is safe even when there is evidence of risky sexual behavior (Masaro, Dahinten, Johnson, Ogilvie, & Patrick, 2008).

Third, we may need to have information on HIV testing. If we have engaged in high-risk behavior, we may want to be tested for our own peace of mind and that of our partner. If we test positive for HIV, we need to make important decisions regarding our health, sexual behavior, and lifestyle. Actually, research has shown that people living with HIV who know of their infection, in contrast to those living with HIV who don't know they are infected, are more likely to take precautions to prevent HIV transmission. The researchers noted that the increase from 2001 to 2004 in the proportion of people living with HIV who were aware of their infection and took precautions can be credited with preventing nearly 6,000 new HIV infections during that 30-year period (Pinkerton, Holtgrave, & Galletly, 2008).

Finally, if we are sexually active with more than one long-term, exclusive partner, we need to start using condoms correctly and consistently. Although Americans have responded to the threat of AIDS by purchasing more condoms, rates of condom use remain low among many segments of the population. Many people remain unconvinced regarding either their own vulnerability to HIV or the usefulness of condoms in preventing its transmission. Male latex and polyurethane condoms, when used consistently and correctly, can greatly reduce the risk of HIV and other STIs. But the effectiveness of condoms has been disputed lately, leaving some people confused. (To help clarify the current beliefs about condoms among the leading federal health authorities, the position of the CDC is presented in the box "Preventing STIs: The Role of Male Condoms, Female Condoms, and Nonoxynol-9" in Chapter 15.) Female condoms and nonoxynol-9 are discussed relative to HIV/STI prevention.

Saving Lives Through Prevention

Prevention Education   The Centers for Disease Control and Prevention (2008gg) reports that HIV prevention efforts across the United States have been successful. One analysis measures the annual rate of HIV transmission in the

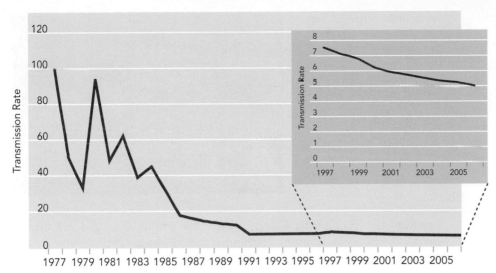

● **FIGURE 16.9**

Annual Transmission Rates per 100 People Living With HIV, 1977–2006. (*Source:* Holtgrave, Hall, Rhodes, & Wolitski, 2008.)

United States. This measure—the **HIV transmission rate**—represents the annual number of new HIV infections transmitted per 100 individuals living with HIV, (Holtgrave, Hall, Rhodes, & Wolitski, 2008). The researchers found that the HIV transmission rate has declined dramatically since the early days of the epidemic. For example, in 1980, when the disease was still undetected, the transmission rate was 92%, meaning that there were 92 transmissions per 100 individuals living with HIV at that time (see Figure 16.9). Following the identification of AIDS, and later HIV, and the implementation of prevention programs and HIV testing, the transmission rates began to decline. Over the past decade, as prevention efforts were expanded and improved medical treatments for HIV became available, the transmission rate declined by 33% (from an estimated 8 transmissions per 100 individuals living with HIV in 1997 to 5 in 2006). Five transmissions per 100 individuals living with HIV in 2006 means that more than 95% of those living with HIV did not transmit the infection that year.

The findings of the analysis of HIV transmission rates add to several recent signs of success in HIV prevention. Stable HIV incidence in recent years, as well as dramatic declines in mother-to-child transmission and declines in new infections among injection drug users and heterosexuals, also indicates progress against this disease. Despite these successes, the fight against HIV is far from over. Too many people—both HIV-infected and uninfected individuals—have not yet been reached by prevention efforts that we know to be most effective.

A review of 18 meta-analyses of sexual risk reduction interventions found significant increases in condom use and reductions in unprotected sex (Noar, 2008). Another meta-analytic review of HIV prevention interventions was conducted to see if they not only decreased sexual risk behavior but may have inadvertently increased sexual behavior. This analysis of 174 studies of HIV risk reduction interventions showed that HIV prevention programs did not increase the frequency of sexual activity. Some studies that were behavioral theory–based showed that HIV prevention interventions reduced the frequency of sexual activity and the number of sex partners (Smoak, Scott-Sheldon, Johnson, Carey, & SHARP research team, 2006).

Obstacles to Prevention HIV/AIDS is still seen by many people as a disease of "marginalized" groups, those who are outside the mainstream of

> *Ignorance breeds passivity, pessimism, resignation, or a sense that AIDS is someone else's problem.*
>
> —Paul Farmer, MD (1959–)

Bono, lead singer of the Irish rock band U2, is in the company of public figures Mariah Carey, Bill Clinton, Elton John, Nelson Mandela, and Brad Pitt who have established charities that help fight HIV/AIDS.

American life. People who are not White, not middle class, and not heterosexual are often viewed with suspicion by people who are. People who are gay or lesbian are often ignored or reviled even within their own ethnic communities. People who use drugs are written off as useless, worthless, and criminal. Sex workers are frequently blamed for spreading STIs, even though they undoubtedly contract these diseases from their clients, who more than likely have or will spread them to their partner or partners.

One effect of AIDS has been to make gay men more vulnerable to hate-motivated violence. Men who have been victims of vicious incidents of gay-bashing report that their attackers accuse them of causing AIDS. Assigning

Community outreach programs provide information about prevention and assistance available to those at high risk for HIV.

blame for AIDS to certain groups not only stigmatizes people in those groups but also keeps the blamers from scrutinizing their own risk behavior. This denial is one of the biggest obstacles AIDS prevention specialists face. And it affects not only adults but their children as well.

Needle Exchange Programs   Needle exchange programs (NEPs), especially those that provide information about risks and HIV prevention, also play an important role. However, these programs are controversial because some people believe that they endorse or encourage drug use. Others feel that because the drug use already exists, saving lives should be the first priority. Actually, several studies have shown that needle exchange programs can reduce injection drug risk behavior, such as needle sharing. For example, a study conducted in Chicago between 1997 and 2000 of 901 injection drug users found that NEPs significantly reduced the odds of receptive needle sharing by 60% and the odds of lending used needles by 45%. Also, there was a 30% reduced likelihood for sharing other drug injection paraphernalia and a twofold increase in the likelihood of always bleaching used needles. The researchers concluded that, compared to nonusers, NEP users engaged in less HIV-related injection risk, a difference that persisted over time (Huo & Ouellet, 2007).

Although needle exchange programs are illegal in some areas, they are often allowed to continue as long as the workers keep a low profile. Needle exchange activists believe that high priority should be given to legalizing and expanding these programs, which are cost-effective and have the potential of saving thousands of lives.

HIV Testing

Free or low-cost and anonymous or confidential HIV testing is available in many areas, including local health departments, clinics, offices of private physicians, hospitals, and sites specifically set up for that purpose. For information on where to find an HIV testing site, visit the National HIV Testing Resources Web site at http://www.hivtest.org or call CDC-INFO 24 hours/day at 1-800-CDC-INFO (232-4636) or 1-888-232-6348 (TTY), in English, en Español. Both of these resources are confidential.

Who Should Get Tested?   Screening for HIV infection is a major HIV control strategy. The CDC has promoted HIV testing, and the number of people who have had one HIV screening test in their lifetime has increased. However, an estimated 1 in 5 individuals living with HIV is unaware of their infection and may be unknowingly transmitting the virus to others. Knowing one's HIV status can reduce the number of new infections. Research shows that the majority of people who know they are infected take steps to prevent the transmission of HIV to others (Marks, Crepaz, & Janssen, 2006).

A person participating in any of the following behaviors should definitely get an HIV test. If the person continues with any of these behaviors, he or she should get tested every year.

- Injected drugs or steroids or shared drug equipment
- Had unprotected sex (didn't use a condom) with men who have sex with men, numerous partners, or anonymous partners
- Exchanged sex for drugs

- Was diagnosed with or treated for hepatitis, tuberculosis, or an STI, like syphilis
- Had unprotected sex with someone who had any of the above behaviors

If a person has had sex with someone whose history of sex partners and/or drug use is unknown or if a partner has had numerous partners, then he or she has a chance of being infected with HIV. New partners (both individuals) should get tested for HIV, and learn the results, before having sex for the first time. HIV testing is important for women who plan to become pregnant as medical care and certain drugs given during pregnancy can lower the chance of passing HIV to the child.

Most HIV tests are antibody tests that measure the antibodies the body makes against HIV. It takes some time for the immune system to produce enough antibodies to be detected by the antibody test; this is called the **"window period,"** which can vary from person to person. Almost everyone infected with HIV develops antibodies to HIV within 2–8 weeks after exposure (the average is 25 days); 97% will develop antibodies within the first 2–3 months; and, in very rare cases, it can take up to 6 months to develop antibodies to HIV. Therefore, if the initial negative HIV test was conducted within the first 3 months after possible exposure, repeat testing should be considered after the exposure occurred to account for the possibility of a false-negative result. Between the time of a possible exposure and the receipt of test results, a person should consider abstaining from sexual contact with others or use condoms and/or dental dams during all sexual encounters (CDC, 2007n).

What a person can do if he or she tests positive for HIV is discussed later in this chapter. Having an HIV-negative test does not mean that one's partner is also HIV-negative. An HIV test result reveals only the HIV status of the person taking the test. HIV is not necessarily transmitted every time there is an exposure. Therefore, taking an HIV test oneself should not be viewed as a method to find out if one's partner has HIV. A person should ask about the HIV status of his or her partner and what risk behaviors the partner engaged in both currently and in the past. Certainly it is advisable to encourage the partner to get an HIV screening test.

In most cases the **EIA (enzyme immunoassay),** performed on blood drawn from a vein, is the most common screening test used to detect the presence of antibodies to HIV. A reactive (positive) EIA is then followed up with a confirmatory test such as the **Western blot** to make sure of a positive diagnosis. Other EIA tests that use other body fluids to screen for antibodies for HIV include

- *Oral fluid tests.* These tests use oral fluid (not saliva) collected from the mouth using a special collection device and if positive require a follow-up confirmatory Western blot using the same oral fluid sample.
- *Urine tests.* These tests use urine, but are somewhat less accurate than blood and oral fluid tests. If positive, they require a follow-up confirmatory Western blot using the same urine sample.

A rapid test is a screening test that produces very quick results, in about 20 minutes, whereas other HIV tests take a few days for results. This means that the person tested can find out the results at the same visit, which cannot be done for the other screening tests. The rapid test has become very valuable to HIV control efforts because failure to return for HIV test results is very common (Sullivan, 2004). Rapid tests use blood or oral fluid to look for the presence of antibodies to HIV. As is true for all screening tests, a reactive rapid HIV test must be confirmed with a follow-up confirmatory test before final diagnosis of infection can be made. The rapid test has similar accuracy rates as traditional EIA screening tests.

Another type of test is an RNA test, which detects HIV directly. The time between HIV infections and RNA detection is 9 to 11 days. RNA tests, which are more costly and used less often than antibody tests, are used in some parts of the United States (CDC, 2007o).

In 1997, the first consumer-controlled test kit (popularly known as "home testing kits") was licensed by the Food and Drug Administration. Only the Home Access HIV-1 Test System is currently licensed; the accuracy of other home testing kits cannot be verified. The Home Access HIV-1 Test System can be found in most local drug stores or purchased on the Internet. This kit is not a true home test, but a home collection kit. The testing procedure involves pricking a finger with a special device, placing drops of blood on a specially treated card, and then mailing the card to a licensed laboratory to be tested. Customers are given an identification number to use when phoning in for the results. Callers may speak to a counselor before taking the test, while waiting for the test result, and when the result is given. All individuals receiving a positive test result are provided referrals for a follow-up confirmatory test, as well as information and resources for treatment and support services.

Counseling for the Tested   Most people who go for an HIV test are anxious. Even though the vast majority of test results are negative, there is still the understandable fear that one has "drawn the short straw." For many people, there are probably also feelings of ambivalence or guilt about the risky behaviors that led them to this situation. Because of these kinds of responses, which are normal, counseling is a key part of the testing process. It is important for people being tested to understand what their risks for HIV actually are and to know what the results mean. It is also important for everyone, no matter what the results of their tests are, to understand the facts of transmission and prevention. For the majority who test negative, practicing abstinence or safer sex, remaining sexually exclusive, avoiding injection drug use, and taking other preventive measures can eliminate much of the anxiety associated with HIV. (These measures reduce the risk of other STIs as well.)

Counseling is vital for individuals who are HIV-positive. Early treatment and positive health behaviors are essential to maintaining good health and prolonging life. Pregnancy counseling should be made available for women. It is also essential that people know they can pass the virus on to others.

Treatments

When AIDS first surfaced in the United States, there were no drugs to combat the underlying immune deficiency and few treatments existed for the opportunistic diseases that resulted. Researchers, however, have developed drugs to fight both HIV infection and its associated infections and cancers. HIV treatment is the use of anti-HIV medications to keep an HIV-infected person healthy. Treatment can help people at all stages of HIV disease. Although anti-HIV medications can treat HIV infection, they cannot cure it.

Anti-HIV medications, also called **antiretroviral medications,** are used to control the reproduction of the virus and to slow the progression of HIV disease.

A person does not necessarily need to take antiretroviral medications just because he or she is infected with HIV. When to take antiretroviral medications depends on one's overall health, the amount of virus in the blood (called "viral load"), and how well the immune system is working. Treatment usually begins if the HIV-infected person is experiencing severe symptoms of HIV infection or has been diagnosed with AIDS, has a CD4 count of 350 cells/millimeter (especially if 200 cells/mm or less), or is pregnant. HIV-infected people who have not started antiretroviral medications should have a viral load test every 3 to 4 months and a CD4 count every 3 to 6 months.

Because HIV can become resistant to the drugs used to fight HIV infection, health-care providers must use a combination treatment to effectively suppress the virus. When multiple drugs (three or more) are used in combination, it is referred to as **highly active antiretroviral therapy, or HAART.** HAART is now the recommended treatment for HIV infection and can be used by people who are newly infected with HIV as well as people with AIDS. The Food and Drug Administration approved, in 2006, the first one-a-day three-drug combination HIV pill. Researchers have credited HAART as being a major factor in significantly reducing the number of deaths from AIDS in this country. One study found that HAART increases HIV-positive people's life expectancy by an average of 13 years (Kaiser Daily HIV/AIDS Report, 2008). Another study found that from the time of entering anti-HIV medical care, including HAART, the projected lifetime expectancy is about 24 years (Schackman et al., 2006). While HAART is not a cure for AIDS, the viral load should decrease if HAART is effective. In general, the viral load is the most important indicator of how well the treatment is working. If HIV is not suppressed completely, drug resistance can develop.

HAART has greatly improved the health of many people with AIDS and reduces the amount of the virus in the blood to nearly undetectable levels. An undetectable viral load does not mean that the HIV infection is gone; it simply means that the test is not sensitive enough to detect the small amount of HIV left in the blood. HIV is less likely to be transmitted when the viral loads are very low or undetectable.

Click on "Undetectable: The New Face of AIDS" to hear an AIDS activist speak about the side effects of highly active antiretroviral therapy (HAART).

Once anti-HIV treatment begins, it may need to be continued for the rest of the person's life. Although newer treatments are easier to take, starting and continuing treatment may mean a significant adjustment to one's lifestyle. Because of the potential side effects of HAART, health experts recommend that anyone on anti-HIV medication be routinely seen and followed by their health-care provider (National Institute of Allergy and Infectious Diseases, 2008; U.S. Department of Health and Human Services, 2008b).

The search for a cure for AIDS continues. Learning more about the genetics of the small number of HIV-infected individuals who remain healthy may lead to new therapies that can help others. Gene therapy, in which the immune system is reconstructed with genetically altered resistant cells, is one potentially promising approach. For HIV/STI prevention, researchers are working on topical microbicides, chemical or biological substances that can kill or neutralize viruses and bacteria that may be present in semen or cervical or vaginal secretions. The goal is to develop a microbicidal gel, cream, film, or suppository that individuals can apply to the vagina prior to intercourse. A major value of microbicides is that women can have much more control of HIV/STI prevention, particularly when they have limited ability to get their male partners to use condoms. A rectal HIV microbicide is also currently in development.

The Names Project Foundation created the AIDS Memorial Quilt as a poignant and powerful tool in preventing HIV infection. Each square has been lovingly created by friends and families of people who have died of AIDS. The quilt now contains more than 40,000 panels.

As a cream or gel, or maybe a douche or an enema, a rectal microbicide could offer protection when condoms are used and a back-up protection in the event of condom breakage or slippage. Also, the rectal microbicide could be a safe and effective alternative for couples who are unwilling or unable to use condoms (International Rectal Microbicide Advocates, 2008). Work has also begun to develop an STI microbicide that would be topically used for penile cleaning before and after sex.

Development of an effective and safe vaccine for HIV is the ultimate goal, but many biological and social challenges have to be overcome. Vaccines tested have failed to achieve expectations (Sternberg, 2005b). While some progress has been achieved, it will still be many years before an HIV vaccine is licensed and widely available (HIV Vaccines and Microbicides Resource Tracking Working Group, 2007). Microbicides and a vaccine would provide another barrier to HIV transmission, but individual practice of safe sex would remain paramount.

Living With HIV or AIDS

People infected with HIV or diagnosed with AIDS have the same needs as everyone else—and a few more. If you are HIV-positive, in addition to dealing with psychological and social issues you need to pay special attention to maintaining good health. If you are caring for someone with HIV or AIDS, you also have special needs.

If You Are HIV-Positive

A positive antibody test is scary to just about anyone. Yet a positive test result is valuable news: It is news that may make it possible to actually save your life. If you don't learn about your status in this way, you probably will not know until a serious opportunistic infection announces the presence of HIV. At that

The evidence demonstrates that we are not powerless against the epidemic, but our response is still a fraction of what it needs to be.

—Peter Piot, MD
(1949–)

point, many of your best medical options have been lost, and you might have spread the virus to others who would not otherwise have been exposed. But remember, although HIV infection is serious, people with HIV are living longer, healthier lives today, thanks to new and effective treatments. Fortunately, people with HIV who are taking HAART can go a long time before their immune systems are damaged enough to allow an opportunistic infection to occur.

Staying Healthy Longer   It is important to find a physician who has experience working with HIV and AIDS, and—even more importantly, perhaps—who is sensitive to the issues confronted by individuals infected with HIV. Begin treatment promptly once your doctor tells you to. Keep your appointments and follow the doctor's instructions. If your doctor prescribes medicine for you, take the medicine just the way he or she tells you since taking only some of your medicine gives your HIV infection more chance to fight back. If you get sick from your medicine, call your doctor for advice; don't make changes to what your doctor has prescribed on your own or because of advice from friends. In addition to appropriate medical treatment, factors that can help promote your continuing good health include good nutrition, plenty of rest, exercise, limited (or no) alcohol use, and stress reduction. People with HIV or AIDS should stop smoking tobacco because it increases susceptibility to pneumonia. They should also get immunizations to prevent infections such as pneumonia and flu.

In addition, if you decide to have sexual contact with another person, it means practicing safer sex, even if your partner is also HIV-positive. Researchers caution that one can become reinfected with different HIV strains. Moreover, STIs of all kinds can be much worse for people with an impaired immune system. HIV doesn't mean an end to being sexual, but it does suggest that different ways of expressing love and sexual desire may need to be explored. If you are living with HIV or AIDS, you may need many kinds of support: medical, emotional, psychological, and financial. Your doctor, your local health department and social services departments, local AIDS service organizations, and the Internet can help you find all kinds of help.

It is recommended that women who are HIV-positive have Pap tests every 6–12 months. Cervical biopsies may also be necessary to determine whether cervical dysplasia or cancer is present.

Addressing Your Other Needs   The stigma and fear surrounding HIV and AIDS often make it difficult to get on with the business of living. Among gay and bisexual men, social support is generally better for Whites than for Blacks; in Black communities, there tends to be less affirmation from primary social support networks and less openness about sexual orientation. Women, who usually concern themselves with caring for others, may not be inclined to seek out support groups and networks. But people who live with HIV and AIDS say that it's important not to feel isolated. If you are HIV-positive, we encourage you to seek support from AIDS organizations in your area.

Partner Notification   Both current and past partners should be notified so that they can be tested and receive counseling. Actually, in many states, HIV-infected people are required by law to notify current and recent sexual and needle-sharing partners. AIDS counselors and health-care practitioners currently encourage those with HIV to make all possible efforts to contact past and current partners. In some cases, counselors try to make such contacts, with their clients' permission.

Final Thoughts

As we have seen, HIV/AIDS remains a major public health challenge, in the United States and globally. HIV continues to take a severe toll on many communities in the U.S., with gay and bisexual men of all races, African Americans, and Latinos bearing the heaviest burden. Not only is HIV/AIDS a medical problem, but barriers such as stigmatization, discrimination, limited prevention education messages, and gender inequity impede progress to controlling the epidemic. We must do more—as individuals, in our communities, and as a nation—to expand our prevention efforts to people at risk and stop the spread of HIV. As we know, HIV can be avoided. We hope that this chapter has provided you with the information and motivation that will serve as your vaccine against HIV/AIDS.

Summary

What Is AIDS?

- *AIDS* is an acronym for *acquired immunodeficiency syndrome.* For a person to receive an AIDS diagnosis, he or she must have a positive blood test indicating the presence of *HIV (human immunodeficiency virus)* antibodies and have a T-cell count below 200; if the T-cell count is higher, the person must have 1 or more of over 20 diseases or conditions associated with AIDS to be diagnosed with the disease.

- A host of symptoms are associated with HIV/AIDS. Because these symptoms may be indicative of many other diseases and conditions, HIV and AIDS cannot be self-diagnosed; diagnosis by a clinician or physician is necessary.

- *Leukocytes*, or white blood cells, play a major role in defending the body against invading organisms and cancerous cells. One type, the *macrophage*, engulfs foreign particles and displays the invader's *antigen* on its own surface. *Antibodies* bind to antigens, inactivate them, and mark them for destruction by *killer T cells*. Other white blood cells called *lymphocytes* include *helper T cells*, which are programmed to "read" the antigens and then begin directing the immune system's response. The number of helper T cells in an individual's body is an important indicator of how well the immune system is functioning.

- *Viruses* are primitive entities; they can't propel themselves independently, and they can't reproduce unless they are inside a host cell. Within the HIV's protein core is the genetic material (RNA) that carries the information the virus needs to replicate itself. A *retrovirus* can "write" its RNA (the genetic program) into a host cell's DNA.

- Although HIV begins replication right away within the host cells, it is not detectable in the blood for some time—often years. HIV antibodies, however, are generally detectable in the blood within 2–8 weeks (the average is 25 days). A person's *serostatus* is HIV-negative if antibodies are not present and HIV-positive if antibodies are detected. "T-cell count," or "CD4 count," refers to the number of helper T cells that are present in a cubic milliliter of blood.

- When a person is first infected with HIV, he or she may experience severe flulike symptoms. During this period, the virus is dispersed throughout the lymph nodes and other tissues. The virus may stay localized in these areas for years, but it continues to replicate and to destroy T cells. As the number of infected cells goes up, the number of T cells goes down. In advanced AIDS, the T-cell count drops to under 200, and the virus itself is detectable in the blood.

The Epidemiology and Transmission of HIV

- The number of adults and adolescents living with HIV in the United States has grown to 1.1 million. Worldwide, more than 33 million people are now living with HIV. Rates of new infections are rising most dramatically in sub-Saharan Africa.

- HIV is not transmitted by casual contact.

- Activities or situations that may promote HIV transmission include sexual transmission through vaginal or anal intercourse without a condom; fellatio without a condom; cunnilingus without a latex or other barrier; the sharing of needles contaminated with infected blood; in-utero infection from mother to fetus, from blood during delivery, or in breast milk; the sharing of sex toys without disinfecting them; accidental contamination when infected blood enters the body through mucous membranes (eyes or mouth) or cuts, abrasions, or punctures in the skin (relatively rare); or blood transfusions (very rare).

- Certain physiological or behavioral factors increase the risk of contracting HIV. In addition to anal intercourse, numerous sex partners, and injection drug use, these factors include having an STI (especially if genital lesions are present) and multiple exposures to HIV.

AIDS Demographics

- HIV/AIDS is often linked with poverty, which has roots in racism and discrimination. In the United States, African Americans and Latinos have been disproportionately affected by HIV and STIs in comparison to other racial/ethnic groups.

- Certain groups have been particularly impacted by the AIDS epidemic in the United States: racial/ethnic minorities (particularly African Americans), men who have sex with men; women; and young adults.

- Women face unique issues related to HIV. As the number of infected women rises, the number of infected children is also expected to rise.

- Because young people often have a sense of invulnerability, they may put themselves at great risk without really understanding the consequences that may result from their sexual behavior.

Prevention and Treatment

- To protect ourselves and those we care about from HIV, we need to be fully knowledgable of what constitutes risky behaviors and how to avoid them, develop communication skills so that we can talk with our partners, and get information on HIV testing. If we are sexually active with more than one long-term, exclusive partner, we need to use condoms correctly and consistently.

- Free or low-cost and anonymous or confidential HIV testing is available in many areas. HIV screening tests look for antibodies to the virus. A new HIV test in which the results are available in about 20 minutes is now used at many testing sites.

- Antiretroviral medications—the combination of three or more of these drugs is called *highly active antiretroviral therapy (HAART)*—are available for treatment of HIV/AIDS. Many people on the HAART regimen have an increase in quality of life and longevity.

Living With HIV or AIDS

- An HIV or AIDS diagnosis may be a cause for sadness and grief, but it also can be a time for reevaluation and growth. Those whose friends or family members are living with HIV, or who are themselves HIV-positive, need information and practical and emotional support.

- Early detection of HIV can greatly enhance both the quality and longevity of life. Appropriate medical treatment and a healthy lifestyle are important. People with HIV or AIDS also need to practice safer sex and consider seeking support from AIDS organizations.

Questions for Discussion

- What behaviors or measures have you taken or will you take to prevent yourself from contracting HIV?

- Despite an increasing AIDS epidemic, some people continue to practice risky sexual and injection drug use; many of them are not receptive to HIV prevention messages. What do you suggest as strategies to reach these individuals?

- Individuals who are diagnosed with an HIV infection react in many ways. How do you think you would react?

- What would be your most important concern if you just learned that you had been infected with HIV?

Sex and the Internet

Frequently Asked Questions on HIV/AIDS

The U.S. Centers for Disease Control and Prevention (CDC) provides information about HIV infection and AIDS on its Web site. One section is titled "Questions and Answers (Q & A)." Go there (http://www.cdc.gov/hiv/resources/qa/index.htm) and answer these questions:

- What are the categories of questions?
- Are there questions that address issues you are curious about?
- Choose a few questions and look at the responses. Do they seem adequate?
- Are there questions you have that are not included?
- What did you learn about HIV/AIDS from looking at this site?

Also, note that in this section one can sign up to get free e-mail updates. All you have to do is click on "Get E-Mail Updates on HIV/AIDS Questions and Answers" and enter your e-mail address.

Suggested Web Sites

CDC National Prevention Information Network
http://www.cdcdnpin.org
Claims to house the nation's largest collection of information resources on HIV/AIDS, STI, viral hepatitis, and TB prevention.

Centers for Disease Control and Prevention
http://www.cdc.gov/hiv/dhap
Provides information on HIV/AIDS.
http://www.cdc.gov/std/
Provides information on STIs.

U.S. Government
http://twitter.com/AIDSgov
U.S. Government's social network and outreach to bloggers about HIV prevention and treatment.

Joint United Nations Programme on HIV/AIDS
http://www.unaids.org
Contains epidemiological information on HIV/AIDS worldwide, as well as perspectives on HIV/AIDS-related issues.

Kaiser Family Foundation
http://www.kff.org
Offers fact sheets and new releases on STIs and HIV/AIDS.

National Institutes of Health
http://www.nih.gov
Provides current information about HIV/AIDS.

Rural Center for AIDS/STD Prevention
http://www.indiana.edu/~aids
Provides information about issues related to HIV/STI prevention in rural communities in the United States.

Suggested Reading

Behrmann, G. (2004). *The invisible people: How the U.S. has slept through the global AIDS pandemic, the greatest humanitarian catastrophe of our time.* New York: Free Press. A true story of politics, bureaucracy, disease, and negligence, the book illustrates how the United States failed to act.

Epstem, H. (2008). *The invisible cure: Why we are losing the fight against AIDS in Africa.* New York: Picador. An exploration of the AIDS problem in Africa through the lenses of medicine, politics, and sociology amid the catastrophic failure to reverse the epidemic.

Halkitis, P. N., Gomez, C. A., & Wolitski, R. J. (Eds.). (2005). *HIV & sex: The psychological and interpersonal dynamics of HIV-seropositive gay and bisexual men's relationships.* Washington, DC: American Psychological Association. The editors and contributors explore how gay and bisexual men live with HIV.

Pisani, E. (2008). *The wisdom of whores: Bureaucrats, brothels, and the business of AIDS.* New York: W. W. Norton. A "flame-throwing" epidemiologist talks about sex, drugs, mistakes, ideologies, and hopes of international AIDS prevention.

Shilts, R. (1987). *And the band played on: People, politics, and the AIDS epidemic.* New York: St. Martin's Press. The fascinating story behind the "discovery" of AIDS, complete with real heroes and, unfortunately, real villains.

Weeks, B. S., & Alcams, I. E. (2006). *AIDS: The biological basis.* Boston: Jones and Bartlett. The text provides the necessary background information to understand the biology of HIV and AIDS while also providing information on critical epidemiological patterns and research developments.

For links, articles, and study material, go to the McGraw-Hill Web site, located at **www.mhhe.com/yarber7e.**

17

Sexual Coercion: Harassment, Aggression, and Abuse

TALK ABOUT SEXUAL ASSAULT

MAIN TOPICS

Sexual Harassment

Harassment and Discrimination Against Gay, Lesbian, Bisexual, and Transgender People

Sexual Aggression

Child Sexual Abuse

Although sexuality permits us to form and sustain deep bonds and intimate relationships, it may also have a darker side. For some people, sex is linked with coercion, degradation, aggression, and abuse. In these cases, sex becomes a weapon—a means to exploit, humiliate, or harm others. In this chapter, we first examine the various aspects of sexual harassment, including the distinction between flirting and harassment and the sexual harassment that occurs in schools, colleges, and the workplace. Next, we look at harassment, prejudice, and discrimination directed against gay men and lesbian women. Then we examine sexual aggression, including date rape and stranger rape, the motivations for rape, and the consequences of rape. Finally, we discuss child sexual abuse, examining the factors contributing to abuse, the types of abuse and their consequences, and programs for preventing it.

> *Being forced is poison for the soul.*
> —Ludwig Borne
> (1786 1837)

● Sexual Harassment

Sexual harassment refers to two distinct types of behavior: (1) the abuse of power for sexual ends and (2) the creation of a hostile environment. In terms of abuse of power, sexual harassment consists of unwelcomed sexual advances, requests for sexual favors, or other verbal or physical conduct of a sexual nature as a condition of instruction or employment (Frazier, Cochran, & Olson, 1995). Refusal to comply may result in reprisals. Only a person with power over another can commit the first kind of harassment. In a **hostile environment,** someone acts in sexual ways that interfere with a person's performance at school or in the workplace. Such harassment is illegal.

What Is Sexual Harassment?

The Civil Rights Act of 1964 first made various kinds of discrimination, including sexual harassment, illegal in the workplace. In 1980, the U.S. Office of Equal Employment Opportunity Commission (EEOC) issued guidelines regarding both verbal and physical harassment in the work and education environments. The EEOC defined sexual harassment as unwelcome sexual advances, requests for sexual favors, and other verbal or physical conduct of a sexual nature when this conduct (1) explicitly or implicitly affects an individual's employment, (2) unreasonably interferes with an individual's work performance, or (3) creates an intimidating, hostile, or offensive work environment. A major component of the EEOC guidelines is that the behavior is unwanted and unwelcome and might affect employment conditions. The sexual aggression does not have to be explicit, and even the creation of a hostile work environment that can affect work performance constitutes sexual harassment. Also, it is unlawful for an employer to retaliate against an individual for filing a discrimination charge or opposing employment practices that discriminate based on sex (U.S. Equal Employment Opportunity Commission, 2008a; U.S. Merit Systems Protection Board, 1995). Further, the victim does not have to be the person harassed but could be anyone affected by the conduct. In fiscal year 2007, 12,510 sexual harassment charges were filed with the EEOC, down from a high of 15,889 in 1997 (U.S. Equal Employment Opportunity Commission, 2008b). (Fiscal year for the federal government is October 1 to September 30.)

Sexual harassment is a mixture of sex and power; power may often be the dominant element. In school and the workplace, men and women are devalued by calling attention to their sexuality. For women especially, sexual harassment may be a way to keep them "in their place" and make them feel vulnerable.

Sexual harassment, particularly in the workplace, creates a stressful and hostile environment for the victim.

There are other forms of behavior that, although not illegal, are considered by many to be sexual harassment. These include unwanted sexual jokes and innuendos and unwelcome whistles, taunts, and obscenities directed from a man or group of men to a woman walking past them. As with all harassment, these apply to male-female, male-male, and female-female interactions. They also include a man "talking to" a woman's breasts or body during conversation or persistently giving her the "once-over" as she walks past him, sits down, or enters or leaves a room. Clinical psychologist Elizabeth Powell (1996) lists the following as examples of sexual harassment:

- Verbally harassing or abusing someone
- Exerting subtle pressure for sexual activity
- Making remarks about a person's clothing, body, or sexual activities
- Leering at or ogling a person's body
- Engaging in unwelcome touching, patting, or pinching
- Brushing against a person's body
- Making demands for sexual favors accompanied by implied or overt threats concerning one's job or student status
- Physically assaulting someone

Such incidents may make women (and men) feel uncomfortable and vulnerable. They have been described, in fact, as "little rapes." The cumulative effect of these behaviors is to lead women to limit their activities, to avoid walking past groups of men, and to stay away from beaches, concerts, parties, and sports events unless they are accompanied by others. Sometimes, charges of sexual harassment are ignored or trivialized, and blame often falls on the victim. Sexual harassment more commonly occurs in school or the workplace, as well as in other settings, such as between patients and doctors or mental health and sex therapists.

Flirtation Versus Harassment

There is nothing wrong with flirtation per se. A smile, look, or compliment can give pleasure to both people. But persistent and unwelcome flirtation can be sexual harassment if the flirtatious person holds power over the other or if the flirtation creates a hostile school or work environment. Whether flirtation is sexual harassment depends on three factors:

- *Whether you have equal power.* A person's having power over you limits your ability to refuse, for fear of reprisal. For example, if a professor or teaching assistant in your class asks you for a date, you are placed in an awkward position. If you say no, will your grade suffer? Will you be ignored in class? What other consequences might occur? Or if your boss asks for a date, you may be similarly concerned about losing your job, being demoted, or having your work environment become hostile if you refuse.

- *Whether you are approached appropriately.* "Hi babe, nice tits, wanna get it on?" and "Hey stud, love your buns, wanna do it?" are obviously offensive. But approaches that are complimentary ("You look really nice today"), indirect ("What do you think of the class?"), or direct ("Would you like to have some coffee?") are acceptable because they do not pressure you. You have the opportunity to let the overture pass, respond positively, or politely decline. Sometimes, it is difficult to distinguish the intent of the person doing the approaching. One way to ascertain the intent is to give a direct "I" message and ask that the behavior cease. If the person stops the behavior, and especially if an apology follows, the intent was friendly; if the behavior continues, it is the beginning of sexual harassment. If he or she does not stop, you should contact a trusted supervisor, an academic advisor/counselor, or a resident assistant.

- *Whether you wish to continue contact.* If you find the other person appealing, you may want to continue the flirtation. You can express interest or flirt back. But if you don't, you may want to stop the interaction by not responding or by responding in a neutral or discouraging manner.

The issue is complicated by several factors related to culture and gender. Differing cultural expectations may lead to misinterpretation. For example, when a Latino, whose culture encourages mutual flirting, says "*muy guapa*" ("good looking") to a Latina walking by, the words may be meant *and* received as a compliment. But when a Latino says the same thing to a non-Latina, he may be dismayed at her negative reaction. He perceives her as uptight, and she perceives him as rude, but each is misinterpreting the other because of cultural differences.

Three significant gender differences may contribute to sexual harassment. First, men are generally less likely to perceive activities as harassing than are women (U.S. Merit Systems Protection Board, 1995). The difference in perception often is for the more subtle forms of harassment, as both men and women believe that overt activities such as deliberate touching constitute sexual harassment. Second, men tend to misperceive women's friendliness as sexual interest (Johnson, Stockdale, & Saal, 1991; Stockdale, 1993). Third, men are more likely than women to perceive male-female relationships as adversarial. Given all this, not surprisingly, 85% of the harassment claims filed in 2007 were by women. Interestingly, the percentage of males filing sexual harassment claims increased from 9.1% in 1992 to 16% in 2007 (U.S. Equal Employment Opportunity Commission, 2008b).

Power differences also affect perception. Personal questions asked by an instructor or supervisor, for example, are more likely to be perceived as sexual harassment than they would be if a student or co-worker asked them. What needs to be clarified is the basis of the relationship: Is it educational, business, or professional? Is it romantic or sexual? Flirtatious or sexual ways of relating are inappropriate in the first three contexts.

Harassment in School and College

Sexual harassment in various forms is widespread. It does not necessarily begin in adulthood; it may begin as early as middle childhood.

Harassment in Elementary and High School   It's a "time-honored" practice for boys to "tease" girls: calling them names, spreading sexual gossip, and so on. If such behavior is defined as teasing, its impact is discounted; it is just "fun." But if the behavior is thought of as sexual harassment, then the behaviors may be viewed in a new light. Such behavior, researcher Carrie Herbert (1989) found, leads girls to "become more subordinated, less autonomous, and less capable of resisting. This behavior controls the girls through intimidation, embarrassment, or humiliation."

According to a national study of sexual harassment among 2,064 8th-through 11th-graders, 83% of girls and 79% of boys reported experiencing some type of sexual harassment in school, the vast majority being peer-to-peer harassment (American Association of University Women Educational Foundation, 2001). More than 1 in 4 students experienced sexual harassment often, no matter whether the school was urban, suburban, or rural. Nearly 9 in 10 students (85%) reported that students harassed other students at their schools. Further, nearly 40% of students reported that teachers and other school employees sexually harassed students in their schools. Most of the harassment occurred within the classroom or hallways. Being subjected to sexual comments, jokes, gestures, or looks; being touched, grabbed, or pinched in a sexual way; and being intentionally brushed up against in a sexual way were the most common types of harassment. Thirty-three percent of the girls and 12% of the boys no longer wished to attend school because of the harassment. Other outcomes of the harassment included not wanting to talk as much in class, finding it hard to pay attention in school, staying home from school or cutting a class, and getting lower grades on tests. Feeling embarrassed and self-conscious, being less self-confident, and feeling afraid were the most common emotional consequences of the harassment. Both girls and boys experienced the consequences of harassment, although the impact was greater for the girls. Almost all students (96%) said they knew what sexual harassment is; the definitions given by boys and girls did not differ substantially.

Among students, sexual harassment occurs most often when boys are in groups. Their motives may be designed to heighten their group status by denigrating girls—rather than based on any specific animosity toward a particular girl. Harassment is usually either ignored by adults or regarded as normal or typical behavior among boys—"boys will be boys." Girls are frequently blamed for the harassment because they do not "stand up for themselves" or they take the incidents "too seriously" (Herbert, 1989).

Harassment in College   Sexual harassment on college and university campuses has become a major concern in recent years. In 2005, the American Association of University Women (AAUW) (2006) conducted the most comprehensive survey to date of sexual harassment on college campuses. The online survey of 2,036 undergraduates aged 18–24 included students enrolled in public and private two-year and four-year colleges. Sixty-two percent of female students and 61% of male students reported that they had been verbally or physically sexually harassed while in college. The students reported several types of harassment (see Figure 17.1); sexual comments and jokes were the most common. Among female students who experienced sexual harassment, one third said they felt afraid and one fifth indicated they were disappointed in their college experience because of the sexual harassment. Although more than two thirds of the female students and more than one third of the male students who had experienced sexual harassment felt very or somewhat upset by it, only 7% reported the incident to a faculty member or other college employee. Slightly more than one half of the women surveyed and about one third of the women reported they had sexually harassed someone, largely because they thought it was funny. Lesbian, gay, bisexual, and transgender (LGBT) students (73%) experienced more sexual harassment than heterosexual students (61%) and were harassed more often (18% vs. 7%).

Two major problems in dealing with issues of sexual harassment in college are gender differences in levels of tolerance and attribution of blame. Women

● FIGURE 17.1

Types of Sexual Harassment Experienced by College Students. The figures are based on a 2005 survey of college undergraduates in the United States. (*Source: From Drawing the Line: Sexual Harassment on Campus* (2005) with permission from the AAUW Educational Foundation.)

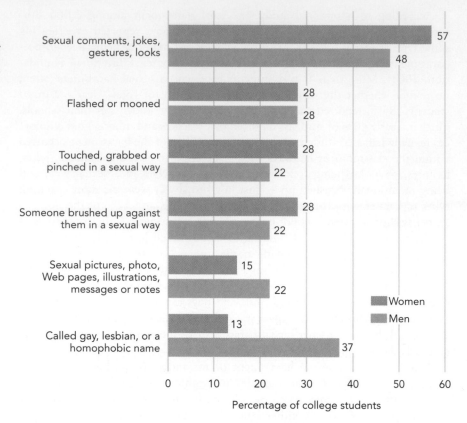

are often blamed for not taking a "compliment" and for provoking unwanted sexual attention by what they wear or how they look. These attitudes are widely held, especially among men.

Because of sexual harassment, many students, especially women students, find it difficult to study; others worry about their grades. If the harasser is an instructor controlling grades, students fear reporting the harassment. They may use strategies such as avoiding courses taught by the harasser or choosing another advisor. In extreme cases, the emotional consequences may be as severe as for rape victims. However, many students view the dating of students by professors as unethical behavior rather than harassment (Quatrella & Wentworth, 1995).

Most universities and colleges have developed sexual harassment policies, most of which prohibit romantic/sexual relationships between students and professors. A fundamental principle of these policies is that the student-professor relationship cannot be truly consensual given the professor's considerable power over the student's academic standing and career plans. Although such policies help make students aware of harassment issues, their effectiveness depends on educating students about what constitutes harassment. The AAUW (2006) states that sexual harassment is disruptive to the college experience, shaping the behaviors that students will take with them into their work careers and into the broader society. Further, the AAUW contends, "A campus environment that encourages—even tolerates—inappropriate verbal and physical contact and that discourages reporting these behaviors undermines the emotional, intellectual and professional growth of millions of young adults." The AAUW continues to note in their research that sexual harassment on the college campus takes a particularly heavy toll on women students, making it more difficult to acquire the education they need for themselves and any future family.

Harassment in the Workplace

Issues of sexual harassment are complicated in the workplace because the work setting, like college, is one of the most important places where adults meet potential partners. As a consequence, sexual undercurrents or interactions often take place. Flirtations, romances, and "affairs" are common in the work environment. The line between flirtation and harassment can be problematic—especially for men. Many women do not realize they were being harassed until much later. When they identify the behavior, they report feeling naive or gullible, as well as guilty and ashamed. As they learn more about sexual harassment, they are able to identify their experiences for what they were—harassment (Kidder, Lafleur, & Wells, 1995).

According to an Employment Law Alliance (ELA) survey of 1,000 American workers in 2000, 21% of the women had been sexually harassed at work, in contrast to 7% of the men (Hirschfeld, 2002). The study also focused on romantic relationships at work, a potential sexual harassment issue. Twenty percent indicated they knew of a romantic relationship between a supervisor and a subordinate at work, and nearly two thirds said that romantic relationships at work caused favoritism and poor morale. Over one half said employees were likely to be retaliated against if they rejected romantic relationships with their supervisors. Another ELA survey of 826 employees found that 7% indicated that they had been involved in a romantic relationship with a supervisor or subordinate and 43% noted that they believed it hurt productivity (Hirschfeld, 2004). Stephen Hirschfeld (2004), CEO of the ELA, notes that more corporations are developing directives that impose bans on workplace romantic relationships even if the relationships are consensual; Hirschfeld cautions corporations not to go overboard in their zeal to create a secure workplace and inadvertently infringe upon an employee's civil liberties.

A study of sexual harassment in federal offices found that 44% of women and 19% of men had experienced some form of unwanted sexual attention during the preceding 2 years (U.S. Merit Systems Protection Board, 1995). Sexual remarks, jokes and teasing, sexual looks and gestures, deliberate touching and cornering, and pressuring for dates were the most common forms of sexual harassment experienced. For many of the survey respondents, the unwanted attention they experienced lasted a month or more.

Sexual harassment tends to be most pervasive in formerly all-male occupations, in which sexual harassment is a means of exerting control over women and asserting male dominance. Such male bastions as the building trades, the trucking industry, law enforcement, and the military have been especially resistant to the presence of women. For example, the U.S. Department of Veterans Affairs found that 22% of women and 1% of men had suffered sexual trauma, which includes assault and harassment, in the military (Kaye & Estrada, 2008).

Sexual harassment can be perpetrated by both fellow employees and supervisors. Recognizing this, the U.S. Supreme Court ruled that employers are liable for their supervisors' behavior even if the companies were unaware of their actions (Sward, 1998). Although most sexual harassment situations involve men harassing women, men can be the victims of harassment, from either a woman or another man. The U.S. Supreme Court has ruled that a man can file legal action against another man for sexual harassment (Solomon, 1998).

Sexual harassment can have a variety of consequences for the victim, including depression, anxiety, shame, humiliation, and anger, as will be discussed later in the chapter.

● Harassment and Discrimination Against Gay, Lesbian, Bisexual, and Transgender People

Researchers have identified two forms of discrimination or bias based on sexual orientation: heterosexual bias and anti-gay prejudice.

Heterosexual Bias

Heterosexual bias, also known as **heterosexism** and widely (and silently) accepted in society, media, and the family, involves the tendency to see the world in heterosexual terms and to ignore or devalue homosexuality (Griffin, 1998; Herek, Kimmel, Amaro, & Melton, 1991). Heterosexual bias may take many forms. Examples of this type of bias include the following:

Click on "Learning to Be Straight" to hear students discussing heterosexual bias and privilege.

- *Ignoring the existence of lesbian, gay, bisexual, and transgender people.* Discussions of various aspects of human sexuality may ignore gay, lesbian, bisexual, and transgender people, assuming that such individuals do not exist, are not significant, or are not worthy of inclusion. Without such inclusion, discussions of human sexuality are really discussions of *heterosexual* sexuality.

- *Segregating gay, lesbian, bisexual, and transgender people from heterosexual people.* When sexual orientation is irrelevant, separating certain groups from others is a form of segregation, as in proposals to separate HIV-positive gay men (but not other HIV-positive individuals) from the general population.

- *Subsuming gay, lesbian, bisexual, and transgender people into a larger category.* Sometimes, it is appropriate to make sexual orientation a category in data analysis, as in studies of adolescent suicide rates. If orientation is not included, findings may be distorted (Herek et al., 1991).

Prejudice, Discrimination, and Violence

Anti-gay prejudice is a strong dislike, fear, or hatred of gay, lesbian, bisexual, and transgender people because of their sexual orientation. **Homophobia** is an irrational or phobic fear of gay, lesbian, bisexual, and transgender people. Not all anti-gay feelings are phobic in the clinical sense of being excessive and irrational, but they may be unreasonable or biased. The feelings may, however, be within the norms of a biased culture.

As a belief system, anti-gay prejudice justifies discrimination based on sexual orientation. Gay, lesbian, bisexual, and transgender people are discriminated against in terms of housing, employment opportunities, adoption, parental rights, family acceptance, and so on. And they are the victims of violence, known as **gay-bashing** or **queer-bashing.**

The level of anti-gay prejudice experienced by gay men, lesbian women, and bisexual individuals was revealed in a 2000 telephone interview survey of 405 randomly selected adults, aged 18 years and older in 15 major U.S. metropolitan areas (Kaiser Family Foundation, n.d). Thirty-four percent of the respondents said that their family or a family member had refused to accept them because of their sexual orientation, with lesbian women (50%) being accepted less than gay men (32%) or bisexual individuals (26%). Seventy-four percent reported having experienced prejudice and discrimination based on their sexual orientation, with lesbian women (85%) having experienced more discrimination than gay men (76%) and bisexual individuals (60%). And 74% reported having been the target of verbal abuse, such as slurs or name-calling, because of their sexual orientation.

Several colleges have reported a form of discrimination called **"biophobia,"** in which some bisexual students, feeling shunned by support groups for gay and lesbian students, are forming their own organizations (Morgan, 2002). Bisexual students have said that many of the student groups set up as havens for gay, lesbian, bisexual, and transgender students have "succumbed to the very kinds of intolerance and discrimination that they were chartered to fight" in their antipathy toward those who identify as bisexual. Typical criticisms of bisexual students are that they are confused about their sexual identity, that they are "riding the fence," and that by being bisexual they have access to "heterosexual privilege." Apparently, many bisexual students have been disappointed at not getting the support from the gay-student groups that they anticipated.

Effects on Heterosexuals   Anti-gay prejudice adversely affects both heterosexuals and gay, lesbian, bisexual, and transgender people. First, it creates fear and hatred, negative emotions that cause distress and anxiety. Second, it alienates heterosexuals from their gay family members, friends, neighbors, and coworkers. Third, it limits their range of behaviors and feelings, such as hugging or being emotionally intimate with same-sex friends, for fear that such intimacy may be perceived as "homosexual." Fourth, among men, it may lead to exaggerated displays of masculinity to prove that one is not gay.

Discrimination and Antidiscrimination Laws   As mentioned, gay, lesbian, bisexual, and transgender people are discriminated against in many areas and experience high levels of stress as a result. For example, the efforts of medical and public health personnel to combat HIV/AIDS were inhibited initially because AIDS was perceived as the "gay plague" and was considered by some to be justified "punishment" of gay men for their "unnatural" sexual practices (Altman, 1985). The fear of HIV/AIDS has contributed to increased anti-gay prejudice among some heterosexuals. Anti-gay prejudice influences parental reactions to their gay and lesbian children, often leading to estrangement.

While public opinion overwhelmingly supports equal employment opportunities for homosexual individuals, gay men and lesbian women have been seeking legislation to protect themselves from discrimination based on their sexual orientation. For example, the Civil Rights Act of 1964 protects employees from being sexually harassed in the workplace by people of the same sex as well as by the other sex (U.S. Equal Employment Opportunity Commission, 2008a). Such legislation guarantees lesbian women and gay men equal protection under the law.

Violence Against Gay Men and Lesbian Women   Violence against gay men and lesbian women has a long history. At times, such violence has been

During the Middle Ages, gay men (called sodomites) were burned at the stake as heretics (above left). In Germany in 1933, the Nazis burned Magnus Hirschfeld's library and forced him to flee the country (above right). Gay men and lesbian women were among the first Germans the Nazis forced into concentration camps, where over 50,000 of them were killed. Today, violence against gay men and lesbian women, known as gay-bashing, continues (right). The pink triangle recalls the symbol the Nazis required lesbian women and gay men to wear, just as they required Jews to wear the Star of David.

think
about it

Public Opinion About Gay and Lesbian Rights and Issues

The American public has ambivalent opinions about most issues concerning gay men and lesbian women. The results of two recent national opinion polls are highlighted here. Subsequent polls may reveal changes in public opinion as issues related to gay/lesbian rights, such as the legalization of same-sex marriage, become even more important on the political agenda.

The Gallup Poll has conducted research on the public opinions related to homosexual individuals and gay rights for the past quarter century and continues to periodically conduct surveys on this issue. Going to the Web site (Gallup.com) is a great way to find out the latest results of the American public's opinion on gay men and lesbian women's rights and issues.

Gallup's 2008 Values and Beliefs Poll

More than 1,000 adults nationally (1,107), aged 18 and older, were interviewed by telephone in May 2008 (Gallup Poll, 2008). Here is what the poll found regarding five important topics concerning issues related to gay men and lesbian women (using the poll's terminology). Results were also compared to prior surveys.

- Opinions about the morality of homosexual relations were evenly divided: 48% considering the behavior morally acceptable and 48% saying it is morally wrong. In 2001, 40% indicated that homosexual relations were morally acceptable, with 53% indicating the behavior was morally wrong.

- 55% believed that homosexual relations between consenting adults should be legal, with 40% indicating it should not be legal. Support for the legality of homosexual relations has advanced and receded over the years (beginning with 43% in support in 1977 and 50% in July 2003, shortly after the U.S. Supreme Court struck down the Texas sodomy law [see Chapter 18]).

- 57% indicated that homosexuality should be considered an acceptable alternative lifestyle, with 40% disagreeing. In 1983, 34% indicated it was acceptable and 51% indicated it was not acceptable.

- 89% believed that homosexuals should have equal rights to job opportunities, with 8% not agreeing. Support for this issue has steadily increased to being nearly universal since 1978, when only 56% agreed.

- 40% indicated that marriages between same-sex couples should be recognized as valid by the law, with the same rights as traditional marriage, and 56% believed such marriages should not be valid. Support of this issue has

changed from 27% and 68%, respectively, from 1997, but opinions have changed little since 2004.

From the survey results, the Gallup Poll stated that, since 2001, Americans have generally become more supportive of gay rights. The poll also noted that:

> Americans have shifted from frowning on homosexuality as an alternative lifestyle and being divided over whether it should be legal to now supporting gay rights on both fronts. At the same time, the country remains highly ambivalent about the morality of homosexual relations, and as a result, support for legalizing gay marriage lags far behind the less culturally sensitive matters of gays having equal job rights.

USA Today/Gallup Poll

After same-sex marriage was approved in California (but later overturned; see Chapter 18), a 2008 USA Today/Gallup Poll found that 6 in 10 adult Americans (63%) indicated that same-sex marriage is "strictly a private decision" between the two people (Grossman, 2008). A majority of respondents at every level of education and income indicated this belief, although more of those of younger age (18 to 29 years) did so. Commenting on the results, Mark Rozell, professor of public policy at George Mason University said that "After Massachusetts [legalized same-sex marriage in 2003], the public has seen that the decision there has not affected people's lives as much as was feared" (quoted in Grossman, 2008).

> ### Think Critically
> - What is your opinion about the issues addressed in the two polls?
> - Does your opinion seem to be similar to that of most of your friends or family?
> - Have your opinions of these issues changed over time? If so, what changed them?
> - Should the results of opinion polls be used in shaping public policy concerning gay men and lesbian women?

SOURCES: Gallup Poll. (2008). Americans divided on morality of homosexuality. Available: http://www.gallup.com/poll/108115/Americans-Evenly-Divided-Morality-Homosexuality (Last visited: 7/29/08); Grossman, C. L. (2008). Most say gay marriage private choice. Available: http://usatoday/printthis.clickability.com/pt/cpt?action-cpt+tile=Most+say+gay+marriage (Last visited: 7/29/08).

sanctioned by religious institutions. During the Middle Ages, leaders of the religious court called the Inquisition condemned "sodomites" to death by burning. In the sixteenth century, England's King Henry VIII made sodomy punishable by death. In our own times, homosexuals were among the first victims of the Nazis, who killed 50,000 in concentration camps. Because of worldwide violence and persecution against lesbian women and gay men, the Netherlands, Germany, and Canada in 1992 granted asylum to men and women based on their homosexuality (Farnsworth, 1992).

Today, gay men and lesbian women are increasingly targets of violence. A 2000 survey of 405 individuals in 15 major U.S. metropolitan areas found that 32% said they had been the target of physical violence against either them or their property, because, some believed, they were a gay, lesbian, or bisexual person (Kaiser Family Foundation, n.d.). In 2007, 2,430 violent incidents involving gay, lesbian, transgender, or bisexual people were reported, representing a 24% increase over the total number of victims reported in 2006. Further, 21 murders related to sexual orientation were reported in 2007 (National Coalition of Anti-Violence Programs, 2008). Besides murder, the incidents included sexual assault/rape, robbery, vandalism, assault/attempted assault, intimidation, and verbal harassment. The brutal murder of Matthew Shepard, a gay University of Wyoming student, in 1998; the beating and strangulation of Gwen Araujo, a 17-year-old transsexual female, in 2002; and the fatal classroom shooting of 15-year-old Lawrence King, who identified as gay, in 2008, are three murders that have received national media attention. A federal bill called The Matthew Shepard Act has been proposed that would expand the federal hate crime law to include crimes motivated by a victim's actual or perceived gender, sexual orientation, or gender identity. This bill has yet to be passed at the printing of this edition of this textbook. A May 2007 Gallup Poll found that 68% of Americans favored this expansion of the law (Gallup Poll, 2007).

Personal Sources of Anti-Gay Prejudice Anti-gay prejudice in people may come from several sources (Marmor, 1980a): (1) a deeply rooted insecurity concerning a person's own sexuality and gender identity, (2) a strong fundamentalist religious orientation, and (3) simple ignorance concerning homosexuality. The literature also indicates fairly consistent gender differences in attitudes toward lesbian women and gay men (Herek, 1984). Heterosexuals tend to have more negative attitudes toward homosexual individuals of their own sex than toward those of the other sex. Heterosexual men tend to be less tolerant of gay men and lesbian women than heterosexual women are (Burn, 2000; Whitley & Kite, 1995).

Ending Anti-Gay Prejudice

As of January 2008, 32 states and the District of Columbia have a law that addresses hate crimes based on sexual orientation, and 12 states and the District of Columbia have a law that addresses hate crimes motivated by sexual orientation or gender identity (Human Rights Foundation, 2008) (see Figure 17.2). Although legislation to prohibit discrimination is important for ending prejudice, education and positive social interactions are also important vehicles for change.

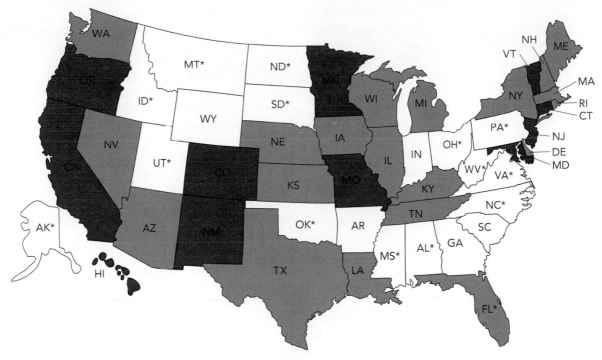

All but five states (Arkansas, Georgia, Indiana, South Carolina, and Wyoming) have laws addressing the scourge of hate crimes, but there is variation in the list of protected classes. The laws that address hate or bias crimes against GLBT people are as follows:

■ States that have a law that addresses hate or bias crimes based on sexual orientation and gender identity. (12 states and D.C.)

■ States that have a law that addresses hate or bias crimes based on sexual orientation. (32 states and D.C.)

*Laws lack GLBT inclusion:
States that have a law that addresses hate or bias crimes based, but do not address sexual orientation or gender identity. (13 states)

● **FIGURE 17.2**
States With Hate Crime Laws Protecting People Based on Sexual Orientation and Gender Identity, 2008. (*Source:* © 2009 The Human Rights Campaign Foundation. Reprinted by permission.)

● Sexual Aggression

In recent years, we have increasingly expanded our knowledge about sexually aggressive behavior and its consequences. We have expanded our focus beyond stranger rape and examined the consequences of sexually aggressive behavior on survivors. Earlier, researchers had focused primarily on **rape,** usually defined as penile-vaginal penetration performed against a *woman's* will through the use or threat of force. They assumed that rape was committed by strangers for the purpose of sexual gratification. In their work, researchers generally examined the sexual psychopathology of male offenders and the characteristics of women that "precipitated" rapes, such as acting docile, living alone, and dressing in a certain way (White & Farmer, 1992).

In the 1970s, feminists challenged the belief that rape is a form of sexual deviance. Instead, they argued, rape is an act of violence and aggression against women, and the principal motive is power, not sexual gratification (Brownmiller, 1975). As a result of feminist influence, the focus of research shifted.

Contemporary research now views rape as a category of sexual aggression. **Sexual aggression** refers to sexual activity, including petting, oral-genital sex, anal intercourse, and penile-vaginal intercourse, performed against a *person's* will through the use of force, argument, pressure, alcohol or drugs, or authority. Sexual aggression includes both women *and* men as victims. It also includes gay men and lesbian women, who traditionally had been excluded from such research because of rape's heterosexual definition (Muehlenhard et al., 1992). **Sexual coercion** is a broader term than "rape" or "sexual aggression." It includes arguing, pleading, and cajoling, as well as force and the threat of force. **Sexual assault** is a term used by the criminal justice system to describe forced sexual contact that does not necessarily include penile-vaginal intercourse, and so does not meet the legal definition of rape. Thus, for example, individuals could be prosecuted for engaging in forced anal intercourse or for forcing an object into the anus.

The Nature and Incidence of Rape

Rape is a means of achieving power or expressing anger and hatred. Rape *forces* its victim (the less pejorative term, "survivor," is preferred by many health professionals) into an intimate physical encounter with the rapist against her or his will. The survivor does not experience pleasure; she or he experiences terror. In most cases, the survivor is a woman; sometimes, the survivor is a man. In most cases, however, the assailant is a man. The weapon in rape is the penis (which may be supplemented by a knife or a gun); the penis is used to attack, subordinate, and humiliate the victim. History reveals that rape occurs more frequently when women are devalued and the negative outcomes of rape are perceived to be low by the assailant (Lalumiere, Harris, Quinsey, & Rice, 2005).

Rape is not only a specific behavior but also a threat. As small girls, women are warned against taking candy from strangers, walking alone down dark streets, and leaving doors and windows unlocked. Men may fear assault, but women fear assault *and* rape. As a result, many women live with the possibility of being raped as a part of their consciousness. Rape and the fear of rape are facts of life for women; this is not true for men.

The actual prevalence rates of rape in the United States are unknown, because most survivors do not report the crime. According to the Rape, Abuse, and Incest National Network (2008a), someone in the United States is sexually assaulted every 2 minutes. The U.S. Justice Department's National Crime Victimization Survey (NCVS) (2007) states that the total number of reported rapes/sexual assaults of persons aged 12 and older was 272,350 in 2006. Since 1993, rape/sexual assault has dropped by nearly 70% (U.S. Department of Justice, 2006). (The NCVS defines rape as "forced sexual intercourse including both psychological coercion as well as physical force. Forced sexual intercourse means penetration by the offender[s]. Includes attempted rapes, males as well as female victims, and both heterosexual and homosexual rape. Attempted rape includes verbal threats of rape.") This decrease also reflects an overall downward trend in criminal victimization that began in 1994. The 2005 NCVS (2006) found that 92% of the sexual crime survivors were female; for every 1,000 women aged 12 and older, 1.4 were raped or sexually assaulted, as opposed to 0.1 per 1,000 men. The rate of rapes/sexual assaults for 2005 was three times greater among Blacks (1.8 per 1,000) than for Whites (0.6 per 1,000), and 73% of female survivors knew their assailant (see Figure 17.3) whereas virtually none of the male survivors knew their assailant.

> The fear of sexual assault is a special fear; its intensity in women can best be likened to the male fear of castration.
>
> —Germaine Greer
> (1939–)

Click on "Behind Closed Doors" to hear campus activists talk about factors that lead to rape.

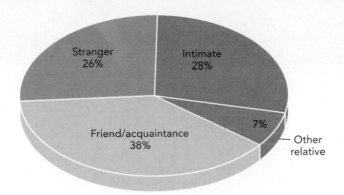

● **FIGURE 17.3**

Type of Relationship With Offender of Female Survivors of Rape and Sexual Assault.
(*Source:* Data from U.S. Department of Justice, 2006.)

Stranger
26%

Intimate
28%

Friend/acquaintance
38%

7%

Other relative

A large-scale survey reported that 1.3% of the male respondents and nearly 22% of the females had been forced to have sex by a man. At the same time, only 2.8% of the men in the survey reported forcing a woman to have sex (Laumann, Gagnon, Michael, & Michaels, 1994). A *Details* magazine study of college students found that 29% of the females and 11% of the males had ever had a date, sexual partner, or friend physically force them into unwanted sexual behavior (Elliott & Brantley, 1997). The Centers for Disease Control and Prevention (CDC) found that nationwide 11% of female students and 5% of male students in grades 9–12 had ever been forced to have sexual intercourse when they did not want to (CDC, 2008hh). A nationally representative telephone survey of 8,000 women and 8,000 men about their experiences with rape and other violence was cosponsored by the National Institute of Justice and the CDC (Tjaden & Thoennes, 1998). Using a definition of rape that included forced vaginal, oral, or anal intercourse, the survey found that 1 in 6 women and 1 in 33 men had experienced an attempted or completed rape as a child and/or as an adult. The study found that rape is primarily a crime against youths: More than half (54%) of the surveyed female rape survivors were under 18 years old when they experienced their first rape (22% were under 12 years old when they experienced their first rape).

A community study comparing Latino and Anglo rape rates found a significantly lower incidence among Latinos. The researchers speculate that the lower rate may be attributed to machismo, which requires Latino men to be protective of women (Sorenson & Siegel, 1992). The lower rate, however, may also be attributed to Latinas' greater reluctance to report rape because of the strong emphasis on female virginity and purity in Latino culture. The National Violence Against Women Survey found that Hispanics/Latinas were less likely to report rape victimization than non-Latinas (Tjaden & Thoennes, 1998).

Myths About Rape

Our society has a number of myths about rape, which serve to encourage rather than discourage it. According to one myth, women are to blame for their own rapes, as if they somehow "deserved" them or were responsible for them. In fact, in a large national sample, two thirds of the women who were raped worried that they might be blamed for their assaults (National Victim Center and Crime Victims Research and Treatment Center [NVC], 1992).

Preventing Sexual Assault

There are no guaranteed ways to prevent sexual assault or coercion. Each situation, assailant, and targeted woman or man is different. But rape education courses may be effective in reducing the rape myths that provide support for sexual aggression.

To reduce the risk of date rape, consider these guidelines:

1. When dating someone for the first time, even if you have established a relationship over the Internet, go to a public place such as a restaurant, movie, or sports event.

2. Share expenses. A common scenario is a date expecting you to exchange sex for his or her paying for dinner, the movie, drinks, and so on.

3. Avoid using drugs or alcohol if you do not want to be sexual with your date. Such use is associated with date rape.

4. Avoid ambiguous verbal or nonverbal behavior, particularly any behavior that might be interpreted as "teasing." Make sure your verbal and nonverbal messages are identical. If you only want to cuddle or kiss, for example, tell your partner that those are your limits. Tell him or her that if you say no you mean no. If necessary, reinforce your statement emphatically, both verbally and physically (by pushing him or her away).

5. If your date becomes sexually coercive despite your direct communication, consider physical denials such as pushing, slapping, and kicking.

To reduce the risk of stranger rape, consider the following guidelines. But try to avoid becoming overly vigilant; use reasonable judgment. Do not let fear control your life.

1. Do not identify yourself as a person living alone, especially if you are a woman. Use initials on the mailbox and in the telephone directory.

2. Don't open your door to strangers; keep your house and car doors locked. Have your keys ready when you approach your car or house. Look in the back seat before getting into your car.

3. Avoid dark and isolated areas. Carry a whistle or airhorn, and take a cell phone when you are out by yourself. Let people know where you are going.

4. If someone approaches you threateningly, turn and run. If you can't run, resist. Studies indicate that resisting an attack by shouting, causing a scene, or fighting back can deter the assailant. Fighting and screaming may reduce the level of the abuse without increasing the level of physical injury. Most women who are injured during a rape appear to have been injured *before* resisting (Ullman & Knight, 1991). Trust your intuitions, whatever approach you take.

5. Be alert to possible ways to escape. Talking with an assailant may give you time to find an escape route.

6. Take self-defense training. It will raise your level of confidence and your fighting abilities. You may be able to scare off the assailant, or you may create an opportunity to escape. Many women take self-defense training following an incidence of sexual aggression to reaffirm their sense of control.

If you are sexually assaulted (or the survivor of an attempted assault), report the assault as soon as possible. You are probably not the assailant's first victim. As much as you might want to, do not change clothes or shower. Semen and hair or other materials on your body or clothing may be very important in arresting and convicting a rapist. You may also want to contact a rape crisis center; its staff members are knowledgeable about dealing with the police and the traumatic aftermath of rape. But most importantly, remember that you are not at fault. The rapist is the only one to blame.

Belief in rape myths is part of a larger belief structure that includes gender-role stereotypes, sexual conservatism, acceptance of interpersonal violence, and the belief that men are different from women. Men are more likely than women to believe rape myths (Kalof & Wade, 1995). Sex researchers Sandra Byers and Raymond Eno (1991) found that acceptance of rape-supportive myths among college men is associated with the use of physical force, verbal coercion, and belief in "uncontrollable physical arousal."

Ethnicity and gender also appear to influence the acceptance of rape myths. One study found that White and African American women are less likely than men of either group to accept rape myths, interpersonal violence, gender-role stereotyping, and adversarial relationships. Furthermore, African

American women's attitudes toward these behaviors and beliefs are significantly less traditional than those of White women (Kalof & Wade, 1995). Another study showed that Latino and White women are less accepting of rape myths and show more empathy toward individuals raped than their male counterparts (Jimenez & Abreu, 2003).

The following list of 11 common rape myths can clarify misunderstandings about rape:

- *Myth 1: Rape is a crime of passion.* Rape is an act of violence and aggression and is often a life-threatening experience. While sexual attraction may be one component, power, anger, and control are the dominant factors resulting in gratification. Actually, most rapists have access to other, willing sexual partners but choose to rape (University of Minnesota, 2005).

- *Myth 2: Women want to be raped.* It is popularly believed that women have an unconscious wish to be raped. Also, some people believe that many women mean "yes" when they say "no." This myth supports the misconception that a woman enjoys being raped because she sexually "surrenders," and it perpetuates the belief that rape is a sexual behavior rather than a violent one.

- *Myth 3: Women ask for it.* Many people believe that women "ask for it" by their behavior. One study found that provocative dress on the part of the victim of a date rape resulted in a greater perception that the victim was responsible and that the rape was justified (Cassidy & Hurrell, 1995). Despite some attempts to reform rape laws, women continue to bear the burden of proof in these cases. No one, female or male, ever deserves to be raped, and regardless of what a person says, does, or wears, she or he does not cause the rape. Actually, most rapes are premeditated and planned by the perpetrator. Opportunity is the critical factor in determining when a rapist will rape (University of Minnesota, 2005).

- *Myth 4: Women are raped only by strangers.* Women are warned to avoid or distrust strangers as a way to avoid rape; such advice, however, isolates them from normal social interactions. Furthermore, studies indicate that 73% of all rapes of women are committed by nonstrangers such as acquaintances, friends, dates, partners, husbands, or relatives (U.S. Department of Justice, 2006).

- *Myth 5: Women could avoid rape if they really wanted to.* This myth reinforces the stereotype that women "really" want to be raped or that they should curtail their activities. Women are often warned not to be out after dark alone. Approximately two thirds of rapes/sexual assaults occur between 6 P.M. and 6 A.M., but nearly 6 out of 10 occur at the victim's home or the home of a friend, relative, or neighbor (Greenfeld, 1997). Women are also approached at work, on their way to or from work, or at their place of worship, or they are kidnapped from shopping centers or parking lots at midday. Restricting women's activities does not seem to have an appreciable impact on rape. Men are often physically larger and stronger than women, making it difficult for women to resist. Sometimes, weapons are used and physical violence occurs or is threatened. And assailants catch their victims "off guard" because they choose the time and place of attack.

- *Myth 6: Women cry rape for revenge.* This myth suggests that women who are "dumped" by men accuse them of rape as a means of revenge. FBI crime statistics show that only about 2% of rape reports are false;

Just because a woman is dressed provocatively does not mean she is inviting rape.

think
about it

Adult Female Sexual Abuse of Male Children and Teens

Although most people think of child sexual abuse as a female child victim and an adult male offender, adult female sexual contact with young boys is actually fairly common. The U.S. Department of Justice (2002) reports that in the United States in 2001, 1.2% of those charged with forcible rape and 8% charged with sexual offenses were female. Studies of sexual contact between young boys and adult women are not common. But a study of almost 1,600 male and female college students and prison inmates revealed that 16% of male college students and 46% of male prison inmates had sexual contacts with women when they were 12 years old or younger and the women were in their 20s.

There are no data on whether more adult women are sexually abusing children now than in the past. Like all types of sexual assaults, most of these assaults are not reported. However, the number of women arrested for having sex with young boys, mostly teenagers, has seemingly increased—certainly there appears to be more media attention on courtroom cases of these crimes that many people are now starting to consider as heinous as abuse of girls. The traditional view that these young male victims were willing, and even lucky, is eroding. One widely covered case was that of Mary Kay Letourneau, who, when she was a 34-year-old grade-school teacher, had a sexual relationship in the summer of 1996 with a former sixth-grade student of hers when he was 13 years old. They had two children in the late 1990s and married in 2005 (Koch, 2005).

Historically, there has been a negation of women as potential sexual aggressors. Criminologist Myriam Denov (2003) states that "traditional sexual scripts, particularly the perception of females as sexually passive, harmless, and innocent, appear not only to have influenced broader societal views concerning sexuality and sexual abuse but also to have permeated the criminal law, victim reporting practices, and professional responses to female sex offending." Denov also notes that implicit denial of sexual aggression by women contributes to under-recognition of the problem.

Richard Gartner (cited in Koch, 2005), New York psychologist and author of *Betrayed Boys*, notes that since boys are scripted to take sex when it is offered, many have difficulty believing that they are victims. Though young boys may be easily sexually aroused, they are also emotionally immature and often uncomfortable. Gartner states that as adults boy survivors have difficulty developing age-appropriate relationships and are more likely to suffer depression, anxiety, and drug addiction.

Female sexual abuse of male children and boys differs from male sexual abuse of female children in that intercourse is less common. Teen boys are less likely to have sex with older women than teen girls with older men, and women offenders usually focus on one child and experience a falling-in-love courtship (Shoop, cited in Koch, 2005).

Think Critically

- Do you think that adult female sexual abuse of young males is an unrecognized problem?
- Do you think that a teen boy who is sexually assaulted by an adult female is "lucky" or an unfortunate victim?
- Would it be harder for a teen boy to report the crime to the police than it would be for a teen girl? Why or why not?

---

this rate is lower than the rate for most other crimes. False reporting is unlikely because of the many obstacles women face before an assailant is brought to trial and convicted.

- *Myth 7: Rapists are crazy or psychotic.* Very few men who rape are clinically psychotic. The vast majority are psychologically indistinguishable from other men, except that rapists appear to have more difficulty handling feelings of hostility and are more likely to express their anger through violence. Studies on date rape find that rapists differ from nonrapists primarily in a greater hostility toward women, acceptance of traditional gender roles, and greater willingness to use force (Cate & Lloyd, 1992).

- *Myth 8: Most rapists are a different race than their victims.* Most rapists and their victims are members of the same ethnic group.
- *Myth 9: Men cannot control their sexual urges.* This myth is based on the belief that men, when subjected to sexual stimuli, cannot control their sexual feelings. This also implies that women have some responsibility for rape by provoking this "uncontrollable" sexuality of men through their attire or appearance (Cowan, 2000). Men, like women, can learn to appropriately and responsibly express their sexuality.
- *Myth 10: Rape is "no big deal."* About 1 in 3 women who are injured during rape or physical assault require medical care. Rape victims can also experience negative mental health outcomes and are more likely to engage in harmful behaviors to cope with the trauma, such as drinking, smoking, or using drugs.
- *Myth 11: Men cannot be raped.* Men can be victims of sexual violence from either men or women. This issue is discussed in more detail later in this section.

Forms of Rape

Rapists may be dates, acquaintances, partners, husbands, fathers, or other family members, as well as strangers.

Date Rape The most common form of rape is sexual intercourse with a dating partner that occurs against the victim's will, with force or the threat of force. It is known as **date rape.** Sometimes, the term **acquaintance rape** has been used interchangeably with the term "date rape." However, Rana Sampson (2003), an expert on crime control, says that they are different. That is, most acquaintance rapes do not happen during a date; they occur when two people just happen to be in the same place. Thus "date rape" is not the appropriate term to describe the acquaintance rapes of college women as date rapes account for only 13% of college rapes (Fisher, Cullen, & Turner, 2000). Because some of the rape literature uses the terms "date rape" and "acquaintance rape" interchangeably, the discussion often does not differentiate these two types of rape and may actually be talking about one or both. Actually, some of the following discussion about date rape may also be applicable to acquaintance rape; however, we discuss some of the specific aspects of acquaintance rape among college students in a later section.

One study found that women are more likely than men to define date rape as a crime. Men are less likely than women to agree that the assailant should have stopped when the woman asked him to. Disturbingly, respondents considered date rape less serious when the woman was African American (Foley, Evancic, Karnik, & King, 1995).

Date rapes are usually not planned. Two researchers (Bechhofer & Parrot, 1991) describe a typical date rape:

> He plans the evening with the intent of sex, but if the date does not progress as planned and his date does not comply, he becomes angry and takes what he feels is his right—sex. Afterward, the victim feels raped while the assailant believes that he has done nothing wrong. He may even ask the woman out on another date.

Alcohol and/or drugs are often involved in date rapes (see the box "Date/Acquaintance Rape Drugs: An Increasing Threat"). Men who believe in rape

*Undismayed, he plucks the rose
In the hedgerow blooming.
Vainly she laments her woes,
Vainly doth her thorns oppose,
Gone her sweet perfuming.*

—German art song

Confusion over whether consent for sex has been given may lead to a strong disagreement between partners.

myths are more likely to see alcohol consumption as a sign that females are sexually available (Abbey & Harnish, 1995).

To draw attention to the date rape problem and other sexual coercions by men, many college campuses have held "Take Back the Night" rallies, at which survivors of school assault share their stories and offer support for other survivors. Also, many colleges provide extensive prevention education on rape, as well as escort services for participants in late-night activities on campus.

Incidence   Lifetime experience of date rape ranges from 13% to 27% for women, according to various studies (Rickert & Wiemann, 1998). If the definition is expanded to include attempted intercourse as a result of verbal pressure or the misuse of authority, then women's lifetime incidence increases significantly. Among college students, the most likely assailant is a peer (Bridgeland, Duane, & Stewart, 1995).

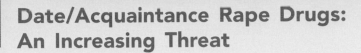

think
about it

Date/Acquaintance Rape Drugs: An Increasing Threat

So-called date rape drugs have become an increasing threat, particularly for young people. These drugs are placed in beverages so that the person consuming the drink will be incapacitated, thus compromising his or her ability to give consent and increasing the person's vulnerability to sexual contact. They also can minimize the resistance and memory of the victim. Although described commonly as "date rape" drugs, the drugs are not only used during dates but also by acquaintances; hence, the more accurate term is "date/acquaintance rape drugs." The drugs are also sometimes used during gang rapes.

Drugging an unwilling or unknowing person is a crime. In 1996, the Drug-Induced Rape Prevention and Punishment Act was passed, making it a felony to distribute controlled substances, such as those classified as date/acquaintance rape drugs, to someone without that person's knowledge and with the intent to commit violence, including rape, against that person (Woodworth, 1996).

Briefly, here are some of the major date/acquaintance rape drugs (Rape, Abuse and Incest National Network, 2008b):

- *Alcohol.* Although many people may not think of alcohol as a date/acquaintance drug, alcohol is the most frequently used substance in drug-facilitated assault. Certainly it is easily accessible in many social situations and very common on college campuses. The relationship of alcohol use and sexuality is discussed in several places in this textbook.
- *Rohypnol.* Also known as "roofies," "roach," "forget pill," "Mexican valium," and "mind erasers," Rohypnol is not approved for medical use in the United States but is becoming an increasingly popular street drug. This small white tablet quickly dissolves in liquid. Alcohol increases the effects of Rohypnol.
- *GHB.* Also known as "grievous bodily harm," "easy lay," "liquid ecstasy," and "bedtime scoop," GHB has not been approved for sale by the FDA since 1990. GHB is sold on the street as a clear, odorless liquid and white crystalline powder, but since it is made in home labs its effects can be unpredictable. Alcohol increases the effects of GHB.

- *Benzodiazepines.* The legal form of Rohypnol, these drugs are prescribed as anti-anxiety and sleeping medications in the United States. Put into a drink in powder or liquid form, they markedly impair or eliminate functions that typically allow a person to resist an assault. Alcohol increases the effects of benzodiazepines.
- *Ketamine.* Also known as "Special K," "Vitamin K," and "K," ketamine is an anesthetic typically used by veterinarians. A fast-acting liquid, ketamine causes individuals to feel detached from their bodies and unable to fight back or remember what happened.
- *Ecstasy.* Also known as "X-TC," "X," and "E," ecstasy is the most common club drug. Illegal in the United States, ecstasy is a hallucinogenic and stimulant with psychedelic effects. Available in powder or liquid form, ecstasy causes people to feel extreme relaxation, sensitivity to touch, and less able to perceive danger.

To protect yourself from date/acquaintance rape drugs, it is essential that you watch what you drink at parties or on dates. Do not take any drinks (soda, coffee, or alcohol) from someone you do not know well and trust, and refuse open-container beverages. Never leave your drink unattended, and go to parties with a friend and leave with a friend. If you think you've been drugged, call 9-1-1 or get to an emergency room. If possible, try to keep a sample of the beverage. If you are a victim of drug-facilitated assault, do not blame yourself. The sexual assault was not your fault; the offender is solely to blame and is the one who took advantage of your diminished capacity (Ellis, 2002; Monroe, 1997; Rape, Abuse and Incest National Network, 2000b).

Think Critically

- How common is the use of rape/acquaintance rape drugs on your campus? In what type of situations does it occur?
- What can a person do to avoid being vulnerable to date/acquaintance rape?

Confusion Over Consent There is confusion about what constitutes consent. As we saw in Chapter 8, much sexual communication is nonverbal and ambiguous. The fact that we don't usually give verbal consent to sexual activity indicates the significance of nonverbal clues. Nonverbal communication is imprecise, however, and can be misinterpreted easily if not reinforced verbally. For example, men frequently mistake a woman's friendliness for sexual interest. They often misinterpret a woman's cuddling, kissing, and fondling as a desire to engage in sexual intercourse (Gillen & Muncher, 1995). A woman must make her boundaries clear verbally, and men need to avoid misinterpreting clues. One study of young heterosexual adults found that women with intercourse experience, more often than men and more often than women without intercourse experience, emphasized the value of consent and preferred explicit verbal communication to obtain it (Humphreys, 2004). In 2003, Illinois became the first state to pass a law explicitly stating that people have a right to withdraw their consent to sexual activity at any time. The law specified that, no matter how far the sexual interaction has progressed, a "no" means no when someone wants to stop (Parsons, 2003).

Our sexual scripts often assume "yes" unless a "no" is directly stated (Muehlenhard et al., 1992). This makes individuals "fair game" unless they explicitly say "no." But the assumption of consent puts women at a disadvantage. Because men traditionally initiate sex, a man can initiate sex whenever he desires without the woman explicitly consenting. A woman's refusal of sex can be considered "insincere" because consent is always assumed. Such thinking reinforces a common sexual script in which men initiate and women refuse so as not to appear "promiscuous." In this script, the man continues, believing that the woman's refusal is "token." Some common reasons for offering "token" refusals include a desire not to appear "loose," unsureness of how the partner feels, inappropriate surroundings, and game playing, which few women (and men) actually engage in. Because some women sometimes say "no" when they mean "coax me," male-female communication may be especially unclear regarding consent. Studies of college students found that more women than men reported sexual teasing, a form of provocation implying a promise of sexual contact but followed with refusal, and that they were more likely to agree that various forms of sexual violence are justified in situations in which the woman is perceived as "leading a man on" or giving mixed signals (Locke & Mahalik, 2005; Meston & O'Sullivan, 2007). However, contemporary beliefs of most people and the law say that if a rape survivor did not explicitly consent to sex, it is rape, even though the survivor flirted with the perpetrator, had been drinking, or experienced sexual arousal or orgasm during the incident (Peterson & Muehlenhard, 2007).

Postrefusal Sexual Persistence   Men are more likely than women to think of male-female relationships as a "battle of the sexes." Because relationships are conflictual, they believe, refusals are to be expected as part of the battle. A man may feel he should persist because his role is to conquer, even if he's not interested in sex. Researcher Cindy Struckman-Johnson and her colleagues (2003) investigated college students' pursuit of sexual contact with a person after he or she has refused an initial advance, a behavior they call **postrefusal sexual persistence.** They believe that all postrefusal behaviors are sexually coercive in that the other person has already communicated that he or she does not consent to the sexual behavior. The researchers examined tactics in four areas: (1) sexual arousal (e.g., kissing and touching, taking off clothes), (2) emotional manipulation and deception (e.g., repeatedly asking, telling lies), (3) exploitation of the intoxicated (e.g., taking advantage of and purposely getting a target drunk), and (4) physical force (e.g., blocking a target's retreat, using physical restraint) (see Figure 17.4). The researchers found that postrefusal sexual persistence was fairly common: Nearly 70% of the students had been subjected to at least one tactic of postrefusal sexual persistence since the age of 16, and

Experienced the tactic

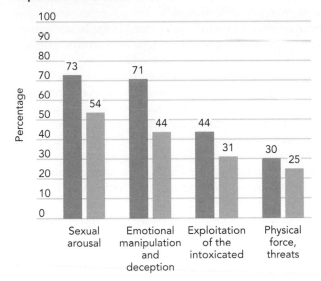

Perpetrated the tactic

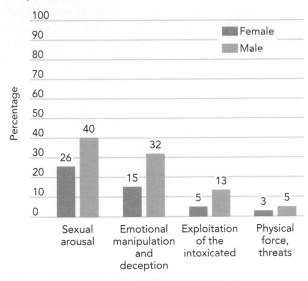

one third indicated that they had used a tactic. More women (78%) than men (58%) reported having been subjected to such tactics since age 16, and more men (40%) than women (26%) reported having used such tactics.

● FIGURE 17.4

Percentage of College Men and Women Experiencing Postrefusal Sexual Persistence Tactics.
(*Source:* Adapted from Struckman-Johnson, Struckman-Johnson, & Anderson, 2003.)

A Date-Raper Profile   A review of research (Baumeister, Catanese, & Wallace, 2002; Hanson & Morton-Bourgon, 2005; Koss & Dinero, 1989; Malamuth, Sockloskie, Koss, & Tanaka, 1991; Muehlenhard & Linton, 1987) found that sexually coercive men, in contrast to noncoercive ones, tend to share several characteristics:

- They hold traditional beliefs about women and women's roles.
- They grew up in a violent home environment.
- They have an antisocial orientation.
- They display hostility toward women.
- They believe in rape-supportive myths.
- They accept general physical violence.
- They express anger and dominance sexually.
- They report high levels of sexual activity.
- They use exploitative techniques.
- They report alcohol and drug use.
- They report early sexual experiences.
- They tend to be narcissistic, having low empathy and a sense of entitlement.

One study examined the patterns of sexually coercive behavior among samples of 266 Asian American men and 299 European American men for over one year. Men were classified into various groups including sexually coercive and noncoercive based on their sexual history. The researchers found that the strongest predictor of sexual coercive behavior was past sexual coercion. Also, the men who were persistently sexually coercive were higher than the other groups in delinquency and hostile masculinity (Hall, DeGarmo, Eap, Teten, & Sue, 2006).

Acquaintance Rape Sampson (2003) notes that acquaintance rape accounts for the vast majority of college rapes and that there are various types of acquaintance rape, such as party rape (can also include gang rapes), rape in a nonparty and nondate situation (e.g., while studying together), rape by a former intimate, and rape by a current intimate. Environmental factors that may contribute to the possibility of acquaintance rape include alcohol and drugs, availability of a private room in a fraternity or off-campus house, loud music that can drown out a person's calls for help, and a cover-up by the house's residents. By contrast, the date rape usually occurs as the two people are getting to know each other and the rape may occur in a car or residence after the date. Stranger rape, which is much less common than acquaintance rape on college campuses, usually occurs in isolated parts of campus, such as campus garages; in these cases, the victim may not have consumed any alcohol and no prior relationship (or even acquaintance) exists between the survivor and the rapist.

Sampson (2003) outlines several factors found in research of acquaintance rape that might increase a woman's vulnerability. Noting that a woman's condition or behavior does not cause rape, these factors include frequently drinking enough to get drunk, drinking so much that she cannot resist forceful sexual advances, using drugs, having previously been a survivor of sexual assault, being single, participating in social activities with sexually predatory men, being in an isolated site, miscommunicating about sex, and holding less conservative attitudes about sexual behavior. According to the Rape, Abuse, and Incest National Network (2008c), a person is more vulnerable to acquaintance rape when, over time, he or she becomes used to or more comfortable with the offender's intrusion into his or her personal space. Consequently, the victim may no longer consider the intrusive behavior threatening or may suppress feelings of fear. The offender then uses the victim's trust to isolate the victim from others. The Network advises that a person finding himself or herself in a threatening situation should listen to his or her instinctual sense or fear and discomfort and leave the situation.

Stranger Rape As mentioned previously, NCVS reports that in 30% of cases involving women and 100% of cases involving men who were raped or sexually assaulted, the rape was committed by a stranger (U.S. Department of Justice, 2006). A typical stranger-rape scenario does not necessarily involve an unknown assailant hiding in the bushes or a stairwell on a dark night. Rather, it is likely to involve a chance meeting with a man who seems friendly and congenial. The woman relaxes her guard because the man seems nice and even protective. He casually maneuvers her to an isolated place—an alley, park, apartment, or house—where the offender quickly and brutally assaults the woman.

Stranger rapes are more likely to involve guns or knives than date or acquaintance rapes. And a stranger rape is more likely to be taken seriously by the police because it reflects the rape stereotype better than does date, acquaintance, or marital rape (Russell, 1990).

> The husband cannot be guilty of rape committed by himself upon his lawful wife, for by their mutual matrimonial consent and contract, the wife gives herself in kind unto the husband which she cannot retract.
>
> —Sir Matthew Hale
> (1609–1676)

Marital Rape By 1993, marital rape had become a crime in all 50 states, although the majority still have exceptions, usually with regard to the use of force. Laws against marital rape, however, have not traditionally been widely enforced. A review of marital rape literature found that marital rape is experienced by 10–14% of all married women and 40–50% of battered married women (Martin, Taft, & Resick, 2007).

Many people discount rape in marriage as a "marital tiff" that has little relation to "real" rape. Women are more likely than men to believe that a husband would use force to have sexual intercourse with his wife. White women are more likely than African American women to identify sexual coercion in marriage as rape (Cahoon, Edmonds, Spaulding, & Dickens, 1995). When college students were asked to describe marital rape, they created "sanitized" images: "He wants to and she doesn't, so he does anyway," or "They are separated, but he really loves her, so when he comes back to visit, he forces her because he misses her." The realities are very different.

Marital rape survivors experience feelings of betrayal, anger, humiliation, and guilt. Following their rape, many wives feel intense anger toward their husbands; others experience constant terror because they are living with their assailant. A minority feel guilt and blame themselves for not being better wives. Others develop negative self-images and view their lack of sexual desire as a reflection of their own inadequacies rather than as a consequence of abuse. Many do not report rape, thinking that no one will believe them. Some do not even recognize that they have been legally raped.

Gang Rape Among adults, gang rape disproportionately occurs in tightly knit groups such as fraternities, athletic teams, street gangs, and military units. Gang rape may be perpetrated by strangers or acquaintances. It may be motivated not only by the desire to wield power but also by male-bonding factors (Sanday, 1990). It is a common form of adolescent rape, most often occurring with strangers (Holmes, 1991). When gang rape takes place on campus, the attackers may know the woman, who may have been invited to a party or apartment, and alcohol is often involved (O'Sullivan, 1991; Sampson, 2003). The assailants demonstrate their masculinity and "share" a sexual experience with their friends. Gang sexual assaults are typically more violent than rapes committed individually. Hence, the victims of gang rape are more traumatized and are more likely to contemplate suicide (Gidyez & Koss, 1990).

Click on "Sarah Recalls Being Date Raped" to hear Sarah talk about the acquaintance rape she experienced during spring break in Florida.

Statutory Rape Consensual sexual contact with a person younger than a state's **age of consent**—the age at which a person is legally deemed capable of giving informed consent—is termed **statutory rape.** The laws rarely are limited just to sexual intercourse but, instead, include any type of sexual contact. Today, the laws are applied to both female and male victims. It may not matter whether the offender is the same age as, older than, or younger than the survivor. If a victim is younger than a certain age—varying from age 16 to age 18 in most states—the court ignores the consent. Further, in some states, factors such as age differences between partners, the age of the survivor, and the age of the defendant are considered (Glosser, Gardiner, & Fishman, 2004). The enforcement of statutory rape laws, however, is generally sporadic or arbitrary. (To learn the age of consent law in a particular state, check the Web site http://www.sexlaws.org.)

Male Rape Sexual assaults against males may be perpetrated by other men or by women. Most rapes of men are by other men. In some states, the word "rape" is used only to define a forced act of vaginal sexual intercourse, whereas forced anal intercourse is termed "sodomy." More recently, states have started using gender-neutral terms such as "sexual assault" or "criminal sexual conduct," regardless of whether the victim is a man or a woman. To be specific, we have chosen the term "male rape."

According to the U.S. Department of Justice (2006), in 2005, 15,130 men aged 12 and older in the United States were raped or sexually assaulted. According to the Rape, Abuse, and Incest National Network (2006), 10% of sexual assault survivors are men. Experts, however, believe that the statistics vastly underrepresent the actual number of males who are raped (National Victim Center, 1997a). Though society is becoming increasingly aware of male rape, the lack of tracking of sexual crimes against men and the lack of research about their effects on survivors are indicative of the attitude held by society at large—that although male rape occurs it is not an appropriate topic for discussion.

There are also many reasons male victims do not come forward and report being raped. Perhaps the main reason is the fear of many that they will be perceived as homosexual. Male sexual assault has nothing to do with the sexual orientation of the attacker or the survivor, just as a sexual assault does not make the victim gay, bisexual, or heterosexual. Male rape is a violent crime that affects heterosexual men as often as gay men (National Victim Center, 1997a). Furthermore, the sexual orientation of the survivor does not appear to be of significance to half of the offenders, and most assailants in male rape are heterosexual (Groth & Birnbaum, 1979; Groth & Burgess, 1980).

Although many people believe that the majority of male rape incidents occur in prison, research suggests that the conditions for male rape are not unique to prison. Rather, all men, regardless of who or where they are, should be regarded as potential victims. It is believed that 10–20% of all men will be sexually violated at some point in their lifetime ("Men Can Stop Rape," 2000).

In the aftermath of an assault, many men blame themselves, believing that they in some way granted permission to the rapist. One study of 358 men who had been sexually assaulted by another male found that those exposed to non-consensual sex were about 3 times more likely to abuse alcohol and have attempted suicide than those who had not been victimized (Ratner et al., 2003). Male rape survivors suffer from fears similar to those felt by female rape victims, including the belief that they actually enjoyed or somehow contributed or consented to the rape. Some men may suffer additional guilt because they became sexually aroused and even ejaculated during the rape. However, these are normal, involuntary physiological reactions connected to the parasympathetic fear response and do not imply consent or enjoyment. Another concern for male rape survivors is society's belief that men should be able to protect themselves and that the rape was somehow their own fault.

Research indicates differences in how gay men and heterosexual men react in the aftermath of rape. Gay men may have difficulties in their sexual and emotional relationships with other men and think that the assault occurred because they are gay. Heterosexual men often begin to question their sexual identity and are more disturbed by the sexual aspect of the assault than by the violence involved (Brochman, 1991).

Although they are uncommon, there are some instances of women sexually assaulting men. Despite being threatened with knives and guns, the men were able to have erections (Sarrel & Masters, 1982). After the assault, the men suffered rape trauma syndrome similar to that experienced by women (discussed later). They experienced sexual difficulties, depression, and anxiety. Most felt abnormal because they did respond sexually during the assault. And because they were sexually assaulted by women, they doubted their masculinity. However, no matter whether the male was sexually assaulted by a female or a male, many of these survivors believe that the rape threatens the very essence of their masculinity and manhood (Ellis, 2002).

Sexual Coercion in Gay and Lesbian Relationships   There is considerable sexual coercion in gay and lesbian relationships. One study found that 57% of gay men and 45% of lesbian women had experienced some form of sexual coercion. Thirty-three percent of the gay men and 32% of the lesbian women reported unwanted fondling, with 55% of the gay men and 50% of the lesbian women having experienced unwanted penetration. The coercive tactics used against both groups, such as threats of force, physical restraint, and use of alcohol, were similar (Waldner-Haugrud & Gratch, 1997).

Motivations for Rape

Most stranger rapes and some acquaintance or marital rapes can be characterized as anger rapes, power rapes, or sadistic rapes (Groth, Burgess, & Holmstrom, 1977; McCabe & Wauchope, 2005).

Anger Rape   Anger rapists are physically violent, displaying anger overtly such as by using a knife or force, and their victims often require hospitalization (McCabe & Wauchope, 2005). Victims are often forced to perform certain sexual behaviors, such as fellatio, on the assailant. Clinical psychologist Nicholas Groth (1979) describes anger rape in this way:

> The assault is characterized by physical brutality. Far more actual force is used . . . than would be necessary if the intent were simply to overpower the victim and achieve sexual penetration. . . . His aim is to hurt and debase his victim, and he expresses contempt for her through abusive and profane language. . . .

Power Rape   Power rapes are acts of dominance and control. Typically, the rapist wishes not to hurt the victim, but to dominate him or her sexually. The rape may be triggered by what the rapist regards as a slight to his or her gender identity. The rapist attempts to restore his or her sense of power, control, and identity by raping. He or she uses sex to compensate for a sense of sexual inadequacy, applying only as much force as is necessary to rape the victim (McCabe & Wauchope, 2005).

Sadistic Rape   A violent fusion of sex and aggression, sadistic rapes are by far the most brutal. A sadistic rapist finds "intentional maltreatment of his/her victim intensely gratifying and takes pleasure in her/his torment, anguish, distress, helplessness and suffering" (Groth & Birnbaum, 1978). Bondage is often involved, and the rape may have a ritualistic quality. The victim is often severely injured and may not survive the attack. Although sadistic rapes are overwhelmingly the most brutal, they are also by far the least frequent.

The Aftermath of Rape

Most rape survivors report being roughed up by the rapist, and about 90% report some physical injury (Rape Network, 2000), although the vast majority do not sustain serious injury.

It is important that rape survivors gain a sense of control over their lives to counteract the feelings of helplessness they experienced during their rape. They need to cope with the depression and other symptoms resulting from their trauma.

Rape crisis centers help sexual assault survivors cope with the effects of rape trauma.

Although White and African American women experience rape at more or less the same rate, the African American woman's experience may be somewhat different. As clinical psychologist and sex researcher Gail Wyatt (1992) writes, "In American culture, rape and sexual vulnerability have a unique history because of the sexual exploitation of slaves for over 250 years." Historically, there were no penalties for the rape of Black women by Whites. Because Whites believed that African American women were "promiscuous" by nature, they believed as well that Black women could not actually be raped. There are three important consequences of this stereotype. First, African American women who are raped assume that they are less likely to be believed than White women, especially if the rapist is White. Second, African American women are less likely to report the rape to the police, whom they view as unsympathetic to Blacks in general and to raped Black women in particular. Third, African American women are less likely to seek treatment and support to help the healing process.

Singer Tori Amos, herself a rape survivor, founded the Rape, Abuse, and Incest National Network (RAINN), an organization that operates a national toll-free hotline for victims of sexual assault (see the section "Sex and the Internet, at the end of chapter).

Rape Trauma Syndrome   Rape is a traumatic event, to which the survivor may have a number of responses, and each survivor's response will vary depending on the situation (Rape, Abuse, and Incest National Network, 2008d). The emotional changes undergone as a result of rape are collectively known as **rape trauma syndrome.** Rape survivors are likely to experience depression, anxiety, restlessness, and guilt. These responses are consistent with **posttraumatic stress disorder (PTSD),** a group of characteristic symptoms that follow an intensely distressing event outside a person's normal life experience. PTSD is an official diagnostic category of the American Psychiatric Association (2000). Anyone who has been raped can develop PTSD. The following description of the aftermath of rape is presented in the context of outcomes for women. In general, the impact of rape on male victims has been underestimated and overlooked in research. However, male rape survivors often experience significant physical and psychological trauma from the assault, including long-term effects of anxiety, depression, self-blame, loss of self-image, emotional distancing, feelings of anger and vulnerability, and self-harming behaviors (Ellis, 2002; Rogers, 1997; Walker, Archer, & Davies, 2005).

Helping Someone Who Has Been Raped

The mission of the organization Men Can Stop Rape is to mobilize men to use their strength for creating cultures free from violence, especially men's violence against women. One of their fact sheets provides suggestions on helping people who say they were raped:

Supporting survivors: When someone says, "I was raped":

1. *Believe the person.* It is not your role to question whether a rape occurred, but to be there to ease the pain.

2. *Help the person explore the options.* Don't take charge of the situation and pressure rape survivors to do what you think they should do. That's what the rapist did. Give them the freedom to choose a path of recovery that is comfortable for them, even if you'd do it differently. Remember, there is no one right way for a survivor to respond after being assaulted.

3. *Listen to the person.* It is critical that you let survivors in your lives know that they can talk to you about their experience when they are ready. Some may not wish to speak with you immediately, but at some point during the healing process, it is likely that they will come to you for support. When that happens, don't interrupt, or yell, or inject your feelings. Your caring but silent attention will be invaluable.

4. *Ask before you touch.* Don't assume that physical contact, even in a form of a gentle hug, will be comforting to survivors. Many survivors, especially within the first few weeks after assault, prefer to avoid sex or simple touching even with those they love and trust. One way to signal to survivors that you are ready to offer physical comfort is to sit with an open posture and a hand palm up nearby.

5. *Recognize that you have been assaulted, too.* We can't help but be hurt when someone we love is made to suffer. Don't blame yourself for the many feelings you will likely have in response to learning that someone close to you has been raped. Sadness, confusion, anger, helplessness, fear, guilt, disappointment, shock, anxiety, desperation, compassion—all are common reactions for survivors and their significant others.

6. *Never blame them for being assaulted.* No one ever deserves to be raped—no matter what they wore, how many times they had sex before, if they were walking alone at night, if they got drunk, if they were married, or if they went to the perpetrator's room. Even if survivors feel responsible, say clearly and caringly that being raped wasn't their fault.

7. *Get help for yourself.* Whether you reach out to a friend, family member, counselor, religious official, or whomever, make sure you don't go through the experience alone. Most rape crisis centers offer counseling for significant others and family members because they realize that the impact of rape extends far beyond the survivors. Keeping your feelings inside will only make you less able to be there for the survivors. Remember, getting help when needed is a sign of strength, not weakness.

SOURCE: Reprinted by permission of Men Can Stop Rape. (http://www.mencanstoprape.org)

Rape trauma syndrome consists of two phases: an acute phase and a long-term reorganization phase. The acute phase begins immediately following the rape and may last for several weeks or more. In the first few hours after a rape, the woman's responses are characterized by feelings of self-blame and fear. She may believe that she was somehow responsible for the rape: She was wearing something provocative, she should have kept her doors locked, she should have been suspicious of her attacker, and so on. Self-blame, however, only leads to deeper depression (Frazier, 1991).

A woman who has been raped may be wracked by fears: that the attacker will return, that she may be killed, that others will react negatively. There are often signs of tension, such as difficulty concentrating, hypervigilance, nausea, gastrointestinal problems, headaches, irritability, sleeplessness, restlessness, and jumpiness (Krakow et al., 2000). The woman may also feel humiliated, angry, embarrassed, and vengeful. In general, women are more likely than men to display these varied symptoms following rape (Fergusson, Swain-Campbell, & Horwood, 2002; Sorenson & Siegel, 1992).

Following the acute phase, the rape survivor enters the long-term reorganization phase. The rape is a crisis in a person's life and relationships. About 3 months after their rapes, 60% of the women in one study reported depression, and 40% rated their depression as severe (Mackey et al., 1992). In a national sample of women, those with histories of sexual assault in both childhood and adulthood had significantly greater odds of lifetime suicide attempts (Ullman & Brecklin, 2002).

Long-term stress reactions are often exacerbated by the very social support systems and staff designed to assist people. These systems and individuals have sometimes proved to be more psychologically damaging to survivors than the rape itself (National Organization for Victim Assistance, 1992), a phenomenon known as secondary victimization. Examples of these support systems and individuals include the criminal justice system, the media, emergency and hospital room personnel, social workers, family and friends, employers, and clergy. Nevertheless, the most important thing you can do to help someone you care about who suffers from symptoms of PTSD is to help her or him get professional help.

Effects on Sexuality   Typically, both men and women find that their sexuality is severely affected for at least a short time after a rape (Meana, Binik, Khalife, & Cohen, 1999; Rape, Abuse & Incest National Network, 2008e). Some begin avoiding sexual interactions, because sex reminds them of the rape. Those who are less depressed, however, have fewer sexual difficulties. Two common sexual problems are fear of sex and lack of sexual desire. Both White and African American women report similar sexual problems (Wyatt, 1992).

● Child Sexual Abuse

Child sexual abuse, by both relatives and nonrelatives, occurs widely. **Child sexual abuse** is *any* sexual interaction (including fondling, sexual kissing, and oral sex, as well as vaginal or anal penetration) between an adult and a prepubescent child. A broad definition also includes nonphysical contact, such as people exposing their genitals to children or having children pose nude or stimulate themselves while being filmed or photographed. It does not matter whether the child is perceived by the adult to be engaging in the sexual activity voluntarily. Because of the child's age, he or she cannot give informed consent; the activity can only be considered as self-serving to the adult. The topic of child sexual abuse has received increased national attention due to the allegations of child molestation against clergy in the Catholic Church. The revelation of widespread child sexual abuse by priests, bishops, and cardinals has rocked the nation, resulting in resignations, lawsuits, imprisonments, and even deaths. Since 1950, more than 4,000 priests in the United States have been accused of molesting minors, and the Catholic Church has paid out over $2 billion in settlements (Simpson, 2008).

There are no reliable annual surveys of sexual assaults on children. The U.S. Justice Department's annual National Crime Victimization Survey does not include victims aged 12 and younger. It is also difficult to know how many children are sexually abused because many cases are not reported. Further, because of the stigma of sexual abuse and the enormous emotional distress caused by abuse, many victims keep the abuse a secret. One research study found that the amount of time between the end of sexual abuse and the victim revealing the abuse averaged 14 years (Roesler, 2000). Twelve percent of men and 17% of women who participated in the National Health and Social Life Survey (Laumann et al., 1994) reported that they had been sexually touched when they were children. A 10-year review of published research on child sexual abuse found that the prevalence rate of being sexually abused as a child was 17% and 8% for adult women and men, respectively (Putnam, 2003). Worldwide, sexual contact between an adult and a child has been reported by about 20% of women and 5–10% of men (Freyd et al., 2005). At least 90% of child sexual abuse is committed by men (Finkelhor, 1994). There has been a dramatic drop in reported child sexual abuse in recent years in the United States, declining over 50% since 1992 ("Sex Crimes Against Children Declining," 2008; U.S. Department of Health and Human Services, 2006). Possible reasons for the decline include fear among professionals and the public about the legal consequences of false reporting and abatement of the problem resulting from prevention programs (Jones & Finkelhor, 2003).

According to the congressionally mandated Third National Incidence Study of Child Abuse and Neglect (Sedlak & Broadhurst, 1996), girls are sexually abused 3 times as often as boys; however, boys are more likely to be seriously injured or killed during such assaults. The risk of being sexually abused does not vary among races, but children from lower-income groups and from single-parent families are more frequently victimized, as are children who have experienced parental inadequacy or unavailability, conflict, harsh punishment, and emotional deprivation (Finkelhor, 1994; Putnam, 2003). Every incident of child sexual abuse causes the victim a loss of trust and sense of self.

Child sexual abuse is generally categorized in terms of kin relationships. **Extrafamilial abuse** is sexual abuse by unrelated people. **Intrafamilial abuse** is sexual abuse by biologically related people and step-relatives. Figure 17.5 shows the type of relationship between the child survivor and the perpetrator. As shown, nonparent relatives were the most common offenders (30%) and parents were the least common (3%) (Snyder & Sickmund, 2006). The abuse may be pedophilic or nonpedophilic. (As explained in Chapter 10, pedophilia refers to an adult's sexual attraction to children.) **Nonpedophilic sexual abuse** refers to an adult's sexual interaction with a child that is not sexually motivated, the most important nonsexual motives are the desire for power and affection. One cannot determine who

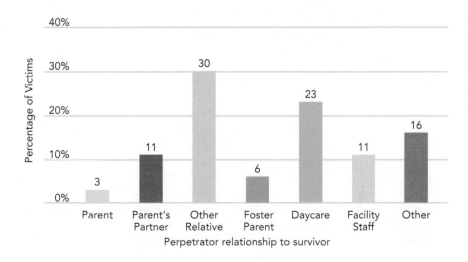

● **FIGURE 17.5**

Relationship Between the Child Survivor and the Perpetrator of Sexual Abuse. (*Source:* Snyder, H. N., Sickmund, M. [2006]. *Juvenile Offenders and Victims: 2006 National Report.* Washington, DC: U.S. Department of Justice.)

is a child molester from appearance—child molesters look like ordinary people. But, research has shown that child molesters, in general, differ from nonmolesters. They are usually heterosexual males (Valente, 2005) and often have, for example, lower intelligence, more-difficult family histories, less-developed social skills, lower self-esteem, and lower life satisfaction than nonmolesters (Finkelhor, 1990; Hunter, Figueredo, & Malamuth, 2003; Milner & Robertson, 1990).

The victimization may involve force or the threat of force, pressure, manipulation, and loss of trust or innocence. Genital fondling and touching are the most common forms of child sexual abuse (Haugaard & Reppucci, 1998). The most serious or harmful forms of child sexual abuse include actual or attempted penile-vaginal penetration, fellatio, cunnilingus, and anilingus, with or without the use of force. Other serious forms of abuse range from forced digital penetration of the vagina to fondling of the breasts (unclothed) or simulated intercourse without force. Less serious forms range from kissing to intentional sexual touching of the clothed genitals or breasts or other body parts, with or without the use of force.

Forms of Intrafamilial Sexual Abuse

The incest taboo is nearly universal in human societies. **Incest** is generally defined as sexual intercourse between people too closely related to legally marry (usually interpreted to mean father-daughter, mother-son, or brother-sister combinations). Sexual abuse in families can involve blood relatives, most commonly uncles and grandfathers, and step-relatives, most often stepfathers and stepbrothers. In grandfather-granddaughter abuse, the grandfathers frequently have sexually abused their children as well.

It is not clear what type of familial sexual abuse occurs most frequently (Peters et al., 1986; Russell, 1986). Some researchers believe that father-daughter (including stepfather-daughter) abuse is the most common; others think that brother-sister abuse is most common. Still other researchers believe that incest committed by uncles is the most common (Russell, 1986). Mother-son sexual relations are considered to be rare (or are underreported).

Father-Daughter Sexual Abuse One of the most traumatic form of sexual victimization is father-daughter abuse, including that committed by stepfathers. One study indicated that 54% of the girls sexually abused by their fathers were extremely upset (Russell, 1986). In contrast, 25% who were abused by other family members reported the same degree of emotional upset. Over twice as many abused daughters reported serious long-term consequences. Another study of 40 men (14 natural fathers and 26 stepfathers) and 44 children (18 biological daughters and 26 stepdaughters) examined both the fathers' and daughters' recollections and interpretations of the incestuous activity (Phelan, 1995). Both fathers and daughters reported that the sexual contact grew out of existing family interactions, but their thoughts surrounding the events were different. Many of the fathers indicated that their thoughts were dominated by ideas of sexual gratification, control, power, and anger. However, the daughters indicated they experienced disbelief, confusion, guilt, and anger. Many of the fathers said they completely misread their daughter's reaction to the sexual activity. Fathers indicated that they knew what they were doing was wrong, but few noted that they were worried about potential legal outcomes.

In the past, many people have discounted the seriousness of sexual abuse by a stepfather because there is no *biological* relationship. The emotional consequences are just as serious, however. Sexual abuse by a stepfather still represents a violation of the basic parent-child relationship.

Brother-Sister Sexual Abuse There are contrasting views concerning the consequences of brother-sister incest. Researchers generally have expressed little interest in it. Most have tended to view it as harmless sex play or sexual exploration between mutually consenting siblings. The research, however, has generally failed to distinguish between exploitative and nonexploitative brother-sister sexual activity. One study found that brother-sister incest can represent a devastating violation of individual boundaries (Canavan, Myers, & Higgs, 1992). A study of women attending support groups for incest survivors concluded that the outcomes of brother-sister incest are equally serious as those of father-daughter incest (Rudd & Herzberger, 1999). Sibling incest needs to be taken seriously (Adler & Schultz, 1995).

Feminist researcher Diane Russell (1986) suggests that the idea that brother-sister incest is usually harmless and consensual may be a myth. In her study, the average age difference between the brother (age 17.9 years) and sister (10.7 years) is so great that the siblings can hardly be considered peers. The age and gender difference represents a significant power difference. Furthermore, not all brother-sister sexual activity is "consenting"; considerable physical force may be involved. In most instances, the brother initiates the sexual contact and is the dominant person during the sexual contact.

Children at Risk

Incest does not discriminate; it occurs in all types of families. Nevertheless, not all children are equally at risk for sexual abuse. Although any child can be sexually abused, some groups of children are more likely to be victimized than others. A review (Finkelhor & Baron, 1986) of the literature indicated that children at higher risk for sexual abuse include females, preadolescents (particularly those aged 10–12), children with absent or unavailable parents, children whose relationships with their parents are poor, children whose parents are in conflict, and children who live with a stepfather. Finkelhor (1994) notes that the most significant risk factors are children separated from their parents and children whose parents have such serious problems that they cannot attend to or supervise their children. The result is emotionally deprived children who are vulnerable to the ploys of sexually abusive individuals.

Effects of Child Sexual Abuse

Until recently, much of the literature on child sexual abuse was anecdotal, case studies, or small-scale surveys of nonrepresentative groups. Nevertheless, numerous well-documented consequences of child sexual abuse hold true for both intrafamilial and extrafamilial abuse. These include both initial and long-term consequences. Many child sexual abuse survivors experience symptoms of posttraumatic stress disorder (Day, Thurlow, & Wolliscroft, 2003; Paolucci, Genuis, & Violato, 2001).

In recent years, some women and men have stated that they were sexually abused during childhood but had repressed their memories of it. They later recovered the memory of it, often with the help of therapists. When these recovered memories surfaced, those accused often expressed shock and denied the abuse ever happened. Instead they insisted that those memories were figments of the imagination. The question of whom to believe has given rise to a vitriolic "memory war": recovered memories versus false memories. Each side has its proponents, and the fierce controversy about the nature of memories of abuse continues today.

Initial Effects The initial consequences of sexual abuse occur within the first couple of years or so and appear in many of the children survivors. Typical effects include the following (Anderson, 1995; Briere & Elliott, 1994; Calam, Horne, Glasgow, & Cox, 1998; Carlson, McNutt, & Choi, 2003; Wonderlich et al., 2000):

- *Emotional disturbances,* including fear, sadness, self-hatred, anger, temper tantrums, depression, hostility, guilt, and shame
- *Physical consequences,* including difficulty in sleeping, changes in eating patterns, and headaches
- *Sexual disturbances,* including significantly higher rates of open masturbation, sexual preoccupation, exposure of the genitals, and indiscriminate and frequent sexual behaviors that might lead to pregnancy and STIs
- *Social disturbances,* including difficulties at school, truancy, running away from home, and early marriages by abused adolescents (a large proportion of homeless youths are fleeing parental sexual abuse)

Long-Term Effects Although there can be some healing of the initial effects, child sexual abuse may leave lasting scars on the adult survivor. These adults often have significantly higher incidences of psychological, physical, and sexual problems than the general population. Abuse may predispose some women to sexually abusive dating relationships.

Long-term effects of child sexual abuse include the following (Dube et al., 2005; Jumper, 1995; Meston, Rellini Heiman, 2006; Najman, Dunne, Purdie, Boyle, & Coxeter, 2005; Noll, Trickett, & Putnam, 2003; Sachs-Ericsson, 2005; Shinozaki, Passov, Kung, Alarcon, & Mrazek, 2009):

- *Depression,* the symptom most frequently reported by adults sexually abused as children
- *Self-destructive tendencies,* including suicide attempts and thoughts of suicide
- *Somatic disturbances and dissociation,* including anxiety and nervousness, insomnia, chronic pain, eating disorders (anorexia and bulimia), irritable bowel syndrome, feelings of "spaciness," out-of-body experiences, and feelings that things are "unreal"
- *Health risk behaviors,* including tobacco use, alcoholism, obesity, and unsafe sexual behaviors that may result in STIs and pregnancy
- *Negative self-concept,* including feelings of low self-esteem, isolation, and alienation
- *Interpersonal relationship difficulties,* including problems in relating to both sexes and to parents, in responding to their own children, and in trusting others
- *Revictimization,* in which women abused as children are more vulnerable to rape and marital violence
- *Sexual problems,* in which survivors find it difficult to relax and enjoy sexual activities or in which they avoid sex and experience hypoactive (inhibited) sexual desire and lack of orgasm

A study of 534 women and 643 men attending a public STI clinic examined whether the severity of sexual abuse in childhood impacted sexual risk behavior in adulthood. The study found that penetration by itself (i.e., without force) and penetration with force were associated with greater sexual risk behavior. Specifically, those reporting childhood sexual abuse involving penetration and/or force also reported more lifetime sexual partners and more previous STI diagnoses. Also, men experiencing sexual abuse with force and penetration reported a greater number of episodes of sex trading (exchanging sex for money, drugs, etc.), and women who were abused with penetration, regardless of whether force was involved, reported the most episodes of sex trading. Hence, the more severe childhood sexual abuse was associated with riskier adult sexual behavior (Senn, Carey, Vanable, Coury-Doniger, & Urban, 2007).

Gay men and lesbian women who were sexually abused as children or adolescents may have additional issues to deal with. This is especially true if they were in the process of becoming aware of their sexual orientation at the time of the abuse. They may have avoided telling anyone about the abuse because of their orientation and their fear of being blamed if their homosexuality were suspected by a family member or caseworker. The community may be unsupportive. The survivor's age and stage in the coming-out process are particularly significant (Arey, 1995; Burke, 1995). The abuse may create or intensify self-directed homophobia.

Sexual Abuse Trauma   The consequences of child sexual abuse may involve a traumatic dynamic that affects the child's ability to deal with the world. Angela Browne and David Finkelhor (1986) suggest a model of **sexual abuse trauma** that contains four components: traumatic sexualization, betrayal, powerlessness, and stigmatization. These consequences affect abuse survivors not only as children but also as adults.

Traumatic Sexualization   Traumatic sexualization refers to the process by which the sexually abused child's sexuality develops inappropriately and he or she becomes interpersonally dysfunctional. Sexually traumatized children learn inappropriate sexual behaviors (e.g., manipulating an adult's genitals for affection), are confused about their sexuality, and inappropriately associate certain emotions (e.g., loving and caring) with sexual activities. Childhood sexual abuse may be associated with the reasons some women later become prostitutes (Simons & Whitbeck, 1991).

Adult survivors may experience flashbacks, suffer from sexual difficulties, and develop negative feelings about their bodies. A fairly common confusion is the belief that sex may be traded for affection.

Betrayal   Children feel betrayed when they discover that someone on whom they have been dependent has manipulated, used, or harmed them. They may also feel betrayed by other family members, for not protecting them from abuse.

As adults, survivors may experience depression as a manifestation, in part, of extended grief over the betrayal of trusted figures. Some may find it difficult to trust others; others may feel a deep need to regain a sense of trust and become extremely dependent. For adolescents, antisocial or delinquent behavior may be a means of protecting themselves from further betrayal. Anger may express a need for revenge or retaliation, while distrust may manifest itself in social isolation and avoidance of intimate relationships.

Powerlessness   Children experience a basic sense of powerlessness when their bodies and personal space are invaded against their will. This powerlessness is reinforced as the abuse is repeated.

In adulthood, powerlessness may be experienced as fear or anxiety, with the person feeling unable to control events and having impaired coping abilities. This feeling of ineffectiveness may be related to the high incidence of depression and despair among survivors. Powerlessness may also be related to increased vulnerability or revictimization through rape or marital violence; survivors feel incapable of preventing subsequent victimization. Other survivors may attempt to cope with their earlier powerlessness by attempting to control or dominate others.

Stigmatization   Stigmatization—the guilt and shame associated with sexual abuse that are transmitted to abused children and then internalized by them—is communicated in numerous ways. The abuser blames the child or, through his secrecy, communicates a sense of shame. If the abuser pressures the child to keep the abuse a secret, the child may also internalize feelings of shame and guilt. Children's prior knowledge that their family or community considers such activities deviant may contribute to their feelings of stigmatization.

As adults, survivors may feel extreme guilt or shame about having been sexually abused. They may have low self-esteem because they feel that the abuse made them "damaged merchandise." They also feel different from others because they mistakenly believe that they alone have been abused.

Treatment Programs

As stated earlier in this section, survivors of childhood sexual abuse suffer both immediate and long-term negative outcomes. It is vital that they receive adequate support and therapy involving both cognitive and behavioral approaches. Therapy should be available and considered for the child following the sexual abuse, as well as when the child becomes an adolescent and then an adult (McDonald et al., 2005). It is common now to deal with child sexual abuse by offering therapy programs that function in conjunction with the judicial system, particularly when the offender is an immediate family member, such as a father. The district attorney's office may work with clinicians in evaluating the existing threat to the child in the home and deciding whether to prosecute or to refer the offender for therapy—or both. The goal is not simply to punish the offender but also to try to help the survivor and the family come to terms with the abuse. Many of these clinical programs work on several levels simultaneously; that is, they treat the individual and the family as a whole. Sex abusers also need treatment. This is important not only to assist these individuals in developing healthier child and adult relationships, but also to avoid any future abuse episodes.

Preventing Child Sexual Abuse

Programs focusing on preventing child sexual abuse have been developed; however, they have been hindered by several factors. In confronting these problems, child abuse prevention (CAP) programs have been very creative. Most programs include group instruction in schools, either as a component of regular classroom instruction or as an after-school program (Daro, 1994). These programs typically address three audiences: children, parents, and professionals. CAP programs

One objective of child sexual abuse prevention programs is to teach children the difference between "good" touching and "bad" touching.

aimed at children use plays, puppet shows, films, videotapes, books, and comic books to teach children that they have rights: to control their own bodies (including their genitals), to feel "safe," and to not be touched in ways that feel confusing or wrong. The CAP programs stress that children are not at fault when such abuse does occur. These programs generally teach children three strategies (Gelles & Conte, 1991): (1) to say "no," (2) to get away from the assailant or situation, and (3) to tell a trusted adult about what happened (and to keep telling until they are believed).

Many schools include instruction about the prevention of child sexual abuse.

Other programs focus on educating parents, who, it is hoped, will in turn educate their children. These programs seek to help parents discover abuse or abusers by identifying warning signs. Parents seem reluctant in general to deal with sexual abuse issues with their children, according to Finkelhor (1986). Many do not feel that their children are at risk, are fearful of unnecessarily frightening their children, and may also feel uncomfortable talking with their children about sex in general, much less about such taboo subjects as incest. In addition, parents may not believe their own children's reports of abuse or may feel uncomfortable confronting a suspected abuser, who may be a partner, uncle, friend, or neighbor.

CAP programs also seek to educate professionals, especially teachers, physicians, mental health workers, and police officers. Because of their close contact with children and their role in teaching children about the world, teachers are especially important. Professionals are encouraged to watch for signs of sexual abuse and to investigate children's reports of such abuse. Signs that may indicate the presence of child sexual abuse are nightmares or other sleep problems, depression or withdrawal from family or friends, statements from the child that there is something wrong with her or him in the genital area, unusual interest in or avoidance of all things related to sexuality, secretiveness, and refusal to go to school (American Academy of Child & Adolescent Psychiatry, 2008).

In 1997, the U.S. Supreme Court ruled in favor of what is now referred to as Megan's Law. Enacted in 1995, the law calls for schools, day-care centers, and youth groups to be notified about moderate-risk sex offenders in the community. For high-risk offenders, the law requires that the police go door-to-door notifying neighborhood residents. It also requires sex offenders who have been paroled or recently released from prison to register with local authorities when moving to a community. The law is named for Megan Kanka, a 7-year-old who was raped and murdered by a twice-convicted sex offender who lived across the street from her. Although parts of the law have been challenged, the Supreme Court has rejected objections (Carelli, 1998). Actually, the Court ruled in 2003 that photos of convicted offenders may be posted on the Internet (CNN.com/Law Center, 2003). Most communities see the law as a welcome victory for their children.

In efforts to further prevent child sexual abuse, most states and many communities have enacted laws directed toward sex offenders to, for example, extend prison sentences, require offenders to register with the police, restrict where the person can live (not near schools or playgrounds), improve public notification of their whereabouts, and order electronic monitoring (Koch, 2006). All states have Internet registries of sex offenders. For many of the attempts to make identity of sex offenders easily accessible to the public, constitutional and safety issues relative to the rights of the offender have been raised. For example, a man who shot two sex offenders to death in April 2006 indicated that he got their names from the state's online sex offender registry

("Maine Killers Use of Sex-Offender List," 2006). Actually, Human Rights Watch, in its report *No Easy Answers,* states that state and federal laws designed to monitor released offenders and protect the public may be counterproductive—they may actually cause more harm than good. The report notes that laws restricting where sex offenders can live and requiring public notification of their crimes have not been shown to reduce sex crimes. Further, no other country in the world governs where sex offenders can live. Human Rights Watch says that, according to U.S. Justice Department Statistics, only 5.3% of sex offenders re-offend in 3 years (Human Rights Watch, 2007; Rozas, 2007). As you can see, efforts to protect children from sexual abuse can involve several components, not all of which may be compatible and many that are controversial.

Final Thoughts

Sexual harassment, anti-gay harassment and discrimination, sexual aggression, and sexual abuse of children represent the darker side of human sexuality. Their common thread is the humiliation, subordination, or victimization of others. But we need not be victims. We can educate ourselves and others about these activities; we can work toward changing attitudes and institutions that support these destructive and dehumanizing behaviors.

Summary

Sexual Harassment

- *Sexual harassment* includes two distinct types of illegal harassment: the abuse of power for sexual ends and the creation of a *hostile environment*. Sexual harassment may begin as early as middle childhood. In college, 6 in every 10 female students and male students have experienced some form of sexual harassment (verbal or physical) from other students, faculty members, or administrators.

- In the workplace, both fellow employees and supervisors may engage in sexual harassment. In many instances, harassment may not represent sexual attraction as much as an exercise of power.

Harassment and Discrimination Against Gay, Lesbian, Bisexual, and Transgender People

- Researchers have identified two forms of discrimination or bias against gay, lesbian, bisexual, and transgender people: heterosexual bias and anti-gay prejudice. *Heterosexual bias* includes ignoring, segregating, and submerging gay, lesbian, bisexual, and transgender people into larger categories that make them invisible.

- *Anti-gay prejudice* is a strong dislike, fear, or hatred of gay, lesbian, bisexual, and transgender people. It is acted out through offensive language, discrimination, and violence. Anti-gay prejudice is derived from a deeply rooted insecurity concerning a person's own sexuality and gender identity, a strong fundamentalist religious orientation, or simple ignorance.

Sexual Aggression

- *Rape* forces its victim into intimate sexual contact against her or his will. *Sexual aggression* refers to any sexual activity against a person's will through the use of force, argument, pressure, alcohol/drugs, or authority. *Sexual coercion,* a broader term than "rape" or "sexual aggression," includes arguing, pleading, and cajoling, as well as force or the threat of force. *Sexual assault* is the term used by the legal system for criminal sexual contact that does not meet the legal definition of rape.

- Myths about rape encourage rape by blaming women. Men are more likely than women to believe rape myths.

- *Date rape* and *acquaintance rape* are common forms of rape. Alcohol or drugs are often involved. There is also considerable sexual coercion in gay relationships; there is less coercion in lesbian relationships.

- The majority of reported rapes are by strangers. Stranger rapes are more likely to involve guns or knives than date or acquaintance rapes.

- In every state, a husband can be prosecuted for raping his wife. Marital rape survivors experience feelings of betrayal, anger, humiliation, and guilt.

- Gang rape may be perpetrated by strangers or acquaintances. It may be motivated by a desire for power and by male-bonding factors.

- Most male rape survivors have been raped by other men. Because the motive in sexual assaults is power and domination, sexual orientation is often irrelevant.

- Most stranger rapes (and some acquaintance and marital rapes) can be characterized as anger rapes, power rapes, or sadistic rapes.

- The emotional changes undergone as a result of rape are collectively known as *rape trauma syndrome.* These survivors may experience depression, anxiety, restlessness, and guilt. The symptoms following rape are consistent with *posttraumatic stress disorder (PTSD).* Rape trauma syndrome consists of an acute phase and a long-term reorganization phase. Women find their sexuality severely affected for at least a short time after being raped.

Child Sexual Abuse

- *Child sexual abuse* is any sexual interaction between an adult and a prepubescent child. *Incest* is sexual contact between individuals too closely related to legally marry.

- The initial effects of abuse include physical consequences and emotional, social, and sexual disturbances. Child sexual abuse may leave lasting scars on the adult survivor.

- *Sexual abuse trauma* includes traumatic sexualization, betrayal, powerlessness, and stigmatization. Treatment programs use both cognitive and behavioral psychotherapy to assist the survivor.

- Child abuse prevention (CAP) programs that focus on skills training, such as self-protective behaviors, appear to be the most effective. CAP programs generally teach children to say "no," to get away from the assailant or situation, and to tell a trusted adult about what happened.

Questions for Discussion

- If you are a college student, how common is sexual harassment on your campus? What makes it sometimes difficult to determine the difference between flirting and sexual harassment?

- Why do you think people commit rape? Are they mainly motivated by need for sexual gratification, by need for power and control, or by other reasons?

- What do you think you could do to help someone who has been raped? What resources or organizations would you recommend?

- Have you observed anti-gay prejudice? If so, what could have been done to prevent it, if anything?

- What do you think can be done to prevent child sexual abuse?

The Rape, Abuse, and Incest National Network

The Rape, Abuse, and Incest National Network (RAINN) is the nation's largest anti-sexual-assault organization and operates a national toll-free hotline for survivors of sexual assault (1-800-656-HOPE). RAINN offers free, confidential counseling and support 24 hours a day. Founded by singer Tori Amos, RAINN also has an information-filled Web site: http://www.rainn.org. Go to the RAINN site and answer the following questions:

- What type of information is provided?
- What are some of the RAINN highlights?
- What is in the "Latest News" section?
- What types of programs and events does RAINN offer?
- How can one support or volunteer for RAINN?

Suggested Web Sites

Feminist Majority Foundation
http://www.feminist.org
Discusses its latest projects and gives information about feminist issues.

Human Rights Campaign
http://www.hrc.org
Offers the latest information on political issues affecting lesbian, gay, bisexual, and transgender Americans.

National Clearinghouse on Child Abuse and Neglect Information
http://nccanch.acf.hhs.gov
Serves as a resource for professionals and others seeking information on child abuse and neglect and child welfare.

National Coalition Against Domestic Violence
http://www.ncadv.org
Provides information about domestic violence and suggestions for getting help.

National Sexual Violence Resource Center
http://www.nsvrc.org
A project of the Pennsylvania Coalition Against Rape; is a resource for information about rape and links to other sites.

U.S. Department of Justice, Bureau of Justice Statistics
http://www.ojp.usdoj.gov/bjs
Gives statistics and information on legal and enforcement issues related to victimization crime, as well as press releases.

U.S. Equal Employment Opportunity Commission
http://www.eeoc.gov
Provides information on federal laws prohibiting job discrimination and gives directions for filing a charge.

Suggested Reading

Fetner, T. (2008). *How the religious right shaped lesbian and gay activism.* Minneapolis: University of Minnesota Press. Descriptions of the two movements are significantly shaped by their rivals.

Koenig, L. J., Doll, L. S., O'Leary, A., & Pequegnat, W. (Eds.). (2004). *From child sexual abuse to adult sexual risk: Trauma, revictimization, and intervention.* Washington, DC: American Psychological Association. Examines the relation between child sexual abuse and adult sexual health outcomes in men and women.

Lalumiere, M. L., Harris, G. T., Quinsey, V. L., & Rice, M. E. (2005). *The causes of rape: Understanding individual male propensity for sexual aggression.* Washington, DC: American Psychological Association. Examines why some men are prone to rape, offers probable causes for this inclination, and provides a comprehensive review of scientific studies of coercive sex.

Maltz, W. (2001). *The sexual healing journey.* New York: HarperCollins. A comprehensive guide designed to help survivors of sexual abuse improve their relationships and discover the joys of sexual intimacy.

Raine, N. V. (1999). *After silence: Rape and my journey back.* New York: Three Rivers Press/Crown. An award-winning book that describes the long-term aftereffects of rape through an account of the author's own experience as a rape victim.

Sandy, P. R. (2007). *Fraternity gang rape: Sex, brotherhood, and privilege on campus.* New York: New York University Press. Discusses the nature of fraternity gang rape and how Greek life in general contributes to a culture that promotes the exploitation of women on college campuses.

Scarce, M. (1997). *Male on male rape.* New York: Plenum. One of few resources for survivors of male rape, written from the perspective of a rape survivor.

Schewe, P. A. (2002). *Preventing violence in relationships: Interventions across the lifespan.* Washington, DC: American Psychological Association. Focuses on building healthy relationships and preventing family violence.

For links, articles, and study material, go to the McGraw-Hill Web site, located at **www.mhhe.com/yarber7e.**

18

Sexually Explicit Materials, Prostitution, and Sex Laws

MAIN TOPICS

"My boyfriend and I sometimes use X-rated movies while we have sex. We have learned some new techniques from them, and they really help us get turned on. Some of our friends had recommended that we get them. At first, we were a little hesitant to use them, but now watching the movies has become a regular part of our sex. But I wonder if something is wrong with us having to use the movies. And, at times, I still feel uncomfortable using them. I sure haven't told any of my friends about them."

—21-year old female

"I was only sixteen when I traveled to Peru with Carlos, who was twenty-nine. We were in Lima for two days, and while we were there, Carlos took me to a hotel so we could both have sex with prostitutes. At the time, I did not really understand what was happening until after it occurred. Carlos knew that I was a virgin and thought this would be a fantastic way for me to become a 'man.' I felt embarrassed, dirty, and ashamed of myself."

—24-year-old male

"She (my aunt) actually started molesting me when I was six. She would come home late at night, drunk, and carry me into her bed so that she could perform oral sex on me. She molested me until I was twelve years old. She was a prostitute, so later in my molestation she tried to include her tricks, but I cried my way out of it every time."

—26-year-old female

> Since the human body is perfect in all forms, we cannot see it often enough.
>
> —Kenneth Clark
> (1903–1983)

MONEY AND SEX are bound together in the production and sale of sexually explicit material and in prostitution. Money is exchanged for sexual images or descriptions contained in films, electronic media, magazines, books, music, and photographs that depict people in explicit or suggestive sexual activities. Money is also exchanged for sexual services provided by streetwalkers, call girls, escorts, massage parlor workers, and other sex workers. The sex industry is a multibillion-dollar enterprise with countless millions of consumers and customers. As a nation, however, we feel ambivalent about sexually explicit material and prostitution. Many people condemn it as harmful, immoral, and exploitative and wish to censor or eliminate it. Others see it as a harmless and even beneficial activity, an erotic diversion, or an aspect of society that cannot (or should not) be regulated; they believe censorship and police action do greater harm than good.

In this chapter, we examine sexually explicit material, including depictions of sex in popular culture, the role of technology in the distribution of sexually explicit material, the effects of sexually explicit material, and censorship issues. We then examine prostitution, focusing on females and males working in the sex industry, the legal issues involved, and the impact of HIV and other STIs. We then discuss current laws dealing with private, consensual sexual behavior among adults and end the chapter with gay marriage.

• Sexually Explicit Material in Contemporary America

Studying sexually explicit material objectively is difficult because such material often triggers deep and conflicting feelings we have about sexuality. Many people enjoy sexually explicit material, others find it degrading, and still others may simultaneously feel aroused and guilty.

Pornography or Erotica: Which Is It?

As sexual themes, ideas, images, and music increasingly appear in art, literature, and popular culture, the boundaries blur between what is socially acceptable and what is considered erotic or obscene. Thus, we are confronted with questions like these: Is Eminem's crotch grabbing or Madonna and Britney Spears kissing at the 2004 MTV video music awards obscene or expressive (see photo on page 609)? Is the explicit talk show of Dr. Drew prurient or informative? Is the titillating satellite radio show of Howard Stern vulgar or entertaining?

Much of the discussion about sexually explicit material concerns the question of whether such material is, in fact, erotic or pornographic—that is, whether viewing it causes positive or harmful outcomes. Unfortunately, there is a lack of agreement about what constitutes erotica or pornography. Part of the problem is that "erotica" and "pornography" are subjective terms, and the line separating them can be blurred. **Erotica** describes sexually explicit material that can be evaluated positively. (The word "erotica" is derived from the Greek *erotikos,* meaning "a love poem.") It often involves mutuality, respect, affection, and a balance of power and may even be considered to have artistic value. **Pornography** represents sexually explicit material that is generally evaluated negatively and might include anything that depicts sexuality and causes sexual arousal in the viewer. ("Pornography" is a nineteenth-century word derived from the Greek *porne,* meaning "prostitute," and *graphos,* meaning "depicting.") Webster's *New World Collegiate Dictionary* defines pornography as "writing, pictures, etc. intended to arouse sexual desire." Sexually explicit materials are legal in the United States; however, materials that are considered to be obscene are not. Although the legal definition of **obscenity** varies, the term generally implies a personal or societal judgment that something is offensive; it comes from the Latin word for "filth." Often, material depicting the use of violence and aggression or degrading and dehumanizing situations is deemed obscene. Because such a determination involves a judgment, critics often point to the subjective nature of this definition. (Obscenity and the law are discussed in detail later in the section.)

The same sexually explicit material may evoke a variety of responses in different people. "What I like is erotica, but what you like is pornography" may be a facetious statement, but it's not entirely untrue. It has been found that people view others as more adversely affected than themselves by sexually explicit material (Gunther, 1995). Judgments about sexually explicit material tend to be relative.

Because of the tendency to use "erotica" as a positive term and "pornography" as a negative term, we will use the neutral term "sexually explicit material" whenever possible. **Sexually explicit material (SEM)** is material such as photographs, videos, films, magazines, and books whose primary themes, topics, or depictions involve sexuality that may cause sexual arousal; the genitals or intimate sexual behaviors typically are shown. Sometimes, however, the context of studies we are citing may require us to use either "erotica" or "pornography" rather than "sexually explicit material." This is especially true if the studies use those terms or are clearly making a positive or negative evaluation.

Sexually Explicit Material and Popular Culture

In the nineteenth century, technology transformed the production of sexually explicit material. Cheap paper and large-scale printing, combined with mass literacy, created an enormous market for books and drawings, including sexually

> How can you accuse me of liking pornography when I don't even have a pornograph?
> —Groucho Marx
> (1890–1977)

> The difference between pornography and erotica is lighting.
> —Gloria Leonard
> (1940–)

> Obscenity is whatever happens to shock some elderly and ignorant magistrate.
> —Bertrand Russell
> (1872–1970)

Click on "Technology and Sexual Fantasy" to see how various communications and entertainment media have incorporated elements of sexual titillation.

explicit material. Today, technology is once again extending the forms in which this material is conveyed.

In recent decades, sexually explicit material, especially soft-core (material that portrays sexual behaviors in a highly suggestive rather than an explicit way), has become an integral part of popular culture. *Playboy, Penthouse,* and *Hustler* are among the most widely circulated magazines in America. The depiction of sexual activities is not restricted to books and magazines, however. Various establishments offer live entertainment. Bars, for example, feature topless dancers. Some clubs or adult entertainment establishments employ erotic dancers who expose themselves and simulate sexual behaviors before their audience, and some even have "live sex shows." The Internet, cable and satellite television sex channels, and video/VCR/DVD revolutions have been so great that homes have largely supplanted adult theaters or "porno" movie houses as sites for viewing sexually explicit films.

The sexually explicit material industry is big business in the United States, with an estimated revenue of $12.6 billion in 2005 of which $4.3 billion was for sales and rentals of DVDs alone (Schultz, 2005). Frank Rich (2001), in his article "Naked Capitalists" in *The New York Times Magazine,* describes the magnitude of the "porn" industry:

> The $4 billion that Americans spend on video pornography is larger than the annual revenue accrued by either the N.F.L., the N.B.A. or Major League Baseball. But that's literally half of it: the porn business is estimated to total between $10 billion to $14 billion annually in the United States when you toss in porn networks and pay-for-view movies on cable and satellite, Internet Web sites, in-room hotel movies, phone sex, sex toys and that archaic medium of my own occasionally misspent youth, magazines.

The availability of in-home sexually explicit films has had a profound effect on *who* views erotic films. In the past, adult movie houses were the domain of men; relatively few women entered them. Most explicit DVDs or films, as well as books and magazines, have been marketed to heterosexual men. But with erotic films available for viewing in the privacy of the home, women and couples have become consumers of sexually explicit material. The inclusion of women in the audience has led to the production of **femme porn,** sexually explicit material catering to women and heterosexual couples. Compared to other types of porn, femme porn typically involves women in its production and has story lines that depict emotional intimacy and greater equality between the sexes, is less male centered, avoids violence, and is more sensitive to women's erotic fantasies (Milne, 2005).

Undoubtedly, the total money spent on sexually explicit films continues to be high. And the amount may increase even more if what is happening in Europe—the availability of explicit films on cell phones—becomes widespread in the United States. Cell phone pornography was a $775 million industry in 2007 in Europe and is projected to grow to $1.5 billion by 2012. The global market may reach $3.5 billion in 2010. Accessing explicit film clips via cell phone has several advantages such as the small size and portability of the phone and the ease of concealing it. Unlike in Europe, cell phone pornography is not yet widely available in the United States. However, media authorities predict that it will become available for free soon, and some adult industry companies have been pushing hard for this way of expanding their market. In the U.S., phone carriers are concerned about political, religious, and parental opposition, as well as the need to develop cell phone systems to shield minors from the explicit clips ("Porn to Spice Up Cell Phones," 2008). It will be interesting to

Erotic or pornographic? The kiss that occurred on national television between Madonna and Britney Spears raised the question about what is acceptable viewing on home entertainment. What do you think?

Click on "Sharon: A Telephone Sex Worker" to hear Sharon talk about her work at a firm that offers explicit telephone sex.

see how the societal and parental issues related to the availability of explicit films on cell phones will evolve in the next few years. (For more about other types of sexually oriented forms of mass media, see Chapter 1.)

Internet Sex Site Use by College Students

Internet sites containing sexually explicit materials are so common that, according to estimates, they comprise more than 1 in every 10 sites, accounting for about 25% of daily search-engine requests (Ropelato, 2006). In this section, we present research on Internet sex site use among college students, who, for the most part, are within the age group—18 to 25 years—that uses sexually explicit material most often (Buzzell, 2005). With the dramatic increase in computer technology and availability, college students have ample access to sexually explicit Web sites. Studies of college students help us understand the prevalence of and factors related to sex site use by this population.

A study of Canadian university students published in 2002 found that Internet use to view sexually explicit material was more common among men than women (72% versus 22%) (Boies, 2002). A study published in 2008 that assessed U.S. college students' viewing of sexually explicit media, including the Internet, movies, and/or magazines, found a similar gap by gender: 87% for men, 31% for women (Carroll et al., 2008). (For more information about the findings of this study, see the box "College Students

think
about it

College Students and the Viewing of Sexually Explicit Media

Accessibility to and acceptability of sexually explicit media is becoming more widespread in our increasingly technological world. In contrast to the 1980s, when one would have to go to a store and ask for "porn" magazines (often located behind the counter) or visit an adult theater (located in a "seedy" area of town), young people today can, with the press of a key, acquire sexually explicit materials easily via the Internet. In fact, today's young people are the first generation to have access to sexual images on a wireless, handheld device and be able to distribute them to others. With the omnipresence of computers and the Internet in homes and on college campuses plus the nearly universal use of cell phones, the use of sexually explicit materials may be a prevalent part of young adulthood meriting research (Arnett, 2006; Carroll et al., 2008; Fackelmann, 2007).

Family life researcher Jason Carroll of Brigham Young University and his colleagues assessed, via an online questionnaire, the levels of pornography use and acceptance of pornography among 813 university students (313 men, 500 women; mean age 20 years) recruited from six college sites across the United States (Carroll et al., 2008). Pornography was defined as media (such as Internet, movies, and/or magazines) portraying nudity and sexual behaviors used or intended to increase sexual arousal. The data set also captured whether or not a sample of fathers and mothers of the participating college students agreed that pornography is an acceptable expression of one's sexuality. Here's what the researchers found:

- About two thirds (67%) of the college men and one half (49%) of the college women agreed that viewing pornography is an acceptable way to express one's sexuality.

- Nearly 9 in 10 (87%) of the men reported using pornography, with about one fifth reporting daily or every-other-day use and nearly half (48%) reporting weekly or more frequent use.

- Nearly one third (31%) of the women reported using pornography, with two thirds (67%) of those reporting pornography use indicating they used pornography once a month or less often. Only 3% reported pornography use weekly or more often.

- For men, significant connections were found between use of pornography and greater number of lifetime sexual partners and more acceptance of premarital, casual, and extramarital sexual behavior. Further, the men who used pornography had higher levels of alcohol drinking and binge drinking than the non-users.

- For women, higher acceptance and use of pornography was significantly related to greater acceptance of casual sexual behavior, greater number of sexual partners in the past 12 months and lifetime, and alcohol use, binge drinking, and cigarette use.

- For both the men and the women, greater acceptance of pornography was related to being more accepting of nonmarital cohabitation and having a greater desire for later marriage and parenthood, financial independence between spouses, and lower levels of child-centeredness.

- Only about one third (37%) of the fathers and one fifth (20%) of the mothers of the college students in the study agreed that pornography is an acceptable expression of one's sexuality.

The researchers concluded that, for college men, pornography use is as common as drinking. They state that "it appears that a sizable number of emerging young men 'binge' on pornography, with similar frequency and intensity that define binge drinking on American college campuses." They therefore questioned whether, similar to binge drinking behaviors, the pornography use would taper off and not lead to lasting negative effects or whether the high use would be the genesis for problematic behavior in the future.

The researchers concluded that the most notable finding was the marked difference in pornography use and acceptance among the college men and women in the study. And they wondered if the large disparity of pornography acceptance and use between the men and women would impact their future serious romantic relationships. For example, once men were in relationships, would they decrease or stop pornography use or continue to use pornography, but covertly? Would women in the same circumstance start or increase their pornography use? The researchers did note that both the pornography users and the non-users had a high desire to eventually marry and become parents.

Think Critically

- How common is Internet pornography use on your campus?
- Why do you think men and women differ in their use and acceptance of pornography?
- How do you think pornography use might impact a future romantic relationship?

SOURCES: Arnett, J. J. (2006). Emerging adulthood: Understanding the new way of coming of age. In J. J. Arnett & J. L. Tanner (Eds.), *Emerging adults in America: Coming of age in the 21st century* (pp. 3–20). Washington, DC: American Psychological Association; Carroll, J. S., Padilla-Walker, L. M., Nelson, L. J., Olson, C. D., Barry, C. M., & Madsen, S. D. (2008). Pornography acceptance and use among emerging adults. *Journal of Adolescent Research, 23*, 6–30.

and the Viewing of Sexually Explicit Media" on the previous page.) The Canadian study also found that:

- 82% reported that the viewing of SEM online was sexually arousing, yet 57% indicated that the viewing disturbed them;
- 65% reported that the viewing of SEM satisfied curiosity;
- 63% said that they learned new sex techniques from the viewing of SEM and 44% said that they believed it improved their sexual relationship offline; and
- 83% of the men and 55% of the women reported masturbating while viewing the SEM.

Further research on the variables used in these studies would be valuable so that we would have more updated information about the factors related to college student use of Internet sex sites, particularly given the dramatic increase of Internet technology and its availability to young people.

Content and Themes   Many of the themes found in sexually explicit material are also found in the mainstream media. Music videos, TV shows, and movies, for example, contain sexual scenes and innuendos, images of the subordination of women, and acts of violence. They differ primarily in their levels of explicitness. When researchers analyzed the contents of sexually explicit media, they found four common themes: diverse sexual activity, high levels of sexual desire, pleasure as the purpose of sexual activity, and many readily available sexual partners (Schlosser, 1997).

Many "mainstream" sexually explicit films target a male, heterosexual audience and portray stereotypes of male sexuality: dominant men with huge, erect

> The older one grows, the more one likes indecency.
>
> —Virginia Woolf
> (1882–1941)

The performances of pop music artists are often highly sexual; Beyoncé Knowles uses sexuality as an integral theme in her videos and concerts, as do many pop music artists.

penises, able to "last long" and satisfy eager and acquiescent women who are driven mad by their sexual prowess. The major theme of the films is cookbook sex; they show fellatio, cunnilingus, vaginal and anal sex, climax with the man ejaculating on the woman's body, and the woman typically faking an orgasm. The focus is typically on the physical beauty of the woman "star," with three-somes (two women and one man) or group sex often featured. The male actors may not even be "good-looking" (Cassell, 2008; Paul, 2006). One criticism is that films like these do not represent the unique individuality of sexual expression nor how women experience erotic fulfillment. Very little focus is on relationships, emotional intimacy, nonsexual aspects of life, or the woman's sexual satisfaction. Rarely are lovers shown massaging each other's shoulders or whispering "I love you." Nor do lovers ask each other questions such as "Is this okay?" or "What can I do to help you feel more pleasure?" (Castleman, 2004). Some sex therapists criticize these films as reinforcing an unhealthy and unrealistic image of sexuality: that men are all-powerful and that women are submissive objects, deriving all sexual satisfaction from male domination.

As touched on previously, however, there is evidence that some sexually explicit films are moving away from impersonal sex to more romantic views of sexual encounters. This trend may be the result of women's becoming an increasingly large segment of the market. Women traditionally place sexual relationships within a more romantic or relational context. One study found that women who viewed videos targeted at a female audience were more aroused, absorbed, and positive about such videos than they were toward impersonal videos (Mosher & Maclan, 1994).

Gay and lesbian sexually explicit films differ somewhat from straight, heterosexual-focused films. Gay porn typically features attractive, young, muscular, "well-hung" men, and focuses on the eroticism of the male body. Lesbian-explicit films usually depict realistic sexual interactions with a range of body types and both butch (notably masculine in manner or appearance) and femme styles (Blue, 2003). Sex between men is rarely shown in heterosexual films, presumably because it would make heterosexual men uncomfortable. But heterosexual videos may sometimes portray sex between women because many heterosexual men find such depictions sexually arousing.

With few exceptions, most studies are of material featuring White heterosexuals. As a result, we have very little empirical evidence about sexually explicit material directed toward ethnic groups such as African Americans and Latinos, or toward gay men and lesbian women. Such research is limited or nonexistent, but needed.

The Effects of Sexually Explicit Material

There are a number of concerns about the effects of sexually explicit material: Does it cause people to engage in "deviant" behavior? Is it a form of sex discrimination against women? And, finally, does it cause violence against women?

Sexual Expression
People who read or view sexually explicit material usually recognize it as fantasy; they use it as a release from their everyday lives. Exposure to such material temporarily encourages sexual expression and may activate a person's *typical* sexual behavior pattern.

Sexually explicit material deals with fantasy sex, not sex as we know it in the context of human relationships. This sex usually takes place in a world in

> Western man, especially the Western critic, still finds it very hard to go into print and say: "I recommend you go and see this because it gave me an erection."
>
> —Kenneth Tynan
> (1927–1980)

which people and situations are defined in exclusively sexual terms. People are stripped of their nonsexual connections.

People are interested in sexually explicit material for a number of reasons. First, they enjoy the sexual sensations erotica arouses; it can be a source of intense pleasure. Masturbation or other sexual activities, pleasurable in themselves, may accompany the use of sexually explicit material or follow it. Second, since the nineteenth century, sexually explicit material has been a source of sexual information and knowledge. Eroticism generally is hidden from view and discussion. When sexuality is discussed in the family, in schools, or in public, it is typically discussed moralistically, rationally, or objectively. And most discussions are in the context of sexual intercourse; other sexual behaviors are not discussed. Because the erotic aspects of sexuality are rarely talked about, sexually explicit material can fill the void. Third, sexually explicit material, like fantasy, may provide an opportunity for people to rehearse sexual activities. Fourth, reading or viewing sexually explicit material to obtain pleasure or to enhance one's fantasies or masturbatory experiences may be regarded as safer sex.

Sex therapist Barbara Keesling (2006) states that she often recommends the use of sexually explicit materials to women who experience low sexual desire and sexual arousal problems. She notes that "women can sometimes learn to become more aroused by retraining themselves in the ability to feel physical arousal at the sight of sexually explicit images." Keesling also states that since some women may "shut down" because of their belief that some sexually explicit material may be disgusting, they should try to find material that is both acceptable and arousing to them. Men are cautioned that sexually explicit materials are typically all-genital and that such focus can wreak havoc on their sexual expression in bed—they should not buy into the idea that sex should occur like it does in most adult films. Medical writer Michael Castleman (2004) suggests the following for men, although his advice could also apply to women:

> Stop trying to imitate what you see in pornography—the rushed, mechanical sex that's entirely focused on the genitals. Instead, cultivate the opposite of porn: leisurely, playful, creative, whole-body, massage-based lovemaking that includes the genitals, but is not obsessed with them.

Sexually explicit material may perform an additional function for those who are HIV-positive or have AIDS or another STI. Because having these diseases can create anxieties about transmissions to others, sexually explicit material permits infected individuals to explore their own sexuality with masturbatory images and scenes while refraining from potentially risky sexual encounters with a partner.

Variation in Personal Response

Why does one person evaluate sexually explicit material negatively and another positively? The answer seems to lie in the individual's emotional response to the material. A person's erotophobic/erotophilic attitudes affect his or her response to sexually explicit material (see Chapter 9). Erotophilic people tend to respond positively to such material; erotophobic people do not. Sociologist Ira Reiss (1990) writes:

> Our reactions to sexually arousing films or books provide insight into our personal sexual attitudes. What we really are reacting to is not the objective material but rather a projection of our own innermost feelings concerning the type of sexuality presented. We may feel that sexuality being portrayed is too revealing, too embarrassing, too suggestive, or too private.

The only thing pornography has been known to cause is solitary masturbation.

—Gore Vidal
(1925–)

Obscenity is best left to the minds of man. What's obscene to one may not offend another.

—William O. Douglas
(1898–1980)

Some contemporary video games have strong, suggestive sexual messages.

My reaction to porno films is as follows: After the first ten minutes, I want to go home and screw. After the first twenty minutes, I never want to screw anything as long as I live.

—Erica Jong
(1942–)

What's wrong with appealing to prurient interests? We appeal to killing interest.

—Lenny Bruce
(1925–1966)

Sexual Aggression In 1970, the President's Commission on Pornography and Obscenity concluded that pornography did not cause harm or violence. It recommended that all legislation restricting adult access to it be repealed as inconsistent with the First Amendment.

In the 1980s, President Ronald Reagan established a new pornography commission under Attorney General Edwin Meese. In 1986, the Attorney General's Commission on Pornography stated that "the most prevalent forms of pornography" were violent; it offered no evidence, however, to substantiate its assertion (U.S. Attorney General's Commission on Pornography [AGCOP], 1986). There is, in fact, no evidence that the majority of sexually explicit material is violent; actually, very little contains aggression, physical violence, or rape (Garcia & Milano, 1991; Scott & Cuvelier, 1993).

In the 1970s, feminists and others working to increase rape awareness began to call attention to the violence against women portrayed in the media. They found rape themes in sexually explicit material especially disturbing, arguing that those images reinforced rape myths. Again, however, there is no evidence that nonviolent sexually explicit material is associated with actual sexual aggression against women. Even the conservative commission on pornography agreed that nonviolent sexually explicit material had no such effect (AGCOP, 1986). It did assert that "some forms of sexually explicit materials bear a causal relationship . . . to sexual violence," but it presented no scientific proof.

Researchers have studied the relationship between violent sexually explicit material and aggression and negative attitudes toward women. Most studies have been experimental; that is, male college students were exposed to various media, and factors related to their attitudes about, for example, the rape of women were measured. In studying male responses to depictions of rape, researchers have found that realistic portrayals of rape tend not to be arousing to men and may actually produce negative emotional responses (Bauserman, 1998). This is in contrast to the responses that are elicited to "rape myths," or unrealistic portrayals in films in which women become aroused and participate willingly. In a national sample of men enrolled in postsecondary education, researchers reported that men having the highest levels of hostility, sexual "promiscuity," and pornography use were the most likely to report a history of sexual aggression against women. But the researchers noted that we cannot conclude from this analysis that pornography use causes or is an outcome of aggressive sexual tendencies (Malamuth, Addison, & Koss, 2001).

Sometimes, the consumption of sexually explicit films and sexual assault are linked in the popular media, but with no evidence. An analysis of the trend of sexual assaults in the United States from 1995, when Internet pornography availability began to increase, to 2005 revealed a steady decline in the number of sexual assaults. The scientists who analyzed the trend of assaults concluded that "after a full decade of the easiest availability of every type of erotic, degrading and violent pornographic material, no increase in rates of reported sexual assault was found" (Whitty & Fisher, 2008). A study of 1,023 Australian consumers of sexually explicit materials (in magazines, DVDs, novels, and the Internet) found no association between consumption of sexually explicit media and negative attitudes toward women (McKee, 2007). However, a relationship was found between greater negative attitudes toward women and being older, voting for a right-wing political party, residing in a rural area, being less educated, and being a man.

Contact with sexually explicit material is a self-regulated choice, and research on factors related to such self-directed behavior is very limited: "Existing findings by and large fail to confirm fears of strong antisocial effects of self-directed exposure to sexually explicit media" (Fisher & Barak, 2001). Despite some of these more recent findings, whether violent sexually explicit material causes sexual aggression toward women remains a fractious issue.

Sex Discrimination   Since the 1980s, feminists have been divided over the issue of sexually explicit material. One segment of the feminist movement, which identifies itself as antipornography, views sexually explicit material as inherently degrading and dehumanizing to women. Many in this group believe that sexually explicit material provides the basis for women's subordination by turning them into sex objects. They argue that sexually explicit material inhibits women's attainment of equal rights by encouraging the exploitation and subordination of women.

Feminist and other critics of this approach point out that it has an antisexual bias that associates sex with exploitation. Sexually explicit images, rather than specifically sexist images, are singled out. Furthermore, discrimination against and the subordination of women in Western culture have existed since ancient times, long before the rise of sexually explicit material. The roots of subordination lie far deeper. The elimination of sexual depictions of women would not alter discrimination against women significantly, if at all. Sex researchers William Fisher and Clive Davis, in their review of research on the impact of sexually explicit materials, state that sexual scientists are against any anti-woman attitudes and aggression that some people may fear would result from experience with pornography. They suggest that remedies for such attitudes and behavior linked to pornography could be achieved through education, policies and laws, and social change, for example (Fisher & Davis, 2007). However, they also state,

> The inconsistent evidence connecting pornography with harm would indicate that efforts to fight pornography as a way of combating anti-woman attitudes and anti-woman aggression would not effectively bring about the sought-after result.

Leonore Tiefer (2004), clinical associate professor of psychiatry at the New York University School of Medicine and sex therapist who is a primary spokesperson for newer views of women's sexuality, states that sexually explicit materials can contribute to women's sexual power. She notes that empowerment, not protection, is the path to sexual growth in women. Tiefer states that

> if we accept that women's sexuality has been shaped by ignorance and shame and is just beginning to find new opportunities and voices for expression, then now is exactly the wrong time to even think about campaigns of suppression. Suppressing pornography will harm women struggling to develop their own sexualities.

Child Pornography   Child pornography is a form of child sexual exploitation. Children used for the production of sexually explicit materials, who are usually between the ages of 6 and 16, are motivated by friendship, interest in

Censorship can't eliminate evil; it can only kill freedom.
—Garrison Keillor
(1942–)

Click on "Arthur, Attorney for First Amendment Issues," to hear an attorney talk about cases in which people have been arrested for images involving children that they downloaded from the Internet.

sexuality, offers of money, or threats. Younger children may be unaware that their photographs are being used sexually. A number of these children are related to the photographer. Many children who have been exploited in this way exhibit distress and poor adjustment; they may suffer from depression, anxiety, and guilt. Others engage in destructive and antisocial behavior.

Digital cameras and cell phones with cameras, plus the ability to download photographs onto computers, have made this into what some call the "golden age of child pornography." Children and teenagers have been reported taking pictures of each other and posting them on the Internet or sending them to each other, a practice called "sexting." The fact that the possession of such images is a crime does not deter people from placing or viewing them on the Internet. Laws governing obscenity and child pornography already exist and, for the most part, can be applied to cases involving the Internet to adequately protect minors. Unlike some sexually explicit material, child pornography has been found to be patently offensive and therefore not within the zone of protected free speech. Internet child pornography is common. One study, reported in 2007, found that child pornography was far-reaching across the world. The investigation indentified over 2,000 e-mail addresses in at least 77 countries, including the United States, of customers who paid to view film clips of young boys and girls being sexually abused. The authorities noted that the customers are hard to trace since many have multiple addresses (Johnson, 2007).

Censorship, Sexually Explicit Material, and the Law

To censor means to examine in order to suppress or delete anything considered objectionable. **Censorship** occurs when the government, private groups, or individuals impose their moral or political values on others by suppressing words, ideas, or images they deem offensive. Obscenity, as noted previously, is the state of being contrary to generally accepted standards of decency or morality. During the first half of the twentieth century, under American obscenity laws, James Joyce's *Ulysses* and the works of D.H. Lawrence were prohibited,

> *Congress shall make no law . . . abridging the freedom of speech, or of the press . . .*
> —First Amendment to the Constitution of the United States

> *A dirty book is seldom a dusty one.*
> —Anonymous

Two of the most heavily censored books in America are Leslea Newman's *Heather Has Two Mommies*, and Michael Willhoite's *Daddy's Roommate* (shown here). These books are opposed because they depict a lesbian couple family and a gay couple family, respectively.

think about it

Sexually Explicit Materials: Helpful or Harmful?

Visual depictions of sexual behavior and genitals have always been a part of society. Because of the Internet, there has been an explosion in the number of and access to sexually explicit images. These materials add to the abundance of existing books and magazines such as *Playboy, Penthouse, Hustler,* and *Playgirl,* as well as explicit films available via mail and at video rental stores and "adult" bookstores. Some videos, such as *The Better Sex Video Series,* are touted as sex education tools designed to increase sexual skills and enhance sexual pleasure for couples. The widespread availability of sexually explicit materials has heightened concerns about their impact. The fundamental question remains: Are sexually explicit materials helpful or harmful?

Some people believe that sexually explicit materials are useful or, at the least, harmless. They contend that the materials provide information about sexual expression, enhance a couple's sexual behavior, provide an outlet for sexual expression, and offer entertainment; thus, they should be readily available to adults. Others feel that sexually explicit materials cause sexual criminality, lead to moral decay and societal breakdown, demean and objectify women, and damage children; therefore, access should be restricted. The debate over sexually explicit materials has forced us to confront core issues related to freedom of speech, definitions of "erotica" versus "pornography," protection of children, the impact of sexual information, the rights of citizens, censorship, and the role of government in "protecting" its citizens. Various efforts have been made by the federal government to restrict access to sexually explicit materials, and some statutes have received Supreme Court support.

Think Critically

- Do you think sexually explicit materials are helpful or harmful? Does your answer vary based on the content of such materials or the audience exposed to the materials?
- Should the federal government regulate access to such materials? If so, what types of materials, and what audiences?
- Should any attempts to limit or deny access to sexually explicit materials on the Internet be made, given that national laws cannot extend to other countries?

Havelock Ellis's *Studies in the Psychology of Sex* was banned, nude paintings were removed from gallery and museum walls, and everything but chaste kisses was banned from the movies for years.

U.S. Supreme Court decisions in the 1950s and 1960s eliminated much of the legal framework supporting literary censorship on the national level. But censorship continues to flourish on the state and local levels, especially among schools and libraries. The women's health book *The New Our Bodies, Ourselves* has been a frequent object of attack because of its feminist perspective and descriptions of lesbian sexuality. More recently, two children's books have been added to the list of most censored books: Leslea Newman's *Heather Has Two Mommies* and Michael Willhoite's *Daddy's Roommate*. Both books have come under attack because they describe children in healthy lesbian couple and gay couple families. Judy Blume's books for teenagers, J. D. Salinger's *The Catcher in the Rye,* and the *Sports Illustrated* swimsuit issue are regular items on banned-publications lists. And exhibits of the photographs taken by the late Robert Mapplethorpe have been strenuously attacked by the more conservative groups for "promoting" homoeroticism.

Obscenity Laws   Sexually explicit material itself is not illegal, but materials defined as legally obscene are. It is difficult to arrive at a legal definition of obscenity for determining whether a specific illustration, photograph, novel, or

> ❝ *If a man is pictured chopping off a woman's breast, it only gets an "R" rating; but if, God forbid, a man is pictured kissing a woman's breast, it gets an "X" rating. Why is violence more acceptable than tenderness?*
>
> —Sally Struthers (1948–)

film is obscene. Traditionally, U.S. courts have considered material obscene if it tended to corrupt or deprave its user. Over the years, the law has been debated in a number of court cases. This process has resulted in a set of criteria for determining what is obscene:

- The dominant theme of the work must appeal to prurient sexual interests and portray sexual conduct in a patently offensive way.
- Taken as a whole, the work must be without serious literary, artistic, political, or scientific value.
- A "reasonable" person must find the work, when taken as a whole, to possess no social value.

The problem with these criteria, as well as the earlier standards, is that they are highly subjective. For example, who is a reasonable person? Most of us would probably find that a reasonable person has opinions regarding obscenity that closely resemble our own. (Otherwise, we would think that he or she was unreasonable.) However, there are many instances in which "reasonable people" disagree about whether material has social value. In 1969, the U.S. Supreme Court ruled, in *Stanley v. Georgia,* that private possession of obscene material in one's home is not illegal (Sears, 1989). This does not, however, apply to child pornography.

As we saw earlier, our evaluation of sexually explicit material is closely related to how we feel about such material. Our judgments are based not on reason but on emotion. Justice Potter Stewart's exasperation in *Jacobelis v. Ohio* (1965) reveals a reasonable person's frustration in trying to define pornography: "But I know it when I see it."

The Issue of Child Protection

In 1988, the United States passed the Child Protection and Obscenity Enforcement Act, which supports stiff penalties for individuals involved in the production, distribution, and possession of child pornography. Since then, the development and distribution of child pornography, as well as minors' access to online pornography, has been the focus of the U.S. Congress, resulting in the passing of numerous legislative acts. As you can see in Table 18.1, the bills have most often been turned down by the courts, usually based on protection of free speech; however, there have been a few instances of the courts upholding the law.

The Communications and Decency Act of 1996 tried to address the problem of sexual exploitation of children and teens over the Internet by making it a crime to send obscene or indecent messages to minors via e-mail, chat rooms, and Web sites (Biskupic, 2004). In 1997, the U.S. Supreme Court ruled that the statute was not constitutional because it violated the First Amendment's guarantee of free speech. In two subsequent rulings, the Court rejected the law that made it a crime to send an indecent message online to a person under age 18 and the ban on computer-generated "virtual" child pornography and other fake images of sex, saying that the law could have banned works of art (Biskupic, 2002, 2003a, 2004). However, in 2008, the U.S. Supreme Court upheld the Child Obscenity and Pornography Act of 2003, a law that made it a crime to produce or possess sexually explicit images of children as well as to "pander" to willing audiences through advertising, presenting, distributing, or soliciting such material. The 2003 law applies even if the material consists solely of computer-generated images or digitally altered photographs of adults, and even if the offer of material is fraudulent (e.g., the material does not exist) (Greenhouse, 2008; Mears, 2008).

> " I would like to see an end to all obscenity laws in my lifetime. I don't know that it will happen, but it's my goal. If I can leave any kind of legacy at all, it will be that I helped expand the parameters of free speech.
>
> —Larry Flynt
> (1942–)

1996	The Communications Decency Act is passed by Congress, banning the posting or sending of obscene or indecent messages on the Internet to persons under age 18.
1998	The Child Online Protection Act (COPA) is passed by Congress, targeting material "harmful to minors" only on commercial Web sites. The age of those protected is lowered to under 17. COPA is challenged by the American Civil Liberties Union and online publishers on the grounds that it violates free-speech rights.
1999	The Communications Decency Act is rejected by the U.S. Supreme Court, calling it too vague and broad.
2000	COPA is struck down by a U.S. appeals court citing the statute's attempt to set "community standards" for the Internet. COPA defined materials that should be banned as those that "the average person, applying contemporary community standards, would find . . . designed to appeal to . . . the prurient interest."
2002	The Supreme Court rules that the use of community standards does not, by itself, make COPA too broad.
2003	A U.S. appeals court again rejects COPA, saying that the law is not the least restrictive way the government can shield minors from online porn.
2004	COPA is not permitted to take effect by ruling of the U.S. Supreme Court. The justices suggest that the law is likely unconstitutional and that software computer filters may be a less restrictive way to screen sexually explicit materials. The statute is sent back to a lower court.
2007	U.S. district court judge issues a permanent injunction against COPA, stating that it violates the First and Fifth Amendments of the U.S. Constitution. The federal government appeals the ruling.
2009	COPA ends as the U.S. Supreme Court turns away the government's final attempt to revive the law.

SOURCE: Adapted from "Congress' Attempts at Limits Have Faced Several Obstacles," *USA Today,* June 30, 2004, p. 6A (Years 1996–2004). Reprinted with permission.

Justice Antonin Scalia, writing for the majority, noted, "Offers to provide and obtain child pornography are categorically excluded from the First Amendment" (quoted in Greenhouse, 2008). Free-speech proponents question whether mainstream movies or innocent photographs of babies and young children, for example, might now be subject to prosecution.

Another law intended to keep adult material away from Net-surfing children is the Child Online Protection Act (COPA). Passed in 1998, it sought to require Internet users to give an adult ID before accessing a commercial site containing "adult" materials (Miller, 2000). The law has been blocked twice by the U.S. Supreme Court. Table 18.1 provides a summary of congressional efforts to protect children from online pornography and subsequent court rulings. In its 2004 ruling, the U.S. Supreme Court stated that the use of filtering software on home computers might be the best method of shielding kids from porn while preserving the rights of adults. Justice Kennedy wrote for the majority, stating that the Court presumes that any government attempts to limit explicit materials on the Web are unconstitutional (Biskupic, 2004). In 2007, COPA was again struck down. A U.S. district court judge ruled that the defendant (the federal government) had failed to show that COPA is the least restrictive, most effective alternative in achieving the goal of shielding minors from online pornography and that COPA is impermissibly vague and overboard. The judge also noted that "perhaps we do the minors harm if First Amendment protections, which they will inherit fully, are chipped away in the name of their protection" (U.S. District Court, Eastern District of Pennsylvania, 2007). In January 2009, COPA ended more than a decade after Congress had approved it. The U.S. Supreme Court rejected the government's final effort to revive the law by turning away the appeal without comment ("Internet pornography law dies quietly in Supreme Court," 2009).

In 2003, the U.S. Supreme Court upheld a provision of the Children's Internet Protection Act that requires public libraries receiving federal funding

> " To slurp or not to slurp at the fountain of filth is a decision to which each of us is entitled.
>
> Stephen Kessler

to put antipornography Internet filters on their computers or lose funding. More than 95% of the nation's libraries offer Internet access. The Court rejected arguments that filters violate library patrons' First Amendment free-speech rights and said that adults should be able to ask librarians to disable the filters. Opponents of Internet filters contend that filtering software is so imprecise that it blocks constitutionally protected sexual material and medical information (Locy & Biskupic, 2003). They note that, for some young people, the Internet is their only source of valuable information about sexual health, sexually transmitted infections, birth control, and pregnancy. This contention was confirmed in a research study on blocking filters and searching for health information in the *Journal of the American Medical Association* (Richardson, Resnick, Hansen, Derry, & Rideout, 2002); it concluded that an unintended outcome of Internet filtering software is the blocking of "legitimate" information.

With millions of children accessing the Internet from home, serious questions must be asked about their access to certain kinds of information, pictures, graphics, videos, animation, and interactive experiences. Government censorship, academic freedom, constitutionally protected speech, child safety concerns, public health dilemmas—these and other troublesome issues are at the core of the Internet–free-speech debate (Portelli & Meade, 1998).

Our inability to find criteria for objectively defining obscenity makes it potentially dangerous to censor such material. We may end up using our own personal standards to restrict speech otherwise guaranteed by the First Amendment. By enforcing our own biases, we could endanger the freedom of others.

> Murder is a crime. Describing murder is not. Sex is not a crime. Describing sex is.
>
> —Bill Margold
> (1943–)

> I may disagree with what you say but I will defend to the death your right to say it.
>
> —Voltaire
> (1694–1778)

• Prostitution

The exchange of sexual behaviors such as intercourse, fellatio, anal intercourse, discipline and bondage, and obscene insults, for money and/or goods, is called **prostitution.** More recently, instead of the term "prostitute," the terms "sex worker" and "commercial sex worker" have often been used, particularly by prostitutes, to identify themselves and other sex-related work they might do such as phone sex, exotic dancing, Internet sex, and acting in sexually explicit videos. Many individuals who enter prostitution do so for monetary gains; hence, prostitution can represent a form of work. However, given that some research shows negative aspects of prostitution and that some prostitutes are coerced by a third party, some feminists are uncomfortable with connoting prostitution as a type of sex work and are hesitant to "celebrate the existence of a market for commoditized sex" (Davidson, 2002). We have decided to use the term "prostitution/prostitute," to distinguish it from other types of "sex work." Yet, we recognize that "sex work" is a preferred term by many prostitutes and is becoming more frequently used to describe prostitution.

Boys and girls as well as men and women, including transvestites and transsexuals, work as prostitutes. By far the most common form of prostitution is women selling sex to men. The second most common is male prostitutes making themselves available to men. Less common is males selling sex to females. Prostitution between two women is rare. A growing international market of child sex slaves has fueled the economies of developing countries and spawned a multibillion dollar industry commonly referred to as "sex travel" (see "Think About It" Forced Against Their Will: International Child and Teen Prostitution).

Male customers of female prostitutes, called "johns," represent a wide range of occupations, ethnicities, ages, and marital statuses. Men go to prostitutes for many reasons. Some want to experience a certain sexual behavior that their partner is unwilling to try, or they may not have a regular partner. Some desire to have sex with someone having a certain image, such as sexy or very athletic looking. Some like the anonymity of being sexual with a prostitute: No courting is required, there are no postsex expectations, and it is less entangling than having an affair. Sometimes, young men go to a prostitute as their first sexual experience (Weitzer, 2005). Curiously, in a study of 140 men from large cities in the Midwest and on the West Coast who have used prostitutes, only one third reported that they enjoyed sex with a female prostitute, and 57% reported that they had tried to stop using prostitutes. The study also found that the common impression that men seek prostitutes when sexually dissatisfied with marital sex was only mildly supported, and the data did not support the notion that men seek "unusual" sexual behaviors such as bondage with a female prostitute. Nearly 30% indicated that they had used alcohol prior to visiting a prostitute (Sawyer, Metz, Hinds, & Brucker, 2001–2002).

Females Working in Prostitution

Determining the number of women who are prostitutes is difficult for many reasons, including different definitions of prostitution as well the secrecy often involved with the accepting of money for sex. Some studies of female prostitutes and their male clients can give us an idea of the prevalence of female prostitutes, although the numbers may not reflect the true prevalence because the stigma associated with prostitution may result in underreporting. According to sex researchers Samuel Janus and Cynthia Janus (1993), 5% of the women and 20% of the men in their representative study reported exchanging sex for money. Sociologist Edward Laumann and his colleagues (1994) report that 16% of the men surveyed ever paid for sex. A more recent study of a representative sample of men from around the world found that, on average, about 9–10% of the men had purchased sex from a female prostitute in the past 12 months (Carael, Slaymaker, Lyerla, & Sarkar, 2006). And a study of 2,665 British men completing a health-screening questionnaire found that 10% (267) reported paying for sex over the decade 1990 to 2000, with 96% of these reporting paying women and 4% paying men (Groom & Nandwani, 2006).

Sex as Work   Many women who accept money or drugs for sexual activities do not consider themselves prostitutes. Prostitutes often identify themselves as "working girls" or "sex workers," probably an accurate description of how they perceive themselves in relation to sex. Common, but more pejorative, terms are "whore" and "hooker." They are usually sex workers not because they like anonymous sex and different partners per se, but because they perceive it as good-paying work. They generally do not expect to enjoy sex with their customers and avoid emotional intimacy. They separate sex as a physical expression for which they are paid from sex as an expression of intimacy and pleasure. One prostitute (quoted in Zausner, 1986) describes her feelings about sex:

> I don't think about sex when I'm working. You have to be a good actress to make men think that you like it when you don't. I only enjoy sex if I'm with someone I care about.

Entrance Into Prostitution   Many women begin working as prostitutes in their younger years, even in their early teens (Albert, Warner, Hatcher, Trussell,

Identifying women as sexual beings whose responsibility is the sexual service of men is the social base for gender specific slavery.

—Kathleen Berry

Forced Against Their Will: International Child and Teen Prostitution

It is estimated that 4 million people worldwide are bought and sold each year—into marriage, prostitution, or slavery. About 800,000 of these people, of whom about 80% are women and girls and up to 50% are minors, are trafficked across national borders. Most who are trafficked to the United States to work as female prostitutes or servants are from Latin America, Southeast Asia, and Eastern Europe. Worldwide income from sex trafficking of children and women is estimated to be between at least $7 billion and $10 billion per year (U.S. Department of State, 2003, 2007). With prosecutions lacking and profits soaring, this pathological phenomenon shows no signs of abating.

Families may sometimes feel they have little choice but to send their children into deplorable situations because, for example, they are simply too poor to feed their children (McCormick & Zamora, 2000). Increased trade across borders, lack of education (including sexuality education) of children and their parents, inadequate legislation, lack of or poor law enforcement, the eroticization of children by the media—all have contributed to commercial sexual exploitation of children (Chelala, 2000). In eastern and southern Africa, children who are orphaned as a result of AIDS may lack the support they need from other family members. Children from industrialized countries may be fleeing abusive homes. In Southeast Asia, attitudes and practices perpetuate the low status of girls (Sternberg, 2005a).

Sex trafficking of children and young teens is not limited to countries other than the United States. The FBI estimates that over 100,000 children and young women have been trafficked into the United States. These victims, both girls and boys, range in age from 9 to 19, with the average being 11. Many of these children and young teens are runaways or kids who have been abandoned, whereas others are from "good families" or lured or coerced by skillful predators who promise jobs, money, clothing, and modeling careers. Pimps move these young people from state to state, which makes this a federal matter. The FBI has initiated a project called Lost Innocence, which specializes in child and teen sex trafficking (Fang, 2005; "Teen Girls Tell Their Stories," 2006).

Children who enter sexual servitude at an early age suffer profound physical and psychological consequences. They can become malnourished, be at an increased risk for STIs including HIV/AIDS, and suffer feelings of guilt and inadequacy, to name just a few of the effects.

In the United States, the Trafficking Victims Protection Act of 2000 made human trafficking within the U.S. a federal crime. Further, the law allows women trafficked into the U.S. to receive permanent residence status after 3 years from the issuance of a temporary residence visa (Victims of Trafficking and Violence Protection Act of 2000, 2000). Also, according to U.S. law, Americans caught paying children for sex while in foreign countries can be prosecuted in the United States ("California: Sex Tourists," 2006). Education, social mobilization and awareness building, legal support, social services, psychosocial counseling, and prosecution of perpetrators are but a few of the strategies that have been used to address this problem. Much more must be done to protect the endangered lives and well-being of the world's children.

Think Critically

- What, in your opinion, contributes to the demand for child sex workers?
- What more do you think could be done to address sex trafficking worldwide?
- What, if any, additional laws should the United States enact to prevent the trafficking of children and young women into the United States?

& Bennett, 1995; Dittman, 2004). In one study 75% of the women prostitutes were under the age of 25 (Potterat, Woodhouse, Muth, & Muth, 1990). Analysis of the National Longitudinal Study of Adolescent Health, a nationally representative sample of 13,294 U.S. adolescents, found that 3.5% of these adolescents (32.1% of whom were girls) had even exchanged sex for drugs or money (Edwards, Iritani, & Hallfors, 2006).

Childhood sexual abuse is often a factor in both adolescent girls' and boys' entrance into prostitution, for two reasons (Simons & Whitbeck, 1991; Widom & Kuhns, 1996). First, sexual abuse increases the likelihood that a preadolescent or adolescent will become involved in deviant street culture and activities.

Physically and sexually abused youths are more likely to be rejected by their conventional peers and to become involved in delinquent activities. Second, one major reason young people flee home is parental abuse—generally sexual abuse for girls and physical abuse for boys.

Girls usually are introduced into prostitution by pimps, men upon whom prostitutes are emotionally and financially dependent. Prostitutes give their pimps the money they earn; in turn, pimps provide housing, buy them clothes and jewelry, and offer them protection on the streets. Although girls meet their pimps in various ways, pimps most frequently initiate the contact, using both psychological and physical coercion. Many girls and young women are "sweet-talked" into prostitution by promises of money, protection, and companionship. Adolescent prostitutes are more likely than adults to have pimps.

Once involved with pimps, women are frequently abused by them. The women also run the risk of abuse and violence from their customers. Prostitutes who solicit customers on the streets (called **streetwalkers**) are especially vulnerable.

Personal Background and Motivation   Adult prostitutes are often women who were targets of early male sexual aggression, had extensive sexual experience in adolescence, were rejected by peers because of sexual activities, and were not given adequate emotional support by their parents. There are high rates of physical and sexual abuse (including intrafamilial abuse) and neglect in their childhoods (Widom & Kuhns, 1996). Their parents failed to provide them with a model of affectionate interaction. As a result, as the girls grew up, they tended to be anxious, to feel lonely and isolated, and to be unsure of their own identity. Another common thread running through the lives of most prostitutes is an economically disadvantaged background. However, there is a wide range of motivations and backgrounds among those who enter this "oldest profession." As one ex-prostitute notes (quoted in Queen, 2000):

> When I began sex work, I did not expect the range of education and life experience I found in my colleagues. Like many people, I believed prostitution was mainly engaged in by women who have no options. But I ended up working with women who were saving to buy houses, put kids through school, put themselves through school, start businesses.

Research has shown that adolescent prostitutes describe their general psychological state of mind as very negative, depressed, unhappy, or insecure at the time they first entered prostitution. Many had run away from home and engaged in sexual risk behaviors. There were high levels of drug use, including alcohol, methamphetamines, marijuana, cocaine, and heroin, and many of those who became drug addicts later turned to prostitution to support their drug habit (Edwards, Iritani, & Hallfors, 2006; Miller, 1995; Potterat, Rothenberg, Muth, Darrow, & Phillips-Plummer, 1998). Their emotional state made them particularly vulnerable to pimps.

No single motive seems to explain why someone becomes a prostitute. It is probably a combination of environmental, social, financial, and personal factors that leads a woman to this profession. When women describe the most attractive things about life in the prostitution subculture, they describe them in monetary and material terms. One prostitute notes, "I said to myself how can I do these horrible things and I said money, money, money" (quoted in Weisberg, 1990). Compared with a minimum-wage job, which may be the only alternative, prostitution appears to be an economically rational decision.

Prostitutes are aware of the psychological and physical costs. A 15-year longitudinal study of 130 sex workers found that sex work was associated with higher incidences of illness—including STIs, mental health problems, and substance abuse—and death (Ward & Day, 2006). Prostitutes fear physical and sexual abuse, AIDS and other STIs, harassment, jail, and legal expenses. They are aware as well of the damage done to their self-esteem from stigmatization and rejection by family and society, negative feelings toward men and sex, bad working conditions, lack of a future, and control by pimps (Weisberg, 1990). Many do not enjoy being a prostitute, and one international study found that nearly 90% wanted out of prostitution (Farley et al., 2003).

In many countries, the availability of prostitutes has become part of the tourist economy, with the money paid to prostitutes an important part of the national income ("Asia," 1996; Baker, 1995; Sternberg, 2005a). In developing countries such as India, Thailand, and the Philippines, where social and economic conditions combine with a dominant male hierarchy and acceptance of a sexual double standard, prostitution is seen by many people in those countries as a necessary and accepted occupation.

Prostitutes exhibit a range of feelings toward their customers. Some may project onto others their feelings of being deviant. If customers regard prostitutes as bad, the women feel that the so-called respectable people who come to them are worse—hypocrites, freaks, weirdos, and perverts who ask them to perform sexual behaviors that the women often consider degrading. Prostitutes encounter such people frequently and may generalize from these experiences. Other prostitutes, however, are accepting of and nonjudgmental toward their customers. "My customers are people like everyone else," reports one prostitute (quoted in Zausner, 1986). "If they're nice to me and don't try to fuck with me, then I like them."

Forms of Female Prostitution   Female prostitutes work as streetwalkers, in brothels, in massage parlors, as call girls or escorts, and solicit heavily on the Internet. Some academics believe that the great majority of prostitutes in the United States live indoor and, for the most part, unnoticed lives (Queen, 2000).

Streetwalkers   Estimates vary, but approximately 10% of American prostitutes are streetwalkers (Queen, 2000). Streetwalking is usually the first type of prostitution in which adolescents become involved; it is also the type they prefer, despite its being at the bottom of the hierarchy of prostitution and having the greatest cultural stigma. Many advertise by dressing provocatively and hanging out at locales noted for prostitution. Women working as streetwalkers are often high school dropouts or runaways who fled abusive homes and went into prostitution simply to survive. Not all streetwalkers come out of desperate situations, however; some are married and have satisfactory sexual relationships in their private lives. Because streetwalkers make their contacts through public solicitation, they are more visible and more likely to be arrested. Without the ability to easily screen their customers, streetwalkers are more likely to be beaten, robbed, or raped. One study found that more than 90% of street prostitutes had been sexually assaulted (Miller & Schwartz, 1995). The study also found that people often consider prostitutes to be "unrapable" or even deserving of being raped. Streetwalkers are also susceptible to severe mental health problems. A qualitative study of 29 street youths engaged in the sex trade found that they had a high suicide attempt rate (Kidd & Kral, 2002).

> Prostitutes are degraded and punished by society; it is their humiliation through their bodies—as much as their bodies—which is being purchased.
>
> —Phyllis Chester
> (1940–)

Because of their inability to screen clients or control their working conditions, streetwalkers are the most likely of prostitutes to be victimized.

Streetwalkers suffer more occupational hazards such as assault, kidnapping, threats by a weapon, robbery, and rape than the so-called indoor prostitutes of the brothels, massage parlors, and escort services or independent call girls, or Internet purveyors. Streetwalkers have less control over working conditions such as freedom to refuse clients and particular sexual behaviors, are more likely to have been coercively trafficked into prostitution, have less access to protective services, and depend more on pimps than indoor workers do (Weitzer, 2005).

In contrast to other types of prostitutes, streetwalkers' sexual activity with clients typically is less varied and shorter (Hock, 2007). Fellatio was their most common activity; less than one quarter of their contacts involved sexual intercourse. In a study of men arrested for soliciting female prostitutes in three western U.S. cities, fellatio was the most common behavior experienced in prior contact with a prostitute (Monto, 2001).

Brothels Brothels, also called "houses of prostitution," "whorehouses," and "houses of ill repute," can be found in most large cities but, in the United States, are legal only in most counties in Nevada. Prostitution in brothels has higher status than streetwalking, and it is safer. Indeed, protection from violence is a major advantage of Nevada's legal brothels; they are the safest of all environments in which women sell consensual sex for money (Brents & Hausbeck, 2005). Several safety precautions, such as panic buttons, listening devices, and management surveillance, are used in Nevada brothels (Weitzer, 2005). Further, the Nevada brothel prostitutes are required to have regular medical and STI exams of which one outcome is less STI transmission. A major attraction of brothels is their comfortable and friendly atmosphere. In brothels, men can have a cup of coffee or a drink, watch television, or casually converse with the women. Many customers are regulars. Sometimes, they go to the brothel simply to talk or relax rather than to engage in sex. Male brothels, often called "stables," are common in Southeast Asia and in some large cities in the United States. These stables are where male prostitutes are available for sex with male customers, although there are also some male brothels for female customers called "stud farms."

Prostitution is legal and subject to government regulation in most counties in Nevada.

Masseuses There are relatively few brothels today; most have been replaced by massage parlors. The major difference between brothels and massage parlors is that brothels present themselves as places specifically dedicated to prostitution, whereas massage parlors try to disguise their intent. Most massage parlors provide only massages. However, some massage parlors are fronts to prostitution and offer customers any type of sexual service they wish for a fee, which is negotiated with the masseuses. But most are "massage and masturbation only" parlors. These so-called M-and-M parlors are probably the most widespread; their primary service is the "local," "hand finishing," or "relief" massage in which there is only masturbation. By limiting sex to masturbation, these parlors are able to avoid legal difficulties, because most criminal sex statutes require genital penetration, oral sex, discussion of fees, and explicit solicitation for criminal prosecution. Women who work M-and-M parlors are frequently referred to as "hand whores"; these women, however, often do not consider themselves prostitutes, although they may go into prostitution later. Many masseuses run newspaper ads for their services and work on an out-call basis, meeting customers at their hotel rooms or homes.

Call Girls Call girls have the highest status among prostitutes, experience less social stigma than other prostitutes, and have among the safest working environments as they can experience more control over their working conditions and who they have as customers than streetwalkers. They are usually better educated than other prostitutes, often come from a middle-class background, and dress fashionably. A call girl's fee is high—much higher than those of a streetwalker or masseuse. She operates through contacts and referrals; instead of the street, she takes to the telephone or computer and arranges to meet her customers at the customer's residence or at his or her hotel room. The call girl is the one, not the agency, who arranges for the sex, thus providing the agency some protection from prosecution. Another major difference between call girls and streetwalkers is that streetwalkers usually have fleeting interactions with customers whereas call girls are much more likely to provide "emotional work," such as counseling and befriending their customers (Lever & Dolnick, 2000; Lucas, 1998). Further, call girls often have interactions that resemble a dating experience involving conversation and receiving gifts, hugs, kisses, massages, and oral sex from the clients (Weitzer, 2005).

Call girls often work for escort services that advertise through newspapers and the Web. Escort agencies supply attractive escorts for social occasions and never advertise that they provide sexual services, although most do. Agencies usually specialize in one type of sex, that is, female-for-male, male-for-male, female-for-female, or male-for-female. Some offer transsexual prostitutes. Not all escorts work through an agency; some are independent and communicate with clients themselves ("Prostitution," n.d.).

Males Working in Prostitution

Although there has been extensive research into prostitution, most of it concerns female prostitution. Most research on male prostitution focuses on street hustlers, the male equivalent of streetwalkers. There are other kinds of male prostitutes, such as call boys, rent boys, masseurs, and prostitutes who work out of gay bars, who have not been extensively investigated. Male sex workers represent varied backgrounds ranging from those with few literacy skills to middle-class and wealthy men working in varied conditions such as the street, clubs, and escort agencies. Increasingly, they are utilizing escort agencies and making their availability known through the Internet (Minichiello, Marino, & Browne, 2000). Few males who work as prostitutes are gigolos—heterosexual men providing sexual services for women in exchange for money. Their customers are usually wealthy, middle-aged women who seek sex, a social "companion," or a young man. The gigolo phenomenon illustrates that women, like men, will pay for sex. Another type of male prostitute is kept boys—young men financially supported for sexual services by an older "sugar daddy." The overwhelming majority of male prostitutes sell their sexual services to other males. Young male prostitutes are called "chickens," and the customers who are attracted to them are known as "chickenhawks."

Street hustlers, like female prostitutes, are often young adults with drug, alcohol, and health issues.

The most common types of sexual behaviors male prostitutes engage in are fellatio, either alone or with other activities (99%); anal sex (80%); and oral stimulation of the anus (63%) (Morse, Simon, Balson, & Osofsky, 1992). Male sex workers are usually expected to ejaculate during the sexual encounters. Because of the refractory period, the number of clients seen by male sex workers in a short period of time is limited, in contrast to female sex workers. Women usually do not have orgasms during sex with a client; further, women do not have a refractory period.

In female adolescent prostitution, the pimp plays a major role: He takes the girl's money and maintains her in the life. In contrast, there is usually no pimp role in male prostitution (Calhoun & Weaver, 1996). Most males are introduced to prostitution through the influence of their peers. A typical male begins when a friend suggests that he can make "easy money" on the streets. Hustlers sometimes live alone or with roommates, whereas female streetwalkers usually live with their pimps. However, one interview study of 90 street-based male sex workers (mean age 32 years) found that they had high levels of homelessness. These men also had contact with the criminal justice system for drug and property offenses, and a high rate of attempted suicide (Kidd & Kral, 2002; Ross, Timson, Williams, Amos, & Bowen, 2007).

Male prostitution is shaped by three subcultures: the peer delinquent subculture, the gay subculture, and the transvestite subculture. The **peer delinquent subculture,** an antisocial street subculture, is characterized by male and female prostitution, drug dealing, panhandling, theft, and violence. Young people in this culture sell sex for the same reason they sell drugs or stolen goods—to make money. Teenage hustlers may not consider themselves gay, because they are selling sex rather than seeking erotic gratification. Instead, they may identify themselves as a bisexual or heterosexual person. They may find their customers in urban "sex zones"—adult bookstores, topless bars, and adult movie houses—which cater to the sexual interests of people of all sexual orientations. And they are more likely to work the street than bars. Recall that earlier in this section we mentioned that 3.5% of 13,294 adolescents of a nationally representative study reported that they had exchanged sex for drugs or money. Two thirds of these youth (67.9%) were boys. For both genders, the odds of having exchanged sex for money or drugs were higher for those who had used drugs, had run away from home, and were depressed (Edwards, Iritani, & Hallifors, 2006).

In contrast to male delinquent prostitutes, gay male prostitutes engage in prostitution as a means of expressing their sexuality *and* making money (Weisberg, 1990). They identify themselves as gay and work primarily in gay neighborhoods or gay bars. Many are "pushed-away" children who fled their homes when their parents and peers rejected them because of their sexual orientation (Kruks, 1991). The three most important reasons they give for engaging in prostitution are money, sex, and fun/adventure.

Very little is known about male transvestite prostitutes (Boles & Elifson, 1994). They are a diverse group, distinct from other male and female prostitutes (Elifson, Boles, Posey, & Sweat, 1993), and they can be found in most major cities. Their clients are heterosexual, bisexual, and gay men. Many of their heterosexual clients believe that the transvestites are women, but others are aware that the prostitutes are transvestites.

Another type of male prostitute is the **she-male,** a male who has undergone breast augmentation. The she-male's client may mistakenly believe that the he is a she. Often, the client is another she-male or a male who knows that the prostitute is genitally a male (Blanchard, 1993).

Prostitution and the Law

Arrests for prostitution and calls for cleanups seem to be a communal ritual practiced by influential segments of the population to reassert their moral, political, and economic dominance. The arrests are symbolic of community disapproval, but they are not effective in ending prostitution.

Female prostitution is the only sexual offense for which women are extensively prosecuted; the male patron is seldom arrested. Prostitutes are subject to arrest for various activities, including vagrancy and loitering, but the most common charge is for solicitation. **Solicitation**—a word, gesture, or action that implies an offer of sex for sale—is defined vaguely enough that women, and men, who are not prostitutes occasionally are arrested on the charge because they act "suspiciously." It is usually difficult to witness a direct transaction in which money passes hands, and such arrests are also complicated by involving the patron.

There are periodic attempts to repeal laws criminalizing prostitution because it is perceived as a victimless crime: Both the prostitute and the customer engage in it voluntarily. Other people, especially feminists, want to repeal such laws because they view prostitutes as being victimized by their pimps, their customers, the law enforcement system, and social stigmas (Barry, 1995; Bullough & Bullough, 1996; Valera, Sawyer, & Schiraldi, 2001).

Reformers propose that prostitution be either legalized or decriminalized. Those who support legalizing prostitution want to subject it to licensing and registration by police and health departments, as in Nevada and parts of Europe. Those who propose decriminalization want to remove criminal penalties for engaging in prostitution; prostitutes would be neither licensed nor registered. Many reformers believe that prostitutes should be accorded the same political and legal protections and rights of all citizens (Davidson, 2002). Some prostitutes have organized groups like the North American Task Force on Prostitution (NTFP) and COYOTE (Call Off Your Old Tired Ethics) to push for decriminalization and support. NTFP's goals include the repeal of existing prostitution laws, ensuring the rights of prostitutes and other sex workers, promoting the development of social support services for sex workers, and ending the public stigma associated with sex work.

Whatever one's opinion about decriminalizing adult prostitution, the criminalization of adolescent prostitution needs to be reevaluated. Treating juvenile prostitutes as delinquents overlooks the fact that in many ways adolescent prostitutes are more victims than criminals. As researchers and concerned others examine such social problems as the sexual and physical abuse of children, running away, and adolescent prostitution, they are discovering a disturbing interrelationship. The law, nevertheless, does not view adolescent prostitution as a response to victimization and an attempt to survive on the streets. Instead, it treats it as a criminal behavior and applies legal sanctions. A more appropriate response might be to offer counseling, halfway houses, alternative schooling, and job training.

The Impact of HIV/AIDS and Other STIs

Prostitution has received increased attention as a result of the HIV/AIDS epidemic. Numerous studies have documented a high frequency of many

> I regret to say that we of the FBI are powerless to act in cases of oral-genital intimacy, unless it has in some way obstructed interstate commerce.
>
> —J. Edgar Hoover (1895–1972)

> Driven underground, prostitution became integrated into the underworld of crime. Like the prohibition of liquor, the criminalization of prostitution became a self-fulfilling prophecy. Like the birth control movement—which also began with the aim of elevating women's status—the antiprostitution movement resulted in the professional and official victimization of poor women.
>
> —Ruth Rosen (1945–)

> Upon these women we have no right to turn our backs. Their wrongs are our wrongs. Their existence is part of our problem. They have been created by the very injustice against which we protest.
>
> —Carrie Chapman Catt (1859–1947)

STIs, including HIV, among female, male, and male-to-female transgender prostitutes in the United States (e.g., Cohan et al., 2006; Edwards, Iritani, & Hallfors, 2006). There are several reasons female and male prostitutes are at higher risk than the general population. First, many prostitutes are injection drug users, and injection drug use is one of the primary ways of transmitting HIV infection. Prostitutes exchanging sex for crack in crack houses are also at high risk for HIV infection as well as other STIs. Second, prostitutes are at higher risk for STI/HIV infection because they have numerous partners. Third, prostitutes do not always require their customers to use condoms. Male prostitutes are at even greater risk than female prostitutes because of their high-risk sexual practices, especially anal intercourse, and their high-risk gay/ bisexual clientele (see Chapter 17 for discussion of anal intercourse and HIV risk) (Estcourt et al., 2000; Nemoto et al., 2004; Williams et al., 2003). What can we learn from all of the above? That clients of prostitutes are putting themselves, *as well as their partners,* at high risk for HIV and other STIs if they do not use condoms.

● Sexuality and the Law

A basic tenet of our society is that all Americans are equal under the law. But state laws relating to sexuality vary from one state to another, with people having widely differing rights and privileges ("SIECUS Looks," 1999). Though most Americans don't give much thought to the government's decision making concerning their sexual lives, they generally agree that sexual behavior is private and that what occurs in their bedrooms is their own business. They may even think that sexuality-related laws are for other people, not themselves. As a result, most Americans don't think about how their lives can be impacted by the law depending on where they live or visit.

Legalizing Private, Consensual Sexual Behavior

Laws related to various aspects of human sexuality, such as HIV/AIDS, child sexual abuse, prostitution, and hate crimes based on sexual orientation and gender identity, have been discussed throughout the book. In this section and the box "The Invalidation of State Antisodomy Laws: A Triumph for Equality and a Path to Gay Marriage?" we discuss laws related to two specific sexuality-related areas: private, consensual sexual behavior between adults and same-sex marriage.

Historically, the United States has enacted laws that criminalize certain sex-related behaviors, such as rape, incest, sexual assault, public indecency, and prostitution. For the most part, there has been a strong consensus among Americans as to the need for and value of such laws. However, one area of sexual behavior, referred to as **sodomy,** has provoked considerable debate. Sodomy has had several definitions, including any sexual behaviors between members of the other or the same sex that cannot result in procreation (some of which were considered "crimes against nature") and sexual behaviors considered to be "homosexual acts." Oral and anal sex are the behaviors typically considered to be sodomy. Rooted in sixteenth-century English laws prohibiting nonprocreative sex, the first American antisodomy law was passed in 1610 in colonial Virginia; the penalty was death. In 1873, South Carolina became

The Invalidation of State Antisodomy Laws: A Triumph for Equality and a Path to Gay Marriage?

The historic ruling in June 2003 by the U.S. Supreme Court that overturned state antisodomy laws directed toward both same-sex and other-sex partners has been hailed as one of the most significant advances in terms of individual rights in America and the Court's most far-reaching decision for gay men and lesbian women. In reversing a 1986 ruling that upheld antisodomy laws, the Court said that the Constitution's guarantee of individual liberty extends to consensual sex between same-sex people in the confines of their homes. The Court's ruling invalidated antisodomy laws in the 13 states that still had them.

For gay men in particular, not only did the decriminalization of same-sex behavior bring relief, but it also helped validate them as human beings and reduce some of the stigmas they face. Many people think the ruling changes the legal landscape by opening the door for legal attacks on other laws that discriminate against gay men and lesbian women. Individuals can, for example, be fired from their jobs, denied the opportunity to adopt children, denied custody of their own children, and denied housing because of their sexual orientation.

Some criticized the Court's ruling, claiming that it hurts the "natural family," validates immoral behavior, and will lead to sexual chaos and more cases of AIDS. In the dissenting opinion, Justice Antonin Scalia said that the ruling would lead to government-sanctioned gay marriages (Biskupic, 2003a, 2003b). As of the printing of this textbook, seven countries—Belgium, Canada, Netherlands, Norway, South Africa, Spain, and Sweden—have extended marriage to include same-sex couples, and several countries have civil unions or domestic partnerships for same-sex couples (Gibbs, 2008; Human Rights Campaign, 2008a; Johnson, 2009).

The right of gay men and lesbian women to legally marry has become a major source of controversy. In November 2003, the Massachusetts Supreme Court became the first state to give marriage licenses to gay and lesbian couples. In May 2008, the California Supreme Court became the second state to declare that gay and lesbian couples have a constitutional right to marry. However, in the November 2008 election, the voters of California overturned the ruling by voting for a constitutional amendment banning same-sex marriage, a decision supported by the California Supreme Court in May 2009. (McKinley & Goodstein, 2008; Schwartz, 2009). In October 2008, the Connecticut Supreme Court ruled that gay couples have the right to marry (Human Rights Campaign, 2008c; McFadden, 2008). By June 2009, four more states permitted same-sex marriage, increasing the total to six:

in April 2009 the Iowa Supreme Court unanimously ruled to allow same-sex marriage and Vermont lawmakers overrode the government's veto of a bill legalizing same-sex marriage in the state, in May 2005 Maire lawmakers approved same-sex marriage, and in June 2009 the New Hampshire legislators recognized same-sex marriage (Crary, 2009; Evans & Gillers, 2009; Goodnough, 2009; "New Hampshire to allow gay marriages," 2009). In efforts to extend many of the benefits of marriage to same-sex couples, a few states have enacted laws for civil unions or domestic partnerships—but not marriage—for gay and lesbian couples. At the printing of this book, seven states—California, Hawaii, Maine, New Hampshire, New Jersey, Oregon, and Washington—and the District of Columbia offered civil unions or domestic partnerships with spousal benefits (Human Rights Campaign, 2009a, 2009b; "Lessons Learned on Gay Marriage," 2008).

In fear that some states might legalize gay marriages, Congress in 1996 passed the Defense of Marriage Act, which defined marriage as a union between one man and one woman. By mid-2008, 27 states had subsequently adopted their own version (Human Rights Campaign, 2008b, 2008c). (To learn the status of individual state laws relative to same-sex marriage, check the Human Rights Campaign Web site: http://www.hrc.org.) The controversy surrounding same-sex marriage continues in the United States. Public opinion polls show nearly equal proportions of Americans support or oppose a U.S. constitutional amendment defining marriage as between a man and a woman (see the box "Public Opinion About Gay and Lesbian Rights and Issues" in Chapter 17).

Think Critically

- Do you agree with the Supreme Court ruling overturning state antisodomy laws? Why or why not?
- Do you think the ruling will lead to the legalization of same-sex marriages?
- Do you support or oppose same-sex marriage? Why?
- What are your thoughts about other areas in which gay men and lesbian women are discriminated against? For example, should they be able to adopt children, have custody of their own children, and be protected from being fired at work?

the last state to repeal capital punishment for sodomy. More recently, sodomy laws had been used to target individuals participating in same-sex behaviors (Greenberg, 2003; "Social Evolution Changed," 2003).

Every state had laws banning sodomy until 1961, when Illinois repealed its sodomy ban. By mid-2003, only 13 states had sodomy laws, of which nine states had laws prohibiting sodomy between both same-sex and other-sex partners, and four states outlawed sodomy between same-sex partners only. Civil rights activists and the gay community protested that the laws violated individual rights, were rarely enforced, and provided grounds for other types of discrimination based on sexual orientation. Other groups, particularly those that believe homosexuality is immoral, fought to retain the laws.

In 2003, in *Lawrence et al. v. Texas,* the U.S. Supreme Court struck down, by a decisive 6–3 vote, the Texas law that banned sex between people of the same gender. Considered by many as a "watershed moment" in American culture, the verdict reversed the Supreme Court's 1986 ruling in *Bowers v. Hardwick* that upheld a state's right (Georgia) to criminalize sodomy. The Court said that the *Bowers* ruling was incorrect then and is incorrect today. This landmark ruling also invalidated the antisodomy laws in the 13 remaining states that have them.

The Texas case originated in 1998 when John Geddes Lawrence and Tyron Garner were discovered having sex by a Harris County sheriff's officer who had entered Lawrence's residence while responding to a false report about an armed intruder. They were fined $200 each (Biskupic, 2003b) for violating state law prohibiting oral and anal sex between same-sex partners. In writing for the majority, Justice Anthony Kennedy (Supreme Court of the United States, 2003a) stated that

> the case does involve two adults who, with full and mutual consent from each other, engaged in sexual practices common to a homosexual lifestyle. The petitioners [Lawrence and Garner] are entitled to respect for their private lives. The State cannot demean their existence or control their destiny by making their private sexual conduct a crime. The right to liberty under the Due Process Clause gives them the full right to engage in their conduct without intervention of the government.

Kennedy also declared that the criminalization of homosexual conduct is an invitation in and of itself for discrimination against homosexuals in the public and private spheres (Supreme Court of the United States, 2003a). In a dissenting opinion, Justice Antonin Scalia stated that the Court "has largely signed on the so-called homosexual agenda" (Supreme Court of the United States, 2003b).

The *Lawrence et al. v. Texas* ruling by the U.S. Supreme Court is considered a milestone ruling for gay rights advocates. In recent years there have been several court rulings significant to gay rights issues. A highlight of milestone court rulings in the United States at the time this book went to press is shown in Table 18.2. These rulings have largely dealt with private consensual sexual behavior among gay men and lesbian women and rights relative to marriage. Certainly there will be future court rulings concerning the civil rights of gay men and lesbian women as this issue remains contentious in the United States. To keep current on legal issues related to gay men and lesbian women, such as parenting and military service, go to the Human Rights Campaign Web site: http://www.hrc.org.

Table 18.2 • Milestone Court Rulings on Gay Rights in the United States	
1986	U.S. Supreme Court backs Georgia antisodomy law.
1993	Hawaii's top court says state constitution's guarantee of equal protection could give same-sex couples marital rights.
1996	President Clinton signs federal Defense of Marriage Act. It defines marriage as a "legal union between one man and one woman" and says states do not have to recognize same-sex marriages from other states.
1996	Supreme Court rejects Colorado ban on laws protecting gays from discrimination.
1998	Hawaii amends state constitution to reserve marriage for opposite-sex couples.
2000	Vermont allows civil unions between same-sex couples, giving them most of the benefits of marriage.
2003	U.S. Supreme Court rejects Texas law that banned sex between adults of same sex.
2003	Massachusetts' top court says same-sex couples have a right to marry.
2005	California Supreme Court issues the first-of-its-kind ruling that recognizes co-parenting rights of same-sex couples.
2006	New York's and Washington's highest courts reject gay marriage.
2006	New Jersey Supreme Court rules that gay couples have the same rights as heterosexual couples but lets the state legislature decide whether to permit same-sex marriage.
2007	Maryland Court of Appeals upholds ban on same-sex marriage.
2008	California becomes second state to allow gay marriage when the California Supreme Court strikes down a state ban on same-sex marriage. California voters later approves a constitutional amendment banning same-sex marriage.
2008	Connecticut Supreme Court rules that same-sex couples have the right to marry.
2009	Iowa Supreme Court votes unanimously to permit gay marriage.
2009	California Supreme Court upholds a ban on same-sex marriage, ratifying voters' decision in 2008.

SOURCES: From Biskupic, J. (2006, March 24). Milestones in gay rights. *USA Today*, p. 4A (Years 1986–2003). Reprinted with permission. Collins, D. (2008, October 11). Connecticut court OKs: gay marriages. *Indianapolis Star*, p. A3; Evans, T., & Gillers, H. (2009, April 4). Iowa court nixes ban on gay marriage. *Indianapolis Star*, pp. A1, A11. Human Rights Campaign. (2008e). *Civil unions*. http://www.hrc.org/issues/marriage/civil_unions.asp. Kornblum, J. (2008, May 16). Court address gay civil rights. *USA Today*, p. 3A; Schwartz, J. (2009, May 27). Court upholds California's ban on gay marriage, *The New York Times*, p. A1, A20.

Advocating Sexual Rights

Policymakers and advocates of free speech continue to scrutinize states' sexuality laws and enforcement practices and to monitor and report on them. One such advocacy group is the Sexuality Information and Education Council of the United States (SIECUS), which states (1999):

> SIECUS advocates for the right of individuals to make responsible sexual choices The right is composed of a variety of specific rights—the right to information, the right to sexual health services, the right to engage in sexual behaviors in private with another consenting adult, the right to live according to one's sexual orientation, and the right to obtain and use materials that have a sexual theme or content.

In many ways, sexuality-related laws reflect an ambivalence about sexuality in America's culture. For some sexuality-related issues, there is not a consensus, although laws have been enacted. This is particularly evident with issues relating to sexuality education and abortion. Although some laws seem to be based on sexuality as something from which we must be protected, in other cases, the absence of laws speaks loudly. For example, many states have yet to protect against sexual harassment and discrimination based on sexual orientation, and every state has work to do in developing laws that support sexual rights and sexual health. Recall that in Chapter 1 we presented the World Association for Sexual Health's Declaration of Sexual Rights, which identifies 11 sexual rights. As discussed in various chapters of this book, the expression of many of these rights has been hampered by laws and social restriction. Further legal protection of fundamental sexual rights is needed for people to fully attain individual sexual health.

Click on "It's Elementary" to hear children discussing gay marriage.

Final Thoughts

The world of commercial sex is one our society approaches with ambivalence. Society simultaneously condemns sexually explicit material and prostitution, yet provides both to customers. Because of conflicting attitudes and behaviors, our society rarely approaches the issues surrounding sexually explicit material and prostitution with disinterested objectivity. Now, in every state, adults can legally participate in consensual sexual behavior with other adults, no matter what their sexual orientation is; but other fundamental sexual rights remain hampered by laws or social restriction.

Summary

Sexually Explicit Material in Contemporary America

- There is a lack of agreement about what constitutes *erotica, pornography,* and *obscenity* because they are subjective terms. The term *sexually explicit material* is a more neutral term.

- Millions of people spend billions of dollars on sexually explicit material each year in the United States.

- The increasing availability of erotic films in the privacy of the home via DVDs, pay-for-view television, and the Internet has led to an increase in women viewers. The inclusion of women in the audience has led to *femme porn.*

- The legal guidelines for determining whether a work is obscene are that the dominant theme of the work must appeal to prurient sexual interests and portray sexual conduct in a patently offensive way; taken as a whole, the work must be without serious literary, artistic, political, or scientific value; and a reasonable person must find the work, when taken as a whole, to possess no social value. Obscene material is not protected by law.

- People who read or view sexually explicit material usually recognize it as fantasy. They use it as a release from their everyday lives. Sexually explicit material temporarily encourages sexual expression, activating a person's typical sexual behavior pattern. People are interested in sexually explicit material because they

enjoy sexual sensations, it is a source of sexual information and knowledge, it enables people to rehearse sexual activities, and it is safer sex.

- Child pornography is a form of sexual exploitation that, because of the Internet, has become a worldwide problem. U.S. courts have prohibited its production, sale, and possession.

- Some feminists believe that sexually explicit material represents a form of sex discrimination against women because it places them in what they believe to be a degrading and dehumanizing context. Other feminists believe that opponents of sexually explicit material have an antisex bias.

- In 1970, the President's Commission on Pornography and Obscenity concluded that pornography does not cause harm or violence. Over the years, there has been a heated debate over the effects of sexually explicit material. There is no definitive evidence, however, that nonviolent sexually explicit material is associated with sexual aggression against women, nor is there evidence that sexually violent material produces lasting changes in attitudes or behaviors.

Prostitution

- *Prostitution,* also called sex work, is the exchange of sexual behaviors for money and/or goods. Both men and women work as prostitutes. Women are generally introduced into this type of sex work by pimps.

Adolescent prostitutes describe their psychological state as negative when they first entered prostitution. Streetwalkers run the risk of abuse and violence from their customers. Prostitutes report various motives for entering prostitution, including quick and easy money, the prostitution subculture, and the excitement of "the life." Fellatio is the most common sexual behavior of streetwalkers.

- Prostitutes solicit on streets and work in brothels and massage parlors. Some masseuses have intercourse with clients, but most provide only masturbation. Call girls (escorts) have the highest status among prostitutes.

- Most research on male prostitution focuses on street hustlers. Male prostitution is shaped by the *peer delinquent,* gay male, and transvestite subcultures. The three most important reasons given for engaging in prostitution are money, sex, and fun/adventure.

- Arrests for prostitution are symbols of community disapproval; they are not effective in curbing prostitution. Female prostitution is the only sexual offense for which women are extensively prosecuted; the male patron is seldom arrested. Decriminalization of prostitution is often urged because it is a victimless crime or because prostitutes are victimized by their pimps, customers, police, and the legal system. Some people advocate regulation by police and health departments.

- Prostitutes are at higher risk for HIV/AIDS than the general population because many are injection drug users, have multiple partners, and do not always require their customers to use condoms. Female and male prostitutes and their customers may provide a pathway for HIV and other STIs into the general heterosexual community.

Sexuality and the Law

- In 2003, the U.S. Supreme Court overturned state anti*sodomy* laws in the 13 remaining states that had them, making it legal for consenting adult gay men and lesbian women, as well as heterosexual individuals, to have sex in private. At the time of the printing of this book, marriage between same-sex individuals is now legal in six states: Connecticut, Iowa, Maine Massachusetts, New Hampshire, and Vermont. Seven states and the District of Columbia offer civil unions or domestic partnerships for same-sex couples.

Questions for Discussion

- Imagine that you were assigned to argue that the federal government should regulate sexually explicit material. What would you say? Imagine the converse: that sexually explicit material should be available freely to adults in the marketplace. How would you advocate that position?

- Do you think that sexually explicit materials are helpful, harmful, or neutral? What place, if any, do they have in a society? Explain your position on this issue.

- Do you think that prostitution should be legalized/regulated (i.e., licensed and/or registered by health and police departments) or decriminalized (i.e., no criminal penalties and no licensing or registration) or neither? Defend your stance.

- Do you believe that gay marriage will ever be legalized in every state in the United States? Why or why not?

Sex and the Internet

American Civil Liberties Union

Protection of our First Amendment rights is part of the mission of the American Civil Liberties Union (ACLU). But what exactly is this organization, what does it do, and how can it help you? To find out, click to the ACLU's home page (http://www.aclu.org) and find one topic related to this chapter or text that interests you. This could include Internet issues, free speech, HIV/AIDS, lesbian and gay rights, privacy, reproductive rights, or women's rights. After reading information related to this topic, answer the following:

- What new information or news release did you find related to this topic?

- What is the history or background of laws related to it?

- What is the ACLU's stance?

- What is your position, and why?

Suggested Web Sites

National Coalition Against Censorship
http://www.ncasc.org
Provides action alerts, censorship news, and frequently asked questions about censorship.

Prostitutes' Education Network
http://www.bayswan.org
Provides information and resources related to prostitution.

Prostitution Research and Education
www.prostitutionresearch.com
Advocates for alternatives to prostitution, including emotional and physical health care for sex workers.

U.S. Supreme Court
http://www.supremecourtus.gov
Lists U.S. Supreme Court decisions by year and volume. Type in "sodomy" in the search box to locate the Court's ruling on the *Lawrence et al. v. Texas* case.

Suggested Reading

Angell, J. (2004). *Call girl.* Sag Harbor, New York: Permanent Press. A revealing memoir of a university professor who is also a call girl.

Delacoste, F., & Alexander, P. (Eds.). (1998). *Sex work: Writing by women in the sex industry* (2nd ed.). Pittsburgh: Cleis Press. A collection of short, personal stories by women who work as prostitutes, masseuses, topless dancers, models, and actresses, many of whom regard themselves as feminists.

Flowers, R. B. (2001). *Runaway kids and teenage prostitution: America's lost, abandoned, and sexually exploited children.*
Westfield, CT: Greenwood Press. A concise text that examines the correlations between runaway children and teenage prostitution in the United States from a criminological, sociological, and psychological perspective.

Jeffreys, S. (1998). *The idea of prostitution.* North Melbourne, Australia: Spinifex Press. Argues that the involvement of women in prostitution is a variety of male sexual violence and a violation of women's human rights.

Kempadoo, K., & Doezema, J. (Eds.). (1998). *Global sex workers: Rights, resistance, and redefinition.* New York: Routledge. A collection of essays on the sex workers' rights movement around the world.

Ringal, N. J., & Daly, R. (2003). *Love for sale: A world history of prostitution.* New York: Grove Press. A panoramic tracing of the global history of prostitution.

Spector, J. (Ed.). (2006). *Prostitution and pornography: Philosophical debate about the sex industry.* Stanford, CA: Stanford University Press. This anthology examines the debates about the sex industry, discussing the ways prostitution, pornography, and other forms of commercial sex are made subject to legislation.

Strosser, N. (2000). *Defending pornography.* New York: New York University Press. A lucid, broad exploration of the long debate over pornography.

Weitzer, R. (Ed.). (2000). *Sex for sale: Prostitution, pornography, and the sex industry.* New York: Routledge. Examines sex work and the sex industry.

> For links, articles, and study material, go to the McGraw-Hill Web site, located at
> **www.mhhe.com/yarber7e.**

Glossary

abortifacient   A device or substance that causes an abortion.

abortion   The expulsion of the conceptus, either spontaneously or by induction.

abstinence   Refraining from sexual intercourse.

acculturation   The process of adaptation by an ethnic group to the attitudes, behaviors, and values of the dominant culture.

acquaintance rape   A nonconsensual sexual encounter by two people who just happen to be in the same place and know each other.

acquired immunodeficiency syndrome (AIDS)   A chronic disease caused by the human immunodeficiency virus (HIV), in which the immune system is weakened and unable to fight opportunistic infections such as *Pneumocystis carinii* pneumonia (PCP) and Kaposi's sarcoma.

adolescence   The social and psychological state that occurs between the beginning of puberty and full adulthood.

afterbirth   The placenta, the remaining section of the umbilical cord, and the fetal membranes.

agape   In John Lee's typology of love, altruistic love.

age of consent   The age at which a person is legally deemed capable of giving consent.

AIDS   *See* acquired immunodeficiency syndrome.

alveoli   (singular, *alveolus*) Small glands within the female breast that begin producing milk following childbirth.

amenorrhea   The absence of menstruation, unrelated to aging.

amniocentesis   A process in which amniotic fluid is withdrawn by needle from the uterus and then examined for evidence of possible birth defects.

amnion   An embryonic membranous sac containing the embryo and amniotic fluid.

amniotic fluid   The fluid within the amniotic sac that surrounds the embryo or fetus.

ampulla   The widened part of the fallopian tube or the vas deferens.

anabolic steroids   A class of natural and synthetic hormones that are derivatives of the male hormone testosterone. They promote the growth of several tissues, especially muscles and bones.

anal eroticism   Sexual activities involving the anus.

anal intercourse   The insertion of the erect penis into the partner's anus.

anal stage   In Freudian theory, the period from age 1 to 3, during which the child's erotic activities center on the anus.

analingus   The licking of the anal region.

anatomical sex   Identification as male or female based on physical sex characteristics such as gonads, uterus, vulva, vagina, and penis.

androgen   Any of the male hormones, including testosterone.

androgen-insensitivity syndrome or **testicular feminization**   A genetic, hereditary condition passed through X chromosomes in which a genetic male is born with testes but is unable to absorb testosterone; as a result, the estrogen influence prevails, and his body tends toward a female appearance, failing to develop male internal and external sex organs.

androgyny   The unique and flexible combination of instrumental and expressive traits in accordance with individual differences, situations, and stages in the life cycle.

anodyspareunia   Pain occurring during anal intercourse.

anorexia nervosa   An eating disorder characterized by the pursuit of excessive thinness.

antibody   A cell that binds to the antigen of an invading cell, inactivating it and marking it for destruction by killer cells.

anti-gay prejudice   A strong dislike, fear, or hatred of gay men and lesbian women because of their same-sex behavior.

antigen   A molecular structure on the wall of a cell capable of stimulating the immune system and then reacting with the antibodies that are released to fight it.

antiretroviral medications   Drugs designed to control the reproduction of HIV and slow the progression of HIV disease.

anus   The opening of the rectum, consisting of two sphincters, circular muscles that open and close like valves.

anxious/ambivalent attachment   A style of infant attachment characterized by separation anxiety and insecurity in relation to the primary caregiver.

Apgar score   The cumulative rating of the newborn's heart rate, respiration, color, reflexes, and muscle tone.

aphrodisiac   A substance that supposedly increases sexual desire or improves sexual function.

areola   A ring of darkened skin around the nipple of the breast.

artificial insemination (AI)   *See* assisted reproductive technology.

asexuality   The state of having no sexual attraction for either sex or no sexual contact with another person by choice.

assigned gender   The gender ascribed by others, usually at birth.

assisted reproductive technology (ART)   A procedure in which a woman's ovaries are stimulated and her eggs surgically removed, combined with sperm, and returned to her body. Commonly referred to as artificial insemination.

attachment   The emotional tie between an infant and his or her primary caregiver.

attitude   The predisposition to act, think, or feel in certain ways toward particular things.

atypical sexual behavior   Sexual activity that is not statistically typical of usual sexual behavior.

autoerotic asphyxia   A form of sexual masochism linking strangulation with masturbation.

autoeroticism   Sexual self-stimulation or behavior involving only the self; includes masturbation, sexual fantasies, and erotic dreams.

autofellatio   Oral stimulation of the penis by oneself.

avoidant attachment   A style of infant attachment characterized by avoidance of the primary caregiver as a defense against rejection.

bacterial vaginosis (BV)   A vaginal infection commonly caused by the bacterium *Gardnerella vaginalis*.

Bartholin's gland   One of two small ducts on either side of the vaginal opening that secretes a small amount of moisture during sexual arousal. Also known as vestibular gland.

basal body temperature (BBT) method   A contraceptive method based on a woman's temperature in the morning upon waking; when her temperature rises, she is fertile.

B cell   A type of lymphocyte involved in antibody production.

behavior   The way a person acts.

benign prostatic hypertrophy (BPH)   Enlargement of the prostate gland, affecting many men over age 50.

benign tumor   A nonmalignant (noncancerous) tumor that grows slowly and remains localized.

bestialists   People who have sexual contact with animals.

bias   A personal leaning or inclination.

biased sample   A nonrepresentative sample.

binge eating disorder   An eating disorder characterized by rapid eating, eating to the point of discomfort or beyond, continual eating, and eating when not hungry. Also called compulsive overeating.

biopsy   Surgical removal of tissue for diagnosis.

biphobia   Fear of, discrimination against, or hatred of bisexual individuals.

birth canal   The passageway through which an infant is born; the vagina.

birth control   Any means of preventing a birth from taking place, including contraception and abortion.

bisexuality   An emotional and sexual attraction to members of both sexes.

blastocyst   A collection of about 100 human cells that develops from the zygote.

bondage and discipline (B&D)   Sexual activities in which one person is bound while another simulates or engages in light or moderate "disciplinary" activities such as spanking and whipping.

Braxton-Hicks contractions   Uterine contractions during the last trimester of pregnancy that exercise the uterus, preparing it for labor.

breast self-examination (BSE)   A method of checking one's own breasts for lumps or suspicious changes.

bulimia   An eating disorder characterized by episodes of uncontrolled overeating followed by purging (vomiting).

calendar (rhythm) method   A contraceptive method based on calculating "safe" days depending on the range of a woman's longest and shortest menstrual cycles.

candidiasis   A yeast infection caused by the fungus *Candida albicans*. Also known as moniliasis.

capacitation   The process by which a sperm's membranes become fragile enough to release the enzymes from its acrosomes.

caring   Making another's needs as important as one's own.

castration anxiety   In Freudian theory, the belief that the father will cut off the child's penis because of competition for the mother/wife.

celibacy   Not engaging in any kind of sexual activity.

censorship   The suppression of words, ideas, or images by governments, private groups, or individuals based on their political or moral values.

cervical cancer   Invasive cancer of the cervix (ICC).

cervical dysplasia or **cervical intraepithelial neoplasia (CIN)**   A condition of the cervical epithelium (covering membrane) that may lead to cancer if not treated.

cervical mucus method   A contraceptive method using a woman's cervical mucus to determine ovulation.

cervicitis   The swelling (inflammation) of the cervix, usually the result of an infection.

cervix   The end of the uterus, opening toward the vagina.

cesarean section (C-section)   The delivery of a baby through an incision in the mother's abdominal and uterine walls.

chancre   A round, pea-sized, painless sore symptomatic of the first stage of syphilis.

child-free   Individuals or couples who choose not to have children.

child sexual abuse   Any sexual interaction (including fondling, erotic kissing, oral sex, and genital penetration) between an adult and a prepubertal child.

chlamydia   An STI caused by the *Chlamydia trachomatis* organism. Also known as chlamydial infection.

chorion   The embryo's outermost membrane.

chorionic villus sampling (CVS)   A procedure in which tiny pieces of the membrane that encases the embryo are removed and examined for evidence of possible birth defects.

cilia   Tiny, hairlike tissues on the fimbriae and ampulla that become active during ovulation, moving the oocyte into the fallopian tube.

CIN *See* cervical dysplasia.

circumcision The surgical removal of the foreskin which covers the glans penis. *See also* clitoridectomy.

clinical research The in-depth examination of an individual or group by a clinician who assists with psychological or medical problems.

clitoral hood A fold of skin covering the glans of the clitoris.

clitoridectomy The surgical removal of the clitoris and all or part of the labia. Also known as female genital cutting and female circumcision, or female genital mutilation.

clitoris (plural, *clitorides*) An external sexual structure that is the center of arousal in the female; located above the vagina at the meeting of the labia minora.

cloning Reproduction of an individual from a single cell taken from a donor or parent.

coercive paraphilia Sexual behavior involving victimization and causing harm to others.

cognitive development theory A child development theory that views growth as the mastery of specific ways of perceiving, thinking, and doing that occurs at discrete stages.

cognitive social learning theory A child development theory that emphasizes the learning of behavior from others, based on the belief that consequences control behavior.

cohabitation The practice of two people sharing living space and having a sexual relationship.

coitus Penile-vaginal sex.

coitus interruptus The removal of the penis from the vagina prior to ejaculation. Also called withdrawal.

colostrum A yellowish substance containing nutrients and antibodies that is secreted by the breasts 2–3 days prior to actual milk production.

coming out The public acknowledgment of one's sexual orientation, such as gay, lesbian, or bisexual.

commitment A determination, based on conscious choice, to continue a relationship or a marriage.

communication A transactional process in which symbols such as words, gestures, and movements are used to establish human contact, exchange information, and reinforce or change attitudes and behaviors.

conceptus In medical terminology, the developing human offspring from fertilization through birth.

condom or **male condom** A thin, soft, flexible sheath of latex rubber, polyurethane, or processed animal tissue that fits over the erect penis to prevent semen from being transmitted and to help protect against STIs. *See also* female condom.

conflict A communication process in which people perceive incompatible goals and interference from others in achieving their goals.

congenital adrenal hyperplasia A condition in which a genetic female with ovaries and a vagina develops externally as a male as a result of a malfunctioning adrenal gland. Previously known as adrenogenital syndrome.

contraception The prevention of conception.

contraceptive film A small, translucent tissue that contains spermicide and dissolves into a sticky gel when inserted into the vagina.

contraceptive foam A chemical spermicide dispensed in an aerosol container.

contraceptive patch A reversible method of birth control that releases estrogen and progestin to protect against pregnancy for 1 month.

control group A group that is not being treated in an experiment.

coprophilia A paraphilia in which a person gets sexual pleasure from contact with feces.

corona The rim of tissue between the glans and the penile shaft.

corpora cavernosa The hollow chambers in the shaft of the clitoris or penis that fill with blood and swell during arousal.

corpus luteum The tissue formed from a ruptured ovarian follicle that produces important hormones after the oocyte emerges.

corpus spongiosum A column of erectile tissue within the penis enclosing the urethra.

correlational study The measurement of two or more naturally occurring variables to determine their relationship to each other.

Cowper's gland or **bulbourethral gland** One of two small structures below the prostate gland that secrete a clear mucus into the urethra prior to ejaculation.

cross-dressing Wearing the clothing of a member of the other sex.

crura (singular, *crus*) The internal branches of the clitoral or penile shaft.

cultural equivalency perspective The view that attitudes, behaviors, and values of diverse ethnic groups are basically similar, with differences resulting from adaptation to historical and social forces such as slavery, discrimination, or poverty.

cunnilingus Oral stimulation of the female genitals.

cybersex Expressions of sexuality while responding to words or images on a computer.

cystitis A bladder infection affecting mainly women that is often related to sexual activity, although it is not transmitted from one partner to another.

date rape Sexual penetration with a dating partner that occurs against the victim's will, with force or the threat of force.

delayed ejaculation A sexual function difficulty characterized by a male not being able to ejaculate easily during intercourse.

delayed labor Pregnancy that has gone beyond 2 weeks of full term.

demographics The statistical characteristics of human populations.

dependent variable In an experiment, a factor that is likely to be affected by changes in the independent variable.

DHT deficiency A genetic disorder in which some males are unable to convert testosterone to the hormone dihydrotestosterone (DHT), required for the normal development of external male genitals; usually identified as girls at birth, the children begin to develop male genitals in adolescence.

diabetes mellitus   A chronic disease characterized by excess sugar in the blood and urine due to a deficiency of insulin.

diaphragm   A rubber cup with a flexible rim that is placed deep inside the vagina, blocking the cervix, to prevent sperm from entering the uterus.

dilation   Gradual opening of the cervix.

dilation and evacuation (D&E)   A second-trimester abortion method in which the cervix is slowly dilated and the fetus removed by alternating curettage with other instruments and suction.

disinhibition   The phenomenon of activating behaviors that would normally be suppressed.

disorders of sex development (DSD)   Congenital conditions in which development of chromosomal, gonadal, or anatomical sex is atypical.

domestic partnership   A legal category granting some rights ordinarily reserved to married couples to committed, cohabiting heterosexual, gay men, and lesbian women couples.

domination and submission (D/S)   Sexual activities involving the consensual acting out of fantasy scenes in which one person dominates and the other submits.

dominatrix   In bondage and discipline, a woman who specializes in "disciplining" a submissive partner.

doulas   Specially trained individuals who offer birthing mothers emotional support and help in managing pain during the birth process.

drag   Cross-dressing, often with comic intent.

drag queens   Gay men who cross-dress to entertain.

dysmenorrhea   Pelvic cramping and pain experienced by some women during menstruation.

dyspareunia   A female sexual functioning difficulty characterized by painful intercourse.

eating disorder   Eating and weight management practices that endanger a person's physical and emotional health.

ectoparasitic infestation   Parasitic organisms that live on the outer skin surfaces, not inside the body.

ectopic pregnancy   A pregnancy in which the fertilized ovum is implanted in any tissue other than the uterine wall. Most ectopic pregnancies occur in the fallopian tubes. Also known as a tubal pregnancy.

effacement   Thinning of the cervix during labor.

egocentric fallacy   An erroneous belief that one's own personal experiences and values are held by others in general.

EIA (enzyme immunoassay)   A test used to detect antigen-soliciting molecules specifically related to autoimmune disorders and cancer.

ejaculation   The process by which semen is forcefully expelled from the penis.

ejaculatory duct   One of two structures within the prostate gland connecting with the vasa deferentia.

ejaculatory inevitability   The point at which ejaculation is imminent in the male.

Electra complex   In Freudian theory, the female child's erotic desire for the father and simultaneous fear of the mother.

embryo   The early form of life in the uterus between the stages of blastocyst and fetus.

embryonic membranes   The embryo's membranes include the amnion, amniotic fluid, yolk sac, chorion, and allantois.

emergency contraception (EC)   The use of hormones or a copper IUD to prevent a pregnancy from occurring.

emission   The first stage of ejaculation, in which sperm and semen are propelled into the urethral bulb.

endometriosis   A disease caused by endometrial tissue (uterine lining) spreading and growing in other parts of the body; a major cause of infertility.

endometrium   The inner lining of the uterine walls.

epidemic   A wide and rapid spread of a contagious disease.

epidemiology   The study of the causes and control of disease epidemics.

epididymis   The coiled tube, formed by the merging of the seminiferous tubules, where sperm mature.

epididymitis   Inflammation of the epididymis.

epidural   A method of anesthetic delivery during childbirth in which a painkilling drug is continuously administered through a catheter in the woman's lower back.

episiotomy   A surgical procedure during childbirth that enlarges the vaginal opening by cutting through the perineum toward the anus.

erectile dysfunction   A sexual function difficulty characterized by not having or maintaining an erection during intercourse. Previously referred to as impotence.

erection   The process of the penis becoming rigid through vasocongestion; an erect penis.

erogenous zone   Any area of the body that is highly sensitive to touch and associated with sexual arousal.

eros   In John Lee's typology of love, the love of beauty.

erotica   Sexually explicit material that is evaluated positively.

erotic aid or **sex toy**   A device, such as a vibrator or dildo, or a product, such as oils or lotions, designed to enhance erotic responsiveness.

erotophilia   A positive emotional response to sexuality.

erotophobia   A negative emotional response to sexuality.

estrogen   The principal female hormone, regulating reproductive functions and the development of secondary sex characteristics.

ethnic group   A group of people distinct from other groups because of cultural characteristics transmitted from one generation to the next.

ethnicity   Ethnic affiliation or identity.

ethnocentric fallacy or **ethnocentrism**   The belief that one's own ethnic group, nation, or culture is innately superior to others.

exhibitionism   A paraphilia involving recurrent, intense urges to expose one's genitals to a nonconsenting person.

experimental research   The systematic manipulation of an individual or the environment to learn the effect of such manipulation on behavior.

expressiveness   Revealing or demonstrating one's emotions.

expulsion   The second stage of ejaculation, characterized by rapid, rhythmic contraction of the urethra, prostate, and muscles at the base of the penis, causing semen to spurt from the urethral opening.

extradyadic involvement (EDI)   Sexual or romantic relationship outside of a primary marital or dating dyad.

extrafamilial abuse   Child sexual abuse by someone unrelated to the child.

fallacy   An error in reasoning that affects one's understanding of a subject.

fallopian tube   One of two uterine tubes extending toward an ovary.

familismo   Emphasis on family among Hispanics/Latinos.

Family and Medical Leave Act (FMLA) (Public Law 103-3)   Allows an employee to take unpaid leave for the birth and care of a newborn child, during his or her own illness, or to care for a sick family member.

feedback   The ongoing process in which participants and their messages create a given result and are subsequently modified by that result.

fellatio   Oral stimulation of the penis.

female condom   A soft, loose-fitting, disposable polyurethane sheath with a diaphragm-like ring at each end that covers the cervix, vaginal walls, and part of the external genitals to prevent conception and to help protect against sexually transmitted infections.

female genital cutting (FGC)   The surgical removal of the clitoris and all or part of the labia. Also known as clitoridectomy, female circumcision, or female genital mutilation.

female impersonators   Men who dress as women.

female orgasmic disorder   The absence of or delay in orgasm for women following typical sexual excitement.

female sexual arousal disorder   The persistent or recurring condition of a woman attaining or maintaining the level of vaginal lubrication and swelling associated with sexual excitement.

feminism   Efforts by both men and women to achieve greater equality for women.

femme porn   Sexually explicit material catering to women and heterosexual couples.

fertility awareness–based (FAB) method   One of several contraceptive methods based on a woman's knowledge of her body's reproductive cycle, including calendar (rhythm), basal body temperature (BBT), cervical mucus, and symptothermal methods.

fetal alcohol effect (FAE)   Moderate alcohol consumption by pregnant women resulting in some intellectual and behavior deficits.

fetal alcohol syndrome (FAS)   Chronic ingestion of alcohol by pregnant women resulting in unusual facial features, congenital heart defects, defective joints, and behavioral and intellectual impairment in children.

fetishism   A paraphilia in which a person is sexually attracted to certain objects.

fetus   The stage of life from 8 weeks of gestation to birth.

fibrocystic disease   A common and generally harmless breast condition in which fibrous tissue and benign cysts develop in the breast.

fimbriae   Fingerlike tissues that drape over the ovaries, but without necessarily touching them.

follicle-stimulating hormone (FSH)   A hormone that regulates ovulation.

follicular phase   The phase of the ovarian cycle during which a follicle matures.

foreskin   The portion of the sleevelike skin covering the shaft of the penis that extends over the glans penis. Also known as prepuce.

45, X (Turner syndrome)   A chromosomal disorder affecting females born lacking an X chromosome, resulting in the failure to develop ovaries.

frenulum   The triangular area of sensitive skin on the underside of the penis, attaching the glans to the foreskin.

frotteurism   A paraphilia involving recurrent, intense urges to touch or rub against a nonconsenting person for the purpose of sexual arousal.

gamete   A sex cell containing the genetic material necessary for reproduction; an oocyte (ovum) or sperm.

gay-bashing or **queer-bashing**   Violence directed against gay men or lesbian women because of their sexual orientation.

gender   The social and cultural characteristics associated with being male or female.

gender identity   A person's internal sense of being male or female.

gender identity disorder (GID)   A strong and persistent cross-gender identification and persistent discomfort about one's assigned sex.

gender presentation   The way in which we present our gender to others, whether it be through bodily habits or personality.

gender role   The attitudes, behaviors, rights, and responsibilities that society associates with each sex.

gender-role attitude   Beliefs about appropriate male and female personality traits and activities.

gender-role behavior   The activities in which individuals engage in accordance with their gender.

gender-role stereotype   A rigidly held, oversimplified, and overgeneralized belief about how each gender should behave.

gender schema   A set of interrelated ideas used to organize information about the world on the basis of gender.

gender theory   A theory that a society is best understood by how it is organized according to gender.

gender variation   A person's inability or unwillingness to conform to societal gender norms associated with his or her biological sex.

genetic sex   Identification as male or female based on chromosomal and hormonal sex characteristics.

genital herpes   An STI caused by the herpes simplex virus (HSV).

genitals The reproductive and sexual organs of males and females. Also known as genitalia.

genital stage In Freudian theory, the period in which adolescents become interested in genital sexual activities, especially sexual intercourse.

genital warts An STI caused by the human papillomavirus (HPV).

gestation Pregnancy.

GIFT (gamete intrafallopian transfer) An ART procedure that transfers gametes into the woman's fallopian tubes through small incisions in her abdomen.

glans clitoris The erotically sensitive tip of the clitoris.

glans penis The head of the penile shaft.

gonad An organ (ovary or testis) that produces gametes.

gonadotropin A hormone that acts directly on the gonads.

gonadotropin-releasing hormone (GnRH) A hormone that stimulates the pituitary gland to release follicle-stimulating hormone (FSH) and luteinizing hormone (LH), initiating the follicular phase of the ovarian cycle.

gonorrhea An STI caused by the *Neisseria gonorrhoeae* bacterium.

Grafenberg spot (G-spot) According to some researchers, an erotically sensitive area on the upper front wall of the vagina midway between the introitus and the cervix.

gynecomastia Swelling or enlargement of the male breast.

halo effect The assumption that attractive or charismatic people possess more desirable social characteristics than others.

Hegar's sign The softening of the uterus above the cervix, indicating pregnancy.

helper T cell A lymphocyte that "reads" antigens and directs the immune system's response.

hepatitis A viral disease affecting the liver; several types of the virus can be sexually transmitted.

herpes simplex virus (HSV) The virus that causes genital herpes.

heterosexual bias or **heterosexism** The tendency to see the world in heterosexual terms and to ignore or devalue homosexuality.

heterosexuality Emotional and sexual attraction between members of the other sex.

highly active antiretroviral therapy (HAART) An aggressive anti-HIV treatment usually including a combination of protease inhibitors and reverse transcriptase inhibitors whose purpose is to bring viral load infection down to undetectable levels.

HIV *See* human immunodeficiency virus.

HIV transmission rate The annual number of new HIV infections transmitted per 100 people living with HIV.

homoeroticism Sexual attraction, desire, or impulses directed toward members of the same sex; homosexuality.

homologous structure A similarity in structures that perform the same function.

homophobia An irrational or phobic fear of gay men and lesbian women. *See also* anti-gay prejudice, heterosexual bias.

homosexuality Emotional and sexual attraction between members of the same sex.

hormone A chemical substance that acts as a messenger within the body, regulating various functions.

hormone replacement therapy (HRT) The administration of estrogen, often with progestin, in the form of pills, vaginal cream, or a small adhesive patch. Also known as menopausal hormone use, postmenopause hormone therapy (PHT), or hormone therapy for menopause.

hostile environment As related to sexuality, a work or educational setting that interferes with a person's performance because of sexual harassment.

hot flash An effect of menopause consisting of a period of intense warmth, flushing, and perspiration, typically lasting 1–2 minutes.

human chorionic gonadotropin (HCG) A hormone secreted by the developing placenta and needed to support a pregnancy.

human immunodeficiency virus (HIV) The virus that causes AIDS.

human papillomavirus The virus that causes genital warts.

hymen A thin membrane partially covering the introitus prior to first intercourse or other breakage.

hypoactive sexual desire (HSD) or **inhibited sexual desire** A sexual function problem characterized by low or absent sexual desire.

hypospadias A hormonal condition in which the opening of the penis, rather than being at the tip, is located somewhere on the underside, glans, or shaft or at the junction of the scrotum and penis.

hysterectomy The surgical removal of the uterus.

hysterotomy A late-pregnancy abortion method in which the fetus is removed through an incision in the woman's abdomen; an extremely rare procedure.

implant A contraceptive device inserted under the skin that protects against pregnancy for up to 3 years. Implanon is the most common among them.

implantation The process by which a blastocyst becomes embedded in the uterine wall.

incest Sexual intercourse between individuals too closely related to legally marry, usually interpreted to mean father-daughter, mother-son, or brother-sister activity.

incidence The number of new cases of a disease within a specified time, usually 1 year.

independent variable In an experiment, a factor that can be manipulated or changed.

induction A type of reasoning in which arguments are formed from a premise to provide support for its conclusion.

infertility The inability to conceive a child after a year of unprotected intercourse, or the inability to carry a child to term.

infibulation The stitching together of the sides of the vulva or vaginal opening; part of the process of female circumcision or female genital mutilation.

informed consent Assent given by a mentally competent individual at least 18 years old with full knowledge of the purpose and potential risks and benefits of participation.

infundibulum The tube-shaped ends of the fallopian tubes.

inhibited ejaculation A sexual function problem in which the male does not ejaculate despite an erection and continued stimulation.

instrumentality Being oriented toward tasks and problem solving.

interfemoral intercourse Movement of the penis between the partner's thighs.

internalized homophobia Negative attitudes and affects toward homosexuality in other persons and toward same-sex attraction in oneself.

intersex A variety of conditions in which a person is born with a reproductive sexual anatomy that doesn't fit the typical definitions of male or female.

intimate love Love based on commitment, caring, and self-disclosure.

intrafamilial abuse Child sexual abuse by biologically and step-related individuals.

intrauterine device (IUD) A T-shaped device inserted into the uterus through the cervical os to prevent conception or implantation of the fertilized egg.

introitus The opening of the vagina.

in vitro fertilization (IVF) An ART procedure that combines sperm and oocyte in a laboratory dish and transfers the blastocyst to the mother's uterus.

involuntary ejaculation The male not being able to control the moment of his ejaculation.

jealousy An aversive response that occurs because of a partner's real, imagined, or likely involvement with a third person.

Kaplan's tri-phasic model of sexual response A model that divides sexual response into three phases: desire, excitement, and orgasm.

Kaposi's sarcoma A rare cancer of the blood vessels that is common among people with AIDS.

Kegel exercises A set of exercises designed to strengthen and give voluntary control over the pubococcygeus and to increase sexual pleasure and awareness.

killer T cell A lymphocyte that attacks foreign cells.

Klinefelter syndrome A condition in which a male has one or more extra X chromosomes, causing the development of female secondary sex characteristics.

klismaphilia A paraphilia in which a person gets sexual pleasure from receiving enemas.

labia majora (singular, *labium majus*) Two folds of spongy flesh extending from the mons pubis and enclosing the labia minora, clitoris, urethral opening, and vaginal entrance. Also known as major lips.

labia minora (singular, *labium minus*) Two small folds of skin within the labia majora that meet above the clitoris to form the clitoral hood. Also known as minor lips.

lactation The production of milk in the breasts (mammary glands).

lanugo The fine, downy hair covering the fetus.

laparoscopy A form of tubal ligation using a viewing lens (the laparoscope) to locat the fallopian tubes and another instrument to cut or block and close them.

latency stage In Freudian theory, the period from age 6 to puberty in which sexual impulses are no longer active.

leukocyte White blood cell.

Leydig cell Cell within the testes that secretes androgens. Also known as an interstitial cell.

libido The sex drive.

lifetime risk The risk within one's lifetime of a disease.

limbic system A group of structures in the brain associated with emotions and feelings; involved with producing sexual arousal.

lochia A bloody vaginal discharge following childbirth.

Loulan's sexual response model A model that incorporates both the biological and the affective components into a six-stage cycle.

low-birth-weight infants Those born weighing less than 2,500 grams, or 5.5 pounds.

ludus In John Lee's typology of love, playful love.

lumpectomy Breast surgery that removes only the malignant tumor and surrounding lymph nodes.

luteal phase The phase of the ovarian cycle during which a follicle becomes a corpus luteum and then degenerates.

luteinizing hormone (LH) A hormone involved in ovulation.

lymphocyte A type of leukocyte active in the immune response.

machismo In Latino culture, highly prized masculine traits.

macrophage A type of white blood cell that destroys foreign cells.

male condom *See* condom.

male erectile disorder The persistent or recurring difficulty of a man attaining or maintaining an adequate erection until completion of sexual activity.

male impersonators Women who dress as men.

male orgasmic disorder The persistent delay in or absence of orgasm for men following typical sexual excitement.

malignant tumor A cancerous tumor that invades nearby tissues and disrupts the normal functioning of vital organs.

mammary gland A mature female breast.

mammogram A low-dose X-ray of the breast.

mammography The use of X-rays to detect breast tumors before they can be seen or felt.

mania In John Lee's typology of love, obsessive love.

mastectomy The surgical removal of part or all of the breast.

Masters and Johnson's four-phase model of sexual response A model that divides sexual response into four phases: excitement, plateau, orgasm, and resolution.

masturbation Stimulation of the genitals for pleasure.

medication abortion A two-drug regimen used to terminate early pregnancy. Previously known as RU-486.

menarche The onset of menstruation.

menopausal hormone therapy (MHT) The administration of estrogen (often along with progestin) to relieve the symptoms of menopause. Also known as hormone replacement therapy (HRT).

menopause The complete cessation of menstruation.

menorrhagia Heavy or prolonged bleeding that may occur during a woman's menstrual cycle.

menses The menstrual flow, in which the endometrium is discharged.

menstrual cycle The more-or-less monthly process during which the uterus is readied for implantation of a fertilized ovum. Also known as uterine cycle.

menstrual phase The shedding of the endometrium during the menstrual cycle.

menstrual synchrony Simultaneous menstrual cycles that occur among women who work or live together.

metastasis The process by which cancer spreads from one part of the body to an unrelated part via the bloodstream or lymphatic system.

miscarriage The spontaneous expulsion of the fetus from the uterus. Also called spontaneous abortion.

Mittelschmerz A sharp twinge that may occur on one side of the lower abdomen during ovulation.

mons pubis In the female, the mound of fatty tissue covering the pubic bone; the pubic mound. Also known as mons veneris.

mons veneris The pubic mound; literally, mountain of Venus. Also known as mons pubis.

myotonia Increased muscle tension.

necrophilia A paraphilia involving recurrent, intense urges to engage in sexual activities with a corpse.

neonate A newborn.

neural tube defect screening A test on a pregnant woman's blood during the second trimester to measure the level of alpha-fetoprotein; test results reveal possible defects of the spine, spinal cord, skull, and brain.

neurosis A psychological disorder characterized by anxiety or tension.

nocturnal orgasm or **emission** Orgasm and in males, ejaculation while sleeping; usually accompanied by erotic dreams. Also known as wet dream.

noncoercive paraphilia Harmless and victimless paraphilia sexual behavior.

nongonococcal urethritis (NGU) Urethral inflammation caused by something other than the gonococcus bacterium.

nonoxynol-9 (N-9) The sperm-killing chemical in spermicide.

nonpedophilic sexual abuse An adult's sexual interaction with a child that is motivated not by sexual desire but by nonsexual motives such as for power or affection.

nonspecific urethritis (NSU) Inflammation of the urethra with an unspecified, nongonococcal cause.

normal sexual behavior Behavior that conforms to a group's typical patterns of behavior.

nulliparous woman A woman who has never given birth.

nymphomania A pseudoscientific term referring to "abnormally high" or "excessive" sexual desire in a woman.

objectivity The observation of things as they exist in reality as opposed to one's feelings or beliefs about them.

obscenity That which is deemed offensive to "accepted" standards of decency or morality.

observational research Studies in which the researcher unobtrusively observes people's behavior and records the findings.

Oedipal complex In Freudian theory, the male child's erotic desire for his mother and simultaneous fear of his father.

oocyte The female gamete, referred to as an egg or ovum.

oogenesis The production of oocytes; the ovarian cycle.

oophorectomy The removal of one or both ovaries.

open marriage A marriage in which both partners agree to allow each other to have openly acknowledged and independent relationships with others, including sexual ones.

opinion An unsubstantiated belief in or conclusion about what seems to be true according to an individual's personal thoughts.

opportunistic infection (OI) An infection that normally does not occur or is not life threatening, but that takes advantage of a weakened immune system.

oral contraceptive (OC) A series of pills containing synthetic estrogen and/or progesterone that regulate egg production and the menstrual cycle. Commonly known as "the pill."

oral-genital sex The touching of a partner's genitals with the mouth or tongue.

oral stage In Freudian theory, the period lasting from birth to age 1 in which infant eroticism is focused on the mouth.

orgasm The climax of sexual excitement, including rhythmic contractions of muscles in the genital area and intensely pleasurable sensations; usually accompanied by ejaculation in males beginning in puberty.

orgasmic platform A portion of the vagina that undergoes vasocongestion during sexual arousal.

os The cervical opening.

osteoporosis The loss of bone density that can lead to weaker bones.

ovarian cycle The more-or-less monthly process during which oocytes are produced.

ovarian follicle A saclike structure in which an oocyte develops.

ovary One of a pair of organs that produces oocytes.

ovulation The release of an oocyte from the ovary during the ovarian cycle.

ovulatory phase The phase of the ovarian cycle during which ovulation occurs.

ovum (plural, *ova*) An egg; an oocyte; the female gamete.

oxytocin A hormone that stimulates uterine contractions during birth, and possibly orgasm.

Pap test A method of testing for cervical cancer by scraping cell samples from the cervix and examining them under a microscope.

paraphilia A mental disorder characterized by the American Psychiatric Association as recurrent, intense, sexually arousing fantasies, sexual urges, or behaviors generally lasting at least 6 months and involving nonhuman objects, the suffering or humiliation of oneself or one's partner, or children or other nonconsenting persons.

parous woman   A woman who has given birth.

partialism   A paraphilia in which a person is sexually attracted to a specific body part.

participant observation   A method of observational research in which the researcher participates in the behaviors being studied.

pathological behavior   Behavior deemed unhealthy or diseased by current medical standards.

pedophilia   A paraphilia characterized by recurrent, intense urges to engage in sexual activities with a prepubescent child.

peer delinquent subculture   An antisocial youth subculture.

pelvic floor   The underside of the pelvic area, extending from the top of the pubic bone to the anus.

pelvic inflammatory disease (PID)   An infection of the fallopian tube (or tubes), caused by an organism such as *C. trachomatis* or *N. gonorrhoeae*, in which scar tissue may form within the tubes and block the passage of eggs or cause an ectopic pregnancy; a leading cause of female infertility. Also called salpingitis.

penis   The male organ through which semen and urine pass.

penis envy   In Freudian theory, female desire to have a penis.

perimenopause   A period of gradual changes and adjustments a woman's body goes through prior to menopause, before menstruation stops completely.

perinatal HIV transmission (mother to child)   Women who transmit HIV to their babies during pregnancy or labor and delivery.

perineum   An area of soft tissue between the genitals and the anus that covers the muscles and ligaments of the pelvic floor.

persistent sexual arousal syndrome (PSAS)   Sexual arousal in women that does not resolve in ordinary ways but continues for hours, days, or weeks.

Peyronie's disease   A painful male sexual disorder, resulting in curvature of the penis, that is caused by fibrous tissue and calcium deposits developing in the corpora cavernosa of the penis.

phallic stage   In Freudian theory, the period from age 3 through 5 during which both male and female children exhibit interest in the genitals.

pheromone   A sexually arousing chemical substance secreted into the air by many kinds of animals.

placenta   The organ of exchange between mother and fetus.

Plan B   Also referred to as "emergency contraception." A backup method of preventing pregnancy that, if taken 72 hrs (3 days) after unprotected intercourse, can reduce the chances of pregnancy.

pleasuring   Erotic, nongenital touching.

plethysmograph   A device attached to the genitals to measure physiological response.

PLISSIT model   A model for sex therapy consisting of four progressive levels: **P**ermission, **L**imited **I**nformation, **S**pecific **S**uggestions, and **I**ntensive **T**herapy.

Pneumocystis carinii **pneumonia (PCP)**   An opportunistic lung infection caused by a common, usually harmless organism, frequently occuring among people with AIDS.

polyamory   The practice or lifestyle of being open to having more than one loving intimate relationship at a time, with the full knowledge and consent of all partners involved.

pornography   Sexually explicit material that is generally evaluated negatively.

postpartum depression   A form of depression thought to be related to hormonal changes following the delivery of a child.

postpartum period   The period (about 3 months) following childbirth, characterized by physical stabilization and emotional adjustment.

postpartum psychosis   A serious and rare postpartum mental illness thought to be biologically based and related to hormonal changes.

postrefusal sexual persistence   Continued requests for sexual contact after being refused.

posttraumatic stress disorder (PTSD)   A group of characteristic symptoms, such as depression, that follow an intensely distressing event outside a person's normal life experience.

pragma   In John Lee's typology of love, practical love.

pregnancy-induced hypertension   Condition characterized by high blood pressure, edema, and protein in the urine.

premature birth   Birth that takes place prior to 27 weeks of gestation.

premature ejaculation or **rapid ejaculation**   A sexual function difficulty characterized by not being able to control or delay ejaculation as long as desired, causing distress.

premenstrual dysphoric disorder   Severe premenstrual symptoms, sufficient enough to disrupt a woman's functioning.

premenstrual syndrome (PMS)   A set of severe symptoms associated with menstruation.

prepuce   The foreskin of the penis.

prevalence   Overall occurrence; the total number of cases of a disease, for example.

priapism   Prolonged and painful erection due to the inability of blood to drain from the penis.

progesterone   A female hormone that helps regulate the menstrual cycle and sustain pregnancy.

proliferative phase   The buildup of the endometrium in response to increased estrogen during the menstrual cycle.

prostaglandins   A type of hormone with a fatty-acid base that stimulates muscle contractions.

prostate gland   A muscular gland encircling the urethra that produces about one third of the seminal fluid.

prostate-specific antigen (PSA) test   A blood test used to help diagnose prostate cancer.

prostatitis   Inflammation of the prostate gland.

prostitution   The exchange of sex for money and/or goods.

protection from harm   A basic entitlement of all participants in research studies, including the right to confidentiality and anonymity.

proximity   Nearness in physical space and time.

psychoanalysis   A psychological system developed by Sigmund Freud that traces behavior to unconscious motivations.

psychosexual development   Development of the psychological components of sexuality.

puberty   The stage of human development when the body becomes capable of reproduction.

pubic lice   *Phthirus pubis,* colloquially known as crabs; tiny lice that infest the pubic hair.

pubococcygeus   A part of the muscular sling stretching from the pubic bone in front to the tailbone in back.

queer theory   Identifies sexuality as a system that cannot be understood as gender neutral or by the actions of heterosexual males and females. It proposes that one's sexual identity and one's gender identity are partly or wholly socially constructed.

random sample   A portion of a larger group collected in an unbiased way.

rape   Sexual penetration against a person's will through the use or threat of force.

rape trauma syndrome   The emotional changes an individual undergoes as a result of rape.

refractory period   For men, a period following ejaculation during which they are not capable of having ejaculation again.

relaxin   A hormone produced by the placenta in the later months of pregnancy that increases flexibility in the ligaments and joints of the pelvic area. In men, relaxin is contained in semen, where it assists in sperm motility.

representative sample   A small group representing a larger group in terms of age, sex, ethnicity, socioeconomic status, orientation, and so on.

repression   A psychological mechanism that keeps people from becoming aware of hidden memories and motives because they arouse guilt or pain.

reproduction   The biological process by which individuals are produced.

retrograde ejaculation   The backward expulsion of semen into the bladder rather than out of the urethral opening.

retrovirus   A virus capable of reversing the normal genetic writing process, causing the host cell to replicate the virus instead of itself.

reverse transcriptase   An enzyme in the core of a retrovirus enabling it to write its own genetic program into a host cell's DNA.

root   The portion of the penis attached to the pelvic cavity.

RU-486   *See* medication abortion.

sadomasochism (S&M)   A popular, nonclinical term for domination and submission.

satyriasis   An excessive, uncontrollable sexual desire in a man.

scabies   A red, intensely itchy rash appearing on the genitals, buttocks, feet, wrists, knuckles, abdomen, armpits, or scalp, caused by the barely visible mite *Sarcoptes scabiei.*

schema   A set of interrelated ideas that helps individuals process information by organizing it in useful ways.

scientific method   A systematic approach to acquiring knowledge by collecting data, forming a hypothesis, testing it empirically, and observing the results.

script   In sociology, the acts, rules, and expectations associated with a particular role.

scrotum   A pouch of skin that holds the two testicles.

secondary sex characteristics   The physical changes that occur as a result of increased amounts of hormones targeting other areas of the body.

secretory phase   The phase of the menstrual cycle during which the endometrium begins to prepare for the arrival of a fertilized ovum; without fertilization, the corpus luteum begins to degenerate.

secure attachment   A style of infant attachment characterized by feelings of security and confidence in relation to the primary caregiver.

self-disclosure   The revelation of personal information that others would not ordinarily know because of its riskiness.

semen   The ejaculated fluid containing sperm. Also known as seminal fluid.

seminal vesicle   One of two glands at the back of the bladder that secrete about 60% of the seminal fluid.

seminiferous tubules   Tiny, tightly compressed tubes in which spermatogenesis takes place.

sensate focus   The focusing on touch and the giving and receiving of pleasure as part of the treatment of sexual difficulties.

serial monogamy   A succession of monogamous (exclusive) marriages or relationships.

seroconversion   The process by which a person develops antibodies.

serosorting   Having sex with a partner one believes has the same HIV status (negative or positive) as one's own HIV status.

serostatus   The absence or presence of antibodies for a particular antigen.

sex   Identification as male or female based on genetic and anatomical sex characteristics.

sex flush   A darkening of the skin or a rash that temporarily appears as a result of blood rushing to the skin's surface during sexual excitation.

sex information/advice genre   A media genre that transmits information and norms about sexuality to a mass audience.

sexism   Discrimination against people based on their sex rather than their individual merits.

sexologist   A specialist in the study of human sexuality.

sex reassignment surgery   A process that brings a person's genitals in line with his or her gender identity and diminishes the serious suffering the person experiences.

sex selection   Pre- and post-implantation methods that allow couples to choose whether to have a boy or a girl. (Also marketed as "family balancing.")

sex surrogates   In sex therapy, sex partners who assist clients having sexual difficulties without spouses or other partners.

sexual abuse trauma A dynamic marked by traumatic sexualization and feelings of betrayal, powerlessness, and stigmatization exhibited by children and adults who have been sexually abused.

sexual aggression Any kind of sexual activity performed against a person's will through the use of force, argument, pressure, alcohol or drugs, or authority.

sexual assault Legal term for forced sexual contact that does not necessarily include penile-vaginal intercourse.

sexual aversion disorder A sexual function disorder characterized by a consistently phobic response to sexual activities or the idea of such activities.

sexual coercion A broad term referring to any kind of sexual activity initiated with another person through the use of argument, pressure, pleading, or cajoling, as well as force, pressure, alcohol or drugs, or authority.

sexual diary The personal notes a study participant makes of his or her sexual activity and then reports to a researcher.

sexual double standard A standard applied more leniently to one sex than to another.

sexual dysfunction An impaired physiological response that prevents an individual from functioning sexually, such as erectile difficulties or absence of orgasm. Also called sexual function dissatisfaction or sexual function problems.

sexual fluidity Situation-dependent flexibility in the gender of a woman's sexual attraction.

sexual function dissatisfaction A condition in which an individual or couple, not based on a medical diagnosis, decide they are unhappy with their sexual relationship and that they have a problem. Also known as sexual function difficulties or sexual dysfunction.

sexual function enhancement Improvement in the quality of one's sexual function.

sexual harassment The abuse of power for sexual ends; the creation of a hostile work or educational environment because of unwelcomed conduct or conditions of a sexual nature.

sexual health Physical, mental, and social well-being related to sexuality.

sexual identity One's self-label or self-identification as a heterosexual, homosexual, or bisexual person.

sexual intercourse The movement of bodies while the penis is in the vagina. Sometimes also called vaginal intercourse or penile-vaginal intercourse.

sexual interest An inclination to behave sexually.

sexuality The emotional, intellectual, and physical aspects of sexual attraction and expression.

sexually explicit material (SEM) Material such as photographs, films, magazines, books, or Internet sites, whose primary themes, topics, or depictions involve sexuality or cause sexual arousal.

sexually transmitted infections (STIs) Infections most often passed from person to person through sexual contact.

sexual masochism A paraphilia characterized by recurrent, intense urges to engage in real (not fantasy) sexual behaviours in which the person is humiliated, harmed, or otherwise made to suffer.

sexual orientation The pattern of sexual and emotional attraction based on the gender of one's partner.

sexual orientation uncertainty Being unsure of the gender of one's sexual attraction.

sexual response cycle Sequence of changes and patterns that take place in the genitals and body during sexual arousal.

sexual sadism A paraphilia characterized by recurrent, intense urges to engage in real (not fantasy) sexual behaviors in which the person inflicts physical or psychological harm on a victim.

sexual script A "blueprint" for sexual behaviors.

sexual strategies theory Postulates that men and women have different short-term and long-term mating strategies.

sexual variation Sexual variety and diversity in terms of sexual orientation, attitudes, behaviors, desires, fantasies, and so on; sexual activity not statistically typical of usual sexual behavior.

shaft The body of the penis.

she-male A male who has undergone breast augmentation.

smegma A cheesy substance produced by several small glands beneath the foreskin of the penis and hood of the clitoris.

social construction The development by society of social categories such as masculinity, femininity, heterosexuality, and homosexuality.

social construction theory Views gender as a set of practices and performances that occur through language and a political system.

socioeconomic status Ranking in society based on a combination of occupational, educational, and income levels.

sodomy Term used in the law to define sexual behaviors other than penile-vaginal intercourse, such as anal sex and oral sex.

solicitation In terms of prostitution, a word, gesture, or action that implies an offer of sex for sale.

sonogram A visual image created by ultrasound.

spectatoring The process in which a person becomes a spectator of his or her sexual activities, thereby causing sexual function difficulties.

sperm The male gamete. Also known as a spermatozoon.

spermatic cord A tube suspending the testicle within the scrotal sac, containing nerves, blood vessels, and a vas deferens.

spermatogenesis The process by which a sperm develops from a spermatid.

spermicide A substance that is toxic to sperm.

spirochete A spiral-shaped bacterium.

sponge A contraceptive device consisting of a round polyurethane shield with a pouch in the center that covers the cervix.

spontaneous abortion The natural expulsion of the conceptus, commonly referred to as miscarriage.

squeeze technique A technique for the treatment of early or involuntary ejaculation in which the partner squeezes the erect penis below the glans immediately prior to ejaculation.

status An individual's position or ranking in a group.

statutory rape Consensual sexual intercourse with a female under the age of consent.

stereotype A set of simplistic, rigidly held, overgeneralized beliefs about a person or group of people.

sterilization A surgical procedure that makes the reproductive organs incapable of producing or "delivering" viable gametes (sperm and eggs).

storge In John Lee's typology of love, companionate love.

strain gauge A device resembling a rubber band that is placed over the penis to measure physiological response.

streetwalker A prostitute who solicits on the streets.

sudden infant death syndrome (SIDS) A phenomenon in which an apparently healthy infant dies suddenly while sleeping.

surrogate motherhood An approach to infertility in which one woman bears a child for another.

survey research A method of gathering information from a small group to make inferences about a larger group.

sweating The moistening of the vagina by secretions from its walls.

swinging A wide range of sexual activities conducted between three or more people. Typically, swinging activities occur when a married or otherwise committed couple engages with another couple, multiple couples, or a single individual.

symptothermal method A fertility awareness method combining the basal body temperature and cervical mucus methods.

synthesis A whole formed by combining or integrating.

syphilis An STI caused by the *Treponema pallidum* bacterium.

tantric sex A sexual technique based on Eastern religions in which a couple shares "energy" during sexual intercourse.

T cell Any of several types of lymphocytes involved in the immune response.

telephone scatologia A paraphilia involving recurrent, intense urges to make obscene telephone calls.

tenting The expansion of the inner two thirds of the vagina during sexual arousal.

teratogen A toxic substance that causes birth defects.

testicle or **testis** (plural, *testes*) One of the paired male gonads inside the scrotum.

testosterone A steroid hormone associated with sperm production, the development of secondary sex characteristics in males, and the sex drive in both males and females.

testosterone replacement therapy Treatment that is indicated when both clinical symptoms and signs suggestive of androgen deficiency and decreased testosterone levels are present.

toxic shock syndrome (TSS) A potentially life-threatening condition caused by the *Staphylococcus aureus* bacterium and linked to the use of superabsorbent tampons and other devices that block the vagina or cervix during menstruation.

transgender Individuals whose appearance and behaviors do not conform to the gender roles ascribed by society for people of that sex.

transition The end of the first stage of labor, when the infant's head enters the birth canal.

transsexual A person whose genitals and gender identity as male or female are discordant; postsurgical transsexuals have surgically altered their genitals to fit their gender identity.

transvestic fetishism A paraphilia in which a heterosexual male cross-dresses for sexual arousal.

transvestism A clinical term referring to the wearing of clothing of the other sex, usually for sexual arousal.

triangular theory of love A theory developed by Robert Sternberg emphasizing the dynamic quality of love as expressed by the interrelationship of three elements: intimacy, passion, and decision/commitment.

tribidism A behavior in which one partner lies on top of the other and moves rhythmically for genital stimulation.

trichomoniasis A vaginal infection caused by *Trichomonas vaginalis*. Also known as trich.

trust Belief in the reliability and integrity of another person, process, thing, or institution.

tubal ligation The cutting and tying off (or other method of closure) of the fallopian tubes so that ova cannot be fertilized.

Turner syndrome (45, X) A chromosomal disorder affecting females born lacking an X chromosome, resulting in the failure to develop ovaries.

two-spirit In many cultures, a male who assumes female dress, gender role, and status.

ultrasound The use of high-frequency sound waves to create a visual image, as of the fetus in the uterus.

umbilical cord The cord connecting the placenta and fetus, through which nutrients pass.

unrequited love Love that is not returned.

urethra The tube through which urine (and in men, semen) passes.

urethral bulb The expanded portion of the urethra at the bladder.

urethral opening In females, the opening in the urethra, through which urine is expelled.

urethral orifice In males, the opening in the urethra, through which semen is ejaculated and urine is excreted.

urethritis Inflammation of the urethra.

urophilia A paraphilia in which a person gets sexual pleasure from contact with urine.

uterus A hollow, thick-walled, muscular organ held in the pelvic cavity by flexible ligaments and supported by several muscles. Also known as womb.

vacuum aspiration A first-trimester form of abortion using vacuum suction to remove the conceptus and other tissue from the uterus.

vagina In females, a flexible, muscular organ that begins between the legs and extends diagonally toward the small of the back. It encompasses the penis during sexual intercourse and is the pathway (birth canal) through which an infant is born.

vaginal ring A vaginal form of reversible, hormonal birth control. Commonly referred to as NuvaRing.

vaginismus   A sexual function difficulty characterized by muscle spasms around the vaginal entrance, preventing the insertion of a penis.

vaginitis   Any of several kinds of vaginal infection.

value judgment   An evaluation as "good" or "bad" based on moral or ethical standards rather than objective ones.

variable   An aspect or factor that can be manipulated in an experiment.

varicocele   A varicose vein above the testicle that may cause lowered fertility in men.

vas deferens (plural, *vasa deferentia*)   One of two tubes that transport sperm from the epididymis to the ejaculatory duct within the prostate gland.

vasectomy   A form of surgical sterilization in which each vas deferens is severed, thereby preventing sperm from entering the seminal fluid.

vasocongestion   Blood engorgement of body tissues.

vernix   The waxy substance that sometimes covers an infant at birth.

vestibule   The area enclosed by the labia minora.

virus   A protein-coated package of genes that invades a cell and alters the way in which the cell reproduces itself.

voyeurism   A paraphilia involving recurrent, intense urges to view nonconsenting others while they are engaged in sexual activities.

vulva   The collective term for the external female genitals.

vulvodynia   Chronic vulvar discomfort or pain often involving burning, stinging, irritation, or rawness of the female genitalia, but there is no infection or skin disease of the vulva or vagina causing these symptoms.

Western blot   A test to determine whether antibodies are specific to HIV.

window period   The variable amount of time it takes for the immune system to produce enough antibodies to be detected by an antibody test.

yolk sac   The producer of the embryo's first blood cells and the germ cells that will develop into gonads.

ZIFT (zygote intrafallopian transfer)   An ART procedure whereby a woman's eggs are fertilized in the laboratory and then transferred to her fallopian tubes.

zoophilia   A paraphilia involving recurrent, intense urges to engage in sexual activities with animals. (Also referred to as bestiality.)

Bibliography

Abbey, A. (2002). Alcohol-related sexual assault: A common problem among college students. *Journal of Studies on Alcohol, 14,* 118–128.

Abbey, A., Clinton-Sherrod, A. M., McAussian, P., Zawacki, T., & Buck, P. O. (2003). The relationship between the quality of alcohol consumed and the severity of sexual assaults committed by college men. *Journal of Interpersonal Violence, 18,* 813–833.

Abbey, A., & Harnish, R. J. (1995). Perception of sexual intent: The role of gender, alcohol consumption, and rape supportive attitudes. *Sex Roles, 32*(5–6), 297–313.

Abel, G. (1989). Paraphilias. In H. I. Kaplan & B. Sadock (Eds.), *Comprehensive textbook of psychiatry, Vol. 1* (5th ed.), Baltimore: Williams & Wilkins.

Abma, J. C., Martinez, G. M., Mosher, B. S., & Dawson, B. S. (2004). Teenagers in the United States: Sexual activity, contraceptive use, and childbearing, 2002. *Vital Health Statistics, 23.* Available: http://www.ncbi.nlm.nig.gov (Last visited 6/1/06).

Absi-Semaan, N., Crombie, G., & Freeman, C. (1993). Masculinity and femininity in middle childhood: Developmental and factor analyses. *Sex Roles, 28*(3–4), 187–202.

Abu-Nasr, D. (2005, October 9). Gay Arabs defy laws, extremists by coming out. *San Francisco Chronicle,* p. A19.

Ackard, D. M., Kearney-Cooke, A., & Peterson, C. B. (2000). Effect of body image on women's sexual behaviors. *International Journal of Eating Disorders, 28,* 422–429.

Adler, N. A., & Schultz, J. (1995). Sibling incest offenders. *Child Abuse & Neglect, 19*(7), 811–819.

AGOG News Release. (2007, September 1). AGOG advises against cosmetic vaginal procedures due to lack of safety and efficacy data. Available: http://www.accg.org/from_home/publications/press_releases/nr09-01-07-1.cfm (Last visited 1/17/08).

Ahlborg, T., Dahlof, L. G., & Hallberg, L. (2005). Quality of the intimate and sexual relationship in first-time parents six months after delivery. *Journal of Sex Research, 42*(2), 167–174.

Ahrendt, D. (2001). Ergogenic aids: Counseling the athlete. *American Family Physician, 63*(5), 913–1013.

Ahrons, C. (2004). *We're still family.* New York: HarperCollins.

Ainsworth, M., et al. (1978). *Patterns of attachment: A psychological study of the strange situation.* Hillsdale, NJ: Erlbaum.

Albert, A. E., Warner, D. L., Hatcher, R. A., Trussell, J., & Bennett, C. (1995, March 21). *Condom use among female commercial sex workers in Nevada's legal brothels.* Paper available from Family Planning Program, Emory University School of Medicine, Atlanta.

Alcott, W. (1868). *The physiology of marriage.* Boston: Jewett.

Alison, L., Santtila, P., Sandnabba, N. K., & Nordling, N. (2001). Sadomasochistically oriented behavior: Diversity in practice and meaning. *Archives of Sexual Behavior, 30,* 1–12.

Allen, E. S., Atkins, D., Baucom, D. H., Snyder, D., et al. (2005). Intrapersonal, interpersonal, and contextual factors in engaging in and responding to extramarital involvement. *Clinical Psychology: Science and Practice, 12,* 101–130.

Allen, E. S., & Baucom, D. H. (2006). Dating, marital, and hypothetical extradyadic involvements: How do they compare? *Journal of Sex Research, 48*(4), 307–317.

Allen, J. (2004, March 7). Male enhancement ads might not deliver on promises. *The Indianapolis Star,* p. J8.

Allina, A. (2005a, May/June). FDA committee says no to testosterone patch. *National Women's Health Network,* p. 10.

Allina, A. (2005b, July/August). The truth behind the new Depo label. *National Women's Health Network,* p. 4.

Allport, G. (1958). *The nature of prejudice.* Garden City, NY: Doubleday.

Altman, D. (1985). *AIDS in the mind of America.* Garden City, NY: Doubleday.

Amaro, H., Raj, A., & Reed, E. (2001). Women's sexual health: The need for feminist analyses in public health in the decade of behavior. *Psychology of Women Quarterly, 25,* 324–334.

Amato, P. (2003). Reconciling divergent perspectives: Judith Wallerstein, qualitative family research, and children of divorce. *Family Relations, 52*(4), 332–339.

Amato, P. R. (2000). The consequences of divorce for adults and children. *Journal of Marriage and Family, 62,* 1269–1287.

America's children: Key national indicators of well-being. (2007). Available: http://www.nichd.nih.gov/publications/pubs/upload/report2007.pdf (Last visited 6/4/08).

American Academy of Child and Adolescent Psychiatry. (2008). Facts for families: Child sexual abuse. Available: http://www.aacp.org/cs/roots/facts_for_families/child_sexual_abuse (Last visited 10/7/08).

American Academy of Pediatrics. (2000). Evaluation of the newborn with developmental anomalies of the external genitalia. *Pediatrics, 106*(1), 138–142.

American Academy of Pediatrics. (2001). Sexuality, contraception, and the media. *Pediatrics, 107*(1), 191–194.

American Academy of Pediatrics. (2002). Coparent or second parent adoption by same-sex parents. *Pediatrics, 109*(2), 339–341.

American Academy of Pediatrics. (2007). Parenting corner Q&A: Circumcision. Available: http://www.aap.org/publiced/BR_Circumcision.htm (Last visited 4/2/09).

American Academy of Pediatrics Section on Breastfeeding. (2003). Policy statement: Breastfeeding and the use of human milk. *Pediatrics, 115,* 496.

American Association of Retired Persons. (2005). Sexuality at midlife and beyond: 2004 update of attitudes and behaviors. Available: http://www.aarp.org (Last visited 2/8/06).

American Association of University Women. (2006). Drawing the line: Sexual harassment on campus. Available:http://www.aauw.org/newsroom/presskits/DTL_Press_Conf_060124/DTL_012406.cfm (Last visited 1/10/06).

American Association of University Women Educational Foundation. (2001). *Hostile hallways: The AAUW survey on sexual harassment in America's schools.* Washington, DC: Author.

American Cancer Society. (2003). All about prostate cancer. Available: http://www.cancer.org/docroot/CRI/CRI_2_3x.asp?dt=36 (Last visited 5/3/03).

American Cancer Society. (2005a). All about breast cancer. Available: http://www.cancer.org/docroot/CRI/CRI_2x.asp?sitearea=8dt=5 (Last visited 1/10/06).

American Cancer Society. (2005b). Effects of cancer treatment on female sexual desire and response. Available: http://www.cancer.org/docroot/MIT_7_2x_Cancer_Treatments_Effects_On_Female_Sexual_Desire_And_Response.asp?sitearea=MT (Last visited 6/9/06).

American Cancer Society. (2005c). All about cervical cancer. Available: http://www.cancer.org/docroot/1rn/1rn_0.asp (Last visited 1/10/06).

American Cancer Society. (2005d). All about ovarian cancer. Available: http://www.cancer.org/docroot/CRI/CRI_2x.asp? sitearea=8dt=33 (Last visited 1/11/06).

American Cancer Society. (2005e). All about uterine sarcoma. Available: http://www.cancer.org/CRI/CRI_2x.asp?sitearea=8dt =63 (Lasted visited 1/11/06).

American Cancer Society. (2005f). All about vaginal cancer. Available: http://www.cancer.org/CRI/CRI_2x.asp?sitearea=8dt=55 (Last visited 1/10/06).

American Cancer Society. (2005g). All about prostate cancer. Available: http://www.cancer.org/docroot/CRI/CRI_2x.asp? sitearea=8dt=36 (Last visited 1/13/06).

American Cancer Society. (2005h). All about testicular cancer. Available: http://www.cancer.org/docroot/CRI/CRI_2s.asp?sitearea=8dt=41 (Last visited 1/19/06).

American Cancer Society. (2005i). All about penile cancer. Available: http://www.cancer.org/docroot/CRI/CRI_2x.asp?sitearea=8dt=35 (Last visited 1/19/06).

American Cancer Society. (2005j). All about male breast cancer. Available: http://www.cancer.org/docroot/CRI/CRI_2x.asp?sitearea=8dt=28 (Last visited 1/19/06).

American Cancer Society. (2005k). All about anal cancer. Available: http://www.cancer.org/docroot/CRI/CRI_2x.asp?sitearea=8dt=47

American Cancer Society. (2006a). Detailed guide: Prostate cancer surgery. Available: http://www.cancer.org/docroot/CRI/content/CRI_2_4_4X_Surgery_36.asp (Last visited 1/19/06).

American Cancer Society. (2006a). Staying sexually healthy after being treated for cancer. Available: http://www.cancer.org/docroot/MIT/content_7_2x_Staying_Sexually_Healthy_After_Being_Treated_for_Cancer (Last visited 9/24/08).

American Cancer Society. (2007a). *Breast Cancer Facts and Figures 2007–2008.* Atlanta, GA: Author.

American Cancer Society. (2007b). Breast reconstruction after mastectomy. Available: http://www.cancer.org/docroot/CRI/content/CRI_2_6x_Breast_Reconstruction_AfterMastectomy (Last visited 9/25/08).

American Cancer Society. (2007c). Detailed guide: Prostate cancer—surgery. Available: http://www.cancer.org/docroot/CRI/content/CRI_2_4_4x_Surgery_36.asp?sitearea= (Last visited 4/24/08).

American Cancer Society. (2008a). Overview: Breast cancer. Available: http://www.cancer.org/docroot/CRI/CRI_2_1x.asp?dt=5 (Last visited 9/22/08).

American Cancer Society. (2008b). Overview: Cervical cancer. Available: http://www.cancer.org/docroot/CRI/CRI_2_1x.asp?dt=8 (Last visited 9/25/08).

American Cancer Society. (2008c). Overview: Ovarian cancer. Available: http://www.cancer.org/docroot/CRI/CRI_2_1x.asp?dt=33 (Last visited 9/25/08).

American Cancer Society. (2008d). Detailed guide: Uterine sarcoma. Available: http://www.cancer.org/docroot/CRI/CRI_2_3x.asp?dt=63 (Last visited 9/25/08).

American Cancer Society. (2008e). Detailed guide: Vaginal cancer. Available: http://www.cancer.org/docroot/CRI/CRI_2_3x.asp?dt=55 (Last visited 9/26/08).

American Cancer Society. (2008f). Overview: Prostate cancer. Available: http://www.cancer.org/docroot/CRI/CRI_2_1x.asp?dt=36 (Last visited 9/26/08).

American Cancer Society. (2008g). Overview: Testicular cancer. Available: http://www.cancer.org/docroot/CRI/CRI_2_1x.asp?dt=41 (Last visited 9/29/80).

American Cancer Society. (2008h). Detailed guide: Penile cancer. Available: http://www.cancer.org/docroot/CRI/CRI_2_3x.asp?dt=35 (Last visited 9/30/08).

American Cancer Society. (2008i). Detailed guide: Breast cancer in men. Available: http://www.cancer.org/docroot/CRI/CRI_2_3x.asp?dt=28

American Cancer Society. (2008j). Overview: Anal cancer. Available: http://www.cancer.org/CRI/CRI-2-1x.asp?dt=47

American College Health Association. (2006). *American College Health Association–National College Health Assessment: Reference Group Executive Summary, Spring 2006.* Baltimore: Author.

American College of Obstetricians and Gynecologists. (2006a). Late childbearing. Available: http://www.acog.org/publications/patient_education/bp060.cfm (Last visited 10/14/08).

American College of Obstetricians and Gynecologists. (2006b). ACOG recommends restricted use of episiotomies: News release. Available: http://www.acog.org/from_home/publications/press_releases/nr03-31-06-2.cfm (Last visited 11/24/08).

American College of Obstetricians and Gynecologists. (2007). New recommendations for Down syndrome: Screening should be offered to all pregnant women. Available: http://www.acog.org/from_home/publications/press_releases/nr01-02-07.cfm (Last visited 10/14/08).

American Diabetes Association. (2001). A guide for women with diabetes. Available: http://www.diabetes.org (Last visited 5/2/03).

American Psychiatric Association. (2000). *Diagnostic and statistical manual of mental disorders* (4th ed., text revision). Washington, DC: Author.

American Psychiatric Association Work Group on Eating Disorders. (2006). Practice guideline for the treatment of patients with eating disorders. *American Journal of Psychiatry, 157* (Suppl. 1), 1–39.

American Psychological Association. (2000). *Guidelines for psychotherapy with lesbian, gay, and bisexual clients.* Washington, DC: Author.

American Social Health Association. (1998a). STD statistics. Available: http://www.ashastd.org/std/stats/html (Last visited 12/5/00).

American Social Health Association. (1998b). *Sexually transmitted diseases in America: How many cases and at what cost?* Menlo Park, CA: Kaiser Family Foundation.

American Social Health Association. (1998c). Chlamydia: What you should know. Available: http://sunsite.unc.edu/ASHA/ std/chlam.html#intro (Last visited 2/14/98).

American Social Health Association. (2006). Crabs: Questions and answers. Available: http://www.ashastd.org/learn/learn_crabs_facts .cfm (Last visited 1/11/06).

American Social Health Association. (2006a). STD/STI statistics. Available: http://www.ashastd.org/learn/learn_statisticss.cfm (Last visited 10/14/08).

American Social Health Association. (2008). NGU (nongonococcal urethritis). Available: http://www.ashastad.org/learn/learn_ngu .cfm (Last visited 10/22/08).

American Society of Plastic Surgeons. (2008). 2000/2006/2007 national plastic surgery statistics. Available: http:/www.plastic surgery.org/media/statistics/index.cfm (Last visited 9/10/08).

American Society for Reproductive Medicine. (2008). Assisted reproductive technologies: A guidebook for patients. Available: http://www. asrm.org/Patients/patientbooklets/ART.pdf (Last visited 10/25/08).

Anderson, C. (1995). Childhood sexually transmitted diseases: One consequence of sexual abuse. *Public Health Nursing, 12*(1), 41–46.

Anderson, S. E., & Must, A. (2005). Interpreting the continued decline in the average age at menarche: Results from two nationally representative surveys of U.S. girls studied 10 years apart. *Journal of Pediatrics, 147*(6), 735–760.

Angier, N. (2007, April 10). Search for the female equivalent of Viagra is helping to keep lab rats smiling. *New York Times*, p. D4.

Ann, C. C. (1997). A proposal for a radical new sex therapy technique for the management of vasocongestive and orgasmic dysfunction in women: The AFE zone stimulation technique. *Sexual and Marital Therapy, 12*, 357–370.

Annon, J. (1974). *The behavioral treatment of sexual problems.* Honolulu: Enabling Systems.

Annon, J. (1976). *Behavioral treatment of sexual problems: Brief therapy.* New York: Harper & Row.

APA Online. (2007, February 19). Sexualization of girls is linked to common mental health problems in girls and women—eating disorders, low self-esteem and depression; an APA task force reports. Available: http://www.apa.org/releases/sexualization.html (Last visited 7/7/08).

Aral, S. O. (1994). Sexual behavior in sexually transmitted disease research: An overview. *Sexually Transmitted Diseases, 21*, S59–S64.

Arey, D. (1995). Gay males and sexual child abuse. In L. A. Fontes (Ed.), *Sexual abuse in nine North American cultures: Treatment and prevention.* Thousand Oaks, CA: Sage.

Armstrong, M. L., Roberts, A. E., Owen, D. C., & Koch, J. R. (2004). Contemporary college students and body piercing. *Journal of Adolescent Health, 35*, 58–61.

Arndt, W. B., Jr. (1991). *Gender disorders and the paraphilias.* Madison, CT: International Universities Press.

Arnett, J. J. (2006). Emerging adulthood: Understanding the new way of coming of age. In J. J. Arnett & J. L. Tanner (Eds.), *Emerging adults in America: Coming of age in the 21st century* (pp. 3–20). Washington, DC: American Psychological Association.

Aron, A., & Aron, E. (1991). Love and sexuality. In K. McKinney & S. Sprecher (Eds.), *Sexuality in close relationships.* Hillsdale, NJ: Erlbaum.

Aron, A., Dutton, D. G., & Aron, E. N. (1989). Experiences of falling in love. *Journal of Social and Personal Relationships, 6*, 243–257.

Ashton, A. K. (2007). The new sexual pharmacology: A guide for the clinician. In S. Leiblum (Ed.), *Principles and practice of sex therapy* (4th ed., pp. 509–542). New York: Guilford.

Asia: Child prostitution in Cambodia. (1996). *The Economist*, 338.

Ayling, K., & Ussher, J. M. (2008). "If sex hurts, am I still a woman?" The subjective experience of vulvodynia in heterosexual women. *Archives of Sexual Behavior, 37*, 294–304.

Baca-Zinn, M. (1994). Feminist rethinking from racial-ethnic families. In M. Baca-Zinn & B. Thorton-Dill (Eds.), *Women of color in U.S. society.* Philadelphia: Temple University Press.

Bacon, C. G., Mittleman, M. A., Kawachi, I., Giovannucci, E., Glasser, D. B., & Rimm, E. B. (2003). Sexual function in men older than 50 years of age: Results from the Health Professionals Follow-Up Study. *Annals of Internal Medicine, 139*, 161–168.

Bada, H. S., Das, A., Bauer, C. R., Shankaran, S., Lester, B. M., Gard, C., et al. (2005). Low birth weight and preterm births: Etiologic fraction attributable to prenatal drug exposure. *Journal of Perinatology, 10*(6), 631–637.

Bailey, J., Dunne, M., & Martin, N. (2000). Genetic and environmental influences on sexual orientation and its correlates in an Australian twin sample. *Journal of Personality and Social Psychology, 78*, 524–536.

Bailey, J. M., & Pillard, R. C. (1991). A genetic study of male sexual orientation. *Archives of General Psychiatry, 48*(12), 1089–1096.

Bailey, J. M., Pillard, R. C., Neale, M. C., & Agyei, Y. (1993). Heritable factors influence sexual orientation in women. *Archives of General Psychiatry, 50*(3), 217–223.

Bailey, J. V., Farquhar, C., & Owen, C. (2004). Bacterial vaginosis in lesbians and bisexual women. *Sexually Transmitted Diseases, 31*(11), 691–694.

Bailey, R. (2007). Male circumcision for HIV prevention in young men in Kisumu, Kenya: A randomized controlled trial. *The Lancet, 369*, 643–656.

Bajracharya, S., Sarvela, P., & Isberner, F. R. (1995). A retrospective study of first sex intercourse experiences among undergraduates. *Journal of American College Health, 43*(4), 169–177.

Baker, C. P. (1995). Child chattel: Future tourists for sex. *Insight on the News, 11*, 11.

Balsam, K. F., Beauchaine, T. P., Rothblum, E. D. & Solomon, S. E. (2008). Three-year follow-up of same-sex couples who had civil unions in Vermont, same-sex couples not in civil unions, and heterosexual married couples. *Developmental Psychology, 44*(1), 102–116.

Bancroft, J. (2002). The medicalization of female sexual dysfunction: The need for caution. *Archives of Sexual Behavior, 31*, 451–455.

Bancroft, J., Herbenick, D., & Reynolds, M. (2003). Masturbation as a marker of sexual development. In J. Bancroft (Ed.), *Sexual development in childhood.* Bloomington: Indiana University Press.

Bancroft, J., & Janssen, E. (2000). The dual control model of male sexual response: A theoretical approach to centrally mediated erectile dysfunction. *Neuroscience and Biobehavioral Reviews, 24*, 571–579.

Bancroft, J., Loftus, J., & Long, S. (2003). Distress about sex: A national survey of women in heterosexual relationships. *Archives of Sexual Behavior, 32*, 193–208.

Bancroft, J., & Vukadinovic, Z. (2004). Sexual addiction, sexual compulsivity, sexual impulsivity, or what? *Journal of Sex Research, 41*, 225–234.

Bandura, A. (1977). *Social learning theory.* Englewood Cliffs, NJ: Prentice Hall.

Barbach, L. (2001). *For each other: Sharing sexual intimacy* (Rev. ed.). Garden City, NY: Doubleday.

Barclay, L. (2008, September 18). Gardasil approval expanded to prevention of HPV-related vulvar, vaginal cancer. *Medscape Medical News.* Available: http://www.medscape.com/viewarticle/580720 (Last visited 9/26/08).

Bardia, A., et al. (2006). Recreational physical activity and risk of postmenopausal breast cancer based on hormone receptor status. *Archives of Internal Medicine, 166*, 2478–2483.

Barrow, G., & Smith, P. (1992). *Aging, ageism, and society.* St. Paul, MN: West.

Barry, K. (1995). *The prostitution of sexuality: The global exploitation of women*. New York: University Press.

Bartholow, B. N., Vamshidar, G., Ackers, M., McLellan, E., Gurwith, M., Durham, M., & Greenberg, A. E. (2006) Demographic and behavioral change contextual risk groups among men who have sex with men participating in a phase 3 HIV vaccine efficacy trial: Implications for HIV prevention and behavioral/biomedical intervention trials. *Journal of Acquired Immune Deficiency Syndromes, 43,* 594–602.

Bartky, S. L. (1990). *Femininity and domination: Studies in the phenomenology of oppression*. New York: Routledge.

Basson, R. (2002). A model of women's sexual arousal. *Journal of Sex and Marital Therapy, 28,* 1–10.

Basson, R., Berman, J., Burnett, A., Derogatis, L., Ferguson, D., Fourcroy, J., et al. (2001). Report of the International Consensus Development Conference on Female Sexual Dysfunction: Definitions and classifications. *Journal of Sex and Marital Therapy, 27,* 83–94.

Basson, R., Leiblum, S., Brotto, L., Derogatis, L., Fourcroy, J., Fugl-Meyer, K., et al. (2003). Definitions of women's sexual dysfunctions reconsidered: Advocating expansion and revision. *Journal of Psychosomatic Obstetrics and Gynecology, 24,* 221–229.

Basson, R., Leiblum, S., Brotto, L., Derogatis, L., Fourcroy, J., Fugl-Meyer, K., et al. (2004). Revised definitions of women's sexual dysfunction. *Journal of Sexual Medicine, 1,* 40–48.

Bauer, C. R., Langer, J. C., Shankaran, S., Bada., H. S., Lester, B., Wright, L. L., et al. (2005). Acute neonatal effects of cocaine exposure during pregnancy. *Archives of Pediatrics and Adolescent Medicine, 159*(9), 824–834.

Baumeister, R., Wotman, S. R., & Stillwell, A. M. (1993). Unrequited love: On heartbreak, anger, guilt, scriptlessness, and humiliation. *Journal of Personality and Social Psychology, 64,* 377–394.

Baumeister, R. F., Catanese, K. R., & Wallace, H. M. (2002). Conquest by force: A narcissistic reactance theory of rape and sexual coercion. *Review of General Psychology, 6,* 92–135.

Bauserman, R. (1998). Egalitarian, sexist, and aggressive sexual materials: Attitude effects and viewer responses. *Journal of Sex Research, 35*(3), 244–253.

Bayles, F. (2003, November 20). Gay-marriage ruling gives little time to prepare. *USA Today,* p. 8A.

Bearman, P. S., & Bruckner, H. (2001). Promising the future: Virginity pledges and first intercourse. *American Journal of Sociology, 106*(4), 859–912.

Bechhofer, L., & Parrot, A. (1991). What is acquaintance rape? In A. Parrot & L. Bechhofer (Eds.), *Acquaintance rape: The hidden crime*. New York: Wiley.

Bell, A., Weinberg, M., & Hammersmith, S. (1981). *Sexual preference: Its development in men and women*. Bloomington: Indiana University Press.

Belzer, E. G. (1984). A review of female ejaculation and the Grafenberg spot. *Women and Health, 9,* 5–16.

Bem, D. J. (1996). Exotic becomes erotic: A developmental theory of sexual orientation. *Psychological Review,103,* 320–335.

Bem, D. J. (2000). Exotic becomes erotic: Integrating biological and experiental antecedents of sexual orientation. In A. R. D'Augelli & C. L. Patterson (Eds.), *Lesbian, gay, and bisexual identities and youth: Psychological perspectives* (pp. 52–68). New York: Oxford University Press.

Bem, S. L. (1975). Androgyny vs. the tight little lives of fluffy women and chesty men. *Psychology Today, 9*(4), 58–59ff.

Bem, S. L. (1983). Gender schema theory and its implications for child development: Raising gender-aschematic children in a gender-schematic society. *Signs, 8*(4), 598–616.

Benotsch, E. G., Kalichman, S., Lawrence, A., & Nordling, N. (2002). Men who have met sex partners via the Internet: Prevalence, predictors, and implications for HIV prevention. *Archives of Sexual Behavior, 31,* 177–183.

Beral, V. (2007). Ovarian cancer and hormone replacement therapy in the Million Women Study. *The Lancet, 369* (9574), 1703–1710.

Berenson, A. (2005, December 4). Sales of impotence drugs fall, defying ads and expectations. *New York Times,* pp. 1, 34.

Berger, A. A. (1991). Of mice and men: An introduction to mouseology; or anal eroticism and Disney. *Journal of Homosexuality, 21*(1–2), 155–165.

Berning, J. M., Adams, K. J., Stamford, B. A., Finewman, I., & Maud, P. J. (2004). Prevalence and perceived prevalence of anabolic steroid use among college-aged students. *Medicine and Science in Sports and Exercise, 36,* S350.

Berry, D. A., Cronin, K. A., Plevritis, S. K., Fryback, D. G., Clarke, L., Zelen, M., et al. (2005). Effect of screening and adjuvant therapy on mortality from breast cancer. *New England Journal of Medicine, 17,* 1784–1792.

Bertone-Johnson, E. R., Hankinson, S. E., Bendich, A., Johnson, S. R., Willett, W. C., & Manson, J. E. (2005). Calcium and vitamin D intake and risk of incident premenstrual syndrome. *Archives of Internal Medicine, 165,* 1246–1252.

Best, K. (2007, December 17). Kiss and tell: Smooches make or break a relationship. *Indianapolis Star,* p. E1.

Bieschke, K. J., Perez, R. M., & Debord, K. A. (Eds.). (2007). *Handbook of counseling and psychotherapy with lesbian, gay, bisexual and transgender clients*. Washington, DC: American Psychological Association.

Billy, J. O., Tanfer, K., Grady, W. R., & Klepinger, D. H. (1993). The sexual behavior of men in the United States. *Family Planning Perspectives, 25*(2), 52–60.

Binson, D., Michaels, S., Stall, R., Coates, T. J., Gagnon, J. H., & Catania, J. A. (1995). Prevalence and social distribution of men who have sex with men: United States and its urban centers. *Journal of Sex Research, 32,* 245–254.

Biskupic, J. (2002, April 17). "Virtual" porn ruling hinged on threat to art. *USA Today,* p. A3.

Biskupic, J. (2003a, March 4). Case tests Congress's ability to make libraries block porn. *USA Today,* p. A3.

Biskupic, J. (2003b, June 27). Gay sex ban struck down. *USA Today,* p. A1.

Biskupic, J. (2003c, June 27). Decision represents an enormous turn in the law. *USA Today,* p. A5.

Biskupic, J. (2004, June 30). It may be up to parents to block Web porn. *New York Times,* p. 6A.

Blackless, M., Charuvastra, A., Derryck, A., Fausto-Sterling, A., Lauzanne, K., & Lee, E. (2000). How sexually dimorphic are we? Review and synthesis. *American Journal of Human Biology, 12,* 151–166.

Blackwood, E. (1984). Sexuality and gender in certain Native American tribes: The case of cross-gender females. *Signs, 10,* 27–42.

Blanchard, R. (1993, March). The she-male phenomena and the concept of partial autogynephilia. *Journal of Sex and Marital Therapy, 19*(1), 69–76.

Blanchard, R., & Bogaert, A. F. (2004). Proportion of homosexual men who owe their sexual orientation to fraternal birth order: An estimate based on two national probability samples. *American Journal of Human Biology, 16,* 151–157.

Blanchard, R., Cantor, J., Bogaert, A., Breedlove, S., & Ellis, L. (2006). Interaction of fraternal birth order and handedness in the development of male homosexuality. *Hormones and Behavior, 49,* 405–414.

Blanchard, R., & Hucker, S. (1991). Age, transvestism, bondage, and concurrent paraphilic activities in 117 fatal cases of autoerotic asphyxia. *British Journal of Psychiatry, 159,* 371–377.

Blechman, E. A. (1990). *Emotions and the family: For better or for worse.* Hillsdale, NJ: Erlbaum.

Blue, V. (2003). *The ultimate guide to adult videos: How to watch adult videos and make your sex life sizzle.* San Francisco: Cleis Press.

Blum, D. (1997). *Sex on the brain.* New York: Viking Press.

Blumberg, E. S. (2003). The lives and voices of highly sexual women. *Journal of Sex Research, 40,* 146–157.

Blumstein, P., & Schwartz, P. (1983). *American couples.* New York: McGraw-Hill.

Bodansky, V., & Bodansky, S. (2006). *To bed or not to bed.* Alameda, CA: Hunter House.

Bogaert, A., Friesen, C., & Klentrou, P. (2002). Age of puberty and sexual orientation in a national probability sample. *Archives of Sexual Behavior, 31,* 73–81.

Bogaert, A. F. (2004). Asexuality: Prevalence and associated factors in a national probability sample. *Journal of Sex Research, 41*(3), 279–287.

Bogart, L., & Thornton, S. (2005). Are HIV/AIDS conspiracy beliefs a barrier to HIV prevention among African Americans? *Journal of Acquired Immune Deficiency Syndromes, 38*(2), 213–218.

Bogle, K. A. (2008). *Hooking up: Sex, dating, and relationships on campus.* New York: New York University Press.

Boies, S. C. (2002). University students' use of and recreations to online sexual information and entertainment: Links to online and offline sexual behavior. *Canadian Journal of Human Sexuality, 11,* 77–89.

Bolan, G., Ehrhardt, A. A., & Wasserheit, J. N. (1999). Gender perspectives and STDs. In K. K. Holmes et al. (Eds.), *Sexually transmitted diseases.* New York: McGraw-Hill.

Boles, J., & Elifson, E. W. (1994, July). The social organization of transvestite prostitution and AIDS. *Social Science and Medicine, 39*(2), 85–93.

Bolin, A. (1997). Transforming transvestism and transsexualism: Polarity, politics, and gender. In B. Bullough, V. L. Bullough, & J. Elias (Eds.), *Gender bending.* New York: Prometheus Books.

Bonilla, L., & Porter, J. (1990). A comparison of Latino, Black, and non-Hispanic attitudes toward homosexuality. *Hispanic Journal of Homosexuality, 12,* 439–452.

Boonstra, H. D. (2007) The case for a new approach to sex education mounts; will policymakers heed the message? *Guttmacher Policy Review, 10*(2). Available: http://guttmacher.org/pubs/gpr/10/2/gpr100202.html (Last visited 6/9/08).

Boonstra, H. D., Gold, H. D., Richards, C. L., & Finer, L. B. (2006). Abortion in women's lives. New York: Guttmacher Institute. Available: http://www.guttmacher.org/pubs/2006/05/04/AiWL.pdf (Last visited 9/18/08).

Borneman, E. (1983). Progress in empirical research on children's sexuality. *SIECUS Report,* 1–5.

Borrello, G., & Thompson, B. (1990). A note regarding the validity of Lee's typology of love. *Journal of Psychology, 124*(6), 639–644.

Boston Women's Health Book Collective. (2005). *Our bodies, ourselves.* New York: Touchstone.

Bostwick, H. (1860). *A treatise on the nature and treatment of seminal disease, impotency, and other kindred afflictions* (12th ed.). New York: Burgess, Stringer.

Bower, B. (1996, August 10). From exotic to erotic: Roots of sexual orientation found in personality, childhood friendships. *Science News, 150,* 88–89.

Bowman, C. G. (1993). Street harassment and the informal ghettoization of women. *Harvard Law Review, 106*(3), 517–580.

Boyd, C. J., McCabe, S. E., & d'Arcy, H. (2003). Ecstasy use among college undergraduates: Gender, race and sexual identity. *Journal of Substance Abuse Treatment, 24,* 209–215.

Boyer, C. B., Shafer, M., Wibbelsman, C. J., Seeberg, D., Teitle, E., & Lovell, N. (2000). Associations of sociodemographic, psychosocial, and behavioral factors with sexual risk and sexually transmitted diseases in teen clinic patients. *Journal of Adolescent Health, 27,* 102–111.

Braverman, P., & Strasburger, V. (1994, January). Sexually transmitted diseases. *Clinical Pediatrics,* 26–37.

Brendgen, M., Wanner, B., & Vitaro, F. (2007). Peer and teacher effects on the early onset of sexual intercourse. *American Journal of Public Health, 97*(11), 2070–2075.

Brennan, K., & Shaver, P. R. (1995). Dimensions of adult attachment, affect regulation, and romantic relationship functioning. *Personality and Social Psychology Bulletin, 21*(3), 267–283.

Brenner, M. G. (2005). You can provide efficient, effective, and reimbursable breastfeeding support—Here's how. *Contemporary Pediatrics.* Available: http://www.contemporarypediatrics.com (Last visited 12/21/05).

Brents, B., & Hausbeck, K. (2005). Violence and legalized brothel prostitution in Nevada. *Journal of Interpersonal Violence, 20,* 270–295.

Breslow, N., Evans, L., & Langley, J. (1985). On the prevalence and roles of females in the sadomasochistic subculture: Report on an empirical investigation. *Archives of Sexual Behavior, 14,* 303–317.

Brewster, A. M., et al. (2008). Residual risk of breast cancer recurrence 5 years after adjuvant therapy. *Journal of the National Cancer Institute, 100,* 1171–1183.

Bridgeland, W. M., Duane, E. A., & Stewart, C. S. (1995). Sexual victimization among undergraduates. *College Student Journal 29*(1), 16–25.

Bridges, A. (2006, June 9). World's 1st cancer vaccine targets cervical disease. *Indianapolis Star,* p. A1, A11.

Bridges, A. (2006, August 24). FDA eases limits on Plan B sales. *San Francisco Chronicle.* Available: http://www.sfgate.com (Last accessed 8/24/06).

Briere, J. N., & Elliott, D. M. (1994). Immediate and long-term impacts of child sexual abuse. *The Future of Children, 4,* 54–69.

Brizendine, L. (2006). *The female brain.* Northridge, CA: Morgan Road.

Brochman, S. (1991, July 30). Silent victims: Bringing male rape out of the closet. *The Advocate,* pp. 38–43.

Brock, G., Nehra, A., Lipshultz, L., Karlin, G., Gleave, M., Seger, M., et al. (2003). Safety and efficacy of Vardenafil for the treatment of men with erectile dysfunction after radical retropubic prostatectomy. *Journal of Urology, 170,* 1278–1283.

Brotto, L. A., Chik, H. M., Ryder, A. G., Gorzalka, B. G., & Seal, B. N. (2005). Acculturation and sexual function in Asian women. *Archives of Sexual Behavior, 6,* 613–626.

Brown, G. R. (1995). Cross-dressing men often lead double lives. *Menninger Letter,* pp. 4–5.

Brown, J. D. (2002). Mass media influences on sexuality. *Journal of Sex Research, 39*(1), 42–46.

Brown, J. D., & Keller, S. N. (2000). Can the mass media be healthy sex educators? *Family Planning Perspectives, 32*(5), 255–257.

Brown, P. L. (2006, December 2). Supporting boys or girls when the line isn't clear. *New York Times,* p. A1.

Browne, A., & Finkelhor, D. (1986). Initial and long-term effects: A review of the research. In D. Finkelhor (Ed.), *Sourcebook on child sexual abuse.* Beverly Hills, CA: Sage.

Brownmiller, S. (1975). *Against our will: Men, women, and rape.* New York: Ballantine Books.

Bruckner, H., & Bearman, P. S. (2005). After the promise: The STD consequences of adolescent virginity pledges. *Journal of Adolescent Health, 36,* 271–278.

Brydoy, M., Fossa, S. D., Klepp, O., Bremnes, R. M., Wist, E. A., Wentzel-Larsen, T., et al. (2005). Paternity following treatment for testicular cancer. *Journal of the National Cancer Institute, 97,* 1580–1588.

Bullough, B., & Bullough, V. L. (1996). Female prostitution: Current research and changing interpretations. *Annual Review of Sex Research, 7,* 158–180.

Bullough, V. (1991). Transvestism: A reexamination. *Journal of Psychology and Human Sexuality, 4*(2), 53–67.

Bullough, V. L. (2004). Sex will never be the same: The contributions of Alfred C. Kinsey. *Archives of Sexual Behavior, 33,* 277–286.

Bullough, V. L., & Bullough, B. (1993). *Cross dressing, sex and gender.* Philadelphia: University of Pennsylvania Press.

Burke, M. (1995). Lesbians and sexual child abuse. In L. A. Fontes (Ed.), *Sexual abuse in nine North American cultures: Treatment and prevention.* Thousand Oaks, CA: Sage.

Burn, S. M. (2000). Heterosexuals' use of "fag" and "queer" to deride one another: A contributor to heterosexism and stigma. *Journal of Homosexuality, 40,* 1–11.

Buss, D. M. (1994a). *The evolution of desire: Strategies of human mating.* New York: Basic Books.

Buss, D. M. (1994b). The strategies of human mating. *American Scientist, 82*(3), 238–249.

Buss, D. M. (1998). Sexual strategies theory: Historical origins and current status. *Journal of Sex Research, 35,* 19–31.

Buss, D. M. (1999). *Evolutionary psychology: The new science of the mind.* Boston: Allyn & Bacon.

Buss, D. M. (2000). *Dangerous passion: Why jealousy is as necessary as love and sex.* New York: Simon & Schuster.

Buss, D. M. (2003). Sexual strategies: A journey into controversy. *Psychological Inquiry, 14,* 219–226.

Buss, D. M., & Schmitt, D. P. (1993). Sexual strategies theory: An evolutionary perspective on human mating. *Psychological Review, 100*(2), 204–232.

Buss, D. M., Shackelford, T. D., Kirkpatrick, L. A., & Larsen, R. J. (2001). A half century of mate preferences: The cultural evolution of values. *Journal of Marriage and Family, 63,* 491–503.

Bussey, K., & Bandura, A. (1999). Social cognitive theory of gender development and differentiation. *Psychological Review, 106,* 676–713.

Butler, J. (1993). *Bodies that matter: On the discursive limits of sex.* New York: Routledge.

Butts, J. D. (1992). The relationship between sexual addiction and sexual dysfunction. *Journal of Health Care for the Poor and Underserved, 3*(1), 128–135.

Buzzell, T. (2005). Demographic characteristics of persons using pornography in three technological contexts. *Sexuality & Culture, 9,* 28–48.

Byard, R. W., & Botterill, P. M. B. (1998). Autoerotic asphyxial death—accident or suicide? *American Journal of Forensic Medicine and Pathology, 19,* 377–380.

Byers, E. S. (2005). Relationship satisfaction and sexual satisfaction: A longitudinal study of individuals in long-term relationships. *Journal of Sex Research, 42*(2), 113–118.

Byers, E. S., & Demmons, S. (1999). Sexual satisfaction and sexual disclosure within dating relationships. *Journal of Sex Research, 36,* 180–189.

Byers, E. S., & Eno, R. J. (1991). Predicting men's sexual coercion and aggression from attitudes, dating history, and sexual response. *Journal of Psychology and Human Sexuality, 4*(3), 55–70.

Byne, W., Tobet, S., Mattiace, L. A., Lasco, M. S., Kemether, E., Edgar, M. A., et al. (2001). The interstitial nuclei of the human anterior hypothalamus: An investigation of variation with sex, sexual orientation, and HIV status. *Hormones and Behavior, 409,* 86–92.

Cabello Santamaria, F. (1997). Female ejaculation: Myth and reality. In J. J. Baras-Vass & M. Perez-Concillo (Eds.), *Sexuality and human rights: Proceedings of the 13th World Congress of Sexology* (pp. 325–333). Valencia, Spain.

Cahoon, D., Edmonds, E. M., Spaulding, R. M., & Dickens, J. C. (1995). A comparison of the opinions of Black and White males and females concerning the occurrence of rape. *Journal of Social Behavior and Personality, 10*(1), 91–100.

Cain, V. S., Johannes, C. B., Avis, N. E., Mohr, B., Schocken, M., Skurnick, J., et al. (2003). Sexual functioning and practices in a multi-ethnic study of midlife women: Baseline results from SWAN. *Journal of Sex Research, 40*(3), 266–276.

Calam, R., Horne, L., Glasgow, D., & Cox, A. (1998). Psychological disturbance and child sexual abuse: A follow-up study. *Child Abuse and Neglect, 22,* 901–913.

Calderone, M. S. (1983). Childhood sexuality: Approaching the prevention of sexual disease. In G. Albee et al. (Eds.), *Promoting sexual responsibility and preventing sexual problems.* Hanover, NH: University Press of New England.

Calhoun, T., & Weaver, G. (1996). Rational decision-making among male street prostitutes. *Deviant Behavior: An Interdisciplinary Journal, 17,* 209–227.

California: Sex tourists can be prosecuted in U.S. (2006, January 26). *New York Times,* p. A19.

Camp, S. (2005). Quote cited by Nadeau, J. (2005). Teen sex is common worldwide. Available: http://www.agi-usa.org/media/nr/2005/11/08/index.html (Last visited 1/16/06).

Campos-Outcalt, D., & Hurwitz, S. (2002). Female-to-female transmission of syphilis: A case report. *Sexually Transmitted Diseases, 29,* 119–120.

Canavan, M. M., Myers, W. J., & Higgs, D. C. (1992). The female experience of sibling incest. *Journal of Marital and Family Therapy, 18,* 129–142.

Cann, A., Mangum, J. L., & Wells, M. (2001). Distress in response to relationship infidelity: The roles of gender and attitudes about relationships. *Journal of Sex Research, 38*(3), 185–190.

Cantor, J. M., Blanchard, R., Paterson A. D., & Bogaert, A. F. (2002). How many gay men owe their sexual orientation to fraternal birth order? *Archives of Sexual Behavior, 3,* 63–71.

Caplan, A. L. (1992). Twenty years after: The legacy of the Tuskegee syphilis study. When evil intrudes. *Hastings Center Report, 22*(6), 29–32.

Carael, M., Slaymaker, E., Lyerla, R., & Sarkar, S. (2006). Clients of sex workers in different regions of the world: Hard to count. *Sexually Transmitted Infections, 82*(Suppl 3), iii26-iii33.

Carelli, R. (1998, February 24). High Court turns down Megan's Law challenges. *San Francisco Chronicle,* p. A1.

Carey, B., & O'Connor, A. (2005, February 15). How to get those at risk to avoid risky sex? *New York Times,* p. D1.

Carlsen, E., Petersen, J., Anderson, A. M., & Skakkebaek, N. E. (2004). Effects of ejaculatory frequency and season on variations in semen quality. *Fertility and Sterility, 82*(2), 358–366.

Carlson, B. E., McNutt, L., & Choi, D. Y. (2003). Childhood and adult abuse among women in primary health care: Effects on mental health. *Journal of Interpersonal Violence, 18,* 924–941.

Carnes, P. (1983). *Out of shadows.* Minneapolis: CompCare.

Carnes, P. (1991). Progress in sex addiction: An addiction perspective. In R. T. Francoeur (Ed.), *Taking sides: Clashing views on controversial issues in human sexuality* (3rd ed.). Guilford, CT: Dushkin.

Carrier, J. (1992). Miguel: Sexual life history of a gay Mexican American. In G. Herdt (Ed.), *Gay culture in America: Essays from the field.* Boston: Beacon Press.

Carroll, J., Volk, K. D., & Hyde, J. J. (1985). Differences in males and females in motives for engaging in sexual intercourse. *Archives of Sexual Behavior, 14,* 131–139.

Carroll, J. S., Padilla-Walker, L. M., Nelson, L. J., Olson, C. D., Barry, C. M., & Madsen, S. D. (2008). Pornography acceptance and use among emerging adults. *Journal of Adolescent Research, 23,* 6–30.

Carroll, R. (1999). Outcomes of treatment for gender dysphoria. *Journal of Sex Education and Therapy, 24,* 128–136.

Caspi, A., Williams, B., Kim-Cohen, J., et al. (2007). Moderation of breast feeding effects on the IQ genetic variation in fatty acid metabolism. National Academy of Sciences. Available: http://www.pnas.org/cgi/content/full/0704292104/DC1 (Last visited 11/22/08).

Cassell, C. (1984). *Swept away.* New York: Simon & Schuster.

Cassell, C. (2008). *Put passion first: Why sexual chemistry is the key to finding and keeping lasting love.* New York: McGraw-Hill.

Cassidy, L., & Hurrell, R. M. (1995). The influence of victim's attire on adolescents' judgments of date rape. *Adolescence, 30*(118), 319–404.

Castleman, M. (2004). *Great sex: A man's guide to the secret principles of total-body sex.* New York, NY: Rodale Books.

Cate, R. M., & Lloyd, S. A. (1992). *Courtship.* Newbury Park, CA: Sage.

Cates, J. R., Herndon, N. L., Schulz, S. L., & Darroch, J. E. (2004). *Our voices, our lives, our futures: Youth and sexually transmitted diseases.* Chapel Hill: School of Journalism and Mass Communication, University of North Carolina at Chapel Hill.

Cates, W., Chesney, M. A., & Cohen, M. S. (1997). Primary HIV infection—a public health opportunity. *American Journal of Public Health, 87*(12), 1928–1930.

Caughey, A. B., Hopkins, L. M., & Norton, M. E. (2006). Chorionic villus sampling compared with amniocentesis and the difference in the rate of pregnancy loss. *Obstetrics & Gynecology, 108*(3, Part 1), 612–618.

Centers for Disease Control and Prevention. (1981). Pneumocystis pneumonia—Los Angeles. *Morbidity and Mortality Weekly Report, 30,* 250–252.

Centers for Disease Control and Prevention. (1992). 1993 revised classification system for HIV infection and expanded surveillance case definition for AIDS among adolescents and adults. *Morbidity and Mortality Weekly Report, 41,* 961–962.

Centers for Disease Control and Prevention. (1996a). Ten leading nationally notifiable diseases—United States, 1995. *Morbidity and Mortality Weekly Report, 45,* 883–884.

Centers for Disease Control and Prevention. (1996b). Surveillance report: U.S. AIDS cases reported through December 1995. *HIV/AIDS Surveillance Report, 7*(2), 1–10.

Centers for Disease Control and Prevention. (2000a). CDC statement on study result of products containing nonoxynol-9. *Morbidity and Mortality Weekly Report, 49,* 717–718.

Centers for Disease Control and Prevention. (2000b). Bacterial vaginosis (BV). Available: http://www.cdc.gov/nchstp/dstd/Fact_Sheets/FactsBV.htm (Last visited 12/12/01).

Centers for Disease Control and Prevention. (2001). Chlamydia disease information. Available: http://www.cdc.gov/nchstp/dstd/Fact_Sheets/Factschlamydiainfo.htm (Last visited 12/12/01).

Centers for Disease Control and Prevention. (2002a). Youth risk behavior surveillance—United States, 2001. *Morbidity and Mortality Weekly Report, 51,* 1–64.

Centers for Disease Control and Prevention. (2002b). *Sexually transmitted disease surveillance, 2001.* Atlanta: U.S. Department of Health and Human Services.

Centers for Disease Control and Prevention. (2003a). HIV prevention strategic plan through 2005. Available: http://www.cdc.gov/hiv/partners/psp.htm (Last visited 12/10/05).

Centers for Disease Control and Prevention. (2003b). Advancing HIV prevention: New strategies for a changing epidemic. *Morbidity and Mortality Weekly Report, 52,* 329–332.

Centers for Disease Control and Prevention. (2003c). HIV and its transmission. Available: http://www.cdc.gov/hiv/pubs/facts/transmission.htm (Last visited 12/4/05).

Centers for Disease Control and Prevention. (2003d). Can I get HIV from kissing? Available: http://www.cdc.gov/hiv/pubs/faq/faq17.htm (Last visited 12/4/05).

Centers for Disease Control and Prevention. (2003e). HIV/STD risks in young men who have sex with men who do not disclose their sexual orientation—Six U.S. cities. *Morbidity and Mortality Weekly Report, 52,* 81–85.

Centers for Disease Control and Prevention. (2004a). Trends in reportable sexually transmitted diseases in the United States, 2003—national data on chlamydia, gonorrhea and syphilis. Available: http://www.cdc.gov/std/status03/trends2003.htm (Last visited 10/15/08).

Centers for Disease Control and Prevention. (2004b). *Hypospadias trends in two U.S. surveillance systems.* Washington, DC: Office of Enterprise Communications.

Centers for Disease Control and Prevention. (2004c). Trends in primary and secondary syphilis and HIV infections in men who have sex with men—San Francisco and Los Angeles, California, 1998–2002. *Morbidity and Mortality Weekly Report, 53*(26), 575–578.

Centers for Disease Control and Prevention. (2004d). HIV transmission among Black women—North Carolina, 2004. *Morbidity and Mortality Report, 54,* 217–222.

Centers for Disease Control and Prevention. (2005a). Mean gestational age, by plurality. Available: http://www.cdc.gov/nchs/births.htm (Last visited 10/15/08).

Centers for Disease Control and Prevention. (2005b). *Sexually transmitted disease surveillance, 2004.* Atlanta: U.S. Department of Health and Human Services.

Centers for Disease Control and Prevention. (2005c). Chlamydia. Available: http://www.cdc.gov/std.healthcomm/fact_sheets (Last visited 11/1/05).

Centers for Disease Control and Prevention. (2005d). Gonorrhea. Available: http://www.cdc.gov/std.healthcomm/fact_sheets (Last visited 11/1/05).

Centers for Disease Control and Prevention. (2005e). Syphilis. Available: http://www.cdc.gov/std.healthcomm/fact_sheets (Last visited 11/1/05).

Centers for Disease Control and Prevention. (2005f). HIV prevalence, unrecognized infection, and HIV testing among men who have sex with men—five US cities, June 2004–April 2005. *Morbidity and Mortality Weekly Report, 54,* 597–601.

Centers for Disease Control and Prevention. (2006a). Recommendations to improve preconception health and health care—United

States: A report of the CDC/ATSDR Preconception Care Work Group and the Select Panel on Preconception CARE. *Morbidity and Mortality Weekly Report, 55*(RR-6), 1–23.

Centers for Disease Control and Prevention. (2006b). Methamphetamine use and HIV risk behaviors among heterosexual men—preliminary results from five California counties, December 2001–November 2003. *Morbidity and Mortality Weekly Report, 55*(10), 273–277.

Centers for Disease Control and Prevention. (2006c). Can I get HIV from oral sex? Available: http://www.cdc.gov/hiv/resources/qa/qa19.htm (Last visited 11/14/08).

Centers for Disease Control and Prevention. (2006d). Can I get HIV from kissing? Available: http://www.cdc.gov/hiv/resources/qa/qa17.htm (Last visited 11/14/08).

Centers for Disease Control and Prevention. (2006e). HIV/AIDS among women who have sex with women. Available: http://www.cdc.gov/hiv/topics/women/resources/factsheets.htm (Last visited 11/4/08).

Centers for Disease Control and Prevention. (2007a). Youth risk behavior surveillance—United States, 2007. Available: http://www.cdc.gov/HealthyYouth/yrbs/index.htm (Last visited 6/5/08).

Centers for Disease Control and Prevention. (2007b). Assisted reproductive technology success rates for ART cycles. Available: http://www.cdc.gov/ART/ART2005 (Last visited 11/22/08).

Centers for Disease Control and Prevention. (2007c). 2007 national diabetes fact sheet. Available: http://www.cdc.gov/diabetes/pubs/factsheet07.htm (Last visited 9/16/08).

Center for Disease Control and Prevention. (2007d). Use of mammograms among women aged ≥ 40 years—United States, 2000–2005. *Morbidity and Mortality Weekly Report, 56*(3), 49–51.

Centers for Disease Control and Prevention. (2007e). Sexually transmitted disease surveillance. Available: http://www.cdc.gov/std/stats/toc2006.htm (Last visited 10/15/08).

Centers for Disease Control and Prevention. (2007f). Male latex condoms and sexually transmitted diseases. Available: http://www.cdc.gov/condomeffectiveness/latex.htm (Last visited 10/12/08).

Centers for Disease Control and Prevention. (2007g). Sexually transmitted diseases treatment guidelines, 2006. Available: http://www.cdc.gov/std/treatment/2006/clinical.htm (Last visited 10/20/08).

Centers for Disease Control and Prevention. (2007h). Chlamydia Available: http://www.cdc.gov/std/chlamydia/STDFact-Chlamydia.htm (Last visited 10/13/08).

Centers for Disease Control and Prevention. (2007i). Trichomoniasis. Available: http://www.cdc.gov/std/trichomonas/STYDFact-Trichomoniasis.htm (Last visited 10/13/08).

Centers for Disease Control and Prevention. (2007j). Living with HIV/AIDS. Available: http://www.cdc.gov/hiv/resources/brochures/livingwithhim.htm (Last visited 11/14/08).

Centers for Disease Control and Prevention. (2007k). How can I tell if I'm infected with HIV? What are the symptoms? Available: http://www.cdc.gov/hiv/resources/qa/qa5.htm (Last visited 11/14/08).

Centers for Disease Control and Prevention. (2007l). HIV and its transmission. Available: http://www.gov/hiv/resources/factsheets/transmission.htm (Last visited 11/14/08).

Centers for Disease Control and Prevention. (2007/m). Mother-to-child (perinatal) HIV transmission and prevention. Available: http://www.cdc.gov/topics/perinatal/resources/factsheets/perinatal.htm (Last visited 11/4/08).

Centers for Disease Control and Prevention. (2007n). Deciding if and when to get tested. Available: http://www.cdc.gov/hiv/topics/testing/resources/qa/be_tested.htm (Last visited 11/14/08).

Centers for Disease Control and Prevention. (2007o). How HIV tests work. Available: http://www.cdc.gov/hiv/testing/resources/qa/tests_work.htm (Last visited 11/14/08).

Centers for Disease Control and Prevention. (2008a). Youth risk behavior surveillance—United States, 2007. *Morbidity and Mortality Weekly Report, 57* (SS-4).

Centers for Disease Control and Prevention. (2008b). 2005 assisted reproductive technology success rates: National summary and fertility clinic report. *Morbidity and Mortality Weekly Report, 57*(NSS-5), 1–23. Available: http://www.cdc.gov/ART/ (Last visited 10/25/08).

Centers for Disease Control and Prevention. (2008c). Male circumcision and risk for HIV transmission and other health consequences: Implications for the United States. Available: http://www.cdc.gov/hiv/resources/factsheets/circumcision.htm (Last visited 10/16/08).

Centers for Disease Control and Prevention. (2008d). Breast feeding in the United States: Findings from the National Health and Nutrition Examination Survey, 1999–2006. Available: http://www.cdc.gov/nchs/data/databriefs/db05.htm (Last visited 6/5/08).

Centers for Disease Control and Prevention. (2008e). Nonoxynol-9 spermicide contraception use. *Morbidity and Mortality Weekly Report, 51*, 389–392.

Centers for Disease Control and Prevention. (2008f). *HIV/AIDS Surveillance Report.* Available: http://www.cdc.gov/hiv/topics/surveillance/resources/reports/2006report/default.htm (Last visited 10/14/08).

Centers for Disease Control and Prevention. (2008g). 2006 Disease Profile. Available: http://www.cdc.gov/nchhstp/publications/index.htm (Last visited 10/10/08).

Centers for Disease Control and Prevention. (2008h). Nationally representative CDC study finds 1 in 4 teenage girls has a sexually transmitted disease. Available: http://www.cdc.gov/stdconference/2008/media/release-11march2008.htm (Last visited 10/21/08).

Centers for Disease Control and Prevention. (2008i). The role of STD detection and treatment in HIV prevention. Available: http://www.cdc.gov/std/hiv/STDFact-STD&HIV.htm (Last visited 10/13/08).

Centers for Disease Control and Prevention. (2008j). Gonorrhea. Available: http://www.cdc.gov/std/Gonorrhea/STDFact-gonorrhea.htm (Last visited 10/13/08).

Centers for Disease Control and Prevention. (2008k). Syphilis. Available: http://www.cdc.gov/std/syphilis/STDFact-Syphilis.htm (Last visited 10/13/08).

Centers for Disease Control and Prevention. (2008l). Genital HPV infection. Available: http://www.cdc.gov/std/HPV/STDFact-HPV.htm (Last visited 10/13/08).

Centers for Disease Control and Prevention. (2008m). Genital herpes. Available: http://www.cdc.gov/std/Herpes/STDFact-Herpes.htm (Last visited 10/13/08).

Centers for Disease Control and Prevention. (2008n). Hepatitis A. Available: http://www.cdc.gov/hepatitis/HepatitisA.htm (Last visited 10/22/08).

Centers for Disease Control and Prevention. (2008o). Hepatitis B. Available: http://www.cdc.gov/hepatitis/HepatitisB.htm (Last visited 10/22/08).

Centers for Disease Control and Prevention. (2008p). Hepatitis C. Available: http://www.cdc.gov/hepatitis/HepatitisC.htm (Last visited 10/22/08).

Centers for Disease Control and Prevention. (2008q). Bacterial vaginosis. Available: http://www.cdc.gov/std/by/STDFact-Bacterial-Vaginosis.htm (Last visited 10/13/08).

Centers for Disease Control and Prevention. (2008r). Candidiasis. Available: http://www.cdc.gov/nczved/dfbmd/disease_listing/candidiasis_gi.html (Last visited 10/23/08).

Centers for Disease Control and Prevention. (2008s). Pubic "crab" lice. Available: http://www.cdc.gov/lice/public/factsheet.html (Last visited 10/23/08).

Centers for Disease Control and Prevention. (2008t). Pelvic inflammatory disease. Available: http://www.cdc.gov/std/PID/STDFact-PID.htm (Last visited 10/13/08).

Centers for Disease Control and Prevention. (2008u). HIV prevalence estimates—United States, 2006. *Morbidity and Mortality Weekly Report, 57*(39), 1073–1076.

Centers for Disease Control and Prevention. (2008v). HIV/AIDS statistics and surveillance: Slide sets. Available: http://www.cdc.gov/hiv/topics/surveillance/resources/slides (Last visited 11/19/08).

Centers for Disease Control and Prevention. (2008w). Factsheet: HIV/AIDS among African Americans. Available: http://www.cdc.gov/hiv/topics/as/resources/factsheets/aa.htm (Last visited 12/16/08).

Centers for Disease Control and Prevention. (2008x). Hispanics/Latinos. Available: http://www.cdc.gov/hiv/hispanics/index.htm (Last visited 12/16/08).

Centers for Disease Control and Prevention. (2008y). HIV/AIDS among Asians and Pacific Islanders. Available: http://www.cdc.gov/hiv/resources/factsheets/API.htm (Last visited 11/14/08).

Centers for Disease Control and Prevention. (2008z). HIV/AIDS among American Indians and Alaska Natives. Available: http://www.cdc.gov/resources/factsheets/aian.htm (Last visited 11/4/08).

Centers for Disease Control and Prevention. (2008aa). HIV/AIDS among women. Available: http://www.cdc.gov/hiv/topics/women/resources/factsheets/women.htm (Last visited 12/18/08).

Centers for Disease Control and Prevention. (2008bb). HIV/AIDS surveillance report: cases of HIV infection and AIDS in the United States and dependent areas, 2006:Vol. 18. Available: http://www.cdc.gov/hiv/topics/surveillance/resources/reports/2006report/default.htm (Last visited 12/19/08).

Centers for Disease Control and Prevention. (2008cc). HIV/AIDS surveillance in adolescents and young adults (through 2006). Available: http://www.cdc.gov/hiv/topics/surveillance/resources/slides/adolescents/index.htm (Last visited 12/18/08).

Centers for Disease Control and Prevention. (2008dd). HIV/AIDS among youth. Available: http://www.cdc.gov/hiv/resources/factsheets/youth.htm (Last visited 11/4/08).

Centers for Disease Control and Prevention. (2008ee). HIV/AIDS among persons aged 50 and older. Available: http://www.cdc.gov/hiv/topics/over50/resources/factsheets/over50.htm (Last visited 11/4/08).

Centers for Disease Control and Prevention. (2008ff). Cases of HIV infection and AIDS in urban and rural areas of the United States, 2006. Available: http://www.cdc.gov/hiv/topics/surveillance/resources/reports/2008supp_vol13no2 (Last visited 12/18/08).

Centers for Disease Control and Prevention. (2008gg). HIV transmission rates in the United States: Dramatic declines indicate success in U.S. HIV prevention. Available: http://www.cdc.gov/hiv/topics/surveillance/resources/factsheets/transmission.htm (Last visited 12/8/08).

Centers for Disease Control and Prevention. (2008hh). Youth risk behavior surveillance—United States, 2007. Available: http://www.cdc.gov/HealthyYouth/yrbs/pdf/yrbss07.mmwr.pdf

Centers for Disease Control and Prevention. (2009a). Condoms and STDs: Fact sheet for public health personnel. Available: http://www.cdc.gov/condom effectiveness/latex.htm (Last visited 4/14/09).

Centers for Disease Control and Prevention. (2009b). Refocusing national attention on the HIV crisis in the United States. Available: http://www.cdc.gov/hiv/aaa/refocusing.htm (Last visited 4/7/09).

Central Intelligence Agency. (2008). The world factbook: Rank order—infant mortality rates. Available: https://www.cia.gov/library/publications/the-world-factbook/rankorder/2091 rank.html (Last visited 10/25/08).

Chambers, W. C. (2007). Oral sex: Varied behaviors and perceptions in a college population. *Journal of Sex Research, 44,* 28–42.

Chan, C. (1992). Cultural consideration in counseling Asian American lesbians and gay men. In S. Dworkin & F. Gutierrez (Eds.), *Counseling gay men and lesbians: Journey to the end of the rainbow.* Alexandria, VA: American Association for Counseling and Development.

Chelala, C. (2000, November 28). The unrelenting scourge of child prostitution. *San Francisco Chronicle,* p. A27.

Chesson, H. W., Blandford, J. M., Gift, T. L., Tao, G., & Irwin, K. L. (2004). The estimated direct medical cost of sexually transmitted diseases among American youth, 2000. *Perspectives on Sexual and Reproductive Health, 36*(1), 11–19.

Chia, M., & Abrams, R. C. (2005). *The multi-orgasmic woman: Sexual secrets every woman should know.* London: Rodale International.

Childless by choice. (2001, November). *American Demographics,* 44–50.

Child Trends Inc. (2007). Unpublished analysis of Early Childhood Longitudinal Birth Cohort data on pregnancy and intention and parental relationship outcomes. Washington, DC: Child Trends Inc.

Christenson, P., & Ivancin. M. (2006, October). The reality of health: Reality television and the public health. Available: http://kff.org/entmedia/upload/7567.pdf (Last visited 1/10/08).

Christopher, F. S., & Sprecher, S. (2000). Sexuality in marriage, dating, and other relationships: A decade review. *Journal of Marriage and Family, 62,* 999–1017.

Chromosomal anomalies. (2004). Available: http://www.humpath.com (Last visited 4/26/06).

Clark, J. (2003). Furor erupts over NIH "hit list." *British Medical Journal, 327,* 1065.

Cloud, J. (2008, January 28). Are gay relationships different? *Time,* pp. 78–80.

CNN.com/Law Center. (2003, March 5). Supreme Court upholds sex offender registration laws. Available: http://www.cnn.com/2003/law/03/05/scotus.sex.offenders.ap/index (Last visited 3/5/03).

Cochran, S. D., Mays, V. M., Bowen, D., Gage, S., Bybee, D., Roberts, S. J., et al. (2001). Cancer-related risk indicators and preventive screening behaviors among lesbians and bisexual women. *American Journal of Public Health, 91,* 591–597.

Cohan, D., Lutnick, A., Davidson, P., Cloniger, C., Herlyn, A., Breyer, J., et al. (2006). Sex worker health: San Francisco style. *Sexually Transmitted Infections, 82,* 418–422.

Cohen, A. B., & Tannenbaum, H. J. (2001). Lesbian and bisexual women's judgments of the attractiveness of different body types. *Journal of Sex Research, 38,* 226–232.

Cohen, E. (2007, February 15). Loving with all your . . . brain. Available: http://www.cnn.com/2007/HEALTH/02/14/love.science/index.html (Last visited 7/25/08).

Cohen-Kettenis, P. T. (2005). Gender change in 46, XY persons with 5a-reductase-2 deficiency and 17b-hydroxysteroid dehydrogenase-3 deficiency. *Archives of Sexual Behavior, 34,* 399–410.

Coleman, E. (1987). Sexual compulsivity: Definition, etiology, and treatment considerations. *Journal of Chemical Dependency Treatment, 1,* 189–204.

Coleman, E. (1991). Compulsive sexual behavior: New concepts and treatments. *Journal of Psychology and Human Sexuality, 4,* 37–52.

Coleman, E. (1996). *What sexual scientists know about compulsive sexual behavior.* Allentown, PA: Society for the Scientific Study of Sexuality.

Coleman, E., Colgan, P., & Gooren, L. (1992). Male cross-gender behavior in Myanmar (Burma): A description of the Acault. *Archives of Sexual Behavior, 21*(3), 313–321.

Coleman, E., Raymond, N., & McBean, A.. (2003). Assessment and treatment of compulsive sexual behavior. *Minnesota Medicine, 86*(7), 42–47.

Coleman, L. M. (2001). *Young people, "risk" and sexual behavior: A literature review.* Report prepared for the Health Development Agency and the Teenage Pregnancy Unit. Brighton, England: Trust for the Study of Adolescence.

Coleman, L. M., & Cater, S. M. (2005). A qualitative study of the relationship between alcohol consumption and risky sex in adolescents. *Archives of Sexual Behavior, 34,* 649–661.

Collier, M. J. (1991). Conflict competence within African, Mexican, and Anglo American friendships. In S. Ting-Toomey & F. Korzenny (Eds.), *Cross-cultural interpersonal communication.* Newbury Park, CA: Sage.

Collins, D. (2008, October 11). Connecticut court OKs gay marriage. *Indianapolis Star,* p. A3.

Condy, S., Templer, D. E., Brown, R., & Veaco, L. (1987). Parameters of sexual contact of boys with women. *Archives of Sexual Behavior, 16*(5), 379–394.

Connell, P., McKevitt, C., & Low, N. (2004). Investigating ethnic differences in sexual health: Focus groups with young people. *Sexually Transmitted Infections, 80,* 300–305.

Connell, R. W. (1995). *Masculinities.* Berkeley: University of California Press.

Contraception Report. (2001). Adolescent issues: Sexual behavior and contraception use. Available: http://www.contraceptiononline .org/contrareport/ (Last visited 12/30/02).

Contraceptive use. (2006, February 7). Centers for Disease Control and Prevention. Available: http://www.cdc.gov/nchs/fastats/ usecontr.htm (Last visited 6/3/06).

Cook, R. L., & Clark, D. B. (2005). Is there an association between alcohol consumption and sexually transmitted diseases? A systematic review. *Sexually Transmitted Diseases, 32,* 156–164.

Cooper, A. (1985). Sexual enhancement programs: An examination of their current status and directions for future research. *Archives of Sexual Behavior, 21*(4), 387–404.

Cooper, C. (2000, June/July). Abortion: Take back the right. *Ms.,* pp. 17–21.

Cooper, M. L. (2002, March). Alcohol use and risky sexual behavior among college students and youth: Evaluating the evidence. *Journal of Studies on Alcohol Supplement, 14,* 101–117.

Cortese, A. (1989). Subcultural differences in human sexuality: Race, ethnicity, and social class. In K. McKinney & S. Sprecher (Eds.), *Human sexuality: The societal and interpersonal context.* Norwood, NJ: Ablex.

Cosby, B. (1968, December). The regular way. *Playboy,* pp. 288–289.

Couch, M., Dowsett, G. W., Duterrtrc, S., Keys, D., & Pitts, M. (2006). Looking for more: A review of social and contextual factors affecting young people's sexual health. Melbourne, Australia: The Australian Research Centre in Sex, Health & Society, La Trobe University. Available: http://www.latrobe.edu.au/arcshs/assets/ downloads/reports/looking_for_more.pdf (Last visited 6/6/08).

Cowan, G. (2000). Beliefs about the causes of four types of rape. *Sex Roles, 42,* 807–823.

Crary P. (2009, May 11). 5 years on, gays enjoy security of marriage. *USA Today,* p. 2A.

Crawford, M., & Popp, D. (2003). Sexual double standards: A review and methodological critique of two decades of research. *Journal of Sex Research, 40*(1), 13–26.

Crepaz, N., Hart, T. A., & Marks, G. (2004). Highly active antiretroviral therapy and sexual risk behavior: A meta-analytic review. *Journal of the American Medical Association, 292,* 224–236.

Crooks, R., & Baur, K. (2005). *Our sexuality* (9th ed.). Belmont, CA: Thomson Wadsworth.

Crooks, R., & Baur, K. (2008). *Our sexuality* (10th ed). Belmont, CA: Thomson Wadsworth.

Crosby, R. A., & DiClemente, R. J. (2004). Use of recreational Viagra among men having sex with men. *Sexually Transmitted Infections, 80,* 466–468.

Crosby, R. A., DiClemente, R. J., & Salazar, L. F. (2006). *Research methods in health promotion.* San Francisco: Jossey-Bass.

Crosby, R. A., DiClemente, R. J., Wingood, G. M., Lang, D., & Harrington, K. F. (2003). The value of consistent condom use: A study of STD prevention among African American adolescent females. *American Journal of Public Health, 93,* 901–902.

Crosby, R. A., Sanders, S. A., Yarber, W. L., Graham, C. A., & Dodge, B. (2002). Condom use errors and problems among college men. *Sexually Transmitted Diseases, 29,* 552–557.

Crosby, R. A., & Yarber, W. L. (2001). Perceived versus actual knowledge about correct condom use among U.S. adolescents: Results from a national study. *Journal of Adolescent Health, 28,* 415–420.

Cross, S. E., & Madson, L. (1997). Models of the self: Self-construals and gender. *Psychological Bulletin, 122,* 5–37.

Cross, S. E., & Markus, H. R. (1993). Gender in thought, belief, and action: A cognitive approach. In A. E. Beall & R. J. Sternberg (Eds.), *The psychology of gender.* New York: Guilford Press.

Cummings, J. (1987, June 8). Disabled model defies sexual stereotypes. *New York Times,* p. 17.

Cupach, W. R., & Comstock, J. (1990). Satisfaction with sexual communication in marriage. *Journal of Social and Personal Relationships, 7,* 179–186.

Curtin, S. C., & Martin, J. A. (2000, August 8). Birth: Preliminary data for 1999. Washington, DC: *National Vital Statistics Reports.*

Cutler, W. (1999). Human sex-attractant pheromones: Discovery, research, development, and application in sex therapy. *Psychiatric Annals, 29,* 54–59.

Damon, W., & Rosser, B. R. S. (2005). Anodyspareunia in men who have sex with men. *Journal of Sex and Marital Therapy, 31,* 129–141.

Darling, C. A., & Davidson, J. K. (1986). Enhancing relationships: Understanding the feminine mystique of pretending orgasm. *Journal of Sex and Marital Therapy, 12,* 182–196.

Darling, C. A., Davidson, J. K., & Cox, R. P. (1991). Female sexual response and the timing of partner orgasm. *Journal of Sex and Marital Therapy, 17*(1), 11.

Darling, C. A., Davidson, J. K., & Jennings, D. A. (1991). The female sexual response revisited: Understanding the multiorgasmic experience in women. *Archives of Sexual Behavior, 20,* 527–540.

Daro, D. A. (1994). Prevention of child sexual abuse. *The Future of Children, 4,* 198–223.

Darroch, J. E., Landry, D. J., & Oslak, S. (1999). Age differences between sexual partners in the United States. *Family Planning Perspectives, 31*(4), 199–207.

Datta, S. D., et al. (2007). Gonorrhea and chlamydia in the United States among persons 14 to 39 years of age, 1999 to 2002. *Annals of Internal Medicine, 147,* 89–97.

Davidson, J. K., & Darling, C. A. (1986). The impact of college-level sex education on sexual knowledge, attitudes, and practices: The knowledge/sexual experimentation myth revisited. *Deviant Behavior, 7,* 13–30.

Davidson, J. K., Sr., & Darling, C. A. (1989). Self-perceived differences in the female orgasmic response. *Family Practice Research Journal, 8,* 75–84.

Davidson, J. O. (2002). The rights and wrongs of prostitution. *Hypatia, 17,* 84–98.

Davies, S., Katz, J., & Jackson, J. L. (1999). Sexual desire discrepancies: Effects on sexual and relationship satisfaction in heterosexual dating couples. *Archives of Sexual Behavior, 28,* 553–567.

Davila, V. (2008, June 24). For today's seniors, it's never to late for sex education. *San Jose Mercury.*

Davis, A. R., & Castano, P. M. (2004). Oral contraceptives and libido in women. *Annual Review of Sex Research, 25,* 297–320.

Davis, K. E., & Todd, M. J. (1985). Assessing friendship: Prototypes, paradigm cases and relationship description. In S. Duck & D. Perlman (Eds.), *Understanding personal relationships: An interdisciplinary approach.* Newbury Park, CA: Sage.

Day, A., Thurlow, K., & Wolliscroft, J. (2003). Working with childhood sexual abuse: A survey of mental health professionals: *Child Abuse and Neglect, 27,* 191–198.

De Judicibus, M. A., & McCabe, M. P. (2002). Psychological factors and the sexuality of pregnant and postpartum women. *Journal of Sex Research, 39*(2), 94–103.

DeLamater, J., & Friedrich, W. (2002). Human sexual development. *Journal of Sex Research, 38,* 10–14.

DeLamater, J. D., & Sill, M. (2005). Sexual desire in later life. *Journal of Sex Research, 42*(2), 138–149.

Del Carmen, R. (1990). Assessment of Asian-Americans for family therapy. In F. Serafica, A. Schwebel, R. Russell, P. Isaac, & L. Myers (Eds.), *Mental health of ethnic minorities.* New York: Praeger.

Demian, A. S. B. (1994). Relationship characteristics of American gay and lesbian couples: Findings from a national survey. *Journal of Gay and Lesbian Social Services, 1*(2), 101–117.

Denny, D. (1997). Transgender: Some historical, cross-cultural, and contemporary models and methods of coping and treatment. In B. Bullough, V. L. Bullough, & J. Elias (Eds.), *Gender blending.* New York: Prometheus Books.

DeNoon, D. J. (2007, November 27). Higher death risk in men with lower testosterone levels. *WebMD.* Available: http://men.webmd.cm/news/20071127/low-testosterone-early-death (Last visited 1/7/08).

DeNoon, D. J. (2008, October 15). Infant mortality: U.S. ranks 29th. Available: http://www.webmd.com/news/20081015/infant-mortality-us-ranks-29th (Last visited 10/25/08).

Denov, M. S. (2003). The myth of innocence: Sexual scripts and the recognition of child sexual abuse by female perpetrators. *Journal of Sex Research, 40,* 303–314.

Des Jarlais, D. C., Paone, D., Milliken, J., Turner, C. F., Miller, H., Gribble, J., et al. (1999). Audio-computer interviewing to measure risk behavior for HIV among injecting drug users: A quasi-randomized trial. *The Lancet, 353,* 1657–1661.

Diamond, L. (2009). Sexual fluidity: Understanding women's love and desire. Cambridge, MA: Harvard University Press.

Diamond, L. (1998). Development of sexual orientation among adolescent and young adult women. *Developmental Psychology, 34,* 1085–1095.

Diamond, L., Savin-Williams, R. C., & Dube, E. M. (1999). Sex, dating, passionate friendships, and romance: Intimate peer relations among lesbian, gay and bisexual adolescents. In W. Furman, B. B. Brown, & C. Feiring (Eds.), *The development of romantic relationships during adolescence.* New York: Cambridge University Press.

Diamond, L. M. (2005). A new view of lesbian subtypes: Stable verses fluid identity trajectories over an 8-year period. *Psychology of Women Quarterly, 29*(2), 119–128.

Diamond, L. M. (2008). Female bisexuality from adolescence to adulthood: Results from a 10-year longitudinal study. *Developmental Psychology, 44*(1), 5–14.

Diamond, M. (1996). Prenatal predisposition and the clinical management of some pediatric conditions. *Journal of Sex and Marital Therapy, 22*(3), 139–147.

Diamond, M. (2004). Pediatric management of ambiguous and traumatized genitalia. *Contemporary Sexuality, 38*(9), 1–7.

Diamond, M., & Sigmundson, H. K. (1997a). Management of intersexuality: Guidelines for dealing with individuals with ambiguous genitalia. *Archives of Pediatrics and Adolescent Medicine, 151,* 1046–1050.

Diamond, M., & Sigmundson, H. K. (1997b). Sex reassignment at birth: Long-term review and clinical implications. *Archives of Pediatric and Adolescent Medicine, 151,* 298.

Diaz, R. M. (1998). *Latino gay men and HIV: Culture, sexuality and risk behavior.* New York: Routledge.

Dickson, N., van Roode, T., & Paul, C. (2005). Herpes simplex virus type 2 status at age 26 is not related to early circumcision in a birth cohort. *Sexually Transmitted Diseases, 32*(8), 517–519.

Dickson, N. P., van Roode, T., Herbison, P., & Paul, C. (2008). Circumcision and risk of sexually transmitted infections in a birth cohort. *Journal of Pediatrics, 152,* 383–387.

Dick-Read, G. (1972). *Childbirth without fear* (4th ed.). New York: Harper & Row.

DiGioacchino, R. F., Sargent, R. G., & Topping, M. (2001). Body dissatisfaction among White and African American male and female college students. *Eating Disorders, 2*(1), 39–50.

di Mauro, D. (1995). Executive summary. Sexuality research in the United States: An assessment of the social and behavioral sciences. Social Science Research Council. Available: http://www.kinseyinstitute.org/resources/sexrealn.html (Last visited 8/1/06).

Dinh, T., Sternberg, M., Dunne, E. F., & Markowitz, L. E. (2008). Genital warts among 18- to 59-year-olds in the United States, National Health and Nutrition Examination Study, 1999–2004. *Sexually Transmitted Diseases, 35,* 357–360.

Dittman, M. (2004). Getting prostitutes off the street. *Monitor on Psychology, 35*(9), 71.

Division of STD Prevention. (2000). *Sexually transmitted disease surveillance, 1999.* Department of Health and Human Services. Atlanta, GA: Centers for Disease Control and Prevention.

Djerassi, C. (1981). *The politics of contraception.* New York: Freeman.

Docter, R. F., & Prince, V. (1997). Transvestism: A survey of 1032 cross-dressers. *Archives of Sexual Behavior, 26,* 589–606.

Dodge, B., Reece, M., Cole, S. L., & Sandfort, T. G. M. (2004). Sexual compulsivity among heterosexual college students. *Journal of Sex Research, 41*(4), 343–350.

Doheny, K. (2006, May 8). No interest in sex? It could be the drugs. *Los Angeles Times,* p. P8.

Donohue, J., & Gebhard, P. (1995). The Kinsey Institute/Indiana University report of sexuality and spinal cord injury. *Sexuality and Disability, 13*(1), 7–85.

Dorey, G., Speakman, M. J., Feneley, R. C. L., Swinkels, A., & Dunn, C. D. R. (2005). Pelvic floor exercises for erectile dysfunction. *British Journal of Urology, 96,* 595–597.

Downs, M. F. (2007, April 30). Psychologists debate whether people can have an addiction to pornography. *WebMD.* Available: http://www.webmd.com/guide/is-pornography-addictive (Last visited 1/7/08).

Dryfoos, J. (1985). What the United States can learn about prevention of teenage pregnancy from other developed countries. *SIECUS Report, 14*(2), 1–7.

Dube, S. A., et al. (2005). Long-term consequences of childhood sexual abuse by gender of victim. *American Journal of Preventive Medicine, 28,* 430–438.

Ducharme, S. H., & Gill, K. M. (1997). *Sexuality after spinal cord injury: Answers to your questions.* Baltimore: Brookes.

Dunn, M. E., & Trost, J. E. (1989). Male multiple orgasms: A descriptive study. *Archives of Sexual Behavior, 18,* 377–387.

Dunne, E. F., et al. (2007). Prevalence of HPV infection among females in the United States. *Journal of the American Medical Association, 297,* 813–819.

Dunne, M. P. (2002). Sampling considerations. In M. W. Wiederman & B. E. Whitley (Eds.), *Handbook for conducting research on human sexuality.* Mahwah, NJ: Erlbaum.

Durkin, K. (1997). Misuse of the Internet by pedophiles: Implications for law enforcement and probation practice. *Federal Probation, 61,* 14–18.

Dworkin, S. L., & O'Sullivan, L. (2005). Actual versus desired initiation patterns among a sample of college men: Tapping disjunctures within traditional male sexual scripts. *Journal of Sex Research, 42,* 150–158.

Dzokoto, V. A., & Adams, G. (2005). Understanding genital shrinking epidemics in West Africa: Koro, juju, or mass psychogenic illness? *Culture, Medicine, and Psychiatry, 29*(1), 53–78.

Eagly, A. (1987). *Sex differences in social behavior: A social role interpretation.* Hillsdale, NJ: Erlbaum.

Early Breast Cancer Trialists' Collaborative Group. (2005). Effects of chemotherapy and hormonal therapy for early breast cancer on recurrence and 15-year survival: An overview of the randomised trials. *The Lancet, 365,* 1687–1717.

Ecstasy effects. (1996, May 31). Available: http://www.columbia.edu/cu/healthwise/0925.html (Last visited 1/29/98).

Ecstasy: Happiness is . . . a pill? (2000, June 5). *Time,* pp. 64–68.

Edozien, F. (2003, July 8). Fighting AIDS face to face. *The Advocate,* 46–49.

Edwards, J. M., Iritani, B. J., & Hallfors, D. D. (2006). Prevalence and correlates of exchanging sex for drugs or money among adolescents in the United States. *Sexually Transmitted Infections, 82,* 354–358.

Ehrenreich, N., & Barr, M. (2005). Intersex surgery, female genital cutting, and the selective condemnation of cultural practices. *Harvard Civil Rights–Civil Liberties Law Review, 40*(1), 71–140.

Eitzen, D., & Zinn, M. (1994). *Social problems* (6th ed.). Boston: Allyn & Bacon.

Eke, N., & Nkanginieme, K. (2006). Female genital mutilation and obstetric outcome. *The Lancet, 367,* 1799–1800.

Elias, M. (2003, January 15). Women's sex problems may be overstated. *USA Today,* p. A1.

Elias, M. (2004, November 11). Kinsey, as timely as ever. *USA Today,* p. 8D.

Ellen, J. M., et al. (2006). Sex partner selection, social networks, and repeat sexually transmitted infections in young men: A preliminary report. *Sexually Transmitted Diseases, 33,* 18–21.

Ellingson, L. A., & Yarber, W. L. (1997). Breast self-examination, the health belief model, and sexual orientation in women. *Journal of Sex Education and Therapy, 22,* 19–24.

Elliott, L., & Brantley, C. (1997). *Sex on campus: The naked truth about the real sex lives of college students.* New York: Random House.

Ellis, C. D. (2002). Male rape—the silent victims. *Collegian, 9,* 34–39.

Ellis, H. (1900). *Studies in the psychology of sex.* Philadelphia: Davis.

Ellis, L. (1996). Theories of homosexuality. In R. C. Savin-Williams & K. M. Cohen (Eds.), *The lives of lesbians, gays and bisexuals.* Fort Worth, TX: Harcourt Brace.

Ellis, L., Robb, B., & Burke, D. (2005). Sexual orientation in the United States and Canadian college students. *Archives of Sexual Behavior, 34*(5), 569–581.

Ellis, M. (2002, June 10). Women leery as date-rape drug use soars. *Indianapolis Star,* pp. A1, A6.

Ellison, C. (1985). Intimacy-based sex therapy. In W. Eicher & G. Kockott (Eds.), *Sexology.* New York: Springer-Verlag.

Ellison, C. (2000). *Women's sexualities.* Oakland, CA: New Harbinger.

Ellison, C. R. (2000). *Women's sexualities: Generations of women share intimate secrets of sexual self-acceptance.* Oakland, CA: New Harbinger.

Emergency contraception (morning after pill). (2008). Planned Parenthood Federation of America. Available: http://www.plannedparenthood.org/health-topics/emergency-contraception-morning-after-pill.html (Last visited 8/6/08).

Eng, T. R., & Butler, W. T. (Eds.). (1997). *The hidden epidemic: Confronting sexually transmitted diseases.* Washington, DC: National Academy Press.

Epstein, A. (1997, June 10). Justices will rule on issue of same-sex harassment. *The Oregonian,* p. A1.

Especially for fathers. (n.d.). American College of Obstetricians and Gynecologists. Education Pamphlet AP032.

Espín, O. M. (1984). Cultural and historical influences on sexuality in Hispanic/Latin women: Implications for psychotherapy. In C. Vance (Ed.), *Pleasure and danger: Exploring female sexuality.* New York: Routledge & Kegan Paul.

Estcourt, C. S., Marks, C., Rohrsheim, R., Johnson, A. M., Donovan, B., & Mindel, A. (2000). HIV, sexually transmitted infections, and risk behaviors in male commercial sex workers in Sydney. *Sexually Transmitted Infections, 76,* 294–298.

Evans, T., & Gillers, H. (2009, April 4). Iowa nixes ban on gay marriage. *Indianapolis Star,* pp. A1, A11.

Fackeimann, K. (2007, December 13). Study: Young adults now find porn more acceptable. *USA Today,* p. 3D.

Fagan, P. J., Wise, T. N., Schmidt, C. W., & Berlin, F. S. (2002). Pedophilia. *Journal of the American Medical Association, 288,* 2458–2465.

Fagin, D. (1995, February 1). DES moms, gay or bisexual daughters: Study links exposure to sexual orientation. *San Francisco Chronicle.*

Fahey, T., Insel, P., & Roth, W. (2000). *Fit and well: Core concepts in labs in physical fitness and wellness.* Mountain View, CA: Mayfield.

Faludi, S. (1991). *Backlash: The undeclared war against American women.* New York: Crown.

Fang, B. (2005, October 24). Why more kids are getting into the sex trade—and how the feds are fighting back. *U.S. News and World Report,* pp. 30–34.

Farley, M., Cotton, A., Lynne, J., et al. (2003). Prostitution and trafficking in nine countries: An update on violence and post-traumatic stress disorder. In M. Farley (Ed.), *Prostitution, trafficking and traumatic stress* (pp. 33–74). Binghamton, NY: Haworth Press.

Farnsworth, C. H. (1992, January 14). Homosexual is granted refugee status in Canada. *New York Times,* p. A5.

Fausto-Sterling, A. (2000). *Sexing the body: Gender politics and the construction of sexuality.* New York: Basic Books.

FDA News. (2005, November 10). FDA updates labeling for Ortho Evra contraceptive patch. Available: http://www.fda.gov/cder/drug/infopage/orthoevra/default.htm (Last visited 1/2/06).

Feinberg, L. (1996) *Transgender warriors: Making history from Joan of Arc to Rupaul.* Boston: Beacon Press.

Feldman, H., Goldstein, I., Hatzichristou, D., Krane, R., & McKinlay, J. (1994). Impotence and its medical and psychosocial correlates: Results of the Massachusetts Male Aging Study. *Journal of Urology, 151,* 54–61.

Fenigstein, A., & Preston, M. (2007). The desired number of sexual partners as a function of gender, sexual risks, and the meaning of "ideal." *Journal of Sex Research, 44,* 879–895.

Fennell, E. (2003). Turner syndrome. In T. H. Ollendick & C. S. Schroeder (Eds.), *Encyclopedia of clinical child and pediatric psychology* (pp. 687–689). New York: Kluwer Academic/Plenum.

Feray, J. C., & Herzer, M. (1990). Homosexual studies and politics in the 19th century: Karl Maria Kertbeny. *Journal of Homosexuality, 19*(1), 23–47.

Fergusson, D. M., Swain-Campbell, N. R., & Horwood, L. J. (2002). Does sexual violence contribute to elevated rates of anxiety and depression in females? *Psychological Medicine, 32,* 991–996.

Ferrer, F., & McKenna, P. (2000). Current approaches to the undescended testicle. *Contemporary Pediatrics, 17,* 106–112.

Fertility awareness. (2005). Planned Parenthood Federation of America. Available: http://www.plannedparenthood.org/health-topics/birth-control/fertility-awareness-4217.html (Last visited 8/6/08).

Fetters, K., Marks, C., Mindel, A., & Estcourt, C. S. (2000). Sexually transmitted infections and risk behaviors in women who have sex with women. *Sexually Transmitted Infections, 76,* 345–349.

Finer, L. (2006, May 4). Poorest U.S. women increasingly likely to face unintended pregnancies. *Perspectives on Sexual and Reproductive Health, 38*(3).

Finer, L. B. (2007). Trends in premarital sex in the United States, 1954–2003. *Public Health Reports, 122,* 73–78.

Finer, L. B., Darroch, J. E., & Singh, S. (1999). Sexual partnership patterns as a behavioral risk factor for sexually transmitted diseases. *Family Planning Perspectives, 31,* 228–236.

Finer, L. B., et al. (2006) Disparities in unintended pregnancies in the United States, 1994 and 2001. *Perspectives on Sexual and Reproductive Health, 38*(2), 90–96.

Finer, L. B., & Henshaw, S. K. (2003). Abortion incidences and services in the United States in 2000. *Perspectives on Sexual and Reproductive Health, 35*(1), 6–15.

Finkelhor, D. (1986). Prevention approaches to child sexual abuse. In M. Lystad (Ed.), *Violence in the home: Interdisciplinary perspectives.* New York: Brunner/Mazel.

Finkelhor, D. (1990). Early and long-term effects of child sexual abuse: An update. *Professional Psychology: Research and Practice, 21,* 325–330.

Finkelhor, D. (1994). Current information on the scope and nature of child sexual abuse. *The Future of Children, 4,* 31–53.

Finkelhor, D., & Baron, L. (1986). High-risk children. In D. Finkelhor (Ed.), *Sourcebook on child sexual abuse.* Beverly Hills, CA: Sage.

Finz, S. (2000, June 12). Emerging from a secret. *San Francisco Chronicle,* p. A1.

Firestone, R. W., Firestone, L. A., & Catlett, J. (2006). *Sex and love in intimate relationships.* Washington, DC: American Psychological Association.

Fisch, H., Hyun, G., Golden, R., Hensle, T. W., Olsson, C. A., & Liberson, G. L. (2003). The influence of paternal age on Down's syndrome. *Journal of Urology, 169,* 2275–2278.

Fischer, A. R., & Good, G. E. (1994). Gender, self, and others: Perceptions of the campus environment. *Journal of Counseling Psychology, 41*(3), 343–355.

Fisher, B., Cullen, F., & Turner, M. (2000). *The sexual victimization of college women.* Washington, DC: U.S. Department of Justice.

Fisher, D., & Howells, K. (1993). Social relationships in sexual offenders. *Sexual and Marital Therapy, 8,* 123–136.

Fisher, H. (2004). *Why we love: The nature and chemistry of romantic love.* New York: Henry Holt.

Fisher, W. (1986). A psychological approach to human sexuality. In D. Byrne & K. K. Kelley (Eds.), *Alternative approaches to human sexuality.* Hillsdale, NJ: Erlbaum.

Fisher, W. (1998). The Sexual Opinion Survey. In C. M. Davis, W. L. Yarber, R. Bauserman, G. Schreer, & S. L. Davis (Eds.), *Handbook of sexuality-related measures.* Thousand Oaks, CA: Sage.

Fisher, W. A., & Barak, A. (2001). Internet pornography: A social psychological perspective on Internet sexuality. *Journal of Sex Research, 38,* 312–323.

Fisher, W. A., & Davis, C. M. (2007). *What sexual scientists know about pornography.* Allentown, PA: Society for the Scientific Study of Sexuality.

Flaks, D. K., Ficher, I., Masterpasqua, F., & Joseph, G. (1995). Lesbians choosing motherhood: A comparative study of lesbians and heterosexual parents and their children. *Developmental Psychology, 31*(1), 105–114.

Fleming, D. T., & Wasserheit, J. N. (1999). From epidemiological synergy to public health policy and practice: The contribution of other sexually transmitted diseases to sexual transmission of HIV infection. *Sexually Transmitted Diseases, 75,* 3–17.

Fleming, M., & Pace, J. (2001). Sexuality and chronic pain. *Journal of Sex Education and Therapy, 26,* 204–214.

Foa, U. G., Anderson, B., Converse, J., & Urbansky, W. A. (1987). Gender-related sexual attitudes: Some cross-cultural similarities and differences. *Sex Roles, 16*(19–20), 511–519.

Foley, L. A., Evancic, C., Karnik, K., & King, J. (1995). Date rape: Effects of race of assailant and victim and gender of subjects on perceptions. *Journal of Black Psychology, 21*(1), 6–18.

Food and Drug Administration. (2003, Fall). Toxic shock syndrome is so rare you may have forgotten about it. *FDA & You: News for Health Educators and Students, 1.*

Forbes, G. G. (2001). College students with tattoos and piercing: Motives, family experiences, personality factors, and perception by others. *Psychological Reports, 89,* 774–786.

Ford, C., & Beach, F. (1951). *Patterns of sexual behavior.* New York: Harper & Row.

Fortenberry, J. D., Cecil, H., Zimet, G. D., & Orr, D. P. (1997). Concordance between self-report questionnaires and coital diaries for sexual behaviors of adolescent women with sexually transmitted infections. In J. Bancroft (Ed.), *Researching sexual behavior.* Bloomington: Indiana University Press.

Fortenberry, J. D., McFarlane, M., Bleakley, A., Bull, S., Fishbein, M., Grimley, D., et al. (2002). Relationship of stigma and shame to gonorrhea and HIV screening. *American Journal of Public Health, 92,* 378–381.

Forum on Child and Family Statistics. (2008). America's children in brief: Key national indicators of well-being, 2008. Washington, DC: U.S. Government Printing Office. Available: http://www.childstats.gov/pdf/ac2008/ac_08.pdf (Last visited 9/24/08).

Foster-Rosales, A., & Stewart, F. H. (2002). Contraceptive technology. In G. M. Wingood & R. J. DiClemente (Eds.), *Handbook of women's sexual and reproductive health*. New York: Kluwer Academic/Plenum.

Foucault, M. (1978). *The history of sexuality: Vol. 1.* New York: Pantheon.

Fowers, B. J., & Olson, D. H. (1989). ENRICH marital inventory: A discriminant validity and cross-validation assessment. *Journal of Marital and Family Therapy, 15,* 65–79.

Foxman, B., Aral, S. O., & Holmes, K. K. (1998). Interrelationships among douching practices, risky sexual practices, and history of self-reported sexually transmitted diseases in an urban population. *Sexually Transmitted Diseases, 25,* 90–99.

Foxman, B., Sevgi, A., & Holmes, K. (2006). Common use in the general population of sexual enhancement aids and drugs to enhance sexual experience. *Sexually Transmitted Diseases, 33,* 156–162.

Fram, A. (2007, November 2). Birth control and public schools. *Monterey Country Herald,* p. A 2.

Frayser, S. G. (2002). Discovering the value of cross-cultural research on human sexuality. In M. W. Wiederman & B. E. Whitley (Eds.), *Handbook for conducting research on human sexuality*. Mahwah, NJ: Erlbaum.

Frazier, P. A. (1991). Self-blame as a mediator of postrape depressive symptoms. *Journal of Social and Clinical Psychology, 10*(1), 47–57.

Frazier, P. A., Cochran, C. C., & Olson, A. M. (1995). Social science research on lay definitions of sexual harassment. *Journal of Social Issues, 51*(1), 21–37.

Frederick, D. A., & Haselton, M. G. (2007). Why is masculinity sexy? Tests of the fitness indicator hypothesis. *Personality and Social Psychology Bulletin, 33,* 1167–1183.

Frederick, D. A., Peplau, A., & Lever, J. (2008). The Barbie mystique: Satisfaction with breast size and shape across the lifespan. *International Journal of Sexual Health, 20,* 200–210.

Freud, S. (1938). Three contributions to the theory of sex. In A. A. Brill (Ed.), *The basic writings of Sigmund Freud*. New York: Modern Library.

Freyd, J. J., et al. (2005). The science of child sexual abuse. *Science, 308,* 501.

Frost, J. J., & Darroch, J. E. (2008). Factors associated with contraceptive choice and inconsistent method use, United States, 2004. *Perspectives on Sexual and Reproductive Health, 40*(2), 94–104.

Fugh-Berman, A. (2004, September/October). Harmless hormones? Bah, humbug! *National Women's Health Network,* p. 11.

Gagnon, J. H. (1975). Sex research and social change. *Archives of Sexual Behavior, 4,* 112–141.

Gagnon, J. H., & Simon, W. (1973). *Sexual conduct: The origins of human sexuality*. Chicago: Aldine.

Gallup Poll. (2006). Homosexual relations. Available: http://www.poll.gallup.com/content/default.aspex?ci+1651&VERSION (Last visited 3/27/06).

Gallup Poll. (2007). Public favors expansion of hate crime law to include sexual orientation. Available: http://www.gallup.com/poll/27613/Public-Favors-Expansion-Hate-Crime-Law-Include-Sexual-Orientation (Lasted visited 5/21/08).

Gallup Poll. (2008). Americans divided on morality of homosexuality. Available: http://www.gallup.com/poll/108115/Americans-Evenly-Divided-Morality-Homosexuality (Last visited 7/29/08).

Garcia, L., & Milano, L. (1991). A content analysis of erotic video. *Journal of Psychology and Human Sexuality, 3,* 95–103.

Garza-Mercer, F. D. (2006). The evolution of sexual pleasure. In M. Kauth (Ed.), *Handbook of the evolution of human sexuality*. New York: Hawthorn.

Gay, P. (1986). *The bourgeois experience: The tender passion*. New York: Oxford University Press.

Geary, D. C., Vigil, J., & Byrd-Craven, J. (2004). Evolution of human mate choice. *Journal of Sex Research, 41,* 27–42.

Gelles, R. J., & Conte, J. R. (1991). Domestic violence and sexual abuse of children: A review of research in the eighties. In A. Booth (Ed.), *Contemporary families: Looking forward, looking back*. Minneapolis, MN: National Council on Family Relations.

Gender Education and Advocacy. (2001). Gender Variance Model. Available: http://www.gender.org (Last visited 12/21/05).

Gerbner, G., Gross, L., Morgan, M., Signorielli, N., & Shanahan, J. (2002). Growing up with television: Cultivation processes. In J. Bryant & D. Zillman (Eds.), *Media effects: Advances in theory and research* (2nd ed.). Hillsdale, NJ: Erlbaum.

Gergen, K. J. (1985). The social constructionist movement in modern psychology. *American Psychologist, 40,* 266–275.

Gerressu, M., Mercer, C. H., Graham, C. A., Wellings, K., & Johnson, A. M. (2008). Prevalence of masturbation and associated factors in a British national probability survey. *Archives of Sexual Behavior, 37,* 266–278.

Gibbs; W. (2008, June 12). Norway: New rights granted to gays. *New York Times,* p. A12.

Gidyez, C. A., & Koss, M. P. (1990). A comparison of group and individual sexual assault victims. *Psychology of Women Quarterly, 14*(3), 325–342.

Gijs, L. (2007, September). *Gender identity disorders: Sexuality and gender identity*. Paper presented at the XX biennial symposium of the World Professional Association of Transgender Health, Chicago.

Gijs, L., & Brewaeys, A. (2007). Surgical treatment of gender dysphoria in adults and adolescents: Recent developments, effectiveness, and challenges. *Annual Review of Sex Research, 25,* 178–224.

Giles, L. C., Glonek, G. F. V., Luszca, M. A., & Andrew, G. R. (2005). Effect of social networks on 10-year survival in very old Australians: The Australian Longitudinal Study of Aging. *Journal of Epidemiology and Community Health, 59,* 574–579.

Gillen, K., & Muncher, S. J. (1995). Sex differences in the perceived casual structure of date rape: A preliminary report. *Aggressive Behavior, 21*(2), 101–112.

Gilliland, F. D., Berhane, K., McConnell, R., Gauderman, W. L., Vora, H., Rap, E. B., et al. (2000). Maternal smoking during pregnancy, environmental tobacco smoke exposure and childhood lung function. *Thorax, 55,* 271–276.

Gilmore, M. R., Gaylord, J., Hatway, J., Hoppe, M. J., Morrison, D. M., Leigh, B. C., et al. (2001). Daily data collection of sexual and other health-related behaviors. *Journal of Sex Research, 38,* 35–42.

Glazer, H. I., & Gae, R. (2002). The vulvodynia survival guide: How to overcome painful vaginal symptoms and enjoy an active lifestyle. Oakland, CA: New Harbinger.

Global study of sexual attitudes and behaviors funded by Pfizer Inc. (2002). Available: http://www.pfizerglobalstudy.com (Last visited 2/7/06).

Glock, A. (2005, February 6). She likes to watch. *New York Times,* p. 26.

Glosser, A., Gardiner, K., & Fishman, M. (2004). Statutory rape: A guide to state laws and reporting requirements. Available: http://

www.lewin.com/Lewin_Publications/Human_Services/ StateLawsReport.htm (Last visited 3/26/06).

Goldstein, I., & Working Group for the Study of Central Mechanisms in Erectile Dysfunction. (2000, August). Male sexual circuitry. *Scientific American*, pp. 70–75.

Gonzales, V., Washienko, K. M., Krone, M. R., Chapman, L. I., Arredondo, E. M., Huckeba, J. J., et al. (1999). Sexual and drug-use risk factors for HIV and STDs: A comparison of women with and without bisexual experiences. *International Journal of STD and AIDS, 10,* 32–37.

Goodman, A. (1993). Diagnosis and treatment of sexual addiction. *Journal of Sex and Marital Therapy, 19,* 225–251.

Goodnough, A. (2009, April 8). Rejecting veto, Vermont backs gay marriage. *New York Times,* pp. A1, A8.

Gosink, P. D., & Jumbelic, M. I. (2000). Autoerotic asphyxiation in a female. *American Journal of Forensic Medicine and Pathology, 21,* 114–118.

Gottman, J., & Carrere, S. (2000, October). Welcome to the love lab. *Psychology Today,* pp. 42–47.

Gottman, J. M., & Levenson, R. W. (1992). Marital processes predictive of later dissolution: Behavior, physiology and health. *Journal of Personality and Social Psychology, 63,* 221–233.

Gottman, J. M., Levenson, R. W., Gross, J., Frederickson, B. L., McCoy, K., Rosenthal, L., et al. (2003). Correlates of gay and lesbian couples' relationship satisfaction and relationship dissolution. *Journal of Homosexuality, 45,* 23–43.

Goyer, P. F., & Eddleman, H. C. (1984). Same-sex rape of nonincarcerated men. *American Journal of Psychiatry, 141,* 576–579.

Grady, D. (2005, May 13). Therapies cut death risk, breast-cancer study finds. *New York Times,* p. A10.

Graham, C. A., & Bancroft, J. (1997). A comparison of retrospective interview assessment versus daily ratings of sexual interest and activity in women. In J. Bancroft (Ed.), *Researching sexual behavior.* Bloomington: Indiana University Press.

Graham, C. A., Sanders, S. A., Milhausen, R. R., & McBride, K. R. (2004). Turning on and turning off: A focus group study of the factors that affect women's sexual arousal. *Archives of Sexual Behavior, 33*(6), 527–538.

Grant, J. E. (2005). Clinical characteristics and psychiatric comorbidity in males with exhibitionism. *Journal of Clinical Psychology, 66,* 1367–1371.

Gray, R. H., Wawer, M. J., Brookmeyer, R., Sewankambo, N. K., Serwadda, D., Wabwire-Mangen, F., Lutalo, T., Li, X., van Cott, T., Quinn, T. C., & Rakai Project Team. (2001). Probability of HIV-1 transmission per coital act in monogamous, heterosexual, HIV-1-discordant couples in Rakai, Uganda. *The Lancet, 357,* 1149–1153.

Green, B. C. (1998). Thinking about students who do not identify as gay, lesbian, or bisexual, but . . . *Journal of American College Health, 47*(2), 89–92.

Greenberg, J. C. (2003, June 27). Supreme Court strikes down laws against homosexual sex. *Chicago Tribune,* sec. 1, pp. 1, 4.

Greenfeld, L. (1997). *Sex offenses and offenders: An analysis of data on rape and sexual assault.* Washington, DC: U.S. Department of Justice, Bureau of Justice Statistics.

Greenhouse, L. (2008, May 20). Court upholds child pornography law, despite free speech concerns. *New York Times,* p. A17.

Greenwald, J. (2000, October 30). What about the boys? *Time,* p. 74.

Gregor, T. (1985). *Anxious pleasures.* Chicago: University of Chicago Press.

Grello, C., Welsh, D. P., & Harper, M. S. (2006). No strings attached: The nature of casual sex in college students. *Journal of Sex Research, 43*(3), 255–267.

Grello, C., Welsh, D. P., Harper, M. S., & Dickson, J. W. (2003). Dating and sexual relationship trajectories and adolescent functioning. *Adolescent and Family Health, 3,* 103–112.

Gribble, J. N., Miller, H. G., Rogers, S. M., & Turner, C. F. (1999). Interview mode and measurement of sexual behaviors: Methodological issues. *Journal of Sex Research, 36*(1), 16–24.

Griffin, G. (1998). Understanding heterosexism—the subtle continuum of homophobia. *Women and Language, 21,* 11–21.

Grimes, T. R. (1999). In search of the truth about history, sexuality, and Black women: An interview with Gail E. Wyatt. *Teaching of Psychology, 26*(1), 66–70.

Grimley, D. M., Annang, L., Houser, S., & Chen, H. (2005). Prevalence of condom errors among STD clinic patients. *American Journal of Health Behavior, 29*(4), 324–330.

Groom, T. M., & Nandwani, R. (2006). Characteristics of men who pay for sex: A UK sexual health clinic study. *Sexually Transmitted Infections, 82,* 364–367.

Gross, B. (2004). Sleeping dogs—dreams and repressed memories. *Annals of the American Psychotherapy Association, 7,* 43–44.

Gross, M., et al. (1999). Use of Reality "female condoms" for anal sex by US men who have sex with men. *American Journal of Public Health, 89,* 1739–1741.

Grossman, C. L. (2008). Most say gay marriage private choice. Available: http://usatoday/printthis.clickability.com/pt/ cpt?action= cpt&tile=Most+say+gay+marriage (Last visited 7/29/08).

Groth, A. N., & Birnbaum, H. J. (1978). Adult sexual orientation and attraction to underage persons. *Archives of Sexual Behavior, 7,* 175–181.

Groth, A. N., & Birnbaum, H. J. (1979). *Men who rape: The psychology of the offender.* New York: Plenum.

Groth, A. N., & Burgess, A. W. (1980). Male rape: Offenders and victims. *American Journal of Psychiatry, 137*(7), 806–810.

Groth, A. N., Burgess, A. W., & Holmstrom, L. L. (1977). Rape: Power, anger, and sexuality. *American Journal of Psychiatry, 104*(11), 1239–1243.

Gruber, E., & Grube, J. W. (2000). Adolescent sexuality and the media: A review of current knowledge and implications. *Western Journal of Medicine, 172*(3), 210–214.

Gruenbaum, E. (2001). *The female circumcision controversy: An anthropological perspective.* Philadelphia: University of Pennsylvania Press.

Gudelunas, D. (2007). *Confidential to America: Newspaper advice columns and sexual education.* Edison, NJ: Transaction.

Guerrero Pavich, E. (1986). A Chicana perspective on Mexican culture and sexuality. In L. Lister (Ed.), *Human sexuality, ethnoculture, and social work.* New York: Haworth Press.

Gunasehera, H., Chapman, S., & Campbell, S. (2005). Sex and drugs in popular movies: An analysis of the top 200 films. *Journal of the Royal Society of Medicine, 98,* 464–470.

Gunther, A. (1995). Overrating the X-rating: The third person perceptions and support for censorship of pornography. *Journal of Communication, 45*(1), 27–38.

Gur, R., Mozley, L., Mozley, P., et al. (1995). Sex differences in regional cerebral glucose metabolism during a resting state. *Science, 267*(5197), 528–531.

Gurian, M. (1999). *The good son: Shaping the moral development of our boys and young men.* New York: Putnam.

Guthmann, E. (2008, January 20). More men seeking pec perfection and will pay for it. *San Francisco Chronicle,* p. F1.

Guttmacher Institute. (2008a). In brief: Improving contraceptive use in the United States, 2008 Series, No. 1.

Guttmacher Institute. (2008b). Facts on young men's sexual and reproductive health. Available: http://www.guttmacher.org/pubs/fb_YMSRH.html (Last visited 8/8/08).

Guttmacher Institute. (2008c). In brief: Facts on induced abortion in the United States. Available: http://www.guttmacher.org/pubs/fb_induced_abortion.html (Last visited 9/18/08).

Guttmacher Institute. (2008d). State policies in brief: An overview of abortion laws. Available: http://www.guttmacher.org/statecenter/spibs/spib_OAL.pdf (Last visited 9/18/08).

Guttmacher Institute. (2008e). In brief: Facts on contraceptive use. Available: http://www.guttmacher.org/pubs/fb_contr_use.html (Last visited 11/28/08).

Guttmacher Institute. (2008f). State policies in brief: Infant abandonment. Available: www.guttmacher.org/statecenter/spibs/spib_IA.pdf (Last visited 11/22/08).

Hablett, M. (1999). No insurance for "video voyeurs." *New York Law Journal.* Available: http://www.store.law.com/newswire_results.asp?lqry=video+voyeurism (Last visited 2/15/06).

Hader, S. L., Smith, D. K., Moore, S. L., & Holmberg, S. D. (2001). HIV infection in women in the United States: Status at the millennium. *Journal of the American Medical Association, 285,* 1186–1192.

Haignere, C. S., Gold, R., & McDaniel, H. J. (1999). Adolescent abstinence and condom use: Are we sure we are really teaching what is safe? *Health Education and Behavior, 26,* 43–54.

Hall, C. T. (2007, May 6). Gays, lesbians seeking parenthood increasingly turn to infertility clinics. *San Francisco Chronicle,* p. A-1.

Hall, G. C. N., DeGarmo, D. S., Eap, S., Teten, A. L., & Sue, S. (2006). Initiation, desistance, and persistence of men's sexual coercion. *Journal of Counseling and Clinical Psychology, 74,* 732–742.

Hall, H. I., et al. (2008). Estimation of HIV incidence in the United States. *Journal of the American Medical Association, 300*(5), 520–529.

Hall, H. I., Qian, A., Hutchinson, A. B., & Sansom, S. (2008). Estimating the lifetime risk of a diagnosis of the HIV infection in 33 states, 2004–2005. *Journal of Acquired Immune Deficiency Syndromes, 49,* 294–297.

Hall, K. (2004). *Reclaiming your sexual self: How you can bring desire back into your life.* Hoboken, NJ: Wiley.

Halpern-Flesher, B. L., Cornell, J. L., Kropp, R. Y., & Tschann, J. M. (2005). Oral versus vaginal sex among adolescents: Perceptions, attitudes, and behaviors. *Pediatrics, 115,* 845–851.

Hamer, D. H., Hu, S., Magnuson, V. L., & Pattatucci, S. (1993). A linkage between DNA markers on the X-chromosome and male sexual orientation. *Science, 261*(5119), 321–327.

Hamilton, B. E., Martin, J. A., & Ventura, S. J. (2007, December 5). Births: Preliminary data for 2006. *National Vital Statistics Reports, 56*(7). Hyattsville, MD: National Center for Health Statistics.

Hamilton, B. E., Martin, J. A., Ventura, S. J., Sutton, P. D., & Menacker, F. (2005). Births: Preliminary data for 2004. *National Vital Statistics Reports, 54*(8). Hyattsville, MD: National Center for Health Statistics.

Handsfield, H. H., Warren, T., Werner, M., & Phillips, J. A. (2007). Suppressive therapy with valacyclovir in early genital herpes: A pilot study of clinical efficacy and herpes-related quality of life. *Sexually Transmitted Diseases, 34,* 339–343.

Hanson, R. K., & Morton-Bourgon, K. E. (2005). The characteristics of persistent sexual offenders: A meta-analysis of recidivism studies. *Journal of Counseling and Clinical Psychology, 73,* 1154–1163.

Harlow, B. L., & Steward, E. G. (2003). A population-based assessment of chronic unexplained vulvar pain: Have we underestimated the prevalence of vulvodynia? *Journal of the Medical Women's Association, 58,* 82–88.

Harris, G. (2006, June 9). U.S. approves use of vaccine for cervical cancer. *New York Times,* pp. A1, A25.

Harrison. T. (2003). Adolescent homosexuality and concerns regarding disclosure. *Journal of School Health, 73,* 107–112.

Hart, T., & Peterson, J. (2004). Predictors of risky sexual behavior among young African American men who have sex with men. *American Journal of Public Health, 94,* 1122–1123.

Hartman, S. M., Metter, E. J., Tobin, D. J., Pearson, J., & Blackman, M. R. (2001). Longitudinal effects of aging on serum total and free testosterone levels in healthy men. *Journal of Clinical Endocrinology and Metabolism, 86,* 724–731.

Harvey, J. H., Wenzel, A., & Sprecher, S. (2004). *The handbook of sexuality in close relationships.* Mahwah, NJ: Erlbaum.

Hatcher, R. A., Trussell, J., Stewart, F., Cates, W., Stewart, G. K., Guest, F., et al. (1998). *Contraceptive technology.* New York: Ardent Media.

Hatcher, R. A., Trussell, J., Stewart, F., Nelson, A. L., Cates, W., Guest, F., et al. (2007). *Contraceptive technology* (19th ed.). New York: Ardent Media.

Hatfield, E., & Sprecher, S. (1986). Measuring passionate love in intimate relations. *Journal of Adolescence, 9,* 383–410.

Hatfield, E., & Walster, G. W. (1978). *A new look at love.* Latham, MA: University Press of America.

Haugaard, J. J., & Reppucci, N. D. (1998). *The sexual abuse of children: A comprehensive guide to current knowledge and intervention strategies.* San Francisco: Jossey-Bass.

Hazan, C., & Shaver, P. (1987). Romantic love conceptualized as an attachment process. *Journal of Personality and Social Psychology, 52*(3), 511–524.

Heiman, J. R., Talley, D. R., Bailen, J. L., Oskin, T. A., Rosenberg, S. J., Pace, C. R., Creanga, D. L., & Bavendam. (2007). Sexual function and satisfaction in heterosexual couples when men are administered sildenafil citrate (Viagra) for erectile dysfunction: A multicentre, randomized, double-blind, placebo-controlled trial. *BJOG: An International Journal of Obstetrics and Gynaecology, 114,* 437–447.

Heiss, G., Wallace, R., Anderson, G. L., Aragaki, A., Beresford, S., et al. (2008). Health risks and benefits 3 years after stopping randomized treatment with estrogen and progestin. *Journal of the American Medical Association, 299*(9), 1036–1045.

Helms, D. J., et al. (2008). Risk factors for prevalent and incident trichomonas vaginalis among women attending three sexually transmitted disease clinics. *Sexually Transmitted Diseases, 35,* 484–488.

Hennessy, M., Fishbein, M., Curtis, B., & Barrett, D. W. (2007). Evaluating the risk and attractiveness of romantic partners when confronted with contradictory clues. *AIDS and Behavior, 11,* 479–490.

Henshaw, S. K. (1999). Unintended pregnancy and abortion: A public health perspective. In M. Paul et al. (Eds.), *A clinician's guide to medical and surgical abortion* (pp. 11–22). New York: Churchill Livingston

Henshaw, S. K. (2003). U.S. teenage pregnancy statistics with comparative statistics for women. Available: http://www.agi-usa.org/pubs/teen_stats.htm (Last visited 5/30/03).

Herbenick, D., Reece, M., Sanders, S., Ghassemi, A., & Fortenberry, J. D. (2009). Prevalence and characteristics of vibrator use by women in the United States: Results from a nationally representative study. *Journal of Sexual Medicine, 6,* 1857–1866.

Herbert, C. M. H. (1989). *Talking of silence: The sexual harassment of schoolgirls.* London: Falmer Press.

Herdt, G. (1987). Transitional objects in Sambia initiation. Special issue: Interpretation in psychoanalytic anthropology. *Ethos, 15,* 40–57.

Herdt, G., & Boxer, A. (1992). Introduction: Culture, history, and life course of gay men. In G. Herdt (Ed.), *Gay culture in America: Essays from the field.* Boston: Beacon Press.

Herek, G. M. (1984). Beyond homophobia: A social psychological perspective on attitudes toward lesbians and gay men. *Journal of Homosexuality, 10*(1–2), 1–21.

Herek, G. M. (1995). Psychological heterosexism in the United States. In A. R. D'Augelli & C. J. Patterson (Eds.), *Lesbian, gay, and bisexual identities over the lifespan: Psychological perspectives.* New York: Oxford University Press.

Herek, G. M., Kimmel, D. C., Amaro, H., & Melton, G. B. (1991). Avoiding heterosexist bias in psychological research. *American Psychologist, 46*(9), 957–963.

Herzer, M. (1985). Kertbeny and the nameless love. *Journal of Homosexuality, 12,* 1–26.

Hetherington, E. M., & Kelly, J. (2002). *For better or worse: Divorce reconsidered.* New York: W. W. Norton.

Hicks, T. V., & Leitenberg, H. (2001). Sexual fantasies about one's partner versus someone else: Gender differences in incidence and frequency. *Journal of Sex Research, 38,* 43–50.

Higginbotham, E. B. (1992). African-American women's history and the metalanguage of race. *Journal of Women in Culture and Society, 17,* 251–274.

Hill, C. A. (2002). Gender, relationship stage, and sexual behavior: The importance of partner emotional investment within specific situations. *Journal of Sex Research, 39*(3), 228–240.

Hine, D. C. (1989). Rape and the inner lives of Black women in the Middle West: Preliminary thoughts on the culture of dissemblance. *Signs, 14,* 915.

Hirschfeld, M. (1991). *Transvestites: The erotic drive to cross dress.* Buffalo: Prometheus Books.

Hirschfeld, S. (2002). 21% of women surveyed in the latest national poll report having been sexually harassed at work. Available: http://www.employmentlawalliance.com/en/node/1324 (Last visited 5/26/09).

Hirschfeld, S. (2004). Sex in the workplace: Employment Law Alliance Poll finds 24% involved in sexually-explicit computing. Available: http://www.employmentlawalliance.com/en/node/1324 (Last visited 5/26/09).

HIV Vaccines and Microbicides Resource Tracking Working Group. (2007). Building a comprehensive resource: Funding for HIV vaccines, microbicides and other new prevention options, 2000–2006. Available: http://www.hivresourcetracking.org (Last visited 10/11/08).

Hoberman, J. (2005). Testosterone dreams. *American Sexuality Magazine.* Available: http://www.nsrc.sfsu.edu/MagArticle.cfm?Article=527 (Last visited 11/17/05).

Hock, R. R. (2007). *Human sexuality.* Upper Saddle River, NJ: Pearson Education.

Hoffman, V., & Cohen, D. (1999). A night with Venus: Partner assessments and high-risk encounters. *AIDS Care, 11,* 555–566.

Hofschire L. J., & Greenberg, B. S. (2002). Media's impact on adolescents' body dissatisfaction. In J. D. Brown, J. R. Steele, & K. Walsh-Childers (Eds.), *Sexual teens, sexual media* (pp. 125–149). Mahwah, NJ: Erlbaum.

Holman, T. B., & Jarvis, M. O. (2003). Hostile, volatile, avoiding, and validating couple-conflict types: An investigation of Gottman's couple-conflict types. *Personal Relationships, 10*(2), 267–282.

Holmes, R. M. (1991). *Sex crimes.* Newbury Park, CA: Sage.

Holstege, G., Georgiadis, J. R., Paans, A. M., Meiners, L. C., van der Graff, F. H., & Reinders, A. A. (2003). Brain activation during human male ejaculation. *Journal of Neuroscience, 34,* 9185–9193.

Holtgrave, D. R., Hall, H. I., Rhodes, P. H., & Wolitski, R. J. (2008). Updated annual HIV transmission rates in the United States, 1977–2006. *Journal of Acquired Immune Deficiency Syndromes, 50,* 236–238.

Hooker, E. (1957). The adjustment of the overt male homosexual. *Journal of Projective Psychology, 21,* 18–31.

Hudson, J. I., Hiripi, E., Pope, H. G., & Kessler, R. C. (2007). The prevalence and correlates of eating disorders in the National Comorbidity Survey Replication. *Biological Psychiatry, 61,* 348–358.

Hughes, A., Houk, C., Ahmed, S. F., Lee, P. A., & LWPES/ESE Consensus Group (2006). Consensus statement on management of intersex disorders. *Archives of Disease in Childhood, 91,* 554–562.

Hughes, S. M., Harrison, M. A., & Gallup, G. G. (2007). Sex differences in romantic kissing among college students: An evolutionary perspective. *Evolutionary Psychology, 5,* 612–663.

Human Rights Campaign. (2003). Hate crimes. Available: http://www.hrc.org/familynet/chapter.asp?article=550 (Last visited 6/12/03).

Human Rights Campaign. (2008a). International marriage rights. Available: http://www.hrc.org/issues/int_rights_immigration/5023.htm (Last visited 6/5/08).

Human Rights Campaign. (2008b). Working on gay, lesbian, bisexual, and transgender rights: News. Available: http://www.hrc.org/issues/marriage_news.asp (Last visited 11/4/08).

Human Rights Campaign. (2008c). Statewide marriage prohibitions. Available: http://www.hrc.org/state_laws (Last visited 4/30/09).

Human Rights Foundation. (2008d). State hate crimes laws. Available: http://www.hrc.org/maps (Last visited 7/30/08).

Human Rights Campaign. (2009a). Domestic partner. Available: http://www.hrc.org/issues/marriage/domestic_partners.asp (Last visited 4/30/09).

Human Rights Campaign. (2009b). Civil unions. Available: http://www.hrc.org/issues/marriage/civil_unions.asp (Last visited 4/30/09).

Human Rights Watch. (2007). No easy answers. Available: http://www.hrw.reports/2007/us0907 (Last visited 8/17/08).

Humphreys, L. (1975). *Tearoom trade: Impersonal sex in public places.* Chicago: Aldine.

Humphreys, T. P. (2004). Understanding sexual consent: An empirical investigation of the normative script for young heterosexual adults. In M. Cowling & P. Reynolds (Eds.), *Making sense of sexual consent.* Aldershot, England: Ashgate.

Hunter, J. A., Figueredo, A. J., & Malamuth, N. M. (2003). Juvenile sex offenders: Toward the development of a typology. *Sexual Abuse: Journal of Research and Treatment, 15,* 27–48.

Huo, D., & Ouellet, L. (2007). Needle exchange and injection-related risk behaviors in Chicago: A longitudinal study. *Journal of Acquired Immune Deficiency Syndromes, 45,* 108–114.

Hutchinson, K. B., Kip, K. E., & Ness, R. B. (2007). Condom use and its association with bacterial vaginosis and bacterial vaginosis-associated vaginal microflora. *Epidemiology, 18,* 702–708.

Hyde, J. S., & DeLamater, J. D. (2006). *Understanding human sexuality* (9th ed.). New York: McGraw-Hill.

Hyde, J. S., & DeLamater, J. D. (2008). *Understanding human sexuality* (10th ed). New York: McGraw-Hill.

Ickovics, J. R., Beren, S. E., Grigorenko, E. L., Morrill, A. C., Druley, J. A., & Rodin, J. (2002). Pathways of risk: Race, social class, stress, and coping as factors predicting heterosexual risk behaviors for HIV among women. *AIDS and Behavior, 6,* 339–350.

Insel, P. M., & Roth, W. T. (2008). *Core concepts in health* (10th ed., Brief Update). New York: McGraw-Hill.

Institute of Medicine. (1999). *Lesbian health: Current assessment and directions for the future.* Washington, DC: National Academy Press.

InteliHealth. (2005). Health A to Z: Premenstrual syndrome (PMS). Available: http://www.intelihealth.com.html (Last visited 10/11/05).

International Rectal Microbicide Advocates. (2008). Less silence more science: Advocacy to make rectal microbicide a reality. Available: http://www.rectalmicrobicides.org/materials.php (Last visited 12/22/08).

Internet pornography law dies in Supreme Court. (2009, January 22). *Herald Times,* P. E3.

Intersex Society of North America. (2000a). Frequently asked questions. Available: http://www.isna.org/faq.html (Last visited 7/13/00).

Intersex Society of North America. (2000b). How common is intersexuality? Available: http://www.isna.org/frequency.html (Last visited 7/19/00).

Intersex Society of North America. (2005). Suggestions for writing about intersex. Available: http://www.isna.org (Last visited 4/26/06).

Intersex Society of North America. (2006). *Clinical guidelines for the management of disorders of sexual development in children.* Rohnert Park, CA: Author. Available: http://www.dsdguidelines.org/files/clinical.pdf (Last visited 1/25/08).

Intersex Society of North America. (2008). *What is intersex?* Rohnert Park, CA: Author. Available: http://www.isna.org/faq/what_is_intersex (Last visited 2/28/09).

Ionannidis, J. P. (2005). Contradicted and initially stronger effects in highly cited clinical research. *Journal of the American Medical Association, 294,* 218–228.

Irvine, M. (2007, June 4). Porn's influence on young women can be empowering—and embarrassing. *San Francisco Chronicle,* p. A12.

Ishii-Kuntz, M. (1997). Chinese American families. In M. K. DeGenova (Ed.), *Families in cultural context.* Mountain View, CA: Mayfield.

Is NuvaRing right for you? (2003). Planned Parenthood Federation of America. Available: http://www.plannedparenthood.org/BC/030109_NuvaRing.html (Last visited 4/9/03).

Jaakkola, J., & Gissler, M. (2004). Maternal smoking in pregnancy, fetal development, and childhood asthma. *American Journal of Public Health, 94*(1), 136–140.

Jackson, A. B., & Wadley, V. (1999). A multicenter study of women's self-reported reproductive health after spinal cord injury. *Archives of Physical Medical Rehabilitation, 80,* 1420–1428.

Jacobs, A. (2002, January 29). In clubs, a potent drug stirs fear of an epidemic. *New York Times,* p. B1.

Jacobs, S. E., Thomas, W., & Lang, S. (1997). *Two-spirit people.* Chicago: University of Illinois Press.

James, A. B., Simpson, T. Y., & Chamberlain, W. A. (2008). Chlamydia prevalence among college students: Reproductive and public health implications. *Sexually Transmitted Infections, 35,* 529–523.

Janssen, D. F. (2007). First stirrings: Cultural notes on orgasm, ejaculation, and wet dreams. *Journal of Sex Research, 44*(2), 122–134.

Janssen, E. (2002). Psychological measurement of sexual arousal. In M. W. Wiederman & B. E. Whitley (Eds.), *Handbook for conducting research on human sexuality.* Mahwah, NJ: Erlbaum.

Janus, S., & Janus, C. (1993). *The Janus Report on sexual behavior.* New York: Wiley.

Jayson, S. (2007, July 9). Charles Atlas was right: Brawny guys get the girls. *USA Today,* p. D6.

Jessor, R., & Jessor, S. L. (1997). *Problem behavior and psychosocial development: A longitudinal study of youth.* New York: Academic Press.

Jimenez, J. A., & Abreu, J. M. (2003). Race and sex effects on attitudinal perceptions of acquaintance rape. *Journal of Counseling Psychology, 50,* 252–256.

Joensuu, H., Lehtimaki, T., Holli, K., Elomaa, L., Turpeenniemi-Hujanen, T., Kataja, V., et al. (2004). Risk of distant recurrence of breast cancer detected by mammography screening or other methods. *Journal of the American Medical Association, 292,* 1064–1073.

Johnson, C. B., Stockdale, M. S., & Saal, F. E. (1991). Persistence of men's misperceptions of friendly cues across a variety of interpersonal encounters. *Psychology of Women Quarterly, 15*(3), 463–475.

Johnson, K. (2002). Time, patience needed to find right testosterone level with HRT. *Family Practice News, 32*(11), 31.

Johnson, K. (2007, February 8). Investigation of child porn site hits 77 countries. *USA Today,* p. A13.

Johnson, L. A. (2000, March 23). New risks seen with genital herpes. *Monterey County Herald,* p. A6.

Joint United Nations Programme on AIDS/World Health Organization/United Nations Population Fund. (2004). Position statement on condoms and HIV prevention. Available: http://www.who.int/hiv/pub/prev_care/statement/en (Last visited 11/22/05).

Joint United Nations Programme on AIDS and World Health Organization. (2005). AIDS epidemic update: December 2005. Available: http://www.unaids.org/Epi2005/doc/report.html (Last visited 11/22/05).

Joint United Nations Programme on HIV/AIDS. (2008a). 08 Report on the global AIDS epidemic. Available: http:www//unaids/org/en/KnowledgeCentre/HIVData/GlobalReport/2008/2008_Global_report.asp (Last visited 11/17/08).

Joint United Nations Programme on HIV/AIDS. (2008b). 2008 epidemiology slides. Available: http://www.unaids/org/en/knowledgeCentre/HIVData/Epidemiology/epidemiologySlides (Last visited 11/18/08).

Jones, J. H. (1993). *Bad blood: The Tuskegee syphilis experiment* (Rev. ed.). New York: Free Press.

Jones, L. M., & Finkelhor, D. (2003). Putting together evidence on declining trends in sexual abuse: A complex puzzle. *Child Abuse and Neglect, 27,* 133–136.

Jones, R. K., Darroch, J. E., & Henshaw, S. K. (2002b). Contraceptive use among U.S. women having abortions in 2000–2001. *Perspectives on Sexual and Reproductive Health, 34*(6), 294–303.

Jones, R. K., et al. (2008). Abortion in the United States: Incidence and access to services, 2005. *Perspectives on Sexual and Reproductive Health, 40*(1), 6–16

Jossi, F. (2005). Sharp decline in teen pregnancy prompts researchers to ponder what works. *Contemporary Sexuality, 39*(5), 1–6.

Joura, E. A., et al. (2007). Efficacy of a quadrivalent prophylactic human papillomavirus (types 6, 11, 16, and 18) L1 virus-like-particle vaccine against high-grade vulval and vaginal lesions: A combined analysis of three randomized clinical trials. *The Lancet, 369,* 1693–1702.

Jumper, S. A. (1995). A meta-analysis of the relationship of child sexual abuse to adult psychological adjustment. *Child Abuse and Neglect, 19*(6), 715–728.

Kaestle, C. E., & Halpern, C. T. (2007). What's love got to do with it? Sexual behaviors of opposite-sex couples through emerging adulthood. *Perspectives on Sexual and Reproductive Health, 39*(3), 134–140.

Kaestle, C. E., Halpern, C. T., Miller, W. C., & Ford, C. A. (2005). Young age at first intercourse and sexually transmitted infections in adolescents and young adults. *American Journal of Epidemiology, 161,* 774–778.

Kaiser Daily HIV/AIDS Report. (2008, July 28). HAART increases HIV-positive people's life expectancy by average of 13 years, study finds. Available: http://www.kaisernetwork.org/daily_reports/print_report.cfm?DR_ID=53529&dr_cat=1 (Last visited 7/28/08).

Kaiser Family Foundation. (2001a). V-chip study 2000. Available: http://www.kff.org (Last visited 11/22/05).

Kaiser Family Foundation. (2001b). New SexSmarts study on teens and sexually transmitted diseases. Available: http://www.kff.org/content/2001/3148 (Last visited 12/14/01).

Kaiser Family Foundation. (2005, January). U.S. teen sexual activity (Publication #3040-02). Available: http://www.kff.org (Last visited 5/12/05).

Kaiser Family Foundation. (2006). Survey of Americans on HIV/AIDS. Available: http://www.kff.org/hivaids/index.cfm (Last visited 12/15/08).

Kaiser Family Foundation. (n.d.). Inside-out: A report on the experiences of lesbians, gays and bisexuals in America and the public's views on issues and policies related to sexual orientation. Available: http://www.kff.org (Last visited 6/11/03).

Kaiser Family Foundation/Harvard School of Public Health. (2000, February). Health news index. Available: http://www.kff.org (Last visited 1/6/01).

Kalliala, I., Anttila, A., Pukkala, E., & Nieminen, P. (2005). Risk of cervical cancer and other cancers after treatment of cervical intraepithelial neoplasia: Retrospective cohort study. *British Medical Journal, 331,* 1183–1185.

Kalof, L., & Wade, B. H. (1995). Sexual attitudes and experiences with sexual coercion: Exploring the influence of race and gender. *Journal of Black Psychology, 21*(3), 224–238.

Kaplan, A. (1979). Clarifying the concept of androgyny: Implications for therapy. *Psychology of Women, 3,* 223–230.

Kaplan, H. S. (1974). *The new sex therapy.* New York: Brunner/Mazel.

Kaplan, H. S. (1979). *Disorders of desire.* New York: Brunner/Mazel.

Kaplan, H. S., & Horwith, M. (1983). *The evaluation of sexual disorders: Psychological and medical aspects.* New York: Brunner/Mazel.

Kaplan, J., Sadock, B., & Grebb, J. (1994). *Synopsis of psychiatry* (7th ed.). Baltimore: Williams & Wilkins.

Kappy, M. S., Blizzard, R. M., & Migeon, C. J. (Eds.). (1994). *The diagnosis and treatment of endocrine disorders in childhood and adolescence* (4th ed.). Baltimore: Thompson.

Kaufman, M., Silverberg, C., & Odette, F. (2003). *The ultimate guide to sex and disability.* San Francisco: Cleis Press.

Kaunitz, A. M. (1999). Oral contraceptive health benefits: Perception versus reality. *Contraception, 59*(Suppl. 1), 295–335.

Kaunitz, A. M. (2000). Menstruation: Choosing whether, and when. *Contraception, 62,* 277–284.

Kavanaugh-Lynch, M. H. E., White, E., Daling, J. R., & Bowen, D. J. (2002). Correlates of lesbian sexual orientation and the risk of breast cancer. *Journal of the Gay and Lesbian Medical Association, 6,* 91–95.

Kaye, R., & Estrada, I. (2008, March 19). Female veterans report more sexual, mental trauma. Available: http://cnn.site/printthis.clickability.com/pt/ept?action-ept8title=Female+veterans+report (Last visited 3/19/08).

Keele, B. F., et al. (2008). Identification and characterization of transmitted and early founder virus envelopes in primary HIV-1 infection. *Proceedings of the National Academy of Sciences, 105,* 7552–7557.

Keesling, B. (2006). *Sexual healing: The complete guide to overcoming common sexual problems* (3rd ed.). Alameda, CA: Hunter House.

Keiser, L. R., Wilkins, V. M., Meier, K. J., & Holland, C. (2000). *Lipstick and logarithms: Gender, institutional context, and representative bureaucracy.* Paper presented at the American Political Science Association Meeting on August 31–September 2, 2000, Washington, DC.

Kelly, G. F. (2006). *Sexuality today* (8th ed.). New York: McGraw-Hill.

Kelly, M. P., Strassberg, D. S., & Kircher, J. R. (1990). Attitudinal and experiential correlates of anorgasmia. *Archives of Sexual Behavior, 19*(2), 165–167.

Kennedy, H. (1988). *The life and works of Karl Heinrich Ulrichs: Pioneer of the modern gay movement.* Boston: Alyson.

Kenyon, E. B. (1989). The management of exhibitionism in the elderly: A case study. *Sexual and Marital Therapy, 4*(1), 93–100.

Kero, A., Hogberg, U., & Lalos, A. (2004). Wellbeing and mental growth—long term effects of abortion. *Social Science Medicine, 58,* 2559–2569.

Keuls, E. (1985). *Reign of the phallus: Sexual politics in ancient Athens.* Berkeley: University of California Press.

Khaw, K. T., Dowsett, M., Folkerd, E., Bingham, S., Wareham, N., et al. (2007). Endogenous testosterone and mortality due to all causes, cardiovascular disease, and cancer in men. *Circulation, 116,* 2694–2701

Kidd, S. A., & Kral, M. J. (2002). Suicide and prostitution among street youth: A qualitative analysis. *Adolescence, 37,* 411–431.

Kidder, L. H., Lafleur, R. A., & Wells, C. V. (1995). Recalling harassment, reconstructing experience. *Journal of Social Issues, 52*(1), 69–84.

Kigozi, G., et al. (2008). The effect of male circumcision on sexual satisfaction and function, results from a randomized trial of male circumcision for human immunodeficiency virus prevention, Rakai, Uganda. *BJU International, 101,* 65–70.

Kim, G. (2008, January 22). People getting burned out on social ties. *San Francisco Chronicle,* p. B2.

Kim, J., Sorsoli, C. L., Collins, K., Zylbergold, B. A., Schooler, D., & Tolman, D. L. (2007). From sex to sexuality: Exposing the heterosexual script on primetime network television. *Journal of Sex Research, 44*(2), 145–157.

King, P. A. (1992). Twenty years after. The legacy of the Tuskegee syphilis study. The dangers of difference. *Hastings Center Report, 22*(6), 35–38.

Kingsberg, S. (2002). The impact of aging on sexual function in women and their partners. *Archives of Sexual Behavior, 31,* 431–437.

Kinsey, A., Pomeroy, W., & Martin, C. (1948). *Sexual behavior in the human male.* Philadelphia: Saunders.

Kinsey, A., Pomeroy, W., Martin, C., & Gebhard, P. (1953). *Sexual behavior in the human female.* Philadelphia: Saunders.

Kirby, D. (2000). School-based interventions to prevent unprotected sex and HIV among adolescents. In J. L. Peterson & R. J. Di Clemente (Eds.), *Handbook of HIV prevention.* New York: Kluwer Academic/Plenum.

Kirby, D. (2001). Emerging answers: Research findings on programs to reduce teen pregnancy. Washington, DC: The National Campaign to Prevent Teen Pregnancy.

Kirby, D. (2002). Effective approaches to reducing adolescent unprotected sex, pregnancy, and childbearing. *Journal of Sex Research, 39*(7), 51–58.

Kirby, D. (2004, June 21). Party favors: Pill popping as insurance. *New York Times,* pp. E1, E11.

Kirby, D. (2007). Emerging answers, 2007. Research findings on programs to reduce teen pregnancy and sexually transmitted diseases.

Scotts Valley, CA: National Campaign to Prevent Teen and Unplanned Pregnancy.

Kirby, D. (2008). The impact of abstinence and comprehensive sex and STD/HIV education programs on adolescent sexual behavior. *Sexuality Research and Policy, 5*(3), 18–27.

Kirk, G., Singh, K., & Getz, H. (2001). Risk of eating disorders among female college athletes and nonathletes. *Journal of College Counseling, 4,*122–132.

Klein, F. (1993). *The bisexual option* (2nd ed.). New York: Haworth Press.

Kitano, H. H. (1994, November). *Recent trends in Japanese Americans' interracial marriage.* Paper presented at the Center for Family Studies Lecture Series, University of California, Riverside.

Klinetob, N. A., & Smith, D. A. (1996). Demand-withdraw communication in marital interaction: Tests of interspousal contingency and gender role hypotheses. *Journal of Marriage and Family, 58*(4), 945–957.

Kluger, J. (2008, January 16). Why we love. *Time,* pp. 55–60.

Koch, P. B., Palmer, R. F., Vicary, J. A., & Wood, J. M. (1999). Mixing sex and alcohol in college: Female-male HIV risk model. *Journal of Sex Education and Therapy, 24,* 99–108.

Koch, W. (2005, November 30). More women charged in sex cases. *USA Today,* p. A3.

Koch, W. (2006, May 24). States get tougher with sex offenders. *USA Today,* p. A1.

Kohlberg, L. (1966). A cognitive-developmental analysis of children's sex-role concepts and attitudes. In E. E. Maccoby (Ed.), *The development of sex differences.* Palo Alto, CA: Stanford University Press.

Kolodny, R., Masters, W., & Johnson, V. (1979). *Textbook of sexual medicine.* Boston: Little, Brown.

Komisaruk, B. R., Beyer-Flores, C., & Whipple, B. (2006). *The science of orgasm.* Baltimore: Johns Hopkins University Press.

Konrad, A., & Harris, C. (2002). Desirability of the Bem Sex-Role Inventory items for women and men: A comparison between African Americans and European Americans. *Sex Roles: A Journal of Sex Research, 47*(5/6), 259–272.

Kornblum, J. (2008, May 16). Courts address gay civil rights. *USA Today,* p. A3.

Kost, K., et al. (2008). Estimates of contraceptive failure from the 2002 National Survey of Family Growth. *Contraception, 77*(1), 10–21.

Koss, M. P., & Dinero, T. E. (1989). Predictors of sexual aggression among a national sample of male college students. *Annals of the New York Academy of Science, 528,* 133–146.

Koumans, E. H., et al. (2007) The prevalence of bacterial vaginosis in the United States, 2001–2004; Associations with symptomatic, sexual behaviors, and reproductive health. *Sexually Transmitted Diseases, 34,* 864–869.

Krakow, B., Germain, A., Tandberg, D., Koss, M., Schrader, R., Hollifield, M., et al. (2000). Sleep breathing and sleep movement disorders masquerading as insomnia in sexual-assault survivors. *Comprehensive Psychiatry, 41,* 49–56.

Kruks, G. (1991). Gay and lesbian homeless/street youth: Special issues and concerns. Special issue: Homeless youth. *Journal of Adolescent Health, 12*(7), 515–518.

Kunkel, D., Eyal, K., Finnerty, L., Biely, E., & Donnerstein, E. (2005). *Sex on TV 4: A Family Foundation report.* Available: http://www .kff.org/entmedia/upload/sex-on-TV-4-Full-Report.pdf (Last visited 11/17/05).

Kurdek, L. A. (2004). Are gay and lesbian cohabiting couples *really* different from heterosexual married couples? *Journal of Marriage and Family, 66,* 880–900.

LaBrie, J. W., Schiffman, J., & Earleywine, M. (2002). Expectations specific to condom use mediate the alcohol and sexual risk relationship. *Journal of Sex Research, 39,* 145–152.

Lacey, R. S., Reifman, A., Scott, J. P., Harris, S. M., & Fitzpatrick, J. H. (2004). Sexual-moral attitudes, love styles and mate selection. *Journal of Sex Research, 41*(2), 121–128.

Ladas, A., Whipple, B., & Perry, J. (1982). *The G spot.* New York: Holt, Rinehart & Winston.

Lalumiere, M., Blanchard, R., & Zucker, K. (2000). Sexual orientation and handedness in men and women: A meta-analysis. *Psychological Bulletin, 126,* 575–592.

Lalumiere, M. L., Harris, G. T., Quinsey, V. L., & Rice, M. E. (2005). *The causes of rape.* Washington, DC: American Psychological Association.

Lamaze, F. (1970). *Painless childbirth* (Rev. ed.). Chicago: Regnery. (1st ed., 1956).

Landry, D. J., Darroch, J. E., Singh, S., & Higgins, J. (2003). Factors influencing the content of sex education in U.S. public secondary schools. *Perspectives on Sexual and Reproductive Health, 35*(6), 261–269.

Landry, V. (Ed.). (2003). *Contraceptive sterilization: Global issues and trends.* New York: EngenderHealth.

Langstrom, N., & Seto, M. (2006). Exhibitionistic and voyeuristic behavior in a Swedish national population study. *Archives of Sexual Behavior, 35,* 427–435.

Langstrom, N., & Zucker, K. J. (2005). Transvestic fetishism in the general population: Prevalence and correlates. *Journal of Sex and Marital Therapy, 31,* 87–95.

Laqueur, T. (2003). *Solitary sex: A cultural history of masturbation.* Cambridge, MA: MIT Zone.

Laumann, E., Gagnon, J., Michael, R., & Michaels, S. (1994). *The social organization of sexuality.* Chicago: University of Chicago Press.

Laumann, E. O., & Mahay, J. (2002). The social organization of women's sexuality. In G. M. Wingood & R. J. DiClemente (Eds.), *Handbook of women's sexual and reproductive health.* New York: Kluwer Academic/Plenum.

Laumann, E. O., Nicolosi, A., Glasser, D. B., et al. (2005). Sexual problems among women and men aged 40–80 years: Prevalence and correlates identified in the Global Study of Sexual Attitudes and Behaviors. *International Journal of Impotence Research, 17,* 39–57.

Laumann, E. O., Paik, A., Glasser, D. B., et al. (2006). A cross-national study of subjective sexual well-being among older women and men: Findings from the Global Study of Sexual Attitudes and Behaviors. *Archives of Sexual Behavior, 35*(2), 145–161.

Laumann, E. O., Paik, A., & Rosen, R. C. (1999). Sexual dysfunction in the United States: Prevalence and predictors. *Journal of the American Medical Association, 281,* 537–544.

LaVay, S., and Valente, S. M. (2003). *Human sexuality.* Sunderland, MA: Sinauer Associates.

Lee, E. (2008, January 24). Sex education goes online to reach teens. *San Francisco Chronicle,* p. C 1.

Lee, J. A. (1973). *The color of love.* Toronto: New Press.

Lee, J. A. (1988). Love styles. In R. Sternberg & M. Barnes (Eds.), *The psychology of love.* New Haven, CT: Yale University Press.

Lee, J. M., Appugliese, D., Kaciroti, N., Corwyn, R. H., Bradley, R. H., & Lumeng, J. C. (2007, March). Weight status in young girls and the onset of puberty. *Pediatrics, 119*(3), 624–630.

Lehner, T., & Chiasson, M. A. (1998). Seroprevalence of human immunodeficiency virus Type I and sexual behaviors in bisexual African-American and Hispanic men visiting a sexually transmitted disease clinic in New York City. *American Journal of Epidemiology, 147,* 269–272.

Leiblum, S., Brown, C., Wan, J., & Rawlinson, L. (2005). Persistent sexual arousal syndrome: A descriptive study. *Journal of Sexual Medicine, 2,* 331–337.

Leiblum, S. R., & Nathan, S. G. (2001). Persistent sexual arousal syndrome: A newly discovered pattern of female sexuality. *Journal of Sex and Marital Therapy, 27,* 365–380.

Leinwand, D. (2002, September 23). Ecstasy-Viagra mix alarms doctors. *USA Today,* p. A1.

Leitenberg, H., Detzer, M. J., & Srebnik, D. (1993). Gender differences in masturbation and the relation of masturbation experience in preadolescence and early adolescence to sexual behavior and sexual adjustment in young adulthood. *Archives of Sexual Behavior, 22*(2), 87–98.

Leitenberg, H., & Henning, K. (1995). Sexual fantasy. *Psychological Bulletin, 117*(3), 469–496.

Leitzmann, M. F., Platz, E. A., Stampfer, M. J., Willet, W. C., & Giovannucci, E. (2004). Ejaculation frequency and subsequent risk of prostate cancer. *Journal of the American Medical Association, 291,* 1578–1586.

Leland, J. (2000, May 29). The science of women and sex. *Newsweek,* pp. 46–54.

Lemonick, M. D. (2000, October 30). Teens before their time. *Time,* pp. 68–74.

Lenz, R., & Chaves, B. (1981). Becoming active partners: A couple's perspective. In D. Bullard & S. Knight (Eds.), *Sexuality and disability: Personal perspectives.* St. Louis, MO: Mosby.

Lescano, C. M., et al. (2009). Correlates of heterosexual anal intercourse among at-risk adolescents and young adults. *American Journal of Public Health, 99,* 1131–1136.

Lessons learned on gay marriage image on Election Day. (2008, November 11). *USA Today,* p. A10.

Lethbridge-Cejku, M., Schiller, J. S., & Bernadel, L. (2004). Summary statistics for U.S. adults: National Health Interview Survey, 2002. *Vital Health Statistics, 10,* 222.

Lev, A. I. (2007). Transgender communities: Developing identity through connection. In K. J. Bieschke, R. M. Perez, & D. A. Debord (Eds.), *Handbook of counseling and psychotherapy with lesbian, gay, bisexual and transgender clients* (2nd ed., pp. 147–175). Washington, DC: American Psychological Association.

LeVay, S. (1991). A difference in hypothalamic structure between heterosexual and homosexual men. *Science, 253,* 1034–1037.

LeVay, S., & Valente, S. M. (2006). *Human sexuality* (2nd ed.). Sunderland, MA: Sinauer Associates.

Lever, J. (1994, August 23). Sexual revelations. *The Advocate,* pp. 17–24.

Lever, J. (1995, August 22). Lesbian sex survey. *The Advocate,* pp. 23–30.

Lever, J., & Dolnick, D. (2000). Clients and call girls: Seeking sex and intimacy. In R. Weitzer (Ed.), *Sex for sale: Prostitution and the sex industry.* New York: Routledge.

Lever, J., Frederick, D., & Peplau, L. A. (2006). Does size matter? Men's and women's views on penis size across the lifespan. *Psychology of Men & Masculinity, 7,* 129–143.

Levine, L., & Barbach, L. (1983). *The intimate male.* New York: Signet Books.

Levine, M. P. (1987). *How schools can help combat student eating disorders: Anorexia nervosa and bulimia.* Washington, DC: National Education Association.

Levine, M. P., & Troiden, R. (1988). The myth of sexual compulsivity. *Journal of Sex Research, 25*(3), 347–363.

Li, C. K. (1990). "The main thing is being wanted": Some case studies in adult sexual experiences with children. *Journal of Homosexuality, 20*(1–2), 129–143.

Liben, L. S., & Signorella, M. L. (1993). Gender-schematic processing in children: The role of initial interpretations of stimuli. *Developmental Psychology, 29*(1), 141–150.

Lichtenstein, B. (2003). Stigma as a barrier to treatment of sexually transmitted infections in the American Deep South: Issues of race, gender, and poverty. *Social Science and Medicine, 57,* 2435–2445.

Lieblum, S. R. (2002). Reconsidering gender differences in sexual desire: An update. *Sexual and Relationship Therapy, 17*(1), 57–68.

Lindau, S. T., Schumm, L. P., Laumann, E. O., Levinson, W., O'Muircheartaigh, & Waite, L. J. (2007, August 23). A study of sexuality and health among older adults in the United States. *New England Journal of Medicine, 357*(8), 762–774.

Lindberg, L. D., Boggs, S., Porter, L., & Williams, S. (2000). *Teen risk-taking: A statistical report.* Washington, DC: Urban Institute.

Lindberg, L. D., Jones, R., & Santelli, J. S. (2008). Non-coital sexual activities among adolescents. *Journal of Adolescent Health, 43,* 231–238.

Linnehan, M. J., & Groce, N. E. (1999). Psychosocial and educational services for female college students with genital human papillomavirus infection. *Family Planning Perspectives, 31*(3).

Lippa, R. A. (2000). Gender-related traits in gay men, lesbian women, and heterosexual men and women: The virtual identity of homosexual-heterosexual diagnosticity and gender diagnosticity. *Journal of Personality, 68,* 899–925.

Lippa, R. A. (2002). Gender-related traits of heterosexual and homosexual men and women. *Archives of Sexual Behavior, 31,* 83–98.

Lips, H. (2001). *A new psychology of women: Gender, culture and ethnicity* (2nd ed.). Boston: McGraw-Hill.

Lips, H. (2004). *Sex and gender: An introduction* (5th ed.). New York: McGraw-Hill.

Lipscomb, G. H., et al. (1992). Male victims of sexual assault. *Journal of the American Medical Association, 267*(22), 3064–3066.

Liptar, A. (2008a, May 17). Same-sex marriage and racial justice find common ground. *New York Times,* p. A10.

Liptar, A. (2008b, May 17). California court overturns a ban on gay marriage. *New York Times,* pp. A1, A19.

Lloyd, E. (2005). *The case of the female orgasm.* Cambridge, MA: Harvard University Press.

Lloyd, E. A. (2007). A fantastic bonus. *National Sexuality Resource Center.* Available: http://nsrc.sfsu.edu (Last visited 9/27/07).

Locke, B. D., Mahalik, J. R. (2005). Examining masculinity norms, problem drinking, and athletic involvement as predictors of sexual aggression in college men. *Journal of Counseling Psychology, 52,* 279–283.

Locy, T., & Biskupic, J. (2003, June 23). Requirement for library porn filters upheld. *USA Today,* p. A1.

London, S. (2004). Risk of pregnancy-related death is sharply elevated for women 35 and older. *Perspectives on Sexual and Reproductive Health, 36,* 87–88.

Long, V. E. (2003). Contraceptive choices: New options on the U.S. market. *SIECUS Report, 31*(2), 13–18.

LoPiccolo, J. (1991). Counseling and therapy for sexual problems in the elderly. *Clinics in Geriatric Medicine, 7,* 161–179.

Lowenstein, L. (2002). Fetishes and their associated behaviors. *Sexuality and Disability, 20,* 135–147.

Lucas, A. (1998). *The dis-ease of being a woman: Rethinking prostitution and subordination.* Doctoral dissertation, University of California.

Macaluso, M., et al. (2007). Efficacy of the male latex condom and the female polyurethane condom as barriers to semen during intercourse: A randomized clinic trial. *American Journal of Epidemiology, 166,* 88–96.

MacKay, J. (2001). Global sex: Sexuality and sexual practices around the world. *Sexual and Relationship Therapy, 16,* 71–82.

MacKellar, D. A., Vallery, L. A., Secura, G. M., Betha, S., Bingham, T., Celentano, D., Koblin, B. A., Lalota, M., MacFarland, W., Shehan, D., Thiede, H., Torian, L. V., Janssen, R. S., & Young Men's Survey Study Group. (2002). Unrecognized HIV infection, risk behaviors, and perceptions of risk among young men who have sex with men: Opportunities for advancing HIV prevention in the third decade of HIV/AIDS. *Journal of Acquired Immune Deficiency Syndromes, 38,* 603–614.

Mackey, R. A., & O'Brien, B. A. (1999). Adaptation in lasting marriages. *Families in Society: The Journal of Contemporary Human Services, 80*(6), 587–602.

Mackey, T., Sereika, S. M., Weissfeld, L. A., Hacker, S. S., Zender, J. F., & Heard, S. L. (1992). Factors associated with long-term depressive symptoms of sexual assault victims. *Archives of Psychiatric Nursing, 6*(1), 10–25.

Mah, K., & Binik, Y. M. (2001). The nature of human orgasm: A critical review of major trends. *Clinical Psychology Review, 21*(6), 823–856.

Mah, K., & Binik, Y. M. (2002). Do all orgasms feel alike? Evaluating a two-dimensional model of the orgasm experience across gender and sexual context. *Journal of Sex Research, 39*(2), 104–113.

Maine killer's use of sex-offender list. (2006, April 18). *New York Times,* p. A19.

Major, B., Cozzarelli, C., Cooper, I., et al. (2000). Psychological responses of women after first-trimester abortion. *Archives of General Psychiatry, 47,* 777–784.

Malamuth, N. M., Addison, T., & Koss, M. (2001). Pornography and sexual aggression: Are there reliable effects? *Annual Review of Sex Research, 11,* 26–91.

Malamuth, N. M., Sockloskie, R. J., Koss, M. P., & Tanaka, J. S. (1991). Characteristics of aggressors against women: Testing a model using a national sample of college students. *Journal of Consulting and Clinical Psychology, 59,* 670–781.

Manlove, J., Ryan, S., & Franzetta, K. (2003). Patterns of contraceptive use within teenagers first sexual relationship. *Perspectives on Sexual and Reproductive Health, 35,* 246–255.

Mansergh, G., Colfax, G. N., Marks, G., Rader, M., Guzman, R., & Buchbinder, S. (2001). The Circuit Party Men's Health Survey: Findings and implications for gay and bisexual men. *American Journal of Public Health, 91,* 953–958.

March of Dimes. (2008). C-section: Medical reason. Available: http://www.marchofdimes.com/pnhec/240_1031.asp (Last visited 11/24/08).

Marchbanks, P. A., McDonald, J. A., Wilson, H. G., Folder, S. G., et al. (2002). Oral contraceptives and the risk of breast cancer. *New England of Medicine, 346*(26), 2025–2032.

Marchbanks, P. A., McDonald, J. A., Wilson, H. G., et al. (2002). Oral contraceptives and the risk of breast cancer. *New England Journal of Medicine, 346,* 2025–2032.

Marchione, M. (2008, February 13). Study backs "watchful waiting" for men with prostate cancer. *Indianapolis Star,* p. A3.

Marcofty, J. (2007, May 6). Love at first site. Available: http://www.sunjournal.com/story/210883-3/bsection/Love_at_first_site (Last visited: 11/28/08).

Margolies, L., Becher, M., & Jackson-Brewer, K. (1988). Internalized homophobia: Identifying and treating the oppressor within. In Boston Lesbian Psychologies Collective (Eds.), *Lesbian psychologies.* Urbana: University of Illinois Press.

Marks, G., Crepaz, N., & Janssen, R. (2006). Estimating sexual transmission of HIV from persons aware and unaware that they are infected with the virus in the USA. *AIDS, 20,* 1447–1450.

Marmor, J. (Ed.). (1980a). *Homosexual behavior.* New York: Basic Books.

Marmor, J. (1980b). The multiple roots of homosexual behavior. In J. Marmor (Ed.), *Homosexual behavior.* New York: Basic Books.

Marrazzo, J. M., Coffey, P., & Bingham, A. (2005). Sexual practices, risk perception, and knowledge of sexually transmitted disease risk among lesbian and bisexual women. *Perspectives on Sexual and Reproductive Health, 37*(1), 6–12.

Marshall, D. (1971). Sexual behavior on Mangaia. In D. Marshall & R. Suggs (Eds.), *Human sexual behavior.* New York: Basic Books.

Marshall, W. L. (1993). The role of attachments, intimacy, and loneliness in the etiology and maintenance of sexual offending. *Sexual and Marital Therapy, 8,* 109–121.

Marshall, W. L., Marshall, L. E., & Serran, G. A. (2006). Strategies in the treatment of paraphilias: A critical review. *Annual Review of Sex Research, 17,* 162–182.

Marston, C., & Cleland, J. (2003). Relationships between contraception and abortion: A review of the evidence. *International Family Planning Perspectives, 29,* 6–13.

Martin, E. K., Taft, T. T., & Resick, P. A. (2007). A review of marital rape. *Aggression and Violent Behavior, 12,* 3329–3347.

Martin, J. A., Hamilton, B. E., Sutton, P. D., Ventura, S. J., Menacker, F., & Munson, M. L. (2003, December 17). Births: Final data for 2002. *National Vital Statistics Reports, 10,* 1–113.

Martin J. A., Hamilton, B. E., Sutton, P. D., et al. (2005). Births: Final data for 2003. *National Vital Statistics Reports, 54*(2). Hyattsville, MD: National Center for Health Statistics, 2003. Available: http://www.cdc.gov/nchs/data/nvsr/nvsr54/nvsr54_02.pdf (Last visited 6/9/08).

Martin, S. J., Martin, J. A., Curtin, S. C., et al. (2001). Births: Final data for 1999. *National Vital Statistics Reports, 49*(1).

Masaro, C. L., Dahinten, V. S., Johnson, J., Ogilvie, G., & Partrick, D. M. (2008). Perceptions of sexual partner safety. *Sexually Transmitted Diseases, 35,* 566–571.

Mason, T. H., Foster, S. E., Finlinson, H. A,. Morrow, K. M., Rosen, R., Vining, S., et al. (2003). Perspectives related to the potential use of vaginal microbicides among drug-involved women: Focus groups in three cities in the United States and Puerto Rico. *AIDS and Behavior, 7,* 339–351.

Masters, W. H., & Johnson, V. E. (1966). *Human sexual response.* Boston: Little, Brown.

Masters, W. H., & Johnson, V. E. (1970). *Human sexual inadequacy.* Boston: Little, Brown.

Masters, W. H., & Johnson, V. E. (1974). *The pleasure bond.* Boston: Little, Brown.

Masters, W. H., Johnson, V., & Kolodny, R. C. (1992). *Human sexuality* (3rd ed.). New York: HarperCollins.

Matarazzo, H. (2004, December 14). Out, proud, and honest. *The Advocate,* p. 924. Available: http://www.advocate.com (Last visited 5/17/06).

Matich-Maroney, J., Boyle, P. S., & Crocker, M. M. (2007). Meeting the challenge: Providing comprehensive sexuality services to people with intellectual disabilities. In A. F. Owens & M. S. Tepper (Eds.), *Sexual health: Physical conditions.* Westport, CT: Praeger.

Matteson, D. (1997). Bisexual and homosexual behavior and HIV risk among Chinese-, Filipino-, and Korean-American men. *Journal of Sex Research, 34,* 93–104.

Mautner Project. (2005). Harris Interactive Poll: New national survey shows financial concerns and lack of adequate health insurance are top causes for delay by lesbians in obtaining health care. Available: http://www.mautnerproject.org.bluenile.doceus.com/programs_and_services (Last visited 1/16/06).

Maxmen, J., & Ward, N. (1995). *Essential psychopathology and its treatment* (2nd ed.). New York: Norton.

Mayers, L. B., Judelson, D. A., Moriarty, B. W., & Rundell, K. W. (2002). Prevalence of body art (body piercing and tattooing) in university undergraduates and incidence of medical complications. *Mayo Clinic Proceedings, 77,* 29–34.

Mayo Clinic. (2007a). Prostatitis. Available: http://www.mayoclinic.com/health/prostatitis/DS00341 (Last visited 10/1/08).

Mayo Clinic. (2007b). Prostatitis: Can sexual activity make it worse? Available: http://www.mayoclinic.com/health/prostatitis/AN01718 (Last visited 10/1/08).

Mayo Clinic. (2007c). Cervicitis. Available: http://www.mayoclinic.com/print/cervicitis/DS00518:METHOD-print&DSECTION=all (Last visited 10/23/08).

MayoClinic.com. (2008a). Female infertility. Available: http://www.mayoclinic.com/health./female-infertility/DS01053/DSECTION=risk-factors (Last visited 10/25/08).

MayoClinic.com. (2008b). Vaginal birth after C-section. Available: http://www.mayoclinic.com/health/vbac/VB99999/PAGE=VB00003 (Last visited 11/24/08).

Mays, V. M., Cochran, S. D., Bellinger, G., & Smith, R. G. (1992). The language of black gay men's sexual behavior: Implications for AIDS risk reduction. *Journal of Sex Research, 29*(3), 425–434.

Mazur, T., Colsman, M., & Sandberg, D. E. (2007). Intersex: Definitions, examples, gender stability, and the case against merging with transsexualism. In R. Ettner, S. Monstrey, & A. E. Eyler (Eds.), *Principles of transgender surgery* (pp. 235–254). New York: Haworth Press.

McCabe, M. P., & Taleporos. G. (2003). Sexual esteem, sexual satisfaction, and sexual behavior among people with physical disability. *Archives of Sexual Behavior, 32,* 359–369.

McCabe, M. P., & Wauchope, M. (2005). Behavioral characteristics of men accused of rape: Evidence for different types of rapists. *Archives of Sexual Behavior, 34,* 241–253.

McCabe, S. E., Brower, K. J., West, B. T., Nelson, T. F., & Wechsler, H. (2007). Trends in non-medical use of anabolic steroids by U.S. college students. *Drug and Alcohol Dependence, 90,* 243–251.

McCarthy, B., & McCarthy, E. (2003). *Rekindling desire: A step-by-step program to help low-sex and no-sex marriages.* New York: Brunner/Routledge.

McCarthy, B. W. (1998). Integrating Viagra into cognitive-behavioral couples sex therapy. *Journal of Sex Education and Therapy, 23,* 302–308.

McCollum, V. J. C. (1997). Evolution of the African American family personality: Considerations for family therapy. *Journal of Multicultural Counseling and Development, 25,* 219–229.

McConaghy, N. (1993). *Sexual behavior: Problems and management.* New York: Plenum.

McConaghy, N. (1998). Pedophilia: A review of the evidence. *Australian and New Zealand Journal of Psychiatry, 32,* 252–265.

McCormick, E., & Zamora, J. H. (2000, February 13). Slave trade still alive in U.S. *San Francisco Chronicle,* p. A1.

McCormick, N. (1996). Our feminist future: Women affirming sexuality research in the late twentieth century. *Journal of Sex Research, 33*(2), 99–102.

McDonald, A., et al. (2005). Randomized trial of cognitive-behavioral therapy for chronic posttraumatic stress disorder in adult female survivors of childhood sexual abuse. *Journal of Clinical and Consulting Psychology, 73,* 515–524.

McFadden, R. D. (2008, October 11) Gay marriage is ruled legal in Connecticut. *New York Times,* pp. A1, A17.

McKee, A. (2007). The relationship between attitudes towards women, consumption of pornography, and other demographic variables in a survey of 1,023 consumers of pornography. *International Journal of Sexual Health, 19,* 31–45.

McKinley, J., & Goodstein, L. (2008, November 6). Bans in three states on gay marriage. *New York Times,* p. A1.

McNaughton-Collins, M., Joyce, G. F., Wise, M., & Pontari, M. A. (2007). Prostastis. In M. S. Liwin & C. S. Saigal (Eds.), *Urological diseases in America.* U.S. Department of Health and Human Services. Washington, DC: U.S. Government Printing Office.

McNeill, B., Prieto, L., Niemann, Y., Pizarro, M., Vera, E., & Gomez, S. (2001). Current directions in Chicana/o psychology. *Counseling Psychologist, 29,* 5–17.

McNicholas, T., Dean, J., Mulder, H., Carnegie, C., & Jones, N. (2003). Androgyny. *British Journal of Urology International, 91,* 69–74.

McWhirter, D. (1990). Prologue. In D. McWhirter, S. A. Sanders, & J. M. Reinisch (Eds.), *Homosexuality/heterosexuality: Concepts of sexual orientation.* New York: Oxford University Press.

Mead, M. (1975). *Male and female.* New York: Morrow.

Meana, M., Binik, Y. M., Khalife, S., & Cohen, D. (1999). Psychosocial correlates of pain attributions in women with dyspareunia. *Psychosomatics, 40,* 497–502.

Mears, B. (2008). Justices: Child porn is not protected speech. Available: http://site.printthis.clickability.com/pt/cpt?action=cpt&title=Justices%3A+Child+porn (Last visited 5/19/08).

Mehl, M. R., Vazire, S., Ramírez-Esparza, N., Slatcher, R. B., & Pennebaker, J. W. (2007). Are women really more talkative than men? *Science, 317*(5834), 82–92.

Meier, C., Nguyen, T. V., Handelsman, D. J., Schindler, C., Kushnir, M. M., et al. (2008). Endogenous sex hormones and incident fracture risk in older men: The Dubbo osteoporosis epidemiology study. *Archives of Internal Medicine, 168*(1), 47–54.

Melhuus, A. (1996). Power, value and the ambiguous meaning of gender. In A. Melhuus & K. A. Stolen (Eds.), *Machos, mistresses, Madonnas: Contesting the power of Latin American gender imagery.* London: Verso.

Men can stop rape. (2000). Why should men care about violence? Available: http://www.mrpp.org/facts/menissue.html (Last visited 1/19/01).

Menorrhagia. (2005). Available: http://www.mayoclinic.com/health/menorrhagia/DS00394 (Last visited 1/2/06).

Mercer, C. H., Fenton, K. A., Johnson, A. M., Macdowall, W., Erens, B., & Wellings, K. (2005). Who reports sexual function problems? Empirical evidence from Britain's 2000 National Survey of Sexual Attitudes and Lifestyles. *Sexually Transmitted Infections, 81,* 394–399.

Mercer, C. H., Fenton, K. A., Johnson, A. M., Wellings, K., Macdowall, W., McManus, S., et al. (2003). Sexual function problems and help seeking behavior in Britain: National probability sample survey. *British Medical Journal, 327,* 426–427.

Mercer, C. H., et al. (2007). Women who report having sex with women: British national probability data on prevalence, sexual behaviors, and health outcomes. *American Journal of Public Health, 97,* 1126–1133.

Meston, C., & Buss, D. (2007). Why humans have sex. *Archives of Sexual Behavior,* 477–507.

Meston, C. M., Levin, R. J., Spiski, M. L., Hull, E. M., & Heiman, J. R. (2004). Women's orgasm. *Annual Review of Sex Research, 25,* 173–257.

Meston, C. M., & O' Sullivan, L. F. (2007). Such a tease: Intentional sexual provocation within heterosexual interactions. *Archives of Sexual Behavior, 36,* 531–542.

Meston, C. M., Rellini, A. H., & Heimans, J. (2006). Women's history of sexual abuse, their sexuality, and sexual self-schemas. *Journal of Consulting and Clinical Psychology, 74,* 229–236.

Metts, S., & Cupach, W. (1989). The role of communication in human sexuality. In K. McKinney & S. Sprecher (Eds.), *Human sexuality: The social and interpersonal context.* Norwood, NJ: Ablex.

Meyer-Bahlburg, H. F. L. (1994). Intersexuality and the diagnosis of gender identity disorder. *Archives of Sexual Behavior, 23,* 21–40.

Michael, R., Gagnon, J., Laumann, E., & Kolata, G. (1994). *Sex in America: A definitive survey.* Boston: Little, Brown.

Michaels, K. B., Xue, F., Colditz, G. A., & Willett, W. C. (2007). Induced and spontaneous abortion and incidence of breast cancer among young women. *Archives of Internal Medicine, 167,* 814–820.

Middle school to offer birth control. (2007, October, 19). *Monterey County Herald,* p. A-2.

Milhausen, R. R. (2004). *Factors that inhibit and enhance sexual arousal in college men and women.* Doctoral dissertation, Indiana University, Bloomington.

Milhausen, R. R., Crosby, R. A., & Yarber, W. L. (2008). Public opinion in Indiana regarding the vaccination of middle school students for HPV. *The Health Education Monograph, 25*(2), 21–27.

Milhausen, R. R., Yarber, W., Sanders, S., & Graham, C. (2004, November). *Factors that inhibit and enhance sexual arousal in college men and women.* Paper presented at the annual meeting of the Society for the Scientific Study of Sexuality, Orlando, FL.

Miller, J. (1995). Gender and power on the streets: Street prostitution in the era of crack cocaine. *Journal of Contemporary Ethnography, 23,* 427–452.

Miller, J., & Schwartz, M. D. (1995). Rape myths and violence against street prostitutes. *Deviant Behavior, 16*(1), 1–23.

Miller, K. S., Clark, L. F., & Moore, J. F. (1997). Sexual initiation with older male partners and subsequent HIV risk behavior among female adolescents. *Family Planning Perspectives, 29,* 212–214.

Miller, L. (2000, October 17). Panel agrees: Rethink new porn laws. *USA Today,* p. D3.

Millet, G. A., Flores, S. A., Marks, G., Reed, J. B., & Herbert, J. H. (2008). Circumcision status and risk of HIV and sexually transmitted infections among men who have sex with men. *Journal of the American Medical Association, 300,* 1674–1684.

Mills, J. L., & England, K. (2001). Food fortification to prevent neural tube defects. *Journal of the American Medical Association, 285,* 3022.

Milne, C. (2005). *Naked ambition: Women pornographers and how they are changing the sex industry.* Berkeley, CA: Pub Group West.

Milner, J., & Robertson, K. (1990). Comparison of physical child abusers, and child neglectors. *Journal of Interpersonal Violence, 5,* 37–48.

Minichiello, V., Marino, R., & Browne, J. (2000). Commercial sex between men: A prospective diary-based study. *Journal of Sex Research, 37,* 151–160.

Mohler-Kuo, M., Dowdall, G. W., Koss, M., & Wechsler, H. (2004). Correlates of rape while intoxicated in a national sample of college women. *Journal of Studies on Alcohol, 65,* 37–45.

Money, J. (1980). *Love and love sickness: The science of sex, gender difference, and pair bonding.* Baltimore: Johns Hopkins University Press.

Money, J. (1981). Paraphilias: Phyletic origins of erotosexual dysfunction. *International Journal of Mental Health, 10,* 75–109.

Money, J. (1984). Paraphilias: Phenomenology and classification. *American Journal of Psychotherapy, 38,* 164–179.

Money, J. (1990). Forensic sexology: Paraphilic serial rape (biastophilia) and lust murder (erotophonophilia). *American Journal of Psychotherapy, 44*(1), 26–37.

Montagu, A. (1986). *Touching* (3rd ed.). New York: Columbia University Press.

Montgomery, J. P., Mokotoff, E. D., Gentry, A. C., & Blair, J. M. (2003). The extent of bisexual behavior in the HIV-infected men and implications for transmission to their female partners. *AIDS Care, 15,* 829–837.

Monroe, J. (1997). Roofies: Horror drug of the '90s. *Current Health, 2,*(24), 24–33.

Monto, M. A. (2001). Prostitution and fellatio. *Journal of Sex Research, 38,* 140–145.

Moore, K., & Smith, K. (2003). Policies needed to increase awareness of emergency contraception. *SIECUS Report, 31*(2), 9–12.

Morgan, R. (2002, November 29). Bisexual students face tension with gay groups. *The Chronicle of Higher Education,* p. A31.

Morley, J. E., Kaiser, P. E., Perry, M. H., et al. (1997). Longitudinal changes in testosterone, luteinizing hormone and follicle-stimulating hormone in healthy older men. *Metabolism, 46,* 410–413.

Morris, J. F., Balsam, K. F., & Rothblum, E. D. (2002). Lesbian and bisexual mothers and nonmothers: Demographic and the coming-out process. *Developmental Psychology, 16,* 144–156.

Morrow, M. (2002). Rational local therapy for breast cancer. *New England Journal of Medicine, 347,* 1270–1271.

Morse, E. V., Simon, P. M., Balson, P. M., & Osofsky, H. J. (1992). Sexual behavior patterns of customers of male street prostitutes. *Archives of Sexual Behavior, 21,* 347–357.

Moser, C. (2001). Paraphilia: A critique of a confused concept. In P. J. Kleinplatz (Ed.), *New directions in sex therapy: Innovations and alternatives.* Philadelphia: Brunner/Routledge.

Mosher, D. L., & Maclan, P. (1994). College men and women respond to X-rated videos intended for male or female audiences: Gender and sexual scripts. *Journal of Sex Research, 31*(2), 99–113.

Mosher, W. D., Chandra, A., & Jones, J. (2005). Sexual behaviors and selected health measures: Men and women 15–44 years of age, United States, 2002. *Advance Data from Vital Statistics,* No. 362. Hyattsville, MD: National Center for Health Statistics.

Mosher, W. D., Martinez, G. M., Chandra, A., Abma, J. C., & Wilson, S. J. (2004). Use of contraception and use of family planning services in the United States: 1982–2004. *Vital Health Statistics,* No. 350. Hyattsville, MD: National Center for Health Statistics.

Motluk, A. (2003). The big brother effect: The more older brothers you have, the more likely you are to be gay. What's going on? *New Scientist, 177,* 44–47.

Moynihan, R. (2002). The making of a disease: Female sexual dysfunction. *British Medical Journal, 326,* 45–47.

Muehlenhard, C. L., & Linton, M. A. (1987). Date rape and sexual aggression in dating situations: Incidence and risk factors. *Journal of Consulting Psychology, 34,* 186–196.

Muehlenhard, C. L., Ponch, I. G., Phelps, J. L., & Giusti, L. M. (1992). Definitions of rape: Scientific and political implications. *Journal of Social Issues, 48*(1), 23–44.

Mulick, P. S., & Wright, L. W., Jr. (2002). Examining the existence of biphobia in the heterosexual and homosexual populations. *Journal of Bisexuality, 2*(4), 45–64.

Najman, J. M., Dunne, M. P., Purdie, D. M., Boyle, F. M., & Coxeter, P. D. (2005). Sexual abuse in childhood and sexual dysfunction in adulthood: An Australian population-based study. *Archives of Sexual Behavior, 34,* 517–526.

Nakano, M. (1990). *Japanese American women: Three generations, 1890–1990.* Berkeley, CA: Mina Press.

Nanda, S. (1990). *Neither man nor woman: The Hijra of India.* Belmont, CA: Wadsworth.

National Association of People with AIDS. (2002). Get the facts on HIV . . . Latinos and HIV and AIDS. Washington, DC: Author.

The National Campaign to Prevent Teen and Unplanned Pregnancy. (n.d.). Sex and Tech: Results from a Survey of Teens and Young Adults. Available: http://www.thenationalcampaign.org/sextech/. (Last visited 6/17/09).

National Cancer Institute. (2002a). Questions and answers: Use of hormones after menopause. Available: http://www.cancer.gov/newscenter/estrogenplus (Last visited 4/29/03).

National Cancer Institute. (2002b). Lifetime probability of breast cancer in American women. Available: http://cis.nci.nih.gov/fact/5_6.htm (Last visited 5/3/03).

National Cancer Institute. (2002c). What you need to know about cancer of the cervix. Available: http://cancer.gov/cancerinfo/wyntk/cervix (Last visited 5/3/03).

National Cancer Institute. (2004). Understanding prostate changes: A health guide for men. Available: http://www.cancer.gov/cancertopics/understanding-prostate-changes (Last visited 12/29/05).

National Cancer Institute. (2005). What you need to know about prostate cancer. Available: http://www.cancer.gov/cancertopics/wyntk/prostate (Last visited 9/26/08).

National Cancer Institute. (2007). What you need to know about breast cancer. Available: http://www.cancer.gov/cancertopics/wyntk/breast (Last visited 9/22/08).

National Center for Environmental Health. (1995). Smoking men at risk for erectile dysfunction. *Contemporary Sexuality, 29*(2), 8.

National Center for Health Statistics. (2005). Sexual behavior and selected health measures: Men and women 15–44 years of age, United States, 2002. Available: http://www.cdc.gov/nchs/products/pubs/pubd/ad/361-370/ad362.htm (Last visited 1/26/06).

National Center for Health Statistics. (2007). Health, United States, 2007. Available: http://www.cdc.gov/nchs/hus.htm (Last visited 10/14/08).

National Center for Health Statistics. (2008). NCHS data on teenage pregnancy. Available: http://www.cdc.gov/nchs/data/infosheets/infosheet_teen_preg.htm (Last visited 3/1/09).

National Coalition of Anti-Violence Programs. (2008). *Anti-lesbian, gay, bisexual and transgender violence in 2007.* New York: National Coalition.

National Institute of Allergy and Infectious Diseases. (2008). HIV infection and AIDS: An overview. Available: http://www.niaid.nih.gov/factsheets/hivibnf.htm (Last visited 11/14/08).

National Institute of Child Health and Human Development. (2004). NICHHD Study finds no association between oral contraceptive use and breast cancer for women from 35 to 64. Available: http://www.nichd.nih.gov/new/releases/contraceptive_use.cfm (Last visited 8/22/04).

National Institute of Child Health and Human Development. (2007). Fast facts about endometriosis. Available: http://www.nichd.nih.gov/publications/pubs/endometriosis/index/cfm (Last visited 9/30/08).

National Institute of Mental Health. (2007). Eating disorders. Available: http://www.nimh.nih.gov/health/publications/eating-disorders/complete-publication.shtml (Last visited 9/12/08).

National Institute on Aging. (2002). Sexuality in later life. Available http://www.niapublication.org/engagepages/sexuality.asp (Last visited 1/11/06).

National Institute on Aging. (2003). Hormones after menopause. Available: http://www.niapublications.org/engagepages/hormonesafter.asp (Last visited 12/28/05).

National Institute on Aging. (2005). Menopause. Available: http://www.niapublication.org/engagepages/menopause.asp (Lasted visited 1/4/06).

National Institute on Aging. (2006). Hormones and menopause: Tips from the National Institute on Aging. Available: http://niapublications.org/tipsheets/hormones.asp (Last visited 7/10/08).

National Institute on Aging. (2008a). Can we prevent aging? Available: http://www.nia.nih.gov/HealthInformation/Publications/preventaging.htm (Last visited 7/8/08).

National Institute on Aging. (2008b). Sexuality in later life. Available: http://www.nia.nih.gov/HealthInformation/Publications/sexuality.htm (Last visited 9/16/08).

National Institutes of Health. (1997). Arthritis: What we know today. Available: http://www.niams.nih.gov/ne/reports/sci_wrk/1997/lappin.htm (Last visited 5/2/03).

National Institutes of Health. (2002a). News release: Multiples born to older moms fare same as or better than those born to younger moms. Available: http://www.nih.gov/news/pr/sep2002/nichd10.htm (Last visited 11/30/02).

National Institutes of Health. (2002b). News release: Undersize infants score higher on IQ tests if breastfed exclusively. Available: http://www.nih.gov/news/pr/mar2002/nichd-20.htm (Last visited 11/30/02).

National Institutes of Health. (2002c). Postmenopausal hormone therapy: Questions and answers. Available: http://www.nhlbi.nih.gov/health/women/q_a.htm (Last visited 4/26/03).

National Institutes of Health. (2005). Facts about menopausal hormone therapy. Available: http://www.nhlbi.nih.gov/health/women/pht_facts (Last visited 6/7/06).

National Institutes of Health. (2007). News release: Effect of hormone therapy on risk of heart disease may vary by age and years since menopause. Available: http://www.nih.gov/news/pr/apr2007/nhlbi-03.htm (Last visited 7/10/08).

National Institutes of Health. (2008). WHI follow-up study confirms health risks of long-term combination hormone therapy outweigh benefits for postmenopausal women. Available: http://public/nhlbi.nih.gov/newsroom/home/GetPressRelease.aspx?id=2554 (Last visited 7/10/08).

National Institutes of Health. (n.d.). Frequently asked questions about the estrogen-alone findings. Available: http://www.whi.org/faq/faq_ealone.php (Last visited 6/7/06).

National Organization for Victim Assistance. (1992). *Community crisis response team training manual.* Washington, DC: Author.

National Osteoporosis Foundation. (2005). Fast facts. Available: http://www.nof.org/osteoporosis/diseasefacts.htm (Last visited 12/28/05).

National Victim Center. (1995). Posttraumatic stress disorder (PTSD). Available: http://www.nvc.org/ns-search/infolink/INF . . . ch-set\35060\s7g.060c7b&-NS-doc-offset+38& (Last visited 3/10/98).

National Victim Center. (1997a). Male rape. Available: http://www.nvc.org/ns-search/infolink/INF . . . ch-set=\35060\s7g.060c7b&-NS-doc-offset=0& (Last visited 3/10/98).

National Victim Center. (1997b). Incest. Available: http://www.nvc.org/ns-search/infolink/INF . . . ch-set\35060\s7g.060c7b&NS-doc-offset=1& (Last visited 3/10/98).

National Victim Center and Crime Victims Research and Treatment Center. (1992). *Rape in America: A report to the nation.* Charleston, SC: Author.

National Vulvodynia Association. (2008). What is vulvodynia? Available: http://www.nva/org/about_vulvodynia/what_is_vulvodynia.html (Last visited 9/30/08).

National Women's Health Information Center. (2002a). Health information for minority women. Available: http://www.4women.gov/minority/index.html (Last visited 3/3/00).

National Women's Health Information Center. (2002b). Douching. Available: http://www.4woman.gov/faq/douching (Last visited 11/4/05).

National Women's Health Information Center. (2002c). Pelvic inflammatory disease. Available: http://www.gov/faq/stdpids.html (Last visited 12/20/05).

National Women's Health Information Center. (2005). Lesbian health. Available: http://www.4woman.gov/faq/lesbian.htm (Last visited 1/16/06).

Navarro, M. (2004, July 11). Conservative agenda is curtailing sexual health and research, experts Say. *New York Times,* p. 12.

Nelson, A. L. (2000). Whose pill is it, anyway? *Family Planning Perspectives, 32,* 89–90.

Nelson, A. L. (2005). Extended-cycle oral contraception: A new option for routine use. *Treatments in Endocrinology, 4*(3), 139–145.

Nemoto, T., Iwmoto, M., Wong, S., Le, M. N., & Operario, D. (2004). Social factors related to risk for violence and sexually transmitted infections/HIV among Asian massage parlor workers in San Francisco. *AIDS and Behavior, 8,* 475–483.

Ness, R. B., Richter, H. E., Montagno, A., Sweet, R. L., Schubeck, D., Bass, D. C., et al. (2004). Condom use and the risk of recurrent pelvic inflammatory disease, chronic pelvic pain, or infertility following an episode of pelvic inflammatory disease. *American Journal of Public Health, 94*(4), 1327–1329.

New Hampshire to allow gay marriages. (2009, June 4). *USA Today,* p. 34.

New pill to eliminate menstrual periods. (2006). *American Journal of Sexuality Education, 47*(1), 6.

Niccolai, L. M., Farley, T. A., Ayoub, M. A., Magnus, M. K., & Kissinger, P. J. (2002). HIV-infected persons' knowledge of their sexual partners' HIV status. *AIDS Education and Prevention, 14,* 183–189.

Nichols, M. (1987). Lesbian sexuality: Issues and developing theory. In Boston Lesbian Psychologies Collective (Ed.), *Lesbian psychologies: Explorations and challenges.* Urbana: University of Illinois Press.

Nichols, M. (1988). Bisexuality in women: Myths, realities, and implications for therapy. Special issue: Women and sex therapy. *Women and Therapy, 7,* 235–252.

Nicolosi, A., Laumann, E. O., Glasser, D. B., Moreira, E., Paik, A., & Gingell, C. (2004). Sexual behavior and sexual dysfunctions after age 40: The global study of sexual attitudes and behaviors. *Urology, 64,* 991–997.

Nicolosi, A., Moreiba, E., Shirai, J., Bin Mohd Tambi, M., & Glasser, D. (2003). Epidemiology of erectile dysfunction in four countries: Cross-national study of the prevalence and correlates of erectile dysfunction. *Urology, 61,* 201–206.

Noar, S. (2008). Behavioral interventions to reduce HIV-related sexual risk behavior: Review and synthesis of meta-analytic evidence. *AIDS and Behavior, 3,* 335–353.

Noll, J. G., Trickett, P. K., & Putnam, F. W. (2003). A prospective investigation of the impact of childhood sexual abuse on the development of sexuality. *Journal of Consulting and Clinical Psychology, 71,* 575–586.

Noller, P., & Fitzpatrick, M. A. (1991). Marital communication. In A. Booth (Ed.), *Contemporary families: Looking forward, looking back.* Minneapolis, MN: National Council on Family Relations.

North American Menopause Society. (2006). *Menopause guidebook* (6th ed.). Available: http://www.menopause.org (Last visited 7/10/08).

Nusbaum, M., Hamilton, C., & Lenahan, B. (2003). Chronic illness and sexual functioning. *American Family Physician, 67,* 347–354.

Nusbaum, M. R. (2002). Erectile dysfunction: Prevalence, etiology, and major risk factors. *Journal of the American Osteopathic Association, 102*(Suppl. 4), S1–S56.

Oakley, A. (1985). *Sex, gender, and society* (Rev. ed.). New York: Harper & Row.

O'Brien, P., Wyatt, K., & Dimmock, P. (2000). Premenstrual syndrome is real and treatable. *The Practitioner, 244,* 185–189.

O'Donnell, L., Stueve, A., Agronick, G., Wilson-Simmons, R., Duran, R., & Jeanbaptiste, V. (2005). Saving sex for later: An evaluation of a parent education intervention. *Perspectives on Sexual and Reproductive Health, 37*(4). Available: http://www.guttmacher.org/journals/toc/psrh3704toc.html (Last visited 1/17/06).

Office of the Surgeon General. (2001). The Surgeon General's Report on Sexual Behavior. Available: http://www.surgeongeneral.gov/library/sexualhealth/ (Last visited 3/1/03).

Okami, P. (2002). Dear diary: A useful but imperfect method. In M. W. Wiederman & B. E. Whitley (Eds.), *Handbook for conducting research on human sexuality.* Mahwah, NJ: Erlbaum.

Okazaki, S. (2002). Influences of culture on Asian Americans' sexuality. *Journal of Sex Research, 39*(1), 34–41.

Okonofua, F. E., Larsen, U., Oronsaye, F., Snow, R. C., & Slanger, T. E. (2002). The association between female genital cutting and correlates of sexual and gynaecological morbidity in Edo State, Nigeria. *Journal of Obstetrics and Gynaecology, 109,* 1089–1096.

Olivennes, F. (2005). Do children born after assisted reproductive technology have a higher incidence of birth defects? *Fertility and Sterility, 84*(5), 1325–1326.

Ostovich, J. M., & Sabini, J. (2005). Timing of puberty and sexuality in men and women. *Archives of Sexual Behavior, 34*(2), 197–207.

Ostrow, D. E., et al. (2002). Attitudes towards highly active antiretroviral therapy are associated with sexual risk taking among HIV-infected and uninfected homosexual men. *AIDS, 16,* 775–780.

O'Sullivan, C. S. (1991). Acquaintance gang rape on campus. In A. Parrot & L. Bechhofer (Eds.), *Acquaintance rape: The hidden crime.* New York: Wiley.

Ott, M. A., Adler, N. E., Millstein, S. G., Tschann, J. M., & Ellen, J. M. (2002). The trade-off between hormonal contraceptives and condoms among adolescents. *Perspectives on Sexual and Reproductive Health, 24,* 6–14.

Owens, A. F., & Tepper, M. S. (2007). Chronic conditions and disability. In A. F. Owens & M. S. Tepper (Eds.), *Sexual health: Physical conditions.* Westport, CT: Praeger.

Padian, N. S., Shiboski, J. N., & Jewell, N. P. (1991). Female-to-male transmission of human immunodeficiency virus. *Journal of the American Medical Association, 266*, 1664–1669.

Padilla, E. R., & O'Grady, K. E. (1987). Sexuality among Mexican Americans: A case of sexual stereotyping. *Journal of Personality and Social Psychology, 52*, 5–10.

Padma-Nathan, H., Eardley, I., Kloner, R. A., Laties, A. M., & Montorsi, F. (2002). A 4-year update on the safety of sildenafil citrate (Viagra). *Urology, 60*(S2), 67–90.

Paolucci, E. O., Genuis, M. L., & Violato, C. (2001). A meta-analysis of the published research on the effects of child sexual abuse. *Journal of Psychology, 135*, 17–36.

Pardun, D. J., L' Engle, K. L., & Brown, J. D. (2005). Linking exposure to outcomes: Early adolescents' consumption of sexual content in six media. *Mass Communication & Society, 8*, 75–91.

Parker, R., & Gagnon, J. (Eds.). (1995). *Conceiving sexuality: Approaches to sex research in post-modern world.* New York: Routledge.

Parrinder, G. (1980). *Sex in the world's religions.* New York: Oxford University Press.

Parsons, C. (2003, July 29). Sexual consent measure is signed. *Chicago Tribune*, pp. 1, 7.

Paul, E. L., McManus, B., & Hayes, A. (2000). "Hookups": Characteristics and correlates of college students' spontaneous and anonymous sexual experiences. *Journal of Sex Research, 37*(1), 76–88.

Paul, J. P., Pollack, L., Osmond, D., & Catania, J. A. (2005). Viagra (sildenafil) use in population-based sample of U.S. men who have sex with men. *Sexually Transmitted Diseases, 32*, 531–533.

Paul, P. (2006). *Pornified: How pornography is transforming our lives, our relationships, and our families.* New York: Times Books.

Paz-Bailey, G., Koumans, E. H., Sternberg, M., Pierce, A., Papp, J., Unger, E. R., et al. (2005). The effect of correct and consistent condom use on chlamydial and gonococcal infection among urban adolescents. *Archives of Pediatric and Adolescent Medicine, 159*, 536–542.

Peplau, L. A., & Beals, K. P. (2004). The family lives of lesbians and gay men. In A. L. Vangelisti (Ed.), *Handbook of family communication.* Mahwah, NJ: Erlbaum.

Peplau, L. A., & Spaulding, L. R. (2000). The close relationships of lesbians, gay men, and bisexuals. In C. Hendrick & S. S. Hendrick (Eds.), *Close relationships: A sourcebook.* Thousand Oaks: Sage.

Perel, E. (2006). *Mating in captivity.* New York: Harper.

Perry D. G., & Bussey, K. (1979). The social learning theory of sex differences: Imitation is alive and well. *Journal of Personality and Social Psychology, 37*, 1699–1712.

Perry, J. D., & Whipple, B. (1981). Pelvic muscle strength of female ejaculators: Evidence in support of a new theory of orgasm. *Journal of Sex Research, 17*(1), 22–39.

Pertot, S. (2007). *When your sex drives don't match.* New York: Marlowe & Company.

Peters, K. (1992, October 15). Gay activists denounce NAMBLA, attempt to highlight differences. *Spartan Daily*, p. 1.

Peters, S., et al. (1986). Prevalence of child sexual abuse. In D. Finkelhor (Ed.), *Sourcebook on child sexual abuse.* Newbury Park, CA: Sage.

Peterson, Z. D., & Muehlenhard, C. L. (2007). Conceptualizing the "wantedness" or women's consensual and nonconsensual sexual experiences: Implications for how women label their experiences with rape. *Journal of Sex Research, 44*, 72–88.

Petrecca, L. (2007, December 6). That's entertainment: Marketers get inked. *USA Today*, p. 4B.

Pew Research Center. (2007). As marriage and parenthood drift apart, public is concerned about social impact. Available: http://pewresearch.org/pubs/526/marriage-parenthood (Last visited 6/30/08).

Phelan, P. (1995). Incest and its meaning: The perspectives of fathers and daughters. *Child Abuse and Neglect, 19*, 7–24.

Physicians for Reproductive Choice and Health & Guttmacher Institute. (2008). An overview of abortion in the United States. Available: http://www.guttmacher.or/presentation/abort_slides .pdf (Last visited 8/8/08).

Piercing exquisite: Aftercare for navel and nipple piercings. (1998). Available: http://www2.ba.best.com/ardvark/ac-body.html (Last visited 1/15/98).

Pinkerton, S. D., Bogart, L. M., Cecil, H., & Abramson, P. R. (2002). Factors associated with masturbation in a collegiate sample. *Journal of Psychology and Human Sexuality, 14*, 103–121.

Pinkerton, S. D., Holtgrave, D. R., & Galletly, C. L. (2008). Infections preventing by increasing HIV serostatus awareness in the United States, 2001 to 2004. *Journal of Acquired Immune Deficiency Syndromes, 47*, 354–357.

Pistole, M. C. (1995). College students' ended love relationships: Attachment style and emotion. *Journal of College Student Development, 36*(1), 53–60.

Pistole, M. C., Clark, E. M., & Tubbs, A. L. (1995). Love relationships: Attachment style and the investment model. *Journal of Mental Health Counseling, 17*(2), 199–209.

Planned Parenthood. (2008). Insurance coverage for birth control. Available: http://www.plannedparenthood.org/issues-action/ birth-control/insurance-coverage-birth-control-21018.htm (Last visited 8/6/08).

Planned Parenthood of the Mid-Hudson Valley. (2008). Fertility information and support. Available: http://www.plannedparenthood .org/mid-hudson-valley/infertility-support-information-4975.htm (Last visited 10/25/08).

Pogrebin, L. C. (1983). *Family politics.* New York: McGraw-Hill.

Pollis, C. A. (1988). An assessment of the impacts of feminism on sexual science. *Journal of Sex Research, 25*(1), 85–105.

Pope, H. G., Ionescu-Pioggia, M., & Pope, K. W. (2001). Drug use and life style among college undergraduates: A 3-year longitudinal study. *American Journal of Psychiatry, 158*, 1519–1521.

Porn to spice up cell phones. (2008). Available: http: news.zdent .com/2100-9588_22-6228443.html?tage=rbxccndzdl1 (Last visited 6/10/08).

Portelli, C. J., & Meade, C. W. (1998, October/November). Censorship and the Internet: No easy answers. *SIECUS Report.* Available: http://www.siecus.org/pubs/orpt/articles/arti0001.html (Last visited 11/30/00).

Potterat, J. J., Rothenberg, R. B., Muth, S. Q., Darrow, W. W., & Phillips-Plummer, L. (1998). Pathways to prostitution: The chronology of sexual and drug abuse milestones. *Journal of Sex Research, 35*(4), 333–340.

Potterat, J. J., Woodhouse, D. E., Muth, J. B., & Muth, S. Q. (1990). Estimating the prevalence and career longevity of prostitute women. *Journal of Sex Research, 27*, 233–243.

Powell, E. (1996). *Sex on your own terms.* Minneapolis, MN: CompCare.

Prause, N., & Graham, C. A. (2007). Asexuality: Classification and characterization. *Archives of Sexual Behavior, 36*, 341–356.

Price, M., Kafka, M., Commons, M. L., Gutheil, T. G., & Simpson, W. (2002). Telephone scatologia—comorbidity with other paraphilias and paraphilia-related disorders. *International Journal of Law and Psychiatry, 25*, 37–49.

Pritchard, J. (2007, November). Herbal substitutes for Viagra can be harmful to some. *Indianapolis Star*, p. 12.

Prostate screenings gain acceptance. (2000, December 4). *USA Today*, p. D8.

Prostitution. *Wikipedia*. Available: http://en.wikipedia/org/wiki/ Prostitution (Last visited 4/7/06).

Puente, S., & Cohen, D. (2003). Jealousy and the meaning (or non-meaning) of violence. *Personality and Social Psychology Bulletin, 29*, 449–460.

Putnam, F. W. (2003). Ten-year research update review: Child sexual abuse. *Journal of the American Academy of Child and Adolescent Psychiatry, 42*, 269–278.

Qaseem, A., et al. (2007). Screening mammography for women 40 to 49 years of age: Clinical practice guidelines from the American College of Physicians. *Annals of Internal Medicine, 146*, 511–515.

Quatrella, L., & Wentworth, K. K. (1995). Students' perceptions of unequal status dating relationships in academia. *Ethics & Behavior, 5*(3), 249–259.

Queen, C. (2000, November 19). Sex in the city. *San Francisco Chronicle*, pp. 1, 4.

Quinn, T. C., Wawer, M. J., Sewankambo, N., Serwadda, D., Chuanjun, L., Wabwire-Mangen, F., et al. (2000). Viral load and heterosexual transmission of human immunodeficiency virus type 1. *New England Journal of Medicine, 342*, 921–929.

Raffaelli, M., & Ontai, L. L. (2004). Gender socialization in Latino/a families: Results from two retrospective studies. *Sex Roles, 50*, 287–299.

Raffle, A. E., Alden, B., Quinn, M., Babb, P. J., & Brett, M. J. (2003). Outcomes of screening to prevent cancer: Analysis of cumulative incidence of cervical abnormality and modelling of cases and deaths prevented. *British Medical Journal, 326*, 901–906.

Rahman, M., Da Vanzo, J., & Razzaque, A. (2001). Do better family planning services reduce abortion in Bangladesh? *The Lancet, 358*, 1051–1056.

Ramanowicz, M., Shinozaki, G., Passov, V., Kung, S., Alarcon, R., & Mrazek, D. (2009). Psychological impact of child abuse. *Science Daily*. Available: http://www.sciencedaily.com/releases/2009/ 05/090521112831.htm. (Last visited 6/15/09).

Randall, H. E., & Byers, E. S. (2003). What is sex? Students' definitions of having sex, sexual partner, and unfaithful sexual behavior. *Canadian Journal of Human Sexuality, 12*, 87–96.

Rankow, E. (1997). Primary medical care of the gay and lesbian patient. *North Carolina Medical Journal, 58*, 92–97.

Rape, Abuse, and Incest National Network. (2006). Statistics. Available: http://www.rainn.org/statistics/index.html (Last visited 3/31/06).

Rape, Abuse, and Incest National Network. (2008a). How often does sexual assault occur? Available: http://www.rainn.org/get-information/ statistics/frequency-of-sexual-assault (Last visited 7/31/08).

Rape, Abuse, and Incest National Network. (2008b). Drug-facilitated assault. Available: http://www.rainn.org/get-information/types-of -sexual-assault/drug-facilitated-assault (Last visited 7/31/08).

Rape, Abuse, and Incest National Network. (2008c). Acquaintance rape. Available: http://www.rainn.org/get-information/types-of -sexual-assault/acquaintance-rape (Last visited 7/31/08).

Rape, Abuse, and Incest National Network. (2008d). Effects of sexual assault. Available: http://www.rainn.org/get-information/effects -of-sexual assault (Last visited 7/31/08).

Rape, Abuse, and Incest National Network. (2008e) Male sexual assault. Available: http://www.rain.org/get-information/types-of-sexual-assault/male-sexual assault (Last visited 7/31/08).

Rape Network. (2000). Rape is a crime of silence. Available: http:// www.rapenetwork.com/whatisrape.html (Last visited 11/16/00).

Rathus, S. A., Nevid, J. S., & Fichner-Rathus L. (2002). *Human sexuality: A world of diversity*. Boston: Allyn & Bacon.

Rathus, S. A., Nevid, J. S., & Fichner-Rathus, L. (2005). *Human sexuality in a world of diversity* (6th ed.). Boston: Allyn & Bacon.

Ratner, P. A., Johnson, J. L., Shoveller, J. A., Chan, K., Martindale, S. L., Schilder, A. J., et al. (2003). Nonconsensual sex experienced by men who have sex with men: Prevalence and association with mental health. *Patient Education and Counseling, 49*, 67–74.

Ravdin, P. M., et al. (2007). The decrease in breast-cancer incidence in 2003 in the United States. *New England Journal of Medicine, 356*, 1670–1674.

Redoute, J., Stoleru, S., Gregoire, M. C., Costes, N., Cinotti, L., Lavenne, F., et al. (2000). Brain processing of visual sexual stimuli in human males. *Human Brain Mapping, 11*, 343–350.

Reece, R. (1988). Special issues in the etiologies and treatments of sexual problems among gay men. *Journal of Homosexuality, 15*, 43–57.

Reece, M., Herbenick, D., Sanders, S. A., Dodge, B., Ghassemi, A., & Fortenberry, J. D. (2009). Prevalence and characteristics of vibrator use by men in the United States. *Journal of Sexual Medicine, 6*, 1867–1874.

Reefhuis, J., Honein, M. A., Schieve, L. A., Correa, A., et al. (2008). Assisted reproductive technology and major structural birth defects in the United States. *Human Reproduction*. Available: http:// humrep.oxfordjournals.org/cgi/reprint/den387v3 (Last visited 11/22/08).

Regan, P. C., Shen, W., De La Pena, E., & Gossett, E. (2007). "Fireworks exploded in my mouth": Affective responses before, during, and after the very first kiss. *International Journal of Sexual Health, 19*(2), 1–16.

Reimers, S. (2007). The BBC Internet study: General methodology. *Archives of Sexual Behavior, 36*, 147–161.

Reiner, W. G. (2005, May 31). Declaring with clarity: When gender is ambiguous. *New York Times*, p. D-2.

Reiner, W. G., & Gearhart, J. P. (2004). Discordant sexual identity in some genetic males with cloacal exstrophy assigned to female sex at birth. *New England Journal of Medicine, 350*, 333–341.

Reinholtz, R. K., & Muehlenhard, C. L. (1995). Genital perceptions and sexual activity in a college population. *Journal of Sex Research, 32*(2), 155–165.

Reiss, I. (1967). *The social context of premarital sexual permissiveness*. New York: Irvington.

Reiss, I. (1980). A multivariate model of the determinants of extramarital sexual permissiveness. *Journal of Marriage and Family, 42*, 395–411.

Reiss, I. (1989). Society and sexuality: A sociological explanation. In K. McKinney & S. Sprecher (Eds.), *Human sexuality: The societal and interpersonal context*. Norwood, NJ: Ablex.

Reitman, V. (2004, September 12). Viagra users are getting younger and younger. *Indianapolis Star*, pp. J1, J4.

Renshaw, D. C. (1988a). Short-term therapy for sexual dysfunction: Brief counseling to manage vaginismus. *Clinical Practice in Sexuality, 6*(5), 23–39.

Renshaw, D. C. (1988b). Young children's sex play: Counseling the parents. *Medical Aspects of Human Sexuality, 22*(12), 68–72.

Resolve. (2002). Infertility myths and facts. Available: http://www .resolve.org/main/national/coping/demystify/mythfact.htm (Last visited 5/21/03).

Restrictions on minors' access to abortion. (2001). NARAL Foundation. Available: http://www.naral.org/mediasources/fact/ pdfs/restrictions.pdf (Last visited 5/12/03).

Reuters. (2005). Education persuades young women to avoid douching. Available: http://www.nlm.nig.gov/medlineplus/news/fullstory_28864.html (Last visited 1/2/06).

Reynolds, A., & Caron, S. L. (2000). How intimate relationships are impacted when heterosexual men crossdress. *Journal of Psychology and Human Sexuality, 12,* 63–77.

Rhodes, J. C., Kjerulff, K. H., Langenberg, P. A., & Guzinski, G. M. (1999). Hysterectomy and sexual functioning. *Journal of the American Medical Association, 282,* 1934–1941.

Rich, F. (2001, May 20). Naked capitalists. *New York Times Magazine,* pp. 50–56, 80, 82, 92.

Richards, K. (1997). What is a transgenderist? In B. Bullough, V. L. Bullough, & J. Elias (Eds.), *Gender blending.* New York: Prometheus Books.

Richardson, C. B., Resnick, P. J., Hansen, D. L., Derry, H. A., & Rideout, V. J. (2002). Does pornography-blocking software block access to health information on the Internet? *Journal of the American Medical Association, 288,* 2887–2894.

Richtel, M., & Marriott, M. (2005, September 17). Ring tones, cameras, now this: Sex is latest cellphone feature. *New York Times,* p. A1.

Richters, J., de Visser, R., Rissel, C., & Smith, A. (2006). Sexual practices at last heterosexual encounter and occurrence of orgasm in a national survey. *Journal of Sex Research, 48*(3), 217–226.

Rickert, V. I., Sanghvi, R., & Wiemann, C. M. (2002). Is lack of sexual assertiveness among adolescent and young adult women a cause for concern? *Perspectives on Sexual and Reproductive Health, 34,* 178–183.

Rickert, V. I., & Wiemann, C. M. (1998). Date rape among adolescents and young adults. *Journal of Pediatric and Adolescent Gynecology, 11,* 167–175.

Rideout, V. (2007). Parents, children and media: A Kaiser Family Foundation survey. Available: http://kff.or/entmedia/upload/7638.pdf (Last visited 1/10/08).

Ridley, C. A., Cate, R. M., Collins, D. M., Reesing, A. L., Lucero, A. A., Gilson, M. S., & Almeida, D. M. (2006). The ebb and flow of marital lust: A relational approach. *Journal of Sex Research, 43*(2), 144–153.

Riggs, N., Houry, D., Long, G., Markovchick, V., & Feldhaus, K. M. (2000). Analysis of 1,076 cases of sexual assault. *Annals of Emergency Medicine, 35,* 358–362.

Riscol, L. (2003). Bigger, harder, better: Natural sex enhancers or Viagra-era snake oil. *Contemporary Sexuality, 37*(1), 4–6.

Roan, S. (2005, March 3). Toxic shock returns. *Monterey County Herald,* p. A2.

Roberts, D. F. (2000). Media and youth: Access, exposure, and privatization. *Journal of Adolescent Health, 27*(2), 8–14.

Roberts, D. F., Foehr, U. G., & Rideout, V. (2005). *Generation M: Media in the lives of 8–18-year-olds.* Menlo Park, CA: Kaiser Family Foundation.

Roberts, E. (1983). Childhood sexual learning: The unwritten curriculum. In C. Davis (Ed.), *Challenges in sexual science.* Philadelphia: Society for the Scientific Study of Sex.

Robinson, P. (1976). *The modernization of sex.* New York: Harper & Row.

Robson, S. (2004, July 18). You can't do that on television! *New York Times,* sec. 2, p. 1.

Roddy, R. E., Zekeng, L., Ryan, K. A., Tamoufe, U., & Tweedy, K. G. (2002). Effect of nonoxynol-9 gel on urogenital gonorrhea and chlamydial infection. *Journal of the American Medical Association, 287,* 1117–1122.

Roesler, T. A. (October, 2000). Adult's reaction to child's disclosure of abuse will influence degree of permanent damage. *Boston University Child and Adolescent Behavior Newsletter,* pp. 1–2.

Rogers, P. (1997). Post traumatic stress disorder following male rape. *Journal of Mental Health, 6,* 5–10.

Rogler, L. H. (1999). Methodological sources of cultural insensitivity in mental health research. *American Psychologist, 54,* 424–433.

Roisman, G. I., Clausell, E., Holland, A., Fortuna, K., & Elieff, C. (2008). Adult romantic relationships as contexts of human development: A multi-method comparison of same-sex couples with opposite-sex dating, engaged, and married dyads. *Developmental Psychology, 44*(1), 91–101.

Ropelato, J. (2006). Internet pornography statistics. Available: http://internet-filter-review.toptenreviews.com/internet-pornography-statistics.html (Last visited 5/22/08).

Roscoe, W. (1991). *The Zuni man/woman.* Albuquerque: University of New Mexico Press.

Rose, S., & Sork, V. (1984a). Teaching about female sexuality: Putting women on top. *Women's Studies Quarterly, 13*(4), 19–20.

Rose, S., & Sork, V. L. (1984b). Teaching about female sexuality. *Women's Studies Quarterly, 12,* 19–22.

Rosenberg, P. S., & Biggar, R. J. (1998). Trends in HIV incidence among young adults in the United States. *Journal of the American Medical Association, 279,* 1894–1899.

Rosman, J., & Resnick, P. J. (1989). Sexual attraction to corpses: A psychiatric review of necrophilia. *Bulletin of the American Academy of Psychiatry and the Law, 17*(2), 153–163.

Ross, M. W., Essien, E. J., & Torres, I. (2006). Conspiracy beliefs about the origin of HIV/AIDS in four racial/ethnic groups. *Journal of Acquired Immune Deficiency Syndromes, 41,* 342–344.

Ross, M. W., Tikkanen, R., & Mansson, S. A. (2000). Differences between Internet samples and conventional samples of men who have sex with men: Implications for research and HIV interventions. *Social Science and Medicine, 51,* 749–758.

Ross, M. W., Timpson, S. C., Williams, M. L., Amos, C., & Bowen, A. (2007). Stigma consciousness concerns related to drug use and sexuality in a sample of street-based sex workers. *International Journal of Sexual Health, 19,* 57–65.

Rosser, S., Short, B. J., Thurmes, P. J., & Coleman, E. (1998). Anodyspareunia, the unacknowledged sexual dysfunction: A validation study of painful receptive anal intercourse and its psychosexual concomitants in homosexual men. *Journal of Sex and Marital Therapy, 24,* 281–292.

Rowan, E. L. (1988). Pedophilia. In D. Dailey (Ed.), *The sexually unusual.* New York: Harrington Park Press.

Rowan, E. L. (1989). Masturbation according to the Boy Scout handbook. *Journal of Sex Education and Therapy, 15*(2), 77–81.

Royce, C. F. (1998). Condom use by Hispanic and African-American adolescent girls who use hormonal contraception. *Journal of Adolescent Health, 23,* 205–211.

Rozas, A. (2007, September 13). U.S. sex-offender laws are called ineffective. *Chicago Tribune,* p. 3.

Rubin, L. (1990). *Erotic wars.* New York: Farrar, Straus & Giroux.

Rubin, R. (2003a, January 29). Testosterone replacement therapy faces scrutiny. *USA Today,* p. D7.

Rubin, R. (2003b, May 16). Mammograms fare well in study. *USA Today,* p. A1.

Rubin, R. (2005, April 13). FDA panel rejects silicone implants. *New York Times,* p. A3.

Rubin, R. (2007, January 27). Radiation after lumpectomy cuts recurrence. *USA Today*, p. C1.

Rudd, J. M., & Herzberger, S. D. (1999). Brother-sister incest—father-daughter incest: A comparison of characteristics and consequences. *Child Abuse and Neglect, 23,* 15–28.

Rural HIV/STD Prevention Work Group. (2009). *Tearing down fences: HIV/STD prevention in rural America.* Bloomington, IN: Rural Center for AIDS/STD Prevention.

Russell, D. (1984). *Sexual exploitation: Rape, child sexual abuse, and workplace harassment.* Newbury Park, CA: Sage.

Russell, D. E. H. (1986). *The secret trauma: Incest in the lives of girls and women.* New York: Basic Books.

Russell, D. E. H. (1990). *Rape in marriage* (Rev. ed.). Bloomington: Indiana University Press.

Rust, P. C. R. (2002). Bisexuality: The state of the union. *Annual Review of Sex Research, 13,* 180–240.

Ryan, J. (1997, October 30). A painful statement of self-identity. *San Francisco Chronicle,* p. A1.

Rye, B. J., & Meaney, G. J. (2007). Voyeurism: Is it good as long as we do not get caught? *International Journal of Sexual Health, 19,* 47–56.

Sachs-Ericsson, N., et al. (2005). Childhood sexual and physical abuse and the 1-year prevalence of medical problems in the National Comorbidity Survey. *Health Psychology, 24,* 32–40.

Sadker, D., & Zittleman, K. (2005). Gender bias lives, for both sexes. *Education Digest, 70*(8), 27–30.

Saks, B. (2000). Sex receptors: Mechanisms of drug action via biochemical receptors on sexual response of women. *Journal of Sex Education and Therapy, 25,* 33–35.

Salgado de Snyder, V. N., Cervantes, R., & Padilla, A. (1990). Gender and ethnic differences in psychosocial stress and generalized distress among Hispanics. *Sex Roles, 22*(7), 441–453.

Sampson, R. (2003). Acquaintance rape of college students. Washington, DC: U.S. Department of Justice.

Sanchez, Y. M. (1997). Families of Mexican origin. In M. K. DeGenova (Ed.), *Families in cultural context: Strengths and challenges in diversity.* Mountain View, CA: Mayfield.

Sanday, P. (1990). *Fraternity gang rape: Sex, brotherhood and privilege on campus.* New York: New York University Press.

Sanders, S., & Reinisch, J. (1999). Would you say you "had sex" if . . . ? *Journal of the American Medical Association, 281,* 275–277.

Sanders, S. A., Graham, C. A., Yarber, W. L., & Crosby, R. A. (2003). Condom use errors and problems among young women who put condoms on their male partners. *Journal of the American Medical Women's Association, 58,* 95–98.

Sanders, S. A., Reinisch, J. M., & McWhirter, D. P. (1990). Homosexuality/heterosexuality: An overview. In D. P. McWhirter, S. A. Sanders, & J. M. Reinisch (Eds.), *Homosexuality/heterosexuality: Concepts of sexual orientation.* New York: Oxford University Press.

Sandroni, P. (2001). Aphrodisiacs past and present: A historical review. *Clinical Autonomic Research, 11,* 303–307.

Santtila, P., Sandnabba, N. K., Alison, L., & Nordling, N. (2002). Investigating the underlying structure of sadomasochistically oriented behavior. *Archives of Sexual Behavior, 31,* 185–196.

Sarrel, P. M., & Masters, W. H. (1982). Sexual molestation of men by women. *Archives of Sexual Behavior, 11,* 117–131.

Satcher, D. (2001). The surgeon general's call to action to promote sexual health and responsible sexual behavior. Available: http://www.surgeongeneral.gov/library/sexualhealth/call.htm (Last visited 5/17/06).

Saunders, E. B., & Awad, G. (1991). Male adolescent sexual offenders: Exhibitionism and obscene phone calls. *Child Psychiatry and Human Development, 21*(3), 169–178.

Sauvageau, A., & Racette, S. (2006). Autoerotic deaths in the literature from 1954 to 2004: A review. *Journal of Forensic Sciences, 51,* 140–146.

Savin-Williams, R. C. (2005). The new gay teen: Shunning labels. *The Gay and Lesbian Review Worldwide.* Available: http://glreview.com/12.6-williams.php (Last visited 1/17/06).

Sawyer, S., Metz, M. E., Hinds, J. D., & Brucker, R. A. (2001–2002). Attitudes toward prostitution among males: A "Consumers' Report." *Current Psychology, 20,* 363–376.

Sax, L. (2002). How common is intersex? A response to Anne Fausto-Sterling. *Journal of Sex Research, 39*(3), 174–178.

Schackman, B., et al. (2006). The lifetime cost of current human immunodeficiency virus care in the United States. *Medical Care, 44,* 990–997.

Schardt, D. (2004, October). Sex in a bottle: The hard sell. *Nutrition Action Newsletter,* pp. 8–10.

Scheer, S., Peterson, I., Page-Shafer, K., Delgado, V., Gleghorn, A., Ruiz, J., Molitor, F., McFarland, W., Klausner, J., & Young Women's Survey Team. (2002). Sexual and drug use behavior among women who have sex with both women and men: Results of a population-based survey. *American Journal of Public Health, 92,* 1110–1112.

Schiavi, R. C., Schreiner-Engle, P., Mandeli, J., Schanzer, J., & Cohen, E. (1990). Chronic alcoholism and male sexual dysfunction. *Journal of Sex and Marital Therapy, 16*(1), 23–33.

Schlosser, E. (1997, February 10). The business of pornography. *Newsweek,* pp. 42–52.

Schmitt, D. P. (2003). Universal sex differences in the desire for sexual variety: Tests from 52 nations, 6 continents, and 13 islands. *Journal of Personality and Social Psychology, 85,* 85–104.

Schnarch, D. (2002). *Resurrecting sex.* New York: HarperCollins.

School sex education focusing on abstinence. (2000, February). *Nation's Health,* p. 24.

Schultz, G. (2005, December 16). Large increase in porn DVD sales indicates growing pornography addiction. *LifeSiteNews.com.* Available: http://www.lifesite.net/ldn/2005/dec/05121603.html (Last visited 4/6/06).

Schureurs, K. M. (1993). Sexuality in lesbian couples: The importance of gender. *Annual Review of Sex Research, 4,* 49–66.

Schwartz, J. (2007, January 27). Of gay sheep, modern science and the perils of bad publicity. *New York Times,* pp. A1, A16.

Schwartz, J. (2009, May 27). Court upholds California's ban on gay marriage. *The New York Times,* pp. A1, A20.

Schwartz, S. (2000). *Abnormal psychology: A discovery approach.* Mountain View, CA: Mayfield.

Schwimmer, B. (1997). The Dani of New Guinea. Available: http://www.umanitoba.ca/faculties/arts/anthropology/tutor/case_studies/dani/ (Last visited 11/3/05).

Scott, J., & Cuvelier, S. (1993). Violence and sexual violence in pornography: Is it really increasing? *Archives of Sexual Behavior, 22,* 357–370.

Sears, A. E. (1989). The legal case for restricting pornography. In D. Zillman & J. Bryant (Eds.), *Pornography: Research advances and policy considerations.* Hillsdale, NJ: Erlbaum.

Sedlack, A. J., & Broadhurst, D. D. (1996). *Executive Summary of the Third National Incidence Study of Child Abuse and Neglect.* Washington, DC: National Center on Child Abuse and Neglect, National Committee to Prevent Child Abuse.

Seligman, L., & Hardenberg, S. A. (2000). Assessment and treatment of paraphilias. *Journal of Counseling and Development, 78,* 107–113.

Sellers, R. M., & Shelton, J. (2003). The role of racial identity in perceived racial discrimination. *Journal of Personality and Social Psychology, 84*(5), 1079–1093.

Senn, T. E., Carey, M. P., Vanable, P. A., Coury-Doniger, & Urban, M. (2007). Characteristics of sexual abuse in childhood and adolescence influence sexual risk behavior in adulthood. *Archives of Sexual Behavior, 36,* 637–645.

Severson, K. (2003, January 8). Breast milk may help control growing appetite. *San Francisco Chronicle,* p. A8.

Sex crimes against children declining. (2008, April 17). *USA Today,* p. D8.

Shackelford, T. K., Goetz, A. T., LaMunyon, C. W., Quintus, B. J., & Weekes-Shackelford, V. A. (2004). Sex differences in sexual psychology produce sex-similar preferences for a short-term mate. *Archives of Sexual Behavior, 33,* 405–412.

Shamloul, R. (2005). Treatment of men complaining of short penis. *Urology, 65*(6), 1183–1185.

Shaver, P. (1984). *Emotions, relationships, and health.* Newbury Park, CA: Sage.

Shaver, P., Hazan, C., & Bradshaw, D. (1988). Love as attachment: The integration of three behavioral systems. In R. Sternberg & M. Barnes (Eds.), *The psychology of love.* New Haven, CT: Yale University Press.

Shelton, J. N., & Sellers, R. M. (2000). Situational stability and variability in African Americans' racial identity. *Journal of Black Psychology, 26*(1), 27–50.

Shevell, T., Malone, F. D., Vidaver, J., Porter, T. F., Luthy, D. A., Comstock, C., et al. (2005). Assisted reproductive technology and pregnancy outcomes. *Obstetrics and Gynecology, 106*(5 Pt. 1), 1039–1045.

Shilts, R. (1987). *And the band played on: Politics, people, and the AIDS epidemic.* New York: St. Martin's Press.

Shlay, J. C., McClung, M. W., Patnaik, J. L., & Douglas, J. M. (2004). Comparison of sexually transmitted disease prevalence by reported level of condom use among patients attending an urban sexually transmitted disease clinic. *Sexually Transmitted Diseases, 31*(3), 154–160.

Shon, S., & Ja, D. (1982). Asian families. In M. McGoldrick, J. K. Pearce, & J. Giordano (Eds.), *Ethnicity and family therapy.* New York: Guilford Press.

Shumaker, S. A., Legault, C., Rapp, S. R., Thal, L., Wallace, R. B., Ockene, J. K., et al. (2003). Estrogen plus progestin and the incidence of dementia and mild cognitive impairment in postmenopausal women. *Journal of the American Medical Association, 289,* 2651–2662.

SIECUS. (2001). Issues and answers: Fact sheet on sexuality education. *SIECUS Report, 29*(6).

SIECUS. (2002). Sexuality in middle and later life. Available: http://www.siecus.org/pubs/fact/fact0018.html (Last visited 12/30/02).

SIECUS. (2004). *Guidelines for comprehensive sexuality education* (3rd ed.). New York: Author.

SIECUS looks at states' sexuality laws. (1999, January 19). *SIECUS Report.* Available: http://www.siecus.org/policy/Sreport/srep0004.html (Last visited 11/30/00).

Siegel, K., & Schrimshaw, E. W. (2006). Diminished sexual activity, interest, and feelings of attractiveness among HIV-infected women in two eras of the AIDS epidemic. *Archives of Sexual Behavior, 35,* 437–449.

Sieving, R., Bearinger, L., Remafedi, G., Taylor, B. A., & Harmon, B. (1997). Cognitive and behavioral predictors of sexually transmitted disease risk behavior among sexually active adolescents. *Archives of Adolescent and Pediatric Medicine, 151,* 243–251.

Simon, R. I. (1997). Video voyeurs and the covert videotaping of unsuspecting victims: Psychological and legal consequences. *Journal of Forensic Science, 42,* 884–889.

Simons, R. L., & Whitbeck, L. B. (1991). Sexual abuse as a precursor to prostitution and victimization among adolescent and adult homeless women. *Journal of Family Issues, 12*(3), 361–380.

Simpson, J., Collins. W. A., Tran, S., & Haydon, K. (2007). Attachment and the experience and expression of emotion in romantic relationships: A developmental perspective. *Journal of Personality and Social Psychology, 92*(2), 355–367.

Simpson, V. L. (2008, April 18). Pope meets with victims of sex abuse by priests. *Indianapolis Star,* p. A12.

Simpson, W. S., & Ramberg, J. A. (1992). Sexual dysfunction in married female patients with anorexia and bulimia nervosa. *Journal of Sex and Marital Therapy, 18*(1), 44–54.

Singh, D., Meyer, W., Zambarano, R. J., & Hurlbert, D. F. (1998). Frequency and timing of coital orgasm in women desirous of becoming pregnant. *Archives of Sexual Behavior, 27*(1), 15–29.

Slater, L. (2006, February). Love: The chemical reaction. *National Geographic,* pp. 34–49.

Slater, P. (1974). *Earthwalk.* New York: Doubleday.

Slowinski, J. (2007). Sexual problems and dysfunctions of men. In A. Owens & M. Tepper (Eds.), *Sexual health: State-of-the art treatments and research.* Westport, CT: Praeger.

Smith, R. A., Saslow, D., Sawyer, K. A., Burke, W., Costanza, M. E., Evans, W. P., et al. (2003). American Cancer Society guidelines for breast cancer screening: Update 2003. *CA: A Cancer Journal for Clinicians, 53,* 141–169.

Smith, T. W., Uchino, B. N., Berg, C. A., Florsheim, P., Pearce, G., Hawkins, M., Hopkins, P. N., & Yoon, H. C. (2007). Hostile personality traits and coronary artery calcification in middle-aged and older married couples: Different effects for self-reports versus spouse ratings. *Psychosomatic Medicine, 69,* 441–448.

Smoak, N. D., Scott-Sheldon, L. A. J., Johnson, B. T., Carey, M. P., & SHARP Research Team. (2006). Sexual risk reduction interventions do not inadvertently increase the overall frequency of sexual behavior: A meta-analysis of 174 studies with 116,735 participants. *Journal of Acquired Immune Deficiency Syndromes, 41,* 374–384.

Snyder, H. N., & Sickmund, M. (2006). *Juvenile offenders and victims: 2006 national report.* Washington, DC: U.S. Department of Justice.

Snyder, P. (1974). Prostitution in Asia. *Journal of Sex Research, 10,* 119–127.

So, H., & Cheung, F. M. (2005). Review of Chinese sex attitudes and applicability of sex therapy for Chinese couples with sexual dysfunction. *Journal of Sex Research, 42*(2), 93–101.

Social evolution changed nature of sodomy. (2003, June 27). *Chicago Tribune,* p. A4.

Society for Reproductive Technologies. (2008). Success rates. Available: http://www.sart.org/Guide_SuccessRates.html (Last visited 10/25/08).

Solomon, J. (1998, March 16). An insurance policy with sex appeal. *Newsweek,* p. 44.

Sonfield, A. (2004). Meeting the sexual and reproductive health needs of men worldwide. New York: Alan Guttmacher Institute. Available: http://agi-usa.org/pubs/ito-intl/pdf (Last visited 12/12/05).

Sorenson, S. B., & Siegel, J. M. (1992). Gender, ethnicity, and sexual assault: Findings from a Los Angeles study. *Journal of Social Issues, 48*(1), 93–104.

Sowell, R. L., Seals, B. F., Phillips, K. D., & Julious, C. H. (2003). Disclosure of HIV infection: How do women decide to tell? *Health Education Research, 18*, 32–44.

Sprecher, S. (2002). Sexual satisfaction in premarital relationships: Associations with satisfaction, love, commitment, and stability. *Journal of Sex Research, 39*(3), 190–196.

Sprecher, S., Harris, G., & Meyers, A. (2008). Perceptions of sources of sex education and targets of sex communication: Sociodemographic and cohort effects. *Journal of Sex Research, 45*(1), 17–26.

Sprecher, S., Hatfield, E., Cortese, A., Potapova, E., & Levitskaya, A. (1994). Token resistance to sexual intercourse and consent in unwanted sexual intercourse: College students' experiences in three countries. *Journal of Sex Research, 31*(2), 125–132.

Sprecher, S., & McKinney, K. (1993). *Sexuality.* Newbury Park, CA: Sage.

Springen, K. (2005, February 7). The miscarriage maze. *Newsweek,* pp. 63–64.

SSSS signs letter to President Bush opposing abstinence-only funding. (2002). Available: http://www.sexscience.org/sex_sci43-1.htm (Last visited 3/18/02).

Stack, S., & Gundlach, J. H. (1992). Divorce and sex. *Archives of Sexual Behavior, 21*(4), 359–368.

Stall, R., Hays, R., Waldo, C., Ekstrand, M., & McFarland, W. (2000). The gay '90s: A review of research in the 1990s on sexual behavior and HIV risk among men who have sex with men. *AIDS, 14,* S1–S14.

Standards of care for gender identity disorders, sixth version. (2001, February). The Harry Benjamin International Gender Dysphoria Association. Available: http://www.hbigda.org (Last visited 2/21/03).

Staples, R. (1991). The sexual revolution and the Black middle class. In R. Staples (Ed.), *The Black family* (4th ed.). Belmont, CA: Wadsworth.

Staples, R. (2006). *Exploring Black sexuality.* Boulder, CO: Rowman & Littlefield.

Staples, R., & Johnson, L. B. (1993). *Black families at the crossroads: Challenges and prospects.* San Francisco: Jossey-Bass.

Stayton, W. R. (1996). A theology of sexual pleasure. In E. Stuart & A. Thatcher (Eds.), *Christian perspectives on sexuality and gender.* Grand Rapids, MI: Eerdmans; Herefordshire, England: Gracewing.

Stein, M. D., Freedberg, K. A., Sullivan, L. M., Savetsky, J., Levenson, S. M., Hingson, R., et al. (1998). Sexual ethics: Disclosure of HIV-positive status to partners. *Archives of Internal Medicine, 158,* 253–257.

Stein, R. (2008, February 14). On this you can rely: A kiss is fundamental. *Indianapolis Star,* p. A4.

Steinauer, J., & Autry, A. (2007). Extended cycle combined hormonal contraception. *Obstetrics and Gynecology Clinics of North America, 34*(1), 43–55.

Steingraber, S. (2007). The falling age of puberty in U.S. girls: What we know, what we need to know. San Francisco, CA: Breast Cancer Fund. Available: http://www.breastcancerfund.org (Last visited 6/4/08).

Sternberg, R. (1986). A triangular theory of love. *Psychological Review, 93,* 119–135.

Sternberg, R., & Grajek, S. (1984). The nature of love. *Journal of Personality and Social Psychology, 47,* 312–327.

Sternberg, R. J., & Barnes, M. L. (1989). *The psychology of love.* New Haven, CT: Yale University Press.

Sternberg, S. (2005a, February 24). In India, sex trade fuels HIV's spread. *USA Today,* pp. D1–D2.

Sternberg, S. (2005b, February 10). Routine HIV screening cost-effective, studies say. *New York Times,* p. 9D.

Sternberg, S. (2008, October 27). Early HIV treatment radically boosts survival. *USA Today,* p. D7.

Stevenson, M. R. (2002). Conceptualizing diversity in sexuality research. In M. W. Wiederman & B. E. Whitley (Eds.), *Handbook for conducting research on human sexuality.* Mahwah, NJ: Erlbaum.

Stewart, E. G., & Spencer, P. (2002). *The V Book: A doctor's guide to complete vulvovaginal health.* New York: Bantam Books.

St. Louis, M. E., Wasserheit, J. N., & Gayle, H. D. (1997). Editorial: Janus considers the HIV pandemic—harnessing recent advances to enhance AIDS prevention. *American Journal of Public Health, 87,* 1012.

Stirn, A., & Hinz, A. (2008). Tattoos, body piercings, and self-injury: Is there a connection? Investigations on a core group of participants practicing body modification. *Psychotherapy Research, 18,* 326–333.

Stobbe, M. (2008, January 16). Against the trend, U.S. births way up. *Associated Press News.*

Stockdale, M. S. (1993). The role of sexual misperceptions of women's friendliness in an emerging theory of sexual harassment. *Journal of Vocational Behavior, 42*(1), 84–101.

Stoller, R. J. (1982). Transvestism in women. *Archives of Sexual Behavior, 11*(2), 99–115.

Stoller, R. J. (1991). *Pain & passion: A psychoanalyst explores the world of S&M.* New York: Plenum.

Storms, M. D. (1980). Theories of sexual orientation. *Journal of Personality and Social Psychology, 38,* 783–792.

Storms, M. D. (1981). A theory of erotic orientation development. *Psychological Review, 88,* 340–353.

Strage, M. (1980). *The durable fig leaf.* New York: Morrow.

Strassberg, D. S., & Lowe, K. (1995). Volunteer bias in sex research. *Archives of Sexual Behavior, 24*(4), 369–382.

Strauss, L. T., Gamble, S. B., & Parker, W. Y. (2007). Abortion surveillance—United States, 2004. *Morbidity and Mortality Weekly Report, 56,* SS-9.

Strauss, L. T., Herndon, J., Chang, J., Parker, W. Y., Bowens, S. V., & Berg, C. J. (2005). Abortion surveillance—U.S., 2002. Washington, DC: Centers for Disease Control and Prevention. Available: http://www.cdc.gov/mmwr/preview/mmwrhtml/ss5407a1.htm (Last visited 2/21/06).

Strider, W. (1997). Making sense of the Pap test. *Women's Health Digest, 3*(4), 250–251.

Strote, J., Lee, J. E., & Wechsler, H. (2002). Increasing MDMA use among college students: Results of a national survey. *Journal of Adolescent Health, 30,* 64–72.

Struckman-Johnson, C., Struckman-Johnson, D., & Anderson, P. B. (2003). Tactics of sexual coercion: When men and women won't take no for an answer. *Journal of Sex Research, 40,* 76–86.

Stuebe, A. M., Rich-Edwards, J. W., Willett, W. C., Manson, J. E., & Michels, K. B. (2005). Duration of lactation and incidence of Type 2 diabetes. *Journal of the American Medical Association, 294*(20), 2601–2610.

Stulhofer, A. (2006). Letter to the editor: How (un)important is penis size for women with heterosexual experience? *Archives of Sexual Behavior, 35*(1), 5–6.

Suarez, T., & Miller. T. (2001). Negotiating risks in context: A perspective on unprotected anal intercourse and barebacking among men who have sex with men—where do we go from here? *Archives of Sexual Behavior, 30,* 287–300.

Suarez-Al-Adam, M., Raffaelli, M., & O'Leary, A. (2000). Influence of abuse and partner hypermasculinity on the sexual behavior of Latinas. *AIDS Education and Prevention, 12,* 263–274.

Sue, D. (1979). Erotic fantasies of college students during coitus. *Journal of Sex Research, 15,* 299–305.

Sulak, P. J., Scow, R. D., Preece, C., Riggs, M. W., & Kuehl, T. J. (2000). Hormone withdrawal symptoms in oral contraceptive users. *Obstetrics and Gynecology, 95*(2), 261–266.

Sullivan, A. (2000, April 2). The he hormone. *New York Times Magazine,* pp. 46–51, 58–59, 69–70.

Sullivan, P. S. (2004). Failure to return for HIV test results among persons at high risk for HIV infection. *Journal of Acquired Immune Deficiency Syndromes, 35,* 511–518.

Suppression of menstruation with extended OC regimens. (2002, October). *The Contraception Report, 13*(3), 8–11.

Supreme Court of the United States. (2003a, June 26). John Geddes Lawrence and Tyron Garner, Petitioners *v.* Texas. Majority opinion.

Supreme Court of the United States. (2003b, June 26). John Geddes Lawrence and Tyron Garner, Petitioners *v.* Texas. Minority opinion.

Swan, S. H., Elkin, E. P., & Fenster, L. (2000). The question of declining sperm density revisited: An analysis of 101 studies published 1934–1996. *Environmental Health Perspectives, 108,* 961–966.

Sward, S. (1998, June 27). High Court widens employer liability for sex harassment. *San Francisco Chronicle,* pp. A1, A15.

Sybert, V. P., & McCauley, E. (2004). Medical progress: Turner's syndrome. *New England Journal of Medicine, 351,* 1227–1238.

Symons, D. (1979). *The evolution of human sexuality.* New York: Oxford University Press.

Taberner, P. V. (1985). *Aphrodisiacs: The science and the myth.* Philadelphia: University of Pennsylvania Press.

Tabrizi, S. N., Fairley, C. K., Bradshaw, C. S., & Garland, S. M. (2006). Prevalence of *Gardnerella vaginalis* and *Atopobium vaginae* in virginal women. *Sexually Transmitted Diseases, 33,* 663–665.

Tam, L. W. (2001, November/December). What is postpartum depression? *The Network News,* pp. 4–5.

Tanfer, K., Cubbins, L. A., & Billy, J. O. G. (1995). Gender, race, class and self reported sexually transmitted disease incidence. *Family Planning Perspectives, 27,* 196–202.

Tannen, D. (1990). *You just don't understand: Women and men in conversation.* New York: Ballantine Books.

Tanner, L. (2002, February 4). Doctors back gay adoptions. *Monterey County Herald,* p. A7.

Tanner, L. (2005, July 17). Latest research findings: Research is often wrong. *Indianapolis Star,* p. A23.

Taylor, L. D. (2005). Effects of visual and verbal sexual television content and perceived realism on attitudes and beliefs. *Journal of Sex Research, 42,* 130–137.

Teen girls tell their stories of sex trafficking and exploitation in U.S. (2006, February 9). ABC News. Available: http://abcnews.go.com/Primetime/story?id=15967788page=1 (Last visited 3/30/06).

Tejada-Vera, B., & Sutton, P. D. (2008). Births, marriages, divorces and deaths: Provisional data for January 2008. *National Vital Statistics Reports, 57*(3).

Templeman, T., & Stinnett, R. (1991). Patterns of sexual arousal and history in a "normal" sample of young men. *Archives of Sexual Behavior, 20*(2), 137–150.

Tepper, M. S., & Owens, A. F., (2007). Current controversies in sexual health: Sexual addiction and compulsion. In. A. F. Owens & M. S. Tepper, *Sexual health: State-of-the-art treatments and research.* Westport, CT: Praeger.

Thables, V. (1997). A survey analysis of women's long-term post-divorce adjustment. *Journal of Divorce and Remarriage, 27*(3–4), 163–175.

Thayer, L. (1986). *On communication.* Norwood, NJ: Ablex.

Thomas, S. B., & Quinn, S. C. (1991). The Tuskegee syphilis study, 1932 to 1972: Implications for HIV education and AIDS risk education programs in the Black community. *American Journal of Public Health, 81*(11), 1498–1504.

Thompson, I. M., Pauler, D. K., Goodman, P. J., Tangen, C. M., Lucia, M. S., Parnes, H., et al. (2004). Prevalence of prostate cancer among men with a prostate-specific antigen level ≤ ng per milliliter. *New England Journal of Medicine, 350,* 2239–2246.

Tiefer, L. (2001). A new view of women's sexual problems: Why new? Why now? *Journal of Sex Research, 38*(2), 89–110.

Tiefer, L. (2004). *Sex is not a natural act and other essays* (2nd ed.). Boulder, CO: Westview Press.

Tjaden, P., & Thoennes, N. (1998). *Prevalence, incidence, and consequences of violence against women: Findings from the National Violence Against Women Survey.* Washington, DC: National Institute of Justice.

Tjaden, P., & Thoennes, N. (2008, November). Prevalence, incidence, and consequences of violence against women: Findings from the National Violence Against Women Survey. *National Institute of Justice Center for Disease Control and Prevention Research in Brief,* p. 12.

Tolman, D. L., Striepe, M. I., & Harmon, T. (2003). Gender matters: Constructing a model of adolescent sexual health. *Journal of Sex Research, 40*(1), 4–12.

Tolson, J. (2000, March 13). No wedding? No ring? No problem. *U.S. News & World Report,* p. 48.

Torabi, M. R., & Yarber, W. L. (1992). Alternate forms of the HIV Prevention Attitude Scale for Teenagers. *AIDS Education and Prevention, 4,* 172–182.

Traeen, B., Nilsen, T. S., & Stigum, H. (2006). Use of pornography in traditional media and on the Internet in Norway. *Journal of Sex Research, 43*(3), 245–254.

Treas, J., & Giesen, D. (2000). Sexual infidelity among married and cohabiting Americans. *Journal of Marriage and Family, 62,* 48–60.

Trujillo, C. M. (1997). Sexual identity and the discontents of difference. In B. Greene (Ed.), *Ethnic and cultural diversity among lesbians and gay men.* Thousand Oaks, CA: Sage.

Truong, H. M., et al. (2006). Increases in sexually transmitted infections and sexual risk behavior without a concurrent increases in HIV incidence among men who have sex with men in San Francisco: A suggestion of HIV serosorting? *Sexually Transmitted Infections, 82,* 461–466.

Trussell, J. (2007). Contraceptive efficacy. In R. A. Hatcher et al. (Eds.), *Contraceptive technology* (19th Rev. ed). New York: Ardent Media.

Tufts University. (2002, December). Better sex life not found over the counter. *Tufts University Health and Nutrition Letter, 20*(10).

Tully, C. T. (1995). In sickness and in health: Forty years of research on lesbians. In C. T. Tully (Ed.), *Lesbian social services: Research issues.* New York: Harrington Park Press/Haworth Press.

Tunuguntla, H. (2005). Management of andropause: The male menopause. *Clinical Geriatrics.* Available: http://www.hmpcommunica-tions.com/cg/displayArticle.cfm?articleID=article4922 (Last visited 12/16/05).

Turner, A. N., et al. (2008). Male circumcision and women's risk of incident chlamydial, gonococcal, and trichomonal infections. *Sexually Transmitted Diseases, 35,* 689–695.

Tuttle, T. M., Habermann, E. B., Grund, E. H., Morris, T. J., Virnig, B. A (2007). Increasing use of contralateral prophylactic mastectomy for breast cancer patients: A trend toward more aggressive surgical treatment. *Journal of Clinical Oncology, 33,* 5203–5209.

TV parental guidelines. (2000, May 29). Available: http://www.rvguidelines.org/default.htm (Last visited 12/8/00).

Uba, L. (1994). *Asian Americans: Personality patterns, identity, and mental health.* New York: Guilford Press.

Uhlenhuth, K. (2003, March 10). Hormone attention turns to men. *Monterey Country Herald,* p. 2.

Ullman, S. E., & Brecklin, L. R. (2002). Sexual assault history and suicidal behavior in a national sample of women. *Suicide and Life-Threatening Behavior, 32,* 117–130.

Ullman, S. E., & Knight, R. A. (1991). A multivariate model for predicting rape and physical injury outcomes during sexual assaults. *Journal of Consulting and Clinical Psychology, 59*(5), 724–731.

U.N. Demographic Yearbook, 2001. New York: United Nations, 2003. Available: http://www.un.org/issues/m-women.html (Last visited 1/22/06).

Undersize infants score higher on IQ tests if breastfed exclusively. (2002). National Institutes of Health. Available: http://www.nih.gov/news/pr/mar2002/nichd_20.htm (Last visited 11/30/02).

Understanding your treatment options. (2002). Resolve. Available: http://www.resolve.org/main/national/treatment/options/index.jsp?name=treatment&tag=options (Last visited 8/22/03).

United Nations General Assembly. (1993). Standard rules on the equalization of opportunities for persons with disabilities. Available: http://www.un.org/esa/socdev/enable/rights/wgrefa14.html (Last visited 1/10/06).

University of Minnesota. (2005). List of rape myths. Available: http://www.d.umn.edu/cla/faculty/jhamlin/3925/myths.html (Last visited 3/28/06).

U.S. Attorney General's Commission on Pornography (AGCOP). (1986). *Final report.* Washington, DC: U.S. Government Printing Office.

U.S. Bureau of the Census. (2001). Marital status of the population 15 years and over by sex, and race and Hispanic origin. Available: http://www.census.gov/population/socdemo/race/black/pp1-142/tab02.txt (Last visited 2/6/03).

U.S. Bureau of the Census. (2006). *Statistical abstract of the United States* (126th ed.). Washington, DC: U.S. Government Printing Office.

U.S. Census Bureau. (2005a). America's families and living arrangements: 2004. Table A1. Available: http://www.census.gov/population/www/socdemo/hhfam/cps2004.html (Last visited 5/19/06).

U.S. Census Bureau. (2005b). American Community Survey, 2004. Available: http://factfinder.census.gov (Last visited 2/1/06).

U.S. Census Bureau. (2008). *Statistical abstract of the United States.* Washington, DC: U.S. Government Printing Office. Available: http://www.census.gov/compendia/statab/2008edition.html (Last visited 7/1/08).

U.S. Department of Health and Human Services. (2000a). *Vital and health statistics: Trends in pregnancies and pregnancy rates by outcome: Estimates for the United States, 1976–96.* Series 23, No. 56. Washington, DC: Centers for Disease Control and Prevention/National Center for Health Statistics.

U.S. Department of Health and Human Services. (2000b). *Healthy people 2010.* Washington, DC: Author.

U.S. Department of Health and Human Services. (2000c). The Development Disabilities Assistance and Bill of Rights Act of 2000. (Available: http://www.acf.hhs.gov/programs/add/ddact/DDACT2.html (Last visited 9/17/08).

U.S. Department of Health and Human Services. (2002). Emergency department trends from the drug warning network: Preliminary estimates January–June 2001 and revised estimates 1994–2000. Available: http://www.samhsa.gov (Last visited 6/18/03).

U.S. Department of Health and Human Services. (2006). *Child mistreatment 2005.* Washington, DC: U.S. Government Printing Office.

U.S. Department of Health and Human Services. (2008a). ADD fact sheet: Available: http://www.acf.hhs.gov/programs/add/Factsheet.html (Last visited 9/16/08).

U.S. Department of Health and Human Services. (2008b). HIV and its treatment: What you should know. Available: http://www.aids.gov/treatment/overview/index.html (Last visited 12/22/08).

U.S. Department of Justice. (2002). *Criminal victimization 2001: Changes 2000–01 with trends 1993–2001.* Washington, DC: Bureau of Justice Statistics.

U.S. Department of Justice. (2005). *Criminal victimization, 2004.* Washington, DC: Bureau of Justice Statistics.

U.S. Department of Justice. (2006). *Criminal victimization, 2005.* Washington, DC: Bureau of Justice Statistics.

U.S. Department of Justice. (2007). *Criminal victimization, 2006.* Washington, DC: Bureau of Justice Statistics.

U.S. Department of Labor (2005). Compliance Assistance—Family and Medical Leave Act (FMLA). Available: http://www.dol.gov/esa (Last visited 10/11/05).

U.S. Department of State. (2003). *Trafficking in persons report, June 2003.* Available: http://www.state.gov/g/tip/rls/tiprpt/2003/21262.htm (Last visited 6/16/08).

U.S. Department of State. (2007). *Trafficking in persons report, June 2007.* Available: http://www.state.gov/g/tip/ris/tiprpt/2007 (Last visited 6/16/08).

U.S. District Court, Eastern District of Pennsylvania. (2007). Attorney General of the United States: Final Adjudication Lowell A. Reed, Jr., March 22, 2007. Available: http://www.paed.uscourts.gov (Last visited 6/12/08).

U.S. Equal Employment Opportunity Commission. (2008a). Sexual harassment. Available: http://www.eeoc.gov/types/sexual_harrassment.html (Last visited 7/28/08).

U.S. Equal Employment Opportunity Commission. (2008b). Sexual harassment charges EEOC & FEPAs combined: FY 1997–FY 2007. Available: http://www.eeoc.gov/stats/harass/html (Last visited 7/28/08).

U.S. Food and Drug Administration. (2003). New device approval: Essure system—P020014. Available: http://www.fda.gov/cdrh/mda/docs/p020014.html (Last visited 8/22/03).

U.S. Food and Drug Administration. (2006). Breast implant questions and answers. Available: http://www.fed.gov/cdrh/breastimplants/qa2006.html (Last visited 9/10/08).

U.S. House of Representatives, Committee on Government Reform—Minority Staff, Special Investigations Division. (2004). The content of federally funded abstinence-only education programs. Prepared for Rep. Henry A. Waxman.

U.S. Merit Systems Protection Board. (1995). *Sexual harassment in the federal workplace: Trends, progress, continuing challenges.* Washington, DC: Author.

U.S. Preventive Services Task Force. (2008). Screening for prostate cancer: U.S. Preventive Services Task Force Recommendation Statement. *Annals of Internal Medicine, 149,* 185–191.

Vaginal births after cesarean births—California 1996–2000. (2002, November 8). *Morbidity and Mortality Weekly Report, 51*(44), 996–998.

Valdiserri, R. O. (2004). Mapping the roots of HIV/AIDS complacency: Implications for program and policy development. *AIDS Education and Prevention, 16,* 426–439.

Valdiserri, R. O. (2005). A future free of HIV: What will it take? *Journal of Public Health Management Practice, 11,* 1–3.

Valente, S. M. (2005). Sexual abuse of boys. *Journal of Child and Adolescent Psychiatric Nursing, 18,* 10–16.

Valera, R., Sawyer, R., & Schiraldi, G. (2001). Perceived health needs of inner-city street prostitutes: A preliminary study. *American Journal of Health and Behavior, 25,* 50–59.

Valleroy, L. A., Mackeller, D. A., Behel, S. K., Secura, G. M., & Young Men's Survey. (2003). The bridge for HIV transmission to women from 23- to 29-year-old men who have sex with men in 6 U.S. cities. National HIV Prevention Conference, July 2003, Atlanta, GA. Abstract M2-B0902.

Vandeweil, H. B. M., Jaspers, J. P. M., Schultz, W. C. M. W., & Gal, J. (1990). Treatment of vaginismus: A review of concepts and treatment modalities. *Journal of Psychosomatic Obstetrics and Gynecology, 11,* 1–18.

Van Voorhis, B. J. (2006). Outcomes from assisted reproductive technology. *Obstetrics and Gynecology, 107*(1), 183–200.

Vega, W. (1991). Hispanic families. In A. Booth (Ed.), *Contemporary families: Looking forward, looking back.* Minneapolis, MN: National Council on Family Relations.

Velez-Blasini, C. J. (2008). Evidence against alcohol as a proximal cause of sexual risk taking among college students. *Journal of Sex Research, 45,* 118–128.

Venners, S. A., Wang, X., Chen, C., Wang, L., Chen, D., Guang, W., et al. (2004). Paternal smoking and pregnancy loss: A prospective study using a biomarker of pregnancy. *American Journal of Epidemiology, 159*(10), 993–1001.

Ventura, S. (2007, December 5). Teen birth rate rises for first time in 15 years. *National Center for Health Statistics, 56*(7). Hyattsville, MD: National Center for Health Statistics. Available: http://www.cdc.gov/nchs/pressroom/07newsreleases/teenbirth.htm (Last visited 6/9/08).

Ventura, S. J., Abma, J. C., Mosher, W. D., & Henshaw, S. (2004). Estimated pregnancy rates for the United States, 1990–2000: An update. *National Vital Statistics Reports, 52*(23). Hyattsville, MD: National Center for Health Statistics.

Ventura, S. J., Abma, J. C., Mosher, W. D., & Henshaw, S. K. (2008, April 14). Estimated pregnancy rates by outcome for the United States, 1990–2004. Hyattsville, MD: Centers for Disease Control & Prevention, National Vital Statistics.

Ventura, S. J., Matthews, T. J., & Hamilton, B. E. (2001). Births to teenagers in the United States, 1940–2000. *National Vital Statistics Report, 49*(10). Hyattsville, MD: National Center for Health Statistics.

Victims of Trafficking and Violence Protection Act of 2000. (2000). Available: http://www.state.gov/documents/organization/10492.pdf (Last visited 6/16/08).

Vitale, A. (2005). Rethinking the gender identity disorder terminology in the *Diagnostic and Statistical Manual of Mental Disorders IV.* Presented at the 2005 HBIGDA Conference, Bologna, Italy. Available: http://www.avitale.com/hbigdatalk2005.htm (Last visited 12/12/05).

Wald, A., et al. (2005). The relationship between condom use and herpes simplex virus acquisition. *Annals of Internal Medicine, 143,* 707–713.

Waldner-Haugrud, L., & Gratch, L. V. (1997). Sexual coercion in gay/lesbian relationships: Among gay and lesbian adolescents. *Violence and Victims, 12,* 87–98.

Walker, J., Archer, J., & Davies, M. (2005). Effects of rape on men: A descriptive analysis. *Archives of Sexual Behavior, 34,* 69–80.

Wallerstein, J. S., Lewis, J., & Blakeslee, S. (2000). *The unexpected legacy of divorce.* New York: Hyperion.

Walter, C. (2008 February/March). Affairs of the lips. *Scientific American Mind,* pp. 24–29. Available: http://www.sciAmMind.com (Last visited 7/25/08).

Ward, H., & Day, S. (2006). What happens to women who sell sex? Report of a unique occupational cohort. *Sexually Transmitted Infections, 82,* 413–417.

Warner, J. (n.d.) Why women lose interest in sex. *WebMD.* Available: http://www.webmd.com/sex-relationships/features/why-women-lose-desire-for-sex (Last visited 3/2/08).

Warren, C. S., Gleaves, D. H., Cepeda-Benito, A., Fernandez, M. D., & Rodriguez-Ruiz, S. (2005). Ethnicity as a protective factor against internalization of a thin ideal and body dissatisfaction. *International Journal of Eating Disorders, 37,* 241–249.

Webb, P. (1983). *The erotic arts.* New York: Farrar, Straus & Giroux.

Weeks, J. (1986). *Sexuality.* New York: Tavistock/Ellis Horwood.

Weeks, J. D., & Kozak, I. J. (2001). Trends in the use of episiotomy in the United States: 1980–1998. *Birth, 28*(3), 152–160.

Weinberg, M. S., Williams, C. J., & Moser, C. (1984). The social constituents of sadomasochism. *Social Problems, 31,* 379–389.

Weingert, P., & Kantrowitz, B. (2007, January 15). The new primetime. *Newsweek,* pp. 38–60.

Weinstock, H., Berman, S., & Cates, W. (2004). Sexually transmitted diseases among American youth: Incidence and prevalence estimates, 2000. *Perspectives on Sexual and Reproductive Health, 36*(1), 6–10.

Weis, D. L. (2002). The need to integrate sexual theory and research. In M. W. Wiederman & B. Whitley, Jr. (Eds.), *Handbook for conducting research on human sexuality.* Mahwah, NJ: Erlbaum.

Weisberg, D. K. (1990). *Children of the night.* New York: Free Press.

Weiss, H. A., Thomas, S. L., Munabi, S. K., & Hayes, R. J. (2006). Male circumcision and risk of syphilis, chancroid, and genital herpes: A systematic review and meta-analysis. *Sexually Transmitted Infections, 82,* 101–110.

Weitzer, R. (2005). New directions in research in prostitution. *Crime, Law and Social Change, 43,* 211–235.

Wells, B. (1986). Predictors of female nocturnal orgasm. *Journal of Sex Research, 23,* 421–427.

Wells, B. E., Bimbi, D. S., Tider, D., Van Ora, J., & Parson, J. T. (2006). Preventive health behaviors among lesbian and bisexually identified women. *Women and Health, 44,* 1–13.

Wessells, H., Lue, T. F., & McAninch, J. W. (1996). Complications of penile lengthening and augmentation seen at one referral center. *Journal of Urology, 155,* 1617–1620.

West, S. L., Vinikoor, L. C., & Zolnoun, D. (2004). A systematic review of the literature on female sexual dysfunction prevalence and predictors. *Annual Review of Sex Research, 15,* 40–172.

What Is priapism? (1997, March 28). Available: http://www.columbia.edu/cu/healthwise/1133.html (Last visited 1/29/98).

Whipple, B. (2002). Review of Milan Zaviacic's book: *The human female prostate: From vestigial Skene paraurethral glands and ducts to woman's functional prostate. Archives of Sexual Behavior, 31,* 457–458.

Whipple, B., & Komisaruk, B. (1999). Beyond the G spot: Recent research on female sexuality. *Psychiatric Annals, 29,* 34–37.

Whipple, B., Ogden, G., & Komisaruk, B. R. (1992). Physiological correlates of imagery-induced orgasm in women. *Archives of Sexual Behavior, 21*(2), 121–133.

White, J. W., & Farmer, R. (1992). Research methods: How they shape views of sexual violence. *Journal of Social Issues, 48,* 45–59.

Whitehead, M., & Holland, P. (2003, January 25). What puts children of lone parents at a health disadvantage? *The Lancet, 361,* 271–272.

Whiteman, M., Hillis, S. D., Jamiesons, D. J., et al. (2008). Inpatient hysterectomy surveillance in the United States, 2000–2004. *American Journal of Obstetrics and Gynecology, 198*(1), 34.

Whitley, B. E., Jr., & Kite, M. E. (1995). Sex differences in attitudes toward homosexuality: A comment on Oliver and Hyde (1993). *Psychology Bulletin, 117*(1), 146–154.

Whitty, M., & Fisher, W. A. (2008). The sexy side of the Internet. In A. Barak (Ed.), *Internet sexuality.* New York: Oxford University Press.

Widom, C. S., & Kuhns, J. B. (1996). Childhood victimization and subsequent risk for promiscuity, prostitution, and teenage pregnancy: A prospective study. *American Journal of Public Health, 86*(11), 1607–1612.

Wiederman, M. W. (1996). Women, sex, and food: A review of research on eating disorders and sexuality. *Journal of Sex Research, 33,* 301–311.

Wiederman, M. W. (1999). Volunteer bias in sexuality research using college student participation. *Journal of Sex Research, 36,* 59–66.

Wiederman, M. W., Maynard, C., & Fretz, A. (1996). Ethnicity in 25 years of published sexuality research: 1971–1995. *Journal of Sex Research, 33*(4), 339–343.

Williams, C. J., & Weinberg, M. S. (2003). Zoophilia in men: A study of sexual interest in animals. *Archives of Sexual Behavior, 32,* 523–535.

Williams, M. L., Timpson, S., Klovdal, A., Bowen, A. M., Ross, M. W., & Keel, B. (2003). HIV risk among a sample of drug-using male sex workers. *AIDS, 17,* 1402–1404.

Williams, T., Pepitone, M., Christensen, S., & Cooke, B. (2000, March 30). Finger-length ratios and sexual orientation. *Nature, 404,* 455–456.

Wilson, C., Murphy, S., & Aguirre, M. (2008). Breastfeeding support as a primary prevention strategy for Type 2 diabetes mellitus. Available: http://www.aap.org/NACH/Wilson.pdf (Last visited 4/2/09).

Wilson, P. (1986). Black culture and sexuality. *Journal of Social Work and Human Sexuality, 4*(3), 29–46.

Wilson, S., & Delk, J., II. (1994). A new treatment for Peyronie's disease: Modeling the penis over an inflatable penile prosthesis. *Journal of Urology, 152,* 1121–1123.

Wind, R. (2008, July 31). Media Center: Publicly funded family planning clinics prevent 1.4 million unintended pregnancies each year, save $4.3 billion in public funds. Available: http://www.guttmacher.org/media/nr/2008/07/31/index.html (Last visited 8/8/08).

Wingood, G. M., DiClemente, R. J., Bernhardt, J. M., Harrington, K., Davies, S. L., Robillard, A., et al. (2002). A prospective study of exposure to rap music videos and African American female adolescents' health. *American Journal of Public Health, 93,* 437–439.

Winters, S. J., Brufsky, A., Weissfeld, J., Trump, D. L., Dyky, M. A., & Hadeed, V. (2001). Testosterone, sex hormone–binding globulin, and body composition in young adult African-American and Caucasian men. *Metabolism: Clinical and Experimental, 50,* 1242–1247.

Wise, T. N., & Meyer, J. K. (1980). The border area between transvestism and gender dysphoria: Transvestitic applicants for sex reassignment. *Archives of Sexual Behavior, 9,* 327–342.

Wolff, C. (1986). *Magnus Hirschfeld: A portrait of a pioneer in sexology.* London: Quartet Books.

Wolitski, R. (2005). The emergence of barebacking among gay men in the United States: A public health perspective. *Journal of Gay and Lesbian Psychotherapy, 9,* 13–38.

Women's hormones—testosterone, the other female hormone. (2002, September). *Harvard Women's Health Watch, 10,* 1.

Wonderlich, S. A., et al. (2000). Relationship of childhood sexual abuse and eating disturbances in children. *Journal of the American Academy of Child & Adolescent Psychiatry, 39,* 1277–1283.

Wood, J. M., Koch, P. B., & Mansfield, P. K. (2006). Women's sexual desire: A feminist critique. *Journal of Sex Research, 43,* 236–244.

Wood, M. L., & Price, P. (1997). Machismo and marianismo: Implications for HIV/AIDS risk reduction and education. *American Journal of Health Sciences, 13*(1), 44–52.

Woodworth, T. W. (1996). DEA congressional testimony. Available: http://www.usdoj.gov/dea/ (Last visited 2/6/97).

Working Group for a New View of Women's Sexual Problems. (2001). A new view of women's sexual problems. In E. Kaschak & L. Tiefer (Eds.), *A new view of women's sexual problems.* New York: Haworth Press.

World Health Organization. (1992). *Reproductive health: A key to a brighter future.* Biennial report, 1990–1991. Geneva, Switzerland: Author.

World Health Organization. (2006). Defining sexual health. Available: http://www.who.int/reproductive-health/publications/sexualhealth (Last visited 9/10/08).

World Health Organization. (2007). New data on male circumcision and HIV prevention: Policy and programme implications. Available: http://www.who.int/hiv/pub/meetingreports/mc_montreauz_march 07/en (Last visited 10/16/08).

World Health Organization. (2008). Eliminating female genital mutilation: An interagency statement: OHRHR, UNAIDS, UNDP, UNECA, UNESCO, UNFPA, UNHCR, UNICEF, UNIFEM, WHO. Available: http://www.who.int/reproductive-health/publications/fgm/fgm_statement_2008 (Last visited 9/30/08).

Worth, H., & Rawstorne, P. (2005). Crystallizing the HIV epidemic: Methamphetamine, unsafe sex, and gay diseases of the will. *Journal of Sex Research, 34,* 483–486.

Worthington, R. L. (personal communication, January 31, 2008).

Worthington, R. L., Navarro, R. L., Savoy, H. B., & Hampton, D. (2008). Development, reliability, and validity of the Measure of Sexual Identity Exploration and Commitment (MoSIEC). *Developmental Psychology, 44,* 22–33.

Wyatt, G. E. (1992). The sociocultural context of African American and White American women's rape. *Journal of Social Issues, 48*(1), 77–91.

Xavier, C., Xavier, B. F., Munoz, N., Meijer, C. J. L. M., Shah, K. V., deSanjose, L., et al. (2002). Male circumcision, penile human papillomavirus infection, and cervical cancer in female patients. *New England Journal of Medicine, 346,* 1105–1112.

Xu, F., Markowitz, L. E., Sternberg, M. R., & Aral, S. O. (2007). Prevalence of circumcision and herpes simples virus type 2 infection in men in the United States: The National Health and Nutrition Examination Survey (NHANES), 1999–2004. *Sexually Transmitted Diseases, 34,* 479–484.

Yarber, W. L. (1996). Rural adolescent HIV/STD health risk behavior: The accuracy of estimates of five groups. *Health Education Monograph Series, 14,* 41–46.

Yarber, W. L. (2003). *STDs and HIV: A guide for today's teens.* Reston, VA: American Association for Health Education.

Yarber, W. L., Crosby, R. A., & Sanders, S. A. (2000). Understudied HIV/STD risk behaviors among a sample of rural South Carolina women: A descriptive pilot study. *Health Education Monograph Series, 18,* 1–5.

Yarber, W. L., Graham, C. A., Sanders, S. A., Crosby, R. A., Butler, S. M., & Hartzell, R. M. (2007). "Do you know what you're doing?" College students' experiences with male condoms. *American Journal of Health Education, 38,* 322–331.

Yarber, W. L., Milhausen, R., Crosby, R. A., & DiClemente, R. J. (2002). Selected risk and protective factors associated with two or more lifetime sexual intercourse partners and non-condom use during last coitus among U.S. rural high school students. *American Journal of Health Education, 33,* 206–213.

Yarber, W. L., Milhausen, R. R., Crosby, R. A., & Torabi, M. R. (2005). Public opinion about condoms for HIV and STD prevention: A midwestern telephone survey. *Perspectives on Sexual and Reproductive Health, 37*(3), 148–154.

Yarber, W. L., Milhausen, R. R., Huang, B., & Crosby, R. A. (2008). Do rural and non-rural single, young adults differ in their risk and protective HIV/STD behaviors? Results from a national survey. *Health Education Monograph, 25,* 7–12.

Yarber, W. L., Sanders, S. A., Graham, C. A., Crosby, R. A., & Milhausen, R. R. (2007, November). *Public opinion about what behaviors constitute "having sex": A state-wide telephone survey in Indiana.* Paper presented at the annual meeting of the Society for the Scientific Study of Sexuality, Indianapolis, IN.

Yarber, W. L., Torabi, M. R., & Veenker, C. H. (1989). Development of a three-component sexually transmitted disease attitude scale. *Journal of Sex Education and Therapy, 15,* 36–49.

Yarnall, K. S. H., McBride, C. M., Lyna, P., Fish, L. J., Civic, D., Grothaus, L., et al. (2003). Factors associated with condom use among at-risk women students and nonstudents seen in managed care. *Preventive Medicine, 37,* 163–170.

Yates, A., & Wolman, W. (1991). Aphrodisiacs: Myth and reality. *Medical Aspects of Human Sexuality, 25,* 58–64.

Yawn, B. P., & Yawn, R. A. (1997). Adolescent pregnancy: A preventable consequence? *The Prevention Researcher.* Eugene, OR: Integrated Research Services.

Young, K. (1998). *Caught in the net: How to recognize the signs of Internet addiction and a winning strategy for recovery.* New York: Wiley.

Zak, A., & McDonald, C. (1997). Satisfaction and trust in intimate relationships: Do lesbians and heterosexual women differ? *Psychological Reports, 80,* 904–906.

Zausner, M. (1986). *The streets: A factual portrait of sex prostitutes as told in their own words.* New York: St. Martin's Press.

Zaviacic, M. (2002). *The human female prostate: From vestigial Skene paraurethral glands and ducts to woman's functional prostate.* Bratislava, Slovakia: Slovak.

Zilbergeld, B. (1992). *The new male sexuality.* New York: Bantam Books.

Zilbergeld, B. (1999). *Male sexuality* (Rev. ed.). Boston: Little, Brown.

Zimmerman, R. (2002, September 25). Some makers, vendors drop N-9 spermicide on HIV risk. *The Wall Street Journal Online.*

Zuckerman, M. (1994). *Behavioral expressions and biosocial bases of sensation seeking.* New York: Cambridge University Press.

Zurbriggen, E. L., & Yost, M. R. (2004). Power, desire, and pleasure in sexual fantasies. *Journal of Sex Research, 41,* 288–300.

Zurenda, L., & Sandberg, D. E. (2003a). Klinefelter syndrome. In T. H. Ollendick & C. S. Schroeder (Eds.), *Encyclopedia of clinical child and pediatric psychology* (pp. 331–333). New York: Kluwer Academic/Plenum.

Zurenda, L., & Sandberg, D. E. (2003b). Congenital adrenal hyperplasia. In T. H. Ollendick & C. S. Schroeder (Eds.), *Encyclopedia of clinical child and pediatric psychology* (pp. 134–136). New York: Kluwer Academic/Plenum.

Credits

Photo Credits

Chapter 1

p. 1, © PureStock/Punchstock; pp. 3, 4, © Joel Gordon; p. 5, © Rudi Von Briel/PhotoEdit; p. 7, © VH1 Television/Photofest; p. 8, ABC-TV/The Kobal Collection/Ron Tom; p. 9, © Jeff Snyder/FilmMagic/Getty Images; p. 10, © Focus Features/Courtesy Everett Collection; p. 11T, © Joel Gordon; p. 11B, © Chris Jackson/Getty Images; p. 14, Kelsey McNeal/© ABC/Courtesy Everett Collection; p. 15, © The Granger Collection, New York; p. 16, © Erich Lessing/Art Resource, NY; p. 17, © Jagadeesh NV/Reuters/Landov; p. 18, Smithsonian Institution, National Anthropological Archives. Neg. # 85-8666; p. 21TL, © Donna Binder; p. 21TR, © Cleo/PhotoEdit; p. 21BL, © The McGraw-Hill Companies, Inc./Christopher Kerrigan, photographer; p. 21BR, © Alán Gallegos/AG Photograph

Chapter 2

p. 28, © Bonnie Kamin/PhotoEdit; p. 36, © David Ryan/Lonely Planet Images; p. 38, © Mark Thornton/Getty Images; p. 42, © Joel Gordon; p. 43, © Irven DeVore/Anthro-Photo; p. 44, © Mary Evans Picture Library; p. 45, © Mary Evans Picture Library/Sigmund Freud Copyrights; p. 46T, © Hulton-Deutsch Collection/Corbis; p. 46B, Photo by Bill Dellenback. Reprinted by permission of the Kinsey Institute for Research in Sex, Gender and Reproduction; p. 47, © Matthew Peyton/Getty Images; p. 49, © John Chiasson/Getty Images; p. 51, © Bruce Powell; p. 56T, © AP/Wide World Photos; p. 56B, Photo of Dr. Evelyn Hooker courtesy of "Changing Our Minds: The Story of Dr. Evelyn Hooker"; p. 57, © 1978 Raymond Depardon/Magnum Photos; p. 59, © PureStock/Punchstock; p. 60, © Bob Daemmrich/Stock Boston; p. 62, © Dex Image/PunchStock

Chapter 3

p. 67, © Hans Neleman/Stone/Getty Images; p. 71, Georgia O'Keeffe, (1887–1986). *Black Iris,* 1926. Oil on canvas, H. 36, W. 29-7/8 inches (91.4 × 75.9 cm). Alfred Stieglitz Collection, 1969 (69.278.1). Photo: Malcom Varon. Image copyright © The Metropolitan Museum of Art/Art Resource, NY. © 2009 Georgia O'Keeffe Museum/Artists Rights Society (ARS), New York; p. 73, © Susan Lerner 1999/Joel Gordon Photography; p. 79, Photograph by Imogen Cunningham, © 1978, 1998 The Imogen Cunningham Trust; p. 81, © C. Edelmann/La Villete/Photo Researchers, Inc.; p. 86, © The McGraw-Hill Companies, Inc./Jill Braaten, photographer; p. 95, © Joel Gordon

Chapter 4

p. 104, © Terje Rakke/Riser/Getty Images; p. 108, © Joel Gordon; p. 111TL, © Bachmann/PhotoEdit; p. 111TR, © Luca I. Tettoni/Corbis; p. 111B, © Purestock/Getty Images; p. 117, © CNRI/Science Photo Library/Photo Researchers, Inc.

Chapter 5

p. 125, © Jonathan Ferrey/Getty Images; p. 128, *Lisa Lyon,* 1981 © Copyright The Estate of Robert Mapplethorpe/A+C Anthology;

p. 129, © Tom McCarthy/PhotoEdit; p. 131, © Monica M. Davey/AFP/Getty Images; p. 135, trbfoto/Brand X Pictures/Jupiterimages; p. 136, © Brendan Smialowski/Getty Images; p. 137, © David Young-Wolff/PhotoEdit; p. 142, © AP/Wide World Photos; p. 145, © Custom Medical Stock Photo; p. 152, Courtesy Dr. Daniel Greenwald; p. 152BL, © AP/Wide World Photos; p. 152BR, © China Photos/Getty Images

Chapter 6

p. 157, Ryan McVay/Getty Images; p. 160T, © Lisa Gallegos/AG Photograph; p. 160B, © Christine DeVault; p. 166L, Rob Melnychuk/Getty Images; p. 166M, © Lindsay Hebberd/Corbis; p. 166R, © Inge Yspeert/Corbis; p. 167T, © Andrew Lichtenstein/The Image Works; p. 167B, © PureStock/Superstock; p. 169, © Bob Daemmrich/Stock Boston; p. 171, © R. Hutchings/PhotoEdit; p. 177, © Fox Searchlight/The Kobal Collection/Doane Gregory

Chapter 7

p. 184, © Lyn Balzer and Tony Perkins/Riser/Getty Images; p. 188, © Purestock/PunchStock; p. 192, © Justin Sullivan/Getty Images; p. 194, Getty Images/Digital Vision; p. 197T, © AP/Wide World Photos; p. 197B, © Ian Waldie/Getty Images; p. 199, © Jason LaVeris/FilmMagic/Getty Images; p. 201, © Royalty-Free/Corbis; p. 203, © Noel Hendrickson/Digital Vision/Getty Images; p. 206, © Cindy Charles/PhotoEdit; p. 208, © Jean Mounicq/ANA, Paris; p. 211, © Rhoda Sidney/PhotoEdit

Chapter 8

p. 220, © Reggie Casagrande/PhotoDisc/Getty Images; p. 222, © Barbara Stitzer/PhotoEdit; p. 224, © Michael Newman/PhotoEdit; p. 226, © David Young-Wolff/PhotoEdit; p. 229, © Joel Gordon; p. 233T, © Jonathan Nourok/PhotoEdit; p. 233B, © Strauss/Curtis/Offshoot Stock; p. 239, © Ghislain & Marie David de Lossy/The Image Bank/Getty Images; p. 244, © Sonda Dawes/The Image Works; p. 247, © Digital Vision; p. 248, © Bill Aron/PhotoEdit; p. 253, © Ron Chapple

Chapter 9

p. 259, © Royalty-Free/Corbis; p. 262TL, © Jon Feingersh/Blend Images/Getty Images; p. 262TML, © ICHIRO/Taxi Japan/Getty Images; p. 262TMR, © Bigshots/The Image Bank/Getty Images; p. 262TR, © Jose Luis Pelaez/Iconica/Getty Images; p. 262BL, © Vladimir Pcholkin/Photographer's Choice/Getty Images; p. 262BML, © Marcy Maloy/Digital Vision/Getty Images; p. 262BMR, © Yukmin/Asia Images/Getty Images; p. 262BR, © Dan Hallman/PhotoDisc/Getty Images; pp. 269, 273, 274, © Joel Gordon; p. 282, © Tom & Dee Ann McCarthy/Corbis

Chapter 10

p. 296, © Image Source/SuperStock; p. 303, © Roberto Soncin Gerometta/Lonely Planet; p. 304, © Movie Star News; p. 305, © Markus Morianz; p. 306, © Joel Gordon; p. 308, © Columbia/Courtesy Everett Collection; p. 312, © David McNew/Getty Images; p. 318, Everett Collection

Chapter 11

p. 323, Keith Brofsky/Getty Images; pp. 328, 329, © Joel Gordon; p. 333, Don Farrall/Getty Images; p. 336, © Michael Keller/Corbis; p. 337, © Joel Gordon; p. 338, © Royalty-Free/Corbis; p. 339, © Joel Gordon; pp. 341, 342, © McGraw-Hill Companies Inc./Jill Braaten, photographer; p. 343, © Joel Gordon; p. 344, © The McGraw-Hill Companies, Inc./Christopher Kerrigan, photographer; p. 345, © Joel Gordon; p. 349, Courtesy Conceptus Incorporated

Chapter 12

p. 361, © Brand X Pictures/PunchStock; p. 365, Photo by Lennart Nillson/Bonnier Alba AB. From *Behold Man*. Little Brown and Company; p. 369, © age fotostock/SuperStock; p. 375, © Louie Psihoyos/Corbis; p. 376, © Custom Medical Stock Photo; p. 383T, Big Cheese Photo/JupiterImages; p. 383B, © Rachael Epstein/PhotoEdit; p. 386, © David Young-Wolff/PhotoEdit; p. 389T, © Roger Tully/Stone/Getty Images; p. 389B, Huichol People, Nayarit or Jalisco Mexico. The Husband Assists in the Birth of a Child, mid 20th Century. Yarn, 23 3/4 × 23 3/4 in. Fine Arts Museums of San Francisco, Gift of Peter F. Young, 74.21.14; p. 390, © Jose Luis Pelaez, Inc./Corbis

Chapter 13

p. 397, © Michael Schwarz/The Image Works; p. 399, © Zed Nelson/Reportage/Getty Images; p. 401T, © Christopher LaMarca/Redux; p. 401B, © Bubbles Photolibrary/Alamy; p. 404, © The McGraw-Hill Companies, Inc./Lars A. Niki, photographer; p. 406, © PNC/Lifesize/Getty Images; p. 409, © AP/Wide World Photos; p. 411, © Robert W. Ginn/PhotoEdit; p. 414T, © Spencer Grant/Index Stock Imagery; pp. 414B, 418T, © Joel Gordon; p. 418B, © Custom Medical Stock Photo; p. 421, © 1980 Hella Hammid. All rights reserved; p. 422, © Susan Lerner/Design Conceptions; p. 430, © Joel Gordon; p. 431, © Robert Laberge/Getty Images; p. 432, © Catherine Leroy/Sipa Press; p. 435, © Getty Images

Chapter 14

p. 440, © Robert De Viset/Jupiter Images; p. 443, © Kristin Gerbert/zefa/Corbis; p. 459, © Creatas/PunchStock; p. 462, © Altrendo Images/Getty Images; p. 466, © Bob Bachmann/PhotoEdit; p. 468, © Apply Pictures/Alamy; pp. 469, 480, © Joel Gordon; p. 484, © Elena Dorfman/Offshoot Stock

Chapter 15

p. 489, © Joel Gordon; p. 498, © Creatas Images/PictureQuest; p. 505, Courtesy of the Centers for Disease Control and Prevention, Atlanta; p. 507L, © SPL/Photo Researchers, Inc.; pp. 507R, 510T© Custom Medical Stock Photo; p. 510B, © ISM/Phototake; p. 512L, Courtesy of the Centers for Disease Control and Prevention, Atlanta; p. 512R, © Custom Medical Stock Photo; p. 516, Courtesy of the Centers for Disease Control and Prevention, Atlanta; p. 518, © AP/Wide World Photos; p. 520, © Royalty-Free/Corbis

Chapter 16

p. 526, © Joel Gordon; p. 530, © A. Ramey/PhotoEdit; p. 531, © Custom Medical Stock Photo; p. 538, © AP/Wide World Photos; p. 542, © Michael Newman/PhotoEdit; p. 546, © Jes Aznar/AFP/Getty Images; p. 554T, © Adam Berry/Bloomberg News/Landov; p. 554B, © Jonathan Nourok/PhotoEdit; p. 559, © Mark Phillips/Photo Researchers, Inc.

Chapter 17

p. 564, © Sonda Dawes/The Image Works; p. 566, © Digtial Vision; p. 574TL, © Scala/Art Resource; p. 574TR, © UPI/Bettmann/Corbis; p. 574B, © James D. Wilson/Woodfin Camp and Associates; p. 581, Ryan McVay/Getty Images; p. 584, © Stockbyte/Getty Images; p. 592T, © Rhoda Sidney/PhotoEdit; p. 592B, © Fotex/Shooting Star; p. 600, Network Publications; p. 601, © BananaStock/PunchStock

Chapter 18

p. 605, © Joel Gordon; p. 609, © Kevin Kane/WireImage/Getty Images; pp. 611, 614, © AP/Wide World Photos; p. 616, © Michael Wilhoite from Daddy's Roommate, Alyson Wonderland, 1990; p. 625, © The McGraw-Hill Companies, Inc./Christopher Kerrigan, photographer; p. 626, © AP/Wide World Photos; p. 627, © Fred Wood/Summer Productions **Think About It Boxes** Young people in café, © Stockbyte/Getty Images; Young woman thinking, © Glow Images/Getty Images; Group of teenagers walking, © Susan Wides/Uppercut Images/Getty Images; Couple with a piggy bank, © Asia Images Group/AsiaPix/Getty Images

Subject Index

Note: Page references followed by italicized "*f*" or "*t*" refer to figures or tables, respectively.

child sexual abuse (continued)
  long-term effects of, 598–599
  pedophilia vs., 316
  perpetrators of, 198, 595–596, 595f
  powerlessness after, 600
  prevalence of, 594–595
  prevention of, 600–602
  rape, 579
  repressed memories of, 597–598
  sexual abuse trauma, 599
  stigmatization after, 600
  traumatic sexualization, 599
  treatment programs for victims of, 600
Chinese Americans, sexuality in, 62
chlamydia (Chlamydia trachomatis)
  ectopic pregnancy and, 374
  HIV infection and, 501
  HPV infection and, 423
  prevalence of, 491, 492f, 493f, 501
  symptoms of, 502–504, 502t
  transmission of, 499, 502
chocolate, 90
cholesterol, estrogen and, 212
chorion, 364, 364f
chorionic villus sampling (CVS), 376, 376f
Christina (methamphetamine), 409, 544,
    545–546
chronic illness, sexuality and, 412
chronic pelvic pain, 492, 517
churches, 196. See also Catholic Church
Cialis (tadalafil), 480, 482
cilia, on fimbriae, 77
CIN (cervical intraepithelial
    neoplasia), 422–424, 529
circumcision, female, 432
circumcision, male
  debate over, 387
  penile cancer and, 431, 433
  procedure for, 106, 106f, 108f
  sexually transmitted infections and, 387, 499
Civil Rights Act of 1964, 566, 573
civil unions, 15, 227, 631
"the clap." See gonorrhea
class. See socioeconomic status
clinical research, 38–39
clitoral hood, 70f, 71
clitoral tumescence, 99
clitoridectomy, 432
clitoris, 70–71, 70f, 99–100
clomiphene citrate, 425
cloning, 381–382
CMV (cytomegalovirus), 515, 530
cocaine, 373, 409
cognitive-behavioral approach in sexual
    difficulties, 473–477
cognitive development theory, 133–134
cognitive social learning theory, 132–133
cohabitation
  acceptance of, 193, 199–200, 199f
  advantages of, 200
  extradyadic involvements in, 239
  of same-sex couples, 200–201
college newspapers, sex advice in, 31
college students
  alcohol use and sexuality, 405–407
  casual sex among, 264
  chlamydia in, 501

condom-use mistakes by, 519
confusion over consent by, 585–586
on definitions of "having sex," 280–281
gay, lesbian, or bisexual identity formation
    in, 191
Internet sex sites used by, 609–612
on kissing, 284
masturbation by, 170, 276–277
nonmarried sexuality among, 194–195
on pornography, 610
reasons for having sex, 196
sexual activity in, 53–54
sexual arousal factors in, 467
sexual bias in colleges, 136
sexual harassment of, 569–571, 570f
sexual scripting by, 270
sexual variations among, 301, 302f
single, 194–195
voyeurism and, 310
colostrum, 390
combined genital and subjective arousal
    disorder, 445
comedy series, sex and, 7
"coming out," 38, 192
commercial sex workers. See prostitution
commitment
  definition of, 242
  intimacy and, 240
  in triangular theory of love, 230, 230f,
    231–232
communication
  conflict and, 253–255
  cultural context of, 242–243
  directing sexual activity, 248–249
  feedback, 252–253, 252f
  first move and beyond, 247–248
  halo effect, 246–247
  Health Protective Sexual Communication
    Scale, 551
  initiating sexual activity, 249, 251
  interest and opening lines, 247
  misinterpretation, 248
  nonverbal, 244–246, 585
  obstacles to, 250
  partner satisfaction and patterns of, 251
  during pregnancy, 368–369
  psychological context of, 244
  in same-sex couples, 227
  self-disclosure, 240, 242, 246, 250–251
  sexually transmitted infections and, 521,
    551–552
  sexual scripts, 249, 586
  social context of, 243
  trust and, 251–252
  vocabulary for sexual activity, 242
communication loop, 252–253, 252f
Communications Decency Act, 13, 618, 619t
compromise, 241
compulsive overeating, 403–404
computers. See Internet
conception. See fertilization
conceptus, 329
conceptus development, 364–367, 364f,
    365f, 366f
condoms, female, 341–342, 341f, 496
condoms, male
  adolescent use of, 53, 328–329

advantages of, 341
alcohol consumption and, 407
in anal intercourse, 340, 341, 521, 539
college student use of, 54, 407
effective use of, 339, 340
inconsistent and incorrect use of, 495, 519
latex and synthetic, 340
lubricants for, 340
possible problems with, 341
in same-sex sexual activity, 52
sexuality programs on, 178
sexually transmitted infection
    prevention, 339, 495–496, 511, 514
spermicidal, 340
statistics on, 52, 339
women and, 340
confidentiality, in research, 37
conflict, about sex, 253–254, 253f
conflict resolution, 241, 243, 254–255
Confucianism, 62
congenital adrenal hyperplasia, 146t, 150
Consensus Development Panel on Female
    Sexual Dysfunction, 444–445
consummate love, 232
contraception. See also birth control
  birth control vs., 329
  emergency, 54, 350–351
contraceptive film, 344, 344f
contraceptive foam, 344
contraceptive patch, 335–336
control groups, 57
COPA (Child Online Protection Act),
    619, 619t
Copper T 380A, 345
coprophilia, 298t, 304
corona, of the penis, 106, 106f
corpora cavernosa
  calcium deposits and fibrous tissue
    in, 459–460
  location of, 71, 106, 106f, 109f
corpus luteum, 77, 83, 87f
corpus spongiosum, 106, 106f, 109f
correlational studies, 43
couvade, 130
Cowper's glands, 109f, 110–111, 120, 120f
COYOTE (Call Off Your Old Tired
    Ethics), 629
"crabs," 515–516
cramps, 88, 91
cranberry juice, 76
cremaster muscle, 109
critical thinking
  biases, 35
  egocentric fallacy, 35–36
  ethnocentric fallacy, 362
  opinions, 34–35
  on pop psychology, 32
  on sex advice columns, 31
  stereotypes and, 35
  value judgments vs. objectivity, 342
cross-dressing. See transvestites
crura (singular, crus), 70f, 71, 106
cryptorchidism, 109
crystal (methamphetamine), 409, 544,
    545–546
C-section, 389
culdoscopy, 348

women. *See also* gender differences
  abortions and, 354–355, 354*f*
  breast augmentation in, 400
  cancer in, 415–426, 433
  changes during pregnancy, 368–371,
    370*f. See also* pregnancy
  cultural views on sexuality of, 46
  cunnilingus, 285–287, 286*f*, 456–457,
    483, 521, 540
  distress about sex by, 450
  dyspareunia in, 445, 458–459
  eating disorders in, 401, 404
  faking orgasms, 97, 463
  female genital cutting, 432
  female orgasmic disorder, 454–455, 455*t*
  feminist research perspective, 54–55
  health-care needs, 85
  "highly sexual," 299–301
  HIV and, 546–547
  hormones in. *See* reproductive
    hormones, female
  infertility in, 378–379
  initiating sexual activity, 249, 251
  kissing and, 284
  male condom use and, 340
  masturbation by, 273*f*, 277–278, 461
  menopausal hormone therapy,
    212–215, 213*t*
  menopause in, 98, 211–215, 213*t*
  negative attitudes toward, 615
  norms on sexual activity in, 226
  orgasms in, 454–455, 455*t*, 456–458,
    477, 478*t*
  pedophilia, 317
  persistent sexual arousal syndrome in, 454
  physical causes of sexual dysfunction
    in, 461
  secondary sex characteristics, 113
  on sex and love, 225
  sex organs of, 68–80, 70*f*, 72*f*, 73*f*, 76*t*, 78*f*
  sex trafficking of, 622
  sexual aggression. *See* rape; sexual
    aggression
  sexual arousal disorder in, 452–453
  sexual assaults by, 590–591
  sexual attractiveness in, 261–262, 267
  sexual dysfunction prevalence
    in, 447–449, 448*f*, 449*f*
  sexual fantasies of, 271–272
  sexuality differences among, 446
  in sexually explicit films, 612
  sexual physiology of, 81–91, 81*f*, 83*f*,
    84*f*, 87*f*
  sexual response of, 49, 91–100, 93*f*, 94*t*
  with spinal cord damage, 410–411
  sterilization of, 348–349, 348*f*
  STI consequences in, 492–493, 516–518
  vaginismus in, 445, 458, 477
  vaginitis in, 76, 76*t*, 492, 503*t*, 513–514
  Viagra use by, 482
  Victorian views on sexuality of, 14–15,
    15*f*, 45, 46
Women's Health Initiative, 214
women's orgasmic disorder, 445
women's sexual disorders. *See also* sexual
    function difficulties
  definitions of, 445–446
  female sexual arousal disorder, 452–453
  new view of, 446–447
women's sexual interest/desire disorder, 445
Working Group for a New View of Women's
    Sexual Problems, 442–443, 446–447
workplace laws, 571–572, 573
World Health Organization (WHO), 399,
    443, 499

Xhosa people, 166*f*
X-rays, during pregnancy, 372
X syndrome (Turner syndrome), 146*t*,
    148, 148*f*
X-TC (ecstasy), 409, 585

yeast infection, 76, 413, 514
yohimbe, 470
yolk sac, 364
young people. *See* adolescents
Youth Risk Behavior Survey (YRBS),
    52–53

zoophilia, 298*t*, 309
Zuni people, 18, 18*f*
zygote intrafallopian transfer (ZIFT), 381
zygotes, 116, 363–364, 363*f*

Name Index